ITALY

THE ROUGH GUIDE

written and researched by

**ROS BELFORD, MARTIN DUNFORD,
CELIA WOOLFREY & MARK ELLINGHAM**

With additional contributions by
Jonathan Buckley, Tim Jepson, Jules Brown,
Robert Andrews, Hilary Robinson, Monica Levy,
Roberto Perretta, John-Paul Thomson, Kate Calvert,
Jeremy Tarry, Jean-Marc Salmon, Yvonne Newman, Phil
Cheesman and Mike Ivy

Edited by
Martin Dunford
with Jonathan Buckley

THE ROUGH GUIDES

ITALY

THE ROUGH GUIDE

ROUGH GUIDE CREDITS

Series Editor: Mark Ellingham
Editorial: Martin Dunford, John Fisher, Jack Holland, Jonathan Buckley,
  Greg Ward, Richard Trillo, Kate Berens
Production: Susanne Hillen, Gail Jammy, Andy Hilliard, Vivien Antwi

The authors would like to **thank**: Seena Smith for listings on Genova, Dan Goldstein for his piece on the World Cup, Jules Brown for editing, Mick Sinclair and Kate Berens for proof-reading. Also to Justin Ratcliffe, Bridget Bouch, Alfredo Trentelange, Bjarne Stig Hansen, Pat and Colin Belford, Lola Perrin, Jean Barclay, Anja Stanley, Fiona Cochran, Floriano and Germania Biagini, Michael Benis, Jonathan Degani, Luisa Segnana, Maurizio and Maurizio, Philip Dallas Say, Rachel Hedley, Kate and Flo Austin, Jerry Peakin, Al Spicer, Chris Botterill, Letizia and Jacopo Volpi, Giovanna Iannaco, Susan Madocks and Natania Jansz.

Many thanks, too, for assistance with research to: Paula Greco and the Italian State Tourist Office, Davide Jouve, Dino Treggiani, Gillian Ania, Giorgio and Flavio, Floriana Morresi, Alessandria of Francavilla al Mare, Cesare Mancabelli and the Mantova Lega per l'Ambiente, the EPTs of Pésaro, Ancona, Macerata and Áscoli Piceno, Gambino d'Angella and Anna Rosa Cavassoli of the Genova AAST, Gian Guido d'Amico of the Rapallo AAST.

The publishers and authors have done their best to ensure the accuracy and currency of all the information in **The Rough Guide: Italy**; however, they can accept no responsibility for any loss, injury, or inconvenience sustained by any traveller as a result of information or advice contained in the guide.

First published and reprinted (twice) by Harrap Columbus Ltd 1990.
This reprint published by Rough Guides Ltd, 149 Kennington Lane, London SE11 4EZ.
Distributed by Penguin Books, 27 Wrights Lane, London W8 5TZ.

Typeset in Linotron Univers and Century Old Style, to an original design by Andrew Oliver.
Printed in the UK by Cox & Wyman, Reading, Berks

Illustrations in Part One and Part Three by Ed Briant; Basics illustration by Paul Leith
Contexts illustration by Tommy Yamaha

992pp
includes index

British Library Cataloguing in Publication Data
A catalogue record for this book is available from the British Library.

ISBN 1-85828-012-5 (previously published by Harrap Columbus Ltd, under ISBN 0-7471-0104-3)

CONTENTS

Introduction vi

INTRODUCTION

O f European countries, **Italy** is perhaps the hardest to classify. It is a modern, industrialised nation, with companies like *Fiat* and *Olivetti* market-leaders in their field. It is the harbinger of style, its designers leading the way with each season's fashions. But it is also, to an equal degree, a Mediterranean country, with all that implies. Agricultural land covers much of the country, a lot of it, especially in the south, still owned under almost feudal conditions. In the towns and villages all over the country, life stops during the middle of the day for a siesta, and is strongly family-orientated, with an emphasis on the traditions and rituals of the Catholic church – which, notwithstanding a growing scepticism among the country's youth, still dominates people's lives here to an immediately obvious degree.

Above all Italy provokes reaction. Its people are volatile, rarely indifferent to anything, and on one and the same day you might encounter the kind of disdain dished out to tourist masses worldwide, and an hour later be treated with almost embarrassing hospitality. If there is a single national characteristic, it's to embrace life to the full: in the hundreds of local festivals taking place across the country on any given day, to celebrate a saint or the local harvest; in the importance placed on good food; in the obsession with clothes and image; and above all in the daily domestic ritual of the collective evening stroll or *passeggiata* – a sociable affair celebrated by young and old alike in every town or village across the country.

It's important to remember that Italy wasn't a unified state until 1861, and this is borne out by the regional nature of the place. Italians often feel more loyalty to their region than the nation as a whole – something manifest in different cuisines, dialects, landscape, and often varying standards of living. There is also, of course, the country's enormous cultural legacy: Tuscany alone has more classified historical monuments than any country in the world; there are considerable remnants of the Roman empire all over the country, notably of course in Rome itself; and every region retains its own relics of an artistic tradition generally acknowledged to be the world's richest.

Yet there's no reason to be intimidated by the art and architecture. If you want to lie on a beach, there are any number of places to do it: unlike, say, Spain, development has been kept relatively under control, and many resorts are still largely the preserve of Italian tourists; other parts of the coast, especially in the south of the country, are almost entirely undiscovered. Beaches are for the most part sandy, and doubts about the cleanliness of the water have been confined to the northern part of the Adriatic coast. Mountains, too, run the country's length – from the Alps and Dolomites in the North right along the Apennines, which form the spine of the peninsula – and are an important reference-point for most Italians: skiing and other winter sports are practised avidly, and in the five national parks, protected from the national passion for hunting, wildlife of all sorts thrives.

Italy North by South

Italy breaks down into nineteen regions, which in turn divide into different provinces. Some of these regional boundaries reflect long-standing historic borders, like Tuscany, Lombardy or the Veneto; others, like Friuli-Venezia Giulia or Molise, are more recent administrative divisions, often established in recognition of relatively modern distinctions. But the sharpest division is between north and south. The North is one of the most advanced industrial societies in the world, a region of extraordinary economic dynamism and home to the largest communist party in Western Europe, whose stronghold spreads across the central part of the peninsula. Its people speak Italian with the cadences of France or Germany; its "capital", Milan, is a thoroughly European city. The South, known as *il mezzogiorno*, begins somewhere between Rome and Naples, and is by contrast one of the economically most depressed areas in Europe. Its rate of unemployment (about twenty percent) is more than twice that of the North, its gross regional product about a third. And its history of absolutist regimes often seems carried over into the present by the presence of the Mafia, and the remote hand of central government in Rome. Its people are dark-skinned and speak with the cadences of the Mediterranean, the dialect down here sounding almost Arabic in some places; indeed its "capital" city, Naples, is often compared with Cairo.

This economic backwardness of the South is partly the result of the historical neglect to which it was subjected by various foreign occupiers. But it is also the result of the deliberate policy of politicians and corporate heads to industrialise the north while preserving the underdeveloped south as a convenient reservoir of labour. Italy's industrial power and dynamism, based in the North, has been built with exploited southerners who emigrated to the "Industrial Triangle" – Turin, Milan, Genova – in their millions during the Fifties and Sixties. Even now, Milan and Turin have very sizeable populations of *meridionali*, southerners, working in every sector of the economy.

This north-south divide is something you'll come up against time and again, wherever you're travelling. To a northerner the mere mention of Naples – a kind of totem for the South – can provoke a hostile response. And shops in the north have been known to sell such things as a poster-map (now banned) depicting the South as "The Dark Continent", Sicily as "Gheddafiland", Puglia as the "Turkish Principality". The same poster showed in Turin a concentration camp for *terroni* ("those of the land"), the offensive northern nickname for southern immigrants. You'll also notice graffiti on the walls of northern cities, saying "Terroni Go Home"; or posters for the *Liga Lombarda*, a party from Lombardy which campaigns against southern immigration to the North. And the antagonism cuts both ways. After the Naples football club won the national championship in 1987 for the first time, fans paraded through the city's streets, chanting "We're better than the North" and waving flags of the American Confederacy.

Having said all this, it would be wrong to imagine a country in a state of civil unrest, and Italy's north-south divide is more manifest in deep-rooted bigotry than direct action. Furthermore, even in its desperate economic conditions, the South does have productive industries, and it has contributed much to the country as a whole. Many of the nation's leaders, statesmen and bureaucrats are southerners by birth (prime ministers Aldo Moro and Ciriaco De Mita), as well as many of its greatest writers and philosophers – Verga, Pirandello, Sciascia, Vico, Croce and Gramsci, to name just a few.

Where to go

The **North** is the "discovered" Italy. The regions of **Piemonte** and **Lombardy**, in the northwest, make up the richest – and most cosmopolitan – part of the country, and the two main centres, Turin and Milan, are its wealthiest large cities. In their southern reaches, these regions are flat and scenically dull, especially Lombardy, but in the north the presence of the mountains shapes the character of each: skiing and hiking are prime activities, and the lakes and mountains of Lombardy are long-established tourist territory. **Liguria**, the small coastal province to the south, has long been known as the "Italian Riviera" and is accordingly crowded with sun-seeking holidaymakers for much of the summer season. But it's a beautiful stretch of coast, and its capital, Genova, is a bustling port with a long seafaring tradition.

Much of the most dramatic mountain scenery lies within the smaller northern regions. In the far northwest, the tiny bilingual region of **Val d'Aosta** is home to some of the country's most frequented ski resorts, and is bordered by the tallest of the Alps – the Matterhorn and Mont Blanc. Moving east, **Trentino-Alto Adige**, another bilingual region, and one in which the national boundary is especially blurred, marks the beginning of the Dolomites mountain range, where Italy's largest national park, the Stelvio, lies amid some of its most memorable landscapes.

The Dolomites stretch into the northeastern regions of the **Veneto** and **Friuli-Venezia Giulia**, though here the interest is of course Venice itself: a unique city, and every bit as beautiful as its reputation would suggest – though this means you won't be alone in appreciating it. If the crowds are too much, there's also the arc of historic towns outside the city – Verona, Padua and Vicenza, all centres of interest in their own right though rather overshadowed by their illustrious neighbour. To the south, the region of **Emilia-Romagna** has been at the heart of Italy's postwar industrial boom and has a standard of living on a par with Piemonte and Lombardy, though oddly enough it's also the country's principal stronghold of the Communist Party. Its coast is popular among Italians, and Rimini is about Italy's brashest, tackiest seaside resort. You'd do better to ignore the beaches altogether and concentrate on the ancient centres of Ravenna, Ferrara and Parma. And Bologna, the capital, is one of Italy's liveliest but least appreciated cities.

Central Italy perhaps represents the most commonly perceived image of the country, and **Tuscany**, with its classic rolling countryside and the art-packed towns of Florence, Pisa and Siena, is one of its most visited regions. Neighbouring **Umbria** is similar in all but its relative emptiness, though it gets fuller every year, as visitors flock into towns such as Perugia, Spoleto and Assisi. Further east still, **Marche** could in time go the same way, but for the moment is comparatively untouched, its highlights being the ancient towns of Urbino and Áscoli Piceno. South of Marche, the hills begin to pucker into mountains in the twin regions of **Abruzzo** and **Molise**, Italy's first really remote area if you're travelling north to south, centring on Italy's highest peak – the Gran Sasso d'Italia. Molise, particularly, is a taster of the South, as is **Lazio** to the west, in part a poor and desolate region whose often rugged landscapes contrast with the more manicured beauty of the other central regions. Lazio's real focal point, though, is **Rome**, Italy's capital, and the one city in the country which owes allegiance neither to the North *or* South, its people proudly aloof from the rest of the country's squabbles. There's nowhere quite like Rome: it's a tremendous city just to *be*, and in terms of historical sights outstrips everywhere else in the country by a long way.

The **South** proper begins south of Rome, with the region of **Campania**, which is as far as many tourists get. Naples is a petulant, unforgettable city, the spiritual heart of the Italian south, and on hand nearby are some of Italy's finest ancient sites in Pompeii and Herculaneum, not to mention its most spectacular stretch of coast around Amalfi. **Basilicata** and **Calabria**, which make up the instep and toe of Italy's boot, are harder territory but still rewarding, the emphasis less on art, more on the landscape and quiet, unspoilt coastlines. **Puglia**, too, the "heel" of Italy, has underrated pleasures: the landscape of its Gargano peninsula, the souk-like quality of its capital Bari, and the Baroque glories of Lecce in the far south. As for **Sicily**, the island is really a law unto itself, a wide mixture of attractions ranging from some of the finest preserved Hellenistic treasures in Europe, to a couple of Italy's fanciest beach resorts in Taormina and Cefalù, not to mention some gorgeous upland scenery. Come this far south and you're closer to Africa than Milan, and it shows, in the people, the architecture, and the cooking – *couscous* featuring on many menus in the west of the island.

Climate and when to go

Italy's **climate** is one of the most hospitable in the world, with a general pattern of warm, dry summers and mild winters. There are, however, marked regional variations, ranging from the more temperate northern part of the country to the firmly Mediterranean south. **Summers** are hot and dry along the coastal areas, especially as you move south, cool in the major mountain areas – the Alps and Apennines. **Winters** are mild in the south of the country, Rome and below, but in the north they can be at least as cold as Britain, sometimes worse, especially across the plains of Lombardy and Emilia-Romagna, which can be very inhospitable places indeed in January.

As for **when to go**, if you're planning to visit fairly touristed areas, especially beach resorts, avoid July and August, when the weather can be too hot and the crowds at their most congested; August is when the Italians go on holiday so expect the crush to be especially bad in the resorts then, not to mention a slightly artificial scene in the major historic cities – Rome, Florence, Venice – when the only people around are fellow-tourists. Really, the nicest time to visit, both for the weather and crowds, is April to late June, or September and October – though if you're planning to swim bear in mind that only the south of the country may be warm enough outside the summer months.

AVERAGE TEMPERATURES (°C)

	Jan	Feb	Mar	Apr	May	June	July	Aug	Sept	Oct	Nov	Dec
Ancona	5.7	5.8	9.4	13.6	17.6	22.3	24.9	24.3	21.1	16.6	12.6	7.4
Bari	8.4	8.5	10.8	13.9	17.5	21.9	24.5	24.3	21.7	18.2	14.8	10.2
Bologna	2.5	3.4	8.6	13.8	18.1	23.3	26.0	25.4	21.3	15.2	9.7	3.9
Florence	5.6	5.8	9.9	13.3	17.4	22.1	25.0	24.5	21.2	15.8	11.2	6.0
Genova	8.4	8.7	11.5	14.5	17.8	21.9	24.6	25.0	21.8	18.1	13.3	9.5
Milan	1.9	3.8	8.6	13.2	17.3	22.2	24.8	23.9	20.3	13.7	8.5	3.0
Naples	8.7	8.7	11.4	14.3	18.1	22.3	24.8	24.8	22.3	18.1	14.5	10.3
Palermo	10.3	10.4	13.0	16.2	18.7	23.0	25.3	25.1	23.2	19.9	16.8	12.6
Rome	7.4	8.0	11.5	14.4	18.4	22.9	25.7	25.5	22.4	17.7	13.4	8.9
Trieste	5.3	4.8	8.6	12.9	17.1	21.2	24.0	23.8	20.8	15.6	11.0	6.3
Venice	3.8	4.1	8.2	12.6	17.1	21.2	23.6	23.3	20.4	15.1	10.5	5.0

°C = (°F - 32) multiplied by 5/9

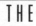

PART ONE

THE

BASICS

GETTING THERE

The easiest way to get to Italy from Britain is to fly, and prices for charter flights compare well with those for the long railway journey. Deals change all the time, however, and prices really depend on where you want to fly to. The main destinations are Milan, Turin, Pisa, Bologna, Rome, Naples and Palermo, and costs broadly reflect the distance and popularity of the place you're travelling to – flights to Milan, for instance, can be a great deal cheaper than those to Palermo.

BY PLANE

A **scheduled flight** is the most obvious option: the main airlines flying the Italian routes are *British Airways* and *Alitalia*, who between them during summer fly direct from **London** Heathrow to Milan (around 8 times daily), Naples (4 weekly), Pisa (3 daily), Rome (6–7 daily), Turin (4 daily) and Venice (3 daily); *British Airways* also fly from **Manchester** to Milan up to 3 times a day, and to Rome once a week.

The cheapest **ticket** you'll find is an Apex return fare, which ranges in cost from £162 to Milan, £174 to Rome, to £183 to Naples between April and September; add around £20 for each for July–September prices. Restrictions on Apex tickets are that you must book a minimum of 14 days in advance, you must stay a Saturday night abroad, and there are no refunds. **Other sched-**

uled options include *Air Europe*'s summer daily service to Rome (from £146 return, Apex), and *British Island Airways'* almost daily summer services to either Palermo or Catania (from about £150 return) – good if you're heading for Sicily first.

Usually **direct charter** flights are a better bargain, though you'd be advised to book some weeks in advance in peak season. *Pegasus Holidays*, and *Pilgrim Air* (see boxes overpage for addresses) both offer daily summer departures from London to most major Italian destinations, with current summer season prices working out at around £120 return to Milan during June, £140 to Naples – though you can cut these by about 10 percent by booking at least 12 weeks in advance. *Pilgrim*'s hybrid **air-coach** arrangement, making the outward journey by plane, the return by coach, is a very cheap way of working things, with fares starting at £69 return. On the negative side, it's only open to people staying in Italy for between 6 and 12 nights, and the coach journey takes 24 hours. *Quo Vadis* offer a similar arrangement, called *Italbreaks* and starting at £60 a head.

You can sometimes get flights even cheaper than this by going to a specialist **agent** – last summer's bargains were from about £90 return to Milan. There are usually dozens of sources. Look in the classified sections in the Sunday newspapers – the *Sunday Times* especially, and, if you live in London, *Time Out* magazine and the *Evening Standard*. Or contact one of the big youth/student travel specialists like *STA Travel* or *Campus Travel*, good for cheap deals if you're under 26 or a student. There are also a number of specialist Italian agents (addresses below), who will normally have a range of fares to a wide array of gateway cities.

Most agents offer **"open-jaw"** deals, whereby you can fly into one Italian city and back from another – a good idea if you want to make your way across the country, and generally no more expensive than a standard charter return. Consider also a **package deal** (see below), which takes care of flights and accommodation for an all-in price. Package operators can also be a source of cheap one-off flights.

AIRLINES AND AGENTS

Alitalia, 27 Piccadilly, London W1 (☎081-745 8286).

British Airways, 156 Regent Street, London W1 (☎081-897 4000).

CTS Travel, 33 Windmill Street, London W1 (☎071-636 5915/6).

Inter-Air, Liberty House, 222 Regent Street, London W1 (☎071-439 6633).

Italflights, 125 High Holborn, London WC1 (☎071-405 6771).

Campus Travel, 52 Grosvenor Gardens, London SW1 (☎071-730 3402).

Mundus Travel, 5 Peter Street, London W1 (☎071-437 2272, ☎071-437 7387/8).

Italy Sky Shuttle (Pilgrim Air), 227 Shepherds Bush Rd, London W6 7AS (☎081-748 1333).

Quest-Ultra (ex-Quo Vadis), 243 Euston Road, London NW1 (☎071-387 6122).

Rapid Air Travel Service, London House, 26–40 Kensington High Street, London W8 (☎01-937 6042).

STA Travel, 86 Old Brompton Road, London SW7 (☎071-937 9921).

RAIL TICKET OFFICES

British Rail European Travel Centre, Victoria Station, London SW1 (☎071-834 2345).

Eurotrain, 52 Grosvenor Gardens, London SW1 (☎071-730 8518).

FERRY COMPANIES

Any travel agent can provide up-to-date schedules and make advance bookings – essential in season, if you're driving. Or contact the **ferry companies** direct: for the latest cross-Channel details ring the numbers below.

Sally Lines, ☎01-409 2240.
Sealink, ☎01-834 8122.

P&O European Ferries, ☎01-734 4431.
Hoverspeed, ☎01-554 7061.

BY TRAIN

Travelling by **train** to Italy won't save much money, certainly not if you're over 26, but it can be a more pleasurable way of getting to the country, giving the opportunity to stop off in other parts of Europe on the way. An ordinary **return fare** on the fastest route (via Switzerland), currently costs £133 and the journey takes 18 hours – though bear in mind that the daily service delivers you there at 4am; the slower route, via Paris, costs £10 less and takes about 6 hours longer. Tickets are valid for two months, costing £150–170 to Rome, at least a 24-hour journey, and around £180 to Palermo – a full 42 hours from London.

If you're **under 26**, *Eurotrain* (address above), the student and youth agents and some high street travel agents can sell you a discounted *BIJ* ticket from London to any Italian destination, again valid for up to two months and giving as many stopovers as you like. Fares range from about £110 return to Milan to £150 to Naples. You can also arrange connecting fares at a discount from outside London, or – if you prefer – qualify for reduced price tickets if you join the train at the Channel ports. *Eurotrain* also sell *Explorer* tickets – like a railpass, but offering a set route through Europe to Milan, Rome or Venice; prices from £123.

All in all, if you are planning a trip through Europe, and travelling around Italy once you're there, it might be a better idea to invest in an *InterRail* pass if you're under 26. This costs £145, is valid for one month's unlimited rail travel throughout Europe, and gives discounts on cross-Channel services and some ferry routes in Europe. Once in Italy, the rail system is comprehensive and efficient, and much the best way of getting around the country. *InterRail* passes are available from British Rail stations and youth/student travel agents, and you need to have been resident in Europe for at least six months to qualify for one.

Whichever method you plump for, it's well worth **reserving** a **seat** (currently £1.50) or **couchette bed** (around £8) for your trip to Italy – something you should do well in advance.

BY COACH

It's difficult to see why anyone would want to travel to Italy by **coach**. But if you do have a phobia about trains and planes, there are direct services to Turin, Milan, Bologna, Florence and Rome. The Milan service takes around 27 hours, and Rome a gruelling 36 hours. Run by *National Express Eurolines* (☎01-730 0202), coaches leave at least three times weekly in summer: tickets to Milan cost about £106 return, to Rome £122 return, with small reductions for under-26s and students.

BY CAR/HITCHING: THE FERRIES

There's no one fixed route to Italy if you're travelling under your own steam. The best cross-Channel options for most drivers and hitchers will be the standard **ferry/hovercraft** links between Dover and Calais or Boulogne (with *Hoverspeed*, *P&O* or *Sealink*), Folkestone and Boulogne (*Sealink*) or Ramsgate and Dunkerque (*Sally Lines*).

From northern France, the Alpine route, via Germany and Switzerland, is probably the shortest as the crow flies, but can be pretty arduous; most drivers hotfoot it to the south of France and then switch east into northern Italy. Certainly this is a preferable option for **hitchers**: getting rides south is notoriously difficult from the Channel ports and you're most likely to pick up a lift in the direction of Paris. From here the N7 road provides a direct – and reasonably hitchable – route south to Provence.

PACKAGES AND ORGANISED TOURS

Italy stands somewhat apart from other European package destinations: it's not especially cheap and has avoided the big hotel build-ups that have blighted parts of Spain and Greece. And it's as much a venue for specialist interest and touring holidays as sun-sand-sea packages.

That said, there's no shortage of **travel-plus-accommodation** deals on the market, and if you're keen to stay in one (or two) places, they can work out very good value, especially if you live some way outside London. Many companies offer travel at rates as competitive as you could find on your own, and any travel agent can fill you in on all the latest offers. All the usual companies – *Thomson*, *Horizon*, etc – go to Italy, but there are a number of specialist operators too. It's obviously cheapest to travel **out of season**, something we'd recommend anyway as the resorts and sights are much less crowded, and the weather, in the south anyway, is often warm enough to swim. Prices start at around £320 per person per week for half-board in a hotel during May in one of the cheaper Adriatic resorts, about £400 for the same in Amalfi or Sorrento. In **high season** (Easter, July and August), all these prices shoot up considerably, and you can expect to pay £500–600 for a week's half-board in Amalfi, though your travel agent might come up with good, last-minute deals.

Some operators organise **specialist holidays** to Italy – walking tours, art and archaeology holidays, Italian food and wine jaunts – but they don't come cheaply either: accommodation, food, local

SPECIALIST OPERATORS

Citalia, 50–51 Conduit Street, London W1 (☎071-434 3844 or ☎071-686 5533). Hotel and villa packages all over Italy.

Italiatour, 21 Fleet St, London EC4 (☎071-353 9684). Package deals, city breaks, winter sun holidays and specialist Italian cuisine tours.

Italian Escapades, 227 Shepherds Bush Rd, London W6 7AS (☎081-748 2661). "Design-it-yourself" package holidays all over Italy. City breaks, self-catering, fly-drive.

Magic of Italy, 227 Shepherds Bush Rd, London W6 7AS (☎081-748 7575). Hotel and villa pack-

ages in Tuscany, Umbria, Amalfi Coast, Sicily and Sardinia. City-breaks, fly-drive and fly-coach tours.

Quest-Ultra (ex-Quo Vadis), 243 Euston Road, London NW1 (☎071-387 6122). Sea-and-sun packages, city breaks, self-catering, fly-drive.

Sunvil Holidays, Sunvil House, 7 & 8 Upper Square, Old Isleworth, Middx TW7 7BJ (☎081-568 4499). Hotel and villa packages, city breaks and fly-drives.

Time Off, Chester Close, Chester Street, London SW1 (☎071-235 8070). Short break specialists offering holidays in Milan, Florence, Venice and Rome.

transport and the services of a guide are nearly always included, and a week's half-board holiday can cost anything from £500 to £700 per person. There are also many operators selling **short-break deals** to Italian cities: for these, reckon on spending from about £200 per person for three nights in Florence in a two-star hotel, upwards of £250 between March and October.

If you want to hire a car in Italy, it's well worth checking with tour operators before you leave as some **fly/drive deals** work out very cheaply. *Italian Escapades* (see above) have good prices – from about £150 a week per person – but check out also *Quo Vadis*, *Sunvil* and *Italiatour*, who all offer some kind of fly-drive deal.

FROM EIRE

The only **airline** that flies direct to Italy is *Aer Lingus*, who fly to Milan about five times weekly, and Rome once a week. A scheduled Apex fare to Milan is IR£290, to Rome a little over IR£300. As always, you'll be better off going through an agent, especially if you're a student or under 26. *USIT* (address below) offer youth fares from Dublin to Milan for IR£210 return, to Rome for around IR£260 return. They also have cheap

deals available with *Air France* from Dublin, Shannon or Cork – from around IR£120 return to Turin or Venice, IR£140 to Naples – though these normally entail overnighting in Paris.

If you don't want to fly, you can always take the **train**. The current *BIJ* fare from Dublin to Rome, using the Rosslare–Le Havre crossing, is IR£185 return – a two-day journey each way.

FROM AUSTRALIA & NEW ZEALAND

From Australia or New Zealand, the only direct flights are to **Rome**. From Australia, you can fly direct from Melbourne or Sydney to Rome, at a price of around Aus$2300 return; from New Zealand, there are flights from Auckland to Rome for about NZ$1100 return. From Rome you can pick up connecting flights to anywhere in Italy. Alternatively, from either country it might be a better idea to pick up whatever deal you can get to **London** and take a cheap charter to Italy from there.

The best agent in both countries is the long-established *STA Worldwide*, who have offices at 1a Lee Street, Sydney 2000, Australia (☎02-212 1255 and 64 High Street, Auckland, New Zealand (☎9-390 458), as well as in Melbourne, Canberra, Perth and Wellington.

ADDRESSES IN IRELAND

Aer Lingus, 42 Grafton Street, Dublin 2 (☎01-794764), or at Dublin airport (☎01-370 011).

Dan-Air, no Dublin office but reservations on ☎01-428 311/417/831.

Ryan Air, College Park House, Nassau Street, Dublin 2 (☎01-797 444 or ☎01-770 444).

USIT, 7 Angelsea Street, Dublin 2 (☎01-778 117).

RED TAPE AND VISAS

British and other EC citizens can enter Italy, and stay as long as they like, simply on production of a valid passport. The temporary *British Visitor's Passport* (£7.50), available over the counter at post offices, is valid for one year; a full ten-year passport currently costs £25 and you should allow around a month for delivery. Citizens of Eire, Australia and New Zealand need only a valid passport, too, but are limited to stays of three months. All other nationals should consult the relevant embassies about visa requirements.

Legally, you're required to register with the police within three days of entering Italy, though if you're staying at a hotel this will be done for you. After the recent scares about terrorism, some policemen are more punctilious about this than ever, though others would be amazed and baffled by any attempt to register yourself down at the local police station while on holiday. If you're going to be staying for some time and working, you may as well do it; see p.37 for more details.

ITALIAN EMBASSIES AND CONSULATES

UK: 38 Eaton Place, London SW1 (☎01-235 9371); 6 Melville Crescent, Edinburgh (☎031-226 3169); 79 Oxford Street, Manchester (☎061-228 7041).

EIRE: 12 Fitzwilliam Square, Dublin 2 (☎01-762 401).

AUSTRALIA: 6169 Macquarie St, Sydney 2000, NSW (☎02-278 442); 34 Anderson St, Yarra, Melbourne, Victoria (☎03-267 5744).

NEW ZEALAND: 34 Grant Road, Wellington (☎04-735 339).

COSTS, MONEY AND BANKS

The days are long gone when Italy was a relatively cheap country to visit: the economic boom and the glut of visitors in the more touristy cities have conspired to make prices roughly on a par with the UK, and in certain cases even more expensive. Generally you'll find the poorer South much less expensive than the wealthier, more European North: as a broad guide, expect to pay most in Venice, Milan, Florence and Bologna, less in Rome, while in Naples and Sicily prices come down to fairly reasonable levels.

AVERAGE COSTS

Most **basic things** are inexpensive compared with Britain: a pizza or plate of pasta with a beer (the staple cheap meal in a restaurant) will set you back around £3–4 on average, though in some of the larger, more visited cities – Florence and Venice, for example – it can be difficult to find venues for this; Rome or Naples, on the other hand, are no problem at all. Buses and trains are cheap too, the journey from Rome to Milan, for instance, costing just £20 for a second-class return – an eight-hour, six-hundred-kilometre trip. Drinking, by contrast, is pricey: soft drinks or coffee all cost around the same price, if not more than in Britain, a large glass of beer can cost up to £3, even more if you decide to sit down. And room rates *start* at a bottom-line of £10 for a double room in a one-star hotel, though again in Florence or Venice you won't find anything under £15–20. Overall, in central Italy, if you're watching your budget – camping, hitching a little, buying food from shops and markets – you could get by on around £10 a day; a more realistic **average daily budget** – staying in one-star hotels, taking trains and eating one cheap meal out a day – would be approaching £25, perhaps a few pounds less in the south of the country.

Bear in mind, too, that **time of year** can make a big difference. During the height of summer, in July and especially August when the Italians take their holidays, hotel prices can escalate; outside the season, however, you can often negotiate much lower rates. There are few **reductions** or discounts for students or young people over 18: only a handful of museums accept ISIC cards, and buses and trains never do – though *Alitalia*'s domestic routes are subject to a 25 percent reduction if you're under 26 or a student.

MONEY AND BANKS

The Italian unit of **money** is the *Lira* (plural *Lire*), always abbreviated as L: the rate right now is around L2200 to the pound sterling. Notes come in denominations of L1000, L2000, L5000, L10,000, L50,000 and L100,000, coins as L50, L100, L200 and L500. Smaller denomination coins still float around and you might be given them as change – though a lot of places will give you sweets instead.

The easiest and safest way to carry your money is as **travellers' cheques**, available for a small commission (1 percent of the amount ordered) from any British high street bank and some building societies, whether or not you have an account. You'll usually – though not always – pay a small commission, too, when you **exchange money** using travellers' cheques – again around 1 percent of the amount changed, although some banks will make a standard charge per cheque regardless of its denomination. Alternatively, most banks can issue current account holders with a **Eurocheque card** and chequebook, with which you can get cash from the majority of banks in Italy (including from cash-dispensing machines, which can help to avoid the queues); you'll pay a few pounds service charge but usually no commission on transactions. Major **credit cards** – *Visa, Access, American Express* – are also accepted in many shops, and for cash in many banks. It's an idea to have at least some Italian money for when you first arrive, and you can buy *Lire* in advance from British banks, though you're not supposed to exceed L400,000 (around £170).

In Italy, the best place to change money or travellers' cheques is at a **bank**; major banking chains include the scandal-ridden *Banco Nazionale del Lavoro, Banco d'Italia, the Banco di Roma* and *Cassa Risparmio*. **Banking hours** are normally Monday to Friday mornings from 8.30am until 1pm, and for an hour in the afternoon (usually 3–4pm), though there are local variations on this. Outside banking hours, the larger hotels will change money or travellers' cheques, though if you're staying in a reasonably large city the rate is invariably better at those times at the railway station exchange bureaux – normally open evenings and weekends.

HEALTH AND INSURANCE

EC nationals can take advantage of Italy's health services under the same terms as the residents of the country. You'll need form E111, which in theory you can get by applying on form SA30 by post, one month in advance, to any DSS office in Britain. In practice it can often be issued over the counter at a main DSS office (not an Unemployment Benefit office).

HEALTH PROBLEMS

If you need treatment, go to a **doctor** (*médico*); every town and village has one. Take your E111 with you: this should enable you to get free treatment and prescriptions for medicines at the local rate – about 10 percent of the price of the medicine. If you're looking for repeat medication, take any empty bottles or capsules with you to the doctors – the brand-names often differ.

An Italian **chemist** (*farmacia*) is well-qualified to give you advice on minor ailments, and to dispense prescriptions, and there's generally one open all night in the bigger towns and cities. They work on a rota system, and you should find the address of the one currently open on any *farmacia* door. There's usually a phone number you can ring for addresses – see the city *Listings* sections in *The Guide*. If you are taken **seriously ill** or involved in an accident, hunt out the nearest hospital and go to the *Pronto Soccorso* (casualty) section; in a real emergency phone ☎113 and ask for *ospedale* or *ambulanza*. Major railway stations and airports often have first-aid stations with qualified doctors in hand. Try to avoid going to the **dentist** (*dentista*) while you're in Sicily. These aren't covered by the *mutua* or health service, and for the smallest problem they'll make you pay through the teeth.

INSURANCE

Whatever happens you should take out ordinary **travel insurance** before you leave, especially if you're a non-EC citizen. Ask about policies at any bank or travel agency, or use a specialist, low-priced firm like *Endsleigh* (97 Southampton Row, London WC1; ☎01-436 4451), who offer two weeks' basic cover for around £13. For medical treatment and drugs, keep all the bills and claim the money back later. If you have anything stolen (including money), register the loss immediately with the local police – without their report you won't be able to claim.

INFORMATION AND MAPS

Before you leave, it's well worth dropping in at the Italian State Tourist Office (*ENIT*) and picking up a selection of their free maps and brochures, though don't go mad – much of what they have is available in Italy itself. Worth grabbing are any accommodation listings they may have for the area you're interested in, town plans and maps of the regions, and the very useful annual *Travellers Handbook*, which can be an indispensable reference on all aspects of the country.

IN ITALY

Most Italian towns, main railway stations and airports have a tourist office: either an **EPT** (*Ente Provinciale Turismo*) – a provincial branch of the state organisation – or an **AAST** (*Azienda Autonoma di Soggiorno e Turismo*): a smaller local outfit. The Italian tourist system is reorganising right now and you'll notice a number of other acronyms – APT, AAT, IAT are just three – but all offer much the same mix of general advice and bumph, free maps and accommodation lists, though rarely do they book accommodation. Very small or out-of-the-way villages may have a tiny office known as a **Pro Loco**, which gives much the same service. Only in the larger cities and more touristed areas are the staff likely to speak much English. Opening hours vary, but larger city offices are likely to be open Monday–Saturday 9am–1pm and 4–7pm, and sometimes for a short period on Sunday morning; smaller offices may open weekdays only, while Pro Loco times are notoriously erratic – sometimes for only a couple of hours a day, even in summer.

A further source of information, at any rate in larger cities, is the **Tuttocittá** booklet, given away as supplement to the main telephone directories. This carries listings and phone numbers of essential services, adverts for restaurants and shops, together with indexed maps of the appropriate city. Most bars with phones have a copy, as do hotels, or you can get a look at one in a SIP or AAST public telephone office.

MAPS

As for **maps**, the **town plans** we've printed should be fine for most purposes, and most tourist offices give out maps of their local area for free. But if you want an indexed town plan, *Studio FMB* cover the country's towns and cities for £3.25 each; *Falk* also do decent plans of the major cities for £3.95. For **road maps**, the *Automobile Club d'Italia* issue a reasonable free map, available from the State Tourist Office – though this isn't of very much use for the individ-

ual regions; the clearest and best-value large-scale road map of Italy is the *Michelin* 1:1,000,000 (£2.40). Or there are the *TCI* 1:800,000 *North* and *South* maps – £4.95 each. *TCI* also do maps of the individual regions (1:200,000) for £4.95 each. For **hiking**, you'll need at least a scale 1:100,000 map, better 1:50,000. There are a number of different series: the *Studio FMB* maps of northern Italian mountain areas are the clearest (£3.25 each); for the whole country there's also the *Kompass* series (£3.50 each). All of these maps are available in Britain from *Stanfords*, 12 Long Acre, London WC2 (☎01-836 1321), or *Robertson McCarta*, 122 Kings Cross Road, London WC1 (☎01-278 8278). In Italy, the *Club Alpino Italiano*, Via Foscolo 3, Milan, is a source of hiking maps.

GETTING AROUND

The easiest way of travelling around Italy is by train. The Italian train system is cheap, reasonably comprehensive, and in the north of the country at least, fairly efficient – far preferable to the fragmented, localised and sometimes grindingly slow buses. We've detailed train, bus and ferry frequencies in the "Travel Details" section at the end of each chapter of the guide, and where it actually is a better idea to take a bus we've said as much in the text.

TRAINS

Operated by Italian State Railways, *Ferrovie dello Stato* (*FS*), there are five **types of train** in Italy. *Super Rápido Inter City* and *Rápido* are the fastest, often first class only, stopping only at major cities and charging a supplement of around 30

percent on top of the normal fare. More common are the *Espresso* and *Diretto* routes, of which the former stop at most larger stations, and the latter only slightly less selectively. Both are perfectly comfortable and not at all slow. A *Locale*, on the other hand, stops just about everywhere and is usually worth avoiding if you can manage it. In summer it's often worth making a **seat reservation** on the main routes, something which you'll find yourself obliged to do anyway on many more expensive *Rápido* trains. On these you can either pay the supplement in advance or, if time is short, simply board the train and pay the ticket-collector.

Fares are very reasonable, calculated by the kilometre and thus easy to work out for each journey. The state tourist board's *Travellers Handbook* gives the prices per kilometre but as a rough guide, the single second-class fare from Milan to Bari, one of the longest journeys you're ever likely to make, currently costs about L50,000. Reductions are available to kids under 12 and people over 65 (around 50 percent). **Sleepers** are available on most services, and prices vary according to the length of journey and whether or not you're sharing. Generally, expect to pay an extra L10–20,000 on a journey on the scale of, say, Rome to Turin.

As with most other European countries, you can cut costs greatly by using a **railpass**. *InterRail* gives free travel on the whole *FS*

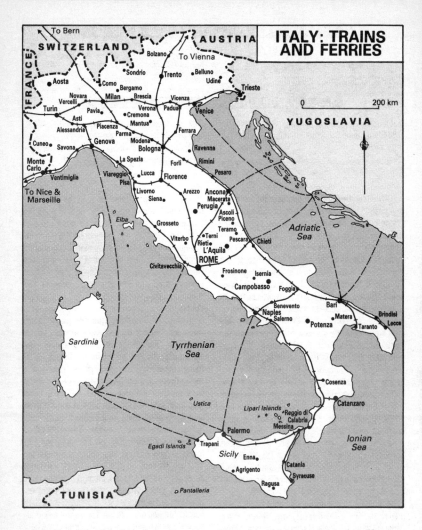

ITALY: TRAINS
AND FERRIES

network (though you'll be liable for supplements on the fast trains – see *Getting There*), and there are two specific Italian passes available. The *Biglietto turistico libera circolazione* (travel-at-will ticket) entitles you to unlimited travel on the entire FS network, including *Rápido* services, for a period of between 8 and 30 days – at a price ranging from £65 to £112. A *Chilometrico* ticket, valid for up to five people at once, gives three thousand kilometres' worth of free travel on a maximum of 20 separate journeys – cost £60.

Passes are available in advance from FS agents in Britain, or in Italy from all larger city railway stations.

If you're travelling as a family, it might also be worth investing in a *Rail Europe Family Card*, which is valid in Italy on all services and entitles a maximum of eight people to reductions of up to 50 percent for all the adults bar one (who pays full fare) and 75 percent for all kids under 12. Further details can be obtained from the state tourist office.

ITALIAN STATE RAILWAYS AGENTS IN THE UK

CIT, 50 Conduit St, London W1 (☎01-434 3844).

Ultima Travel, 424 Chester Rd, Little Sutton, South Wirral, L66 3RB (☎051-339 6171).

Wasteels Travel, 121 Wilton Rd, London SW1 (☎01-834 7066).

MAJOR ITALIAN BUS COMPANIES

Autostradale, Piazzale Castello 1, Milan (☎02/801.161). Services around Lombardy, Liguria and the lakes.

Lazzi, Via Mercadente 2, Florence (☎055/363.041). Services around Tuscany and central Italy.

SITA, Viale del Cadorna, Florence (☎(☎055/278.611). Services all over Italy.

Obviously **timings and route information** are posted up at railway stations (some in the larger cities accessible by way of increasingly fancy technology), and we give a rough idea of frequencies and journey-times in the "Travel Details" sections at the end of each chapter. But if you're going to be doing a lot of moving about by train, it might be sensible to invest in a **timetable**. *Rápido* and *Espresso* routes are covered by a little national pocket book, *Principali Treni*, issued twice yearly by FS and free from most railway stations, while stations also often hold free leaflets detailing individual routes. You can purchase full timetables detailing the entire nationwide FS network, also published twice-yearly, from station tobacconists for around L8000; in addition, FS publish this in two volumes – Sud Centro Italia and Nord Centro Italia – if you're going to be travelling around a more confined area. In all cases pay attention to the timetable notes, which may specify the dates between which some services run (*Si effetua dal . . . al . . .*), or whether a service is seasonal (*periodico*); *feriale* is the word for daily, *festivo* means a train only runs on Sundays and holidays.

In addition to the routes operated by FS, there are a number of **privately-run lines**, using separate stations though charging similar fares. Where they're worth using, these are detailed in the text.

BUSES

Trains don't go everywhere and sooner or later you'll have to use **regional buses** (*autobus* or *pullman*). Almost everywhere is connected by some kind of bus service, but schedules can be sketchy, and are drastically reduced – sometimes non-existent – at weekends, something the time-table won't always make clear. Bear in mind also that in rural areas schedules are often designed with the working and/or school day in mind, meaning a frighteningly early start if you want to catch that day's one bus out of town, and occasionally no buses at all during school holidays. Even if there are plentiful buses, bear in mind that the journey will be long and full of stops and starts.

There isn't a national **bus company**, though there are a few that do operate services beyond their own immediate area (see above). **Bus terminals** can be anywhere in larger towns, though often they're sensibly placed next door to the railway station; wherever possible we've detailed their whereabouts in the text, but if you're not sure ask for directions to the *autostazione*. In smaller towns and villages, most buses pull in at the central piazza. **Timetables** are worth picking up if you can find one, from the local company's office, bus stations or on the bus. You buy **tickets** on the bus, though on longer hauls you can try and buy them in advance direct from the bus company; seat reservations are, however, not possible. On most routes it's usually possible to flag a bus down if you want a ride: the convention, when it stops, is to get on at the back, off at the front. If you want to get off, ask *posso scéndere?*; the next stop is *la próssima fermata*.

City buses are always cheap, usually a L600–800 flat fare. Invariably you need a ticket *before* getting on. Buy them in *tabacchi* or from the kiosks at bus terminals and stops, and cancel in the machine at the back of the bus. The whole thing works on a basis of trust, though in most cities checks are regularly made, and hefty spot-fines issued to offenders.

CARS, HITCHING AND CYCLING

Travelling **by car** in Italy is relatively painless. The roads are good, the motorway, or *autostrada*, network very comprehensive, and the notorious Italian drivers rather less erratic than their reputation suggests – though their regard for the rules of the road is sometimes lax to say the least. Basically, avoid driving in cities as much as possible, which the congestion and lack of concern for other drivers can make a nightmare.

Most motorways are toll-roads. Take a ticket as you come on and pay on exit; the amount due flashed up on a screen in front of you. Rates aren't especially high but they can mount up on a long journey: as a general reference, you'll pay around L13,500 for a medium-sized car from Milan to Bologna.

As for **documentation**, if you're bringing your own car you need a valid driving licence *plus* an Italian translation (available from the state tourist office, see *Information and Maps*, above), and an international green card of insurance. It's compulsory to carry your car documents and passport while you're driving, and you may be required to present them if stopped by the police – not an uncommon occurrence. **Rules of the road** are straightforward: drive on the right; at junctions, where there's any ambiguity, give precedence to vehicles coming from the right; observe the speed limits (50kph in built up areas, 110kph on country roads and on motorways during the week, 130kph on motorways at weekends); and *don't* drink and drive.

If you **break down**, dial ☎116 at the nearest phone and tell the operator where you are, the type of car and your registration number: the nearest office of the *Automobile Club d'Italia* (*ACI*), the Italian AA/RAC equivalent, will be informed and they'll send someone out to fix your car – though it's not a free service, and could work out very expensive if you need a tow. For peace of mind, you might prefer to join the *ACI* outright, and so qualify for their discounted repairs scheme. Write to *ACI*, via Marsala 8, 00185 Rome. Any *ACI* office in Italy can tell you where to get **spare parts** for your particular car: see the city *Listings* sections for details of local addresses.

Car hire in Italy is pricey, currently around £180 per week for a *Ford Fiesta* with unlimited mileage. All the major firms are represented, and addresses are detailed in the city *Listings*

sections, though you might find Italian and locally-based firms cheaper than the multinationals. You can book with two Italian firms, *Maggiore* and *Italy by Car*, through agents in Britain: *Transhire*, Silver House, 31–35 Beak Street, London W1 (☎01-437 0951), *Quo Vadis*, 243 Euston Rd, London NW1 (☎01-387 6122), or *Pilgrim Air*, 227 Shepherds Bush Rd, London W6 (☎01-748 1333). You can also arrange it in conjunction with your flight or holiday, something which can make things cheaper – see *Getting There*.

At about L1500 a litre, Italy is also one of the most expensive countries in Europe in which to buy **petrol**, though if you take your own car you're entitled to **petrol coupons** worth 15 percent off and concessions on the motorway tolls; information from the Italian State Tourist Office.

Never leave anything visible in the car when you leave it, including the radio. If you're taking your own vehicle, consider installing a detachable car-radio, and always depress your aerial or else you might find it snapped off. Most cities and ports have **garages** where you can leave your car, a safe enough option which costs from around L4000 a day. At least your car is unlikely to be stolen if it's got a right-hand drive and a foreign number-plate: they're too conspicuous to be of much use to thieves.

Hitchhiking (*autostop*) is average to good in Italy, though less practised in the south of the country. Getting around exclusively by hitching would be a chore, but for the odd short hop along a quiet country road, and long hauls between major cities, it's a feasible alternative. Remember that it's illegal to hitch on motorways – to do so would be to risk a spot-fine; stand on a slip-road or at one of the service stations. Bear in mind also that women should be wary of hitching alone, particularly in the South, where male machismo predominates: pairs are best and always ask where the car is headed (*Dovè diretto?*) before you commit yourself. If you want to get out, say *Mi fa scéndere?*.

Cycling isn't a particularly popular pastime in Italy, and some parts of the country aren't especially well suited to it. The plains of the north are perfect for cycling, but down south and in the central and far northern mountains you need a decent machine and plenty of stamina: a mountain-bike would be good bet, though you can expect to be a real curiosity in some rural places. On the islands and in major resorts and in the larger cities it's usually possible to **hire** a bike, but generally facilities for this are few and far between and you may well be better off bringing your own.

An alternative is to tour by **motorbike** though again there are few places to hire one. **Mopeds** and **scooters**, on the other hand, are relatively easy to find: everyone in Italy, from kids to grandmas, rides one of these, and although they're not really built for any kind of long-distance travel, for shooting around towns and islands they're ideal. We've detailed outlets in the text, but roughly speaking you should expect to pay around L50,000 a day for a machine. Crash helmets are compulsory these days, though in the south at least it's a law which seems to be largely ignored.

However you get around on the roads, bear in mind that the **traffic** can be appalling – every Italian seems to have at least two cars – and although Italians aren't the world's worst drivers they don't win any safety prizes either. The secret really is to make it very clear what you're going to do, using your horn as much as possible, and then do it with great determination. Just walking around, too, don't assume that as a pedestrian you're safe, and *never* step off the pavement without looking first: Italian drivers aren't keen on stopping when they can simply swerve, and even on pedestrian crossings you can undergo some close calls. Again, the answer is to be bold, and stride straight out with great determination.

PLANES

ATI, the domestic arm of *Alitalia*, operate **flights** all over Italy, connecting all the major cities and islands. Really, though, it's only advisable to take a plane within Italy if you want to cover a large

distance quickly: prices are quite high, pricier than even the most expensive express train, and the larger cities are all linked by fast rail night-services with sleeping cars (see above). But if you need to take a plane, it's worth knowing that passengers between 12 and 25 qualify for a 25 percent discount on normal fares, as do students – though the former must produce proof of their age (a passport should do) and the latter a note from the college stating they're in full-time education. There are also reductions of up to 50 percent for families travelling together, and sometimes 30 percent if you travel at night; *Alitalia* have full details. Sample fares are Venice–Naples L156,000, Naples–Palermo L105,000.

FERRIES AND HYDROFOILS

Operated by a number of different private companies, Italy has a well-developed network of **ferries** and **hydrofoils**. Large car ferries connect the major islands of Sardinia and Sicily with the mainland ports of Genova, Civitavecchia, Naples, and the smaller island groupings – the Tremiti islands, the Bay of Naples islands, the Pontine islands, for example – are usually linked a variety of nearby mainland towns. There are also plentiful international links with Yugoslavia, Malta, Corsica, Spain, Tunisia, Egypt and Israel. Fares are reasonable, though on some of the more popular serices – to Sardinia, certainly – you should book up well in advance in summer, especially if you're taking a vehicle across. Bear in mind also that frequencies are drastically reduced outside the summer months, while some services may stop altogether. You'll find a broad guide to journey times and frequencies in the "Travel Details" section at the end of each chapter; for full up-to-date schedules, and prices, contact the local tourist office or one of the addresses below.

MAJOR FERRY COMPANIES: AGENTS AND ADDRESSES

Aliscafi Snav, Via Carraciolo 13, Naples (☎081/684.288). Hydrofoils to destinations around the Bay of Naples.

Caremar, Molo Beverello, Piazza Municipio, Naples (☎081/5551.5384). Ferries to destinations around the Bay of Naples.

Navarma, c/o Serena Holidays, 40–42 Kenway Rd, London SW5 (☎01-373 6548/9). Ferries to Elba.

Siremar, Via F. Crispi 120, Palermo (☎091/582.688). Ferries to islands off Sicily and Naples.

Tirrenia, c/o Serena Holidays, 40–42 Kenway Rd, London SW5 (☎01-373 6548/9). Ferries to Sardinia, Sicily, Corsica, Malta, Tunisia.

SLEEPING

Accommodation in Italy is strictly regulated, and while never especially cheap, is at least fairly reliable: hotels are star-rated and required to post their prices clearly in each room. Most tourist offices have details of hotel rates in their town or region, and you can usually expect them to be broadly accurate. If they're not, demand to know why, and don't hesitate to report discrepancies to the EPT/AAST. Whatever happens, establish the *full* price of your room *before* you accept it. In the major cities – Venice, Rome, Florence especially – booking ahead is often a good idea, particularly during July or August. We've given phone numbers throughout the guide for this. The phrases at the end of the book should help you get over the language barrier, but in many places you should be able to find someone who speaks at least some English.

HOTELS

The cheapest type of hotel accommodation is a *locanda* – a basic but usually clean guesthouse costing between L15,000 and L25,000 a night for a double room, without bath/shower. These are rare in the north of the country and in the larger cities, but are reasonably plentiful in the south,

> Please note: All **hotel prices** in the guide are for the cheapest double room, without private bath, during summer, unless otherwise stated.

especially outside the main tourist areas. Ordinary hotels, either known as *alberghi* or *pensioni* (there's no real difference between the two), come more expensive, rated on a system of one to five stars, and starting on average at about L25,000 per night for a double room without private bath. Prices, as ever, vary greatly between the poor south and the wealthy north: in Florence, for example, it's difficult to find anything for much under L35,000; Palermo, on the other hand, has hotels with rooms for under L20,000. Two-star hotels cost upwards of L35–40,000 and facilities won't always be that much better; with three-star places you begin to notice a difference, though in them you'll be paying a minimum of L60,000.

In very busy places it's not unusual (as well as finding everywhere full) to have to stay for a minimum of three nights, and many proprietors will add the price of breakfast to your bill whether you want it or not; try to resist this – you can always eat more cheaply in a bar. You can cut costs slightly by cramming three into a double room, but on average most hotels will charge you an extra 35 percent for this. Note also that people travelling alone may often be clobbered for the price of a double room even when taking a single; check in the tourist office's listings for the officially quoted price. Again, whenever you feel you're being ripped off, don't be afraid to wave the official literature at the proprietor, or to mutter dire threats about the tourist authorities – it usually has some effect.

> One peculiar Italian institution is the *albergo diurno* or **day hotel**, which is not as sleazy as it sounds but in fact an establishment providing bathrooms, showers, cleaning services, hairdressers and the like for a fixed rate. You'll often find them at railway stations and they're usually open daily 6am–midnight. Useful for a fast clean-up if you're on the move.

YOUTH HOSTELS

There are **youth hostels** spread all over Italy, around 50 in all, though at an average of around L10,000 a night for a dormitory bed, they don't represent a massive saving on the cheapest double hotel room. That's especially true once you add on the bus fare you're likely to have to fork out to reach one. If you're travelling on your own, on the other hand, hostels can work out a lot cheaper, and many have facilities – cheap restaurants, kitchens, etc – that enable you to cut costs further. In a few cases, too – notably Castroreale in Sicily, and Verona and Montagnana in the Veneto – the hostels are beautifully located and far preferable to any hotel.

Virtually all of the Italian hostels are member of the official *International Youth Hostel Federation*, and strictly speaking you need to be a member of that organisation in order to use them. Many hostels however allow you to join on the spot, or simply charge you extra. In Britain the *YHA* head office is at 14 Southampton St, London WC2 (☎01-836 8542), and membership currently costs £4 if you're under 21, £7 otherwise. Whether or not you're a member, you'll need to book ahead in the summer months, most efficiently by contacting the hostels direct at least 15 days in advance. We've listed most of the hostels in the guide, or you can get a full list from the Italian youth hostels association's travel section, *Associazione Italiana Alberghi per la Gioventù*, Palazzo della Civiltà del Lavoro, Quadrato della Concordia, 00144 EUR Roma (☎06/462.342; fax ☎474.1256).

In some cities – Rome is one – it's also possible to stay in **student accommodation** vacated by Italian students for the summer. This is usually confined to July and August, but accommodation is generally in individual rooms and can work out a lot cheaper than a straight hotel room. Again you'll need to book in advance: we've listed possible places in the text and you should contact them as far ahead as possible to be sure of a room.

CAMPING

Camping is not as popular in Italy as it is some European countries, but there are plenty of sites, and most of them are well-equipped. The snag is that they're expensive, and, once you've added the cost of a tent and vehicle, don't always work out a great deal cheaper than staying in a hotel or hostel. Local tourist offices have details of nearby sites, and prices range from L3000–5000 per person daily, plus L4000–7000 for each caravan or tent, plus around L4000 for each vehicle. If you're camping extensively it might be worth

investing in the *TCI*'s *Campeggi e Villaggi Turistiei*, available from *Robertson McCarta* (address on p.10), though this costs L25,000. If you don't need something this detailed, you can obtain an abridged version free of charge from *Centro Internazionale Prenotazioni, Federcampeggio*, Casella Postale 23, 50041 Calenzano, Florence (☎055/882.391). This is also the place to book places on campsites in advance.

VILLAS, *AGRITURISMO* AND *RIFUGI*

If you're not intending to travel around a lot it might be worth considering renting a **villa or farmhouse** for a week or two. These don't come cheap, but most are of a very high standard, and often enjoy marvellous locations. Reckon on paying around £300 a week for the average four-bedded Tuscan farmhouse, rather less in less popular regions such as Umbria or Marche. Tour operators with a selection of farmhouses and villas on their books include *Chapter Travel*, 102 St John's Wood Terrace, London NW8 (☎01-586 9451); *Villas Italia*, 227 Shepherds Bush Road, London W6 (☎01-740 9988); and *Cuendet* – a long-standing Tuscan specialist whose villas are bookable through *Chapter Travel*.

Agriturismo is a way of doing things more cheaply, not unlike the French *gîte* system, whereby farmers let out their unused buildings to tourists through a centralised booking agency. Under this system, which is as yet fairly undiscovered, it's possible to find places for as little as L4000 per person per night, though around L10,000 is more usual. For a full list of properties write to *Agriturist*, Corso V. Emanuele 101, Rome (☎06/651.2342).

Finally, if you're planning on hiking and climbing, there is the **rifugi** network, consisting of about 500 mountain huts, owned by the *Club Alpino Italia*, that non-members can stay in for around L11,000 a night; there are also private *rifugi* which charge around double this. Most are fairly spartan, with bunks in unheated dorms, but their sitings can be magnificent, and usually leave you well-placed to continue your hike next day. They are obliged to take you if you turn up on the offchance, but often it's better to book in advance, either through the local tourist office or the *Club Alpino Italia*, Via Foscolo 3, Milan (☎70202.3085) – who can also provide a full list of huts.

FOOD AND DRINK

Though it has long been popular primarily for its cheapness and convenience, Italian food is finally beginning to wrest some of the attention it deserves as one of the world's great cuisines. The Southern Italian diet especially, with its emphasis on fresh and plentiful fruit, vegetables and fish, is one of the healthiest in Europe, and there are few national cuisines that can boast so much variety in both ingredients and cooking methods. Wine, too, is becoming more respected, as the Italian industry's devotion to fizzy pop and characterless plonk is replaced by a new pride and a better product.

THE BASICS OF ITALIAN CUISINE

Though the twentieth century has done much to blur the **regional differences** of Italian food, they are still there – and often highly evident, the French influence strong in Piemonte, Austrian flavours in Alto Adige, even Greek in Calabria. Also, save for the Chinese restaurants which crop in every town, and the ubiquitous burger bar, Italy has remained largely untouched by the latter-day boom in non-indigenous eating, partly due to its lack of any substantial colonial legacy but also because of the innate chauvinism of Italian eating habits – a match for the French every time. Instead, the exotic option here is sampling cooking from other parts of the country. Milan tends to be the favourite melting-pot, with restaurants

specialising in food from all regions; Rome is the only city where there's any real choice of foreign food.

Because of the feeling that every Italian cherishes at heart, that Italian food is the best in the world and that mama's is always the perfect example, many restaurants are simply an extension of the home dining table. Adventure is not common on the menu. There has been some limited experimentation with new, "trendier" ingredients like wholewheat pasta and brown rice, but the best you'd get if you asked a waiter for any such thing would be a raised eyebrow; request a wholewheat pizza and you'd certainly be laughed out of sight. Vegetarian restaurants, too have been slow to catch on, the first ones appearing relatively recently, where else but in Milan.

Perhaps the most striking thing about eating in Italy is how deeply embedded in the culture it really is. Food is celebrated with gusto, and meals are traditional affairs of many courses, that can seem to last forever, starting with an antipasto, followed by a risotto or a pasta dish, leading on to a fish or meat course, cheese, and finished with fresh fruit and coffee. Even everyday meals are a miniaturised version of the fully-blown affair. Shopping for food is a serious matter. Supermarkets have yet to make any real impact on the dominance of the traditional store in town centres and foodstores of every description abound. Street markets, too, can be exhilarating, selling bountiful, fresh and flavoursome produce. The Italians as yet haven't adopted the heavy cropping methods which result in completely tasteless produce. Even a simple raw tomato can be a revelation.

Foods like bread and cheese are still made with an eye on quality rather than mass production; bread is almost entirely still made by small bakeries and white sliced is rare. Bread tends to get heavier, crustier and more salty the further south you go (for eating with salty hams, salami and cheeses there is "pane senza sale"). Cheese *is* often factory-produced, large firms like the Milan-based *Galbani* marketing common varieties like *Bel Paese*, *Gorgonzola* and *Taleggio*. But cheese making also remains in the hands of local farmers working to traditional recipes: local tastes are much in evidence.

BREAKFAST, SNACKS AND ICE CREAM

Most Italians start their day in a bar, their **breakfast** consisting of a coffee with hot milk, a *cappuccino*, and the ubiquitous *cornetto* – a jam, custard or chocolate-filled croissant, which you usually help yourself to from the counter; unfilled croissants are hard to find. Breakfast in a hotel (*prima colazione*) will be a limp affair, usually worth avoiding.

At other times of the day, **sandwiches** (*panini*) can be pretty substantial, a bread stick or roll packed with any number of fillings. There are sandwich bars in larger towns and cities (*panino-*

teche), and in smaller places grocer's shops (*alimentari*) will normally make you up whatever you want; you'll pay L1500–L3000 each. Bars may also offer *tramezzini*, ready-made sliced white bread with mixed fillings – less appetising than the average *panino* but still tasty, and slightly cheaper at around L1000 a time. Toasted sandwiches (*toste*) are common too: in a *paninoteca* you can get whatever you want toasted; in ordinary bars it's more likely to be a variation on cheese or ham with tomato.

If you want hot takeaway food there are a number of options. It's possible to find slices of pizza (*pizza rustica*) pretty much everywhere (buy

REGIONAL CUISINE

Piemonte

Piemontese cooking gives away the region's close links with France with dishes like *fonduta* (fondue) and its preference for using butter and cream in cooking. As in most of the North, olive oil and tomatoes are relatively uncommon, though immigrants from the south to towns like Turin have brought their cooking with them. Piemonte is perhaps most famous for its truffles, the most exquisite of which come from around the town of Alba – and are ferociously expensive. Their most usual use is a few thin slices to top a dish of pasta or a risotto.

Liguria

Liguria belongs geographically to the North, but its benign Mediterranean climate belongs further south. Its capital Genova is synonymous with pesto, the sauce made from pine nuts, basil, olive oil, pecorino and parmesan. It is usually served with linguine or trenette (long, thin pasta), but can be found with gnocchi and even in soups. Genova's links with Sardinia have also led to the adoption of pecorino in all its strengths as Liguria's favourite cheese. Seafood can be very good – Liguria is all coastline – and the region produces some fine olive oils as well as abundant quantities of chick peas. The latter are often ground to flour and made into *farinata*, a sort of cross between a pizza and an omelette. *Focaccia* – flat bread – is common too, often flavoured with olives, sage or rosemary. Pastries are excellent – Genova is famous for its *pandolce* (sweet bread), laced with dried fruit and pine nuts.

Lombardy

The cooking of Lombardy varies even from town to town. Polenta and rice are widely eaten, but the Alpine foothills and lakes contrast sharply with the rural plains of the Po valley and the rich urban food of Milan. *Risotto alla Milanese* is perhaps Milan's most renowned culinary export, bright yellow from saffron. *Ossobucco* (shin of veal) is another Milanese favourite, as are *biscotti* – hand-made biscuits flavoured with nuts, vanilla and lemon and sold by weight at specialist shops all over the city. *Panettone*, the soft, eggy cake with sultanas, also originated here, though now it's available all over Italy. Stuffed pastas and veal are – as in Piemonte – also popular, and again wild fungi are to be found. Some dishes, like *pizzocheri* (buckwheat noodles from the Valtellina) can be peculiarly local. Lombardy is also perhaps Italy's largest cheese-making region. As well as *Gorgonzola* and *Bel Paese* there are numerous local cheeses – the parmesan-like *Grana Padano* and the smooth rich *Mascarpone* (used in sweet dishes) are the best-known.

Trentino-Alto Adige

Trentino-Alto Adige, as its name suggests, is really two regions: Alto Adige with its unreservedly Austrian traditions, and Trentino, which mixes mountain influences with more Italian flavours from the south. Polenta is common to both, but while dishes such as *gnocchi* (small dumplings made from potato, flour and sometimes spinach and ricotta) are found in Trentino, Alto Adige turns out the decidedly Germanic *speck* (smoked pork), *knodel* (dumplings), *sauerkraut* and all manner of sweet tarts and cakes, often flavoured with apples and plums.

it by the *etto* – 100g), and you can get most of the things already mentioned, plus pasta, chips, even full hot meals, in a **távola calda**, a sort of stand-up snack bar that's at its best in the morning when everything is fresh. Some are self-service and have limited seating too. The bigger towns have these, and there's often one inside larger railway stations. Another alternative is a **rosticceria**. Here the speciality is spit-roast chicken but *rosticcerie* often serve fast foods such as slices of pizza, chips and hamburgers.

Other sources of quick snacks are obviously **markets**, some of which sell takeaway food from stalls, including *focacce* – oven-baked pastries topped with cheese or tomato or filled with spinach, fried offal or meat – and *arancini* or *suppli*: deep-fried balls of rice with meat (*rosso*) or butter and cheese (*bianco*) filling. **Supermarkets**, also, are an obvious stop for a picnic lunch: the major departments store chains, *Upim* and *Standa*, often have food halls.

Italian **ice cream** (*gelato*) is justifiably famous: a cone (*un cono*) is an indispensable accessory to the evening *passegiata*. Most bars have a fairly good selection, but for real choice go to a **gelateria**, where the range is a tribute to the Italian imagination and flair for display. You'll sometimes have to go by appearance rather than

The Veneto/Friuli-Venezia Giulia

The Veneto vies with Lombardy for the crown of risotto making, while Venice specialises in fish and seafood, together with odd ingredients like pomegranates, pine nuts and raisins, harking back to its days as a port and merchant city. The risottos tend to be more liquid than those to the west, usually with a seafood base although peas (*bisi* in dialect) are also common, as are other seasonal vegetables – spinach, asparagus, pumpkin. The red salad leaf raddichio also has its home in the Veneto, as does the renowned Italian dessert, *tiramisu*. Polenta is eaten too, but is more common in neighbouring Friuli-Venezia-Giulia, the poorest of the northern regions, with a dialect that's almost a language of its own and culinary influences from both Austria and Yugoslavia. Pork in all forms features strongly, together with heavy soups of beans, rice and root vegetables. *Gnocchi* are also served in an unusual sweet-sour sauce.

Emilia-Romagna

Emilia-Romagna has a just reputation for harbouring the richest, most lavish food in Italy, its most famous specialities – parmesan cheese, egg pasta, parma ham and wine vinegar – quintessentially Italian in their appeal. Bologna is regarded as the gastronomic capital of Italy, and Emilia is the only true home of pasta in the North, in the form of *lasagne*, *tortellini* stuffed with ricotta cheese and spinach, pumpkin or pork, and other fresh pastas served with *ragù* (meat sauce), cream sauces or simply with butter and parmesan. Modena and Parma specialise in *bollito misto* – boiled meats; *alla parmigiana* usually denotes something cooked with parmesan. Romagna's cuisine owes more to the South. While ingredients such as butter, cheese, mushrooms, chestnuts and meat feature in Emilia, Romagna tends more to onions, garlic, olive oil and fish.

Tuscany

Tuscan cooking has been a seminal influence in Italian cuisine generally. It emphasises simplicity: meat is kept plain, often grilled, and Florentines will often profess to liking nothing better than a good *bistecca alla fiorentina* – rare grilled steak. Beans of all types are popular, white cannellini beans and chick peas most of all. They turn up in salads, with pasta (*tuoni e lampo*) or just dressed with olive oil. Chick peas can also be found in *torta di ceci*, similar to the *farinata* found in Liguria. Spinach is the essential Tuscan vegetable, often married with ricotta to make gnocchi, used as a pasta filling, and in *crespoline* (pancakes) or between two chunks of *focaccia* and eaten as a street or bar snack. *Alla fiorentina* can often mean with spinach and cheese, but don't bank on it. Soups are very popular, ranging from simple vegetable broths to thick bean *minestre*. And the region is home to Italy's most delicate olive oils. Siena is best known for its sweets – things like almond macaroons and *panforte di Siena*, a rich fruit bread.

Abruzzo/Molise

Pasta in Abruzzo often comes as the curious *maccheroni alla chitarra*, long strings cut by pressing the dough over a wired frame; typically it's eaten with a tomato and pecorino or a lamb sauce. Abruzzo food tends to be characterised by hot, strong flavours – *spaghetti aglio, olio e peperoncini* (with oil, garlic, chili) is a favourite. Hot peppers bring their fire to all sorts of dishes. Cheeses are the ubiquitous pecorino and *scamorza*, a spun cheese similar to mozzarella, and often smoked.

attempting to decipher their exotic names, many of which don't even mean much to Italians: often the basics – chocolate, strawberry, chocolate – are best. There's no problem locating the finest *gelateria* in town – it's the one that draws the crowds, and we've noted the really special places in the text.

PIZZA

Pizza is now a worldwide phenomenon, but Italy remains the best place to eat it. The creations served up here – especially in the city where pizza started, Naples – are wholly different from the soggy concoctions that have taken over the UK fast-food market. Everywhere in Italy pizza comes thin and flat, not deep-pan, and the choice of toppings is fairly limited – none of the pineapple and sweetcorn variations that have taken off in Britain and America. It's also easier, especially in the south of the country, to find pizzas cooked in the traditional way, in wood-fired ovens (*forno a legna*), rather than the squeaky-clean electric ones, so that the pizzas arrive blasted and bubbling on the surface, and with a distinctive charcoal taste.

Pizzerias range from a stand-up counter selling slices (*pizza rustica* – see above) to a fully-fledged sit-down restaurant, and on the whole they don't sell much else besides pizza, soft drinks and beer. Some straight restaurants often have pizza on the menu too. A basic cheese and tomato pizza (a *margherita*) costs around L2000–3000 (sometimes less in the south, often more in the north), a fancier variety L4000–5000, and it's quite acceptable to cut it into slices and eat it with your fingers. Check the food glossary for the different kinds of pizza.

Lazio

Lazio means only one thing – Rome. And Roman cooking, like Tuscan, is essentially simple: pasta (cut shapes like *bucatini* and *penne* are favourites), served with sauces like *all'amatriciana* (cured pork and tomato), *alla carbonara* (egg and bacon), *all'arrabbiate* (hot pepper and tomato). *Fettuccine* and *gnocchi alla romana* (made with semolina and baked with tomato sauce) are also very common, not to mention all kinds of offal. *Saltimbocca*, the favourite antipasto, is veal fried with raw ham; *zampetti* are calves' trotters. Two of the most popular sauces are not used for pasta but with vegetables – *all'agro* (olive oil and lemon juice or vinegar) and *agrodolce* (sweet-sour). Pasta itself is often topped with *pecorino romano*, a hard, salty cheese with a hot, raucous flavour. Other cheeses are sheep's milk ricotta and provatura. The most common vegetables are artichokes, aubergines, courgettes and salads like *misticanza* (wild salad leaves). Rome is also one of the best places outside Naples to eat *pizza rustica*, baked on traditionally wood fires and often topped with just one embellishment – tomato, pepper, courgette, mushroom, even potato.

Umbria/Marche

Landlocked, hilly Umbria is the only area outside Piemonte where truffles are abundant, and they find their way onto eggs, pasta, fish and meat. Pork, mushrooms, game and birds are all important in Umbrian food – pork made into hams, sausage and salami, and most famously into *la porchetta*, whole suckling pig stuffed with rosemary or sage, roasted on a spit and any vegetarian's nightmare. Perugia is renowned for its pastries and chocolates. Marche is very much a rural region, its food a mixture of seafood from the long coastline and country cooking form its interior, based on locally-grown produce – tomatoes, fennel, mushrooms. Like Umbria, truffles feature, and porchetta is stuffed with garlic and fennel.

Campania

The flavour of Naples dominates the whole of Campania. Nowhere in Italy is street-food so much part of the culture. Naples is the home of the true pizza, rapidly baked in searing hot wood-fired brick ovens and running with olive oil. Pizza Napolitana simply doesn't exist: in Naples *every* pizza is Neapolitan, and the crucial one is the *marinara*, not, as you might think, anything to do with seafood but topped with just tomato, garlic and a leaf or two of basil. Street food also comprises fried pizzas topped with a smear of tomato and a square of mozzarella; calzone – a stuffed fried pizza with ham or cheese or vegetables. *Friggitorie* sell other fried food – heavenly *krocche* (potato croquettes), *arancini* and *fiorilli* – courgette flowers in batter. Naples is also the home of pasta and tomato sauce, made with fresh tomatoes and laced with garlic. It's a curious aspect of Neapolitan sauces that garlic, onion and parmesan are rarely combined. Aubergines and courgettes turn up endlessly in pasta sauces, as does the tomato-mozzarella pairing, the latter particularly good with gnocchi (the regions to the north and of Naples are both big mozarella-

MEALS: LUNCH AND DINNER

Full **meals** are often elaborate affairs, generally served in either a **trattoria** or a **ristorante**. Traditionally, a trattoria is a cheaper and more basic purveyor of homestyle cooking (*cucina casalinga*), while a ristorante is more upmarket, with aproned waiters and tablecloths, though these days there's a fine line between the two. The main differences you'll notice now are to do with opening times: often trattorias, at least in rural areas, will be open lunchtime – there won't be a menu and the waiter will simply reel off a list of what's on that day. In large towns both will be open in the evening, but there'll be more choice in a ristorante, which will always have a menu and sometimes a help-yourself antipasto buffet. In either, pasta dishes go for around L3000–5000, and there's never any problem just having this;

the main fish or meat courses will normally be anything between L8000 and L12000. Bear in mind that almost everywhere you'll pay a cover charge on top of your food – the *pane e coperto* – of around L1500 a head.

Other types of eatery include places, common in tourist resorts, that bill themselves as everything – trattoria-ristorante-pizzeria – and perform no function very well, serving mediocre food that you could get much cheaper elsewhere. Look out also for spaghetterias, restaurant-bars which serve basic pasta dishes and are often the hangout of the local youth. Osterias are common too, basically an old-fashioned restaurant specialising in home cooking, though be careful of places that label themselves as "hosterias" – an affectation on a par with the English "Ye Olde".

Traditionally, a meal (lunch is *pranzo*, dinner is *cena*) starts with **antipasto** (literally "before the

producing areas). Seafood in Naples is also particularly good. Here, they love squid, octopus and mussels – clams join up with garlic and oil for *spaghetti alla vongole*, mussels are prepared as *zuppa di cozze*. Pastries are exceptionally good, too. Absolutely not to be missed is the *sfogliatella*, a flaky pastry case stuffed with ricotta and candied peel, and the Easter cake, *pastiera*, made with ricotta and wheat berries.

Calabria and Basilicata

The food of Calabria is similar to that of Campania but tends to have a rougher approach. Greek influence still pervades in the form of aubergines, swordfish and sweets incorporating figs, almonds and honey; otherwise it's the common trademarks of the South – plenty of pasta, pork and cheeses such as mozzarella, caciocavallo, mature provolone and pecorino. Basilicata is another poor region, mountainous and sparsely populated and relying on pasta, tomatoes, bread, olives and pork. A fondness for spicy food shows in the popularity of all types of peppers, and, unusually in Italy, ginger (*zenzero*) – which is thrown into many dishes. Strong cheeses, like matured ricotta – to match the strength of other dishes – are favoured.

Puglia

Puglia is the land of the grape – and the wine lake. In recent years the region has exploited its hot, fertile plains to become the wealthiest part of the South and while much of its wine may be fairly basic, its olive oils are gaining much respect. Its cooking, particularly in coastal areas, has a lingering Arab-Greek feel, though bread, pasta and seafood tend to be the staples. Puglians are fond of preserved vegetables: tomatoes are sun dried and salted or boiled and bottles; mushrooms, artichokes and aubergines are submerged in oil – *sott'olio*. Hams and pork sausage feature prominently, but in the coastal areas – Bari, Taranto, Brindisi – seafood dominates, shellfish often eaten raw. Pasta in Puglia is usually *orechiette*, or "little ears".

Sicily

Sicily's food has been tinkered with by the island's endless list of invaders, from Greeks, Arabs, Normans and Spanish, even the English. Sicily is famous for its sweets, like the rich *cassata* ice cream dish, and *cannoli* – fried pastries stuffed with sweet ricotta and rolled in chocolate. Dishes like orange salads evoke North Africa; couscous is a more obvious pointer. Just as in Naples, street food is all over, things like rice balls, potato croquettes, fritters and dinky-sized pizzas made to be clutched in a hand. Rice, brought by the Arabs, is more often found here than in the rest of Italy. Naturally, fish like anchovies, sardines, tuna and swordfish are abundant, teamed often with the ever-popular pasta in dishes like *spaghetti con le sarde*. Cheeses are pecorino, provola, caciocavallo and, of course, the sheep's milk ricotta which goes into so many of the sweet dishes.

meal"), a course generally served only in ristoranti and consisting of various cold cuts of meat, seafood and various cold vegetable dishes. *Prosciutto* is a common antipasto dish, ham either cooked (*cotto*) or just cured and hung (*crudo*) and served alone or with mozarella cheese. A plateful of various antipasti from a self-service buffet will set you back around L5000, a item chosen from the menu a couple of thousand less. Bear in mind that if you're moving onto pasta, let alone a main course, you may need quite an appetite to tackle this. The next course, **il primo** consists of a soup or pasta dish, and it's fine to just eat this and nothing else. This is followed by **il secondo** – the meat or fish course, usually served alone, except for perhaps a wedge of lemon or tomato. Watch out when ordering fish, which will either be served whole or by weight: 250g is usually plenty for one person, or ask to have a look at the fish before it's cooked.

Vegetables or salads – **il contorno** – are ordered and served separately, and often there won't be much (if any) choice: potatoes will invariably be chips, salads either green (*verde*) or mixed (*mista*). If there's no menu, the verbal list of what's available can be bewildering; if you don't understand, just ask for what you want. Everywhere will have pasta with tomato sauce (*pomodoro*) or meat sauce (*al ragù*). Afterwards you nearly always get a choice of fresh fruit (*frutta*) and a selection of desserts (*dolci*) – sometimes just ice cream, but often more elaborate items, like, in Sicily, *cassata* – ice cream made with ricotta, *zuppa inglese* – spongecake or trifle, or fresh fruit salad (*macedonia*). The favourite way to finish an Italian meal in Britain, *zabaglione*, is sadly rarely available at any but the most upmarket places.

Italy isn't a bad country to travel in if you're a **vegetarian**. There are several pasta sauces and pizza varieties without meat, and if you eat fish and seafood you should have no problem at all. Salads, too, are fresh and good, and filling. The only real problem is one of comprehension: Italians don't *understand* someone not eating meat, and stating the obvious doesn't always get the point across. Saying you're a vegetarian (*Sono vegetariano/a*) and asking if a dish has meat in (*c'è carne dentro?*), might still turn up a poultry or *prosciutto* dish. Better is to ask what a dish is made with before you order (*com'è fatto?*), so that you can spot the non-meaty meat. Being a

vegan you'll have a much harder time, though pizzas without cheese are a good standby, vegetable soup is usually just that and the fruit is excellent.

At the **end of the meal** ask for the bill (*il conto*). In many trattorias this doesn't amount to much more than an illegible scrap of paper, and if you want to be sure you're not being ripped off, ask to have a receipt (*ricevuta*), something all bars and restaurants are legally bound to provide anyway. As well as the cover charge, service (*servizio*) will often be added, generally about 10 percent. If service isn't included you should perhaps tip about the same amount, though trattorias outside the large cities won't necessarily expect this.

DRINKING: WHERE AND HOW TO DO IT

Although many Italian children are brought up on wine, there's not the same emphasis on dedicated drinking as there is in Britain. You'll rarely see drunks in public, young people don't devote their nights to getting wasted, and women especially are frowned upon if they're seen to be over-indulging. Nonetheless there's a wide choice of alcoholic drinks available, often at low prices; soft drinks come in multifarious hues, thanks to the abundance of fresh fruit; and there's also mineral water and crushed-ice drinks: you'll certainly never be stuck if you want to slake your thirst.

Where to drink

Bars are less social centres than functional places, and are all very similar to each other – brightly-lit places, with a chrome counter, a *gaggia* coffee machine and a picture of the local football team on the wall. You'll come here for **ordinary drinking**: a coffee in the morning, a quick beer, a cup of tea, but people don't generally idle away the day or evening in bars. Indeed in some, more rural places it's difficult to find a bar open much after 9pm. Where it does fit into the general Meditteranean pattern is that there are no set licensing hours and children are always allowed in; there's often a telephone and you can buy snacks and ice creams as well as drinks.

Whatever you're drinking, the **procedure** is the same. It's cheapest to drink standing at the counter (there's often nowwhere to sit anyway), in which case you pay first at the cash desk (*la* *cassa*), present your receipt (*scontrino*) to the barperson and give your order. If you don't know how much a drink costs, there's always a list of prices (*listino prezzi*) behind the bar. It's customary to leave an extra L50 or L100 on the counter for the barperson, though no one will object if you don't. If there's waiter service, just sit where you like, though bear in mind that to do this will cost perhaps twice as much, especially if you sit outside (the difference is shown on the price list as *tavola*).

Coffee, tea, soft drinks

One of the most distinctive smells in an Italian street is that of fresh **coffee**, usually wafting out of a bar (most trattorias and pizzerias don't serve hot drinks). It's always excellent: the basic choice is either small and black (*espresso*, or just *caffé*), or white and frothy (*cappuccino*), but there are other varieties. If you want your *espresso* watered down ask for a *caffé lungo*; with a shot of alcohol – and you can ask for just about anything in your coffee – is *caffé corretto*; with a drop of milk is *caffé macchiato*. Although most places let you help yourself, some will lace your black coffee with sugar; if you don't want it, you can make sure by asking for *caffé senza zucchero* – though the barperson will think you're mad. Many places also now sell decaffeinated coffee (ask for *Hag*, even when it isn't); while in summer you'll probably want to have your coffee cold (*caffé freddo*). For a real treat ask for *caffé granita*, cold coffee with crushed ice, usually topped with cream.

If you don't like coffee, there's always **tea**. In summer you can drink this cold too (*te freddo*) – excellent for taking the heat off. Hot tea (*te caldo*) comes with lemon (*con limone*) unless you ask for milk (*con latte*). **Milk** itself is drunk hot as often as cold, or you can get it with a dash of coffee (*latte macchiato*) and sometimes as milk shakes – *frappe*.

Alternatively, there are various **soft drinks** (*analcoliche*) to choose from. A *spremuta* is a fresh fruit juice, squeezed at the bar, usually orange, lemon or grapefruit. You might need to add sugar to the lemon juice (. . . *di limone*) but the orange (. . . *di limone*) is invariably sweet enough on its own, especially the crimson-red variety, made from blood oranges. There's also crushed-ice *granitas*, big in Sicily and coming in several flavours other than coffee. Otherwise there's the usual range of fizzy drinks and concen-

trated juices: *Coke* is as prevalent as it is everywhere; the homegrown Italian version, *Chinotto*, is less sweet – good with a slice of lemon. **Tap water** (*acqua normale*) is quite drinkable, and you won't pay for it in a bar. **Mineral water** (*acqua minerale*) is a more common choice, either still (*senza gas* or *naturale*) or sparkling (*con gas* or *frizzante*) – about L500 a glass.

Beer and spirits

Beer (*birra*) is always a lager-type brew which usually comes in one-third (*piccolo*) or two-third (*grande*) litre bottles. Commonest and cheapest are the Italian brands, *Peroni* and *Dreher*, both of which are very drinkable; if this is what you want, either state the brand name or ask for *birra nazionale* – otherwise you may be given the more expensive imported beer. In most bars you have a choice of this or draught beer (*alla spina*), measure for measure more expensive than the bottled variety. You may also come across darker beers (*birra nera* or *birra rossa*), which have a sweeter, maltier taste and in appearance resemble stout or bitter.

All the usual **spirits** are on sale and known mostly by their generic names. There are also Italian brands of the main varieties: the best Italian brandies are *Stock* and *Vecchia Romagna*. A generous shot of these costs about L1200, much more for imported stuff. The homegrown Italian firewater is **Grappa**, originally from Bassano di Grappa in the Veneto but now available just about everywhere. It's made from the leftovers from the winemaking process (skins, stalks and the like) and is something of an acquired taste; should you acquire it, it's probably the cheapest way of getting plastered there is.

You'll also find **fortified wines** like *Martini, Cinzano* and *Campari*; ask for a Campari-Soda and you'll get a ready-mixed version from a little bottle; a slice of lemon is a *spicchio di limone*, ice is *ghiaccio*. You might also try *Cynar* – believe it or not, an artichoke-based sherry often drunk as an aperitif. There's also a daunting selection of **liqueurs**. *Amaro* is a bitter after-dinner drink, *Amaretto* much sweeter with a strong taste of marzipan, *Sambuca* a sticky-sweet aniseed concoction, traditionally served with a coffee bean in it and set on fire (though only tourists are likely to experience this these days). *Strega* is another drink you'll see behind every bar – the yellow stuff in tall, elongated bottles: about as sweet as it looks but not unpleasant.

A LIST OF FOODS AND DISHES

Basics and snacks

Aceto	Vinegar	Grissini	Bread sticks	Patatine fritte	Chips
Aglio	Garlic	Maionese	Mayonnaise	Pepe	Pepper
Biscotti	Biscuits	Mermellata	Jam	Pizzetta	Small cheese and
Burro	Butter	Olio	Oil		tomato pizza
Caramelle	Sweets	Olive	Olives	Riso	Rice
Cioccolato	Chocolate	Pane	Bread	Sale	Salt
Focaccia	Oven-baked snack	Pane integrale	Wholemeal bread	Uova	Eggs
Formaggio	Cheese	Panino	Bread roll/	Yogurt	Yoghurt
Frittata	Omelette		sandwich	Zúcchero	Sugar
Gelato	Icecream	Patatine	Crisps	Zuppa	Soup

Pizzas

Calzone	Folded pizza with cheese, ham and tomato.	Margherita	Cheese and tomato.
		Marinara	Tomato.
Capricciosa	Literally "capricious"; topped with whatever they've got in the kitchen, usually including baby artichoke, ham and egg.	Napoli/ Napolitana	Tomato, anchovy and olive oil.
		Quattro formaggi	"Four cheeses", usually including mozzarella, fontina and gruyère.
Cardinale	Ham and olives.		
Funghi	Mushroom; tinned, sliced button mushrooms unless it specifies fresh mushrooms, funghi freschi.	Quattro stagioni	"Four seasons"; the toppings split into four separate sections, usually including ham, green pepper, onion, egg, etc.
Frutta di mare	Seafood; usually mussels, prawns, squid and clams.		

Antipasti and starters

Antipasto misto	Mixed cold meats and cheese.	Melanzane in parmigiana	Aubergine in tomato and parmesan cheese.
Caponata	Mixed aubergine, olives, tomatoes.	Peperonata	Green and red peppers stewed in olive oil.
Caprese	Tomato and mozzarella cheese salad.	Pomodori ripieni	Stuffed tomatoes.
Insalata di mare	Seafood salad.		
Insalata di riso	Rice salad.	Prosciutto	Ham.
Insalata russa	Russian salad; diced vegetables in mayonnaise.	Salame	Salami.

The first course (Il primo): soups, pasta . . .

Brodo	Clear broth.	Pastina in brodo	Pasta pieces in clear broth.
Cannelloni	Large tubes of pasta, stuffed.	Penne	Smaller version of rigatoni.
Farfalle	Literally "butterfly"-shaped pasta.	Ravioli	Ravioli.
		Rigatoni	Large, grooved tubular pasta.
Fettucine	Narrow pasta ribbons.	Risotto	Cooked rice dish, with sauce.
Gnocchi	Small potato and dough dumplings.	Spaghetti	Spaghetti.
		Spaghettini	Thin spaghetti.
Lasagne	Lasagne.	Stracciatella	Broth with egg.
Maccheroni	Tubular spaghetti.	Tagliatelle	Pasta ribbons, another word for fettucine.
Minestrina	Any light soup.		
Minestrone	Thick vegetable soup.	Tortellini	Small rings of pasta, stuffed with meat or cheese.
Pasta al forno	Pasta baked with minced meat, eggs, tomato and cheese.	Vermicelli	Very thin spaghetti ("little worms").
Pasta fagioli	Pasta soup with beans.		

... and pasta sauce (salsa)

Arrabiata	Spicy tomato sauce, with chillies.	*Parmigiano*	Parmesan cheese.
Bolognese	Meat sauce.	*Peperoncino*	Olive oil, garlic and fresh chillies.
Burro	Butter.	*Pesto*	Green basil and garlic sauce.
Carbonara	Cream, ham and beaten egg.	*Pomodoro*	Tomato sauce.
Funghi	Mushroom.	*Ragù*	Meat sauce.
Matriciana	Cubed pork and tomato sauce.	*Vóngole*	Clam and tomato sauce.
Panna	Cream.		

The second course (Il secondo): meat (carne) ...

Agnello	Lamb	*Involtini*	Meat slices, rolled and stuffed	*Pollo*	Chicken
Bistecca	Steak			*Polpette*	Meatballs
Cervello	Brain	*Lingua*	Tongue	*Rognoni*	Kidneys
Cinghiale	Wild boar	*Maiale*	Pork	*Salsiccia*	Sausage
Coniglio	Rabbit	*Manzo*	Beef	*Saltimbocca*	Veal with ham
Costolette	Chops	*Mortadella*	Salami-type cured meat	*Spezzatino*	Stew
Cotolette	Cutlets			*Tacchino*	Turkey
Fegatini	Chicken livers	*Ossobuco*	Shin of veal	*Trippa*	Tripe
Fegato	Liver	*Pancetta*	Bacon	*Vitello*	Veal

... fish (pesce) and shellfish (crostacei)

Acciughe	Anchovies	*Gamberetti*	Shrimps	*Sgombro*	Mackerel
Anguilla	Eel	*Gámberi*	Prawns	*Sógliola*	Sole
Aragosta	Lobster	*Granchio*	Crab	*Tonno*	Tuna
Baccalà	Dried salted cod	*Merluzzo*	Cod	*Triglie*	Red mullet
Calamari	Squid	*Ostriche*	Oysters	*Trota*	Trout
Céfalo	Mullet	*Pescespada*	Swordfish	*Vóngole*	Clams
Cozze	Mussels	*Pólipo*	Octopus		
Dentice	Dentex	*Sarde*	Sardines		

Vegetables (contorni) and salad (insalata)

Asparagi	Asparagus	*Cetriolo*	Cucumber	*Orígano*	Oregano
Basílico	Basil	*Cipolla*	Onion	*Patate*	Potatoes
Bróccoli	Broccoli	*Fagioli*	Beans	*Peperoni*	Peppers
Cápperi	Capers	*Fagiolini*	Green beans	*Piselli*	Peas
Carciofi	Artichokes	*Finocchio*	Fennel	*Pomodori*	Tomatoes
Carciofini	Artichoke hearts	*Funghi*	Mushrooms	*Radicchio*	Chicory
Carotte	Carrots	*Insalata verde/ mista*	Green salad/ mixed salad	*Spinaci*	Spinach
Cavolfiori	Cauliflower			*Zucchini*	Courgettes
Cávolo	Cabbage	*Melanzane*	Aubergine		

Some terms and useful words

Affumicato	Smoked	*Al dente*	Firm, not overcooked	*Milanese*	Fried in egg and breadcrumbs
Arrosto	Roast				
Ben cotto	Well done	*Ferri*	Grilled without oil	*Pizzaiola*	Cooked with tomato sauce
Bollito/lesso	Boiled				
Brasato	Cooked in wine	*Fritto*	Fried	*Ripieno*	Stuffed
		Grattuggiato	Grated	*Sangue*	Rare
Cotto	Cooked (not raw)	*Alla griglia*	Grilled	*Allo spiedo*	On the spit
		Al Marsala	Cooked with Marsala wine	*Surgelati*	Frozen
Crudo	Raw			*Úmido*	Steamed/stewed

Sweets (dolci), fruit (frutta), cheeses (formaggi) and nuts (noce)

Amaretti	Macaroons	Gorgonzola	Soft blue-veined cheese	Pere	Pears
Ananas	Pineapple			Pesche	Peaches
Anguria/ Coccómero	Water melon	Limone	Lemon	Pignoli	Pine nuts
		Macedonia	Fruit salad	Pistacchio	Pistachio nut
Arance	Oranges	Mándorle	Almonds	Provolone	Hard strong cheese
Banane	Bananas	Mele	Apples	Ricotta	Soft white sheep's cheese
Cacchi	Persimmons	Melone	Melon		
Ciliegie	Cherries	Mozzarella	Bland soft white cheese used on pizzas	Torta	Cake, tart
Fichi	Figs			Uva	Grapes
Fichi d'India	Prickly pears			Zabaglione	Dessert made with eggs, sugar and marsala wine
Fontina	Northern Italian cooking cheese	Néspole	Medlars		
		Parmigiano	Parmesan cheese		
Frágole	Strawberries	Pecorino	Strong hard sheep's cheese	Zuppa Inglese	Trifle
Gelato	Icecream				

Drinks

Acqua minerale	Mineral water	Latte	Milk	Vino	Wine
Aranciata	Orangeade	Limonata	Lemonade	Rosso	Red
Bicchiere	Glass	Selz	Soda water	Bianco	White
Birra	Beer	Spremuta	Fresh fruit juice	Rosato	Rosé
Bottiglia	Bottle	Spumante	Sparkling wine	Secco	Dry
Caffè	Coffee	Succo	Concentrated fruit juice with sugar	Dolce	Sweet
Cioccolata calda	Hot chocolate			Litro	Litre
Ghiaccio	Ice	Tè	Tea	Mezzo	Half
Granita	Iced drink, with coffee or fruit	Tónico	Tonic water	Quarto	Quarter
				Salute!	Cheers!

ITALIAN WINE

Just as Italy's food has suffered from stereotyped images, so too has its **wine**. *Lambrusco* has soared to second place in the best-seller list in Britain, while cheapo *Soaves* and *Chianti* continue to shift units. All of which is a fair indication of the methods that until now have permeated the Italian wine industry – high yields, low prices, ship 'em out and never mind the quality.

The nice thing about travelling to Italy, though, is that the best wines are kept mostly for the home market. Nudged along by the DOC laws (see below), standards have been steadily increasing in recent years. Many producers have been turning their hands to making higher quality wines, and besides the finer tuning of established names such as *Barolo* and *Orvieto*, there's a good deal of experimentation going on everywhere. Southern winemakers are no longer content to see nearly all of their produce going north to beef up table-wine blends, while in Tuscany, Trentino-Alto Adige and Friuli, French grape varieties such as chardonnay, sauvignon and the pinots are joining old Italian favourites with startling success.

They don't waste drinking time in Italy with dialogue or veneration, however; neither is there much time for the snobbery associated with "serious" wine drinking in France or Britain. Light reds such as those made from the *dolcetto* grape are hauled out of the fridge in hot weather, while some full-bodied whites are drunk at near room temperature. Wine is invariably drunk with meals. It's also still very cheap, though unless your aim is to get legless as cheaply as possible, it's wise to avoid the very cheapest plonk. In restaurants you'll invariably be offered red (*rosso*) or white (*bianco*) – rarely *rose*. If you're unsure about what to order, don't be afraid to try the local stuff: sometimes served straight from the barrel, particularly down south, and often very good, and cheap at just L2000–3000 a litre. Bottled wine is pricier but still very good value; expect to pay around L8000 a bottle in a restaurant, less than half that from a shop or supermarket. One peculiarity is that bars don't tend to serve wine by the glass: where they do, it'll cost around L1000.

REGIONAL WINES

The North

Piemonte rivals Tuscany as producer of Italy's finest reds. Its big names are the names of tradition – *Barolo, Barbaresco, Barbera*. These wines need ageing, and *Barolo* in particular can be very expensive. More suitable for everyday drinking are wines made from the *dolcetto* grape, notably *Dolcetto d'Alba*; drunk young and lightly chilled. Probably the most famous is the sparkling *Asti Spumante* ("Spumante" is the Italian for wines made by the champagne method) – a sweet wine, though there has been a trend in recent years to make dry spumanti. In contrast to the traditional grapes and names of Piemonte, the three northeastern regions – **Trentino-Alto Adige**, **Veneto** and **Friuli-Venezia Giulia** – have been very successful at developing wines with French and German grape varieties. Merlot, cabernet, pinot bianco, pinot grigio, müller-thurgau, riesling, chardonnay and gewürztraminer from these regions are all likely to be good, and Alto Adige in particular produces excellent fresh, aromatic whites at reasonable prices.

Names more familiar to British supermarket shelves – *Bardolino, Valpolicella* and *Soave* – are all from the Verona region and like so many Italian wines always taste better near their region of origin. **Emilia-Romagna** is synonymous with *Lambrusco*, which you could easily be forgiven for taking to be a different wine altogether from stuff you buy in Britain. Buy only DOC *Lambrusco* – it's still ridiculously cheap – and amaze yourself. **Lombardy** and **Liguria** are not well known for their wines, which is a pity, because both produce some attractive brews. Milan supermarket shelves bulge with basic wines from the *Oltrepò Pavese*, and the northern areas of Valtellina and and around Brescia make good wines such as the red *Franciacorta* and the white *Cá del Bosco*, a sparkler. Liguria only really produces two wines, the crisp, dry *Cinque Terre* and the sweet *Sciacchetra* – made from partially dried grapes and prohibitively expensive.

Central Italy

Tuscany dominates central Italian winemaking, and *Chianti* can be very good, but beware of bottles that seem too cheap. It's worth genning up on vintages for reds, but most recent *Chiantis* are fairly reliable. Tuscany's two other prime reds, *Brunello di Montalcino* and *Vino Nobile di Montepulciano* can be Italy's most expensive wines – not the sort of thing you'd knock back at a trattoria. *Rosso di Montalcino* offers a more pocket-friendly option. Two common whites are *Vernaccia di San Gimignano* and the fresh *Galestro*. Tuscany is also renowned for *Vin Santo*, a sweet, strong wine into which biscuits are traditionally dipped.

Lazio, **Umbria** and **Marche** are best known for their fresh, dry whites. Umbria's *Orvieto*, once predominantly a medium sweet wine has been revived in a dry style, though the original abboccato is still available. Lazio's wine comes chiefly from the Roman hills, the best known *Est! Est! Est!* and *Frascati*, both of which can be unreliable. The best reds of these regions tend to come, like *Rosso Conero*, from Marche, though its own white, *Verdicchio dei Castelli di Jesi*, is worth a tipple.

Abruzzo produces few wines. Red wine here will almost certainly be *Montepulciano d'Abruzzo*, a strong, earthy wine; white will be *Trebbiano d'Abruzzo*. *Cerasuola* is a rosé version of Montepulciano. In **Molise** the wines are similar but the names change – *Biferno* and *Pentro*, both in white and red.

The South

Other than the odd pocket of quality, Southern wines don't enjoy a good reputation. **Puglia** perhaps sums the region up, the largest producer of wine in the country, most of which is basic stuff that goes to strengthen table wines from the North or ends up in five-litre flagons selling for a few thousand lire. There are however a number of DOC wines and one or two producers have begun to produce better wines, such as the red and rose *Castel del Monte*.

The volcanic slopes of Vesuvius in **Campania** are among the most ancient wine-producing areas in Italy, though again there's not much of note. Whites from Ischia and Capri are reliable everyday drinks, and *Lacryma Christi*, red and white, from the slopes of Vesuvius, can be reasonable. The best choices for a Campanian white are *Greco di Tufo* and *Fiano di Avellino*; for a red the only choice is *Taurasi*, a rich wine that commands high prices at riserva level. The grape that produces Taurasi, *aglianico*, makes another pedigree appearance further south in **Basilicata**. *Aglianico del Vulture* is that region's only DOC, but other wines worth trying are the sweet, sparkling *Malvasia* and *Moscato*. *Cirò* is the success story of **Calabria**, an old wine which has been given some modern touches, and now shifts bottles outside its home territory. Not surprisingly, given its far-south position, Calabria also turns out sweet whites such as *Greco di Bianco*.

Sicily is of course associated mainly with the fortified *Marsala*. but the island has also made a name for itself as a producer of quality everyday wines such as *Corvo* and *Regaleali*. These names (red and white) have no classification but Corvo in particular is found all over Italy – a tribute to its quality.

The *Denominazione d'Origine* System

This is the key to understanding what to look for in Italian wine, but it shouldn't be seen as any sort of guarantee. The denomination is a certification of origin, not of quality, and while it may mean a wine will be drinkable, stick to it too rigidly and you could be missing out on an awful lot.

Denomination zones are set by governmental decree. They specify where a certain named wine may be made, what grape varieties may be used, the maximum yield of grapes per hectare and how long the wine should be aged. *Vino da tavola* is simply wine that does not conform to the DOC laws; it's not necessarily wine you'd sooner pour down the sink than drink. *Denominazione d'Origine Controllata* (DOC) guarantees the origin of the wine and that the wine has been made to the specification of the rules for the zone in which it's produced. *Denominazione d'Origine Controllata e Garantita* (DOCG) is the only designation at the moment that actually has any real meaning. Wines sold under this label not only have to conform to the ordinary DOC laws, but are also tested by government-appointed inspectors. There are only half a dozen or so such wines.

Though it's undoubtedly true that the DOC system has helped lift standards, the laws have come under fire from both growers and critics for their rigidity, constraints and anomalies. *Chianti* for instance, can be a quaffable lunchtime drink, a wine of pedigree to be treated with reverence, or – in the case of some of the 1984 harvest – it can be appalling. All have a DOC. Some claim too that the restrictions of the DOCG are losing their credibility. With big reds such as *Barolo* the ageing term can destroy all the fruitiness of the wine, while the entry of *Albana di Romagna*, a somewhat ordinary white, to DOCG status, with others to follow, has caused consternation. Increasingly, producers eager to experiment have begun to disregard the regulations and make new wines that are sometimes expensive and among Italy's best wines, though they're still offically labelled "da tavola" (the nickname "super vini da tavola" has emerged). The Sicilian *Corvo*, red and white, is perhaps the best known non-DOC label, a modern wine which goes for a little over twice the price of ordinary table plonk, and Tuscany produces some excellent table wines.

COMMUNICATIONS : POST, PHONES AND THE MEDIA

Post office opening hours are usually Monday–Saturday around 8am until 6.30pm; smaller towns won't have a service on a Saturday and everywhere the post offices close at noon on the last day of the month. If you want stamps, you can buy them in *tabacchi* too, as well as in some gift shops in the tourist resorts. Rates to Britain are L750 for a letter, L550 for a postcard. Letters can be sent poste restante to any Italian post office, by addressing them "Fermo Posta" followed by the name of the town. When picking something up take your passport, and make sure they check under middle names and initials – and every other letter when all else fails – as filing is diabolical.

TELEPHONES

Public **telephones**, run by SIP, the state telephone company, come in various forms, usually with clear instructions printed on them (in English too). For the most common type, you'll need L100 or L200 coins, or a token known as a *gettone* (L200), available from SIP offices, *tabacchi*, bars and some news-stands – they're also in common use as currency. Other phones take L500 coins, handy for long-distance calls. **Phone cards** (*schede telefoniche*), also, are gradually coming in, available for L2000, L5000 and L10,000 from

INTERNATIONAL TELEPHONE CODES

For direct **international calls**, dial the country code (given below), the area code (minus its first 0), and finally the number.

UK: 0044	AUSTRALIA: 0061
EIRE: 00353	NEW ZEALAND: 0064

CODES FOR MAJOR ITALIAN CITIES

Bari ☎080	Florence ☎055	Milan ☎02	Palermo ☎091	Turin ☎011
Bologna ☎051	Genova ☎010	Naples ☎081	Rome ☎06	Venice ☎041

For a **full list of Italian telephone codes** in Britain, dial 100 and ask for Freephone BTI between 8am and 10pm, Mon–Fri.

tabacchi or newsstands and apparently soon valid for all phone booths. If you can't find a phone box, **bars** will often have a phone you can use (look for the yellow phone symbol), though these tend only to take *gettoni*. Alternatively, especially if you're phoning home and don't want to be bothered with piles of change, you could find a **SIP (or AAST) office** – listed in the larger towns – or a bar that has *cabine a scatti*: soundproofed kiosks that enable you to pay for your call afterwards. You also make metered calls from higher-geared hotels, but this may cost you 25 percent more. To make an international **reversed charge** call, dial the international operator (☎10) and ask for a call *cárico a destinatario*; say *Vorrei telefonare all'Inghilterra, cárico a destinatario*.

NEWSPAPERS

The **Italian press** is fairly regionally-based, but there are some newspapers that are available all over the country. The centre-left *La Repubblica* and authoritative right-slanted *Corriere della Sera* are the two most widely-read and available. *L'Unità*, the Communist party organ, has hit hard times of late, its declining appeal matched by the dip in its readership – many of whom have turned to the fresher, more radical *Il Manifesto* as an alternative. *Paese Sera*, also, is a left-wing daily read widely in the south.

Of provincial newspapers, *La Stampa* is the daily of Turin, *Il Messagero* of Rome – both rather stuffy, establishment sheets. *Il Mattino* is the more readable organ of Naples and the Campania area, while other southern editions include the *Giornale della Sicilia* and *La Gazzetta del Sud*. The most avidly read paper of all is with-

out question the pink *Gazzetta dello Sport*, essential reading for the serious sports fan – of which there are many. **English newspapers** can be found for around L2000 a time in all the larger cities and most of the more established resorts, usually a day late; *The Guardian's* European edition is often available the day of publication. In the remoter parts of the South, however, expect papers to be delayed by a couple of days, sometimes more.

THE AIRWAVES: TV AND RADIO

If you get the chance, try and watch some Italian **TV**, if only to size up the pros and cons of deregulation. The three state-run channels, *RAI 1*, *2* and *3*, controlled under law by the *DC*, *PSI* and local networks respectively, have of late been facing a massive onslaught by independent operators, especially those owned by the Euromogul Berlusconi, whose *Canale 5* is one of the more successful of the new arrivals. Although the stories of stripping housewives are way overplayed, the output is pretty bland across the board, with the accent on ghastly quiz shows and soaps, with a heavy smattering of American imports, though the *RAI* channels do carry less advertising and try to mix the dross with above-average documentaries and news coverage.

The situation in **radio** is even more anarchic, with the FM waves crowded to the extent that you continually pick up new stations whether you want to or not. This means there *are* generally some good stations if you search hard enough, but on the whole the *RAI* stations are again the more professional – though even with them daytime listening is virtually undiluted dance music.

BUSINESS HOURS, HOLIDAYS AND TOURIST SIGHTS

Most shops and businesses in Italy open from Monday to Saturday from 8 or 9am until around 1pm, and from about 4pm until 7 or 8pm, though in the north especially some offices work to a more standard European 9am–5pm day. Everything, except bars and restaurants, closes on Sunday, though you might find fish shops in some coastal towns and pasticcerias or bakers open until Sunday lunchtime.

The other factors that can disrupt your plans are **national holidays** and local **saint's days**. Local religious holidays don't generally close down shops and businesses, but they do mean that accommodation space may be tight. The country's official national holidays, on the other hand, close everything, except bars and restaurants down. These are:

January 1

January 6 (Epiphany)

Easter Monday

April 25 (Liberation Day)

May 1 (Labour Day)

August 15 (*Ferragosto*; Assumption of the Blessed Virgin Mary)

November 1 (*Ogni Santi*; All Saints)

December 8 (Immaculate Conception of the Blessed Virgin Mary)

December 25

December 26

CHURCHES, MUSEUMS, AND ARCHAEOLOGICAL SITES

The rules for visiting **churches** are much as they are all over the Mediterranean. Dress modestly, which usually means no shorts and covered shoulders for women, and try to avoid wandering around during a service. Most churches open in the early morning, around 7 or 8am for Mass, and close around noon, opening up again at 4 or 5pm, closing at 7pm. In more obscure places, some churches will only open for early morning and evening services, while others are closed at all times except Sundays and on religious holidays.

Another problem you'll face – and this applies to the whole country – is that lots of churches, monasteries, convents and oratories are **closed for restoration** (*chiuso per restauro*). We've indicated in the text the more long-term closures, though you might be able to persuade a workman or priest/curator to show you around even if there's scaffolding everywhere.

Museums generally open daily from 9am until 1 or 2pm, sometimes (though rarely) for a couple of hours in the afternoon on selected days, and are often closed on Mondays. They also often close early on Sunday, usually around noon, and for smaller museums, certainly, opening hours are severely cut back during winter. The opening times of **archaeological sites** are more flexible: most sites open every day, often Sunday included, 9am until late evening – frequently specified as one hour before sunset. In winter, times are again drastically cut, if only because of the darker evenings; 4pm is a common closing time. Again they are sometimes closed on Monday. **Admission prices** for museums varies between L2000 and L4000 (the Uffizi in Florence, the Roman forum, and excavations at Pompeii are exceptions to this rule, where the charge is L5000), although under-18s and over-60s get in free on production of documentary proof – student cards are no longer accepted at most places though it's worth a try. Some sites, churches and monasteries are nominally free to get in, though there'll be a custodian around to open things up and show you around, who you are expected to tip – L1000 per person should do it. Otherwise expect to pay much the same as you would in a museum.

FESTIVALS AND ANNUAL EVENTS

Italy has few national festivals, but there is no shortage of celebrations, saints' days being the usual excuse for some kind of binge. All cities, small towns and villages have their local saint, who is normally paraded through the streets amid much noise and spectacle. There are no end of other occasions for a *festa* – either to commemorate a local miracle or historic event, or to show off the local products or artistic talent. Many happen at Easter, or in May, September or around Ferragosto (August 15); the local AAST/EPT will have details and exact dates.

Recently there's also been a revival of **carnival** (*carnevale*), the last fling before Lent, although the anarchic fun that was enjoyed in the past has generally been replaced by elegant, self-conscious affairs, with ingenious costumes and handmade masks. Venice has the most famous carnival – a well-organised event that is so popular it sometimes closes off the entire city centre – and there are other, equally large and perhaps more fun events such as at Viareggio in Tuscany and Acireale in Sicily. And smaller towns will often put on some kind of parade. Carnival usually lasts for the five days before Ash Wednesday; because it's connected with Easter the dates can change from year to year – count on some time between the end of February and end of March.

RELIGIOUS AND TRADITIONAL FESTIVALS

Perhaps the most widespread local event in Italy is some kind of **religious procession**, some of which can be very dramatic affairs. Many – perhaps all – have strong pagan roots, marking important dates on the calendar and only relatively recently sanctified by the church. One of the best-known takes place in the small village of **Cocullo** in the Abruzzi mountains, on May 6 (Saint Dominic Abate's day), when a statue of the saint, swathed in snakes, is carried through the town – a ritual that certainly dates back to pre-Christian times. **Good Friday**, for obvious reasons, is also a popular time for processions. In many towns and villages models of Christ taken from the Cross are paraded through towns accompanied by white-robed, hooded figures singing penitential hymns. The west coast of Sicily sees many of these, as do other places across the South – **Táranto**, **Reggio**, **Bari**, **Brindisi**. On the following Saturday a procession of flagellants makes its way through **Nocera Tirinese** in Calabria. Later on in the year, big *presepi* (nativity scene) markets mark the days leading up to **Christmas** in **Naples** and **Verona** (in Naples especially *presepi* are a popular local craft), and there's a similarly large-scale *Mercato di Sant'Ambrogio* in **Milan**. At **Epiphany** (January 6) a toy and sweet fair, dedicated to the good witch *Befana*, lasts until dawn around the fountains of Piazza Navona in **Rome**. On the same day a procession of the *Rei Magi* (Three Kings) passes through **Milan**, and there are live tableaux at **Rivisondoli** in Abruzzo. There are other, less obviously purely events of celebration, marking miracles, the most famous of which is the *Festa di San Gennaro* in **Naples**, where much superstition surrounds the miraculous liquefaction of the saint's blood three times a year.

Other ritual celebrations bear less of the Church's imprint, and a Communist mayor and local bishop will jointly attend a town's saint's day celebration, where the separate motivations to make some money, have a good time and pay some spiritual dues all merge. Superstition and a desire for good luck are part of it too. In **Gubbio** there's a mad race to the Church of San Ubaldo

(May 5) with the *Ceri* – three phallic wooden pillars each 8m high. Similar obelisks are carried around in other places. On September 3 a ninety-foot tall *Macchina di Santa Rosa*, illuminated with tiny oil lamps, is paraded through the streets of **Viterbo**, and at **Nola**, near Naples, around June 22, eight *gigli* (lilies) are carried through the streets. Phallic though these may seem, the giant towers are more likely to be associated with an ancient, goddess-worshipping culture.

The number of practising Catholics in Italy is dwindling, and until recently many *feste* were dying out. But there has been a revival of interest in many festivals over the last decade or so, especially in **pilgrimages**. These are as much social occasions as spiritual journeys, some of them more important to people than Christmas,

and they still attract massive crowds. As many as a million pilgrims travel through the night, mostly on foot, to the **Shrine of the Madonna di Polsi** in the inhospitable Aspromonte mountains in Calabria. And there are other shrines and sanctuaries all over the country, mostly in inaccessible hilltop locations, some of them visited regularly by families from the surrounding area keen for a day out, others just the subject of a once-a-year trek. **Other traditions** survive: on the **Day of the Dead** (All Saints Day) in November, children receive presents, given on behalf of dead relatives, to make them feel that the people they were close to are still thinking of them. There are festivals which evoke local pride in tradition too, medieval contests like the *Palio* horserace in **Siena** perpetuating allegiances to certain

FESTIVALS DIARY

AGRIGENTO	Almond blossom festival	*Feb*
ALBA	*Giostra delle Centro Torri* Palio and costume parade	*1st Sun in Oct*
AMALFI	*Sant'Andrea*'s day	*June 27*
AOSTA	*Fiera di Sant'Orso* Thousand-year-old fair	*End of Jan*
AREZZO	*Giostra del Saracino* Jousting by knights in armour	*1st Sun in Sept*
ASCOLI PICENO	*Torneo della Quintana* Jousting	*1st weekend in Aug*
ASSISI	Holy Week celebrations	*Easter*
	Calendimaggio spring festa	*1st week in May*
ASTI	Bareback riders from villages around take part in *Palio*	*3rd Sun in Sept*
BARI	*Sagra di San Nicola* Pilgrims follow a boat carrying the Saint's image for a ceremony out at sea, in honour of the 47 sailors who saved his bones from raiders.	*May 7–8*
BRISIGHELLA	Medieval festival	*End of June*
CAGLIARI	*Sagra di Sant Efisio* Thousands of pilgrims accompany the Saint's statue in carts, on horseback or on foot.	*May 1*
CAMOGLI	*Sagra del Pesce* Procession of boats, with a fish fry-up.	*2nd Sun in May*
CAMPOBASSO	*Sagra dei Misteri*	*Beginning of June*
COCULLO	*Festa di San Domenico Abate* Procession through the village with a statue of the saint swathed in snakes.	*May 6*
DIANO MARINA	*Festival del Mare* Fireworks	*Aug 15*
DOLCEACQUA	*Festa di San Sebastiano* Saint's day celebrated with a tree covered with communion hosts carried through town.	*Jan 20*
ENNA	Celebrations for Holy Week	*Easter*
FAVIGNANA (off Sicily)	*La Mattanza* Ritual slaughter of tuna.	*May/June*
FELTRE	Medieval *Palio*	*1st weekend in Aug*
FLORENCE	*Scoppio del Carro* Firework display in the Piazza del Duomo	*Easter Sun*
	Festa di San Giovanni, Fireworks and the *Gioco di Calcio Storico* – a rough-and-tumble football game played between the four quarters of the city in medieval costume.	*June 24 and 28*
FOLIGNO	*Torneo della Quintana* Six hundred medieval knights, in jousting contest	*2nd weekend in Sept*
GENOVA	*Festa di San Giovanni*	*June 24*

competing clans; *Palio* races take place in a few other centres, Alba and Asti in Piemonte for example, though most have been revived more to support the tourist indiustry than anything else and can't compete with the seriousness and vigour of Siena's contest. Other towns put on crossbow and flag twirling contests, marching bands in full medieval costume accompanying the event with enthusiastic drumming.

FOOD FESTIVALS

Food-inspired *feste* are more low-key affairs than the religious events, but no less enjoyable for it, usually celebrating the local speciality of the region to the accompaniment of dancing, music from a local brass band and noisy fireworks at the end of the evening. There are literally hundreds of food festivals, sometimes advertised as *sagre*, and every region has them – look in the local papers or ask at the tourist office during summer and autumn and you're bound to find something going on. Most are modest affairs, meant for the locals and little-publicised. But there are a few exceptions. In **Tivoli**, near Rome, the town's fountains run with wine on the second Sunday in October; the same happens in **Citta della Pieve**, in Umbria, in April, during the *Festa dell Fontane*, and at nearby **Panicale**. Other notable events are **Orvieto**'s wine festival each June, **Bolzano**'s in the second half of March, and the truffle fair and *palio* in **Alba** on the first Sunday in October. Generally, the smaller they are, though, the better, giving you a chance to join in the dancing and sample the cooking.

GUBBIO	*Festa dei Ceri*	*May 5*
	Crossbow matches against San Sepolcro	*Last Sun in May*
LA SPEZIA	Rowing contests in *Palio del Golfo*	*Aug*
LAVAGNA	*Torta di Fieschi* Blind-Date-style festa, commemorating medieval wedding	*Aug 14*
LUCCA	Torchlight processions as part of *Luminaria di Santa Croce*	*Aug 14*
LUNGRO (Calabria)	Albanian celebrations	*Easter*
MAROSTICA	Human chess game (every even year)	*2nd weekend in Sept*
MASSA MARITIMA	Crossbow competition	*May 24*
MILAN	*Mercato di Sant'Ambrogio*	*December*
NAPLES	*Festa di San Gennaro*	*1st Sat of May*
	Gathering in the cathedral to witness the liquefaction of the saint's blood	*Sept 16, Dec 19*
NOCERA TIRINESE	Flagellants' procession through the village	*Easter Sat*
NORCIA (Umbria)	Crossbow matches and processions	*March 20–21*
NOVOLI (Lecce)	Bonfires in honour of *Sant'Antonio Abate*	*Jan 17*
ORVIETO	*Corpus Domimi* procession	*Beginning of June*
PIANA DEGLI ALBANESI	Byzantine celebrations	*Easter and Epiphany*
PISA	*Luminaria* , Festival of Lights	*June 16–17*
PISTOIA	*Giostra dell Órso* Joust of the Bear	*July 25*
PORTO CESAREO	*Luminaria* Festival of lights	*Aug 22*
ROME	*Befana* Toy and sweet fair in Piazza Navona	*Jan 6 (Epiphany)*
	Festa de 'Noantri Dancing, songs and floats in Trastevere's piazzas	*July 16–24*
SAN SEPOLCRO	Crossbow matches against Gubbio	*2nd weekend in Sept*
SIENA	*Palio* in medieval Campo	*July 2, Aug 16*
TAGGIA	*Festa della Maddalena* with Dance of Death in main piazza	*Sun nearest July 22*
VENICE	*Carnevale* Feb/March	*Feb/March*
	Il Redentore gondola procession, fireworks, to commemorate the end of a sixteenth-century plague.	*3rd week in July*
	Regatta	*1st Sun in Sept*
VENTIMIGLIA	Regatta and processions	*Aug 9–10*
VIAREGGIO	*Carnevale*	*Feb/March*
VITERBO	Procession of the *Macchina di Santa Rosa*	*Sept 3*

ARTS FESTIVALS

The home-town pride that sparks off many of the food festivals also expresses itself in some of the **arts festivals** spread across Italy, particularly in the central part of the country – based in ancient amphitheatres or other ruins or marking the work of a native composer, and sometimes going on for as long as a month. Perhaps the most prestigious is the **Venice** film festival in August and September. **Spoleto**'s summer *Festival dei Due Mondi* (Festival of the Two Worlds) is also becoming well-known, the two-month long event a mixture of classical concerts, films, ballet, street theatre and performance art, with its venue the open spaces of the ancient walled town. The *Sferisterio* in **Macerata** in Marche, and the Roman arena in **Verona** are two equally dramatic places to hear music in the summer months. Similarly there's the *Panatenee*

Pompeiane music festival, held in the ruins of **Pompeii** during the last week of August. **Bologna**'s summer festival often tries something different, with live bands playing in its medieval palace courtyards, and screenings of soap opera or art movies in unexpected places. Other festivals remember a particular composer: Puccini's music is celebrated from the end of July to mid-August in Torre del Lago, near **Viareggio**, Rossini's in **Pésaro** from mid-August to September. And it's worth noting the dates of the Italian **opera season**, which begins in December and runs through until May or June. The principal opera houses are *la Scala* in Milan, the *Teatro dell'Opera* in Rome, *La Fenice* in Venice, the *Teatro Comunale* in Florence and the *Teatro San Carlo* in Naples. But there are also other, smaller venues that have regular performances of opera throughout these months.

ARTS FESTIVALS

CITTA DI CASTELLO	Chamber Music Festival	Aug & Sept
FIESOLE	*Estate Fiesolana* (music, cinema, ballet, theatre)	Mid-June to Aug
FLORENCE	*Maggio Musicale Fiorentino*	May & June
LUCCA	Opera and theatre festival at Barga	Last half of July
MESSINA	International Film Festival	July
NAPLES	International Music Festival	Last half of May
	Neapolitan song contest at Piedigrotta	First half Sept
PERUGIA	Umbria Jazz Festival	July & Aug
RAVENNA	*Basilica di San Vitale* Organ music recitals	July & Aug
ROME	Opera at Baths of Caracalla	July & Aug
	concerts at Campidoglio, in July, the Basilica of Maxentius, all summer, and the *Accademia Nazionale di Santa Cecilia* and *Accademia Filarmonica Romana* in winter.	
SIENA	*Settimane Musicale* (musical weeks)	Aug
SORRENTO	International Cinema Convention	October
STRESA	*Settimane Musicale* (Lago Maggiore)	end of Aug
SYRACUSE	Greek drama in ancient theatre	May & June
TAORMINA	International film festival	July & Aug
	concerts and plays in the Greek theatre	
TORINO	*Settembre Musica*	Sept
UMBÉRTIDE	Rock festival	Summer
VENICE	International Film Festival	Aug & Sept
VERONA	International Film Festival	June
VITERBO	Baroque Music Festival	Mid-June to July

TROUBLE AND THE POLICE

Despite what you hear about the Mafia, most of the crime you're likely to come across in Italy is of the small-time variety, prevalent in the major cities and the south of the country, where gangs of *scippatori* or "snatchers" operate. Crowded streets or markets, and packed tourist sights, are the places to beware; *scippatori* work on foot or on scooters, disappearing before you've had time to react. As well as handbags, they whip wallets, tear off visible jewellery and, if they're really adroit, unstrap watches.

You can **minimise the risk** of this happening by being discreet: don't flash anything of value, keep a firm hand on your camera, and carry shoulderbags, as Italian women do, slung across your body. It's a good idea, too, to entrust money and credit cards to hotel-managers. Never leave anything valuable in your car and try and park in carparks on well-lit, well-used streets. On the whole it's common sense to avoid badly-lit areas completely at night, and deserted inner-city areas by day. Confronted with a robber, your best bet is to submit meekly: it's an excitable situation where panic can lead to violence – though very few tourists see anything of this.

THE POLICE

If it comes to the worst, you'll be forced to have some dealings with the **police**. In Italy these come in many forms, their power split ostensibly to prevent any seizure of power. You're not likely to have much contact with the **Guardia di Finanza**, responsible for investigating smuggling, tax evasion and other finance-related felonies; and the **Polizia Urbana**, or town police, are mainly concerned with directing the traffic and punishing parking offences; the **Poliza Stradale** patrol motorways. You may, however, have dealings with the **Carabinieri**, with their military-style uniforms and white shoulder belts, who deal with general crime, public order and drug control. These are the ones Italians are most rude about, but a lot of jokes about how stupid they are stem from the usual north-south prejudice. Eighty percent of the Carabinieri are from southern Italy – joining the police is one way to climb out of the poverty trap – and they are posted away from home so as to be well out of the sphere of influence of their families (the Carabinieri is actually part of the army). The **Polizia Statale**, the other general crimefighting branch, enjoy a fierce rivalry with the *Carabineri*, and are the one you'll perhaps have most chance of coming into contact with, since it's to them that **thefts** should be reported. You'll find the address of the **Questura** or police station in the local *Tuttocittà* supplement, and we've included details in the major city listings. The *Questura* is also where you're supposed to go to obtain a *permesso di soggiorno* **if you're staying** for any length of time, or a **visa extension** if you require one (see p.37).

In any brush with the authorities, your experience will depend on the individuals you're dealing with. Apart from **topless bathing** (permitted, but don't try anything more daring) and **camping rough**, don't expect a soft touch if you're picked up for any offence, especially if it's **drugs**-related: it's not unheard-of to be stopped and searched if you're young and carry a rucksack. Drugs are generally frowned upon by everyone above a certain age, and universal hysteria about *la droga*, fuelled by the serious problem of heroin addiction all over Italy, means that any distinction between the "hard" and "soft" variety has become blurred. Theoretically everything is illegal above the possession of a few grams of cannabis or marijuana "for personal use", though there's no agreed definition of what this means. In general the south of Italy is more intolerant than the north, and in any case, if found with suspicious substances you can be kept in gaol for as long as it takes for them to analyse the stuff, draw up reports and wait for the bureaucratic wheels to grind – which could be several weeks, and sometimes months. For the nearest **British consulate** see *Listings* in the Rome, Milan and Naples accounts – though bear in mind that they're unlikely to be very sympathetic, or to do anything more than put you in touch with a lawyer.

EMERGENCIES

In an **emergency**, note the following national emergency telephone numbers.

☎112 for the police (*Carabinieri*).

☎113 for any emergency service (*Soccorso Pubblico di Emergenza*).

☎115 for the fire brigade (*Vigili del Fuoco*).

☎116 for road assistance (*Soccorso Stradale*).

SEXUAL HARASSMENT AND WOMEN IN ITALY

Italy has a reputation for sexual harassment against women that is well known and well founded. Generally it's worse the further south you travel, where if you're travelling on your own, or with another woman, you can expect to be tooted and hissed at in towns every time you step outside the hotel door. You're also likely to attract unwelcome attention in bars, restaurants and on the beach. This persistent pestering is not usually made with any kind of violent intent, but it's annoying and frustrating nevertheless. There are a few things you can do to ward it off, though you'll never be able to stop the car-horns and hisses (the equivalent of a wolf-whistle).

Indifference is often the most effective policy, as is looking as confident as possible, a purposeful stride and directed gaze both good ways of fending off unwelcome attention. Frotteurs on buses can be a problem. To deter them, either keep your back to the wall or station yourself next to a middle-aged woman, and remonstrate noisily if someone starts rubbing up against you. Hopefully the other woman will be your ally, and give him/them a mouthful. Flashers in parks are another common occurence, and it's best to avoid hidden, leafy places. Parks are often a pick-up place, so your motives for sitting quietly in the sun may be misconstrued. This doesn't mean it's impossible to go there, just that it's more relaxing if you pick a spot where there are other people

around. If all else fails, you could try hurling a few well-chosen examples of the vernacular, like *lasciátemi in pace* ("leave me alone"), *sei fesso?* ("are you stupid ?"), *testa di cazzo* ("dickhead") or – as a last resort – *va fan culo* ("fuck off"). Failing that, don't hesitate to approach a policeman. Obviously, travelling with a man cuts out much of the more intense hassle, though even this won't deter the more determined onslaughts.

As you might guess from the prominence of the Virgin Mary in churches in Italy, women are certainly not absent from the Italian landscape, it's just that most of them are mothers. A few decades ago in the north, customs were very rigid, and are still in the south. The gap between marriage and motherhood is usually very small, about nine months, while unmarried women are carefully closeted indoors, their only escape the evening *passeggiata* – needless to say, well-chaperoned.

Hardly surprising, then, that women tourists, radiating freedom and independence, are assumed to be easy numbers, and that Italian women have found it so hard to break the strict rules governing their conduct.* The degree of freedom enjoyed by them varies from place to place: it's probably greatest in Milan and the North, where the situation can sometimes be on a par with Britain, and narrowest in Calabria, Basilicata and Sicily – although Rome can be a nightmare, whistling and catcalling part of the capital's experience for women.

CONTACTS

There are women's groups all over Italy: the largest are affiliated to the PCI, Italy's communist party, but campaigns against rape, for better access to abortion and towards increasing womens' skills and resources demonstrate the need for an independently active movement. There are contacts, bookshops and documentation centres in the major cities, but Italy's decen-

---

* The problem of women is closely linked to the problems of Italian men, specifically to the traditional adoration of the male-child that lingers on into adult life. After all, it is said that Jesus Christ himself was an Italian: he thought he was the son of God, lived at home till he was thirty, and thought his mother was a virgin.

tralised nature means that there are few national organisations.

Feminist papers like *Effe, Quotidiano Donna* and *Noi Donne* are good sources of infomation on the **women's movement**, or contact **ISIS**, Via Santa Saba 5, 00153 Rome (☎06/574.6479), who act as a gathering group for women's organisations across the country as well as internationally. **Radio Donna** in Rome is a women's radio station (the only one in Italy), restarted after a neo-Fascist firebombing in 1979.

ARCI-Co-ordinamento Donne is the main co-ordinating body for the women's section of the communist youth section, ARCI. They are based at Via F. Carrara 24, Rome (☎06/35.791); other branches in the major cities are listed under *ARCI Provinciale* in the phone book. Rome, Bologna and Milan are the places with most action, although this is fairly limited – *il riflusso*, the general term to describe the fall-off in political activity since

the Seventies, has affected the women's movement as it has others. *Centro Documentazione Donne* Via Galliera 8, 40121 Bologna (☎051/233.863), the *Centro Documentazione sul Studi sul Feminisme (CDSF)* Via San Francesco di Sales 1a, 00165 Rome (☎06/686.4210) and the *Centro Studi Storiche sul Movimento di Liberazione delle Donne* Via Romagnosi 3, 20121 Milan (☎02/869.3911) can all put you in touch with local groups – though for a more immediate idea of what's happening, visit the women's bookshops in each of these cities (see *Listings*).

Women's organisations also tend to share activities with **lesbian** groups. The *CDSF*, above, publishes a bimonthly newsletter called *Bolletino del Connessione Lesbiche Italiane*. There's also a national *Lesbian Line*, based in Florence, that's open every Wednesday and Saturday 8.30–10pm (☎055/240.384), for information, advice and help.

FINDING WORK

All EC citizens are eligible to work in Italy. The two main bureaucratic requirements are a *libretto di lavoro* and *permesso di soggiorno*, respectively a work and residence permit, both available from the *Questura* (see *Trouble and Police* above). For the first you must have a letter from your employers saying they are prepared to take you on, for the second (which is also necessary if you want to buy a car or have a bank acount in Italy) you'll need a passport, passport-photos, and a lot of patience.

TEACHING

The obvious choice is to **teach English**, for which the demand has expanded enormously in recent years. You can do this in two ways: freelance private lessons, or through a language school. **Private lessons** generally pay best, and you can charge up to £10 an hour, though there's scope for bargaining. Advertise in bars, shop windows and local newspapers, and, most importantly, get the news around by word-of-mouth that you're looking for work, emphasising your excellent background, qualifications and experience. An advantage of private teaching is that you can start at any time of the year (summer especially is a good time for schoolchildren and students who have to retake exams in September); the main disadvantage is that it can take weeks to get off the ground, and you need enough money to support you until then. You'll find the best opportunities for this kind of work in the tourist resorts and the bigger towns and cities.

Teaching in schools, you start earning immediately. It usually involves more hours per week, often in the evening, at a lower rate per hour, though the amount you get depends on the school. Don't accept anything less than £5 an hour, while the bigger schools should pay much more than this. For the less reputable places, you can get away without any qualifications and a bit of bluff, but you'll need to show a TEFL certificate for more professional language schools. For these, it's best to apply in writing from Britain (look for the ads in the *Guardian* and *TES*, and contact the *Italian Cultural Institute* at 39 Belgrave Square, London SW1; ☎01-235 1461), preferably before the summer, though you can also find openings in September. If you're looking on the spot, sift through the yellow pages and do the rounds on foot, asking to speak to the *direttore* or his/her secretary; don't bother to try in August when everything is closed. The best teaching jobs of all are with a university as a *lettore*, a job requiring fewer hours than the language schools and generally providing a fuller pay-packet. Universities require English language teachers in most faculties and you can write to the individual faculties (addressed to *Ufficio di Personale*). Strictly speaking you could get by without any knowledge of Italian while teaching, though some definitely helps.

OTHER OPTIONS

If teaching's not up your street, there's the possibility of **courier work** in the summer, especially around the seaside resorts. These are good places for finding **bar/restaurant work** too – not the most lucrative of jobs, though you should make enough to keep you over the summer. You'll have to ask around for both types of work, and some knowledge of Italian is essential. **Au pairing** is another option: contact *Au Pairs Italy*, 46 The Rise, Sevenoaks, Kent TN13 1RJ (☎0732-461522) for more information.

DIRECTORY

ADDRESSES Usually written as the street-name followed by the number – eg Via Roma 69. *Interno* refers to the flat-number – eg interno 5 (often abbreviated as int.).

AIRPORT TAX None to pay.

BARGAINING Not really on in shops and restaurants, though you'll find you can get a "special price" for some rooms and cheap hotels if you're staying a few days, and that things like boat/bike hire and guided tours (especially out of season) are negotiable. In markets, you'll be taken for an imbecile if you don't haggle for everything except food.

BEACHES You'll have to pay a few hundred lire for access to most of the better beaches (referred to as lidos), a few thousand to hire a sun-bed and shade and use the showers all day. During winter most beaches look like rubbish dumps, which is what they are: it's not worth anyone's while to clean them until the season starts at Easter.

BRING ... Photographic films, which are cheaper in Britain – and wait until you get home to have them developed. An alarm clock for early morning buses is also useful, as is mosquito repellent and antiseptic cream, not to mention sun tan lotion. If you're considering visiting a lot of hot, exposed archaeological sites, a water bottle is handy. And if you're camping don't forget a torch.

CAMPING GAZ Easy enough to buy for the small portable camping stoves, either from a hardware store (*ferramenta*) or camping/sports shops. You can't carry canisters on aeroplanes.

CIGARETTES The state monopoly brand – *MS* – are the most widely-smoked cigarettes, strong and aromatic, and selling for a little over L2000 for a packet of twenty. Younger people tend to smoke imported brands these days – all of which are slightly more expensive. You buy cigarettes from *Tabacchi*, recognisable by a sign displaying a white 'T' on a blue background.

CONTRACEPTION Condoms (*profilatici*) are available over the counter from all chemists and some supermarkets; the Pill (*la píllola*) is available on prescription only.

DEPARTMENT STORES There are two main nationwide chains, *Upim* and *Standa*, branches of which you'll see virtually everywhere. Neither is particularly posh, and they're good places to stock up on toiletries and other basic supplies; both stores sometimes have a food hall attached.

DISABLED TRAVELLERS Facilities aren't particularly geared towards disabled travellers in Italy, though people are helpful enough. Disabled drivers should contact *Radar*, 25 Mortimer Street, London W1 (☎01-637 5400) to obtain a badge enabling them to park more freely. A list of tour operators who specialise in holidays for the disabled is available from the Italian State Tourist Office; see *Information and Maps* for addresses.

ELECTRICITY The supply is 220V, though anything requiring 240V will work. Most plugs are two round pins: a travel plug is useful.

GAY LIFE Homosexuality is legal in Italy, and the age of consent is sixteen. Attitudes are most tolerant in the northern cities: Bologna is generally regarded as the gay capital, and Milan, Turin and to a lesser extent Rome all have well-developed gay nightlifes. There are a few *spiagge gay* (gay beaches) dotted along the coast, and two women-only holiday centres in Umbria. Away from the big cities, activity is more covert. You'll notice, in the south especially, that overt displays of affection between (all) men – linking arms in the *passegiata*, kissing in greeting, etc – are common. The line of what's acceptable, however, is finely drawn – in 1982 two gay men received an eight-month jail sentence for kissing in a Sicilian street. The national gay organisation, ARCI-gay, at Piazza di Porta Saragozza 2, PO Box 691, 40100 Bologna (☎051/436.700), affiliated to the youth section of the Communist Party, has branches in most big towns; *Babilonia* is the national gay magazine, published monthly by *Babilonia Edizioni*, PO Box 11224, 20110 Milano. For information on the situation for lesbians, see the note in *Women in Italy*.

KIDS Children are revered in Italy and will be made a fuss of in the street, and welcomed and catered for in bars and restaurants. Hotels normally charge around 30 percent extra to put a bed or cot in your room, though kids pay less on trains. The only hazards really, travelling with kids in Italy, are the summer heat and sun.

LAUNDERETTES Coin-operated launderettes are very rare outside large cities, and even there numbers are sparse; see the *Listings* headings of the main city sections for addresses. More common is a *lavanderia*, a service-wash laundry, but this will be expensive. Although you can usually get away with it, washing clothes in your hotel room has been known to cause problems, since in some parts of the country the plumbing can't cope with all the water. It's better to ask if there's somewhere you can wash your clothes.

LEARNING ITALIAN One way of spending time in Italy is to combine a holiday with learning the language. There are a great many places where you can do this, usually offering courses of varying levels of intensity for between one and three months. Reckon on paying around £250 for a 4-week course, plus accommodation, which will normally be with an Italian family. For details, contact the *British Institute of Florence*, Palazzo Lanfredini, Lungarno Guicciardini 9, 50100 Florence, or *Università Italiana per Stranieri*, Palazzo Gallenga, Palazzo Fortebraccio 4, 06100 Perugia – both of which run regular courses.

PUBLIC TOILETS Almost unheard-of outside railway and bus stations, and usually the only alternative is to dive discreetly into a bar or restaurant. Carry a supply of your own paper around and don't expect anywhere to be spotless.

TAKE HOME ... Top of the list of many Italian goodies worth taking home is a *caféteria* – the many-sided coffee-makers that cost a fortune in Britain but are actually very cheap in Italy; *Upim* and *Standa* usually have a good selection. Obviously clothes and shoes make a tempting souvenir, too, but don't expect any bargains; in Milan, especially, prices are sky-high, though if you're in the market for designer threads, this is as cheap a place as any.

TAMPONS From chemists and supermarkets everywhere, slightly more expensive than in Britain.

TIME Italy is always one hour ahead of Britain except for one week at the end of September when the time is the same.

VACCINATIONS None required.

WAR CEMETERIES Anzio and Cassino are just the best known of a number of fiercely contested battles on Italian soil during World War II. Information and a list of Allied cemeteries from the *Commonwealth War Graves Commission*, 2 Marlow Road, Maidenhead, Berkshire (☎0628-34221).

WATER Safe to drink everywhere, though bottled mineral water is always more pleasant.

CLOTHING AND SHOE SIZES

Dresses

British	8	10	12	14	16	18
Italian	36	38	40	42	44	46

Women's Shoes

British	3	4	5	6	7	8	9	10
Italian	35	36	37	38	39	40	41	42

Men's Shoes

British	5	6	7	8	9	10	11	12
Italian	39	40	41	42	43	44	45	46

Sweaters

British	32	34	36	38	40	42	44	46
Italian	38	40	42	44	46	48	50	52

Shirts and Collars

British	14	14½	15	15½	16	16½	17	17½
Italian	36	37	38	39	40	41	42	43

PART TWO

THE

GUIDE

CHAPTER ONE

PIEMONTE AND VAL D'AOSTA

F ringed by the French and Swiss Alps and grooved with mountain valleys, there are no less "Italian" regions than **Piemonte** and **Val d'Aosta**, in the extreme northwest of the country. French was spoken in Piemonte until the end of the last century, and Val d'Aosta remains bilingual. **Piemonte** especially is one of Italy's wealthiest regions, known for its fine wines and food and home to key Italian corporations like *Fiat* and *Olivetti*. The mighty Po River, Italy's longest, begins here, and the towns of its vast plain – which stretches right across northern Italy – are rich on both manufacturing and rice, grown on sweeping paddy fields. The region is a paradise for gastronomes and connoisseurs of vintage wines: the rolling vine-clad hills of Le Langhe and Monferrato produce classy wines like *Barolo, Bardolino, Barbera* and *Nebbiolo*, as well as the famous fizzy *Asti Spumante*. *Martini* and *Cinzano* are produced in and around Turin – a fusion of the region's wines with the wild herbs that grow on its mountains; and the food is Italy's richest, with much meat and game, cooked with wine or cream and butter and often enhanced with shavings of the pricey regional delicacy – white truffles.

Turin, on the main rail and road route from France to Milan, is the obvious first stop, and the one place in the region that (if you're not skiing) repays a lengthy visit – it's Italy's second industrial city, but retains a splendid Baroque core and is well placed for days out. Appealing historic towns are otherwise thin on the ground. **Alba** and **Saluzzo** are the most enticing, the former a good base for visiting the wine *cantinas*, the latter convenient if you want to explore the western valleys. **Asti** only really comes to life during its famous medieval *palio*. For the rest, winter sports and walking are the main activities – although, except for the ascent of **Monviso** in the far west, hikers will find more challenges and more spectacular views in the adjoining region of **Val d'Aosta**. Cut off from Switzerland and France by the highest of the Alps – **Monte Rosa**, the **Matterhorn** and **Mont Blanc** – and with a **national park** around the **Gran Paradiso** mountain, this is serious skiing and hiking country. **Aosta** itself repays a visit, and the countryside is sprinkled with **castles**.

PIEMONTE

Many of the dishes in **Piemonte**'s swankiest restaurants derive from the tables of the Piemontese aristocracy, in particular the Savoy dukes and kings who ruled the region from the eleventh century, making Turin their capital in 1574. Their

presence is clearly visible today in the grandiose architecture of central Turin, and in their ostentatious hunting palace at Stupenigi just outside the city.

Piemonte – and the Savoys – were at the heart of the Italian Unification movement in the nineteenth century, which under King Vittorio Emanuele II and the Piemontese statesman, Camillo Cavour, succeeded in dragging the various regions of Italy together under Savoy rule. Rome became the new capital, much to the disquiet of the Piemontese aristocracy and bourgeoisie, who acted quickly to save the region's not inconsiderable influence, setting up industries (*Fiat* and *Olivetti* were two) that were destined to change the face of Italian as well as Piemontese society. These days Piemonte is second only to Lombardy in national wealth and power.

Getting around Piemonte is fairly easy. The network of trains and buses is comprehensive, and hitching is rarely necessary. You can get to most places from Turin; Alba makes a good base for exploring Le Langhe, Saluzzo for the western valleys.

Turin (Torino)

"Do you know Turin?" said Nietzsche, "It is a city after my own heart . . . a princely residence of the seventeenth century, which has only one taste giving commands to everything, the court and its nobility. Aristocratic calm is preserved in everything: there are no nasty suburbs." Although **TURIN**'s traffic-choked streets are no longer calm, and its suburbs are as nasty as any in Italy, the city centre's gracious Baroque avenues, opulent palaces, sumptuous churches and splendid collections of Egyptian antiquities and Northern European paintings are still here – a pleasant surprise to those who might have been expecting satanic factories and little else.

Turin's suburbs were built by a new dynasty – **Fiat** (*Fabbrica Italiana di Automobili Torino*) – whose owner, Gianni Agnelli, is reckoned to be the most powerful man in Italy. Although the only sign of Agnelli's power appears to be the number of *Fiats* which cram Turin's streets (as they do those of every other Italian city), *Fiat* owns *Lancia* and *Alfa Romeo* too, accounting for sixty percent of the Italian car market. But there are other, more hidden, branches of the Agnelli empire. Stop for a *Cinzano* in one of the city's many fin-de-siècle cafés and you're drinking an Agnelli vermouth; buy any of three major newspapers – *La Stampa*, *Corriere della Sera* or *La Repubblica* – and you're reading newsprint repectively owned, controlled and managed by the Agnelli family. Support the Juventus football team, and you're supporting the Agnellis who own it; or go for a *Club Med* skiing holiday at the nearby resort of Sestriere, and you'll sleep in hotels built by Agnelli's grandfather. More sinister still, the Agnellis have major stakes in international arms companies, one of which supplied both Iran and Iraq during the Gulf War. This concentration of power is a peculiarly Italian phenomenon, with Agnelli and his friends seen as a stabilising force in a country where governments change rapidly. Foreign governments often take more notice of Agnelli than they do of Italy's elected leaders: as Henry Kissinger said in 1988, Gianni Agnelli "is the permament establishment". Terrorists too recognised where the roots of Italian power lay – the Red Brigade was founded on the factory floors of *Fiat*, and *Fiat* executives were as much targets as were politicians.

Some history

The Torinese are accustomed to absolutism. From 1574 Turin was the seat of the Savoy Dukes, who persecuted Piemonte's Protestants and Jews, censored the press and placed education in the extreme hands of the Jesuits. The Savoys gained a royal title in 1713, and a few years later acquired Sardinia, which whetted their appetite for more territory. The second monarch, Carlo Emanuele III (who promised to "eat Italy like an artichoke"), teamed up with the liberal politician of the Risorgimento, Cavour, who used the royal family to lend credibility to the Unification movement. In 1860 Garibaldi handed over Sicily and Southern Italy to Vittorio Emanuele, and though it was to take a further ten years for him to seize the heart of the artichoke – Rome – he was declared King of Italy.

The capital was moved to Rome in 1870, leaving Turin in the hands of the Piemontese nobility, a provincial backwater where a tenth of the 200,000 population worked as domestic servants, with a centre donned out in turn-of-the-century finery, its cafés, decorated with chandeliers, carved wood, frescoes and gilt, only slightly less ostentatious than the rooms of the Savoy palaces. World War I brought plenty of work, but also brought food shortages and, in 1917, street riots which spread throughout the North, establishing Turin as a centre of labour activism. Gramsci led occupations of the *Fiat* factory here, going on to found the Communist Party.

By the Fifties Turin's population had soared to 700,000, the increase mainly made up of migrant workers from the poor South, who were housed in shanty towns outside the city and shunned as peasants by the Torinese. Blocks of flats were eventually built for the workers – the bleak Mirafiori housing estates – and by the Sixties *Fiat* was employing 130,000 workers, with a further half million dependent on the company in some way. Not surprisingly, Turin became known as Fiatville.

Arriving, information and getting around

Turin's main **railway station**, Porta Nuova, is on Corso Vittorio Emanuele, at the foot of Via Roma – convenient for the city centre and hotels. Some trains also stop at Porta Susa, west of the centre on Corso Inghilterra, close to the main **bus station** on the corner of Corso V. Emanuele. Turin's **airport**, Caselle, is 15km north of the city, connected with the main bus station by regular bus – a 45-minute journey.

There are two **EPT**s – the main one on Piazza San Carlo (Mon–Fri 9am–noon & 3–7pm, Sat 9am–noon; ☎535.181) and a smaller one at the railway station. They have maps, hotel lists and assorted bumph.

Most of Turin's sights are within walking distance of Porta Nuova station, although if you're pushed for time the **tram and bus** network provides a fast and efficient way of getting around. Tickets must be bought before you board – L700 from *tabacchi* (the one in Porta Nuova is open long hours). Free route **maps** are available from the transport office in the subway outside Porta Nuova. Of **routes** you might use a lot, tram #4 goes north through the city from Porta Nuova, along Via XX Settembre to Piazza della Repubblica. Other useful routes are tram #1 between Porta Susa and Porta Nuova, bus #60 between the two stations via the main bus station, tram #15 from Porta Nuova to Via Pietro Micca, bus #61 from Porta Nuova across the river and bus #34 from Porta Nuova to the Museo dell'Automobile.

Finding a place to stay

Many of Turin's **cheap hotels** are in the seedy quarter off Via Nizza – convenient for clubs, restaurants and Porta Nuova station but not an advisable choice for solo women as it's red light territory. Somewhat safer, but – except for one *pensione* – more expensive, are the streets opposite Porta Nuova, close to Piazza Carlo Felice. There are also a number of fairly reasonably priced hotels to the west of Piazza Castello. Wherever you decide to make for, bear in mind that demand on hotels is high and it's a good idea to phone in advance.

Hostels and campsites

Ostello Torino, Via Alby 1 (☎683.738). Official YHA hostel, with beds in clean modern dormitories for L11,000, breakfast included; other meals L8000. Closed Jan. Bus #52 from Corso Vittorio Emanuele.

Riviera sul Po (☎638.706). The most convenient of the city's campsites, on the far side of the river, south of the youth hostel. Open year round. Bus #67 from Corso Vittorio Emanuele.

Hotels

AROUND PIAZZA CARLO FELICE

Bologna, Corso Vittorio Emanuele 60 (☎510.191). A clean, worn-at-the-seams two-star hotel with doubles without bath for L38,500.

Campo di Marte, Via XX Settembre 7 (☎545.361). A fairly large two-star hotel with doubles without bath for L38,500. As the owners can't be relied on to keep reservations, treat it as a last resort.

Pensione Lagrange, Piazza Lagrange 1 (☎538.861). A clean, if basic hotel, with a motherly owner, just off Piazza Carlo Felice. Much used by itinerant workers; doubles without bath cost L33,000.

BEHIND VIA NIZZA

Castagnole, Via Berthollet 3 (☎669.8678). Recently refurbished and extremely clean, with doubles without bath for L33,000.

Moderno, Via San Pellico 11 (☎669.8158). Clean and quiet. Doubles without bath L30,000.

Principe Tommaso, Via Principe Tommaso 8 (☎669.86.12). Fairly good rooms on the lower floor, but those above are cramped. Doubles without bath L33,000.

Hotel Bellavista, Via Galliari 15 (☎687.989). Odd owner, but the rooms are fine. Doubles without bath for L33,000.

Lux, Via Galliari 9 (☎657.257). A seedy hotel – but by no means the seediest in the area – with doubles without bath for L25,000.

AROUND PIAZZA CASTELLO

Pensione Azelea, Via dei Mercanti 16 (☎543.172). A clean and simple *pensione* used by Torinese students. Beware the obsessively appearance-conscious owner. Assuming she'll take you, it's excellent value, with beds in doubles costing between L5000 and L11,000 per person, and evening meals for L7000.

Pensione Europa, Piazza Castello 99 (☎544.238). Great position in an eighteenth-century palazzo, with many an ex-contessa living permanently in the antique-furnished rooms. Book well in advance (around a month if possible). Doubles without bath for L38,500.

> The Turin area telephone code is ☎011

TURIN

CORSO REGINA MARGHERITA

PIAZZA DELLA REPUBBLICA

Consolata

VIA S. CHIARA

VIA DEL CARMINE

PIAZZA SAVOIA

VIA DELLA CONSOLATA

VIA MILANO

Duomo

Palazzo Reale

Museo del Cinema

S. Lorenzo

PIAZZA DELLO STATUTO

VIA GARIBALDI

VIA BARBAROUX

VIA S. FRANCESCO D'ASSISI

VIA DEI MERCANTI

VIA P. MICCA

PIAZZA CASTELLO

Armeria Reale

CORSO FRANCIA

CORSO S. MARTINO

CORSO SICCARDI

Porta Susa Train Station

PIAZZA XVIII DICEMBRE

VIA CERNAIA

VIA S. TERESA

Palazzo Madama

VIA ROMA

VIA ACCADEMIA DELLE SCIENZE

Palazzo Museo del Riso

Museo Egizio and Galleria Sabauda

PIAZZA S. CARLO

CORSO INGHILTERRA

CORSO BOLZANO

CORSO VINZAGLIO

CORSO G. FERRARIS

PIAZZA SOLFERINO

VIA XX SETTEMBRE

VIA LAGRANGE

CORSO MATTEOTTI

Main Bus Station

LARGO VITTORIO EMANUELE II

PIAZZA CARLO FELICE

Galleria d'Arte Moderna

CORSO VITTORIO EMANUELE II

CORSO STATI UNITI

Porta Nuova Train Station

VIA GA

VIA BER

VIA S. P

CORSO DUCA DEGLI ABRUZZI

CORSO GALILEO

CORSO RE UMBERTO

VIA SACCHI

VIA NIZZA

CORSO M

VIA BELFIORE

CORSO EINAUDI

CORSO SOMMEILLER

To Stupenigi

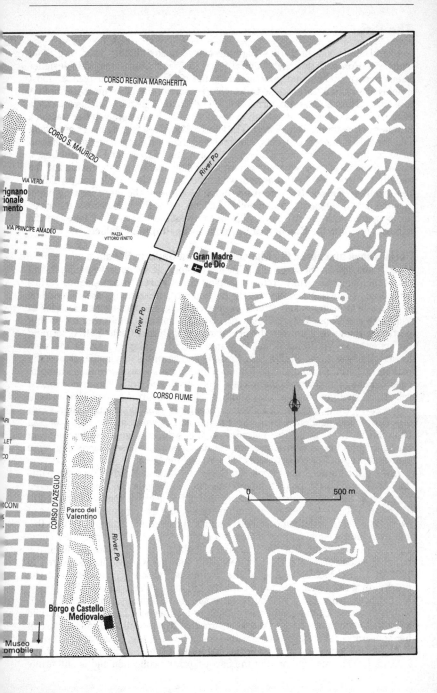

The City

The grid street-plan of Turin's Baroque centre makes finding your way about easy. **Via Roma** is the city's central spine, a grand affair lined with designer shops and ritzy cafés and punctuated by the city's most elegant piazzas, most notably Piazza San Carlo, close to which are some of the city's most prestigious museums. **Piazza Castello** forms a fittingly grand, if hectic, conclusion to Via Roma, with its royal palaces awash in a sea of traffic. From here you can walk in a number of directions. To the west, **Via Pietro Micca** leads to a cluster of elegant pedestrianised shopping streets, more relaxed than Via Roma and a good area to head to during the evening *passeggiata*. North lies **Piazza della Repubblica**, a vast and rather squalid square given over to a daily market. To the southeast, the shabby porticoes of **Via Po** forge down to the river, a short walk along which is the extensive **Parco del Valentino**, home to some of the city's best nightlife. Beyond lies the engaging Automobile Museum, while the hills **across the river** are peppered with the Art Deco villas of the wealthiest Torinese. Make specific trips out here – to the **Basilica di Superga** or the **Stupinigi Palace**.

Porta Nuova and north: the Museo Egizio and Galleria Sabauda

Cars, trams and buses surge along Turin's aristocratic avenues, whipping in and out of the pompous, grimy arches. Stepping out of **Porta Nuova** station, Turin's measured symmetry is immediately in evidence, though the area around is seedy, with prostitutes and street-hasslers cruising the once-elegant arcades of Via Nizza and Corso Vittorio Emanuele. Directly opposite, embraced by curving porticoes, things pick up with the neat gardens of **Piazza Carlo Felice**, forming the gateway to Via Roma – still very much the stomping ground of the well-heeled. Halfway down, **Piazza San Carlo** is known with some justification as the parlour of Turin, a grand and stylish open space, flanked with symmetrical porti-coed buildings housing opulent cafés and decorated with buttermilk stucco reliefs and rhythmic rows of grey shutters. Holding court is an equestrian statue of the Savoy Duke, Emanuele Filiberto, raising his sword in triumph after secur-ing Turin's independence from the French and Spanish at the battle of San Quintino in 1574, while the entrance to the square is guarded by the twin Baroque churches of **San Carlo** and **Santa Cristina**, whose languishing nude statues represent Turin's two rivers – the Po and the Dora.

Around the corner from Piazza San Carlo, the **Museo Egizio** (Tues–Sat 9am–2pm & 3–7pm; L3000) holds a superb collection of Egyptian antiquities, gathered together in the late eighteenth century under the aegis of Carlo Emanuele III. There are gorgeously decorated mummy cases, and an intriguing assortment of everyday objects, including castanets, sandals, a linen tunic dating from 2300 BC, and even food – eggs, pomegranates and grain, recognisable despite their shriv-elled, darkened state. But the undoubted highlight is the **Tomb of Kha**, the burial chamber of a 1400 BC architect, Kha, and his wife Merit, discovered in 1906 at Deir-el-Medina, home of the architects, masons and painters of the nearby royal necropoli. The tomb contains the tools of his trade – cubits, a case for balances, pens and a writing tablet – and more ordinary daily items: a bed with a headrest, clothes, generous rations of food, even a board game to while away the posthumous hours. And to ensure that Merit continued to take care of her appearance, she was provided with a cosmetic case, wig, comb, and tweezers.

Above the museum, the **Galleria Sabauda** (Tues–Sat 9am–2pm & 2.30–7.30pm; L3000) was built around the Savoys' private collection and is still firmly stamped with their taste – a middling miscellany of Italian paintings, supplemented by a fine collection of Dutch and Flemish works. Of the Italian paintings, the most interesting is the fifteenth-century *Archangel Raphael and Tobias* by Antonio and Piero Pollaiolo, an ultra-realistic work which amply demonstrates the Pollaiolo brothers' studies in anatomy. Among the first artists to do this, the brothers were once considered ahead of their time, as a look at the rarefied, almost ethereal painting of the same subject by their contemporary, Filippino Lippi, shows.

The Northern European collection is more engaging. Alongside a number of French paintings, there are debauched peasant scenes by Flemish artists – notably works by Pieter Breughel, David Teniers Jnr, and a bucolic *Amarilli and Mirtillo* by Van Dyck. Take a look too at the intriguing *Vanity of Human Life* by Jan Breughel. On a more elevated level, Hans Memling's *Passion of Christ*, tells the story of Christ's final days in a Renaissance city setting.

Piazza Castello and around

Via Roma continues north through the heart of Turin, passing some of the key monuments of the Savoys and the Italian Unification. The **Museo del Risorgimento** (Tues–Sat 9am–6pm, Sun 9am–noon; L3000, free on Sun), housed in the double-fronted **Palazzo Carignano**, birthplace of Vittorio Emanuele II, is worth a brief visit even if you usually give such things a miss; this was, after all, the centre of the movement, and the first capital of Italy proper before it was moved to Rome. The first meetings of the Italian parliament were held in the palace's circular Chamber of the Subalpine Parliament, and the building was the powerbase of leaders like Cavour, who ousted the more radical Garibaldi to an early retirement on the island of Caprera near Sardinia. It's ironic then, that the most interesting sections of the museum are those dedicated to Garibaldi: portraits showing him as a scruffy, long-haired revolutionary, some of his clothes – an embroidered fez, a long stripey scarf and one of the famous red shirts – adopted during his exile in South America, where he trained himself by fighting in various wars of independence. These shirts became the uniform of his army of a thousand volunteers who seized southern Italy and Sicily from the Bourbons.

What Vittorio Emanuele II made of the eccentrically dressed revolutionary who secured half the kingdom for him is undocumented, but you feel sure that his residence, the **Palazzo Reale** (Tues–Sun 9am–1.30pm; guided tours only; L3000) at the head of the sprawling, traffic-choked **Piazza Castello**, wouldn't have impressed Garibaldi – a *nouveau riche* residence with a dull apricot facade hiding glitzy rooms gilded virtually top-to-bottom and decorated with bombastic allegorical paintings. Around the rooms you'll find comical collections of Chinoiserie, with lions, cockerels and fat laughing Chinamen, a thousand-piece dinner set and a particularly tasteless vase of Meissen porcelain encrusted with golf balls and flashy birds. If this isn't enough, look in also on the seventeenth-century church of **San Lorenzo**, concealed behind the left wing of the palace. Designed by Guarini, also responsible for the Palazzo Carignano, it's scalloped with chapels, crowned by a complex dome supported on overlapping semi-circles, and lined with multicoloured marble, frescoes and stucco festoons and statuettes.

Really, you'd do better to save your energy for a wander around the gardens, or a visit to the **Palazzo Madama**, across the square from the Palazzo Reale – an altogether more appealing building with an ornate Baroque facade by the early eighteenth-century architect, Juvarra, who also redesigned the piazza and many of the streets leading off it. Inside, the originally fifteenth-century palace incorporates parts of a thirteenth-century castle and a Roman gate, though it's currently closed for restoration and likely to remain so for some time. If it has opened by the time you read this, look in for some of the building's original furniture and frescoes, and the **Museo Civico dell'Arte Antico** – a collection that includes everything from early Christian gold jewellery and Oriental ceramics to a famous *Portrait of an Unknown Man* by Antonello da Messina and an inlaid Gothic commode.

Opposite the Palazzo Madama is the **Armeria Reale** (Tues–Fri 9am–2pm & 2.30–7pm, Sat 9am–2pm; guided tours; L3000), a collection of armour and weapons spanning seven centuries and several continents started by King Carlo Alberto in 1837. Pride of place is given to his stuffed horse, which stands among cases of guns and swords. There's also a gallery of suits of armour and a blood-curdling collection of oriental arms, including gorgeously jewelled Turkish sheaths and intimidating Japanese masks.

Around the corner from the Palazzo Reale, the **Museo del Cinema** has also been closed for some time, and there are no signs of reopening in the near future. But the otherwise dull fifteenth-century **Duomo**, across the square, houses what has been called "the most remarkable forgery in history" – the **Turin Shroud**, a piece of cloth imprinted with the image of a man's body that has been claimed as the shroud in which Christ was wrapped after his crucifixion. One of the most famous medieval relics, it made world headlines in 1989 after carbon-dating tests carried out by three universities all concluded it was a fake, made between 1260 and 1390 – although no one is any the wiser about how the medieval forgers actually managed to create the image. You can't see the shroud itself, just a photographic reproduction, on which the face of a bearded man, crowned with thorns, is clearly visible, together with marks supposed to have been left by a double-thonged whip, spear wounds and bruises that could have been caused carrying a cross. The true shroud is kept in a locked chapel built by Guarini in 1668 and topped by a fantasy spire – the church's only other remarkable feature.

The only relics of Turin's days as a small Roman colony are visible from outside the duomo: the scant remains of a **theatre** and the impressive **Porta Palatina** – two sixteen-sided towers flanking an arched passageway. Beyond, the massive **Piazza della Repubblica** is another Juvarra design, though his grand plan for it is marred nowadays by seedy market buildings. The daily market here is at its best on Saturdays, when the *Balon*, or flea market, is held, home to fortune tellers (Turin is the reputed centre of Italian occult practices) and black marketeers.

Behind Piazza della Repubblica, Turin's most elaborate church, the **Santuario della Consolata**, was built to house an ancient statue of the Madonna, Maria Consolatrice, the protector of the city. Designed by Guarini, and with an impressive decorative altar by Juvarra, there are shops crammed with votive objects outside its pink and white neoclassical facade, which the more devout Torinese buy to offer to the statue, housed in an ancient crypt below the church.

Down to the river: Parco del Valentino and the Museo dell'Automobile
The scruffy porticoes of Via Po lead down to the river from Via Roma, ending just before the bridge in the vast arcaded **Piazza Vittorio Veneto**. Turn off halfway down, along Via Montebello, to the **Mole Antonelliana** whose bishop's hat dome, topped by a pagoda-like spire balancing on a mini-Greek temple, is the

city's most distinctive landmark. Designed as a synagogue in the nineteenth century by the eccentric architect Antonelli – who landed the town of Novara (p.67) with a similar eccentricity – it's something of a white elephant today, as Turin's Jews now worship in the newer oriental-style synagogue behind Via Nizza. But it's used for occasional exhibitions, and by tourists who want a bird's eye view of the city (daily 9am–7pm, closed Monday; L3000).

Along the river from Piazza Vittorio Veneto, you're most likely to visit the riverside **Parco del Valentino** at night – it holds some of the best of Turin's clubs. But it also makes a pleasant place to wind down after the hum of the city centre, its curving lanes, formal flower beds and fake hills covering 500,000 square metres – one of Italy's largest parks. Within the grounds are two castles, one real, the other a fake. The ornate **Castello Valentino** was another Savoy residence, mainly used for wedding feasts and extravagant parties, and nowadays seat of the university's faculty of architecture. The **Castello e Borgo Medioevale** (Tues–Sun 9am–6pm; L2500) dates from an industrial exhibition held in 1884, and is a synthesis of the best houses and castles of medieval Piemonte and Val d'Aosta, built with the same materials and techniques as the originals. You may baulk at the bogusness of the thing, and it can't help but feel a little like Disneyland, but it actually conjures up a picture of life in a fifteenth-century castle far better than many of the originals, kitted out with painstaking replicas of intricately carved Gothic furniture. The castle is based on those at Fénis (p.73) and Verrès (p.71); and the frescoes are reproductions of those at Manta (see below, *Saluzzo*).

A longish walk from here, along the river, takes you to the **Museo dell'Automobile** (Tues–Sun 9am–12.30pm & 3–7pm; L4000; bus #34 from Via Nizza) – Italy's only motor museum. Even if you know nothing about cars, this has some appeal – you'll spot models you haven't seen since your childhood and others familiar from films, as the museum traces the development from the early cars, handcrafted for a privileged minority, to the mass-produced family version. There's one of the first *Fiats*, a bulky 1899 model, close to a far sleeker version, built only two years later and, just three decades later, the first small *Fiat* family-targeted vehicle, a design which was still on the streets in the Sixties. Look also at the gleaming *Isotta Franchini* driven by Gloria Swanson in *Sunset Boulevard*, still with the initials of Norma Desmond, the character she played, on the side. The pride of the collection, the 1907 *Itala* which won the Peking to Paris race in the same year, is currently being prepared to try again. You can read of its adventures in Luigi Barzini's book *Peking to Paris*.

Out from the centre: the Basilica di Superga and Stupenigi Palace

South of the river, Turin fades into decrepit suburbs, beyond which lie the wooded hills that conceal the fancy villas of Turin's industrialists, including that of Gianni Agnelli. For a taste of the views enjoyed by Turin's mega-rich you can take a bus (#70) up to the **Parco della Rimembranza**, with 10,000 trees planted in honour of the Torinese victims of World War I and crowned with an enormous light-flashing statue of Victory. Alternatively, head out to the grandiose Baroque **Basilica di Superga**, from which there are fine views across the city to the Alps (tram #15 followed by a shuttle bus).

The basilica, built (again) by Filippo Juvarra, stands high on a hill above the rest of the city, a position that is the key to its existence. In 1706 King Vittorio Amadeo climbed the hill in order to study the positions of the French and Spanish armies who had been besieging the city for four months, vowing that he would erect a temple to the Madonna here if aided in the coming battle. Turin was spared, and the king immediately set Juvarra to work, flattening the top of the hill and producing over the next 25 years the circular basilica you see today. An elegant dome, pierced by windows and supported on pairs of white columns is flanked by delicately scalloped onion-domed towers and rises above a Greek temple entrance, though the most striking thing about the building these days is the graffiti – names dating back to the beginning of the century scratched into the interior pillars. Many Torinese come here not to pay homage to the Virgin, nor even to the splendid tombs of the Savoys, but to visit the tomb of the 1949 Torino football team, all of whom were killed when their plane crashed into the side of the hill. If you happen to go to a Torino–Juventus match, the sinister chant from the Juventus supporters, "Superga, Superga" can still be heard.

The other nearby attraction worth making a trip out of town for is the Savoys' luxurious hunting lodge, **La Palazzina di Caccia di Stupenigi** (summer 10–11.50am & 3–5.20pm; winter 10–11.50am & 2–4.20pm; closed Mon & Fri; L3000), out to the west of the city beyond the bleak Mirafiori suburbs, purpose-built for workers at the nearby *Fiat* plant. This is another Juvarra creation and perhaps his finest work, a symmetrical fantasy with a generous dash of Rococo, built in the 1730s. To get here, take bus #41 from Corso Vittorio Emanuele.

Much of the exterior of the palace is rather the worse for wear, but the interior is as luxurious as it ever was, the most extravagant room, the oval *Salone Centrale*, a dizzying triumph of optical illusion that merges fake features with real in a superb trompe d'oeil. Other rooms are decorated with hunting motifs: Diana, goddess of hunting bathes on bedroom ceilings, hunting scenes process across walls, and even the chapel is dedicated to Saint Uberto, patron saint of the hunt. And everywhere there are opulent wall-coverings – gilded brocades, hand-painted silk, carefully inked rice paper – and delicate eighteenth-century furniture, including gilded four-posters, inlaid desks and cabinets, even a marvellous marble bath, decorated with a relief of an imperial eagle, installed by Pauline Bonaparte.

Eating

Turin cuisine, influenced by the French, is guaranteed to raise cholesterol levels. Among local dishes you'll find, the classic winter dish, *bagna cauda*, is a sauce of oil, butter, cream, garlic and anchovies into which chunks of fried beef and raw vegetables are dipped. The sweets, many of them invented in the Savoy kitchens to tempt the royal palates and increase their waistlines, include such decadent delights as *spumone piemontese*, a mousse of marscapone cheese with rum, *panne cotta*, smooth, rich cooked cream, and light pastries like *lingue di gatto* (cat's tongues) and *baci di dama* (lady's kisses).

That said, most of the cheaper eating places serve the kind of food you can find anywhere in the country; there are snack bars and takeaways on Via Nizza, some tempting delicatessens on Via Lagrange and a superb *rosticcerie* on Corso Vittorio Emanuele for d-i-y lunches.

Snacks, pastries and ice cream

Bon Bon Fabrika, Via Lagrange, corner Via Maria Vittoria. The best ice cream in town, close to the Museo Egizio and Galleria Sabauda.

Cossolo, central branch at Via Roma 68. City-wide chain selling mini pizzas, *foccacia* and a wide range of sandwiches.

Fragola; **Lo Zodiaco**, Via Barbaroux. Cheap takeaway pizza.
Pizzeria Esedra, Via Berthollet. Eat in or takeaway pizza.
Zucca, Via Roma 294. Tiny biscuits, glistening pastries and ice cream cakes.

Restaurants and self-service
Da Amelia, Via Mercanti 6. Good, reasonably priced food lunchtimes and evenings.
Brek, Piazza Carlo Felice. Slick, high quality self-service, with tables inside and out.
Cucina Toscana, Via Galliari 16. Tiny trattoria packed with locals. Full meals for L12,000.
Peppino, Via Mercanti 9a. Full meals at lunchtime and evenings for L10,000.
Il Punto Verde, Via Belfiore 15f. Vegetarian food at reasonable prices.
Ristorante da Romano, Via Galliari. Full meals for L12,000.
Snack Bar Bambi, Via Corte d'Apello. Full lunchtime meals for L10,000.
Torino 1, Via Lagrange 43b. Cheap, functional and basic food until around 9pm.
Trattoria Bellezia, Via Bellezia. Good range of homely food at fairly reasonable prices. Very popular.
Trattoria Toscana, Via Vanchiglia 2 (off Piazza Vittorio Veneto). Good food at fairly reasonable prices.

Cafés

You'd be missing out on one of Turin's most hallowed institutions if you visited the city without at least looking in on its fin-de-siècle **cafés**. With aperitifs running at L5000 in the swankiest, the prices are steep, but the atmosphere more than compensates.

Baratti and Milano, Piazza Castello. Genteel Torinese sip leisurely teas at 5pm in a rarefied ambience of mirrors, chandeliers and carved wood.
Caffè San Carlo, Piazza San Carlo. Altogether more glitzy, with gilt pilasters and an immense chandelier; reputedly a favoured hangout of politicians and industrialists.
Confetteria, Piazza della Consolata. Marble-topped tables and dark wood-panelled walls overlooked by the Consolata sanctuary.
Elena, Piazza Vittorio Veneto 5. Scruffy old fashioned café frequented by students.
Florio, Via Po 8. Once the haunt of Cavour, now visited mostly for its ice cream.
Mulussano, Piazza San Carlo. A gorgeous, intimate café, supposedly the haunt of the in-crowd.
Pepino, Piazza Carignano 8. Ritzy café with summer garden, again famed for its ice creams.

Nightlife

One of the best things about Turin is its **nightlife**. There's a large and varied mix of clubs here – slick and trendy, arty, or even world-music orientated – and many birrerias have dance floors or live music. Virtually all clubs officially require membership, but most will let you join temporarily.

Birrerias
La Contea, Corso Q. Sella 132 (☎812.2307). Across the river. African, Latin American, blue-grass and country.
Divina Commedia, Via San Donato 47 (☎488.336). Set out on three floors – Heaven, Purgatory and Hell – with music appropriate to each. Frequent gigs.
Doctor Sax, Lungo Po Cadorna 4 (☎878.416). By the river. Punk, rock and jazz among the graffiti.

La Gaia Scienza, Via Guastalla 22 (☎870.821). Birreria popular with students.

Incontro, Imbarco Valentino. On the river in Parco Valentino, an unpretentious and scruffy club/birreria with an easy atmosphere. Music ranges from Italian "New Wave" to live jazz.

Roar Roads, Via Carlo Alberto 3 (☎839.6764). Noisy, lively, central and popular.

Clubs and discos

AEIOU, Via Spanzotti. Urban angst prevails; wear black.

African Club, Via Principe Pommaso 5/d. African and reggae.

Hiroshima Mon Amour, Via Belfiore 24 (☎650.5287). Affiliated with the ecology movement. Films, alternative theatre, and concerts.

Studio Due, Via Nizza 32. Disco with mostly student crowd.

Polaroid, Piazza Statuto. Frenetic yuppie disco – neon lights, perspex dance floor and aeroplane seats.

Pontes, Via Montebello 21. South American music.

Triangolo Rosa, Via Garibaldi. Mixed gay and straight disco.

Tuxedo, Via Belfiore 8 (☎658.690). Sleek, comfortable and friendly. Dance music spiked with rock and reggae.

Listings

Airport Caselle (☎577.8361/2/3/4; ☎57.781 midnight–6am). Buses from Corso Inghilterra bus station (every 30min 5.45–9am & 5–10.30pm; every 45min 9am–4.30pm). There are also plans to build a rail-link.

Books If you've run out of reading matter, *Libreria Luxembourg*, Via C. Battisti 7, has an excellent range of British and American paperbacks.

Buses Most inter-city and all international buses leave from the station on Corso Inghilterrra (bus #60 from Via Nizza near Porta Nuova station or from Porta Susa station). Buses to Saluzzo and Cuneo leave from the top of Corso Marconi, near the junction with Via Nizza.

Carparks Porta Nuova and Piazza Reale (daily 7am–8pm), Piazza Bodoni – all unstaffed and closed 2–5am.

Car problems Breakdown (☎116); traffic police (☎26.091); 24-hour petrol stations at Piazza Statuto, Corso Vittorio Emanuele 125, Corso M. d'Azelgio 40, Piazza Zara, Corso Francia 401, Corso Vercelli 266, Via O. Vigliani 174.

Car rental *Hertz*, Porta Nuova (☎659.658) and Corso Marconi 19 (☎650.4504); *Avis*, Caselle Airport (☎470.1528), Porta Nuova (☎659.800) and Corso Turati 15 (☎501.107).

Chemists All-night chemists are the *Alleanza Cooperativa Torinese*, on Via Nizza (☎659.259) and *Boniscontro*, Corso Vittorio Emanuele 66 (☎538.271).

Exchange Out of banking hours at Porta Nuova station (Mon–Fri 7–9am, noon–1.50pm & 3.05–8.50pm; Sat, Sun & holidays 7.40–10am, 11am–1.15pm, 3.05–5pm & 6–8.50pm.

Football Turin's two teams, *Juventus* and *Torino*, play on alternate Sundays at the Stadio Comunale, Corso Sebastopoli 123 (☎390.292), reachable from Porta Nuova station by taking tram #2 and bus #58. Tickets from L10,000.

Hospital *Maria Vittoria*, Via Cibrario 72; emergency medical attention (☎5747).

Laundry *Alba*, Via San Secondo 1; *Aleotti M*, Via Berthollet 18; *Peretti*, Corso Vittorio Emanuele 73.

Markets Piazza della Repubblica is the scene of a daily fruit, veg, clothes and bric-a-brac market, and a flea market, *Balon*, takes place on Saturday mornings in the streets around. Secondhand, ethnic and designer cast-offs on Via Crocetta, Via Cassini and Via Marco Polo, Tues–Fri mornings and all day Sat.

Newspapers British newspapers from the newsagents in Porta Nuova station. Good range of UK magazines at *Feltrinelli*, Piazza Castello 9.

Police ☎113. Main police station at Corso Vinzaglio 10 (☎512.444).

Post Office Central post office, Via Alfieri 10.

Shopping Via Roma for designer staples; trendier, less expensive fare in the pedestrianised streets bordered by Via Pietro Micca, Via Monte Pietá, Via dei Mercanti and Via San Francesco d'Assisi.

Taxis Main ranks at the stations and airport, or dial ☎5730, ☎5737, ☎5744, ☎5748.

Telephones *SIP* at Via Arsenale 13, open 24hr. Other offices at the corner of Via Barbaroux and Via XX Settembre (8am–9.30pm), on Via Roma 18 (8am–10pm) and at Porta Nuova (8am–10pm).

West of Turin: the Susa Valley

The main route to France from Turin runs through the **Susa Valley**, passing the region's main ski resorts. The one real sight, the **Sacra di San Michele**, a forbidding fortified abbey anchored atop a rocky hill, is an easy day trip from Turin. **Susa** itself, reached by a minor branch of the railway was once a modest Roman town and is now a modest provincial town – a pleasant stopover but with not much else to lure you.

Sacra di San Michele

Closest town to the **Sacra di San Michele** is AVIGLIANA, half an hour by train from Turin and connected with the abbey by infrequent bus. It's a grotty sort of place, though, and if you don't mind walking it's much nicer to push on to the next stop on the train route, SANT'AMBROGIO, a small village at the foot of San Michele's hill, from where it's a steep 60–90-minute hike to the abbey.

The walk is worth it, both for the views and the undeniably spooky atmosphere which surrounds the glowering abbey, reached by a long flight of stairs hewn into the rock – the *Scalone dei Morti* (Stairs of the Dead). Corpses used to be laid out here for local peasants to come and pay their respects – a morbid tone that's continued with the abbey buildings proper, from the Romanesque entrance arch carved with signs of the zodiac to the Gothic-Romanesque abbey church – nothing special architecturally, but a gloomy enough setting if you're in the mood for weaving Gothic horror stories.

Susa

A further 25km down the valley, **SUSA** is a possible stopover if it's late, a likeable, rather scruffy old town with a very cheap **hotel**, the *Rosa*, at 46 Via Roma (☎0122/2470), with doubles for just L10,000; phone ahead to book. If it's full, the *Sole* (☎0122/2474), on Piazza IV Novembre, is twice the price but still a bargain.

While most of Italy was under the Romans, Susa and western Piemonte remained in the hands of the Gauls. The best known of its Gaulish leaders, Cottius, was much admired by the Romans, with whom he reached a peaceful arrangement, and there are a handful of Gaulish/Roman remains scattered around the town centre, notably in **Piazza San Guisto**, where there's a redoubtable defensive gate. The adjacent Romanesque **Cattedrale** has a fine campanile, but its most interesting features are the external frescoes – a *Crucifixion* and an *Entry into Jerusalem*. Just above the piazza, Cottius erected the **Arco di Augosto** in honour of the Roman emperor, its top decorated with a processional frieze and giving views down into a small park laid out around the remains of some **Roman Baths**. For a complete round-up of the town's ancient origins, look in on the **museum** housed in the crumbling medieval castle above the town (July & Aug Wed–Sun 9.30am–12.30pm, also 2–5pm on Thurs, Sat & Sun; Sept–June Tues–Sat 9.30am–12.30pm, also 2–5pm Thurs & Sat).

Skiing: the Piemontese resorts

Close to the French border are Piemonte's principal purpose-built ski resorts – well used by British tour operators and really far cheaper if you take a package. The snow is in any case notoriously unreliable, and resorts have been known to close down mid-season, though Sestriere has lately protected itself against the weather by installing Europe's largest artificial snow-machine.

Of the main three resorts, **BARDONECCHIA** is a weekenders' haunt, a modern resort with small chalet-style hotels. **SAUZE D'OULX**, a little way south, is known as the Benidorm of the Alps, and attracts hordes of young Brits who treat skiing as a hangover cure. Apart from a few winding streets of old houses, it's a vast, ugly sprawling place, and its lift-passes are expensive, at L171,000 per week. Linked by lift to Sauze d'Oulx, **SESTRIERE** was the dream resort of Mussolini and the *Fiat* baron, Agnelli, though it's now very overdeveloped. Agnelli conceived of an aristocratic mountain retreat, favoured by the young and beautiful, though he was not unaware of the fast-growing tourist industry. The story goes that he insisted the height of the sinks be raised to prevent "common tourists" from pissing in them. The bland resort now dribbles over a bleak mountain, dominated by two cylindrical towers, both now owned by *Club Med*. Apart from the advantage of its snow-machine, there's little appeal to the place at all.

Saluzzo and the western valleys

A flourishing medieval town, and later the seat of one of Piemonte's few Renaissance courts, **SALUZZO**, 57km south of Turin, retains much of its period appeal. Flaking ochre-washed terraces and Renaissance houses with painted trompe l'oeil landscapes line stepped cobbled streets climbing up to a castle, now a prison. A pleasant place to stay and wander, the bus services from Saluzzo make it a convenient base for excursions into the Po, Varaita and Maira valleys, which cut through the foothills of the Monviso mountain towards France.

There are a few things around town worth seeing. Just below the castle, the Gothic church of **San Giovanni** has a number of thirteenth- and fourteenth-century frescoes and the tomb of the leading light of Renaissance Saluzzo, Marchese Ludovico II, anachronistically depicted like a medieval knight beneath a fancily carved canopy. Close by, the Gothic **Casa Cavassa** is a fifteenth-century palace with an arcaded courtyard that doubled as home for one of Ludovico's ministers and now houses the town's **Museo Civico**. Inside are period furniture and paintings, including the gorgeously gilded *Madonna della Misericordia*, with the Madonna sheltering Ludovico, his wife and the population of Saluzzo in the folds of her tumbling cloak.

That's about all there is to the town centre, but just to the south of Saluzzo, a five-minute bus ride from outside the train station, there's the **Castello di Manta** – a medieval fortress that was transformed into a refined residence by the Saluzzo marquises in the fifteenth century. Though from the outside it's as plain and austere as Saluzzo's castle, it's worth visiting for the late Gothic frescoes in the Baronial Hall. One of these illustrates the myth of the fountain of youth, elderly people processing towards the magical waters while others impatiently rip off their clothes to plunge in. The other, the Nine Heroes and Nine Heroines, contains idealised chivalrous courtiers and exquisite damsels, with china-pale faces and elaborate costumes, standing beneath stylised trees with coats of arms hanging from the branches.

Saluzzo practicalities

The **AAST** is housed in the Municipio, a couple of streets below the Casa Cavassa (Mon–Fri 8.30am–12.30pm & 2.30–3.30pm, Sat 8.30am–noon) and has details of the variable opening times of the museum and Castello di Manta (see below). Of Saluzzo's **hotels**, the *Luna* on Via Martiri della Libertá (☎0175/43.707) is cheap and convenient, with doubles without bath for L25,000, and the *Perpoin* (☎0175/42.552), at the top of the same street, has doubles with bath for L36,900. Most of the town's **restaurants** are along Via Martiri della Libertá and the main street, Corso Italia.

Valle Po

West of Saluzzo, close to the French border lies the source of the river Po, which flows right across industrial northern Italy, gathering the waste from its thousands of factories before finally discharging into the Adriatic. The Alpine-style resort of **CRISSOLO** lies towards the end of the valley, and you can hike (or take a minibus in summer) to the **Pian del Re**, a grassy plain around the source of the Po, walking on to the entrance of the **Pertuis de la Traversette**, a 75-metre-long tunnel (currently closed) built by Saluzzo's Marquis Ludovico, to ease the trading route into France for his mule trains. According to one theory, the pre-tunnel pass was used by Hannibal and his elephants.

Crissolo is also a good base for climbing **Monviso**, Piemonte's highest mountain, reachable by way of a long rocky scramble in about six hours from the *Quintino Sella rifugio*, two to three hours beyond the Pian de Re. Even if you don't want to scale the summit, the walk to the *rifugio* is lovely, passing a series of **mountain lakes**; or, if you prefer, it's possible to do a **circuit of the lakes**, turning off the main trail just before Lago Chiaretto, from which a path leads past Lago Superiore and back to Pian del Re. There are also **caves** near Crissolo, **Grotta del Rio Martino** above the town, with stalactites and a subterranean lake and waterfall. The quick route here takes half an hour from Crissolo but is steep; the slower, easier route takes an hour. Unless you're an experienced caver, it's advisable to go with a guide from the **AAST** on the main square in Crissolo.

Practical details

Crissolo's **hotels** are all on the main street. The *Albergo Serenella* (☎0175/94.944) is open year round and charges L18,000 per person in high season and L15,000 in low season for clean and modern rooms with bath. *Club Alpino* (☎0175/94.925) is seasonal and has doubles without bath for around L30,000; the owners will give advice and make suggestions for walks, and perhaps even guide you around the caves. Most of Crissolo's **restaurants** are in the hotels, so you may find taking half-board a better deal.

There's also a small seasonal hotel at Pian del Re, the *Pian del Re* (☎0175/94.967), with doubles without bath for L26,000. The *Quintino Sella rifugio* is open June to September, and sometimes in winter; at all times it's advisable to phone in advance (☎0175/94.943 summer, ☎0175/94.158 winter.)

Val Varaita

To the south of the Valle Po, **Val Varaita**'s only draw is the rustic-style furniture that has been produced here since the eighteenth century, when the locals decided to capitalise on the vogue among Torinese and Genovese aristocrats for building country villas in the area. The industry continues to flourish, these days patronised by wealthy Torinese weekenders, and has brought much needed prosperity to the area, though sadly its distinctly un-rustic factories and the 1980s equivalent of the country villa – fake Alpine apartment blocks – have ruined the look of the place irreparably.

Val Maira

Val Maira, further south still, is a quiet and narrow valley, its drama heightened if you take the bus from Cuneo (see below), recklessly hurtling around craggy cliffs, the driver seemingly oblivious to the sheer drops below. There's not much beyond this, though the villages, with their traditional rubble and wood houses perched high above the river, are very picturesque, particularly **ELVA**, in the hills above **STROPPO** (hitch or ask in the cafés for the unofficial taxi driver). If you're walking get a **map** from Saluzzo before heading out. The best base is the small village of **PRAZZO**, where there's a hotel, the *Impero* (☎0171/99.124), which has modern, comfortable doubles without bath for L22,000, and a good traditional restaurant. There are no hotels at Stroppo, just a **campsite** near the turn-off for Elva.

Cuneo and around

There's not much to bring you to **CUNEO**, the main town of southern Piemonte and provincial capital. Its severely geometric modern centre has less appeal than its extensive bus and rail connections, and the old town – what there is left of it – is dark and gloomy. Even its one "sight", the museum (weekdays only) in the restored Gothic church of **San Francesco** behind the bus station, is only of limited interest: the collection ranges from medieval frescoes to a folk section with traditional costumes, kitchen utensils and an ancient bike.

The valleys

What does bring people to Cuneo is the area to the south of the town, where the valleys form a popular area of sulphurous spas and summer and winter resorts. **Valle Stura** is much visited by botanists for its many rare species of flowers; the **Valle del Pesio** shouldn't be missed in spring, when a waterfall, known for obvious reasons as the *Piss del Pesio*, is in full pelt. Trains to France run through the verdant **Valle Vermenagna**, where it's possible to visit the **Palanfre Parco Naturale** from VERNANTE. Again, the appeal is mainly botanical, with over 650 species of trees and flowers growing at some 3000m above sea level.

Mondoví: frescoes, a sanctuary and some caves

Half an hour by train from Cuneo, **MONDOVÍ** is a peculiar town. Split into two, the lower half – Breo – is sleepily suburban, while the upper half, Piazza, is an uneasy combination of crumbling medieval and exuberant Baroque. Neither are especially exciting, but the town gives access to some interesting attractions nearby – some fifteenth-century frescoes, a sanctuary and some caves.

Time in Mondoví is best spent in Piazza, built around a large square on which stand a turretted medieval palace and an exotic Baroque church, the seventeenth-century **Chiesa della Missione**, whose interior is decorated with an incredible trompe l'oeil by Andrea Pozzo, a cloudy heaven with angels seemingly suspended in mid-air. If you've time, you can laze around in the **Belvedere**, to the north of Piazza, a garden occupying the site of a thirteenth-century church destroyed except for its campanile in the last century. The campanile was used by a physicist in the eighteenth century to establish various topographical measurements. Though you can't climb up, the views from the gardens are fine, stretching north to the hills of Le Langhe and south to the foothills of the Alps.

San Fiorenzo

One of the attractions of Mondoví is its vicinity to the hamlet of **BASTIA**, 10km northeast, where the church of **San Fiorenzo** – from the outside a modest rustic structure – holds some brilliantly coloured late-Gothic frescoes. Completed around 1472, at least four artists worked on them, and they're absorbing pieces of work, with lively, if predictable scenes from the lives of Christ and various saints, including a stunning Hell, infested with vicious monsters.

Buses run to Bastia from the train station at Mondoví but are badly timed for returning – though hitching along the main road (28bis) is fairly easy.

The Santuario di Vicoforte

A twenty-minute bus ride (from the train station) east of Mondoví, the **Santuario di Vicoforte** is another popular trip from the town, an imposing Baroque church crowned by what is claimed as the world's largest elliptical dome. It's at its liveliest on Sundays – like most Italian sanctuaries as much a place for a good day out as for devotions, purpose-built arcaded crescents housing restaurants, pastry and souvenir, even clothes shops.

According to legend the sanctuary owes its existence to a hunter who while out in the woods discovered a pillar painted with a picture of the Madonna and Child – said, according to a second legend, to have been erected as a votive offering by a poor baker whose bread wouldn't rise. In fact, the sanctuary was begun in 1598 on the orders of King Carlo Emanuele I, and eventually finished in 1890. The frescoed pillar is nowhere to be seen, and the 36-metre dome is rather a disappointment. But the kitschy **museum** provides some compensation: a haphazard collection of ecclesiastical bric-a-brac laid out in a labyrinth of rooms around the dome and towers. The exhibits range from gaudy treasures to ceremonial costumes and photos of those cured by a visit here.

Grotta di Bossea
March–Nov 10am–noon & 2–6pm
Twenty-four kilometres south of Vicoforte, the **Grotta di Bossea** is the third of Mondovì's surrounding attractions, a long-established underground tourist target filled with contorted stalactites and stalagmites, waterfalls and lakes and a subterranean scientific laboratory, set up to monitor the caves' population – which includes seven unique species. On display is the skeleton of the *Ursius Spelaeus*, an undergound monster over three metres long and two metres high which lived here between 25,000 and 40,000 years ago. Sadly, reaching the caves without your own transport is virtually impossible, although it's often possible to hitch at weekends when the caves are busiest.

Alba and the Le Langhe hills

The town of **Alba** and the surrounding Le Langhe hills mean two things to the Italians: white truffles and red wine. The region supplies some of the finest of both – the truffles are more delicate and aromatic than the black variety found further south, and the wines range from the "King of Italian reds", **Barolo**, to the light and fragrant **Nebbiolo**. There are a number of wine museums and *cantinas* in the hill-villages around Alba, best those at Barolo, Annunziata and Grinzane di Cavour – all accessible direct by bus from Alba (though to hop from one to the other you'll need to hitch).

Although these big *cantinas* all sell wine, you'll get a better deal at one of the smaller family-owned *cantinas* scattered around the region. Most of the area's very different wines all come from the same grape, Nebbiolo, and the final taste is dependent on the soil: sandy soil produces the grapes for the light red, **Nebbiolo**, calcium and mineral-rich soil those for the more robust **Barolo**.

Alba

Whether or not you want to taste wine, **ALBA** repays a visit, its central core of redbrick medieval towers, Baroque and Renaissance palaces and cobbled streets lined with gastronomic shops one of Piemonte's most alluring. And if you come in October, there's a chance to see the town's hilarious annual donkey race – a skit on nearby Asti's prestigious *Palio*.

Of things to see, the late-Gothic **Duomo** on the central Piazza Risorgimento has been gaudily restored, and holds some fine Renaissance stalls, inlaid with cityscapes, musical instruments, and fake cupboards whose contents seem to be on the verge of falling out. But Alba is primarily a place to stroll and eat. **Via Vittorio Emanuele**, the main drag, leads up to the centre from Piazza Savona, a fine, bustling street, with the most tempting of Alba's local produce on display – wines, truffles, cheeses, weird and wonderful varieties of mushroom, and the wickedly sticky *nocciola*, a nutty, chocolatey cake. **Via Cavour** is another pleasant medieval street with plenty of wine shops, behind which the **donkey race** and displays of medieval pageantry attract the crowds during the October festival. There's also an annual **truffle festival** at the same time, when you could blow your whole budget on a knobbly truffle or a meal in one of the many swanky restaurants.

Practical details

The **APT** (Tues–Sat 9am–noon & 3.30–6.30pm, closed Sat afternoons, all day Mon & Sun) has maps of the town and information on the surrounding area. Aside from October, when **room** rates soar, there are doubles without bath for L28,000 at the *Piemonte* on Piazza Rosetti (☎0173/43.967), just behind the duomo, and the *Corona Grossa* at the top of Viale Torino (☎0173/43.964) – turn left out of the train station and keep on walking. The best places to sample Albanese cooking are *Osteria dell'Arco*, on Vicolo dell'Arco, off Via Vittorio Emanuele, and the *Corona Grossa*'s restaurant – though neither are cheap. If you want to save money, try the *spaghetteria* on Via Vittorio Emanuele.

Around Alba: the Le Langhe hills

Eight kilometres south of Alba, the castle of **Grinzane di Cavour** was rented by the Cavour family in the nineteenth century and served as a weekend retreat for Camillo Cavour. Nowadays it's the seat of Piemonte's regional *enoteca*, or winery, and has a pricey restaurant specialising in local specialities. The upstairs **folk museum** (Wed–Mon 9am–noon & 2–6pm; closed Jan) holds various bits of Cavour trivia (most intimate Camillo's wooden bedside toilet) and a surprisingly engaging display of agricultural equipment, ranging from a ferret trap and grappa distillery, to winter boots made of hay and a contraption for cleaning the cocoons of silkworms. In the afternoons there are wine-tasting sessions – L500 will buy you two glasses – and although there are inevitably some extremely expensive wines, many are affordable if you're interested in buying.

A few kilometres southwest of Grinzane, in the heart of the Le Langhe hills, **BAROLO** is the best known name among Italian wines, its peach, apricot and ochre-washed houses set among extensive vineyards. It's a small village but is very geared up to the steady stream of wealthy gastronomes and wine connoisseurs that come here. You can visit the *Cantina Marchesi di Barolo* (Fri–Wed 10am–12.30pm & 3–6.30pm) in a flaking turreted castle, or, at a price (around L56,000 a double), indulge yourself with a night and a meal at the *Hotel Barolo* (☎0173/55.191), whose restaurant – an imperious place with a stiff dress code – is renowned hereabouts.

Just north of Barolo, **LA MORRA** is an earthy old village, with good views over the undulating vineyards from outside the *Belvedere* restaurant and hotel, where there's a *cantina* (Wed–Fri 11am–12.30pm & 2.30–5.30pm, closed Jan & Feb) in which you can taste and buy wine. There are also some good food shops, with a wide range of local cheeses, and if you're there on a Monday, you can pick up bargains at the market.

The *cantina* has maps of walks through the vineyards, best of which is the one to **ANNUNZIATA**, about half an hour down the hill, where there's a private **wine museum**, the *Museo Ratti* (Mon–Fri 8.30am–noon & 2.30–6pm, Sat & Sun phone in advance: ☎0173/50.185), housed in a Renaissance abbey next to the firm's *cantina*. Laid out in a musty cellar, this is mainly of appeal to dedicated wine buffs, although there are a number of intriguing exhibits – a massive barrel for treading grapes, a primitive wine tanker, consisting of an elongated barrel on a rickety cart, and a collection of Roman wine jugs found in the area. Best of all, there's a letter from an Arctic explorer, congratulating the Ratti on the fact that their Barolo had stood up to the rigours of travel and climate on an expedition to the North Pole.

Wine at the *Ratti cantina* is expensive, and you can only buy it in lots of six. It's far cheaper and sold in single bottles at the small family *cantina*, Oberto Severino, a kilometre or so up the road back towards La Morra. As for staying over, there are two **hotels** in La Morra – the *Italia* (☎0173/50.310) on the main road, and the *Belvedere* (☎0173/50.190), above the restaurant on Piazza Castello.

Asti and around

The wine connection continues in **ASTI**, 30km north of Alba and the capital of Italy's sparkling wine industry – though for most of the year Asti itself is fairly sedate, a small town, not unattractive, that only livens up in mid-September, for its annual *Palio*. In the run-up to the event there are street banquets and a medieval market, and on the day of the race itself, the third Sunday in September, there's a thousand-strong procession of citizens dressed as their fourteenth-century ancestors, before the frenetic bare-backed horse race around the arena of the Campo del Palio – followed by the awarding of the *Palio* (banner) to the winner and all night feasting and boozing. It's taken nothing like as seriously as Siena's more famous event (see *Tuscany*, Chapter Eight), and has to some extent been revived for tourists. But if you're in the area at the right time you'd be mad to miss it.

The rest of the year the Campo del Palio is a vast, bleak carpark, and there's frankly not a lot to see. The arcaded **Piazza Alfieri** is official centre of the town, behind which the church of **San Secondo** is dedicated to the city's patron saint, built on the site of the saint's martyrdom in the second century. Not surprisingly, there's nothing left of the second-century church but there is a fine sixth-century crypt, its columns so slender that they seem on the verge of toppling over. As for the rest of the church, it's a slick early Gothic construction, with neat redbrick columns topped with tidily carved capitals and in the left aisle a polyptych by one of Asti's Renaissance artists, Gandolfino d'Asti. The *Palio* banners are also kept here, housed in a heavily ornate Baroque chapel.

The main street, **Corso Alfieri**, slices through the town from the square, on the right of which the church of **San Pietro** (Tues–Sat 9am–noon & 3–6pm, Sun 10am–noon; ring for the custodian) has a circular twelfth-century **baptistry**, now used as an exhibition space and a **museum**, housed in what was a pilgrim's hospice, displaying an odd – and badly labelled – assortment of Roman and Egyptian artefacts. At the other end of the Corso, the **Torre Rossa** is a medieval tower with a chequered top, built on the foundations of the Roman tower in which San Secondo, a Roman soldier, was imprisoned before being killed.

Asti practicalities

Asti's **APT** (Mon–Sat 9am–12.30pm & 3–6pm, closed Sat afternoon and all day Sun) is on Piazza Alfieri, and has information on the *Palio* and maps of the town. If you're intending to go to Asti on the *Palio* weekend, book a **room** well in advance. At other times there should be little problem. The classiest of the affordable options is the 200-year-old *Hotel Reale* on Piazza Alfieri (☎0141/50.240), with doubles without bath for L35,000. The *Cavour*, on Piazza Marconi (☎0141/50.222), outside the train station, is convenient and has doubles without bath for L40,000. The town's cheapest option is *Del Mercato*, on Campo del Palio (☎0141/32.142), where doubles without bath cost L29,600 – though this is rather unfriendly.

Most of Asti's **restaurants** are expensive, but there's a cheap pizzeria, the *Rosalba*, next to the Torre Rossa, and the trattorias at the hotels *Genova* and *Del Mercato* are reasonable. If you're into Asti Spumante, or want to sample the other wines of the region, there are **wine festivals** in late August and September – details from the **APT**.

Near Asti: the Abbazia di Vezzolano

Although ALBA is a better base for visiting vineyards and wine museums, **COSTIGLIOLE D'ASTI**, a short bus ride south of Asti, is the centre of Asti Spumante production, and has an *enoteca* and predictably pricey gastronomic restaurant in its castle (Tues–Sun 10am–noon and 2.30–5.30pm).

If you have your own transport or the patience to hitch, the **ABBAZIA DI VEZZOLANO**, isolated deep in a valley to the northwest of Asti, displays some of the area's best late-Romanesque architecture. According to legend the abbey was founded by Charlemagne, who had a religious vision on the site in the eighth century. Outside it has a fancily arcaded and sculpted facade and a secluded Romanesque cloister. Inside, there's a stone rood screen carved with expressive scenes from the life of Mary, and a row of naive, rustic-looking saints.

Alessandria, Acqui Terme and Casale Monferrato

Immediately east of Asti, the area around Alessandria is scattered with castles, though all are privately owned and only occasionally opened to the public. The one attraction of the modern, industrial provincial capital, **ALESSANDRIA**, was a museum of Borsalino hats (the kind with the dented crown, favoured by American prohibition era gangsters), but this has now closed, and there is no real reason to step out of the station.

ACQUI TERME, to the south, is a dreary spa town, with a steaming sulphurous spring, *La Bollente*, gurgling up in its scruffy main piazza, and a polluted river flowing through the centre. The efficacy of Acqui's spas earned the attention of Romans from Pliny to Seneca, but there's only one substantial relic from its Roman heyday – four arches of an aqueduct below the main bridge. There is also a small **museum**, with mosaics from the Roman spa, in a dilapidated castle above the railway station, but it's of limited interest.

North of Asti, **CASALE MONFERRATO** has the dubious distinction of being cement capital of Italy, and it's also home to the country's most sumptuous **synagogue** – a leftover from the days when there was a sizeable Jewish population in Piemonte, most of whom had fled from Spain in the sixteenth century to escape persecution. Casale was home to nearly two hundred Jewish families, who lived here in peace until Mussolini's racial laws (brought in mainly to appease Hitler) forced many to leave. The synagogue lies down an alley off Via Saloman Olmer, the first left off the main Via Roma (Sun & holidays 10am–noon & 3–5.30pm, at other times ring next door), a rich, gold-encrusted affair with a voluptuously curving pulpit and a "museum of treasures" laid out in the closed-off women's gallery.

Eastern Piemonte: Vercelli and Novara

A less typical Italian landscape than the area **east of Turin** would be difficult to imagine. The vast paddy fields here produce more rice than anywhere in Europe, on a deadly flat plain across which road and rail cut on their way to Milan. For about half the year the fields are flooded (with warm water in winter), and they're at their most evocative in autumn when the weak sun filters through the mists, making the stalk-spiked waters gleam.

Whatever time of year you're here, the novelty soon wears off, and most people are only too glad to leave the area. You'd do well to follow their example, either hurrying through to Milan or Turin, or heading north, via the towns of Novara and Vercelli, to the Val Sesia – which winds up towards Monte Rosa on the Swiss border.

Vercelli

The centre of Piemonte's – indeed Europe's – rice-growing region is **VERCELLI**, usually full of businesspeople come to wheel and deal over prices in the *Borsa di Riso* or rice stock exchange. There its appeal really ends, although if you've time to spare between trains, the **Basilica of Sant'Andrea**, just across from the station, is worth a studied peek, built in the thirteenth century by a cardinal funded with revenues from a Cambridgeshire monastery, granted him by King Henry III as a reward for helping to establish him on the English throne. As the revenues were vast, it took only nine years to complete – an incredible feat at a time when churches frequently took over a century to build – and today it's an important church architecturally, one of the first in Italy to incorporate Gothic elements: pointed arches, slender columns shooting up to the vaults, and tall slim conical-roofed bell-towers flanking the facade.

Otherwise Vercelli's most atmospheric spot is **Piazza Cavour**, just off the main Corso Libertà, surrounded by pleasantly scruffy arcades and the scene of the Tuesday market. Close by, on Via Borgogna, the large **Museo Borgogna** (summer Tues & Thurs 3–5pm; winter 2.30–4.30pm; all year Sun 10am–noon) holds the work of relatively unknown local artists together with the odd Bruegel and Jan Steen and some frescoes taken from local churches.

Vercelli practicalities

Finding a **room** in Vercelli can be a problem, the hotels often full with rice-trade reps and the overspill from Turin's industrial fairs; it's advisable to phone in advance. Cheapest is the *Rondinella*, Corso Gastaldi 15 (☎0161/53.835), outside the bus station and a couple of minutes' walk to the right of the train station – doubles without bath only L20,000. The *Albergo Valsesia*, on Via G. Ferraris (☎0161/53.842), is very scruffy, but convenient, with doubles without bath for L33,500 and full meals for L12,000.

Novara

NOVARA, twenty minutes further down the train line towards Milan, makes for a more elegant, unhurried stopover than Vercelli, its main street, Corso Cavour, neatly paved with half-moon cobbles and lined with *pasticcerias* and old fashioned tea rooms. That said, there's not much left of historic Novara: the medieval **Broletto** houses an open-air cinema in summer, and the **Duomo** is an overblown neoclassical creation which dwarfs all around to Lilliputian proportions; inside are bits and pieces from earlier churches – a fifth-century **Baptistry** with tenth-century frescoes of the Apocalypse, and a frescoed twelfth-century chapel – both open only in the morning. A couple of blocks north, the weird three-tiered dome of the church of **San Gaudenzio** with its syringe-like spire dominates the whole town. It was built by Antonelli, a nineteenth-century architect responsible for a similar monstrosity, the *Mole* in Turin.

Novara's most convenient **hotel** is the *Moderno* (☎0321/29.864) opposite the train station, with doubles without bath for L35,000, and there's a fairly reasonable **pizzeria**, *Le Tre Laterne*, on Via dei Tornelli, just off Piazza Gramsci at the end of Corso Cavour.

Northern Piemonte: Biella, Varallo and Valsesia

The main attraction of northern Piemonte is really the mountains, especially the dramatic Alpine **Valsesia**, which winds up to the foot of Monte Rosa on the Swiss border. On the way, stop off at two of the region's most visited sanctuaries, the **Santuario d'Oropa** near **Biella**, or **Sacro Monte** at **Varallo**. From here you're well poised either for Piemonte's mountains or those of Val d'Aosta, a few kilometres west.

Biella and the Santuario d'Oropa

A short train ride northwest from Novara, **BIELLA** is best known for its wool industry, its periphery choked with mills and the hilltop upper town with the mansions and villas of wool barons. It's not an especially rewarding place, but it does give access to the **Santuario d'Oropa**, a forty-minute bus ride northwest at the foot of Monte Mucrone. Founded in the fourth century by Saint Eusebio to house a black statue of the Madonna and Child, this is an odd sort of attraction, and can't really compete with the sanctuary at Varallo for sensation. But it's the most venerated of Piemonte's shrines, the main church an immense neo-Baroque concoction, and it's a good starting-point also for **walks** into the surrounding mountains. A cable car runs regularly up Monte Mucrone as far as the (closed) *Albergo Savoia*, where a network of marked trails begin. One of the nicest and easiest is to the **Lago Mucrone**, a small mountain lake, while if you want views without too much effort you can simply walk back down to the sanctuary in about an hour. If all this seems too easy, hike up to the summit of Monte Mucrone itself – a two-hour trek.

Though you should definitely move on if you can, you may need to **stay overnight** in Biella. Be warned that the two cheap hotels are a bit seedy, best the *Monte di Varallo* at the far end of Via Italia (☎015/22.366), with doubles for L28,000. Off Via Italia, *La Grande Muraglia*, Via B. Bona 15 (☎015/22.669), has grotty doubles with outside loos for L20,000.

Varallo and Sacro Monte

Some fifty kilometres by train north of Novara, **VARALLO** marks the beginning of northern Piemonte's more picturesque reaches, a gateway to the region, surrounded by steep wooded hills and filled with Art Deco villas and Baroque palazzi. It's a pretty place in itself, very pleasant for a short visit, but most people come to see the sanctuary of **Sacro Monte**, just outside the town and connected by bus five times daily from the train station.

If you've only come for Sacro Monte you could make straight there from the station; if you want to see the town first – and it is worth a quick wander – the centre is a five-minute walk to the right along Corso Roma. On the way you pass the church of **San Gaudenzio**, spectacularly anchored to a creeper-covered cliff and surrounded by arcades. It's less impressive inside, though there's a polyptych by the sixteenth-century Varallo-born artist Gaudenzio Ferrari, responsible for much of the work at Sacro Monte. The main street, **Corso Umberto I**, lined with shuttered and balconied palaces, winds through the town from here towards the river Serio. There's more work by Gaudenzio Ferrari in the church of **Madonna delle Grazie**, where an entire wall is covered with colourful and detailed scenes from the life of Christ.

If you want to **stay over** in Varallo, the *Albergo Monte Rosa* (☎0163/51.100) is a brisk five-minute walk to the left of the train station. It's rambling, friendly and very clean, and a double without bath costs L35,000. The **AAST** is on the corner of Corso Roma and Piazza Garibaldi (Tues–Fri 8.30am–noon & 2.30–6.30pm, Sat 8.30am–noon & 2.30–6pm, Sun 9am–noon).

Sacro Monte

Sacro Monte crowns the hill above Varallo, a complex of 44 chapels, each housing a 3D tableau of painted statues against frescoed scenery representing a scene from the life of Christ. Founded in the fifteenth century by a friar anxious to popularise Catholicism in a region in which heresy was rife, the emphasis is on sensationalism and spectacle, calculated to work upon the emotions of the uneducated. The sanctuary is at its best when busy – to get a measure of its continuing popularity, you need to visit on a Sunday, when it's full of families, pensioners and nuns, all of whom picnic in the shady grounds after finishing their pilgrimage.

It's inevitably a bizarre spectacle, depicting the whole range of key biblical episodes from the Fall to Christ's birth, life and death. And the tableaux don't pull any punches: the *Massacre of the Innocents* (no. 11) has a floor littered with dead babies, while Herod's army prepare to spear, hack and slash more. And the chapels (nos. 30–41) that retell the events of Christ's passion are flagrant emotional manipulation, with crazed flagellators, spitting soldiers and a series of liberally blood-splattered Christs. By the time you reach the *Road to Calvary* (no. 36) you almost flinch at the sight of a flaked-out Christ being viciously kicked. Dominating the central piazza of the sanctuary, the Baroque **Basilica** offers some relief, the highlight the cupola – a nice piece of optical trickery, encrusted with figures perched on bubblegum clouds.

Valsesia

From Varallo the road follows the river Sesia to the foot of multi-peaked **Monte Rosa**, whose massive bulk heads four Italian valleys and spreads north into

Switzerland. **Valsesia**, the most easterly valley, is also the most dramatic – worth going for the ride even if you don't want to hike or ski.

Flanked by dark pine-wooded slopes crowned with a toothed ridge of rock, the road winds up the valley, the perspective changing at every turn. Well touristed (mainly by Italians and Germans), traditional houses with slate roofs and wood-slatted balconies mingle with Alpine-style villas and apartments. The villages are crowded for much of the summer, and with weekend skiers in the winter. September is the quietest month, when many of the hotels close, but the weather up the mountains is unpredictable then, and hiking can be hazardous.

The Valsesia villages were founded in the thirteenth century by religious sects from the Swiss Valais, known as Walser, in search of land and the freedom to worship. There are reckoned to be around 3000 true Walsers in the valleys of Monte Rosa, and in most bars and shops you'll still hear people speaking a dialect based on ancient German. If you want to see how these isolated communities lived and worked, there's a **Walser Museum** (July & Aug only 2–6pm), a traditionally furnished seventeenth-century house in the hamlet of **PEDEMONTE**, ten minutes' walk out of Alagna.

ALAGNA, at the head of the valley, right below Monte Rosa, is the most convenient place to stay, whether you want to ski or hike. Popular and predominantly modern, it has a cluster of wood-slatted Walser houses to the south, with a tiny network of overgrown tracks winding in between them. Some houses still function as farms, with hay hanging to dry on the slats and wood stacked behind, while others are holiday homes, spilling with geraniums.

There are lots of **walks** among the foothills, all of which are well marked from Alagna. If you're interested in seeing more than mountain scenery, there's a path along to **RIVA VALDOBBIA** five kilometres back down the valley, whose church facade is covered with a colourful late-sixteenth-century fresco of *The Last Judgment*. However, the toughest and most spectacular hikes are those on **Monte Rosa** itself. If you can afford it, it's possible to save time and energy by taking the cable car (return trip around L23,000) up to Punta Indren (3260m), from where you can walk to one of the many *rifugi*; most of these are open from June to September, but check at the tourist office in Alagna before setting out. Failing that, you could walk down into the next valley, Val Gressoney in Val d'Aosta (see below).

All these walks involve a good deal of scree-crossing and some sobering drops, and none are to be taken lightly – you'll need a good **map** (*Studio FMB* publishes a map of the four Monte Rosa valleys showing all paths, *rifugi* and pistes) and you should check on the weather before setting out. There's also an ambitious long-distance circuit of Monte Rosa, starting at Alagna, taking in Val Gressoney, Val d'Ayas and Zermatt across the Swiss border: you'll need five days if you make use of ski-lifts and cable cars, and a good deal longer than that if you don't.

Skiing in the area is organised by *Monterosa Ski* who have an office in Alagna. A day pass costs L27,000, and equipment is available for hire in the village. However, the runs are narrow, and though experienced skiers can cross into Val Gressoney, it involves walking as well as off-piste skiing.

Alagna's cheapest **hotel** is the *Alagnese*, in the centre of the village (☎0163/91.325), large and old-fashioned with doubles without bath for L30,000, and a bar which does snacks. Most of the local restaurants are pricey, but there are plenty of food shops.

VAL D'AOSTA

Fringed by Europe's highest mountains, Mont Blanc, the Matterhorn and Monte Rosa, veined with valleys and studded with castles, **Val d'Aosta** is undeniably picturesque. The central Aosta valley cuts right across the region, following the river Dora to the foot of Mont Blanc on the French border. Along the river are most of the feudal castles for which Val d'Aosta is famed – the majority built by the Challant family who ruled the region for seven centuries. Although the castles are pretty from the outside, and easily accessible by bus or train, few are absorbing enough to warrant a special trip into the region. But as skiing and walking country Val d'Aosta is unsurpassed.

Val d'Aosta is the least Italian of all the regions. Its landscape and architecture are Swiss, the official language French, and in some valleys the locals, whose ancestors emigrated from Switzerland, still speak a dialect based on German. In fact, although Italian is more widely spoken than French, bilingualism is an essential part of Val d'Aosta's identity, which is quite distinct from other parts of the north – a distinctiveness reflected in the greater administrative and financial autonomy of the region.

Aosta, the regional capital, is the only town of any size, and though in itself unspectacular makes a good base for much of the area. As for the countryside, the main valley is for the most part rather bland, and it's in the more scenic tributary valleys that you'll want to spend most of your time. The eastern valleys are the most touristed, with ski resorts and narrow, winding roads that can get choked with holiday traffic. If you're walking, the best valleys to head for are those in the west, inside the protected zone of Italy's largest national park, the **Gran Paradiso**. The valleys here can also be busy – the mountain *rifugi* as well as the hotels get packed in summer – but development is restrained.

Getting around

Getting around on **public transport** demands patience. Buses run from Piemonte along the main valley past most of the castles, but buses into many of the tributary valleys are rare. The road branches off at Aosta into Switzerland via the Grand St Bernard Pass (where you can stop to take clichéd photos of the famous dogs) and forks again some 30km further west at Pré-St-Didier: both branches run into France – the southern via the Petit-St-Bernard pass to Chambéry, the northern to Chamonix through the Mont Blanc tunnel. Because of the border posts, the road is much used by long-distance lorries – useful for hitching, but something of an earache and eyesore. Trains are less regular and run only as far as Pré-St-Didier, but by using a combination of the two, and hitching into the less touristed tributary valleys, you can get just about everywhere.

The road to Aosta and the eastern valleys

The tributary valleys in **eastern Val d'Aosta** have suffered most from the skiing industry, although experienced mountain hikers may be allured by the challenge of climbing Monte Rosa and the Matterhorn from **Valtournenche**. Less ambitious walkers will find most to do in the **Valgressoney**, which still has a number of traditional villages settled by the Swiss Walsers, while in the main Aosta valley there are two of the region's more interesting castles, **Issogne** and **Fénis**.

Val Gressoney

The **Val Gressoney** is the first of the Val d'Aosta valleys, but you could be forgiven for thinking you'd stepped into an ad-man's Switzerland. The grass is velvety green, the river Lys crystal clear, the traditional houses wood-slatted and the modern ones gleaming Alpine chalets, while the craggy head of the valley is overlooked by one of Monte Rosa's shimmering glaciers. As you might expect from such natural advantages, the valley gets busy, especially at weekends and holidays: the walking is good, though the skiing less so, with pistes laid out on rocky slopes.

At the mouth of the valley, **PONT-ST-MARTIN** was named for the single-spanned Roman bridge that dominates the village. According to legend it was donated by the Devil in exchange for the first soul that crossed it. However, Saint Martin tricked him by sending a dog over, thus securing a bridge for the villagers and his own immortalisation in the village's name. Pont-St-Martin's usefulness as a bus and train terminus outweighs its attractiveness, and there's little reason to hang around. Buses run fairly regularly up the valley, but if there isn't one due, hitching is easy.

The valley comes into its own at **GRESSONEY-ST-JEAN** and **GRESSONEY-LA-TRINITÉ**. These are popular but attractive resorts, especially La Trinité which is close to the head of the valley. It's quieter and cheaper than St Jean, with some good, homely hotels, and makes a convenient starting-point for walks. If you want to do more than wander along the river, a track leads up to the lovely mountain lake, **Gabiet**, in two to three hours (you can go part way by ski-lift), from where you can continue over the mountain into the Valsesia, doing the descent by cable car if you're tired. Valgressoney's Walser settlements can also be reached by footpaths from Trinité, one of the nicest of which is **BIEL**, with some eighteenth-century houses (maps available from the tourist office). The Walsers still speak their German dialect, and French and Italian too, and the trilingual signs you'll see are not only for the benefit of tourists.

La Trinité's **AAST** (daily 7am–7pm) is on the main piazza, across the river from the bus stop. Close by, the *Albergo Castore* (☎0125/366.131) is a clean and traditional hotel, charging L34,000 for a double without bath (L38,000 during the skiing season and from mid-July to mid-August). The *Pensione Monterosa* (☎0125/366.120), near the entrance of the village, is slightly cheaper but closes out of season. There's a **campsite** at STAFFAL, 5km further up the valley, connected with Trinité by shuttle bus in the skiing season – it's the starting point for the ski-lifts across to Champoluc, in the next valley, Val d'Ayas. There are also a couple of other campsites just beyond Gressoney-St-Jean.

Verrès and Issogne

Buses and trains continue up the main valley to **VERRÈS**, an undistinguished village overlooked by the gloomy cube of its virtually impregnable fourteenth-century **fortress** (March–Nov 9.30am–noon & 2–5.30pm, guided tours every half hour; Dec–Feb 9.30–11.30am & 2–4pm, guided tours every hour; closed Wed; L2000). This is a stark, primitive place, built by the lord of the town, Ibelto di Challant, primarily as a military stronghold. The spartan soldiers' quarters gives some idea of the conditions under which they lived; the Challants' quarters are barely more comfortable, although their fortress does go down in the history books as one of the first to install a toilet. If you need a **room** in Verrès for the night, there are some very basic ones in the *Hotel Ghibli* (☎0125/929.316), three minutes' walk from the railway station, though they charge a steep L35,000 for a ropey double without bath.

Issogne

The castle at **ISSOGNE** (March–Nov 9.30am–noon & 2–5.30pm, guided tours every half hour; Dec–Feb 9.30–11.30am & 2–4pm guided tours every hour; L2000) is of greater interest, another residence of the Challants but a far more comfortable and civilised dwelling than its counterpart at Verrès. Few buses go there, but it's only a short walk from the bus stop outside VERRÈS. Set unceremoniously in the centre of Issogne village, from the outside the castle resembles a municipal building, and you'll probably wonder why you bothered to come. But the well-preserved interior is one of Val d'Aosta's best examples of a late-Gothic ducal residence – with an arcaded courtyard, some vivid frescoes and coffered-ceilinged rooms furnished with ornate Gothic furniture.

In the centre of the courtyard is an unusual fountain – a wrought iron pomegranate tree with water spurting from the lower branches. The courtyard's walls are patched with painted coats of arms, and in the shelter of one of the arcades is a colourful and bustling fresco of a medieval high street. From here, guided tours take you through kitchens, a beautifully furnished dining room, a couple of chapels with ornate polyptychs, and into the Countess of Challant's bedroom, whose bedside chair conceals a commode.

After seeing the castle, it's worth paying the L2000 extra to see the castle's **exhibition of costume** – well researched reconstructions of those worn in the courtyard frescoes.

Val d'Ayas

Branching off the main valley, and headed by the huge mass of Monte Rosa, **Val d'Ayas** is one of the region's most beautiful valleys, large, open and flanked by thickly wooded slopes. Sadly it's also overwhelmed by visitors, and the tourist-geared villages are chock-full of trippers and skiers at the weekend and in season, and completely dead at other times of the year.

The main ski resort, **CHAMPOLUC** at the head of the valley, is connected by a series of ski-lifts to STAFFAL in the Val Gressoney. It's also the base for the tough ascent (4hr minimum; route 62) of the **Testa Grigia** (3315m) – although you can cheat on this by taking the funicular and ski-lift part of the way. From the top there's a superb view across the peaks of the Matterhorn to Mont Blanc; however unless you can afford a guide (ask at the tourist office in Champoluc) the climb is strictly for the experienced.

BRUSSON, further down the valley, is a better base for less demanding walks. There's a trail (3hr 30min; route 6) up to seven mountain lakes, starting with a long climb through a dense wood up to a waterfall – the water drops thirty metres, and is most impressive in spring when the snow is melting.

Hotel *Beau Site* (☎0125/300.144), on the edge of Brusson, is clean, simple and has a good restaurant. Doubles without bath cost L35,000. In Champoluc the central hotels are expensive, but *Cre-Forné* (☎0125/307.197) at Crest (connected with Champoluc by funicular) has doubles without bath for L25,000. There are also **campsites** between Brusson and Champoluc.

Valtournenche and the Matterhorn (Cervino)

VALTOURNENCHE, headed by the Matterhorn, or Cervino as the Italians call it, should be one of the most spectacular of Italy's mountain valleys. Instead it's the most depressing. The international ski resort of Breuil-Cervinia is brutally ugly, and even the Matterhorn is a let-down, tribes of skiers ensuring that its glacier is grubby for much of the year.

Breuil-Cervinia
BREUIL-CERVINIA was one of Italy's first ski resorts, built in the prewar years as part of Mussolini's drive for a healthy nation. In its day the ski-lifts, soaring to 3500m, broke all records, and its grand hotels ensured the patronage of Europe's wealthy. Today the wealthy are cossetted in modern monstrosities outside the resort, leaving the tacky streets of the purpose-built town for packaged hordes attracted by a large skiing area with lots of easy runs.

Frankly, the only reason to come here is to climb the **Matterhorn** (4476m). You'll need the *FMB* map which covers Valtournenche and the Monte Rosa valleys, and to be well equipped. There are two *rifugi* on the way, *Duca degli Abruzzi* (0166/949.119), 2 hours 15 minutes from Breuil, and the *Rifugio M Carrel* (no phone) – where most people stay the night – 4 hours beyond. Both are open all year. From the Carrel *rifugio* it's a tough climb to the summit, even with the ropes that have been fitted along the more dangerous stretches of the route.

The less agile members of the smart set now head to **ST VINCENT**, a spa resort near the industrial town of Chatillon at the mouth of the valley. There's a famous **casino** here, but a distinct lack of Monte Carlo glitz on the streets. If you end up with time to spare between buses, the parish **church** (*Parrochiale*) is quite interesting, with the excavations of the baths of a Roman villa around the outside, some lively frescoes inside.

Nus and the Castello di Fénis

NUS, further up the main valley from Chatillon, is a small, pretty village over-looked by a ruined castle, that makes a good base for the castle of **Fénis** 2km away (March–Nov 9.30am–noon & 2–5.30pm, guided tours every half hour; Dec–Feb 9.30–11.30am and 2–4pm guided tours every hour; closed Tuesday; L2000). Backed by wooded hills and encircled by two rows of turreted walls, the castle is a fairytale cluster of towers decorated with scalloped arcades. These defences were primarily aesthetic, with the real job of protecting the valley being left to the less prettified fortresses of nearby Nus and Quart, while the Fénis branch of the Challant counts concentrated on refining their living quarters with fine Gothic frescoes.

The best of these is in the courtyard, above the elaborate twin staircase that leads to the upper storeys. A courtly Saint George rescues a damsel-in-distress from the clutches of a tremendous dragon, overlooked by a tribe of protective saints brandishing moral statements on curling scrolls. There are further frescoes in the Baronial Hall upstairs, which has been closed for some time. It's due to reopen this year, but the authorities are reluctant to subject the frescoes to troops of tourists.

There's a **hotel** in Fénis, *La Chatelaine* (☎0165/764.264), at the foot of the castle, but it closes out of season. Doubles without bath cost between L32,000 and L37,500. Five minutes' walk from the castle there's a **campsite**, *Les Chataigniers*, open from April to October. However, as Nus has a railway station, and is close to the main road for buses, you may find it more convenient to sleep there. The *Florian* (☎0165/767.968), on the main street, has clean and comfortable doubles with bath for L33,000 (L42,000 in July, Aug and late Dec to mid-Jan).

Aosta and around

AOSTA is well used to tourists. Until recently, as the capital of a duty-free region it was patronised by a steady stream of French, Swiss and Italians in search of cheap booze. Baskets of liqueurs and vermouths still line the main street, but the prices have risen and are no longer the town's main draw.

Aosta was founded by the Romans in 25 BC, after disposing of the local tribe by auctioning them off in a slave market. It was primarily a military camp, unlikely to have been particularly splendid, and in any case little survives from the era. More remains of medieval Aosta, but the town's key attraction is its position. Encircled by the **Alps**, and with access to the lovely valleys of the **Gran Paradiso National Park**, the ski resorts of **Mont Blanc**, and a sprinkling of castles in between, it's an ideal base or jumping-off point for exploring the northwest of the region, before heading on to Switzerland or France.

The Town

Centre of town is **Piazza E. Chanoux** and its smart pavement cafés, from where Via Porta Pretoriana and Via Sant'Anselmo lead east, forming the main axis of the town centre and the principal street for window-shopping and people-watching. At the far end, the **Porta Pretoria** is one of the town's most impressive sights, two parallel triple-arched gateways which formed the main entrance into the Roman town. The space in between was for soldiers to keep a check on visitors to the town, and a family of medieval nobles later made their home above it, building a tower which now houses temporary exhibitions.

North of the gate there are further relics of the Roman occupation in the **Teatro Romano** (daily 9.30am–noon & 2.30–6.30pm; closes at 4.30pm in winter), of which an impressive section of the four-storeyed facade remains, 22m high and pierced with arched windows. Only the lower section of the auditorium or *cavea* has survived, however, and theatrical performances now take place in summer on a platform overlooking the theatre. Close by, the medieval **Torre Fromage** is now a contemporary art exhibition-space.

Outside the main town walls, off Via Sant'Anselmo, the church of **Sant'Orso** houses a number of tenth-century frescoes behind its dull facade, hidden up in the roof where you can examine them at close quarters from specially constructed walkways – though you'll need to find the sacristan to get up there. If you can't find him, content yourself with the fifteenth century choir stalls, carved with a menagerie of holy men and animals, ranging from bats and monkeys to a tonsured monk. There are even better carvings on the eye-level capitals of the intimate Romanesque cloisters – mostly scenes from the story of Christ, with emphasis on donkeys and sheep.

At the end of the street, the **Arco di Augusto** was erected in 25 BC to celebrate the seizure of the territory from the local Salassi tribe, and to honour Emperor Augustus for whom the town *Augusta Praetoria* – was named (Aosta is a corruption of Augusta). Though the arch loses something islanded in a sea of traffic and topped by an ugly eighteenth-century roof, it's a sturdy-looking monument, the mountains behind only adding to its measure of dignity. Beyond is a well-preserved **Roman bridge**, its single arch spanning the dried-up bed of the river Buthier.

Back in the centre of town, the **Forum** is the misleading name for another Roman relic, a vaulted passage under the actual forum area, the purpose of which is unclear (summer daily 10am–noon & 2.30–6pm; winter daily 10am–noon & 2.30–4.30pm). The Cattedrale, next door, looks unpromising from the outside, but it masks a Gothic interior with even more fantastically carved choir stalls than Sant'Orso's, with a mermaid, lion and snail among the saints. Remains of a fourth-century baptistry are visible through the floor; better are the mosaics on the presbytery pavement showing the two rivers of earthly paradise and Christ, holding the sun and moon, surrounded by the symbols of the months. There are more treasures in the church's **museum** – gold-, silver- and gem-encrusted reliquaries and equally ornate chalices, crucifixes and caskets for relics.

Aosta practicalities

Aosta's **EPT** is on Piazza E. Chanoux and has maps and other information on the town and around (June–Sept daily 9am–1pm & 3–8pm; Oct–May Mon–Sat 9am–1pm & 3–8pm, Sun 9am–1pm). You can get to most places within the region by **bus** from the **terminus** at Piazza Narbonne, but some of the more remote valleys are served by only one bus a week out of season. **Trains** run west along the main valley only as far as Pré Saint Didier. The best bet is to arm yourself with the combined bus and train timetable from the EPT and use both.

First choice for a **room** is *La Belle Epoque* on Via d'Avise, off Via E. Aubert (☎0165/362.276), new, clean and comfortable with doubles without bath at around L35,000. *Juventus*, Via E Aubert 33 (☎0165/34.088), is scruffier, but has doubles without bath for only L27,000 in low season, rising to L38,000 in the high season. The *Hotel Pila*, Via Paravera 12b (☎0165/43.398), is good value, with clean doubles with bath for between L26,000 and L36,000, again depending on the time of year, though it's a ten-minute walk from the centre of town on the far side of the railway line. Finding **somewhere to eat** is no problem, as most pizzerias and restaurants have prices outside – the best street is Via E. Aubert. If you want to save money, there's a popular **self-service restaurant** at the railway station, and numerous foodstores and takeaway pizza places.

West from Aosta: three castles

Both road and railway run west from Aosta through the main valley, passing a number of **castles**. All of these are easy to reach on public transport, and after visiting you can catch a bus or hitch into the valleys of the Gran Paradiso National Park.

Castello di Sarre

First of the castles is the thirteenth-century **Castello di Sarre** (July–mid-Sept Wed–Mon 10–11am & 2.30–4.30pm; June Sat & Sun only; L2000), accessible by bus or train from Aosta. From the main road walk from the bus stop and take the unmarked turning just before the toll-booth. From the train station, it's a ten-minute walk up a hill covered with apple orchards. Sarre is the former hunting lodge of Vittorio Emanuele II, who actually bought the castle by mistake. He had set his sights on the castle of Aymaville opposite, but the agent sent to buy the castle was confused about the direction in which the river flowed, and ended up buying Sarre instead.

Vittorio Emanuele made the best of a bad job, permanently stamping the halls of the castle with his astounding taste in interior decor, pushing the hunting-lodge motif to its limits, with horns of wild ibex lining the main gallery, thousands of white chamois skulls studding the stuccoed festoons and horn-sprouting medallions that surround the stuffed heads of ibex. Pride of place is given to the first ibex that the king killed. The custodian claims that many died a natural death, but this was hardly the impression that Vittorio Emanuele, in his guise as macho huntsman, intended. The rest of the castle is well patronised by diehard Italian monarchists come to pay their respects to Savoy family trees, portraits and photographs and walls plastered with magazine features on the now exiled Italian royals.

Castello di Saint-Pierre and Castello Sarriod de La Tour

Five minutes further along the rail line, the **Castello di Saint-Pierre** (April–Oct 9am–noon & 3–7pm, closed Tues except in July & Aug; L2000) perches on a rocky cliff, a crenellated and turreted castle that dates from the twelfth century but is mostly the result of a restyling in the eighteenth century. There's a small **natural history museum** inside with an array of stuffed birds, and unless this appeals you'd do well to press on.

A short walk along the main road beyond Saint-Pierre, set on a low hill above the river, and invisible from the road, **Sarriod de La Tour** (May–Sept Wed–Mon 9.30am–noon & 3–7pm; L2000) is less a castle than a medieval tower with farm buildings built around it. It's a refreshingly rustic place, with some appealing frescoes, and an archaeological museum laid out in its warren of rooms.

The Gran Paradiso National Park

For some of Val d'Aosta's most beautiful mountains and valleys you need to make for the south of the region, down to the **Parco Nazionale di Gran Paradiso** – Italy's second largest national park, spread around the valleys at the foot of 4061-metre-high Gran Paradiso mountain.

Oddly enough the park owes its foundation to Vittorio Emanuele II, who donated his extensive hunting park to the state in 1922, ensuring that the population of ibex that he and his hunters had managed to reduce to near-extinction survived. There are now around 3500 ibex here and about 6000 chamois, living most of the year above the tree line, but descending to the valleys in winter and spring. The most dramatic sightings are during the mating season in November and December, when if you're lucky you can see pairs of males fighting it out for the possession of a female. You might also see golden eagles nesting, and there are a number of rare types of alpine flower – most of which can be seen in the Botanical Garden in the Cogne valley.

The park's three valleys – **Cogne**, **Valsaveranche** and **Val de Rhêmes** are popular, but tourist development has been cautious and well organised. The hotels are good (you get far more for your money than you would in one of the nearby towns), the campsites not too vast, and there are lots of mountain *rifugi* and well marked footpaths. Though primarily a summer resort for walkers, the cross-country skiing is also good, and every winter a 45km *Gran Paradiso Trek* is organised at Cogne (write ahead to the local tourist office for details). The starting-point for the ascent of Gran Paradiso itself is **Pont** in the Valsavarenche, while **Cogne** has a good range of walks ranging from easy strolls to long mountain trails.

There are regular buses throughout the year from Aosta to Cogne, but Valsavarenche and Val de Rhêmes are served only by buses in summer. At other times hitching into either of these valleys is easiest from the village of INTROD, about 2km from VILLENEUVE which is on the main bus route and a walkable distance from the castles of Saint-Pierre and Sarriod de la Tour.

Val di Cogne

The **Val di Cogne** is the principal, most popular and most dramatic section of the park. Its lower reaches are narrow, the road running above the fast-flowing Grand

Eyvia river overlooked by sheer wavy-ridged mountains. Further on, the valley broadens out around the main village, **COGNE**, which is surrounded by gentle green meadows and glacier-covered mountains rising beyond.

The **AAST** (daily 9am–12.30pm & 3–6pm, Sun and holidays 9am–12.30pm) in the centre of the village has maps with English descriptions of walks. One of the easiest and most scenic is along the gorgeous riverside trail that winds along the valley of the Valnontey tributary, the glaciers in view for most of the way. **VALNONTEY** itself is a small village and starting-point for the walk up to the *Rifugio V. Sella* (open from Easter to September; ☎0165/74.310; extremely popular – avoid summer weekends and early August). The path passes the **Botanical Garden** (June–Sept) then zigzags up through a forest and down to the *rifugio*, set on a grassy mountain plain. At the small mountain Lake Lausan, half an hour's walk from the *rifugio*, you may well spot some **ibex**, especially at sunset and sunrise. Hardened hikers, who can cope with a stretch of climbing, can walk over the **Colle de Lausan** to the Val de Rhêmes.

There's a **campsite**, *Vallee de Cogne*, close to Cogne village, and two sites at Valnontey – *Lo Stambecco* and *Gran Paradiso*. The first is open all year, the others from June to September. Most **hotels** close from mid-September to mid-November, and some from April to mid-May as well. They also get booked up quickly in high season, and it's advisable to call ahead. Cogne's cheapest hotels are *Stambecco* (☎0165/74.068), just off the road to Valnontey (doubles without bath L20,000–36,000 depending on the season), and on the main entrance road, *Du Soleil* (☎0165/74.033) – which charges around L35,000. **Restaurants** are pricey, but there are a couple of **takeaways** and plenty of *salumerie* which will make up sandwiches.

Valsavarenche

Although not as spectacular as the Val di Cogne, **Valsavarenche**, the next valley west, has its own kind of beauty, attracting seasoned walkers rather than gentle amblers. The most popular route is the **ascent of Gran Paradiso**, from **PONT** at the end of the valley – reckoned to be the easiest of the higher Alps to climb but nevertheless a climb rather than a hike, with no path marked beyond the *Rifugio Vittorio Emanuele* (April 15–Sept 30; 2hr 30min from Pont). It's obligatory to phone (☎0165/95.710) before setting out to check there's room.

If you feel safer walking along footpaths, the best of the hikes are from the main village of **DEGIOZ**, otherwise known as *Valsavarenche*, up to the *Rifugio Orvielles* (2hr 30min) and then on to a series of high mountain lakes. This takes seven hours, but you can shorten it a bit by taking the path marked #3a down to Pont. Less taxing is the two-hour walk from Pont towards the glacier **Grand Etret** at the head of the valley, although the first stretch is boring.

The only **hotel** in Degioz, the *Parco Nazionale* (☎0165/95.706), is expensive (doubles with bath only; L48,000), but the seasonal *Edelweiss* (☎0165/95.702), in the hamlet of Bien about twenty-five minutes' walk away, charges L25,000–30,000 for doubles without bath, depending on the time of year.

Pont has the best **campsite**, *Pont Breuil*, open from June to September, with a fairly well stocked site shop (there's no other for miles). Best of all, in June ibex come down to graze on the grassy meadow around the tents – so have your camera at the ready in the early morning. Pont also has a bar and a couple of hotels: *Gran Paradiso* (☎0165/95.714) is the cheap one, charging L30,000 for doubles without bath.

There are **places to eat** in Degioz, but at Pont you'll have to cook for yourself, or ask at one of the hotels.

Val di Rhêmes

The least touristed but most open of the valleys, **Val di Rhêmes** is also headed by glaciers. The best place to stay is **BRUIL**, a small hamlet outside Rhêmes Notre Dame at the end of the valley, from which most of the walks start. There's a fairly easy path along the river to a waterfall, the *Cascata di Goletta*, at its most spectacular after the spring snow-melt, and from here you can continue to the *Rifugio Benevolo* and the mountain lake of Goletta (open late March–May, weekends in June & July–Sept). There are only five beds, so phone (☎0165/96.113) before setting out.

The *Della Pineta* (☎0165/96.101) and *Pellaud* (☎0165/96.110) **hotels** in Bruil charge around L30,000 for a double without bath – but out of season you can get a double with bath at the *Galisia* (☎0165/96.100) for the same price.

Arvier and Valgrisenche

Valgrisenche, a few kilometres west from Val di Rhêmes, is the wildest and least inaccessible of Val d'Aosta's valleys. The only buses from Aosta into the valley are at 7am and 6pm in summer, and at 5.30am in winter, although buses and trains stop year-round at **ARVIER** at the mouth of the valley – one of the regions' most appealing villages, with a medieval core of twisting streets and stone houses alongside a gorge spanned by a Roman bridge. Arvier also has Val d'Aosta's oldest hotel, and produces *L'Enfer d'Arvier*, reckoned to be the region's best wine.

The **hotel**, *Col du Mont* (☎0165/99.001), dates from the nineteenth century and is clean, comfortable and friendly, as well as atmospheric, with doubles without bath for between L25,000 and L37,000 depending on the season. It's closed right through from October to June, so in this period try the *Beau Sejour* (☎0165/99.016), which has doubles with bath for L34,000 and a popular restaurant and bar below.

Hitching into the Valgrisenche from here is difficult: there's little traffic, especially out of season; if you have no joy, try asking around in Arvier's bars. The effort, though, is worth it. A narrow valley, with rocky snow-dusted ridges rising above dark pine woods, Valgrisenche is stunning, though the upper reaches are defaced by the concrete dam of a reservoir.

A good starting-point for **walks** is the hamlet of **BONNE** above the reservoir. These include the 4–5-hour ascent of the glaciated Testa del Rutor (3486m) via the *Rifugio Scavarda* (two hours along the path; open July 1–Sept 30). There are many other walks, but none of them is easy – you should be sure to have the *Kompass* Gran Paradiso map. The cheapest **hotel** is the *Perret* (☎0165/97.107) in Bonne (closed June & Nov) with a restaurant, bar and doubles without bath for L37,500.

The Northwest: around Mont Blanc

Dominated by the year-long snowy peaks of **Mont Blanc** (Monte Bianco to the Italians), the northern reaches of Val d'Aosta are scenically stunning but also very popular. The most sensational views are from the cable cars that glide and swoop (at times alarmingly so) across the mountain to Chamonix in France. However, the trip is expensive, even if you take a bus or hitch back to Italy through the 11km-long Mont Blanc tunnel, and the service is often suspended because of bad weather.

La Thuile and Testa d'Arpy

If the cable car seems too pricey, you can walk up to the **Testa d'Arpy** from the sprawling resort of **LA THUILE**, on the road to the Petit St Bernard pass into France, for sweeping views of the peaks and glaciers of Mont Blanc. Buses run from Pre-St-Didier at the end of the Val d'Aosta railway line to La Thuile, from where it's just over two hours' walk by path or road to the *La Genzianella* hotel at the top of the Colle San Carlo. From here a path leads through woods to Testa d'Arpy in around ten minutes, a natural balcony with a bird's eye view up the valley to Mont Blanc. It's well worth having a good map (FSB *Monte Bianco*) – not so much to find your way as to identify the peaks and glaciers spread out before you.

As for La Thuile, it's an over-developed resort, and it makes sense to pass through quickly, after calling in at the **AAST** for maps, and to sleep up in the mountain at *La Genzianella* (☎0165/884.137). Doubles without bath cost between L27,000 and L36,500 depending on the season – but phone in advance to check that there's room. Of the other walks starting from the hotel the most interesting is the forty-five-minute hike to **Lago d'Arpy**, from where a path leads down into La Thuile.

Courmayeur and Mont Blanc

COURMAYEUR is the smartest and most popular of Val d'Aosta's ski resorts, much used by British package operators. The skiing is good, though there's little to challenge experts, the scenery magnificent; but, predictably, what remains of the old village is enmeshed in a web of ersatz Alpine chalets and après-ski hangouts.

If you want a week of skiing, you'll probably save money by taking a package anyway; if you've come to hike or take the big-dipping cable cars across to Chamonix, the most convenient place to stay is **LA PALUD**, 5km outside Courmayeur. There are only three buses a day, but hitching is okay: don't get disheartened at the number of cars of smart city skiers whizzing past you – most local people will stop.

The **cable car** starts at La Palud and travels in three stages via Punta Hellbronner and Aiguille du Midi – where there's a restaurant perched on a dizzying granite needle rock – to Chamonix. To be sure of good views, you'll need to set out before 9am since it's usually cloudy by midday; be sure also to get there in plenty of time, especially on summer weekends, as it's much used by summer skiers. The first car leaves at 8am, the last at 4.20pm, but the regularity depends on the weather. Incidentally, even if it's blazing hot in the valley, the temperature plunges to freezing-point at the top, so take some warm clothes.

There are good walks along the two valleys at the foot of the Mont Blanc glaciers, both of which have seasonal **campsites** accessible by bus from Courmayeur. Val Ferret to the west is the more interesting option – you can walk back from Frebouze over Monte de la Saxe, with some stunning views of Mont Blanc en route.

If you do end up having to **spend a night** in Courmayeur, the cheapest hotel is the *Agip* (☎0165/842.427) – a motel above the Agip petrol station on the main road, with doubles without bath for L28,000. One of the nicest places **to eat** is at the *Turistica*, off Courmayeur's main street, which also has some (more expensive) rooms.

The cheapest hotels in La Palud are the *Funivia* (☎0165/89.924) and *La Quercia* (☎0165/89.931), both with doubles without bath for around L36,000. Since they close out of season, you may have to take a double with bath for between L43,000 and L45,000 at the extremely comfortable *Vallee Blanche* (☎0165/89.933).

travel details

Trains

From Turin to Vercelli (25 daily; 45min–1hr 10min); Novara (27 daily; 1hr–1hr 15min); Milan Centrale (19 daily; 1hr 30min–1hr 45min); Aosta (change at Chivasso; 13 daily; 1hr 45min–4hr 55min); Cuneo (9 daily; 1hr–1hr 30min); Asti (33 daily; 30min–1hr); Modane (8 daily; 1hr 25min–2hr 25min).

From Cuneo to Limone Piemonte (14 daily; 30min).

From Alba to Asti (change at Castagnole delle Lanze; 8 daily; 40min–1hr 10min).

From Asti to Casale Monferrato (6 daily; 50min).

From Novara to Varallo (9 daily; 1hr 10min–1hr 30min); Biella (10 daily; 1hr–1hr 10min).

From Verrès to Aosta (14 daily; 30min–1hr 10min); Turin (change at Chivasso; 13 daily; 1hr 10min–1hr 45min).

From Aosta to Pré-St-Didier (9 daily; 50min).

Buses

From Turin Corso Marconi to Saluzzo (up to 10 daily; 1hr 20min); Cuneo (up to 8 daily; 2hr 10min–2hr 45min).

From Turin Corso Inghilterra to Aosta (up to 12 daily; 2–3hr); Ivrea (up to 12 daily; 1hr–1hr 15min); Gressoney La Trinité (up to 4 daily; 2hr 10min–3hr 10min); Champoluc (2 daily; 3hr 15min–3hr 30min); Cervinia (1 daily; 2hr 15min);

Courmayeur (up to 7 daily; 3–4hr 10min); Chamonix/Geneva (1 daily; 3hr 15min/4hr 30min); Lugano via Novara (1 daily; 3hr); Locarno (1 daily; 4hr).

From Biella to Ivrea (6 daily; 2hr 25min); Santuario di Oropa (9 daily; 40min).

From Saluzzo to Cuneo (up to 17 daily; 1hr); Val Varaita (up to 3 daily; 45min–1hr 15min); Crissolo (up to 3 daily; 1hr 30min– 2hr).

From Cuneo to Dronero (Val Maira) (up to 20 daily; 35min); Valle Stura (up to 7 daily; 1hr–1hr 20min).

From Alba to Barolo (up to 6 daily; 30min); Grinzane (hourly).

From Pont St Martin to Gressoney La Trinité (7 daily; 1hr 20min).

From Verrès to Champoluc (up to 6 daily; 1hr 10min).

From Chatillon to Breuil Cervinia (up to 6 daily; 1hr–1hr 30min).

From Aosta to Cogne (5 daily; 50min); Pont Valsavarenche (3 daily in summer; 1hr 10min); Rhêmes St Georges (3 on weekdays Sept–June; 45min; July & Aug 2 daily, going on to Rhêmes Notre Dame; 1hr); Valgrisenche (mid-June–mid-Sept 2 daily; mid-Sept–mid-June Mon, Tues & Sat only); Courmayeur (up to 20 daily; 1hr).

From Pré-St-Didier to La Thuile (7 daily; 25min); Courmayeur (15 daily; 10–25min).

Cable cars

La Palud/Chamonix (☎0165/89.925) every 20 min: June 1–July 1 8.30am–5pm; July 2–July 29 7am–5.20pm; July 30–Aug 28 7am–6.20pm; Aug 29–Sept 11 7.30am–5.20pm; Sept 12–Nov 30 8am–4.20pm.

Breuil/Matterhorn (☎0166/948.421) Summer hourly 8am–5pm; winter hourly 8.45am–5pm.
Champoluc/Crest (☎0125/307.146) 8am–12.50pm & 2–5.50pm.
Cogne/Gran Paradiso (☎0165/74.008) Summer 9am–12.30pm & 2–6pm; winter 9am–4.30pm.

LIGURIA

Liguria – also known as the **Italian Riviera** – has two parts: the narrow, commercially developed strip of coast, and a mountainous hinterland of isolated villages, terraced for olives and vines. Approaching from Nice and Monaco, there's an unexpected change as you cross the border: the Italian Riviera has more variety of landscape and architecture than its French counterpart, and is generally less frenetic – though it's still extremely crowded in summer. An autostrada (A12) sweeps the length of the province through to Tuscany, and a main railway line follows the same route – rapid bursts of daylight between tunnels give a glimpse of the string of resorts along the coast, silver olive groves and a brilliant sea.

Chief town of the province is **Genova**. Heavy industry and a manic traffic system make the city off-putting if you're just travelling through, but Genova is worth spending time in for its old town round the port. The city makes a neat division between two distinct stretches of coastline. To the west is the **Riviera del Ponente** – packed out with Italian families who book a year ahead to stay in their favourite hotel. This side of the coast has become one long ribbon of hotels, but there are places to head for: **Noli** and **Albenga** are both medieval towns; **Finale Ligure** is a pleasant resort; and **San Remo**, flanked by hillsides covered with glasshouses, is a major centre for flower growers who trade at the early morning market.

Southeast, towards Tuscany, on the **Riviera del Levante**, the coast is more rugged. Umbrella pines grow horizontally on cliff faces, and in the evening there's a glassy calm over the bays and inlets. Walks on **Monte Portofino** and in the **Cinque Terre** take you high enough through *macchia* and vineyards for views over wide gulfs. The mix of mountains and fishing villages reachable only by boat appealed to the Romantics, who "discovered" the Riviera in the eighteenth century, preparing the way for other artists and poets, and the first package tourists earlier this century. Now the whole area explodes into a nightmarish ruck every July and August, with people coming to resorts like **Portofino** and **Santa Margherita Ligure** strictly for pose value.

One way to avoid this is to travel into the hinterland. Minor roads and mule tracks link villages, built spiral-fashion around hill tops, originally as protection against Saracen invasion. Further up into the mountains, the **Alta Via dei Monti Liguri** runs for 440km along the ridges, from **Ventimiglia** near the border with France, to **Ceparana**, north of La Spezia. *Club Alpino Italiano* offices in the major towns have information on refuges, and there's a guide to the trail by the *Centro Studi Unioncamere Liguri* on sale in bookshops. Base yourself at **Monesi** near Monte Saccarello, **Alberola** in the mountains near Genova, or **Santo Stefano d'Aveto** on the border with Emilia Romagna for walking or skiing. This is one of the few areas of Liguria where hiring a car is an advantage: bus links with larger towns on the coast are good, but you need to change a few times to reach the

LIGURIA

more out-of-the-way places. You'll also be able to get to some of the mountain restaurants, which are often the best places for sampling **Ligurian cooking**. Recipes make something out of nothing – a legacy of past hardships, which have bred a reserve in the Ligurian character and given them an undeserved reputation amongst other Italians for meanness.

GENOVA

GENOVA is "a place that grows upon you every day . . . it abounds in the strangest contrasts; things that are picturesque, ugly, mean, magnificent, delightful and offensive, break upon the view at every turn", wrote Dickens in 1844, and the description still fits. It's a marvellously eclectic city and it would be a big mistake to pass it by completely. At the heart of everything is the port, surrounded by a warren of alleyways which make up the medieval centre, a district which has more zest than all the coastal resorts put together.

Genova made its money at sea, through trade, colonial exploitation and legalised piracy. By the thirteenth century it was one of the five Italian maritime republics and the implacable enemy of two of the others – Venice and Pisa. Later, Genova had bigger threats from outside to worry about: France and Austria invaded in the seventeenth and eighteenth centuries, at the same time as the city lost its position as financial capital of Europe. During the Unification era, Genova had a relatively free press and recognised at least some civil liberties. Political refugees came from more reactionary parts of Italy and the city was a base for radical thought. **Mazzini**, one of the main protagonists in Italy's unification was born here, and in 1860 **Garibaldi**, whose family came from nearby, set sail for Sicily with his "Thousand" from the city's harbour. Genova is also where Italy's industrial revolution began, its trade routes to the Middle East, north Africa, and Spain opening the city to diverse cultures. The port is now in economic decline, but Genova remains a focus for many of Italy's immigrants.

The core of the city, between the two stations and the waterfront, is full of interest: food shops in the portals of former palaces, carpenters' workshops sandwiched between designer furniture outlets, everything surrounded by a crush of people and the inpenetrable Genovese dialect – a mixture of Neapolitan, Calabrese and Portuguese. There are enough buildings and art collections to keep you busy for several days. Worth seeking out are small medieval churches such as **San Donato** and **Santa Maria di Castello**, the **Cattedrale di San Lorenzo** with its fabulous treasury, as well as the Renaissance palaces which contain Genova's **art collections**, with many paintings by the Flemish masters, and Oriental and pre-Columbian art. But it's not all culture. Other attractions include live music, theatre and cinema, ritzy bars, clubs, and an active political scene.

Arriving and staying

Trains arrive from Savona at Stazione Principe, in Piazza Acquaverde (☎262.455) and from La Spezia and Rome at Stazione Brignole, on Piazza Verdi (☎586.350). Trains from Milan and Turin usually stop at both, but if you do have to travel between the two, take bus #37. The **airport** (☎26.901) is 6km away at Sestri Ponente – buses into Genova link up with flight arrivals. Buses out to the airport leave from both Piazza della Vittoria and Via Petrarca one hour before scheduled flight departures. The old town is closed to traffic, but **buses** leave for other points from both stations. A **tourist ticket** from one of the *ATM* kiosks here gives you an unlimited number of journeys on any route for L1000 a day. Out of town, the *Tigullio Line* (☎313.851) operates from Piazza della Vittoria.

The most central (and helpful) of the tourist offices is the **AAST** at Via Porta degli Archi 10/5, tucked in at an angle near the flight of steps. The central **EPT** is at Via Roma 11 (Mon–Thurs 8am–2pm & 4–6pm, Fri & Sat 8am–1pm); there are also **EPT** offices at Stazione Brignole (Mon–Fri 9am–noon & 3–6pm, Sat 9am–noon), Stazione Principe (Mon–Sat 8am–8pm) and the airport.

You may stop over in Genova before taking a **ferry** to the Italian islands or further afield. *Corsica Line* and *Sardinia Ferries* are at Piazza Dante 5/a (☎593.301). For crossings to Sardinia and Sicily contact *Tirrenia* at Ponte Colombo (☎258.041). There are also occasional round-trips calling at several Mediterranean ports including Piraeus and Barcelona. All boats leave from the *Stazione Marittima*, ten minutes' walk downhill from Stazione Principe. See "Travel Details" on p.118 for schedules and journey-times.

Genova has a confusing system of street numbers – buildings are divided into two categories: the first, consisting of residential buildings and offices, is distinguished by blue or black number plates; the second, comprising shops and restaurants, has red plates. This means that there can be two number 17s, for example, in the same long street; under a thick layer of grime, it's sometimes hard to tell the difference.

Orientation

Genova spreads outwards from its **old town** around the port in a confusion of tiny alleyways (*carrugi*), bordered by **Via Gramsci** along the waterfront, and by **Via Balbi** and its continuations to the north. The **newer part** of Genova starts to the right of **Piazza de Ferrari** – from here **Via XX Settembre** runs a straight course through the commercial centre of the city, to the area around **Stazione Brignole**. Finding your bearings takes time: useful reference points are the two railway stations. Away from the centre, past Stazione Brignole, is the beach area of **Albaro**. **Boccadasse**, further along, is a small fishing port, now part of the city. Inland, the higher districts of Genova are mainly residential. The rest of the city sprawls for 35km in a narrow strip round the arch of the bay, east towards **Nervi** and west to **Pegli**, both former resorts swallowed up by suburbs.

Finding a place to stay

There are plenty of cheap **hotels** in the city centre, but many are grimy and depressing, and you need to look hard to find the exceptions. Good areas to try are the roads bordering the old town, and Piazza Colombo and Via XX Settembre, near Stazione Brignole. *Pensione Mediterranee*, just north of the old town at Via Cairoli 14/4 (☎206.531), is particularly good, with rooms from L23,000, or there are *pensioni* in the apartment buildings on Via Balbi, close to Stazione Principe. Other possibilities near Stazione Brignole are *Carletto*, Via Colombo 16/4 (☎546.412), and *Hotel Ricci*, Piazza Colombo 4/8 (☎592.746), both of which have

The Genova area telephone code is ☎010

GENOVA

rooms at around L40,000. There's a batch of places round the corner, on Via XX Settembre: at no. 23, the *Soana* (☎562.814) starts at L35,000; at no. 19 *Bel Soggiorno* (☎581.418) has rooms from L42,000); while *Mirafiori* (☎542.245) and *Bruxelles Margherita* (☎589.191) are both in the L30,000 range.

The **youth hostel** at Albaro has closed indefinitely, but for a place with similar prices – around L12,000 a head – try the tiny *Caffaro*, off Piazza Portello at Salita San Gerolamo 7 (☎296.434).

The City

The layout of Genova's **old town** reflects its medieval politics. From the thirteenth to the fourteenth century, families marked out certain streets and squares as their territory, even extending their domain to include churches – to pray in someone else's chapel was to risk being stabbed in the back. The maze of alleyways was the battleground of long-running feuds between the Doria, Spinola, Grimaldi and Fieschi families, the city's major dynasties. Nothing really changed until the election in 1339 of Genova's first **Doge**, when all four clans were excluded from government.

The Palazzo Ducale, Gesù and Cattedrale

From 1384 to 1515, except for brief periods of foreign domination, the Doge ruled the city from the **Palazzo Ducale** in Piazza Matteotti. The present black and white striped building, with its huge vaulted atrium, was built in the sixteenth century – its wide steps up from the courtyard designed with the doge's grand processions in mind. The dour **Gesù** church across the square, designed by Pellegrino Tibaldi at the end of the sixteenth century, contains a mass of marble and gilt stucco, lurking among which are Guido Reni's *Assumption* and two paintings by Rubens: the *Circumcision* and *Miracles of St Ignatius*.

Traffic files down to the port past the blackened walls of the Gothic **Cattedrale di San Lorenzo** (open all day). Master craftsmen from France constructed the central portal, which is surrounded by twisting, fluted columns and topped with alternating black and white stripes. The statue of Saint Lawrence holding a sundial is known locally as "the knife-grinder". Inside is the Renaissance chapel of Saint John the Baptist, whose remains once rested in the thirteenth-century sarcophagus. After a particularly bad storm priests carried his casket through the city to placate the sea, and a commemorative procession takes place each June 24 in honour of the saint. His reliquary is in the treasury **museum** (Tues–Sat 9.30–11.45am & 2–5pm) along with a polished quartz plate on which, legend says, Salome received his severed head. Also on display, and also from the first century AD, is a glass dish said to have been given to Solomon by the Queen of Sheba, and used at the Last Supper. Artefacts from Byzantine and later times include delicate jewelled crosses and arm-shaped reliquaries.

Around Piazza di Sarzano

Uphill from Piazza Matteotti, past a row of restaurants and bars, is the old entrance to the city, a twin-towered stone gate called the **Porta Soprana**. Between here and the waterfront lies a district of monasteries and convents, small squares, wasteground and building sites – this part of town was heavily

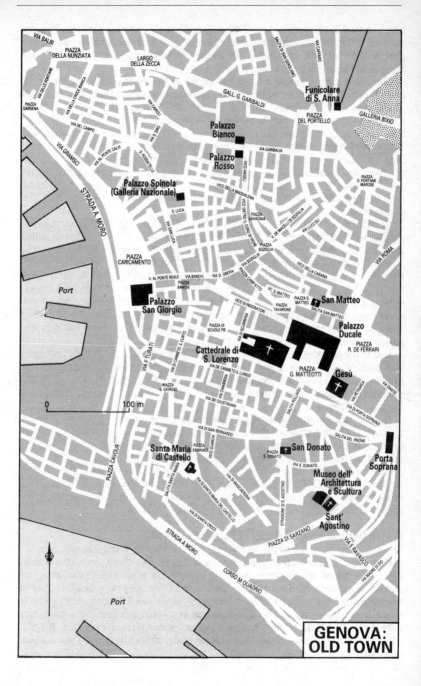

GENOVA: OLD TOWN

bombed by Allied forces in World War II, and is only just being rebuilt. The ivy-covered brick house next to the gate belonged to Columbus's father, who was a cloth weaver by trade but served also as the official gatekeeper; Christopher was the first in his family to go to sea.

Genova is now spending a lot of money on its public buildings, including the church of **Sant'Agostino**, whose mosaic spire makes a good landmark off Piazza di Sarzano. The adjoining building houses the **Museo dell'Architettura e Scultura Ligure** (Tues–Sat 9am–1pm & 3–6pm, Sun 9am–12.45pm; L2000), built around the original triangular cloister of the thirteenth-century monastery, with Roman and Romanesque fragments from other churches, as well as wood carvings and ancient maps of Genova. The alleyways around here are cramped and rundown and outsiders run a gauntlet of stares and the occasional catcall as they go; the warnings you read in guide books on the danger to single women, though, are often overdone – trust your instincts and go where you feel comfortable.

Heading down to the port, along Via di Santa Croce and then Salita Santa Maria on the right, you come across **Santa Maria di Castello**, a basilica church dating back to the twelfth century, and one of the oldest churches in the city. The attached Dominican convent was built in the fifteenth century, when the church itself was altered along Gothic lines. The **museum** inside (Wed & Sat 3–5pm) has paintings by Lodovico Brea, including a *Coronation of Our Lady*, richly coloured and packed with portraits of sixteenth-century Genovese. The church served as a hostel for Crusaders on their way to the Holy Land, led by Guglielmo *Testa di Maglio* (Hammerhead) Embriaco, whose tower has been incorporated into a seven-storey house nearby.

Just to the north of Santa Maria is Via San Bernardo, a long, straight thorough-fare built by the Romans, and now one of Genova's busiest pedestrian streets: grocers and bakers trade behind the grand portals of palazzi, altered in the fifteenth and sixteenth centuries with the addition of vaulted ceilings, balustraded loggias and frescoes.

Piazza San Donato, just off Via San Bernardo, is a quiet square surrounded by busy shopping streets, with one of the most attractive churches in the old town, **San Donato**. The black and white marble bands on the outside, like the others throughout the city, were a sign of prestige – families could use them only if they had a permit, awarded for "some illustrious deed to the advantage of their native city". The Doria family went one step further in **Piazza San Matteo** (the other side of Via San Lorenzo), by carving testimonials to their worthiness on the stripes of the twelfth-century church and adjoining palaces.

Piazza Caricamento to Piazza di Fontane Marose

The sea once came up to the vaulted arcades of **Piazza Caricamento**; now the waterfront is blocked off by containers and fences, but there's constant activity here, with buses arriving and departing outside the small café-restaurants, and porters hurrying into the square's market from the alleyways behind. There's been a market here since the twelfth century, when small boats used to come to shore from galleys at anchor, and fruit and veg stalls still line the arcade, now interspersed with fly pitches selling sunglasses and pirated cassettes. It's also where some of the city's prostitutes wait for trade, although it's not a place where other women get hassled.

Customs inspectors, and then the city's elected governors, set up in the **Palazzo San Giorgio**, on the edge of the square. In 1408 it was taken over by the *Banco di San Giorgio*, a syndicate established to finance the war against Venice. The *Sala dei Protettori* (Hall of the Bank's Protectors) and *Sala Manica Lunga* (Hall of the Long Sleeve), in the medieval wing, are open to the public. In the sixteenth century the bank steered the city from trading to banking, turning Genova into a major financial capital. It's from this period that most of the grand palaces date, and although Genova produced no outstanding artists of its own, it could afford the best portrait painters and decorators of the time, as its surviving buildings prove.

Behind Piazza Caricamento is a thriving commercial zone centred on **Piazza Banchi**, a small square of secondhand bookstalls which was once the heart of the medieval city. Off one side runs Via Soziglia, an alleyway with a good mixture of bars and places to eat – among them *Kainguti*, an Austrian-built *salon*, selling cakes and ice cream under chandeliers. Further along there's a shop specialising in secondhand period clothing, and a sign (*Mercato dei Pulci*) pointing to the flea-market in **Piazza Lavagna**. From Piazza Soziglia it's a short stroll up to Piazza di Fontane Marose, where the city's sixteenth-century streets and palaces begin (see below).

Another exit from Piazza Banchi is the long, medieval Via San Luca. This street was in Spinola family territory, and when the last of the family died, in 1958, their palace became the **Galleria Nazionale di Palazzo Spinola** (Tues–Sat 9am–6.30pm, Sun 9am–1pm; L2000) – it's towards the far end, off Piazza Pelliceria. The Sicilian master Antonello da Messina's *Ecce Homo* might still be away for restoration, but *The Adoration of the Magi* by Joos Van Cleve, sawn into planks when stolen from the church of San Donato in the 1970s, is worth tracking down.

The **Museo del Risorgimento** (Tues–Sat 9.30–11.45am & 2–5pm) is in this part of the old town, at Via Lomellini 11. **Giuseppe Mazzini** was born here in 1805, and at the age of sixteen saw political refugees begging in the streets on their way through Genova to exile. He became the archetypal romantic hero, always dressed in black, in mourning for the failed revolution of 1821. It was his ideology which lay behind the radical revolutionary movement, and after a spell in jail he formed "Young Italy", a group dedicated to a unified country and a free sovereign state. Esoteric though his writings were, his fundamental beliefs inspired an enormous following – at one time there were 200,000 political exiles from other parts of Italy in Genova and Turin, amongst whom Mazzinian ideals were strong. Pictures, documents and relics from Mazzini's life are on display in the museum.

Via Garibaldi and Genova's palaces

When newly made fortunes encouraged Genova's merchant bankers to move out of the cramped old town in the mid-sixteenth century, artisans' houses were pulled down to form the Strada Nuova, later named **Via Garibaldi**. To walk along it is to stroll through a Renaissance architect's drawing pad – sculpted facades, stucco work and medallions decorate the exterior of the three-storey palazzi, while the big courtyards are almost like private squares. Take a look, for instance, at no. 7, the sixteenth-century **Palazzo Podestà**, with its grotto and fountain. Snooty antique shops use the ground floors of some, but most of the palaces have become business and administrative offices.

Two palaces on Via Garibaldi have been turned into art galleries. **Palazzo Bianco** (Tues–Sat 9am–1pm & 3–6pm, Sun 9am–12.45pm; L2000) holds a collection of paintings by Genovese artists and others who stayed here briefly, including Van Dyck and Rubens, and there's a good general collection of Flemish art too. Look for the portrait of Andrea Doria by Jan Matsys: ruler of Genova in 1528, Doria made his reputation and fortune attacking Turkish fleets and Barbary pirate ships in the Mediterranean, but life in the streets of Genova required as much skill and fortitude – he survived many plots on his life, several instigated by the Fieschi family.

A collection of paintings including works by Titian, Caravaggio and Dürer is to be found across the road in **Palazzo Rosso** (Tues–Sat 9am–1pm & 3–6pm, Sun 9am–12.45pm; L2000), but it's the decor which really impresses – fantastic chandeliers, mirrors, an excess of gilding, and frescoed ceilings. A vast array of nativity figures is a diverting speciality.

The other Genovese palace worth a visit is the **Palazzo Reale** (Tues, Thurs, Sat & Sun 9am–1pm; L2000) a kilometre or so away in Via Balbi. Covered galleries and arched windows which today look out over container ships, once had a direct view of the sea, and the building has the feel of a summer pleasure palace – a sprung wooden floor in the ballroom, sugared-almond decor and figures floating around on rococo ceilings. A small collection of paintings is spread through the upper storey.

The Harbour

Quaysides and railway tracks line the major basins of Genova's harbour as far west as the airport. Shipbuilding and steel-making started here at the beginning of the century, and were the mainstay of Italy's industrial revolution; recent world recession, though, has put many out of work. The Stazione Marrittima, a *fin-de-siècle* building from which steamers once left for New York and Buenos Aires, is now the ferry terminal for shorter trips to Corsica, Sardinia and Sicily. A trip around the harbour gives you a view of the **Lanterna** (Lighthouse) built in 1544, and the **Molo Vecchio**, where condemned prisoners were blessed and then hanged. **Tours**, run by the *Co-operative Battellieri* (☎265.712), leave every afternoon at about 2pm and cost L3500.

The **Ponte dei Mille** (Bridge of the Thousand), in front of the ferry terminal, was named after an episode during the Unification. It was from here that Giuseppe Garibaldi, ex-mercenary and spaghetti salesman, and the ultimate guerilla leader of the nineteenth century, persuaded his one thousand Red Shirts to set off for Sicily in two clapped-out paddle steamers, armed with just a few rifles and no ammunition. Their mission – to support a local revolution and unite the island with the mainland states – greatly annoyed some northern politicians, who didn't want anything to do with the undeveloped south. Reactionaries weren't the only ones to express dismay at Garibaldi's strategy – Mazzini himself called the unified Italy which eventually resulted a "lifeless mosaic . . . governed by a few rich men", in which the majority was excluded from the political process, and the people remained in thrall to the Catholic church.

Via XX Settembre

Genova's commercial nucleus is **Via XX Settembre**, with big department stores, shops selling designer clothes, and pavement cafés under gentle neon in the arcades – one of these, *Tonitto*, is a favourite haunt of Genovese young bloods.

Shops in the side streets around Stazione Brignole and Piazza Colombo are good for local food specialities, as is the covered **Mercato Orientale** (Mon–Sat), half-way down Via XX Settembre in the old cloisters of an Augustinian monastery.

In front of the small park outside the train station is **Piazza della Vittoria**, a dazzling white square built during the Fascist period, and the departure point for buses out of town. Uphill from the station, at Piazza Corvetto, buses plunge into the tunnel running underneath **Villetta di Negro**, a hill of artificial waterfalls and grottoes, topped by the **Museo d'Arte Orientale E. Chiossone** (Tues–Sat 9am–1pm & 3–6pm; L2000) which holds a collection of Oriental art including eighteenth-century sculpture and paintings, and samurai armour. Piazza Corvetto is a major confluence of traffic and people – watch it all from the park benches, or from inside the grand **Caffè Mangini** on the corner of Via Roma, built by the Austrians in the nineteenth century. Mainly residential streets zig-zag up the hills, though at Corso Solferino 39 there's an interesting collection of Pre-Columbian artefacts in the **Museo Americanisto F. Lunardi** (Tues–Sat 9.30–noon & 3–5.30pm, Sun 3–5.30pm only; L2000). Bus #33 takes you there from Stazione Brignole.

Out of the centre: Albaro, Boccadasse, the Heights and the Staglieno

For a spot of relaxation, head for the suburb of **Albaro**, at the end of **Corso Italia**, a broad street which runs along the seafront beyond the *Fiera* exhibition area (bus #41 from Stazione Principe). This is the place to jog, stroll, pose, or to watch the sun set from a café table. The private **beaches** charge a small fee and provide changing areas and showers; if you don't like the look of the sea, there's an **open-air pool** at Via O. de Gaspari 39.

From Albaro, you can walk or take bus #31 from Piazza de Ferrari to **Boccadasse**. Once an outlying fishing port, this village is now part of the city and there are boats pulled up on the pebble beach, nets hanging out to dry, stretched between windows, and some arty shops to browse around.

When Genova ran out of building space, plots for houses were hewn out of the hillside behind, like the steps of an amphitheatre. You see how it was done as you're slowly taken past people's front windows by the **funicular** which runs from Piazza del Portello, between the two road tunnels, up to Sant'Anna. There's also a wood-panelled lift which does the same journey, leaving from Galleria Garibaldi; use ordinary bus tickets for both.

The view from the heights of Righi is much hyped, but the trip by funicular is more absorbing than anything you'll see when you arrive – and as often as not the thing won't be working anyway. Far more worthwhile is an outing to the **Staglieno cemetery**, across the valley from Righi. It's a veritable city of the dead, with neoclassical porticoes and marble steps leading up to a pantheon bounded by tombs and cypress trees. One of the most sentimental monuments is the statue of Caterina Campdonico, a seller of nuts, whose life savings went to reproduce her slight, bent figure. Carved below is a poem telling how she sold her nuts in sunshine and in rain so as to gain her daily bread and propel her image into future ages.

Evelyn Waugh called the Staglieno "a museum of mid-nineteenth-century bourgeois art", yet it's the melancholy atmosphere that really stays with you. It is still Genova's major burial ground, and people come here to pay their respects to the dead and to weed the graves. To get here, take bus #34 from Piazza Annunziata or Piazza Corvetto, or bus #14, #48 or #50 from Stazione Brignole.

Eating, drinking and entertainment

You could spend several days checking out the scores of places to **eat**, from basic trattorie to elegant nineteenth-century *caffè*. The cheapest, around the port, are often open only at lunchtime. On first impressions life after dark looks sparse – the Genovese tend to entertain at home, and if they go out, it's to somewhere like the theatre or opera. A few small **clubs and bars** have music (often live) and, during student term-time especially, small cinema clubs operate; in summer, you'd do best to head down to Albaro for the seafront cafés.

Eating

Best known of Ligurian specialities is *pesto*, made with basil, pine-nuts, oil and parmesan and used as a sauce for pasta or stirred into minestrone. Another is *torta pasqualina*, a spinach and cheese pie with eggs, widely served as fast food. Piazza Caricamento is especially good for **snacks**, with deep-fried seafood to take away. All over the place in the old town you'll see shops selling *farinata*, a kind of chickpea pancake. Chickpeas also feature in *zuppa di ceci*, found on practically every Genovese menu, but rarely outside Liguria. For more substantial informal fare, *Café Royal* on Via di Macelli di Soziglia does steak and salad, and some appetising *panini* are turned out at the studenty place at Via Balbi 15r.

Some of the best and cheapest places for full **meals** are in the old town, too. A well known place for local cooking is *Sâ Pesta*, Via Giustiniani 16r (closed Sat evening and all Sun) – get there before 7.30pm as they shut early. *Corona di Ferro*, Vico Inferiore del Ferro 11 (leading onto Via di Macelli di Soziglia), has a set menu for L15,000, while at *Trattoria Luciano e Mimma*, Corso M. Quadrio 4 (on the edge of the port), you can eat three courses for L9000 – in season they serve a starter which is an acquired taste: *fave* (broad beans that you shell yourself), eaten with an aperitif. Both these places are open only at lunchtime. Close to here, on Salita Santa Maria di Castello, is the reasonably priced *Puci dei Trilli* (closed Wed evening), and there's a trattoria-pizzeria, *Florida*, just down the hill from Stazione Principe.

Trattoria Lombarda, Via San Bernardo, serves **Sardinian** food and wine, and gets very busy – a meal will cost around L20,000 per person. Highly regarded for **Ligurian** specialities is *Genio*, Salita San Leonardo 61 (closed Sun; booking advisable, ☎546.463) – take Via Fieschi off Piazza Dante, Salita San Leonardo is the first set of steps on the left. A gourmet treat of seafood (including razor clams), home-made pasta and pudding comes to around L30,000 a head. Near Stazione Principe is a very good **Chinese** restaurant – the *Hong Kong Trattoria* in Via San Carlo.

Bars and clubs

There are plenty of **bars** along the waterfront on the seamy Via Gramsci, in between the stripjoints and brothels, but more relaxed places to drink can be found on the side roads off Via XX Settembre – try *All'Insieme* on Via Ceccardi (running south to Piazza Dante), or, nearer Stazione Brignole, *Cin-Cin* on Via Cesearea and the *American Bar* on Via Maragliano. If you're dying for a Guinness, hit the *Brittania Pub* in Vico Casana, just off Via San Lorenzo – though it's open all day, the pub's only lively at night, when it's fraternised by Genova's foreign population as well as by Italians.

The city's well off for clubs and music too. *Panteca Volante* is a friendly, smoky club-cum-bar with live music most nights, hidden away at the Stazione Principe end of Via Balbi – take the set of steps just past *Farmacia Pescetto* up to the tiny Piazza Santa Brigida. *Psycho Club*, Scaletta Carmagnola 7, is an "alternative" club in an alleyway near Piazza de Ferrari – the third on the left, up Via XXV Aprile. The *Centro Sociale Occupato Autogestita*, an arts centre on Via Madre di Dio, has **jazz, reggae and world music** most Fridays and Saturdays; go down the steps and alleys from Piazza di Sarzano – the centre is in an old church next to the dual carriageway. For jazz, try the *Louisiana Jazz Club* at Piazza Matteotti 20 (right inside the Palazzo Ducale) on Thursday nights, and there's live **bluegrass** on Mondays out at Nervi (see below), at *The Patio*, Via Oberdan 22.

Other entertainment

For other entertainment, check the local daily paper, *Il Secolo XIX*, or *L'Agenda*, free from the AAST and EPT offices. Genova's two main **theatres**, *Teatro Duse* and *Teatro Politeama*, are on Via Martin Piaggio and Via Bacigalupo respectively. Major British and American **bands** usually play at the *Teatro Verdi* in Piazza Oriani, Sestri Ponente (frequent trains and buses) – watch for posters around the city. Genova's **opera** is based at *Teatro Margherita*, Via XX Settembre 16a, where there's also **dance** and **classical music**; look in the local paper for details. The monthly **student magazine**, *La Rosa Purpurea del Cairo*, has information on music, theatre and cinema: it's available in term-time from Via Terralba 4/r (take Via Tolemaide and Corso Aldo east from Piazza Verdi).

Listings

Airlines Most are around Via XX Settembre, between Piazza Dante and Corvetto. *Alitalia*, Via XII Ottobre 188r (reservations ☎5493; passenger information ☎531.091); *British Airways*, c/o *Airsima*, Via E. Vernazza 23 (☎541.411); *TWA*, Via XII Ottobre 184/r (☎293.858).

Airport information ☎26.901.

Banks Next to Stazione Principe in Piazza Acquaverde, along Via Balbi and at the airport. Open Mon–Fri 8am–1.15pm & 2.45–3.45pm.

Books English language paperbacks from *Bozzi*, Via Cairoli 2a/r. *British Library*, Piazza della Vittoria 15, open Mon–Fri 10am–noon & 4–7pm.

Bus information For city services, *ATM* (☎59.971); for provincial services *Tigullio* (☎313.851).

Car Rental *Gianfranco & Co*, Via Malta 64/r (☎562.141); *Hertz* (☎564.412); *Avis* (☎255.598).

Chemists All night service, ☎192. Central are *Pescetto*, Via Balbi 185/r (☎262.697), near Stazione Principe, and *Ghersi*, Corso Buenos Aires 74/r (☎541.661), close to Stazione Brignole.

Consulates *UK*, Via XII Ottobre 2 (☎564.833); *USA*, Piazza Portello 6 (☎282.741).

Cycling *Amici della Bicicletta*, Vico dei Caprettari 3/1 (☎281.141) is a campaigning group which arranges weekend trips and mountain bike off-road rides. Details also in window of *Olmo*, Via Caeserea 67.

Doctor On duty Sundays and at night, ☎354.022.

Football Genova's premier side, the sporadically successful *Sampdoria*, play at the *Luigi Ferraris* stadium, reached by *KV* and *KM* bus from Stazione Brignole; tickets from L10,000. They share the stadium with the recently promoted *Genoa*, who are expected to struggle for their place in the top league.

Hospital *Galliera*, Mura Cappuccine 14 (☎56.321). For ambulance ☎595.951.

Launderette *Sprint*, Via Caprera 28/r.

Left Luggage At both train stations; L2000 for 24hr.

Police Emergencies ☎113. Central Office on Via Diaz (☎53.661).

Post Office Via Dante, behind Piazza de Ferrari (Mon–Fri 8.15am–8pm, Sat 8am–1pm). Sub-post office at Stazione Principe, open same hours.

Swimming pool Open air pool at Via de Gaspari 39, Albaro.

Taxi ☎26.96.

Telephones *SIP* at both train stations (daily 8.15am–9.15pm), and at Via XX Settembre 139 (24hr).

Train information ☎28.4081.

Travel Agencies For *BIJ* and ferry tickets *D. G. Viaggi*, Piazza San Matteo 3r and *Guimar*, Via Balbi 192/r.

Women's Group Legal advice and reference library open to all women at *UDI*, Via Cairoli 14/7 (☎298.703); Tues–Thurs 4–7.30pm.

Around Genova

Genova has spilled over the old city limits to spread around the bay, with good bus and train connections to some of its outlying parts. Popular at weekends are the parks and seaside promenade at **Nervi**, or at **Pegli** in the opposite direction, towards Savona. If you can, head **inland**, through terraced hills. They are green and lush in spring, when the blossom is out and the vines are sprouting. Several small villages make good targets, or it's possible from here to join the long distance trail across the Ligurian mountains.

Nervi

Genova's mainly residential suburbs extend east to **NERVI** (take a train or #17 bus), spread around a small harbour with one or two bars along the front. There are usually some people fishing off the rocks, or paddling along in canoes but the bulk of Nervi's visitors come for the *passeggiata*, which winds around the headland and through the gardens underneath the cliff. The **Parco Municipale**, by the main road, has an open-air cinema from June to September and a highly acclaimed ballet festival in summer. Semi-suburban though Nervi is, you still feel a long way from city life among the orange trees and the lush villa gardens.

Pegli

Out to the west of Genova, near the airport, is the city's heavy industry, concentrated in the suburb of **Sestri Ponente**, a grim collection of blast furnaces, smelting works and housing blocks. Trains and the slow #3 buses from Stazione Principe pass through here to **PEGLI**, once a seaside town and a retreat from the city, but now engulfed by it. Although there are better places to swim further along the coast, Pegli has its own attractions, notably the **Villa Durazzo-**

Pallavicini, which the local Communist party are fighting to preserve from declining into ruin. Set in grounds landscaped in nineteenth-century style, with fake waterfalls and pagodas, it houses the **Museo Civico di Archeologia Ligure** (Tues–Sat 9am–1pm & 2–5pm; L2000). Items unearthed from cave burials in the hills along the west coast include the skeleton of a "Young Prince" with seashell crown and ceremonial dagger.

North from Genova

Many Genovese escape the city in summer by heading for the hills inland. A branch line runs north from Genova to CASELLA, 12km from **Lago di Val Noci**. A small road deviates from the route to the lake and ascends the Val Brevanna to the mountainous **Parco Naturale dell'Antola**. Along the way are ancient communes which the Spinola and Malaspina families, the bishops of Tortona, and the Republic of Genova contested in medieval times. Here and there you'll see the crumbling outer walls of a castle built by one of these factions on the edge of small villages.

There are two routes over the mountains from Genova: one to Tortona in Piemonte and the other to Piacenza in Emilia Romagna. The principal rail line follows the one to **Tortona** and Milan, tracking the autostrada (A7) and the SS35, passing through hillsides planted with fruit trees and vines. The *Alta Via dei Monti Liguri* dips down to the Tortona road at the Passo di Giovi, just before **BUSALLA**, a way station between Genova and the Po valley for hundreds of years. Should you want to explore the mountain trail, there are two **hotels** in Busalla: *Vittoria* at Via Veneto 177 (☎932.907), with rooms at L22,000, and *Appennino*, Piazza Borzino 8 (☎934.0780), at around L13,000. Several trains stop there daily.

The road to **Piacenza** goes through **TORRIGLIA**, the main town of an agricultural *comune* encircled by hills; if you want to travel through the isolated land to the north, base yourself at one of its hotels: the *Aurelio* at Piazza E. Piaggio 20, with rooms at L36,000, or *Della Posta*, at Via Matteotti 39 (☎944.050), costing around L24,000. Further along the road lies the village of **MONTEBRUNO**, with its richly decorated fifteenth-century Santuario dell'Assunta (containing a Byzantine carving of the Madonna), and its mushroom-shaped chocolates called *funghetti*. Ancient copper mines, first worked in the eleventh century and revived at the beginning of this, lie on the outskirts of **ROVEGNO** just before the border with Emilia Romagna.

WEST OF GENOVA:
THE RIVIERA DEL PONENTE

You get the most positive impression of the coast west of Genova – the **Riviera del Ponente** – as you speed along the autostrada, from where the marinas and resorts are mere specks in a panorama of glittering sea and acres of glasshouses. Close up, the seaside towns from Genova to the French border are fairly functional places, whose occasionally attractive centres are packed with hotel and apartment blocks. Yet these resorts have their good points – chiefly the sandy beaches, lower prices and lack of pretentiousness. An exceptionally mild climate means that flowering plants grow everywhere all year round, and much of the hillsides are draped with rush matting to protect the lucrative plantations of carnations and lilies.

If you can put up with the emphasis on family fun, head for resorts such as **Finale Ligure** or **Alassio**; if not, there are the medieval ports of **Noli** and **Albenga**, and grand, crumbling **San Remo** makes a good base for travelling into the **mountain areas** behind the coast. Here, stone villages and agricultural communes reveal the more private side of the province. Walkers can explore sections of the *Alta Via dei Monti Liguri* or loop through hill towns like Baiardo, Apricale and Dolceacqua. And close to the French border, worth a stop before you cross, are the spectacular gardens of **La Mortola**.

Pegli to Savona, Spotorno and Noli

The resorts between Pegli and the large industrial port of Savona are inevitably affected by their proximity to two big cities. The railway, autostrada and trunk road all hug the coast, so ARENZANO, VARAZZE and CELLE LIGURE present an uninspiring face to the world. **SAVONA** itself is a modern city of concrete and steel architecture, and bits of the city which were bombed in the last war are now open spaces enlivened with sculpture. Via Paleocapa, an arcade of art nouveau buildings, leads down to the port and the alleys of the main shopping area. "Vecchia Savona", a type of blue and white faience first made in the seventeenth century, is produced here and at ALBISOLA, a small resort 5km away.

It doesn't take much persuasion to leave the coast and head for the hills. **SASSELLO** is the most interesting of the small towns: on August 11 the streets are decorated with rose petals for the procession of the Corpus Domini, and locally produced amaretti biscuits and pecorino cheese are on sale.

Continuing west from Savona, the train emerges from the long tunnels at SPOTORNO, a soulless place with the saving grace of a long sandy beach between it and **NOLI**, 3km to the west. A tiny village now, Noli was once an autonomous maritime republic – on festivals the last flag of the Republic of Noli is flown from the **Torre Comunale**, one of three red-brick towers in the town. Remains of the castle and walls spread over the hill while some of its thirteenth-century palaces have been converted into hotels with noisy, popular restaurants. (If money's really tight, better to eat at the stalls along the seafront, among the palms and oleanders.) The grid of old streets is a lively place to wander and its position – near several small beaches – makes it a genuinely appealing place to stop for a day or so. Not far from the train station is the beautiful Romanesque church of **San Paragorio** (Tues–Sun 10am–noon & 3.30–5pm), notable for its original crypt, fifteenth-century frescoes, a thirteenth-century bishop's throne of inlaid wood, and a twelfth-century *Volto Santo* (True Likeness) of Christ on the Cross.

The Via Aurelia continues round the bay past a couple of small headlands, where the sea is inviting and the inlets accessible from the road. At nearby **VARIGOTTI** there are cheaper **places to stay** than in Noli – first choice is *Pensione Faia* (☎019/698.115) which has rooms at L25,000, though you must take full pension in July and August. An alternative is to **camp** at *Camping Valentino* (☎019/698.004) or to make for the youth hostel at Finale Ligure, less than twenty minutes away by bus.

Finale Ligure

With nearly one hundred hotels in and around its centre, **FINALE LIGURE** is
overtly committed to tourism, yet it manages to remain an attractive place. There
are three parts to the town: Finale Marina, next to the sea, has a promenade lined
with palms, and narrow shopping streets behind; Finale Pia is the district on the
Genova side; and a couple of kilometres from the sea is the old town of
Finalborgo, set on a slight hill. The bare rock faces behind the coast are particularly good for **climbing**, and are a favourite with free climbers, who gather at
Bar Gelateria Centrale in Finalborgo's Piazza Garibaldi at weekends. For kit and
information on local routes go to *Sport Alp*, at Via Nicotera 23 (☎019/970.549), or
Rockstore, further up the valley at FEGLINO (5 buses a day).

However, the area's wider fame comes not from its cliffs but from the *Grotte
delle Arene Candide*, some of Europe's most important caves for prehistoric
remains. They are closed for excavation, but some finds are on display at the
Museo Archaeologico in the cloisters of Santa Caterina in Finalborgo (Tues–Sat
10am–noon & 3–6pm, Sun 9am–noon).

Above all, Finale Ligure is a pleasant **place to stay**. Outstanding among Finale
Marina's central **hotels** is the friendly and lively family-run *Cirio* on Via Pertica,
in the old part of town (☎019/692.310); half pension, with bathroom, costs from
L30,000 in high season – and there's also a small apartment (no kitchen) for four
people in an annexe. Further along, in the same price bracket and run on similar
lines, is *Ferrando*, at Via Barrili 31 (☎019/692.355). Cheapest option of all is the
youth hostel, which occupies an ex-castle high above the train station in Via
Generale Caviglia (☎019/690.515), it's open from mid-April to mid-October, and
costs L9000 per night. There are plenty of other possibilities in which all meals
are included, ranging around the L35,000 mark for full pension, often with
reductions for half pension available. Get a list with prices from the **AAST** on the
seafront at Piazza Vittorio Veneto 29 (daily summer 9am–noon & 3.30–7pm;
winter 9am–noon and 3–5pm).

If you're not **eating** at the place you're staying, there's very good Ligurian food
at *Da Giovanni*, Via Roma 9 (☎019/692.245; closed Sat except July and Aug) – get
there early or book. In Finalborgo, *Au Quatre*, Via Fiume 38, is a relaxed trattoria
with good food and music, which stays open until midnight.

Into the hills

It is worth finding transport and heading further inland. There you'll see small
villages clinging to a hill, surrounded by woods; crumbling farmhouses and
terraces banked up with stones growing vines. Away from the roads, you sometimes come across the occasional ox pulling a cartload of hay – the area certainly
feels remote. Best of all is the food: soft cheeses preserved in oil, local wines and
fruit. **Buses** inland are sporadic, but there are a few **footpaths** which take you
away from the coast. One of these starts from VERZI, 5km behind Finale Pia, and
includes a section of the old *Via Aurelia*, which traverses a handful of Roman
bridges along the Val Ponci. A half-day walk will bring you back down into
Varigotti (basic map available from the AAST), from where buses run half-hourly
to Finale Marina.

The most popular trip is to the grottoes at **TOIRANO** (daily 9.30–11.30am & 2.30–6pm; 50-min tour L5000), set halfway up a rocky hillside just outside the village. Evidence suggests that 12,500 years ago bears and hunters penetrated this network of caves. The prehistoric human footprints in what was once mud are helpfully circled with chalk, and there's a mass of bones in the underground bear cemetery of the *Grotta della Bàsura*. The second set of caves, the *Grotta di Santa Lucia*, contains remarkable stalagmite and stalactite formations.

Buses for Toirano leave from outside Finale Ligure station and turn off the main coastal road at BORGHETTO SAN SPIRITO, a route which takes you through **BORGIO VEREZZI**, a couple of kilometres from Finale Ligure. In the nineteenth century an artist called Brilla created an extraordinary grotto of artificial rock formations here, inside the **Santuario del Buon Consiglio**; it's open on the first Saturday of the month at 4pm, and on April 25 for the *Festa della Madonna*.

Albenga

Following the coast westwards, buses and trains take you past nurseries of artichokes and petunias, interspersed with garden gnome shops and caravan sites, before arriving at the small market town of **ALBENGA**, which sits in the middle of an exposed alluvial plain. The pebbly beach isn't worth going out of your way for, but the pleasingly business-like **old town** within the medieval walls merits a visit.

The nucleus of red-roofed buildings and thirteenth- to fourteenth-century brick **tower houses** is centred on Piazza San Michele, and dominated by the **Cattedrale**. The main part of the church was built in the eleventh century and enlarged in the early fourteenth, but it has a fifth-century baptistery, constructed on the orders of Constantius III. The curator of the unengrossing **Museo Civico Ingauno** (Tues–Sun 9am–noon & 3–6pm; L2000), in the adjacent Torre Comunale, guides visitors round the baptistery, leading them across planks over the waterlogged floor. Ten-sided on the exterior yet octagonal within, the building contains fragmentary mosaics in which the Apostles are represented by twelve doves. The amphorae stacked against the walls, out of the way of the rising damp, supported the roof until the beginning of this century, and, being hollow, also augmented the acoustics.

A little way up the road from Piazza San Michele is the frescoed **Palazzo Vescovile** (Bishop's Palace), which houses the cathedral treasury (Tues–Sun 9am–noon). At the opposite end of the Piazza is the Renaissance **Palazzo Peloso-Cepolla** (Tues–Sun 9am–noon & 3–6pm; L2000), whose tower holds items from the wreck of a Roman galley dug up from the offshore mud of Isola Gallinara in the 1950s. The first-century Roman port, *Album Ingaunum*, lies many layers under the present town, its centre marked by the thirteenth-century **Loggia dei Quattro Canti**, where Via delle Medgalie crosses Via Bernardo Ricci.

The bulk of the **bars and restaurants** are in the vicinity of the cathedral. For takeaway snacks, try *Puppo*, on Via Torlaro, or *Da Charlotte*, in the square adjacent to the cathedral. There's a good *osteria* in Piazza dei Leoni, behind the baptistery, while just outside the walls, at Viale Pontelungo, is the popular trattoria *Lanterna Verde* (both closed Sun).

The **EPT** (Mon–Sat 9am–noon & 3–7pm, July & Aug also Sun 9am–noon) is at Viale Martiri della Libertà 17, the road running between the bus and train stations. **Hotels** are concentrated here and by the sea; *Bucaniere*, right on the front (☎0182/50.220), and *Italia*, at Viale Martiri della Libertà 10 (☎0182/50.405), both have rooms at around L36,000. The more attractive **campsites** lie west of Albenga: about five minutes away by the bus to Alassio is the seafront *Camping Delfino*, with straw pergolas over pitches, and five minutes further on the same bus brings you to *Camping Sant'Anna*, set on terraces overlooking the railway and road, close to a pebble beach with pines and clear water.

Inland from Albenga

A few kilometres inland from Albenga, the village of **VILLANOVA D'ALBENGA** exports violets to the rest of Europe; religious decorations made from the flowers decorate the town in the second week of September.

Several buses a day make the journey west along the terraced, semi-wooded Arroscia valley to the ancient market town of **PIEVE DI TECO**. Formed in 1233 around a parish church, a well and a mill, it has expanded into porticoed streets of workshops and palaces, and become a small industrial centre. The main reason for coming here is to make connections with **buses** further inland, but if you're here on August 15, the skittle games led by women, in commemoration of a narrow escape from a fourteenth-century Piemontese attack, are worth checking out, as is the hooded procession on the night of Good Friday.

A long bus ride further up the valley brings you to **PONTEDASSIO**, complete with a **Museo Storico degli Spaghetti**, and the village of **MENDATICA**, founded in the seventh century by refugees from the north, fleeing Lombard invasion. The latter makes a centre for trails onto Monte Saccarello, and has some cheap hotels: *La Campagnola*, at Via San Bernardo 28 (☎0183/38.745), charges just L15,000, and *Il Torchietto*, at Piazza Roma 10 (☎0183/38.729), only a little more.

Alassio to Cervo

After Albenga the terrain becomes more mountainous, and the railway line and road stick next to the sea as far as **ALASSIO**, a once-beautiful resort ruined by its reputation. At peak times, with the crowds packing the gardens, promenade and sandy beach, it takes on a nightmarish quality.

You can still enjoy the beach – one of the best on the Riviera – if you move further down to **LAIGUEGLIA**, an ex-fishing port with a couple of porticoed streets to wander, a large Baroque church and choice accommodation. *Hotel Mariella*, Via Dante 190 (☎0182/49.356), with rooms from L30,000, combines wonderfully kitsch elegance with excellent food. Slightly higher prices are charged by the Sixties-style *Windsor Hotel*, at Via XXV Aprile 7 (☎0182/49.000), right next to the beach. If money is in short supply, stay at *Pensione Rita*, at no. 120 on the main Via Roma (☎0182/49.400), which has rooms from L22,000.

A walk up the steps from the junction of Via Mimosa and Via Roma takes you away from the coast through a cluster of holiday homes to the old Roman road near the top of the hill. From here, follow the *strada privata* into the woods and take the signposted path for the ruins of the **Castello di Andora** and what's rated as the best Romanesque **church** on the Riviera (45-min walk). Even if you never get to the church and castle, the walk along muletracks between olive groves and woods is one of the most appealing parts of this bit of coast, with plenty of shaded places to spend the afternoon. From the castle you can either backtrack, or walk on through the outskirts of ANDORA to its train station.

Cervo and beyond

With so high a density of tourists along the coast, it's inevitable that the hillside fishing village of **CERVO**, on the other side of Capo Mele from Andora, has become primped and preened. Overlooking the houses is the rich Baroque church of **San Giovanni Battista**, dedicated to the local coral fishermen. The piazza in front of the church provides a dramatic setting for evening chamber orchestra performances in July and August, while workshops in the steep alley-ways around the church sell a range of arty objects.

Down the coast a whole clump of towns have *Diano* in their names, from the Roman cult of Diana. Like other parts of the hinterland, the hills are dotted with villages, many with their own particular products – special sweets, sheep and goat's milk cheese, olive oil, and mushrooms and chestnuts in season. From Cervo the resorts of SAN BARTOLOMEO AL MARE and DIANO MARINA – catering largely for British package tourists, and to be avoided – merge into one before a precipitous headland and the port of Imperia.

Imperia

In 1923 Mussolini joined the two towns of ONEGLIA and PORTO MAURIZIO to create the new provincial capital of **IMPERIA**. The two halves lie on opposite sides of the River Impero: Oneglia, to the east, is marked out by large olive oil storage tanks on the harbour front, while Porto Maurizio works its way up the hillside in a series of zig-zags from the marina and beach. The main drag through town is Corso Matteotti; at no. 22 is the **AAST** (summer Mon–Sat 8am–2pm & 4–7pm; winter mornings only), which can supply a timetable for all the province's buses, many of which stop outside (buy tickets from the café next door). Shopping streets run parallel with Corso Matteotti, and there's a large indoor food market over the brow of the hill.

Admittedly, once you've seen this and climbed the steps round the old quarter, you've seen the sights, but Imperia is a useful place if you're looking for a **room** when everywhere else is booked up. The best area to look is between Corso Matteotti and the sea. *Ariston*, at Via Privata Rambaldi 7 (☎0183/61.694), is the most appealing of the hotels, offering doubles with bathroom for L45,000. Further down the hill, many places do bed, breakfast and evening meal – *Pensione Irene*, at Via Rambaldo 30 (☎0183/62.996), and *Pensione Paola*, at Via Pirinoli 34 (☎0183/650.343), both offer full pension from L28,000 per person, or a double room for the same price.

North to Dolcedo

From Imperia, an intensively cultivated valley leads inland: palm trees stand like strange oases engulfed by glasshouses, and ranged on the slopes are olive trees with nets spread underneath to catch the crop. The bus for PRELA (every half hour) passes a couple of hilltop towns before reaching **DOLCEDO**, where a series of medieval bridges cross the River Prino, and vaulted arcades line the banks. This part of Liguria has been called "Riviera dei Fiori" – cultivated on every slope between Imperia and San Remo, and protected by glass or straw canopies, they're picked at night before being transported to San Remo flower market.

San Remo

SAN REMO's heyday as a classy resort was earlier this century, when wealthy Europeans paraded up and down the Corso Imperatrice and filled the large hotels overlooking the sea. Some of these buildings, especially near the railway station, are crumbling and grey, but others are still in pristine condition, and San Remo remains a showy town, a place with a good bit more life in it than the bland resorts further up the coast.

The main road, Corso Matteotti, runs west from the central Piazza Colombo, lined with discos, cocktail bars, gelaterias, cinemas and a selection of Paris-Milan boutiques. Neon signs down sidestreets point to private clubs and by-the-hour hotels, mixed in with a handful of expensive restaurants.

San Remo's lush gardens and parks attracted, among others, a colony of wealthy Russian exiles, who lived here at the end of the nineteenth century, ruled over by Maria Alexandrovna, consort of Tsar Alexander II. This community paid for the onion-domed **Russian Orthodox church** in Via Nuvolini, built in the 1920s. Other relics from the same era include a ruined Art Nouveau house, complete with stained glass irises and majolica tiles, close to the junction of Via Fratelli Asquascati and Corso degli Inglese.

If you can drag yourself out of bed in time, the Via Garibaldi **flower market** is a unique experience. You have to get there before 6.30am – you'll know when you're close by the waiters running around with trays of espresso, and woven boxes for flowers attached to the sardine-can vans and Vespas outside. It's strictly for trade – lilies are bunched in fifties, for example – but no one minds bystanders as long as they don't get in the way.

An archway leads off from Piazza Colombo through to Piazza Cassini, from where you can walk up to the **old town**, called *La Pigna* (Fir Cone) because of the layering of the streets up the hill. **Monte Bignone**, 1300m high, towers over *La Pigna* and the rest of the town – a cable car from Corso Inglese, next to the market, travels up to the summit.

There isn't a lot to do in terms of galleries or museums, and even the small **beach** by the railway station is a bit mucky, but the attraction of the place is its seediness. The blue-movie cinemas (packed with American naval ratings), the shops selling "Souvenir of San Remo" shell lamps, the trolley buses, the ageing cafés overlooking the marina – they all give the place some welcome sleaze after the overwhelming respectability of the rest of the coast. San Remo is also well placed for trips **inland**: the bus service is fairly good, but more options open up if you have your own wheels – bikes and Vespas are for hire at the marina. For advice on hiking, visit the *Club Alpino Italiano* office on Piazza Cassina, behind the Red Cross Ambulance depot (Tues & Fri 9.30–10.30pm, Wed & Sat 6–7pm). Maps showing refuges, footpaths and gradients are available from *Libreria Cauda*, Via Gioberti 17.

Arrival, information and finding a place to stay

The **train station** is in the western corner of town, next to the sea. An **accommodation** service operates in the station (daily 7.45am–7.45pm; closed Sun in winter), and you can also get assistance across the road at the **AAST**, Via Nuvolini 1 (Mon–Sat 8am–7pm, Sun 9am–1pm). The **bus station** is in front of Piazza Colombo, five minutes' walk from the train station; buy tickets from the tobacconist's opposite. Orange **trolley buses** for transport around the town, and to Taggia (see below), stop at the train station.

Finding a **place to stay** is no problem, except, like everywhere else, in August. There's a concentration of hotels along Corso Mombello five minutes' walk to the right of the station – among many choices is *Mombello* at no. 49 (☎0184/86.528), with rooms at L35,000. The two other main streets which converge at the station are Via Roma and Corso Matteotti; Via Gioberti, between the two, is another place to look. At no. 3 is *Diana* (☎0184/80.621), from L15,000, and there are two more at no. 25 – *Olimpia* (☎0184/80.093) and *Venise* (☎0184/80.110), both with doubles at L21,000.

Most of the Liberty-style hotels are four- and five-star, but an exception is *Hotel San Remo*, set back from the road at Corso Garibaldi 123 (☎0184/84.591), which charges from L45,000. Similar in style and price is the nearby *Villa Italia*, Via XX Settembre 45 (☎0184/86.080). Both are booked well in advance.

Eating, drinking and nightlife

For **picnic** food walk along Via Palazzo, off Piazza Colombo, where four or five large shops sell spit-roasted chickens, salami, cheese and ornate delicacies in aspic. Up in the old town, in the first street on the right as you enter from Piazza Cassini, is *Osteria della Costa*, specialising in an excellent rabbit stew – there are only a few tables, so get there around 8pm. For substantial fresh salads try *Shaker Bar*, Corso Matteotti 152, which is open all day. On Via Palazzo itself is *Cantine San Remo*, a bar with hot food at noon and early evening. At the end of the road and to the right you can't miss Piazza Eroi San Remesi, a carpark surrounded on all sides by large pizzeria-restaurants, with tourist menus at L10,000 and upwards.

In the evening Piazza Colombo and Corso Matteotti are packed with *ragazzi* hanging around, eating ice cream, and later putting money down on the *Totocalcio* lottery. The *Bar-Gelateria* at Corso Garibaldi 49 may not be at the centre of the action, but the cones are worth the walk.

For entertainment, if you want to gross out, go to the nightly cabaret at the Liberty-style **Casino**, or, if you're around in February, the annual "Festival of Song", which is arguably more extreme than the Eurovision song contest. Fortunately, there's no shortage of other clubs and bars. For **live bands**, go to *Pipistrello*, a cellar bar at Piazza Borea d'Olmo 8 – to get there, turn down Via Goffredo Mameli, opposite the *Ariston* Cinema on Corso Matteotti.

Inland from San Remo

Just outside San Remo are two small hilltop towns, both much visited, but each rather different. **BUSSANA VECCHIA** makes you want to turn round and go back home as soon as you get there. Destroyed by an earthquake in 1887, the houses are kept in an artificial state of ruin, and you can't move for rip-off galleries masquerading as artists' workshops. A far more satisfactory trip is to take the trolley bus outside San Remo station to the more sleepy **TAGGIA** (every 20min).

Its long echoing alleyways are distinguished by the variety of carved slate portals with which the different families adorned their houses – some of them chipped off as fortunes dipped; the overriding sound is of cicadas in the fields around. The town's principal attraction is a collection of work by Ligurian artists in the cloister of the **San Domenico** (Fri–Wed 9am–noon & 3–6pm), but more thrilling is the ancient *festa* of the Magdalene, held on the Sunday closest to July 22 – it culminates in a "Dance of Death" performed by two men, traditionally from the same two families, accompanied by the local brass and woodwind band.

Baiardo

The other side of Monte Bignone, past CERIANA, becomes a landscape of terraced meadows and woods. **BAIARDO** makes the best centre if you plan to stay in the region – it's a hill town with wide views over several valleys, reachable by bus from San Remo. No more than a few houses around a church, the village is a very relaxing place, with mule tracks and footpaths meandering through the fields and vineyards. The most central places to stay are *Pensione Colombo* (☎0184/93.034), with rooms at L20,000, and *Hotel Pineta* (☎0184/93.014), at around L29,000 – the *Pineta* also has an excellent small restaurant with dishes based on local produce such as wild boar. At Pentecost, Baiardo holds the *Festa della Barca*, when a maypole topped with a small tree is set up for dancing.

Seven and a half kilometres west of Baiardo, you pass the village of APRICALE clinging to a pinnacle of rock, with PERINALDO perched even higher in the distance. At ISOLABONA, a couple of kilometres from Apricale, you can pick up buses for Dolceacqua, Bordighera and Ventimiglia (see below).

Triora

Further into the mountains, along the heavily cultivated Argentina valley, is the tiny village of **TRIORA**. The bus trip is worth it in itself, following the rock-strewn course of the Argentina, passing small settlements with ancient bridges, and farms linked to the main road across the valley by a rope and pulley system. Triora itself is literally the end of the road, spectacular for its setting in sight of Monte Pietradura, which stays snowcapped until April. A couple of bends below the village, a mule track leads down one mountainside and up another to **MOLINI DI TRIORA** (which the bus passes earlier), named after the mills which used to line the river. (You can still buy the special flat bread of the town.) In 1588, two hundred women in this isolated community were denounced as witches. Thirty were tortured, fourteen burned at the stake, and one woman committed suicide before she could be executed. The **Museo Etnografico** in Triora (June–Sept afternoons only) has documents from the trial and other exhibits on peasant life.

From Bordighera to the French Border

The plantation of palms surrounding the long-established resort of **BORDIGHERA** is the town's special resource – during Holy Week the Vatican uses the fronds of Bordigheran palms to the exclusion of all others. The monopoly was secured in unusual circumstances by a sea captain from the town who was visiting Rome in 1586. An obelisk which was being raised in Saint Peter's Square threatened to topple, but nobody dared disobey the pope's order for complete silence during the ceremony – nobody, that is, except the Bordigheran, whose shouted warning earned him the reward of the exclusive contract.

A cluster of medieval buildings make up the old town – several alleyways of restaurants and small shops, and the Romanesque **Capello di Sant'Ampelio**. This part of Bordighera is really tiny and off the beaten track, a steep walk, or four-kilometre bus-ride, away from the train station and seafront. To the east along Via Arziglia are the Winter Gardens and plantations of palm and mimosa (40min walk); the sea glitters hundreds of feet below. The mild climate has long been an attraction. Katherine Mansfield rented a villa in the hills after she had been asked to leave her hotel in San Remo, where her ill-health made the other guests nervous.

Dolceacqua

Buses run regularly from Bordighera to the hilltop village of **DOLCEACQUA**, visited chiefly for its excellent *Rossesse* wine, probably the best in Liguria, and olive oil. You see piles of black olives in the village at harvest, spread out on cloths on the ground before processing. The modern half of Dolceacqua is linked with the old part of town by a single-spanned medieval bridge over the River Nervia, and the stone alleyways are topped by a ruined castle once belonging to the Doria family, who apparently exercised the *droit de seigneur* with local brides. A theatre festival is staged in the castle every July and August, as well as summer concerts. Dolceacqua is also the scene of a more ancient festival on the Sunday nearest to January 20. A laurel tree hung with coloured communion wafers like Christmas decorations is carried through the village as part of the procession of Saint Sebastian, the origins of which are rooted in ancient fertility rites. From Dolceacqua, there are regular buses to Ventimiglia.

Ventimiglia and La Mortola

Eleven kilometres from France, **VENTIMIGLIA** is a typical border town, with a string of duty-free shops near the station, and French spoken as often as Italian. It can seem on the dreary side, but livens up on Fridays when a giant **food and clothes market** takes over the town from Via della Repubblica down to the seafront. Across the river is the old quarter, where the Lombard-Romanesque **Cattedrale** and Baptistry are separated from the eleventh-century church of **San Michele** by echoing alleyways and stone piazzas. If you're stopping over for market day, there are plenty of **hotels**: the *Lido*, on the seafront below the old town at Via Marconi 11 (☎0184/351.473), has rooms at L28,000, while closer to the station is *Villa Franca*, Corso Repubblica 12 (☎0184/351.871), charging around L36,000.

From the junction of Via Martiri della Libertà and Via Cavour several buses a day leave for the gardens of **La Mortola**, set on a hillside near the frontier. This (daily 10am–4pm) is expensive at L8500, but worth it, especially if you take something to eat and spend the afternoon here. Seven thousand species or more once grew in this botanical garden; now three-quarters have gone, but even on the brink of ruin it's a powerfully atmospheric place, with hidden corners and pergola-covered walks. The steeply terraced site covers 45 acres down to the sea, laid out so that vistas of grottoes and wild vegetation unfold before you. At its centre is the Islamic-style mausoleum of Sir Thomas Hanbury, the garden's creator.

A half-hour walk further up the road is the **frontier post** at Ponte San Luigi. A scramble down the hillside brings you to the **Balzi Rossi**, a significant prehis-

toric site, but visually not much more than an unengrossing crevice of rock
(Tues–Sun 9am–1pm & 2.30–6.30pm; L2000). Close by is the main road to
France, which crosses the border at Ponte San Ludovico.

EAST OF GENOVA:
THE RIVIERA DEL LEVANTE

The stretch of coast east from Genova, dubbed the **Riviera del Levante** (Riviera
of the Rising Sun), is not the place to come for a relaxing beach holiday. Getting a
tan in the most popular towns involves fighting for a small piece of pebble beach
or concrete jetty, while the waterfront restaurants and cafés are the arenas for
some highly competitive posing. Ports which once survived on the trades of navigation, fishing and coral diving, have now experienced a solid thirty years of tourism; the coastline is still wild and extremely beautiful in parts, but inevitably the
sense of remoteness has gone. It's pointless protesting against the stranglehold
tourism has over the Riviera. Once you've accepted that wandering around ex-
fishing villages with hordes of others is inevitable, you appreciate the major
attractions this area still has to offer.

Away from the resorts, the cliffs and inlets are covered with pines and olive
trees, best seen along the footpaths of **Monte Portofino**, on the way to **San
Fruttuoso**, a short way east of Genova. The nearby harbour towns of **Camogli**
and **Santa Margherita Ligure**, painted up with trompe l'oeil balustrades and
shutters, are favourite subjects for arty picture postcards, but for more nightlife
head further along the coast to **Rapallo** and **Sestri Levante**. After Sestri, the
road heads inland, bypassing the **Cinque Terre** – five fishing villages shoe-
horned into inlets along the cliffs, the middle three of which are accessible only
by train or boat. The main Genova to La Spezia line then disappears in a series of
tunnels, to emerge at the wide Golfo di Spezia. From the naval and shipbuilding
port of **La Spezia** itself, there's transport to Tuscany or across the Apennines to
Parma, and ferries to Bastia in Corsica.

Recco and Camogli

Allied bombing in 1944 virtually destroyed **RECCO**, and the town which has
sprung up in its place is unremarkable except for the grey concrete flyover which
hurdles the centre. People come here specifically to eat – some of the best
restaurants in the province are within two or three kilometres of the town
centre. Specialities include *foccaccia al formaggio* (a superior version of foccaccia,
with cheese), *trofie* (twirly pasta with pesto) and *pansoti* (a spinach-filled pasta
with walnut sauce).

If your wallet is fat enough, book a table at *Manuelina*, Via Roma 300 (☎0185/
74.128; closed Wed) – it's on the main road running north from the flyover. A
more budget-conscious menu is on offer at the *Foccaceria* next door. *Da-ö
Vittorió*, at Via Roma 160 (☎0185/74.029; closed Thurs), rivals *Manuelina* in quality and will similarly set you back around L45,000 per head. For snacks, call in at
La Baracchetta (closed Tues), a hut with tables at the base of the cliffs, or at
Pizzeria del Ponte, Via Marconi 11 (by the flyover), for their *pasta e carne*.

Camogli

CAMOGLI – just around the headland from Recco – was the "saltiest, roughest, most piratical little place", according to Dickens when he visited in 1884; and crumbling arcades next to the harbour and dark flights of steps up past houses, to the centre of town, still have "a smell of fish, and seaweed, and old rope" although the town's livelihood is now more based on tourists than the sea. In its day Camogli was an important seafaring town; something of a nursery for navigators, it supported a fleet of 700 vessels, a force which was larger than Genova's and once saw off Napoleon's fleet. The town's name, a contraction of *Casa Moglie* (House of Wives), comes from the days when voyages took years, and the women ran the port while the men were away. Camogli declined in the age of steam, but not before its seamanship was exploited by the French to conquer Algiers in the 1830s, and the foundation of the first maritime mutual insurance company here in the nineteenth century. These days the harbour is busy with ferries to San Fruttuoso, Portofino and Santa Margherita.

Punta Chiappa, across the bay, was once famous for the "ever changing colours of the sea", as guidebooks will tell you, but is now murky in places with rubbish from the yachts moored off the promontory. The flat rocks are still a popular place to bask, and plenty of people swim from here. It's also the starting point for trails around the edge of **Monte Portofino**, and is accessible by ferry or by taking the path from San Rocco church, on the edge of Camogli. From Punta Chiappa it takes three hours to walk to San Fruttuoso and five to Portofino, along wild and beautiful clifftops.

For **places to stay**, try *La Camogliese* , Via Garibaldi 55 (☎0185/771.402), with rooms at L35,000, or the slightly cheaper *Augusta*, Via P. Schiaffino 100 (☎0185/770.592), on the edge of town as you come in by bus. The **restaurants** along the front are either expensive or bland – a better deal is *Da Fallù*, a seafood café on Salita Priaro, the flight of steps up from the harbour. The daily fruit and veg **market** takes place a few yards along the main road, in a building like a Fifties toy garage; of the food shops along the seafront, *Revello's* is the best – with queues for their *foccaccia* straight from the oven and the extravagant choux pastry *camogliese*.

On the second Sunday in May, the **Sagra del Pesce** takes place: basically a great fry-up at the harbour. The Camogliese celebrate the abundance of the sea and hope for the same the following year by giving the fish away free. Recently it's hit problems: the authorities have said that the giant frying pan is a health hazard, and there have been allegations that frozen fish are defrosted out at sea and then brought in to be sold as fresh. Less controversial is the *Stella Maris*, on the first Sunday in August: a procession of boats which heads off after dark to Punta Chiappa as part of a festival to placate the sea gods.

The Headland of Monte Portofino

PORTOFINO, at the extremity of the Monte Portofino headland, manages to be both attractive and offputting at the same time. The tiny resort is a microcosm of wealthy urban life transplanted to the seaside. Once you've surveyed the expensive restaurants and lace shops by the water there's not much more to do other than watch everyone else do the same. The thing is, it is very beautiful: the slopes surrounding the bay are covered in cypress and olive trees, and a **footpath to San Fruttuoso** (about 2hr 30min over the cliffs) passes through vineyards and orchards, at the end of the steep flight of steps inland. Shorter walks lead to the lighthouse and the castle and church of San Giorgio, said to contain relics of the saint. Three kilometres out of the village, on the corniche road, the sparkling cove at **PARAGGI** is a good place for a swim – not exactly remote, but less formal than Portofino, with a couple of bars set back from the beach.

Staying in Portofino is expensive, even out of season – it's better to take the bus to the nearby towns of Santa Margherita Ligure and Rapallo.

Monte Portofino

At 612m, **Monte Portofino** is big enough to be interesting without demanding any hiking expertise. The trails cross slopes of wild thyme, pine and holm oak, enveloped in the constant buzz of cicadas, and loop around the headlands which fringe its base. Monte Portofino represents a goldmine for developers, but for the moment there's a ban on any building work; rumour has it that fires are started deliberately to sabotage its national park status. You can reach the coastal paths by foot from Camogli or Portofino, or take a bus to RUTA, from where you can either slog on foot to the summit, or catch another bus to Portofino Vetta (see below), from where it's twenty minutes' walk to the top. On very clear days you can see as far as Corsica, or so it's said; even routinely, though, the view over successive headlands is fantastic. Not many people walk the trails, maybe because their early stages are fairly steep – but they aren't particularly strenuous, levelling off later, with plenty of places to stop.

PORTOFINO VETTA itself consists of a patch of *RAI* transmitters, a sedate hotel and a self-proclaimed "Most Important Fresco Museum in the World", none of which offer much incentive to stay.

San Fruttuoso

More rewarding than the haul to the top are the coastal paths to **SAN FRUTTUOSO** which start from Portofino Vetta (1hr 15min), Camogli (3hr) or Portofino itself (2hr 30min). What happens when you arrive depends on the time of year. If it's a summer weekend, ferries crammed with tourists will be shuttling every half-hour between the small inlet and Portofino, Santa Margherita Ligure and Rapallo in one direction, and Camogli in the other. Out of season, however, San Fruttuoso is peaceful, and an excellent place for doing nothing – wandering through the recently restored abbey, the only sounds are the waves on the beach outside. There are a couple of shack-type restaurants on the beach selling **beer** and **seafood**, but nowhere to stay.

The **Abbazia di San Fruttuoso di Capodimonte**, which fills the width of the bay, was originally built as a home for the relics of Saint Fructuosus, brought here after the Moorish invasion of Spain in 711. Destroyed by Saracen raids, it was rebuilt as a Benedictine abbey in 984. Among the tombs is that of one Maria Aregna, killed trying to save survivors of a warship bound for the Crimea, which had caught fire near the bay. Some of the Doria family, who gave their name to the sixteenth-century defence tower on the headland, are buried here too.

Off the headland, a bronze statue of Christ (*Cristo degli Abissi*) has been lowered eight fathoms down onto the seabed, in commemoration of divers who have lost their lives at sea. Unless you're a diver yourself you can't get down deep enough to see much of this, but there's a replica in a fish tank inside the Gothic church which adjoins the abbey.

Santa Margherita Ligure

SANTA MARGHERITA LIGURE is a small resort which makes you feel churlish for not enjoying it. It's thoroughly attractive, with palm trees along the front and trompe l'oeil paintings on the walls, and it threatens to drive you mad with boredom after about half a day. Trendy young Italians cruise the streets in convertibles, or whizz around the harbour on jet skis, while the rest of the family sunbathes on the miniscule pebble beach and concrete jetties, or crams the many restaurants and *gelaterie*. Nonetheless, you might well want to stay in Santa Margherita, as it's on the Genova to La Spezia line and makes a convenient base for visiting Monte Portofino and the other coastal towns. The cheap **hotels** are friendly and pleasant. Try *Albergo Annabella* on Via Costasecca, just off Piazza Mazzini (☎0185/286.531), which has rooms at L25,000, or *Albergo Fasce*, a little further up the road in Via L. Bozzo (☎0185/286.435), at L40,000. *Hotel La Piazzetta*, next to the seafront at Via Gramsci 1 (☎0185/286.010) costs around L35,000.

The Friday morning **market** takes place in Via Palestro, in the shadow of the **Basilica di Santa Margherita**, which has a rich interior of gilt and rococo paintings. Nearby, the **EPT** on Via XXV Aprile (Mon–Sat 8–11.45am & 3.15–5.45pm, plus Sun morning in summer) has free footpath maps of the area.

If you carry on towards Rapallo, the road cuts the corner of the first headland and drops down to a patch of beach in the bay of **SAN MICHELE DI PAGANA**. For the truly dedicated, the church here has a *Crucifixion* by Van Dyck, but the beach bars and clear water are a stronger attraction.

The Golfo di Tigullio: Rapallo, Chiávari and Lavagna

After the rocks and inlets which fringe Monte Portofino, the coast flattens out to form the **Golfo di Tigullio**, stretching for 28km in a wide arc. There are no quiet parts – most of the level land next to the sea has been developed, and the gulf is bracketed by the commercialised resorts of Rapallo and Sestri Levante. Chiávari and Lavagna are smaller towns, with buses into the hinterland – to the basilica at San Salvatore, and, further into the mountains, to the resort of Santo Stefano d'Aveto.

Most of the train journey between Rapallo and Chiávari is through tunnels, so for an idea of what lies in between you need to take the local bus, which follows the mad coast road around several headlands. It's fairly densely built-up, although some of the villas and gardens are spectacular, surrounded by wisteria, fig trees and mini olive groves. The overriding attraction, however, is the sea, which takes on a transparent quality outside the big resorts. Brilliant turquoise coves appear and disappear in a matter of seconds as the bus takes another bend, and occasional signs point *al mare* – jump off if the fancy takes you, though you probably won't be alone when you get there.

Rapallo

RAPALLO crowds around the first bay along in the gulf, a highly developed resort with acres of glass-walled restaurants and plush hotels. Earlier this century Rapallo was a backwater, and writers in particular came for the bay's extraordinary beauty, of which you now get an inkling only early in the morning or at dusk. Caricaturist and ferocious critic of British Imperialism, Max Beerbohm lived in Rapallo for the second half of his life, and attracted a vast coterie; Ezra Pound wrote the first thirty of his *Cantos* here between 1925 and 1930. (Just to be contrary, Ernest Hemingway came to visit and said the sea was flat and boring.) The striking landmarks now are the large marina and the castle stuck out at the end of a small causeway – once a prison, now an exhibition space.

The town does have an existence separate from its tourist trade, particularly around the **old town**, a grid of cobbled streets behind the stone Saline Gate – this is the commercial centre, and venue for the **market** which overflows Piazza Cile every Thursday.

The best **places to stay** in Rapallo are along the front, within sight and smell of the sea and the palm and orange trees. *Pensione Bandoni*, Via Marsala 24 (☎0185/50.423), has rooms at L40,000, some of them with balconies. Almost next door, *Hotel Rapallo* (☎0185/60.380) charges around L55,000, breakfast and bathroom included. A double room at the luxurious *Astoria*, away from the main drag at Via Gramsci 4 (☎0185/273.533), will cost you L95,000, and is worth every lira. At the other end of the scale, *Da Beppino*, by the station at Corso Assereto 15 (☎0185/50.352), should give you change from L20,000. There's a campsite, *Rapallo* (☎0185/60.260), 1km before Santa Maria di Campo and the autostrada, at Via San Lazzaro 6.

Da Beppino's **restaurant** offers the cheapest meal in town, in double-quick time (closes 8.30pm). For a costly blowout, try *Zi Teresa* at Corso Italia 33, (closed Wed), or sample less expensive Ligurian food at *Michelitto*, Via San Massimo 33, near the golf course (closed Tues) – take the bus for Santa Maria di Campo and get off at the junction with Via San Massimo, or take the bus for San Massimo itself. There are some pub-type **bars** too, like *Taverna Paradiso*, Via Venezia 72, between the station and the castle.

The **AAST** at Via Diaz 9 (daily 8.30am–12.30pm & 3.30–6.30pm) provides sketchy maps of the footpaths which head up to **MONTALLEGRO**, in the hills behind Rapallo. The less energetic could take the cable car from Via Castegneto, ten minutes' walk inland from the castle. A bus makes the same journey, passing through **SAN MAURIZIO DI MONTI**, where there are a couple of cheap restaurants specialising in Ligurian home cooking. The **Santuario di Montallegro**, at the top, has a superb setting, overlooking the steep, green valley, with every available space planted with terraces of olives and vegetables. It was founded in 1557 when a Byzantine icon of the Madonna appeared miraculously in the hands of one Giovanni Chichizola; a commemorative *festa* is held during the first three days of July, with the coffer of the Madonna carried through town, and a fireworks contest culminating in the mock burning of the castle.

Chiávari and around

Paths lead down from the main Rapallo to Chiávari road to some small coves – take the bus and get off when you see signs pointing to the sea. The traffic drives murderously fast around the switchbacks swooping inland around **ZOAGLI**, a village which began making patterned velvets in the Middle Ages, and later supplied most of Europe. They still make some of them – notably the red and gold *Genovese Palm* – for use in interior decoration. The area as a whole is famed for textiles. Further up in the hills is the small town of LORSICA, which still produces brilliant damasks – many of those you see in Genova's palaces came from here.

In contrast to the rock faces and inlets which have gone before, **CHIÁVARI** faces a flat bit of coastline, featureless but for the boulder and cement breakwaters separating the marina from the sand and pebble beach. Called Clavarium (Keys) by the Romans for the access it gave them to the valleys behind the coast, Chiávari is still a good starting point for trips into the mountains. The **bus** and **train** stations are next door to each other, just off Chiávari's main street, Corso della Libertà, which bisects a grid pattern of medieval arcades lined with food shops and macramé outlets. The craft was brought back from the East by local sailors, and its name is derived from the Chiávari dialect.

Off the Corso, at Via Costaguta 2, is the **Civico Museo Archeologico** (Tues–Thurs 9am–1pm, Fri–Sun 2–7.30pm; free) with graphics explaining such recondite matters as the intricacies of the triple flint arrowhead, backed by finds from a vast seventh- to eighth-century necropolis on the outskirts of town.

Lavagna

Occupying the other bank of the River Entella, **LAVAGNA** is a smaller, plainer version of Chiávari. Its name means "blackboard" in Italian, after the slate quarried from caves on Monte San Giacomo and used on the outside of most of Liguria's striped churches. Nothing much happens in Lavagna, with the major exception of August 14 each year, when the town hosts its own version of *Blind Date*. Hundreds of people turn up to claim their piece of the giant wedding cake set up in the main square – called the *Torta dei Fieschi* after a thirteenth-century wedding between Opizzone Fieschi and Bianca dei Bianchi. You take a ticket, which matches up with a ticket held by someone else in the large crowd; finding your partner, according to the tourist office, "at times leads to enduring relationships".

The **Basilica di San Salvatore dei Fieschi**, a couple of kilometres north (accessible by bus from Lavagna or Chiávari), is a beautiful complex of Romanesque-Gothic buildings, adorned with pagan symbols under the eaves. Half hidden off the main road, the basilica, in its own walled square, looks down on a valley of farms and fruit trees.

Inland to Santo Stefano d'Aveto

Two routes lead inland to **SANTO STEFANO D'AVETO**: from Rapallo and from Chiávari. Both pass through isolated villages and hillsides terraced up to the snowline, with vines on the lower slopes and strange grass-hut-style canopies for covering hay. It's good countryside for hiking – especially around REZZOAGLIO and CERISOLA – and botanists will enjoy *La Riserva dell Agoraie*, a reserve of three small lakes on the northern slopes of Monte degli Abeti (1543m), with its rare plant species, and 2500-year-old trees preserved in the icy water. Santo Stefano itself, the largest of the mountain resorts, is a centre for walking and skiing, with a brace of one-star **hotels** – *Genovese*, Piazza del Mercato 9 (☎0185/980.50), with rooms at L25,000, and *San Lorenzo*, Via Marconi 26 (☎0185/980.08), a few thousand lire dearer.

Sestri Levante to the Cinque Terre

From Lavagna the road sweeps round the bay to **SESTRI LEVANTE**, one of the most commercialised resorts this side of Genova. It consists of two bays separated by a narrow isthmus: the "Bay of Fables" (nearer the train station), said to be so named by Hans Christian Andersen, and the "Bay of Silence". Marconi conducted some of his first short-wave radio experiments at the castle between the bays in 1897, sending radio waves 19km out to warships off La Spezia. On the Bay of Fables side, the beach is wide and sandy but is packed with sunbeds and overlooked by ranks of hotels which will probably send you in the opposite direction. The Bay of Silence, on the other hand, might not exactly live up to its name in high season, but is far more pleasant, with a narrow beach and lots of fishing boats.

On the headland there are a couple of small churches, including the restored Romanesque church of San Nicolò; the adjacent park of cork-oaks and other Mediterranean plants is open between May and September (closed noon–4pm). The most attractive **places to stay** are on the headland as well. *Pensione Jolanda*, Via Pozzetto 15 (☎0185/41.354), has rooms with balconies at around L30,000; another possibility in the same range, near the Bay of Silence, is the *San Pietro* on Via Palestro (☎0185/41.279). Back on the main drag, and closer to the sea, is *Locanda Trattoria L'Approdo* at Piazza Francesco Bo 17 (☎0185/47.367), which costs around L40,000.

Via XXV Aprile, which runs through the narrow peninsula and widens out onto Corso Colombo, is where you'll find the best places to **eat and drink**. *Ristorante Polpo Mario*, at no. 18, specialises in fish, and *Buon Geppin* on Corso Colombo (closed Mon) has good fish antipasti. For **takeaway food**, from Ligurian specialities to chips and ketchup, visit the place at no. 61/63 Via XXV Aprile, which is open restaurant hours every day. On the same road, there's a selection of wines from Liguria and the rest of Italy at *Enoteca Il Leudo* (daily until 8pm).

The **nightlife** is good in Sestri, too – plenty of bars stay open until 3am, and the video bar *Ca di Ferrae*, on Via Nazionale, has **live music** on Fridays.

Inland from Sestri

Travelling inland from Sestri, buses go to **VARESE LIGURE**, a market town in the upper Val di Vara, built in a circle around a fifteenth-century castle and medieval hog-backed bridge over the River Gresino. Varese's Augustinian nuns have traditionally made an income from *scivette* – marzipan flowers. A special kind of grappa comes from here too. To see the rest of the valley you really need your own transport. If you do have a car, you can continue along 13km of switchback road to the **Passo di Cento Croci** (1053m), and loop back down to the coast, or else cross the border and make for Bedonia and Borgo Val di Taro in Emilia Romagna.

Along the Coast

Once out of Sestri Levante, past the headland and the shipyards at RIVA TRIGOSO, the rail line and coastal road disappear into a set of tunnels which last almost until La Spezia. Getting around by **bus** takes time – its route loops onto the coast at the family resorts of MONEGLIA and DÉIVA MARINA, then cuts inland, where it passes red marble quarries, olive groves and burnt-out patches of forest before coming back down to the coast at **LEVANTO**, the last town before the Cinque Terre, – an unpretentious small town with a long stretch of sand backed by beach bars. The big day here is Wednesday, when the huge general **market** draws people in from miles around.

The Cinque Terre

If you're travelling on a fast train, you'll speed through the five villages of the **Cinque Terre** without seeing much more than a few tantalising glimpses of sheer cliffs and bright turquoise water as the train dashes from one tunnel to the next. However, the stopping services on the Genova to La Spezia line call at each of the five (hourly in both directions), and until the completion of the *Litoranea delle Cinque Terre*, rail is the most convenient way of getting to the villages – though there is a ferry service from La Spezia. Their comparative remoteness, and the drama of their position on tiny cliff-bound inlets, make a visit to the area a real attraction rather than just a convenient stopover on the way to Tuscany or Rome.

Purely fishing ports originally, the Cinque Terre now also produce large quantities of wine from steeply terraced vineyards, some of which are accessible only by boat. Fishing, wine-making and olive-growing are the major occupations, though tourism is an equally visible recent addition.

RIOMAGGIORE, closest to La Spezia and one of the larger villages, is the best place to head. Its bizarre charm lies in it being wedged impossibly into a hillside, with no two buildings on the same level. Along the cliff path which winds its way to **MANAROLA**, lemon trees flourish in every back yard, and in spring – before the sun has turned everything except the vines to dust – the cliffs are covered with wild flowers. From Manarola a less crowded and more spectacular path passes rock-cut steps leading down to the water all the way to **MONTEROSSO** (12km), largest and least charming of the villages, and the only one with a recognisable beach. **CORNIGLIA** and **VERNAZZA** are much the same as Riomaggiore, but on a smaller scale. A word of warning – if you follow the Italians' example and dive into the sea from the rocks, watch out for power boats whizzing past.

Reasonably priced **hotels** aren't too difficult to find – Monterosso and Riomaggiore present the best opportunities – but don't expect anything dirt-cheap, and bank on encountering problems in August. If you ask around in the villages, you'll probably be able to find a **room** in a private house. The **restaurants** are just overdecorated ordinary trattorias with inflated cover charges to match; the only relief in Monterosso (the worst offender) is, improbably enough, a beatnik café. **Bars**, on the other hand, tend to be reasonable even in the most obvious locations.

The Golfo di Spezia

Even though La Spezia itself is a major naval and shipbuilding town, the **Golfo di Spezia** is impressive, its sweep of islands and headlands being too big for heavy industry to dominate. When everywhere else is booked up, La Spezia usually still has cheap rooms, but if you have the choice, make for the small resorts outside, linked by bus along twisting roads: Portovénere, sitting astride a spit of land on one side of the gulf, or San Terenzo, Lérici or Tellaro, lining the coast on the other.

La Spezia

Most travel guides either bypass **LA SPEZIA** or dismiss it with a few curt comments, and on the face of it it's easy to see why. It's pretty well a blank as far as art and architecture are concerned, and nobody comes here to admire the things it does have: a huge mercantile port, the largest naval base in Italy, and unsightly petrochemical and quarrying industries. Still, with its bustling market and purposeful inhabitants, La Spezia is a real town, where people do things other than cater for tourists. Although its main attraction is undoubtedly the stunning beauty of the surrounding villages – particularly the Cinque Terre to the north – its cheap hotels and restaurants make it a good base for exploration.

Sweeping around the curve of the gulf – one of Europe's best natural harbours – La Spezia is crammed between the hills and the sea. This position proved an early attraction, its strategic importance reflected in the number of Genovese castles which stud the hills. These were the town's first fortifications, yet it wasn't until Napoleon arrived that a large naval and military base developed here. The naval presence made it a prime target in World War II and the results were predictable – most of the town centre had to be rebuilt after Allied bombing and is rather drab, with the exception of the modern Cattedrale (completed in 1974), its boldly minimalist white tower curving up against a hilly background.

In fact, the nearest La Spezia comes to anything traditional is the church of **Santa Maria**, whose facade displays attractively restrained black and white stone banding. Nestling modestly in the corner of Piazza Giulio Beverini, it was originally constructed in the 1300s and rebuilt in the seventeenth century after the city walls were expanded.

Close to the church is the town's principal *raison d'être* – the **Arsenale**, which was finished in 1869 and occupies a huge swathe of the southern part of town. The entrance is in Piazza Chiodo, but a visit requires a convoluted written application to the director of the complex. The **Museo Navale** (Tues–Thurs & Sat 9am–noon & 2–6pm; L2000), in the same square, contains battle relics, models and figureheads from the sixteenth century onwards. The **Museo Civico** (Tues–Sat 9am–1pm & 3–7pm, Sun 9am–1pm) at Via Curtatone 9 (between the Stazione Centrale and the Arsenale) holds archaeological remains from eastern Liguria; the most striking are the simple *stele* – faces sculpted on stone slabs in the Bronze and Iron Ages.

Practicalities

The **train station**, at the top end of town, is one of the main convergence points for **buses**; others are Piazza Cavour (the market place) and Piazza Chiodo. The last of these is the departure point for *ATC* buses to the Val di Magra, the Val di Vara and Tuscany (information ☎0187/503.123).

Ferries operate daily in summer between La Spezia and Bastia in Corsica – they're run by *Corsica Ferries*, on the Molo Italia (☎0187/21.282). Boat services to Lérici, Portovénere and its islands (Palmária and Tino), and the Cinque Terre are run by *Collegamenti Marittimi* (☎0187/503.123) and *Battellieri del Golfo* (☎0187/ 28.066) both on Banchina Revel, and *Navigazione Golfo dei Poeti* on Molo Italia (☎0187/508.334). See "Travel Details" for rough frequencies.

For a list of **hotels** and a map, head for the **EPT** at Via Mazzini 47, by the seafront (most buses go near there). Rooms are reasonably priced, the cheaper hotels tending to be near the station – but get there early in high season. *Firenze*

& *Continental* (☎0187/31.248) and *Parma* (☎0187/20.754) are just to the left of the station on Via Fiume, both costing around L35,000; the low budget option is *Flavia*, Vicolo dello Stagno 7 (☎0187/27.465), some L10,000 cheaper.

The daily covered **market** in Piazza Cavour is a good place to buy something for a picnic; it's a huge affair on Saturday mornings. **Restaurants** cluster in the area between Via del Prione and the Arsenale, to the right as you face the sea, the prices kept low by the naval clientele, many of them conscripts doing National Service. *Farinata* is available from many take-away places, also at one or two pizzerias – try the *Giulio* in Via San Agostino, just off Via del Prione. Seafood and pesto dominate trattoria menus – *Da Sandro* at Via del Prione 268 does a good line in both, while *La Posta*, at Via Don Minzoni 24 (☎0187/34.419; closed Sat & Sun), is hard to beat, though the price per head can reach L50,000.

Portovénere

PORTOVÉNERE sits on the small peninsula that encloses the gulf. The bus ride from La Spezia is a frenetic affair, with some hair-raising bends, but it gives fine views of the bay and the islands of Palmária and Tino. The village is tiny, its houses perched on the cliff and along the concrete harbour, which spreads out at the end of the promontory to the medieval church of San Pietro. One of the rocky coves around its base is called "Byron's window" so called because the poet once swam across the gulf from here to visit Shelley at San Terenzo (see below).

Portovénere is firmly on the tourist trail and doesn't cater for people travelling on a budget; the only cheapish **place to stay** is *Genio*, next to the tourist office (☎0187/900.611), with rooms at L45,000. There is, though, a very good place to **eat**: *L'Antica Osteria del Carrugio* at Via Capellini 66 (closed Thurs) – it's in the shadow of the Genovese castle, built to defend the coast from the Pisans on the other side of the bay.

The most frequent island **boat trips** are to the *Grotta Azzurra* on Palmária and the remains of a Romanesque abbey on Tino, though it's considerably cheaper if you leave from La Spezia. Boats also run the width of the bay to Lérici.

San Terenzo and Lérici

Dockyards, foundries and bars line the coast road to the east before La Spezia gives way to some small resorts. At **SAN TERENZO** there's a good sand **beach**, but if you want to stay, most of the hotels insist on you taking either full or half-pension; about the best deal you'll get is *Leonella* along the seafront (☎0187/970.969), at L40,000 per person. Next door but one is **Casa Magni**, where **Shelley** spent some productive months in 1822, before setting off to meet Leigh Hunt at Livorno, "full of spirits and joy", according to Mary Shelley's account; on the way back, his boat *Ariel* went down and Shelley drowned, aged thirty.

LÉRICI, in the next bay, is a fairly conventional resort of seafront bars, trattorias and gift shops. The Pisans built the castle in the twelfth century, to keep out the Genovese, who were established at Portovénere on the other side of the gulf. Paths skirt the castle and cross the headland to a small cove, an alternative to the beach next to the main road on the town side. Next to the marina are stalls selling fresh coconut, a couple of bars filled with yacht crews, and some pricey restaurants. Piazza Garibaldi, behind it, acts as the **bus terminus** (for services to

Sarzana, see below). The converted Genovese palace on Piazza Garibaldi, the *Albergo Italia* (☎0187/966.566), is a good **place to stay**, with rooms in the L40,000 range. If this is full, try *Albergo Luisa*, Via Gerrini 36 (☎0187/967.400), which is a shade less expensive.

To Tellaro

The five-kilometre stretch of coast to Tellaro, though close to some heavily developed resorts, seems worlds apart – the water is improbably clear and the coves and inlets are irresistible places to bask. If you don't feel like walking, a bus service does the trip. Look out for the huge signs about halfway there saying *Eco del Mare* and *spiaggia libera a 200m*; the path takes you down to a shingle and sand **beach**, surrounded by wooded slopes. Nearest affordable hotel on the Tellaro road is *Pensione Delfino* (☎0187/ 965.049), at around L40,000. Next inlet along from here is sparklingly clear FIASCHERINO, accessible along Via D.H. Lawrence (he lived here just before World War I). One of the most pleasant **campsites** on the Riviera is here – take the steps inland from the carpark, turn right and *Campeggio Gianna* (☎0187/966.411; Easter–late Sept) is in front of you, set on a terraced and shaded hillside.

Ten minutes' walk from Fiascherino is the quiet fishing village of **TELLARO**, where the road ends in a cluster of bars and a couple of **places to stay** – try *Delle Ondine* (☎0187/965.131), with rooms at L23,000. The rest of the village is comparatively untouched by tourism, with stone houses packed tightly on the spur of rock over the slipway, and alleyways stalked by cats. There's no beach, but you can swim off the flat rocks at the bottom of the cliff on the other side of the slipway.

Inland to Sarzana and Luni

Immediately beyond the gulf, the hills end suddenly and give way to the flatlands of the Magra estuary (the *Bocca di Magra*), an important habitat for birds. The River Magra was once the border between Liguria and Etruria, and later between the Pisans and Genovese; thus AMÉGLIA, one of the few villages here, is well fortified and set on a hill above the plain. Nearby **SARZANA** is an unremarkable lowland town, whose medieval quarter includes a fifteenth-century citadel. A reason to visit, though, is to eat at *La Scaletto*, ten minutes' walk from Piazza Martiri della Liberta, where **buses** from Lérici stop. Check out, too, the Romanesque church of **Sant'Andrea**, rebuilt with a rococo interior, and the **Cattedrale di Santa Maria Assunta**, which contains a twelfth-century panel painting of the Crucifixion by Maestro Guglielmo.

Still on the plain, towards the border with Tuscany, are the remains of a Roman colony at **LUNI**, the name of which comes from a cult of the moon goddess. The shipbuilding colony, founded in 177 BC, was eventually destroyed by war and malaria; finds from villas in the Bocca di Magra are on display in the **museum** (summer daily Tues–Sun 9am–noon & 4–7pm; winter 9am–noon & 2–5pm). The ruined amphitheatre in the *Zona Archaeologico* (same hours as museum) is a venue for theatre and music in summer – the Sarzana to Carrara bus passes it.

travel details

Trains

From Genova to Tortona and Milano (virtually hourly; 2hr); Pisa (every 2hr; 2hr 30min; change for Florence in just over 1hr); Rome (every 2hr; 6hr); Naples (9 daily; 8hr); Piacenza/Bologna (8 daily; 1hr 30min/3hr); La Spezia, (via Nervi, Santa Margherita, Rapallo, Chiàvari, Sestri Levante, Levanto; 8 daily; 1hr 30min); slower trains to La Spezia stopping everywhere including Cinque Terre (virtually hourly; 2hr 10min); Ventimiglia, via Savona, Albenga, Alassio, Imperia, San Remo, Bordighera, (virtually hourly; 2hr 30min); Casella (10 daily; 55min); Busalla (9 daily; 25min).

Buses

From Genova to Torriglia (virtually hourly; 1hr 10min); Montebruno (5 daily; 1hr 35min); Rovegno (5 daily; 1hr 50min).

From Rapallo to Santa Margherita (every 20min; 10min); Montallegro (every couple of hours; 40min); Chiavari/Lavagna (hourly; 30min).

From Rapallo, Santa Margherita and Camogli to Portofino Vetta (3 daily; 40min).

From Camogli to Ruta (hourly; 25min).

From Santa Margherita to Paraggi and Portofino (virtually every 30min; 15min).

From Chiavari to Santo Stefano d'Aveto (6 daily; 1hr 55min); Rezzoaglio (6 daily; 1hr 25min).

From Sestri Levante to Varese Ligure (Mon–Sat only; 11 daily; 1hr); Levanto (every couple of hours; 1hr).

From La Spezia to Portovenere (half-hourly; 20min); San Terenzo and Lerici (every 10min; 20min).

From Lerici to Tellaro (virtually every 30min; 10min); Ameglia (10 daily; 35min); Sarzana (half-hourly; 30min).

From Sarzana to Luni and Carrara (virtually hourly between 6am and 6pm).

From Riviera del Ponente, coastal route, stopping everywhere between Savona and Finale Ligure (hourly), Finale Ligure and Andora (every 15–20min), Andora and San Remo (half-hourly).

From Savona to Sassello (8 daily; 1hr).

From Finale Ligure to Ponti Romani (2 daily; 23min); Toirano (4 daily; 25min).

From Albenga to Villanova (8 daily; 15 min); Pieve di Teco (several daily; 1hr. Change for Mendatica – 3 daily; 45min).

From Imperia Oneglia to Pontedassio (4 daily; 15min).

From San Remo to Baiardo (4 daily; 1hr 15min); Apricale (3 daily; 40min).

From Ventimiglia to Dolceacqua (11 daily – less on Sunday; 15min); Triora and Molini di Triora (3 daily; 1hr 30min); La Mortola (9 daily; 15min); Ponte San Ludovico, for Balzi Rossi (6 daily; 20min).

Ferries

From Genova to **Sardinia**: Porto Torres (1 daily; 12hr 30min), Olbia and Arbatax (1 daily; 13hr); **Sicily**: Palermo (1 daily; 25hr) – *Tirrenia* line. Palermo (1 daily; 22hr) – *Grandi Traghetti S.p.A.*); **Corsica**: Bastia (2 daily; 5hr) – *Corsica Ferries.* Other services to Tunis, Naples and Barcelona.

From Genova to **Cagliari** (2 daily; 18hr).

From La Spezia to **Bastia** (2 daily; 5hr) – *Corsica Ferries.*

CHAPTER THREE

LOMBARDY AND THE LAKES

Lombardy, Italy's richest and most developed region, often seems to have more in common with its northern European neighbours than with the rest of Italy. Given its history, this is hardly surprising: it was ruled for almost two centuries by the French and Austrians and takes its name from the northern Lombards, who invaded the region and ousted the Romans. As a border region, accessible through numerous mountain passes, Lombardy has always been vulnerable to invasion, just as it has always profited by being a commercial crossroads. It was long viewed by northerners as the capital of Italy – emperors from Charlemagne to Napoleon came to Lombardy to be crowned king – and northern European business magnates continue to take Lombardy's capital, Milan, more seriously than Rome, the region's big businesses and banks wielding political as well as economic power across the nation.

The region's landscape has paid the price for economic success: industry chokes the peripheries of towns, sprawls across the Po plain in the south, and even spreads its polluting tentacles into the northern lakes and mountain valleys. Nonetheless Lombardy has its attractions: the upper reaches of its valleys are largely unspoilt, and there's good walking to be had in the mountains; its towns and cities all retain wanderable medieval cores; and the stunning scenery and lush vegetation of the lakes makes it easy to forget that the water is polluted.

As for Lombardy's people, from the cossetted snobs of the provincial towns to Milan's workaholics, they hardly fit the popular image of Italians. In fact, they don't have much time for at least half their compatriots: urban northerners are dismissive of the south, derisive of Rome and all too ready to exploit the so-called *terrone* (literally earth-people) – a highly insulting term for southern Italians who leave their poverty-stricken villages to find work in the north.

Milan is a natural gateway to the region, and where you may well arrive, dominating the plain that forms the southern part of Lombardy. The towns across here – **Pavia**, **Cremona**, **Mantua** – flourished during the Middle Ages and Renaissance, and retain their historical character today, albeit circled by burgeoning suburbs. To the north, Lombardy is quite different, the lakes and low mountains of the edge of the Alps sheltering fewer historic towns – though **Bergamo** and **Brescia** are notable exceptions. This has long been popular tourist territory, particularly around the lakes of **Maggiore**, **Como** and **Garda**, and is the heartland of Lombardy's monied classes – though the chocolate-box image of the lake scenery is these days tarnished by encroaching industry. **Public transport** in the region is good, the main cities, towns and lakes connected by train, with buses running to villages and up into the mountains. Hitching is rarely necessary, but can save time in the remoter areas where buses run infrequently.

MILAN AND
SOUTHERN LOMBARDY

Much of Lombardy's wealth concentrates in the cities and towns of the broad Po plain, which forms the southern belt of the region. It's a wealth which is obvious throughout the area, in the well preserved medieval towns and the ugly industrial estates that surround them, not to mention the pollution – the Po is Italy's most polluted river, and air-pollution in Milan is sometimes so dangerous that the traffic police don gas masks.

Despite all this, the area is well worth exploring. **Milan** may be polluted, and the majority of its buildings modern and ugly, but it's an upbeat city, with some great classical and contemporary art galleries and a splendid cathedral, as well as world famous designer boutiques and a lively nightscene. As a first taste of Italy it can be both daunting and disappointing; given time, though, and taken on its own, contemporary terms, it can be a stimulating place to be. **Pavia**, to the south, is a pretty medieval town and makes a cheaper – and rather more peaceful – alternative base for this part of Lombardy, its cobbled streets and ancient churches taking a firm back seat in terms of sights to its **Certosa**, just outside. Heading east, **Cremona** was the birthplace of the violin and home of Stradivari, and has a neat, well preserved centre – though it's not the kind of place you'd want to stay long. **Mantua**, in the far eastern corner of the region, is by contrast Lombardy's most visually appealing city, at least from a distance, though what you really come for are the remains of the powerful Gonzaga family who ruled here for 300 years from their extravagant Palazzo Ducale. Their later Palazzo Te, on the outskirts of the city, is also a must, containing some of the finest (and most steamily erotic) fresco-painting of the Renaissance.

Milan (Milano)

The dynamo behind the country's "economic miracle", **MILAN** is a city like no other in Italy. It's foggy in winter, muggy in summer, sees itself as Europe's New York, and is closer in outlook as well as distance to London than Palermo. This is no city of peeling palazzi, cobbled piazzas and *la dolce vita*, but one in which time is money, the pace fast, and where consumerism and the work-ethic rule the lives of its power-dressed citizens.

Because of this most people pass straight through, and if it's summer and you're keen for sun and sea this might well be the best thing you can do; the weather, in August especially, can be off-puttingly humid. But at any other time of year it's worth giving Milan a bit more of a chance. It's a historic city in its way, with enough churches and museums to keep you busy for a week: the Accademia Brera, duomo and the church of Santa Maria delle Grazie. And the contemporary aspects of the place represent the leading edge of Italy's fashion and design industry. Take time to designer window-shop and visit the city's private galleries; and sample a nightlife scene which is probably the country's best and most varied, centring in part on the decaying Navigli quarter. Perhaps in defiance of the ugliness of much of the city, the visual quality of life matters in Milan. Fashion and design are taken with a passion that goes beyond the fact that they are multi-million pound industries – five minutes on a metro or city centre street will prove the point. Street-fashion, as understood in Britain, is virtually non-existent – label-conscious Italian youth dresses to conform not rebel.

Some history

Milan first stepped into the historical limelight in the fourth century when Emperor Constantine issued the **Edict of Milan** here, granting Christians throughout the Roman Empire the freedom to worship for the first time. The city, under its charismatic bishop, Ambrogio (Saint Ambrose), swiftly became a major centre of Christianity – many of today's churches stand on the sites, or even retain parts, of fourth-century predecessors.

Medieval Milan rose to prominence under the ruthless regime of the Visconti dynasty, who founded what is still the city's most spectacular building, the florid late-Gothic **Duomo**, and built the first, heavily fortified nucleus of the **Castello** – which, under their successors, the Sforza, was extended to house what became one of the most luxurious courts of the Renaissance. This was a period of much building and rebuilding, notably under the last Sforza, Lodovico, who employed the architect **Bramante** to improve the city's churches, and **Leonardo da Vinci** to paint *The Last Supper* and design war-machines to aid him in his struggles with foreign powers and other Italian states. Leonardo's inventions didn't prevent Milan falling to the French in 1499, marking the beginning of almost four centuries of foreign rule. Later, the Austrian Hapsburgs took control, during their time commissioning the **Teatro della Scala** and founding the **Brera** art gallery, which was filled, during Milan's short spell under Napoleon, with paintings looted from churches and private collections.

Mussolini made his mark on the city too. Arrive by train and you emerge into the massive white megalith of the central **station** built on his orders; the main tourist office is housed in one half of the pompous twin **Arengario**, from which he would address crowds gathered in Piazza Duomo. And with stark irony it was on the now major road junction of **Piazzale Loreto** that the dead dictator was strung up for display to the baying mob.

Arrival

Milan has two airports, both used by domestic and international traffic. Linate is the closest, just 7km from the city centre, to which buses leave Stazione Centrale every twenty minutes from 5.40am until 8.40pm (a half-hour journey; L2000). The other airport, **Malpensa**, 50km away towards Lago Maggiore, takes considerably longer to reach and buses are less frequent – they leave Stazione Centrale two and a half hours before each international flight. Tickets for both from *Agenzia Doria* (open 7am–11pm) on the ground floor of Stazione Centrale. There are also **urban transport buses** (#73) until around midnight from Linate to Piazza San Babila (connecting with MM1). Tickets currently cost L800, to be bought before you get on the bus from the airport newsagent or, if you have change, from the ticket machine at the bus stop.

Almost all international **trains** pull in at the main Stazione Centrale (☎67.500), northeast of the city centre on Piazza Duca d'Aosta – MM2. Other stations include **Garibaldi, Lambrate** and **Nord**, all on MM2 and serving various stations in the Milan region – Bergamo, Pavia, Como and the other western lakes, though these often also stop at Centrale.

International and long-distance **buses** arrive at and depart from Piazza Castello, in front of the Castello Sforzesco. Information and tickets from the *Autostradale* bus office on the piazza, or *Zani Viaggi* (☎867.131) on the corner of Piazza Castello and Foro Buonaparte.

Arriving **by car**, the city is encircled by a multi-laned toll road, the *Tangenzianale*, from which there are exits onto the autostradas for Venice, Turin and the Lakes, and the *Autostrada del Sole* for Bologna, Florence, Rome and the south. Driving in the city is best avoided: the streets are congested and parking close on impossible. Parking in prohibited zones is not worth it: you'll be fined if caught and have your car impounded by the police (see *Listings* for carparks).

The Milan area telephone code is ☎02

Information and getting around

Information and **city maps** are available from Milan's main APT offices, conveniently located at the **Stazione Centrale** (daily 9am–12.30pm & 2–6pm; ☎669.0432) and on **Piazza Duomo** (Mon–Fri 8.45am–12.30pm & 1.30–6pm, Sat 9am–12.30pm & 1–5pm; ☎809.662). Their *Tutta Milano* is a useful and fairly comprehensive information booklet, worth buying (L2000) if you're going to be in the city for any time, as is the guide *Key to Milan*, available in better bookshops. For **what's on** listings the Thursday pullouts in either *Corriere della Sera* or *La Repubblica*.

The city council also has an **information office** in the Galleria Vittorio Emanuele (Mon–Sat 8am–11pm, Sun in summer; ☎870.545). They have (often more reliable) details of cultural events and will book tickets for theatre and concerts.

Orientation and city transport

Milan's street-plan resembles a spider's web, with roads radiating out from the central Piazza Duomo. The bulk of the city is encircled by three concentric ring roads, though the suburbs and industrial estates are now spilling out towards a fourth ring, the *tangenzianale*, which links the main autostradas. The city centre is, however, fairly compact, and most of what you'll want to see within the first or second rings – each of them marking ancient city boundaries.

In spite of this, the streets can be smoggy and packed, and at some point you'll want to make use of the **public transport** system – an efficient network of trams, buses and metro. The **metro** is easiest to master (and the fastest and most useful), at present made up of two lines, the red MM1 and green MM2, with a third, yellow MM3 under construction and due for completion in the early 1990s. MM1 runs from the northeast suburbs through the centre by way of Piazza Duomo and Piazza Cairoli; MM2 connects the three main railway stations, Centrale, Garibaldi and Lambrate, and runs out to Stazione Porta Genova near the Navigli; the forthcoming MM3 will run from the Stazione Centrale through

Line 3 due for completion early 1990s.

Piazza Cavour and Via Manzoni to the southeast suburbs. The lines join at Loreto and Cadorna. Though the system is not comprehensive, it's adequate for sightseeing, though you any need to use a **tram** or **bus** to get to your hotel: the system is well organised and integrated with the metro. Buses, trams and the metro run from around 6am to midnight, after which **night buses** take over, following the metro routes until 1am.

For all **public transport enquiries** the information office at the Duomo metro station is helpful, and has free route maps. **Tickets**, valid for 75 minutes, cost L800 and can be used for one metro trip and as many bus and tram rides as you want. Tickets are on sale at tobacconists, bars and at the metro station newsagents; most outlets close at 8pm so buy a few tickets in advance. Some stations have automatic ticket machines though only the newer ones give change. If you *are* stranded without a ticket, a used ticket will get you through the automatic ticket barriers, though if you're caught, pleading a foreigner's ignorance won't cut much ice. You can avoid the situation by buying a **24-hour ticket** (L2800) from the Centrale or Duomo metro stations.

Finding a place to stay

Milan is more a business than a tourist city, and its **accommodation** is geared to the expense-account traveller. The frequent commercial fairs (most significantly in April and October) mean that hotels can be packed out of season, and good value cheap hotels hard to find, most low-priced places charging by the hour. If you want to be sure of a room in any of the places listed below, book in advance; if you haven't, the best bet is to head straight for the APT at Stazione Centrale or Piazza Duomo (Mon–Sat 9am–12.30pm & 2.15–6pm), who can officially only give you a list of hotels with prices but in fact will book you a room free of charge. If you arrive at Linate airport, try *SEA Viaggi*.

The area between Stazione Centrale, Viale V. Veneto and Corso Buenos Aires is home to most of the city's **cheaper hotels**, though many cater to the area's considerable red light trade; keep to the fringes and you should, however, be fine – though women alone might want to avoid even these streets at night. Better value than the hotels are the city's **hostels**, though most of these are run by monks and nuns and have 10.30pm curfews. There are also three **campsites** outside the city – inconvenient if you're relying on public transport, but okay if you have a car. Incidentally, if you want to see Milan but are not bothered about being there at night, you could save money by staying in nearby Pavia and visiting Milan on day-trips.

Hostels

ACISJF, Corso Garibaldi 121 (☎659.5206). Not far from the Castello and Parco Sempione. Run by nuns, and taking women only aged 18–25 in rooms of up to four beds. Open 7am–10.30pm with an extension to midnight on Thursday and Saturday. Meals available. Bed and breakfast L13,000. MM Moscova.

La Casa, Via Lattuada 14 (☎546.9251). Off Viale Monte Nero (just behind Piazza Medaglio d'Oro). Open year-round to men and women, all rooms with private bathroom; doubles for L50,000. Tram #29 or #30.

Ostello Piero Rotta, Via Salmoiraghi 2 (☎367.095). Official YHA hostel housed in a large modern building with a garden, out in the northwest suburbs near the San Siro stadium. Open 7–9am and 5–11pm, midnight curfew. Reserve in summer, IYHF card required. L13,500. MM1 direction Molino Dorino, get off at Lotto.

Pensionata Alessandri, Via Panizza 5 (☎469.0604). In the Cittá Studi. Open June and July only for short-term residents, but you can occasionally find a room between September and May. Landlady is extremely fussy, prefers women, and may turn you away whatever your sex if you look scruffy. 10.30pm curfew. If you reckon you can put up with the regime, best book in advance. L25–30,000. MM Conciliazione.

Pensionato Bertoni, Via Cicognara 17 (☎742.0826). Modern building off Via Sidoli in the Cittá Studi. Singles for men only available June, September and October. L20,000 per person. Bus #54, #62, #90 or #91.

Hotels and pensions

AROUND THE STATION

Arno, Via Lazzaretto 17 (☎652.782). Off Viale Tunisia not far from Stazione Centrale. Packed from March to July and charges extra for shower, soap and towels. At the same address is the similar *Pensione Eva* (☎659.2898). L38,000. Tram #4 or #11.

Arthur, Via Lazzaretto 14 (☎204.6294). For directions see above. Clean, spacious rooms with a touch of fading splendour. Breakfast available. L38,000.

Canna, Viale Tunisia 6 (☎224.133). Small friendly *pensione* on fifth floor. Some rooms have terraces. Breakfast available. L32,000. Tram #5 or #11.

Parva Domus, Piazza Argentina 4 (☎204.1138). On the sixth floor overlooking Corso Buenos Aires. Quiet, small and popular; book in advance. On the seventh floor is the slightly bigger and equally popular *Pensione Londra* (☎228.400). Doubles for L43,000. MM Loreto.

CITY CENTRE

Antica Locanda Solferino, Via Castelfidardo 2 (☎656.905). Between the Giardini Pubblici and Parco Sempione, a fairly recently converted hotel favoured by models and lefty intellectuals. Book in advance. Doubles with bath around L76,000. MM Moscova.

Brera, Via Pontaccio 9 (☎873.509). Via Pontaccio runs from the top of Via Brera along to the Castello. Doubles L40,000.

Carobbio, Via Medici 3 (☎805.9958). Great location halfway between Piazza Duomo and the Ticinese quarter. Doubles for around L43,000. Tram #8, #15 or #19.

Dante, Via Dante 14 (☎866.471). Small, clean *pensione* with a range of options, from dorm beds to double rooms for around L32,000. Very popular so book in advance. MM Duomo or Cairoli.

Pensione Rovello, Via Rovello 19A (☎873.956). Off Via Dante, which runs between the Castello Sforzesco and Piazza Duomo. Doubles for L30,000. MM Duomo or Cairoli.

Vecchia Milano, Via Borromei 4 (☎875.042). On the north side of Piazza Cordusio, doubles with bath for around L70,000. MM Cordusio.

CITTÀ STUDI

Città Studi, Via Saldini 24 (☎744.666). A good deal if you get one of the rooms without bathroom, but otherwise expensive at L45,000 a double. Bus #61, #90 or #91.

San Francisco, Viale Lombardia 55 (☎236.1009). Recently renovated hotel with doubles for L50,000. Bus #56.

Camping

Agip Metanopoli, Viale Emilia, San Donato Milanese (☎537.2159). Way outside the city in a location that's hardly picturesque. Bus (direction San Giuliano, Melegnano and Lodi) from Piazza Medaglie d'Oro, near Porta Romana, to San Donato – a thirty-minute ride; night service until around midnight. Open all year.

Autodromo, Parco di Monza, Monza (☎039/387.771). In the park nearby the renowned Formula One circuit. Open May to the end of September. Direct bus from Stazione Centrale.

Il Bareggino, Via Corbettina, Bareggio (☎901.4417). Bus from Piazzale Loreto, direction Magenta. The bus stops on the main road, after which it's a 1km walk. Open all year.

The City

Historic Milan lies at the centre of a web of streets, the main Corsos zeroing in from the main ring roads or *cerchie* to **Piazza del Duomo** – the city's main orientation point and centre of the district enclosed by the inner **Cerchia dei Navigli**, which follows the route of the medieval city walls. Within here are most of the city sights, and the swankiest designer shops and most elegant cafés. Visits to **art galleries and museums**, the **Duomo** and other churches can be punctuated with window-shopping at *Armani, Gigli* and *Krizia* in the so-called *Quadrilatero d'Oro*, or sipping overpriced drinks among the designer-dressed clientele of the pavement cafés of the **Galleria Vittorio Emanuele** or around the **Accademia di Brera** art gallery. The second cerchia, **Viali**, skirts behind the centre's two large parks – the **Parco Sempione** and **Giardini Pubblici** – to the canalsides of the **Navigli** in the south, following the tracks of defensive walls built during the Spanish occupation. Within lies the **Castello Sforzesco**, and the church of **Santa Maria delle Grazie**, which has Milan's most famous painting, Leonardo's *The Last Supper*. What follows is roughly a wedge by wedge account of the city. Milan is not a wanderable place, so make a judicious selection, walking a little but where necessary hopping between places by way of the metro or other public transport.

Piazza del Duomo

Unquestioned hub of the city is **Piazza del Duomo**, a large mostly pedestrianised square that's rarely quiet at any time of day. Harassed Milanese hurry out of the metro station deftly avoiding the pigeon-feed sellers and ice cream vendors; designer-dressed kids hang out on the steps of the cathedral; harassed tourguides gather together their flocks; and well preserved women stiletto-click across the square to glitzy cafés.

Having taken in the streetlife, you can turn your attention to the **Duomo**, the world's largest Gothic cathedral, begun in 1386 under the Viscontis and taking nearly five centuries to complete. The finishing touches to the facade were finally added in 1813, and from the outside at least it's an incredible building, notable as much for its decoration as its size and with a front that's a strange mixture of Baroque and Gothic. The marble, chosen specially by the Viscontis, comes from the quarries of Candoglia near Lago Maggiore, and continues to be used in renovation today – the fabric not surprisingly under severe attack from Milan's polluted atmosphere.

Inside the duomo, a green, almost subterranean half-light filters through the stained-glass windows, lending the marble columns a bone-like hue that led the French writer Suarés to compare the interior to "the hollow of a colossal beast". By the entrance, the brass strip embedded in the pavement with the signs of the zodiac alongside is Europe's largest sundial, laid out in 1786. A beam of light still falls on it through a hole in the ceiling, but changes in the Earth's axis mean that it's no longer accurate, so don't bother trying to set your watch by it. To the right, the sixteenth-century statue of San Bartolomeo, with his flayed skin thrown like a toga over his shoulder, is one of the church's more gruesome statues, with veins, muscles and bones sculpted with anatomical accuracy, the draped skin retaining the form of knee, foot, toes and toenails.

At the far end of the church, suspended high above the chancel, a large crucifix contains the most important of the duomo's holy relics – a nail from Christ's

To Stazione Centrale ↑

VIA TURATI

VIA MANIN

Spazio Baj &
Museo del Cinema

To
Palestro
Metro
Station

VIA FATEBENEFRATELLI

PIAZZA
CAVOUR

VIA PALESTRO

Padiglione d'Arte
Contemporanea

TACCIO

VIA BRERA

Museo del
Risorgimento

Civica Galleria
d'Arte Moderne

Accademia
Brera

VIA MANZONI

VIA S. SPIRITO

VIA GESU

VIA DELLA SPIGA

VIA SENATO

CORSO VENEZIA

Museo
Poldi-Pezzoli

VIA SANT'ANDREA

NI ETTO

VIA VERDI

Casa
di Manzoni

VIA MORONE

VIA MONTE NAPOLEONE

La Scala

Palazzo
Marino

PIAZZA
DELLA SCALA

Cordusio
★
PIAZZA
CORDUSIO

VIA SANTA MARGHERITA

Galleria Vittorio
Emanuele

PIAZZA
SAN BABILA

San Babila
★

VIA MERCANTI

CORSO VITTORIO EMANUELE

Palazzo della
Ragione

Palazzo dei
Giureconsulti
Duomo ★

Duomo

VIA CANTU

VIA SPADARI

PIAZZA
MERCANTI

PIAZZA
DEL DUOMO

Arengario
EPT

San Satiro

VIA MAZZINI

Museo del
Duomo

Cimac

VIA FRANCESCO SFORZA

VIA LARGA

Ospedale
Maggiore

CORSO ITALIA

CORSO DI PORTA ROMANA

San
Nazaro

cross, which was crafted to become the bit for the bridle of Emperor Constantine's horse. The cross is lowered once a year, on September 14, the Feast of the Cross, by a device invented by Leonardo da Vinci. Close by, beneath the presbytery, the **Scurolo di San Carlo** (daily 9am–noon & 2–6pm; L1000) is an octagonal crypt designed to house the remains of Saint Charles Borromeo, the zealous sixteenth-century cardinal who was canonised for his unflinching work among the poor of the city and whose reforms antagonised the higher echelons of the corrupt Church. He lies here in a glass coffin, clothed, bejewelled, masked and gloved, wearing a gold crown attributed to Cellini. Borromeo was also responsible for the large altar in the north transept, erected in order to close off a door which allowed the locals to use the cathedral as a short cut to the market.

The **treasury**, adjacent to Borromeo's resting-place, has extravagant evangelistery covers, Byzantine ivory-work and heavily embroidered vestments. After seeing this, stroll back towards the entrance and the cathedral's fourth century **baptistry** (Tues–Sun 10am–noon & 3–5pm), where Saint Ambrose baptised Saint Augustine in AD 387. Augustine had arrived in Milan three years earlier with his illegitimate son, and after sampling various religions, pagan and Christian, was eventually converted to Christianity by Ambrose, then the city's bishop. Back outside, an elevator takes you up to the cathedral **roof**, where you can walk around the forest of tracery, pinnacles and statues while enjoying fine views of the city and on clear days even the Alps. Highlight is the central spire, its lacy marble crowned by a gilded statue of the Madonna looking out to the city over the bodies of the duomo roof sunbathers.

Across the way from the cathedral, the **Museo del Duomo** (Tues–Sat 9.30am–12.30pm & 3–5.30pm), housed in a wing of Palazzo Reale on the southern side of the piazza, holds casts of a good many of the three thousand or so statues and gargoyles that spike the duomo. You can also see how it might have ended up, in a display of entries for a late nineteenth-century competition of new designs for the facade. The scheme all came to nothing, – partly because the winner died, but mostly because the Milanese had grown attached to the duomo's distinctive hybrid frontage.

In the same building, the **Civico Museo di Arte Contemporanea** (Tues–Sun 9.30am–12.20pm & 2.30–5.20pm; free) has a wide-ranging collection of twentieth-century art, tastefully displayed with as much eye to colour schemes as chronology. The early twentieth century is well represented, with works by De Chirico, Boccioni, Morandi and de Pisis, but there's also a challenging selection of more recent artists, notably the bright canvases of the Lucio Fontana, slit and perforated in order to hint at the infinity of space beyond.

South of Piazza del Duomo

South of Piazza del Duomo is a relatively sparse area, with few real targets and unalluring streets. But the church of **San Satiro**, on the busy shopping street of Via Torino, is a study in ingenuity, commissioned from Milan's foremost Renaissance architect, Bramante, in 1476. Originally the oratory of the adjacent ninth-century church of San Satiro, Bramante transformed it to a long-naved basilica by converting the long oblong oratory into the transept and adding a trompe l'oeil apse onto the back wall.

Five minutes away, just off Via Torino, the **Pinacoteca Ambrosiana** (Sun–Fri 9.30am–5pm; L4000) was founded by another member of the Borromeo family, Cardinal Federico Borromeo, in the early seventeenth century. The cardinal collected ancient manuscripts, assembling one of the largest libraries in Europe, though what you come here for now is his art collection, stamped with his taste for Jan Breughel, sixteenth-century Venetians and some of the more kitschy followers of Leonardo. Among many mediocre works, there is a rare painting by Leonardo da Vinci, *Portrait of a Musician*, a cartoon by Raphael for the *School of Athens* and a Caravaggio considered to be Italy's first ever still-life. The museum's quirkiest exhibit, however, is a lock of Lucrezia Borgia's hair – put for safe-keeping in a glass phial ever since Byron (having decided that her hair was the most beautiful he had ever seen) extracted one as a keepsake from the library downstairs where it used to be kept unprotected.

Cutting across Via Torino and Via Mazzini to Corso di Porta Romano, one of the city's busiest radial roads, the church of **San Nazaro** is something of a minor sight, but the severe octagonal chapel which serves as its vestibule was the family church of one of the city's better-known traitors – the condottiere Giangiacomo Trivulzio, who led the French attack on Milan to spite his rival Lodovico Sforza and was rewarded by being made the city's French governor. The tombs of he and his family are contained in niches around the walls, the inscription above Giangiacomo's reading "He who never rested now rests: silence".

Behind San Nazaro, the **Ospedale Maggiore** was once known locally as the *Ca' Granda* (Big House), an ambitious project by the Florentine architect Filarete to unite the city's numerous hospitals and charitable institutions on one site. His hopes of introducing Renaissance architecture to Milan were dampened by local architects who, as soon as Filarete returned to Florence, introduced the late-Gothic elements clearly visible on the facade. To get a clearer idea of Filarete's intentions, step inside to look at the courtyards – eight small ones formed by two crucifixes, separated by a ninth rectangular one. Today the building houses the city's university.

North of Piazza del Duomo

Almost as famous a Milanese sight as the duomo is the gaudily opulent **Galleria Vittorio Emanuele**, a cruciform glass-domed gallery designed in 1865 by Giuseppe Mengoni, who was killed when he fell from the roof a few days before the inaugural ceremony. Though the prices in its cafés are extortionate, it's worth splashing out once to indulge in some people-watching – eke your drink out for long enough and you'll see what seems like the whole population of the city shove or stroll through depending on the time of day. In one of the lulls take a look at the circular mosaic of the signs of the zodiac beneath the glass cupola – it's considered good luck to stand on Taurus's testicles.

The left arm of the gallery leads towards **Piazza dei Mercanti**, the commercial centre of medieval Milan and the city's financial hub until the turn of the century, when the *Borsa* or Stock Exchange – then housed in the sixteenth-century **Palazzo dei Giureconsulti** on Via Mercanti – was moved north to Piazza degli Affari. The medieval palaces of the square were once the seats of guilds and other city organisations; now it's one of the city's more peaceful spots, dominated by the **Palazzo della Ragione** built in the early thirteenth century to celebrate Milan winning autonomy from the emperor. The upper storey was added four centuries later, by another imperial figure, Empress Maria Theresa.

The main branch of Galleria Vittorio Emanuele leads through to Piazza della Scala and the world-famous **La Scala** opera house, designed by Piermarini and opened in 1778 with an opera by Antonio Salieri – a well-known name then, though more famous now (thanks to Peter Schaffer's play *Amadeus*) for his rivalry with Mozart than for his music. As much the social as the cultural centre of Milan's elite, Sixties protests have since led to a more open official policy on the arts in Milan, though La Scala remains as exclusive a venue as it ever was, with ticket prices sky-high. The small **museum**, with its composers' death masks, plaster casts of conductors' hands, and a rugged statue of Puccini in a capacious overcoat, may be the only chance you get to see the interior.

Another big-name nineteenth-century figure lived only a block away from La Scala on Via Morone, just off the busy street that now bears his name. The **house of Alessandro Manzoni** (Tues–Fri 9am–noon & 2–4pm; free), who wrote *the* great Italian novel of the last century, *The Betrothed*, now contains a small museum of memorabilia, though it won't mean much if you haven't read the book.

The star attraction of Via Manzoni, however, is the **Museo Poldi Pezzoli** (Tues & Wed 9.30am–12.30pm & 2.30–6pm, Thurs 9.30am–12.30pm & 2.30–5.30pm, Fri–Sun 9.30am–12.30pm & 2.30–5.30pm; L4000), comprising pieces assembled by the nineteenth-century collector, Gian Giacomo Poldi Pezzoli. Much of this is made up of rather dull rooms of clocks, watches, cutlery and jewellery, but the *Salone Dorato* upstairs contains a number of intriguing paintings, including a portrait of a portly *San Nicola da Tolentino* by Piero della Francesca, part of an altarpiece on which he worked spasmodically for fifteen years. San Nicola looks across at two works by Botticelli, one a gentle *Madonna del Libro*, among the many variations of the Madonna and Child theme which he produced at the end of the fifteenth century, the other a mesmerising *Deposition*, painted towards the end of his life in response to the monk Savonarola's crusade against his earlier, more humanistic canvases. Also in the room is one of Italy's most famous portraits, *Portrait of a Young Woman* by Pollaiuolo, whose anatomical studies are evidenced in the subtle suggestion of bone-structure beneath the skin of this ideal Renaissance woman.

The Brera district and Accademia di Brera

North of La Scala **Via Brera** sets the tone for the city's arty quarter with its small galleries and art shops. There's nothing resembling an artist's garret, however: Via Brera and the streets around it are the terrain of the rich, reflected in the café prices and designer styles of those who can afford to sit outside them. Nevertheless, the streets to the west of Via Brera, and the shopping quarter to the southeast, are well worth a stroll, if only to observe the better-heeled Milanese searching out the perfect objet d'art for their designer pads.

The Brera district gives its name to Milan's most prestigious art gallery, the **Accademia Brera** at the far end of Via Brera (Tues–Sat 9am–6pm, Fri & Sat 9am–1.30pm, Sun 9am–12.30pm; L4000) – originally set up by Napoleon, who filled the building with works looted from the churches and aristocratic collections of French-occupied Italy, opening the museum to the public in 1809. It's a fine gallery, Milan's best by far, but it's also very large, and unless you're keen on making several exhaustive visits you need to be very selective, dipping into the collection guided by your own personal tastes.

Not surprisingly most of the museum's paintings are Italian and predate this century. The Brera does display modern work, including paintings by Modigliani, De Chirico and Carrà, but it's the Renaissance which provides the museum's core. There's a good representation of Venetian painters – works by Bonifacio and, a century later, Paolo Veronese, the latter weighing in a depiction of *Supper in the House of Simon* that got him into trouble with the Inquisition, who considered the introduction of frolicking animals and unruly kids unsuitable subject matter for a religious painting. Tintoretto's *Deposition* was more starkly in tune with requirements of the time, a scene of intense concentration and grief over Christ's body, painted in the 1560s; and Gentile Bellini's *St Mark Preaching in St Euphemia Square* introduces an exotic note, the square bustling with turbaned men, veiled women, camels and even a giraffe. There are also paintings by Gentile's follower, Carpaccio, namely *The Presentation of the Virgin* and *The Disputation of St Stephen*, while the *Pietà* by Gentile's more talented brother, Giovanni, has been deemed "one of the most moving paintings in the history of art".

Look out also for a painting by Giovanni Bellini's brother-in-law, Mantegna's *The Dead Christ*: an exercise in virtuosity really, but an ingenious one – Christ, lying on a wooden slab, viewed from the wrinkled and pierced soles of his feet upwards. Although a contemporary of Mantegna, Crivelli's work, nearby, is quite different, his paintings creating a fairyland for his pale, perfect Madonnas, hermetically sealed from the realities of time and decay.

The rooms that follow hold yet more quality work. Piero della Francesca's chill *Madonna with Angels, Saints and Federigo da Montefeltro* is the most famous painting here. But take a look too at Raphael's *Marriage of the Virgin*, whose lucid, languid Renaissance mood is in sharp contrast to the grim realism of Caravaggio's *Supper at Emmaus* – set in a dark tavern and painted a century later. Less well known but equally realistic are the paintings of Lombardy's brilliant eighteenth-century realist, Ceruti – known as *Il Pitochetto* (The Little Beggar) for his unfashionable sympathy with the poor, who stare out with reproachful dignity from his canvases. As his main champion, Roberto Longhi, said, his figures are "dangerously larger than life", not easily transformed into "gay drawing room ornaments".

Northeast from the duomo: parks and more galleries

At the top of Via Brera, Via Fatebenefratelli heads east to Milan's **Museo del Risorgimento** on Via Borgonuovo (March–Oct 9.30am–12.30pm & 2.30–5.30pm; Nov–Feb 9.30am–12.30pm & 2.30–5pm; closed Mon; free), which charts the course of Italian Unification through a well presented combination of paintings, proclamations, cuttings and photographs – though like most Italian Unification museums you need a keen knowledge of Italian (and Italian history) to appreciate it.

Continuing along Via Fatebenefratelli, the heavily-trafficked Piazza Cavour marks the corner of the city's oldest public park, the **Giardini Pubblici**, designed by Piermarini shortly after completing La Scala. Re-landscaped in the nineteenth century to give a more rustic look, its shady avenues and small lake are ideal for recuperating from Milan's twin doses of culture and carbon monoxide fumes.

On the left side of the park the Palazzo Dugnani houses Milan's **Museo del Cinema** in its basement (Tues–Fri 3–6pm; L2000), with an unlabelled collection of cameras, film-cutting apparatus and other equipment from the early days of cinema. The curator will do his best to persuade you to buy a catalogue, but the free leaflets are perfectly adequate, and in any case the museum isn't exactly a must.

More engaging is the upstairs **Spazio Baj** (Tues–Sun 9.30am–12.30pm & 2.30–5.30pm; free), given over entirely to the work of the twentieth-century Milanese artist, Enrico Baj, and a light-hearted change from the city's more serious museums. The primary-coloured Meccano sculptures in the entrance set the mood for the gallery, which includes a portrait entitled *Homme Sans Lollipop*, a head of a robotic general made of military bric-a-brac suspended in plastic, and a series of *Personaggi* – collages using paint, glitter, card, braid and badges. There are also aquatints for the *Hunting of the Snark* and illustrations for *Paradise Lost* – in which Adam's graffitied heart quite literally bleeds in a Picasso-meets-Disney hell inhabited by ET-like monsters.

If your taste is for more conventional modern art, the **Civica Galleria d'Arte Moderne** (Wed–Mon 9.30am–12.30pm & 2.30–5.30pm; free), across the road from the park in the Villa Reale, is one of Milan's most palatable galleries, housed in Napoleon's former in-town residence, which now doubles as the civic registry office. The main building holds nineteenth-century Italian art and sculpture – striking political works by the painter Giuseppe Pellizza da Volpedo, canvases by the self-styled romantic *scapigliati* (wild-haired) movement of the late nineteenth century, impressive sculptures by Marino Marini together with a less arcane selection of paintings by Corot, Millet and various French Impressionists. Also worth a look are the works of the Futurists – Boccioni, Balla and Morandi.

In the grounds the **Padiglione d'Arte Contemporanea** (Wed–Mon 9.30am–6.30pm; free) is a venue for temporary and often prestigious exhibitions of national and international contemporary art. Overlooking the gardens, in a light airy annexe, the small **Collezione Vismara** has Picasso's *Battle of the Centaurs* – a spontaneously simple charcoal complete with finger smudges – and minor but appealing works by Matisse, Dufy and their Italian contemporaries.

Facing Corso Venezia on the right side of the Giardini Pubblici, the **Museo Civico di Storia Naturale** (Tues–Sun 9.30am–12.30pm & 2.30–5.30pm; free) completes the round of museums, with a fairly predictable natural history collection. It's reckoned to be Italy's best, though really the stuffed animals and dinosaur-bits are best reserved for one of Milan's rainy afternoons.

The West: Castello Sforzesco

At the far end of Via Dante, **Castello Sforzesco** rises imperiously from the mayhem of Foro Buonaparte, a congested and distinctly un-forum-like road and bus terminus laid out by Napoleon in self-tribute. He had a vision of a grand new centre for the Italian capital, laid out along Roman lines, but he only got as far as constructing an arena, a triumphal arch and these two semi-circular roads before he lost Milan to the Austrians a few years later. The arena and triumphal arch still stand behind the castle in the **Parco Sempione**, a notorious hangout for junkies and prostitutes, while the emperor's grandiose plans for the area in front live on in name alone.

The redbrick castle, the result of numerous rebuildings, is with its crenellated towers and fortified walls one of Milan's most striking landmarks. Begun by the Viscontis, it was destroyed by mobs rebelling against their regime in 1447, and rebuilt by their successors, the Sforzas. Under Lodovico Sforza the court became one of the most powerful, luxurious and cultured of the Renaissance, renowned for its ostentatious wealth and court artists like Leonardo and Bramante. Lodovico's days of glory came to an end when Milan was invaded by the French in 1499, and from then until the end of the nineteenth century the castle was used as a barracks by successive occupying armies. A century ago it was converted into a series of museums.

The castello's buildings group around three courtyards, one of which, the Corte Ducale, formed the centre of the residential quarters which now contain the **Museo d'Arte Antica** and the **Pinacoteca** (Tues–Sun 9.30am–12.15pm & 2.30–5.15pm; free). The Museo d'Arte Antica holds fragments of sculpture from Milan's demolished churches and palaces, a run-of-the-mill collection saved by the inclusion of Michelangelo's *Rondanini Pietà*, which the artist worked on for the last nine years of his life. It's an unfinished but oddly powerful work, with much of the marble unpolished and a third arm (indicating a change of position for Christ's body) hanging limply from a block of stone to his right.

The first room of the **Pinacoteca**, upstairs, contains a cycle of monochrome frescoes illustrating the Griselda story from Boccaccio's *Decameron* – a catalogue of indignities inflicted by a marquis on his wife in order to test her fidelity. It was intended as a celebration of the patience and devotion of one Bianca Pellegrini, and if you decide to push on into the first room of the main picture gallery, you'll see what she looked like: Bianca was used as a model for the Madonna in a polyptych by Benedetto Bembo. In the same room are works by Bellini, Crivelli and Lippi, and one of Mantegna's last works, a dreamy evocation of the *Madonna in Glory among Angels and Saints*. There are also lots of paintings by Vincenzo Foppa, the leading artist on the Milanese scene before Leonardo da Vinci, in the next room; look out too for the polyptych by De' Tatti in which the castle makes an appearance as a fanciful setting for the crucifixion, and for Arcimboldi's bizarre *Primavera* – a portrait of a woman composed entirely of flowers, heralded as a sixteenth-century precursor of surrealism.

The castle's other museums are housed in the Sforza fortress, the **Rocchetta**, to the left of the Corte Ducale. Of these, the **museum of applied arts** is of limited interest, containing wrought-iron work, ceramics, ivory and musical instruments. The small, well displayed **Egyptian collection** in the dungeons is rather better, with impressive displays of mummies and sarcophagi, and papyrus fragments from *The Book of the Dead*. There's also a small and deftly lit **prehistoric collection**, which has as its centrepiece an assortment of finds from the Iron Age burial grounds of the Golasecca civilisation, south of Lago Maggiore.

Santa Maria delle Grazie and around

Apart from Parco Sempione, good for a wander or lakeside picnic, the area around the Castello Sforzesco has little to detain you, and there are more interesting pickings to the south, beyond the busy streets of the financial district, skirted by Corso Magenta. The **Museo Archaeologico** (Wed–Mon 9.30am–12.20pm & 2.30–5.20pm; free), in the ex-Monastero Maggiore at Corso Magenta 15, is well worth a visit. The displays of glass phials, kitchen utensils and jewellery from Roman Milan are compelling, and though there's a scarcity of larger objects, there is a colossal head of Jove, found near the castle, a torso of Hercules and a smattering of mosaic pavements unearthed around the city.

But what really brings visitors into this part of town is the church of **Santa Maria delle Grazie** – famous for its mural of the *Last Supper* by Leonardo da Vinci. First built as a Gothic church by the fifteenth-century architect Solari, Santa Maria delle Grazie was partially rebuilt under a dissatisfied Lodovico Sforza by the more up-to-date Bramante, who tore down Solari's chancel and replaced it with a massive dome supported by an airy Renaissance cube. Lodovico also intended to replace the nave and facade, but was unable to do so before Milan fell to the French, leaving an odd combination of styles – Solari's Gothic vaults, decorated in powdery blues, reds and ochre, illuminated by the light that floods through the windows of Bramante's dome. A side door leads into Bramante's cool and tranquil cloisters, outside of which there's a good view of the sixteen-sided drum the architect placed around his dome.

Leonardo's **Last Supper** covers one wall of the church's refectory (daily 9am–1.15pm & 2–6.15pm, Sun and holidays mornings only; L4000), one of the world's great paintings and most resonant images. Henry James likened it to an "illustrious invalid" which people visited with "leave-taking sighs and almost death-bed or tip-toe precautions"; and certainly it's hard, when you visit the painting, decayed and faded on the refectory wall and partially obscured by restorers' scaffolding, not to feel that it's the last time you'll see it. That the work survived at all is something of a miracle. Leonardo's decision to use oil paint rather than the more usual faster-drying – and longer-lasting – fresco technique led to the painting disintegrating within five years of its completion. A couple of centuries later Napoleonic troops billetted here used the wall for target practice. And in 1943 a bomb destroyed the building, amazingly leaving only the *Last Supper*'s wall standing. Well-meaning restoration over the centuries also means that little of Leonardo's original colouring has survived, but today's restorers are removing the work of their predecessors and protecting the wall from damp – a task due to be completed in the early 1990s.

Despite all this the painting still retains its power. Leonardo spent two years on it, searching the streets of Milan for models. When the monks complained that the face of Judas was still unfinished, Leonardo replied that he had been searching for over a year among the city's criminals for a sufficiently evil face, and that if he didn't find one he would use the face of the Prior. Whether or not Judas' face is modelled on the Prior's is unrecorded, but Leonardo's Judas does seem, as Vasari wrote, "the very embodiment of treachery and inhumanity".

A couple of blocks south, the **Museo Nazionale della Scienza e della Tecnica** (Tues–Sun 9am–5pm; L4000) is dedicated to Leonardo and inspired by his inventions, with reconstructions of some of his wackier contraptions, including the famous flying machine. Less compelling are the general sections of physics, astronomy, telecommunications and musical instruments, all incomprehensible to non-scientists. There are also, if you're interested in such things, collections of steam trains, aeroplanes and even an ocean liner.

The nearby church of **Sant'Ambrogio** was founded in the fourth century by Milan's patron saint. Saint Ambrose, as he's known in English, is even today an important name in the city: the Milanese refer to themselves as Ambrosiani, have named a chain of banks after him, and celebrate his feast day, December 7, with the opening of the Scala season and a big street market around the church. Ambrose's remains still lie in the church's crypt, but there's nothing left of the original church in which his most famous convert, Saint Augustine, first heard him preach.

The present church, the blueprint for many of Lombardy's Romanesque basilicas, is, however, one of the city's loveliest, reached through a colonnaded quadrangle with column capitals carved with rearing horses, contorted dragons and an assortment of bizarre predators. Inside, to the left of the nave, a freestanding Byzantine pillar is topped with a "magic" bronze serpent, flicked into a loop and symbolising Aaron's rod. An ancient tradition held that on the Day of Judgment it would crawl back to the Valley of Jesophat. Look, too, at the pulpit, a superb piece of Romanesque carving decorated with reliefs of wild animals and the occasional human, most of whom are intent upon devouring one another. There are older relics further down the nave, notably the ciborium, reliefed with the figures of saints Gervasius and Protasius – martyred Roman soldiers whose clothed bodies flank that of Saint Ambrose in the crypt. A nineteenth-century autopsy revealed that they had been killed by having their throats cut. Similar investigations into Saint Ambrose's remains restored the reputation of the anonymous fifth-century artist responsible for the mosaic portrait of the saint in the Capella di San Vittorio in Ciel d'Oro (to the right of the sacristry). Until then it was assumed that Ambrose owed his skew-whiff face to a slip of the artist's hand, but the examination of his skull revealed an abnormally deep-set tooth, suggesting that his face would indeed have been slightly deformed.

Outside (entrance to the left of the choir) is Bramante's unfinished **Cortile della Canonica**. The side that Bramante did complete, a novel concoction incorporating knobbled "tree trunk" columns and a triumphal arch, was shattered by a bomb in the last war and reconstructed from the fragments. The second side was added only in 1955 and leads to a modest museum whose only memorable exhibit is Saint Ambrose's bed.

South of the centre: Navigli and Ticinese
Flanking the city's two canals, just south of the *Cerchia Viali*, the streets of the **NAVIGLI** quarter feel a long way from the city centre, their peeling houses and waterside views much sought after by the city's would-be Bohemians. A thriving inland port from the fifteenth century until the 1950s, the Naviglio Pavese – which links Milan with Pavia – and the Naviglio Grande – which runs to the west – are part of a network of rivers and canals covering the whole of Italy's northern plain, making ports or even naval bases of land-locked cities. They were also much used by travellers: the ruling families of the north used them to visit one another, Prospero and Miranda escaped along the Navigli in *The Tempest*, and they were still being used by Grand Tourists in the eighteenth century; Goethe, for example, describes the discomfort and hazards of journeying by canal. These days there's not much to do other than browsing in its artists' studios and antique shops, but it's a peaceful area, good for idle strolling, and at night its bars and clubs are among the city's best.

Back towards the centre, the **TICINESE** is another arty district, though as yet less a prey to the yuppie invasion than Navigli. On the edge of the quarter, at the bottom of Corso di Porta Ticinese, the nineteenth-century **Arco di Porta Ticinese** is an Ionic gateway on a noisy traffic island built to celebrate Napoleon's victory at Marengo – and, after his demise, dedicated to peace. Walking up the Corso, the only obvious signs of trendification are a scattering of secondhand clothes shops and the occasional club, and the musty decadence makes it one of Milan's more intriguing areas.

Ticinese also boasts two important churches. The first, **Sant'Eustorgio**, was built in the fourth century to house the bones of the Magi, said to have been brought here by Saint Ambrose. It was rebuilt in the eleventh century and virtually destroyed by Barbarossa in the twelfth century, who seized the Magi's bones and deposited them in Cologne Cathedral. Some of them were returned in 1903 and are kept in a Roman sarcophagus in the right transept. The main reason for visiting the church, however, is to see the **Portinari Chapel** commissioned from the Florentine architect Michelozzi in the 1460s by one Portinari, an agent of the Medici bank, to house the remains of Saint Peter the Martyr. Peter, one of Catholicism's less attractive saints, was banned from the Church for allegedly entertaining women in his cell, then cleared of the charge and given a job as an Inquisitor. His death was particularly nasty – he was axed in the head by a member of the sect he was persecuting – but the martyrdom led to almost immediate canonisation and the dubious honour of being deemed Patron of Inquisitors. The simple geometric design of the chapel has been credited with being Milan's first real building of the Renaissance, although it was Bramante who really developed the style. Inside, you are treated to scenes from the life of Saint Peter in frescoes by Foppa and reliefs carved on the sides of his elaborate tomb.

Further up the Corso, the fourteenth-century Porta Ticinese and sixteen Corinthian columns scavenged from a Roman ruin stand outside the church of **San Lorenzo**. It's an evocative spot – an odd contrast with the backdrop of grubby bars and rattling trams – and *the* place to hang out at night before hitting the Navigli and Ticinese clubs and bars. San Lorenzo, apparently considered by Leonardo da Vinci to be the most beautiful church in Milan, was founded in the fourth century, when it was the largest centrally planned church in the western Roman Empire. The current structure is a sixteenth-century renovation of an eleventh-century rebuilding, a shaky edifice under threat from the vibrating tramlines outside. Inside, the most interesting feature is the **Capella di San Aquilino** (usually locked, but the sacristan will open it), much of which has survived from the fourth century. There are fragments of fourth-century mosaics on the walls, including one in the left apse where the tiles have crumbled away revealing the artist's original sketches. Behind the altar steps lead down to what is left of the original foundations, a jigsaw of fragments of Roman architecture looted from an arena.

Eating

Food in workaholic Milan, at lunchtime at least, is more of a necessity than a pleasure, with the city centre dominated by *paninotece* and fast-food outlets. Don't despair, though: there are plenty of good value restaurants here, and although pricier than the rest of Italy, you can easily pay less than L20,000 for a full meal.

Food markets and supermarkets

For real low-budget eating, there are **streetmarkets** every day except Sunday scattered through the city, selling all the cheese, sausage and fruit you need for a picnic lunch. A complete list is given daily in the *Corriere della Sera* under the heading "Mercati". The most central **supermarkets** are *Standa* at Via Torino 37 and in Piazza Castello, and *Esselunga* at Viale Piave 38, near Porta Venezia.

Paninotece, fast food and self service

Brek, Via del Duca 5. Good value self-service restaurant with an excellent choice of salads and freshly cooked main courses.

Cantinetta, Via Santa Maria Segreta 6. Excellent sandwiches and home-produced wine.

China Express, Piazza Beccaria 4 (☎705.015). Self-service Chinese fast food in the city centre.

Ciao. Citywide chain with good, reasonably priced food. Branches at Via Dante, on the corner with Via Meravigli, Corso Europa 12, Corso Buenos Aires and Via Fabio Filzi, near Stazione Centrale.

Italy & Italy. Another chain, good for spaghetti, pizza and sparkling wine. Branches at Largo Carrobio, Corso Buenos Aires 7 and Corso Venezia 7.

Lunico, Via Palermo 20. Elaborate sandwiches and salads served to a predominantly young clientele.

Latteria Unione, Via Unione 6, near the church of San Satiro on Via Torino (lunchtime only). Good for vegetarians.

Pagnotta, Via Bergamini 7, near the Universitá Statale. Packed with students and offering affordable meals as well as sandwiches.

Restaurants and pizzerias

Abele, Via Temperanza 5. A warm, smoky atmosphere, and open until late. Risottos a speciality. MM Pasteur. Evenings only, closed Mon.

Artisti, Corso di Porta Ticinese 16. Near the San Lorenzo columns, a lunchtime favourite with workers and usually crowded with locals at night. Tram #8, #15, #19. Closed Sun.

La Bruschetta, Piazza Beccaria 12. Always packed, so expect a long wait. Good location, good pizza, good prices . . . and a free *bruschetta* (bread rusk served with tomato, garlic and olive oil) when you eventually get a table. MM San Babila or Duomo.

Da Franco, Via Donatello 5. Tiny trattoria much frequented by students from the nearby architecture faculty. Menu always includes some fish. Last orders at 9.30pm. MM Loreto or Piola. Closed Sat & Sun.

Da Maria, Via Grubicy de Dragon, corner Viale Montello. Reliable traditional cuisine on the edge of the designer shopping quarter, so expect a few trendy clients. MM Moscova. Closed Sat evening and all day Sun.

Mergellina, Via Molino delle Armi 48. Average pizza but the prices are hard to beat. Tram #15, bus #96 or #97. Closed Tues & Wed lunchtime.

Officina, Viale Monza 140. Next door to the ex-HQ of the socialist party and still known as the socialist trattoria. More interestingly there's a waiter reputed to be Mel Smith's brother. Good spicy food, great atmosphere and gets very crowded. MM Turro. Evenings only, closed Mon.

Osteria Strippoli, Via Boccaccio 15. Self-service trattoria near Santa Maria delle Grazie specialising in hors d'oeuvres that can be a meal in themselves, grilled meat and sausage. It's also famous for its Pugliese wines. MM Cadorna or Conciliazione. Closed Sun.

Pasta e Fagioli, Via Venini 54. Speciality, as the name suggests, is pasta and beans, but give their *scamorza* a go too – mozzarella grilled to a pleasant gooiness on the fire. MM Loreto. Closed Wed.

Pattaya, Via Murtori 10. Good, reasonably priced Thai food in a simple, friendly atmosphere. Tram #29 or #30.

Da Rino Vecchia Napoli, Via Chevez 4. Off the beaten track, but worth the effort of getting there: Rino won the European Pizza Championship a few years ago. Good prices and massive choice. Tram #33 or bus #56.

Rondine, Via Spartaco 2. Off the beaten track, but with a chef from one of the most famous city restaurants. Traditional dishes along with some more creative ones in simple, homely surroundings. Try to get there early. Bus #84. Closed Sun.

Spontini, Via Spontini, corner Corso Buenos Aires. One kind of pizza only: tomato, cheese and anchovies on a thick, soft base served in various sized portions. Great value, and open lunchtime for lasagne as well as pizza. MM Lima or Loreto. Closed Mon and Tues lunchtime.

Stalingrado, Via Biondi 4. Long-standing politically orientated eatery that caters to a young clientele and is also open as a pub. Reasonable prices and small outside eating area for the summer. Bus #61 or #78. Closed Sun.

Stella d'Oro, Via Vonizetti 3. A Milanese institution. Prices are good, though. Bus #60 or #62. Closed Sat.

Ungherese, Largo La Foppa 5. Home-style Hungarian food in small, unpretentious surroundings, though not cheap. MM Moscova. Closed Sun.

Veneta, Corso di Porta Romana 103. Friendly place that specialises in Venetian food, notably *Fegato alla Veneziana*, very thin slices of liver and onions cooked in olive oil. Tram #13, #29, #30. Closed Sun.

Cafés, bars and pubs

As well as the traditional cafés of the Galleria Vittorio Emanuele, there's a hip, late-night café scene in the Navigli and Ticinese quarters, and a swankier one in the Brera. Be warned, though, whether hip, swanky or elegant, none are cheap. Many serve food as well, and some are open day and night.

Bar Magenta, Via Carducci 13. Twenties' decor, extremely trendy, and usually packed. Good for sandwich lunches as well as late-night drinks.

Berlin Café, Via Gian Giacomo Mora 9. Ersatz Berlin in a tiny street off Corso di Porta Ticinese.

La Briosca, Via Ascanio Sforza. Crammed with large parties of guitar-strumming neo-hippies.

Camparino, Piazza Duomo 21. Probably Milan's oldest bar, and the original inventor of Campari. Prices are high even by Milanese standards.

Chimera Magazine Café-Book, Via Cicco Simonetta 11. Café/bookshop with a mixed gay/straight crowd. Occasional concert and exhibition. Open weekdays only.

Osteria del Pallone, Via Gorizia, corner Alzaio Naviglio Grande. Booze or ice cream in tasteful setting – twenty years ago all Milan's osterias looked like this.

Pois, Colonne di San Lorenzo. Once Milan's hippest bar; if you're used to student-poseur hangouts, the clientele will look familiar.

Portnoy Café, Via De Amicis, corner with Corso di Porta Ticinese. The only café in Milan with poetry readings.

Racana Pub, Via Sannio 18 (☎589.027). Run by a Brit. Go there if you're missing real ale and basket meals. Out of the centre, though – bus #90 or #91.

Resentin Caffè, Via Mercato 24. Thirty-five kinds of grappa and a good selection of wine. Also serves coffee and has newspapers and magazines for browsing.

Nightlife: live music and clubs

Milan's **nightlife** centres on two areas – the streets around the Brera gallery and in canalside Navigli and the adjacent Ticinese Quarter. Clubs are hippest mid-week, particularly on Thursdays – at weekends out-of-towners flood in and any self-respecting Milanese trendy either stays at home or hits a bar. Most clubs have obscure door policies, often dependent on the whim of the bouncer; assuming you get in, expect to pay up to L20,000 entrance, which usually includes your first drink. As for live music, Milan scores high in jazz, but the rock and disco scene is pretty unoriginal. Drinks everywhere, incidentally, are very overpriced, so get most of your boozing done before you go.

Live music

Capolinea, Via Lodovico Il Moro 119 (☎470.524). Founded in 1969, a jazz milestone where all the best performers, Italian and foreign, have played. Named for the terminal (capolinea) of tram #19.

Club Due, Via Formentini 2 (☎873.533). Piano bar upstairs and jazz in the smoky cellar. Cocktails, champagne and wine, and pasta served until 2.30am.

Leoncino, Corso Garibaldi 50 (☎802.315). Brazilian basement club with rum cocktails, milkshakes and coconut cakes; live music currently Wed and Thurs.

Magia Music Meeting, Via Salutati 2 (☎481.3553). Small basement venue for new bands.

Patuscino, Via Madonnina 21 (☎807.264). Trio with singer everyday. Crowded, noisy, expensive, and open till the small hours.

Scimmie, Via Ascanio Sforza 49 (☎839.174). One of Milan's most popular venues, with a different band every night and jazz-fusion predominating. Small, noisy and smoky.

Zelig, Viale Monza 140 (☎255.1774). Just outside the "socialist café" – pretentious and appallingly overpriced.

Clubs and discos

Hollywood, Corso Como 15 (☎659.8996). Near the former Alitalia air terminal and with an airport theme – staff dressed as flight attendants, etc. Popular with a media crowd.

Plastic Killer, Viale Umbria 120 (☎743.674). Gothic hangout.

Prego, Via Besenzanica 3 (☎4407.5653). Currently has a wrecked Chevrolet on the roof – and sometimes has gigs. At present Sixties revival on Wednesdays, R&B and rock Friday to Sunday.

Rolling Stone, Corso XXII Marzo 32 (☎733.172). Enormous hall, very loud music, sometimes used as a venue by big-name rock bands. Tuesday nights a swing band play 1940s music.

There are comprehensive **What's On** listings in the local pages of *Corriere della Sera* and *La Repubblica* on Thursdays. You can also get information, and book theatre seats, at the **Ufficio Informazione del Comune**, run by the city council in Galleria Vittorio Emanuele (Mon–Sat 9am–10pm).

Opera, theatre and cinema

Many of Milan's tourists have just one reason for coming to the city: **La Scala**, one of the world's most prestigious opera houses. The season starts on December 7 and runs through to July, and there's also a season of classical concerts from September to November. Not surprisingly, seats for the opera sell out months in advance. You can book good (ie extremely expensive) seats in advance from CIT in London (☎01-434 3844), though they'll charge you a hefty commission fee. More cheaply, write direct to *Botteghino*, La Scala, Via dei Filodrammatici 2, enclosing the price of a ticket in an international reply-paid coupon – this will be returned if the seats you want aren't available. There is also often a reasonable chance of picking up a seat in the gods on the day – get there an hour or so before the performance starts.

Of Milan's **theatres**, the *Piccolo Teatro*, Via Rovello 2 (☎872.352), is the classical theatre, with a traditional repertoire, and is reckoned to be one of Italy's best. *Teatro dell'Elfo*, Via Ciro Menotti 11 (☎716.791), bus #60, puts on more original plays. As for **film**, there are twenty cinemas on Corso Vittorio Emanuele, and the *Angelicum*, Piazza Sant'Angelo 2 (☎659.2748; bus #61), shows films in the original language, usually English, often before their British release (Wed–Sat; screenings at 9.15pm).

Fashion, design and shopping

Milan is the European capital of **fashion**, and to leave it without looking in the windows of its designer boutiques would be to miss out on a crucial aspect of the city. In the few hundred square yards bordered by Via Montenapoleone, Via

Sant'Andrea, Via Spiga and Via Borgospesso – the *Quadrilatero d'Oro* – are the shops of all the big designer names, along with design studios and contemporary art galleries. On the peripheries are youth-orientated shops, like *Emporio Armani* and *Oaks by Ferre*, whose clothes are nevertheless priced well beyond the means of most people. You can, however, get designer cast-offs at the (early) Saturday morning market on Viale Papiniano.

Probably the most outrageous shop you can visit is that of **Francesco Moschino**, Corso Venezia 41 – the city's so-called "fashion philosopher", where his claims that fashion is "the stupidest, most absurd and amusing thing around" are fully realised. More likely to tempt you to run up a massive credit card debt are the covetable unstructured jackets at **Armani** on Via Sant'Andrea. Other designers worth checking out are **Romeo Gigli**, **Krizia** and **Gianni Versace**, all on Via Spiga, and **Valentino** on Via Santo Spirito.

If you're on a budget, and can't make the Papinaio market, there are a couple of **secondhand shops** worth checking out: *Zeus*, Via Vigévano, in the Navigli quarter, though this is pricey; *Surplus*, Corso Garibaldi 7; or one of the few on Corso Ticinese. There are also a number of **warehouses** selling last season's lines at half-price. Try *Gastone*, Via Vanzetti 20, or *Niki Blocchista*, Via Fontane 19, Zona Tribunale.

If the Milanese are hung up on image, they're almost equally obsessive about the furniture and objects with which they surround themselves. **Design** is big news, and the Milanese elite avid consumers. Cover versions of chairs by Le Corbusier, Mackintosh and Gio Ponti, who designed the Pirelli tower, are being snapped up at *Cassina* on Via Durini; while *Alessi*, better known for stainless steel cutlery, have produced *the* watch of the late Eighties. Designed by architect, Aldo Rossi the face snaps out of its leather strap in order to snap into a post-modern watch and chain. *Alessi* are also responsible for the Eighties' sleekest *cafétiere*, while *SICC*, at *Pakowa* on Piazza San Babila, have attempted to give the vacuum flask street-cred – designing a stainless steel model with a shoulder strap.

It's also to the golden rectangle that the rich head when they want to buy that final, indispensible wall-accessory – a few billion lire worth of **contemporary art**. Milan rivals New York as the centre of the contemporary art market, and many of the galleries have small semi-permanent exhibitions for those who are not in the running to buy. There's little point in listing all the galleries here, but of the few you might want to visit, *Studio Marconi*, on Via Tadino, is Milan's most prestigious gallery; *Galleria Tega*, on Via Senato, often has classy contemporary work; *Galleria Artcentro*, on Via Brera, exhibits abstract paintings and work from the Thirties and Forties *Aeropittura* school – a style championed by Mussolini and Goebbels. Perhaps more fun, and less intimidating for aimless browsing, is the **antiques market**, on the third Sunday of each month, in the Brera district. Prices are high, and if you're seriously into buying, the **bric-a-brac market** along the banks of the Naviglio Grande, on the last Sunday of the month, is a better bet.

Women's Milan

By Italian standards, Milan is not a difficult city for **women**. It is the centre of the Italian women's movement, and there are a number of places to make contact with other women. The *Libreria delle Donne* at Via Dogana 2, close to the Duomo, sells feminist literature and has information on womens' groups, events and publications. If you understand Italian, there's a weekly broadcast on Radio Popolare, Monday at 8.30pm (FM 10105 and 107.6), dealing with women writers.

Cicip e Ciciap (which roughly means gossip) at Via Gorani 9, closed Monday, is a women-only **café/bar/restaurant** with occasional exhibitions and readings. There's also a women-only **disco** at *Sottomarino Giallo* (Yellow Submarine), Via Donatello 2 (Tues–Sun 10pm–2.30am).

The Gay Scene

Milan is also something of a focus for **gays**, with Italy's only gay bookshop, the *Babel Bookshop*, Via Sammartini 21 (☎669.2986). Run by a Milan-based gay publishing house, *Babilonia*, it issues a monthly magazine of the same name and makes for a good meeting-place for gay men. Italian-speakers can get more info from the weekly gay programme, *L'altro martedi*, broadcast Tuesday evenings on Radio Populare (FM 101.5 and 107.6).

As for **gay bars**, *Querelle*, Via de Castillia 20, offers snacks and music nightly except Monday, as well as exhibitions and book discussions. *After Dark*, Viale Certosa 134 (Wed–Mon 10pm–2am), is a disco/restaurant, with a mainly young crowd. Membership cards are required, and they're pretty selective. *Contatto*, on Corso Sempione, is a private club/disco, which also shows gay videos. It's open every day from 11pm until 6am, members only, and closed to women and trans-vestites. *Nuova Idea*, Via de Castiesa 30, is the biggest gay disco in Italy (Tues–Sun 9am–1pm); *No Ties*, Foro Buonoparte 68 (Wed–Sun 11pm–3am), is a disco-cum-restaurant whose theme is the prohibition of ties.

Listings

Airlines *British Airways*, Piazza Diaz 7 (☎809.041/809.892); *Alitalia*, Via Albricci 7 (☎62.81); *Aer Lingus*, Galleria Passarella 2 (☎783.565); *American Airlines*, Piazza della Repubblica 28 (☎655.7720); *Air Canada*, Via Pisacane 44 (☎270.829); *Qantas*, Piazza Velasca 4 (☎807.441).

Airport enquiries Flight information for both Linate and Malpensa airports on ☎7485.2200.

Bike hire Via Washington 60, MM Wagner or bus #60 from Stazione Centrale. Open 9.30am–12.30pm & 3–7.30pm, closed Mon.

Books Foreign books at the *American Bookstore*, Largo Cairoli, the *International Bookshop*, Via Senato 28, or the *English Bookshop*, Via Mascheroni 12.

Bus enquiries ☎801.161.

Car hire The international companies have offices at both airports, but local firms are cheaper – try *Auto Lord*, Via dal Re 6 (☎321.840); tram #14 from Piazza Castello. Otherwise look in the Yellow Pages or *Tutta Milano*.

Carparks Central carparks include *Autosilo Diaz*, Piazza Diaz 6, just south of Piazza Duomo, but there are also a number near the Stazione Centrale: *Autosilo Comunale*, Via Pirelli 39; *Autosilo SISP*, Piazza IV Novembre 5, at the side of the station; *Repubblica*, Piazza Repubblica 14, at the end of Via Pisani.

Consulates *Australia*, Via Turati 40 (☎659.8727); *Canada*, Via V. Pisani 19; *UK*, Via San Paolo 7 (☎869.3442); *USA*, Largo Donegani 1 (☎652.841).

Dentist Piazzale Loreto 9 (☎282.9808). Mon–Fri 9am–noon, 2.30–6pm & 7–11.30pm, Sat & Sun 9am–noon, 2.30–6pm & 8–11.30pm.

Doctors English-speaking doctors: Dr A. Ferrario, Via Tibaldi 17 (☎835.8494, 4–7pm only); Dr B. Sturlese, Via Sant'Eufemia 19 (☎805.783); Dr G. Dabbah, Via Pirandello 4 (☎469.6223).

Exchange Out of normal banking hours you can change money and travellers cheques at the Stazione Centrale office (Mon–Sat 7.30am–7pm, Sun 9.30am–2.30pm).

Football Milan's two teams are *Inter Milan* and *AC Milan*, who play on alternate Sundays at the Guiseppe Meazza stadium. Tickets from L10,000; MM Cadorna.

Hospital 24-hour casualty at the Fatebenefratelli hospital, Corso Porta Nuova 23 (☎63.631) and Ospedale Maggiore Policlinico, Via Francesco Sforza 35 (☎581.655) – a short walk from Piazza Duomo.

Laundry There's a coin-operated launderette in the Brera district, Via Anfiteatro 9. Otherwise the *tintoria* on Via Tadati, off Via Casati, which is off Corso Buenos Aires, does a full wash and dry for L11,000.

Left Luggage Office at Stazione Centrale. Fixed rate of around L2000; closed 2.30–4pm.

Pharmacy 24-hour service in Stazione Centrale. Rotas published in *Corriere del Sera*, and usually on *farmacia* doors.

Police Phone ☎113. Head office at Via Fatebenefratelli 11 (☎62.261), near the Brera.

Post Office Via Cordusio 4, off Piazza Cordusio, not the building marked Poste, but around the corner. Mon–Fri 8am–8pm, Sat 8am–2pm, closed Sun. Telephones 7am–12.45pm.

Swimming pools *Cozzi*, Viale Tunisia 35 (☎659.9703); *Lido di Milano*, Piazzale Lotto 15 (☎36.61.00) – open-air.

Telephones International calls either from the post office (see above) or the SIP office in Galleria V. Emanuele II, open 8am–9.30pm.

Train enquiries ☎67.500.

South of Milan: Pavia and Vigévano

Furthest west of the string of historic towns that spread across the Lombardy plain, **Pavia** and **Vigévano** are close enough to Milan to be seen on a day trip, but still retain clear identities of their own. Pavia, certainly, should not be missed if you're in Milan for any length of time, and conversely could also serve as a feasible and perhaps more palatable base for seeing the larger city. Vigévano is more of a backwater, and as such hardly a place to stay, but its central Renaissance square and ramshackle castle could make a pleasant half-day out from either Pavia or Milan.

Pavia

Medieval **PAVIA** was known as the city of a hundred towers. And although only a handful remain – one of the best collapsed last year, killing four people – the medieval aspect is still strong, with numerous Romanesque and Gothic churches tucked away in a wanderable web of narrow streets and cobbled squares. The town is not, however, stranded in the past – its ancient university continues to thrive, ensuring an animated streetlife and reasonably lively nightscene.

Pavia reached its zenith in the Dark Ages when it was capital of the Kingdom of the Lombards. After their downfall it remained a centre of power, and the succession of emperors who ruled North Italy continued to come to the town to receive the Lombards' traditional iron crown. This all came to an end in the fourteenth century when Pavia was handed over to the Viscontis and became a satellite of Milan. The Viscontis, and later the Sforzas, did however found the university and provide the town with its prime tourist attraction – the Certosa di Pavia.

Arriving and finding a place to stay

Regular trains make the half-hour journey between Pavia and Milan, but connections from Pavia to the other cities of the Lombardy plain are infrequent and slow. Once here, getting around is no problem: the centre is small and walkable and buses #3 and #6 connect the railway station with the main Corso. The **EPT** is on Corso Garibaldi (June–Aug Mon–Fri 8.30am–1.30pm & 3–6pm, Sat 9am–noon; Sept–May Mon–Fri 8.30am–12.30pm & 2.30–6pm; Sat 9am–noon).

Pavia's hotels tend to get filled with the overspill from Milan's commercial fairs, and finding **somewhere to stay** can be more difficult than you might imagine. Out of the university term you can rent a **room** for a minimum of a week in a private house – details from the EPT. Of the **hotels**, pleasantest is *Albergo Regisole*, Piazza Duomo 2 (✆0382/24.739), with doubles for L30,000: it's clean, the management are friendly, and it's in a superb position opposite the duomo. Cheaper but pretty seedy are the *Splendid*, Via XX Settembre 11 (✆0382/24.703); the *Roma*, Via Roma 13 (✆0382/29.320); and the *Cannon d'Oro*, Strada Nuova 7 (✆0382/21.093).

Of the town's two **campsites**, both open from May to September, the *Ticino*, Via Mascherpa 10 (✆0382/20.015), has a swimming pool (take bus #4 from the train station). The other, the *Lido* (✆0382/332.69), is on Via Varazza on the far side of the river Ticino; bus #3 or #6 to Strada Nuova, then bus #1 or #8 across the river, followed by a longish walk).

The Town

It's Pavia as a whole which appeals, rather than any specific sight. Just wandering around town is the nicest way to spend time here: pick any sidestreet and you're almost bound to stumble on something of interest – a lofty medieval tower, a pretty Romanesque or Gothic church, or just a silent, sleepy piazza. Getting lost is difficult, as long as you bear in mind that the centre is quartered by the two main streets.

One piazza that is neither sleepy nor silent is the central **Piazza della Vittoria**, a large cobbled rectangle surrounded by tatty buildings housing bars, *gelaterie* and restaurants. Steps lead down to an **underground market** (8.30am–12.30pm & 3.30–7.30pm) – a rather tacky affair, worth visiting only if you can't afford to buy food anywhere else. At the square's right end the **Broletto**, medieval Pavia's town hall, abuts the rear of the rambling and unwieldy **Duomo**: an early Renaissance sprawl of protruding curves and jutting angles that was only finally completed in the 1930s. The west front of the duomo, facing Piazza del Duomo, is now undergoing restoration, following the collapse of the adjacent Torre Civica in March 1989 which killed four people.

Best of the town's churches is the Romanesque **San Michele**, a five-minute walk away on Via Cavallotti. The friezes and capitals on its broad sandstone facade are carved into a menagerie of snake-tailed fish, griffons, dragons and other beasts, some locked in a struggle with humans, representing the fight between good and evil. Look in also on the church of **San Pietro in Ciel d'Oro**, on the other side of the centre at the top of Strada Nuova, dating from 1132 and containing a superb fourteenth-century altarpiece. Nearby, the **Castello** (April–Sept 10am–12.15pm & 2.30–5.15pm; Oct–March 10am–noon & 2–4pm; Aug, Dec & Jan 9am–1pm only) was initiated by Galeazzo II Visconti in 1360, and added to by the Sforzas. The austere exterior originally housed luxurious apartments, the majority of which were in the wing of the quadrangle destroyed by the French in 1527. But the castle was used as a barracks until 1921, and although it's been restored the rooms that remain are hardly stunning. Inside there's an **art gallery** holding a handful of Venetian paintings, an **archaeology museum** with Roman jewellery, pottery, and glassware, and a **museum of sculpture** displaying architectural fragments, mosaics and sculptures rescued from the town's demolished churches – most impressive of which are the reconstructed eleventh- and twelfth-century portals. Otherwise you'll see the castle at its best on summer evenings, when its courtyard is used for concerts, opera and dance (details from the EPT).

The Certosa di Pavia

May–Aug Tues–Sun 9–11.30am & 2.30–8pm; March–April & Sept–Oct Tues–Sun 9–11.30am & 2.30–5pm; Nov–Feb Tues–Sun 9–11.30am & 2.30–4pm; free.

Ten kilometres from Pavia, the **Certosa di Pavia** is one of the most extravagant monasteries in Europe, commissioned by Gian Galeazzo Visconti in 1396 as the family mausoleum. Visconti intended the church here to resemble Milan's late-Gothic cathedral. It took a century to build, and by the time it was finished tastes had changed – and the Viscontis had been replaced by the Sforzas. But the architect appointed to finish the building, Amadeo, did so in style, festooning the facade with a fantasia of inlaid marble, twisted columns and friezes that say more about the wealth of the families that financed the complex than the contemplative Carthusian order it was built for.

The monastery lies at the end of a tree-lined avenue, part of a former Visconti hunting range that stretched all the way from Pavia's castello. You can see the **church** unaccompanied, a Gothic building on the inside though no less splendid than the facade, its paintings, statues and vaults combining to create an almost ballroom glamour; look out for the tombs of Lodovico Il Moro and Gian Galeazzo Visconti, masterpieces of the early Renaissance. But to visit the rest of the monastery you need to join a **guided tour** (in Italian) which takes just over an hour, led by one of the monks released from the Carthusian strict vow of silence. The **small cloister** is the first stop, with fine terracotta decoration and a geometric garden around a fountain. Further on, the **great cloister** is less appealing, but offers some insight into life in the complex, surrounded on three sides by the

The Certosa di Pavia is actually reachable from both Milan and Pavia, either by bus or by train. Buses are most frequent, hourly from Piazza Castello in Milan or from outside Pavia's train station, dropping you a fifteen-minute walk from the Certosa. By train, turn left out of the station and walk around the Certosa walls until you reach the entrance – also a fifteen-minute walk.

monks' cells, each consisting of two rooms, a chapel, garden and loggia, with a bedroom above. The hatches to the side of the entrances are to enable food to be passed through without any communication. There is also a **refectory** for occasional communal eating, with a pulpit from which the Bible is read throughout the silent meal – the only diversion the frescoed ceiling. The final call is the Certosa **shop**, stocked with the famous (Chartreuse) liqueur, honey, chocolate and souvenirs. Give yourself time before leaving to sample the different varieties of liqueur at the kiosk outside the entrance – yellow is strong, green stronger.

Practicalities: eating, drinking and nightlife

Bar Haiti on Corso Cavour makes for a good start to the day – snatch a coffee at the bar or linger over *cappuccino* and pastries. For a **breakfast** on the move, there are savoury breads and pizzas as well as sweet pastries at *Medagliani* (branches on Corso Cavour and Corso Garibaldi), while the town's most tempting aromas waft out of the basement *Pasticceria Demetrio* on Via Guidi, between Piazzale Stazione and Corso Mazzini.

For a quick lunch, the *Bar Vittoria*, Strada Nuova 8, is a good **paninoteca**, with at least a hundred varieties of sandwich and plenty of space to sit down. For a more substantial feed in more subdued surroundings, try the *Bar del Senatore* on Via del Senatore off Corso Cavour.

Pavia prides itself on its cuisine, with the result that many of its **restaurants** are expensive. However, there are exceptions: *Pizzeria Toscana*, Via Cardano 6, off Strada Nuova, sells its pizza by the metre; *Piedigrotta*, near the church at the far end of Via Teodolinda, does good, reasonably-priced pizza and pasta. More expensive, but in a great position on the far bank of the Ticino, is the *Osteria della Malora*.

Posters around town will fill you in on what's happening in the evening – there's a foreign film season during term-time, and **Settembre Pavese**, a festival of processions, concerts and folksy events, in the first half of September. Otherwise try one of the two central clubs: *Café Insomnia* on Vicolo San Sebastiano, off Strada Nuova, or *Docking* at Via Rezia 42.

Vigévano

An hour by bus to the west of Pavia, **VIGÉVANO** is Lombardy at its most comfortably wealthy, a smug little town of boutiques, antique dealers and – most significantly – shoe shops. The shoe industry is Vigévano's mainstay and there are signs of the bedrock of the town's prosperity all over the centre. If you go on a Sunday, Italy's only **Shoe Museum** is open on Corso Cavour, with a collection of some of the weirdest and wackiest excesses of shoe-design in the country.

As for the town itself, most of it is pretty unremarkable, and there'd be little reason to visit were it not for the **Piazza Ducale**, which is something special, surrounded on three sides by well preserved and delicately frescoed arcades, the embodiment of Renaissance harmony. Designed by Bramante and heavily influenced by Leonardo, even the Baroque front of the duomo doesn't spoil the proportions, deftly curved to conceal the fact that the church is set at a slight angle to the square.

Otherwise the **Castello** (Tues–Sun 9.30am–12.30pm & 2.30–5.30pm) is about all Vigévano has to offer. A Visconti and later Sforza stronghold, it's been in the throes of restoration for over ten years, but its semi-dilapidated state is part of the attraction – it's largely unsupervised, especially in the mornings, which means you can go just about wherever you want, scrambling up rickety flights of steps to the upper floors, or down dank passages to the dungeons. The oldest part of the castle is the Rocca Vecchia, a fort built by the Visconti to defend the road to Milan, to which it is connected by a covered walkway. The Sforzas retained the castle's military function, but added the elegant Palazzo Ducale, still mostly unrestored, the Loggia delle Dame, an open walkway for the noblewomens' evening *passeggiata*, and the Falconiera, another open gallery used for the training of falcons but now holding the castle's most absurd sight – the tiles of a military bathroom dating from its conversion this century into a barracks. On the right of the courtyard, the stables, designed by Leonardo, offer some insight into how the Sforza troops lived and worked – cathedral-like quarters for the horses, and a loft above for soldiers and hay.

Cremona

A cosy provincial town situated bang in the middle of the Po plain, **CREMONA** is known for its violins. Ever since Andrea Amati established the first violin workshop here in 1566, and his son Nicola and pupils Stradivari and Guarneri continued and expanded the industry, Cremona has been a focus for the instrument, attracting both tourists and musicians worldwide. Today around a hundred violin-makers maintain the tradition started by the Amati family: there's an internationally famous school of violin-making here, and there are frequent classical concerts, as well as a string festival held every third October (next in 1991).

For non-musicians, however, Cremona can be something of a non-event. There's a staleness about the town which can fast become deadening. Treat it as a day-trip from Milan, or as a stopover en route to the richer pickings of Mantua or Bergamo – time to wind down, but not long enough to get bored.

Practicalities: arrival, information and sleeping

Cremona's centre is in walking distance of the **train station** on Via Dante, and there are regular buses to the two out-of-town sights – the church of San Sigismondo to the east and the Museo della Civiltà Contadina in the western suburbs. Most inter-city **buses** stop at the train station.

The **EPT** (Mon–Sat 9am–12.30pm & 3–7pm, Sun 9.30am–12.30pm) is on the main square opposite the duomo, and has maps, leaflets and details of classical concerts. They also have lists of violin-makers' workshops (*Botteghe Liutarie*) and will be able to tell you if the school of violin-making in Palazzo Raimondi is open for visits.

The cheapest **hotel** is the *Concordia*, Via Pallavicino 4 (☎0372/20.412) near the junction with Corso Matteotti, with doubles at L23,000 – but you'll need to book about a week in advance. Doubles cost L25,000 at the *Brescia*, Via Brescia 7 (☎0372/434.615), just off Piazza Libertá, a ten- to fifteen-minute walk or bus #4 or #5 from the train station, though again you'll need to book in advance. The best bet if you're arriving on spec is the *Touring*, Via Palestro 3 (☎0372/21.390), near the junction with Corso Garibaldi, which has doubles for L25,000. Finally there's a **campsite** (open May–Sept) on Via Parco Po Europa (☎0372/27.137). Take bus #1 (direction Cadorna and Viale Po) from the train station.

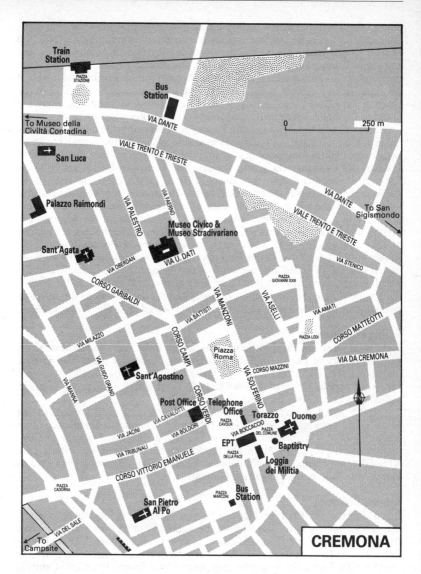

The City

If you've come for the violins, first stop should perhaps be the pilastered Palazzo Affaitati on Via Palestro, which holds the **Museo Stradivariano** (Tues–Sat 9.30am–12.15pm & 3–5.45pm, Sun 9.30am–12.15pm; L1000, free Sun) containing models, paper patterns, tools and acoustic diagrams from Stradivari's workshop. Hanging impotently in glass cases are violins, violas, viols, cellos and guitars, many of which have elaborately carved scrolls. They have to be played regularly to keep them in trim, and you could try asking the custodian when the next work-out is due. In the same building (entrance around the corner in Via U. Dati), the **Museo Civico** (same hours) has more violins – by Andrea Amati and his son, and pupils Guarneri and Stradivari. There's also a bizarre collection of Garibaldi memorabilia, including a lock of his hair, shavings from his beard and a stub of his cigar; and a fragment of the Great Wall of China among the porcelain in the Oriental collection. Also, among a small assortment of paintings, there's a disputed Caravaggio of an anguished Saint Francis contemplating a skull.

A little way south of the museums, **Piazza del Comune** is the medieval heart of the city, a grave, disjointed square, its west side formed by the turreted redbrick **Loggia dei Militia** – medieval headquarters of the town's militia – and the arched **Palazzo del Comune**. The gawky Romanesque **Torazzo** (Mar 15–Nov 30 Mon–Sat 10.30am–noon & 3–6pm, Sun 10am–12.30pm; L2000) claims, at 110m, to be Italy's highest medieval tower, linked to the **Duomo** by way of a Renaissance loggia – a mixed-looking church, with a west facade made up of Classical, Romanesque and fancy Gothic features. It is most notable for the western rose window and the early sixteenth-century frescoes inside, though these are difficult to see in the gloomy light. The church of **San Pietro al Po**, southwest of the square on Via Tibaldi, has better (and more visible) frescoes, indeed its walls are coated with paintings and intricate stuccos, also dating from the sixteenth century. It's all pretty excessive, but there's sophisticated optical trickery in the trompe l'oeil work of Antonio Campi in the transept vaults. Look in also on the refectory next door for Bernadino Gatti's hearty fresco of the feeding of the two thousand.

Eating and drinking

Pizza is, as ever, the cheapest **food**. The *Bottega della Pizza*, Corso Mazzini 65, and the bakery at Corso Garibaldi 143 both sell takeaway pizza. The *Pizzeria Stagnino*, Corso Garibaldi 85, and the *Pizzeria La Pendola* on Via Pallavicino are cheap and popular places to sit down and eat. There's also, if you prefer to picnic, a good street market on Tuesdays and Thursdays.

The city also has loads of traditional trattorias serving local specialities like *bollito misto*, a mixture of boiled meats eaten with *mostarde* – a Cremonese relish consisting of fruit suspended in a sweet mustard syrup. The *Trattoria da Cerri*, Piazza Giovanni 23, off Via Aselli, and the *Ristorante Centrale* on Via Solferino, are typical, but not cheap. More affordable is the always busy *Trattoria della Pace* on Piazza della Pace, behind Piazza del Comune.

Around Cremona

If you liked the church of San Pietro al Po, you'll love that of **San Sigismondo** on the eastern edge of town (bus #3 from the station; #2 or #3 from Piazza Libertà). Built by Francesco and Bianca Sforza in 1441 to commemorate their wedding – Cremona was Bianca's dowry – its Mannerist decor is among Italy's best, ranging from Camillo Boccaccino's soaring apse fresco to the *Pentecost* by Giulio Campi in the third bay of the nave, plagiarised from Mantegna's ceiling in the Camera degli Sposi at Mantua. Other highlights include Giulio's *Annunciation* on the entrance wall, in which Gabriel is seemingly suspended in mid-air, and the gory John the Baptist in the second left chapel, by his younger brother Antonio.

There's a rather different attraction in the opposite direction (bus #3 from the station), the **Museo della Civiltà Contadina** (Tues–Sat 9.30am–12.15pm & 3–5.45pm Sun 9.30am–12.15pm; L1000), stuck on the edge of an industrial estate in the outskirts of town at Via Castelleone 51 and possible contender for Italy's muddiest museum. A display of agricultural history laid out in an old farm, it's a scruffy place, and sporadic labelling (in Italian only) makes working out the uses of the various pieces of agricultural apparatus virtually impossible. But the farm itself, with its row of tiny workers' cottages, the larger houses of the foreman and *padrone*, the immense stable, and the small chapel, built so that time wasn't wasted in travelling to church, is sufficient to give you a good picture of the strict hierarchy and slave-like existence that governed the lives of Italian agricultural labourers over several centuries.

Mantua and around

Aldous Huxley called it the most romantic city in the world; and with an Arabian nights skyline rising above its three encircling lakes, **MANTUA** (MANTOVA) is undeniably evocative. It was the scene of Verdi's *Rigoletto*, and its history is one of equally operatic plots, most of them perpetuated by the Gonzagas, one of Renaissance Italy's richest and most powerful families, who ruled the town for three centuries. Its centre of interlinking cobbled squares retains its medieval aspect, and there are two splendid palaces: the Palazzo Ducale, containing Mantegna's stunning fresco of the Gonzaga family and court, and Palazzo del Te, whose frescoes by the flashy Mannerist, Giulio Romano, have entertained and outraged generations of visitors with their combination of steamy erotica and illusionistic fantasy.

But hazy sunsets reflected in tranquil lakes, and the town's melodramatic history, are only half the story. Outside the few traffic-free streets of the historic centre the roads are lined with grimy fascist-era buildings and jammed with cars, while the outskirts have been desecrated by chemical, plastics and paper works that are reputedly responsible for lining the bed of the largest lake, Superiore, with mercury. Nevertheless, the core of the city is still appealing, especially on Thursdays when Piazza Mantegna, Piazza dell'Erbe and the streets around are filled with a large market.

The state of these same streets aroused the ire of a visiting pope in 1459, who complained that Mantua was muddy, marshy, riddled with fever and intensely hot. His host, Lodovico II Gonzaga, was spurred into action: he could do little about the heat (Mantua can still be unbearably hot and mosquito-ridden in summer) but he did give the city an elaborate facelift, ranging from paving the squares and repainting the shops, to engaging Mantegna as court artist and calling in the prestigious architectural theorist, Alberti, to design the monumental church of Sant'Andrea – one of the most influential buildings of the early Renaissance. Lodovico's successors continued the tradition of artistic patronage, and although most of the thousands of works of art once owned by the Gonzagas are now scattered around Europe, the town still has plenty of relics from the era.

Arriving and finding a place to stay

Getting around Mantua is no problem: the centre is a ten-minute walk from both the bus and train stations. If you're heading straight for Palazzo Te there are buses from outside the train station; take any that stop at **Risorgimento** or **Repubblica** – routes are listed on the bus stops.

The only really **cheap accommodation** is at the official **youth hostel** (☎0376/372.465), known as Sparafucile's Inn, where the hired assassin Sparafucile is supposed to have killed Rigoletto's daughter. It's now known for its mosquitos and cold showers. The other cheap option is the **campsite** in its grounds. Both are open from April to mid-October 15; take bus #2 or #9 from outside *Upim* on Piazza Cavalotti. **Hotels** get booked up quickly in summer, so it's advisable to phone ahead. There are two one-star hotels in the centre: *Roma Vecchia*, Via Corridoni 20 (☎0376/322.100), near Piazza Martiri Belfiore, and *Rinascita*, Via Concezione 4 (☎0376/320.607), about five minutes' walk from the train station. Both have doubles for L28,000. The other central hotels are more expensive – *Bianchi Stazione* (0376/321.504) and *ABC Moderno* (0376/322.329) are both directly in front of the train station and have doubles for L35,000. If you have no luck at any of these you'll either have to take a room way out in the suburbs or pay over the odds for one in the centre. The **EPT** (Mon–Sat 9am–12.30pm & 3–5pm, Sun 9am–12.30pm), around the corner from Sant'Andrea, has a list.

Eating and drinking

For inexpensive **food**, try the *Piedigrotto*, Corso Libertá 15, *Bella Napoli*, Piazza Cavalotti 14, or *Da Gigi*, Via Oberdan 4, off Corso Umberto, all of which have good, well priced pizza. For cheap, filling food in an institutional atmosphere try one of the mensas: *Al Punto* (noon–2.30pm & 7.30–9.15pm, closed Sun) on Via Solferino, near the train station, has complete meals for L9,500; *Self-Service Virgiliana*, Piazza Virgiliana 57, is slightly cheaper, but is only open weekday lunchtimes (noon–2pm).

For more interesting eating, Mantuan specialities include such delights as donkey stew and pasta stuffed with pumpkin, which you can try at *Due Cavallini* (closed latter half of July) on Vicolo Salnitro 5, off Corso Garibaldi – an affordable place with full meals for around L17,000. *Trattoria del Lago*, Piazza Arche 5, hasn't much atmosphere but is cheaper: it serves traditional dishes such as *agnoli in brodo* – pasta stuffed with cheese and sausage in broth. Unusually, there's also a macrobiotic restaurant, *Aratro* (8.30am–2.30pm & 4.30–7.30pm) at Vicolo Albergo 4, off Via Cavour.

Mantuan evenings are best spent in one of its two **birrerias**: *Birreria Oblo*, Via Arrivabene 50, has a great selection of beers, almost matched by a good range of sandwiches, while *Lioncino Rosso*, just through the bridge behind Piazza Broletto, has an unpretentious pubby atmosphere.

The City

Historic Mantua centres on four interlinking squares – Piazza Mantegna, Piazza dell'Erbe, Piazza Broletto and Piazza Sordello. Coming from the station, Piazza Mantegna is the first you see, a small, wedge-shaped open space dominated by the facade of Alberti's **Sant'Andrea**, an unfinished basilica that says a lot about the ego of Lodovico II Gonzaga who commissioned it. He felt that the existing medieval church was neither impressive enough to represent the splendour of his state, nor large enough to hold the droves of people who flocked to Sant'Andrea every Ascension Day to see the holy relic of Christ's blood which

Lago di Mezzo

Lago
Superiore

VIALE MINCIO

PIAZZA
VIRGILIANA

To the
Youth
Hostel

VIA ALBERTO PITENTINO

VIA CONCEZIONE

VIA CAVOUR

Duomo

**Palazzo
Ducale**

VIA SOLFERINO E SAN MARTINO

PIAZZA
DORE E
LEONI

Torre della
Gabbia

PIAZZA SORDELLO

Sant'Andrea

VIA BROLETTO

Broletto

EPT

Train
Station

PIAZZA
MANTEGNA

VIA ARDIGO

Teatro
Bibiena

CORSO VITTORIO EMANUELE II

CORSO
CAVALOTTI

PIAZZA
MARCONI

Rotonda

Palazzo
Della
Ragione

PIAZZA
UMBERTO I

PIAZZA
DELL'ERBE

LUNGOLAGO DEI GONZAGA

CORSO D. LIBERTA

VIA ROMA

VIA BERTANI

Lago
Inferiore

Bus
Station

VIA STOPI

Fish
Market

VIA POMPONAZZO

PIAZZA MARTINI
BELFIORI

VIA CORRIDONI

VIA CARDUCCI

VIALE PAVE

VIA AMEDEO

Canal

VIA TRIESTE

Casa di
Giulio Romano

VIA DELLA CONCILIAZIONE

VIA DOGANA

VIA POMA

Palazzo di
Giustizia

Casa di
Mantegna

VIA ACERBI

VIA GIULIO ROMANO

VIA L. SAURO

VIA CHIASSI

PIAZZALE
GRAMSCI

VIALE DELLA REPUBBLICA

VIA LUNGO
24 MAGGIO

San
Sebastiano

CORSO GARIBALDI

VIALE MONTELLO

VIA LUNGO
VENETO

VIALE RISORGIMENTO

VIALE TE

Palazzo Te

MANTUA

had been found on the site. The relic is still here, and after years of dispute about its authenticity (it was supposed to have been brought to Mantua by the soldier who pierced Christ's side) Pope Pius II settled the matter in the fifteenth century by declaring it had miraculously cured him of gout.

Work started on the church in 1472, with the court architect, Luca Fancelli, somewhat resentfully overseeing Alberti's plans. There was a bitchy rivalry between the two, and when, on one of his many visits, Alberti fell and hurt a testicle, Fancelli gleefully told him that "God lets men punish themselves in the place where they sin." Inside, the church is roofed with one immense barrel vault, echoing the triumphal arch of the facade, giving it a rather cool and calculated feel. The octagonal balustrade at the crossing stands above the crypt where the holy relic is kept in two vases, copies of originals designed by Cellini and stolen by the Austrians in 1846. To see them, ask the sacristan. There are also wall-paintings designed by Mantegna and executed by students, one of whom was Correggio; Mantegna himself is buried in the church, his tomb, in one of the north aisle chapels, topped with a bust of the artist that's said to be a self-portrait.

Opposite Sant'Andrea, sunk below the present level of Piazza dell'Erbe, Mantua's oldest church, the eleventh-century **Rotonda**, narrowly escaped destruction under Lodovico's city-improvement plans, only to be partially demolished in the sixteenth century and used as a courtyard by the surrounding houses. Rebuilt at the beginning of this century, it still contains traces of twelfth- and thirteenth-century frescoes, but getting inside can be a problem – it's supposed to be open for a couple of hours daily, but don't count on it, especially out of season.

Piazza dell'Erbe itself is one of the town's most characteristic squares, with a small daily market, and cafés and restaurants sheltering in the arcades below the thirteenth-century **Palazzo della Ragione**. The dark underpassage beneath the redbrick **Broletto**, or medieval town hall, leads into Piazza Broletto, with two reminders of how "criminals" were treated under the Gonzagas. The bridge to the right has metal rings embedded in its vault, to which victims were chained by the wrists, before being hauled up by a pulley and suspended in mid-air. And on the far left corner of the square the medieval **Torre della Gabbia** has a cage attached in which prisoners were displayed. The Broletto itself is more generous to deserving Mantuans, and is dedicated to the city's two most famous sons: Virgil, a statue of whom overlooks the square, and Tazio Nuvolone, Italy's most celebrated racing driver, whose career is mapped in a small museum (Tues–Sun 9am–noon & 3–6pm; L1000).

If you've time, it's worth making a short diversion up Via Accademia to the eighteenth-century **Teatro Scientifico** or **Bibiena** (Mon–Sat 9am–noon & 3.30–6pm; L300), designed by Antonio Bibiena, whose brother designed the Bayreuth Opera Houses. This is a much smaller theatre, at once intimate and splendid, its curving walls lined with boxes calculated to make their inhabitants more conspicuous than the performers. A thirteen-year-old Mozart gave the inaugural concert here: his impression is unrecorded, but his father was fulsome in his praise for the building, writing that he had never in his life seen anything more beautiful. Concerts are still given – details from the theatre or tourist office.

Beyond Piazza Broletto, Piazza Sordello is a large, sombre square, headed by the Baroque facade of the **Duomo** and flanked by grim crenellated palaces built by the Gonzaga's predecessors, the Bonalcosi. The duomo conceals a rich interior designed by Giulio Romano after the church had been gutted by fire. As for the palaces, the two on the left are now owned by the successors of Baldassare Castiglione, a relative of the Gonzagas, who made himself unpopular at the Mantuan court by setting his seminal handbook of Renaissance behaviour, *The Book of the Courtier*, in the rival court of Urbino. Opposite, the **Palazzo del Capitano** and **Magna Domus** were taken by Luigi Gonzaga when he seized Mantua from the Bonalcosi in 1328, the beginning of three hundred years of Gonzaga rule.

The Palazzo Ducale

Tues–Sat 9am–5pm, Sun & Mon 9am–2pm; L4000

The Palazzo del Capitano and Magna Domus form the core of the **Palazzo Ducale**, an enormous complex that was once the largest palace in Europe. At its height it covered 34,000 square metres, had a population of over a thousand, including an entourage of dwarfs, and when it was sacked by the Hapsburgs in 1630 eighty carriages were needed to carry the two thousand works of art contained in its five hundred rooms. Only a proportion of these rooms are open to visitors, and to see them you have to take a guided tour. These are fairly indiscriminate; save your energy for the rooms that deserve it.

At the time of Luigi's coup of 1328, the Gonzagas were a family of wealthy local peasants, living outside the city on vast estates with an army of retainers. On seizing power Luigi immediately nominated himself Captain of the People – an event pictured in one of the first paintings you'll see on your tour – and the role quickly became a hereditary one, eventually growing in grandeur to that of Marquis. During this time the Gonzagas did their best to make Mantua into a city which was a suitable reflection of their increasing influence, commissioning sought-after Renaissance artists like Mantegna to depict them in their finery. Lodovico II's grandson, Francesco II, further swelled the Gonzagan coffers by hiring himself out as a mercenary for various other Italian city-states – money his wife, Isabella d'Este, spent amassing a prestigious collection of paintings, sculpture and objets d'art. Under Isabella's son, Federico II, Gonzaga fortunes reached their height, his marriage to the heiress of the duchy of Monferrato procuring a ducal title for the family, while continuing the policy of self-glorification by commissioning an out-of-town villa for himself and his mistress. Federico's descendants were for the most part less colourful characters, one notable exception being Vincenzo I, whose debauchery and corruption provided the inspiration for Verdi's licentious duke in *Rigoletto*. After Vincenzo's death, the now bankrupt court was forced to sell many of the family treasures to England's King Charles I (many of the works are still in the Victoria and Albert Museum) just three years before it was sacked by the Hapsburgs.

The first rooms of the palace hold little of interest, save a damaged fresco by Pisanello, discovered in 1969 behind two layers of plaster. It's thought to depict either an episode from an Arthurian romance or the (idealised) military exploits of the first marquis, Gianfrancesco Gonzaga. Whatever its subject, it's a powerful piece of work, charged with energy, in which faces, costumes and landscape are minutely observed.

Less tasteful is the *Salone dei Fiume* (Room of the Rivers) in which Baroque trompe l'oeil goes over the top to create a mock garden complete with painted creepers and two ghastly fountains surrounded by stalactites and stalagmites. The *Sala dei Specchi* (Hall of the Mirrors), further on, has a notice outside signed by Monteverdi, who worked as court musician to Vincenzo I and gave frequent concerts of new works – notably the world's first modern opera, *L'Orfeo*, written in 1607. Vincenzo also employed Rubens, whose *Adoration of the Magi* in the Salone degli Arcieri shows the Gonzaga family of 1604, including Vincenzo with his handlebar moustache. The picture was originally part of a tryptych, but Napoleonic troops carried off two-thirds of it after briefly occupying the town in 1797 and chopped the remaining third into saleable chunks of portraiture. Although most have been traced, and some returned to the palazzo, there are still a few gaps.

The private apartments of Isabella d'Este, an even more voracious collector than Vincenzo, are on the ground floor. Though they once housed works by Michelangelo, Mantegna and Perugino, only the unmoveable decorations remain – inlaid cupboards and intricately carved ceilings and doors. A ruthless employer, Isabella would threaten her artists and craftsmen with the dungeon if she thought they were working too slowly, and had no compunction about bullying Mantegna on his death-bed to give her a piece of sculpture she particularly coveted. She was more deferential to Leonardo da Vinci, however, who did two drawings of her, but ignored her suggestion that one be converted into a portrait of Christ. Isabella also collected dwarfs, whose job it was to cheer her up while her husband was away fighting. For centuries it was assumed that the suite of miniature rooms beyond Isabella's apartments were built for the dwarfs; in fact it's a scaled-down version of the St John Lateran basilica in Rome, built for Vincenzo.

The Castello di San Giorgio, beyond, contains the palace's real treasure, Mantegna's frescoes of the Gonzaga family, the painter's most famous works, splendidly restored in the so-called *Camera degli Sposi* and depicting the Marquis Lodovico and his wife Barbara with their family. They're naturalistic pieces of work, giving a vivid impression of real people, of the relationships between them and of the tensions surrounding something that is happening, or about to happen. In the main one Lodovico discusses a letter with a courtier while his wife looks on; their youngest daughter leans on her mothers" lap, about to bite into an apple, while an older son and daughter (possibly Barbarina) look towards the door, where an ambassador from another court is being welcomed – lending some credence to the theory that negotiations are about to take place for Barbarina's marriage. The other fresco, *The Meeting*, takes place out of doors against a landscape of weird rock formations and an imaginary city with the Gonzagan arms above the gate. Divided into three sections by fake pilasters, it shows Gonzagan retainers with dogs and a horse in attendance on Lodovico who is welcoming his son Francesco back from Rome, where he had just become the first Gonzaga to be made a cardinal. In the background are the Holy Roman Emperor Frederick III, and the King of Denmark – a selection which apparently annoyed the Duke of Milan, who was incensed that the "two most wretched men in the world" had been included while he had been omitted. Lodovico's excuse was that he would have included the Duke, had he not objected so strongly to Mantegna's uncompromising portrait style.

Finally, if you have time before the guide sweeps you out, have a look at the ceiling, a nice piece of trompe l'oeil, in which two women, peering down from a balustrade, have balanced a tub of plants on a pole and appear to be on the verge of letting it tumble into the room – an illusionism that was to be crucial in the development of the Gonzaga's next resident artist of any note, Giulio Romano, whose Palazzo Te should not be missed.

The walk to Te

The court artists Mantegna and Giulio Romano both lived outside the Palazzo Ducale, and you can still see their houses if you walk the twenty minutes to Palazzo del Te rather than taking the bus.

The **Casa di Giulio Romano** is on Via Poma, overshadowed by the monster-studded Palazzo di Giustizia – designed by Romano, and, like much of his Mantuan work, meant to impress the sophisticated, who would have found the licence taken with the classical rules of architecture witty and amusing. A five-minute walk away on busy Via Acerbi, the **Casa di Mantegna** was also designed by the artist, both as a home and private museum, and it's now used as a contemporary art-space and conference centre. If it's open, pop in and take a look at the unusual circular courtyard. Across the road, the church of **San Sebastiano** was the work of Alberti, and is famous as the first Renaissance church to be built on a central Greek cross plan. It's now a neglected, rather seedy place, however, described as "curiously pagan" by Nicholas Pevsner. Lodovico II's son was less polite: "I could not understand whether it was meant to turn out as a church, a mosque or a synagogue." If you want to look inside, keys are available between 3pm and 5pm at Palazzo Te.

The Palazzo del Te

Oct–March Tues–Sun 9.30am–12.30pm & 2.30–5pm; April–Sept Tues–Sun 9am–12.30pm & 2.30-5.30pm; L2500

The later of Mantua's two Gonzaga palaces, the **Palazzo del Te** was designed for playboy Federico Gonzaga and his mistress, Isabella Boschetta, by Giulio Romano – the artist/architect's greatest work and a renowned Renaissance pleasure dome. When the palace was built, Te – or Tejeto, as it used to be known – was an island connected to the mainland by bridge, an ideal location for an amorous retreat away from Federico's wife and the restrictions of life in the Palazzo Ducale. Built around a square courtyard originally occupied by a labyrinth, there are modest but appealing collections of **modern art** and a small **Egyptian museum** here these days, though the main reason for visiting is to see Giulio's amazing decorative scheme.

A tour of the palace is like a voyage around Giulio's imagination, a sumptuous world where very little is what it seems. In the Sala dei Cavalli, dedicated to the prime specimens from the Gonzaga stud-farm (which was also on the island), portraits of horses stand before an illusionistic background in which simulated marble, fake pilasters and mock reliefs surround views of painted landscapes through non-existent windows. The function of the *Salotta di Psiche*, further on, is undocumented, but the sultry frescoes, and the proximity to Federico's bedroom, might give a few clues, the ceiling paintings telling the story of Cupid and Psyche with some dizzying "sotto in su" (from the bottom up) works by Giulio, among others clumsily executed by his pupils. On the walls, too, are racy pieces, covered with orgiastic wedding-feast scenes, at which drunk and languishing gods in various states of undress are attended by a menagerie of real and mythical beasts. Don't miss the severely incontinent river-god in the background, included either as a punning reference to Giulio's second name, Pippi (The Pisser), or as encouragement to Federico who according to his doctors suffered from the "obstinate retention of urine". Other scenes show Mars and Venus having a bath, Olympia about to be raped by a half-serpentine Jupiter and Pasiphae disguising herself as a cow in order to seduce a bull – all watched over by the giant Polyphemus, perched above the fireplace, clutching the pan-pipes with which he sang of his love for Galatea before murdering her lover.

Polyphemus and his fellow giants are revenged in the extraordinary *Sala dei Giganti* beyond – "the most fantastic and frightening creation of the whole Renaissance" according to the critic Frederick Hartt, showing the destruction of the giants by the gods. As if at some kind of advanced disaster movie, the destruction appears to be all around, cracking pillars, toppling brickwork, and screaming giants, mangled and crushed by great chunks of architecture, appearing to crash down into the room. Stamp your feet and you'll discover another parallel to twentieth-century cinema – sound-effects like those used in the film *Earthquake* that Giulio created by making the room into an echo chamber.

Around Mantua: Sabbioneta

There's not much to see within easy reach of Mantua, and the countryside – the Mantuan plain – is for the most part flat and dull. Closest real attraction is at **GRAZIE**, a ten-minute bus ride west, where the church of **Santa Maria delle Grazie** has an interior chock-full of weird votive offerings, wax and wooden mannequins in clothes petrified with age standing in niches, surrounded by wooden hearts, breasts, hands and feet nailed up by the recipients of miracle-cures. There's even a stuffed crocodile hanging from the ceiling. Alongside the church, a path leads down to the marshes, rich in rare birds and wildlife, viewable at closer quarters by booking a rowing-boat trip (☎0376/653.735 or ☎0376/311.56) the day before.

Further out, fifty minutes by bus from Mantua, **SABBIONETA** is a more interesting target, an odd little place with the air of an abandoned film set, where imperious Renaissance palaces gaze blankly over deserted and dusty piazzas. The town is the result of the obsessive dream of Vespasiano Gonzaga, member of a minor branch of the Mantuan family, to create the ideal city, but it has now been abandoned by all but the oldest inhabitants, a handful of agricultural workers and the tourist board.

Sabbioneta was an anachronism even as it was being built. In the sixteenth century it was no more than an agricultural village, nominal capital of an insignificant state on the Mantuan border struggling to maintain its independence from the foreign powers who had colonised most of Lombardy. Unperturbed, its ruler, Duke Vespasiano, was keen to create an ideal state on the model of ancient Athens and Rome, and he uprooted his subjects from their farm cottages, forcing them to build and then inhabit the new city, which held a Greek and Latin Academy and a Palladian theatre as well as a couple of ducal residences. After Vespasiano's death, Sabbioneta returned to – and has remained in – its former state: a small agricultural village like hundreds of others throughout Italy.

To get inside any of the town's buildings you have to take a **guided tour**. These are arranged by the **AAST** (daily 9.30am–noon & 2.30–5.30pm) at Via Gonzaga 31, by the main piazza and bus-stop, and they start with the **Palazzo del Giardino**, Vespasiano's private residence, decorated with frescoed models of civilised behaviour, ranging from Roman emperors to the Three Graces. Next stop is the **Teatro Olimpico**, copied from Palladio's theatre of the same name in Vicenza, in which the only spectators are pallid marble gods, fake-bronze emperors and ghostly painted courtiers. The **Palazzo Ducale**, around the corner, holds painted wooden statues of four of the Gonzagas, including Vespasiano (with the ruffle and beard), sitting imperiously on horseback. What remains of the palace's decor is likewise concerned with the show of strength – frescoed elephants and friezes of eagles and lions. Close by, the **Chiesa dell'Incoronata** is remarkable mainly for its trompe l'oeil roof, which appears to be three times higher in than out – perhaps an apt comment on Vespasiano, a bronze statue of whom sits beneath, dressed as a Roman emperor and looking reluctant to leave his dream city.

NORTHERN LOMBARDY: LAKES AND MOUNTAINS

"One can't describe the beauty of the Italian lakes, nor would one try if one could." So wrote Henry James, a sentiment that hasn't stopped generations of writers trying to describe the region in pages of purple prose. In fact, the lakes just about deserve it: their beauty *is* extravagant, and it's not surprising that the most melodramatic and romantic of Italy's opera composers – Verdi, Rossini and Bellini – rented lakeside villas to work in. British and German Romantic poets also gushed about the area, and in doing so introduced them firmly to northern European imaginations. The result: a massive influx every summer of ageing packaged tourists from cooler climes, come to savour the Italian dream, and to take large gulps at what Keats called "the beaker of the warm south".

To literally drink the lake's waters would be inadvisable, as they are heavily polluted – Como is known by locals as the "toilet of Italy" and even small lakes like **Iseo** have their pockets of industry. This doesn't deter the flocks of sailors and windsurfers, and resisting the temptation to swim is difficult in high summer. **Garda** is the cleanest lake, but as long as you guard against swallowing any water, and avoid any obviously polluted stretches, you should be okay. If swimming and watersports don't appeal, **Maggiore** and **Como** have most to offer – luxuriant botanic gardens and sumptuous villas on the lake-shores and islands.

The hilly terrain between the lakes is sliced up by **mountain valleys**: their lower reaches are almost inevitably choked with industry, and their rivers frequently reduced to a trickle by hydro-electric works, but the upper reaches are in parts unspoilt, with plenty of possibilities for hikes. There are also a handful of small ski resorts.

The two cities of the north, **Bergamo** and **Brescia**, are also worth visiting, Bergamo in particular, its old walled city on the hill one of Italy's loveliest town centres, and a good base for seeing Lago Como or Lago d'Iseo and the mountainous countryside in between. Brescia, further east, is best known for its arms industry, but has an interesting old centre, and is conveniently placed for trips into the mountains, or as a stopover between Lago d'Iseo and Lago di Garda.

Though included in this chapter for convenience, Lombardy actually shares the lakes with its neighbours: the eastern shore of Lago di Garda is shared by Trento and the Veneto; small, quiet Lago d'Orta is in Piemonte, as is the western shore of Maggiore, whose northern tip is in Switzerland. Inter-regional rivalry means that information from a Lombardian tourist office will cover only those parts of a lake in its territory, and that maps of Maggiore and Garda will frequently show another region's shore as a blank.

Lago Maggiore and Lago d'Orta

For generations of overland travellers, **LAGO MAGGIORE** has been the first taste of Italy. Road and railway from Switzerland run along its shores and, weary of the journey and the cool grandeur of the Alps, the first glimpse of Maggiore's limpid waters, gentle green hills and the hint of exotic vegetation can seem a promising taster of the country. In fact a good deal of Maggiore is dull, with the mountains set well back from its shores in its Italian stretches, and much of its southern reaches somewhat nondescript, particularly along the eastern shore.

Still, its orange blossom, vines, clear air and the verbena that flourishes on its shores continue to draw the tourists, and to stay in the most popular resorts – Pallanza, Stresa and Baveno – you'll need to book in advance in peak season. The lake has always been a favourite with the British: Queen Victoria stayed at the Villa Clara at Baveno – described by Edward Hutton in an early-twentieth-century guidebook as "a replica of the Wimbledon or Putney residence of a retired trades-man" – while Robert Southey reckoned the Villa Borromeo on Isola Bella, now Maggiore's biggest tourist attraction, to be "one of the most costly efforts of bad taste in all Italy."

The western shore

The southern reaches of the west shore of the lake are drab, but you'll have more chance of finding a room in high season. **ARONA**, uninteresting in itself, is on the main railway line, and its cheap *locande* make it a useful base for visiting the rest of the lake. The one sight here is a 100-foot-high copper statue of Saint Charles Borromeo who was born in the now ruined Castle of Arona. It's hollow, and if you don't suffer from claustrophobia you can climb up into its empty head.

If you decide to stay in Arona, the campsite, *Lido* (☎0322/3383), is right on the shore (a short walk from the railway station). The cheapest *locande* – with doubles for L20,000 – are *Antico Gallo* (☎0322/3137) and *Ponte* (☎0322/45.317). Tourist information at Corso Bagni 8.

Stresa and the islands

The Maggiore of the tourist brochures begins at **STRESA**, whose popularity as a resort began in 1906 with the construction of the Simplon Tunnel. Its elegant promenade is now well trodden by elderly Brits and Germans, for whose benefit the shops are stocked with schmaltzy souvenirs and the cafés with overpriced drinks. However, with its Edwardian hotels, eighteenth-century villas, luxuriant gardens, views across to the Isole Borromee, and a prestigious international classical music festival in late August and early September, Stresa retains an undeniable air of refinement.

After wandering along the promenade to see the *Grand Hotel des Iles Borromees*, a location used by Hemingway in *Farewell to Arms*, take a boat from Piazza Marconi or Piazzale Lido (further up) across to the **Isole Borromee** (round-trip L7000; admission L5000 for each palace). Of the Borromean islands **Isola Bella** (mid-March–Oct daily 9am–noon & 12.30–5.30pm) is the best-known and most gloriously excessive of all the lakes' gardens, though three centuries ago it was little more than a barren rock. In the seventeenth century Count Carlo III Borromeo decided to create an island paradise for his wife Isabella, and commissioned the architect, Angelo Crivelli, to transform it into a sumptuous

Baroque oasis. Tons of soil were brought across from the mainland, a villa, fountains and statues built, white peacocks imported, and ten terraces of orange and lemon trees, camellias, magnolias, box trees, laurels and cypresses carved out. The centrepiece, however, is a four-tiered confection of shell-, mirror- and marble-encrusted grottoes, topped with a Disneyesque unicorn, mini-obelisks, stone poseurs and cute cherubs. There's more kitsch, and some ritzy rooms and furniture, in the villa – with more artificial grottoes and a collection of eighteenth-century marionettes in the cellar.

Hemingway's favourite, **Isola dei Pescatori**, once an island of fishermen, is now a tourist-trap suffused with fake charm, and there's no need to hang around for longer than it takes to catch a ferry to **Isola Madre** (same hours as Isola Bella; admission expensive), larger and less visited than Isola Bella, with a small tasteful palazzo stacked with portraits of the Borromeos in a luxuriant but less contrived garden. Tiny **San Giovanni**, the third Borromean island, has a villa once owned by Toscanini, but is closed to the public.

When you tire of islands, you can take a cable car from Stresa up **Monte Mottarone**, hardly the most sensational of hills, but undeserving of Ruskin's derision – he called it "the stupidest of mountains" and thought the views of the Alps dull. Ruskin's mood, or the weather, must have been bad, for the views stretch from Monte Rosa, on the Val d'Aosta/Swiss border, across to the Adamello by Lago di Garda. Its wooded western slopes are now a favourite destination for family outings and at weekends the roadside is lined with avid picnickers. These apart, it's a pleasant and easy stroll down to small, but beautiful, Lago d'Orta (see below).

If you want to **sleep** in Stresa, the best deal is at the relatively unknown *Locanda del Baffo* (☎0323/30.507), Via Anna Maria Bolongar 57, with doubles at L28,000. Otherwise try *Mon Toc* (☎30.282) in Via Duchessa di Genova up the hill from the station, with doubles for L25,000. **Food** is good value at most of the *pensioni*, while the *Taverna del Papagallo*, Via Principessa Margherita 46, has reasonably priced pizzas.

Further north

BAVENO, north of Stresa along a villa-lined road, is a quieter resort with a beach backed by craggy mountains. Queen Victoria stayed at the Villa Clara (now Castello Branca) in 1879, establishing Baveno as a fashionable resort among the pre-jet set, although predictably it's now been colonised by British package operators. From here you can reach the tiny Lake Mergozzo, an arm of Maggiore, cut off from the rest of the lake by silt, or take the lovely road up to Monte Camoscio.

The best value **hotels** are *La Ripa* (☎0323/24.589), off the lakeside road driving into Baveno (booking vital), or the quiet, modern *Ortensie* (☎0323/24.502), open June to September; both charge L28,000 for a double.

Further up the lake is **PALLANZA**, which along with the industrial quarters of SUNA and INTRA makes up the town of **VERBANIA**, whose name recalls *Verbanum* – the name used by the Romans for the whole, verbena-shored lake. Verbania's winter climate is the mildest on the lake, which enabled a retired Scottish soldier, Captain Neil McEachern, to create in the Thirties the most botanically prestigious garden of all the lakes, at the **Villa Táranto** (April–Oct daily 8.30am–6.30pm; L1000). The grounds contain 20,000 species of plant, including giant Amazonian lilies, lotus blossoms, Japanese maple, and *melia azederach*, a sacred Indian tree, laid out with cool geometric accuracy around fountains and pools.

The eastern shore

There is little of great interest on the eastern side of the lake, although any of the smaller centres make feasible bases for the rest of the lake, or for hiking into the hills behind. The small resort of **MACCAGNO**, at the northern end, is undistinguished but fairly quiet, and has a **campsite** among trees on the waterfront used by dinghy sailors – *Camping Park* (☎0332/560.203; May–Sept only). There are also a couple of reasonably cheap **hotels** – *Pensione Paradiso* in Via Verdi (☎0332/560.128) has doubles for L28,000; slightly cheaper is the *Maccagno* (☎0332/560.141) on the main road, which charges L27,000 for a stark old-fashioned double. The best all-in deal is the *Italia* (☎0322/560.182) which does full board for L40,000.

LUINO, an industrial town and tourist centre, is marginally bigger than Maccagno, but as it's even less attractive there's little point in visiting unless it's to shop at its sizeable Wednesday market. Head instead to **LAVENO** (also accessible by car ferry from Intra) which specialises in bizarre attractions. At Christmas there's a floodlit underwater crypt, and, even if you're not into ceramics – its main industry – a visit to its entertainingly kitschy **museum** (daily 10am–noon and 2–6pm; L1000), 3km down the road at CERRO, is a must. The collection reaches the height of tastelessness in the gilded green aspidistra containers, a lavatory bowl decorated inside with pastoral scenes and an Art Nouveau bidet perched on a stand of leaves.

From Laveno a cablecar climbs up to the **Sasso del Ferro** for great views of the Alps. On its southern slopes, but visible only from the lake, is the **Santuario di Santa Caterina del Sasso**. In the early twelfth century a wealthy money-lender, Alberto Besozzi, was sailing on the lake when his boat sank. He prayed to Saint Catherine of Alexandria and was safely washed up on shore, afterwards giving up usury and becoming a hermit in a cave on the hillside. When his prayers averted a plague the locals built a church which became popular with pilgrims, especially after a boulder fell on the roof but was miraculously wedged just above the altar instead of the falling on the priest saying mass. The boulder finally crashed through in 1910, and the church remains closed for fear of further rockfalls.

Towards the foot of the lake, **ANGERA** is a sizeable village with a small, quiet beach dominated by an imposing twelfth-century castle, the **Rocca** (April–Oct 9.30am–noon & 2–5pm), more appealing for the character it gives the shore than for the self-congratulatory Visconti frescoes inside – battle scenes celebrating their seizure of the Rocca from the Torriani family. Little did the Viscontis know that just over 100 years later they would lose the castle to the pious and powerful Borromeo family, who ended up owning much of the lake and producing Milan's saint, Charles Borromeo.

Lago d'Orta

The locals call **Lago d'Orta** "Cinderella", capturing perfectly the reticent beauty of this small lake with its deep blue waters and intriguing island. Tourism, centring on Orta San Giulio, is fairly low-key, and although in high season the odd motor boat may shatter the peace, it's nothing compared to the international pizzazz of the larger lakes.

Orta San Giulio and the hinterland

The main town, **ORTA SAN GIULIO**, peaceful and traffic-free, rises up a wooded hill from its lakeside piazza, bordered by pastel-washed houses and pavement cafés, and the faded frescoed facade of its Palazzo Commune. Above the town is the **Sacro Monte**, 21 phoney Renaissance chapels dedicated to Saint Francis and containing some awful tableaux of painted terracotta statues acting out scenes from the saint's life against frescoed B-movie backgrounds.

Orta's **APT** is on Piazza Motta, up the hill from the Palazzo del Commune. **Accommodation** can be a problem in high season as there are few hotels – cheapest are *Amici Miei*, Via Olino 4 (☎0322/90.444), with doubles at L35,000, and *Antico Agnello* (☎90.259), off Piazza Motta, which has doubles without bath for L29,700 but is closed out of season. Life is easier for campers: there are three **campsites** nearby – *Orta* (☎0322/90.267), *Cusio*, near the train station (☎0322/90.290), and *Miami* (☎0322/90.197). Finding **cheap food** can also be a problem, especially out of season – the best bet is the pizzeria *Elesir Amaro* on Via Giacomo Giovanetti.

The villages above the town also have **places to stay**. There are three *locande* at **ARMENO**, at the foot of Monte Mottarone – *Madonna di Luciago* (☎0322/900.192), *Mottarone* (☎0322/900.195) and *Tre Montagnette* (☎0322/900.197). From here you can hitch or walk along the lovely road to **GIGNESE**, which has a **museum** (summer only) documenting the history of (believe it or not) the umbrella, and is connected by bus with Stresa on Lago Maggiore. More fun, walk up Monte Mottarone and take the cable car down to Maggiore.

Isola San Giulio

Orta's highlight is the **Isola San Giulio**, a tiny island-village dominated by a severe white seminary and the tower of its twelfth-century basilica. Steamboats leave every half-hour between 9am and 6.30pm from Orta San Giulio. The San Giulio of the town and island was a priest who in AD 390 decided to found a sanctuary on the island. The locals refused to row him over, as the island was supposedly seething with monsters and snakes, and Giulio is supposed to have crossed on foot using his staff as a rudder and his cloak as a sail. Once there, he banished the snakes, founded his sanctuary and earned himself a sainthood. The **Basilica** (Tues–Sun 9.30am–12.30pm & 2.30–7pm, Mon 2.30–7pm) has a redoubtable black marble pulpit, carved with venomous-looking griffons and serpents, recalling the myth. The massive vertebrae in the sacristry is said to have belonged to one of the island's dragons; scientists reckon it's a whalebone.

The Varesotto

The **Varesotto** is the least attractive but richest of the lake provinces – a major industrial region which produces everything from shoes and silk to helicopters. Its three lakes are badly polluted and, lying blandly on the plain, cannot compete with nearby Maggiore and Como for scenic splendour. The provincial capital, Varese, is worthy of a place on your itinerary only if you have to make train or bus connections, or want to visit the province's more interesting pickings at Castiglione Olona or Castelseprio.

Varese

VARESE is a gracious purpose-built town of gardens, marble Fifties villas and rectangular Fascist-era buildings, fringed with shoe factories. Its inhabitants are every bit as obsessed with style as the Milanese, and look almost as perfect as the window-display mannequins in the designer shops that line the main street, Corso Matteotti.

Centre of town is Piazza Monte Grappa, where there's an **AAST** office (Mon–Fri 8.30am–12.30pm & 2–6.45pm, Sat 9am–noon & 3–6pm). They may point you to the city's main attraction, the formal gardens (open until 5pm in winter and 6pm in summer) around the long, pink **Palazzo Estense**, built in the eighteenth century for the Este Dukes of Modena. Otherwise, if you're in Varese in April or October a considerable proportion of the crowds here will be Americans and Europeans come to attend the fashion shows of Milan; in fact the town's proximity to Milan means that most of its **hotels** are aimed at an expense account clientele. However, there are a couple of cheap options. The *Bologna* at Via Broggi 7, on the corner of Via G. Verati (☎0332/234.362), has doubles for L25,000. Further out, the *Stadio*, Via Bolchini 24 (☎0332/224.069), has rooms for up to four at L15,000 per head, and a restaurant next door that does a set meal for L9000.

Around Varese: Castiglione Olona and Castelseprio

One of the best excursions you can make from Varese is to **CASTIGLIONE OLONA**, a Renaissance-style village just twenty minutes by bus from Varese's Piazza Kennedy (#B45), built by Cardinal Branda Castiglione in the fifteenth century and inspired by the architecture he had seen in Florence. Masolino, a pupil of Masaccio, created the limpid frescoes you can see in the hilltop **Collegiata** and its **baptistry**. And there are more frescoes in the **Casa dei Castiglioni** on the sleepy main square, including one of Vezprem, Hungary, as described to Masolino by the cardinal, who was bishop there for a while. Castiglione Olona livens up on the first Sunday in the month, when an antiques market is held.

Further along the #B45 bus route, **CASTELSEPRIO** is less attractive but worth visiting for its intriguing seventh-century church, **Santa Maria Foris Portas**, which has exotic Byzantine-style frescoes of *Christ's Infancy*, discovered during the last war by a partisan hiding in the church.

North of Varese: hiking

More attractive than the three lakes near Varese is **Lago di Ghirla**, a tarn deep in a valley, the Valganna, near the Swiss border. There's a **campsite** on the side away from the B37 road and plenty of opportunities for stiff hikes.

If you're into walking, there are a number of country and forest **treks** to the north of Varese, the most interesting of which is the haul across to MACCAGNO on Lago Maggiore. The walk starts at PORTO CERESIO at the foot of Lago Lugano near the Swiss border and takes ten days; you could, though, pick it up at any point along the route. The booklet *Via Verde Varesina*, available only in Italian from local bookstores, is useful for information on how to get to starting-points on public transport, and for places to eat and stay over. The maps, however, are poor, and unless you can read its route descriptions you'll need to buy another.

Lago di Como

Of all the Italian lakes, it's the forked **Lago di Como** which comes most heavily praised. Wordsworth thought it "a treasure which the earth keeps to itself", though what he would think of the place now is anyone's guess: the lake is still surrounded by abundant vegetation but its sapphire waters are heavily polluted, and crowded with either elderly British package tourists or young Italian windsurfers. Its main centres have a distinct air of parochial England: there are Anglican churches, *belle epoque* villas and hotels with lush gardens in which you wouldn't be surprised to see the heroine of a nineteenth-century novel sketching beneath a parasol; less romantically, you'll also find toast and marmalade on many a breakfast menu.

Como Town

COMO is the least English of the resorts, juggling its traditional Campari elegance with the burger-and-shake culture of the windsurfers. Its position at the tip of the lake is picturesque enough, but as the nearest resort to Milan and a popular stopoff on the main road into Switzerland, it's both heavily touristed and, on the outskirts at least, fairly industrialised. The main industry is a rarefied one – Como is the main silk-supplier for Milan's fashion designers – but it doesn't make its factories any more endearing, and you may feel inclined to bypass the place altogether for one of the lake's more attractive resorts.

The Town

Historically, though, Como has much of interest, and it's worth spending a couple of hours checking out its two fine churches, before catching a boat elsewhere.

Lakeside Piazza Cavour, where you'll find the **APT**, is centre of the Como tourist scene. The punters sit outside the rip-off pavement cafés, looking out over the water, watching the steamers arrive and depart and vaguely gazing at the little white **temple** in the lakeside park to the left of the piazza. This is dedicated to Como's most useful son, Alessandro Volta, a pioneer in electricity who gave his name to the volt. If you're interested in such things, there are some of the instruments he used to conduct his experiments inside.

Afterwards, head up Via Plinio to the **Broletto**, prettily striped in pink, white and grey, and with a fifteenth-century balcony designed for municipal orators. Next door, the splendid **Duomo** was begun at the end of the fourteenth century and is reckoned to be Italy's best example of Renaissance-Gothic fusion, its fairy-tale pinnacles and rose windows contrasting with restrained Renaissance doors flanked by two honorary saints – the Elder and Younger Plinys, both of whom were born in Como. There was nothing unusual in the Christianisation of Classical figures in the Renaissance, but the presence, especially of Pliny Jnr, does seem somewhat inappropriate, since his only connection with Christianity was to order the assassination of two deaconesses.

The second of Como's churches, the Romanesque **Sant'Abbondio**, left along Via Regina from the main railway station, struggles to hold its own in a dreary industrial suburb. Built in the eleventh century, it was stripped of later encrustations in the nineteenth century and returned to its original simplicity. Once inside you can forget the brutal surroundings as you wander down the serene aisles to the apse with its colourful fourteenth-century frescoes, the most appealing of which depicts the Magi dreaming of Christ under striped and patterned blankets.

If you have time, head down to the shore to the right of Piazza Cavour and take a **funicular** (roughly every half hour) up to BRUNATE, a small hilltop resort with great views up the lake that's a good starting point for hikes.

Practical details

Como's smartness means that **cheap accommodation** is a problem. However, there's a **youth hostel** (open from 5pm, curfew 11pm; ☎031/558.722) at Via Bellinzona 2; take bus #1, #2 or #6 from the centre, or walk for twenty minutes left along Via Borgo Vico from the main train station. This is friendly and reasonably convenient, though it gets full in high summer. Officially it's closed between mid-November and mid-March, but you might get in if you're persistent. They also sell tickets for the local pool and hire out **bikes** at L5000 per day. A cheap alternative for **women** who can put up with a 10pm curfew (11pm in the summer and on Saturday) is the *Ostello per la Protezione della Giovane* (open from 5.30pm; ☎031/558.449) back down at Via Borgo Vico 182, which has doubles for L7000 a head.

Of the town's **hotels**, the *Sole*, Via Borgo Vico 91 (☎031/559.854), has clean doubles off a tiny old courtyard for L29,000. Other possibilities are the *Agnello*, Via Crespi 6 (☎031/263.336), beyond Como Lago station walking towards the funicular, with doubles for L30,000; or, just behind it, *Sant'Antonio*, Via Coloniola 10 (031/262.042), which is slightly smarter but charges only L28,000 a double. For a taste of fin-de-siècle gentility, the place to stay is the *Terminus*, Lungo Lario Trieste 14 (☎031/267.042), right on the lake front just east of Piazza Cavour. Rooms go for between L32,000 and L49,000 for a double at present, though renovation, and the raising of prices, is on the cards.

To mingle with the descendents of the Terminus' original clientele, head for Como's swankiest café-pasticceria, *Belli's* on Via Vittorio Emanuele, or for ice cream, *Bolla's* on Via Pietro Boldoni. For the rest, Como has some great, good value **trattorias and pizzerias** and, if your budget's really tight, a number of takeaways. *Il Golosone* on Via Bernardo Luini and *Geral's* in Via Bianchi Giovini are two of the best, while if you're yearning for junk food *Burgy's* in Via Plinio will fix you up with burgers and shakes. The *Grotta Azzuma*, Borgo Vico 161, is a good value pizzeria.

The western shore

The **western** shore of Lago di Como may no longer be as chic as when Greta Garbo stayed at the *Villa d'Este* hotel, near **CERNOBBIO**, the first port of call by steamer from Como. However, the hotel is still one of Europe's most luxurious, and it still manages to fill itself with guests willing to pay L500,000 a night for the chance to wander like Garbo among the statues, fountains and grottoes of its extravagant gardens.

Villa Pliniana and Isola Comacino

If your pockets aren't up to this, content yourself with glimpses of its gardens from the steamer. At **TORNO** on the other shore, where the steamer also stops, the **Villa Pliniana** was built in the sixteenth century on the site of one of Pliny the Younger's many villas. A spring behind it feeds a pool, and still gushes out at six-hour intervals as Pliny Jnr described it. Rossini composed here, and Shelley tried to rent the place, describing it as magnificent but in ruins with "ill-furnished apartments".

If you're not into villas, stay on the steamer until you reach **OSPIDALETTO**, from where boats cross to **Isola Comacino**, the lake's only island. Now virtually abandoned save for a few artists, this was a haven for political refugees during the Middle Ages, until the citizens of Como invaded and razed it to the ground. Today you can spend a pleasant few hours wandering among the ruins of its nine churches, but bring food, as the only restaurant is expensive.

The Tremezzina

Sheltered by a headland, the shore above Isola Comacina, known as the **Tremezzina**, is where Como's climate is at its gentlest, the lake at its most tranquil and the vegetation at its most lush. Lined with cypresses and palms, it's lovely at any time, but unbeatable in spring, awash with the colours of azaleas, rhododendrons, magnolias and camellias.

LENNO, in the south of the Tremezzina, is site of another of Pliny the Younger's villas, from which, he reported, he could fish from his bedroom window. Just inland at **MEZZEGRA** in 1944, two families of evacuees staying at the Villa Belmonte witnessed a rather different scene from their windows. A car drew up and a burly man in a black beret, nervously clutching the lapels of his coat, got out, followed by a woman and a tall pale man with a machine gun. The burly man was Mussolini, the woman his mistress, Claretta Petacci, and the tall man the partisan leader, Waltger Audasio. Audasio pulled the trigger and Claretta flew at him, grasping the barrel of the gun; Audasio shot twice more, but the trigger jammed. He took his driver's machine gun and pointed it at Mussolini who said "Shoot me in the chest"; Audasio shot first at Claretta, killing her outright, and then complied with Mussolini's last request.

More in keeping with the Tremezzina's usual character is the **Villa Carlotta** (April–Sept 9am–6pm; Mar & Oct 9am–noon & 2–4.30pm; L4000) between the next two steamer halts, **TREMEZZO** and **CADENABBIA**. These are the most English of Como's resorts, consisting almost entirely of villas and hotels, and suffocated by packaged tourists in season. Villa Carlotta, pink, white and Neoclassical, was built by a Prussian princess for her daughter, Carlotta, and now houses a collection of pompous eighteenth-century statues, by Canova among others, including a frieze of Alexander entering Babylon commissioned by Napoleon – though he was exiled before he could pay for it. The bill was picked up by a count, who in return got himself included as a member of Alexander's army (he's at the end, along with the artist). The villa's greatest attraction, however, is the fourteen-acre garden, a beautifully ordered collection of camellias, rhododendrons and azaleas.

Tremezzo has a couple of reasonable **hotels**, *La Darsena* (☎0344/40.423) right on the water's edge with doubles for L28,000 – their restaurant is good, so full-board at L32,000 is good value. About 3km up the hill, turning just by the petrol station, *Bel Sit* (☎0344/40.462) is indeed beautifully situated and has doubles at L36,500, though in season you need to have booked a long time in advance.

Further north, **MENAGGIO** is less geriatric than Tremezzo, and is a good choice if you want to do more than potter about; it's also a starting-point for trips to **LUGANO** in Switzerland (the round-trip currently costs L8000). There's a **youth hostel**, *La Primula*, at Via IV Novembre (☎0344/32.356) to the left of the main road as you approach from the south, with beds for L8000 a head: the rooms overlook the lake, and if it's full and the weather good you can sleep on the balcony. They also offer discounts on **windsurfer hire** and **swimming** at the local Lido, and have **maps of walks** in the local hills. Outside July and August the *Ristorante Alpino* on Via Carlo Comozzi (☎0344/32.082) has doubles at L26,000, or the *Lario* (☎0344/32.368), on the left as you enter the old town from the south, has doubles at L34,000. The best options for **eating** are the *Vapore*, just beyond the tourist office, or the *Trattoria da Gino*, much patronised by locals and with good food on a set menu for L13,500.

The north

The next major steamer stop is **GRAVEDONA**, not particularly pretty but one of the few towns on the lake as old as Como. Wordsworth set off on a moonlight hike from here, got lost and, stuck on a rock in the middle of nowhere, was unable to sleep because he was "tormented by the stings of insects". Medieval Gravedona, along with nearby Dongo and Sorico, formed part of an independent republic, victimised in the fifteenth century by the inquisitor Peter of Verona for daring to doubt that the pope was God's earthly representative. The people got rid of Peter by hacking him to death, but the pope rewarded him for his devotion to duty by swiftly canonising him and deeming him Patron of Inquisitors. There's a prophetic twelfth-century carving in the lakeside church of **Santa Maria del Tiglio** (open July–Sept, at other times get the key from the green house on the road) – a centaur pursuing a deer, an early Christian symbol for the persecution of the Church.

If you want to stay over, the *Locanda Serenella* (☎0344/80.060) and the *Serenella* **campsite**, beyond the church and down towards the lake, are open July to September. Beyond Gravedona the lake sides flatten out and the building gets more haphazard, although as the winds are good for **sailing** and **windsurfing** there are a number of **campsites** and cheap, modern **hotels** to the north of **DOMASO** – a not unattractive small town. There's also a **youth hostel** (March–Oct) down a side road immediately beyond the bridge, right on the water.

The eastern shore, Lecco and the central zone

The **eastern shore** of the lake, stretching from the flat marshes of the north to Como's left branch, **Lago Lecco**, overshadowed by the saw-like ridge of Monte Resegone, is often sunless and consequently less visited than the western shore. The triangle of land between the two branches – the **Central Zone** – is lusher and sunnier, busy on the coast but with plenty of quiet villages and three small lakes inland. There are fewer places to stay, however, and those that there are are not easily accessible, except Colico, Bellano and Varenna on the main shore and Bellagio on the central triangle, which are all served by steamer and hydrofoil.

The north

At the top end of the lake's eastern shore, **COLICO** is the final stop for Como steamers, a small industrial centre whose only attraction is a restored eleventh-century abbey, the **Abbazia di Piona**, on the tip of the promontory just above the steamer landing. From here, steamers and hydrofoils head back down the eastern shore, stopping off at **BELLANO**, a tiny town of silk and cotton mills, near to which is a steep gorge with walkways suspended above a roaring river (Easter–Sept Thurs–Tues 9.30am–12.30pm & 1.20–5.30pm).

Further south, **VARENNA** is the main village on the east shore. The gardens of its **Villa Monastero** (daily 9am–noon & 2–5pm, 7pm in high season) are less opulent and less visited than those on the west bank, with statues sheltered by citrus trees. Varenna's greatest attraction, however, is a natural one, the **Fiumelatte**, at 250m Italy's second shortest river, whose foaming waters are milk-white. Nobody has managed to discover the secret of its colour, nor why it suddenly begins to gush out at the end of March, and stops just as abruptly at the end of October. Another option, if you're feeling energetic, is to walk up to the **Castello di Vezio**, supposedly founded by the Lombard Queen Theodolinda, for tremendous views.

Hotels in Varenna are not cheap, but if you want to stay, the *Cavallino* by the steamer landing (0341/830.223) has doubles at L34,000, but there's little chance of a room in high season. The nearby *Olivedo* (☎0341/830.115) is more stylish but costs L43,000 for a double.

The central zone: Bellagio

The views from the triangle of land between the lake's two forks are superb, especially from Como's most refined resort, **BELLAGIO**, a small town of ochre-washed balconied hotels and a small sailing harbour backed by cypresses. The **Villa Serbelloni**, on the hill above, was built on the site of another of Pliny's, and is perhaps the best place to appreciate Bellagio's genteel English air. Now owned by the Rockefeller Foundation and used mostly for medical conferences, it was once a favourite haunt of European monarchs, and it's not hard to imagine them gliding among the grottoes and statues of the extravagant garden and gushing over the views of the two branches of the lake. The sumptuously frescoed interior is closed to visitors, but there are guided tours around the gardens at 10am and 4pm (except Monday) between April 15 and October 15. At the foot of the hill is a classy hotel, also called Villa Serbelloni, whose guests numbered Churchill, recovering from the war in late 1945, and John F. Kennedy. Close to Bellagio's Lido, the Neoclassical **Villa Melzi** contains a collection of Egyptian sculpture, and is surrounded by cypress terraces and exotic gardens.

Bellagio's best bet for affordable accommodation is the *Giardinetto*, Via Roncati 12 (☎031/950.168), with meticulously clean doubles for L30,000 and a garden where you can picnic. Or there's the *Roma*, Via Salita Grande 6 (☎031/950.424), with good views of the lake for a pricey L50,000; a triple without bath is L40,000.

Lecco

If you have to go to **LECCO**, approach it if you can by the early morning boat from Bellagio rather than by bus or train from Varenna or Bellano. As you sail into the Lecco fork the sun-soaked slopes of the west coast seem a world away, and Lecco's industrial spread broods in the shadows of plunging granite mountains. Not very enticing perhaps, but Lecco has the advantage of being close to some good hiking territory in the nearby mountains, and boasts good public transport connections. Trains run to Milan and Bergamo, and back up the eastern shore by way of Varenna, to Sondrio in the Valtellina. In the town most people pass the time in Lecco's **Basilica**, which boasts a set of fourteenth-century Giottesque frescoes, and the birthplace of Alessandro Manzoni, author of the great nineteenth-century novel *I Promessi Sposi* ("The Betrothed"). The **Villa Manzoni** on Via Amendola, is open as a museum (Tues–Sat 10am–12.30pm & 2.30–5.30pm, Sun 10am–3pm).

Above Lecco at the end of the road to MALNAGA a **funivia** – and paths #1, #7 and #18 – climb up to the **Piani d'Erna**, from where trails lead further into the mountains. Alternatively, buses from outside the train station run up to **Piani Resinelli**, another starting-point for hikes. The best place to stay if you are hiking is the **youth hostel** at Via Filanda 9 in the small village of Germandeo (☎0341/494.509) – close to the funivia and the beginnings of the Piani d'Erna trails. An alternative if you need a stopover in the centre is the hotel above the restaurant-bar *Brambilla* (☎0341/368.330) on Via Pescatori, off Via Corti (bus #1), where rather grimy doubles and triples cost L30,000. For **food**, the sandwiches and hot meals at the *Alpinista*, at the top of Via Fratelli Cairoli, are good value.

The Valtellina: Sondrio and Bormio

Unless you're a keen skier, or are heading for eastern Switzerland or Trentino, there's little to draw you to the **Valtellina**, one of Italy's less appealing Alpine valleys. Cut through by road and railway, it's mined for minerals and iron ore and is prone to landslides – the last, in 1987, partially destroyed the railway, killing several people.

The railway has since been reconstructed, and runs up from Lake Como to the region's main centre, **SONDRIO**, a modern and undistinguished town, well known for its wine, which is on sale in many of the shops. The **Museo Valtellinese** (Mon–Fri 9am–noon & 2.30–5pm) is a museum of local traditions, with small art and archaeological sections. But you'd do better to head straight for **BORMIO**, close to the Swiss and Trentino borders. Once an important stopover on the trade routes between Venice and Switzerland, this still retains cobbled streets and frescoed palaces from the fifteenth and sixteenth centuries. It's also a prestigious ski resort (it hosted the 1985 World Alpine Ski Championships) and one of Europe's largest areas for summer skiing. Close by, the huge national park, the **Parco Nazionale di Stelvio**, is a good place for walks and challenging climbs as well as skiing. For details contact the **AAST**, Via Stelvio 10. If you're keen to stay, most of the hotels are expensive, only the *Daniela* (☎0342/904.572) and *Serena* (☎0342/902.429) offering double rooms for less than L30,000.

Bergamo

Just 50km north of Milan, yet much closer to the mountains in look and feel, **BERGAMO** is a city with a split identity, made up of two distinct parts – **Bergamo Bassa**, the lower, modern centre, and **Bergamo Alta**, clinging to the hill 1200 feet above the Lombardian plain. Bergamo Bassa is no great shakes, a mixture of faceless suburbs and pompous Neoclassical town planning; but Bergamo Alta is one of northern Italy's loveliest city centres, a favourite retreat for the work-weary Milanese, who flock here at weekends seeking solace in its fresh mountain air, wanderable streets and the lively, easy-going pace of its life.

Bergamo owes much of its magic to the Venetians, who ruled the town for over 350 years, building houses and palaces with fancy Gothic windows, and adorning many a facade and open space with the Venetian lion – symbol of the republic. The most striking feature, however, is the ring of gated walls. Now worn, mellow and overgrown with creepers, these kept alien armies out until 1796, when French Revolutionary troops successfully stormed the city, throwing off centuries of Venetian rule.

Arriving and finding a place to stay

The **train station** is right at the end of Bergamo Bassa's central avenue, on Piazzale Marconi, with the **bus station** just to the right on Via B. Bono. Buses #1 and #3 run from Piazzale Marconi along the central avenue and up to Bergamo Alta. Alternatively you can get off the bus at the **funicular station** at the foot of the hill, and make the ascent by cable car for no extra charge. **Tickets**, as ever, should be bought before you get on the bus – they're on sale at the bag shop near the bus stop.

Unless you intend to explore the area around Bergamo, there's little point in visiting the **EPT** at Viale Vittorio Emanuele 4 (Mon–Fri 9am–12.30pm & 3–6.30pm, Sat 9am–noon), which has more information on the province than the town. Wait instead until you get to Piazza Vecchia in the heart of the upper city, where the **AAST** has maps and information on the city.

For a **place to stay**, there's a clean and modern **youth hostel** at Via G. Ferraris 1 (☎035/342.349; closed Nov 15–Feb 15), a fifteen-minute ride from Porta Nuova. Take bus #14, direction S. Colombana, and get off the stop after the modern church and the *Red Mountain* café. The price – around L8000 with a YHA card – includes a stingy breakfast, with unremarkable dinners at L7000 extra.

Bergamo's **cheaper hotels** are in Bergamo Bassa. Closest to the upper city is *Mammagrande*, Via N. Sauro 7 (☎035/218.413; bus #9a, #9b, #9c from Porta Nuova), near the Accademia Carrara, which has doubles for L23,000. Cheaper, with doubles for L20,000, is the *Antica Trattoria della Brianza*, Via Broseto 61a (☎035/253.338), a fifteen-minute walk to the west of the train station; bus #11 from Porta Nuova – get off at the Esso garage. Also west of the station is the *Valentina*, Via Quarenghi 35 (☎035/237.177), with doubles at L23,000, a friendly, family-run hotel with a pizzeria. Take Via Bonimelli from the station and walk for ten minutes. Closer to the station, though often fully booked, is the *Sant'Antonio*, Via Papa Giovanni 23 (☎035/210.284), which charges L26,000 for a double.

The City

However you get to Bergamo, you'll arrive in **BERGAMO BASSA**, which spreads north from the railway station in an uneasy blend of Neoclassical ostentation, Fascist severity and tree-lined elegance. At the heart of things, the mock-Doric temples of the **Porta Nuova** mark the entrance to **Sentierone**, a spacious piazza with gardens, surrounded by nineteenth-century arcades and frowned down upon by the **Palazzo di Giustizia**, built in the bombastic rectangular style of the Mussolini era. This is the liveliest part of the lower city, busy most of the day and especially during the evening *passeggiata*, but it has no great appeal, and you'd be wise to save your energy for **BERGAMO ALTA**, easily walkable utilising the **funicular** at the top end of Viale Vittorio Emanuele II, or by taking a #1 or #3 bus from the train station – both of which leave you on Piazza Mercato delle Scarpe.

Bergamo Alta

From Piazza Mercato delle Scarpe, Via Gombito leads up to **Piazza Vecchia**, enclosed by a harmonious miscellany of buildings, ranging from wrought-iron-balconied houses containing cafés and restaurants to the opulent Palladian-style civic library. Stendhal rather enthusiastically dubbed the square "the most beautiful place on earth", and certainly it's a striking open space, the most imposing building the medieval **Palazzo della Ragione**, a Venetian-Gothic style structure that stretches right across the piazza, lending a stagey feel to things, especially at night when the wrought-iron lamps are switched on. Court cases used to be heard under the open arcades that form the ground floor, and, following a guilty verdict, condemned criminals exhibited there. The piazza itself was scene of more joyous celebrations in 1797, when the French formed the Republic of Bergamo. A "tree of liberty" was erected, and the square, carpeted with tapestries, was transformed into an open-air ballroom in which – as a symbol of the new democracy – dances were led by an aristocrat partnered by a butcher.

To the right of the Palazzo della Ragione is the entrance to the massive **Torre della Civica**, which you can ascend by lift (Sat 10am–12.45pm & 3–5.50pm, Sun and holidays 10am–5.50pm). Its fifteenth-century bell, which narrowly escaped being melted down by the Germans to make arms during World War II, still tolls a 180-peal curfew at 10pm every night. Afterwards, walk through the palazzo's arcades to the **Piazzetta del Duomo** and the **Duomo** on the left – though this is of less interest than the church of **Santa Maria Maggiore** in front, a rambling Romanesque church garnished with a scalloped Gothic porch crowned by two loggias sheltering statues of saints. Inside, Santa Maria is an extraordinarily elaborate church, its ceiling marzipanned with ornament in the worst tradition of Baroque excess, encrusted with gilded stucco, painted vignettes and languishing statues. There's a piece of nineteenth-century kitsch too – a monument to Donizetti, the Bergamo-based composer of highly popular romantic comedies with memorable melodies and predictable plots who died from syphilis here in 1848. As the town's most famous son, his death was much grieved, and bas-relief *putti* stamp their feet and smash their lyres in misery over the event. More subtly, the intarsia landscapes on the choir stalls – designed by Lotto, and executed by a local craftsman – are remarkable not only for their intricacy, but for the incredible colour-range of the natural wood.

Even the glitziness of Santa Maria is overshadowed by the Renaissance decoration of the **Cappella Colleoni** next door. Built onto the church in the 1470s, the chapel is a gorgeously extravagant confection of pastel-coloured marble carved into an abundance of miniature arcades, balustrades and twisted columns, and capped with a mosque-like dome. Commissioned by Bartolomeo Colleoni, a Bergamo mercenary in the pay of Venice, it was designed by the Pavian sculptor Amadeo – responsible for the equally excessive Certosa di Pavia. The interior is almost as opulent, with a ceiling frescoed in the eighteenth century by Tiepolo sheltering Colleoni's sarcophagus, encrusted with reliefs and statuettes, and topped with a gleaming gilded equestrian statue. There's also the more modest tomb of his daughter, Medea, who died aged 15.

Take a look, too, at the nearby **Baptistery**, removed from the interior of Santa Maria Maggiore in the seventeenth century when christenings were transferred to the duomo. After some time in storage it was eventually reconstructed outside the **Aula della Curia** (Bishop's Court), to the right of the Capella Colleoni, which contains thirteenth- and fourteenth-century frescoes of the life of Christ, including an odd scene in which Christ judges the damned, holding a dagger, Damocles-like, in his teeth. Behind, at the back of Santa Maria Maggiore, is the bulging and recently restored **Tempietto di San Croce**, dating from the tenth century.

Leading out of Piazza Vecchia, **Via Colleoni** also remembers Bartolomeo Colleoni, a narrow street but one of the upper city's main pedestrian thoroughfares, lined with pastry shops selling marzipan birds (*ucelli*) and leading to the brink of Bergamo Alta. At no. 9–11 is a charitable institution set up by Colleoni to provide dowries for poor women – the Venetians ruled that no woman could marry without one – that now holds a small **museum** inside, open Wednesday from 10am until noon. At the end of Via Colleoni, Piazza Mascheroni lies at the entrance to the **Cittadella**, a military stronghold built by Barnabo Visconti that originally occupied the entire western headland. The remaining buildings now house a small theatre and two **museums**, of **archaeology** (Tues–Fri 9am–noon & 3–5pm, Sat 3–6pm) and **natural history** (Tues–Sun 9am–noon & 2–5pm) – both only of interest to specialists.

There are good views from here across the **Colle Aperto** (open hill) to Bergamo Bassa, though for really outstanding views you need to walk up to the **Castello** perched on the summit of San Vigilio, which rises up from Porto San Alessandro. A funicular operates in summer but the walk is pleasant, up a steep narrow road overlooking the gardens of Bergamo's most desirable properties, and past pricey bars and restaurants. The castle itself is closed for restoration, but you can get into the grounds, and there's a maze of underground passages to explore that used to run right down to Bergamo Alta.

Returning to the Colle Aperto, you can either walk back through the city, or follow the old **walls** around its circumference – the whole circuit takes a couple of hours. The most picturesque stretch is between the Colle Aperto and Porta San Giacomo, from which a long flight of steps leads down into the lower city. Alternatively, returning through the upper city to Piazza Mercato delle Scarpe, you can climb up to the grounds of the **Rocca**, where there's a small Unification museum – worth a look before delving into the twisting streets of the **medieval quarter** below.

The Accademia Carrara

Just below the upper town, close to the city walls, the **Accademia Carrara** (Wed–Mon 9.30am–12.30pm & 2.30–5.30pm; L2000) is one of Bergamo's most important sights, and among Lombardy's top quality collections of art. You can walk down here from the old city, along the steep Via Porta Dipinta and through the Porta Sant'Agostino, to see portraits by Pisanello and Botticelli, works by Giovanni Bellini and Crivelli, Carpaccio and Lotto – all carefully and imaginatively displayed with the layperson in mind. There are also paintings by the Lombard realists Foppa and Bergognone, Spanish-style portraits by Moroni, an elegant idealised *St Sebastian* by Raphael and canvases by Titian and Palma il Vecchio. Don't miss either the room dedicated to works by the twentieth-century Bergamo-born sculptor Giacomo Manzù, best known for his stylised bronzes of cardinals.

Eating and drinking

The cheapest place to **eat** in Bergamo is the *ACLI mensa* in the *Sant'Antonio* hotel basement, which charges L8000 for a full meal. Otherwise, restaurant prices tend to be aimed at well-heeled tourists, for whom one of Bergamo's attractions are the local bird specialities (hunting and eating the wildlife around Bergamo is a major local sport). If you're on a tight budget, the best bet is as ever takeaway pizza or a supermarket: there's a pizza place on Via Gombita and a large super-market on Via Tiraboschi near Porta Nuova. For sit-down eating, there's a self-service restaurant open lunchtimes only on Via San Alessandro, a steep street packed with birrerias and clothes shops, climbing from the lower to the upper city. Among ordinary restaurants you might try are *Trattoria Bernabo* on Piazza Mascheroni, outside the cittadella, which isn't too expensive; and Via Previtali, Via San Bernadino and Via Quarenghi, to the west of the train station, have a number of reasonably cheap pizzerias and trattorias. For entertainment while you eat or drink, the *Half Moon Video Bar* on Via N. Sauro (bus #9a, #9b or #9c from Porta Nuova) plays videos all night. For drinking in more traditional surround-ings head for the birreria on Piazza Mercato delle Scarpe.

Around Bergamo

Industrial development has done a pretty thorough job of ruining much of the countryside around Bergamo, particularly in the **Valle Seriana** northwest of the town, where factories and apartment blocks compete for space with forests and mountains, and rivers have been reduced to streams by hydro-electric power. Persevere, however: the upper reaches of the valley are still fairly unspoilt, and easily accessible by bus from Bergamo.

Clusone

CLUSONE is the first stop worth making, a picturesque hilltop village, whose **Chiesa dei Disciplini** (above the village centre, a ten-minute walk from the bus station) draws people from all over. There's little of interest inside the church, but the two fifteenth-century frescoes on its outside wall more than compensate – in a good state of repair and making a strong political statement beyond their obvious moral message. The upper fresco, *The Triumph of Death*, concentrates on the attitude of the wealthy towards death, with three noblemen returning from the hunt, discovering an open tomb containing the worm-infested corpses of the Pope and Emperor. A huge skeleton, representing Death, balances on the edge of the tomb, while other skeletons take aim at people gathered around the tomb – incorruptible figures, uninterested in the bribes being offered them. The *Dance of Death* below continues the moral tale, contrasting the corrupt upper classes with a procession of contented commoners, each dancing his way towards death quite happily, above an inscription inviting those who have genuinely served God to approach without fear and "join the dance".

Clusone itself is worth a wander, especially on Mondays when the steep curving streets are taken over by a market selling local sausage and cheeses. The **AAST** is on Piazza della Orologia, named for the fiendishly complicated sixteenth-century clock on the tower of the Palazzo Comunale. If you have the time and patience, you can work out the date, the sign of the zodiac, the duration of the night and the phase of the moon. The tourist office has information on local walks and hotels; of the five one-star hotels, the cheapest is the *Gamberino* on Via Cifrondi (☎0346/21.215).

Val Cavallina

From Clusone you can take a bus to Lago d'Iseo or further up the **Valle Seriana**, though this is of little interest unless you're a committed skier. Similarly the **Val Cavallina**, which has also suffered from industrial development, much of it ruined by small factories and tacky housing. The holiday area around Lago Endine isn't too bad, but you're more likely to pass through the valley only on your way up to Lago Iseo.

Beyond the lake, to the northwest, **Cantoniera della Presolana** is a large ski-resort with some swanky hotels, dating back to the turn-of-the-century. It has fifteeen slopes, an ice rink, ski and sled hire, and, surprisingly, a number of reasonable one-star hotels. **Val di Scalve**, beyond Presolana, is famous for the **Gorge of the Dezzo**, a narrow chasm forged by the torrents of the river Scalve, whose overhanging rocks are spectacular even if the river has been reduced to a miserable trickle by hydro-electric works.

Val Brembana

Northeast of Bergamo the **Val Brembana** follows a mountain-fringed route that was well-trodden in the Middle Ages by caravans of mules transporting minerals from the Valtellina to the cities of the plain. The road is now frequented mostly by weekend skiers heading up to FOPPOLO, and by less energetic Italians en route to **SAN PELLEGRINO TERME** to take the waters. San Pellegrino has been Lombardy's most fashionable spa since the turn-of-the-century, and it's from this period that its extravagant main buildings – the grand hotels and casino – date. When you tire of mock-Baroque, take the funicular up to **SAN PELLEGRINO VETTA** for fantastic views of the Alps.

Lago d'Iseo and the Val Camonica

Lago d'Iseo raises your expectations. Descending from Clusone, the road passes through steep gorges, thick forests and stark angular mountains, at the foot of which lies the lake. The fifth largest of the northern lakes, and the least known outside Italy, you'd imagine it to be more undiscovered than the others but the apartment blocks, harbourside boutiques, ice cream parlours and heavy industry of **LOVERE** put paid to any notions that Iseo might have escaped either tourist exploitation or industrialisation. This doesn't deter the Italians, who flock to Lago d'Iseo's resorts for its fish restaurants, watersports and low-key hikes, but unless any of these appeal, or you want to use it as a base for the ascent of Monte Gugliemo or for exploring the prehistoric rock carvings in the Val Camonica, there's little point in hanging around.

There is *one* retreat, the traffic-free **Monte Isola**, accessible by **ferry** (hourly) from Iseo town at the south of the lake. Italy's largest lake-island, over 3km long and rising to 600m, its attractively decaying villages are populated mostly by poets, artists and fishermen. As there's a large campsite, and space in its hotels for 200 people, you're unlikely to get much solitude in high season; but out of season it's well worth a visit, either to be utterly lazy or to take a walk right round the edge of the island, for great views across the lake. There are a couple of **cheap hotels**: the *Bellavista* (☎030/988.106) in the village of SIVIANO on the northwest corner of the island, with doubles at L26,000, and the *Castello* (☎030/988.154) at MENZINO in the southwest, with doubles for L30,000. The **campsite** is at CARZANO on the northeast tip of the island and is open year round.

The attractions of **ISEO** town are purely practical. **Trains** from Brescia stop here, as do buses, and there's a cheap hotel: the *Locanda Mirolte* (☎030/980.136) on Via Mirolte above the *Il Cenacolo* bar, with doubles for L21,000. Iseo's **AAST** has maps and details of walks, the most worthwhile of which is the hike from MARONE, halfway along the eastern side of the lake, up a steep and winding road to the village of ZONE. The reward is the extraordinary rock formations – soaring pinnacles formed by the erosion of the debris brought down by the glacier that gouged out the lake basin. If they look strangely familiar, it could be because Leonardo is said to have visited them, reproducing their peaks in his *Virgin of the Rocks* in the Louvre.

From Zone a track leads up to **Monte Gugliemo** (1949m), the ascent taking about three and a half hours. There's a *rifugio* near the summit: ask around in Zone before you leave to check it's open; if the warden's not there you'll be given the key.

Val Camonica: prehistoric rock carvings

Like Lago d'Iseo, the **Val Camonica** would be outstandingly beautiful were it not for the indiscriminate scattering of light industry that mars its lower reaches. Road and railway run up from the lake, following the river Oglio through the spa town of BOARIO to **CAPO DI PONTE**, whose **National Park** (Tues–Sun 9am–sunset; L2000), a fifteen-minute walk from the town, contains prehistoric rock carvings spanning an incredible 8000 years – remnants from the culture of the Camuni tribe who holed up here to escape northern invaders from 5000 BC until the Romans colonised the area several thousand years later, together with the even older works that inspired the Camuni's art. There are carvings throughout the valley, but the most concentrated group is in the park, beginning with the **Great Rock** in front of the site's shop, where a set of stick-and-blob figures gives a taste of Camuni life over a 1000-year period. There are hunters, agricultural workers, a religious ceremony presided over by priests, and a Bronze Age burial in which the corpse is surrounded by his weapons and tools. To see how the civilisation developed into the Iron Age, head for Rock 35, carved with a blacksmith, and Rock 23, with a four-wheeled wagon transporting an urn. Carvings in other parts of the valley include some in the hamlet of **BEDOLINO** outside **CEMMO**, about 2km above Capo di Ponte on the other side of the Oglio, where there's a rock with a carving of a **Bronze Age map** showing huts, fields, walls, streams and canals.

Brescia and around

BRESCIA is unfairly famed for two things: its arms industry, and a piazza reckoned to be Fascism's most chilling and brutal piece of town planning. Unsurprisingly, it's not the kind of city that's on most travellers' itineraries – most are in a hurry to get to Venice or up to the lakes. But there is more to Brescia than its reputation might lead you to expect – a substantial Roman temple, a generous sprinkling of medieval and Renaissance buildings and a stunningly simple Romanesque cathedral. It also has a slick and energetic streetlife, at its best on Corso Palestro during the evening *passeggiata*, that points to Brescia's status as one of the wealthier Italian cities.

Arriving, getting around and sleeping

Brescia is on the main Milan–Verona railway line, giving you access to the cities of the Veneto, as well as those of Lombardy. Local trains run up to Lecco, Lago d'Iseo, and the Camonica valley, and there's also a daily train to Pisa. The rest of the province, including the main resorts of Garda and several more distant destinations, is covered by direct buses, which leave from the two bus terminals outside the **train station** – south of the centre, a short bus ride or fifteen-minute walk from the city centre. For information, use the **EPT** office at Corso Zanardelli 34 (Mon–Thurs 8.30am–12.30pm & 3–6.30pm, Fri 8.30am–12.30pm & 3–5pm).

Brescia has plenty of hotels, but the best deal for **women only** is at a convent at Via Fratelli Bronzetti 17 (☎030/55.837), though this has a 10pm curfew; the advantages, however, are that it's convenient and you have access to a kitchen. The cheapest ordinary **hotel**, *Ai Giardini*, Via Rubuffone 13 (☎030/292.250), has doubles for just L14,000 but is some way out – take bus #Q from the train station or any that runs through Porta Venezia. Other hotels include the *Calzavellia* on Via Calzavellia, off Corso Mameli (☎030/43.341), the *Cavallino* at Corso Garibaldi 31 (☎030/40.213), or, nearer the station, the *Albergo Stazione* on Vicolo Stazione off Viale Stazione (☎030/52.128) – all of which have rooms for under L30,000.

The City

Brescia's centre is grouped around the four piazzas beyond the main Corso Palestro. **Piazza Mercato** is a sprawling cobbled square of more interest to the stomach than the eye – there's a weekday market, a supermarket, and small shops selling local salamis and cheeses nestling under its dark porticoes. **Piazza Vittoria** is quite different, a disquieting reminder of the Fascist regime embodied in the oppressive austerity of Piacentrini's gleaming marble rectangles. Behind the belittling facades lie the **post office** to the north, a **bank** to the south and, in the arcades, boutiques, *gelaterie* and *pasticcerie*, ensuring that the square is well-frequented in the *passeggiata* hour.

Alongside the post office, Via 24 Maggio leads to Brescia's pretttiest square, **Piazza della Loggia**, dating back to the fifteenth century, when the city invited Venice in to rule and protect it from Milan's power-hungry Viscontis. The Venetian influence is clearest in the fancily festooned **Loggia**, in which both Palladio and Titian had a hand, and in the **Torre dell'Orologio**, modelled on the campanile in Venice's Piazza San Marco. On the top left-hand corner is the **Porta Bruciata**, a defensive medieval tower-gate that was the scene in 1974 of a Red Brigade attack in which eight people were killed and over a hundred injured.

At the other side of Porta Bruciata, a small side street leads to **Piazza del Duomo**, one of the few squares in Italy to have two cathedrals – though, frankly, it would have been better off without the second, a heavy Mannerist monument that took over 200 years to complete. The old twelfth-century cathedral, or **Rotonda**, is quite a different matter, a simple circular building of local stone, whose fine proportions are sadly difficult to appreciate from the outside as it is sunk below the current level of the piazza. Inside, glass set into the transept pavement reveals the remains of Roman baths (a wall and geometrical mosaics) and the apse of an eighth-century basilica which burned down in 1097. Most interesting is the fine red marble tomb of Berardo Maggi, a thirteenth-century Bishop of Brescia, opposite the entrance, decorated on one side with a full-length relief of the cleric, on the other by reliefs showing other ecclesiasts and dignitaries processing through a lively crowd of citizens to celebrate the peace Maggi had brought to the town's rival Guelf and Ghibelline factions.

Behind Piazza del Duomo, Via Mazzini leads to Via Musei, along which lie the remains of the Roman town of *Brixia*, though there's not a lot to see. There's a **theatre**, currently in the process of excavation and visible only through a wire fence. But the most substantial monument is the **Capitolino** (Tues–Sun 10.15am–1pm & 2–6pm), a Roman temple built in AD 73, now partially reconstructed with red brick. Behind the temple are three reconstructed *celle*, probably temples to the Capitoline trinity of Jupiter, Juno and Minerva, which now house fragments of carved funerary monuments and mosaic pavements. Look also at the excellent **museum** upstairs, which has a well displayed collection of jewellery, glassware, sculptures and bronzes, fragments of mosaic pavements and a life-sized winged Victory.

Further along Via dei Musei, the **Abbey of San Salvatore** thrived from the eighth to the eighteenth century and now contains a **modern art gallery** in its main building and a **museum of Christian Art** in its church of **Santa Giulia**. The latter is currently only open for temporary exhibitions, but its prize exhibits include a fourth-century ivory chest carved with lively biblical scenes and an eighth-century crucifix presented to the convent by Desiderius, King of the Lombards – made of wood overlaid with silver and encrusted with over 200 gems and cameos. Look also at the remains of the Byzantine **Basilica of San Salvatore**, visible through a glass screen at the back of the church.

Behind the museum, Via Piamarta climbs up the **Cydnean Hill**, the core of early Roman *Brixia*, mentioned by Catullus, though again the remains are scanty. There are a few fragments of a gate opposite the sixteenth-century church of **San Pietro in Oliveto**, so-called because of the olive grove surrounding it, and the hill itself is crowned by the **Castello** – a monument to Brescia's various over-lords, begun in the fifteenth century by Luchino Visconti and added to by the Venetians, French and Austrians over the years. The resultant confusion of towers, ramparts, halls and courtyards makes a good place for an atmospheric picnic, and holds Italy's largest **museum of arms**, a **model railway museum** and a small **zoo**.

More appealing perhaps is Brescia's main art gallery, the **Pinacoteca Tosio-Martinengo** (Tues–Sun 10.15am–1pm & 2–6pm; L2000), though its collection is mainly made up of the works of minor local artists. The works of the sixteenth-century artist, Romanino, are worth a look, heavily influenced by Titian – as are those of the seventeenth-century realist Ceruti, who, unusually for his time, specialised in painting the poor (see *Milan*, the Accademia Brera).

Eating, drinking and nightlife

Brescia is well endowed with **restaurants**, though none are especially cheap. If you're flat broke, *BarBar*, opposite the Rotonda, is a good place to fill up on bar snacks for free; and there is a good concentration of pizzerias and takeaways on Corso Mameli, near the university. *Bersaglieri*, on Corso Magenta, is the city's best pizzeria, cheap and with vegetarian pizza on a wholemeal (*integrale*) base; while for a relatively unusual evening meal there's the natural (not vegetarian) food at *Altamira*, just off Piazza Duomo.

For **evenings** there are plenty of bars and ice cream parlours around the centre, after which the best place to hit is the *Arancia Meccanica* (Clockwork Orange), a student hangout on Via Sovera at the start of Corso Mameli, which has live music most Friday nights.

Around Brescia

With Lago di Garda and the mountains of Val Trompia so easily accessible from Brescia, there seems little point in making do with the distinctly run-of-the-mill attractions of the countryside closest to the city. But if you're keen on wine you might want to make for the area between Brescia and Lago d'Iseo, known as the **Franciacorta** – a hilly wine-producing district, rising from the bland built-up lowlands around the city, that got its name from the religious communities that lived there from the eleventh century onwards. These communities and their land were exempt from tax and known as the *Corti Franche*, or free courts. The wine-producers soon moved in, attracted by the possibility of owning vineyards in a duty-free haven, and though the Franciacorta is no longer tax-free, the extremely drinkable, if little-known wine continues to flow – and is available from shops all over the region.

With a further half-day to spare in Brescia, you could also head out to the **Badia di Rodengo** (daily 9am–noon & 3–6pm, until 8pm in summer), just outside the village of the same name, which has a sumptuously frescoed church, with some gorgeous stucco-work and a generous dash of trompe l'oeil, and another room decorated with scantily-clad figures surging into a cloudy heaven. The most interesting thing about a visit here is the insight you get into the lives of the five monks who live here – their primitive kitchen, tatty library and silently austere corridors. Entrance is free, although if Don Antonio shows you round he'll probably ask you to send him stamps for his collection; if you wish, the

Getting to the abbey, bear in mind that express buses take the autostrada – keep a sharp lookout for the yellow signs as the drivers are apt not to stop; the abbey is a ten-minute signposted walk from the bus-stop. If your bus is a local one, get off in Rodengo village centre and walk back along the main road towards the motorway.

monks will put you up and feed you for no charge, although you should bear in mind that they're pretty poor themselves.

Val Trompia, Lago d'Idro and Lago di Ledro

You may be able to ignore the arms industry in Brescia, but its impact is unavoidable when you pass through the **Val Trompia**, directly north of the city. The industry dates back over 400 years, started by the Venetians, keen to utilise the rich iron ore deposits of the area, to whom it became so indispensable that during the sixteenth century restrictions were actually placed on people's movements out of the region. The centre of today's (much diminished) arms industry is **GARDONE VAL TROMPIA**, where the *Beretta* company has its headquarters.

The valley beyond Gardone is crammed with industry as far as LAVONE, and hiking becomes a possibility only at **BOVENGNO**. From this small village paths lead up to Monte Muffetto (4hr) and, even better, to Monte Crestoso and its tiny tarns (5hr 30min), though you'll need a tent, as there are no *rifugi*. If you're without a tent, there are two *rifugi* further on – *Croce Domini* (1992m) at the head of the valley, and *Bonardi* (1743m) above the lovely Passo del Maniva. From either base you can walk down to Lago d'Idro or climb Monte Colombino, again with a couple of tarns. The map to get is the *Kompass* Carta Turistica, *Le Tre Valli Bresciane*. There are also a few cheap hotels at the ski resorts of COLLIO and SAN COLUMBANO, with doubles at around L20,000; if its not full, the tiny *Belvedere* (☎030/927.259) has doubles for just L13,000.

From close to the *rifugio Croce Domini* a steep track climbs over into the broad Valle della Berga and up to **BAGOLINO** on the road to Lago d'Idro. Bagolino is quiet, preserving many of its medieval houses and a church, **San Rocco**, that has a startlingly realistic cycle of fifteenth-century frescoes. If you want to avoid Idro's unremarkable resorts, this is the place to stay: the *Cavallino* hotel (☎0365/99.103) has doubles for L34,000, and buses run reasonably frequently to and from the lake.

LAGO D'IDRO is a reasonably pretty lake, except for its marshy upper reaches where the effect is spoiled by a sand-dredger. Tourism is family-orientated, but as there's no road running along the upper reaches of the east shore, you should be able to find a quiet beach there. Although bathing in the lake is thought to induce a skin-rash, few people are able to resist its cool, clear waters; there are also walks in the area if you want to do more than swim and laze around. Marked paths climb up into the hills from the east shore, and from ANFO on the west shore a track leads past the *rifugio Rosa di Baramone* to Bagolino. Again, you'll need the Kompass map mentioned above.

Idro's resorts are uniformly bland, but if you want to stay over, *Da Parida* (☎0365/809.026) at ANFO has doubles for L26,000, and *Miralago* (☎0365/83.138) at CRONE, on the bus route, 2km from Idro town, charges around the same. Of the **campsites**, the most convenient are the two at Anfo and a couple at Vantone on the east shore – both on the bus route from Brescia.

Northeast from Ildro, via Ponte Caffaro, you reach the point where the Austrian border ran through until 1918. From here a road leads to **Lago di Ledro** in the Val Sabbia, only 2km long and slightly less wide, and with a beauty straight out of a Swiss-kitsch postcard. Quieter than Ildro, and far preferable, there are a couple of **campsites** here and a hotel, the **Mezzolago** (☎0464/508.181), which charges L40,000 for a double room and is open all year.

Lago di Garda

Lago di Garda is the largest and least polluted of the Italian lakes, and also the most popular. Tourism is relatively recent – beginning only this century when the road around its shores was completed – and it has little of the precious respectability that hangs over the Victorian-era resorts of Como and Maggiore. Indeed, the only celebrity English visitor to spend much time around the lake was D.H. Lawrence, whose *Twilight in Italy* details many of the lake's attractions.

For all that, Lake Garda is now firmly entrenched in the pages of UK tour brochures, and its resorts each year invaded by a fair number of packaged Brits, as well as Germans, French and Italians attracted by the great windsurfing and Garda's gentle climate. Winters are mild, summers tempered by breezes – the northern *sover*, which blows down the lake from midnight and through the morning, and the *ova*, blowing from the south in the afternoon and evening. Along the so-called Riviera Bresciana, on the most sheltered stretch of the western shore, are lush groves of olives, vines and citrus trees – fruits used for Garda's main products: olive oil, citrus syrups and *Bardolino*, *Soave* and *Valpolicella* wines. Scenically the shores of the lake are extremely varied: the rich vegetation of its middle reaches gives way to the rugged north, where the lake narrows and is tightly enclosed by craggy mountains; the southern shores, 16km at their widest, are backed by a gentle plain.

Desenzano, Sirmione and the southern shore

Within easy striking distance of the Milan–Venice autostrada and railway, the **southern shore** of Lake Garda is predictably well-touristed. **DESENZANO DEL GARDA**, the lake's largest town, is a major railway junction and the best starting-point for visiting Garda. But it has little to detain you: buses out tend to connect with trains, and there are several ferries daily to Riva on the northwest corner of the lake.

A short but infrequent train-ride from Desenzano, **SAN MARTINO DELLA BATTAGLIA** was the site of a famous battle, when Napoleon III and Vittorio Emanuele II defeated the Austrians in 1859. The **Torre di San Martino** (summer Wed–Mon 9.30am–1pm & 2–7pm; winter 9.30am–12.30pm & 1.30–5pm) was built in 1893 to commemorate the victory, and has paintings and sculptures of the leading figures plus a good view of the battlefield and Lake Garda from the top. Behind it is a battle museum.

Horrified by the extent of the slaughter, a Swiss man, Henry Dunant, was inspired to found the Red Cross, writing a short book, *A Memory of Solferino* suggesting the formation of "relief societies for the purpose of having care given to the wounded in wartime, by zealous, devoted and thoroughly qualified volunteers". Dunant bankrupted himself over founding the Red Cross, and was discovered in the last years of his life in a home for impoverished men. He was awarded the first ever Nobel prize, but never moved from the home. There's a monument to Dunant and the Red Cross 11km southeast of San Martino, at **SOLFERINO** – a paved path along the crest of the hill lined with tablets set into a wall, bearing the names of countries who ratified the Geneva convention. There are also good views from the nearby fortress, and a small **museum** (same hours as Torre di San Martino) of battle memorabilia on the fringes of the village.

Sirmione and around

Back on the shore, **SIRMIONE**, spread along a narrow promontory protruding
4km into the lake, is a more popular spot, in a beautiful setting, though it's these
days suffocated with luxury hotels, souvenir stands and lots of tourists. You're
unlikely to want to stay, and in any case most of the hotels are pricey and usually
full, but it's worth a brief visit to take in the town's handful of sights and laze
around on the surrounding lidos.

Most people make straight for the **Rocca Scaglieri** (daily, summer 9am–1pm
& 3.30–8.30pm; winter 10am–7pm), a fairytale castle with boxy turreted towers
almost entirely surrounded by water, named after the Veronese Scaglieri family
who built it in the thirteenth century when they ruled Garda. There's not much to
see inside, and although the views from its battlements are lovely, they don't
warrant the steep entrance fee.

You can escape the crowds by walking out beyond the town to the peninsula's
triangular and traffic-free hilly head, covered in cypresses and olive groves. The
church of San Piero here has thirteenth-century frescoes inside, and its shady
grounds make for a good picnic-stop. There's also a **lido** on the eastern shore
below the church, and good swimming from the rocks on the west shore.

At the tip of the promontory is the so-called **Grotte di Catullo** (Tues–Sun
9am–sunset). Though touted as Catullus' villa, the white ruins are actually of a
Roman spa: there's a hot sulphur spring 300m under the lake, and people still
come to Sirmione to take the waters. Catullus did, however, retire to the town,
coming all the way from the Black Sea by boat, hauling it overland when necessary so that he could keep it on the lake. The ruins, scattered on the hillside
among ancient olive trees, are lovely, and there are superb views across the lake
to the mountains. There's a small antiquarium with fragments of mosaics and
frescoes, and below the site, a beach.

If you do want to stay in Sirmione, booking ahead is essential in July and
August. If you haven't booked, the **AAST** at Viale Marconi 2 has a list of **rooms** to
rent, but don't count on these being free either. Of the **hotels**, the *Risorgimento*
(☎030/916.325) and *Speranza* (☎030/916.116) on Via Vittorio Emanuele are
centrally located near the castle, and have doubles for around L25,000 out of high
season; *Lo Zodiaco*, Via XXV Aprile 18 (☎030/916.095), a five-minute walk from
the tourist office, has a lakeside garden and doubles from L25,000 to L29,000
depending on the season. The nearest **campsite** is the *Sirmioncino* (☎030/
919.045), a fifteen-minute walk along Via Colombare out of town towards the
mainland – though this too (and its nearby beach) gets extremely crowded.

The western shore

Less built-up, and with reputedly cleaner water than the northern reaches of the
lake, the lower reaches of the **western shore** are studded with campsites which
make for cheap and reasonably convenient bases. If you're not heading for the
campsites, only **SALÓ** is worth a stop, splendidly sited on a bay at the foot of the
luxuriant Riviera Bresciana and a good place to stock up on local produce. Saló
gave its name to Mussolini's short-lived last republic, instituted here after his
rescue from the Abruzzi by the Nazis, but there's not a lot to see in the town.
Better to detour 6km inland to **PUEGNAGO DEL GARDA**, where you can
sample the rose wines – *Grapello* and *Chiaretto* – the **Comincioli** vineyard has
been producing since the sixteenth century.

Gardone Riviera: Il Vittoriale and the village of San Michele

A few miles further up the shore **GARDONE RIVIERA** was once the most fashionable of Garda's resorts, and still retains its symbols of sophistication, though the elegant promenade, lush gardens, opulent villas and ritzy hotels now have to compete with some more recent – and less tasteful – tourist tack. It is famous for the consistency of its climate, and has Garda's most exotic botanical garden, the **Giardino Botanico Hruska** (daily, 8am–7pm; shorter hours in winter), laid out among artificial cliffs and streams.

Highlight of Gardone, and indeed of the whole lake, is **Il Vittoriale** (Tues–Sun 9am–12.30pm & 2–5.30pm; L6000): home of Italy's most notorious and extravagant twentieth-century writer, Gabriele D'Annunzio. Born in 1863, D'Annunzio was no ordinary writer. He did pen some exquisite poetry and a number of novels. But he became better known as a soldier and socialite, leading his own private army and indulging in much-publicised affairs with numerous aristocrats. Later he became a fervent supporter of Mussolini, providing the Fascist party with their (meaningless) war-cry, *eia! eia! alalá*, though Mussolini eventually found his excessive exhibitionism an embarrassment (his boasts of eating dead babies, certainly, were bad publicity), and in 1925 presented him with this villa – ostensibly as a reward for his patriotism, in reality to shut him up.

It didn't take D'Annunzio long to transform Mussolini's Liberty-style gift into the Hollywood studio lookalike you see now. Outside, rammed into the cypress-covered hillside, is the prow of a battleship used in D'Annunzio's so-called "Fiume adventure". Fiume (now Rijeka), on the North Adriatic, had been promised to Italy before they entered World War I, but was eventually handed over to Yugoslavia instead. Incensed, d'Annunzio gathered together his army, occupied Fiume, and returned home a national hero. Inside the villa, you have to take a **guided tour**. These are in Italian only, but the building really speaks for itself, D'Annunzio's personality making itself felt from the start in the two reception rooms – one a chill and formal room for guests he didn't like, the other warm and inviting for those he did. Il Duce was apparently shown to the former, where the mirror has an inscription reputedly aimed at him – "Remember that you are made of glass and I of steel".

Nor was dining with D'Annunzio a reassuring experience: roast baby may not have featured on the menu, but in the glitzy dining room pride of place was given to a gilded and embalmed tortoise who had died of overeating as a warning to greedy guests. In fact D'Annunzio rarely ate with his guests, retreating instead to the *Sala di Lebbroso* where he would lie on a bier surrounded by leopard skins and contemplate death. The rest of the house is no less bizarre: the bathroom has a bathtub hemmed in by over 2000 tacky pieces of bric-a-brac; and the *Sala del Mappamondo*, as well as the huge globe for which it is named, contains an Austrian machine-gun and books including an immense version of *The Divine Comedy*. Suspended from the ceiling of the auditorium adjoining the house is the biplane which D'Annunzio used in a famous flight over Vienna in World War I.

Up in the mountains behind Gardone is the little Alpine village of **SAN MICHELE**. There are six buses daily from Gardone and Saló, but as the views along the road are splendid, it's worth walking. The *Colomber Hotel* (☎0365/21.108), 500m inland, is a good base if you want to do some walking to the springs and waterfalls in the surrounding hills. Doubles with bath cost L34,000. The owners will give some suggestions for **walks**, but for more ambitious hikes, there are maps with footpaths available from *CAI*, Via San Carlo 17, in Saló.

Gargnano and the north

GARGNANO, a twenty-minute bus-ride from Gardone, was during 1944 the headquarters of Mussolini's impotent Republic of Saló – a puppet government set up by the Nazis after they had rescued the Duce from his mountaintop prison in the Abruzzi. The Germans were fearful that Rome might fall to the Allies at any moment, and installed Mussolini this far north for safety. However, by this time the dictator had lost all credibility and he soon sank into depression, and although he installed his mistress, Claretta Petacci, in nearby Il Vittoriale, the cold, damp rooms and heavy Nazi presence in the woods outside put paid to any passion.

Gargnano is more a working town than a resort, with a thirteenth-century church, **San Francesco**, its main sight. The columns in the cloisters are carved with citrus fruits – a reference to the fact that the Franciscans were credited with introducing the cultivation of citrus fruit to Europe.

There are citrus groves aplenty at **LIMONE SUL GARDA**, creating a luxuriant setting for a resort much frequented by packaged tourists. Modern hotels compete with the red-roofed houses of the old town, but its 3km-long beach and relatively cheap one-star hotels could well persuade you to stay. Cheapest are *Degli Ulivi* (☎0365/954.032) and *Monte Baldo* (☎0365/954.021) with doubles for L22,000, but if you arrive in high season, the best bet is to head straight for the **AAST** at Via Mons D. Camboni 15. There's also a **campsite**, *Nanzel*, on the water's edge.

At the northwest tip of the lake, **RIVA DEL GARDA** is the best known of the lake's resorts. The old town is pretty, a maze of cobbled streets and squares, but it's been vastly overdeveloped, with a long string of modern characterless hotels cluttering the shore to the south. Popular and lively, it's much used by UK tour companies as well as Italian windsurfers. There's little point in going unless you're into watersports, or want to use it as a cheap base for exploring the lake and the northern hinterland. As for things to see, the town's most distinctive sight is a severe twelfth-century moated castle (Tues–Sun 9am–noon & 2.30–6pm) housing a small **museum** with a modest collection of prehistoric and Roman finds.

Riva does have one cheap place to stay in its **youth hostel**, Piazza Cavour 10 (☎0464/554.911) – open from the beginning of March to the end of October, with beds for L7000. There are also double beds for about L28,000 at the *Trieste*, Via Fiule 15–17 (☎0464/552.653), or *Villa Minerva*, Viale Roma 40a (☎0464/553.031). A good place to **eat** is the *Vaticano* at Via Santa Maria 8, or there's a vegetarian and macrobiotic restaurant, *Il Tangram*, in Via Don Porto – a little road north of Viale N. Pernici.

The eastern shore

Overlooked by the mountains of the Monte Baldo chain, the main resorts of Garda's **eastern shore** are heavily touristed. But it's worth putting up with the crowds at Torbole if you're a keen windsurfer, while Malcesine has a lovely old centre, and is a good base for escapes by bike or on foot into the mountains. Further south, there is little to appeal: Garda has some old palaces and narrow cobbled streets, but is pleasant only in the early morning when there are just fisherman about. Bardolino, further south, has little other than its famous wine to recommend it.

Torbole

TORBOLE, at the top of the lake, played an important role in the fifteenth-century war between the Viscontis and the Venetians, when a fleet of warships was dragged overland here and launched into the lake. Nowadays it's still the water that dominates. The town – and its *Circolo Verlico* (daily 9am–5pm) – is the centre of Garda's windsurfing scene, with plenty of opportunities for hiring equipment and taking lessons. The **AAST**, on the lake front south of the old port, has full details, but one place you might try is the *Surfcenter Camping Al Port* (open May–Oct). A week's use of a windsurfer and dinghy will set you back about L150,000. If you want to stay there are plenty of **hotels**. The *Nataly*, at the back of Piazza Alpini, has doubles from L25,000, and facilities include a sauna. *Pensione Ischia*, Via Matteotti 24, has a garden with lemons and vines and charges L34,000 for a double. There are also numerous **campsites**.

Malcesine

Backed by green slopes, **MALCESINE**, 14km further south, has a rather different feel, a sedate little town most popular with the over-fifties, many on UK packages. The old town, with its colour-washed palazzi and cobbled streets, is one of Garda's most appealing, though it has its inevitable share of modern hotels, bars and restaurants. Rising straight up from the water is a thirteenth-century turreted **Rocca** (summer daily 9am–1pm & 3–8pm; winter weekends only), built like Sirmione's by the Scaglieri family and worth visiting for its small museum and the views from its tower. For more extensive views, take the **funicular** up 2000-metre-high Monte Baldo: if you're there in winter a chair-lift and six ski-lifts service 11km of ski slopes.

The **AAST** in Via Capitanato, running north along the lake from the port, has maps of signposted walks in the hills behind. Another way of exploring the mountains is by bike – *Ciclo Baldo* at the top of the Monte Baldo funicular rent mountain bikes, rucksack, picnic and insurance for L30,000; from here you can do a panoramic ride down the hill in four to six hours.

Most **accommodation** in Malcesine gets swallowed up by package companies, so the choice is limited. *Garni Catullo* in Via Francesco e Giovanni Priori (☎045/740.0352) has doubles with bath for L34,000, as does *Casa Gaby* (☎045/740.0288) – signposted up a steep path from the main road north along the lake. **Cheap food** is also hard to come by, but *La Pace* overlooking the old port has main courses for L10,000 and under, while the *Pizzeria Da Gigi*, on the main road to the south of the centre, is also good value.

travel details

Trains

From Milan Centrale to Certosa di Pavia (up to 7 daily; 35min); Pavia (up to 30 daily; 20–30min); Arona (8 daily; 50min–1hr); Stresa (10 daily;1hr–1hr 20min); Bergamo (6 daily; 50min); Brescia (32 daily; 45min–1hr 10min); Desenzano (16 daily; 1hr 5min–1hr 45min); Lecco (up to 20 daily; 20–40min); Como (13 daily; 30min); Como (20 daily; 30min).

From Milan Porta Genova to Vigévano (up to 19 daily; 20–35min).

From Milan Lambrate to Certosa di Pavia (up to 13 daily; 30–40min); Pavia (up to 15 daily; 25–40min).

From Milan Porta Garibaldi to Cremona, via Treviglio (up to 5 daily; 1hr 45min–2hr); Varese (28 daily; 1hr–1hr 10min); Arona (10 daily; 40min–1hr 45min); Stresa (8 daily; 1hr – 2hr 15min).

From Lecco to Sondrio (16 daily; 1hr 10min).

From Pavia to Cremona, via Codogno (up to 7 daily; 1hr 40min–2hr 30min); Mantua, via

Codogno (up to 6 daily; 2hr 45min–3hr 15min); Certosa di Pavia (11 daily; 10 min).

From Cremona to Mantua (19 daily; 40min–1hr 5min).

From Bergamo to Lecco (up to 12 daily; 45min); Brescia (up to 14 daily; 1hr).

From Brescia to Iseo (11 daily; 45min); Capo di Ponte (7 daily; 1hr 15min–1hr 40min); Desenzano (17 daily; 20min).

Buses

From Milan to Cremona (up to 8 daily; 2hr).

From Pavia to Vigévano (up to 12 daily; 1hr); Certosa di Pavia (Mon–Sat half-hourly, Sun hourly; 10–15min).

From Cremona to Bergamo (up to 4 daily; 2hr 20min); Brescia (up to 11 daily; 1hr 25min); Iseo (1 daily; 2hr).

From Mantua to Sabbioneta (up to 6 daily; 50min); Peschiera (9 daily; 1hr 10min); Verona (Mon–Sat 6 daily; 1hr 20min).

From Como to Colico (6 daily; 2hr 30min); Bellagio (up to 9 daily; 1hr 15min); Varese (up to 30 daily; 1hr).

From Menaggio to Lugano (up to 9 daily; 1hr).

From Bergamo to Clusone (up to 16 daily; 1hr); Brescia (up to 7 daily; 1hr 15min).

From Sondrio to Bormio (1 daily, Sun 2 daily; 1hr 20min).

From Brescia to Gardone Riviera (15 daily; 1hr); Iseo (3 daily; 3hr); Sirmione (hourly; 2hr); Mantua (Mon–Sat 15 daily, Sun 10 daily; 1hr 40min).

Ferries

From Como to Cernobbio (6 daily; 15min); Lenno (2 daily; 1hr 45min); Bellagio (2 daily; 2hr 10min); Varenna (2 daily; 2hr 30min).

From Lenno to Bellagio (4 daily; 20min); Menaggio (4 daily; 35min); Varenna (4 daily; 50min).

From Desenzano to Sirmione (15 daily; 20min); Pescheria (1 daily; 25min); Garda (2 daily; 55min); Saló (2 daily; 1hr 15min); Gardone Riviera (2 daily; 1hr 30min); Gargnano (2 daily; 2hr 30min); Malcesine (2 daily; 3hr 15min); Riva del Garda (2 daily; 2hr 10min).

From Pescheria to Malcesine (1 daily; 2hr 30min); Torbole (1 daily; 3hr 30min); Riva del Garda (1 daily; 3hr 40min).

Hydrofoils

From Como to Colico (4 daily; 1hr 30min). Stopping at Lenno, Bellagio, Menaggio, Varenna, Dongo, Gravedona, Domaso.

From Pescheria to Riva del Garda (4 daily; 2hr 15min). Stopping at Torbole, Limone, Malcesine, Gargnano, Gardone Riviera, Saló, Garda, Bardolino, Sirmione, Desenzano.

CHAPTER FOUR

TRENTINO-ALTO ADIGE

T
wo quite distinct cultural entities make up the province of **Trentino-Alto Adige**. The northern half – **Alto Adige** – is Italian more in name than affiliation. It's part of the Tyrol, a mountain enclave straddling the border between Austria and Italy, and an area which sees itself as part of the German-speaking world. In **Trentino**, on the other hand, Italian is spoken everywhere, and the food and architecture belong more to Italy than the Alps.

Austria ceded Trentino-Alto Adige to Italy at the end of World War I, a move much resented by many inhabitants of German descent, who have wanted to secede ever since. If some German speakers are unwilling to remain part of Italy, there are right-wing Italian speakers who would be equally pleased to see them go, and there's been friction between the two camps since the Sixties, when Germanic activists bombed power stations, railways and military installations. The government responded by occupying part of the province with troops, an economic disaster for an area dependent on tourism. Talks brought concessions and promises from central government which satisfied some, but not all – another spate of bombings began in the Eighties, provoking a strong response from Italian right-wingers. The fascist *MSI* (*Movimento Sociale Italiano*) surged ahead in the last election to become the most popular party amongst Italian speakers in the province.

The province's resorts can be lethargic, but the landscape of this part of Italy, dominated by the stark and jagged **Dolomites**, is among the most beautiful in the country. Circling the spiked towers of rock which characterise the range, a network of trails follows the ridges, varying in length from a day's walk to a two-week trek. Long-distance trails called *Alte Vie* can be picked up from the small resorts, usually a long bus ride away from the chief towns of **Trento** and **Bolzano**, the transport hubs for the region.

Trento gives access to most of the western Dolomites: the **Pale di San Martino**, a cluster of enormous peaks encircling the rocky "high plain" above San Martino di Castrozza; the **Catinaccio** (or Rosengarten) range between the Val di Fassa and Bolzano; the **Gruppo di Sella**, with its *vie ferrate* (iron ladders across rock walls); and the glacier-topped **Marmolada**. Still in the western Dolomites, but with easier access from Bolzano, are the **Alpe di Siusi**, a magical plateau of grass and wetland, high above the valley. The *alpe* are enclosed by the peaks of **Sasso Lungo** (or Langkofel) and **Sciliar** (or Schlern); to the north is the quieter **Odle** (or Geisler Gruppe).

Even further to the west, on the other side of Trento, are the **Dolomiti di Brenta**, a collection of wild peaks above the meadows of Valle Rendena. The eastern Dolomites start on the opposite side of the Adige valley, past Passo di Campolongo and Corvara, activity focussing on **Cortina d'Ampezzo**, self-styled "Queen of the Dolomite resorts". In summer, avoid the over-populated peaks like the Tre Cime di Lavaredo and head for **Sorapiss** or **Monte Pelmo** to the south, or **Le Tofane** and the mountains of the **Fanes-Sennes-Braies** group to the west. In winter, Cortina comes into its own as an extremely upmarket ski resort with excellent, if expensive, facilities, and a voyeuristic appeal.

Hiking and skiing

Officially the hiking season lasts from June 20 to September 20, although cable cars sometimes close in mid-September. Nearby refuges are the best place to phone for information on cable cars and weather conditions.

The six *Alte Vie* run north–south between the Val Pusteria (Pusertal) and the Veneto, each stage of the routes requiring five to eight hours' walking from one mountain refuge to the next. Some of the initial ascents are strenuous, but once you are up on the ridges the paths level out, and give superb views across the valleys and glaciers. Parts of the trails are exposed, or have snow fields across them, but alternative routes are always available. *Alta Via* 1 is the most popular, so much so that you should think twice about going between mid-July and August because of the crowds, not to mention the summer heat. There aren't many guides in English to the trails – the Belluno **AAST** (Via Matteotti 3) sometimes has guides to *Alte Vie* 1 and 2. The alternative is to use Stefano Ardito's *Backpacking and Walking in Italy* (Bradt) for *Alta Via* 1 and get hold of the Italian *Tamari* guides to the others. The *Alte Vie* are marked on the *Kompass* or *Tobacco* 1:50,000 maps, along with the multitude of other shorter trails which can be followed without guides. (As a rule of thumb, an averagely unfit person takes around three hours to ascend 1000m.) The maps are on sale everywhere in the Dolomites.

Trento's *Snowy Planet* brochure and Bolzano's skiing booklet (published by the provincial tourist offices) give details of chair lifts, altitude and length of runs in each resort, plus maps. *Settimane Biance* (White Weeks) are cheap-rate package deals offering full or half-board and a ski-pass – for specific information on places to stay, and prices, ask for the leaflets published each October. If you take a car and want to ski at more than one resort, the *Superski Dolomiti* – the most comprehensive ski-pass in the world – gives you access to 420 cable cars and chair lifts, and will set you back somewhere in the region of L170,000.

RIFUGI

The most convenient places to stay once you're high up are the **rifugi**. Solidly constructed, usually three-storey buildings, they provide dormitory accommodation, hot meals and a bar, and freezing cold water in the single bathroom. All are open between June and October and some of them operate in the skiing season. It's an idea to phone ahead to see if the place is likely to be packed out by a large party – nobody is ever turned away, but overflow accommodation is either a table in the bar, or somewhere like the hen house. A list of refuges, with phone numbers, is available from the provincial tourist offices in Bolzano and Trento.

For more information on rifugi, see *Basics*, "Sleeping".

To Landeck

AUSTRIA

SWITZERLAND

Passo di Résia
Palla Bianca
3738 m

L'Altissima
3479 m
Parco Naturale
Gruppo di Tessa

Málles

Madonna
di Senáles

Glorenza

Val Martello

Passo di Stelvio
2758 m

Ortles
2905 m

Gioveretto
3438 m

Val d'Ultimo

S. Gertrude

Parco Nazionale
dello Stelvio

Cevedale
3769 m

Bagni di Rabbi

To St-Moritz

Peio Terme

Malé

Cles

Val di Sole

Tuenno

Val di Non

Lago di
Tovel

Madonna
di Campiglio

Presanella
3558 m

Brenta
3150 m

Mezzo-
Lombardo

Paganella
2125 m

Parco Naturale
Adamello-Brenta

Carisolo

Molveno

Adamello
3554 m

L O M B A R D Y

Lago di
Molveno

To Bormio

Sténico

Bondone

Tione di Trento

A22

Fol
Rover

Riva d. Garda

Torbole

To Verona (A22)

To Brescia

Lago
di Garda

TRENTINO

Unlike Alto Adige to the north, where you sometimes wonder if you've crossed the border into Austria, Trentino is unmistakably Italian. The main centres are **Trento** and **Rovereto**, established in the Middle Ages as market towns in a predominantly wine-growing area. Both make useful bases for travelling into the mountains, where countless trails cross the awesome terrain. One of the more unusual is the *Sentiero della Pace* (Path of Peace), which snakes across the province along the World War I front. A long campaign of attrition took place in these peaks, claiming 460,000 dead and 947,000 wounded on the Italian side alone. The trail occasionally enters galleries carved through rock, or old fortifications pitted with bullet holes; route details are available in Trento at Via Torre Verde 27.

Up in the mountains, a traditional way of life still exists for some. In the summer months, farmers base themselves in a *malga* (hut) on the upper pastures and cut timber and hay, bringing their animals and wood down to the village as soon as winter starts. First snowfall is the starting signal for Trentino's other major industry, tourism – the area is criss-crossed with ski-lifts and runs, and offers facilities for less conventional winter sports, like ice-yachting on the lakes.

Trento

Small provincial towns don't usually buzz with activity and excitement, and Trento is no exception. The relaxed pace of life is a virtue though: after somewhere like Venice – three hours away by train – it's a relief to be treated like a human being. Straddling the Adige valley, Trento is overshadowed by Monte Bondone, from where the green roof of the Duomo and the Castello di Buonconsiglio stand out above the other stone buildings.

Trento was known as *Tridentum* to the Romans, a name celebrated by the eighteenth-century Neptune fountain in Piazza Duomo. A ring of arcades, shops and cafés encircles this central piazza, from which radiate streets lined with frescoed palaces, many of them built in the sixteenth century when Trento was an important market town.

Information, transport and finding a place to stay

The **EPT** at Corso III Novembre 132 (Mon–Fri 8.30am–noon & 2–4pm) is the main information centre for the area, with details on mountain refuges, transport, hiking or skiing possibilities, and *agriturism* (farm holidays) in the province as a whole. There are two **tourist offices** which specifically cover the city – in Piazza Duomo (Mon 3.30–7pm, Tues–Sat 9am–noon & 3.30–7pm, Sun 9am–noon) and at Via Alfieri 4, across the park from the train station (Mon–Fri 9am–noon & 3.30–7pm, Sat 9am–noon); both have copies of *Viva Trento*, the monthly guide to life in the town.

A reason for stopping in Trento is the bus service to the mountains. The main **bus** and **train stations** are almost next door to each other at Piazza Dante and Via Pozzo and there's a second combined station called Trento Malé ten minutes' walk away, with trains up to Cles and the Val di Non, and buses to Madonna di Campiglio and Molveno. Tickets and information from the office on Via G. Segantini (☎0461/823.671).

The best options for **places to stay** are *Albergo Mostra*, Piazza Mostra 12 (☎0461/980.223), with doubles for L32,000, or *Al Cavallino Bianco*, Via Cavour 29 (☎0461/26.868), at L39,000. A **youth hostel** should be open on Via Manzoni by the beginning of 1990, charging L10,000 a night including breakfast. The **camp-site**, near the river at Via Lung'Adige Leopardi (☎0461/823.562), charges L4800 per person and L6650 per tent; it's about twenty minutes' walk out of town, or take bus #2 from the station.

The Town

From the tenth to the eighteenth century, Trento was a bishopric ruled by a dynasty of princes, the most powerful of whom was Bernardo Clesio, who in the fifteenth century built up much of the town's collection of paintings and other works of art. Many of these are held in the **Castello di Buonconsiglio**, venue for the Council of Trent in the sixteenth century, when the Catholic church, threatened by the Reformation in northern Europe, met to plan its counter meas-ures. The meetings spanned a total of eighteen years; in the meantime, events outside Italy moved apace, and the meetings were more useful, in the end, for settling internal arguments and reinforcing the pope's authority.

Behind a thick outer wall there are two castles – the thirteenth-century Castelvecchio and the extension built in 1530 called the Magno Palazzo (both open Tues–Sun 9am–noon & 2–5pm; L2000). Several rooms frescoed with classi-cal subjects by the Dossi brothers and Romanino lead off a quiet inner courtyard; upstairs is the **Museo Provinciale d'Arte** where the highlight of the collection is the *Ciclo dei Mesi* (Cycle of the Months), hidden at the end of a narrow passageway in the Torre d'Aquila (ask at the ticket desk for a plan). These fifteenth-century frescoes show details from farming and courtly life; soldiers confined to barracks – the castle's role in the nineteenth century – added their own touches by scribbling on the borders and drawing in beards.

The ditch around the castle was the place of execution for two celebrated Trentese – Cesare Battisti and his comrade Fabio Filzi. Born in 1875, Battisti was a man of his times, a combination of romantic idealist and guerrilla fighter. He set up the Socialist-Irredentist newspaper *Il Popolo* to as a forum for protest against Austrian rule, and used Italy's entry into World War I as an opportunity to step up his campaign to eject Austrian forces from the Tyrol. The strategem was unsuc-cessful: in 1916 he led an attempt to take Monte Pasubio to the south of Trento, but he was arrested by the Austrians, and shot as a traitor. You can visit his and Filzi's cells in the castle, as well as a small museum to the Risorgimento and Liberation of Trentino.

The three most important meetings of the Council of Trent took place in the **Duomo** between 1545 and 1563. The building itself was begun in the thirteenth century, but completed in the century of the Council. Inside, the arched, colon-naded steps flanking the nave are a dramatic touch to an otherwise plain building. There are fresco fragments in the nave and an enormous carved marble balda-chin over the altar – a replica of the one in Saint Peter's – but a more interesting part lies under the church, where a medieval crypt and foundations of an early Christian basilica (built over the tomb of Saint Vigilio, the third Bishop of Trento) were discovered in 1977.

The **Museo Diocesano Trentino** (daily 9am–noon & 2–6pm; L2000), in the neighbouring **Palazzo Pretorio**, holds large annotated paintings of the sessions of the Council of Trent and some carved altarpieces from the church of San Zeno in the Val di Non. Hidden away in cell-like side rooms are some ornate reliquaries, and an impressive cycle of fifteenth-century Flemish tapestries. The building is appealing in itself, too, with its fishtail battlements and heavy studded doors, and a view from the upper floor of the frescoed palaces around the square.

Eating, drinking and nightlife
Trento town centre is not that good for places to eat, but there are two or three cheapish and lively places on Via Santa Croce, while *Albergo Accademia*, at Vicolo Collico 1 (closed Mon), has an expensive **restaurant** with a sophisticated version of local cooking. In summer, you can eat outside under a pergola at *Alla Mora*, Via Roggia Grande 8 (closed Mon). There's also a student *mensa* at Via Belenzani 18 – meals L6000, no ID necessary. If you can find transport, *Ristorante Quattro Stagioni* in San Vito di Cognola (closed Mon) – a few kilometres above the city – is popular, with good homemade pasta. One of the best ways to sample **local cooking** is to head for the *Strada di Vino*, an *agriturism* route which tracks through vineyards parallel to the main Trento to Bolzano road. Unfussy restaurants along the way serve *canederli* (bread dumplings in clear broth), potato pancakes with homemade salami and cheese, and local wines. Back in Trento itself, *birrerie* like *Due Giganti* at Via Simonino 20 (closed Sat) serve both **snacks** and full meals.

Trento doesn't resound with **nightlife**, but there are a couple of good bars open late. *Boston Bar* on Viale San Francesco d'Assisi is centre of the social whirl – American beer, loud music, and packed out all evening. *Al Picaro* on Via San Giovanni specialises in malt whiskies and beers, and has an occasional noticeboard offering lifts or tickets to various parts of Italy.

Around Trento

From Ponte San Lorenzo, near Trento's bus station, a cable car brings you to SARDAGNA, on the lower slopes of the towering Monte Bondone. There's some skiing in winter, and a scattering of holiday homes belonging mostly to Trentese. Campers might come here as an alternative to the site by the river: *Camping Mezavia* (☎0461/474.78), is two hours' trek from the top of the cable car . Equally popular with people who live nearby are the resorts of LAVARONE and FOLGARIA to the south, but if you've come from further afield, the attraction of the more distant and dramatic mountain groups will probably be stronger.

The railway line south from Trento runs between the scree-covered slopes of the Adige valley, where the only sight for miles might be a station platform in the middle of nowhere, or the blank fortifications of a castle or World War I stronghold. **Castel Beseno** is one of the few castles which have been restored and is open to the public – it hangs on an outcrop above the village of CALLIANO, 9km north of Rovereto.

Rovereto and Monte Pasubio
Fifty minutes south of Trento by train, **ROVERETO** is the largest town in the area between Trento and Verona. The gilded lion of Saint Mark over the gateway into the old town dates from the fifteenth century, when Rovereto was an outpost of the Venetian empire, as do the extensions to the castle, now the **Museo della Guerra** (Aug daily 8am–7pm; summer 8am–noon & 2–7pm; winter 9am–noon & 2–6pm).

Along the dark stone streets of the old town is the **Museo Depero** (9am–noon & 2–7pm; free), a collection of Futurist art ranging from Fortunato Depero's advertising designs (*Campari* posters among others), to semi-abstract work. Cassettes and word-pictures complement the more conventional stuff – including an evocative one of the New York subway.

Some of the most bloody engagements of World War I took place around **Monte Pasubio**, to the southeast of Rovereto. The recently created *Sentiero della Pace* (Path of Peace) follows the front, from the Órtles mountains east across the ranges to Marmolada, the trail littered with old bullets and barbed wire. The opposing armies dug fortresses in the rock and cut tunnels into the glaciers, but protection from enemy fire did not ensure safety – in the winter of 1916, one of the hardest in living memory, around 10,000 soldiers died in avalanches. Historian GM Trevelyan, commander of a British Red Cross ambulance unit in the campaign, described one fortress as "four storeys of galleries, one above the other, each grinning with cannon and machine guns. There were also medieval-looking wooden machines for pouring volleys of rock down the gullies by which the enemy might attempt to ascend . . . Our work lay, of course, at the foot of the teleferiche, or aerial railways which fed the war on those astonishing rock citadels: the sick and wounded came down the wires in cages, hundreds of feet in the air." The *Campana dei Caduti*, made out of melted-down cannon, tolls every evening in memory of the dead of both sides, from the *Colle di Miravalle* outside town.

The Dolomiti di Brenta and the Val di Non

The saw-toothed peaks and glaciers of the **Dolomiti di Brenta**, northwest of Trento, give these ranges a rougher character than the rest of the Dolomites, yet throughout these groups you can choose your level of walking. At around 3000m the paths are easy to follow but strenuous, while less demanding trails circle the side valleys. Less exploited by the tourist industry, the Dolomiti di Brenta are best approached via the small resorts of Madonna di Campiglio or Molveno.

Climbers come here for the towers of Cima Tosa and Cima Brenta, the original reason for *vie delle bochette* – iron ladders knocked into the rock to give access to these ascents. For these *vie ferrate* you need karabiners and ropes, but no special skills are necessary for the ordinary trails, and there are enough marked foot-paths for two or three days' high-altitude walking. Trento's EPT gives a free guide to the Brenta Dolomites, in English, with details on the location of *vie delle bochette* and how long they should take.

Around the Valle Rendena

Buses to Madonna from Trento skirt Monte Bondone and wind their way past a series of patchy hills and villages, turning into the Valle Rendena at TIONE DI TRENTO, where a more remote landscape of pasture and forest begins. This quiet valley is a good place to rest up, with a couple of small campsites reasonably close to villages – one of these is *Faè della Val Rendena* (☎0465/57.178) between Pinzolo and Sant'Antonio di Mavignola. Small churches like the lone Sant'Antonio just before BORZAGO are decorated with fresco cycles by Baschenis, one of the many Bergamese artists who worked in the area. At CARISOLO, the church of Santo Stefano has frescoes of the Seven Deadly Sins on an outside wall, and others inside depicting the legend of Charlemagne's passage through the Val di

Campiglio on the way to his coronation in Rome. Before Madonna several turnings off the main road lead high up into the Adamello range, the most beautiful being the **Val di Genova**. The valley begins 4.5km from Carisolo, and a steep, unmetalled road takes you past several waterfalls, spectacular in spring when the snow begins to melt – most impressive is the **Cascata di Nárdis**, where several channels spill down the granite rock walls of the mountainside. From here, it's another 13km to Bédole (1614m). *Rifugio Città di Trento* (☎0465/51.193) is at 2449m, three hours hike from Bédole, and within reach of the Adamello glaciers.

A more restful turning off the Valle Rendena at CADERZONE takes you up to Malgra Campo; from here path no. 230 leads to the small lakes of **San Giuliano** and **Garzono** (two and a half hours' walk). There's a small refuge between the two – ask for keys at the bar in Caderzone.

Madonna di Campiglio

The major village in the valley is **MADONNA DI CAMPIGLIO**, an upmarket ski resort, with plenty of chair lifts and runs for all levels of skiing. **Buses** from Trento run to the main square, not far from the tourist office. In summer, climbing and walking in the Dolomiti di Brenta are superb, and you may want to stay at Madonna, if only to reach the trail heads. The best way to approach these is by cable car from Carlo Magno, 3km north of the village centre. Services run from there to Grostè (daily 8.30am–1pm & 2–5.30pm; L10,000 one way) – see below. Another possibility from Carlo Magno is to take *Funivia Cinque Laghi* west, to *Rifugio Pancugolo* (2064m) in the Presanella group, where the paths include a five-hour route via **Lago Ritorto** and **Lago Gelato** back down to the valley.

Out of the skiing season, Madonna tends to be deserted except for a sprinkling of walkers. Most **hotels** here expect you to want a full- or half-pension arrangement, and off-season there are good deals to be had in some of the three-star places – ask around when you get there. There are cheaper places off the main road and east of the sports centre: follow the yellow signs pointing to *Rifugio Valesinalla* for *Garni Bucaneve* (☎0465/41.271), with bed and breakfast for L23,000 per person. On the same road, *Norma Garni* (☎0465/41.110) and *Gianna* (☎0465/41.106) are slightly more expensive, at L30,000.

Near Madonna is the smaller ski resort of PINZOLO; ski-lift passes cover both villages, but Pinzolo has its own centre, around the church of San Vigilio, decorated with a sixteenth-century fresco of the *danse macabre*.

Trails from Grostè

With the *Kompass* or *Tobacco* maps, you can plan your own routes. A couple of good trails start at Grostè (2437m), reached by cable car from Carlo Magno in the valley. *Rifugio Graffer* (2261m; ☎0465/41.358), by the cable car exit, is close to the trails, and has overnight accommodation. From the cable car , trail no. 316 sets out across boulder-strewn slopes towards refuges *Sella* and *Tuckett* (☎0465/41.226) – this is the place to eat a large meal and bask on the verandah, thousands of feet above the valley.

Trail 328, which later becomes no. 318 (called the *Sentiero Bogani*), starts just past the refuges – there are difficult boulders to negotiate, and then an easy path which has been blasted out of the side of the rock walls. A Madonna and shrine in a small overhang commemorate the lives lost in these peaks, but by this time, about four hours from Grostè, *Rifugio Brentei* (2182m; ☎0465/41.244) is in sight, midway between Cima Brenta and Cima Tosa. Some difficult ascents are a short distance from the refuge, but it's more than likely that by this stage you won't be capable of anything other than staring across the vast ravine at the Adamello glaciers in the distance.

Next day, if you can cope with snow fields, trek up to the Bocca di Brenta and cross over the ridge to meet trail no. 319 down to Molveno (3hr 30min). Otherwise, return to Madonna, via trails 318 and 316 (3hr 30min).

Molveno

The lakeside village of **MOLVENO**, surrounded by the peaks of the Brenta Alta, makes a cheaper base to stay than Madonna. The tourist office will help you find a bed for the night for around L15–20,000 per person, but the cheapest places go quickly, particularly in high season. *Campeggio Spiaggia Lago di Molveno* (☎0461/586.978), on the water's edge, charges L4800 per person and L7350 per tent – it's a good site, but the number of caravans is a potential drawback.

There are few easy trails from Molveno into the Brenta massif – paths often disappear into nothing but *vie ferrate* across the rocks; fortunately these are all marked on maps, so you just need to plan your route. If you decide to approach the Brenta group from this side, a cable car runs from the village to Pradel (1500m), from where trails lead through the beeches and pines of the Val delle Seghe in the shadow of Croz dell'Altissimo (2339m). An easy circular route winds back to Molveno (2hr 30min), or technically more demanding paths take you higher up, past *Rifugio Tosa* (2439m) and *Rifugio Tommaso Pedrotti* (2491m; ☎0461/47.316).

The most prodigious of nineteenth-century climbers, Francis Fox Tuckett, opened up a difficult new route to Cima Brenta from Molveno, now known as the *Bochetta di Tuckett*. As ice axes hadn't been invented, he negotiated snow fields with a ladder and alpenstock, carrying with him joints of meat and bottles of wine for mountaintop breakfast. The landscape where he "roamed amongst toppling rocks, and spires of white and brown and bronze coloured stone" is almost unchanged but for the *Bochetta*, which descends from the pass down to the *Tuckett* and *Sella* refuges (see above). More paths skirt Cima Tosa and lead down to PINZOLO via *Rifugio Dodici Apostoli* (2489m; ☎0465/51.309).

Val di Non

The steep Val di Non, where apple orchards cover every available terraced slope, skirts the northern edges of the Brenta group. You see the best of the valley by car, taking the turning for TUENNO off the N43 from Trento to **CLES**, at the head of the Val di Non; if you're reliant on public transport, Cles is served by buses and trains on the Trento to Malé line. Lying on the shore of the artificial Lago di Santa Giustina, Cles presents a strange mixture, with a hydroelectric dam on the lake to the northeast and several castles around. One which merits a visit is turretted **Castel Cles**, which has good frescoes by Fogolino.

Across the lake from Cles is the **Santuario di San Romedio**, a 45-minute walk uphill from SANZENO. The place is a popular pilgrimage shrine, as it's the legendary home of Romedius, a hermit who lived with his bear on the side of the cliff. The sanctuary is a complex of several churches built between the eleventh and eighteenth centuries; the two upper chapels are said to be the saint's retreat.

From Cles, the **Stelvio National Park** is an hour or so's drive via MALÉ and BAGNI DI RABBI or PEJO TERME – both are off the N42, though if you're relying on buses, access to the park is much easier from Merano.

East of Trento

To the east of Trento, the Val Sugana and the Val di Fiemme are joined by road, making a wide loop. Halfway around, a group of stunning pinnacles and bare peaks called the **Pale di San Martino** appears – formed as a coral reef sixty million years ago, their rock is so pale it glares even at dawn. The nearest resort to the Pale is San Martino di Castrozzo, the terminus for buses travelling the loop in both directions.

Val Sugana

Most people take the bus along the Val Sugana to get to a market in one of its modern and busy towns. There's nothing to see between the towns except rows of fruit trees and vineyards, and later, as the Brenta valley closes in to become a narrow gorge, a succession of hydroelectric plants. What makes the trip interesting is the terrain to the north, in particular the Cima d'Asta, a mountain dotted with bright blue, icy tarns, and crossed by the *Sentiero della Pace*. You reach the westerly part of this from PANAROTTA, in the mountains above Lago di Caldonazzo, from where the trail – at this point an ancient ridgeway path and wartime patrol route – follows a course across the peaks towards Passo di Rolle (see below).

If you're travelling by bus from Trento to San Martino you have no choice but to travel the long way round via Fonzaso in the Veneto. By car, though, there's a short cut if you turn off at BORGO VALSUGANA, and cut through the foothills; this lane climbs through an increasingly alpine landscape, to rejoin the main road at Imer (see below).

Imer and Fiero di Primiero

IMER and **MEZZANO** (a couple of kilometres north) might be archetypal tourist villages decked out with geraniums and credit card stickers, but these trappings scarcely irritate thanks to the splendour of the landscape around. The Pale are just about visible in the distance, and out to the east is the peak of Sass de Mura, but the valley itself is wide, with haymeadows spreading either side of the main road. Away from the tourism, the valley makes a good place to rest up, with easy paths into the foothills. One possibility is the path from Imer along the lush Val Noana to the reservoir under the slopes of **Monte Pavione** (3hr 30min round trip). As far as accommodation goes, self-sufficiency is an advantage, as you compete with coach parties if you look for a cheap hotel. An alternative to alpine-style hotels in the villages is *Camping Calavise*, a couple of kilometres (well sign-posted) off the main valley road (☎0439/67.468).

FIERO DI PRIMIERO is a larger resort and market town, 4.5km from Imer. It's a major crossroads in the area, from where buses run up to the beginning of the Val Canali and to Passo Cereda (1369m). The mountains around Fiero were worked for silver from the thirteenth century, and local miners paid for the town's fifteenth-century church. Now the ranges are crossed by trails – *Alta Via* no. 2 dips down to the main road here, and, travelling south, regains altitude around the slopes of Monte Cimonega (2381m).

Trails to the north of Passo Cereda take you up into the Pale. One path follows a long ridge of rock before passing down into Val Canali, described by Amelia Edwards in the nineteenth century as the most "lonely, desolate and tremendous scene . . . to be found this side of the Andes". There's now a bar and some places to camp at the head of the glen, but the valley has kept its feeling of isolation. *Rifugio Treviso* (☎0439/62.311) in Val Canali is the only overnight stop.

A stiff ascent from the refuge brings you onto the **Altopiano delle Pale** at Passo di Pradidali, where eagles can be seen circling above the barren plateau, and the silence is broken every so often by a trickle of falling stones. Once you are at this altitude, there are many possibilities for linking up with other trails across the stark upland. *Rifugio Pedrotti all Rosetta* (2581m) is the nearest place with accommodation (a 2hr 30min hike north).

San Martino and around

The road into San Martino twists and turns, and seems like it's in the middle of nowhere until the resort's new hotels appear around the corner. After Cortina d'Ampezzo, San Martino is one of the smarter Dolomite resorts, but it has a more relaxed atmosphere in the cafés and a generally unpretentious way of going about things. The **AAST** next to the bus stop may help with finding a cheapish bed and breakfast; the alternative is to camp in the village site, *Sass Maor* (☎0439/68.347) – it charges L10,000 for a pitch, and L6000 per person in high season.

A number of trails head off into the mountains, the strongest attraction being the Pale themselves. Chair lifts and cable cars from San Martino (8.30am–12.30pm & 1–4.45pm; L12,000 single, L17,000 day return) take you up to *Rifugio Pedrotti-Rossetta* at 2581m (☎0439/68.308 or 62.567), perched on the edge of the Altopiano. At the refuge there's accommodation, a restaurant and bar.

Up on the tops, either make for *Rifugio Pradidali* (2278m; ☎0439/67.290) a walk and descent of three hours, or climb up to **Cima della Vezzana** (3192m), the highest point in the group, with views down across the whole range – the path is difficult in places, and the round trip takes about five hours. If you prefer the relative security of a guided trek, the *Gruppo Guide Alpine*, next door to the AAST in San Martino, runs graded excursions most days in July and August.

The Parco Naturale Paneveggio

Out of San Martino, traffic files up to **Passo di Rolle**, a beautiful stretch of high moorland dotted with avalanche breaks and a few sheep. There are only two buses a day, but hitching is easy. At the pass, a chair lift takes you up to *Baita Segantini*, a log cabin bar from where you can see **Cimon della Pala**'s summit. It takes half an hour or so to walk back down to the pass, where there are several more bars and restaurants.

The Passo di Rolle falls within the **Parco Naturale Paneveggio**, an area of firs, rowan and larch that once provided timber for the Venetian fleet and wood for Stradivarius' violins. Skirted by nature trails, it has a visitors' centre 7km on from the pass, outside PANEVEGGIO village, with displays on the wildlife of the area. The remoter parts of the park are where to see live specimens of the white alpine hare and the marmot – a creature resembling a large guinea pig, which stands up on its hind legs to act as sentinel for the burrow, and emits a distinctive screech. After a few days trekking in the Pale, you may want to take it easy, and Paneveggio's fields are good for sunbathing and sleep. There's an unusually pleasant campsite next to Lago Paneveggio – the entrance is at the end of the track marked "Area della Sosta", just past the village, and the maximum stay is 24 hours.

If you're travelling by bus, there are two main choices from Paneveggio – either finish the round trip back to Trento, or break your journey at Predazzo in the Val di Fiemme if you want to travel into the mountainous Val di Fassa (see below).

Val di Fiemme

Once out of the confines of the park, **PREDAZZO** is the first town you come to in the Val di Fiemme. Hotel hoardings are ubiquitous, and even the tiniest villages hereabouts have a plan of the mountain ranges with chairlifts marked, but behind the modern Dolomites industry is an ancient region that until the seventeenth century was virtually autonomous. A local parliament met at **CAVALESE**'s *Banco de la reson*, a circle of stone benches surrounded by trees, and the *Magnifica Communità* of Cavalese is still relatively powerful, administering extensive communal land. Nearby, the **Palazzo della Communità** was the Bishop of Trento's summer palace; the building is covered in frescoes, and surrounded by cobbled streets with a handful of bars and *pasticcerie*. The European witchhunt pandemic reached this valley in 1505, when eleven women were burnt at the stake in the village of DOSS DE LE STRÌE.

Predazzo is on the way to the Val di Fassa (see below), so a night here saves going back to Trento and retracing your steps. *Cimon* (☎0462/51.691) has the cheapest **rooms** at L32,000 and upwards, while one or two small hotels in Cavalese charge from L20,000 – the tourist office has details.

TESERO, 4km away, is like a smaller version of Cavalese – people drive through on their way to the mountains, or stop to take the cable car up to Lago Lagorai or the dozens of smaller lakes in the chain. Otherwise, Tesero's main attractions are a couple of *gelaterie* and the parish church, frescoed with *Cristo della Domenica* (Sabbath Christ) and symbols of everything banned on a Sunday. In Tesero, bed and breakfast is offered by Signora Maria Canal (☎0462/84.178) at L16,000 per person.

To get to the **Catena dei Lagorai**, a group of lakes hidden in the mountains to the south of the valley, you can either walk from any of the small villages along the main road or take the cable car from Cavalese. Once you're up on the ridges, either follow the paths towards Passo di Rolle, or go west. A day or two of walking westward (via refuges) brings you to the Val dei Mócheni, which was colonised in medieval times by German farmers travelling south, and has kept its own language and gothic script. The first farmers were joined later by speculators searching for the rich seams of copper and silver which lay in the mountains.

The Catinaccio and Sella groups

Trails from the Val di Fassa take you up into ranges whose scale is unbelievable at times. These mountains make up the centre of the western Dolomites, with a number of possibilities for walking across onto the Alpe di Siusi, or towards the high Sella, Gardena and Pordoi passes. The main villages in the Val di Fassa are Moena, Vigo di Fassa and Canazei, none of which has more than a couple of thousand inhabitants, except in the winter and summer seasons, when tourists pack out the many guest houses. All three give access to the mountains and are popular with German parties, who come here for the classic Dolomite walks across the western edge of the valley, into dramatic areas such as the famous **Catinaccio (Rosengarten)** range. Wilderness is not the key word in the valley – especially on the lower slopes, where the sound of overhead wires tells you another chairlift is on its way – but once you gain altitude you reach a completely different world.

Catinaccio

The long belt of sheer rock walls and towers which makes up the Catinaccio (Rosengarten) range gets its German name from the roses which legend says used to grow here. King Laurens, who was captured in the mountains, put a spell on the roses so that no-one would see them again by day or night, but forgot to include dawn and dusk in his curse, which is when the low sun gives the rock a roseate glow. The trails across the range are for all levels of hiking, but the going gets tough on the ridges, from where you can see as far as the Stubaier Alps, on the border with Austria. The most popular approach to **Catinaccio** is from **VIGO DI FASSA**, a bus stop on the Trento to Canazei route with a dozen or so hotels in the L45–60,000 range.

The trek to **Torri di Vajolet** from Vigo di Fassa is the preferred route up onto the range; the cable car from the village to *Rifugio Ciampedie* deals with most of the ascent – from there a well-beaten trail leads through the woods to *Rifugio Gardeccia*. Then it's a steep walk up to the refuge under the Torri, though the severity of the ascent doesn't discourage hordes of summer Sunday walkers. A stiff zigzagging climb from here brings you to *Rifugio Re Alberto* (3hr from Ciampedie), which looks the size of a Monopoly house in comparison with the peaks above it, and there's alternative accommodation nearby at *Rifugio Passo Santner* (☎0471/642.230).

Paths lead **south** across the range and eventually down to Passo di Costalunga and the Lago di Carezza, from where you can catch a bus to Bolzano. There are more choices to the **north**, where there are a number of trails onto Monte Sciliar (Schlern), with variations in height of no more than around 500m. *Rifugio Bolzano al M. Pez* (☎0471/616.024) near the summit of Monte Sciliar is a good two days' trek from *Rifugio Re Alberto* – stop overnight at *Tierser Alplhütte* (☎0471/72.952), in between the two. From Sciliar paths descend onto the wetland plateau of the Alpi di Siusi (see below).

Canazei and Pradel

From **CANAZEI**, a relatively modern town at the head of the Val di Fassa, you head for the high passes – the Gruppo di Sella for hard trails, or the easier Viel del Pan, opposite Marmolada. Bus connections are virtually non-existent, so to get to most places you have to use cable cars or hitch. From Canazei the switchback road climbs relentlessly for 12km and is often busy with coachloads of tourists heading for the Great Dolomites Road, or cyclists making the thousand-metre ascent.

Halfway up, the cable car at PRADEL leads to **Passo di Sella** (2240m), one of the most impressive of the Dolomite passes. Paths climb from here onto the jagged peaks of the **Sasso Lungo** (Langkofel) and follow the ridges down onto the Alpi di Siusi. Even up on the summits, saxifrage grows between cracks in the rock, and the silence is broken every so often by the buzzing of a beetle. It takes two days to walk from the Sella pass, via *Rifugio Vicenza* (☎0471/77.315) into the Val Gardena (Grödnertal), where there are buses to Bolzano.

Just past Pradel the road forks. The right-hand turning takes you up to **Passo Pordoi** (2242m), an astonishing vantage point between the Gruppo di Sella and Marmolada, at 3246m the highest Dolomite. The ranges and peaks in every direction are more like North America than Europe, with tough grass over the lower slopes, and massive outcrops of grey rock. A small road winds downwards to Passo Folzarego, and ultimately Cortina d'Ampezzo, but Passo Pordoi itself is where many of the trails start. It's also another occasion for joining *Alta Via* no. 2, which dips down to the main road here. Most of the tourist coaches stop at this point, so a collection of rip-off cafés and stalls have grown up around the two hotels which mark the start of the trails.

The Gruppo di Sella

The Sella mountain group lies to the north of Passo Pordoi, with many fairly difficult trails. If you're a complete beginner, there's a choice of two paths: either stick to the *Alta Via* no. 2, which crosses from one edge of the massif to the other, or break away at Sass de Mesdi, from where a trail circles down to the Sella pass. Both routes take a couple of days, with overnight stops at *Rifugio Franco Cavazza* (Pisciaduhutte; ☎0471/836.292) or *Rifugio Boe* (Boe Hutte; ☎0471/83.217). The Sella group is an excellent place to walk, with views across the ranges down to Passo Gardena (Sellajoch, 2137m), from where Corvara and the Val Badia are within striking distance, as are the Odle (Geisler) group across the valley (see below). Buses are few and far between so hitching is the better option; otherwise, pick up buses to Bolzano from SELVA, 11km away in the Val Gardena.

Viel del Pan

Much less ambitious walking from Passo Pordoi starts just past *Albergo Savoia*, again following the route of *Alta Via* no. 2, but in the opposite direction. A narrow path cut into the turf traverses the mountainside opposite Marmolada, where Austrian battalions hid under the glacier in 8km of gallery during World War I.

From the seventeenth century this path was on the grain-smuggling route called the Viel del Pan – "trail of bread" in Venetian dialect – and it remained busy enough in the nineteenth century for the Guardia di Finanza to set up armed patrols along it. The contrast between the glacier on Marmolada and the peaks of the Sella group – 360 degrees of mountain – is superb. The path descends to **Lago Fedaia**, from where there are irregular buses in summer back to Canazei – otherwise you have to hitch. *Rifugio Castiglioni* (☎0462/61.117) is on the edge of the reservoir. On the northern side of the ridge lies ARABBA, a tiny resort with small family-run hotels in the centre and in the pastures around. It's a quiet village for the moment, but foundations for more hotels and another cable car are being carved out of the mountain. The only bus service from here goes to Corvara.

Ladini country – Corvara and Fanes Park

The **Ladino** language – a derivation of Latin traceable to the Roman legions who passed through on their way to subdue Celtic tribes – is unique to the Alps, being especially prevalent in the area around the Sella group: the Val di Fassa, the Val Badia, the Val Gardena and Livinallongo. A peaceful tribe, the Ladini were constantly threatened with invasion by Germanic tribes from the north, and others from the Po valley, and their epics recount a history of battles, treachery and reversals of fortunes. Christianity later emerged as a major threat, but the Ladini absorbed and transformed the new religion, investing the new saints with the powers of more ancient female divinities. The rudimentary Castello di Thurn at SAN MARTINO DI BADIA, a bleak outpost of the bishop princes of Bressanone, is testimony to the Church's attempt to keep the Val di Badia under its control. In 1452, Bishop Nicolo Cusano railed against a woman from the Val di

Fassa who said she had met the goddess Diana in the woods, and there was a strong pagan undercurrent to the cult of Santa Giuliana, whose sword-wielding image is painted onto the plaster of houses in the Fassa and Badia valleys.

Relative isolation until recent years has kept the 40,000 Ladino-speaking people together as a culturally distinct group, even though their territory has been cut in three by the Veneto, Trentino and Alto Adige provincial boundaries. These days, however, the central town of the Ladini, **CORVARA**, is primarily a ski resort, and the most visible sign of the language is a page or two in the Ladino tongue in local newspapers. The mountainous Fanes park (see below), where most of the Ladini legends are based, has excellent trails within a bus ride of Corvara. The **AAST** has details of **rooms** from L18,000 per person; from outside the office a few buses creak in and out on their way to Brunico and Belluno.

The Parco Naturale Fanes-Sennes-Braies

The best way to see the Fanes-Sennes-Braies park is to walk the section of *Alta Via* no. 1 that runs through it, a hike taking three to four days, with overnight stops at refuges. The *Alta Via* trail starts at **Lago di Braies** (Pragser Wildsee), a deep-green lake surrounded by pines, 8km off the main road through the Val Pusteria (see below). It's an extraordinary place – legend says the lake is a gateway to underground caverns – but avoid it in July and August, when crowds descend on the trails. For the beginning of the *Alta Via* take the DOBBIACO (TOBLACH) bus from Brunico and ask the driver to drop you at the turn off between MONGUELFO (WELSBERG) and VILLABASSA (NIEDERDORF), around thirty minutes later. If you have less time to spend in the park, then aim for the upper slopes of **Alpe di Fanes**, where you pick up some of the best ridge-way paths. Access is by bus from either Corvara or Brunico to LONGEGA (ZWISCHENWASSER), and from there a walk of 4km to SAN VIGILIO DI MAREBBE, in a side valley. The AAST here can advise on routes up onto the mountains. A regular jeep taxi service (L7000) runs from San Vigilio to *Rifugio Fanes* (☎0474/51.097) and *Rifugio Lavarella* (☎0474/51.038), both at around 2000m on the Alpe di Fanes Piccola. Footpaths cross the grassy plateaus, past small tarns, and the rocks of **Ciastel de Fanes**, home of Dolasilla, the mythical princess of the Ladini. The lakes are fed by underground streams, which you can sometimes hear, flowing deep beneath your feet.

Several day-trip targets in the park mean it's overrun at weekends in summer. One is the **Plan de Corones**, surrounded by jagged peaks and reached by cable car from Brunico. Here, legend has it, Dolasilla was crowned at the top of the mountain with the *raiëta* – a crystal that harnessed powerful forces.

Merano and around

MERANO, an hour north by train from Bolzano (see p.208), lies close to two great mountain ranges. Less than 10km away is the **Giogaia di Tessa (Texelgruppe)**, the trails on its northern flank characterised by steep traverses across pastureland, with old snow still on the slopes in summer; watercourses irrigate the south-facing slopes, planted below with vines, peach and apple trees. Further west are the Ortles mountains, straddling the border with Val d'Aosta – an unbelievable spread of glaciers and rocky spurs. Both offer isolated trails, away from the tourist routes, with buses to most villages.

The sedate spa town of Merano sits on a bend in the River Passirio, surrounded by a ring of mountains and, incongruously, by semi-tropical plants. Mild spring and autumn weather attracted Central Europeans at the turn of the century, and a resort of *fin de siècle* hotels, neat gardens and promenades evolved. The town's old nucleus is Via dei Portici, close to the Gothic **Duomo** and fifteenth-century castle; around it are plenty of shopping streets, and the Thermal Centre, which still provides radioactive water cures. The alpenstock-wielding over-sixties have colonised the riverside promenades and the hills around, but you still may decide to stay in Merano for bus connections to the Parco Naturale di Tessa to the north, or the Ortles mountains in the Parco Nazionale dello Stelvio to the southwest (see below for both). **Buses** arrive and leave directly outside the train station (☎0473/42.002 for information). The **Azienda di Soggiorno, Cura e Turismo** at Corso Libertà 45 (Mon–Fri 8am–12.30pm & 3–6.30pm, Sat 9am–noon & 3–5pm) has details on the clutch of centrally located **hotels** – expect to pay upwards of L15,000 per person. For **hiking**, consult the Alpine Association at Via Galilei 45 (Mon–Fri 9am–noon), the *Alpenverien Südtirol*, based at *Heidenberger* on the small arcade off Corso Libertà, or the *Club Alpino Italiano* office, Corso Libertà 188.

The Parco Naturale di Tessa (Naturpark Texelgruppe)

The mountain chains around Merano belong to a separate geological period from the Dolomites, being part of the Zillertaler and Ötztaler ranges of the eastern Alps. Their foothills, called the **Giogáia di Tessa (Texelgruppe)**, begin immediately north of the town. Two high-level paths, the north and south sections of the **Meraner Höhenweg**, encircle this massif. The gentler **southern route** (marked as route 24 on signs) overlooks Merano, the built-up Val Venosta (Vinschgau), and the neighbouring peaks, and is crowded even out of season. Total walking time is 24 hours, and every few kilometres there's a dairy farm offering bed and breakfast, or a refuge for overnight stops. **Buses** go from Merano to the beginning of the route at Hof Unterpferl in KATHARINABERG, and to ULFAS, just west of SANKT LEONHARD, where it ends – plus several points along the way, including **Castel Tirolo**, where a cable car ascends to a couple of refuges and souvenir shops at HOCHMUTER. The castle's tenth-century frescoed chapel is worth the visit, if you can fight your way through the crowds of other tourists who pack the lanes around.

The **northern** stretch of the Meraner Höhenweg is an entirely different trail, running at a higher altitude but still below snow line, through isolated pastures and rocky terrain. The comparative scarcity of refuges makes it necessary to plan overnight stops in advance. The first section of the trail (KATHARINABERG–MONTFERT–EISHOF) is a walk of four hours; you then pick up the path from Eishof to *Rifugio Stettiner* (3hr 30min); STETTINER to PFELDERS (3hr 30min) is the last part. For **places to stay** in **Katharinaberg**, try *Katharinabergerhof* (☎0473/89.171), with bed and breakfast from L20,000 per person, or *Schnalsburg* (☎0473/89.145), from L16,000 per person. Among the guest houses in **Pfelders** are *Edelweiss* (☎0473/85.713), from L15,000 per person, and *Panorama* (☎0473/85.727) from L18,000, both for bed and breakfast.

From *Rifugio Stettiner* there's another option: the **Pfelderer Höhenweg**, which runs east to the Zwickauer Shelter, crosses the path here, and traverses the pastures of Obere Schneid. There are some sheer drops down to the valley, and you need crampons above the snowline, but this is an excellent walk, with a hint of how isolated these small valleys were until recently. If you don't feel equipped for this, but want to extend the route, continue past Pfelders to ULFAS (4hr), and from there on to VIPITENO (2–3 days), where you either link up with the main Bolzano to Innsbruck railway, or carry on eastwards along the **Pfunderer Höhenweg** (see below).

A bus travels north along the Val Passiria to SANKT LEONHARD, skirting the edge of the Texelgruppe, and taking you away from Merano's ski resorts on the slopes of Punta Cervina (Hirzer Spitze). A network of paths cross the summer pastures around Sankt Leonhard: one of these leaves SANKT MARTINO, 4.2km south of Sankt Leonhard, and makes the steep ascent (2hr 30min), to **PFANDLERALM**, the home village of Andreas Hofer. Originally an innkeeper, wine merchant and cattle dealer, he fought for the Tyrol's return to Austria after it had been ceded to Bavaria in 1805. After successful uprisings against occupying Bavarian and Napoleonic troops, he became self-styled commander-in-chief of the South Tyrol, commanding strong popular support. However, larger political forces overtook him. When the Tyrol was ceded to the French by Austria's Emperor Francis I, Hofer wavered between resistance and acceptance; arrested in 1810, he was then executed under Napoleon's orders in Mantua. At Pfanderalm a memorial to him stands on the edge of the meadow.

The other road out of Sankt Leonhard follows the Val Passiria west to MOSO (MOOS), at the head of the Val di Plan (Pfelderer Tal). From Moso the old military road leads to SANKT MARTIN AM SCHNEEBERG (2hr). An eerie trail leads through a peat gulley to *Schneeberghütte* (no accommodation), surrounded by spoil heaps and ruined buildings – the remains of Europe's highest mining settlement (2355m), opened in 1660 within sight of the glaciers on Austria's Pan di Zucchero (Zuckerhütl) mountain.

Parco Nazionale dello Stelvio

The Parco Nazionale dello Stelvio is one of Italy's major national parks – it covers the whole Ortles range, topped by one of Europe's largest glaciers (the *Ghicciaio dei Forni*) and crossed by the Passo dello Stelvio, which misses being the highest pass in the Alps by twelve metres. Like other places in the Alps, the park has felt the effects of tourism, being criss-crossed by ski-lifts, but it's still a remarkable place. People come here for the high trails and glacier skiing in summer, or to spot species such as the red and roe deer, elk, chamois, golden eagles and ibex. One of the best valleys for wildlife is the sheer sided Val Zebrù, off the Valfurva – the smallest of the valleys, it's accessible from Bormio. There are buses to the park's various points of access but perhaps the place to head for first is SILANDRO (SCHLANDERS), with its visitors' centre and information on refuges and trails.

The valleys

Three main valley roads thread their way into the foothills of the Ortles range: Val d'Ultimo (Ultental), Val Martello (Martelltal) and Val di Solda (Suldental). A traditional place of hiding in an area renowned for mountain warfare, the isolated **Val d'Ultimo (Ultental)** was opened up this century, and buses now run from Merano to the village of SANKT GERTRUD. Around the lower slopes are startling green pastures and some ancient larches, but the main attraction of coming here lies higher up, where trails lead over rock-strewn moorland to *Rifugio Canziani* (*Höchster Hütte*; 3hr; no accommodation), dramatically surrounded by the glaciers and peaks of **Zufrittspitze**. If you're feeling less energetic, the valley is still a good place for some shorter walks, using the village as base. *Innerlahn* (☎0473/79.167) is one of a handful of **hotels** in the village, with bed and breakfast from L11,000.

Further west, **Val Martello** (Martelltal) is equally beautiful, its lower slopes covered with silver birches. A bus travels from Merano to Silandro, and another from Silandro into Val Martello, passing the ruins of Castel Montani, and an aviary for falcons at MORTER. At the head of the valley, PARADISO DEL CEVEDALE (2088m) is one of the busiest bases for climbers and cross-country skiiers, lying close to Monte Cevedale (Zufall Spitze; 3757m) and refuges *Corsi* (*Zufall Hütte*; 2265m) and *Casati* (3266m). Other trails lead through high passes to Val d'Ultimo and Val di Solda.

One of the main roads through the park is the awe-inspiring route over the **Passo di Stelvio** (2758m) towards Bormio. A bus from Merano makes the journey to the pass (open between June and October), passing the **Val di Solda** on the way. The village of SOLDA, at its head, is another major climbing centre, but you don't have to be experienced to attempt some of the trails. There are easy paths (2hr) up to *Rifugio Città di Milano* (*Schaubach Hütte*; 2581m; ☎0473/75.402), or more difficult trails to *Rifugio Payer* (☎0473/75.410), a fantastic viewpoint and base for the ascent of **Ortles** (3905m). The Passo di Stelvio marked the frontier between Italy, Switzerland and Austria until 1918, and **Pizzo Garibaldi** (**Dreisprachenspitze**), a spur of rock fifteen minutes' walk from the pass is the symbolic meeting place for the three main languages of the area. The road continues from Passo di Stelvio down through switchbacks and startling gradients to Bormio (see below).

ALTO ADIGE (SÜD TIROL)

Austria officially begins at the Brenner pass, but it can feel as though the border is some way south, around **Bolzano**, where the villages are Tyrolean in looks, and German is spoken everywhere. Despite the promises of autonomy that have been reiterated since 1946, **Alto Adige** (Süd Tirol) remains part of Italy, and ample funds have been fed into the provincial administration by successive governments to placate the Germanic inhabitants. Unemployment is low compared with the national average, and per capita income high. Central government aid has done nothing to endear the German-speaking majority to the right-wing *MSI* (*Movimento Sociale Italiano*), who have condemned as anti-Italian such reforms as a measure to increase the intake of German-speakers into lucrative civil service positions. The *MSI* have held rallies in Bolzano, and in 1987 managed to elect their first-ever local deputy – a lawyer who has declared Mussolini "a great man". Since then they've actively encouraged neo-Fascist sympathisers to move into the province to swell their numbers.

Their opposition is the *SVP* – the *Süd-Tiroler Volkspartei* – some of whom want to secede from Italy, while others will settle for a better deal within the Italian state. Sympathisers with the more radical secessionists have been implicated in some of the bombing campaigns of recent years, outbreaks of violence that persuaded then President Cossiga to take his holiday elsewhere.

Travelling around is not as eventful as it might sound from all this, and there are certainly few hints of any tension to outsiders. Quite the reverse in fact, as even the big towns have a leisurely pace of life, and the high valleys are utterly peaceful. Although you can get close to some mountainous land around Bolzano, the Dolomites region proper only begins to pay dividends once you head east, high up into the ranges between here and **Cortina d'Ampezzo**. Alternatively, make for the glacial ranges to the west, in the Ortles group, in sight of the Swiss and Austrian Alps.

Bolzano (Bozen)

Lying on the junction of the rivers Talvera (Talfer) and Isarco (Eisack) near the southern limit of the province, **BOLZANO** is Alto Adige's chief town. For centuries a valley market town and way station, Bolzano's fortunes in the Middle Ages vacillated as the Counts of Tyrol and the Bishops of Trento competed for power. The town passed to the Habsburgs in the fourteenth century, then at the turn of the nineteenth century Bavaria took control, opposed by Tyrolese patriot and military leader, Andreas Hofer. His battle in 1809 to keep the Tyrol under Austrian rule was only temporarily successful, as in the same year the Austrian Emperor ceded the Tyrol to the Napoleonic kingdom of Italy. More changes followed, as Bolzano was handed back to Austria until after World War I, whereupon it passed to Italy.

Bolzano looks part of the German-speaking world. Around Piazza dell'Erbe (Obst Platz), site of a daily fruit and vegetable market, spread the dark streets of the old town, where oriel windows overhang eleventh-century arcades in Via dei Portici (Laubenstrasse). Along here are a number of restaurants serving *speck*, *gulasch* and *knödel*, as well as bakers selling rich *sachertorte* and black bread. In both winter and summer, the place is a busy tourist resort, but even so, Bolzano's pavement cafés and generally relaxed pace of life make the city a good, if uneventful, place to rest up, or use as a base for trips into the mountains. An unmissable pleasure is the local wine: a wine-producing area since Roman times, Bolzano is at the head of the *Strada di Vino* (*Südtiroler Weinstrasse*) which runs south to Trento and is especially well known for its Chardonnay.

Orientation, information and finding a place to stay

Piazza Walther is Bolzano's centre. The **APT** is at no. 8 (Mon–Fri 8.30am–12.30pm & 2–6pm, Sat 9am–12.30pm), and the **EPT** is off the square at Piazza Parrochia 11/12 (Mon–Fri 8.30am–12.30pm & 2–5.30pm) – their "Alpine Desk" (Mon–Fri 9am–noon & 3–5.30pm) has information on weather conditions and advisability of routes. Another source of hiking information is the *Club Alpino Italiano* at Piazza Erbe 46. The **bus station**, at Via Perathoner 4, serves most of the small villages and resorts in the province; the **train station** is five minutes' walk away.

For **places to stay**, try *Albergo Colleggio* (*Kolpinghaus*), at Via dell'Ospedale 3 (Spitalgasse; ☎0471/971.170), a couple of minutes' walk from Piazza Walther – it's a hostel with rooms at L23,000 per person. *Croce Bianco* (*Weisses Kreuz*; ☎0471/27.552) and *Figl* (☎0471/978.412) are both on Piazza del Grano (Kornplatz), with doubles from L35,000. They are less gloomy than most of Bolzano's cheap hotels. One way of escaping the summer humidity is to stay in the hills above town at Colle (Kohlern). A cable car runs there from Via Campiglio (Kamillerweg), a twenty-minute walk from the train station; *Klaus*, Colle 14 (☎0471/971.294), costs L32,000 including breakfast and is one of several hotels on the same road.

The town and environs

The town's favoured meeting places are the pavement cafés of Piazza Walther and around its statue of the *minnesinger* (troubadour) Walther von der Vogelweide. Converted into a cathedral as recently as 1964, the **Duomo** (Dom), on the edge of the square, resembles a parish church: built in the fourteenth and fifteenth centuries, and restored since bombing in World War II, it has a striking green and yellow mosaic roof, and elaborately carved spire.

A couple of streets away, the **Chiesa dei Domenicani** (Dominican monastery) has frescoes of fifteenth-century courtly life painted on the walls of the decaying cloisters, framed by a growth of stone tracery. The Cappella di San Giovanni, built at the beginning of the fourteenth century; retains frescoes by painters of the Giotto school, including a *Triumph of Death* underneath a starry vault. Bolzano's Gothic quarter ends the other side of the River Talvera (Talfer), where Piazza della Vittoria (Siegesplatz), with its epic triumphal arch, was built by Mussolini in 1928.

A couple more churches in the town centre are worth seeking out. The fourteenth-century **Franciscan church** on Via dei Francescani is embellished with a carved wooden altarpiece by Hans Klocher, and has elegant, frescoed cloisters from the same period. The other church is in the leafy suburb of Gries, on the left bank of the Talvera at the end of Corso Libertà. The Gothic **Parrocchiale** in the main square, overshadowed by a Baroque church nearby, contains a richly carved and painted fifteenth-century altarpiece by Michael Pacher.

Bolzano is hemmed in by mountains terraced high with vineyards, across which lead a couple of "promenades" from the valley basin. The *Passeggiata del Guncinà* starts at the end of Via Knoller (Knollerstrasse) near Gries' Parrocchiale, while the other, the *Passeggiata Sant'Osvaldo*, begins at Via Renico (Rentscherstrasse) behind the train station, traverses some hillside terraces, and brings you down to the path next to the River Talvera. Another good place to aim for relatively close to town is the thirteenth-century **Castello Róncolo (Schloss Runkelstein)**, reachable by bus #1 from the station. Frescoes of courtly life show people hunting, dancing and generally having a good time, as well as a group of knights on horseback (summer daily 10am–noon & 3–6pm; winter 3–6pm).

Monte Renòn (Rittner) gives a taste of the high peaks around Bolzano. A cable car ascends from Via Renòn (Rittnerstrasse) to Soprabolzano (Oberbozen), from where footpaths lead to some of the other small villages, past a forest of eroded earth pillars, half an hour's walk north of COLLALBO. If you're feeling energetic, you can attempt the summit (2260m) for a glimpse of the Dolomites to the east. A good time to come up here is in summer, around Saint Bartholomew's day (August 24), when hundreds of farmers from outlying villages congregate on Renòn for the annual horse fair.

Eating, drinking and nightlife

Wurstel and *apfel strudel* are the commonest **street food**, from stalls on Kornplatz and the cafés of Via dei Portici. **Restaurants** along this street include *Weisse Traube* (*Uva Bianca*), offering a set lunch for L6000. Along Via dei Bottai (Bindergasse) is *Cavallino Bianco* (*Weisses Rossel*), a bierkeller with a menu heavy on Tyrolean specialities (closed July). There's a choice of both Italian and local cooking (including smoked deer and carpaccio) at the excellent, but expensive, *Grifone* (*Greif*) in Piazza Walther.

In the early evening, buskers play on the Portici, where *Bar Gibó* and *Spaghetti Express* (round the corner on Via Goethe) are the places with the most pizzazz. Other than this, **nightlife** is sparse, and the streets empty after about 9pm, but there are a few bars in the town centre and one or two cinemas. *Filmclub Aktuell* (*Filmclub-Filmrunde*) at Dr. Streitergasse 20 shows a selection of European and Hollywood offerings, dubbed into Italian or German. The *Casa della Cultura* (*Kulturhaus*), Via Sciliar 1 (Schlernstrasse), puts on theatre; occasional bands playing at the sports stadium are well postered around town.

Travelling onwards

The major **bus** route out of Bolzano is to **Cortina d'Ampezzo**, a journey involving several changes (via the Val Pusteria). An alternative, more impressive, way is the *Grande Strada delle Dolomiti* (Great Dolomites Road). No public transport travels this route, but it's hitchable and takes you through the Costalungo, Pordoi and Falzarego passes. As the name suggests, it runs through the heart of the Dolomite ranges, but you really need to strike out along some of the trails, away from the stream of tourist coaches, to enjoy the massive extent of the peaks.

Bus drivers will usually take bikes in the storage spaces at the side of the bus. *Velo Sport* at Via Grappoli 56 (Weintraubengasse) hires mountain bikes at L25,000 per day, L35,000 per weekend.

An alternative approach to the **Catinaccio** range (see above), takes you from Bolzano through a narrow, sheer gorge of black porphyry called Val d'Ega (Eggental) – buses from Bolzano make the journey, past the lake at CAREZZA AL LAGO (KARERSEE), and on to Passo Costalunga (Karerpass). A cable car from the lake and trails from the pass lead up into the mountains.

It's worth noting that provincial bus companies stick fairly rigidly to towns within their territory, so that some places which look like they should be easy to get to from Bolzano, often are not. For example, there are more frequent buses to Canazei from Trento, and this is the case for other towns in the northern part of Trentino.

The Alpe di Siusi (Seiser Alm)

The grassy plateaux of the **Alpe di Siusi**, to the north of Bolzano, are unusual because of their extent – over sixty square kilometres – and their incongruous position, high above the rest of the valley at the base of **Sciliar** (Schlern). The valley roads give you little idea of what lies above.

The bus from Bolzano goes to SIUSI, from where another service ascends to the Alpe. On the way, the road climbs through a series of loops past the Hauenstein forest, the ruins of a castle which was once the home of Osvald of Wolkenstein – the last *minnesinger* of the South Tyrol – and the onion-domed church of **San Valentino** (**Saint Valentiskirchlein**). Buses terminate at SALTRIA (SALTNER), at the heart of the wetlands, an area virtually untouched, apart from some logging in the woods. Horses graze on the tough grass which grows up here, picking their way between the bogs and streams; small huts and clumps of pine are dotted across the plateau. Paths lead off the Alpe di Siusi to refuges in the peaks, or there are two hotels that are more or less the only buildings at Saltria: *Brunelle* (☎0471/72.940) is the simpler, with half-pension at L33,000 per person.

Sciliar (Schlern) and Sasso Lungo (Langkofel)

The National Park which spreads over this area is named after **Sciliar (Schlern)**, a flat-topped, sheer mountain which splits into two peaks, Cima Euringer and Santner. Trails lead onto Schlern from TIRES (TIERS), FIÈ AM SCILIAR (VÖLS AM SCHLERN) or SIUSI (SEIS) all involving long, steep climbs up to the summit (2563m). Just before the top is *Rifugio Bolzano al Monte Pez* (*Schlernhaus*; ☎0471/616.024; open June to end of Sept), one of the original alpine huts from the 1880s. The cable car from HOFERALP, above UMS (UMES DI FIÈ), cuts out

1000m of ascent. In summer, paths can be crowded, but the day-trippers tend to disappear back down into the valley by evening, when the teeth of **Sasso Lungo** (**Langkofel**) become blunted by cloud.

Trails onto Sasso Lungo spring from the path between Saltria and **Monte Pana**, above Santa Cristina in the Val Gardena (see below). Half a day's walking brings you to *Rifugio Vicenza* (*Langkofelhütte*; ☎0471/77.315; open end of June to Sept 25) – from here, paths lead across the mountain down to **Passo di Sella** (Sellajoch).

Val Gardena (Grödnertal)

Trails and chair lifts connect the Alpe with the Val Gardena (Grödnertal), a valley of squeaky-clean guest houses and a continuous stream of tourist coaches. The main village in the valley, ORTISEI (SAINT ULRICH), for centuries has been a big producer of hand-carved wooden toys, several families each perpetuating a particular design. Three thousand woodcarvers in the valley still make furniture and religious statues, but Ortisei, like the neighbouring villages of SANTA CRISTINA and SELVA (WOLKENSTEIN), is now mainly a ski resort. Within reach from these is the **Sella Ronda**, a route of ski-runs and lifts encircling the Gruppo Di Sella that make up the heart of the Dolomite skiing area. The massive circuit takes at least a day to complete. **Buses** make the journey back to Bolzano, and it's possible to hitch in the other direction towards the Passo di Sella or Passo di Gardena.

Val Isarco and Val Pusteria

The attraction of the four-hour bus trip from Bolzano to Cortina d'Ampezzo isn't so much what you see of the **Isarco** (Eisack) and **Pusteria** (Pusertal) valleys, but the access it gives to the beginning of the *Alte Vie* and quieter routes into the Val di Funes (Villnöss), the Odle group, and the isolated ridges to the north of Val Pusteria. Largely untouched by tourism, these are great places to walk. In the side valleys dippers dart in and out of the streams and the sawing of timber cuts through the air. Higher up, you're likely to see marmots, and chamoix give away their presence with a tumbling of stones.

The Val Isarco and around

CHIUSA (KLAUSEN), the main village of the southern Val Isarco, is served by trains from Bolzano and Bressanone (Brixen), and buses which continue into the **Val di Funes**, a little to the north. SANTA MADDALENA (SANKT MAGDALENA), surrounded by tracts of pasture, lies 10.5km into the valley, at the base of Le Odle (see above). This quiet village is a good place for an overnight stop: its **hotels** include *Oberkantiol* (☎0472/40.002; open Easter–Nov), which charges from L15,000 per person including breakfast, and cheaper rooms are available in private houses. Another bus climbs halfway up the mountain to ZANSERALM, where it's one hour's walk to *Rifugio Genova* (☎0472/40.132; open July–Sept) at 2301m. The level paths take you above the larch forests which fill the valley, and give fantastic views of the peaks. A four-hour circular trail called the *Sentiero delle Odle* (*Adolf Munkel Weg*) traverses the grass slopes beneath the teeth of the range, from Zanseralm via SAINT RENON to BROGLES-ALM, and back down to the valley. *Alta Via* no. 2 is a short walk from Saint Renon.

Bressanone (Brixen)

Alta Via no. 2 can also be picked up in the foothills above **BRESSANONE (BRIXEN)**, whose bishops – in constant rivalry with the neighbouring Counts of Tyrol – ruled the area as an independent state for a thousand years. The complex of buildings which made up their base is still the focus of the town, ten minutes' walk from the train and bus stations.

The **Duomo**, modernised in the eighteenth century, is the most imposing building in the main square – the interesting part lies to the side, in the cloisters, which were frescoed in the fourteenth century. A small room off the quadrangle contains the **cathedral treasury** (daily 10am–noon & 1–5pm; L1000), where vestments belonging to Bressanone's bishop princes are hung. Their strong influence in the region is evident from the present given by Emperor Henry II to Bishop Albuino: a tenth-century Byzantine silk cloak, spread with the stylised eagle that was the Bishop's personal emblem. The bishop's palace, next to the duomo, is now the **Museo Diocesano** (daily 10am–5pm; L3000), furnished in predictably grand style, with an overwhelming collection of crib scenes in the crypt.

The **tourist office** (Mon–Fri 8am–noon & 2.30–6pm, Sat 9am–noon), opposite the bus station, has information on trails around the town and further afield.

Places to stay in the old town include *Schwarzer Adler*, Via Portici Minori 2 (Kleine Lauben; ☎0472/223.27), with rooms from L40,000 and *Gasthof Grauer Bär*, Mercato Vecchio 27 (Altenmarktgasse; ☎0472/22.472), similarly priced. There are two **campsites** 5km north in VARNA (VAHRN): at Brennerstrasse 13 (☎0472/23.216) and Oberdorf 130 (☎0472/32.169). Several buses travel here on weekdays, fewer at weekends. For **eating**, the narrow streets around the edge of Piazza Duomo (Dom Platz) have some old-established Tyrolean restaurants, and there's a *mensa* at Via Vescovado 2. For picnic food, try the shops in the old arcades or the Monday market on Goethestrasse.

Val Pusteria (Pusertal)

The road through the Val Pusteria (Pusertal), a wide valley of maize fields and hay meadows, sweeps around the northern edge of the Dolomites. Most of the *Alte Vie* start from points along the main road through the valley, served by bus from Brunico. *Alta Via* no. 1 starts from Lago di Braies (Pragser Wildsee), *Alta Via* no. 3 from Villabassa (Niederdorf), no. 4 from San Candido (Innichen) and no. 5 from Sesto (Sexten). Less well known trails lie to the north, for example the *Alta Via Val di Fundres* (Pfunderer Höhenweg), details of which are given below.

Brunico (Bruneck)

An influx of people from the surrounding villages arrives daily in the market town of Brunico (Bruneck), which is also the transport centre of the region, with buses along the valley and to most of the small places higher up in the hills. A stopping train makes the journey along the Val Pusteria to the end of the line at DOBBIACO; buses from Brunico to Cortina d'Ampezzo also go through Dobbiaco. The **tourist office** at Via Europa, above the **bus station** gives details of **places to stay** from L12,000 per person in the small villages around the town. The more central *Blitzburg*, Via Europa 10 (☎0474/85.723), has rooms for L50,000, and *Corona* (*Krone*) at Via Ragen di Sopra 8 (Oberagen;☎0474/85.267) charges from L21,000 per person. Brunico was home of painter and sculptor Michael Pacher: if you have some spare time between buses, his *Vine Madonna* in San Lorenzo (Saint Lorenzen) parish church, is 4km southwest from the town centre.

Alta Via di Fundres (Pfunderer Höhenweg)

The high-level **Alta Via di Fundres** (**Pfunderer Höhenweg**) follows the ridges north of Brunico. Although it's in the lower part of the Zillertaler Alps, the path gives a feeling of the high mountains, with views across to the glaciers of Gran Pilastro (Hochfeiler) on the Austrian border. It's an exhilarating area, often with snow, ice and scorching sun in the same day. Access to the path is at Kleines Tor (2374m) on Monte Sommo (Sambock), a steep climb along path no. 29 from SELVA DEI MOLINI (MÜHLWALD), 24km from Brunico. The walk takes four to five days, with overnight stops in refuges or *bivacci*.

From Kleines Tor the path drops down to the Winnebach valley, then climbs to *Fritz Walde Hütte*. A steep path crosses the Hochsagescharte Col (2650m), drops to Passenjoch (2410m) and then, after a westerly descent to *Gampes Hütte* (2223m), makes a spectacular traverse across steep pasture that eventually descends to the Eisbrugger valley. The end of the route at VIPITENO (STERZING) is reached via BODEN and the Weitenber valley. Early on the last day you can be descending across pasture just emerging from snow, and in the evening be eating pizza in town, listening to kids roar around on motorbikes. It's possible to do half of the walk by joining the path above FUNDRES, or the top of the Val di Valles (Valser Tal), where there's accommodation at *Brixner Hütte* (☎0472/57.131; open late June to late Sept).

Dobbiaco (Toblach) and around

In the eastern part of the Val Pusteria, civilisation and streams of car-borne German tourists resume at **DOBBIACO**, a stultifying resort and spa town at the junction of roads into the Val di Sesto (Sextental), and the Val di Landro (Höhlenstein Tal). The latter takes you south past Lago di Dobbiaco onto the Alemagna, the pilgrims' route from Germany to Rome. The Val di Landro bus rounds the outer peaks of the Cristallo mountain group, where the road is flanked by forest on either side, before emerging at Cortina d'Ampezzo.

Cortina d'Ampezzo

The 1956 Winter Olympics were staged at **CORTINA D'AMPEZZO** (it still has the *Pista Olimpica di Bob*), an event which began the tranformation of the town from a small resort to a city in the mountains. Its raison d'être is the skiing season – roughly Christmas to Easter – when the population rises from 8000 to around 50,000, packing out the designer-clothes and antiques shops as well as the slopes around the city. Cortina is the Italian equivalent of Saint Moritz, attracting actors, artists, and anyone who's rich: if you don't wear mink, you'll feel in a minority and the city encourages a kind of Hollywood existence – taking sleighs down the mountain after a meal at *Il Meloncino*, or hiring jeeps to get to places for off-piste skiing.

The setting is stunning, surrounded by a great circle of mountains which includes Pelmo and Antelao, the Marmarole, Sorapiss, Cristallo and the Tofane. The bad news is that staying here is prohibitively expensive, unless you manage to book a room at the only two cheap places in town: *Albergo Cavallino*, Corso

Italia 142 (☎0436/2614), at L48,000 including breakfast, and *Battochio*, at Via Franchetti 4 (☎0436/2430), at L45,000. Women who write far enough in advance may be able to get a bed in one of the convent hostels. The names and addresses to try are: Rev. Suore Canossiane, *Casa Regina Mundi*, Località Crignes 18 (☎0436/2660); Rev. Suore Francescane, *Casa San Francesco*, Località Cianderies 7 (☎0436/2279); Rev. Suore Missionaire dell'Eucarestia, Via XXIX Maggio 2 (☎0436/4662); and Rev. Suore Orsoline S. Cuore, Via Faloria (☎0436/3267).

In summer, there's the option of camping. *Cortina* (☎0436/24.83), *Dolomiti* (☎0436/2485) and *Rochetta* (☎0436/5063) are all 2km to the south, at CAMPO, while *Olympia* (☎0436/5057) is at FIAMES, 5km north. It must be said, though, that Cortina in summer deserves to be given a wide berth. The resort's interest lies in the people who come here to show off, and out of season the place is dead. It does have a summer hiking season of sorts, between the beginning of July and mid-September when the cable cars operate, but the ranges are less crowded from the side which lies away from the city, and are better approached from smaller resorts.

Cortina's **APT** offices are at Piazzetta San Francesco 8 and Piazza Roma. Their hiking map is good, with refuge phone numbers and an indication of how long trails take to walk. Apart from the tortuous **bus** routes via Bolzano and Belluno, there are long distance **coaches** to Cortina from Milan, Padua and Bologna; information from the **bus station** on Via Marconi, above town.

Around Cortina

Cortina is better known for trips by road and cable car than for mountain trails, with many drivers heading for the *Grande Strada delle Dolomiti* and its passes. In summer there are buses to the small lake at MISURINA, and the TRE CIME, three mountain peaks to the north of the city – both extremely busy areas in high season. The alternatives are to head south by bus towards Belluno, passing through Titian's home town of PIEVE DI CADORE, with many paintings attributed to him in the Parrocchiale. (The one most likely to be authentic is in the third chapel on the left.) Unless you hitch, it's difficult to reach the most interesting mountains in these parts. One bus route can be recommended, running from Belluno to Arabba and Corvara (see above), via Álleghe. The lake at Álleghe was created after a huge rock avalanche in the eighteenth century – a common occurance in the area. Álleghe gives access to the rock walls of Monte Civetta (3220m), a superb sight late in the day when the sun is low. *Rifugio Sonino*, three and a half hours' walk from Álleghe, next to the small Lago Coldai (2208m), has overnight accommodation.

travel details

Trains
From Trento to Verona (virtually hourly; 1hr 5min), Bolzano (virtually hourly; 35min), Bologna (12 daily; 3hr 10min), Rovereto (virtually hourly; 14min), Venice (7 daily; 3hr 45min).
From Bolzano to Chiusa (every 2 hours; 27min), and on to Bressanone (38min), change at Fortezza (46min) for Brunico. To Merano (virtually hourly; 40min).
From Merano to Silandro (7 daily; 37min).

From Fortezza to Brunico (9 daily; 39min) and on to Monguelfo (1hr 5min) Villabassa (1hr 11min) Dobbiaco (1hr 18min) and San Candido (1hr 22min).
Connections from Trento and Bolzano with fast trains to Hamburg, Munich and Innsbruck.

Buses
From Trento to Calliano and Rovereto (virtually hourly Mon–Sat; 7 daily Sun; 40min); Madonna di

Campiglio (4 daily; 2hr 10min); Molveno (Trento-Malé line 6 daily; 2hr); Cles (Trento-Malé line 12 daily, 9 on Sun; 1hr) and on to Malé (another 20min); Belluno (1 daily Mon–Sat; 2hr 40min); Canazei via Cavalese, Predazzo & Vigo di Fassa (3 daily; 2hr 37min); San Martino via Imer, Mezzano, Fiero di Primiero (3 daily Mon–Sat & 1 on Sun; 3hr).

From Fiero di Primiero to Castelpietra and Passo Cereda (2 daily Mon–Sat; 25min).

From San Martino to Passo di Rolle, Paneveggio, Predazzo (with connections for Trento) (2 daily Mon–Sat; 1hr 15min).

From Corvara to Belluno via Arabba & Alleghe (2 daily, 1 on Sun; 2hr 45min); Longega (6 daily Mon–Fri, 2 at weekend; 45min) & Brunico (1hr 7min). Connections from Longega to San Vigilio di Marebbe (6 daily Mon–Fri, 9 on Sat & 1 on Sun; 10min).

From Brunico to San Vigilio di Marebbe (4 daily Mon–Fri, 3 on Sat, 1 on Sun; 35min); San Candido via Monguelfo, Villabassa and Dobbiaco (8 daily Mon–Fri & 5 at weekends; 50min).

From Bolzano to Selva and Val Gardena (4 daily Mon–Fri & 2 at weekends; 1hr 28min); Cortina d'Ampezzo (4 daily; 3hr 35min); Fiero di Primiero via Predazzo & San Martino (1 daily Mon–Sat; 3hr 45min); Val d'Ega, Carezza al Lago & Passo Costalunga (2 daily Mon–Fri; 4 at weekend; 1hr) and on to Vigo di Fassa & Canazei (1 daily Mon–Fri; 2 at weekend; 1hr 55min); Merano (2 daily Mon–Sat & 1 on Sun; 40min); Silandro (4 daily Mon–Sat & 1 on Sun; 1hr); Corvara (2 daily Mon–Fri; 1hr 15min); Siusi (8 daily; 45min).

From Siusi to Saltria (6 daily; 1hr); Tires (4 daily Mon–Sat; 43min).

From Chiusa to Santa Maddalena (4 daily Mon–Sat; 35min).

From Merano to Santa Caterina (3 daily; 53min); San Leonardo (10 daily Mon–Sat & 5 on Sun; 48 min) and on to Moso (1h 10min); Santa Gertrude (5 daily Mon–Fri; 2 at weekend; 1hr 25min); Passo di Stelvio (1 daily; 3hr); Solda (2 daily in summer); Silandro (8 daily Mon–Fri & 5 at weekend; 1hr 5min).

From Silandro to Rifugio Genziana in Val Martello (2 daily Sun; 1hr 16min);

From Moso to Plata near Ulfas (3 daily; 7min).

From Cortina d'Ampezzo to Dobbiaco (5 daily; 45min); Pieve di Cadore (7 daily Mon–Sat & 5 on Sun; 50min) and on to Belluno (1hr 55min); Calalzo (18 daily; 1hr) with train connections from Calalzo to Belluno (10 daily; 1hr).

CHAPTER FIVE

VENICE AND THE VENETO

The first-time visitor to **Venice** arrives with a heavy freight of expectations, many of which turn out to be well-founded. All the photographs you've seen of the **Palazzo Ducale**, of the **Basilica di San Marco**, of the **Piazza San Marco** (simply known as "the Piazza"), the **Rialto Bridge**, the palaces along the **Canal Grande** – they've simply been recording the extraordinary truth. Everything you've heard about the city turns out to be right as well. It is deluged with tourists, the annual influx exceeding Venice's population two-hundredfold. A couple of years ago things got so bad that entry into the city was barred to those who hadn't already booked a room. And it is expensive – the price of a good meal anywhere else in Italy will get you a lousy one in Venice, and its hoteliers make the most of a situation where demand will always far outstrip supply.

As soon as you begin to explore Venice, though, every day will bring its surprises. Wandering away from the centre, you enter an urban landscape so rich that you can't walk for a minute without coming across something that's worth a stop. Major sights such as the **Scuola di San Rocco**, the **Accademia**, the **Ca' d'Oro**, the colossal church of **I Frari** and the equally stupendous **San Zanipolo**, are scattered all over the city, and there's hardly a parish whose church doesn't offer something of interest, whether it be an altarpiece or an architectural detail. And although it's true that Venice can be unbearably crowded, things aren't so bad beyond the magnetic field of San Marco and the kitsch-sellers of the vicinity, and in the off-season it's still possible to have parts of the centre virtually to yourself. As for keeping your costs down – Venice has plenty of markets apart from the celebrated Rialto, there are *some* inexpensive eating places, and you *can* find a bed for the night without spending a fortune.

Tourism is far from being the only strand to the economy of **the Veneto** – it has Italy's most productive vineyards, and at Marghera, just over the lagoon from Venice, it has the largest industrial complex in the country. But it is important, and the region has more tourist accommodation than any other region in Italy. After Venice, it's **Padua** and **Verona** that are the main attractions, with their masterpieces by Giotto, Donatello and Mantegna, and a profusion of great buildings from Roman times to the Renaissance. None of the other towns of the Veneto can match the cultural wealth of these two former rivals to Venice, but there are nonetheless plenty of places between the plains of Polesine in the south and the mountains in the north that justify a detour – the Palladian city of **Vicenza**, for instance, or the fortified settlements of **Montagnana**, **Cittadella** and **Castelfranco**, or the idyllic upland town of **Ásolo**.

For outdoor types, much of the Veneto is dull – flatlands interrupted by gentle outcrops around Padua and Vicenza. The interesting terrain lies in its northern part, especially in the area above **Vittorio Veneto**, where the wooded slopes of the foothills – excellent for walking – soon give way to the savage precipices of the eastern Dolomites.

VENICE (VENEZIA)

Small groups of fishermen and hunters were living on the mudbanks of the Venetian lagoon at the start of the Christian era, but it was with the barbarian invasions of the fifth century and after that sizeable communities began to settle on the mudbanks. The first mass migration was provoked by the arrival in the Veneto of **Attila the Hun**'s hordes in 453, and the rate of settlement accelerated a century later, when, in 568, the **Lombards** (or Longobards) swept into northern Italy.

The loose confederation of island communes that began to develop in the sixth century owed political allegiance to Byzantium, and until the end of the seventh century its senior officials were effectively controlled by the Byzantine hierarchy of Ravenna. But with the steep increase in the population of the islands which resulted from the strengthening of the Lombard grip on the Veneto in the later seventh century, the ties with the Empire grew weaker, and in 726 the settlers chose their own leader of the provincial government – their first **doge**.

The control of Byzantium soon became no more than nominal, and the traders and boatmen of the lagoon signalled their independence through one great symbolic act – the theft of the body of **Saint Mark** from Alexandria in 828. Saint Mark displaced Byzantium's Saint Theodore as the city's patron, and a basilica was built alongside the doge's castle to accommodate the relics. These two buildings – the **Basilica di San Marco** and the **Palazzo Ducale** – were to remain the emblems of the Venetian state and the repository of power within the city for almost one thousand years.

Before the close of the tenth century the Venetian **trading networks** were well established through concessions granted by Byzantium in the markets of the East, and the exploitation of the waterways of northern Italy to distribute the goods from the Levant. By the early twelfth century Venetian merchants had won exemption from all tolls within the Eastern Empire and were profiting from the chaos that followed the **First Crusade**, which had been launched in 1095. Prosperity found expression in the fabric of the city: the present-day Basilica and many of its mosaics are from this period; and at the end of the century the Piazza was brought to something close to its modern shape. The **Fourth Crusade**, diverted to Constantinople by the Venetians, set the seal on their maritime empire. They brought back shiploads of treasure (including the horses of San Marco) from the **Sack of Constantinople** in 1204, but more significant was the division of the territorial spoils, which left "one quarter and half a quarter" of the Roman Empire under Venice's sway, and gave the Republic a chain of ports that stretched almost without a break from the lagoon to the Black Sea.

For almost all the fourteenth century, the defeat of Genoa – Venice's main rival in the eastern markets – preoccupied Venice's rulers, who finally secured the Republic's economic and political supremacy after the defeat of the Genoese in the **War of Chioggia** (1379–80).

It was during the Genoese campaigns that the **constitution** of Venice arrived at a state that was to endure until the fall of the Republic, the largest step in this evolution being the **Serrata del Maggior Consiglio** of 1297, a measure which basically restricted participation in the government of the city to those families already involved in it. A revolt of disgruntled aristocrats in 1310 led to the creation of the **Council of Ten** to supervise internal security – intended to be an emergency measure, it was made permanent in 1334, and became the most secretive and most feared state institution.

Venetian foreign policy was predominantly eastward-looking from the start, but a degree of intervention on the mainland was necessary to maintain its continental trade routes. By the middle of the fifteenth century, Venice was in possession of a mainland empire that was to survive virtually intact until the coming of Napoleon.

But while Venice was advancing at home, the **Ottoman Turks** were emerging as a threat to the colonial empire. Constantinople fell to the Sultan's army in 1453, and with their capture of the main fortresses of the Morea (Peloponnese) in 1499, the Turks gained control of the access to the Adriatic.

Distrust of Venice's ambitions on the mainland and fear of Turkish expansion provoked the formation of the **League of Cambrai** in 1508. Headed by Pope Julius II, Louis XII, Emperor Maximilian and the King of Spain, it pitted almost every power in Europe against the Venetians, in a pact that set out to destroy Venice's empire as a prelude to conquering the Turks. When the fighting finished in 1516, Venice's subtle diplomacy had ensured that it still possessed nearly all the land it had held a decade before but many of the cities of the Veneto had been sacked, great swathes of the countryside ruined, and the Venetian treasury bled almost dry.

Worse was to come. After Vasco Da Gama's voyage to India via the Cape of Good Hope, the slow and expensive land routes across Asia to the markets and docks of Venice could now be bypassed by the merchants of northern Europe. The economic balance of Europe now began to tilt in favour of the Portuguese, the English and the Dutch.

After the **Sack of Rome** in 1527 the whole Italian peninsula, with the sole exception of Venice, came under the domination of Charles V. Hemmed in at home, Venice saw its overseas territory further whittled away by the Turks as the century progressed: by 1529 the Ottoman Empire extended right along the southern Mediterranean to Morocco, and even the great naval success at **Lepanto** in **1571** was quickly followed by the surrender of Cyprus.

At the start of the seventeenth century a row with Rome, concerning the extent of papal jurisdiction within the Republic, culminated in 1606 with the excommunication of the entire city. After a year of arguments the **Papal Interdict** was lifted, damaging the prestige of the papacy throughout Europe. Relations with the **Hapsburgs** were no easier. The Austrian branch caused trouble by encouraging pirate raids on Venetian shipping, and in 1618 the more devious Spanish wing attempted to subvert the Venetian state by a wildly ambitious plot that has always been known as **The Spanish Conspiracy**. But the **Turks** caused the most lasting damage, taking the one remaining stronghold in the eastern Mediterranean, Crete, in 1669.

Venice in the eighteenth century became a political nonentity, reduced to pursuing a policy of unarmed neutrality. At home, the economy remained healthy, but the division between the upper stratum of the aristocracy and the ever-increasing poorer section was widening, and all attempts to dampen discontent within the city by democratising its government were stifled by the conservative elite.

Politically moribund and constitutionally ossified, Venice was renowned not as one of the great powers of Europe, but rather as its playground, a city of casinos and perpetual festivals. **Napoleon** brought the show to an end. On May 12, 1797 the *Maggior Consiglio* met for the last time, voting to accede to Napoleon's demand that it dismantle the machinery of government. In October, Napoleon relinquished Venice to the Austrians, but returned in 1805 to join the city to his Kingdom of Italy, and it stayed under French rule until after Waterloo. It then passed back to the Austrians again, and remained a Hapsburg province until united with the Kingdom of Italy in 1866.

During the French occupation a large number of buildings were demolished to facilitate urban improvement schemes and modernisation projects were continued under the Austrians. They created most of the *rii terrà* (infilled canals), constructed two new bridges across the Canal Grande, and built a rail link with the mainland.

Yet Venice in the nineteenth century was almost destitute. Eclipsed as an Adriatic port by Trieste (the Austrians' preference), Venice achieved large-scale expansion in the area of **tourism**, with the development of the **Lido** as Europe's most fashionable resort. It was the need for a more substantial economic base that led, in the wake of World War I, to the construction of the industrial complex on the marshland across the lagoon from Venice, at **Marghera**, a processing and refining centre to which raw materials would be brought by sea. In 1933 a road link was built to carry the workforce between Venice and the steadily expanding complex, but it was not until after World War II that Marghera's growth accelerated. The factories of Marghera are essential to the economy of the province, but they have caused terrible problems too: apart from polluting the environment of the lagoon, they have siphoned many people out of Venice and into the cheaper housing of Mestre, making Mestre-Marghera today more than three times larger than the historic centre of Venice, where the population has dropped since the last war from around 170,000 to about 80,000. No city has suffered more from the tourist industry than Venice – about 20 million people visit the city each year, and around half of those don't even stay a night – though without them Venice would barely exist at all.

Arriving, information and getting around

Flights to Venice arrive at either **Treviso** airport, 30km from Venice, or at the city's **Marco Polo** airport, on the edge of the lagoon. From the former, buses run to Treviso train station, from where there are regular train services to Venice. Coaches and (exorbitant) water taxis link Marco Polo to the city centre but the cheapest option by far is the *ACTV* bus #5, which runs hourly and costs just L600. All road traffic comes into the city at **Piazzale Roma**, at the head of the Canal Grande; two *vaporetto* (water bus) services run between the Piazzale and the San Marco area – the same services call at Santa Lucia **train station**, the next stop along the Canal Grande (see below). If you're coming right into Venice by **car**, you'll have to park in either the Piazzale Roma multi-storey carpark, or on the adjoining Tronchetto, a vast artificial island created specifically for the purpose. The queues for both can be huge – a better option in summer is to park in Mestre's municipal carpark, then take a bus over the causeway.

The main **EPT** information office (summer daily 8.30am–7pm; winter 8.30am–2pm) is under the Piazza's arcades, at the end farthest from the Basilica; smaller offices operate at the train station (daily 8am–8pm) and, in summer only, at Piazzale Roma. The free map distributed by the EPT is fine for general orientation, but not much else. Far more useful is the English-Italian magazine *Un Ospite di Venezia*, produced weekly in summer and monthly in winter, which gives up-to-date information on exhibitions, special events and *vaporetto* timetables – it's free from the main office, and from the receptions of the posher hotels.

The transport system

Venice has two interlocking street-systems – the canals and the pavements – and contrary to what you might expect, you'll be using the latter for most of the time. The public transport boats operate along just two of the city's canals – the Canal Grande and the Rio Nuovo–Rio Ca' Fóscari (which cuts through to the Canal Grande from Piazzale Roma). Otherwise they skirt the city centre, connecting points on the periphery and the outer islands. In most cases the speediest way of getting around is **on foot**. Distances between major sights are extremely short (you can cross the whole city in an hour), and once you've got your general bearings you'll find that navigation is not as daunting a prospect as it seems.

The Venice area telephone code is ☎041

VENICE

S. Michele

Miracoli

S.S. Giovanni
e Paolo

S. Francesco
della Vigna

S. Maria
Formosa

CASTELLO

S. Marco

PIAZZA
SAN MARCO

Palazzo
Ducale

Pieta

Arsenale

S. Pietro di Castello

EASTERN DISTRICTS

S. Giorgio
Maggiore

Giardini
Pubblici

S. Elena

The water buses

A **water bus** can be the quickest way of getting between two points, though, and even in cases where it would be quicker to walk, a canal trip is often the more pleasant way of covering the distance. The lack of clear numbering on many of the boats is confusing at first, but in fact the routes are pretty straightforward.

There are two basic types of boat: the **vaporetti**, which are the lumbering workhorses used on the Canal Grande stopping service and other slow routes, and the **motoscafi**, smaller vessels employed on routes where a bit of speed is needed. **Tickets** are available from most landing stages and from shops displaying the *ACTV* sign. Flat-rate fares apply for each service – L2000 for the #2 and #4, L1500 for other lines within the city. In the remoter parts of the city, though, you may not be able to find anywhere to buy a ticket (particularly after working hours); as tickets bought on board are subject to a surcharge, and the spot-fine for not having a valid ticket is L15,000, it's a good idea to buy a block of ten (*un blochetto*). A *Biglietto Turistico* gives you unlimited travel for a 24-hour period, but as it costs L8000 you'd have to spend a hell of a lot of time on the boat to make it cost effective. If you think you'll be making more than half a dozen trips, it's worth investing in a *Carta Venezia*. This also costs L8000, and entitles you to travel for L500 per journey (L600 on the *diretto*), as well as on all *ACTV* road buses – and it's valid for three years, so will be useful on your next visit too. Take a small photo and your passport to the *ACTV* office in Corte dell'Albero, near the Sant'Angelo stop on the Canal Grande.

Timetables are posted at each stop, and details of the more important lines are included in each issue of *Un Ospite di Venezia*. The city centre services run through the night, at greatly reduced frequency after about 1am.

USEFUL WATER BUS SERVICES

#1: the so-called *accelerato*, perversely the slowest of the water buses; it starts at the Piazzale Roma, calls at all but one of the stops on the Canal Grande, works its way along the San Marco waterfront to Santa Elena, then goes over to the Lido.

#2: known as the *diretto*, the quickest way to get between San Marco and Piazzale Roma or the train station; from the Rialto it goes to the top of the Canal Grande, along the Rio Nuovo and Rio Fóscari, then off to the Lido via San Marco. Stops only six times along the Canal Grande, as against the #1's fourteen stops.

#4: known as the *turistico*; a limited-stop summer service along the Canal Grande and across to the Lido.

#5: known as the *circolare*, this comes in two forms. The *destra* goes from the Fondamente Nuove, through the Arsenale to San Zaccaria, zigzags between La Giudecca and the Záttere, goes up to Piazzale Roma and the station, along the Canale di Cannaregio, back to the Fondamente Nuove, then over to the cemetery and Murano. The *sinistra* does the same in reverse – so if you jump on a #5, make sure you know which way round the city it's going. Be warned that the #5 sometimes shoots off up the Canal Grande instead of heading over to San Giorgio Maggiore and La Giudecca; called the *barrato*, this version of the service is more common in winter – look for the sign on the side of the boat reading "Diretto – Piazzale Roma".

#8: shuttles between the Riva degli Schiavoni, San Giorgio, La Giudecca and the Záttere.

#12: runs to the northern islands from the Fondamente Nuove.

Traghetti

As there are only three bridges along the Canal Grande – at the train station, Rialto and Accademia – the *traghetti* (gondola ferries) which cross it can be useful time-savers. Costing just L300, they are also the only cheap way of getting a ride on a gondola – though it's *de rigeur* to stand in a *traghetto* rather than sit. In summer most of the Canal Grande *traghetti* run from early morning to around 7–9pm daily.

In addition to these, some *vaporetti* and *motoscafi* operate as *traghetti* across the Canal Grande and over to the nearer islands: for example, if you want go from San Zaccaria over to San Giorgio Maggiore, you need only pay the L1000 *traghetto* fare. If your journey is a single-stop trip across a body of water, check if a *traghetto* fare applies – it'll be shown on the tariff list on the ticket booth.

Gondolas

The **gondola** is no longer a form of transport but rather an adjunct of the tourist industry. To hire one costs L50,000 an hour for up to five passengers, then L25,000 for every additional 25 minutes; between 8pm and 8am the rate goes up to L60,000. Even though the tariff is set by the local authorities, it's been known for some gondoliers to try to extort a little more. If you do decide to go for a ride, be sure to establish the charge before setting off.

Finding a place to stay

If you arrive with nowhere to stay and don't want to spend your first hours hunting for a bed, there are plenty of **booking offices**: at the **train station** (daily 8am–9pm); on the **Tronchetto** (9am–8pm); at **Piazzale Roma** (9am–9pm); at **Marco Polo airport** (summer 9am–7pm; winter noon–7pm); and at the **autostrada's Venice exit** (8am–8pm). They only deal with hotels and take a L10,000 deposit, deductable from your first night's bill.

Hotels

High season is approximately from mid-March to late October, plus two weeks around Christmas and New Year and the period of the Carnevale (the ten days in February up to Shrove Tuesday). At any time during these periods it's wisest to book a hotel room well in advance, and for July and August it's virtually obligatory.

During the winter it's possible to bargain for a reduced-rate room, but many hotels close down from November to February, so you might have to put in a bit of leg-work before finding somewhere.

Breakfast should be optional, but many hotels get around this regulation by saying that the price of the room includes breakfast. If it's at all possible, get a room without breakfast, as even in the humblest places a jug of coffee and a puny croissant can put L9000 on your bill. Your money is better spent joining the locals in a nearby café.

Unless specified otherwise, the prices quoted below are the **minimum** for a double, excluding the cost of breakfast, which you might not be able to avoid. In the peak season, expect to pay at least ten percent more.

San Marco

Casa Petrarca, Calle delle Colonne, San Marco 4394 (☎700.430). With doubles from L32,000, the cheapest near the Piazza – but phone first, as they only have six rooms. Extremely hospitable, with English-speaking staff.

Fiorita, Campiello Nuovo, San Marco 3457 (☎523.4754). Just nine rooms, so again it's important to book. Welcoming management, and there's a nearby *traghetto* across the Canal Grande. L32,000.

San Samuele, Piscina S. Samuele, San Marco 3358 (☎522.8045). Another friendly place, with rooms distinctly less shabby than some at this end of the market. L37,000.

Dorsoduro

Antico Capon, Campo S. Margherita, Dorsoduro 3004 (☎528.5292). Situated on one of the city's most atmospheric squares, in the heart of the student district. L38,000.

Montin, Fondamenta di Borgo, Dorsoduro 1147 (☎522.7151). Famed for its restaurant, though the food is on a different price-scale to the accommodation. Only seven rooms. L35,000.

San Polo

Ca' Fóscari, Calle della Frescada, Dorsoduro 3888 (☎522.5817). Tucked away in a micro-alley near San Tomà, near the university. Quiet, well decorated and relaxed. Despite its size (ten rooms), you can sometimes find a room even when all other hotels are booked out. L33,000.

Stefania, Fondamenta Tolentini, S. Croce 181 (☎520.3757). A few minutes from the Piazzale Roma, so has an international clientele. Big rooms, some with bizarre murals. L32,000.

Sturion, Calle del Sturion, S. Polo 679 (☎523.6243). Needs to be booked in advance, as it's popular with Italian families. One of the few bargains along the Canal Grande. L30,000.

Tivoli, Crosera S. Pantalon, Dorsoduro 3638 (☎523.7752). The biggest cheap hotel in the immediate vicinity, with 24 rooms – so often has space when the rest are full. L36,000.

Cannaregio

Alle Guglie, Rio Terrà S. Leonardo, Cannaregio 1523 (☎717.351). Miniscule place, with one bathroom between four rooms; the cheapest around. L22,000.

Casa Carettoni, Lista di Spagna, Cannaregio 130 (☎716.231). By a long way the most comfortable one-star in the vicinity. L40,000.

Eden, Rio Terrà Maddalena, Cannaregio 2357 (☎720.228). One to try if you're travelling alone, as it has singles from L20,000. Doubles from L30,000.

Castello

Al Piave, Ruga Giuffa, Castello 4838 (☎528.5174). Not the most picturesque of places, but clean. L38,000.

Albergo Bernardi Semenzato, Calle dell'Oca, Cannaregio 4366 (☎522.7257). The owners speak good English, and are concerned for the welfare of impecunious young people visiting the city. Singles from L19,000, doubles from L30,000 – around L2000 extra for shower.

Caneva, Ramo della Fava, Castello 5515 (☎522.8118). On the approach to the busy Campo San Bartolomeo, yet very peaceful; has a private inner courtyard and overlooks the Rio della Fava. L28,000.

Doni, Fondamenta del Vin, Castello 4656 (☎522.4267). Behind San Marco, heading towards San Zaccaria; most of the eleven rooms look over the Rio del Vin or over the courtyard.

Arsenale

Sant'Anna, Corte del Bianco, Castello 269 (☎528.6466). Good for families with children, as it has rooms for three or four people and is fairly near the Giardini Pubblici. Although it's in one of the remotest parts of the city, beyond the far end of Via Garibaldi, it's been discovered in recent years, so book well in advance. L32,000.

Toscana-Tofanelli, Via Garibaldi, Castello 1650 (☎523.5722). Spartan, but a terrific site, and with a very good trattoria. One of the best deals for someone travelling alone, with singles at L18,000; doubles from L32,000.

Hostels

Venice's **hostels**, most of which are run by religious foundations, are generally comfortable, well-run and inexpensive – and even in the high season they will have a place or two to spare. Each year the tourist office produces a simple typed list of all hostel accommodation in the city; if the places listed below are full, ask for a copy at the San Marco branch.

Archie's House, Rio Terrà San Leonardo, Cannaregio 1814/b (☎720.884). Archie himself is easy-going but runs a tight ship: no one under 21, no rowdy behaviour, and payment in advance. Prices vary depending on the size of the group, the time of year and the number of nights you stay. Expect to pay L13,000–17,000. No breakfast.

Domus Cavanis, Rio Terrà Foscarini, Dorsoduro 912 (☎528.7374). Catholic-run (so separate male and female rooms); open June–Sept; L27,000 each for the double rooms. Full dinners L8000.

Domus Civica, Calle Campazzo, San Polo 3082 (☎721.103). A student house in winter, open to women travellers June–July and Sept–Oct. Most rooms are double with running water; showers free; no breakfast; reception 7.30–11.30am; 11.30pm curfew. Around L22,000 per person.

Foresteria Valdese, Santa Maria Formosa, Castello 5170 (☎528.6797). Difficult to find – go from Campo Santa Maria Formosa along the Calle Lunga, and it's at the foot of the bridge at the far end. Two large dorms, and a couple of rooms for two to four people, plus a self-catering flat for three to six people, which is very pleasant and usually heavily booked. Registration 11am–1pm and 6–8.30pm. L20,000 per person for a room; L16,000 for a dorm, including breakfast and shower.

Ostello Venezia, Fondementa delle Zitelle, Guidecca 86 (☎523.8211). The official *YHA* hostel, in a superb location looking over to San Marco from the island of Giudecca. The waiting room opens at noon in summer and 4pm in winter for the 6pm registration, and it's a good idea to get there early; from October to May you can reserve a place by phone. Curfew at 11.30pm, chucking-out time 9am. If it's full, don't panic: they use a local school with camp-beds as an annexe. L12,000 includes breakfast and sheets. Full (and excellent) meals at L8000. *IYHF* card necessary, but you can join on the spot.

Camping

All the **campsites** require boat rides. There are a number along the **Litorale del Cavallino**, stretching from the Punta Sabbioni to Jésolo, accessible on *vaporetto* #14, from the Riva degli Schiavoni to the Punta. But these are expensive, and the boat trip takes forty minutes. Two are *Marina di Venezia* (Via Montello 6, ☎966.146; April–Sept; minimum stay 3 days) and *Miramare* (Lungomare Dante Alighieri 29, ☎966.150; April–Sept).

The **Lido** is a shorter ride away; its 150-place *San Nicolò* site is at Riviera San Nicolò 65 (☎767.415); an International Camping Card is necessary.

There's an all-year site at **Fusina** (*Mestre Fusina*, Via Moranzani, ☎969.055), but the direct *vaporetto* (#16) only operates in the summer; at other times you have to get the bus to the Mestre and change there.

Some travellers used to spread their sleeping bags on the forecourt of the train station in summer, but this was banned a couple of years ago, leading to the *Scuola San Caboto*, Cannaregio 1104/f (☎716.629), opening its doors to take in the displaced *saccopelisti*, as they're called. The school charges L5000 for sleeping in its garden under the stars, L8000 with your tent, L6500 with their tent, L10,000 dorm-style in the school buildings. It's open 7pm to midnight, and you have to be out by 9am. Follow the signs from the Ponte delle Guglie, on the Canale di Cannaregio.

Recently there's been a resurgence of the *saccopelisti*, but the makeshift campground has shifted to the opposite bank of the canal, next to San Simeone Piccolo. The situation changes each year – the tourist office at the station will tell you if San Caboto has been joined by other refuges for sleeping-baggers.

The City

The 118 islands of central Venice are divided into six districts known as *sestieri*, and the houses within each *sestiere* are numbered in a sequence that makes sense solely to the functionaries of the post office – this explains how buildings facing each other across an alleyway can have numbers which are separated by hundreds.

The *sestiere* of **San Marco** is the zone where the majority of the essential sights are clustered, and is accordingly the most expensive and most crowded district of the city. On the east it's bordered by **Castello**, and on the north by **Cannaregio** – both of which become more residential, and poorer and quieter, the further you go from the centre of the city. On the other side of the Canal Grande, the largest of the *sestieri* is **Dorsoduro**, which stretches from the fashionable quarter at the southern tip of the canal to the docks in the west. **Santa Croce**, named after a now demolished church, roughly follows the curve of the Canal Grande from Piazzale Roma to a point just short of the Rialto, where it joins the smartest and commercially most active of the districts on this bank – **San Polo**.

To the uninitiated, the boundaries of the *sestieri* seem arbitrary, and they are of little use as a means of structuring a guide. So, although in some instances we've used *sestiere* as broad indicators of location, the boundaries of our sections have been chosen for their practicality, and do not, except in the case of *San Marco*, follow the city's official divisions.

San Marco

The section of Venice enclosed by the lower loop of the Canal Grande – a rectangle smaller than 1000 metres by 500 – is, in essence, the Venice of the travel brochures. The plush hotels are concentrated here, as are the swankier shops and the best-known cultural draws of the city. But small though this area is, you can still lose the hordes within it.

Piazza San Marco

"The finest drawing-room in Europe" was how Napoleon described the **Piazza San Marco** (the only *piazza* in Venice, all other squares being *campi* or *campielli*). Less genteel phrases might seem appropriate on a suffocating summer afternoon, but you can take some slight consolation from the knowledge that the Piazza has always been congested. Neither is the influx of foreigners a modern phenomenon – its parades, festivities and markets have always drawn visitors from all over the continent and beyond, the biggest attraction being a huge international trade fair known as the **Fiera della Sensa**, which kept the Piazza buzzing for the fortnight following the Ascension Day ceremony of the marriage of Venice to the sea. The coffee shops of the Piazza were a vital component of eighteenth-century high society, and the two survivors from that period – *Florian* and *Quadri* – are still the smartest and most expensive in town: an espresso in *Florian* will set you back L5000, plus a L3000 supplement for the thrill of hearing the band's rendition of *My Way* or the best of Lloyd-Webber.

Most of the landscape of the Piazza dates from the great period of urban renewal which began at the end of the fifteenth century and went on for much of the following century. The one exception – excluding San Marco itself – is the **Campanile**, which began life as a lighthouse in the ninth century and was modified frequently up to the early sixteenth. The present structure is in fact a reconstruction: the original tower collapsed on July 14, 1902 – a catastrophe which injured nobody and is commemorated by faked postcard photos of the very instant of disaster. The collapse reduced to rubble the **Loggetta** at the base of the Campanile, but somehow it was pieced together again; built between 1537 and 1549 by Sansovino, it has served as a meeting-room for the nobility, a guardhouse and the place at which the state lottery was drawn. At 99 metres, the Campanile is the tallest structure in the city, and from the top you can make out virtually every building, but not a single canal. (Opens daily at 9.30am, closes between 3.30 and 7.30pm, depending on season; closed Dec 25 and all Jan; L3000.)

The other tower in the Piazza, the **Torre dell'Orologio** (summer Tues–Sat 9am–noon & 3–6pm, Sun 9am–noon; winter Tues–Sat 9am–noon & 3–5pm, Sun 9am–noon), was built between 1496 and 1506. A staircase takes you up past the innards of the clock and onto the terrace on which the so-called *Moors* stand; horologists will probably find the climb worthwhile, but the panorama can't compete with the Campanile's, and you can watch the Moors strike the hour perfectly well from the ground.

Away to the left stretches the **Procuratie Vecchie**; begun around 1500 by Coducci, this block housed the offices of the **Procurators of Saint Mark**, a committee of nine men whose responsibilities included the upkeep of the Basilica and other public buildings. A century or so after taking possession, the Procurators were moved to the opposite side of the Piazza, into the **Procuratie Nuove**. Napoleon converted these apartments and offices into a royal palace and then, having realised that the building lacked a ballroom, remedied the deficiency by smashing down the church of San Geminiano in order to connect the two Procuratie with a new wing for dancing.

Generally known as the **Ala Napoleonica**, this short side of the Piazza is partly occupied by the **Museo Correr** (Wed–Mon 10am–4pm, Sun 9am– 12.30pm; L3000), an immense triple-decker museum with a vast **historical collection** – coins, weapons, regalia, prints, mediocre paintings – much of which is generally heavy going unless you have an intense interest in Venetian history. The **Quadreria** on the second floor is no rival for the Accademia's collection, but does set out clearly the evolution of painting in Venice from the thirteenth century to around 1500 (though not all of its pictures are by Venetians), and contains some gems. The *Pietà* by Cosmé Tura, the *Transfiguration* and *Dead Christ Supported by Angels* by Giovanni Bellini stand out, along with a **Carpaccio** picture usually known as *The Courtesans*, although its subjects are really a couple of late-fifteenth-century bourgeois ladies dressed in a manner at which none of their contemporaries would have raised an eyebrow. There's also an appealing

SAN MARCO

exhibition of the applied arts in Venice, featuring the original blocks and a print of Jacopo de'Barbari's astonishing aerial view of Venice, engraved in 1500. The final part of the Correr – the **Museo del Risorgimento** (also on the second floor) is rarely open, a fact which should grieve only worshippers of Daniele Manin, to whose rebellion against the Austrians five of the fifteen rooms are devoted.

The Piazzetta

The **Piazzetta** – the open space between San Marco and the Molo (the waterfront pavement) – was the area where the politicians used to gather before meetings; known as the *broglio*, its wheeling and dealing probably gave rise to the English word "imbroglio". Facing the Palazzo Ducale is Sansovino's masterpiece and the most consistently admired Renaissance building in the city – the **Libreria Sansoviniana** (or Biblioteca Marciana). Work was well advanced on the building when, in December 1545, a severe frost resulted in a major collapse, a setback which landed the architect in prison for a while. Completion came in 1591, two decades after Sansovino's death.

Part of the building is given over to the **Museo Archeologico** (Tues–Sat 9am–2pm, Sun 9am–1pm; L2000), accessible through a door in the loggia. In many cities a collection of Greek and Roman sculpture as comprehensive as this one would merit a strong recommendation; in Venice you needn't feel guilty about leaving it for a rainy day. Attached to the library, with its main facade to the lagoon, Sansovino's first major building in Venice, the **Zecca** (Mint), was built between 1537 and 1545 on the site of the thirteenth-century mint. By the beginning of the fifteenth century the city's prosperity was such that the Venetian coinage was in use in every European exchange, and the doge could with some justification call Venice "the mistress of all the gold in Christendom".

The Piazzetta's two **columns** were brought here from the Levant at the end of the twelfth century, in company with a third, which fell off the barge and still lies somewhere just off the Molo. The figures perched on top are Saint Theodore, patron saint of Venice when it was dependent on Byzantium, and chimera, customised to look like the Lion of Saint Mark. Public executions were carried out between the columns, the techniques employed ranging from straightforward hanging to burial alive, head downwards. Superstitious Venetians avoid passing between them.

Sometimes the heads of freshly dispatched villains were mounted on the **Pietra del Bando**, the stump of porphyry at the other end of the Piazzetta, against the corner of San Marco. Its routine use, however, was as one of the two stones from which the laws of the Republic were proclaimed (the other is at the Rialto). The two square pillars near to it were probably stolen from Constantinople during the most infamous incident in Venice's history – the Fourth Crusade of 1204. Plenty more came back with the fleet from that expedition, as a visit to Venice's cathedral, San Marco, will show.

The Basilica di San Marco

The **Basilica of San Marco** is the most exotic of Europe's cathedrals, and no visitor can remain dispassionate when confronted by it. Herbert Spencer found it loathsome – "a fine sample of barbaric architecture", but to John Ruskin it was a "treasure-heap . . . a confusion of delight". Delightful or not, it's certainly confusing, increasingly so as you come nearer and the details emerge; some knowledge of the history of the building helps bring a little order out of chaos.

NOTE: Although San Marco is often open from 6.30am, tourists are asked to observe the following hours: Mon–Sat 9.30am–5.30pm, Sun & holidays 2–5.30pm. Sections of the Basilica will almost certainly be closed for restoration: current projects involve the Baptistry and Cappella Zen.

THE STORY OF THE BASILICA

According to the **legend of Saint Mark's annunciation**, the Evangelist was moored in the lagoon, on his way to Rome, when an angel appeared and told him that his body would rest there. (The angel's salute – *Pax tibi, Marce evangelista meus* – is the text cut into the book that the Lion of Saint Mark is always shown holding.) The founders of Venice, having persuaded themselves of the sacred ordination of their city, duly went about fulfilling the angelic prophecy, and in 828 the body of Saint Mark was stolen from Alexandria and brought here.

Modelled on Constantinople's Church of the Twelve Apostles, the shrine of Saint Mark was consecrated in 832, but in 976 both the church and the Palazzo Ducale were ruined by fire during an uprising against the doge. The present Basilica was originally finished in 1094, and embellished over the succeeding centuries. The combination of ancient structure and later decorations is, to a great extent, what makes San Marco so bewildering, but the picture is made yet more complicated by the addition of ornaments which were looted from abroad, are sometimes older than the building itself and in some cases have nothing to do with the Church. Every trophy that the doge stuck onto his church (and bear in mind this church was not the cathedral of Venice but the doge's own chapel) was a proof of Venice's secular might and so of the spiritual power of Saint Mark. Conversely, the Evangelist was invoked to sanctify political actions and rituals of state – the doge's investiture was consecrated in the church and military commanders received their commissions at the altar.

THE EXTERIOR, NARTHEX AND LOGGIA DEI CAVALLI

Of the exterior features that can be seen easily from the ground, the **Romanesque carvings** of the **central door** demand the closest attention – especially the middle arch's figures of *The Months and Seasons* and outer arch's series of *The Trades of Venice*. The carvings were begun around 1225 and finished in the early fourteenth century. Take a look also at the mosaic above the doorway on the far left – *The Arrival of the Body of St Mark* – which was made around 1260 (the only early mosaic left on the main facade) and includes the oldest known image of the Basilica.

From the Piazza you pass into the vestibule known as the **narthex**, decorated with the first of the church's **mosaics**: Old Testament scenes on the domes and arches, together with *The Madonna with Apostles and Evangelists* in the niches of the bay in front of the main door – dating from the 1060s, and the oldest mosaics in San Marco.

A steep staircase goes from the church's main door up to the **Museo Marciano** and the **Loggia dei Cavalli** (L2000). Apart from giving you an all-round view which it's difficult to leave, the Loggia is also the best place from which to inspect the **Gothic carvings** along the apex of the facade. The **horses** outside are replicas, the genuine articles having been removed to a room inside, allegedly to protect them from the risks of atmospheric pollution – although some cynics have insisted that the rescue mission had more to do with the marketing strategies of *Olivetti*, who sponsored the operation. Thieved from the Hippodrome of Constantinople, they are Roman works of the second century (the only such classical group, or *quadriga*, to have survived) and are made of a bronze which is nearly one hundred percent copper.

THE INTERIOR

With its undulating floor of patterned marble (twelfth-century), its plates of eastern stone on the lower walls, and its 4000 square metres of **mosaics** covering every other inch of wall and vaulting, the interior of San Marco is the most opulent of any cathedral. One visit is not enough – there's too much to take in at one go, and the shifting light reveals and hides parts of the decoration as the day progresses; try calling in for half an hour at the beginning and end of a couple of days.

The majority of the mosaics were in position by the middle of the thirteenth century; some date from the fourteenth and fifteenth centuries, and others were created in the sixteenth to replace damaged early sections. A thorough guide to them would take volumes, but an inventory of the very best might include these. On the west wall, above the door – *Christ, the Virgin and St Mark* (thirteenth-century); west dome – *Pentecost* (early-twelfth-century); arch between west and central domes – *Crucifixion, Resurrection* (the latter a fifteenth-century copy); central dome – *Ascension*; east dome – *Religion of Christ foretold by the Prophets*; between windows of apse – *Four Patron Saints of Venice*; north transept's dome – *Acts of St John the Evangelist*; arch to west of north transept's dome (and continued on upper part of adjacent wall) – *Life of the Virgin and Life of the Infant Christ*; wall of south aisle – *The Agony in the Garden*; west wall of south transept – *Rediscovery of the Body of St Mark*. This last scene refers to the story that the body of Saint Mark was hidden during the rebuilding of the Basilica in 1063 and was not found again until 1094, when it miraculously broke through the pillar in which it had been buried.

From the south transept you can enter the **Sanctuary** (L1000), where, behind the altar, you'll find the most precious of San Marco's treasures – the **Pala d'Oro** (Golden Altar Panel). Commissioned in 976 in Constantinople, the Pala was enlarged, enriched and rearranged by Byzantine goldsmiths in 1105, then by Venetians in 1209 (to incorporate some less cumbersome loot from the Fourth Crusade) and again (finally) in 1345. The completed screen holds 83 enamel plaques, 74 enamelled roundels, 38 chiselled figures, 300 sapphires, 300 emeralds, 400 garnets, 15 rubies, 1300 pearls and a couple of hundred other stones.

In a corner of the south transept is the door of the **Treasury** (L2000), a dazzling warehouse of chalices, reliquaries, candelabra and so on – a fair proportion of which owes its presence here to the great Constantinople robbery of 1204.

The **Baptistery** (entered from the south aisle) was altered to its present form by the fourteenth-century Doge Andrea Dandolo, whose tomb (facing the door) was thought by Ruskin to have the best monumental sculpture in the city. Dandolo also ordered the creation of the **mosaics** depicting *Scenes from the Lives of Christ and John the Baptist*, works in which the hieratic formality of Byzantine art is blended with the rich detail of the Gothic.

The adjoining **Cappella Zen** was created between 1504 and 1521 by enclosing the Piazzetta entrance to the narthex, in order to house the tomb of Cardinal Giambattista Zen, whose estate was left to the city on condition that he was buried within San Marco. The late-thirteenth-century **mosaics** on the vault show

Scenes from the Life of St Mark. The chapel is sometimes known as the *Chapel of the Madonna of the Shoe*, taking its name from the *Virgin and Child* by Antonio Lombardo (1506) on the high altar.

Back in the main body of the church, there's still more to see on the lower levels of the building. Don't overlook the **rood screen**'s marble figures of *The Virgin, St Mark and the Apostles*, carved in 1394 by the dominant sculptors in Venice at that time, Jacobello and Pietro Paolo Dalle Masegne. The **pulpits** on each side of the screen were assembled in the early fourteenth century from miscellaneous panels (some from Constantinople); the new doge was presented to the people from the right-hand one. The tenth-century **Icon of the Madonna of Nicopeia** (in the chapel on east side of north transept) is the most revered religious image in Venice; it used to be one of the most revered in Constantinople. A beautiful mid-fifteenth-century mosaic cycle of *Scenes from the Life of the Virgin*, one of the earliest Renaissance works in Venice, is to be seen in the adjacent **Cappella della Madonna dei Mascoli**. And on the north side of the nave stands a marble kiosk fabricated from a variety of rare marbles to house a painting of the *Crucifix* on the altar; this arrived in Venice in 1205, and in 1290 achieved its current exalted status by spouting blood after an assault on it.

The Palazzo Ducale
April–mid-Oct Mon–Sat 8.30am–6pm, Sun 9am–1pm; mid-Oct–March daily 8.30am–2pm; L5000.

The **Palazzo Ducale** was far more than the residence of the doge – it was the home of all of Venice's governing councils, many of its courts, a sizeable number of its civil servants and even its prisons. The government of Venice was administered through an intricate system of elected committees and councils – a system designed to limit the power of any individual – but for the last 500 years of the Republic's existence only those families listed in the register of noble births and marriages known as the *Libro d'Oro* (Golden Book) were entitled to play a part in the system.

At the head of the network sat the **doge**, the one politician to sit on all the major councils of state, and the only one elected for life; he could be immensely influential in steering policy and in making appointments, and restrictions were accordingly imposed on his actions to reduce the possibility of his abusing that influence – his letters were read by censors, for example, and he couldn't receive foreign delegations alone. The privileges of the job far outweighed the inconveniences, though, and men campaigned for years to increase their chances of election.

Like San Marco, the Palazzo Ducale has been rebuilt many times since its foundation in the first years of the ninth century. It was with the construction of a new hall for the Maggior Consiglio (Great Council) in 1340 that the Palazzo began to take on its present shape. The hall was constructed parallel to the waterfront and was inaugurated in 1419; three years later, it was decided to extend the building along the Piazzetta, copying the style of the fourteenth-century work – the slightly fatter column on the Piazzetta side, under a tondo of *Justice*, is where the two wings meet.

The principal entrance to the Palazzo – the **Porta della Carta** – is one of the most ornate Gothic works in the city. It was commissioned in 1438 by Doge Francesco Fóscari from Bartolomeo and Giovanni Bon, but the figures of Fóscari and his lion are replicas – the originals were pulverised in 1797 by the head of the stonemason's guild, as a favour to Napoleon.

The passageway into the Palazzo ends under the **Arco Fóscari**, also commissioned from the Bons by Doge Fóscari but finished a few years after his death by Antonio Rizzo and Antonio Bregno. In 1483 a fire demolished most of the wing in front of you, and led to more work for Rizzo – he designed the enormous staircase (*Scala dei Giganti*) and much of the new wing. Reconstruction continued under Pietro Lombardo, Spavento and Scarpagnino, and finally Bartolomeo Monopola, who completed the courtyard in about 1600 by extending the arcades along the other two sides.

Parts of the Palazzo Ducale can be marched through fairly briskly. Acres of canvas cover the walls, but many of the paintings are just wearisome exercises in self-aggrandisement. But other sections you will not want to rush, and, if you're there in the high season, it's a good idea to buy your ticket within half an hour of opening. A word of warning – restoration work is continually in progress in the Palazzo Ducale, and there's never any indication before you go in as to which bits are under wraps; it's a distinct possibility that some of the highlights will be hidden from view on the day you go.

One of the first rooms in the palace is the **Anticollegio**, the room in which embassies had to wait before being admitted to the presence of the doge and his cabinet. As regards the quality of its paintings, this is one of the richest rooms in the Palazzo Ducale: four pictures by **Tintoretto** hang on the door walls, and facing the windows is **Veronese**'s characteristically benign *Rape of Europa*.

The cycle of paintings on the ceiling of the adjoining **Sala del Collegio** is also by Veronese, and he features strongly again in the most stupendous room in the building – the **Sala del Maggior Consiglio**. Veronese's ceiling panel of *The Apotheosis of Venice* is suspended over the dais from which the doge oversaw the sessions of the city's general assembly; the backdrop is the immense *Paradiso* painted at the end of his life by **Tintoretto**, with the aid of his son, Domenico. At the opposite end there's a curiosity: the frieze of portraits of the first 76 doges (the series continues in the *Sala dello Scrutinio* – through the door at the far end) is interrupted by a painted black veil, marking the place where **Doge Marin Falier** would have been honoured had he not conspired against the state in 1355 and been beheaded for his crime.

From here you descend quickly to the underbelly of the Venetian state, crossing the **Ponte dei Sospiri** (Bridge of Sighs) to the **prisons**. Before the construction of these cells in the early seventeenth century all prisoners were kept in the *Piombi* (the Leads), under the roof of the Palazzo Ducale, or in the *Pozzi* (the Wells) in the bottom two storeys; the new block was occupied mainly by petty criminals. If you want to see the Piombi, and the rooms in which the day-to-day administration of Venice took place, you should go on the **Itinerari Segreti del Palazzo Ducale**; a guided tour through the warren of offices and passageways that interlocks with the public rooms of the building. It's not cheap (L5000), and the guide speaks only Italian, but if you can afford it and can understand even a little of the language, it's well worth the price. Tickets can be booked by phoning ☎520.4287; posters at the entrance to the Palazzo give times.

North of the Piazza

The **Mercerie**, a chain of glitzy streets that starts under the Clock Tower and finishes at the Campo San Bartolomeo, is the most direct route between the Rialto and San Marco and has therefore always been the main land thoroughfare of the city and a prime site for its shopkeepers. For those immune to the charms of window-shopping there's little reason to linger until you reach the church of **San Salvatore,** an early sixteenth-century church cleverly planned in the form of three Greek crosses placed end to end. It has a couple of Titian paintings – an altarpiece of the *Transfiguration* (1560) and an *Annunciation* (1566), whose awkward angel is often blamed on the great man's assistants. The end of the south transept is filled by the tomb of Caterina Cornaro, who for a while was Queen of Cyprus before being manoeuvred into surrendering the island to Venice (see "Asolo", below).

The **Campo San Bartolomeo** is at its best in the evening, when it's as packed as any bar in town. For a crash-course in the Venetian character, hang around the statue of Goldoni for a while at about 7pm. If the crush gets a bit too much, you can retire to the nearby **Campo San Luca**, another after-work social centre but not as much of a pressure-cooker as San Bartolomeo.

Beyond the Campo San Luca is the **Campo Manin**, on the south side of which is a sign for the spiral staircase known as the **Scala del Bovolo** (*bovolo* means "snail shell" in Venetian dialect), a piece of flamboyant engineering dating from around 1500. The **Museo Fortuny** (Tues–Sun 9am–7pm; L5000) is also close at hand, similarly tucked away in a spot you'd never accidentally pass, but signposted with small eye-level posters. In addition to making his famous silk dresses (fine enough to be threaded through a wedding ring), **Mariano Fortuny** (1871–1949) was a painter, architect, engraver, photographer, theatre designer and sculptor; the museum reflects his versatility, but you'll probably come out regretting that the museum doesn't have more of the frocks.

West of the Piazza

Although it too has its share of fashionable shops – much of the broad Calle Larga XXII Marzo, for example, is dedicated to the beautification of the well-heeled and their dwellings – the area to the **west of the Piazza** is less frenetic than the streets to the north. None of the first-division tourist sights are here, but the walk from the Piazza to the Accademia bridge, through a succession of campi each quite unlike its predecessor, isn't lacking in worthwhile diversions.

Heading west from the Piazza, you soon reach the hypnotically dreadful **San Moisè** (daily 3.30–7pm), runaway winner of any poll for the ugliest church in Venice. The facade sculpture, featuring a species of camel unknown to zoology, was created in 1668 by Heinrich Meyring; and if you think this is in dubious taste, wait till you see his altarpiece of *Mount Sinai with Moses Receiving the Tablets*.

Halfway along the Calle Larga XXII Marzo, on the right, is the Calle del Sartor da Veste, which takes you over a canal and into the Campo San Fantin, where the Renaissance church of **San Fantin** has a graceful domed apse by Sansovino. Across the campo is Venice's largest and oldest theatre, **La Fenice**, opened in December 1792. On a good day the staff will allow you a look at the auditorium, a luxuriant confection of gilt, plush and stucco, fitted out in 1836 after the place had been wrecked by fire. The opera house sets the tone of the neighbourhood, which has some of the priciest restaurants and most pretentious boutiques in town.

Back on the main road to the Accademia, another very odd church awaits – **Santa Maria Zobenigo** (or del Giglio). You can stare at this all day and still not find a single Christian image. The statues are of the five Barbaro brothers who financed the rebuilding of the church in 1678; Virtue, Honour, Fame and Wisdom hover respectfully around them; and the maps in relief depict the towns they graced in the course of their exemplary military and diplomatic careers.

The tilting campanile that soon looms into view over the vapid church of San Maurizio belongs to Santo Stefano, which stands at the end of the next campo – the **Campo Francesco Morosini** (or Santo Stefano). Large enough to hold several clusters of tourists and natives plus a kids' football match or two, the Campo Morosini is always lively but never feels crowded, and has, in *Paolin*, one of the best icecream places in Venice. **Campo Sant'Angelo** (or Anzolo), on the other side of the church, is almost as capacious, and is bounded by some beautiful palaces, but has the feel of a crossroads rather than a meeting place.

To those few non-Venetians to whom his name means anything, Francesco Morosini is known as the man who lobbed a missile through the roof of the Parthenon towards the end of the seventeenth century. He lived at the Canal Grande end of the campo (no. 2802) and is buried in **Santo Stefano**, an originally thirteenth-century church, rebuilt in the fourteenth and altered again in the first half of the fifteenth; the Gothic **doorway** and the **ship's keel roof** both belong to this last phase. The best paintings are in the sacristy – *The Agony in the Garden*, *The Last Supper* and *The Washing of the Disciples' Feet*, all late works by **Tintoretto**.

Dorsoduro

Some of the finest architecture in Venice, both domestic and public, is to be found in the *sestiere* of **DORSODURO**, a situation partly attributable to the stability of its sandbanks (*Dorsoduro* means "hard back"). Yet for all its attractions, not many visitors wander off the strip that runs between the main sights of the area – the Ca' Rezzonico, the Accademia and the Salute. The *sestiere* has a bafflingly complex border, so for clarity's sake we have taken the curve of the Grand Canal–Rio di Ca' Fóscari–Rio Nuovo as the boundary between Dorsoduro and the rest of central Venice.

The Galleria dell'Accademia

Tues–Sat 9am–2pm, Sun 9am–1pm; L4000.

The **Galleria dell'Accademia** is one of the finest specialist collections of European art, following the history of Venetian painting from the fourteenth to the eighteenth century. When it was established in 1807, its exhibits came largely from churches and convents that were then being suppressed; indeed, the buildings that the Accademia has occupied since then include two former religious buildings – the church of Santa Maria della Carità, rebuilt by Bartolomeo Bon in the 1440s, and the incomplete Convento dei Canonici Lateranensi, partly built by Palladio in 1561.

TO THE EARLY RENAISSANCE

The gallery is laid out in a roughly chronological succession of rooms going anti-clockwise. The first room at the top of the stairs is the fifteenth-century assembly room of the Scuola, and houses works by the earliest known individual Venetian painters. **Paolo Veneziano** (from the first half of the fourteenth century) and his follower **Lorenzo Veneziano** are the most absorbing, but take a look too at **Jacobello Alberegno**'s *Polyptych of the Apocalypse*, with its wrathful Old Testament God, seven-headed beast and many-eyed lamb.

Room 2 moves on to works from the late fifteenth and early sixteenth centuries, with large altarpieces that are contemplative even when the scenes are far from calm. **Carpaccio**'s strange and gruesome *Crucifixion and Glorification of the Ten Thousand Martyrs of Mount Ararat* (painted around 1512) and his *Presentation of Jesus in the Temple* accompany works by **Giovanni Bellini** and **Cima da Conegliano**.

In the west room you can observe the emergence of the characteristically Venetian treatment of colour in works from the early Renaissance, but there's nothing here as exciting as the small paintings in rooms 4 and 5, a high point of the collection. Apart from an exquisite *St George* by **Mantegna**, and a series of **Giovanni Bellini** *Madonnas*, this section contains one of the most mysterious of Italian paintings, **Giorgione**'s *Tempest* (1500) – frustratingly it's been covered in glass, so it catches reflections.

HIGH RENAISSANCE

Room 6 introduces one of the heavyweights of Venetian painting, Jacopo Robusti, called **Tintoretto**. The *Madonna dei Camerlenghi* (1566), with its sumptuously painted velvets, shows facial types still found in Venice today. Another big name represented here is **Titian** (Tiziano Vecellio), with a not particularly interesting *John the Baptist* (early 1540s). One of the most compelling paintings in the gallery is in room 7, the *Young Man in his Study* by **Lorenzo Lotto** (1528).

Room 10 is dominated by epic productions, and an entire wall is filled **Paolo Veronese's** *Christ in the House of Levi*. Originally called *The Last Supper*, this picture provoked a stern reaction from the Court of the Holy Office: it was too irreverent for such a holy subject, they insisted – why were there "Germans and buffoons and such-like things in this picture? Does it appear to you fitting that at our Lord's last supper you should paint buffoons, drunkards, Germans, dwarfs, and similar indecencies?" Veronese fielded all their questions and responded simply by changing the title, which made the work acceptable. The pieces by **Tintoretto** in here include three legends of Saint Mark: *St Mark Rescues a Slave* (1548), which was the painting that made his reputation, *The Theft of the Body of St Mark* and *St Mark Saves a Saracen* (both 1560s). All of these show Tintoretto's love of energy and drama – from the physical or psychological drama of the subject matter, emphasised by the twisting poses of the people depicted, to the technical energy of his brush-strokes, perception of colour and use of light. Opposite is an emotional late **Titian**, a *Pietà* (1570s) thought to be intended for his own tomb in the Frari.

THE EIGHTEENTH CENTURY

Room 11 contains a number of works by **Giambattista Tiepolo**, the most prominent painter of eighteenth-century Venice, including two shaped fragments rescued from the wreckage of the Scalzi (1743–45), and *The Translation of the Holy House of Loreto* (1743), a sketch for the same ceiling.

The following stretch of seventeenth- and eighteenth-century paintings isn't too enthralling – the highlights portraits by **Rosalba Carriera** and interiors by **Pietro Longhi** in room 17. Carriera's work popularised the use of pastel as a medium; look for her moving *Self-Portrait in Old Age* (1740s), executed just before she went blind. Longhi is not the most brilliant of painters in the Accademia, but his illustrative work is fascinating for the insights it gives to eighteenth-century Venice. (For more, including the famous *Rhinoceros*, go to the Ca' Rezzonico.)

THE VIVARINIS, THE BELLINIS AND CARPACCCIO

Around the corner and to the right are more works from the fifteenth and early sixteenth centuries. Pieces by the Vivarini family feature strongly, **Alvise Vivarini**'s *Santa Chiara* is outstanding. **Giovanni Bellini** is represented by four triptychs painted with workshop assistance for this church in the 1460s. The extraordinary *Blessed Lorenzo Giustinian* is by his brother, **Gentile**; one of the oldest surviving Venetian canvases, and Gentile's earliest signed work, it was possibly used as a standard in processions, which would account for its state.

The magnificent cycle of pictures painted around 1500 for the Scuola di San Giovanni Evangelista, mainly illustrating the miracles of the Relic of the Cross, is displayed in room 20, off a corridor to the left. All of the paintings are replete with fascinating local details, but particularly rich are **Carpaccio**'s *Cure of a Lunatic*, and **Gentile Bellini**'s *Recovery of the Relic from the Canale di San Lorenzo* and *Procession of the Relic in the Piazza*. The next room contains a complete cycle of pictures by **Carpaccio** illustrating the *Story of Saint Ursula*, painted for the Scuola di Sant'Orsola at San Zanipolo (1490–94). Restored in the mid-1980s, the paintings form one of Italy's most unforgettable groups. The legend is that Hereus, a British prince, proposed marriage to Ursula, a Breton princess. She accepted on two conditions: that Hereus convert to Christianity, and that he should wait for three years, while she went on a pilgrimage. The pilgrimage, undertaken with a company of 11,000 virgins, ended with a massacre near Cologne by the Huns – as Ursula had been warned in a dream.

Finally, in room 24 (the former hostel of the Scuola), there's **Titian**'s *Presentation of the Virgin* (dating from 1539). It was painted for the place where it hangs, as was the triptych by **Antonio Vivarini** and **Giovanni d'Alemagna** (1446), another of the oldest Venetian canvases.

The Guggenheim and the Salute

Within five minutes' walk of the Accademia, beyond the Campo San Vio, is the unfinished Palazzo Venier dei Leoni, home of **The Guggenheim Collection** (April–Oct Sun, Mon & Wed–Fri noon–6pm, Sat noon–9pm; L5000, but free Sat 6–9pm; open in winter for special exhibitions), and of Peggy Guggenheim for thirty years until her death in 1979. Her private collection is an eclectic, quirky choice of (mainly) excellent pieces from her favourite modernist movements and artists. Prime pieces include Brancusi's *Bird in Space* and *Maestra*, De Chirico's *Red Tower* and *Nostalgia of the Poet*, Max Ernst's *Robing of the Bride*, sculpture by Laurens and Lipchitz, paintings by Malevich and collages by Schwitters.

Continuing along the line of the Canal Grande, you come to Santa Maria della Salute, better known simply as the **Salute** (daily 8am–noon & 3–5pm), built to fulfil a Senate decree of October 22, 1630, that a new church would be dedicated to Mary if the city were delivered from the plague that was ravaging it – an outbreak that was to kill about a third of the population. Work began in 1631 on **Baldessare Longhena**'s design, and was completed in 1681, though the church was not consecrated until November 9, 1687, five years before Longhena's death. Thereafter, every November 21, the Signoria headed a procession from San Marco to the Salute, over a specially constructed pontoon bridge, to give thanks for the city's good health (*salute* meaning "health") – and even today the festival of the Salute is a major event on the Venetian calendar.

In 1656, a hoard of **Titian** paintings from the suppressed church of Santo Spirito were moved here and are now housed in the **sacristy** (small entrance fee). The most prominent of these is the altarpiece of *St Mark Enthroned with Saints Cosmas, Damian, Sebastian and Rocco* (the plague saints). The *Marriage at Cana*, with its dramatic lighting and perspective, is by Tintoretto (1561), featuring portraits of a number of the artist's friends.

The **Dogana di Mare** (Customs House), with its Doric facade (1676–82), occupies the spur formed by the meeting of the Canal Grande with the Giudecca canal. The gold ball, noticeable from anywhere on this busy bit of water, is a weathervane, topped by a figure representing either Justice or Fortune.

Along the Záttere to San Sebastiano

Stretching from the Punta della Dogana to the Stazione Marittima, the **Záttere** (Rafts) was originally the place where most of the bulky goods coming into Venice were unloaded – it's now a popular place to stroll on Sundays or for a picnic lunch. Its principal sight is the church of Santa Maria del Rosario, invariably known as the **Gesuati** – worth a call for its paintings by **Giambattista Tiepolo**: three ceiling frescoes of *Scenes from the Life of St Dominic* and an altarpiece of *Madonna with three Dominican Saints*.

A diversion to the right straight after the Gesuati takes you past the **squero di San Trovaso**, the busiest gondola workshop left in Venice, and on to the church of **San Trovaso**. Venetian folklore has it that this church was the only neutral ground between the rival working-class factions of the *Nicolotti* and the *Castellani*, who would celebrate intermarriages and other services here, but had to use separate doors. It is a large dark church, whose paintings are properly visible only in the morning. These include **Tintoretto**'s last works, *The Adoration of the Magi* and *The Expulsion from the Temple*, flanking the high altar.

The church of **San Sebastiano**, right up by the Stazione Marittima (erratic opening hours) was built between 1505 and 1545, and was the parish church of **Paolo Veronese**, who provided most of its paintings and is buried here. He was first brought in to paint the ceiling of the sacristy with a *Coronation of the Virgin* and the *Four Evangelists*, and then the *Scenes from the Life of St Esther* on the ceiling of the church. He then painted the dome of the chancel, which is now destroyed, and with the help of his brother, Benedetto, moved on to the walls of the church and the nuns' choir. The paintings around the high altar and the organ came last, painted in the 1560s.

Ca' Rezzonico and around

From San Sebastiano it's a straightforward walk back towards the Canal Grande along Calle Avogaria and Calle Lunga San Barnaba, a route that deposits you in Campo San Barnaba, just yards from the **Ca' Rezzonico** – now the **Museo del Settecento Veneziano** (Museum of Eighteenth-Century Venice; Sat & Mon–Thurs 10am–4pm, Sun & holidays 9am–12.30pm; L3000). Having acquired the Ca' Rezzonico in 1934, the comune of Venice set about furnishing and decorating it with eighteenth-century items and materials (or their closest modern equivalent), so giving the place the feel of a well-appointed house rather than of a formal museum. On the applied arts side of the collection, the plentiful and outlandish carvings by **Andrea Brustolon** are as likely to elicit revulsion as admiration. As for the paintings, the highlights are **Pietro Longhi**'s affectionate illustrations of Venice social life, and the frescoes painted towards the end of his life by **Giandomenico Tiepolo**. Although painted at a time when this type of work was going out of fashion, these frescoes of clowns and carnival scenes (created originally for his own house) are among Giandomenico's best-known images. Fans of his father's more flamboyant style won't come away disappointed either.

The nearby **Campo Santa Margherita** is a wide but friendly space, with a daily **market** and a clutch of shops that contribute to the quarter's distinctive atmosphere. The **Scuola Grande dei Carmini** (daily 9am–noon & 3–6pm; L2000), on the west of the campo, is a showcase for Giambattista Tiepolo, whose ceiling paintings in the main upstairs hall, painted in the early 1740s, centre on a large panel of *The Virgin in Glory*.

San Polo

For practical reasons, the district we have labelled **SAN POLO** covers an area over twice the size of the *sestiere* of the same name, including a huge chunk of the *sestiere* of Santa Croce and a bit of Dorsoduro and bounded by the Canal Grande and the Rio Nuovo–Rio di Ca' Fóscari (the short-cut used by the *diretto*). You cannot stray unwittingly over either of these canals, which is more than can be said for the boundaries of the *sestieri*.

Rialto

Relatively stable building land and a good defensive position drew some of the earliest lagoon settlers to the high bank (*rivo alto*) above the Canal Grande that was to develop into the **Rialto** district. While the political centre of the new city grew up around San Marco, the Rialto became the commercial zone. In the twelfth century, Europe's first state bank was opened here, and the financiers of the district were the weightiest figures on the international exchanges for the next three centuries and more. The state offices which oversaw all maritime business were here as well, and in the early sixteenth century the offices of the exchequer were installed in the new **Palazzo dei Camerlenghi**, at the foot of the Rialto bridge.

The connection between wealth and moral turpitude was exemplified by the Rialto, where the fleshpots were as busy as the cashdesks. A late-sixteenth-century survey showed that there were about 3000 patrician women in the city, but well over 11,000 prostitutes, the majority of them based in the banking quarter. One Rialto brothel, the *Casteletto*, was especially esteemed for the literary, musical and sexual talents of its staff, and a perennial Venetian bestseller was a catalogue giving the addresses and prices of the city's most alluring courtesans.

It was through the markets of the Rialto that Venice earned its reputation as the bazaar of Europe. Virtually anything could be bought or sold here: Italian fabrics, precious stones, silver plate and gold jewellery, spices and dyes from the Orient. Trading had been going on here for over 400 years when, in 1514, a fire destroyed everything in the area except the church. The possibility of relocating the business centre was discussed but found little favour, so reconstruction began almost straight away, the **Fabbriche Vecchie** (the arcaded buildings along the Ruga degli Orefici and around the Campo San Giacomo) being finished five years after the fire, and Sansovino's **Fabbriche Nuove** (running along the Canal Grande from Campo Cesare Battisti) following about thirty years later.

Today's Rialto market is tamer than that of Venice at its peak, but it's still one of the liveliest spots in the city, and one of the few places where it's possible to stand in a crowd and hear nothing but Italian spoken. There's a shoal of memento-sellers by the church and along the Ruga degli Orefeci; the market proper lies between them and the Canal Grande – mainly fruit stalls around the **Campo San Giacomo**, vegetable stalls and butcher's shops as you go through to the **Campo Battisti**, after which you come to the fish market. (The fish market and many of the stalls close for the day at 1pm, but some stalls reopen in the late afternoon.) There are excellent cheese shops around the junction of **Ruga degli Orefici** and **Ruga Vecchia San Giovanni**; the Ruga Vecchia has a number of good *alimentari* among the kitsch-merchants.

A popular Venetian legend asserts that the city was founded on Friday, March 25, AD 421 at exactly midday; from the same legend derives the claim that the church of **San Giacomo di Rialto** (daily 10am–noon) was founded in that year, and is thus the oldest church in Venice. It might actually be the oldest; what is not disputed is that the church was rebuilt in 1071 and that parts of the present structure date from then – for instance, the interior's six columns of ancient Greek marble have eleventh-century Veneto-Byzantine capitals. As you walk away from the Rialto, following roughly the curve of the Canal Grande, you enter a district which becomes labyrinthine even by Venetian standards. A directionless stroll between the Rio delle Beccerie and the Rio di San Zan Degolà will satisfy any addict of the picturesque – you cannot walk for more than a couple of minutes without coming across a workshop crammed into a ground-floor room or a garden spilling over a canalside wall.

The church of **San Cassiano** (Mon–Sat 9.45–11.30am & 4.30–7pm) is a building you're bound to pass as you wander out of the Rialto. Don't be put off by its barn-like appearance, as it contains three paintings by **Tintoretto**: *The Resurrection*, *The Descent into Limbo* and *The Crucifixion*. The first two have been mauled by restorers, but the third is one of the greatest pictures in Venice, a startling composition dominated not by the cross but by the ladder on which the executioners stand.

Nearby (and signposted from San Cassiano) is the **Ca' Pésaro**, in which you'll find both the **Galleria d'Arte Moderna** (Tues–Sat 10am–4pm, Sun 9.30am–12.30pm; L2000) and the **Museo Orientale** (Tues–Sat 9am–2pm, Sun 9am–1pm; L2000). Pieces bought from the Biennale make up much of the modern collection, and its backbone consists of work by a range of Italian artists, many of whom will be unfamiliar. As for the Oriental galleries, the jumble of lacquer work, armour, screens, weaponry and so forth will appeal chiefly to the initiated.

Campo San Polo and around

The largest square in Venice after the Piazza, the **Campo San Polo** used to be the city's favourite bullfighting arena as well as the site of weekly markets and occasional fairs. Nowadays it's a combination of outdoor social centre and children's sports stadium.

The bleak interior of **San Polo** church (Mon–Sat 7.30am–noon & 4–7pm, Sun 8am–12.15pm) should be visited for a *Last Supper* by Tintoretto and Giandomenico Tiepolo's paintings of the *Stations of the Cross*, a series painted when the artist was only twenty. The sober piety of these pictures may force you to amend a few preconceptions about Giandomenico; nevertheless, it often seems that his interest was less in the central drama than in the society portraits which occupy the edges of the stage.

Calle Madonera, going off the campo in the direction of Rialto, is the beginning of a sequence of busy **shopping streets**, in which you'll find a couple of the best *pasticcerie* in Venice and a host of shoe and clothes shops. Salizzada San Polo and Calle dei Saoneri, on the opposite side of the campo, are effectively a continuation of these streets, which together comprise this side of the Canal Grande's answer to the Mercerie.

I Frari

Mon–Sat 9.30am–noon & 2.30–6pm, Sun 2.30–6pm; small entrance fee to cover cost of lighting.

Admirers of northern Gothic are unlikely to fall in love with the mountain of brick known as **I Frari** (Santa Maria Gloriosa dei Frari, in full), but whatever your artistic predilections, its collection of paintings, sculptures and monuments is certain to get the church onto your list of Venetian highlights. The Franciscans were granted a plot of land here in about 1250, not long after the death of Saint Francis; replacement of their first church by the present structure began in the mid-fourteenth century and took over a hundred years.

As every guide to the city points out, Venice is relatively impoverished as far as major paintings by **Titian** are concerned: apart from the Salute and the Accademia, I Frari is the only building in Venice with more than a single significant work by him. One of these – the *Assumption*, painted in 1518 – you will see almost immediately as you look towards the altar through the fifteenth-century monks' choir, a swirling, dazzling piece of compositional and colouristic bravura for which there was no precedent in Venetian art. The other Titian masterpiece here, the *Madonna di Ca' Pésaro*, is more static, but was equally innovative in its displacement of the figure of the Virgin from the centre of the picture.

Wherever you stand in I Frari, you're in front of something that deserves your attention, but three or four pieces apart from the Titians stand out from the rest. Two funerary monuments embodying the emergence in Venice of Renaissance sculptural technique flank the Titian *Assumption*: on the left the **tomb of Doge Niccolò Tron**, by Antonio Rizzo and assistants, dating from 1476; on the right, the more chaotic **tomb of Doge Francesco Fóscari**, carved shortly after Fóscari's death in 1457 by Antonio and Paolo Bregno. (See "The Canal Grande" for more on Fóscari.) The wooden statue of *St John the Baptist*, in the chapel to the right, was commissioned from **Donatello** in 1438 by Florentine merchants in Padua; recent work has restored its luridly naturalistic appearance. On the altar of the sacristy (the site for which it was created) is a picture which alone would justify an hour in I Frari – the *Madonna and Child with SS Nicholas of Bari, Peter, Mark and Benedict*, painted in 1488 by **Giovanni Bellini**. In the words of Henry James – "it is as solemn as it is gorgeous and as simple as it is deep".

Two massive tombs take up much of the nave. One is the bombastic **monument to Titian**, built in the mid-nineteenth century on the supposed site of his grave. He died in the 1576 plague epidemic, in around his ninetieth year, and was the only casualty of that outbreak to be given a church burial. Opposite is a tomb of similarly pompous dimensions but of redeeming peculiarity, the **Mausoleum of Canova**, erected in 1827 by pupils of the sculptor, following a design he himself had made for the tomb of Titian.

The Scuola di San Rocco, and San Rocco church

At the rear of I Frari is a place you should on no account miss: the **Scuola Grande di San Rocco** (summer daily 10am–1pm & 3–6pm; winter daily 10am–

2pm; L5000). San Rocco (Saint Roch) was attributed with the power to cure the plague and other serious illnesses, so when the saint's body was brought to Venice in 1485, the Scuola began to profit from donations from people wishing to invoke his aid. In 1515 it commissioned this prestigious new building, and soon after its completion in 1560, work began on the decorative scheme that was to put the Scuola's rivals in the shade – a cycle of more than fifty major paintings by **Tintoretto**.

THE TINTORETTO PAINTINGS

To appreciate the evolution of Tintoretto's art you have to begin in the smaller room on the upper storey – the **Sala dell'Albergo**. In 1564 the Scuola held a competition for the contract to paint its first picture. The subject was to be *The Glorification of St Roch*, and Tintoretto won the contest by rigging up a finished painting in the very place for which the winning picture was destined – the centre of the ceiling. The protests of his rivals, who had simply submitted sketches, were to no avail. Virtually an entire wall of the Sala is occupied by the stupendous *Crucifixion*, a painting which reduced Ruskin to a state of dumbfounded wonder – his loquacious guide to the cycle concludes: "I must leave this picture to work its will on the spectator; for it is beyond all analysis, and above all praise." The pictures on the entrance wall – *Christ before Pilate*, *Christ Crowned with Thorns* and *The Way to Calvary* – inevitably suffer from such company, but they deserve close scrutiny, as does the easel painting of *Christ Carrying the Cross*, which is now generally thought to be an early Titian.

Tintoretto finished the Sala in 1567 and eight years later he started on the main upper hall, a project he completed in 1581. The Old Testament subjects depicted in the three large panels of the **ceiling**, with their references to the alleviation of physical suffering, are coded declarations of the Scuola's charitable activities: *Moses Striking Water from the Rock*, *The Miracle of the Brazen Serpent* and *The Miraculous Fall of Manna*. The paintings around the walls, all based on the New Testament, are an amazing feat of sustained inventiveness, in which every convention of perspective, lighting, colour and even anatomy is defied by a mind that was never content with inherited ideas and rarely content with his own. A caricature of the irascible Tintoretto (with a bouquet of paintbrushes) is incorporated into the *trompe l'oeil* carvings by the seventeenth-century sculptor **Francesco Pianta**.

The paintings on the ground floor were created between 1583 and 1587, when Tintoretto was in his late sixties. The turbulent *Annunciation* is one of the most arresting images of the event ever painted, and there are few Renaissance landscapes to match those of *The Flight into Egypt* and the small paintings of *St Mary Magdalen* and *St Mary of Egypt*.

THE CHURCH

Yet more paintings by Tintoretto adorn the neighbouring church of **San Rocco**. On the south wall of the nave you'll find *St Roch taken to Prison*, and below it *The Pool of Bethesda* – though only the latter is definitely by Tintoretto. In the chancel are four large works, notoriously difficult to see well: the best are *St Roch Curing the Plague Victims* (lower right) and *St Roch in Prison* (lower left); the two higher pictures are *St Roch in Solitude* and *St Roch Healing the Animals*, though the second is again a doubtful attribution.

Cannaregio

In the northernmost section of Venice, **CANNAREGIO**, you can go from one extreme to another in a matter of minutes: it is a short distance from the bustle of the **train station** and the execrable **Lista di Spagna** to areas which, although no longer rural (*Cannaregio* comes from *canna*, meaning reed), are still among the quietest and prettiest parts of the whole city. The district also has the dubious distinction of containing the world's first ghetto.

The station area

The first building worth a look in the vicinity of the station is to the left as you come out of it – the **Scalzi** church (or Santa Maria di Nazareth). Built in the 1670s for the barefoot (*scalzi*) order of Carmelites, the interior, by Baldessare Longhena, is a joy for aficionados of the Baroque. There are frescoes by Giambattista Tiepolo in the first chapel on the left and the second on the right, but his major work in the church, the ceiling, was destroyed in 1915 by an Austrian bomb. A couple of fragments, now in the Accademia, were all that was rescued.

Foreign embassies used to be concentrated in this area, so that the Venetian authorities could keep an eye on them all together, and the **Lista di Spagna** takes its name from the Spanish embassy, which used to be at no. 168. The street is now completely given over to the tourist trade, with shops and stalls, bars, restaurants and hotels all plying for the same desperate trade. As with many major train stations, if you are hunting for trinkets, food or a bed, you'll find things cheaper elsewhere.

The church of **San Geremia** is chiefly notable for being the present home of **Saint Lucy**, martyred in Syracuse in 304, stolen from Constantinople by Venetian crusaders in 1204, and ousted from her own Palladian church in 1863 when it was demolished to build the station. Lucy tore her own eyes out after an unwanted suitor kept complimenting her on their beauty, and hence became the patron saint of eyesight: the glass case on the high altar contains her desiccated body. Architecturally, the church's main point of interest is the twelfth-century campanile, one of the oldest left in the city.

The ballroom of the **Palazzo Labia**, next door to the church, contains frescoes by Giambattista Tiepolo and his assistants (1745–50), illustrating the story of Anthony and Cleopatra. The present owners, *RAI* (the state radio service), allow the public in to see them for a couple of hours each week, but the exact times are changeable; for current hours ask at the door or ring ☎781.111. They also record concerts here which the public can attend for free; again ask at the door or phone to reserve tickets in advance.

The **Canale di Cannaregio** was the main entrance to Venice before the road and rail bridges were built; walk along it to get to the church of **San Giobbe**. The physical afflictions with which God permitted Satan to test the faith of Job – he was smitten with "sore boils from the sole of his foot unto his crown" – made Job particularly popular with the Venetians, who suffered regularly from malaria, plague and a plethora of damp-related diseases. The church was built on the site of an oratory by the Venetian Gothic architect Antonio Gambello, later assisted by Pietro Lombardo, who introduced Tuscan Renaissance elements. Lombardo's contribution, his first work in Venice, consists of the doorway and, inside, the statues of *Saints Anthony, Bernardino and Louis* and the chancel. Its best paintings –

Giovanni Bellini's *Madonna Enthroned with Saints* and Carpaccio's *Presentation in the Temple* – have been removed to the drier atmosphere of the Accademia .

The Ghetto
The Venetian **Ghetto** was the first in the world; indeed, the word itself comes from the Venetian dialect *getar* (to found), or *geto* (foundry), which is what this area was until 1390. It was in 1516 that all the city's Jews were ordered to move to the island of the Ghetto Nuovo, an enclave which was sealed at night by Christian curfew guards – whose wages were paid for by the Jews. Distinctive badges or caps had to be worn by all Jews, and there were various economic and social restraints on the community, although oppression was lighter in Venice than in most other parts of Europe (it was one of the few states to tolerate the Jewish religion). When Jews were expelled from Spain in 1492 and Portugal in 1497, many of them came here.

Each wave of Jewish immigrants established their own synagogues with their distinctive rites. The **Scola Levantina**, founded in 1538 and the **Scola Spagnola**, possibly founded about twenty years later, reflect the wealth of these particular groups, who were important traders within the Venetian state; the latter was rede-signed around 1584 by Longhena (the profession of architect was barred to Jews), a project which influenced the alteration of the other synagogues. These two are still used today for services, and can be viewed, with the Scola Tedesca, in an informative and multilingual guided tour, organised by the **Jewish Museum** in Campo Ghetto Nuovo (July–Oct Mon–Sat 10.30am–5pm, Sun 10.30am–1pm; March–June Mon–Sat 10.30am–1pm & 2.30–5pm, Sun 10.30am–1pm; Nov–March Mon–Sat 10am–12.30pm; closed Jewish holidays; L2000, with tour L6000). The collection is mainly of silverware and embroidered and other fabric objects.

The Ghetto looks quite different from the rest of Venice. The Jewish popula-tion rose to about 4000, and even though they were allowed to spread into the **Ghetto Vecchio** and the **Ghetto Nuovissima** there was gross overcrowding. As the Ghetto buildings were not allowed to be more than one third higher than the surrounding houses, the result was a stack of low-ceilinged storeys – the first high-rise blocks. Napoleon removed the gates of the Ghetto in 1797 but the Austrians replaced them in 1798, and Venice's Jews didn't achieve equal rights with other Venetians until Unification with Italy in 1866.

Sant'Alvise, Madonna dell'Orto and around
The area northeast of the Ghetto is one of the most restful parts of Venice. The long *fondamente*, dotted with food shops, bars and trattorias; the red walls and green shutters of the houses; the blue and yellow hulls of the boats – together they make a scene that recalls Henry James' vision of the essence of Venice: "I simply see a narrow canal in the heart of the city – a patch of green water and a surface of pink wall."

A few minutes' north of the Ghetto stands the church of **Sant'Alvise**. Commissioned by Antonia Venier, daughter of Doge Antonio Venier, after the saint appeared to her in a vision in 1388, the church has one outstanding picture, the recently restored *The Road to Calvary* by Giambattista Tiepolo, painted in 1743. His *Crown of Thorns* and *Flagellation*, slightly earlier works, are on the right-hand wall of the nave. Under the nuns' choir, to the right as you enter the church, are eight small tempera paintings, generally known as *The Baby*

Carpaccios thanks to Ruskin's speculative attribution; they do date from Carpaccio's infancy (around 1470), but they're not actually by him.

A circuitous stroll eastwards brings you to the Gothic church of **Madonna dell'Orto** (9am–noon & 3–7pm in summer; closes 5pm in winter). Dedicated to Saint Christopher in about 1350, the church was renamed after a large stone *Madonna* by Giovanni de'Santi, found discarded in a local vegetable garden (*orto*), began to work miracles; brought inside the church in 1377, the figure can still be seen (now heavily restored) in the Cappella di San Mauro. The main sculpture on the **facade** is a fifteenth-century *St Christopher* by the Florentine Nicolò di Giovanni; Bartolomeo Bon designed the portal in 1460, shortly before his death. The **interior** was messed around in the 1860s, and although some of the overpainting was removed during restoration work of the 1930s, its appearance still owes much to the nineteenth-century interference. Scraps of fresco on the arches and the painted beams give an idea of how it must have looked in the sixteenth century. This was the first church in Venice to be given a thorough restoration job after the floods of 1966; the floor was relaid, the lower walls rebuilt, chapels restored to their pre-1864 layout and all the paintings were cleaned. The *St Christopher* over the door was the first Istrian stone work to be restored in Venice.

This is Tintoretto's parish church: he is buried here, in the chapel to the right of the high altar. So too are his son and daughter, Domenico and Marietta. And there are a number of paintings by the artist here, notably the colossal *Making of the Golden Calf* and *The Last Judgment*, which flank the main altar. Others include Tintoretto's *The Presentation of the Virgin in the Temple*, at end of right aisle; *The Vision of the Cross to St Peter* and *The Beheading of St Paul*, on each side of the chancel's *Annunciation* by Palma il Giovane, and two notable works from the end of the previous century: *St John the Baptist and other Saints* by Cima da Conegliano (first altar on the right) and a *Madonna and Child* by Giovanni Bellini (first chapel on the left).

Castello

Our section of **CASTELLO** is bounded in the northwest by the Rio di San Felice and the Sacca della Misericordia, in the southwest by the canal which winds from the side of the post office at the Rialto to the back of San Marco, and in the east by the Rio dell'Arsenale and the Arsenale itself. It is an area where you can study architecture from the sublime to the ridiculous (Santa Maria dei Miracoli and the Gesuiti), immerse yourself in the history and mythology of Venice (Santi Giovanni e Paolo and Santa Maria Formosa), and take a stroll along one of the world's most scenic promenades, the Riva degli Schiavoni.

The northwestern section

Officially, the area to the north of the Ca' d'Oro is still part of the *sestiere* of Cannaregio, but the Rio di San Felice and the Canale della Misericordia form so strong a geographical boundary that it makes more sense to include it with Castello. Just inland from the Fondamente Nuove, the northern edge of this zone, is the **Gesuiti** church, as Santa Maria Assunta is familiarly known (daily 10am–noon & 5–7pm). The Jesuits began work on their church in 1714, and it took fifteen years to inlay the marble walls of the interior and carve its marble "curtains"; with a result that is jaw-droppingly impressive even if you hate Baroque architecture. The *Martyrdom of St Lawrence* by Titian, on the first altar on the left, is a night scene made doubly difficult to see by the lighting arrangements.

Back towards the Canal Grande, the **Strada Nova** – carved through the houses in 1871–72 – is a bustling shopping street where you can buy anything from spaghetti to surgical trusses. Nearly halfway along is the inconspicuous calle named after, and leading to, the **Ca' d'Oro** – a Gothic palace, much altered by restoration, whose best feature, the facade, is in any case best seen from the water (see "The Canal Grande" below). Inside the **Galleria Giorgio Franchetti** (Mon–Sat 9am–2pm; L2000) is a museum put together from the bequest of the man who owned and repaired the house at the start of this century, and from a few state collections. One of the prize exhibits is in the courtyard – Bartolomeo Bon's sculpted well-head; others include a *St Sebastian* by Mantegna and a beautifully carved *Young Couple* by Tullio Lombardo. Big names such as Tintoretto and Titian are here, but not at their best; you'll get more out of pieces from less exalted artists – the views of *The Piazzetta facing San Giorgio* and *Quayside with the Salute* by Francesco Guardi, for instance.

At the eastern end of the Strada Nova is the Campo dei Santi Apostoli, a general meeting-point and crossroads, and the church of **Santi Apostoli**. The exterior is unexceptional, but give the interior a look for the Cappella Corner: the design of the chapel is attributed to Mauro Coducci, the altar painting of the *Communion of St Lucy* is by Giambattista Tiepolo, and the tomb of Marco Corner (father of Caterina Cornaro, see "Ásolo") is attributed to Tullio Lombardo.

The Miracoli and around

The best work of the Lombardo clan is close at hand. From behind Santi Apostoli, it's a relatively clear route to the **Miracoli** church (or Santa Maria dei Miracoli), one of the most attractive buildings in Europe. It was built in the 1480s to house a painting of the Madonna which was believed to have performed a number of miracles, such as reviving a man who'd spent half an hour lying at the bottom of the Giudecca canal. The church is thought to have been designed by Pietro Lombardo; certainly he and his two sons Tullio and Antonio oversaw the building and executed much of the carving. Typically for Renaissance architecture in Venice, richness of effect takes precedence over classical correctness – the Corinthian pilasters are set below the Ionic, so that the viewer can better appreciate the carving on the Corinthian.

The marble-lined interior contains some of the most intricate decorative sculpture to be seen in Venice. The half-length figures of two saints and the *Annunciation* on the balustrade of the raised galleries at the east end are attributed to Tullio Lombardo; the rest of the attributions for the carvings at this end are arguable between the two brothers and their father. Ruskin was greatly distressed by the children's heads carved to the side of the top of the altar steps – "the man who could carve a child's head so perfectly must have been wanting in all human feeling, to cut it off, and tie it by the hair to a vine leaf."

Head towards the Rialto from the Miracoli and you'll pass the cosy church of **San Giovanni Crisostomo**, built around 1500 to designs by Mauro Coducci. It has a magnificent late painting by Giovanni Bellini, *SS Jerome, Christopher and Augustine*, and a fine altarpiece by Sebastiano del Piombo – *St John Chrysostom with SS John the Baptist, Liberale, Mary Magdalen, Agnes, and Catherine*. Round the back of the church is the Corte Seconda del Milion, a minute courtyard hemmed in by ancient buildings, one of which was Marco Polo's family home.

Campo San Zanipolo (Santi Giovanni e Paolo)

After the Piazza, the **Campo San Zanipolo** (a contraction of Santi Giovanni e
Paolo) is the most impressive open space in Venice. Dominated by the huge
brick church from which it gets its name, it also has the most beautiful facade of
any of the Scuole Grandi and one of the finest Renaissance equestrian monuments in Italy.

THE COLLEONI STATUE AND THE SCUOLA GRANDE DI SAN MARCO

The *condottiere* **Bartolomeo Colleoni** began his wayward career in Venice's
army in 1429. In the succeeding years he defected to Milan, re-enlisted for
Venice, fled again, and finally signed up for good in 1455 – whereupon Venice
suffered an outbreak of peace which meant that in the twenty years leading up to
his death in 1475 Colleoni was called upon to fight only once. When he died,
Colleoni left a handsome legacy to the Republic on condition that a monument
should be erected to him in the square before San Marco, an impossible proposition to Venice's rulers, with their cult of anonymity. They got around the problem
with a splendid piece of disingenuousness, interpreting the will in a way that
allowed them to raise the monument before the Scuola Grande di San Marco,
rather than the Basilica, and still claim the money.

The commission for the monument was won by **Andrea Verrocchio** in 1481,
and difficulties dogged this stage of the proceedings too. Having virtually
completed the horse, Verrocchio heard that another artist was being approached
to sculpt the rider, and retaliated by mutilating the work he'd done and galloping
off to Florence. The matter was eventually patched up, and Verrocchio was working again on the piece when he died at the end of June 1488. **Alessandro
Leopardi** was then called in to finish the work and produce the plinth for it,
which he gladly did – even signing his own name on the horse's girth, and titling
himself *del Cavallo*.

An unimprovable backdrop to Colleoni, the **Scuola Grande di San Marco**
has provided a sumptuous facade and foyer for the Ospedale Civile since its
suppression in the early nineteenth century. The facade was started by Pietro
Lombardo and Giovanni Buora in 1487, and finished in 1495 by Mauro Coducci
after a row between Pietro and Buoro and the Scuola. It works better in sections
rather than as a unity: the perspectival panels by Tullio and Antonio Lombardo
don't quite bring off the intended illusion, but only the hardhearted will not be
charmed by them individually.

SAN ZANIPOLO (SANTI GIOVANNI E PAOLO)

The church of San Zanipolo was founded by the Dominicans in 1246, rebuilt and
enlarged from 1333, and finally consecrated in 1430. The sarcophagus of Doge
Giacomo Tiepolo, who originally gave the site to the Dominicans, is on the left of
the door outside.

The **interior** is quite stunning for its sheer size: 290ft long, 125ft wide at the
transepts, 108ft high in the centre. It seems more spacious now than it would
have up to 1682, when the wooden choir, placed similarly to that of the Frari, was
demolished. The simplicity of the design, a nave with two aisles and gracefully
soaring arches, is offset by the huge number of tombs and monuments around
the walls. Contrary to the impression created, not all of the doges are buried
here, just twenty-five of them.

The **west wall** is devoted to the Mocenigo family: above the door is the tomb of Doge Alvise Mocenigo and his wife by Pietro Lombardo (1477); to the right is the monument to Doge Giovanni Mocenigo (d.1485) by Tullio Lombardo; and on the left the superb monument to Doge Pietro Mocenigo (d.1476), by Pietro Lombardo, assisted by his sons.

In the **south aisle**, after the first altar, is the monument to the Venetian military commander Marcantonio Bragadin, to which is attached one of Venice's grisliest stories. In 1571 Bragadin was double-crossed by the Turks to whom he had been obliged to surrender Famagusta: tortured and humiliated for days by his captors, he was eventually executed by being skinned alive. Some years later the skin was brought back to Venice, and today it sits in that urn high up on the wall.

The next altar has a superb **Giovanni Bellini** polyptych, showing *St Vincent Ferrer, with SS Christopher and Sebastian*, and an *Annunciation* and *Pietà* above, still in the original frame. Before you turn into the transept, you'll see a little shrine with the **foot of Saint Catherine of Siena**; most of her body is in Rome, her head is in her house in Siena, one foot's here, and other little relics are scattered about Italy.

The **south transept** has a painting by **Alvise Vivarini**, *Christ Carrying the Cross* (1474) and **Lorenzo Lotto**'s *Saint Antonine* (1542), painted in return for nothing more than his expenses and permission to be buried in the church. Sadly, Lotto was eventually driven from his home town by the jealousies and plots of other artists (including Titian), and died and was buried in the monastery at Loreto.

On the right of the chancel is the tomb of Doge Michele Morosini (d.1382), selected by Ruskin as "the richest monument of the Gothic period in Venice". The tomb of Doge Andrea Vendramin (d.1478), opposite, was singled out as its antithesis – only the half of the effigy's head that would be visible from below was completed by the artist, a short-cut denounced by Ruskin as indicative of "an extreme of intellectual and moral degradation". Tullio Lombardo is thought to have been the culprit, with help from others – maybe his father and brother.

The **Cappella del Rosario**, at the end of the north transept, was virtually destroyed by fire in 1867; its paintings by Tintoretto, Palma il Giovane and others were lost. Of their replacements, the best are **Veronese**'s ceiling panels and *Adoration*.

Funerary sculpture is the main attraction of the **north aisle**. To the left of the sacristy door is the monument to Doge Pasquale Malipiero (d.1462) by Pietro Lombardo, one of the earliest in Renaissance style in Venice.

From Santa Maria Formosa to the Riva

South of San Zanipolo lies Campo di Santa Maria Formosa, an atmospheric square with a small but mouthwatering morning market. The church of **Santa Maria Formosa** was built by San Magno, Bishop of Oderzo in the seventh century, after a dream in which he saw a buxom (*formosa*) figure of the Madonna; the present building is another Coducci effort, dating from 1492. Palma il Vecchio's altarpiece of *St Barbara*, the church's outstanding picture, was admired by George Eliot as "an almost unique presentation of a hero-woman". Bartolomeo Vivarini's *Madonna della Misericordia* (Madonna of Mercy), in a side chapel, is a fine example of one of the warmest Catholic symbols – here she's shown sheltering a group of parishioners under her cloak.

The Renaissance Palazzo Querini-Stampalia, just round the corner from Santa Maria Formosa, houses the **Pinacoteca Querini-Stampalia** (Tues–Sun 10am–2.45pm; L5000). Unless you have a voracious appetite for seventeenth- and eighteenth-century Venetian painting, you'll get most pleasure from earlier pieces such as Palma il Vecchio's portraits of *Francesco Querini* and *Paola Priuli Querini* and Giovanni Bellini's *The Presentation in the Temple*. Apart from that, the main interest is in the eighteenth-century decor of the rooms.

San Zaccaria

The Campo San Zaccaria, a few yards off the Riva degli Schiavoni, has a more torrid past than most – the convent here was notorious for its libidinous goings-on (officials were once sent to close down the nuns' parlour, only to be met with a barrage of bricks), and in 864 Doge Pietro Tradonico was murdered here as he returned from vespers. The towering church of **San Zaccaria**, a pleasing mixture of Gothic and Renaissance, was started by Antonio Gambello and finished after his death in 1481 by Mauro Coducci, who was responsible for the facade from the first storey upwards. Inside is one of the city's most stunning altarpieces, a *Madonna and Four Saints* by Giovanni Bellini. A small fee gets you into the rebuilt remnants of the old church, the Cappella di Sant'Atanasio and Cappella di San Tarasio; here you'll find an early Tintoretto, the *Birth of John the Baptist*, and three wonderful altarpieces by Antonio Vivarini and Giovanni d'Alemagna. Floor mosaics from the ninth and twelfth centuries can be seen through panels in the present floor level, and downstairs is the spooky waterlogged ninth-century crypt.

The principal waterfront of the area, the **Riva degli Schiavoni**, stretches right back to the Molo. It's a favourite walk, particularly as the sun goes down, and many notables have lived or stayed in houses and hotels here. Petrarch and his daughter lived at no. 4145 for a while, Henry James stayed nearby at no. 4161 when he was finishing *The Portrait of a Lady*, and the *Hotel Danieli*, at the far end, has accommodated George Sand, Charles Dickens, Proust, Wagner, the ever-present Ruskin, and Tina Turner.

Halfway along the Riva is the **Pietà** church (Santa Maria della Visitazione), famous as the place where Vivaldi was choirmaster – he was also violin teacher to the attached orphanage. Giorgio Massari won a competition to redesign the church in 1736, and it's possible that he consulted with Vivaldi on its acoustical aspects; building didn't actually begin until 1745, and the facade was even more delayed, only finished in 1906. The church is still used often for concerts, and when the box office is open you can peer over the ropes at the interior, which, in its newly restored form, looks like a wedding-cake turned inside out – and it has one of Venice's most ostentatious ceiling paintings: Giambattista Tiepolo's *The Glory of Paradise*.

The Scuola di San Giorgio and northwards

The ground floor of the **Scuola di San Giorgio degli Schiavoni** would get onto anyone's list of the ten most beautiful rooms in Europe (April–Oct Tues–Sat 9.30am–12.30pm & 3.30–6.30pm, Sun & holidays 9.30am–12.30pm; Nov–March Tues–Sat 10am–12.30pm & 3.30–6pm, Sun & holidays 9.30am–12.30pm; L3000). Venice's resident Slavs (*Schiavoni*), most of whom were traders, set up a scuola to look after their interests in 1451; the present building dates from the early sixteenth century, and the whole interior looks more or less as it would have then. Entering it, you step straight from the street into the superb lower hall, the walls of which are decorated with a cycle by Vittore Carpaccio between 1502 and 1509. Originally painted for the upstairs room, but moved here when the building was rearranged in 1551, the sequence of pictures consists chiefly of scenes from the lives of Saints George, Tryphone and Jerome (the Dalmatian patron saints). Outstanding is *The Vision of St Augustine*, depicting the moment that Augustine was told in a vision of Jerome's death.

The quarter of Venice's Greek community is identifiable from a distance by the alarmingly tilted campanile of **San Giorgio dei Greci**. The Greek presence was strong in Venice from the eleventh century, and grew stronger after Constantinople's capture by the Turks in 1453; by the close of the fifteenth century they had founded their own church, college and school here. The present scuola, designed (like the college) by Longhena in the seventeenth century, now houses the **Museo Dipinti Sacri Bizantini** (Mon & Wed–Sat 9am–12.30pm & 2.30–5pm, Sun & holidays 9am–noon; L2000). Although many of the most beautiful of the exhibited works (mainly fifteenth- to eighteenth-century) maintain the traditions of icon painting in terms of composition and use of symbolic figures rather than attempts at realism, it's fascinating to see how some of the artists absorbed western influences. The **church** contains icons dating back to the twelfth century, and a lot of work by Michael Danaskinàs, a sixteenth-century Cretan artist.

The church of **San Francesco della Vigna** (daily 7–11.45am & 4.45–7pm) takes its name from the vineyard that was here when the Franciscans were given the site in 1253. The present church building was begun in 1534, designed and supervised by Sansovino, but the design was modified during construction, and Palladio was later brought in to provide the facade. Although smaller than the two great mendicant churches of San Zanipolo and I Frari it feels somehow less welcoming – probably a simple matter of the cold colouring added to the more calculated Renaissance architecture. However, there are some fine works of art that make the trek worthwhile – but be sure to have a pocketful of coins for the (necessary) light-boxes. The ones you shouldn't miss are: *SS Jerome, Bernard and Ludovic*, attributed to Antonio Vivarini (left of main door); the sculptures of *Prophets* and *Evangelists* by the Lombardo family (in the chapel left of the chancel); and the *Sacra Conversazione* by **Veronese** (fifth chapel on north side).

The Arsenale and the east of the city

Once the industrial hub of the city and the largest manufacturing site in Europe, this district of Venice – the eastern section of the Castello *sestiere* – is now predominantly a residential quarter and has little to offer of cultural significance. It would be a mistake, however, to leave it entirely unexplored. The absence of tourists is one of its principal attractions (outside even-numbered years, when the Biennale sets up here in summer), and its open spaces – the **Giardini Garibaldi**, **Giardini Pubblici** and **Parco della Rimembranze** – are a good antidote to the claustrophobia that overtakes most visitors to Venice at some point.

The Arsenale

A corruption of the Arabic *darsin'a* (house of industry), the very name of the **Arsenale** is indicative of the strength of Venice's trading links with the eastern Mediterranean, and the workers of these dockyards and factories were the foundations upon which the city's mercantile and military supremacy rested.

Construction of the Arsenale commenced in the early years of the twelfth century, and by the third decade of the fifteenth century it had become the base for some 300 shipping companies, operating around 3000 vessels in excess of 200 tons. The productivity of the Arsenale was legendary: for the visit of Henry III of France in 1574 the *Arsenalotti* built a complete ship while the state reception for the king was in progress.

Expansion of the Arsenale continued into the sixteenth century – Sanmicheli's covered dock for the state barge (the *Bucintoro*) was built in the 1540s, for example, and da Ponte's gigantic rope-factory (the *Tana*) in 1579. By then, though, the maritime strength of Venice was past its peak; militarily as well, despite the conspicuous success at Lepanto in 1571, Venice was on the wane, and the reconquest of the Morea at the end of the seventeenth century was little more than a glorious interlude in a long story of decline. When Napoleon took over the city in 1797 he burned down the wharves, sank the last *Bucintoro* and confiscated the remnant of the Venetian navy.

Under Austrian occupation the docks were reconstructed, and they stayed in continuous service until the end of 1917, when, having built a number of ships for the Italian navy in World War I, they were dismantled to prevent them being of use to the enemy. Since then it has been used by the navy for storage and repairs, but there are plans to extend the naval museum into the Arsenale buildings and to convert other parts into sports halls.

THE ARSENALE BUILDINGS AND MUSEO STORICO NAVALE

There is no public access to the Arsenale complex. You can get a look at part of it, however, from the bridge connecting the Campo Arsenale and the Fondamenta dell'Arsenale; a better view can be had by taking the *vaporetto* #5, which cuts through the oldest part of the Arsenale, taking you past Sanmichel's *Bucintoro* building, alongside which is the mouth of the *Darsena Grande*.

The main **gateway** to the Arsenale, built by Antonio Gambello in 1460, was the first structure in Venice to employ the classical vocabulary of Renaissance architecture. The four **lions** to the side of the gateway must be the most-photographed in the city: the two on the right were probably taken from Delos (at an unknown date), the left-hand one of the pair being positioned here to mark the recapture of Corfu in 1716; the larger pair were brought back from Piraeus in 1687 by Francesco Morosini after the reconquest of the Morea.

Nearby, on the other side of the Rio dell'Arsenale and facing the lagoon, is the **Museo Storico Navale** (Mon–Fri 9am–1pm, Sat 9am–noon; L1000). Chiefly of interest for its models of Venetian craft from the gondola to the *Bucintoro*, the museum gives a comprehensive picture of the working life of the Arsenale and the smaller boatyards of Venice; but if you want to get a taste of the city's history from a single museum visit, then you should give priority to the Correr (see above).

San Pietro di Castello

In 1808 the greater part of the canal connecting the Bacino di San Marco to the broad inlet of the Canale di San Pietro was filled in to form what is now Via Garibaldi, the widest street in the city and the busiest commercial area in the eastern district. Follow your nose along the right-hand side of the street and you'll soon be crossing the Ponte di Quintavalle onto the island of **San Pietro**, once the ecclesiastical centre of Venice, nowadays a place with the air of a village that has seen more prosperous days.

By 775 the settlement here had grown sufficiently to be granted the foundation of a bishopric under the authority of the Patriarch of Grado. From the beginning, the political and economic nucleus of the city was in the Rialto-San Marco area, and the relationship between the church and the geographically remote rulers of the city was never to be close. In 1451 the first **Patriarch of Venice** was invested, but still his seat remained at Castello, and things stayed that way until 1807 (ten years after the Republic had ceased to exist), when the Patriarch was at last permitted to install himself in San Marco.

As with the Arsenale, the history of San Pietro is perhaps more interesting than what you can see. The church is basically a grandiose derivative of a plan by Palladio and has little to recommend it. The most intriguing object inside is the so-called Throne of Saint Peter (in the south aisle), a marble seat made from an Arabic funeral stone cut with texts from the Koran. The lurching campanile, rebuilt by Coducci in the 1480s, was the first tower in Venice to be clad in stone.

Sant'Elena

The island of **Sant'Elena**, the eastern limit of central Venice, was enlarged tenfold during the Austrian administration, partly to form exercise grounds for the troops. Much of the island used to be covered by the meadow of Sant'Elena, a favourite recreation area in the last century, but houses stand there now, leaving just a strip of park along the waterfront. Still, the walk out here is the nearest you'll get to country pleasures in Venice, and the **church of Sant'Elena** is worth a visit.

A church was erected here in the thirteenth century, following the acquisition of the body of Saint Helena (the mother of Constantine), and substantially rebuilt in 1435. The spartan Gothic interior has recently been restored, as have the cloister and campanile (the latter so zealously that it now looks like a power-station chimney), but the main attraction is the doorway to the church, an ensemble created in the 1470s by Antonio Rizzo. The sculptural group in the lunette – a monument to Comandante Vittore Cappello, showing him kneeling before Saint Helena – is the district's one major work of art.

The Canal Grande

The **Canal Grande** is Venice's main thoroughfare. Almost four kilometres long and between thirty and seventy metres wide (but at no point much deeper than five metres), it divides the city in half – three *sestieri* to the west and three to the east. The majority of the most important palaces in Venice stand on the Canal Grande, and the main facades of all of them are on the canalside, many properly visible only from the water. (Palaces are scattered throughout Venice, and you'll rarely come across one that wasn't built to face a canal.) The section that follows is mainly a brief guide to these palaces – the major churches and other public buildings are covered in the appropriate geographical sections.

Left Bank

The first of the major palaces to come into view is the **Palazzo Labia** (completed around 1750). The main facade of the building stretches along the Canareggio canal, but from the Canal Grande you can see how the side wing wraps itself round the campanile of the neighbouring church – such interlocking is common in Venice, where maximum use has to be made of available space. (See "Cannaregio" for details of the interior.)

Not far beyond stands the **Palazzo Vendramin-Calergi**, built by Mauro Coducci at the start of the sixteenth century. This is the first Venetian palace constructed in accordance with the classical rules of Renaissance architecture as formulated by Alberti, and is frequently singled out as the Canal Grande's masterpiece. The round-arched windows enclosing two similar arches are identifying characteristics of Coducci's designs. Richard Wagner died here in 1883; the size of the palace can be gauged from the fact that his rented suite of fifteen rooms occupied just a part of the mezzanine level.

Just after the Rio di San Felice comes the most beguiling palace on the canal – the **Ca' d'Oro**. Incorporating fragments of a thirteenth-century palace that once stood on the site, the Ca' d'Oro was begun in the 1420s and acquired its nickname – "Golden House" – from the gilding that used to accentuate much of its carving. It now houses a large art collection, details of which are given in the "Castello" section.

Close to the far side of the Rio dei Santi Apostoli stands the **Ca' da Mosto**. The arches of the first floor and the carved panels above them are remnants of a thirteenth-century Veneto-Byzantine building, among the oldest structures to be seen on the Canal Grande. From the fifteenth to the nineteenth century this was one of Venice's most famous hotels, the *Albergo del Lion Bianco*.

As the canal turns, the **Ponte di Rialto** (Rialto Bridge) comes into view. The huge building before it, with five arches at water level, is the **Fondaco dei Tedeschi**, once the headquarters of the city's German merchants. Reconstructed in 1505 after a fire and renovated several times since (most recently to accommodate the main post office), it once had frescoes by Giorgione and Titian on its exterior walls, the remains of which are now in the Ca' d'Oro. The bridge itself was built in 1588–91, superseding a succession of wooden and sometimes unreliable structures; until 1854, when an iron bridge was built at the Accademia, this was the only point at which the Canal Grande could be crossed on foot.

Immediately before the next canal is Sansovino's first palace in Venice, the **Palazzo Dolfin-Manin**. It dates from the late 1530s, a period when other projects by him – the library, the mint and the Loggetta – were transforming the city centre. The **Palazzo Loredan** and the **Palazzo Farsetti**, standing side by side at the end of the Fondamenta del Carbon, are heavily restored thirteenth-century palaces; the former was the home of Elena Corner Piscopia, who in 1678 graduated from Padua University, so becoming the first woman to obtain a degree.

Work began on the **Palazzo Grimani** (near side of the Rio di San Luca) in 1556, to designs by Sanmicheli, but was not completed until 1575, sixteen years after his death. Ruskin, normally no fan of Renaissance architecture, made an exception for this colossal palace, calling it "simple, delicate, and sublime".

On the approach to the sharp bend in the canal (the *Volta del Canal*) there stands a line of five buildings, the first four of which belonged to the Mocenigo family. This group consists of: the **Palazzo Mocenigo-Nero**, a late-sixteenth-century building; the double **Palazzo Mocenigo**, built in the eighteenth century as an extension to the Nero house, and home to Byron for a couple of years; and the **Palazzo Mocenigo Vecchio**, a Gothic palace remodelled in the seventeenth century, reputedly haunted by the ghost of the philosopher-alchemist Giordano Bruno, whose betrayal by Giovanni Mocenigo in 1592 led ultimately to his torture and execution. The fifth palace is the **Palazzo Contarini delle Figure**, named after the almost invisible figures above the water entrance.

The vast pristine building round the *Volta* is the **Palazzo Grassi**, built in 1748–72; owned by *Fiat* – hence the lavish renovation – it's now a conference centre and venue for Venice's glossiest exhibitions.

The Santa Maria del Giglio landing stage is virtually in the shadow of one of the Canal Grande's most imposing buildings – Sansovino's **Palazzo Corner della Ca' Grande**. The house that used to stand here was destroyed when a fire lit to dry out a stock of sugar in one of its rooms ran out of control; Sansovino's replacement was built from 1545 onwards.

Opposite the church of the Salute, squeezed into a line of fifteenth- and seventeenth-century buildings, is the narrow **Palazzo Contarini-Fasan**, a Gothic palace with unique wheel tracery on the balconies. It's popularly known as the *House of Desdemona*, for no good reason.

Right Bank

The first attraction on the right bank is the **Fondaco dei Turchi**. Originally a private house, then from the 1620s until 1838 the base for Turkish traders in the city, the Fondaco was savagely restored in the last century. Whatever the short-comings of the work, however, the building's towers and water-level arcade give a reasonably precise picture of a typical Veneto-Byzantine palace. It now houses the Museo di Storia Naturale (Natural History Museum).

A short distance beyond stands Longhena's thickly ornamented **Ca' Pésaro**, finished in 1703, long after the architect's death. Unusually, the Ca' Pésaro has a stone-clad side facade: most houses in Venice have plain brick sides, either because of the cost of stone, or to allow for a later building to be attached. It now contains the Galleria d'Arte Moderna and the Museo Orientale.

There's nothing especially engrossing now until you reach the Rialto markets, which begin with the neo-Gothic **Pescheria** (fish market), built in 1907. The older buildings which follow it, the **Fabbriche Nuove di Rialto** and (set back from the water) the **Fabbriche Vecchie di Rialto**, are by Sansovino and Scarpagnino respectively, and replaced buildings destroyed by fire in 1514. The large building at the base of the Rialto bridge – the **Palazzo dei Camerlenghi** (1525) – used to be the home of the Venetian exchequer.

The cluster of Gothic palaces at the *Volta* constitutes one of the city's architectural glories. The **Ca' Fóscari** (1435), which Ruskin thought "the noblest example in Venice" of late Gothic, was the home of Doge Francesco Fóscari, whose extraordinarily long term of office (32 years) came to an end with his forced resignation, an event partly attributable to the unrelenting feud conducted against him by the Loredan family and its allies. He died in 1457, only weeks after leaving the Palazzo Ducale. Adjoining the Ca' Fóscari are a pair of joined buildings of the same period – the **Palazzi Giustinian**. Wagner wrote the second act of *Tristan* while living here.

A little further on comes Longhena's **Ca' Rezzonico**, as gargantuan as his Ca' Pésaro, but less aggressive. It was begun in 1667 as a commission from the Bon family, but their ambition exceeded their financial resources and they were obliged in 1750 to sell out to the Rezzonico, who completed the palace and even tacked a ballroom and staircase onto the back. Much of the interior of the Ca' Rezzonico is open to the public, as it houses the Museo del Settecento Veneziano. The unfinished **Palazzo dei Leoni** (soon after the Campo San Vio), would have been the largest palace on the canal, but its construction, begun in 1759, never progressed further than the first storey – probably owing to the ruinous cost. The stump of the building and the platform on which it is raised are occupied by the Guggenheim collection of modern art.

The one domestic building of note between here and the **Dogana di Mare** (Customs House) at the end of the canal is the miniature **Palazzo Dario**, two along from the Palazzo dei Leoni. Compared by Henry James to "a house of cards that hold together by a tenure it would be fatal to touch", the palace was built in the late 1480s not for a patrician family but for Giovanni Dario, a civil servant. The multicoloured marbles of the facade are characteristic of the work of the Lombardo family, and the design may actually be by the founder of the dynasty, Pietro Lombardo.

The Northern Islands

The islands lying to the north of Venice – **San Michele**, **Murano**, **Burano** and **Torcello** – are the places to visit when the throng of tourists in the main part of the city becomes too oppressive, and are the source of much of the glass and lace work you will have seen in many shops in Venice.

To get to them, the main *vaporetto* stop is the **Fondamente Nuove**. The *vaporetto* #5, which runs about every fifteen minutes, will take you to San Michele and Murano. For Burano and Torcello there is the *vaporetto* or steamer #12 (every 1hr–1hr 30min), which takes 45 minutes to get to Burano, from where it's a short hop to Torcello. This service can also be caught from Murano, but only from the **Faro** landing stage.

San Michele
The high brick wall around the cemetery island of **San Michele** gives way by the landing stage for the elegant white facade of **San Michele in Isola**, designed by Mauro Coducci in 1469. With this building, Coducci not only helped introduce Renaissance architecture to Venice, but also promoted the use of Istrian stone. Easy to carve yet resistant to water, it had been used as damp-proofing at ground level, but never before for a complete facade; it was to be used on the facades of most major buildings in Venice from the Renaissance onwards.

The main part of the island, through the cloisters, is the city **cemetery** (daily 8.15am–4pm), established by Napoleonic decree and nowadays maintained by the Franciscans, as is the church. The majority of Venetians lie here for just ten years or so, when their bones are dug up and removed to an ossuary and the land recycled. Only those who can afford it stay longer. The cemetery is laid out in sections – ask at the entrance for the little give-away map – the most dilapidated of which is for the Protestants (no. XV), where any admirers can find **Ezra Pound**'s grave. In section XIV are the Greek and Russian Orthodox graves, including the restrained memorial stones of **Igor and Vera Stravinsky** and the more elaborate tomb of **Serge Diaghilev** – always strewn with flowers.

Murano
Chiefly famed now as the home of Venice's **glass-blowing** industry, **Murano**'s main *fondamente* are crowded with shops selling the mostly revolting products of the furnaces. However, don't despair: Murano does have other things to offer.

The glass furnaces were moved to Murano from Venice as a safety measure in 1291, and so jealously did the Muranese guard their industrial secrets that for a long while they had the European monopoly on glass mirror making. The glass-blowers of Murano were accorded various privileges not allowed to other arti-sans, such as being able to wear swords. From 1376 the offspring of a marriage between a Venetian nobleman and the daughter of a glass-worker were allowed to be entered into the Libro d'Oro, unlike the children of other cross-class matches.

Far more interesting than most of the finished products is the performance of their manufacture. There are numerous **furnaces** to visit, all free of charge on the assumption that you will then want to buy something, though you won't be pressed too hard to do so. Many of the workshops are to be found along Fondamenta dei Vereri, traditionally a glassworking centre, as the name suggests.

When the Venetian republic fell to Napoleon in 1797, there were seventeen churches on Murano; today only two are open. The first is **San Pietro Martire**, a Dominican Gothic church begun in 1363, and largely rebuilt after a fire in 1474. Its main attraction is a large and (as ever) elegant Giovanni Bellini: the *Madonna and Child with SS Mark and Augustine, and Doge Barbarigo* (1488); a second Bellini (an *Assumption*) is at present being restored.

THE GLASS MUSEUMS
Close by, along Fondamenta Cavour, you'll find the **Museo Vetrario** (Glass Museum) in the Palazzo Giustinian (Mon, Tues & Thurs–Sat 10am–4pm, Sun & holidays 9am–12.30pm; L3000). The collection includes some Roman pieces, but the earliest surviving Murano glass dates from the fifteenth century. There are perfunctory labels in Italian only, and there is no guide book, yet even so the exhibits often exert their own fascination – how *did* the aristocracy manage to drink in the seventeenth century? A separate room contains a fascinating exhibi-tion on the history of Murano glass techniques, this time fully explained in English. Look out for the extraordinary *Murine in Lanna* – the technique of plac-ing different coloured rods together to form an image in cross-section.

Hang on to your entry ticket as it will also get you into the recently opened **Modern and Contemporary Glass Museum** on Fondamenta Manin (opposite Fondamenta Vereri; same hours as the main museum). Here they have a few pieces of functional glassware that try to look like modernist sculptures, and one or two modernist sculptures that end up looking like giant pieces of functional ware. However, there are some interesting works – like the baby by Alfredo Borbini which looks as though it's carved from lava, and the mirror with gold leaf by Piero Fornasetti.

SANTI MARIA E DONATO
Murano's main draw is the Veneto-Byzantine church of **Santi Maria e Donato**, which was founded in the seventh century and rebuilt in the twelfth (daily 8am–noon & 4–7pm). Its beautiful **mosaic floor**, dated 1141 in the nave, mingles abstract patterns with images of beasts and birds – an eagle carries off a deer; two roosters carry off a fox, slung from a pole. The church was originally dedicated to Mary, but in 1125 was re-dedicated when the relics of Saint Donato were brought here from Cephalonia. Four splendid bones from an unfortunate dragon which was slain by the holy spit of Donato are now hanging behind the altar. Above these, in the apse, is a twelfth-century **mosaic of the Madonna** and fifteenth-century frescoes of the Evangelists. A guidebook to the church is available, proceeds of which go towards restoration work.

Burano

The main route into **Burano** is a narrow street full of lace shops which soon opens out to reveal the brightly painted houses of the village itself – the colours used to be symbolic, but the meanings have got confused through time and now people paint their houses whatever colour takes their fancy.

This is still largely a fishing community, the lagoon's main yield being shellfish of various kinds, such as *vongole* (tiny clams) and small crabs. (The catch can be bought either here, on the Fondamenta Pescheria, or back in Venice, at the Rialto.) It's a solitary business; one or two people have even built themselves vulnerable-looking houses out on the slightly higher mud-flats, constructed largely from material scavenged from the lagoon tips.

As the men of Burano live mainly from the water, so the women are to a large extent dependent on **lace-making**. Making Burano-point and Venetian- point lace is extremely exacting work, both highly skilled and mind-bendingly repetitive, with an enormous toll on the eyesight. Each woman specialises in one particular stitch, and so each piece is passed from woman to woman during its construction. The skills are taught at the **Scuola dei Merletti** (Lace School; Wed–Mon 9am–6pm; L2000). It's in the spacious Piazza Baldessare Galuppi and combines a school with a museum, and is well worth a visit before you buy anything. (Much of the work in the shops is machine produced and imported.) The school was opened in 1872 after the indigenous crafting of lace nearly died out; the museum shows work dating back to the sixteenth century, but most was produced in the last hundred years.

Torcello

Torcello has come full circle: settled as early as the fifth century, the seat of the Bishop of Altinum from 638, and the home of about 20,000 people by the fourteenth century, it was then eclipsed by Venice, and by 1600 was largely deserted. Today the total population of Torcello is about 100, and there is little visible evidence of the island's prime – two churches and a couple of buildings round a dusty square, and pottery shards half-buried in the fields.

The main reason that people come here today is to visit Venice's first cathedral, **Santa Maria Assunta** (summer daily 10am–12.30pm & 2–6.30pm; open until 4.30pm in winter). An early church on the site became a cathedral after the Bishop of Altinum arrived with other emigrants from the mainland. The present Veneto-Byzantine building is on pretty much the same plan as the seventh-century one, but it was largely rebuilt in the 860s and altered again in 1008. Inside, the waterlogged crypt is the only survival of the body of the original church; the baptistery also dates from the seventh century, but circular foundations in front of the main doors are all that remain of it.

The dominant tone of the interior is created by its watery green-grey marble columns and panelling; the mosaic floor is eleventh-century, but two wooden panels lift to reveal the original floor underneath. A stunning twelfth-century mosaic of the Madonna and Child, on a pure gold background, covers the semi-dome of the apse, resting on an eleventh-century mosaic frieze of the Apostles. In the centre of the frieze, below the window, is an image of Saint Heliodorus, the first Bishop of Altinum, whose remains were brought here by the first settlers. It's interesting to compare this image with the gold-plated face mask given to his remains in a Roman sarcophagus in front of the original seventh-century altar.

The church of **Santa Fosca** (same hours as Santa Maria) was built in the eleventh and twelfth centuries to house the body of the eponymous saint, brought to Torcello from Libya some time before 1011 and now resting under the altar. Much restored, the church retains the Greek cross form and a fine exterior apse, and inside, the elegant brick arches and cornerings leading up to its wooden dome. Despite the tourists, both these churches maintain a meditative calm that many of the churches in Venice lack.

In the square outside sits the curious **chair of Attila**. Local legend has it that if you sit in it, you will be wed within a year. Behind it is the **Museo dell'Estuario** (Tues–Sun 10am–12.30pm & 2–5.30pm; L2000), which includes thirteenth-century beaten gold figures, sections of mosaic heads, and pieces of jewellery. It's all nicely laid out, and worth a visit.

The Southern Islands

The section of the lagoon to the south of the city, enclosed by the long islands of the **Lido** and **Pellestrina**, has far fewer outcrops of solid land than the northern half: once past **Giudecca** and **San Giorgio Maggiore** (in effect detached pieces of central Venice), and clear of the smaller islands that dot the water off the middle section of the Lido, you could, on certain days, look in the direction of the mainland and think you were out in the open sea. The nearer islands are the more interesting: the farther-flung settlements of the southern lagoon have played as significant a role in the history of Venice as the better-known northern islands but nowadays they have few things going for them other than the pleasure of the trip.

San Giorgio Maggiore

The prominence of Palladio's church of **San Giorgio Maggiore** (daily 10am–12.30pm & 2.30–4.30pm) almost forces you to have an opinion as to its architectural merits. Ruskin didn't much care for it: "It is impossible to conceive a design more gross, more barbarous, more childish in conception, more servile in plagiarism, more insipid in result, more contemptible under every point of rational regard." Palladio's successors were more impressed, though, and it was to prove one of the most influential Renaissance church designs.

The finely calculated proportions and Counter-Reformation austerity of the interior reminded Ruskin merely of an assembly room; in his opinion, its paintings were what justified opening the door. Two pictures by Tintoretto hang in the chancel: *The Fall of Manna* and *The Last Supper*, perhaps the most famous of all his images. They were painted as a pair in 1592–94, the last years of the artist's life; another Tintoretto of the same date – a *Deposition* – hangs in the Cappella dei Morti, approached through the door on the right of the choir.

On the left of the choir a corridor leads to the **campanile**; rebuilt in 1791 after the collapse of its predecessor, it's one of the two best vantage points in the city – the other being the campanile of San Marco.

The ex-Benedictine monastery next door to the church, now the base of the **Fondazione Giorgio Cini** (a combined arts research institute, craft school and naval college), is one of the architectural gems of Venice. It incorporates a 128-metre-long dormitory, designed by Giovanni Buora around 1494, a double staircase and a library by Longhena, a magnificent refectory by Palladio and two adjoining cloisters, one planned by Giovanni Buora and built by his son, the other designed by Palladio. Exhibitions are regularly held at the Fondazione, and it's possible to visit the monastery at other times by ringing ☎528.9900 to make an appointment, or by persuading the custodian of your interest in Palladian architecture.

Giudecca

In the earliest records of Venice, the island of **Giudecca** was known as *Spina Longa*, a name clearly derived from its shape; the modern name might refer to the Jews (*Giudei*) who were based here from the late thirteenth century, or to the disruptive noble families who, from the ninth century, were shoved onto this chain of islets to keep them quiet (*giudicati* meaning "judged"). Before the banks of the Brenta became the prestigious site for one's summer abode, Giudecca was where the wealthiest aristocrats of early Renaissance Venice built their villas, and in places you can still see traces of their gardens. The present-day suburb is a strange mixture of decrepitude and vitality. The boatyards and fishing quays on the south side are interspersed with half-abandoned factories and roofless sheds, and even the side facing the city presents a remarkable economic contrast: at the western edge is the derelict neo-Gothic fortress of the Mulino Stucky, a flour mill built in 1895, and at the other stands the *Cipriani*, the most expensive hotel in Venice.

The Franciscan church of the **Redentore** (daily 7.30am–noon & 3.30–7pm), designed by Palladio in 1577, is Giudecca's main monument. In 1575–76 Venice suffered an outbreak of bubonic plague which annihilated nearly 50,000 people – virtually a third of the city's population. The Redentore was built in thanks for Venice's deliverance, and every year until the downfall of the Republic the doge and his senators attended a mass in the church on the Feast of the Redentore to renew their declaration of gratitude. The procession walked to the church over a pontoon bridge from the Záttere, a ceremony perpetuated by the people of Venice on the third Sunday in July.

The present state of the Redentore makes an appreciation of its architectural subtleties a bit of an effort – the plaster is dowdy, statues with fairy-light haloes and other additions clutter the place and a rope prevents visitors going beyond the nave. The best paintings in the church, including a *Madonna with Child and Angels* by Alvise Vivarini, are in the sacristy, where you'll be greatly edified by a gallery of eighteenth-century wax heads of illustrious Franciscans, arranged in glass cases all round the room.

San Lazzaro degli Armeni

Visits Thurs & Sun 3–5pm; take the #10 vaporetto from Riva degli Schiavoni – you have to catch one just before 3pm to have any time on the island.

No foreign community has a longer pedigree in Venice than the Armenians – they were established by the end of the thirteenth century, and for around five hundred years have had a church within a few yards of the Piazza (in Calle degli Armeni). They are far less numerous now, and the most conspicuous sign of their presence is the Armenian island by the Lido, **San Lazzaro degli Armeni**, identifiable from the city by the onion-shaped top of its campanile. The Roman Catholic Armenian monastery here was founded in 1717 by Manug di Pietro (known as *Mechitar* – "The Consoler"), and derived its name from the island's past function as a leper colony – Lazarus being the patron saint of lepers.

The Armenian monks have always had a reputation as scholars and linguists, and the monastery's collection of precious manuscripts and books – the former going back to the fifth century – is one of the visit's highlights, along with a Tiepolo ceiling panel and the room in which Byron stayed while lending a hand with the preparation of an Armenian-English dictionary. The tour ends in a computerised printing and typesetting hall, the nerve centre of the polyglot press which has been operating here continuously since 1789. You should leave a donation or buy something from the press – the old maps and prints of Venice are a bargain.

The Lido and the southern lagoon

For about eight centuries, the **Lido** was the focus of the annual hullaballoo of Venice's "Marriage to the Sea", when the doge went out to the Porto di Lido to drop a gold ring into the brine, and then disembarked for mass at San Nicolò al Lido. It was then an unspoilt strip of land, and remained so into the last century. Within thirty years it had become the smartest bathing resort in Italy, and although it's no longer as chic as it was when Thomas Mann set *Death in Venice* here, there's less room on its beaches now than ever before. But unless you're staying at one of the flashy hotels that stand shoulder to shoulder along the sea front, or are prepared to pay a ludicrous fee to hire one of their beach hutches for the day, you won't be allowed to get the choicest Lido sand between your toes. The ungroomed public beaches are at the northern and southern ends of the island – though why anyone should want to jeopardise his or her health in these filthy waters is a mystery.

The Film Festival occupies the Lido's Palazzo del Cinema in late August and early September, but the place has little else to recommend it – although inveterate gamblers in possession of a snappy wardrobe might want to investigate the summer Casino.

FROM THE LIDO TO PELLESTRINA

There are two routes across the lagoon to Chioggia: in July and August a boat goes there from the Riva degli Schiavoni; and throughout the year the #11 bus from Gran Viale Santa Maria Elizabetta (on the Lido) runs down to **Alberoni**, drives onto a ferry for the five-minute hop to **Pellestrina**, drives the 10km to the southern tip of Pellestrina, and then turfs its load onto a steamer for the 25-minute crossing to Chioggia. The boat takes two hours, the bus eighty minutes, and unless you're aiming for a comprehensive knowledge of the lagoon, it's not time well spent.

The fishing village of **Malamocco**, about 5km into the expedition, is the successor of the ancient settlement which in the eighth century was the capital of the lagoon confederation. In 810 the town was taken by Pepin, son of Charlemagne, and there followed one of the crucial battles in Venice's history, when Pepin's fleet, endeavouring to reach the islands that were to become Venice, became jammed in the mudbanks and was swiftly massacred. After the battle, the capital was promptly transferred to the safer islands of Rivoalto. In 1107 the old town of Malamocco was wiped out by a tidal wave. As the boat crosses from Pellestrina Cimitero to Chioggia, you get the best possible view of what could be described as the last great monument of the Republic – the **Murazzi**. This colossal wall of Istrian boulders, 4km long and 14m thick at the base, was constructed at the sides of the Porto di Chioggia to protect Venice from the battering of the sea, and did its job perfectly from the year of its completion (1782) until the flood of November 1966.

CHIOGGIA

In 1379 **Chioggia** was the scene of the most serious threat to Venice since Pepin's invasion, when the Genoese, after copious shedding of blood on both sides, took possession of the town. Protracted siege warfare resulted in the nearly complete destruction of medieval Chioggia before the surrender of the enemy in June 1380. From then until the arrival of Napoleon's ships nobody broke into the Venetian lagoon.

Modern Chioggia is the second largest settlement in the lagoon after Venice, and one of Italy's busiest fishing ports. It's not the most charming of places, and you can see virtually everything worth seeing in a hour's walk along the Corso del Popolo, the principal street in Chioggia's grid-iron lay-out. The main attractions are the **fish market** (Tues–Sat mornings) and the **Duomo**, which was Longhena's first major commission and possesses some good, if grisly, eighteenth-century paintings.

Buses run from the duomo to **Sottomarina**, Chioggia's down-market answer to Venice's Lido. On the beaches of Sottomarina you're a fraction closer to nature than you would be on the Lido, and the resort does have one big plus – after your dip you can go back to the Corso and have a fresh seafood meal that's cheaper than any you'd find in Venice's restaurants and better than most.

The quickest way back to Venice is by bus from the Duomo or Sottomarina to Piazzale Roma, but it's a dispiriting drive and dearer than the island-hop route. It's only twenty minutes quicker too.

Eating and Drinking

Not surprisingly, **fish and seafood** dominate Venice's restaurant menus. Prawns, squid and octopus are typical Venetian *antipasti*, as are Murano crabs and *sarde in saor* (marinated sardines). Dishes like eel cooked in Marsala wine, *baccalà* (salt cod) and *seppioline nere* (baby cuttlefish cooked in its own ink) are other Venetian staples, but the quintessential dish is the **risotto**, made with rice grown along the Po valley.

Pastries and sweets are also an area of Venetian expertise. Look out for the thin oval biscuits called *baicoli*, the ring-shaped cinnamon-flavoured *bussolai* (a speciality of Burano), and *mandolato* – a cross between nougat and toffee, made with almonds. The Austrian occupation has left its mark in the form of the ubiquitous *strudel* and the cream- or jam-filled *krapfen* (doughnuts).

Restaurants and pizzerias

Virtually every **restaurant** in Venice advertises a set-price *Menu Turistico,* which can be a cheap way of sampling Venetian specialities, but the quality and certainly the quantity won't be up to the mark of an à la carte meal. As a general rule, value for money tends to increase with the distance from San Marco; plenty of restaurants within a short radius of the Piazza offer menus that seem to be reasonable, but you'll probably find the food unappetising, the portions tiny and the service abrupt.

(The addresses below are followed by the name of the section in which the street or campo lies. The prices are for a full meal with a quarter-litre of wine.)

Under L20,000

Ai Canottieri, Ponte Tre Archi; Cannaregio. *Primo* around L5000, *secondo* L9000. Has live music occasionally, but as usual bar prices go up to pay the band. Bar and restaurant open 7pm–midnight; closed Sun.

All'Anfora, Lista Vecchia dei Bari; San Polo. An unpretentious local restaurant that's open for breakfast coffee and still going late at night, and where a woman eating alone is welcomed and not patronised. The seafood risotto is good, as is the *spaghetti del doge*. Closed Fri.

Alle Oche, Calle del Tintor (south side of Campo S. Giacomo dell'Orio); San Polo. Has about fifty varieties of pizza to choose from; closed Mon.

Alle Záttere, Campo Sant'Agnese; Dorsoduro. The *Primavera*, with vegetables, is recommended.

Antico Capon, Campo Santa Margherita; Dorsoduro. Wide range of pizzas including such novelties as gorgonzola and walnut; good prosciutto to start. Closed Wed.

Dalla Cea, Calle del Fumo (down from Fdm. Nuove); Cannaregio. A basic trattoria, catering for workers of the area; has a few outside tables under the trellis in the summer. Good *seppie alla griglia*; *menu turistico* at L12,000.

Donna Onesta, Calle della Madonna (near I Frari); San Polo. Popular and very friendly – ask about the day's special dish; substantial meal and fair quantities of wine for a couple of thousand under L20,000. Noon–3.30pm & 6–11pm; closed Sun.

Frigittoria da Bruno, Calle Lunga San Barnaba; Dorsoduro. Similar to *Donna Onesta*, but a bit cheaper, rougher and more homely; go for the *à la carte* meals. 1–2.30pm & 6.15–10.30pm; closed Thurs lunchtime and all Sun.

Isola Misteriosa, Rio Terrà Scozzera (just off Campo S. Margherita); Dorsoduro. Nice food (with some vegetarian options) but small portions, and a touch overpriced. Open 11am–3pm & 6–11.30pm.

Paradiso Perduto, Fondamenta della Misericordia; Cannaregio. Opens around noon, closes midnight or later, depending on how things are going. Fronted by a popular bar, it has a lively relaxed atmosphere, attracting architecture students, arty types and some of the gay community. Bar prices higher when live music is playing – usually Sunday. Full meals start at around L15,000, but go up to L30,000. Closed Wed.

Rosticceria San Bartolomeo, Calle della Bissa; San Marco. Downstairs it's a sort of glori-fied snack-bar, the meals starting from under L10,000 – the trick is to first grab a place at the long tables along the windows, then order from the counter. Good if you need to refuel quickly and cheaply but can't face another pizza. Noon–2.30pm & 4.30–9pm; closed Mon.

San Tomà, Campo San Tomà; San Polo. Outdoor tables on the campo and under a pergola out the back; pizzas are succulent, but the L2000 *coperto* and twelve percent service bump the price up. Also serves delicious home-made pasta. Closed Mon.

Toscana, Via Garibaldi (bottom end); Arsenale. Plain, with a tiny menu, but all dishes are good and cheap. Noon–2pm & 6–8pm; closed Wed.

L20,000–30,000

Al Masceron, Calle Lunga Santa Maria Formosa; Castello. 'Arty' feel and interesting bar food, worth a try if you're confident in Italian and they're not too busy. *Primo* L4000–6000; *secondo* L8000–12,000 11am–3pm & 6–11pm; closed Sun.

Al Milion, Corte del Milion (behind San Giovanni Crisostomo); Castello. Trattoria with bar where you can get snacks. Wide selection of Veneto wines. 10.30am–2.30pm & 5.30–10.30pm; closed Wed.

Antico Molo, Fondamenta degli Ormesini (near the Ghetto); Cannaregio. Originally a family-run, local place, but becoming trendier by the year. Good food, good value. Closed Wed.

Over L30,000

Altanella, Calle dell'Erbe (Giudecca); Southern Islands. Recommended for a treat; beautiful fish dishes, plus a terrace overlooking the island's central canal. Definitely best to book – ☎522.7780. Closed Mon, Tues and all winter.

Locanda Montin, Fondamenta di Borgo; Dorsoduro. Very highly rated, but the quality's more erratic than you'd expect for the money; you'll pay in the region of L30,000 here for what would cost much less in some places. It's always been a place for the literary/artistic set – Pound, Hemingway, Peggy Guggenheim and Visconti, for example – and the restaurant doubles as a commercial art gallery. Often essential to ring for a table – ☎522.7151. Closed Tues, Wed, and for two weeks in Jan and Aug.

Snacks and bars

Stand at a Venetian **bar** any time of the day and you won't have to wait long before someone drops by for a reviving *ombra*, a tiny glass of wine customarily downed in one. Serious wine enthusiasts should sample a few *ombre* in an **enoteca**, a bar where priority is given to the range and quality of the wines (for example, *Al Volto*). Most bars also serve some kind of food, ranging from *tramezzini* to more exotic nibbles called *cicheti*.

Al Volto, Calle Cavalli (near Campo S. Luca); San Marco. Stocks 1300 wines from Italy and elsewhere, some cheap, many not; good snacks too. 9am–1pm & 4.30–9pm; closed Sun.

Cantina del Vino gia Schiavi, Fondamenta Maravegie (opposite S. Trovaso); Dorsoduro. Great wine shop and bar – do some sampling before you buy. 9am–1.30pm & 3.15–8.30pm.

Corner Pub, Calle della Chiesa; Dorsoduro. Looks a bit like a pub, and (like *Vino Vino*) usually has a few hooray art history students from the home counties, but is authentically Venetian nonetheless. 7am–3pm & 6pm–2am; closed Tues.

Da Codroma, Fondamenta Briati; Dorsoduro. The kind of place you could sit for an hour or two with a beer and a book and feel comfortable. Shows work by local artists, and is a venue for poetry readings and live music.

Do Mori, Calle Do Mori (just off Ruga Vecchia S. Giovanni); San Polo. A narrow, standing-only bar, catering mainly for the Rialto porters and traders, and thus frustratingly shut at lunchtime when they all nip home. Delicious snacks and terrific atmosphere. One of the best of a number of authentic bars in the market area. 9am–1pm & 5–8pm; closed Wed afternoon and Sun.

Do Spade, Sottoportego delle Do Spade; San Polo. Impossible to locate from a map – walk past the *Do Mori* and keep going as straight as possible. Larger than *Do Mori*, but a very similar place. 9am–1pm & 5–8pm; closed Sun.

Harry's Bar, Calle Vallaresso; San Marco. Trendiest bar in town since time immemorial; famed in equal measure for its cocktails, its sandwiches and its (celebrity league) prices. 3pm–1am; closed Mon.

Osteria alla Ghiacciaia, Fondamenta di Cannaregio; Cannaregio. Small local bar with an impressive kitchen. One main dish which changes daily – a generous meal for two, with wine, shouldn't top the L15,000 mark. Tends to shut early; closed Sun.

LATE NIGHT BARS

There aren't too many places in Venice for a **late-night drink**; of the places listed under "Restaurants and pizzerias" and "Bars and snacks", the ones staying open late are:

Ai Canottieri, All'Anfora, Al Masceron, Al Milion, Corner Pub, Da Codroma, Harry's Bar, Isola Misteriosa, Paradiso Perduto, VinoVino.

VinoVino, Ponte delle Veste (near La Fenice); San Marco. A wine bar like *Da Codroma*; though more formal and slightly posey. However, the atmosphere improves as the evening passes, and it does stock over 100 wines. 10am–2pm & 5pm–1am; closed Tues.

Cafés, pasticcerie and ice cream

As in every Italian city, the **cafés** are central to social life, and you'll never be more than a couple of minutes from a decent one. In addition to their marvellous local confections, many **pasticcerie** also serve coffee, but will have at most a few bar stools. Strict budgeting is further jeopardised by Venice's **gelaterie**, where ice cream comes in forms that you won't have experienced before, unless you're a seasoned traveller in Italy.

General areas to find good cafés and pasticcerie include **Campo Santa Margherita**, **Crosera San Pantalon**, running just south of San Rocco, and **Campiello Meloni** (between S. Polo and S. Aponal), which has a couple of excellent *pasticcerie* whose doors remain open on Sundays.

Florian, Piazza San Marco. Opened in 1720 by Florian Francesconi, and frescoed and mirrored in a passable pastiche of that period, this has long been the café to be seen in. A simple *cappuccino* will set you back L10,000 if the band's performing and you'll have to take out a mortgage for a cocktail.

Il Golosone, Salizzada San Lio; Castello. *Pasticceria* and bar with a glorious spread of cakes; does a delicious apple *spremute*. Closed Mon.

Marchini, Ponte San Maurizio; San Marco. The most delicious and most expensive of Venetian *pasticciere*, where people come on Sunday morning to buy family treats.

Nico, Zàttere ai Gesuati; Dorsoduro. A high-point of a wander in the area, celebrated for an artery-clogging creation called a *gianduiotto* – a paper cup with a block of praline ice cream drowned in whipped cream. Closed Thurs.

Paolin, Campo Morosini; San Marco. Thought by many to be the makers of the best ice cream in Venice; certainly their pistachio is amazing, and the outside tables have one of the finest settings in the city. Closed Fri.

Takeaways, markets and shops

The campi, parks and canalside steps make **picnicking** a particularly pleasant alternative in Venice, and if you're venturing off to the outer islands it's often the only way of fuelling yourself. Don't try to picnic in the Piazza though – the by-laws against it are strictly enforced.

Takeaway pizza is all over the place, though most of it is pretty miserable fare. For the best and widest range of pizzas and pies go to *Cip Ciap* in Calle Mondo Nuovo (near S. Maria Formosa; Castello; closed Thurs).

Open-air **markets** for fruit and vegetables are held in various squares every day except Sunday; check out Santa Maria Formosa, Santa Margherita, Campiello dell'Anconetta, Rio Terrà San Leonardo and the barge moored by Campo San Barnaba. The market of markets however is the one at the Rialto, where you can buy everything you need for an impromptu feast – it's open Monday to Saturday 8am to 1pm, with a few stalls opening again in the late afternoon.

Virtually every parish has its **alimentari** and most of them are good; one to single out is *Aliani Gastronomia* (Ruga Vecchia S. Giovanni; San Polo) – scores of cheeses, meats and salads that'll have you drooling as soon as you're through the door.

Entertainment

Except when the Carnevale is in full swing (see "Festivals"), Venice after dark can be pretty moribund. That said, the city's calendar of special events is often impressive, though the bias is definitely towards high culture. To find out what's on in the way of concerts and films, check *Un Ospite di Venezia*; for news of events outside the mainstream, check the posters.

Music and theatre

Music in Venice, to all intents and purposes, means classical music – rock bands rarely come nearer than Padua. The top-bracket **music venues** are *La Fenice*, Campo S. Fantin; San Marco (☎521.0161; closed Aug) and the *Teatro Goldoni*, Calle Goldoni; San Marco (☎520.5422; both box offices open 9.30am–12.30pm and 4–6pm). *La Fenice* isn't as expensive as some other opera and ballet houses, but it isn't in the first division any more either. Tickets start at about L15,000, and are usually snapped up promptly. Music performances at the *Goldoni* are somewhat less frequent, but the repertoire here isn't as straitlaced, with a jazz series cropping up on the schedule every now and then.

Classical concerts are also performed at the *Palazzo Prigione Vecchie,* the *Scuola Grande di San Giovanni Evangelista* and the churches of *Santo Stefano*, *I Frari* and *La Pietà*. The state radio service records concerts at the *Palazzo Labia*, to which the public are admitted free of charge, as long as seats are reserved in advance (☎716.666).

Upbeat and downmarket from the theatre and classical concerts, some **bars** have live music: the main ones are *Paradiso Perduto* (usually jazz), *Ai Canottieri* (hot and sweaty dancing) and *Da Codroma*, addresses above. They don't charge for entrance, but a mark-up on the drinks pays for the bands.

Discos

In central Venice, disco-dancers have only one place to go – **El Souk**, in Calle Corfu, two minutes' walk from the Accademia. It's a "Pub American Bar" from 9am to 8pm (closed Sat afternoon & Sun), and a disco from 10pm to 4am (closed Sun). Only those deemed by the doorman to be fit for admission get to pay the entrance charge of L14,000, a fee that includes the price of your first drink. If purple carpets and smoked glass mirrors don't appeal, you'll have to hop over the causeway into Mestre, or cross over to the Lido, where there's a couple of soulless discos.

Exhibitions – and the Biennale

In addition to those permanent museums which hold one-off exhibitions from time to time, Venice has numerous venues for temporary shows, of which the *Fiat*-owned **Palazzo Grassi** maintains the highest production values. There's also the **Venice Biennale** set up in 1895 as a showpiece for international contemporary art, and held every even-numbered year from June to September. Its permanent site in the Giardini Pubblici has pavilions for about forty countries (the largest for Italy's representatives), plus space for a thematic international exhibition. Supplementing this central part of the Biennale is the *Operto* ("Open"), a mixed exhibition showing the work of younger, or less established artists – often more exciting than the main event. The *Operto* takes over spaces all over the city: the salt warehouses on the Záttere, for instance, or the Corderie in the Arsenale. Over and above this, various sites throughout the city host fringe exhibitions, installations and performances, particularly in the opening weeks.

Tickets for the whole Biennale cost L10,000, but it's possible to buy tickets for individual parts of the show. Exhibits from earlier years, plus a fabulous collection of magazines and catalogues from all over the world, are kept in the **archive** in the Palazzo Corner della Regina (close to Ca' Pésaro); entrance is free.

Festivals

Venice celebrates with enthusiasm a number of holidays either not observed elsewhere in Italy, or, like the Carnevale, celebrated to a lesser extent. Although they have gone through various degrees of decline and revival, the form they take now is still related very strongly to their traditional character.

Carnevale

The Venice **Carnevale** occupies the ten days leading up to Lent, finishing on Shrove Tuesday with a masked ball for the glitterati, and dancing in the Piazza for the plebs. It was revived spontaneously in the late Seventies, and after three years gained support from the city authorities, who now organise various pageants and performances. (Details from the San Marco tourist office.) Apart from these events, Carnevale is very much a case of see and be seen. During the day people don costumes and go to the Piazza to be photographed; parents dress up their kids; businessmen can be seen doing their shopping in the classic white mask, black cloak and tricorne hat. In the evening some congregate in the remoter squares, while those who have spent literally hundreds of pounds on their costumes install themselves in the windows of *Florian*'s and pose for a while.

Masks are on sale throughout the year in Venice, but new mask and costume shops suddenly appear during Carnevale, and Campo San Maurizio sprouts a marquee with mask-making demonstrations and a variety of designs for sale.

La Sensa

The feast of **La Sensa** happens in May on the Sunday after Ascension Day – the latter the day on which the doge performed the wedding of Venice to the sea. The ritual has recently been revived – a distinctly feeble procession which ends with the mayor and a gang of other dignitaries getting into a present-day approximation of the *Bucintoro* (the state barge) and sailing off to the Lido. Of more interest is the **Vogalonga** (long row), held on the same day. Open to any crew in any class of rowing boat, it covers a 32-kilometre course from the Bacino di San Marco out to Burano and back; the competitors arrive at the bottom of the Canal Grande anywhere between about 11am and 3pm.

Santa Maria della Salute

Named after the church of the Salute, this centuries-old feast day is a reminder of the devastating plague of 1630–31. The church was built in thanks for deliverance from the outbreak, and every November 21 since then the Venetians have processed over a pontoon bridge across the Canal Grande to give thanks for their good health, or to pray for sick friends and relatives. It offers the only chance to see the church as it was designed to be seen – with its main doors open, and with hundreds of people milling up the steps and round the building.

La Festa del Redentore

Another plague-related festival, this time to mark the end of the epidemic of 1576. Celebrated on the third Sunday in July, the day is centred on Palladio's church of the Redentore, which was built by way of thanksgiving for the city's escape. A bridge of boats is strung across the Giudecca canal to allow the faithful to walk over to the church, and on the Saturday night hundreds of people row out for a picnic on the water. The night ends with a grand fireworks display, after which it's traditional to make for the Lido to watch the sun rise.

The Regata Storica

Held on the first Sunday in September, the **Regata Storica** is the annual trail of strength and skill for the city's gondoliers and other expert rowers. It starts with a procession of richly decorated historic craft along the Canal Grande course, their crews all decked out in period dress. Bystanders are expected to join in the support for the contestants in the main event, and may even be issued with appropriate colours.

Film Festival

The **Venice Film Festival** takes place on the Lido every year in late August and early September. The tourist office will have the festival programme a few weeks in advance, as will the two cinemas where the films are shown – the main **Palazzo del Cinema** (Lungomare G. Marconi) and the **Astra** (Via Corfu). Tickets are available for the general public, but you have to go along and queue for them on the day of performance. Outside the festival season, the *Palazzo* and *Astra* are run as ordinary commercial cinemas.

Listings

Airlines *Alitalia*, Salizzada San Moisè, San Marco 1463 (☎520.0355); *British Airways*, Riva degli Schiavoni, Castello 4191 (☎528.5026); *TWA*, Salizzada San Moisè, San Marco 1475 (☎520.3219).

Airport enquiries Marco Polo airport, ☎66.1111.

Books A good general bookshop is *Goldoni*, Calle dei Fabbri, San Marco. For art books, *Fantoni Libri*, Salizzada San Luca, San Marco. For books on Venice, *Filippi Editore Venezia*, Calle della Bissa, San Marco, and Calle del Paradiso, Castello.

Bus enquiries For *ACTV* land buses ☎528.7886; for information on the city water buses ☎700.310.

Car hire The major companies have offices at Marco Polo airport and at Piazzale Roma in Venice.

Carparks Venice's carparks are at Piazzale Roma and Tronchetto, at the end of the causeway from the mainland. Additional summer facilities at Fusina, linked to Venice by a *vaporetto* service.

Consulates *UK*, Dorsoduro 1051, by the Accademia (☎522.5996). The nearest US consulate is in Milan, while travellers from Ireland, Australia, New Zealand and Canada should contact their Rome consulates.

Exchange Banks are concentrated around Campo San Bartolomeo and along Calle Larga XXII Marzo.

Hospital *Ospedale Civili Riunti di Venezia*, Campo Santi Giovanni e Paolo (☎520.5622).

Laundry *Lavaget*, Fondamenta Pescaria, off Rio Terrà San Leonardo, Cannaregio.

Left Luggage Train station left-luggage desk open 24hr; L1000 per item.

Lost property If you lose something on the train or at the station call ☎716.122; on the *vaporetti* ☎780.310; in the city itself ☎520.8844.

Pharmacies A list of late-night pharmacies is printed in *Un Ospite di Venezia*, and is available by ringing ☎192.

Police Emergency ☎113; the *Questura*, for passport problems, reporting thefts and so on, is on Fondamenta San Lorenzo, Castello (☎520.0754).

Post office Central post office is in the Fondaco dei Tedeschi, by the Rialto bridge (Mon–Sat 8.15am–7pm; telegram office open 24hr); main branch office in Calle dell'Ascensione (Mon–Fri 8.10am–1.25pm, Sat 8.10am–noon).

Public showers *Albergo Diurnale* at the train station and in Calle dell'Ascensione (9am–7.30pm).

Telephones 24-hr booths at train station. *SIP* offices at Rialto post office (8am–8pm) and at Piazzale Roma (8am–9.30pm).

Train enquiries ☎715.555

THE VENETO

Virtually every acre of the Veneto bears the imprint of Venetian rule. In **Belluno**, right under the crags of the Dolomites, the style of the buildings declares the town's former allegiance. A few kilometres away, the Lion of Saint Mark looks over the central square of the hill town of **Feltre**, as it does over the market square of **Verona**, on the Veneto's western edge. On the flatlands of the Po basin (the southern border of the region) and on farming estates all over the Veneto, the elegant **villas** of the Venetian nobility are still standing.

Yet the Veneto is as diverse culturally as it is geographically. The aspects of Verona that make the city so attractive were created long before the expansion of Venice's *terra firma* empire, and in **Padua** (a university seat since the thirteenth century) the civilisation of the Renaissance displays a character quite distinct from that which evolved in Venice. Even in **Vicenza**, which reached its present form mainly during its long period of subservience, the very appearance of the streets is proof of a fundamental independence.

Nowadays this is one of Italy's wealthiest regions. Verona, Padua, Vicenza and **Treviso**, 30km north of Venice, are all major industrial and commercial centres, while intensive dairies, fruit farms and vineyards (around Conegliano, for example) have made the Veneto a leading agricultural producer too.

The Veneto's densest concentration of industry is at **Mestre** and **Marghera**, the grim conurbation through which all road and rail lines from Venice pass before spreading out over the mainland. It's less a city than an economic life-support system for Venice, and the negative impression you get on your way through is entirely justified. Some people trim their holiday expenses by staying in Mestre's cheaper hotels (Venice's tourist offices will supply addresses), but venturing further inland is a more pleasurable cost-cutting exercise.

The Brenta

The southernmost of the three main rivers that empty into the Venetian lagoon, the **Brenta** caused no end of trouble to the earliest settlers on both the mainland and the islands, with its frequent flooding and its deposits of silt. By the sixteenth century, though, the canalisation of the river had brought it under control, and it became a favoured building site for the Venetian aristocracy. Some of these Venetian villas were built as a combination of summer residence and farmhouse – many, however, were intended solely for the former function. The period from mid-June to mid-November was the season of the *villeggiatura*, when the patrician families of Venice would load their best furniture onto barges and set off for the relative coolness of the Brenta.

Around one hundred villas are left standing on the river between Padua and Venice: some are derelict, a large number are still inhabited and a handful are open to the public. Of this last category, two are outstanding – the Villa Fóscari and the Villa Pisani – both of which are easily accessible by bus from Venice. Don't be tempted by the widely advertised trip along the Brenta on board a boat named the *Burchiello* (after the vessel that used to transport the gentry to their summer abodes) – it costs L98,000 and stops longer for lunch than it does at any of the villas.

The Villa Fóscari

The **Villa Fóscari** at **MALCONTENTA** (May–Oct Tues, Sat & first Sun of each month 9am–noon; L5000) was designed in 1559 by Palladio, and is the nearest of his villas to Venice. Most of Palladio's villas fall into two broad groups: those built on cohesive farming estates, with a central low block for living quarters and wings for storage and associated uses (the Villa Barbaro at Masèr and the Villa Emo near Castelfranco); and the large, single-block villas, built for landowners whose fields were dispersed or in some way unsuitable for the construction of a major building. The Villa Fóscari is the masterpiece of this second group, powerfully evoking the architecture of ancient Rome by its heavily rusticated exterior, its massive Ionic portico and its two-storey main hall – a space inspired by the baths of Rome.

The frescoes in the living rooms include what is said to be a portrait of a woman of the Fóscari family who was exiled here as punishment for an amorous escapade, and whose subsequent misery, according to legend, was the source of the name *Malcontenta*. The reality is more prosaic – the area was known by that name long before the Fóscari arrived, either because of some local discontent over the development of the land, or because of the political *malcontenti* who used to hide out in the nearby salt marshes.

The Villa Pisani

The **Villa Pisani** (or Nazionale) at **STRA** (Tues–Sun 9am–1.30pm; L3000), virtually on the outskirts of Padua, looks more like a product of the *ancien régime* than a house for the Venetian gentry. Commissioned by way of celebration when

Alvise Pisani was elected Doge of Venice in 1735, it was the biggest such residence to be built in Venetian territory during that century. It has appealed to megalomaniacs ever since: Napoleon bought it off the Pisani in 1807 and handed it over to Eugène Beauharnais, his stepson and Viceroy of Italy; and in 1934 it was the place chosen for the first meeting of Mussolini and Hitler.

Entry to the suite of rooms on the main floor of the villa is carefully controlled – you're shepherded round in groups of thirty – and most of what you see is unexciting. But then there's the ballroom, its ceiling covered with a fresco of *The Apotheosis of the Pisani Family*, the last major piece painted by Giambattista Tiepolo at the age of 66. It's a dazzling performance, full of blue space and yet still coherent; and if you're trying to puzzle out what's going on – the Pisani family, accompanied by Venice, are being courted by the Arts, Sciences and Spirits of Peace, while Fame plays a fanfare in praise of the Pisani and the Madonna looks on with appropriate pride.

Padua

Extensively reconstructed after the damage caused by bombing in the last war, and hemmed in by the sprawl which has accompanied its development as the most important economic centre of the Veneto, **PADUA** (PADOVA) is not immediately the most alluring city in northern Italy. It is, however, one of the most ancient, and plentiful evidence remains of its impressive lineage.

A Roman municipium from 45 BC, the city thrived until the barbarian onslaughts and the subsequent Lombard invasion at the start of the seventh century. Recovery was slow, but by the middle of the twelfth century, when it became a free commune, Padua was prosperous once again. The university was founded in 1221, and a decade later the city became a place of pilgrimage following the death here of Saint Anthony.

In 1337 the **Carraresi** (the Da Carrara family) established control. Under their domination, Padua's cultural eminence was secured – Giotto, Dante and Petrarch were among those attracted here – but Carraresi territorial ambitions led to conflict with Venice, and in 1405 the city's independence ended with its conquest by the neighbouring republic. Though politically nullified, Padua remained an artistic and intellectual centre: Donatello and Mantegna both worked here, and in the seventeenth century Galileo researched at the university, where the medical faculty was one of the most ambitious in Europe. With the fall of the Venetian Republic the city passed to Napoleon, who handed it over to the Austrians, after whose regime Padua was annexed to Italy 1866.

Information and finding a place to stay

The main **APT** is at the train station (Mon–Sat 8am–8pm, Sun 8am–noon), with another branch at the coach station, a few hundred metres away on Piazzale Boschetti. Both offices have long lists of one-star **hotels** with singles from L15,000 and doubles from L24,000 – Via Papafrava has a number of inexpensive places. A few years ago it was infinitely simpler to find an inexpensive room in Padua than in Venice; the average cost is still lower, but availability can be a problem as ever more people use Padua as a base from which to visit its overcrowded neighbour. If you're here in high season, be prepared for a slightly protracted search.

Budget alternatives are the two **"holiday houses"**, which offer rooms in the summer: *Antonianum*, at Via Donatello 24 (July 15–Sept 30; ☎049/651.444), which charges L12,000 per person; and *Missionary Verbiti*, Via Forcellini 172 (July 1–Sept 30; ☎049/754.411).

The **youth hostel**, at Via A. Aleardi 30 (☎049/875.2219), costs L9500 per night including breakfast. The nearest **campsite** is in Montegrotto Terme (Strada Romana Aponese 104; ☎049/793.400), served by frequent trains, which take around fifteen minutes; a very upmarket site, it boasts a swimming pool and thermal baths.

The City

From the train station, the Corso del Popolo and Corso Garibaldi lead south through a gap in the Renaissance city walls towards the centre of the city, passing after a short distance the **Cappella degli Scrovegni** and **Museo Civico** (summer Tues–Sun 9am–7pm; winter Tues–Sun 9am–5.30pm; joint ticket L5000). For many people the **Giotto frescoes** in the Scrovegni are *the* reason for coming to Padua, and the building is almost invariably full, though the crush is alleviated by a strict time control on large groups.

The chapel was commissioned in 1303 by Enrico Scrovegni in atonement for his father's usury, which was so vicious that he was denied a Christian burial. As soon as the walls were built, Giotto was commissioned to cover them with illustrations of the life of Mary, the life of Jesus and the story of the Passion; the finished cycle, arranged in three tightly-knit tiers and painted against a backdrop of saturated blue, is one of the high points in the development of European art. The Scrovegni series is a marvellous demonstration of Giotto's innovative attention to the inner nature of his subjects – the exchange of looks between the two shepherds in the *Arrival of Joachim* is particularly powerful, as are the *Embrace of Joachim and Anna at the Golden Gate* and the *Visit of Mary to Elizabeth*.

Beneath the main pictures are shown the vices and virtues in human (usually female) form, while on the wall above the door is the *Last Judgment*, with rivers of fire leading from God to Hell. Directly above the door is a portrait of Scrovegni presenting the chapel; his tomb is at the far end, behind the altar with its statues by **Giovanni Pisano**.

The **Museo Civico** is a recently opened home for part of the civic collection. Unfortunately the bulk of the paintings remain on display near the Basilica (see below), leaving a dull show of archaeological odds and ends, generally dire nineteenth-century paintings and sculpture, and an assortment of coins, medals and other metalwork. More rewarding is the helpful information desk, which gives out information on Padua's cultural events.

The Eremitani

The nearby church of the **Eremitani**, built at the turn of the fourteenth century, was almost completely wrecked by an allied bombing raid in 1944 and has been fastidiously rebuilt (generally open Mon–Sat 8.15am–noon & 3.30–6.30pm, Sun 9am–noon & 3.30–6pm). Photographs to the left of the apse show the extent of the damage, the worst aspect of which was the near-total destruction of **Mantegna**'s frescoes of the lives of Saint James and Saint Christopher – the war's severest blow to Italy's artistic heritage.

Produced between 1454 and 1457, when Mantegna was in his mid-twenties, the frescoes were unprecedented in the thoroughness with which they exploited fixed-point perspective – a concept central to Renaissance humanism, with its emphasis on the primacy of individual perception. The extent of his achievement can now be assessed only from the fuzzy photographs and the sad fragments preserved in the chapel to the right of the high altar. On the left wall is the *Martyrdom of St James*, put together from fragments found in the rubble; and on the right is the *Martyrdom of St Christopher* which had been removed from the wall before the war.

Piazza del Santo and the Basilica

Apart from the encampment of stalls selling decorated candles and outsize souvenir rosaries, the main sight of the Piazza del Santo is Donatello's **Monument to Gattamelata** ("The Honeyed Cat"), as the *condottiere* Erasmo da Narni was known. He died in 1443 and this monument was raised ten years later, the earliest large bronze sculpture of the Renaissance. It's a direct precursor to Verrocchio's monument to Colleoni in Venice, but could hardly be more different: Gattemelata was known for his honesty and dignity, and Donatello has given us an image of comparative sensitivity and restraint, quite unlike Verrocchio's image of power through force. The modelling of the horse makes a double allusion: to the equestrian statue of Marcus Aurelius in Rome, and to the horses of San Marco.

Within eighteen months of his death, Saint Anthony had been canonised and his tomb was attracting enough pilgrims to warrant the building of the Basilica di San Antonio, or **Il Santo** (daily: summer 6.30am–7.45pm; winter 6.30am–7pm). It was not until the start of the fourteenth century that the church reached a state enabled the saint's body to be placed in the Cappella del Santo (in the left transept). Plastered with such votive offerings as photographs of limbs healed by the saint's intervention, the shrine is irresistible to the voyeur. The chapel's more formal decoration includes a sequence of nine panels showing scenes from Saint Antony's life; carved between 1505 and 1577, they are the most important series of relief sculpture created in sixteenth-century Italy.

Adjoining the chapel is the Cappella della Madonna Moro (named after its fourteenth-century French altar statue), which in turn lets onto the Cappella del Beato Luca, whose fourteenth-century frescoes include a lovely image of Saint James lifting a prison tower to free a prisoner. Back in the aisle, just outside the Cappella del Santo, is Padua's finest work by Pietro Lombardo, the monument to Antonio Roselli (1467). More impressive still are the high altar's bronze sculptures and reliefs by Donatello (1444–45), the works which introduced Renaissance classicism to Padua. Built onto the farthest point of the ambulatory, the Cappella del Tesoro (8am–noon & 2.30–7pm) houses the tongue and chin of Saint Anthony, kept in a head-shaped reliquary.

The south side of the Piazza

To the left as you leave the Basilica are the **Oratorio di San Giorgio** and **Scuola di Santo** (daily April–Sept 8.30am–12.30pm & 2.30–6.30pm; Feb, March, Oct & Nov 9am–12.30pm & 2.30–4.30pm; Dec–Jan 9am–12.30pm; L1000). The Oratorio was founded in 1377 as a mortuary chapel, its frescoes by **Altichiero di Zevio** and **Jacopo Avanzi** being completed soon after. One wall is adorned with the wonderfully titled *St Lucy Remains Immoveable at an Attempt to Drag Her with the Help of Oxen to a House of Ill Repute*.

The scuola was founded soon after Anthony's canonisation, though this building only goes back as far as the early fifteenth century. The ground floor is still used for religious purposes, while upstairs is maintained pretty much as it would have looked in the sixteenth century, with its fine ceiling and paintings dating mainly from 1509–1515. Four of the pictures are said to be by Titian.

Next door to the Scuola, the **Pinacoteca Civica** (Tues–Sat 9am–1pm, Sun 9.30am–1pm; L2000, free Sun) is an assembly of fourteenth- to eighteenth-century art from the Veneto. Highlights are a crucifix which Giotto painted for the Scrovegni, and a fine *Portrait of a Young Senator* by Bellini.

One way to relax from all this art is to stroll round the corner to the **Orto Botanico**, the oldest botanic gardens in Europe (May–mid-Sept Mon–Fri 9am–1pm & 3–6pm, Sat & Sun 9am–1pm; March, April & mid-Sept–Oct Mon–Sat 9am–1pm, Sun 9.30am–1pm; Nov–Feb Mon–Sat 9am–1pm; L3000). Planted in 1545 by the university's medical faculty as a collection of medicinal herbs, the gardens are laid out much as they were originally, and the specimens on show haven't changed too much either. Goethe came here in 1786 to see a palm tree that had been planted in 1585; the selfsame tree still stands.

The Prato della Valle and Santa Giustina.

A little to the south sprawls the **Prato della Valle**, claimed to be the largest town square in Italy; it's a cheerless area, ringed by over-wide roads, and even the summer funfair does little to make it jollier.

One side is fronted by the sixteenth-century **Basilica di Santa Giustina** (Mon–Sat 7.30am–noon & 3.30–7.30pm, Sun 7am–1pm & 3.30–7.30pm). A pair of fifteenth-century griffons, one holding a knight and the other a lion, are the only notable adornments to the unclad brick facade; the freezing interior has little of interest except a huge *Martyrdom of St Justina* by Paolo Veronese (in the apse), some highly proficient carving on the choir stalls, and the sarcophagus which once contained the relics of Luke the Evangelist (apse of left transept).

More appealing are the vestiges of the church's earlier incarnations. In the right transept a stone arch opens onto the **Martyrs' Corridor**, a composite of fifth- to twelfth-century architectural fragments that leads to the **Sacellum di Santa Maria e San Prosdocimo**, burial place of Saint Prosdocimus. He was the first bishop of Padua back in the fourth century, when the church was founded, and is depicted here on a fifth-century panel. The fifteenth-century **old choir**, reached by a chain of corridors from the left-hand chapel of the right transept, has choir stalls inset with splendid marquetry panels.

To the University

Via Umberto leads towards the **university**, the main block of which is the **Palazzo del Bò** (The Ox – named after an inn that used to stand here). Established in September 1221, the University of Padua is older than any other in Italy except that of Bologna, and the coats of arms which encrust the courtyard and Great Hall attest to the social and intellectual rank of its alumni. The first permanent **anatomy theatre** was built here in 1594, a facility that doubtless greatly helped William Harvey, who went on to develop the theory of blood circulation after taking his degree here in 1602. Galileo taught physics here from 1592 to 1610, declaiming from a lectern that is still on show. And in 1678 Elena Lucrezia Corner Piscopia became the first woman to collect a university degree when she was awarded her doctorate in philosophy here – there's a statue of her in the courtyard. (Guided tours Sept–July Mon–Fri 9.30am, 11.30am, 3.30pm & 5.30pm, Sat 9.30am & 11.30am; Aug Mon–Sat 9.30am & 11.30am.)

The central squares

The area north and west of the university forms the hub of the city. A little way up from the university, on the left, is the **Caffè Pedrocchi**, which used to be the city's main intellectual salon; it's no longer that, but it does have a multiplicity of functions – chic café, concert hall and conference centre.

The **Piazza delle Frutta** and **Piazza delle Erbe**, the sites of Padua's daily markets, are lined by bars, restaurants and shops. Separating them is the extraordinary **Palazzo della Ragione** or **Salone** (Tues–Sun 9.30am–12.30pm & 3.30–7.30pm; L2000) – at the time of its construction in the 1210s this vast hall was the largest room to have been built on top of another storey. Its decoration would once have been as astounding as its size, but the original frescoes by Giotto and his assistants were destroyed by fire in 1420, though some by Giustio de'Menabuoi have survived; most of the extant frescoes are by Nicola Miretto (1425–1440). Mainly used as the city council's assembly hall, it was also a place where Padua's citizens could plead for justice – hence the appellation *della Ragione*, meaning "of reason". The gigantic wooden horse with disproportionately gigantic gonads is modelled on Donatello's *Gattamelata*, and was made for a joust in 1466.

The Duomo and Baptistery

Close by is Padua's **Duomo** (daily 7am–noon & 4–7.30pm), an unlovely church whose architect cribbed his design from drawings by Michelangelo. The adjacent Romanesque **Baptistry**, though, is one of the unproclaimed delights of Padua (April–Sept Mon–Sat 9.30am–12.30pm & 3–6pm, Sun 9.30am–noon; Oct–March 9.30am–noon & 2.30–5.30pm, Sun 9.30am–noon; L2000). Built by the Carraresi in the thirteenth century, it's lined with fourteenth-century frescoes by Giusto de'Menabuoi, a cycle which makes a fascinating comparison with Giotto's in the Cappella degli Scrovegni. The influence of Giotto is plain, but in striving for greater realism Giusto has lost Giotto's monumentality and made some of his figures awkward and unconvincing. Yet many of the scenes are delightful, and the vibrancy of their colours, coupled with the size and relative quiet of the building, make the visit memorable.

Eating, drinking and entertainment

Padua's student population ensures that the city's **bars** have far longer opening hours than are common in Venice – many don't close until 2am – and that new places spring up as often as established ones revamp their image. Currently trendy are *Alla Ventura* (Via SS. Martino e Solferino) and *Al Coccodrillo* (Riviera S. Benedetto 154). For something a bit more hip, try the devil's grotto ambience of *Lucifer Young*, in Via Altinate.

Catering for the midday stampede of ravenous students, Padua's bars generally produce weightier **snacks** than the routine *tremezzini* – slabs of pizza and sandwiches vast enough to satisfy a glutton are standard. A good variety of stand-up meals is offered at the *rosticceria* in Via Daniele Manin (8.30am–1.30pm & 4–8.30pm), but for a more relaxed session at only slightly greater expense, one of the best cheap **restaurants** is *Al Traguardo*, on Piazza Petrarca (closed Tues). Other places to check out include: *Alla Chiesetta*, Via Eremitani 16; *Al Paradiso*, Via Altinate 11; *Da Giovanni*, Via De Cristoforis 1; *Evan's*, Via B. Pellegrino 21; *All'Anfora*, Via N. Tommaseo 13; and *Vecia Padova*, Via Arco Valaresso 20.

Padua's **nightlife** fluctuates in synch with term-time; check the posters up around the city, and particularly around the university, for details of music, theatre and suchlike. Of the local newspapers, the most comprehensive for listings is *La Mattina*. Look out for the *Associazione Cinemauno*, a club which screens arthouse films in the *Esperia* cinema, at Via Chiesanuova 112. Padua's half-dozen regular **discos** are all fairly low-octane places: liveliest are *Ippopotamus*, at Via Savonarola 149, and the flashier *Extra Extra*, Via Ciamician.

South of Padua

A few kilometres to the southwest of Padua the **Colli Euganei** (Euganean Hills) rise abruptly out of the plains, their slopes patched with vineyards between the scattered villages, villas and churches. Between Padua and the hills lie the spa towns of **ÁBANO TERME** and **MONTEGROTTO TERME**, which for much of the year are crowded with people looking for cures or beauty treatment from the radioactive waters and mud baths. Largely composed of big and expensive modern hotels, these really are places to avoid unless you're hell-bent on trying to poach yourself in the hot springs.

A car is a great advantage for exploring the Colli Euganei proper, as buses are few and far between. The **villas** of the region are its major architectural attractions, but many of them remain in private hands and can only be viewed from a distance. An exception is the **Villa Barbarigo**, at **VALSANZIBIO**, which is famous for its extraordinary gardens; laid out in 1699, they feature a maze and fantastical Baroque gateways (mid-March–Oct Tues–Sat 10am–noon & 2–7pm, Sun 2–7pm).

The gem of the Colli Euganei is the medieval village of **ARQUÀ PETRARCA**, most easily reached by bus from Este or Monsélice (see below). The poet **Francesco Petrarca** (Petrarch) spent the last summers of his life here, and this is where he died. His house still stands, and his desk and chair are still intact, as are various parts of the original fabric of the interior – though the frescoes, illustrating his works, were retouched in the seventeenth century (April–Sept Tues–Sat 9.30am–12.30pm & 3.30–7.30pm, Sun 3–7pm; Oct–March Tues–Sat 9.30am–12.30pm & 1.30–4.30pm, Sun 10am–4pm). Petrarch's sarcophagus is in the centre of the village, with one epitaph penned by him and another by his son-in-law, who placed it here.

Monsélice

Situated on a fork in the rail network, the attractive town of **MONSÉLICE** is far more accessible than the villages nearer to Padua. In earlier times it perched on the pimple of volcanic rock round the foot of which it now winds, and you pass through the remnants of its defensive walls on your way from the train station to the central Piazza Mazzini. A little way beyond the square stands Monsélice's main sight – the **Castello di Ezzelino**, or **Ca' Marcello** (guided tours April–Sept Tues, Thurs & Sat 9am, 10.30am, 3.30pm & 5pm, Sun 9am & 10.30am; Oct & Nov Tues, Thurs & Sat 9am, 10.30am, 2.30pm & 4pm, Sun 9am & 10.30am; L3000). Dating back to the eleventh century, the house was expanded in the thirteenth century by Ezzelino da Romano, who added the square tower across the courtyard. The interior was altered by the Carraresi in the fourteenth century, and linking the two main sections is a fifteenth-century bit added by the Marcello family. The castle's immaculate appearance is down to Count Vittorio Cini, who inherited the derelict building after it had been in the tender care of the army during World War I, and sank a fortune into restoring it and furnishing each section in the appropriate style.

The **Duomo Vecchio**, higher up the hill, retains fourteenth-century fresco fragments and has a Romano-Gothic polyptych on the high altar. Just beyond it, a gateway guarded by two Venetian lions gives onto the Via Sette Chiese, a private road leading up to the **Villa Duodo** (grounds open daily Nov–Feb 9am–12.30pm & 1.30–7pm; March–May, Sept & Oct 8am–noon & 1.30–7pm; June–Aug 7am–12.30pm & 3.30–8pm). The seven churches of the road's name are a small-scale version of the seven pilgrimage churches of Rome, arranged as a line of six chapels leading up to the church of **San Giorgio** at the top. Sinners could earn forgiveness by praying their way up to San Giorgio, where rows of martyred saints are arranged in wood and glass cabinets. It's not possible to go up the steps to the **Rocca** – Ezzelino's citadel on the summit – as the area is now a nature reserve for rare birds.

For **information**, the **Pro Loco** is in Piazza Mazzini (daily 8.30am–12.30pm & 5–8pm). Best option for **eating** is the Piazza's *Caffè Grand Italia* (closed Sun).

Este

If you're dependent on public transport, about the best base from which to roam around the Colli Euganei is the ceramics-producing town of **ESTE**, on the southern edge of the range and just an eight-minute train ride from Monsélice. Sporadic buses run up into the hills from here, and there's a central **Pro Loco** in the Piazza Maggiore (Mon–Sat 9am–noon & 4–6pm).

Right out of the Piazza, you come face to face with the ruined **Castello dei Carraresi**, parts of which went to build the nearby sixteenth-century palace that now houses the **Museo Nazionale Atestino** (April–Sept Tues–Sat 9am–1pm & 3–7pm; Oct–March Tues–Sat 9am–1pm & 3–6pm; L2000). The Veneto's outstanding collection of pre-Roman artefacts is installed on the first floor, while much of the ground floor is given over to Roman remains. The room devoted to medieval pieces includes a *Madonna and Child* by Cima that was once stolen from the church of Santa Maria della Consolazione and is now here for safe keeping.

The Baroque **Duomo**, the plan of which anticipates the Pietà in Venice, contains a huge altarpiece of *St Thecla* by GB Tiepolo – not one of his best, maybe because it's set in a scene of pestilence and death, rather than one of his light-filled heavens.

The best one-star **hotel** in town is the *Leon d'Oro*, at Viale Fiume 20 (☎0429/2955), which has doubles from L28,000. For **food**, try *Al Gambrero*, Via d'Azeglio 6, or *Da Piero Ceschi*, Piazza Trento 16.

Montagnana

The pride of **MONTAGNANA**, fifteen minutes down the train line from Este, is its **medieval city walls**, raised by the ubiquitous Ezzelino da Romano after he had virtually flattened the town in 1242. With a circumference of nearly two kilometres and twenty-four polygonal towers spaced at regular intervals, these are among the finest medieval fortifications in the country.

Gates pierce the walls at the cardinal points of the compass, the entrances to the east and west being further reinforced by fortresses. The eastern gate (Porta Padova) is protected by the **Castello di San Zeno**, built by Ezzelino in 1242. Nearby, the **Museo Civico e Archeologico** displays objects uncovered around the town (Tues–Fri 10am–noon & 4–6pm, Sat 9am–noon & 3–6pm, Sun 4–7pm; L1000, under 18 free). On the western side, the **Rocca degli Alberi** was built by the Carraresi in 1362 to keep the roads from Mantua and Verona covered.

The centre of Montagnana is the Piazza Vittorio Emanuele, dominated by the late Gothic **Duomo**; Veronese's altarpiece, a *Transfiguration*, is less engaging than the huge anonymous painting of the *Battle of Lepanto* on the left as you enter – it's said to represent accurately the ships and their positions at one point in the battle.

The helpful **AAST** is in the Piazza (daily 10am–noon & 4.30–7pm). For **accommodation**, *Locanda Baraldo* in Via San Zeno (☎0429/81.673) is the best deal, with doubles at L25,000. The splendid **youth hostel** occupies the Rocca degli Alberi (April–mid-Oct; reception 3–11pm; ☎0429/81.076); it costs L7000 per night, and if you don't have an IYHF card, you can join on the spot. Many of the town's hotels have **restaurants**; for the cheapest meal, try *Pizzeria al Palio*, in Piazza Trieste.

Come to Montagnana on the first Sunday in September and you'll see its **Palio** – a poor relative of the costumed horse races in Siena, but enthusiastically performed, and the day finishes with a firework display.

Rovigo and beyond

ROVIGO is the capital of the fertile and often-flooded zone between between the Adige and the Po, an area known as the *Polésine* (or "Little Mesopotamia"). Trains on their way to Ferrara and Bologna from Venice call here hourly, crossing another line running east to west – though frankly there's little reason for coming to the town except to change trains. Should you be stuck for a couple of hours waiting for a connection, though, there are a couple of places you could visit. Maps are available from the **EPT** office at Via J. H. Dunant 10, to the right off Corso del Popolo as you walk from the station.

The **Pinacoteca dei Concordi** in Piazza Vittore Emanuele (Mon–Fri 10am–noon & 4–6.30pm, Sat 10am–noon; free) features eminent artists of the Veneto – Palma il Vecchio, GB Piazzetta and Rosalba Carriera – in less than breathtaking form. About fifteen minutes' walk in the same direction, in Piazza San Bartolomeo, is the **Museo Civico delle Civiltà in Polésine**, the main archaeological institute for the area. This is more an assemblage of pieces unearthed by the researchers than a regular museum, and you're shown round by one of the staff, whose informed commentary makes up for the uninspiring display techniques.

Fratta Polésine

A trip to **FRATTA POLÉSINE**, 18km southwest of Rovigo, might appeal to the more ardent lovers of **Palladio**'s buildings. The **Villa Badoer** (check opening times with the EPT in Rovigo), designed in the 1560s, is one of his most eloquent flights of architectural rhetoric, with its distinctive curving colonnades linking the porticoed house to the storage spaces at the side. None of the original furnishings is left, but restorers have uncovered the villa's sixteenth-century grotesque frescoes.

Adria and the Po Delta

Heading **eastward** from Rovigo, trains leave every couple of hours for the Po Delta and Chioggia. **ADRIA**, a sleepy town of about 20,000 inhabitants, is all that is left of the port from which the Adriatic Sea got its name. It now sits on a tributary of the Po some 25km inland, owing to heavy silting in the lagoon. The only sight is the **Museo Archeologico** in Piazzale degli Etruschi, which has a collection of Greek and Etruscan pieces dating from the time when Adria was a major port (daily 9am–1pm & 3–6pm).

It's difficult to explore the **Po Delta** properly unless you have a car, though bikes may be hired from *Vittorio Cacciatori* in PORTO TOLLE – to get there you have to get a bus from LOREO, a couple of train stops after Adria. *Cacciatori* also hires out canoes, but if you prefer a less strenuous investigation of the waterways and islets, companies in Porto Tolle and TAGLIO DI PO run half-day cruises for L10,000 per person – an excellent way to observe the waterfowl and other birds of the delta's nature reserve. Resorts on the delta have done a lot to clean up their act in recent years, yet upstream the pollution of the Po continues unabated, spawning hideous blooms of algae in the waters of the upper Adriatic. See *Emilia Romagna*, Chapter Seven, for more on this, and the delta.

Vicenza

Europe's largest producer of textiles and the focus of Italy's "Silicon Valley", **VICENZA** is a very sleek city, where it can seem that every second car is a BMW. Modern prosperity hasn't ruined the look of Vicenza, though. The centre of the city, still partly enclosed by medieval walls, is an amalgam of Gothic and classical buildings that today looks much as it did when the last major phase of construction came to an end at the close of the eighteenth century. This historic core is compact enough to be explored in a day, but the city and its environs really require a short stay to do them justice.

In 1404 Vicenza was absorbed by Venice, and the city's numerous Gothic palaces reflect its status as a Venetian satellite. But in the latter half of the sixteenth century the city was transformed by the work of an architect who owed nothing to Venice and whose rigorous but flexible style was to influence every succeeding generation – Andrea di Pietro della Gondola, alias **Palladio**.

Born in Padua in 1508, Palladio came to Vicenza at the age of sixteen to work as a stonecutter. At thirty he became the protegé of a local nobleman, Count Giangiorgio Trissino, who directed his architectural training, gave him his classicised name, and brought him into contact with the dominant class of Vicenza. Between 1540 and his death in 1580 Palladio created around a dozen palaces and public buildings in Vicenza – projects whose variety will surprise you if you tend to associate Palladianism with blandness. Even if you've been inclined to agree with Herbert Read's opinion that "in the back of every dying civilisation there sticks a bloody Doric column", you might well leave Vicenza converted.

The City

The main street of Vicenza, the **Corso Andrea Palladio**, cuts right through the old centre from the Piazza Castello down to the Piazza Matteotti, and is lined with palaces, all of them now occupied by shops, offices and banks. Palladio's last

CENTRAL VICENZA

To Parco Querini
CONTRA PUSTERIA
CONTRA V. VENETO
C. CANOVE
CONTRA S. CORONA
PIAZZA VENTI SETTEMBRE
Teatro Olimpico
APT
River Bacchiglione
River Bacchiglione
PIAZZA MATTEOTTI
CONTRA PEDAMURO S. BIAGIO
CONTRA PORTI
Palazzo Iseppo Porto
C.S. STEFANO
S. Corona
Museo Civico
Palazzo Colleoni Porto
S. Stefano
VIALE A. GIURIOLO
Palazzo Thiene
C.S. BARBARA
CORSO ANTIONIO FOGAZZARO
CONTRA RIALE
CORSO ANDREA PALLADIO
Palazzo Barbarano
C. MANIN
CONTRA ORATORIO SERVI
CONTRA DELL BARCHE
S. Lorenzo
PIAZZA S. LORENZO
C. MORETTE
CONTRA MOTTORI S. LORENZO
Palazzo Valmarana
C. MONTE
Loggia del Capitaniato
PIAZZA DEI SIGNORI
VIA BATTISTI
CAVOUR
Basilica
PIAZZETTA PALLADIO
PIAZZA DELL'ERBE
C. DI PRECE
PONTE S. MICHELE
Post Office
C. PESCHERIA
Oratorio di San Nicola
Casa Pigafetta
C. PROTI
PONTE S. PAOLO
Duomo
PIAZZA DEL DUOMO
VESCOVADO
River Retrone
Giardino Salvi
PIAZZA DEL CASTELLO
PIAZZALE DE GASPERI
To Train & Coach Stations
CONTRA
C. ORATORIO PROTI
Pal. Porto-Breganze
To Monte Berico
To SS. Felice & Fortunato

palace, the fragmentary **Palazzo Porto-Breganze**, stands on the far side of Piazza Castello; no. 163 on the Corso, the **Casa Cogollo**, is known as the *Casa del Palladio*, though he never lived there and few people think he designed it.

The Museo Civico and Teatro Olimpico

The Corso ends with one of the architect's most imperious buildings, the **Palazzo Chiericati** (begun in 1550), now home of the **Museo Civico** (Tues–Sat 9.30am–noon & 2.30–5pm, Sun 9.30am–noon; L3000, combined ticket for Museo & Teatro Olimpico L5000, reduced to L3000 on Sun). The core of the picture collection is made up by Vicentine artists, none of whose work will knock you flat on your back; but more celebrated names – Memling, Tintoretto, Veronese, Tiepolo – make the visit memorable.

Across the Piazza Matteotti is the one building in Vicenza you shouldn't fail to go into – the **Teatro Olimpico**, the oldest indoor theatre in Europe (March 16–Oct 15 Mon–Sat 9.30am–12.20pm & 3–5.30pm, Sun 9.30am–12.20pm; Oct 16–March 15 Mon–Sat 9.30am–12.20pm & 2–4.30pm, Sun 9.30am–12.20pm; L3000, see "Museo Civico" for combined ticket). Approached in 1579 by the members of the Olympic Academy (a society dedicated to the study of the humanities) to produce a design for a permanent theatre, Palladio devised a covered amphitheatre derived from his reading of Vitruvius and his studies of Roman structures in

Italy and France. He died soon after work commenced, and the scheme was then overseen by Scamozzi, who added to Palladio's design the backstage perspective of an classical city, creating the illusion of long urban vistas by tilting the "streets" at an alarming angle. The theatre opened on March 3, 1585, with an extravagant production of *Oedipus Rex*, and is still used for plays and concerts.

The Basilica and around
At the hub of the city, the **Piazza dei Signori**, stands the most awesome of Palladio's creations – the **Basilica**. Designed in the late 1540s (but not finished until the second decade of the next century), this was Palladio's first public project and secured his reputation. The monumental regularity of the Basilica disguises the fact that the Palladian building is effectively a stupendous piece of buttressing – the Doric and Ionic colonnades enclose the fifteenth-century hall of the city council, an unstable structure which had defied a number of attempts to prop it up before Palladio's solution was put into effect. The vast Gothic hall is often used for exhibitions (Tues–Sat 9.30am–noon & 2.30–5pm, Sun 9.30am–noon; free).

As in the sixteenth century, a daily fruit, vegetable and flower market is pitched at the back of the Basilica, in the **Piazza dell'Erbe**; if you're shopping for picnic food, you'll save money by going down the slope and over the river, where the shops are a good bit cheaper. On Tuesdays a general market spreads along the roads between the Basilica and the Duomo.

A late Palladio building, the unfinished **Loggia del Capitaniato** faces the Basilica across the Piazza dei Signori. Built as accommodation for the Venetian military commander of the city, it's decorated with reliefs in celebration of the Venetian victory over the Turks at Lepanto in 1571.

The churches
The **Duomo** was bombed flat in 1944 and carefully reconstructed after the war; it's a rather gloomy place, chiefly distinguished as one of the few Italian cathedrals to be overwhelmed by its secular surroundings. Far more interesting is **Santa Corona** (summer daily 9.30am–12.30pm & 3.30–6.30pm; winter daily 9.30am–12.30pm & 3–6pm), on the other side of the Corso Palladio (at the Piazza Matteotti end), a Dominican church dating from the mid-thirteenth century. Here you'll find two of the three great church paintings in Vicenza – *The Baptism of Christ*, a late work by Giovanni Bellini, and *The Adoration of the Magi*, painted in 1573 by Paolo Veronese. The third of the trio is Palma Vecchio's typically stolid and voluptuous *Madonna and Child with SS George and Lucy*, which is in the nearby church of **Santo Stefano** (daily 9–11am & 4–6.30pm).

Contrà Porti, Corso Fogazzaro and the parks
Santo Stefano faces a corner of the huge **Palazzo Thiene**, another of Palladio's palaces. It was planned to occupy the entire block down to Corso Palladio, but in the end work progressed no further than the addition of this wing to the existing fifteenth-century house. The facade of the old building is in Contrà Porti, a street which demonstrates the way in which the builders of Vicenza grafted new houses onto old without doing violence to the line of the street; the palaces here span two centuries, yet the overall impression is one of cohesion. Outstanding are the fourteenth-century **Palazzo Colleoni Porto** (no. 19) and Palladio's neighbouring **Palazzo Iseppo Porto**, designed a few years after the Thiene palace. The paral-

lel Corso Fogazzaro completes the itinerary of major Palladian buildings, with the **Palazzo Valmarana** (no. 16), perhaps the most eccentric of Palladio's projects – notice the gigantic stucco figures at the sides of the facade, where you'd expect columns to be.

Contrà Porti takes you towards the Pusterla bridge and the **Parco Querini**, the biggest expanse of green in the city, enlivened by a decorative hillock populated by ducks, rabbits and peacocks. Vicenza's other refuge for the brickwearied, the **Giardino Salvi** (at the end of the road running straight up from the train station), is a more modest and artificial affair of winding gravel paths and fountains.

Out of the city – Monte Bérico and around

In 1426 Vicenza was struck by bubonic plague, during the course of which outbreak the Virgin appeared twice at the summit of **Monte Bérico** – the hill on the southern edge of the city – to announce the city's deliverance. The chapel raised on the site of her appearance became a place of pilgrimage, and at the end of the seventeenth century was replaced by the present **Basilica di Monte Bérico**. Buses climb the hill from the coach station every thirty minutes or so; on foot it takes around twenty-five minutes from the centre of town.

Pilgrims regularly arrive here by the coachload, and the glossy interior of the church is immaculately maintained to receive them; a well-stocked shop in the cloister sells devotional trinkets to the faithful. The sceptical should venture into the church for Montagna's *Pietà* (in the chapel to the right of the apse) and *The Supper of St Gregory the Great* by Veronese (in the refectory). The latter, the prototype of *The Feast in the House of Levi* in Venice's Accademia, was used for bayonet practice by Austrian troops in 1848 – the small reproduction outside the refectory shows what a thorough job they did on it.

The Villa Valmarana

Ten minutes' walk away from Monte Bérico is the **Villa Valmarana "ai Nani"**, an undistinguished house made extraordinary by the decoration painted by Giambattista and Giandomenico Tiepolo (mid-March–April daily 2.30–5.30pm; May–Sept daily 3–6pm; Oct–mid-Nov 2–5pm; plus Thurs, Sat & Sun 10am–noon during all three seasons; open some public holidays – ring ☎0444/221.803 to check; L4000). *Nani*, by the way, means "Dwarves", the significance of which becomes clear when you see the garden wall. To get there, go back down the hill, go along Via M. D'Azeglio for 100m, then turn right into the cobbled Via S. Bastiano, which ends at the villa.

There are two parts to the house: the *Palazzina*, containing six rooms frescoed with brilliant virtuosity by Giambattista (scenes based on Virgil, Tasso and Ariosto – you're handed a brief guide to the paintings at the entrance); and the *Foresteria*, one room of which is frescoed by Giambattista and six by Giandomenico, whose predilections are a little less refined than his father's.

La Rotonda

From the Villa Valmarana the narrow Strada Valmarana descends the slope to one of Europe's most imitated buildings – Palladio's Villa Capra, known to most people as **La Rotonda** (mid-March–mid-Oct Wed 10am–noon & 3–6pm; L5000). This is unique among Palladio's villas in that it was designed not as the main building of a farm but as a pavilion in which entertainments could be held and the landscape enjoyed. Only a tour of the lavishly decorated interior will fully reveal the subtleties of the Rotonda; the grounds – not much more than a belt of grass round the villa – are worth the entrance money only if you need to study the house from point-blank range (grounds open mid-March–mid-Oct Tues & Thurs 10am–noon & 3–6pm; L2000).

Practicalities

The **APT** is alongside the entrance to the Teatro Olimpico in Piazza Matteotti (Mon–Sat 9am–12.30pm & 3–6.30pm, Sun 9am–12.30pm); they provide a passable map of the town and around, and a very good leaflet on the Teatro.

The best deal among the one-star **hotels** is the basic but central *Villa Marzia*, at Via Mure Pallamaio 96 (reception 8am–noon & 5–7pm; closed Sun; ☎0444/227.055), with doubles around L25,000. The *Casa San Raffaele*, Viale X Giugno 10 (☎0444/235.619), has the advantage of a beautiful position on the slope of Monte Bérico, but is little cheaper than the two-stars in the core of Vicenza – L36,000 for a double. The *Milano*, Stradella dei Servi 5 (☎0444/238.643), *Due Mori*, Contrà Do Rode 26 (☎0444/221.886), and *Palladio*, Via Oratorio dei Servi 25 (☎0444/221.072), are all decent two-stars within a few yards of the Piazza dei Signori.

First recommendation for **eating** goes to the *Antica Casa della Malvasia*, Contrà delle Morette 5 (closed Mon), a bustling tavern just off the Piazza; the food is cheap and unpretentious, and the menu changes daily – the bar's excellent too. Equally popular, but rather less basic, is the *Vecchia Guardia*, Contrà Pescheria Vecchia 11 (closed Thurs). The *Due Mori* (attached to the hotel; closed Wed), *Da Anna*, Contrà Porta Nova 41 (closed Tues), and *Giardini*, Via Giuriolo 10 (closed Wed), are big and busy restaurant-pizzerias – fine if you don't want to linger over your food.

Verona and around

With its wealth of Roman sites and streets of pink-hued medieval buildings, the easy-going city of **VERONA** has more in the way of sights than any other place in the Veneto except Venice itself. Unlike Venice, though, it's not a city overwhelmed by the tourist industry, important though that is to the local economy. Verona is the largest city of the mainland Veneto, its economic success largely due to its position at the crossing of the major routes from Germany and Austria to central Italy and from the west to Venice and Trieste.

Verona's initial development as a **Roman** settlement was similarly due to its straddling the main east–west and north–south lines of communication. A period of decline in the wake of the disintegration of the Roman empire was followed by revival under the Ostrogoths, who in turn were succeeded by the Franks – Charlemagne's son, Pepin, ruled his kingdom from here. By the twelfth century Verona had become a city state, and in the following century approached the zenith of its independent existence with the rise of the **Scaligeri** family. Ruthless in the exercise of power, the Scaligeri were at the same time energetic patrons of the arts, and many of Verona's finest buildings date from the century of their rule.

With the fall of their dynasty a time of upheaval ensued, Gian Galeazzo Visconti of Milan emerging in control of the city. Absorption into the Venetian empire came in 1405, and Venice continued to govern Verona until the arrival of Napoleon. Verona's history then shadowed that of Venice: a prolonged interlude of Austrian rule, brought to an end by the unification of Italy in 1866.

Arriving, information and finding a place to stay

Traffic restrictions make walking the most efficient way of exploring the city, and the centre is concentrated enough to make this no great hardship. The only buses you're likely to need are the frequent #1 or #8 services (#51 or #58 in the evening) from the **train station** to the Piazza Brà, the hub of Verona; buy your ticket before you get on board, from just outside the station.

The main **APT** offices are at Via Dietro Anfiteatro 6 and Piazza delle Erbe 42 (both Mon–Sat 9am–12.30pm & 3.30–6.30pm). There's also a small office at the train station.

Accommodation

The *Locanda Catullo*, Via V. Catullo 1, just off Via Mazzini (☎045/800.2786), with doubles from L16,500, and *Albergo Rosa*, Vicolo Raggiri 9, off Piazza delle Erbe (☎045/800.5693), charging L30,000, are clean and centrally placed **hotels**. With many of its rooms overlooking the Piazza delle Erbe, the *Hotel Aurora*, Via Pellicciai 2 (☎045/594.717), is recommended if money's not too much of a problem – doubles start at L40,000.

Verona's **youth hostel**, the *Ostello della Gioventù*, is at Salita Fontana del Ferro 15 (☎045/590.360), a beautiful old building behind the Teatro Romano. It has 100 beds, plus some overspill accommodation, at L10,000 per night including breakfast. The #20 bus goes nearest to the hostel, but by so circuitous a route that it's easier to walk from the centre. Along similar lines are the *Casa del Giovane "Don Bosco"*, Via Provolo 16 (☎045/591.300), and the *Casa della Giovane*, Via Pigna 7 (☎045/596.880). The latter is run by nuns and is for women only; both are in the old centre, have a midnight curfew and cost in the region of L13,000 per night, excluding breakfast.

For **campers**, convenient and pleasant summer campsites are *Campeggio Castel San Pietro*, up behind the Teatro Romano, and the small site right by the hostel.

The City

Coming from the train station, you pass Verona's south gate, the **Porta Nuova**, and come onto the long Corso Porta Nuova, which ends at the battlemented arches that precede the **Piazza Brà**. Here is the mightiest of Verona's Roman monuments, the **Arena**. Dating from the first century AD, the Arena has survived in remarkable condition, despite the twelfth-century earthquake which destroyed all but four of the arches of the outer wall. The interior (Tues–Sun 8am–6.45pm; L3000, free on holidays) was scarcely damaged by the tremor, and nowadays audiences come here to watch gargantuan opera productions where once crowds of around 20,000 packed the benches for gladiatorial contests and the like. Originally measuring 152m by 123m overall, and thus the third largest of all Roman amphitheatres, the Arena is still an awesome sight – and as an added treat offers a tremendous urban panorama from the topmost of the 44 pink marble tiers.

To the Casa di Giulietta and San Fermo

Going north from the Arena, **Via Mazzini** is a narrow traffic-free street lined with generally expensive clothes, shoe and jewellery shops. A left turn at the end leads to the Piazza delle Erbe (see below), while a right takes you into **Via Cappello**, a street named after the family that Shakespeare turned into the Capulets – and there on the left, at no. 23, is the **Casa di Giulietta** (Juliet's House). In fact, although the "Capulets" and the "Montagues" (Montecchi) did exist, Romeo and Juliet were entirely fictional creations. The house itself, constructed at the start of the fourteenth century and in a fine state of preservation, is open to the public (Tues–Sun 8am–6.45pm; L3000).

Via Cappello leads into Via Leone with its Roman gate, the **Porta Leone**, and segment of excavated Roman street, exposed three metres below today's street level. At the end of Via Leone and across the road stands the red brick **Basilica di San Fermo**, a church whose inconsistent exterior betrays the fact that it consists of two churches combined. Flooding forced the Benedictines to superimpose a second church on the one founded in the eighth century. The Gothic upper church has no outstanding works of art but is graceful enough; the Romanesque lower church, entered from the left of the choir, has impressive low vaulting, sometimes obscured by exhibitions.

Piazza delle Erbe and Piazza dei Signori

Originally a major Roman crossroads and the site of the forum, **Piazza delle Erbe** is still the heart of the city. As the name suggests, the market used to sell mainly vegetables; nowadays the range has widened to include clothes, souvenirs, antiques and fast food. The most striking of the variegated buildings around the square are the **Domus Mercatorium** (on the left as you look from the Via Cappello end), which was founded in 1301 as a merchants' warehouse and exchange, the fourteenth-century **Torre del Gardello** and, to the right of the tower, the **Casa Mazzanti**, whose sixteenth-century murals are best seen after dark, under enhancing spotlights.

The neighbouring **Piazza dei Signori** used to be the chief public square of Verona. Much of the right side is taken up by the **Palazzo del Capitano**, which is separated from the Palazzo del Comune by a stretch of excavated Roman street. Facing you as you come into the square is the medieval **Palazzo degli Scaligeri**, residence of the Scaligeri; a monument to more democratic times extends from it at a right angle – the fifteenth-century **Loggia del Consiglio**, former assembly hall of the city council and Verona's outstanding early Renaissance building. The rank of Roman notables along the roof includes Verona's most illustrious native poet, Catullus. For a dizzying view of the city, take a sharp right as soon as you come into the square, and go up the twelfth-century **Torre de Lamberti** (Tues–Sun 8am–6.45pm; L2500 by lift, L1500 on foot).

The Scaligeri Tombs

Passing under the arch linking the Palazzo degli Scaligeri to the Palazzo del Capitano, you come to the little Romanesque church of Santa Maria Antica, in front of which are ranged the **Arche Scaligeri**, some of the most elaborate Gothic funerary monuments in Italy. Over the side entrance to the church, an equestrian statue of **Cangrande I** ("Big Dog"; d.1329) grins on the summit of his tomb's pyramidal roof; the statue is a copy, the original being displayed in the

Castelvecchio (see below). The canopied tombs of the rest of the clan are enclosed within a wrought iron palisade decorated with ladder motifs, the emblem of the Scaligeri – the family name was della Scala, "scala" meaning ladder. (The enclosure is open Tues–Sun 9am–noon & 2.30–6pm). **Mastino I** ("Mastiff"), founder of the dynasty, is buried in the simple tomb against the wall of the church; **Mastino II** is to the left of the entrance, opposite the most florid of the tombs, that of **Cansignorio** ("Top Dog"; d.1375).

Sant'Anastasia and the Duomo

Going on past the Arche Scaligeri, and turning left along Via San Pietro, you come to **Sant'Anastasia**, Verona's largest church. Started in 1290 and completed in 1481, it's mainly Gothic in style, with undertones of the Romanesque. The fourteenth-century carvings of New Testament scenes around the doors are the most arresting feature of its bare exterior; the interior's highlight is Pisanello's delicately coloured fresco of *St George and the Princess* (in the sacristy), a work in which the normally martial saint appears as something of a dandy.

Verona's red and white striped **Duomo** lies just round the river's bend, past the Roman **Ponte Pietra**. Consecrated in 1187, it's Romanesque in its lower parts, developing into Gothic as it goes up; the two doorways are twelfth-century – look for the story of Jonah and the whale on the south porch, and the figures of statues of Roland and Oliver, two of Charlemagne's paladins, on the west. The interior has fascinating architectural details around each chapel and on the columns – particularly fine is the Cappella Mazzanti (last on the right). In the first chapel on the left, an *Assumption* by Titian occupies an architectural frame by Sansovino, who also designed the choir.

To the Castelvecchio

After the Arena, Verona's most impressive Roman remnant is the **Porta dei Borsari** (on the junction of Via Diaz and Corso Porta Borsari), a structure which was as great an influence on the city's Renaissance architects as the amphitheatre. Now reduced to a monumental screen straddling the road, it used to be Verona's largest Roman gate; the inscription dates it at 265, but it's almost certainly older than that.

Some way down Corso Cavour, which starts at the Porta dei Borsari, stands the **Archo dei Gavi**, a first-century Roman triumphal arch. This is your best vantage point from which to admire the **Ponte Scaligero**; built by Cangrande II between 1355 and 1375, the bridge was blown up by the Germans in 1945 – the salvaged material was used for the reconstruction.

The fortress from which the bridge springs, the **Castelvecchio**, was commissioned by Cangrande II at around the same time, and became the stronghold for Verona's subsequent rulers. Opened as the city museum in 1925, it was damaged by bombing in World War II, but opened again after scrupulous restoration in 1964 (daily 8am–11pm; L5000).

The Castelvecchio's collection of paintings, jewellery, weapons and other artefacts flows through a labyrinth of chambers, courtyards and passages that is fascinating to explore in itself. The equestrian figure **Cangrande I**, removed from his tomb, is strikingly displayed on an outdoor pedestal; his expression is disconcerting from close range, the simpleton's grin being difficult to reconcile with the image of the ruthless warlord. Outstanding among the paintings are two works by Jacopo Bellini, two *Madonna*s by Giovanni Bellini, another *Madonna* by

Pisanello, Veronese's *Descent from the Cross*, a Tintoretto *Nativity*, a Lotto portrait and works by GB and GD Tiepolo. The real joy of the museum, however, is in wandering round the medieval pieces, beautiful sculpture and frescoes by the often nameless artists of the late Middle Ages.

San Zeno Maggiore

A little over a kilometre northwest of the Castelvecchio is the **Basilica di San Zeno Maggiore**, one of the most significant Romanesque churches in northern Italy. A church was founded here, above the tomb of the city's patron saint, as early as the fifth century, but the present building and its campanile were put up in the first half of the twelfth century, with additions continuing up to the end of the fourteenth. Its large rose window, representing the Wheel of Fortune, dates from the early twelfth century, as does the magnificent portal, whose lintels bear relief sculptures representing the months – look also for Saint Zeno trampling the devil. Extraordinary bronze panels on the doors depict scenes from the Bible and the Miracles of San Zeno, their style influenced by Byzantine and Ottoman art; most of those on the left are from around 1100, most of the right-hand panels dating from a century later. Areas of the lofty and simple interior are covered with frescoes, some superimposed upon others, some defaced by ancient graffiti. Diverting though these are, the one compulsive image in the church is the high altar's luminous *Madonna and Saints* by Mantegna.

North of the Adige

On the other side of Ponte Garibaldi, and right along the embankments or through the public gardens, is **San Giorgio in Braida**, in terms of its works of art the richest of Verona's churches. A *Baptism* by Tintoretto hangs over the door, while the main altar, designed by **Sanmicheli**, incorporates a marvellous piece by **Paolo Veronese** – the *Martyrdom of St George*.

It's a short walk along the embankments, past the twelfth-century church of **Santo Stefano** and the Ponte Pietra, to the first-century BC **Teatro Romano** (Tues–Sun 9am–noon & 2.30–6pm); much restored, the theatre is now used for concerts and plays. High above it, and reached by a rickety-looking lift, the **Museo Archeologico** occupies the buildings of an old convent; its well-arranged collection features a number of Greek, Roman and Etruscan finds.

Eating, drinking and entertainment

Your money goes a lot further in Verona than it does in Venice: numerous **trattorias** offer full meals for under L15,000, while on almost every street corner there's a bar where a glass of house wine costs as little as L300. **Nightlife** here is more varied too, and genuinely goes on into the night, in contrast to Venice's general late-evening shutdown.

Pizzerias and restaurants

Verona's best **pizzas** are served at *Da Salvatore*, Corso Porta Borsari 39 (closed Mon); other central places worth trying are the *Pizzeria Corte Farina*, Corte Farina 4 (closed Mon), and the *Pizzeria Arena*, Vicolo Tre Marchetti 1 (closed Mon), both of which stay open until 1am. A little out of the centre *Il Posto*, in Via Fincato (closed Tues and all July & Aug), also does excellent pizzas and often has live music.

In the centre of the city, the best value among the **restaurants** is at the *Osteria Cucina al Cristo*, Piazza Pescheria (closed Sun), where a genuine, no-frills meal will cost around L12,000 with wine. Although it is possible to find cheapish places within the historic centre, they're far more plentiful over the river. Especially good is the *Trattoria Ropeton* in Piazza Cisterna, below the youth hostel (closed Tues). On the other side of the Teatro Romano, the *Osteria Fontanina*, Via Madonna Terraglio, is excellent but usually crowded. In the Veronetta district, over the Adige from San Fermo, *Circolo Perbacco*, Via Carducci 48 (closed Wed), specialises in fish and traditional dishes, and *Capitan Trinchetto*, in Lungadige Porta Vittoria (closed Mon), prides itself on its *risotto* and *crostini* starter.

Bars

Two old bars with a selection of wines from all over Italy are the *Bottega dei Vini* in Vicolo Scudo di Francia, just off the north end of Via Mazzini (10.30am–3pm & 6pm–midnight; closed Tues), and the *Osteria delle Vecete* in Via Pellicciai, also near Piazza delle Erbe (10am–2.30pm & 5–9.30pm; closed Sun). The bars in Piazza Brà and Piazza delle Erbe are a little more expensive, but the city-life spectacle is worth the extra few lire. For a marvellous view of Ponte Pietra and the Teatro Romano, sip a glass in the garden of the *Al Ponte* in Via Ponte Pietra (8am–3pm & 5pm–2am; closed Wed). A bar little changed by twentieth-century fashion is the *Osteria de Duomo*, Via Duomo 7a (7am–8pm, Fri also 9pm until late), which is enlivened on Wednesday afternoons and Friday nights by an enthusiastic troupe of folk musicians.

Night-hawks should head for the *Corto Maltese* in Lungadige Porta Vittoria (11am–2am; closed Sun) and the *Campofiore* in Via Campofiore, near the university (8am–3pm & 5pm–2am; closed Sun). The former gets livelier as the night wears on and sometimes has live music downstairs, while the latter is a favourite with Verona's gay population and many heterosexuals – drawn by a relaxed, unoppressive atmosphere which even allows women on their own to drink without being hassled.

Music, theatre, films and discos

Music and **theatre** are the dominant art forms in the cultural life of Verona. In July and August an opera festival takes place in the **Arena**, often featuring a no-expense-spared production of *Aida*; **big rock events** crop up on the Arena's calendar too – Bob Dylan, Sting, Tina Turner and Joe Cocker have all played it in recent years. (The booking office is in arch six of the Arena; tickets can only be reserved by post or in person.) A season of Shakespeare in Italian is the principal summer fare at the **Teatro Romano**; plays by other dramatists are performed here as well, with **jazz**, **blues** and **rock** festivals as frequent additional attractions. Some of the Teatro events are free; for the rest, cheapskates who don't mind inferior acoustics can park themselves on the steps going up the hill alongside the theatre. The Teatro's box office (☎045/594.363) also sells tickets for the Arena and vice versa.

From October to May **English language films** are shown every Wednesday at the *Cinema Stimate* in Piazza Cittadella. The **disco** scene is much more lively than in Venice, with venues coming and going; look in the local paper, *L'Arena*, to find out where they are and what days they're open. For one-off events, check the *Spettacoli* section of *L'Arena* (there's a copy in every bar); alternatively, get a copy of *Verona For You* from the tourist office – though the times and prices are not always dependable.

Treviso

The local tourist board are pitching it a bit high when they suggest that the waterways of **TREVISO** may remind you of Venice, but the old centre of this brisk provincial capital is certainly more alluring than you might imagine from a quick glance on your way to or from the airport. Treviso was an important town long before its assimilation by Venice in 1389, and plenty of evidence of its early stature survives in the form of Gothic churches, public buildings and, most dramatically of all, the paintings of **Tomaso da Modena** (1325–79), the major artist in north Italy in the years immediately after Giotto's death. The general townscape within Treviso's sixteenth-century walls is often appealing too – long porticoes and frescoed house facades give many of the streets an appearance quite distinct from those of other towns in the region.

The City

These features are well preserved in the main street of the centre, **Calmaggiore**, where modern commerce (epitomised by the omnipresent *Benetton*, a Trevisan firm) has reached the sort of compromise with the past that the Italians seem to arrange better than anyone else. Modern building techniques have played a larger part than you might think in shaping that compromise – Treviso was pounded during both world wars and on Good Friday 1944 was half destroyed in a single bombing raid.

The early thirteenth-century **Palazzo dei Trecento**, at the side of the **Piazza dei Signori**, was one casualty of 1944 – a line round the exterior shows where the restoration began. The adjoining **Palazzo del Podestà** is a nineteenth-century structure, concocted in an appropriate style.

Of more interest are the two churches at the back of the block: **San Vito** and **Santa Lucia**: the tiny, dark chapel of Santa Lucia has extensive frescoes by Tomaso da Modena and his followers; San Vito has even older paintings in the alcove through which you enter from Santa Lucia, though they're not in a good state.

The cathedral of Treviso, **San Pietro**, stands at the end of Calmaggiore (7am–noon & 3–7pm). Founded in the twelfth century, San Pietro was much altered in succeeding centuries, and then rebuilt to rectify the damage of 1944. The interior is chiefly notable for the crypt – a thicket of twelfth-century columns with scraps of medieval mosaics – and the Cappella Malchiostro, with frescoes by Pordenone and an *Annunciation* by Titian.

Just over the Sile river from the railway station is the severe Dominican church of **San Nicolò**, which has frescoes dating from the thirteenth to the sixteenth century. Some of the columns are decorated with paintings by Tomaso da Modena and his school, of which the best are the *St Jerome* and *St Agnes* (by Tomaso) on the first column on your right as you enter. Equally striking, but considerably more graceful, is the composite *Tomb of Agostino d'Onigo* on the north wall of the chancel, created in 1500 by Antonio Rizzo (who did the sculpture) and Lorenzo Lotto (who painted the attendant pages).

The figures of Agnes and Jerome are an excellent introduction to Tomaso da Modena, but for a comprehensive demonstration of his talents you have to visit the neighbouring **Seminario**, where the chapter house is decorated with a series of forty *Portraits of Members of the Dominican Order*, executed in 1352. (Mon–Fri 9am–noon; apply for admittance at the caretaker's office opposite the west end of church.)

The Santa Caterina district

Treviso has a second great fresco cycle by Tomaso da Modena – *The Story of the Life of Saint Ursula*, now housed in the deconsecrated church of **Santa Caterina**, on the other side of the centre from San Nicolò. Other frescoes by Tomaso and his school are preserved in its Cappella degli Innocenti. To get into the church you have to make an appointment by ringing the Museo Civico (☎0422/51.337; Tues–Sat 9–11.30am & 2–4.30pm; L1000).

The area around the church is a pleasant one, with its antiques sellers and furniture restorers, and the hubbub of the stalls around the fish market. There are a couple of other churches worth a look, too. To the north of Santa Caterina is the rebuilt thirteenth-century church of **San Francesco**, an airy building with a ship's-keel roof and patches of fresco, including a *Madonna and Saints* by Tomaso da Modena (chapel to north of chancel). To the south, at the end of Via Carlo Alberto – one of the most attractive streets in the town – stands the **Basilica di Santa Maria Maggiore**, which houses the most venerated image in Treviso, a fresco of the Madonna originally painted by Tomaso but subsequently retouched.

The Museo Civico and around

From the centre the recommended route to the **Museo Civico** on Borgo Cavour (Tues–Sat 9am–noon & 2–5pm, Sun 9am–noon; L1000) is along Via Riccati, which has a number of fine old houses. The ground floor of the museum is taken up by the archaeological collection, predominantly late Bronze Age and Roman relics; the picture collection, on the upper floor, is mediocre too, but has a few very special paintings among the dross – a *Crucifixion* by Jacopo Bassano, *Portrait of Sperone Speroni* by Titian and *Portrait of a Dominican* by Lotto.

Practicalities

The **EPT** is in the Palazzo Scotti, Via Toniolo 41; their *Carnet del Turista* lists all hotels, restaurants and museums in the province of Treviso, with prices and opening hours.

There are two one-star hotels in the old town: *Vittoria*, Via San Nicolo 3/b (☎0422/52.285), and *Alla Colomba*, Via Ortazzo 25 (☎0422/542.284); the second is the cheaper, at L20,000 for a double, but it has only four rooms and is closed on Fridays.

Treviso has a number of **restaurants** with good reputations and prices to match. For those on more modest budgets, *All'Oca Bianca*, at Vicolo della Torre 7 (closed Wed), is excellent value. The fare at *Alla Colomba* (see above) is plain, hearty and very inexpensive.

The most popular **bars and cafés** in Treviso are those clustered underneath the Palazzo dei Trecento; also lively, and only a few yards from the Piazza dei Signori, is the bar of *San Vito*, Piazza San Vito 40, where a knowledge of the fortunes of AC Milan will do wonders for your credibility.

Conegliano

North of Treviso, around the amiable town of **CONEGLIANO**, the landscape ceases to be boring. The surrounding hills are patched with vineyards and the production of wine (*Prosecco* in particular) is central to the economy of the district. Italy's first wine-growers' college was set up in Conegliano in 1876, and today there are a couple of well-established wine routes for the tourist to explore: the *Strada del Vino Rosso*, which runs for 68km southeast to ODERZO, and the more rewarding *Strada del Vino Bianco*, a 42-kilometre journey west to VALDOBBIADENE. For details of the two routes, ask at the extremely helpful **AAST**, right in front of the train station at Viale Carducci 32. Access to Conegliano is straightforward, as the regular Venice to Udine trains stop here.

The Town

The old centre of Conegliano, adhering to the slope of the Colle di Giano, is right in front of you as you come out of the station. The most decorative feature of Via XX Settembre – the original high street – is the unusual facade of the **Duomo**: a fourteenth-century portico, frescoed in the sixteenth century, which joins seamlessly the buildings on each side. The interior of the church has been much rebuilt, but retains fragments of fifteenth-century frescoes; the major adornment of the church, though, is the magnificent altarpiece of *The Madonna and Child with Saints and Angels*, painted in 1493 by Giambattista Cima, the most famous native of Conegliano.

Cima's birthplace, no. 24 Via G.B. Cima (at rear of Duomo), has now been converted into the **Casa Museo di G.B. Cima** (Sat & Sun 4–6pm; free), which consists mainly of reproductions of his paintings and archaeological finds made during the restoration of the house.

The **Museo Civico** (summer Tues–Sun 9am–noon & 3.30–7pm; winter Tues–Sun 9am–noon & 2–5.30pm; L1500) is housed in the main tower of the reconstructed Castello, on top of the hill. There are no masterpieces among the paintings, most of which are workshop productions, and the displays of medals, maps, war memorabilia, armour and so forth are no more fascinating than you'd expect. But two aspects of the museum lift it out of the rut: the exhibition on the upper floors devoted to *The Grape in Art*, a maniacally diligent investigation of the grape motif in every art form you could think of; and the view from the roof, after which you'll never look at a Cima painting in the same way again.

Via Settembre XX has all you'll need in the way of cafés, bars and food shops. If you're planning to **stay**, the *Canon d'Oro* at no. 129 (☎0438/22.173) is a good hotel with doubles from L46,000 and an excellent restaurant; it's also officially recognised as an outlet for the best *Prosecco*. Rooms in the *Stadio*, Via Istria 51 (☎0438/22.320), are around L20,000 cheaper – so if money's tight, stay here and put the difference towards a treat at the *Canon d'Oro*.

Vittorio Veneto

The name **VITTORIO VENETO** first appeared on the map in 1866 when, to mark the unification of Italy and honour the first king of the new country (Vittorio Emanuele II), the neighbouring towns of Cèneda and Serravalle (not previously the best of friends) were knotted together and rechristened. A new town hall was built midway along the avenue connecting the two towns, and the railway station constructed opposite, thus ensuring that the visitor steps straight from the train into a sort of no-man's-land.

Cèneda

CÈNEDA, the commercial centre of Vittorio Veneto, is primarily worth a visit for the **Museo della Battaglia**, next to the dull cathedral (May–Sept Tues–Sun 10am–noon & 4–6.30pm; Oct–April Tues–Sun 10am–noon & 2–5pm; L2000 for a combined ticket for the Museo della Battaglia and Serravalle's Museo and church of San Lorenzo) – turn right out of the station and keep going until you see the sign for the centre. The Battle of Vittorio, in October 1918, was the final engagement of World War I for the Italian army (which is why most towns in Italy have a Via Vittorio Veneto), and the museum is dedicated to the climactic battle.

The only other building that merits a look in Cèneda is the church of **Santa Maria del Meschio**, where you'll find a splendid *Annunciation* by Andrea Previtali, a pupil of Giovanni Bellini. If you turn left off the Cèneda–Serravalle road instead going right for the cathedral square, you'll come across it quickly.

Serravalle

SERRAVALLE, wedged in the neck of the gorge between the Col Visentin and the Cansiglio, is an entirely different proposition. Once through its southern gate you are into a town that has scarcely seen a demolition since the sixteenth century. Most of the buildings along Via Martiri della Libertà, Via Roma and Via Mazzini, and around the stage-like Piazza Marcantonio Flaminio date from the fifteenth and sixteenth centuries – the handsomest being the shield-encrusted Loggia Serravallese. This is now the home of the **Museo del Cenedese** (May–Sept daily 10am–noon & 4.30–6.30pm; Oct–April daily 10am–noon & 3–5pm), a jumble of sculptural and archaeological bits and pieces, detached frescoes and minor paintings.

Your time is more profitably spent in **San Lorenzo dei Battuti** (Wed–Mon 3.30–4.30pm; visit arranged through the Museo del Cenedese), immediately inside the south gate, which is decorated with frescoes painted around 1450. Uncovered in 1953 and restored to rectify the damage done when Napoleon's lads used the chapel as a kitchen, this is one of the best-preserved fresco cycles in the Veneto.

Practicalities

The **AAST** is on Piazza del Popolo, in front of the railway station. The cheapest **accommodation** is at Serravalle's miniscule *Alla Giraffa*, Piazza Fontana 10 (✆0438/550.269), which has doubles from L22,000. For **food** in Serravalle, there's the *Trattoria alla Cerve* on Piazza Flaminio, or the bar-pizzeria *Al 128* in Via Roma.

Three **trains** a day call at Vittorio Veneto from Venice; for the rest of the day you should change at Conegliano. Read the timetable carefully when checking connections between Conegliano and Vittorio Veneto – some of the connections are not by rail but by *Autocorsa*, a coach service for which rail tickets alone are valid. The *Autocorsa*, and **buses** for the towns of the surrounding Dolomite foothills, leave from the station behind the Piazza del Popolo.

Belluno

The most northerly of the major towns of the Veneto, **BELLUNO** was once a strategically important ally of Venice, and today is the capital of a province which extends mainly over the eastern Dolomites. Just one train a day connects Venice and Belluno directly, but it's just as quick anyway to go from Venice to Conegliano and change there.

Although the urban centres to the south are not far away, Belluno's focus of attention lies clearly to the north – the network of the *Dolimiti-Bus* company radiates out from here, trains run regularly up the Piave valley to Calalzo, and the tourist handouts are geared mostly to hikers and skiers. (For entries on Cortina d'Ampezzo and the extreme north of the Veneto, see *Trentino-Alto Adige*.) Its position is Belluno's main appeal, but the old centre calls for an hour or two's exploration if you're passing through. Should you decide to stay over, the cheapest **hotel** in Belluno is *Da Mares*, at Via F. Pellegrini 4 (☎0437/22.860), at around L30,000. For **tourist information**, call at *ASVI Viaggi*, Piazza dei Martiri 27e (Mon–Fri 9am–12.30pm & 3.30–7pm, Sat 9am–12.30pm).

The Town

The hub of the modern town, the spot where you'll find its most popular bars and cafés, is the wide **Piazza dei Martiri**, off the south side of which a road leads to the Piazza del Duomo, the kernel of the old town. The sixteenth-century **Duomo**, an amalgam of the Gothic and classical, and built in the pale yellow stone that is a feature of the buildings in Belluno, was designed by Tullio Lombardo; it has had to be reconstructed twice after earthquake damage, in 1873 and 1936. There are a couple of good paintings inside: one by Andrea Schiavone (first altar on right), and one by Jacopo Bassano (third altar on right). The stately **campanile**, designed in 1743 by Filippo Juvarra, offers one of the great views of the Veneto.

Occupying one complete side of the Piazza del Duomo is the residence of the Venetian adminstrators of the town, the **Palazzo dei Rettori**, a frilly late-fifteenth-century building dolled up with Baroque trimmings. A relic of more independent times stands on the right – the twelfth-century **Torre Civica**, all that's left of the medieval castle. Continuing round the Piazza, in Via Duomo, along the side of the town hall, you'll find the **Museo Civico** (Tues–Sat 10am–noon & 3–6pm, Sun 10am–noon; L2000); the collection is strong on the work of Belluno's three best-known artists – the painters Sebastiano and Marco Ricci and the sculptor-woodcarver **Andrea Brustolon** – all of whom were born here between 1659 and 1673.

Via Duomo ends at the **Piazza del Mercato**, a tiny square hemmed in by porticoed Renaissance buildings. The principal street of the old town, **Via Mezzaterra**, goes down to the medieval **Porta Ruga** (veer left along the cobbled road about 50m from the end), from where the view up into the mountains will provide some compensation if you haven't managed to find the campanile open.

Feltre

The historic centre of **FELTRE**, spread along a narrow ridge overlooking the modern town, owes its beguiling appearance to the calamity of 1509, when, in the course of the War of the League of Cambrai, the troops of the Imperial army decided to punish the place for its allegiance to Venice by wiping much of it from the face of the planet. The Venetians took care of the reconstruction, and within a few decades the streets looked pretty much as they do nowadays. You're not going to find architecture students on every street corner, but you'd have to travel a long way to get a better idea of how an ordinary town looked in sixteenth-century Italy.

Only one **train** a day goes directly from Venice to Feltre (it's the one that goes on to Belluno); a more regular service runs from Padua (taking 90min). Connections to Belluno (30min) are quite frequent.

The Town

From the station the shortest route to the old town is to cross straight over into Viale del Piave, over Via Garibaldi (where there's a decent range of bars, restaurants and hotels) and along Via Castaldi, which brings you to the **Duomo** and **Baptistry**, at the foot of the ridge. The main objects of interest in the Duomo are a sixth-century Byzantine cross and a tomb by Tullio Lombardo. At the top of the steps that go past the side of the Baptistry, on the other side of the road, is the town's south gate, under which begins a long covered flight of steps that takes you up into the heart of the old town.

You come out by the sixteenth-century Municipio, the portico of which was designed by Palladio. The keep of the medieval Castello rises behind the platform of the **Piazza Maggiore.**

To the left, the main street of Feltre, **Via Mezzaterra**, slopes down to the fifteenth-century Porta Imperiale. Nearly all the houses here are sixteenth-century, and several have external frescoes by the town's most important painter, Lorenzo Luzzo – better known as *Il Morto da Feltre* (The Dead Man), a nickname prompted by the pallor of his skin. Via L. Luzzo, the equally decorous continuation of Via Mezzaterra on the other side of the Piazza, leads to the **Museo Civico** (Tues–Fri 10am–1pm, Sat 10am–1pm & 4–6pm, Sun 11am–1pm & 4–6pm; L1000), which has a lustrous *Madonna* by Il Morto, paintings by Cima and Gentile Bellini, and a display of Roman and Etruscan finds. Some people think Il Morto's finest work is the *Transfiguration* in the **Ognissanti** church – its hardly ever open, but if you want to try your luck, go out of the Porta Oria (by the Museo), down the dip and along Borgo Ruga for a minute.

Feltre has a more unusual museum – the **Museo Rizzarda** (June–Sept Tues–Sun 10am–1pm & 4–7pm; L1000), at Via del Paradiso 8, parallel to Via Mezzaterra. This holds both the town's collection of modern art and an exhibition of wrought-iron work, mostly by Carlo Rizzarda (1883–1931), the former owner of the house. It might not sound appetising, but the finesse of Rizzarda's pieces is remarkable.

Castelfranco Veneto

CASTELFRANCO VENETO once stood on the western edge of Treviso's territory, and battlemented bricks walls that the Trevisans threw round the town in 1199, to protect it against the Paduans, still encircle most of the old centre (or *Castello*). Of all the walled towns of the Veneto, only two – Cittadella (see below) and Montagnana – bear comparison with Castelfranco, and the place would merit an expedition if it had no other attraction. But Castelfranco was also the birthplace of **Giorgione**, and possesses a painting which on its own is enough to vindicate Vasari's judgement that Giorgione's place in Venetian art is equivalent to Leonardo da Vinci's in that of Florence.

The painting in question – *The Madonna and Child with SS Francis and Liberale*, usually known simply as the *Castelfranco Madonna* – hangs in the **Duomo** (daily 9am–noon & 3–6pm), in a chapel to the right of the chancel. Giorgione is the most elusive of all the great figures of the Renaissance: including the *Castelfranco Madonna*, only six surviving paintings can indisputably be attributed to him, and so little is known about his life that legends have proliferated to fill the gaps – for instance, the story that his premature death (in 1510, aged not more than 34) was caused by his catching the plague from a mistress. The paintings themselves have compounded the enigma, and none is more mysterious than this one, in which formal abstraction is combined with an extraordinary fidelity to physical texture, while the demeanour of the figures suggests a melancholic preoccupation. It was commissioned to commemorate Matteo Costanza, and was originally placed so that the gazes of the three figures were directed at his tombstone, which is now set into the wall to the left.

In a first-floor room of the adjacent **Casa Giorgione** there's a chiaroscuro frieze that's hopefully attributed to the artist (Tues–Fri 9am–12.30pm & 3–6pm, Sat & Sun 9am–12.30pm & 2.30–6pm; free).

Practicalities

Trains connect Castelfranco to Padua, Bassano, Treviso, Vicenza and Trento, making it a good base from which to explore the central Veneto. Information on the town and the surrounding area is available from the **Pro Loco**, at Via Garibaldi 2. The cheapest **rooms** here are at *Alla Speranza*, a few yards beyond the walls at Borgo Vicenza 13 (☎0423/494.480), where doubles start from L25,000. Of the numerous excellent **restaurants**, the most reasonable is *Ai Due Mori* in Vicolo Montebelluna, just inside the walls from the clock tower (closed Wed). *Alla Torre*, a large restaurant-pizzeria at the foot of the clock tower, is as good a place as any for pizza, although its restaurant menu is not cheap.

Around Castelfranco: Cittadella and the Villa Emo

When Treviso turned Castelfranco into a garrison, the Paduans promptly retaliated by reinforcing the defences of **CITTADELLA**, 15km to the west, on the train line to Vicenza. The fortified walls of Cittadella were built in the first quarter of the thirteenth century, and are even more impressive than those of its neighbour. You enter the town through one of four rugged brick gateways; if you're coming from the train station it'll be the Porta Padova, the most daunting of the four, flanked by the **Torre di Malta**. The tower was built as a prison and torture chamber by the monstrous Ezzelino da Romano, known to those he terrorised in this region in the mid-thirteenth century as "The Son of Satan". His atrocities earned for himself a place in the seventh circle of Dante's *Inferno*, where he's condemned to boil eternally in a river of blood. There's not much else to Cittadella, but it's definitely worth hopping off the train for a quick circuit of the walls.

The Villa Emo at Fanzolo

Just 8km northeast of Castelfranco is **FANZOLO**, where you'll find the **Villa Emo** (May–Sept Sat, Sun & holidays 3–6pm; Oct–April same days 2–5pm;closed Easter, Christmas and New Year; L5000), which Palladio designed in the 1560s for Leonardo Emo, one of the first Venetian patricians to switch his financial interests to farming. The main living rooms, as at the Villa Barbaro (see "Ásolo"), are richly frescoed, and though nobody would pretend that GB Zelotti's work is a match for Veronese's in the Barbaro house, few people would complain at having to stare at his creations every morning over breakfast. Two snags, though – the bus service out to the villa is woeful, and the entry charge is inexcusably high.

Bassano del Grappa

Situated on the Brenta river where it widens on its emergence from the hills, **BASSANO** has expanded rapidly this century, though its historic centre remains largely unspoiled by twentieth-century mistakes. It's better known for its manufactures and produce, and for the events of the two world wars (see below), than for any outstanding architecture or monuments. For centuries a major producer of ceramics and wrought iron, Bassano is also renowned for its **grappa** distilleries and delicacies such as *porcini* (dried mushrooms), white asparagus and honey.

The Town
Almost all of Bassano's sights lie between the Brenta and the train station; go much further in either direction and you'll quickly come to recently developed suburbs. Walking away from the station, you cross the orbital Viale delle Fosse to get to **Piazza Garibaldi**, one of the two main squares. Here, the cloister of the fourteenth-century church of San Francesco now houses the **Museo Civico** (Tues–Sat 10am–12.30pm & 2.30–6.30pm, Sun 10am–12.30pm & 3–6.30pm; L1000). Downstairs the rooms are devoted to ceramics, printing (for a long time one of Bassano's chief crafts), and archaeological finds. Upstairs is a collection including paintings by the da Ponte family (better known as the Bassano family), and a number of plaster works by Canova, 2000 of whose drawings are owned by the museum. Most extraordinary – apart from the room devoted to Tito Gobbi, who was born here – are the huge frescoes moved here while the roof of the palace to which they belong was being restored.

Overlooking the other side of the piazza is the **Torre Civica**, once a lookout tower for the twelfth-century inner walls, now a clock tower with spurious nineteenth-century battlements and windows. Beyond the fifteenth-century Loggia (once home of the Venetian military commander), Piazzetta Montevecchio leads to a little jumble of streets and stairways running down to the river and the **Ponte degli Alpini**. The river was first bridged at this point in the late twelfth century, and replacements or repairs have been needed at regular intervals ever since, mostly because of flooding; the present structure was designed by Palladio in 1568, and built in wood in order to make the bridge as flexible as possible.

Nardini, a grappa distillery founded in 1779 (Tues–Sun 8am–8pm), stands at this end of the bridge; it sells the best quality stuff, and has a bar where you can sample before you select your bottle.

Various streets and squares in Bassano commemorate the dead of the two world wars. The major **war memorial**, however, is out of town on **Monte Grappa**. A vast, circular, tiered edifice with a "Via Eroica" leading to a war museum, it holds 12,000 Italian and Austro-Hungarian dead; less a symbol of mourning and repentance than a declaration of future collaboration, it was built by the fascists in 1935. Buses go up there from Bassano during the summer months.

Practicalities

The **APT** is at Viale delle Fosse 9 (Mon–Sat 9am–12.30pm & 3–6.45pm) – from the train station go straight ahead and turn right into the wide Viale. A free magazine called *Bassano Mese* gives up-to-date information about the city's facilities and special events.

Buses to **Masèr**, **Possagno**, **Maróstica** and **Ásolo** (see below) leave regularly from Piazzale Trento, at other end of Viale delle Fosse from the APT; the *Bar Trevizani*, on the Piazzale, deals with tickets and information (Mon–Sat 6.30am–8.30pm, Sun & holidays 8am–noon and 3–7.15pm).

For budget **accommodation**, it comes down to a choice between two places: *Bassanello*, Via P. Fontana 2 (☎0424/35.347), or *Castello*, Piazza Terraglio 20 (☎0424/23.462) – both have doubles at L28,000.

As far as **food** goes, the *Antica Osteria*, Via Matteotti 5 (closed Mon), has good bars snacks, while *Combattini*, Via Gamba 22 (closed Sat), is recommended for a full meal.

Maróstica

Seven kilometres to the west of Bassano, the walled town of **MARÓSTICA** was yet another stronghold of Ezzelino da Romano, whose fortress glowers down on the old centre from the crest of the hill of Pausolino. The Ezzelini controlled Maróstica for quite a while (Ezzelino III was preceded by Ezzelino the Stutterer and Ezzelino the Monk), but it was another despotic dynasty, the Scaligeri of Verona, who constructed the **town walls** and the **Castello Inferiore** (lower castle).

Beyond the castle is Piazza Castello, the central square of the town, onto which is painted the board for the **Partita a Scacchi**, the town's principal claim to fame. The game's origin was an everyday chivalric story of rival suitors, the only unusual aspect being that the matter was decided with chess pieces rather than swords. The game was played with live pieces here in the square, and is re-enacted with great pomp on the second weekend of September of even-numbered years. Fourteenth-century costumes worn for the game are displayed in the Castello Inferiore (Sun 2–6pm; L500).

Ásolo

Known as "la Città dai cento orizzonti" (the city with a hundred horizons), the medieval walled town of **ÁSOLO** presides over a tightly grouped range of 27 gentle peaks in the foothills of the Dolomites. In 1234 Ezzelino da Romano wrested the town from the Bishop of Treviso; on his death in 1259 the townspeople ensured that the dynasty died with him by massacring the rest of his family, who were at that time in nearby San Zenone.

The end of the fifteenth century was marked by the arrival of Caterina Cornaro (see below) – her celebrated court was attended by the likes of Cardinal Bembo, one of the most eminent literary figures of his day, who coined the verb *Asolare* to describe the experience of spending one's time in pleasurable aimlessness. Later writers and artists found the atmosphere equally convivial: Gabriele d'Annunzio wrote about the town, and Robert Browning's last published work – *Asolando* – was written here.

The Town

The Bassano bus drops you at the foot of the hill, from where a connecting mini-bus shuttles up into the town. Memorabilia of Ásolo's celebrated residents are gathered in the **Museo Civico** in Piazza Maggiore (Tues–Sun 8am–noon & 4–8pm; L1500). Especially diverting are the portraits, photos and personal effects of **Elenora Duse**. An actress in the Sarah Bernhardt mould, Duse was almost as well known for her tempestuous love-life as for her roles in Shakespeare, Hugo and Ibsen, and she came to Ásolo to seek refuge from public gossip. Although she died in Pittsburgh while on tour in 1924, her wish was to be buried in Ásolo, and so her body was transported back here, to the church of Sant'Anna. The main interest of the art collection is provided by a pair of dubiously attributed Bellinis, a portrait of Ezzelino painted a good couple of centuries after his death and a brace of large sculptures by Canova.

The *Teatro Duse* occupies part of the **Castello**, most of which is currently being restored. From 1489 to 1509 this was the home of **Caterina Cornaro**, one of the very few women to have played a major part in Venetian history. Born into one of Venice's most powerful families, Caterina was married to Jacques II, King of Cyprus. Within a year of the wedding Jacques was dead, and there followed nearly a decade of political pressure from Venice's rulers, who wanted to get their hands on the strategically vital island. In 1489 she was finally forced to abdicate in order to gain much-needed weapons and ships against a Turkish attack. Brought back to Venice to sign a deed "freely giving" Cyprus to the Republic, she was given the region of Ásolo as a sign of Venice's indebtedness. Eventually Ásolo too was taken away from her by the Emperor Maximilian, and she returned to seek asylum in Venice, where she died soon after, in 1510.

Practicalities

Tourist information is handled by the **Pro Loco** in Via Regina Cornaro, close to the Museo; they give out a map of the town which is quite handy, if not exactly a model of clarity. **Accommodation** is impossible – two luxury hotels and that's all. Ásolo does have a handful of **bars and restaurants**, though. The *Enoteca Marcello Agnoletto* is an excellent wine bar in Via Browning (closed Mon), while *La Papessa* in Via Pietro Bembo (closed Wed) has a good range of pizzas plus a few other interesting dishes.

The Villa Barbaro at Masèr

Of all the villas of the Veneto, the one that's most likely to make you forget the effort of getting to it is the **Villa Barbaro** at MASÈR, a few kilometres northeast of Ásolo (June–Sept Tues, Sat & Sun 3–6pm; Oct–Dec & March–May Tues, Sat & Sun 2–5pm; Jan & Feb Sat & Sun 2–5pm; L5000). Touring the villas of the mainland, you become used to discrepancies between the quality of the architecture and the quality of the decoration, but at Masèr you'll see the best of two of the central figures of Italian civilisation in the sixteenth century – **Palladio** and **Paolo Veronese**, whose careers crossed here and nowhere else.

The villa was built in the 1550s for Daniele and Marcantonio Barbaro, men whose humanist training and diverse cultural interests made the process of designing the house far more of a collaborative venture than were most of Palladio's other projects.

The entire ground floor was given over to farm functions – dovecots in the end pavilions, stables and storage space under the arcades, administrative offices on the lower floor of the central block. It's in the living quarters of the *piano nobile* that the more rarified aspect of the brothers' world is expressed, in a series of **frescoes** by Veronese that has no equal anywhere in northern Italy. The more abstruse scenes are decoded in an excellent guidebook on sale in the villa, but most of the paintings require no footnotes. The walls of the Villa Barbaro are the most resourceful display of *trompe l'oeil* you'll ever see – servants peer round painted doors, a dog sniffs along the base of a flat balustrade in front of a landscape of ruins, a huntsman (probably Veronese himself) steps into the house through an entrance that's a solid wall. (Inevitably it's speculated that the woman facing the hunter at the other end of the house was Veronese's mistress.)

In the grounds in front of the villa stands Palladio's **Tempietto**, the only church by him outside Venice and one of his last projects; commissioned by Marcantonio a decade after his brother's death, it was built in 1580, the year Palladio himself died.

travel details

Trains

From Venice to Padua (every 30min; 30min); Vicenza (30min; 55min); Verona (30min; 1hr 30min); Treviso (30min; 30min); Conegliano (hourly; 50min); Vittorio Veneto (3 daily direct, 6 changing at Conegliano; 1–2hr); Feltre (1 daily; 1hr 30min); Castelfranco Veneto (2hr; 50min); Bassano (10 daily; 1hr); Belluno (1 daily, otherwise change at Conegliano; 2hr); Udine (hourly; 2hr); Monsélice (10 daily; 50min); Rovigo (10 daily; 1hr 30min); Milan (30min; 3hr 30min); Florence (hourly; 4hr 30min), via Bologna (2hr); Trieste (hourly; 2hr 10min).

From Padua to Venice (30min; 30min); Vicenza (hourly; 25min); Verona (hourly; 50min); Rovigo (10 daily; 30min); Monsélice (hourly; 20min); Bologna (10 daily; 1hr 25min); Bassano (10 daily; 1hr 5min); Belluno (10 daily; 2–3hr), via Feltre (1hr 20min–2hr); Milan (hourly; 2hr 25min).

From Monsélice to Venice (10 daily; 50min) via Padua (20min); Montagnana (6 daily; 25min), via Este (10min).

From Rovigo to Venice (10 daily; 90min) via Monsélice and Padua.

From Vicenza to Venice (30min; 55min), via Padua (20min); Milan (30min; 2hr), via Verona (30min); Treviso (hourly; 1hr), via Cittadella (30min); Castelfranco (40min).

From Verona to Venice (30min; 90min), via Vicenza (30min) and Padua (50min); Milan (30min; 2hr); Rome (6 daily; 6hr).

From Treviso to Venice (30min; 30min); Vicenza (hourly; 1hr), via Castelfranco and Cittadella, and Udine (hourly; 90min).

From Conegliano to Venice (hourly; 50min); Udine (hourly; 1hr 10min); Vittorio Veneto (9 daily; 15min), with onward service to Belluno (60–90min from Conegliano).

From Belluno to Calalzo (6 daily; 1hr); Conegliano (8 daily; 60–90min), via Vittorio Veneto (45–75min).

Buses

From Venice regular services to Malcontenta, Strà, Padua, Chioggia, Treviso, Marco Polo airport.

From Padua regular services to Venice, Vicenza, Bassano, Ábano Terme and Montegrotto Terme.

From Vicenza to Bassano (hourly; 1hr), via Maróstica (45min), and regular services all over the Veneto.

From Treviso to Padua (every 30min); Ásolo (hourly); Bassano (every 2hr); and very regular services to Venice.

From Belluno frequent *Dolimiti-Bus* services to Cortina d'Ampezzo and rest of eastern Dolomites.

CHAPTER SIX

FRIULI-VENEZIA GIULIA

The geographical complexity of **Friuli-Venezia Giulia** – over three thousand square miles of alps, limestone plateau, alluvial plain and shelving coastlands – is mirrored in its social diversity. The mountainous north is ethnically and linguistically Alpine; the old peasant culture of Friuli, though now waning, still gives a degree of coherence to the area south of the mountains; **Udine** seems Venetian, and **Grado**, slumbering in its Adriatic lagoons, Byzantine-Venetian; while **Aquileia**, a few miles north of these, is still redolent of its Roman and early Christian past. And **Trieste** itself, the regional capital, is a Habsburg city, developed with Austrian capital to be the empire's great southern port. In spirit and appearance it is more like Ljubljana in Yugoslavia than anywhere else in the region, with the exception of **Gorizia**.

If one thing unites the different parts of the region, it's their remoteness from the conventional image of Italy, a remoteness that becomes stronger as one moves east. This area has always been a drawbridge between the Mediterranean world and Central Europe, that hazy multinational entity that begins, according to Eric Newby at least, at Monfalcone, north of Trieste. It has been invaded – sometimes enriched, often laid waste – from east and west and north, by the Romans, Huns, Goths, Lombards, Nazis and even the Cossacks. Venice in its heyday controlled the coast and plain as far as Udine; Napoleon succeeded the Venetian Republic, to be supplanted in turn by the Habsburgs.

These latter, nineteenth-century transitions were relatively painless. Not so in the twentieth century. Some of the fiercest fighting of World War I took place on the **Carso** (the plateau behind Trieste), where artillery shells splintered the limestone into deadly shrapnel and the hills are still scarred with trenches. Vast war memorials and ossuaries punctuate the landscape: the bones of 60,000 soldiers lie at Oslavia, near Gorizia; 100,000 at Redipuglia; 25,000 in the Udine ossuary.

There was less loss of life in World War II, but just as much terror. Fuelled by widespread and long-standing anti-Slavism, Italian Fascism in Trieste was especially virulent, and the city held Italy's only concentration camp. And one of the strangest sideshows of the war was staged north of Udine: Cossack troops, led by White Russian officers, made an alliance with the Nazis and invaded **Carnia**, on the promise of a Cossack homeland among the Carnian mountains once the Reich was secure. No more invading armies have taken this road, but the last border dispute between Italy and Yugoslavia was not settled until the 1970s, and the region remains one of the most heavily armed in Europe.

While the *friulani* want Italian nationality (if only negatively – they want not to be Yugoslav), they don't care for the baggage of Italian identity. They have their own ways and traditions, are sure of their own value, and perhaps don't much mind whether you like their home or not. The local dialect, called *friulano*, is undergoing something of an official revival – many road signs are bilingual in Italian and *friulano*, while studies of the dialect's history and many local variants are published by the *Società Filologica Friulana* in Udine. (Pier Paolo Pasolini, who grew up in Casarsa, near Pordenone, wrote his early poetry in *friulano*.) Economically the region is in fairly good shape: Udine and Pordenone are thriving, Trieste is focus for container traffic and is becoming a centre of computer technology and electronics. Even the disastrous 1976 earthquake has had some good effects, in that subsequent government grants have given a leg-up to all sorts of small businesses. A few purpose-built resorts have sprouted on the Adriatic coast and in the mountains, but not many places in Friuli-Venezia Giulia have yet acquired the patina of tourism.

Trieste

Backed by a white limestone plateau and facing the blue Adriatic, **TRIESTE** has an idyllic setting, even by Italian standards. The city itself, however, is a strange place: a capitalist creation built to play a role that no longer exists. Trieste was *Tergeste* to the Romans, who captured it in 178 BC, but although signs of their occupancy are scattered through the city (the theatre off Corso Italia, for instance, or the arch by Piazza Barbacan), what strikes you straightaway is its modernity. With the exception of the castle and cathedral of San Giusto, the city's whole pre-nineteenth-century history seems dim and vague beside the massive Neoclassical architecture and confident Baroque of the *borgo teresiano* – the name given to the city centre, after Empress Maria Theresa (1740–80), who initiated the development.

Trieste was constructed largely with Austrian capital to serve as the Habsburg empire's southern port, but its brief heyday drew to a close after 1918, when it finally became Italian and discovered that, for all its good intentions, Italy had no economic use for the place. The city languished for sixty years, and is only now making a new role for itself. Computer-based firms are cropping up round about, while seaborne trade goes through the container port on the south side of Trieste, leaving the quays of the old port to function as carparks.

Lying as it does on the political and ethnic fault-line between the Latin and Slavic worlds, Trieste has long been a city of political extremes. In the last century it was a hotbed of *irredentismo* – an Italian nationalist movement to "redeem" the Austrian lands of Trieste and the Trentino. After 1918 the tensions increased, leading to a strong Fascist presence in Friuli-Venezia Giulia. Yugoslavia and the Allies fought over Trieste until 1954, when the city and a connecting strip of coast were secured for Italy, though a definitive border settlement was not reached until 1975. Tito kept the Istrian peninsula, whose fearful Italian population emigrated in huge numbers – for instance, Fiume (Rijeka) lost 58,000 of its 60,000 Italians. The neo-Fascist *MSI* party has always done well here, and there's even a local anti-Slav party, the *Lista per Trieste*, which is sinking fast in the polls but still publicises "Slav provocation" and other supposed dangers to Italian culture. Yet nationalism provoked the development of its opposite, and there is an intense socialist tradition among Trieste's intellectuals.

Arrival, information and finding a place to stay

Coaches from Trieste's **airport**, at Ronchi dei Legionari, terminate at the city's Piazza Libertà coach station, which is right by the central train station. The **AAST** is in the Castello di San Giusto (Mon–Sat 9am–1pm & 4–7pm), but the office at the station (same hours) is equally helpful and informative. Students can get time-tables and advice at *CTS*, the student travel office at Piazza Dalmazia 3b (Mon–Fri 9am–12.30pm & 4–7pm, Sat 9am–noon).

The cheapest good **hotels** are the *Julia*, Via XXX Ottobre 5 (☎040/68.247), the *Marina*, Via Galatti 14 (☎040/61.168), *Centro*, Via Roma 13 (☎040/64.408), and the *Venezia*, Via Genova 23 (☎040/68.480), all with doubles around L28,000. If you want to push the boat out, try the stylish *Hotel al Teatro,* Capo di Piazza G. Bartoli 1 (☎040/64.123), where you can expect to pay upwards of L50,000.

Women and married couples can put up cheaply at the *Casa Famiglia Mater Dei*, at Strada Guardiella 8 (☎040/54.332), a convent that provides short-stay accommodation. The **youth hostel**, 8km out of the city at Viole Miramare 331 (#6 or #36 bus), has recently been closed for restoration: check with the tourist information office.

The nearest **campsite** is at the Obelisco (☎040/211.655), which is on bus #4 route and the *tranvia* (see "Around Trieste"). The *Pian del Grisa* site at CONTOVELLO (☎040/213.142) is easy to reach; the *Alle Rose* (☎040/299.457) and *Mare Pineta* (☎040/299.264) at SISTIANA are further away, but have excellent views. There's also a campsite at AURISINA CAVE (☎040/ 200.459).

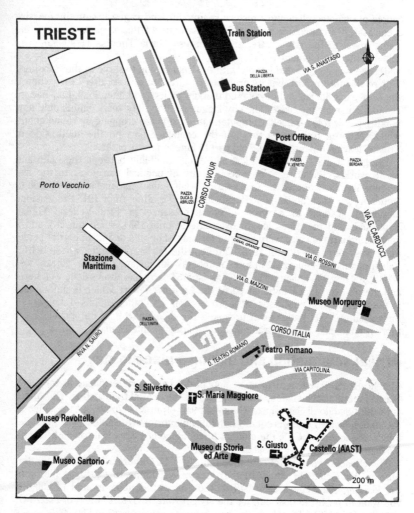

The City

The focal point of the city's pre-modern history, and its prime tourist site, is the hill of San Giusto, with its castle and cathedral. The **Castello** (daily 8am–sunset) is a fifteenth-century Venetian fortress, built near the site of the Roman forum; there's nothing much to see, but a walk round the ramparts is *de rigueur*. Its Museo Civico (Tues–Sun 9am–12.45pm) houses a little collection of antique weaponry. The **Cattedrale di San Giusto** (closed 3–6pm) is a typically Triestine synthesis of styles. In the fourteenth century the three churches on this site were combined into one, as is obvious when you see the nave. The facade is predominantly Romanesque, but includes five Roman columns and a Gothic rose window, and the entrance pillars are fragments from a Roman tomb. Inside, between Byzantine pillars, there are fine thirteenth-century frescoes of Saint Justus, a Christian martyr killed during the persecutions of Diocletian.

Just down the cobbled lane from the cathedral, at Via Cattedrale 15, is the **Museo di Storia ed Arte** (daily 9am–1pm), a collection of cultural plunder that embraces Himalayan sculpture, Egyptian manuscripts and Roman glass. Behind the museum, and accessible from Piazza Cattedrale, is the **Orto Lapidario**, a pleasant modernist environment in which fragments of classical statuary, pottery and inscriptions are arranged on benches and against walls, among the cowparsley and miniature palm trees. The little Corinthian temple on the upper level contains the remains of J.J. Winckelmann (1717–68), the German archaeologist and theorist of Neoclassicism, who was murdered in Trieste by a man to whom he had showed off his collection of antique coins.

Trieste's principal museum is the **Revoltella**, at Via Diaz 27, housed in a Viennese-style palazzo bequeathed to the city by the financier Baron Pasquale Revoltella in 1869. Its combined historical collection and modern art gallery is reputedly excellent, but bureaucratic squabbling – ostensibly over fire regulations – has kept the museum closed for years. A grand re-opening is planned, but the doors are expected to stay shut for some time yet.

The nearby **Museo Sartorio**, in Largo Papa Giovanni XXIII (Tues–Sun 9am–1pm), has ceramics and icons downstairs and oppressive private rooms upstairs, all dark veneers, gothic tracery and bad Venetian oil paintings. A vastly more pleasant domestic interior is the **Museo Morpurgo**, north of San Giusto at Via Imbriani 5 (Tues–Sun 10am–1pm). The palazzo was left to the city by the merchant and banker Mario Morpurgo di Nilma, and its apartments have not really been touched since their first decoration in the 1880s. With its sepia photographs and other memorabilia, it feels less like a museum than like a home whose owners went on holiday and never came back.

The ugliest episode of recent European history is embodied by the **Risiera di San Sabba**, on the southern flank of Trieste in Via Valmaura (Tues–Sun 9am–1pm; on #10 bus route) – once a rice-hulling plant, this was the only concentration camp in Italy. Its crematorium was installed after the German invasion of Italy in September 1943, a conversion supervised by Erwin Lambert, who had designed the death camp at Treblinka. Nobody knows exactly how many people were killed at the *Risiera* before the Yugoslavs liberated the city on May 1, 1945, but 20,000 identity cards were found. Nazism had plenty of sympathisers in this part of Italy: in 1920 Mussolini extolled the zealots of Friuli-Venezia Giulia as model Fascists, and the commander of the camp was a local man. A permanent exhibition at the *Risiera* serves as a reminder of Fascist crimes in the region.

JOYCE IN TRIESTE

From 1905 to 1915, and again in 1919–20, **James Joyce** and his wife Nora lived in Trieste. After staying at Piazza Ponterosso 3 for a month, they moved to the third-floor flat at Via San Nicolò 30. (In 1919 the great poet Umberto Saba bought a bookshop on the ground floor at the same address. The two writers seem never to have met, though they had a common friend in the novelist Italo Svevo.) There is no plaque in Via San Nicolò, but there is one on Via Bramante 4, quoting the postcard that Joyce despatched in 1915 to his brother Stanislaus, whose irredentist sympathies had landed him in an Austrian internment camp. The postcard announced that the first chapter of James's new work, *Ulysses*, was finished.

Drinking and eating

Trieste is still the leading coffee port in the Mediterranean, and one of the pleasures of walking around the *borgo teresiano* is the unexpected scent of roasting coffee which wafts across the streets. The Triestines treat coffee with great seriousness, and there's a plethora of places in which to sample the various imports. As with the rest of Friuli-Venezia Giulia, the cuisine in Trieste bears central European influence – goulash, potato noodles and cheese dumplings featuring on many menus. For less formal meals, a summertime attraction are the *osmizze*, impromptu eating places offering the simplest of local produce at rock-bottom prices.

Cafés and Bars

Trieste's favourite **café** is the *Caffè San Marco*, which has occupied its premises on Via G. Battisti for some eighty years; don't leave without at least a peek at its Liberty-style interior of marble table-tops, mahogany panels, mirrors and gilt. Much of the historic style of the *Caffè Tommaseo* on Piazza Tommaseo – a rendezvous for Italian nationalists in the last century – was lost in a recent refurbishment, but it makes a pleasant if pricey refuge in the summer heat. (Incidentally, if you ask for a cappuccino in Trieste you may well get an espresso with a dash of milk – what's known as a *macchiato* anywhere else in Italy. So ask for a *cappuccino grande* or a *caffè latte*.)

In addition to the conventional cafés, the city centre has many *torrefazioni* – cafés which roast and sell beans, as well as grinding them; try the *Caffè Colombiana* in Via Carducci near the Via Coroneo junction, or the *Crème Caffè* in Piazza Goldoni.

Many of the city's **bars** are as glossy as the top-notch cafés. The bar in the Galleria Protti – which runs north from the Piazza Borsa, inside the *Assicurazioni Generali* building – has a Thirties' nightclub feel, while the *Caffè degli Specchi* in Piazza dell'Unita d'Italia is like the cocktail lounge of a Twenties' Cunard liner. A few bars, including the venerable *Caffè San Marco*, have live music. The *Roxy Bar* and *Nutty Bar* in Via Madonnina, the *Music Club Tor Cucherna* in Via Chiauchiara, the *Tavernetta* in Via Picarda, and the *Birreria Spofford* in Via Rossetti all attract a student clientele.

Gelaterie

For **ice cream**, the best spot is the leafy Viale XX Settembre, where the citizens stroll in the evening. *Pipolo* is superb, but there are many cafés to choose from. The Viale is somewhat less congenial at its Piazza San Giovanni end, a gathering place for young *fascisti*. The *gelateria* at Via della Madonna del Mare 8, and the *Gelateria Viti* on the Passeggio Sant'Andrea (bus #8 from the station), are also excellent.

Snacks

For **snacks** and light meals, the most interesting places in Trieste are the *osterie*, where the landlord draws off wine by the glass from barrels stacked behind the bar. The local sparkling wine called *prosecco*, praised long ago by the Roman Empress Livia, is delicious; and *terrano*, a very sharp red wine grown only on the limestone highlands around the city, should also be tried, though you probably won't want a bottle of the stuff. The *Bar Tevere* in Via Malcanton, just behind the

Piazza d'Italia, is a lively place with simple food; fried sardines or *polpette* in a bread roll, with a glass of *tocai friulano* or *malvasia*, furnish an excellent lunch. There are other *osterie* at Via delle Settefontane 13, Via Veneziana 11, and Via Carducci 34a, where there's an excellent range of bottled wines for sale too.

The *Buffet Pepi* in Via Cassa di Risparmio is a favourite student lunch-stop – offering excellent sausages and bowls of smoking sauerkraut, its cuisine emphasises Trieste's Austrian connections. Round the corner at Via San Nicolò 1b is *La Piola*, a flashier version of the same. Another student hang-out is *Notorious* in Via del Bosco – sandwiches and salads on the ground floor, and a good cheap trattoria on the first floor.

Restaurants and *Osmizze*

For dependable Italian food, try the very popular *Trattoria dell'Antica Ghiacceretta* in Via dei Fornelli, or the *Ai Due Triestini* in Via Armando Diaz. *Trattoria alla Palestra*, Via Madonna del Mare 18, has fine food at reasonable prices, and an English-speaking host. The prestige restaurant is *Antica Trattoria Suban*, at Via Comici 2 – it deserves its reputation, but is pricey.

Seafood can be outstanding in Trieste – it's worth making your way out to Viale Miramare for a meal at *Allo Squero*, at no. 42, or *La Marinella* at no. 323. *Branzino* and *sogliola* – sea bass and sole – are local favourites.

For supper, the thing to do in summer or early autumn is to find an **osmizza**, an informal restaurant where farmers sell their own produce, such as home-cured meats, cheese, olives, bread and wine. A frequent bonus is a stunning view over the bay of Trieste or the limestone hills behind the city. The problem with *osmizze* is that they are temporary, don't advertise, and usually lie off the beaten track – which makes them all the more worth tracking down. Your best bet is to buy a copy of the Slovene newspaper, *Primorski Dnevnik*, preferably the Sunday edition, which usually prints up-to-date lists, and if you can't make head or tail of the Slovene listings, ask someone in a tourist office or a hotel. Otherwise, just take a #44 bus from outside the station, and get off at Contovello or Prosecco, and start asking if there is an *osmizza* nearby. You'll know you are getting warm when you see arrows on clumps of leaves suspended from archways and lamp-posts: they point the way to the nearest *osmizza*.

There is the usual scattering of fast-food places. Decent pizzas can be found at *Il Barattolo* in Piazza Sant'Antonio, or at *2000* and *2001* in Via delle Settefontane. A self-service restaurant chain called *Brek* has outlets in Via San Francesco and Via d'Alviano, and the food is good of its sort.

Listings

Airport information ☎040/773.225.

Boat services From March to September, the steamer *Dionea* plies up and down the Istrian coast, between Grado in the north and Pula in the south. Details from *AGEMAR* travel agency, Piazza Duca degli Abruzzi 1a (☎040/69.021). A day trip on the *Dionea* is recommended for the best view of the city. Boats can also be taken daily to Zadar and Split in Yugoslavia, and three times a month from July to September to Durazzo in Albania. Details again from *AGEMAR*.

Bus information ☎040/68.103.

Car hire *Hertz*, Via Mazzini 1 (☎040/60.650).

Club Alpino Italiano Via Macchiavelli 17 (☎040/60.317), for advice on climbing and skiing.

Consulates *UK*, Vicolo delle Ville 16 (Tues & Fri 9am–12.30pm; ☎040/302.884); *US*, Via Pellegrini 42 (☎040/911.780). If you are going on to Yugoslavia and need a visa (British travellers don't), get it from the Yugoslav consulate at Strada Friuli 54 (☎040/410.125).

Events During the summer the village of Muggia hosts an international theatre festival, and there are programmes of musical events at the castle of San Giusto. The *Verdi* opera house has a summer season. The Festa dell'Unità runs from end of July to mid-August – check the timetable in *Il Piccolo*, Trieste's daily paper, which should also have details of the festivals in the Carso villages (see below).

Gay scene *Fashion* disco in Via Madonna del Mare has a gay night on Wed; the Costa dei Barbari beach is the main meeting place.

Launderette Via Ginnastica 36.

Police Emergencies ☎113; the *Questura* is on Via Teatro Romano (☎040/60.311).

Post office The main post office is in Piazza Vittorio Veneto (Mon–Sat 8am–7.30pm).

Telephones *SIP*, Viale XX Settembre 5 (daily 8am–9.30pm); *ASST*, Via Pascoli 9 (open 24hr daily).

Around Trieste

The **Carso** is the Italian name for the limestone uplands which rise from the Venetian plain south of Monfalcone and eventually merge into the Istrian plateau. The border changes have put most of the Carso within Yugoslavia (its Slovene name is *Kras*), yet even the narrow strip inside Italy, behind Trieste, is geologically, botanically and socially distinct.

Like all limestone country, the Carso is a harsh environment, arid in summer and sometimes snowbound in winter. Its surface is studded with sink-holes, eroded by streams which sometimes reappear miles away on the coast, while in some places – near Aurisina, for instance – it is scarred with World War I trenches. The dour villages of thick-walled houses seem to hunker down against the *bora*, the northeasterly wind which blasts this area at every time of year. (When it's especially fierce, ropes are strung along the steeper streets in Trieste.)

Several bus services run up onto the Carso from Trieste – #42, #43, #44, #45 and #46. A good place to start an exploration is **BORGO GROTTA GIGANTE**, which boasts the world's largest accessible cave – 107 metres deep by 208 metres broad (guided visits: April–Oct every 30min; Nov–March every hr). Whatever the temperature outside, it's a steady 11 or 12°C in the cave, so come prepared. Close to the cave is *Papi Sport*, the only bike-hire place in the area – useful should you not have a car but want to explore more of the Carso. You can make a pleasant round-trip to Borgo by taking the old *tranvia* (cable tramway) from Piazza Oberdan to OPICINA, and then the #45 bus. The *tranvia* runs every twenty minutes between 7.30am and 8pm.

Two walks near the city can be recommended, both needing at least half a day. The **Strada Vicentina** (or *Napoleonica*) is some two miles long, curving along the hillside above the city, between the Obelisco (below Opicina) and the hamlet of BORGO NAZARIO (near PROSECCO). It's a scenic but unstrenuous walk, partly shadowed by trees and partly cut through almost sheer limestone cliffs. Access couldn't be simpler: the Obelisco is a stop on the *tranvia*, and the Borgo Nazario end is near Via San Nazario, where the #42 and #45 buses stop on their way back to Trieste station.

The other walk, through the **Val Rosandra**, is very different. This miniature wilderness of limestone cliffs and sumac trees is the local rock-climbing headquarters. Take bus #40 to SAN DORLIGO DELLA VALLE and follow the road at the back of the square toward the hills. After half a mile or so the tarmac gives way to a path bordered on the right by Roman aqueducts. Half an hour later you see the little church of Santa Maria in Siaris, perched on a spur of rock high on the right. Beyond this is a waterfall, then the tiny hamlet of BOTTEZZA – the last habitation before the Yugoslav border.

From Trieste to Duino

The nearest resort to Trieste on the **Triestine Riviera** – as the twenty kilometres of coastline to Duino are optimistically known – is **BARCOLA**, connected to the city by the #6 bus service. Developed during Trieste's great days at the end of the nineteenth century, it is now really a suburb that comes to life in summer, when all Trieste seems to come here to chat, play cards, sunbathe and swim. Despite the cargo ships and tankers moored in the harbour, the water is moderately clean, and the showers are free.

Miramare
Standing at the tip of a rocky promontory 7km from Trieste, the salt-white castle of **MIRAMARE** is the area's prime tourist attraction, and a dream-castle to rank with Ludwig's in Bavaria. (Take the #36 bus from Trieste or Barcola, or the train from Trieste.) The Archduke Ferdinand Maximilian, Emperor Franz Josef's younger brother, was once forced ashore here by a squall, and resolved to buy the site. He built the castle and laid out its grounds between 1856 and 1870, but never lived to see it completed – having accepted Napoleon III's offer to make him the "Emperor of Mexico", Maximilian was shot in 1867, in the line of imperial duty. His wife Charlotte went mad, and the legend was born that anyone who spends a night in Miramare will come to a bad end.

The kitsch **interior** (Mon 9.30am–1.30pm, Tues–Fri 9.30am–1.30pm & 2.30–6pm, Sat & Sun 9am–12.30pm & 2.30–6pm) is a remarkable example of regal decadence. The "Monarchs' Salon", for instance, is embellished with portraits of the King of Norway, the Emperor of Brazil, the Czar of Russia – anyone, no matter how fraudulent or despotic, as long as he's a monarch. This softens you up for the bedroom and its images of the most important events in the history of this area, pride of place going to the construction of the castle, of course. Other rooms are panelled and furnished like a ship's quarters, reflecting Maximilian's devotion to the Austrian navy.

Sometimes a boat runs between Trieste and Miramare – check with the tourist office. In July and August a *son et lumière* called "Maximilian of Mexico: an Emperor's Tragedy" is performed beside the sea, twice nightly on Tuesday, Thursday and Saturday; the first performance on Tuesday is in English.

Duino and around

The village of **DUINO** (#43 bus from Trieste) is dominated by its sixteenth-century castle, seat of the Princes of Thurn and Taxis down to the present day. It was here that Rilke began the *Duino Elegies*, a work dedicated to his host, the incumbent princess. Access to the castle is granted only to large guided groups, but you can get into the eleventh-century castle (daily 10am–noon & 5–7pm) – now a ruined eyrie above the sea, it commands magnificent views.

The bus from Trieste goes on to **SAN GIOVANNI DEL TIMAVO**, stopping by the Gothic church of San Giovanni in Tuba, built on the site of a fifth-century basilica. A few yards away, the River Timavo surges from the limestone just below road level, the end of a subterranean course of some forty kilometres. The water is icy cold, and emerald-green fronds wave with the current in the deep pool below the spring. Despite the traffic, this is a mysterious spot. The spring is described in Virgil's *Aeneid*, and the Greek historian Strabo says there was a sacred wood here, where white horses were sacrificed to Diomedes, god-hero of the Trojan Wars.

Palmanova, Aquileia and around

Bordered by the Tagliamento in the west and the Isonzo in the east, and drained by other rivers flowing into the sandy, shallow waters at the head of the Adriatic, the triangle of flatlands south of Udine seems unpromising territory for a visitor – mile upon mile of maize fields, punctuated by telegraph poles, streams, level roads and newish villages. Yet the dull fields of this secretive region hide one of the most splendid surviving monuments of early Christendom, and one of Italy's most charming resorts is tucked away in the lagoons to the south. If you don't have your own transport, **buses** are the way to explore the region, the hourly service from Udine to Grado calling at Palmanova, Cervignano railway station, and Aquileia on the way.

Palmanova

Half an hour by train from Udine, **PALMANOVA** is a Venetian fortress built in 1593 in the form of a nine-pointed star, its symmetrical streets converging on a large hexagonal piazza. Guided tours are conducted through the tunnels in the fortifications, and the Museo Civico fills out the story further. Apart from this military curiosity, there is no reason to visit the town.

Aquileia

AQUILEIA was established as a Roman colony in 181 BC, its location at the eastern edge of the Venetian plain – on the bank of a navigable river a few kilometres from the sea – being ideal for defensive and trading purposes. It became the nexus for all Rome's dealings with points east and north, and by 10 BC, when the Emperor Augustus received here Herod the Great, King of Judea, Aquileia was the capital of the *Regio Venetia et Histria* and the fourth most important city in Italy, after Rome, Milan and Capua. In 314 the famous Patriarchate of Aquileia was founded, and under the first patriarch, Theodore, a great basilica was built. Sacked by Attila in 452 and again by the Lombards in 568, Aquileia lost the patriarchate to Grado, which was protected from invasion by its lagoons. It regained its primacy in the early eleventh century under Patriarch Poppo, who rebuilt the basilica and erected the campanile, a landmark for miles around. But regional power inevitably passed to Venice, and in 1751 Aquileia lost its patriarchate for the last time, to Udine. The sea has long since retreated, and the river Natissa is a reed-clogged stream. Aquileia is now a dusty little town of 3000 people, bisected by the main Udine to Grado road, but the remnants of its ancient heyday make it one of northeast Italy's most important archaeological sites.

In 1348 an earthquake destroyed much of Poppo's work on the **Basilica** (daily 8.30am–noon & 3–7pm), but the building is still superb, the Gothic elements of the reconstruction – as in the capitals and arches – harmonising perfectly with the Romanesque. The basilica's glory, though, is Theodore's mosaic pavement, which undulates the full length of the nave like a pattern of brilliant carpets. Rediscovered only this century, the mosaics are amazingly joyful and serene, combining and reconciling Christian and pagan iconography. Look for the blond angel bearing the laurel wreath and palm frond – whether it represents the Pax Romana or Christian Victory, no one can be sure. Other mosaics from Theodore's original basilica, depicting a whole bestiary, have been discovered around the base of the campanile (access from inside the basilica). The ninth-century crypt under the chancel has very beautiful soft-hued frescoes, distinctly Byzantine in form.

A couple of minutes' walk from the basilica, on the main Via Giulia Augusta, is the **Museo Archeologico** (Mon 9am–2pm, Tues–Fri 9am–6.30pm, Sat & Sun 9am–1pm & 3–6.30pm). Items relating to all aspects of Roman life are on show, from surgical needles to statues of the gods. In all likelihood a sculpture school flourished here in the first century, which would account for the fine naturalistic busts, a collection that includes one masterpiece – an almost translucent marble head of Livia Augusta.

The **Museo Paleocristiano** (Mon–Fri 9am–2pm, Sat & Sun 9am–1pm), in the northern part of the town, is recommended solely for those insatiable for Roman remains. The fifteen-minute riverside walk to the museum from the basilica is pleasant though, taking you past what were once the quays of Aquileia; and from the museum you can loop back along the main road, past the forum, to the basilica and the bus stop. If you want to make a picnic there is a grocer's shop at the end of the quays on the right.

The **AAST**, in Piazza Basilica (April–Oct 9am–noon & 3.30–6pm), can provide maps, and lists of the town's meagre accommodation. Cheapest **hotel** is the *Roma*, Via Roma 28 (☎0431/91.008), with doubles from L40,000. *Camping Aquileia*, by the Museo Paleocristiano in Via Gemina, is a luxury site open between May and September (☎0431/91.042); the nearby *Camping Monastero* (☎0431/91.042) is a humbler set-up. Some accommodation might be available in private houses at the bend in the road beyond the campsite.

Grado

Some 11km from Aquileia, isolated among lagoons at the end of a causeway, is the ancient island-town of **GRADO**, through which Aquileia once traded with Syria, Cyprus, Arabia and Asia Minor. Highlight of the small historic centre is the sixth-century cathedral, notable for its Byzantine-influenced capitals and the Venetian fourteenth-century silver *pala* on the high altar. The adjacent church of Santa Maria delle Grazie is from the sixth century too.

Most of Grado, however, is a resort that extends eastwards along the sandy island. The beaches are endless, the water as warm and safe as a bath, and almost as shallow – indeed, the name of the town comes from the gentle angle of its shore. The free beaches are at the western end; if you want a locker, deckchair and shower facilities, you will have to pay a couple of thousand lire to one of the businesses on the Lungomare Adriatico.

Ten coaches per day make the one-hour run to Udine, and there's also a half-hourly bus connection from Cervignano train station, on the Venice to Trieste line. The best way to visit Grado, though, is by boat from Trieste; on Tuesdays, Fridays, Saturdays and Sundays the little steamer *Dionea* calls morning and evening at the Molo Torpediniere on its way from and to the city (see "Listings" in the Trieste section). Boat trips run from Grado to the island of Barbana seven times a day, and on Fridays a round-trip to Venice leaves the Molo Torpediniere at 8am, returning twelve hours later. (Details from *Adriamare*, Piazza Carpaccio 5.)

Grado's **AAST**, at Viale Dante Alighieri 68, has details of the town's **hotels**, the majority of which are fairly expensive, and often insist on your taking full pension. **Campers** have a better deal – sites to try include *Camping al Bosco* (☎0431/80.485), *Camping Punta Spin* (☎0431/80.732) and *Camping Europa* (☎0431/80.877), all towards the eastern end of the island. Of the many places to **eat**, two of the most convivial are *Trattoria de Toni*, in Piazza Duca d'Aosta, and *Enoteca da Pino*, in Via Galilei.

Lignano

A few kilometres westwards across the lagoons lies the purpose-built resort complex of **LIGNANO**. Hemingway used to shoot duck on this sandy, pine-wooded peninsula at the mouth of the Tagliamento, but nowadays it appeals to beachniks only, and is especially popular with German tourists. Its 100,000-plus beds get booked pretty solid in summer – the **AAST** at Via Latisana 42 will winkle out whatever hotel and campsite vacancies there are. If you do get washed up here, the wine and cakes at *Enoteca-bar Scarpa*, Vicolo Marano 9, will cheer you up.

Gorizia

As with other towns in this region, the tranquillity of present-day **GORIZIA** (reached by train from Udine or Trieste) belies the turbulence of its past. The castle which dominates the old centre was the power-base of the dukes of Gorizia, who ruled the area for four centuries. After their eclipse, Venice briefly ruled the town at the start of the sixteenth century, before the Habsburgs took over. It was controlled from Vienna uninterruptedly until August 8, 1916, when the Italian army occupied it – but only until the rout at Caporetto, some 50km north. The border settlement after World War II literally split houses in Gorizia down the middle. Italy kept the town proper but lost its eastern perimeter to Yugoslavia, where the new regime resolved to build its own Gorizia: **Nova Gorica** – "New Gorizia"– is the result. The *NAŠ TITO* (OUR TITO) painted in huge letters on the hill overlooking the town also dates from the period of social-ist construction, though in fact that bit of hillside is Italian territory.

The town's appearance, like that of Trieste, is distinctly Central European, stamped with the authority of Empress Maria Theresa. Numerous parks and gardens – thriving in the area's mild microclimate – further enhance the *fin-de-siècle* atmosphere. Again like Trieste, it's a major shopping town for Slovenes; which explains the large number of electrical goods, clothes and food shops, and the good cafés and restaurants.

One of the finest of its Neoclassical buildings is the **Palazzo Attems** in Piazza De Amicis, which now houses the picture gallery and town archives. The building is closed "per restauro" until further notice, which is a pity, as the gallery has some nice pieces, including an altarpiece by Antonio Guardi. For information on its current status, ask at the **tourist office** at Galleria del Corso 100. The **Museo di Storia e Arte** (Tues–Sun 10am–noon & 3–6pm) is in the Borgo Castello, the quarter built round the castle by the Venetians; the collection of local folkloric items and handicrafts passes a half-hour or so, but the view from the castle is more inspiring.

Probably the strangest sight in Gorizia is the crypt in the Franciscan monastery at **Castagnavizza** – Kostanjevica, rather, for the monastery lies across the border in Nova Gorica. This is the burial place of the last of the Bourbons. After Louis Philippe was ousted by the bloodless revolution of July 1830, the Bourbons were exiled from France; the family eventually arrived in Gorizia in 1836, and the Habsburgs allowed them to stay. To judge by the impassioned entries in the visitors' book, the silence of the crypt is regularly disturbed by French royalists, whose withered bouquets line the walls. The French state must reckon that the republic is now strong enough to withstand any monarchist pressure, for it is apparently expressing interest in obtaining the return of these royal relics. The monastery was also home to Brother Stanislav Skrabec (1844–1918), an important Slovene linguist, and the library of 10,000 books includes a rare copy of the first Slovene grammar, inscribed by its author Adam Bohoric (1584). The easiest approach is to take a taxi up the hill once you have crossed the border; walking is the best way back. Once there, ring the bell; there's no charge, but once inside you should offer a donation.

Cividale

Lying only 17km from Udine and connected to it by rail and coach, **CIVIDALE** is a gem of a town, much prized by the *friulani*, but pretty well unknown to outsiders. It was founded in 50 BC by Julius Caesar where the Natisone valley opens into the plain, and in the sixth century became the capital of the first Lombard duchy. In the eighth century the Patriarch of Aquileia moved here, inaugurating Cividale's most prosperous period.

The Town

The old town lies on the same side as the rail and coach stations, and the visitor need never cross the river; though a walk over the Devil's Bridge is *de rigeur*. Just walking around the town, within the oval ring bisected by Via Carlo Alberto and Corso Mazzini, is a pleasure; the pace of life is provincially serene, and the buildings are interesting. Cividale has been the main market town in the Natisone valley for 200 years, and today you hear Italian, *friulano*, and Slovene dialects spoken in the street. There are some remarkable tourist sights too.

The **Tempietto Longobardo** (Mon 9am–noon, Tues–Fri 9am–noon & 3–6pm, Sat & Sun 9am–1pm), above the Natisone off Piazza San Biagio, is a uniquely fine example of Lombard art. Constructed in the eighth century, largely from older fragments, it was reduced to rubble in the terrible earthquake of 1222, so what you see now is a three-dimensional mosaic in which different styles somehow harmonise. Inside, the exquisite stucco arch around the quartet of female saints, and the luminous, smiling saints themselves, are among the most splendid surviving works of art from the eighth century; the frescoes and stalls all date from the late fourteenth century.

Two other beautiful Lombard pieces are to be found in the **Museo Cristiano**, housed in the precincts of the fifteenth-century **Duomo** (Mon–Fri 9.30am–noon & 3–6.30pm, Sat & Sun 11.30am–noon & 4.30–6.30pm). The *Altar of Ratchis* was carved for Ratchis, Duke of Cividale and King of the Lombards at Pavia, who died as a Benedictine monk at Montecassino in 759; the reliefs of *Christ in Triumph* and the *Adoration of the Magi* are delicate and haunting. The other highlight is the *Baptistery of Callisto*, named after Callisto de Treviso, the first Patriarch of Aquileia to move to Cividale. He lived here from 730 to 756, and initiated the building of the patriarchal palace, the cathedral and this octagonal baptistery, which used to stand beside the cathedral. It's constructed from older Lombard fragments, the columns and capitals dating from the fifth century.

The duomo itself houses a twelfth-century masterpiece of silversmithing: the *pala* (altarpiece) named after Pellegrino II, the Patriarch who commissioned it and donated it to the town; it depicts the Virgin seated between the archangels Michael and Gabriel, who are flanked by 25 saints and framed by saints, prophets, and the patron himself.

Also in Piazza del Duomo is the **Museo Archeologico** (Mon–Fri 9am–1.30pm, Sat & Sun 9am–12.30pm), housing a hotchpotch of local findings and treasures, including fascinating Lombard jewellery and encrusted psalters.

Just a stone's throw from the fifteenth-century Ponte del Diavolo, in Via Monastero Maggiore, is a cellar-like cavern called the *Ipogeo Celtico* (Mon 8am–1pm, Tues–Fri 8am–1pm & 3.30–5.40pm; key from the tourist office in Largo Boiani, or the *Bar al Ponte*). The hypogeum was probably used as a tomb for Celtic leaders, between the fifth and second centuries BC, but there is still some dispute whether it's man-made or merely man-adapted. Either way, the spectral faces carved on the walls make it a weird place.

Practicalities

The **AAST** is on the first floor at Largo Boiani 4. Cividale's least expensive decent hotels are *Al Vescovo*, Via Roma 67 (☎0432/726.015) and the *Belvedere*, Via San Pietro (☎0432/727.057). More comfortable (and pricier), and with exceptional views, is the *Castello*, Via del Castello 18 (☎0432/733.242 or 734.015) – it's couple of kilometres north of the town, on a hill above the road to TARCENTO and FAEDIS. The restaurant is good, and on a sunny day the terrace at the Castello is the best place for a leisurely lunch, well worth the taxi trip from the town centre if you don't feel like walking.

The town's smartest **café** is the *San Marco*, opposite the AAST in the loggia of the town hall – well placed for watching passers-by. Recommended **restaurants** are *Zorutti*, Borgo di Ponte 7, *Alla Frasca*, Via De Rubeis 10, *Al Fortino*, Via C. Alberto 46, and *Da Nardini*, Piazzetta de Portis 6.

Udine

It is fitting that the best artworks in **UDINE** are by Giambattista Tiepolo: his airy brilliance suits this town. Running beside and beneath the streets are little canals called *rogge*, diverted from the Torre and Cormor rivers, and these bright streams reflect light onto the walls and through the roadside greenery. Comfortable and bourgeois, Udine is the second city of Friuli-Venezia Giulia, and some say that although it has less than half the population of Trieste, it will gain the ascendancy sooner or later. Udine seems everything that Trieste is not – delicate, untroubled, successful. Trieste, on the other hand, has a richness of identity beside which Udine can seem as pallid as the pink and white facade of its famous town hall.

Along with Cividale, Tricesimo and Zuglio, Udine was one of the frontier bastions of Imperial Rome, and by the sixth century AD it was far more than a garrison colony. But it was not until the thirteenth century that it started to become a regional centre. Patriarch Bertoldo di Andechs (1218–51) can be seen as the father of Udine – he established two markets (the "old market" in Via Mercatovecchio, and the new one in Piazza Matteotti, still a market place), moved the patriarchate from Cividale to the castle of Udine, and set up a city council. In 1362 the dukes of Austria acquired the place by treaty, but not for long: Venice, now hungry for territory, captured Udine in 1420, after several assaults and sieges. The city was ruled by Venetian governors for almost 400 years – until 1797, when the Venetian Republic surrendered to Napoleon.

Arrival, information and accommodation

Udine's **train and bus stations** are close together in the south of the town, on Via Europa Unita; Via Roma leads from the train station into the centre. The **EPT** is at Via Piave 27 (Mon–Fri 8.30–1pm & 2.30–6pm, Sat 8.30am–1pm). A good, reasonable **hotel** is the *Manin*, Via Manin 5 (☎0432/501.146), with rooms from L32,000; another in the same price range is *Al Vecchio Tram*, Piazza Garibaldi 15 (☎0432/502.516). Two student **hostels** in Via Zoletto (off Via Aquileia) may be able to put you up: *Residenza Grande* (☎0432/26.058) and *Residenza Piccola* (☎0432/299.127). Non-Italian students may be able to stay at the hostel in Via Ungheria: for details ask at the *CTS* (youth travel organisation) at Via Aquileia 50/3 (Mon–Fri 4.30–7pm).

The City

Legend has it that the castle-topped hill at the heart of Udine was built by Attila's hordes, using their helmets as buckets, so that their leader could relish the spectacle of Aquileia in flames, 36km away. The place to start any exploration of Udine is at the foot of the hill, in the **Piazza Libertà**, a square whose architectural ensemble is matched by few cities in Italy. The fifteenth-century **Palazzo del Comune** is a clear homage to the Palazzo Ducale in Venice, and the clock tower facing the palazzo, built in 1527, similarly has a Venetian model – the lion on the facade and the bronze "Moors" who strike the hours on top of the tower are explicit references to the Torre dell'Orologio in Piazza San Marco. The statue at the north end of the square is a bad allegory of *Peace*, donated to the town by Emperor Franz I to commemorate the Habsburg acquisition of Udine.

To walk up to the **Castello**, go through the **Arco Bollani**, designed by Palladio, and onward up the graceful Venetian Gothic gallery, the **Loggia del Lippomano** on the left. The sixteenth-century Castello, built and decorated by local artists, houses an excellent museum containing works by Caravaggio, Carpaccio, Bronzino and Tiepolo; at the moment it's still closed for restoration, after the 1976 earthquake – for a progress report, ask at the EPT.

North from the Piazza Libertà is **Via Mercatovecchio**, once the mercantile heart of the city and now the busiest shopping street. The little chapel of **Santa Maria**, incorporated into the Palazzo del Monte di Pietà in Via Mercatovecchio, is a beauty. Seen through the glass booth from the street, the interior, with its cloudy Baroque frescoes by Giulio Quaglio (1694), has a pristine, subaqueous appearance.

Due west lies the **Piazza Matteotti**, with galleries on three sides and the fine Baroque facade of San Giacomo on the fourth. The square's importance as the centre of public life in Udine is proved by the outside altar on the first-floor balcony of **San Giacomo**; mass was celebrated here on Saturdays so that selling and buying could go on uninterrupted in the market below. As well as being the town's main market, this was the setting for tournaments, plays and carnivals. The fountain in the middle of the square was designed in 1543 by Giovanni da Udine, a pupil of Raphael, who also had a hand in building the castle.

Off the south side of Piazza Libertà is the **Duomo**, a Romanesque construction that was given a Baroque refit in the eighteenth century. Altarpieces and frescoes by Giambattista Tiepolo are the main attraction – they decorate the first two chapels on the right and the chapel of the Sacrament, a little way beyond. A series of frescoes painted by Tiepolo in collaboration with his son, Giandomenico, can be seen in the tiny **Oratorio della Purità** opposite – ask the sacristan in the duomo to show you.

But Udine's outstanding works of art are the Giambattista Tiepolo frescoes in the nearby eighteenth-century **Palazzo Arcivescovile** (Archbishops' Palace; Mon–Fri 9am–noon). Painted in the late 1720s, these luminous and consummately theatrical scenes add up to a sort of rococo epic of the Old Testament. The *Fall of the Rebel Angels* is the first work you see as you climb the staircase to the first floor; other frescoes show *Sarah and the Angel*, *Abraham and the Angels*, *Rachel, Abraham and Isaac* and the *Judgment of Solomon*.

Of the minor sights, perhaps the most enjoyable is the display of local crafts and folk art in the **Museo Friulano delle Arti e Tradizione Popolari** (Tues–Sat 9am–12.30pm & 3–6pm, Sun 9am–12.30pm), housed in the Palazzo Gorgo-Maniago in Via Viola.

Eating and entertainment

Udine has scores of restaurants, one of the most popular being *Da Arturo*, Via Pracchiuso 75 (closed Mon). The unpretentious *Trattoria all'Allegria*, Via Grazzano 18 (closed Mon), does simple local dishes in the dining room beside the bar – the *gnocchi* in butter is delicious. You could also try *Ai Castagni*, Via Barigliara 271, *Al Cacciatore*, Via Cividale 638, or *Alla Ghiacciaia*, Vicolo Portello 2. The self-service *Zenith*, in Via Prefettura, may suit those in a hurry.

Students hang out in the *Manhattan* and *Arcobaleno* **bars** in Viale Palmanova, and in *St James* in Via Grazzano. The *Contarena* **disco**, in Piazza Libertà, is one of the livelier spots. Nightlife is very limited outside the university term-time, but in summer there's a busy programme of cultural events – theatre, music, dance – in and around the town.

North of Udine: the Carnia

The district of moderate peaks in the north of Friuli is known as the **Carnia**, a name given to it by the Celtic tribes who settled here in the fourth century BC. Approaching the area by road or rail from Udine, the gateway to the region is **GEMONA**, a little town that was largely destroyed in the 1976 earthquake, when more than 300 of its inhabitants were killed. The historic centre, on the steep-sided hilltop, has been devotedly reconstructed, and feels disconcertingly like a film set. The cathedral, once a marvellous Romanesque-Gothic specimen, is notable for the enormous fourteenth-century statue of Saint Christopher on the facade.

North of Gemona, around the headwaters of the River Tagliamento, the Carnia begins. High and often sheer limestone peaks are divided by deep, forested valleys which radiate towards the borders with Austria in the north and Yugoslavia in the east. These ranges – the **Alpi Carniche** in the west and the **Alpi Giulie** in the east – are hardly known even within Italy, yet the area has a lot to offer the hiker and climber. (Linguists should get a lot out of it too, as the villagers speak strange variants of *friulano*, German and Slovene.)

There is one high-level **long-distance trail** in the area: the *Traversata Carnica*, which runs between Sesto and Tarvisio, just below the border with Austria. If that sounds too long or strenuous but you still want to see the mountains by foot, head for the **Laghi di Fusine** – two blue-green lakes within the Alpi Giulie national park, in the very northeast corner of Italy. **TARVISIO**, 9km from the lakes, is easily reached by train or coach; then you may have to hitch, but the road to the Yugoslav border is busy, so it shouldn't be a problem. Once there, the walks can be as long or short as you like: the path circuiting the lakes gives impressive views of the north face of Mángart (2677m), or there's the four-hour walk to *Rifugio Zacchi* (1380m) and back. The refuge, which sleeps thirty, is open between July and September, and meals are usually available.

Further information about the national park can be obtained from the *Azienda Regionale delle Foreste*, Via Manzini 41, Udine (☎0432/294.711). General information on hiking and climbing in the Carnia is given out by the *Società Alpina Friulana* (Societa Ospedale Vecchio 3, Udine), and the tourist offices in Tarvisio and Piancavallo.

The Villa Manin and Pordenone

Hourly trains run west from Udine to **CODROIPO**, a peaceful little town that would have nothing to recommend it to the outsider if the huge **Villa Manin** were not just three kilometres to the southeast, where it completely dominates the little village of PASSARIANO. As the only public transport to the Villa from Codroipo consists of three daily buses, the best way to get there is to walk: straight ahead from the station, and bear left in the main square – you could easily pick up a lift.

Built in 1738 and later enlarged for Lodovico Manin, the last doge of Venice, the Villa Manin (Tues–Sun 9.30am–12.30pm & 3–6pm) is Friuli's best-known country house. In 1797 Napoleon stayed here when he signed the Treaty of Campoformio, which gave Venice to Austria. The interior, much of it coated in run-of-the-mill frescoes, is impressive solely in its size. There are plans to develop the villa's tourist potential, but for now it remains a cultural exhibition centre; the arena created by its great frontal galleries is used in summer for open-air concerts. More alluring is the ramshackle park behind the villa (Thurs 2–6pm, Sat & Sun 9.30am–noon & 2.30–6.30pm), where reedy ponds, birdsong and lichen-green statues create a congenial atmosphere for an afternoon doze.

Pordenone

The westernmost of Friuli-Venezia Giulia's three large towns, **PORDENONE** is now the region's main manufacturing centre, specialising in light industries such as electronics, textiles and ceramics. The best way to see its carefully preserved historic centre is to walk along the **Corso Vittorio Emanuele** to the Gothic-Renaissance Palazzo Communale – from the train station go straight ahead along Via Mazzini, then take the second right.

Over the road from the palazzo is the **Museo Civico Ricchieri** (Tues–Sun 9am–12.30pm & 3–6.30pm); it's predominantly a second-string collection of Venetian art, but it does have a clutch of works by the finest local artist, Giovanni Antonio Sacchienze, better known simply as Il Pordenone. (If you want to see more of the master's work in his home town, search out the parish churches of Roraigrande, Torre, Villanova and Valloncello – for information about access, ask at the **EPT**, Piazza della Motta 13.) Many of the paintings in the museum were removed from the **Duomo** after the 1976 earthquake; the building itself, mainly a late Gothic structure, is notable only for its Romanesque campanile, and for some badly damaged frescoes by Pordenone on one of the pillars at the end of the nave.

For a sense of the everyday realities of peasant life in Friuli, visit the **Museo Provinciale della Vita Contadina** (Tues–Sat 9am–noon & 3–6pm, Sat & Sun 9am–noon), a short distance along the river from the duomo in Piazza Giustiniano.

The surrounding area has a lot to offer, though it is not easily accessible without a car. In **SESTO AL REGHENA**, a little way south of Pordenone, is the fortified **Santa Maria in Sylvis**, one of the oldest inhabited abbeys in the world. It was founded by the Lombards in the eighth century, and has some beautiful old bas-reliefs. Further afield, there are fine buildings and more paintings by Pordenone in SPILIMBERGO and VALERIANO.

travel details

Trains

From Trieste to Udine (13 daily; 1hr 15min), via Gorizia or Cervignano; Venice (14 daily; 2hr 10min).

From Udine to Venice (hourly; 2hr), via Pordenone; Trieste (13 daily; 1hr 15min), via Gorizia or Cervignano; Palmanova (12 daily; 30min); Cividale (8 daily; 20min).

Buses

From Trieste to Belluno (1 daily); Cividale (2 daily); Duino (hourly); Gorizia (5 daily); Grado (8 daily); Pordenone (3 daily); Udine (8 daily).

Services to Yugoslavia include: Zagreb (1 daily); Rijeka/Fiume (5 daily); and Ljubljana (1 daily).

From Udine to Palmanova, Cervignano, Aquileia & Grado (hourly; 1hr 15min to Grado); Cividale (8 daily); Trieste (8 daily).

Ferries

From Trieste to Grado (March–Sept 4 daily; 1hr 30min); Porec, Yugoslavia (March–Sept 3 daily; 2hr 30min); Pula, Yugoslavia (1 daily; 4hr 30min); Zadar & Split, Yugoslavia (July–Sept twice monthly); Durazzo, Albania (July–Sept 3 times monthly); Patras, Greece (4–5 monthly).

CHAPTER SEVEN

EMILIA-ROMAGNA

S et between Lombardy and Tuscany, and stretching from the Adriatic coast almost to the shores of the Mediterranean, **Emilia-Romagna** is the heartland of northern Italy. It is two provinces really: Emilia, and the Romagna to the west – the former Papal States, joined together after the Unification. Before the Papacy took charge in the area, it was a patchwork of ducal territories, ruled over by a handful of families – the Este in Ferrara and Modena, the Farnese in Piacenza and Parma, and lesser dynasties in Ravenna and Rimini – who created sparkling Renaissance courts, combining autocracy with patronage of the arts alongside a continual jockeying for power with the Church. Their castles and fortresses remain, preserved in towns with restored medieval centres that – apart from a few notable exceptions – are relatively off the tourist track, many visitors put off partly by the extreme weather (searingly hot in summer, close to freezing in winter), partly by the more immediate pleasures of Tuscany and Umbria.

The region's landscape is a varied one, ranging from the foothills of the Apennine mountains in the south to flat, sunbaked fields of the northern plain, the Pianura Padana, interrupted only by windbreaks of poplars, shimmering in the breeze. The area has grown wheat since Roman times, and nowadays its industry and agri-businesses are among Italy's most advanced – there are currently more pigs than people in the Po Valley, and Emilia also holds some of the most success-ful of the enterprises that have contributed to the country's 1980s boom.

Carving a dead straight route through the heart of Emilia-Romagna, from Piacenza to Rimini on the coast, the **Via Emilia** is a central and obvious refer-ence point, a Roman military road constructed in 187 BC that was part of the medieval pilgrim's route to Rome, and the way east for crusaders to Ravenna and Venice. The towns that grew up along here are among Emilia's most compelling. **Bologna**, the region's capital, is one of Italy's largest cities, but despite having one of the most beautifully preserved city centres in the country, some of its finest food, and inhabitants whose openness and seemingly unflappable tempera-ments contrast markedly with the stressed-out Milanese, it's been relatively neglected by tourists, and most people pass straight through – definitely a mistake. Bologna also gives easy access to towns like **Modena** and **Parma**, each just an hour or so away by train: wealthy provincial towns that form the smug core of Emilia, and hold some of its finest and most atmospheric architecture, as well as giving access to routes south into the **Apennines**. With a car you can dip into the foothills at will from any of these points, sampling some of the cooking and visiting the local festivals; and even by bus it's possible to get a taste of the area, which at its best can be very beautiful, not at all like the functional plain to the north. If you're a keen hiker, there's the *Grand Escursione Apenninica*, a 25-day-long trek following the backbone of the range from refuge to refuge.

The north of Emilia-Romagna is less interesting than the Via Emilia stretch, the Po disgorging into the Adriatic from its bleak **delta** (which it shares with the Veneto), a desolate region of marshland and lagoons that is mainly of appeal to

birdwatchers. The coast south, too, is an overdeveloped and nowadays over-polluted ribbon of settlement, though **Rimini**, at its southern end, provides a spark of interest, with its oddly attractive seaside sleaze concealing a surprisingly historic town centre. But **Ravenna**, just south of the delta, preserves probably the finest set of Byzantine mosaics in the world in its churches and mausoleums; and **Ferrara**, a little way inland, is, as ex-town of the Este family, one of the most important Renaissance centres in Italy.

It's worth remembering that none of this comes cheap: Emilia is a wealthy area that makes few concessions to tourists. Cheaper hotels can be grimy and depressing, with the more comfortable places pitched at business people; and the tone is, rather like Lombardy to the north, well-mannered, well-dressed and comfortable. If you need to economise, though, it would be a shame to stint when it comes to food, which is where the region excels. Emilia-Romagna is the home of quintissentially Italian food like pasta, prosciutto, salami and parmesan cheese. *Lambrusco* comes from here too, though it's a very different affair from the fizzy offerings in the off-licence at home.

Bologna

Emilia's capital, **BOLOGNA** is a boomtown of the Eighties, whose computer-associated industries have brought conspicuous wealth to the old brick palaces and porticoed squares. Previously, it was best known for its food – undeniably the richest in the country and, of course, for its politics. "Red Bologna" has been the Italian Communist party's stronghold and spiritual home since the last war, and it was no chance association that it was this city's railway station that was bombed by fascist groups in 1980 in the postwar nation's worst terrorist atrocity.

After Venice, the city is among the best-looking in the country. The city centre, within the circle of the central ring road, is startlingly medieval in plan, a jumble of red brick, tiled roofs and balconies radiating out from the great central square of Piazza Maggiore. There are enough monuments and curiosities for several days' leisured exploration, but Bologna is really enjoyable just for itself, its university and enlightened local government ensuring that there's always something happening – be it theatre, music, the city's strong summer festival, or just the café and bar scene, which is among northern Italy's most convivial. The only problem is expense: Bologna's latter-day affluence is reflected in a cost of living that is among Italy's highest, exceeding even Florence or Milan; nightlife, particularly, can leave your wallet steamrolled, and finding a low-priced place to stay can be very difficult.

Arrival, information and getting around

Approaching Bologna **by car** takes you through the modern *feira* district, a showcase for North Italian industry, with trade fairs throughout the year and acres of factory space and pollution among its spaghetti-like tangle of autostradas. Bologona's **airport** (☎311.578) is northwest of the centre, linked to the train station by bus #91 (2 an hour). The **train station** (☎246.490) lies on Piazza delle Medaglie d'Oro, near Porta Galleria, the terminus of all inter-city trains; all long-distance buses terminate at the **bus station** (☎235.105), next door on Piazza XX Settembre. For information, there are **EPT** booths at the airport and at the train

station (Mon–Sat 9am–7pm, Sun 9am–1pm) and a main office at 1/d Piazza Nettuno (Mon–Sat 9am–12.30pm & 2–7pm; ☎239.660), with what's-on booklets, maps and other leaflets, as well as a hotel booking facility.

Once you're in the city centre, the best way to **get around** is to walk: the network of porticos and small squares that make up the *centro storico* is more appealing on foot, and small enough to make buses an unnecessary expense. If you want to move quickly, or make a journey out of the centre, buses are, however, fast and frequent. Buy tickets (L600 each) at tabacchi for use on as many buses as you like within one hour. Information from the booth at 1/1 Piazza Re Enzo (☎239.754 or 248.374).

> The Bologna area telephone code is ☎051

Finding a place to stay

In terms of **places to stay**, Bologna is not geared up for tourists, least of all for those travelling on a tight budget: there are few cheap hotels and no feasibly placed campsite. The EPT has hotel lists, and will book rooms for you (see above), or you could just make straight for one of the places listed below.

The most inexpensive option, as ever, is the city's official **youth hostel**, 6km outside the centre of town Via Viadagola 16 (☎519.202), with beds for around L10,000 for *IYHF* members. Bus #93 takes you right to the door, though it stops running at 8.15pm during the week, 2.15pm on Saturday, when you should take bus #19 from Via Irnerio and walk the 1.5km to the hostel (curfew 11.30pm).

One advantage to Bologna is that some of the cheaper **hotels** are reasonably central. *Pensione Fiorita*, Via San Felice 6 (☎229.560), off Via Ugo Bassi, is rundown but good value, with double rooms for L35,000. Behind the station, the *Pensione Neva*, Via Serra 7 (☎369.893), is popular with backpackers in summer and has clean, basic rooms for L33,000, and an excellent *latteria* nearby. *Pensione Farini*, in the shadow of the Due Torre at Via Farini 13 (☎271.969), has double rooms starting at L34,000. Slightly more expensively, the *Orologio*, Via IV Novembre 10 (☎231.253), charges L46,000 for rooms overlooking Piazza Maggiore. Book in advance as it's always packed. Similarly, the *Hotel Accademia* at Via Belle Arti 6 (☎232.218), in the University quarter, has a nice atmosphere and prices around the L50,000 mark.

The City

Bologna's city centre is quite compact, with most things of interest within the main *viale* or ringroad. From the station, **Via dell'Indipendenza** leads into the centre, one of Bologna's main thoroughfares, lined with cinemas and bars and always busy, finishing up at the central squares of **Piazza Maggiore** and **Piazza del Nettuno**. To the right lies the commercial district, bordered by office blocks along Via G. Marconi, to the left the university quarter. One thing you will notice quickly is how well-preserved the *centro storico* actually is: Bologna is a city that takes its history seriously, and it has been determined about restoring the arcades and churches of its centre. This can be frustrating – it's not unusual to find notices on churches suggesting you return in 1994 – but the reward is a city centre that is a joy to stroll through.

Piazza Maggiore and around

Piazza Maggiore is the notional pulse of the city, an obvious place to make for first, with an activity that seems almost constant; its cafés are packed out through the morning for the market, afterwards thinning out just a little before *passeggiata*. It's a quintessentially social place, and together with the adjacent **Piazza Nettuno** hosts, as you might expect, the city's principal secular and religious buildings: the cathedral, Palazzo Re Enzo and Palazzo Comunale – all impressive for their bulk alone, propped up by buttresses and pitted with holes from the original scaffolding. At the centre of Piazza Nettuno, the **statue of Neptune** is a symbol of the city and target for pigeons, styled in extravagant fashion by Giambologna in 1566. On its western side, through a small courtyard, stairs wide enough for a rider on horseback lead to the upper rooms of **Palazzo Comunale** (Mon & Wed–Sat 9am–2pm, Sun 9am–12.30pm; free). Parts of this remain in use as local government offices while other rooms contain galleries of paintings and ornate furniture – worth visiting for the view over the square rather than any particular highlights. Across the square, the **Palazzo Re Enzo** takes name from its time as the prison-home of Enzo, King of Sicily, confined here by papal supporters for two decades after the Battle of Fossalta in 1249. Its ground floor is now the city's tourist office.

On the southern side of Piazza Maggiore, the church of **San Petronio** is the city's largest church and one of the finest Gothic brick buildings in Italy. It was originally intended to have been larger than St Peter's in Rome, but money and land for the side aisle were diverted by the pope's man in Bologna towards a new university, and the architect Antonio di Vicenzo's plans had to be modified. You can see the beginnings of the planned side aisle on the left of the building: when they stopped work they sliced through the arch of a window and left only the bottom third of the facade decorated with the intended marble geometric patterns. There are models of what the church was supposed to look like in the museum (daily 10am–noon, closed Tues & Thurs).

Notwithstanding its curtailment, San Petronio is a fine example of late fourteenth-century architecture. Above the central portal is a beautiful carving of *Madonna and Child* by visiting artist Jacopo della Quercia. Within, the side chapels contain a host of treasures, including some fifteenth-century frescoes of the *Madonna and Child* by Giovanni da Modena, and of *Heaven and Hell* by Jacopo di Paolo. The most unusual feature is the astronomical clock – a long brass meridian line set at an angle across the floor, with a hole left in the roof for the sun to shine through on the right spot.

Across Via dell'Archiginnasio from San Petronio, the **Museo Civico Archaeologico** (Tues–Sat 9am–2pm, Sun 9am–12.30pm) is a rather stuffy museum, and its labelling is as inadequate as any other in Italy. But its displays of Egyptian and Roman antiquities are good ones, and the Etruscan section, drawn from finds from the Etruscan predecessor of Bologna, Felsina, is one of the best outside Lazio. There are reliefs from tombs, vases and a bronze *situla*, richly decorated, from the fifth century BC.

Down the street, Bologna's university – the **Archiginnasio** – was founded at more or less the same time as the Piazza Maggiore was laid out, predating the rest of Europe's universities, though it didn't get a special building until 1565, when Antonio Morandi was commissioned to construct the present building on a site until then reserved for San Petronio. Centralising the university on one site was a way of maintaining control over students at a time when the church felt particularly threatened by the Reformation. You can wander freely into the main court-yard, covered with the coats of arms of its more famous graduates, and perhaps even attend a lecture – Umberto Eco lectures at Bologna on semiotics. It's also possible to visit the main upstairs **library**. But the most interesting of the old university's rooms is the **Teatro Anatomico** (Mon–Fri 9am–7.45pm), the original medical faculty dissection theatre. Tiers of seats surround an extraordinary professor's chair, covered with a canopy supported by figures known as "gli spell-ati" – "the skinned ones". Not many dissections went on, due to prohibitions of the church, but when they did (usually around carnival time), artists and the general public used to turn up as much for the social occasion as for studying the body. *

Outside the old university, **Piazza Galvani** remembers the physicist Luigi Galvani with a statue. One of Bologna's more successful scientists, Galvani discovered electrical currents in animals, thereby lending his name to the English language in the word "galvanise". A few minutes south, down Via Garibaldi, is **Piazza San Domenico**, with its strange canopied tombs holding the bones of medieval law scholars. Bologna was instrumental in sorting out wran-gles between the Pope and the Holy Roman Emperor in the tenth and eleventh centuries, earning itself the title of "La Dotta" (The Learned) and setting the basis for the university's prominent law faculties. The church of **San Domenico** (closed noon–5pm) was built in 1251 to house the relics of Saint Dominic, which were placed in the so-called *Arca di San Domenico*: a fifteenth-century work that was principally the creation of Nicola Pisano – though in reality many artists contributed to it. Pisano and his pupils were responsible for the reliefs illustrating the saint's life, the statues on top were the work of Pisano himself; Nicola dell'Arca was responsible for the canopy; and the angel and figures of saints Proculus and Petronius were the work of a very young Michelangelo.

Back up Via dell'Archiginnasio, off to the right, the **Mercato di Via Clavature** spills out into Via Pescerie Vecchie and Via Draperie, one of the city's most entic-ing sights, and positive proof of Bologna's justified reputation for food. In autumn especially the market is a visual and aural feast, with fat porcini mushrooms, truf-fles in baskets of rice, thick rolls of mortadella, hanging pheasants, ducks and hares, and skinned frogs by the kilo.

East: the University quarter

Bordered by Via Oberdan to the west and Strada Maggiore to the south, the east-ern section of Bologna's *centro storico* preserves many of the older **university** departments, housed for the most part in large seventeenth- and eighteenth-century palaces. This is perhaps the most pleasant part of the city to while away the day – or night – amid a concentration of low-budget bars, restaurants and shops aimed at the student population. It is also the place to scour to find out what's on: posters plaster the walls along Via Zamboni and the lanes off it – Via

---

* Bologna's university was, oddly enough, known for the number of women professors on its staff during the Middle Ages. Bettisia Gozzadini was the first in the thirteenth century, and others followed, not surprisingly to stiff opposition from most men: some women were obliged to wear a veil while teaching, or to lecture from behind a screen. Despite this, the explosion of interest in science at the end of the eighteenth century saw, among others, Maria Gaetana Agnesi lecturing on maths and analytical geometry, and Laura Bassi on experimental physics. Bassi was the first to invent a machine producing electricity.

Dell Moline, Via Delle Belle Arti, Via Mentana – and the bars and cafés are often promoting some happening or other.

Via Rizzoli leads into the district from Piazza Maggiore, ending up at Piazza di Porta Ravegnana, where the Torre degli Asinelli (daily 9am–7pm), next to the perilously leaning Torre Garisenda, are together known as the **Due Torri**, the remains of literally hundreds of towers that were scattered across the city during the Middle Ages. The former makes a good place from which to get an overview of the city centre and beyond, out over the red-tiled roofs across the hazy, flat plains and southern hills beyond.

Walking east from the Due Torri, Via San Stefano leads down to its medieval gateway, past a complex of four – but originally seven – churches, collectively known as **Santo Stefano**. Three of the churches face on to the piazza, of which the striking polygonal church of **San Sepolcro** (closed noon–3.30pm), reached through the church of **Crocifisso**, is about the most interesting. The basin in its courtyard is by tradition the one used by Pilate to wash his hands after he condemned Christ to death, while on the inside the bones of Saint Petronius provide a pleasingly kitsch focus, held in a tomb modelled on the church of the holy sepulchre in Jerusalem. A doorway leads from here through to **San Vitale e Agricola**, Bologna's oldest church, built from discarded Roman fragments in the fifth century; while the fourth church, the **Trinitá**, lies across the courtyard and is home to a small museum (daily 9am–noon & 3.30–6pm) containing a reliquary of Saint Petronius and a handful of dull paintings.

North of Santo Stefano, on Strada Maggiore, the Gothic church of **Santa Maria dei Servi**, is another focus for wanderings in the district, dating from 1386 and with contemporary frescoes inside. Continue north from here and you're on **Via Zamboni**, around and along which are many of the old palaces housing various parts of the university. A large number of these buildings were decorated by members of the Bolognese academies, which were prominent in Italian art after 1600. Tibaldi, better known as an architect, turned his hand to fresco in the main building, the **Palazzo Poggi** at no. 31 (Mon–Fri 9am–12.30pm). His fresco of Ulysses here was influenced by Michelangelo's Sistine Chapel and has played a part in the well-publicised row over the latter's restoration, with art historians using Tibaldi's fresco as proof that they have got Michelangelo's colours right. On the fourth floor of the building, the **Specola** or observatory draws most people here, its small **Museo di Astronomia** home to a number of eighteenth-century instruments and a frescoed map of the constellations – painted just seventy years after Galileo was imprisoned for his heretical statements about the cosmos.

A little way up Via Zamboni, obscured behind a web of corrugated iron and scaffolding in Piazza Rossini, is the church of **San Giacomo Maggiore**, a Romanesque structure, begun in 1267 and enlarged over the centuries which followed. The target here is the Bentivoglio Chapel, decorated with funds provided by one Annibale Bentivoglio to celebrate the family's victory in a local feud in 1488. Lorenzo Costa painted frescoes of the *Apocalypse*, the *Triumph of Death* and a *Madonna Enthroned* as well as the Bentivoglio family – a deceptively pious-looking lot, captured in what was a fairly innovative picture in its time for the careful characterisations of its patrons. Further frescoes by Costa, along with Francesco Francia, decorate the Oratoria di Santa Cecilia (ask the sacristan to unlock it for you); they show gory episodes from the lives of saints Cecilia and Valerian. And there's a tomb of Anton Galeazzo Bentivoglio by Quercia opposite the chapel – one of the artist's last works.

Piazza Rossini is named after the nineteenth-century composer, who studied at the **Conservatorio G.B. Martini** on the square. The library here is among the most important music libraries in Europe, with a number of original manuscripts, some of which are on display to the public along with a few paintings. Further north up Via Zamboni, around Porta San Donato, are many of the university's largest faculties, including that of the **Museo di Anatomia Umana** at Via Irnerio 48. An odd place to visit, perhaps, but it would be a shame to leave Bologna without seeing its highly idiosyncratic (and beautiful) **waxworks** (Mon–Fri 9am–noon & 3.30–7pm). These were used until the nineteenth century for medical demonstration, and they are as startling as any art or sculpture in the city. There were two Italian schools of waxworks: the Florentine method, where they used limbs, organs and bones to make moulds to cast the wax; and the Bolognese, where everything was sculpted, even tiny veins and capillaries, which were rolled like plasticene. The boundaries between "art" and "science" were not rigidly drawn, and in Bologna in the early eighteenth century the workshops of Anna Morandi Mazzolini and Ercole Lelli turned out figures that were much more than just clinical aids. Mazzolini, for example, created a self-portrait in the midst of a brain dissection, pulling back a scalp with wispy hairs attached; other figures, unnervingly displayed in glass cases, are modelled like classical statues, one carrying a sickle, the other a scythe.

Close by, the collection of paintings in the **Pinacoteca Nazionale** at Via Belle Arti 56 (Tues–Sat 9am–2pm, Sun 9am–12.30pm; L2000) may provide some light relief, concentrating mainly (though not exclusively) on the work of Bologna artists. There are canvases by the fourteenth-century local artist, Vitale da Bologna, later works by Francia and Tibaldi, and paintings from the city's most productive artistic period, the early seventeenth century, when Annibale and Agostino Carracci, Guido Reni and Guercino ("the cross-eyed") were active here. Among the gallery's sculptures, Nicolo dell'Arca's *Pietá*, moved here from the church of Santa Maria in Vita, is outstanding, its life-size figures suffused with emotion.

North and west: the Duomo, a museum and the church of San Francesco

There's much less of interest north of Bologna's central piazzas. The city's **Duomo**, on the right out of Piazza Nettuno, was originally a tenth-century building but it's been rebuilt many times amd is these days a fairly dull Baroque church. The **Museo Civico Medioevale e dal Rinascimento** (Mon & Wed–Sat 9am–2pm, Sun 9am–12.30pm; L2000), opposite, is of more interest, housed in the Renaissance Palazzo Fava, decorated with frescoes by Carracci. But its collection, recently moved here from the museum on the other side of the piazza, is no great shakes, including armour, ceramics, numerous tombs and busts of various popes and other dignitaries, and a couple of sculptures by della Quercia. West of Piazza Nettuno is very bare territory, with only the large Gothic church of **San Francesco**, just off Via G. Marconi, to tempt you.

Eating, drinking and nightlife

Eating, drinking and nightclubbing are the mainstays of Bolognese social life, and some of the *osterie* in the city combine all three, staying open well into the night. The city has also tried to curb the general August exodus by mounting a summer arts **festival**, with concerts and videos at night in the courtyards of the civic buildings. **Ferragosto**, too, is a good time to be here, when everyone takes to the hills for all-night revelry in one of the parks outside town. To find out about all of this, get hold of the fortnightly **listings** magazine, *La Mongolfiera*, which has details in Italian but is easily deciphered. *Il Bo*, might also be useful, a weekly with classified ads and some listings, covering a wide area outside Bologna.

Food: snacks, cafés and restaurants

Bologna is known "La Grassa" ("The Fat"), the result of a culinary tradition that's rich in calories rather than experimentation. The stress laid on **food** here can take an extreme form. People travel a long way to eat at the top restaurants, which are said to be the best in Italy, and even the simplest restaurants and the many *osterie* often serve food of a very high standard; certainly the lack of a menu or elaborate decor usually means the place is worth investigating.

For **breakfast**, stop off at *Impero*, Via Indipendenza 39, which does excellent croissants and pastries. At lunchtime, if you want just a **snack** try the *Buffet della Stazione* at the railway station for *tagliatelle* or the dish of the day – unbeatable prices if you eat at the counter. *Altero*, at Via Indipendenza 33 and Via Ugo Bassi 10, is the best place for pizza by the slice. *La Torinese Salata*, under the vaults of the Palazzo del Podestà, Piazza Maggiore, does quiches and stuffed vegetables. *Roberto*, Via Clavature 18, is a small bar with sandwiches or meals at lunchtime. Or there's a *rosticceria* down the street at Via Clavature 7 – you choose what you want and they heat it up; counter seating.

As for **restaurants**, pork, pasta and dairy products are some of the city's tried and tested ingredients, and it would be a pity to come to Bologna and not sample the specialities; if you search around you can have a full meal for L15–20,000. *Boni*, Via Saragozza 88, has very good Emilian cuisine, likewise *Lamma* at Via dei Giudei 4 – a popular place with a pub atmosphere. For family-style Bolognese food go to *Fantoni* at Via del Pratello 11, one of the oldest streets in the city. *Buca San Petronio*, Via Musei 4, serves more elaborate but still traditional food, close to the San Petronio church, and puts a few tables outside in summer. *C'entro*, Via Indipendenza 45, and *Bassotto*, Via Ugo Bassi 8, both open until 2am, serve quality fast food in comfortable surroundings. Way up in the expensive category is *Grassilli*, Via del Luzzo 3 – an experience to remember, though you'll need to book ahead. On a more healthy note, *Clorofilla*, Strada Maggiore 64, specialises in vegetarian cuisine, *crescente ripiena* and lots of salads; *Oggi Si Vola* at Via Urbana 7 is a macrobiotic restaurant and smoke-free zone.

Just for **drinking**, the slickest Bolognese sip their aperitifs at *Mocambo*, a tiny bar in Via d'Azeglio and there are plenty of good bars on and around Via Zamboni, in the student quarter. At *Frulé*, on Via Clavature, where it meets Piazza del Francia, they make very good *frullati*. *La Torinese*, Piazza Re Enzo, is the place for hot chocolate. For good **ice cream**, try *Gianni*, Via Montegrappa 11, off Via Indipendenza, or any of the kiosks along the city walls (March–Oct). There is also *Pino*, on Via Castiglione, the main branch of Bologna's best ice cream chain.

Shops and markets

Some of Bologna's most colourful sights are inside its many **foodstores**, particularly those between Piazza Maggiore and the Due Torri, epitomised by *Tamburini* at Via Caprarie 1, which has a sizeable array of the different ways of eating the fat of Bologna. **Markets**, too, are a feature of the city centre, two of them indoors. The **Mercato delle Erbe**, Via Ugo Bassi 2 (Mon–Sat 7.15am–1pm

& 5–7pm, closed all day Thursday & Saturday afternoon) is the biggest and liveliest, with over a hundred stalls selling edibles in general. The market at **Via Clavature** (same opening hours) runs along the same lines, and there's also an open-air market at Piazza Aldrovandi, along Strada Maggiore – a smaller affair selling food and flowers, closed Tuesday afternoon. For **supermarkets**, go to the Co-op at Via Montebello 2, behind the station – an Emilian chain that symbolises the cooperative traditions behind food production in the region. Finally, there's the open-air **La Montagnola** market, held in Piazza VII Agosto on Fridays and Saturdays, dawn until dusk, which sells just about everything, but is especially good for new and secondhand clothes.

Nightlife: *osterie* and clubs

Osterie have been the mainstay of Bolognese **nightlife** for a few hundred years – pub-like places, open late, where you go more to drink than eat, though you can get snacky (if sometimes pricey) food. *Matusel*, at Via Bertolini 2, close to the university, is a lively and noisy osteria, with reasonably priced full meals. *Orsa*, Via Mentana 1, has jazz during the winter. *Poeti*, Via Poeti 1, off Piazza Cavour, trades on its history; an old palazzo which has been an osteria since the seventeenth century. Its prices are not surprisingly inflated, but it does have occasional live music. *Biassanott*, on Via Piella, is another convivial haunt, open until 4am; *Senzanome*, Via Senzanome 42, serves good meals and has a wide choice of beers and wines. *Marione*, at Via San Felice 137 close to the city gate, is old, smoky and dark, with good wine and snacks. A further choice is *Osteria dell'Infedele*, on Via Gerusalemme, which has good economic food or is fine just for drinking.

There are also a fair number of **discos and clubs** in the city. *Cassero*, Porta Saragozza 2, inside the city gate itself, is a gay club, with a café and bookshop, open daily. *Zelig*, Via Porta Nuova 9, is a club to dress up for. In summer, there's a stage for ballroom dancing in the *Giardini Margherita*. Other places to dance are at *Kinky Club*, Galleria Due Torri 1, though here the door policy is strict – dress smart (Thurs–Sat are gay nights).

Listings

Airport enquiries ☎311.578.

American Express Piazza XX Settembre 6 (☎220.477).

Books English books from *Feltrinelli*, on Via dei Guidei.

Bus enquiries ☎235.105.

Car Hire *Avis* and *Hertz* have offices in the city but *ARICO*, Viale Pietramellara 35 (☎550.130) are half the price.

Cinema *Adriano*, Via San Felice 52, shows films in their original language.

Hospital Casualty at *Ospedale Traumatologico*, Via Boldrini 2 (☎224.965 or 247.367).

Laundry Coin-op launderettes at Via Broccandosso 5B and Via Tibaldi 21.

Pharmacy Night services rotate; look in newspaper for addresses or dial ☎192.

Police In an emergency dial ☎113. Otherwise their main office is Piazza Galileo 7 (☎278.846).

Post Office The city's main post office is on Piazza Minghetti; Mon–Fri 8.15am–7.30pm & Sat 8.15am–1pm.

Swimming pool Try the one at the sports ground (Via Costa 174), open 9.30am–7pm in summer, Sun mornings only in winter.

Taxis ☎534.141 or ☎372.727.

Telephones AAST, Piazza VIII Agosto (24hr); SIP, Via Fossalta 4/E (daily 8am–10pm).

Train enquiries ☎246.490.

Travel agent *CTS,* are at Via delle Belle Arti 20 (☎264.862). Other cheap, student-oriented agents include *Relazione Universitarie,* Via delle Moline 2/G (☎235.097), and *University Viaggi,* Via Zamboni 16E (☎228.584).

Women's Bookshop *Librellula,* Strada Maggiore 3.

On from Bologna: south to Tuscany

In the heat of the summer the need to get out of Bologna becomes pressing, and the hills which start almost as soon as you leave the city gates take you high enough to catch some cooling breezes. The most obvious destination for a short trip is the eighteenth-century **Chiesa di Madonna di San Luca**, close on 4km outside the city but connected by way of the world's longest portico, which meanders across the hillside in a series of 666 arches – a shelter for pilgrims on the trek to the top. Buses #21 or #22 drop you at the start of the route, by Porta Saragozza southwest of the centre, though you'll probably find the walk more rewarding than the church at the end.

Further out, towards Tuscany, the N325 passes through **PONTECCHIO MARCONI**, where the physicist Guglielmo Marconi lived in the late nineteenth century, and from where, in 1895, he sent the first radio message ever to his brother on the other side of the hill. Marconi lies in a specially-designed mausoleum in the village, close to the remains of the boat, Elettra, from which Marconi lit up the warship Sydney while anchored in Genova in 1930. A stop here is also a convenient time to try the *crescente ripiena* (stuffed with cheese and herbs), at SASSO MARCONI, a few kilometres down the road.

The route on from here towards Pistoia is a beautiful one, taking you above the Setta valley, past chestnut groves and small villages. It's a well-trafficked road, though, and the backroads are the greatest attraction, especially in the hills between Bologna and Modena.

MARZABOTTO, a few kilometres on from Sasso Marconi and accessible by direct bus from Bologna, is known for the massacre of 1800 people that took place here during the last war. It also sports the remains of an Etruscan town, **Misa**, just outside (Tues–Sun 8am–dusk). The site marks out the residential areas, the city gates, streets and drains, fragments of foundations from temples, and some tombs remain – evidence of a town of highly-skilled craftsmen, that was much more than just a staging-post between Etruria and the Po valley. The museum (9am–noon & 3–6.30pm) contains a variety of finds, from the remains of the piped water system, to household objects inscribed "mi venelus" ("I belong to Venel") or "mi Sualus" ("I belong to Sualu").

Modena

Though only half an hour away by train, **MODENA** has a quite distinct identity from Bologna. The "spiritual capital" of Emilia it proclaims itself, highlighting the two cities' long and sometimes intense rivalry. Really, though, Modena's claims can seem a little overstated. Like the area's other towns, it's a wealthy place, with the emphasis on food, style and good living. But it's also an unpretentious town, with a medieval centre much like any other in northern Italy.

That said, it's true that Modena does have a number of claims to fame. Pavarotti is a native of the town and gives occasional impromptu concerts in its main square; while the cathedral is considered the finest Romanesque building in the region. On a more contemporary note, its outskirts are fringed with prosperous industry: knitwear and ceramics factories make a healthy profit on the surrounding plain, and Ferrari build their prestige motor cars close by, testing the Formula 1 monsters on the racetrack at nearby Fiorino.

Practical details: arriving and finding a place to stay

Modena's centre, marked by the main Piazza Grande, is a fifteen-minute walk from the **train station** on Piazza Dante, down the wide Corso Vittorio Emanuele II. The **bus station**, for villages on the plain or in the Apennines, is at Via Bacchini, ten minutes' walk from Piazza Grande. The **EPT** is a few doors from the main square at Via Emilia Centro 179 (daily 10am–12.30pm & 3.20–6.20pm).

The most promising area for **places to stay** is between Piazza Grande and the bus station, in the narrow palace-lined streets. Modena's hotel guests are mostly business people so prices tend to be high; the few cheap hotels are often booked up for months on end by people who've come here from other areas for work. One possibility is *Centrale* at Via Rismondo 57 (☎059/ 243.248), with doubles for L39,000. The others are all much of a muchness: *Bonci*, on Via Ramazzini (☎059/ 223.634), *Sole*, Via Malatesta 45 (☎059/214.245), near the station, *La Pace*, Via Paolo Ferrari 47 (☎059/223.447), all have rooms for around L34,000. The nearest **campsite** (*International Camping Modena*; ☎059/332.252) is on Via Cave Ramo, Località Bruciata, halfway between Modena and Reggio Nell'Emilia; bus #19 takes you right there.

The Town

Modena's tight, concentric medieval centre, within the circular viale, is its most interesting section, particularly the patchwork of streets around the duomo on Piazza Grande. The town centre is bisected by the Via Emilia, which crosses the edge of Piazza Grande. Of things to see, top of most people's list are the rich collections of paintings and manuscripts built up by the Este family, who decamped here from Ferrara in 1598, after it was annexed by the Papal states, and ruled the town until the eighteenth century. But really the appeal of Modena is in wandering its labyrinthine centre, finishing up the day with some good food and spirited nightlife. Unlike most other small Emilian towns, Modena has an eclectic nightscene, and bars with live music, bigger name bands at the Palasport and alternative theatre make an overnight stop worth considering – if not, there are late trains back to Bologna.

Piazza Grande

Piazza Grande marks the centre of town, its stone buildings and arcades the focus of much of its life: schoolkids hang around outside the pizza bars, and old men meet in the afternoon for discussion along the barriers fencing off the twelfth-century **Duomo di San Geminiano**, which is sinking, along with the adjacent Torre Ghirlandina, into the pavement. The duomo's facade is sculpted with scenes from the *Jeu d'Adam*, (a medieval mystery play on the Book of Genesis), and it's most intricate parts are probably the work of the twelfth-century sculptor Wiligelmo – though the ones on the building are copies. For the originals you have to go to the **Museo Lapidario** (daily 9am–noon & 3–6pm) on Via Lanfranco. Wiligelmo's life is a mystery, but his skills are acknowledged, unusually, by the stone plaque showing his name and that of the architect, Lanfranco, on the outside of the building. Inside, the duomo is a beautifully simple Romanesque building, the choir set up high, behind a gallery and a pulpit supported on columns resting on the backs of lions and crouched figures. The sculpted details on the column capitals and around doorways are superb, sinuous work – designs so intricate that the eye can hardly follow their lines.

The **Torre Ghirlandina**, begun at the same time as the duomo but completed 200 years later, lurches to one side, and is currently closed to visitors while the work to right it takes place. Until recently it contained the *Seccia Rapita*, a wooden bucket stolen during a raid by the Modenese on Bologna in 1325, and often quoted to show the history of rivalry between the two towns. The Modenese, who supported Re Enzo (the son of the Emperor), swore enmity when the Bolognese took him prisoner after a thirteenth-century battle, liberating the bucket from Bologna until well into the next century in just one attempt to even the score. The seventeenth-century poet Tassoni wrote a mock heroic verse on the subject, which has apparently never lost its significance in people's minds, and it's still the object of occasional rag day stunts.

The Galleria and Biblioteca Estense

Modena is a nice place to do nothing in particular, but if you want some structure to your amblings, head for the **Palazzo dei Musei** (a short walk from Piazza Grande), which, formerly an arsenal, then a workhouse, now houses the city museums and art galleries. The **Biblioteca Estense** (exhibition area open Tues–Sat 10am–1pm; library Sun–Fri 9am–8pm, Sat 9am–2pm), on the first floor, is only partly open to non-students, but what is on display – letters between monarchs, Popes and despots, with great wax seals, filed away for hundreds of years – is of mild interest. And the prize treasure, Borso D'Este's bible (the *Bibbio Borso*), arguably the most decorated book in the world, is worth going through the fairly lengthy procedure of filling out forms and leaving your passport to see. Of more immediate interest is the *Mostra Permanente* (currently being reorganised) – especially the earliest world maps on parchment skins.

The **Museo del Risorgimento** (Tues–Thurs 9am–1pm & 2.30–5.30pm, Fri–Sun 9am–1pm), on the ground floor, is equally evocative. Old wooden cases filled with flags, drums, uniforms, plumed helmets, photographs and political posters, trace the early history of unified Italy from the 1831 revolutions in Modena, Parma and the Papal states, which Duke Francesco IV of Modena put down with savage reprisals, to the disturbances of 1848 and Modena's eventual pact with Piemonte, pesaging the more widespread union of Italian states. Locked away in one of the wooden cases is an impressive goose quill pen, festooned with ribbons – said to be the one used to sign the treaty of union.

Through an archway lined with Roman tombstones – Piazza Matteotti was on the site of a necropolis – a staircase leads off to the right up to the top floor and the **Galleria Estense** (Tues–Sun 9am–7.10pm; L2000,) which is made up of the picture collection of the d'Este family. It contains paintings of the local schools, from the early Renaissance through to the works of the Caraccis, Guercino and Guido Reni, sculptures in terracotta by Nicolo Dell'Arca, as well as portable altars, madonnas and triptychs by lesser-known Emilian artists like Cosimo Tura, who painted the Schifanoia Palace in Ferrara. There's also a bust of Francesco d'Este by Bernini, a portrait of the same man by Velazquez, and Venetian works by Tintoretto and Veronese.

Five minutes' walk away in an undisturbed corner of town, off Via N. Sauro, is another museum, the **Museo Muratoriano** (daily 9am–noon). This contains possessions and works of Ludovico Antonio Muratori, the Jesuit priest, historiographer and intellectual whose ideas helped break the monopoly of the church over education in the eighteenth century.

Eating, drinking and nightlife

Of specific **places to eat**, the *Ristorante Pizzeria Santa Lucia*, Via Taglio 61, and *Trattoria Aldini*, Via Albinelli 40, are both standard restaurants, and there's a cheap *mensa* at the *Centro Sociale S Geminiano*, Via San Geminiano 3 (Sept–July, Mon–Sat 11.50am–12.30pm and 7–9pm). *Fini* on Largo San Francesco has more choice but is pricey; or there's a Chinese restaurant – *Asia*, Via Falloppia 25 – that's normally good value. For picnic food, try *Giusti* in Via Farini, a delicatessen since the seventeenth century.

Wherever you eat, try if you can to sample some of Modena's rather odd, pork-based specialities: *ciccioli* are flaky pork scratchings laid out in bars in the evening; *zampone* shanks of pork, trotter included, boned and stuffed with minced meat. Several hours of simmering softens the rind enough for it to be eaten along with the filling. *Cotechino* is the same kind of thing but stuffed inside an animal bladder.

As for **nightlife**, live **bands** sometimes play at *Wienna* and *Floride*, both on Via Camatta. The *News* **video bar** at Corso Canal Chiaro 26 (go through the brown door and ring bell on right) is a friendly place. And, for women only, there's a **women's centre** (*Casa delle Donne*) at Via dell Gambero 76 (bus #7 out of town towards the *Policlinico*), which has a bar open on Mondays and Fridays, 8–11pm. There's also the large *Palasport*, which hosts visiting British and American bands – tickets from *Fangareggi*, the record shop at Corso Canal Chiaro 3. It's about the only venue of this size in the whole region and you see posters for it as far away as Ferrara and Piacenza.

Around Modena

At first glance the countryside **around Modena** looks bland and uninviting – discount furniture and lighting stores, crumbling farmhouses the size of mansions, and factories. Further north onto the plain, wide vistas of maize fields, rows of pollarded fruit trees, vines strung up from pergolas are broken only occasionally by a line of poplar trees shimmering in the heat.

Its towns, too, are dull and industrial, though you might want to venture out to visit **CARPI**, the region's main centre. The town's central **Piazza dei Martiri** is an enormous and impressive open space, almost worth the trip alone, and the sixteenth-century **Castello del Pio**, a mass of ornamental turrets and towers, holds an interesting museum inside – the **Museo al Deportato**. Occupying forces in World War II held prisoners at a camp in Fossoli 6km to the north, before deporting them to Germany – the camp sheds still stand, dilapidated, in a field – and the museum has displays on the camps and the conditions for the prisoners, neatly putting them into context with information on political and racial exile. The rest of Carpi is unexciting so it's unlikely that you'll want to hang around town. There are trains and buses every hour back to Modena, but if you do want to stay there are cheap **rooms** to be had at *Albergo da Georgio* on Via G. Rocca (☎0531/685.365).

South of Modena

To the **south of Modena** lie the foothills of the Apennines, covered by turkey oak, hornbeam and hazel woods. Narrow roads corkscrew into the mountains, crossing into Tuscany through the Foce delle Radici or at Abetone. From these high passes you can climb by foot onto the *crinale* – the backbone of the Apennine range. Trails lead along the succession of peaks above the treeline, steep slopes on either side, to some glacial lakes, though the routes are most impressive for the views they give across the breadth of Italy on either side.

For many, the main attraction of the small villages in the foothills is **food**. The tourist office can advise you on "gourmet itineraries" to find the real Modenese cuisine, but they're not really necessary: restaurant signs by the side of the road invite you in to try cuisine *"alla tua nonna"* – "like grandma used to make": mortadella, salami or *crescente* (a kind of pitta bread eaten with a mixture of dripping, garlic, rosemary and parmesan). Variations on the same theme include *gnocco fritto* – fried dough diamonds eaten with salami or ham. Higher in the mountains you can still find *ciacci* – chestnut flour pancakes, filled with ricotta and sugar – and walnuts (which should be picked on or around the night of San Giovanni, June 24) that go to make *nocino* liqueur.

But after a while the food becomes a diversion from the scenery, which can be magnificent. It's hard to recommend anywhere in particular to head for. The area is one of small inaccessible villages, and specific tourist targets are very few. Closest to Modena and connected by regular bus, the pastures and cherry orchards around **VIGNOLA** are a possible destination, the venue for a spring festival during April. The castle here is particularly well-preserved, one of many built to defend the crossings along the River Panaro, into the neighbouring state of Bologna. Further out from Modena, the tiny village of **SAN PELLEGRINO IN ALPE**, also connected by bus, has a museum of peasant life that gives the lowdown on the former customs and lifestyle hereabouts.

The area was also a focus for some intense partisan activity during the last war, its mountain farms and haylofts making ideal hideouts. Sabotage of transport and communication links, or harbouring prisoners of war was punishable by death, and the many people shot in reprisals are remembered in the **Museo della Repubblica** in the twelfth-century fortress at **MONTEFIORINO** – seat of the short-lived partisan republic in the summer of 1944. Buses take just under two hours from Modena to the village, which sits on a spur of rock over the rivers Dol and Dragone.

If you're driving, the route over the mountains from Modena to Pisa is a good one, taking the N12 road towards the small resorts around **Monte Cimone** – the highest mountain in the chain, though also one of the most commercialised, spiked with ski-lifts. Further west, places like **Lago di Ninfa**, on the turnoff between Pian del Falco and Passo del Lupo, also tend to be overcrowded at weekends, but it's worth coming at other times, or striking out across the slopes of **Monte Giovo** a few kilometres away. Buses from Modena run to both

PIEVEPELAGO and **SESTOLA**, the area's two main centres – villages which also give access to **Lago Santo** and the small, reed-fringed **Lago Baccio**, high up the mountain at 1554m. You can easily escape the crowds by getting yourself a decent map and following the footpaths. Path #000 weaves around the 1500m mark from Passo delle Radici to Abetone, Passo di Croce d'Arcana, and, a few kilometres further on, **Lago Scaffaiolo**. Path #401 follows the crest down towards FANANO (buses back to Modena) to **Lago Pratignano** – a shallow lake covered with floating plants, in the middle of woods and meadows.

Reggio Emilia

Continuing north up the Via Emilia from Modena, **REGGIO EMILIA** is a quite different place from Modena, a quiet ancient town that makes a good place to rest up for a while. It's admittedly sparse on sights, but it's a pleasant town to wander through and is a feasible jumping-off point for travelling into the Reggiano Apennines.

Some practical details

Reggio is on the main railway line between Bologna and Milan. The **train station** is on Piazza Marconi I, the **bus station** on Via Raimondo Franchetti. The **EPT** (daily 9.30am–12.30pm & 3.30–6pm), is in the main Piazza Prampolini, and there's usually no problem finding a **place to stay**: the *Cairoli* at Piazza XXV Aprile 2 (☎0522/32.307) has doubles for L29,000, and *Ariosto* on Via San Rocco 12 (☎0522/37.320) has doubles with bath for L46,000. Both are within easy walking distance of the centre. It's worth a special journey here just to **eat** at the *Scudo d'Italia* restaurant (closed Sat & Sun), a locally renowned hotel and eatery where you can eat superbly for relatively little. The dark purple *Lambrusco* they serve here is bottled specially by a local *azienda* – worth trying and totally different from the carbonated affair you might be used to. Other places to eat in town are a restaurant specialising in seafood and vegetable dishes on Via Broletto, and *Condor*, at the lower end of Via Spallanzani, which is a good, noisy place to eat pizza. If you're broke, there's a *mensa* a few steps away at *Gioberti*, in the piazza of the same name (noon–2.40pm & 6.30–8.30pm).

The Town

Reggio is built around two central squares, **Piazza Prampolini** and **Piazza San Prospero**, separated by the **Duomo**, and the **Palazzo del Municipio** with its fishtail battlements. Like other towns in the area, the centre is closed to traffic, and bicycles clatter across the cobbles from all directions. Piazza San Prospero comes alive on market days (Tues & Fri), its stalls and the shops selling a staggering array of fruit, veg, salami and cheese, including the local *parmigiano-reggiano*. Around the square, the buildings squeeze up so close to the church of **San Prospero** that they seem to have pushed it off balance and it now lurches to one side. Built in the sixteenth century, its facade is decorated with columns and statues in niches, guarded by six lions in rose-coloured Verona marble – a marked contrast to the unclad octagonal campanile next to it. Via Broletto leads through into **Piazza Prampolini**, skirting the side of the **Duomo**, swathed in green nets and scaffolding while it's being restored. Underneath the marble tacked on in the sixteenth century, it's possible to see the church's Romanesque facade, with statues of Adam and Eve over the medieval portal, although all else that remains of the original building is the apse and enormous crypt. Inside there's a painting of the *Assumption* by Guercino and many tombs, including one for the inventor of the hour glass, Cherubino Sforzani.

At right angles to the Duomo is the sugar-pink **Palazzo del Capitano del Popolo**. The tricolour was proclaimed here as the official national flag of Italy, when Napoleon's Cispadane Republic was formed in 1797. Walking north from here, the **Musei Civici** along Via Spallanzani, on the edge of Piazza della Vittoria, are made up of an eighteenth-century private collection of archaeological finds, fossils and paintings (Mon–Fri 9.30am–12.30pm). In the corner of the square, the **Galleria Parmeggiani** might also be worth a look if it hadn't been closed for the past ten years; there's nothing to suggest it will open soon, but check anyway. It's reputed to contain an important collection of Spanish, Flemish and Italian art as well as costumes and textiles. Assuming it's closed, stroll over to the church of **Madonna della Ghiara**, built in the seventeenth century and decorated with Bolognese School frescoes of scenes from the Old Testament and a *Crucifixion* scene by Guercino.

South of Reggio

The foothills **south of Reggio** are cheese country: you'll see many signs for along the roadside advertising the local *parmigiano-reggiano*, and the village of **CASINA**, about 20km outside reggio on the N63 to La Spezia, holds a popular *Festa Parmigiana* in August, when the vats of cheese mixture are stirred with enormous wooden paddles. The countryside itself is a mixture of lush pastures and scraggy uplands, with some footpaths around, though there's better walking higher up in the mountains.

If you've got your own transport or are prepared to wait a long time for a lift, take the side road leading from Casina to **CANOSSA**. This was the seat of the powerful Da Canossa family, whose most famous member, the Countess Mathilda of Tuscany (*La Gran Contessa*), was a big name here in the eleventh century – unusually so in a society largely controlled by war lords and the clergy. She was known for donning armour and leading her troops into battle herself, and at the age of 43 scandalised the nobility by marrying a youth of seventeen. During the battles between Pope Gregory VII and the Holy Roman Emperor Henry IV, she supported the pope, and helped draw the emperor here barefoot as a penitent to apologise to the pontiff following his excommunication. Henry was apparently left waiting outside in the snow for three days before the castle doors were opened. The remains of the castle (April–Sept Tues–Sun 9am–12.30pm & 3–7pm, Oct–March Tues–Sun 2.30–5pm; L1000) are largely thirteenth-century, but it's the location – on a rocky outcrop looking towards the mountains in one direction and over the neighbouring castle at Rossena, and the towns strung out over the plain in the other – which is impressive.

People from the towns around are fond of coming out here at weekends to eat in the local restaurants, and its a popular area for hiking or cross-country and downhill skiing. In autumn, you see them armed with plastic bags for collecting mushrooms, or filling mineral water bottles with water from the springs off the mountains. There are few specific centres to aim for, though, and you're most likely to travel along these valleys if you're driving across the Apennines to the coast. Two buses a day do the whole journey and more go part of the way – though it's not a trip to do if you're in a hurry. The road is tortuous and the viewpoint constantly changes as you switchback your way across the mountain ridges or through small villages with austere, high-walled houses backing directly onto the roadside. The best times to come are late spring and early summer – in autumn it's foggy more often than not – the fog and low cloud clearing only momentarily for a quick glimpse of chestnut grove or scree-filled riverbed hundreds of feet below.

High in the hills paths lead onto the mountain *crinale*. **CASTELNOVO NEMONTI** in the foothills is a possible base for these. Further on, at **BUSANA**, the road forks to the left, descending through a series of hairpin bends bordered by plenty of falling rock signs, in the Secchia Valley, climbing back up the other side through CINQUECERRI to **LIGONCHIO** – another good starting point for walks away from cable cars and ski lifts, onto nearby **Monte Cusna**. Close by here are the *Prati di Sara*, a windswept expanse of grassland with small tarns and the occasional tree. As you ascend, you have more of a view across the layers of ridges, often half-obscured in the mist. It's possible to stay overnight in some of the refuges which group along the GEA route (*Grand Escursione Apenninica*), a 25-day trek which weaves its way in and out of the border between Emilia and Tuscany. If this seems too much, the *Club Alpino Italiano* office (☎0522/36.685) in Reggio at Corso Garibaldi 14 sometimes organises weekend treks.

Parma

Generally reckoned to have the highest standard of living in Italy, **PARMA** is about as comfortable a town as you could wish for. The measured pace of its streets, the abundance of its restaurants and the general air of provincial afflu- ence are almost cloyingly pleasant, especially if you've arrived from the South. Not surprisingly, if you're travelling on a tight budget, Parma presents a few diffi- culties – the cheap hotels are usually full, and, although the restaurants are excel- lent, food too can cost a bomb. That said, it's a friendly enough place with plenty to see. A visit to the opera can be an experience – the audience are considered one of the toughest outside La Scala, and don't pull any punches if they consider a singer to be performing badly. And the city's works of art include the legacy of two key Renaissance artists – Correggio and Parmigianino.

Arrival and finding somewhere to stay

Parma's **train station** is fifteen minutes' walk from the central Piazza Garibaldi; or take bus #1, #8, #9 or #12. The local **bus station** is next to the river, at the junction of Viale IV Novembre and Viale P. Toschi. The **EPT** is on Piazza Duomo (Mon–Fri 9am–12.30pm & 3–6pm, Sat 9am–12.30pm). Finding a **place to stay** can be tricky. The *IYHF* **Ostello Cittadella** on Via Passo Buole (☎0521/581.546; open April–Oct) charges around L9000 and is open for registration all day, but the dormitories are locked from 10am to 5pm; curfew 11pm, and no breakfast. Take bus #2 (8pm–midnight night bus E). As for **hotels**, there are several places around Piazza Garibaldi; or you many have more luck on the University side of the river (bus #3 from Piazza Garibaldi). *Concari* at Piazzale Santa Croce 9 (☎0521/295.865) is a possibility, with doubles for L27,000, and there there are others along Via Gramsci, the main road out of town. Try *Amorini* at no. 37, (☎0521/93.239), doubles L32,000, or *Il Sole* at no. 15 (☎0521/995.107) – doubles

PARMA

L26,000. Closer to the centre are two more choices: *Farini*, Via Salina 3 (☎0521/344.40) and *Fontana* on Piazza Le Carbone 1 (☎0521-282.563) – both with rooms for L25,000–L31,000. If you want to stay near the station, *Brozzi,* Via Trento 11 (☎0521/771.157) is the least grim choice – doubles for L28,500.

The Town

Piazza Garibaldi is the fulcrum of Parma, its packed-out cafés, along with the narrow streets and alleyways which wind south and west of the piazza, home to much of the town's nightlife. The mustard-coloured **Palazzo del Governatore** flanks the square, behind which the Renaissance church of the **Madonna della Steccata** was built, apparently, using Bramante's original plan for Saint Peter's as a model. Inside there are frescoes by a number of sixteenth-century painters, notably Parmigianino, who spent the last ten years of his life on this work, eventually being sacked for breach of contract by the disgruntled church authorities. A year later he was dead, aged 37, "an almost savage or wild man" who had become obsessed with alchemy, according to Vasari.

Five minutes' walk away – left off Strada Garibaldi – **Piazza Duomo** forms part of the old *centro episcopale*, away from the shopping streets of the commercial centre. The beautiful Lombard-Romanesque **Duomo** (closed noon–3pm), dating from the eleventh century, holds earlier work by Parmigianino in its south transept, painted when the artist was a pupil of Correggio – who painted the fresco of the *Assumption* in the central cupola. Finished in 1534, this is among the most famous of Correggio's works, the Virgin Mary floating up through a sea of limbs, faces and swirling drapery that attracted some bemused comments at the time. One contemporary compared it to a "hash of frogs' legs", while Dickens, visiting much later, thought it a sight "no operative surgeon gone mad, could imagine in his wildest delirium". Correggio was paid for the painting with a sackful of small change to annoy him, since he was known to be a great miser. The story goes that he carried the sack of coins home in the heat, caught a fever and died at the age of 40.

There's more work by Correggio in the cupola of the church of **San Giovanni Evangelista** behind the Duomo – a fresco of the *Vision of St John* at Patmos. And the **Camera di San Paolo** in the former Benedictine Convent off Via Melloni, a few minutes' walk north, was frescoed by Correggio in 1518, the artist portraying the abbess who commissioned the work as the Goddess Diana, above the fireplace.

But your attention is more likely to be drawn to the duomo's octagonal **Baptistery** (daily 9am–1.20pm & 3–7pm; L3000), its rose-coloured Verona marble facing, four storeys high, encircled by a band of sculpture and topped off by some slim turrets. The three elaborately carved portals are often a meeting place in the evening. Bridging the gap between the Romanesque and Gothic styles, this is considered Benedetto Antelami's finest work, built in 1196. Antelami sculpted the frieze which surrounds the building, and was also responsible for the reliefs inside, including a series of fourteen statues representing the months and seasons. Take the spiral staircase to the top for a closer view of the frescoes on the rib-vaulted ceiling – by an unknown thirteenth-century artist. The interior is being painstakingly scrubbed down and restored, and although this is due to finish soon you may find the baptistery closed during some parts of the process.

Walking east from the cathedral square, the **Museo Glauco-Lombardi** at Via Garibaldi 15 (Tues–Sat 9.30–noon & 4–6pm; 3–5pm winter. Sun 9.30am–1pm;

L2000), recalls later times, with a display of memorabilia relating to Marie-Louise of Austria, who reigned here after the defeat of her husband Napoleon at Waterloo, setting herself up here with another suitor (much to the chagrin of her exiled spouse) and expanding the Parma violet perfume industry.

Just across Piazza Marconi from here, it's hard to miss Parma's biggest monument, the **Palazzo della Pilotta**, surrounded by the wide open spaces of its carpark. Begun for Alessandro Farnese in the sixteenth century, World War II bombing reduced this building to a shell, though it's since been rebuilt and now houses a number of Parma's museums. As Paul III, Alessandro Farnese was one of the wiliest Renaissance popes, during his term annexing Parma and Piacenza to the Papal States for his dissolute son, Pierluigi. The palace was built for Pierluigi, but before long he was assassinated and the building left unfinished.

Inside is Parma's main art gallery, the **Galleria Nazionale** (Tues–Sun 9am–7.30pm; L5000, includes entry to Teatro Farnese), a modern, hi-tech display that includes more work by Correggio and Parmigianino, and the remarkable *Apostles at the Sepulchre* and *Funeral of the Virgin* by Caracci – massive canvasses suspended either side of a gantry at the top of the building that overwhelm by their sheer scale. The **Teatro Farnese**, which you pass through to get to the gallery, in the former arms room of the palace, was almost entirely destroyed by bombing in 1944 and has been virtually rebuilt since then. An extended semi-circle of seats three tiers high, made completely of wood, it's a copy of Palladio's *Teatro Olympico* at Vicenza, and as well as being (temporarily) the biggest theatre of its kind, sported Italy's first revolving stage.

Up a floor, the **Museo Nazionale di Antichita** (Tues–Sat 9am–2pm, Sun 9am–1pm; L2000), is less essential a stop but still worth a glance, with finds from the Etruscan city of Velleia and the prehistoric lake villages around Parma, as well as the table top on which the Emperor Trajan notched up a record of his gifts to the poor.

Across the river from the Palazzo della Pilotta, the **Parco Ducale** is a set of formal gardens laid out in the eighteenth century around a sixteenth-century palace built for Ottaviano Farnese. Just south, the **Casa di Toscanini** on Borgo R. Tanzi (daily 8.30am–noon plus Wed & Sat 3–6pm), is just one of a number of sights that recall Parma's strong musical pedigree, the birthplace of the composer who debuted in the *Teatro Regio* here. Further south still, on the same side of the river, the embalmed body of the violinist Niccolo Paganini rests under a canopy in the **Villetta cemetery**.

Eating, drinking, nightlife ... and some musical sights

Parma is not well-known for its nightlife, and the locals tend to prefer long sessions in the various (excellent) **restaurants**, or else dress up and head for the theatre or opera. For local cooking, *Ristorante Aurora* is worth searching for, down the tiny Vicolo Sant'Alessandro. Try also *Café Escandalo* at Via della Repubblica 86; opera *apassionati* eat at *Cannon d'Oro*, Via N. Sauro 3 – expensive but entertaining. More cheaply, on the other side of the Ponte di Mezzo, along Via Massimo d'Aseglio, there are plenty of pizza bars and a student *mensa* on Vicolo Grossardi.

Viale Basetti, next to the river, is the home of one of the top **theatre** companies in Europe, the *Colletivo di Parma*, who perform between October and June at the *Teatro Due*, Viale Basetti 12a (☎0521/208.088), and whose shows draw on a tradition of comedy and political theatre – Dario Fo was a founder member. **Opera**, too, is big in Parma, the *Teatro Regio*, on Via Garibaldi, (☎0521/795.690) renowned for its discerning audiences. It's not unknown for supporters of one singer to gather in cliques during the opera, and discuss his or her virtues with supporters of a rival.

South of Parma

The countryside **around Parma** is a strange mixture: some of the major roads follow bleak gorges, skirting the edge of blank rock walls for miles; others, looking for all the world as if they lead nowhere, emerge into open meadows and orchards, rich farmland stretching far into the distance.

The famous Parma ham (*Prosciutto di Langhirano* and eaten with just butter) comes from the foothills around **LANGHIRANO**, linked by bus with Parma. Tourist brochures say the ham cures so successfully here because of the unique mixture of clear mountain air and sea breezes blowing over the Apennines from Liguria. The town itself has grown into a mass of stainless steel warehouses – there's nothing of interest unless you want to carry a haunch of meat round with you for the rest of your holiday. But the countryside around, particularly near Calestano, is beautiful.

More of a target are any of the **medieval castles** strung out across the foothills. **TORRECHIARA**, also connected with Parma by bus, has a fifteenth-century castle that holds a superb vantage point over the surrounding area. There are frescoes by Bembo in the *Camera d'Oro* (summer Tues–Sat 9am–1pm & 3–6.30pm; winter Tues–Sat 9am–1pm & 2–4pm).

Apart from the rail route, the fast way over the mountains is by **autostrada**, the A15, which snakes its way in and out of a succession of tunnels, giving quick glimpses of lush, hidden valleys, vines and orchards. Women risk life and limb by climbing over the barriers to sell mushrooms on the hard shoulder: they tie plastic bags to the trees, which fill with air and act like crazy dirigible balloons, so you can see them from a distance. Even so, lots of drivers don't, and sail across the three lanes at the last minute, screeching to a halt to inspect the latest fruits.

The slower N62 gives access to the *crinale* of the mountains: the trails are a popular magnet for walkers these days but served a quite different purpose in the last war, when adults and children made the long journey by foot, carrying sacks of salt from the coast to trade for food. The writer Eric Newby was hidden by villagers in these mountains as an escaped prisoner of war in 1943, and his book *Love and War in the Apennines*, chronicling his experiences, best describes the beauty of the region and its stupendous views across the full width of Italy.

CORNIGLIO, reached by bus from Parma, is a centre for hiking or skiing, and there are places to stay in most villages nearby – in Bosco di Corniglio, 10km away, try the *Ghirardini* (☎0521/88.923). More buses squeeze themselves round the tight bends to the small villages of Monchio (11km) Trefiumi (16km) and Prato Spilla (23km from Corniglio), leaving you on the lower slopes of **Monte Malpasso** – glistening with small lakes and tarns.

Take a bus from Corniglio for **LAGDEI**, 14km away, from where a mulepath leads up to Lago Santo – a 45-minute walk; the ski-lift to the same works sporadically. There are **mountain refuges** for overnight stops at Lagdei (☎0521/88.936) and near the summit of Monte Orsaro, is *Rifugio Mariotti* (☎0521/282.344). For more demanding trekking, join the GEA route at RIGOSO (5km from the trail), connected with Parma by three or four buses a day.

Parma to Piacenza

The Via Emilia continues west from Parma, small towns mushrooming out from the edges of the road, but mostly it's just a ribbon of shops and roadside cafés. **FIDENZA**, the first place of any size, has a Lombard-Romanesque cathedral with a richly decorated facade worked on by followers of the Parma master, Antelami. An ancient Roman settlement originally, it was known for centuries as Borgo San Donnino until Mussolini resurrected a modern Italian version of its old Roman name in 1927.

The countryside **to the north** of here is the *bassa*, (the flat, low country where Bertolucci filmed *1900*), cut by drainage ditches and open fields growing wheat and corn, sugar beet and vines. In summer it's scorching hot and almost silent, with an odd, still beauty all of its own, but generally it's seen as a place to pass through on your way to somewhere else. The small towns and villages of the region are quiet and mainly undistinguished. **SORAGNA** is a good place to be on the second Sunday in May, for its *Giostra dei Nasi* ("Festival of the Noses"). The village of **FONTANELLATO**, a few kilometres northeast of Fidenza, was the site of the camp where Eric Newby was imprisoned. Its central square is dominated by the **Rocca San Vitale** (summer Tues–Sun 10am–12.30pm & 3.30–7pm; winter Tues–Sun 9.30am–12.30pm & 3–6pm; L2000), a fifteenth-century moated castle that the Sanvitale family called home until the onset of the last war. Inside there are some ancient pieces of furniture and a fresco by Parmigianino. Further north, **BUSSETO** was the home of Guiseppe Verdi, an appealing little battlemented town that holds few mementoes of the nineteenth-century composer in its **Museo Civico**. There's more Verdi memorabilia in the nearby village of **LE RONCOLE**, where a veritable industry has grown up around the composer's birthplace, with regular opera performances during summer. And Verdi's **villa**, a couple of kilometres outside Busseto at **SANT'AGATAN DI VILLANOVA** is open for guided tours (May–Oct 9.30am–noon & 3–7pm), which include a mock-up of the Milan hotel room where he died.

South of the Via Emilia, there's the same emphasis on food and festivals in the villages as in other parts of the province: local festivals are common, cheese, bilberries, or chestnuts and mushrooms among the themes, and the whole village will turn out for a big party. One *festa* worth travelling for is the *Rodeo del Maiale* (pigs) at **NOCETO** – usually held on the second Sunday in July but check at the Parma tourist office.

With your own transport, the area is well worth dawdling through, though you can easily reach the town of **SALSOMAGGIORE TERME**, 9km from Fidenza, by bus. It's a major local spa town, popular in the region with people anxious to detoxify their systems with its sulphurous springs. The domed *piscina thermale* on Via Valentini (☎0524/79.495) is a relaxed way to join in. Or you can go for the full treatment either at the fabulous art nouveau *Terme Berzieri* (open to the general public in summer) in the town centre, or the more business-like *Terme Zoja*. Some of the grander hotels do treatments too. There are **places to stay**, though it's unlikely you'll want to – the place is unsurprisingly sedate; if you do, the **AAST** at Viale Romagnosi 7, off Piazza del Popolo, will have details.

Striking deeper into the hills, **CASTELL ARQUATO** is a small town with a beautiful medieval piazza, set on a hillside overlooking the Arda Valley. The road continues south from here, through LUGAGNANO, following the line of the river Arda through gentle hills to **BARDI**, overshadowed by its eleventh-century castle on an outcrop of rock (daily June–Sept, restricted openings outside these times; 1 daily bus from Parma).

A side turning from Lugagnano into steeper, narrower lanes takes you to **VELLEIA**, 5km west of RUSTIGAZZO (4 buses a day from Piacenza), where there are the remains of a provincial Roman town, excavated in the eighteenth century. Velleia was the capital of a vast mountainous area inhabited in the first five centuries AD, and named after the Ligurian tribe attracted here by the salt springs in the area. The road continues south through woods of beech to the belt of mountains – the *Apennino Piacentino* – which stretch from BOBBIO down to BORGO.

Just over an hour by bus from Piacenza, is the small town of **BOBBIO**, formerly the mountain refuge of Saint Columbus where he lived until his death. His tomb is in the abbey which he founded in the seventh century, and which has been altered many times since. Pilgrims came here to pay their respects on their way to Rome – the trail came up from VARZI in Lombardy to PASSO DEL PENICE and then down to BOBBIO. There are some interesting hiking trails north of the Passo del Penice – Monte Penice itself is graced by a large transmitter for RAI-TV and is quite touristy. The two maps published by the EPT in Bologna, covering the *Apennino Piacentino – Dal Passo del Mercatello al Passo dello Zovallo* mark trails, gradients and refuges.

Piacenza

PIACENZA marks the end of the Via Emilia, and the border with Lombardy. It's a small, unassuming city, its attractions often passed over in favour of Parma or Modena (or Cremona in Lombardy, see Chapter Three), and despite a small industrial district across the Po, there's a definite feeling of grass growing between the tracks. Travellers are scarce enough to earn a few stares as they cross the main Piazza Cavalli, especially if it happens to be during the dead hours of lunchtime. Most people come to eat, to look at the famous *Fegato di Piacenza* – a bronze Etruscan liver used as a key for divining the future – and then move right on.

Sadly, the one thing you can't see for the moment is the liver: the **Museo Civico**, where it is kept, has been under restoration for the last ten years and it's uncertain when it will reopen. Should it be accessible by the time you read this, the *fegato* is a sheep's liver, and the markings on it are the names of Etruscan deities. The museum also holds a handful of paintings, including work by Botticelli and Mattia Preti, plus various medieval arms and the like.

On **Piazza Cavalli**, the centre of town, there are two more famous works in bronze – a pair of equestrian statues that are often quoted as being among the finest examples of Baroque sculpture. Cast in the early part of the seventeenth century by Francesco Mochi, a pupil of Giambologna, they're impressive works certainly, convincingly poised for action. One of the riders is Alessandro Farnese, a mercenary for Philip II of Spain, the other his son Ranuccio I. Behind the riders, **Il Gotico**, the Palazzo de Comune, is a fine redbrick palace, built in 1280 and an elegant example of Lombard-Gothic architecture – ornate and topped by fishtail battlements. The church of **San Francesco**, also on the square, dates from the same period, with an imposing Gothic interior.

The streets around Piazza dei Cavalli are quiet and mainly residential, scattered with Renaissance and Romanesque churches. The **Duomo**, in a quiet corner of town at the end of Via XX Settembre, has been altered many times since it was built between 1122 and 1233, but it's a grand Lombard-Romanesque church at heart, and has a cupola decorated with frescoes by Guercino. Close by, on Via Scalabrini, the church of **San Antonio** is known as "I Paradiso" for the twelfth-century bas-reliefs on its portal. A couple of minutes from here, the **Galleria Ricci-Oddi** has a collection of nineteenth-century Italian art.

Practical details

Piacenza is considered the gateway to Emilian cooking for people coming from Piemonte and Lombardy, but the best **places to eat** are expensive. If money's tight, there's a *mensa* on Via Vescovado (noon–2.30pm & 7–9.30pm); if it's not, try *Ginetto*, whose menu of Piacentine specialities doesn't come cheap but is well worth the splurge. For **sleeping**, there's a cluster of reasonably-priced hotels opposite the **railway station** on Piazzale Marconi. *Rangoni* at no. 1 (☎0523/21.778) is the most comfortable, with doubles at L26,750; *Datwi* (☎0523/20.823) across the square, and *Moderno* (☎0523/29.296) around the corner at Via Tibiui 29–31, are in the same price bracket. The **EPT** is five minutes' walk from here on Piazzetta dei Mercanti, next to Piazza dei Cavall (daily 9am–12.30pm & 4–6pm, closed Mon, Thurs, Sat afternoons).

The Via Emilia to Rimini

East of Bologna, the Via Emilia takes in much less of interest than it does on its way west, passing through a clutch of small towns – some of them, like Forli, industrialised and mostly post-war, others, like Faenza, with medieval piazzas surrounded by towers and embattlements. Each started life as Roman way-stations, and were under the rule of the Papal States for much of their subsequent history. The lowlands to the north are farmed intensively, and were the heart of the co-operative movement which spawned the now Communist local administration. On the southern side lie hilly vineyards and pastures, and narrow gorges that lead up into the mountains and a couple of ski resorts around Monte Fumaiolo (1407m).

Ímola and Dozza

About 30km out of Bologna, **ÍMOLA** might be worth a short stop if you're heading east, well-known as a centre for machinery and ceramic ware, and for the San Marino Grand Prix, which weaves its way through the streets of the town. It's a pleasant place, with a thirteenth-century castle and some grey-walled Renaissance palaces, but there is nothing extraordinary about it. A big new civic centre and art gallery are currently being built, until which time you can view the city's various art and historical collections in the **Palazzo dei Musei** at Via Emilia 80 – though it's only open on the first and third Sunday of each month (10am–noon). If you're lucky enough to get in, the reward is an extensive display of rare plants and beetles, and a small art gallery holding work by local fifteenth- to eighteenth-century artists. If you're not, the lively *Osteria Cerchi* is a good place to eat.

Back towards Bologna but easiest to reach by bus from Imola, the village of **DOZZA**, set on a hill surrounded by vineyards, is a popular place for a Sunday afternoon outing, with hordes of people descending for the kitsch murals on the outside of the houses, created during the *Biennale del muro dipinto*, held every

other year during the first two weeks of September (the last was in 1989). The
village also has an annual *Sagra dell'Albana*, in honour of the fragrant white wine
produced locally, and you can taste the local product at any time of year in an
enoteca housed in the castle. There's a wine museum there too.

Faenza

FAENZA, 16km east of Imola, gives its name to the faience-ware it has been
producing for the last 500 years. This style of decorated ceramic ware reached its
zenith in the fifteenth and sixteenth centuries and the town is worth a visit for the
vast **Museo delle Ceramiche** alone (summer Tues–Sat 9.30am–1pm & 3.30–
6.30pm, winter Tues–Sat 2.30–5.30pm, Sun 9am–1pm). The museum is on Viale
Baccarini – take Corso D. Baccarini from the station, and it's on the left. Its
massive collection includes early work painted in the characteristic blue and
ochre, and later more colourful work, often incorporating portraits and landscapes. There's a section devoted to ceramics from other parts of the world, too,
including ceramic art by Picasso, Matisse and Chagall.

Faenza is still home to one of Italy's leading ceramics schools, teaching techniques of tin-glazing first introduced in the fourteenth century – the ceramics are
decorated after glazing, and are given a final lead-based, lustrous, wash. The town
is also a major production centre, with small workshops down most of its side
streets; the two **Pro Loco** offices in Piazza del Popolo have details of where to buy.

The rest of Faenza is fairly ordinary, although the town's medieval centre is
appealing enough. The long, crenellated, **Palazzo del Podesta** and the **Piazza
del Popolo** together make up Faenza's medieval heart, linked to **Piazza Martiri
di Libertà**, the main marketplace, through an archway. There's a market here on
Tuesday, Thursday and Saturday mornings, when the trattorias that surround are
packed out with people. If you want to **eat**, try *Al Moro* or the *Osteria del Mercato* –
both good, lively places used by the locals. The former also has accommodation.
Another good time to be here is for the *Palio del Niballo* (jousting and flag twirling), which takes place here on the last two Sundays in July. If you want to **stay** in
Faenza, one of the best central, cheap hotels is the *Albergo Torricelli*, next to the
railway station in Piazzale Cesare Battisti 7 (☎0546/22.287) – rooms at L30,000.

Forlì

FORLÌ, administrative capital of the Romagna, is a mainly modern town with
office blocks and dual carriageways around the centre, but the heart of the town is
closed to traffic, and is an interesting, if low-key place to visit. Benito Mussolini,
who was born a few miles away at Predappio, was editor of the Forlì newspaper
and spokesman of the socialist party's (PSI) radical wing, before he left the town
in 1912 to edit the *Avanti* paper in Milan. It's unlikely that you will want to stay in
Forlì, although you might want to stop off to visit its couple of museums. For some
reason the town is something of a centre for cinema history, with the **Museo
Internazionale del Cinema** at Viale Libertà 37 (open by appointment Wed &
Thurs 4–6pm; ☎0543/30.521), displaying a varied collection of film memorabilia
and cinema-related exhibitions and showing special screenings. The city is also an
important Romagnolo agricultural centre, its **Museo Archaeologico ed
Etnografico**, Corso della Repubblica 72 (Mon–Fri 9am–2pm, Sun 10am–1pm),
giving a good rundown on peasant life early this century and today.

Ferrara

Half an hour by train from Bologna, **FERRARA** was the residence of the Este dukes, an eccentric dynasty that ranked as a major political force throughout Renaissance times. The Este kept the main artists of the day (who all came to stay) in commissions and built a town which despite a relatively small population was – and still is – one of the most elegant urban creations of the period.

When there was no heir the Este were forced to hand over Ferrara to the papacy and leave for good. Life in Ferrara effectively collapsed. Eighteenth-century travellers found a ghost town of empty streets and canals clogged up, infested with mosquitos. Since then Ferrara has picked itself up, the centre of a key fruit-producing area, to which the acres of neat, pollarded trees outside town testify. It's a popular stop for tourists travelling up from Bologna to Venice, but they rarely stay, leaving the city centre enjoyably tourist-free by the evening.

Arrival and finding a place to stay

Ferrara's **train station** is just west of the city walls, ten minutes' walk (or a #1 or #2 bus ride) along Viale Cavour from the centre of town around the Castello. The **bus station** is southwest of the main square, on Corso Isonzo. Through a stone archway, the **AAST** on Piazza Municipio (daily 9am–1pm & 2.30–7pm) has maps and bumph on the town. From the Castello, Corso Porta Reno runs south to the city walls, the town's main shopping street, lined arcades of *pasticcerie*, bars and boutiques. In the opposite direction, Corso Ercole I d'Este leads north to Ferrara's main art galleries and parks, while behind the Duomo, to the east, is the labyrinth of alleyways that make up Ferrara's medieval quarter.

It's in this area that the bulk of Ferrara's cheap **hotels** are to be found. The best of these by far is the *San Paolo*, Via Pescherie Vecchie 10 (☎0532/34.402), which has double rooms for L28,500; if this is full there's the *Casa Artisti*, Via Vittoria 66 (☎0532/35.314), or *Raiti*, Via Dell Scienze 13 (☎0532/464.156) – both of which have rooms for L25,000. When everything else is full, the *Nazionale*, Corso Porta Reno 32 (☎0532/35.210), usually has rooms, for around L36,000. Failing that, try the *Tre Coronne* at Corso Porta Reno 70 (☎0532/35.207), or the *Garibaldi* at no. 77 (☎0532/26.318), both around L25,000.

Ferrara's **campsite**, *Estense*, is off the ringroad just outside the city walls; take bus #3. There's also an *IYHF* **youth hostel** north of Viale Cavour, at Via B. Tisi da Garofalo 5 (☎0532/21.098; open 7–9am & 6–10pm; bus #1, #2, or #9), with beds for around L10,000 for members – though it's only open April to October.

The City

Dominating the centre of town is the bulky **Castello Estense** (summer daily 9.30am–12.30pm & 3–6pm, winter daily 2–5pm; L5000), built in response to a late fourteenth-century uprising and generally held at the time to be a major feat of military engineering. But behind its grim brick walls, the Este court glittered, supporting artists like Pisanello, Jacopo Bellini, Mantegna, and the poets Ariosto and Tasso. The Este dukes were a pragmatic lot, with a range of ways of raising cash, keeping tax levels just ahead of their court expenses, and boosting cashflow by selling official titles, putting up the tolls for traffic along the Po, and supplying troops for the various rulers of Naples, Milan or Florence.

FERRARA

The first of the **Este** to live here was Nicolò II, who commissioned the castle, though later Este were really responsible for its decoration. One of the most famous members of the family was Nicolò III d'Este, who took over in 1393. Nicolò was a well-known patron of the arts, but he was most notorious for his numerous amorous liaisons, and although the 27 children he admitted to siring seems excessive, it's likely that he was responsible for many more beyond his legitimate heir, Ercole. He was also a ruthless man, reputedly murdering his wife Parisina and son by another woman, Ugo, when he discovered that they were having an affair. Two other sons, Leonello and Borso, also became renowned characters, and together with Ercole oversaw some of Ferrara's most civilised years. Leonello was a friend of the Renaissance man, Alberti, and became a caricature of the time by consulting his horoscope before he chose what to wear in the morning. Borso loved hunting and thundered through the woods at Mesola on horseback, dressed in velvet and jewels. Ercole's children, Beatrice and Isabella, married into the Sforza and Gonzaga families, thus sealing the Estes status as one of the most glittering of Renaissance dynasties. Ercole's grandson, Alfonso I, married Lucrezia Borgia, who continued the retinue of artists and poets, patronising Titian and Ariosto – as did the last Este duke, Alfonso II, who invited Tasso and Guarini to his court.

It's hard to credit all this as you walk through the castle now. The **rooms** inside go some way to bringing back the days of Este magnificence, some of them, like the *salone deo giochi* or games room, decorated by Sebastiano Filippi, with frescoes of bacchanalia on the ceiling, and a border of stumpy figures wrestling and throwing the discus. But it's a cold, draughty place on the whole, at its most evocative in the dungeons, where the sound of water from the moat, conjures an image of Este enemies: Ugo and Parisina were incarcerated down here before their execution, and Ferrante and Giulio Este, were detained in the dungeon for most of their lives after attempting to depose Alfonso I.

Just south of the castello, the **Palazzo Comunale**, built in 1243 but since much altered and restored, holds statues of Nicolò III and his other son, Borso, on its facade – though they're twentieth-century reproductions. A little way beyond, Ferrara's **Duomo** is a mixture of Romanesque and Gothic styles, with a carved central portal of St George (the town's patron saint), Madonna and Child and the Last Judgement. The inside has the grandeur of a ballroom, with glittering chandeliers, but it's upstairs, in the **museum** (daily 10am–noon & 3–5pm; "voluntary" admission fee), that the real treasures are kept. The highlight of the collection is a set of bas-reliefs illustrating the labours of the months which formerly adorned the outside of the cathedral. There are also illuminated manuscripts, two organ shutters decorated by Cosimo Tura, one of the Annunciation, another showing Saintt George killing the dragon, and a beautiful *Madonna* by della Quercia.

Ercole I d'Este gave his name to the **Corso** which leads north from the castle. He succeeded to the throne in 1441 after his father died, probably poisoned, and immediately killed off anyone who was likely to be a threat. His reputation for coldness earned him the names "North Wind" and "Diamond", but he certainly got things done, consolidating his power by marrying Eleanor of Aragon, daughter of the Spanish King of Naples, and laying out these northern quarter of the city – the so-called "Herculean Addition" – on a grand scale that led to Ferrara being tagged the first modern city in Europe. He wasn't a puritanical ruler either: writers of the time describe events consisting of many hours of feasting, with sugar castles full of meat set up for the crowd to storm.

The **Palazzo dei Diamanti**, a little way down the Corso on the left, was at the heart of Ercole's town-plan, named after the diamond-shaped bricks that stud its facade. Nowadays it's home to the **Pinacoteca Nazionale** (summer daily 9am–1pm & 4–7pm, winter daily 9.30–1pm & 3–6.30pm; L2000) and the **Museo del Risorgimento e Della Resistenza** (Mon–Sat 9am–12.30pm & 3–6pm, Sun 9am–12.30pm). You can give the latter a miss, but the pinacoteca holds works from the Ferrara and Bologna Schools in rooms with ornately decorated wooden ceilings, notably paintings by Dossi and Garofalo, and Guercino, and a spirited St

Christopher by "Il Bastianino" (Sebastian Filippo). Around the corner on Corso Porta Mare, the **Civico Museo D'Arte Moderna** has a small photographic gallery and the *Documentario della Metafisica* – a collection of transparencies of work by the *Scuola Metafisica*, the proto-surrealist group which Giorgio de'Chirico founded here in 1917.

There are more Renaissance palaces in the southeastern quarter of the city centre, lining the wider streets above the tangled medieval district. Most give nothing away by their anonymous facades – all you get is the occasional glimpse of a roof garden or courtyard inside a closing doorway. But a handful are open to the public, and give an idea of what life must have been like for the privileged few during Ferrara's heyday. The **Casa Romei**, on Via Savaranola (Tues–Sun 8.30am–12.30pm & 3–6.30pm; L2000), is a typical building of the time, with frescoes and graceful courtyards alongside artefacts rescued from various local churches. Just beyond is the house, at no. 19, where the monk Savaranola was born and lived for twenty years; while behind the palace, the church of **Corpus Domini** holds the tombs of Alfonso I and II d'Este and Lucrezia Borgia.

Two minutes away from here, the **Palazzo Schifanoia** ("Palace of Joy"), on Via Scandiana, is one of the grandest of Ferrara's palaces. It belonged to the Este family, and Cosimo Tura set their court in arcadia in the frescoes inside, in the *salone dei mesi*. The blinds are kept closed to protect the colours and the room seems silent and empty in comparison to what's happening on the walls. Borso features in many of the scenes, surrounded by friends and hunting dogs. There are also groups of musicians, weavers and embroiderers with white rabbits nibbling the grass at their feet. The bands above these are decorated with signs of the zodiac, and classical legends.

On nearby Corso della Giovecca, the **Palazzina di Marfisa d'Este** (summer daily 9am–12.30pm & 3–6pm, winter daily 2–5pm, closed Sun afternoon; L2000; students free), has more frescoes – this time by Filippi, and although its gloomy interior is less impressive than the Schifanoia complex, in summer the loggia and orange grove make a retreat from the heat. To the south, the **Palazzo di Lodovico Il Moro** (Mon–Sat 9am–2pm, Sun 9am–1pm; L2000) holds the city's archaeological museum, with finds from Spina, the Graeco-Etruscan seaport and trading colony near Commachio, displayed together with a dugout canoe from one of the prehistoric lake villages in the Po Delta.

Eating and drinking

As in the rest of the country, pizza is the cheapest choice for **eating** in Ferrara. The town has a number of good restaurants but prices are high. There are lots of pizza bars along Via Carlo Mayr: *Pizzeria-Gelateria Giuseppe* at no. 71, has pizzas for L2000–8000 and is open until 1am; there's good takeaway pizza by the slice at *Pizzeria Orcucci*, Via Garibaldi 76. *Bar Trattoria Borgazzi Willman* at Via Regno 31 is basic, offering a four-course meal for L12,000, together with a "Joe Half Lunch" – the brain-numbing *apperativo della casa*. There's a dour student *mensa* at Corso della Giovecca 145 serving up the usual goods lunchtimes and evenings, six days a week, though a better option might be the *Osteria Al Postiglione*, off Corso Martiri di Libertà on the east side of the castello. They do homemade pasta, *fagioli stufati*, and any number of toasted sandwich combinations, as well as lots of different beers and wines (open until 9.30pm).

Listings

Buses Some buses to surrounding towns leave from Rampari San Paolo (☎0532/25.815).

Donkey palio Held every last Sunday in May and based on a thirteenth-century festival in honour of the city's patron saint, Saint George.

Post Office Viale Cavour 27 (☎0532/25.960), open Mon–Fri 8am–7.30pm; Sat 8.15am–noon.

Taxis ☎0532/900.900.

Telephones There's a *SIP* office by the side of the castle at Largo Castello 30; open daily 8am–10pm.

The Po Delta

"So ugly it's beautiful", is one confusing comment made about the **Po Delta**, east of Ferrara – an expanse of marshland and lagoons culminating in small fingers of land poking out into the Adriatic. Most of the traffic is just passing through, and it's not surprising that the tourist authorities have decided on some heavy promotion.

The river Po splits into several channels, reaching the sea through these wetlands. The delta has changed a great deal since Etruscan traders set up the port of Spina here in the fourth to third century BC, when the sea covered much of the land between Comacchio and Ravenna. It's now retreated by 12km, partly due to drainage schemes, and the area becomes a bit less marshy each year – something that's to the advantage of local farmers but a threat to the different varieties of sea and shore **birds** which inhabit the area. The two main lagoons – **Valli di Comacchio** and **Valle Bertuzzi** – have been designated as nature reserves to at least halt the process, and make up one of Europe's most highly-regarded birdwatching areas, providing a habitat for nesting and migrating birds, including herons, egrets, curlews, avocets, and terns.

Another threat to the area's wild (and human) life is **pollution**: 1728 kilos of arsenic are pumped into the river Po every day; and spillages from oil refineries and nearby nuclear plants are a further cause for anxiety. Not surprisingly, the river is banned from being used for swimming, irrigation or drinking water.

Though you might not fancy it having read this, the best way to see the delta is by **boat**. There are a number of people in the surrounding area who run guided tours. Sig. Schiavi Vincensino, Via Vicolo del Farol (☎0533/99.815) or Sig. Dante Passarella, c/o *Ristorante USPA* (☎0533/99.817), both in Gorino, take out boats on Sundays in summer if enough people are interested. Boats also leave from Valle Fole, south of Comacchio; ask at *Larus Viaggi* at Piazza Ugo Bassi 32 in Comacchio for details.

Comacchio

The main town of the region, **COMACCHIO**, is a small fishing town intersected by a network of canals, with a famous local attraction in its triple-bridge or

Trepponti, built in 1634, which crosses three of the canals. Comacchio is an eel-port, and you should try if you can to be here in autumn, when wriggling masses of the creatures are fished out of the canals on their way to the Sargasso Sea. There are one or two restaurants serving fixed price menus of smoked eels (*anguille*), fish risotto, and *fritto misto*, but the best **places to eat** are out of town, and inaccessible unless you've got a car.

The **beach developments** directly east of Comacchio are not particularly invit-ing, especially bearing mind the proximity of the nasty waters of the Po, but it's interesting to see the cantilever nets set up either side of the channels running out to the sea. Incidentally, Comacchio's harbour is named Porto Garibaldi, after the Risorgimento hero who was left on the shore with his wife, Anita, and their companion Leggero, as the last *Garibaldini* were captured off the coast by the Austrian navy.

North of Comacchio: Pomposa Abbey and around

About twenty kilometres north of Comacchio, and connected by buses from the port and direct from Ferrara, the **Abbey of Pomposa** is about all the area has to offer in the way of orthodox sights, a lonely collection of buildings, saved from complete oblivion by the main road to Chioggia and numerous coach parties in summer. At the centre of a complex which includes a Lombard-Romanesque campanile, a chapter house and refectory, is an eighth-century **Basilica** contain-ing frescoes by Vitale di Bologna and the Bolognese school, though the abbey is better-known for one of its monks, Guide d'Arezzo, who in the early eleventh century invented the musical scale here. Only a few hundred years after Pomposa was built, it went into decline, the delta becoming marshier and malarial, and those that weren't killed off by the disease were left to scratch a living from hunt-ing and fishing. The monks finally abandoned their abbey in the seventeenth century.

From Pomposa a minor road leads to Volano, following the **Valle Bertuzzi**, an expanse of water and small islets given over to the *Riserva Natura Pineta di Volano*. On the other side of the estuary is the **Bosco della Mesola**, an ancient wood planted by the Etruscans, now surrounded by fields of peppers and arti-chokes. It has been much reduced in size since it was commercially logged, but it's the only wood for miles around; deer hide out among its oak and juniper trees. It's only open at weekends (8am–dusk), and you can hire bicycles at the gate – reachable by taking a bus from Ferrara to GORO, getting off at stop no. 15 and walking the 2km back down the road to the left-hand turning.

GORO itself, the next port up the coast, is used by deep sea drifters as well as smaller local boats, and is one of the most thriving, if bleakest, harbours along this stretch. Catches are either packed in ice and loaded directly into the container lorries, or else sold at the co-operative a few hundred yards away. In theory it's all strictly for trade but some additional private bargaining does go on at the quayside. The road from Goro inland keeps company with drainage ditches that have a water level higher than the surrounding fields. The main village here is **MÉSOLA**, where a noisy Saturday market invades the courtyard and the porticoes by the castle. From Mésola the road west follows the course of one of the Po's main channels – the *Po di Goro* – which also marks the border with the Veneto.

South of Comacchio: Alfonsine and the Museo del Senio

The countryside around the lagoons of the Valli di Comacchio is a combination of farm and marshland. Buildings are rare and the only sign of life is the odd heron or scavenging bird. **ALFONSINE**, the main centre of the area, is on the Ferrara-Ravenna rail line, although there's little to tempt you off the train. Not much of the pre-1944 town remains after a heavy World War II bombing, and only the **Museo del Senio** (daily 9am–1pm & 2–6pm, closed Sat & Sun afternoons) on Piazza della Resistenza is worth seeing. This documents the war, including the "Gothic Line" held by the Germans across the Apennines, and the role of Italian partisans in their defeat. The many objects and photographs include an esoteric collection of pictures of gates made from leftover anti-slip tank tracking (you still see lots of them around), as well as the bailey bridges used to cross the ditches and canals.

Ravenna and around

When **RAVENNA** became capital of the Western Roman Empire fifteen hundred years ago, it was more by quirk of fate than design. The emperor Honorius, alarmed by armies invading from the north, moved his court from Rome to this obscure town on the Romagna coast because it was easy to defend, surrounded by marshland, and was situated close to the port of Classis – at the time, the biggest Roman naval base on the Adriatic. Honorius' anxiety proved well-founded: Rome was sacked by the Goths in 410, and sunk into a decline only matched by Ravenna's ensuing prosperity, and the town became the Roman capital almost by default. Its days of glory were brief, and it too fell to the Goths in 473. But this short period of fame had made it one of the most sought-after towns in the Mediterranean, and it wasn't long before Byzantine forces took the city from the Goths and made it into an exarchate, under the rule of Constantinople.

The Byzantine rulers were responsible for Ravenna's most glorious era, keen to outdo rival cities with magnificent palaces, churches and art, and the city became one of the most compelling cultural centres in the world. The growing importance of Venice brought some further prosperity, but the sixteenth century saw the sack of the city and its absorption into the Papal States, since when the Adriatic shoreline has receded, and an 11km long canal through a vast industrial complex now links Ravenna's port to the sea. But remnants of the dazzling Byzantine era are still thick on the ground aross the town, not least a set of mosaics that is generally acknowledged to be the crowning achievement of Byzantine art extant anywhere in the world.

Unlike Florence or Venice, these buildings are kept up without much fuss – entrance to most of them is free, and tourism seems incidental to the life of the town, now enjoying the full advantages of jobs in chemical processing plants and oil refineries outside the old walls. Bombs levelled much of Ravenna in the last world war, but enough has survived for a couple of days' unhurried exploration. Churches and mosaics could easily monopolise your time, but foot traffic past the cafés in the main square, and noisy restaurants, make the city an appealing destination just for itself. Nightlife is sparse, but the (albeit largely family-orientated) lido towns a couple of kilometres away provide some excitement in summer, with seafronts to cruise, pizza bars and the occasional disco.

Arriving and finding a place to stay

Ravenna has a compact city centre, and it's only a short walk from the **railway station** on Piazza Farini, on the eastern edge of the centre, along Viale Farini and Via Armando Diaz to the central square, Piazza del Popolo, which with the adjoining streets makes up the *centro storico*. Close by here, at Via San Vitale 2, the **AAST** (daily 8am–1pm & 3–6pm) has maps and assorted bumph on the town.

The slightly unsavoury district around the railway station is unfortunately the best place to find a cheap **place to stay**. There are a couple of possibilities along Via Maroncelli, or go straight to the *Roma* at Via Candiano 26 (☎0544/421.515), which has rooms for LL40,000. *Al Giaciglio*, Via Rocca Brancaleone 42 (☎0544/39.403), is another possibility at L32,000, though a longer walk; while a longer walk still at Via Delle Industrie 37, *Da Danilo* (☎0544/227.99) is another option – doubles at L31,000. There's a **youth hostel**, the *Ostello Dante*, a ten-minute walk out of town at Via Nicolodi 12 (☎0544/420.405), which has beds for L7500 including breakfast, though it's closed between October and March. It has some family rooms and serves evening meals. Take bus #1 from outside station, and ask to be dropped off.

San Vitale and around

In terms of monuments, Ravenna's biggest draw is without question the area ten minutes' walk northwest of the city centre, around the basilica of **San Vitale** (daily 8.30am–7pm), which holds the finest of the mosaics.

San Vitale, which was begun in 525 under the Roman emperor Theodoric and finished in 548 under the Byzantine ruler Justinian, is a fairly typical Byzantine church, and its Eastern-inspired arrangement of void and solid, dark and light, was unique for an Italian building of the time. The Byzantines had a mathematical approach to architecture, calling it the "application of geometry to solid matter", and it shows in the building, based on two concentric octagons, its central dome supported by eight columns, and with eight recesses extending from each side – one of which is a semi-circular apse which glitters with mosaic. The design was the basis for the great church of Aghia Sofia, built 15 years later.

There were definite rules about who appeared where in the **mosaics** – the higher up and further to the east, the more important or holy the subject. The series starts with Old Testament scenes spread across the semi-circular lunettes of the choir; the triumphal arch shows Christ, the Apostles and sons of San Vitale. Further in, on the semi-dome of the apse, a beardless Christ stands between two angels, presenting a model of the church to San Vitale and Bishop Ecclesius. But what could become a rigid hierachy is enlivened by fields and rivers teeming with frogs, herons and dolphins.

Take some L100 and L200 coins for the lights – especially for the mosaics on the side walls of the apse. The two processional panels are the best surviving portraits of the emperor Justinian and his wife Theodora, and a rich example of Byzantine mosaic technique. The small glass *tesserae* are laid in sections, alternate rows set at slightly different angles to vary reflection of light and give an impression of depth. Colour is used emblematically too, with gold backgrounds to denote either holiness or high status. As an extra sign of superiority, Justinian's foot rests on that of his General, Belisarius, who defeated the Goths holding Ravenna and reclaimed the city.

Theodora looks a harsh figure under her finery, and she certainly had a reputation for calculated cruelty, arranging "disappearances" of anyone who went against her. According to the sixth-century chronicler Procopius, in his "Secret History" of the court, her rise to power was meteoric. When young she made a living as a child prostitute and circus performer with her two sisters, and later became a courtesan and an actor in bizarre sex shows. She travelled the Middle East, and when she returned brought herself to the attention of the Emperor, Justinian. To the horror of the court, he rejected the well-brought up daughters of his Roman peers and lived with Theodora, giving her the rank of patrician. He was unable to marry her until his mother, the Empress, was dead and the law changed; the two then embarked on a reign of staggering corruption and legalised looting.

Across the grass from the basilica is the tiny **Mausoleo di Galla Placidia** (daily 8.30am–7pm), named after the half-sister of Honorius, who was responsible for much of the grandeur of Ravenna's early days, though despite the name and three sarcophagi inside, it's unlikely that the building ever held her bones. Galla Placidia was taken hostage when the Goths sacked Rome, and created a scandal for the Roman world by marrying one of her kidnappers, Ataulf, going into battle with him as his army forged south. Later they reigned jointly over the Gothic kingdom; when Ataulf was assassinated the Romans took her back for a ransom of corn, after which she was obliged to marry a Roman General, Constantius. Their son formally became the Emperor Valentinian III at the age of six; as his Regent, she assumed control of the Western Empire.

Inside the building, filtered through thin alabaster windows, the light falls on mosaics which glow with a deep blue lustre, most in an earlier style than those of San Vitale, full of Roman and naturalistic motifs. Stars around a golden cross spread across the vaulted ceiling; the Gospels are four volumes on the shelves of a small cupboard, and there are symbolic representations of the Apostles – the lion of Saint Mark and the ox of Saint Luke are set in the sky at the points in which you expect to see Leo and Taurus. At each end are representations of Saint Lawrence, with the gridiron on which he was martyred, and the Good Shepherd, with one of his flock.

Adjacent to San Vitale on the southern side, housed in the former cloisters of the church, the **National Museum of Antiquities** (Tues–Sun 8.30am–1.30pm) contains various items from this and later periods: fifteenth-century icons, early Byzantine glass, embroidery from Florence. Among the most eye-catching exhibits is a sixth-century statue of Hercules capturing a stag, possibly a copy of a Greek original and a very late example of classically-inspired subject-matter; and the so-called "Veil of Classis", decorated with portraits of Veronese bishops of the eighth and ninth centuries.

The rest of the city centre

Lined with bland, official-looking palaces, **Via di Roma** cuts right through the modern centre of Ravenna, and sees much of its traffic, which threads through the streets in a fiendish one-way system. Halfway up on the right, the basilica of **Sant'Apollinare Nuovo** (daily 8am–noon & 2–7pm) – called Nuovo to distinguish it from the church of the same name at Classe (see below) – is another building of the sixth century, built by Theodoric and with mosaics that rank among Ravenna's most impressive. There are just two of these, running the length of either side of the nave. Each shows ceremonial processions of martyrs – one side male, the other female – bearing gifts for Christ and the Virgin enthroned through an avenue of date palms. Some of the scenery is more specific to Ravenna: you can make out what used to be the harbour at Classe against the city behind, out of which rises Theodoric's palace. As a Goth, Theodoric belonged to the Arian branch of Christianity which didn't accept the absolute divinity of Christ, a heresy which Constantinople stamped out for political as much as theological reasons. Theodoric was painted out of the mosaics and the church re-dedicated to Saint Martin, known for his anti-heretic campaigns.

Five minutes' walk away, north up Via di Roma, the **Arian Baptistry** (daily 8.30am–12.30pm & 2.30–7pm) recalls this struggle, in name at least, with a fine mosaic ceiling showing the twelve apostles and the baptism of Christ. Via Diaz leads from here down to **Piazza del Popolo**, the centre of Ravenna, laid out by the Venetians in the fifteenth century. A few blocks south of the square, the **Tomba di Dante** is a site of local pride, a small greyish building which was put up in the eighteenth century to enclose a previous fifteenth-century tomb. Dante had been chased out of Florence by the time he arrived in Ravenna, and he was sheltered here by the Da Polenta family – then in control of the city – while he finished his *Divine Comedy*. He died in 1381 and was laid to rest in the adjoining church of **San Francesco**, a much-restored building, elements of which date from the fourth century.

A couple of minutes' walk from here, there's another grouping of buildings around **Piazza del Duomo** that have a collective interest. The **Duomo** itself, with its cylindrical tower, was also originally a fifth-century building, but was completely destroyed by an earthquake in 1733, and rebuilt in unexceptional style soon after. It's not particularly worth a second glance, but the **Museo Arcivescovile** (Mon–Sat 9am–noon & 2.30–5pm or 6pm), inside the Bishop's Palace, is interesting, with fragments of mosaics from around the city and the palace's sixth-century *Oratorio Sant'Andrea*, which is adorned with mosaics of birds in a meadow above a Christ dressed in the armour, cloak and gilded leather skirt of a Roman centurion. There are also fragments from the original cathedral, an ornate ivory throne from Alexandria, which belonged to Bishop Maximian in the sixth century, and a circular marble calendar from the same time, used for calculating the date of Easter and related holy days according to the nineteen-year cycle of the Julian calendar.

The **Neonian Baptistery** (daily 9am–noon & 2.30–6pm, Sun 9am–noon), next door, is a conversion from a Roman bath-house, The original floor level has sunk into the marshy ground, and you can still see the remains of the previous building, three metres below. The building was a logical choice: baptisms involved total immersion in those days, and the mixture of styles works well – the marble inlaid designs from the bath-house blend in with the mosaics of prophets on the arches round the sides. Mosaics of the baptism of Christ and portraits of the twelve apostles decorate the dome, which is made of hollow terracotta tubes.

Eating, drinking and entertainment

Ravenna's best **places to eat** are off the cathedral square towards Piazza San Francesco. *Ca' De Ven*, on Via C. Ricci, is a wood panelled *enoteca* with a large selection of Emilia-Romagnan wine, plus food. Back towards the square, on Via Mentana, *Da Renato*, and around the corner, *Guidarello*, on Via R. Gessi, both do traditional local food, specialising in funghi in autumn. There are also *mensas* at the station and Via G. Oberdan 8, as well as a branch of the *Pizza Altero* chain on Via Camillo B Cavour. Besides eating, there's not a lot to do in town. A listings sheet called *ECO 7* covers cinema, concerts and clubs across a fairly widespread area, including some of the Adriatic resorts nearby.

Around Ravenna: Sant'Apollinare in Classe

One stop south of Ravenna by train or bus #4, the remains of the old port of **Classe** (Mon–Fri 9am–noon) are very thin indeed – the buildings have been looted for stone and the ancient harbour has now completely disappeared under the silt of the River Uniti. One building does, however, survive – the church of

Sant'Apollinare in Classe, which was spared because it was the burial-place of Ravenna's patron saint. It's a typical basilical church, quite large in extent, with a beautifully proportioned brick facade concealing an interior holding more fine mosaics. There's a marvellous depiction of the *Transfiguration of Christ* in the apse, flanked by Constantine IV granting privileges to the church of Ravenna, together with Sant'Apollinare pictured in prayer in a naturalistic landscape below.

It's an odd site, with an other-worldly feel quite at odds with its position close to the autostrada. Nearby, the **Pineta di Classe** is a long belt of umbrella pines which runs the length of the coast; the **Pineta San Vitale** runs north. This is closed to visitors during summer due to the fire risk; at other times it's a popular cycling route – though the thick belt of smog that rests over the tops of the trees destroys any bucolic appeal it might have. There's easy access to Ravenna's lido towns of **MARINA ROMEA, MARINA DI RAVENNA** or **PUNTA MARINA** by bus from here. But it's really a grotty part of the coast, and well worth avoiding.

The coast to Rimini

From Ravenna, a slow train runs down to Rimini, past a number of resorts which blur into one after a while. It's not an enticing part of Italy, and if the sea is what you're after you may just as well push on to Rimini — compelling through its sheer excess. But if you're tempted to linger, notwithstanding the problems with algae (see below), **CERVIA** might be the place to do it, a former fishing village that has grown into something of a resort only in the last thirty or so years. On the first Sunday after Ascension, the town's bishop sails out into the Adriatic, accompanied by a flotilla of small boats in a ceremonial "marriage to the sea",

---

THE SLIME FACTOR

Since 1988 the coastline **between Ravenna and Rimini** has become something of a disaster area, its tourist industry gutted by a Northern Adriatic algae slick that started life in the Venetian lagoon and began washing up in rotting, mucus-like strands onto the beaches. It's a pollution-created slick, thought to be the result of the nitrogen and phosphorous output from the fertilisers of the Po Valley mixing with detergents and industrial effluent. Mussel and shellfish beds have been decimated, and the long-term effect on tourism is a serious threat to the local economy. Not surprisingly, few holidaymakers want to share the water with a 45-foot deep stodge of stinking gloop, and even the authorities have admitted that bathing is "impractical".

Nothing effective was done in time to save the 1989 season, and it seems likely – since no one really knows for sure what causes it – that 1990 will be much the same. Business has already dropped off by forty percent, the miles of beach reserves, tennis courts, campsites and hotels empty in comparison with other years. The hoteliers and restauranteurs who helped to make this forty-mile strip into commercial seaside are understandably gloomy. There is nothing else here, they admit, so why come if you can't swim?

The government donated millions of pounds to help with the clean-up last year, and there are plans to erect a floating barrier that will keep the slick away from the beaches, as well as adding water purifiers and anti-pollution systems. Other suggestions have included building swimming pools. But the real question is just how far will Rome go to clean up the hitherto completely unrestrained development of the industrial north – the sacred cow of Italy's economic upsurge.

throwing a wedding ring into the water. Inevitably, it's a ritual kept up for tourists, but its original intention to celebrate the abundance of the sea is given a cruel twist by the burgeoning algae.

CESENATICO, 8km to the south, also grew up on its fishing industry, but has since developed into a large resort, with restaurants lining its central port-canal, designed by Leonardo da Vinci for Cesare Borgia in 1502. Many of the boats here are still primarily fishing vessels, but the port area is rather a glitzy place, with an attendant nightlife. There's a floating **Museo Marittima** on the canal, with a collection of old fishing and trading vessels, but otherwise nothing much to keep you if you don't go in for the grill-pan variety of sunbathing.

Rimini

RIMINI is the least pretentious town in Italy, the archetypal seaside city, with a reputation for good, if slightly sleazy, fun that puts it on a par with Blackpool or Torremolinos. It's certainly brash and high-rise enough to bear the comparison, and there's plenty of money in evidence, but Rimini is never tacky. Rather, it's a traditional family resort, to which some Italians return year after year, to stay in their customary *pensione* and be looked after by a hardworking *padrona di casa* as if they were her own relatives. There's also another, less savoury side to the town. Rimini is known across Italy for its fast-living and chancy nightlife, and there's a thriving hetero- and transsexual prostitution scene alongside the town's more wholesome attractions. The road between the railway station and the beach can be particularly full of kerb-crawlers. Women on their own – at night at any rate – should be wary in this and some other parts of town.

Rimini was 95 percent destroyed in the last war, and the extensive beach operation you see now has been built over the last twenty years. The Adriatic slime slick has hit business badly over the last few years, but a daunting number of holidaymakers still arrive through the city's airport. And it's the crowds, and the town's built-in sleaze factor, that you really come for – though the town does have a much-ignored old centre that is worth at least a morning of your time.

Arrival, information and accommodation

The **railway station** is situated in the centre of Rimini, on Piazzale Cesare Battisti, ten minutes' walk from both the sea and the old centre; the town's main **bus station** is just south of here on Via Clementini. First thing you should do on arrival is head for the **Palazzo del Turismo EPT** in the train station (June–Sept Mon–Sat 8am–8pm, Sun 9am–1pm; Oct–May, Mon–Sat 8am–2pm). They have a list of hotels and will help find a room, except in the peak of the season (first two weeks in August) when, normally, you don't have a chance if you haven't booked ahead. There's also an **AAST** in the Parco dell'Indipendenza on the seafront (June–Sept, Mon–Sat 8am–2pm & 4–7.30pm, Sun 9am–12.30pm; Oct–May Mon–Sat 8am–2pm), which offers the same service, and a lit-up board outside showing vacancies when everything else is closed.

Generally speaking **accommodation** can be a problem. During the season, you have to take full pension at hotels in Rimini, which can make it quite expensive. Out of season, some hoteliers will negotiate a price for room only (around L40,000 for a double without bath), but it's not a particularly pleasant time to be here anyway, and the town is pretty much dead. Try *Annarita*, Via le Misurata 24

(☎0541/259.62) or *Maria Grazie*, Via Don Bosco 11 (☎0541/239.77) both on leafy, residential streets set back from the beach, or *Novella*, Via Dandolo 1 (☎0541/247.24) in the old town. There's a **youth hostel** out near the airport at MIRAMARE, at Via Flaminia 300 (☎0541/373.216), which is open May to September and has beds for under L10,000 a head (bus #9) – though it has an 11pm curfew and you'll need to have booked. You could also **camp**: there are sites next to the railway line at Viserbella (Via Colli), Torre Pedrera (viale Tolemaide) and Rivabella (off the main road), as well as south towards Miramare (Viale Principe di Piemonte).

The City

There are two parts to Rimini. The belt of land east of the railway line is taken up mostly by holiday accommodation, leading down to the main drag of souvenir shops, restaurants and video arcades, which stretches 9km north to the suburbs of Viserba and Torre Pedrera and 7km south to Miramare. Out of season, hotel windows are boarded up and neon signs wrapped in black bin liners to protect against the gales, when Rimini's activity contracts around the Parco dell'Indipendenza and the old town, inland. This is the second, often unseen part of Rimini, a ten-minute walk west from the railway station – stone buildings clustered around the twin squares of Piazza Tre Martiri and Piazza Cavour, bordered by the port-canal and town ramparts.

On the southern edge of the old centre, the **Ponte Tiberio** and the **Arco d'Augustus** sit just inside the ramparts, built at the beginning of the first century AD and BC respectively and testifying to Rimini's importance as a Roman colony. The city passed into the hands of the papacy in the eighth century and was subject to a series of disputes that left it in the hands of the Guelf family of Malatesta. Just north of here, **Piazza Tre Martiri** and **Piazza Cavour** are the two main town squares, the latter with a statue of Pope Paul V and the Gothic **Palazzo del Podestà**, which holds a museum of ethnography inside (Mon, Wed & Fri 8am–1pm, Tues, Thurs & Sat 2–7pm). It's worth a look for its fine collection of Oceanic and pre-Colombian art.

The Malatesta family provide the town's best-known monument, the **Tempio Malatestiano** just east of here on Via 4 Novembre (April–Sept daily 7am–noon & 3.30–7pm; Oct–March erratic hours), a strange-looking building, with an uncompleted facade, but generally held to be one of the masterworks of the Italian Renaissance. Transformed by Leon Battista Alberti in 1450 from a Franciscan Gothic church for Sigismondo Malatesta, a *condittiero* with an unparalled reputation for evil, it's an odd mixture of private chapel and personal monument. His long list of crimes include rape, incest, plunder and looting, not to mention the extreme oppression of his subjects. The temple kept, rather disingenuously, its dedication to Saint Francis, but this didn't fool the pope at the time, Pius II, who condemned its pagan ornaments and emphasis on classical hedonism as "a temple of devil-worshippers".

Pius was angered enough to publicly consign Sigismondo to hell, burning an effigy of him in the streets of Rome. This had no effect of Sigismondo, who treated the church as a private memorial chapel to his great love, Isotta degli Atti. Their initials are linked in emblems all over the church, and the Malatesta armorial bearings – the elephant – appear almost as often. Trumpeting elephants, with their ears flying upwards, or elephants with their trunks entwined, decorate the screens between the side aisles and naves; chubby putti, nymphs and shepherds play, surrounded by bunches of black grapes, in a decidedly unchristian celebration of excess. There are a number of fine artworks to: a *Crucifix* now attributed to Giotto, friezes and reliefs by Agostino and a fresco by Piero della Francesca – though this is currently under restoration. Even now you get the feeling that the authorities are slightly embarassed by the place: no one seems to look after it, or wash the graffiti off the pillars. But it's somehow an appropriate attraction for Rimini, its qualities of extravagance almost an emblem for a town that thrives on excess.

Food, drink and nightlife

As far as **eating** goes, the seafront is the best place to do it cheaply, with hundreds of pizza bars for on-your-feet refuelling. There are also some extremely ritzy places, where Dallas-style dress is obligatory, but most of the interesting restaurants are in the old town. The flashy *Chiesa de Vein*, on Via 4 Novembre, up from the station, offers wine and snacks. A little further along, off Piazza Tre Martiri, *La Greppia*, on Corso d'Augusto, does standard pasta and meat dishes. The *Belvedere*, on Via Molo Levante, and *Bulivon*, Piazza Kennedy 2, are both reliable places for sit-down food. On the other side of the Ponte Tiberio, *Il Colombo* and *Il Lucido*, are pricey fish restaurants. Via Garibaldi, which leads inland from Piazza Tre Martiri, has several pizza-by-the-slice places, and a shop on Via Bonsi selling *piada* – pitta-type bread with hot fillings of mozzarella, tomato and prosciutto. The *mensa* by the railway station at Via Roma 70 is good (Mon–Sat 11.30am–3pm & 6.30–9pm). If you have transport, check out two restaurants in the suburb of Covignano: *Dalla Maria* at Via Grazie 81 and *Grotta Rossa*, Via Grotta Rossa 13. Another restaurant which merits the journey is *Bastian Contrario*, 5km out of town (bus #15/16/18/19) at Via Marecchiese 312.

Rimini's **nightlife** happens along the seafront – an area for cruising, clubbing, playing the fruit machines, and hanging out in the *gelaterie. Ethos-Mama* at Via Risorgimento 25, south of Rimini in Gabbice Mare, and a new club called *Diabolika* (starting around 11pm), play British, US and Spanish House music. People have been known to come here from London and Ibiza – but so far it's a tiny scene. For quieter evenings, *Cinema Astra*, at Via G. D'Annunzio 20, Misano Adriatico, also to the south, shows alternative movies. More sedately still, there's a classical music festival throughout the summer – the *Sagra Musicale Malatestiana* – in the Tempio Malatesta, as well as sporadic film and video weeks. It's also worth checking to see if the film and TV festivals in Riccione (to the south) and Bellaria (north) are running, scheduled respectively for the beginning of June and beginning of July – both appropriate events for Fellini's hometown.

Listings

Airport Take bus #9B from the airport to the railway station.

Doctor Phone ☎113 in an emergency, or there are doctors on 24-hr call on ☎0541/774.037.

Laundry There's a launderette at Via Clementini 2, near the bus station.

Post Office on Piazza G. Cesare (Mon–Fri 8am–noon & 2–7pm, Sat 8am–noon).

Telephones *SIP* at Piazza Ferrari 34 (summer daily 8am–8pm).

Travel Agent *Miramare*, Via Gambalunga 28/c does discount tickets.

Around Rimini: the Republic of San Marino

The countryside around Rimini is attractive: small hilltop towns and lush gentle valleys covered with firs and chestnuts, much of which is connected to the coast by bus. **SANT'ARCANGELO**, 11km inland is worth the short trip for its steep medieval streets and thirteenth-century **fortress** (June–Sept Tues, Thurs & Sat 10am–noon & 4–7pm). Carved into the hillside on the edge of the village are some artificial caves, a dank hideout for early Christians in the seventh century. The beginning of July sees a drama festival here, drawing people from miles around for its street theatre. Others visit for the village's restaurants, of which *Da Lazaroun* at Via del Platano 21 is recommended.

All of which is very different from the region's second tourist attraction after the beach – the **Republic of San Marino**, an unashamed tourist trap which trades on its falsely-preserved autonomy. Said to have been founded around AD 300 by a monk fleeing the persecutions of Diocletian, it has its own mint, produces its own postage stamps, and has an army of around a thousand men. The ramparts and medieval-style buildings, restored this century, are mildly interesting, but really the place is a fake, and worth a visit mainly for the views you get over its tiny knob of territory, and the duty-free whiskey on sale in its shops and bars.

travel details

Trains

From Bologna to Milan, via Modena, Reggio Emilia, Parma and Piacenza (hourly; 2hr 35min); Ferrara (12 daily; 30min); Ravenna (15 daily; 1hr 25min); Florence (hourly; 65min); Rimini, via Imola, Faenza, Forli and Cesena (hourly; 1hr 20min; continues to Ancona).

From Modena to Verona, via Carpi, Suzzara and Mantua (4 daily; 1hr 30min).

From Parma to La Spezia (7 daily; 2hr 15min); Brescia (8 daily; 1hr 45min).

From Fidenza to Cremona, via Busseto (14 daily; 35min); Salsomaggiore (half-hourly; 7min).

From Ferrara to Rimini, via Ravenna (11 daily; 2hr 15min).

Buses

From Bologna to Imola (every 15min; 1hr); Sasso Marconi (3 daily; 35min), continuing to Marzabotto (10min) and Vergato (20min); Porretta Terme (3 daily; 1hr 55min).

From Imola to Dozza (5 daily; 15min).

From Forli to Bertinoro (8 daily; 20min).

From Modena to Abetone, via Pievepelago (5 daily; 3hr 10min); Carpi (7 daily; 40min), continuing to Fossoli (17min); Vignola (5 daily; 40min); Montefiorino (5 daily; 1hr 50min); Sestola (4 daily; 2hr); Fanano (5 daily; 2hr).

From Reggio Emilia to Casina (7 daily; 50min); Castelnuovo ne'Monti (13 daily; 1hr 20min); Busana (4 daily; 1hr 55min); Ligonchio (2 daily; 2hr 45min).

From Parma to Torrechiara (15 daily; 25min), continuing to Langhirano (14min); Calestano (7 daily; 1hr); Corniglio (4 daily; 1hr 40min); Rigoso (5 daily; 2hr 20min); Lagdei (1 daily; 2hr 30min); Monchio (3 daily; 2hr 25min); Fontanellato (9 daily; 30min), continuing to Soragna (10min), Roncole Verdi (7min), Busseto (11min); Bardi (5 daily; 2hr); Noceto (15 daily; 30min); Salsomaggiore (14 daily; 1hr).

From Fidenza to Fontanellato (3 daily; 25min).

From Piacenza to Castell d'Arquato (16 daily; 55min), continuing to Lugagnano (5min); for Velleia, take a Rustigazzo bus (4 daily; 10min); Bobbio (12 daily; 1hr 15min).

From Ferrara to Comacchio (10 daily; 1hr 20min); Bosco della Mesola (3 daily; 1hr 20min), continuing to Goro (10min), Pomposa Abbazia (1 daily; 2hr 45min).

From Ravenna to Classe (half-hourly; 10min); Marina Romea and Marina di Ravenna (15 daily; 20min); Punta Marina (16 daily; 25min); Mesola (2 daily; 2hr).

From Rimini to San Marino (15 daily; 1hr); Sant'Arcangelo (4 daily; 20min).

CHAPTER EIGHT

TUSCANY

I t was in **Tuscany** that the Renaissance came to fruition, and this single fact has given the province an importance quite beyond its political significance. In the fifteenth and sixteenth centuries Tuscan artists such as Masaccio, Donatello and Michelangelo created works that have influenced painters and sculptors down to the present, and every major town in Italy reflects to some extent the ideas of Tuscan architects – Brunelleschi in particular. The country's very language bears the stamp of Tuscany, as the roots of modern Italian spring from the dialect written by Dante, Boccaccio and Petrarch, each of whom was born in the region.

For most visitors, the Tuscan **landscape**, too, is archetypally Italian. Its elements – walled towns, lines of cypress trees, rolling, vineyard-covered hills – are the classic backdrops of Renaissance art, disarmingly familiar from innumerable paintings. If the countryside of Tuscany has a fault, it's the popularity that its seductiveness has brought, and in many respects it's the lesser-known sights that prove most memorable and enjoyable: remote **monasteries** like Sant'Antimo or Monte Oliveto Maggiore, the weird **sulphur spas** of Bagno Vignoni and Saturnia, or the eerily eroded terrain of the **crete** (craters) south of Siena.

Which is not to suggest that you ignore Tuscany's established city attractions. It's true that few people react completely positively to **Florence**, which at present creates the impression that every building worth a look has been encased in scaffolding and tarpaulins. But however unappealing some of the central streets might look, there are plentiful compensations: the Uffizi gallery's masterpieces by Botticelli, Raphael, Titian, and just about every other important artist of the Renaissance; the great fresco cycles in the city churches; or the wealth of Florentine sculpture in the Bargello and Museo dell'Opera del Duomo.

Siena provokes less ambiguous reactions. Radiating from its beautiful Campo – the sloping, shell-shaped market square – this is one of the great medieval cities of Europe, almost perfectly preserved, and with superb works of art in its religious and secular buildings. The Campo is the scene, too, of Tuscany's one unmissable festival – the **Palio** – which sees bareback horse riders careering around the cobbles, amid the brightest display of pageantry this side of Rome.

The other major cities, **Pisa** and **Lucca**, provide convenient entry points to the province, either by air (Pisa's *Aeroporto Galileo Galilei* has flights from Britain) or along the Genova to Rome coastal railway. Both have medieval splendours – Pisa its Leaning Tower and cathedral ensemble, Lucca a string of Romanesque churches – though neither can quite compete with Siena's charm. The places that can are the smaller **hill towns** – the majority of them tucked away to the west or south of Siena. **San Gimignano**, the "city of the towers", is the best known, though too popular today for its own good. Better candidates for the rural Tuscan escape are the wine towns of **Montepulciano** and **Montalcino**, in each of which tourism is yet to overwhelm local character and life.

The one area where Tuscany thoroughly fails to impress is its **coastline**. On the mainland this is almost continuously developed, with overpriced and uninspired beach-umbrella compounds filling every last scrap of sand. There is rather more going for the principal Tuscan **islands** – **Elba** and **Giglio** – though these also are victims of their own allure, and it's not unknown for every last campsite place to be booked through the high season months.

The **season** is in fact a consideration in relation to everywhere remotely well known in Tuscany. Florence, especially, can be a nightmare in summer, with no clear sight-lines in the Uffizi, and scrums thirty-deep round Michelangelo's *David*. Finding **accommodation** here is a major problem from April through to the end of September, and not a great deal easier elsewhere; phoning to book a room is generally essential in Tuscany, at any budget level. Beware that the province is also expensive, even by northern Italian standards, with few hotel rooms below L40,000 a double.

FLORENCE (FIRENZE)

Ever since the nineteenth-century revival of interest in the art of the Renaissance, **FLORENCE** has been one of the holy places for the cult of the beautiful. Close up, however, it does not immediately impress visitors as a beautiful city. The marble-clad **Baptistery** and **Duomo** are stupendous, of course, and the architectural perfection of the latter's dome has been celebrated from the time of its construction to the present. But these colourful monuments, and other photogenic sights such as the Romanesque **San Miniato al Monte** and the towering **Orsanmichele**, are not typical of the city as a whole. The streets of the historic centre are often narrow and dark, their palaces robust and intimidating. Some of the most prominent buildings, left incomplete for centuries, have been fitted with ugly exteriors or simply left blank. Few of the city's squares are places where you'd want to pass an idle hour. The **Piazza della Signoria**, nucleus of political life in Florence, currently resembles a monumental building site, the work having become bogged down amid allegations of corruption and incompetence – as have a number of restoration projects. And despite the imposition of the *zona a traffico limitato* in the central streets, the traffic continues to intimidate.

But Florence is a city of incomparable indoor pleasures, and few people leave here disappointed. Its chapels, galleries and museums are an inexhaustible treasure, embodying the complex, exhilarating and often elusive spirit of the **Renaissance** more fully than any other place in the country. The transformation from the medieval to the modern world-view – a change largely impelled by Florence's artists and thinkers – is plotted stage by stage in the vast picture collection of the **Uffizi**, and charted in the sculpture of the **Bargello** and the **Museo dell'Opera del Duomo**.

The emergence of humanism can similarly be observed in the fabulous fresco cycles of **Santa Croce** and **Santa Maria Novella**, while nothing more eloquently expresses the Renaissance emphasis on harmony and rational design than Brunelleschi's interiors of **San Lorenzo**, **Santo Spirito** and the **Cappella dei Pazzi**. The bizarre architecture of San Lorenzo's **Sagrestia Nuova** and the marble statuary of the **Accademia** (including the *David*) display the full genius of Michelangelo, the greatest Florentine artist and the dominant creative figure of sixteenth-century Italy. Other astonishing individual creations are Fra Angelico's frescoes at **San Marco**, Andrea del Sarto's at **Santissima Annunziata** and Masaccio's at **Santa Maria del Carmine**, while in the enormous **Palazzo Pitti** are gathered half a dozen museums – one of them an art gallery that any city would envy.

The history of Florence

Though the Etruscan people were spread throughout Tuscany from the eighth century BC, there was no Etruscan precursor to Florence – their base in the vicinity was the hill town of Fiesole. The development of Florence itself began with the Roman colony of *Florentia*, established by **Julius Caesar** in 59 BC as a settlement for army veterans; the Roman grid plan is still evident in the streets between the Duomo and Piazza della Signoria. Expansion was rapid, with a steady traffic of trading vessels along the Arno providing the basis of accelerated growth in the second and third centuries AD. In 552, however, the city fell to the barbarian hordes of Totila, and less than twenty years later the Lombards stormed in, subjugating Florence to the duchy they ruled from Lucca.

By the end of the eighth century Charlemagne's Franks had taken control, with the administration being overseen by imperial margraves also based in Lucca. Over the next three hundred years Florence gained pre-eminence among the cities of Tuscany, becoming especially important as a religious centre. In 1078 Countess Mathilda of Tuscia, one of the pope's closest allies in his struggles against the Emperor Henry IV, supervised the construction of new fortifications, and in the year of her death – 1115 – granted Florence the status of an **independent city**. The new *comune* of Florence was essentially governed by a council of one hundred men, the great majority drawn from the increasingly prosperous merchant class. In 1125 the city's dominance of the region was confirmed when it crushed its rival, Fiesole.

GUELPHS AND GHIBELLINES

Agitation from the landed nobility of the surrounding countryside was a constant fact of life in the early years of the republic, and political stability was a long time coming. The governing council was replaced in 1207 by the *Podestà*, an executive official who was traditionally a non-Florentine; around this time the first *Arti* (Guilds) were formed to promote the interests of the traders and bankers. Throughout and beyond the thirteenth century Florence was torn by conflict between the pro-imperial **Ghibelline** faction and the pro-papal **Guelphs**, a feud sparked off by a murder committed in Florence but which soon spread all over Italy. The Guelph-backed regime of the *Primo Popolo*, a government of the mercantile class, was ousted after the Florentine defeat by the Sienese army and its Ghibelline allies in 1260. By the 1280s the Guelphs were back in power through the *Secondo Popolo*, a regime run by the *Arti Maggiori* (Great Guilds). Refinement of the republican system soon followed: the exclusion of the nobility from government in 1293 was the most dramatic measure in a programme of political reforms which invested power in the *Signoria*, a council drawn from the major guilds.

Strife between the so-called "Black" and "White" factions within the Guelph camp marked the start of the fourteenth century, and worse was to come. In the 1340s the two largest banks collapsed, mainly owing to the bad debts of Edward III of England, then in 1348 the **Black Death** destroyed up to half the city's population. Thirty years later, discontent erupted among the industrial workers on whose labour the wool and cloth industries of Florence depended – the rising of the *Ciompi* (wool carders) resulted in the formation of three new guilds and direct representation for the workers. In 1382, though, an alliance of the Guelph party and the *popolo grasso* (the wealthiest merchants) took control of the city away from the guilds, a situation that lasted for four decades.

THE MEDICI

Gradually the balance shifted again, and the political rise of **Cosimo de'Medici** was to some extent due to his family's sympathies with the *popolo minuto*, the members of the lesser guilds. The Medici fortune had been made by the banking prowess of Cosimo's father, Giovanni Bicci de'Medici, and Cosimo used the power conferred by wealth to great effect, becoming the dominant figure in the city's political life, though he rarely held office himself. Through Cosimo's patronage Florence became the centre of artistic activity in Italy, an ascendancy that continued under his son, Piero il Gottoso (the Gouty), and his grandson **Lorenzo il Magnifico**. Papal resentment of Florentine independence found an echo in the

jealousy of the Pazzi family, one of the city's main rivals to the Medici. However, the resulting **Pazzi conspiracy** – in which Lorenzo was wounded and his brother Giuliano murdered – only increased the esteem in which Lorenzo was held.

Before Lorenzo's death in 1492, however, the Medici bank failed, and in 1494 Lorenzo's son Piero was obliged to flee following his surrender to the invading French army of Charles VIII. For a while Florence was virtually under the control of the inspirational and ascetic monk **Girolamo Savonarola**, but he was executed as a heretic in 1498, after which the city functioned as a more democratic republic than that which the Medici had dominated. In 1512, after Florence's defeat by the Spanish, the Medici returned, only to be expelled in the wake of Charles V's pillage of Rome in 1527 – Pope Clement VII was a Medici, and his humiliation by the imperial army provided the spur to eject his deeply unpopular relatives. Two years later the pendulum swung the other way – after a siege by the combined papal and imperial forces, Florence capitulated.

After the assassination of the tyrannous Alessandro de'Medici in 1537, power passed to another Cosimo, a descendant of Cosimo il Vecchio's brother. Under his rule Florence gained control of all of Tuscany; in 1570 he took the title Cosimo I, the first Grand-Duke of Tuscany. Thenceforth the Medici remained in power until 1737, when the last male Medici, Gian Gastone, died.

TO THE PRESENT

Under the terms of a treaty signed by Gian Gastone's sister, Anna Maria, Florence now passed to Francesco of Lorraine, the future Francis I of Austria. Austrian rule lasted until the coming of the French in 1799; after a fifteen-year interval of French control, the Lorraine dynasty was brought back, remaining in residence until the Risorgimento upheavals of 1859. Absorbed into the united Italian state in the following year, Florence became the capital of the Kingdom of Italy in 1861, a position it held until 1875.

The story of Florence since then is distinguished mainly by calamities. In 1944 the city was badly damaged by the retreating German army, who bombed all the bridges except the Ponte Vecchio and blew up much of the medieval city near the banks of the Arno. Even worse was the wreckage caused by the flood of November 1966, which drowned several people and caused damage to buildings and works of art which still has not been fully rectified. These monuments and paintings are the very basis of Florence's survival, a state of affairs which gives rise to considerable discontent. The development of a new industrial city (*Firenze Nuova*) between the northern suburbs and Prato – substantially underwritten by *Fiat* – is the latest and most ambitious attempt to break Florence's ever-increasing dependence on tourism.

Arrival, information and getting around

The nearest international **airport** to Florence is at **Pisa**, which is connected by a regular train service to Florence's Santa Maria Novella train station; the journey takes an hour, and tickets should be bought from the information desk inside the air terminal. If you're coming into the city by car, it's best to leave it some way out of the centre and take a bus into town – there are car parks in the centre (at the train station, for instance), but the recent restrictions on traffic movements and parking within the historic quarter have made these facilities even busier than they used to be.

Orientation is straightforward – it's just ten minutes' walk from the station to Piazza del Duomo, along Via de'Panzani and Via de'Cerretani. The great majority of the major sights are within a few minutes of the Duomo area. Within the city, walking is generally the most efficient way of getting around, but if you want to cover a long distance in a hurry, then take one of the orange *ATAF* buses; tickets valid for 70 minutes cost L800, and can be bought from *tabacchi* and from automatic machines all over Florence. The majority of routes either originate at or pass by the train station.

For **information** about Florence's sights and events, the main **APT** office is on the first floor at Via Tornabuoni 15 (Mon–Sat 9am–1pm; ☎216.544); they hand out an adequate free map, leaflets on a variety of subjects, and a magazine called *Concierge Information*, which gives all the latest opening hours and entrance charges. Information on the province of Florence is available from the **EPT** at Via Manzoni 16 (Mon–Fri 8.30am–1.30pm & 4–6.30pm, Sat 8.30am–1.30pm; ☎247.8141). In the summer, small information desks are to be found in front of the train station (8am–8pm), by the Baptistery in the Loggia di Bigallo (9am–6pm) and in the Chiasso dei Baroncelli, just off Piazza della Signoria (4.30–10.30pm); they provide maps and can answer general queries about the lie of the land, but can't handle accommodation enquiries.

The Florence area telephone code is ☎055

Finding a place to stay

Budget accommodation in Florence is a problem at most times of year – prices tend to be high and standards low, and the city's tourist invasion has scarcely any slack spots. The "Completo" signs are most profuse from March to June and in September – both being favourite periods for Italian school trips, and autumn also being the season of the Florentine fashion shows. Things are not much better in the intervening months, when the sweltering Florentine climate makes the city a pretty unattractive proposition anyway. Basically, between Easter and the start of October you're taking a risk in turning up without a pre-booked room, as it's not unknown for every one- and two-star hotel to be booked solid by the late morning. Should you find yourself roomless, the tourist department's list of hotels (*Elenco degli Alberghi*) contains addresses and phone numbers of hotels in outlying towns, and indicates their accessibility by public transport; in summer you can usually pick up a copy at the train station information booth, but supplies can run out, so it's best to get one from the tourist office in London before travelling.

The quickest way to get a room is to phone round from the station – the desk next to the baggage deposit sells telephone cards (*schede telefoniche*), which makes life far easier than shovelling *gettone* into the phone every few seconds. If this sounds like too much hassle, then the **Informazioni Turistiche Alberghiere** between platforms 9 and 10 (daily 8.30am–9.30pm) will try to make a reservation for you. In high season, though, you could spend a couple of hours queueing, and by the time you get to the front, any cheap rooms that might have been available when you arrived will probably have been taken. Their charges vary with the class of accommodation chosen, ranging from L2000 to L5000, and you pay your first night's bill as deposit.

Hotels

Even at the one-star end, prices in Florence are steep, with a high season average in excess of L35,000. From October to April prices come down a little, one reason for the difference in prices being that breakfast, which should be optional, is virtually compulsory in summer, slapping an extra L5000–10,000 per person onto the bill. The maximum cost of a room should be posted on the back of the door; if it isn't, or if you have any other complaints, contact the EPT.

The major concentrations of one- and two-star hotels are within a few hundred metres of the train station, in particular along and around Via Faenza and the parallel Via Fiume, to the east of the station. Generally more salubrious, if rather noisier, is Via Cavour, the main road from the northern districts into the area round the Duomo. On the other side of the station, Via della Scala has several low-cost hotels that are often more welcoming than those to the east, and Piazza Santa Maria Novella – into which Via della Scala runs – offers a range of options with one of the most scenic sites in the city.

The specific hotels listed below – most of them one-stars – have a slight edge on most of the competition; the prices given are the **minimum summer cost of a double room**, without bathroom but with breakfast, unless otherwise stated.

THE STATION AND MARKET AREAS

Azzi, Via Faenza 56 (☎213.806). With most of its rooms overlooking the garden, the *Azzi* is probably the most pleasant of the six *pensioni* occupying the upper floors of this building; L41,000. The others, all in the same price range, are: **Merlini** (☎212.848); **Armonia** (☎211.146); **Marini** (☎284.824); **Anna** (☎298.322); and **Paola** (☎213.682).

Tony's Inn, Via Faenza 77 (☎284.119). Run by a Canadian woman and her Italian photographer husband, good for homesick Anglophones. L44,000.

Erina, Via Fiume 17 (☎284.343). Located on the third floor of an old palazzo, with seven double rooms; open only from mid-July to mid-September. L34,000.

Desirée, Via Fiume 20 (☎262.382). Now a two-star, the *Desirée* was completely overhauled in 1987 – stained-glass windows, simulated antique furniture, and a bath in every room. L72,000.

Ausonia e Rimini, Via Nazionale 24 (☎496.547). Halfway between the train station and the market; recently refurbished and welcoming. L39,000.

Concordia, Via dell'Amorino 14 (☎213.233). Extremely convenient, being located right in the heart of the market area; it has no private bathrooms and doesn't do breakfast. L34,000.

Mia Casa, Piazza Santa Maria Novella 23 (☎213.061). Pleasantly ramshackle, with very helpful owners – the first choice on this square. L38,000.

Giacobazzi, Piazza Santa Maria Novella 24 (☎294.679). Popular with Italian visitors and has only seven rooms, so usually necessary to book well in advance. L34,000.

La Romagnola (☎211.597) and **Gigliola** (☎287.981), both at Via della Scala 40. Via della Scala, to the south of the train station, has almost as many cheap hotels as the less salubrious Via Faenza on the other side, and these two are the pick of the bunch – a midnight curfew is the only drawback. With a total of 42 rooms, they often have space when the others are full. L33,000.

NORTH AND EAST OF THE DUOMO

Genzianella (☎572.141) and **Savonarola** (☎587.824), both at Via Cavour 112. Two reasonable one-stars. The former doesn't do breakfast, charging from L34,000 for a double; the latter's breakfast can add L9000 to the same basic charge. In the same building there's also the two-star **Benvenuti** (☎573.909), at L56,000.

Panorama Angelico, Via Cavour 60 (☎214.243). In the university quarter; a favourite with school parties. L49,000.

Giglio, Via Cavour 85 (☎486.621). Another serviceable two-star on this major street. L51,000.

Rudy, Via San Gallo 51 (☎475.519). More than a touch quieter than the hotels on the parallel Via Cavour; 1am curfew. L38,000.

Splendor, Via San Gallo 30 (☎483.427). Located in an old palazzo, this peaceful two-star is a good deal if you can get out of breakfast – if you can't, the bill leaps from L47,000 to L61,000.

Brunetta, Borgo Pinti 5 (☎247.8134). Cheap and well-placed, just to the east of the Duomo. L33,000.

Donatello, Via Alfieri 9 (☎245.870). In a quiet area between Piazzale Donatello and Piazza d'Azeglio; strongly recommended – smartly renovated, airy, and run by young management. L41,500. At the same address, **Losanna** (☎245.840) is a small, clean and modest *pensione*; you can avoid breakfast if you make the point clearly when you arrive. L42,500.

Veneto, Via Santa Reparata 33 (☎294.816). Comfortable two-star, though popular for school outings. L59,000.

THE CENTRAL AREA

Zurigo, Via dell'Oriolo 17 (☎2340.644). Ordinary but clean, and just a minute or so from the Duomo. L44,000.

Bavaria, Borgo Albizi 26 (☎2340.313). A little to the south of the *Zurigo*, installed in a sixteenth-century palazzo, with appropriate decor. L39,000.

Brunori, Via del Proconsolo 5 (☎263.648). Noisy and slightly run-down, but with friendly and informative owners; no single rooms. L41,000.

Colore, Via Calzaiuoli 13 (☎210.301). Tiny and welcoming place on the city's main *passeggiata* street. L39,000.

Davanzati, Via Porta Rossa 15 (☎283.414). Situated between Via Tornabuoni and Piazza della Signoria, so right in the thick of things; good value and friendly. L40,000.

Alessandra, Borgo Santi Apostoli 17 (☎283.438). Occupying a sixteenth-century palazzo and furnished in a peculiar mixture of antique and low-budget modern styles, this two-star is frequented by the fashion-show crowd, so booking is essential in September. L49,000.

Cestelli, Borgo Santi Apostoli 25 (☎214.213). A seven-room place right by the Uffizi, fitted with massive pieces of furniture from the 1920s and earlier. L37,000.

SOUTH OF THE RIVER

Sorelle Bandini, Piazza Santo Spirito 9 (☎215.308). Vast rooms, gorgeous decor (including marble fireplaces) and great views from the three-sided loggia make this one of Florence's most attractive options. L46,000.

La Scaletta, Via Guicciardini 13 (☎283.028). From the rooftop terraces you look across the Bóboli gardens in one direction and the city in the other; well worth the slightly higher outlay. L56,000.

Student accommodation

The majority of students at Florence's university are not Florentines, and a number of institutions, most of them run by religious bodies, have sprung up in the city to provide beds for the non-natives. Out of term time (June–Oct) some of these places are open to young tourists, and a couple have a few rooms to spare even during the term. In addition to the houses listed below, there are also a number of *Case dello Studente*, which are run by the university authorities and occasionally made available to visitors; for information on these, ask at the EPT. Prices given over the page are **per person**.

Suore Oblate dello Spirito Santo, Via Nazionale 8 (☎298.202). A few steps from the station. Run by nuns, but open to both men and women from mid-June to October. Very clean and pleasant; beds arranged in single, double and triple rooms; midnight curfew. Under L25,000, including breakfast.

Suore Oblate dell'Assunzione, Via Borgo Pinti 15 (☎248.0582). Not far from the Duomo. Again run by nuns and again open to men and women, this time from mid-June to the end of July and throughout September (although 4–5 beds are available all year round). Single and double rooms; midnight curfew. Under L20,000; no breakfast.

Istituto Gould, Via dei Serragli 49 (☎212.576). Over in Oltrarno, past Ponte alla Carrara. Reception is on the second floor (the doorbell is easily missed); open Mon–Fri 9am–1pm & 3–7pm, all through the year. Recently renovated, the *Gould* is extremely popular, so it's wise to book in advance. L13,000 and upwards; no breakfast.

Pio X – Artigianelli, Via dei Serragli 106 (☎225.044). Probably the cheapest option in town. Don't be put off by the huge picture of Pope Pius X at the top of the steps – the management is friendly and the atmosphere relaxed. It's open all day throughout the year, but whatever the time of year it's best to get there by 9am, as the 35 beds soon get taken. Double, triple and quadruple rooms. L10,000.

Hostels and Camping

Santa Monaca, Via Santa Monaca 6 (☎268.338). In Oltrarno, near the *Istituto Gould*. Privately owned, so no *IYHF* card needed; open for reservations 8–9.30am and after 4pm. Kitchen facilities, free hot showers, and no maximum length of stay. 11.30pm curfew. L13,000 without breakfast. Very popular.

Ostello Villa Camerata, Viale Righi 2 (☎601.451). A 30-min journey on the #17b bus from the train station. Tucked away in a beautiful park, the Villa Camerata is a sixteenth-century house with frescoed ceilings and a wide loggia. Doors open at 2.30pm, and if you can't be there by then, ring ahead to make sure there's a place left. If you don't have an *IYHF* card, you can buy a special guest card that's also valid in other hostels. Films in English every night; curfew at midnight. Breakfast and sheets included in L13,000 charge; optional supper at L7000 (no kitchen facilities).

CAMPSITES

Italiani e Stranieri, Viale Michelangelo 80 (☎681.1977). Open from April to October, this site is always crowded, owing to its superb hillside location. The best way to get there is by taking the #13 bus from the train station. 480 places; kitchen facilities. L4400 per person; L4000 per tent.

Villa Camerata, Viale Righi 2–4 (☎610.300). Basic site, open all year in the hostel grounds. 60 places. L4000 per person; L6500 per tent.

Panoramico, Via Peramonda, outside Fiesole (☎599.069). Beautiful situation on a hill to the north of the city, but involves taking #7 to Fiesole and then another bus out to the site. L7000 per person; L4500 per tent.

FREE CAMPING

Every summer the city authorities open an *Area di Sosta*, an emergency accommodation area that usually amounts to a patch of ground sheltered by a rudimentary roof. Staying there is free, and showers are available for a small charge. At the moment the *Area di Sosta* is at the **Villa Favard**, in Via Rocca Tedalda (☎690.022), reached by the #14a bus.

Don't let the scarcity and expense of beds in Florence tempt you into camping rough outside the city. Over the last few years several Florentines and foreigners have been murdered by a maniac known locally as *Il Mostro*; most of his victims have been campers, and he's still at large.

The City

Greater Florence now spreads several kilometres down the Arno Valley and onto the hills north and south of the city, but the major sights are contained within an area that can be crossed on foot in little over half an hour. A short walk from the train station brings you to the **Baptistery** and **Duomo**; the area from here to **Piazza della Signoria** – site of the **Palazzo Vecchio** and the **Uffizi** – is the inner core, the area into which most of the tourists are packed. A circle drawn so that the Duomo and Uffizi stood on opposite sides of its circumference would gather in the best-preserved of Florence's medieval streets and the majority of its fashionable streets.

Immediately north of the Duomo is the **San Lorenzo** quarter, where market stalls surround one of the city's first-rank churches; within a short radius from here are the monastery of **San Marco**, with its paintings by Fra Angelico, the **Accademia**, home of Michelangelo's *David*, and **Piazza Santissima Annunziata**, generally thought of as Florence's most attractive square.

The Uffizi backs onto the Arno River, over which lies the district known as **Oltrarno**, where the **Palazzo Pitti** exerts the strongest pull, followed by the churches of **Santo Spirito** and the hilltop **San Miniato al Monte**.

Close to the eastern side of Piazza del Duomo stands the **Bargello**, the main museum of sculpture; further eastwards, the area around the Franciscan church of **Santa Croce** forms a nucleus of activity. On the western side of the city, directly opposite the train station, the unmissable attraction is **Santa Maria Novella**, Florentine base of the rival Dominican order.

The Duomo and around

From Santa Maria Novella station, most visitors gravitate towards Piazza del Duomo, following the flow of traffic and beckoned by the pinnacle of Brunelleschi's dome, which dominates the landscape in a way unmatched by any architectural creation in any other Italian city. Yet even though the magnitude of the Duomo is apparent from a distance, the first full sight of the church and the adjacent Baptistery still comes as something of a jolt, the colours of their patterned exteriors making a startling contrast with the dun-coloured buildings around.

The Duomo (Santa Maria del Fiore)

It was some time in the seventh century when the seat of the Bishop of Florence was transferred from San Lorenzo to the ancient church which stood on the site of **Santa Maria del Fiore**, the **Duomo** of Florence. Later generations transformed that building until, in the thirteenth century, it was decided that a new cathedral was required, to reflect more accurately the wealth of the city and to put the Pisans and Sienese in their place. **Arnolfo di Cambio**, entrusted with the project in 1294, designed a massive vaulted basilica focussed on a domed tribune embraced by three polygonal tribunes. Work ground to a halt immediately after his death eight years later, then was resumed under a succession of architects, each of whom roughly followed Arnolfo's plan. By 1418 the nave was finished, the tribunes were complete, and a drum was in place to bear the weight of the dome which Arnolfo had envisaged as the church's crown. The conception was magnifi-

cent: the dome was to span a distance of nearly 140 feet, and rise from a base some 180 feet above the floor of the nave. It was to be the largest dome ever constructed – and nobody had yet worked out how to build the thing.

A committee of the masons' guild was set up to ponder the problem, and it was to them that **Filippo Brunelleschi** presented himself. His arrogant insistence that only he could possibly redeem the situation, and his refusal to say much more about his solution other than that he could build the dome without using scaffolding, did little to endear him to his prospective patrons. In the end, however, they relented, and Brunelleschi was given the commission on condition that he work jointly with Ghiberti – a partnership which did not last long, though Ghiberti's contribution to the project was probably more significant than his colleague ever admitted. On March 25, 1436 – Annunciation Day, and the Florentine New Year – the **completion of the dome** was marked by the consecration of the cathedral, a ceremony conducted by the pope. Yet the topmost piece of the dome – the lantern – was still not in place, and many were sceptical about the structure's capability to bear the weight. Other architects were consulted, but Brunelleschi again won the day; the lantern was completed in the late 1460s, when the gold ball and cross, cast by Verrocchio, was hoisted into place.

Both overblown and pernickety, the main **facade** is a nineteenth-century imitation of a Gothic front, its marble cladding quarried from the same sources as the first builders used – the white stone from Carrara, the red from Maremma, the green from Prato. The south side is the oldest part of the exterior, but the most attractive adornment is the *Porta della Mandorla*, on the other side. It takes its name from the oval frame (or *mandorla*) that contains the relief of *The Assumption of the Virgin*, sculpted by Nanni di Banco around 1420.

THE INTERIOR

The Duomo's interior (daily 10am–5pm) is the converse of the exterior, a vast enclosure of bare masonry. The fourth largest church in the world, it once held a congregation of 10,000 to hear Savonarola preach. The ambience is more that of a great public assembly hall than of a devotional building, and it's not surprising to find that the most conspicuous pieces of painted decoration in the main body of the church are two memorials to *condottieri* on the wall of the north aisle – Uccello's **monument to Sir John Hawkwood**, painted in 1436, and Castagno's **monument to Niccolò da Tolentino**, created twenty years later. Just beyond them, Domenico do Michelino's *Dante Explaining the Divine Comedy*, painted in 1465, gives the recently completed dome a place only marginally less prominent than the mountain of Purgatory.

Judged by mere size, the major work of art in the Duomo is the fresco of *The Last Judgment* that lurks behind the restorers' planks and netting now covering the inside of the dome. A substantial number of Florentines are of the opinion that Vasari and Zuccari's effort does nothing but deface Brunelleschi's masterpiece, and want the paint stripped away. Below the fresco are seven stained glass roundels designed by Uccello, Ghiberti, Castagno and Donatello; they are best inspected from the gallery immediately below them, which forms part of the route to the top of the **dome** (Mon–Sat 10am–5pm; L3000). Most of the climb winds between the brick walls of the outer and inner shells of the dome, and at the summit the view is so stupendous that vertigo shouldn't get a chance to take hold.

When you come back down to earth, be sure to take a look at the entrances to the two **sacristies**, on each side of the altar. The enamelled terracotta reliefs over the doorways are by Luca della Robbia, who also cast the doors of the north sacristy – his only works in bronze. After his brother Giuliano had been mortally stabbed on the altar steps by the Pazzi conspirators, Lorenzo de'Medici took refuge in the north sacristy, the bulk of the new doors protecting him from his would-be assassins.

In the 1960s remnants of the Duomo's predecessor, the church of **Santa Reparata**, were uncovered underneath the west end of the nave. Subsequent excavations have revealed a complicated jigsaw of Roman, paleochristian and Romanesque remains, plus areas of mosaic and patches of fourteenth-century frescoes (daily 10am–5pm; L1500). The explanatory diagrams tend to intensify the confusion – to make sense of it all, refer to the detailed model standing in the further recesses of the crypt. Also discovered in the course of the dig was the tomb of Brunelleschi, the only Florentine ever honoured with burial inside the Duomo – his tombstone can be seen through a grille to the left of the foot of the stairs.

THE CAMPANILE

The **Campanile** was begun in 1334 by Giotto and continued after his death by Andrea Pisano and Francesco Talenti, who rectified the deficiencies of the artist's calculations by doubling the thickness of the walls. Erosion caused by atmospheric pollution has made it necessary to replace the tower's sculptures with copies – the originals are all in the Museo dell'Opera del Duomo (see below).

The first storey, the only part of the tower built exactly as Giotto designed it, is studded with two rows of remarkable bas-reliefs; the lower, illustrating the *Creation of Man* and the *Arts and Industries*, was carved by Pisano himself, the upper by his pupils. The figures of *Prophets* and *Sibyls* in the second-storey niches were created by Donatello and others. The parapet at the top of the tower (summer daily 8.30am–7.30pm; winter daily 9am–5pm; L3000) is a less lofty viewpoint than the dome, but rather more vertiginous.

The Baptistery

The **Baptistery** (daily 10am–6pm), generally thought to date from the sixth or seventh century, is the oldest building in the city. Strangely enough, though its origins are in the depths of the Dark Ages, no building better illustrates the special relationship between Florence and the Roman world. The Florentines were always conscious of their Roman ancestry, and throughout the Middle Ages they chose to believe that the Baptistery was originally a Roman temple to Mars, a belief bolstered by the interior's inclusion of Roman granite columns. The pattern of its marble cladding – applied in the eleventh and twelfth centuries – is clearly classical in inspiration, and the Baptistery's most famous embellishments – its gilded bronze **doors** – mark the emergence of a self-conscious interest in the art of the ancient world.

The south door, originally placed to face the Duomo, was cast in 1336 by Andrea Pisano. In 1401 a competition was held for a commission to make a new set of doors, each entrant being set the task of creating a panel depicting the sacrifice of Isaac. The winning submission came from **Lorenzo Ghiberti**, whose entry can be seen, alongside Brunelleschi's composition, in the Bargello. Ghiberti's north doors, depicting scenes from the life of Christ, the four

Evangelists and the four Doctors of the Church, show a new naturalism and classical sense of harmony, but their innovation is fairly timid in comparison with the sublime **east doors**, of which Michelangelo remarked "they are so beautiful they are worthy to be the gates of Paradise". Unprecedented in the subtlety of their modelling, these Old Testament scenes are a primer of early Renaissance art, using perspective, gesture and sophisticated grouping of their subjects to convey the human drama of each scene. Ghiberti has included a self-portrait in the frame of the left-hand door – his is the fourth head from the top of the right-hand band. The panels are being restored one by one, and placed in the Museo dell'Opera as they are finished; eventually a set of replicas will be installed here in their stead.

The **interior** is equally stunning. Both the semi-abstract mosaic floor and the magnificent mosaic ceiling – including a fearsome platoon of demons at the feet of Christ in judgment – were created in the thirteenth century. To the right of the altar is the **tomb of John XXIII**, the schismatic pope who died in Florence in 1419 while a guest of his financial adviser and close friend, Giovanni di Bicci de'Medici. His monument, draped by an illusionistic marble canopy, is the work of Donatello and his pupil Michelozzo.

The Museo dell'Opera del Duomo

Since the early fifteenth century the maintenance of the Duomo has been supervised from the building at Piazza del Duomo 9, behind the east end of the church; nowadays this also houses the **Museo dell'Opera del Duomo** (summer Mon–Sat 9am–8pm, Sun 10am–1pm; winter Mon–Sat 9am–6pm, Sun 10am–1pm; L3000, free on Sun), the repository of the most precious and fragile works of art from the Duomo, Baptistery and Campanile. As an overview of the sculpture of Florence it's second only to the Bargello, and is far easier to take in on a single visit.

The most arresting works in the first room are a series of sculptures by **Arnolfo di Cambio**, including a glassy-eyed *Madonna*; they were rescued from Arnolfo's unfinished facade for the Duomo, which was pulled down in the sixteenth century. Adjoining rooms are dedicated to Brunelleschi, displaying his death mask, models of the dome and a variety of tools and machines devised by the architect. At the other end of the main room, steps lead up to a display of models of suggested facades for the Duomo, and an assembly of reliquaries that can boast the jaw of Saint Jerome and the index finger of John the Baptist.

On the mezzanine level is **Michelangelo's** anguished and angular *Pietà*, moved here while restoration of the dome is in progress. This is one of his last works, and was intended for his own tomb – Vasari records that the face of Nicodemus is a self-portrait. Dissatisfied with the quality of the marble, Michelangelo mutilated the group by hammering off the left leg and arm of Christ; his pupil Tiberio Calcagni restored the arm, then finished off the figure of the Magdalen, turning her into a vacant supporting player.

Although he's represented on the lower floor as well, it's upstairs that **Donatello**, the greatest of Michelangelo's forerunners, really comes to the fore. Of the figures he carved for the Campanile, the most powerful is that of the prophet *Habbakuk*, the intensity of whose gaze prompted the sculptor to seize it and yell "Speak, speak!" Opposite poles of Donatello's temperament are represented by the haggard wooden figure of Mary Magdalen and his ornate *cantoria* (choir-loft) from the Duomo, with its playground of dancing *putti*. Opposite this is the *cantoria* created at the same time by **Luca della Robbia**, the original panels of which are displayed below the reconstructed loft; the gorgeous groups of earnest young musicians embody the text from Psalm 33 inscribed on the frame: "Praise the Lord with harp. Sing unto Him with the psaltery and an instrument of ten strings."

Pisano's bas-reliefs from the Campanile are on show in one of the two adjoining rooms, while the other contains four of **Ghiberti**'s panels from the "Doors of Paradise" and a dazzling silver-gilt altar from the Baptistery, completed in 1480, more than a century after it was begun.

Piazza della Signoria and around

For several years now, Florence hasn't had a central square. The repaving of the **Piazza della Signoria** has developed into the city's longest-running scandal: first of all the company in charge of the work was hauled up for cleaning a batch of the old slabs so briskly that they resembled nothing so much as the deck of an aircraft carrier, and then some of the stones turned up on the front drives of a number of Tuscan villas. Prosecutions and recriminations are rife, and most Florentines now seem to regard the Piazza's completion as an event of the same order of likelihood as the attainment of stable government.

Even in a state of perfect health, the Piazza della Signoria is not quite adequate to its role: the square is completely subordinated by the colossal Palazzo Vecchio, and the nineteenth-century buildings round the perimeter serve as little more than boundary walls. What little charm it has comes from its peculiar array of statuary, a sculptural miscellany that embodies the city's political volatility. The line-up – arranged in the sixteenth century to accentuate the axis of the Uffizi – starts with Giambologna's equestrian statue of Cosimo I and continues with Ammannati's fatuous *Neptune Fountain*, a copy of Donatello's *Marzocco* (the city's heraldic lion), copies of Donatello's *Judith and Holofernes* and Michelangelo's *David* (both originally installed here as declarations of republican solidarity), concluding with Bandinelli's lumpen *Hercules and Cacus*, a personal emblem of Cosimo I.

The square's grace-note, the **Loggia della Signoria**, was built in the late fourteenth century as a dais for city officials during ceremonies; only in the late eighteenth century did it become a showcase for some of the city's more melodramatic sculpture. In the corner nearest the Palazzo Vecchio stands a figure that has become one of the iconic images of the Renaissance, Benvenuto Cellini's *Perseus*. The traumatic process of its casting is vividly described in Cellini's riproaring autobiography – the project seemed doomed when the molten bronze began to solidify too early, but the ever-resourceful hero saved the day by flinging all his pewter plates into the mixture. Equally attention-seeking is Giambologna's last work, *The Rape of the Sabine*, epitome of the Mannerist obsession with spiralling forms.

The Palazzo Vecchio

Florence's fortress-like town hall, the **Palazzo Vecchio** (Mon–Fri 9am–7pm, Sun 8am–1pm; L4000; last ticket 1hr before closing), was begun in the last year of the thirteenth century as the home of the *Signoria*, the highest tier of the city's republican government. The misshapen plan was not devised by the original architect (thought to be Arnolfo di Cambio), but is rather a product of factional division – the Guelph government refused to encroach on land previously owned by the Ghibellines.

Changes in the Florentine constitution entailed alterations to the layout of the palace, the most radical overhaul coming in 1540, when Cosimo I – recently installed as Duke of Florence – moved his retinue here from the Palazzo Medici. The **Medici** were only in residence for nine years – they moved to the Palazzo Pitti, largely at the insistence of Cosimo's wife, Eleanor of Toledo – but the enlargement and refurbishment instigated by Cosimo continued throughout the period of his rule. Much of the decoration of the state rooms comprises a relentless eulogy of Cosimo and his relations, but in amongst the propaganda are some excellent works of art, including some seminal examples of Mannerism, Cosimo I's court style.

THE INTERIOR

Giorgio Vasari, court architect from 1555 until his death in 1574, was responsible for much of the sycophantic decor in the state apartments. His limited talents were given full rein in the huge **Salone dei Cinquento**, built at the end of the fifteenth century as the assembly hall for the Great Council of the penultimate republic. The production-line heroic murals, painted either by Vasari or under his direction, were executed after the failure of one of Italy's most remarkable decorative projects. Leonardo da Vinci and Michelangelo were employed to paint frescoes on opposite sides of the room; Leonardo's work was abandoned after his experimental technique went wrong, and Michelangelo's project existed only on paper when he was summoned to Rome by Pope Julius II. Michelangelo's *Victory*, facing the entrance door, was sculpted for Julius' tomb, but was donated to the Medici by the artist's nephew; Vasari installed it here to mark Cosimo's defeat of the Sienese.

A door to the right of the entrance to the hall, at the far end, opens onto the bizarre **Studiolo di Francesco I**. Created by Vasari in the 1570s and decorated by several of Florence's prominent Mannerist artists, this windowless cell was created as a retreat for the introverted son of Cosimo and Eleanor. Each of the miniature bronzes and nearly all the paintings reflect Francesco's interest in the sciences and alchemy: the entrance wall (which visitors, allowed no further than the entrance steps, can't actually see) illustrates the theme of "Earth" while the others, reading clockwise, signify "Water", "Air" and "Fire". The outstanding paintings are the two which don't fit the scheme – Bronzino's glacial portraits of the occupant's parents. (The one of Cosimo, over the door, is impossible to see.)

Bronzino's major contribution to the palace can be seen on the floor above, where Eleanor's tiny **chapel** was entirely painted by him in the 1540s. A Mannerist contemporary of Bronzino, Cecchino Salviati, produced what is widely held to be his masterpiece with the fresco cycle in the **Sala d'Udienza**, once the audience chamber of the Republic; the room also has a richly gilded ceiling by Giuliano da Maiano and assistants, and a magnificent inlaid doorway by Giuliano and his brother Benedetto, a partnership responsible for the ceiling of the adjoining **Sala dei Gigli**. Named after the lilies which adorn the room (the city's symbol), this hall was fitted out in the decade after 1475, and features frescoes by Domenico Ghirlandaio. The focus of the room now, however, is Donatello's recently restored *Judith and Holofernes*. Commissioned by Cosimo il Vecchio, the group originally served as a fountain in the Palazzo Medici, but was removed to the Piazza della Signoria after the expulsion of the Medici in 1494, and there displayed as an emblem of vanquished tyranny.

The Uffizi

In 1560 Cosimo I asked Vasari to design a block of government offices to stand on a site then occupied by houses and a church between the Palazzo Vecchio and the river. After Vasari's death, work on the elongated U-shaped building was continued by Buontalenti, who was asked by Francesco I to glaze the upper storey so that it could house his art collection. Each of the succeeding Medici added to the family's trove of art treasures, and the accumulated collection was preserved for public inspection by the last member of the family, Anna Maria Lodovica, whose will specified that it should be left to the people of Florence and never be allowed to leave the city. Last century a large proportion of the sculpture was transferred to the Bargello, while many of the antiquities went to the Museo Archeologico, leaving the **Galleria degli Uffizi** (Tues–Sat 9am–7pm, Sun 9am–1pm; L5000, free on first and third Sat & second and fourth Sun of month; last ticket 45min before closing) as essentially a gallery of paintings supplemented with some classical pieces.

In the case of the Uffizi, superlatives are simply the bare truth – this is the greatest picture gallery in Italy. So many masterpieces are collected here that it's barely possible to skate over the surface in a single visit; it makes sense to limit an initial tour to the first fifteen rooms, where the Florentine Renaissance works are concentrated, and to explore the rest another time. Only two factors impair the pleasure of the Uffizi: the lousy display of some of the paintings (which sometimes means that all you see of a picture is the reflection of your face looking at it), and, of course, the crowds. There's little you can do about the first, but the second problem is easily overcome – be there when the doors open, or go for the last two hours.

FROM CIMABUE TO BOTTICELLI

There are scarcely any dull stretches in the Uffizi. The picture galleries are ranged on the third floor, but some remarkable exhibits are displayed on the ground floor, in rooms that once formed part of the eleventh-century church of San Pier Scheraggio: **Andrea del Castagno**'s frescoes of celebrated Florentines, for instance, and **Botticelli**'s *Annunciation*, at the top of a small flight of steps in the hallway at the foot of the main staircase.

Room 1, housing an assembly of antique sculptures, many of which were used as a sort of source book by Renaissance artists, is often shut. The gestation period of the Renaissance can be studied in the following room, where three altarpieces of the *Maestà* (Madonna enthroned) by **Cimabue**, **Duccio** and **Giotto** dwarf everything around them. A high point in the comparatively conservative art of fourteenth-century Siena (**room 3**) is **Simone Martini**'s *Annunciation*, with its eloquently expansive background of plain gold. Florence's only first-rank Gothic painter, **Lorenzo Monaco**, features amid the collection of other quattrocento artists (**rooms 5 & 6**), with a majestic *Coronation of the Virgin* and an *Adoration of the Magi*; the version of the latter subject by **Gentile da Fabriano** is the epitome of International Gothic, cramming every inch of the flattened picture plane with often highly naturalistic detail.

The *Madonna with SS Francis, John the Baptist, Zenobius and Lucy* is one of only twelve known paintings by **Domenico Veneziano** (**room 7**), whose pupil **Piero della Francesca** is represented with portraits of *Federico da Montefeltro and Battista Sforza*; the portraits are backed by images of the Duke surrounded by the cardinal virtues and his wife by the theological virtues. **Paolo Uccello's** *The Battle of San Romano* – demonstrating the artist's obsessional interest in perspectival effects – once hung in Lorenzo il Magnifico's bed chamber, in company with the depictions of the skirmish now in the Louvre and London's National Gallery. Among the plentiful works by **Filippo Lippi** in **room 8** is his *Madonna and Child with Two Angels*, one of the best-known Renaissance images of the Madonna. Close by there's a fine *Madonna* by **Botticelli**, who in the next room shares centre stage with **Antonio del Pollaiuolo**. The works upon which Botticelli's reputation rests, though, are gathered in the merged **rooms 10–14**: *Primavera, Birth of Venus, Adoration of the Magi* and *The Madonna of the Magnificat*. Even when their meaning remains opaque – and few pictures have occasioned as much scholarly argument as the *Primavera* – these paintings are irresistibly fresh in both their conception and execution, and however many reproductions you've seen of them, the experience of the actual objects always exceeds expectations. Set away from the walls is the huge *Portinari Altarpiece* by Botticelli's Flemish contemporary **Hugo van der Goes**, a work whose naturalism greatly influenced the artists of Florence.

FROM LEONARDO DA VINCI TO TITIAN

Though the Uffizi doesn't own a finished painting that's entirely by **Leonardo da Vinci**, works in **room 15** comprise a full sketch of his career. From his formative years there's the celebrated *Annunciation* (mainly by Leonardo) and the angel in profile that he painted in Verrocchio's *Baptism*, while the incomplete *Adoration of the Magi* encapsulates his later radicalism, with its vortex of figures round Mary and the infant Christ. **Room 18**, the octagonal *Tribuna*, is where the cream of the collection used to be exhibited. It now houses the most important of the **Medici sculptures**, first among which is the *Medici Venus*, a first-century BC copy of the Praxitelean *Aphrodite of Cnidos*. Also in this room are **del Sarto's** flirtatious *Portrait of a Girl* and some chillingly precise portraits by **Bronzino** – especially compelling are *Bartolomeo and Lucrezia Panciatichi* and *Eleanor of Toledo with Giovanni de'Medici*. Vasari's portrait of Lorenzo il Magnifico and Bronzino's of Cosimo il Vecchio are deceptively immediate – each was painted long after the death of its subject.

Perugino and **Signorelli** are the principal artists in **room 19**, and after them comes a room largely devoted to **Cranach** and **Dürer**, including the latter's *Portrait of the Artist's Father*, his earliest authenticated painting. Highlights in the following sequence of rooms are a perplexing *Sacred Allegory* by **Giovanni Bellini**, **Holbein's** *Portrait of Sir Richard Southwell*, several exquisite small panels by **Memling**, and a triptych by **Mantegna**. More first-rate classical pieces are clustered in the short corridor overlooking the Arno.

The main attraction in **room 25** is **Michelangelo's** *Doni Tondo*, his only completed easel painting. Its contorted gestures and virulent colours were studied and imitated by the Mannerist painters of the sixteenth century, as can be gauged from the nearby *Moses Defending the Daughters of Jethro* by **Rosso Fiorentino**, one of the pivotal figures of the movement. Two more pieces by Rosso are on show in **room 27**, along with several works by Bronzino and the mercurial **Pontormo**, a painter whose style seems to have been in a constant state of flux. Separating the two Mannerist groups is a room containing **Andrea del Sarto's** sultry *Madonna of the Harpies* and a number of compositions by **Raphael**, including the lovely *Madonna of the Goldfinch* and *Pope Leo X with*

Cardinals Giulio de'Medici and Luigi de'Rossi – as shifty a group of ecclesiastics as ever was gathered in one frame.

Room 28 is entirely given over to another of the titanic figures of sixteenth-century art, **Titian**. His *Flora* and *A Knight of Malta* are stunning, but most male eyes tend to swivel towards the celebrated *Venus of Urbino*, just about the most fleshly and provocative of all Renaissance nudes.

FROM PARMIGIANINO TO GOYA

A brief diversion through the painters of the sixteenth-century Emilian school follows, centred on **Parmigianino**, whose *Madonna of the Long Neck* is one of the definitive Mannerist creations. **Rooms 31 to 35** feature artists from Venice and the Veneto, with outstanding paintings by **Sebastiano del Piombo** (*Death of Adonis*), **GB Moroni** (*Count Pietro Secco Suardi*), **Paolo Veronese** (*Holy Family with St Barbara*) and **Tintoretto** (*Leda*).

In **room 41**, which is dominated by **Rubens** and **Van Dyck**, it's one of the less demonstrative items that makes the biggest impact – the former's *Portrait of Isabella Brandt*. Rubens' equally theatrical contemporary, **Caravaggio**, has a cluster of pieces in **room 43**, including a howling severed head of Medusa, painted onto a shield. The next room is a showcase for the portraiture of **Rembrandt** – his *Self-Portrait as an Old Man*, painted five years or so before his death, is one of his most melancholic works, its poignancy enhanced by the proximity of another self-portrait from decades earlier. Portraits also seize the attention in the following room of eighteenth-century works, especially the two of Maria Theresa painted by **Goya**. In the hall at the top of the exit stairs squats one of the city's talismans, the *Wild Boar*, a Roman copy of third-century BC Hellenistic sculpture, it was the model for the *Porcellino* fountain in the Mercato Nuovo.

THE CORRIDOIO VASARIANO

A door on the west corridor, between rooms 25 and 34, opens onto the **Corridoio Vasariano**, a passageway built by Vasari to link the Palazzo Vecchio to the Palazzo Pitti through the Uffizi. Winding its way down to the river, over the Ponte Vecchio, through the church of Santa Felicita and into the Giardino di Bóboli, it gives a fascinating series of clandestine views of the city. As if that weren't pleasure enough, the corridor is completely lined with paintings, the larger portion of which comprises a **gallery of self-portraits**. Once past the portrait of Vasari, the series proceeds chronologically, its roll-call littered with illustrious names: Andrea del Sarto, Bronzino, Bernini, Rubens, Rembrandt, Velasquez, David, Delacroix, Ingres.

Visits to the corridor have to be arranged the previous day at the gallery's offices, on the third floor near the entrance; tours are conducted in the morning from Tuesday to Saturday, the precise time varying with staff availability.

The Bargello

To get a comprehensive idea of the Renaissance achievement in Florence, two museum calls are essential: one to the Uffizi and one to the **Museo Nazionale del Bargello** (Tues–Sat 9am–2pm, Sun 9am–1pm; L3000), spaciously installed in the daunting Palazzo del Bargello, in Via del Proconsolo. Nowhere else in Italy is there so full a collection of sculpture from the period, and yet the Bargello is normally uncrowded, the majority of sightseers passing it over in favour of the Accademia up the road.

The palace was built in 1255, immediately after the overthrow of the aristocratic regime, and soon became the seat of the *Podestà*, the chief magistrate. Numerous malefactors were tried, sentenced and executed here – Leonardo da Vinci stood in the street outside to make a drawing of the corpse of one of the Pazzi Conspirators, hung from the windows as an example to all traitors. The building acquired its present name in the sixteenth century, when the chief of police (the *Bargello*) was based here.

THE COLLECTION

The first part of the principal room on the ground floor focuses on **Michelangelo**, within whose shadow every Florentine sculptor of the sixteenth century laboured. His first major sculpture, the lurching figure of *Bacchus*, was carved at the age of 22, seven years before his graceful *Pitti Tondo*. The bust of *Brutus* (1540), Michelangelo's sole work in the genre, is a coded celebration of republican virtue, having been made soon after the murder of the tyrannical Duke Alessandro de'Medici. Works by Michelangelo's followers and contemporaries are ranged in the immediate vicinity, most of them miniature copies of the master's creations.

The shallower and more flamboyant art of **Cellini** and **Giambologna** is exhibited in the farther section of the hall. In an arc round the preparatory model of Cellini's *Perseus* are displayed the original relief panel and four statuettes from the statue's pedestal; the huge *Bust of Cosimo I*, Cellini's first work in bronze, was a sort of technical trial for the casting of the *Perseus*. Close by Giambologna's voluptuous *Florence Defeating Pisa* – a disingenuous pretext if ever there were one – is his best-known creation, the *Mercury*, a nimble figure with no bad angles. Comic relief is provided by the reliably awful **Bandinelli**'s *Adam and Eve*, looking like a grandee and his wife taking an *au naturel* stroll through the estate.

Part two of the sculpture collection is on the other side of the Gothic courtyard, which is plastered with the coats of arms of the Podestà and contains, among many other pieces, six allegorical figures by **Ammannati** from the fountain of the Palazzo Pitti courtyard. If you're in a hurry, the motley array of fourteenth-century pieces and the adjacent collection of seals and other paraphernalia are the sections to skip.

At the top of the courtyard staircase, the first-floor loggia has been turned into an aviary for Giambologna's bronze birds, imported from the Medici villa at Castello. The nearer doorway opens into the fourteenth-century Salone del Consiglio Generale, where the presiding genius is **Donatello**. Vestiges of the Gothic manner are evident in the drapery of his marble *David* (1408), but a new emphasis on the dignity of the human spirit is embodied in the tense figure of *St George*, carved just eight years later for the tabernacle of the armourers' guild at Orsanmichele. His sexually ambiguous bronze *David*, the first freestanding nude figure since classical times, was cast in the early 1430s; the strange jubilant figure known as *Amor* dates from the end of that decade.

The less complex humanism of **Luca della Robbia** is embodied in the glazed terracotta Madonnas set round the walls, while Donatello's master, **Ghiberti**, is represented by his relief of *The Sacrifice of Isaac*, his successful entry in the competition for the Baptistery doors. The treatment of the theme submitted by Brunelleschi, the runner-up, is hung close by.

Most of this floor is occupied by a collection of European and Islamic applied art, of so high a standard that it would constitute an engrossing museum in its own right; the Byzantine and medieval ivories are especially fascinating. The sculptural display resumes upstairs with more works from the della Robbia family, in rooms 14 and 15.

From the first of these rooms there's access to the spectacular **armoury**; adjoining the latter is the **Sala dei Bronzetti**, Italy's best assembly of small Renaissance bronzes – with plentiful evidence of Giambologna's virtuosity at table-top scale. Lastly, room 15 is devoted mainly to Renaissance portrait busts, including **Mino da Fiesole**'s busts of *Giovanni de'Medici* and *Piero il Gottoso* (the sons of Cosimo il Vecchio), **Francesco Laurana**'s *Battista Sforza* (an interesting comparison with the della Francesca portrait in the Uffizi), and the *Woman Holding Flowers* by **Verrocchio**. The centre of the room is occupied by Verrocchio's *David*, clearly influenced by Donatello's treatment of the subject, and a small bronze group of *Hercules and Antaeus* by **Antonio Pollaiuolo**, possessing a power out of all proportion to its size.

Via dei Calzaiuoli and around

With Piazza della Signoria out of commission, **Via dei Calzaiuoli** is without challengers as the cat-walk for the Florentine *passeggiata*. Two distinct economies operate along here: in the daytime its jewellery shops and boutiques trawl in lire by the million, but after dark the mainly Senegalese street traders move in, with their counterfeit *Louis Vuitton* bags and *Lacoste* polo shirts. Every now and then the police half-heartedly move the hawkers on, a futile ritual that sometimes takes into its sweep the buskers, acrobats and dreadful mime artists who perform here on summer evenings. For some reason an exemption seems to have been granted to Via dei Calzaiuoli's nocturnal palmists and tarot-readers, presumably because the Florentine police are as superstitious as the general populace.

ORSANMICHELE

Several of the Bargello's exhibits were removed from the street's dominant building, the church of **Orsanmichele**, which stands foursquare as a military tower one block to the north of Piazza della Signoria. From the ninth century until the thirteenth the church of *San Michele ad hortum* stood here – hence *Orsanmichele*. Towards the end of that century a grain market was raised on the site, which was in turn replaced, after a fire in 1304, with a vast loggia that served as an oratory and a trade hall for the *Arti Maggiori*, the Great Guilds which then governed the city. In 1380 the loggia was walled in and dedicated exclusively to religious functions, while two upper storeys were added for use as emergency grain stores. Not long after, each guild was charged with decorating one of the exterior tabernacles of the building, a scheme which spanned the emergent years of the Renaissance.

At present a full restoration is in progress, so it's unlikely that all the **exterior sculpture** will be visible, but some of the major pieces should be back in their rightful places. Outstanding are the following: on the east side (Via dei Calzaiuoli) – *John the Baptist* by Ghiberti, the first life-size bronze statue of the Renaissance, and *The Incredulity of St Thomas* by Verrocchio; on the north side – the *Four Crowned Saints* by Nanni di Banco (they were four Christian sculptors executed by Diocletian for refusing to make a pagan image), and a copy of Donatello's *St George*; on the west side – *St Matthew* and *St Stephen* by Ghiberti and *St Eligius* by Nanni di Banco; on the south side – a *Madonna and Child*, probably by Giovanni Tedesco.

To get into the square nave of the church it's necessary to circumnavigate the interior's main feature, the vast **tabernacle** by **Orcagna**; carved with delicate reliefs and tiny statues, and studded with coloured marble and glass, this is the only significant sculptural work by the artist. It frames a *Madonna* painted in 1347 by **Bernardo Daddi** as a replacement for a miraculous image of the Virgin that was destroyed by the 1304 fire, and whose powers this picture is said to have inherited. The vaulted halls of the upstairs granary – one of the city's most imposing medieval interiors – are entered via a footbridge from the Palazzo dell'Arte della Lana (Wool Guild); as a rule, they are only accessible when in use as an exhibition space.

PIAZZA DELLA REPUBBLICA
From the back of Orsanmichele it's a brief stroll to the Piazza della Repubblica, created in the last century in an attempt to give Florence the sort of grand public square that is a prerequisite for any capital city. It's an utterly characterless place, impressive solely for its size, while its four large and once-fashionable cafés – *Donnini, Giubbe Rosse, Gilli* and *Paszkowski* – similarly lack the charisma to which they aspire. The last of the quartet recently brought attention to bear on the often-denied racism of Italian society, through its pioneering employment of a black waiter; itself perhaps an instance of radical chic, the move prompted abusive letters and boycotts.

From Piazza della Signoria to Ognissanti

Despite the urban improvement schemes of the last century and the bombings of the last war, several streets in central Florence retain their medieval character, especially in the district to the west of Piazza della Signoria. Forming a sort of gateway to this quarter is the **Mercato Nuovo** (summer daily 9am–7pm; winter Tues–Sat 9am–5pm), whose souvenir stalls are probably the busiest in the city; there's been a market here since the eleventh century, though the present loggia dates from the sixteenth. Usually a small group is gathered round the bronze boar known as *Il Porcellino*, trying to earn some good luck by getting a coin to fall from the animal's mouth through the grill below his head. An aimless amble through the streets beyond the thirteenth-century Palazzo di Parte Guelfa – streets such as Via delle Terme and Borgo Santi Apostoli – will give you some idea of the feel of Florence in the Middle Ages, when every important house was an urban fortress.

Palazzo Davanzati
Although it has been much restored, the fourteenth-century **Palazzo Davanzati** is the city's most authentic example of a house from that period. In the sixteenth century a loggia replaced the battlements on the roof, and the Davanzati stuck their coat of arms on the front, but otherwise the outside of the house looks much as it did when first inhabited. Nowadays the palace houses the **Museo della Casa Fiorentina Antica** (Tues–Sat 9am–2pm, Sun 9am–1pm; L2000), and virtually every room of the reconstructed interior is furnished and decorated in medieval style, using genuine artefacts assembled from a variety of sources.

Merchants' houses in the fourteenth century would typically have had elaborately **painted walls** in the main rooms, and the Palazzo Davanzati preserves some fine examples of such decor – especially in the dining room, where the imitation wall-hangings of the lower walls are patterned with a parrot motif, while the upper part depicts a row of trees. The furnishings are sparse by modern standards, but their quality rather than their quantity is the index of prosperity: the tapestries, ceramics and lacework are all beautiful examples of their craft, none more so than the Sicilian bed cover in the first-floor bedroom, woven with scenes from the story of Tristan. Perhaps the most telling sign of the wealth of the palace's first occupants, however, is the private well, from which water was drawn by a shaft connecting all five floors.

Santa Trìnita

Continuing westward past Palazzo Davanzati, Via Porta Rossa runs into Piazza Santa Trìnita, not so much a square as a widening of the city's most expensive street, Via Tornabuoni. The road crosses the Arno on the city's most stylish bridge, the **Ponte Santa Trìnita**; it was ostensibly designed by Ammannati, but the curve of its arches so closely resembles the arc of Michelangelo's Medici tombs that the credit probably should be his.

The antiquity of the church of **Santa Trìnita** (daily 8am–noon & 4–7pm) is evident in the Latinate pronunciation of its name – modern Italian stresses the last not the first syllable. Founded in the eleventh century, the church was rebuilt between 1250 and the end of the following century, though the inside face of the entrance wall remains from the Romanesque building. The austerity of the architecture is alleviated by a number of works of art, the best of which all date from the fifteenth century. **Lorenzo Monaco** frescoed the fourth chapel on the right and painted its *Annunciation* altarpiece, and the decoration of the Cappella Sassetti (second to the right of the altar) was undertaken by **Ghirlandaio**, who provided an altarpiece of *The Adoration of the Shepherds* and a fresco cycle depicting *Scenes from the Life of St Francis*. Set in Piazza della Signoria, the scene showing Francis receiving the rule of the order includes portraits of Lorenzo il Magnifico and Francesco Sassetti, the patron of the chapel – they are standing in the right foreground, receiving the homage of Lorenzo's sons and his protegé, the philosopher Poliziano. A powerful composition by **Luca della Robbia** – the tomb of Benozzo Federighi, Bishop of Fiesole – occupies a wall of the chapel second to the left of the altar, framed by a ceramic border of flowers and greenery.

Palazzo Strozzi and Palazzo Rucellai

The shops of Via Tornabuoni are effectively out of bounds to those who don't travel first class. *Versace*, *Armani* and company have their outlets here, sharing the territory with jewellery and leather showrooms such as that of *Gucci*, the best-known local firm.

Conspicuous wealth is nothing new on Via Tornabuoni, for looming above everything is the vast **Palazzo Strozzi**, the last, the largest and the least subtle of Florentine Renaissance palaces. Filippo Strozzi bought and demolished a dozen town houses to make space for Giuliano da Sangallo's strong-box in stone, and the construction of it lasted from 1489 to 1536, during which time the supervision of the project passed to Cronaca. A permanent exhibition in the **Museo di Palazzo Strozzi** (Mon, Wed & Fri 4–7pm; free) explains the history of the palace.

Some of Florence's plutocrats made an impression with rather more élan. When Giovanni Rucellai – one of the richest businessmen in the city and an esteemed scholar into the bargain – decided in the 1450s to commission a new house, the architect he turned to was Leon Battista Alberti, the archetypal universal genius of the Renaissance. The **Palazzo Rucellai**, two minutes' walk from the Strozzi house in Via della Vigna Nuova, was the first palace in Florence to follow the rules of classical architecture – its tiers of pilasters, incised into smooth blocks of stone, explicitly evoke the exterior wall of the Colosseum. An even more refined example of Alberti's work, the **Cappella di San Sepolcro** (open Sat 5.30pm Oct–June), is to be seen in the adjoining Cappella Rucellai; designed as the funerary monument to Giovanni Rucellai, it takes the form of a diminutive reconstruction of Jerusalem's Church of the Holy Sepulchre.

The church of San Pancrozio, of which Alberti's chapel once formed a part, has been converted into the swish **Museo Mario Marini** (June–Aug Wed–Mon 10am–1pm & 4–7pm; Sept–May Wed–Mon 10am–6pm; L4000), displaying the works left to the city in the sculptor's will a few years ago. Variations on his familiar horse-and-rider theme predominate.

Ognissanti

In medieval times a major area of cloth production – the foundation of the Florentine economy – lay in the west of the city. **Ognissanti**, the main church of this quarter, was founded in the thirteenth century by a Benedictine order whose particular monastic industry was the weaving of woollen cloth. Three hundred years later the Franciscans took it over, and the new tenure was marked by a Baroque overhaul which spared only the campanile.

The facade of the church is of historical interest as one of the earliest eruptions of the Baroque style in Florence, but the church is made appealing by earlier features – the frescoes by **Domenico Ghirlandaio** and **Sandro Botticelli**. The young face squeezed between the Madonna and the dark-cloaked man in Ghirlandaio's *Madonna della Misericordia*, over the second altar on the right, is said to be that of Amerigo Vespucci – later to set sail on voyages that would give his name to America. Just beyond this, on opposite sides of the nave, are mounted Botticelli's *St Augustine* and Ghirlandaio's more earthbound *St Jerome*, both painted in 1480. In the same year Ghirlandaio painted the bucolic *Last Supper* that covers one wall of the **refectory** (Mon–Sat 9am–noon & 2–4pm), reached through the cloister.

Santa Maria Novella, San Lorenzo and around

Cross the road from the forecourt of the train station, and you're on the edge of a zone free from the hazards of speeding traffic and petrol fumes. On the other side of the church of Santa Maria Novella – whose back directly faces the station – lies a square with something of a lethargic backwater atmosphere, much favoured as a spot for picnic lunches and after-dark loitering. In contrast, a couple of blocks to the east of the station stands Florence's main food market, encircled by scores of street stalls, which spread from the vast market hall to the church of San Lorenzo – like Santa Maria Novella, a monument of major importance.

Santa Maria Novella

From the beguiling green and white patterns of its marble facade, you'd never guess that the church of **Santa Maria Novella** (Mon–Sat 7.15–11.30am & 3.30–5pm, Sun 3.30–5pm) was the Florentine base of the Dominican order, the grim vigilantes of thirteenth-century Catholicism. A church was founded here at the end of the eleventh century, and shortly afterwards was handed over to the

Dominicans, who set about altering the place to their taste. By 1360 the interior was completed, but only the lower part of the facade was finished, a state of affairs that lasted until 1456, when Giovanni Rucellai paid for Alberti to design a classicised upper storey that would blend with the older section while improving the facade's proportions.

The architects of the Gothic interior were capable of great ingenuity too – the distance between the columns diminishes with proximity to the altar, a device to make the nave seem longer from the entrance. **Masaccio**'s extraordinary fresco of *The Trinity* (1428), one of the earliest works in which perspective and classical proportion were rigorously employed, is painted onto the wall halfway down the left aisle. Nothing else in the main part of the church has quite the same impact, but the wealth of decoration at the chancel end is astounding. The **Cappella di Filippo Strozzi** (immediately to the right of the chancel) is covered by a fresco cycle commissioned by Strozzi from **Filippino Lippi** in 1486 and finished fifteen years later, after the artist's sojourn in Rome; Lippi's fantasy vision of classical ruins, in which the narrative often seems to take second place, is one of the first examples of an archaeological interest in Roman ruins. As a chronicle of fifteenth-century life in Florence, no series of frescoes is more fascinating than **Domenico Ghirlandaio**'s pictures behind the high altar; the work was commissioned by Giovanni Tornabuoni – which explains why certain illustrious ladies of the Tornabuoni family are present at the birth of John the Baptist and of the Virgin.

Brunelleschi's *Crucifix*, popularly supposed to have been carved as a lesson to Donatello, hangs in the Cappella Gondi, to the left of the chancel. At the end of the left transept is the raised Cappella Strozzi, whose faded frescoes by **Nardo di Cione** (1350s) include an entire wall of visual commentary on Dante's *Inferno*. The magnificent altarpiece by Nardo's brother Andrea (better known as **Orcagna**), is a piece of propaganda for the Dominicans – Christ is shown bestowing favour simultaneously on both Saint Peter and Saint Thomas Aquinas, a figure second only to Saint Dominic in the order's hierarchy.

THE CLOISTERS
Santa Maria Novella's cloisters (Mon–Thurs & Sat 9am–2pm; Sun 8am–1pm; L2000, free Sun), entered to the left of the church facade, are more richly decorated than any others in Florence. **Paolo Uccello** and his workshop executed the frescoes in the Romanesque **Chiostro Verde** – look out for Uccello's windswept image of the Flood and its aftermath, on the right as you enter. The **Cappella degli Spagnuoli** (Spanish Chapel), once the chapter house, received its new name after Eleanor of Toledo reserved it for the use of her Spanish entourage; its fresco cycle by **Andrea di Firenze**, an extended depiction of the triumph of the Catholic church, was described by Ruskin as "the most noble piece of pictorial philosophy in Italy". His representation of the Duomo was purely speculative – the cycle dates from the 1360s, long before Brunelleschi even won the contract for the dome. The contemporaneous but more exposed decoration of the **Chiostrino dei Morti**, the oldest part of the complex, has not aged so robustly.

The Market
One of the unmissable sights of Florence is the San Lorenzo area's **Mercato Centrale**, built in stone, iron and glass by Giuseppe Mengoni, architect of Milan's Galleria. It opened in 1874, and a century later was given a major overhaul, reopening in 1980 with a new first floor. Butchers, *alimentari*, tripe sellers,

greengrocers (on the first floor), pasta stalls, bars – they're all gathered under the one roof, and all charging prices lower than you'll readily find elsewhere in the city. It's open Monday to Friday from 7am to 2pm, and on Saturdays and days immediately prior to a public holiday it opens additionally from 4 to 8pm. Get there close to the end of the working day and you'll get some good reductions. And for a taste of simple Florentine food at its best, call in at *Ottavino*, a small bar that's the established meeting-place of the market workers – it's on the Via dell'Ariento side, and is open until 1.30pm.

Each day from 8am to 7pm the streets encircling the Mercato Centrale are thronged with stalls selling bags, belts, shoes – everything, in fact, that your wardrobe might need. This is the busiest of Florence's daily **street markets**, and a half-hour's immersion in the haggling mass of customers is a pleasure for all but the irredeemably misanthropic. It's not the cheapest place in town, though – the stalls at Piazza delle Cure, just beyond Piazza della Libertà (every morning; take bus #1), and the enormous Tuesday morning market at the Cascine park, west along the Arno (bus #16), have the real bargains.

San Lorenzo

Founded back in the fourth century, **San Lorenzo** (8am–noon & 3.30–7pm) has a good claim to be the oldest church in Florence, and for the best part of three hundred years was the city's cathedral. As this was the Medici's parish church, it inevitably benefitted from the family's patronage: in 1425 Giovanni Bicci de'Medici commissioned Brunelleschi to rebuild San Lorenzo, a move which started a long association between the family and the building. Although Michelangelo sweated to produce a scheme for San Lorenzo's facade, the bare brick of the exterior has never been clad. It's a stark, inappropriate prelude to the powerful simplicity of Brunelleschi's interior, one of the earliest Renaissance church designs.

Inside, two paintings stand out from the rest – Rosso Fiorentino's *Marriage of the Virgin* (second chapel on the right) and Filippo Lippi's *Annunciation* (in chapel on west side of the left transept). But more striking are the two **bronze pulpits** by **Donatello**. Covered in densely populated and disquieting reliefs, chiefly of scenes preceding and following the Crucifixion, these are the artist's last works, and were completed by his pupils. Close by, at the foot of the altar steps, a large disc of multicoloured marble marks the grave of Cosimo il Vecchio, the artist's main patron.

Further pieces by Donatello (who is buried in the chapel with the Lippi painting) adorn the neighbouring **Sagrestia Vecchia** (Old Sacristy). Much of the decorative work here is by Donatello – the two pairs of bronze doors, the large reliefs of *SS Cosmas and Damian* and *SS Lawrence and Stephen*, and the eight terracotta tondoes. The table of milky marble in the centre of the room is the tomb of Cosimo il Vecchio's parents, Giovanni Bicci de'Medici and Piccarda Bueri.

THE BIBLIOTECA LAURENZIANA

At the top of the left aisle of San Lorenzo a door leads out to the cloister and the staircase going up to the **Biblioteca Laurenziana** (Mon–Sat 9am–1pm; free), a crucial example of Mannerist architecture. Wishing to create a suitably grandiose home for the precious manuscripts assembled by Cosimo il Vecchio and Lorenzo il Magnifico, Pope Clement VII (Lorenzo's nephew) asked Michelangelo to design a new Medici library in 1524.

The startling feature of the building he came up with is the **vestibule**, a room that is almost filled by a flight of steps resembling a solidified lava flow. From this deliberately eccentric space, the visitor passes into the tranquil, architecturally correct **reading room**, from where the illogically placed columns and brackets of the vestibule cannot be seen. Annual exhibitions in the connecting rooms draw on the Medici collection, which includes manuscripts as diverse as a fifth-century copy of Virgil and a treatise on architecture by Leonardo.

THE CAPPELLE MEDICEE
Michelangelo's most celebrated contribution to the San Lorenzo buildings, the **Sagrestia Nuova**, is part of the Cappelle Medicee (Tues–Sat 9am–2pm, Sun 9am–1pm; L4500), the entrance to which is in Piazza Madonna degli Aldobrandini. The larger of the chapels is the Cappella dei Principi (Chapel of the Princes), a marble-plated hall built as a mausoleum for Cosimo I and his ancestors. Morbid and dowdy, it was the most expensive building project ever financed by the family, and epitomises the mentality that thinks magnificence is directly proportional to expenditure.

The Sagrestia Nuova, one of the earliest Mannerist buildings, was begun in 1520 and intended as a tribute to, and subversion of, Brunelleschi's Sagrestia Vecchia. Architectural connoisseurs go into raptures over the complex cornices of the alcoves and other such sophistications, but the lay person will be drawn to the fabulous **Medici tombs**, carved by Michelangelo between 1524 and 1533. To the left is the tomb of **Lorenzo, Duke of Urbino**, the grandson of Lorenzo il Magnifico; he is depicted as a man of thought, and his sarcophagus bears figures of *Dawn* and *Dusk*, the times of day whose ambiguities appeal to the contemplative mind. Opposite is the tomb of Lorenzo il Magnifico's youngest son, **Giuliano, Duke of Nemours**; as a man of action, his character is symbolised by *Day* and *Night*. Contrary to these idealised images, Lorenzo and Giuliano were feeble individuals, and both died young and unlamented. Their effigies were intended to face the equally grand tombs of Lorenzo il Magnifico and his brother Giuliano; the only part of the project realised by Michelangelo is the serene *Madonna and Child*, the last image of the Madonna he ever sculpted.

The Palazzo Medici-Riccardi
On the edge of the square in front of San Lorenzo stands the **Palazzo Medici-Riccardi** (Mon, Tues & Thurs–Sat 9am–12.45pm & 3–4.45pm, Sun 9am–noon; free), built for Cosimo il Vecchio by Michelozzo in the 1440s. With its heavily rusticated exterior, this monolithic palace was the prototype for such houses as the Palazzo Pitti and Palazzo Strozzi, but was greatly altered in the seventeenth century by its new owners, the Riccardi family.

Of Michelozzo's original scheme, only the upstairs **chapel** remains intact; the interior is covered by a colourful narrative fresco of the *Journey of the Magi*, painted around 1460 by Benozzo Gozzoli. The procession is basically a pretext for painting scores of exotic costumes and portraits of the Medici household – a romanticised Lorenzo il Magnifico leads the main cavalcade, while his father, Piero il Gottoso, lags a short way behind. In the crowd at the rear of the entourage is the artist himself, his red beret bearing his name in gold. A second staircase ascends from the courtyard to the **Sala di Luca Giordano**, a gilded and mirrored gallery notable for its *Madonna and Child* by Filippo Lippi, and Luca Giordano's ceiling fresco of *The Apotheosis of the Medici*, an enterprise from which one can only deduce that Giordano had no sense of shame.

San Marco and around

Much of central Florence's traffic is funnelled along **Via Cavour**, the thoroughfare connecting the Duomo area to Piazza della Libertà, a major confluence of the city's peripheral carriageways (the *viale*). Except as a place to catch buses out to Fiesole and other points north, the street has little to recommend it, but halfway along it lies **Piazza San Marco**, the core of the university district. The distinctly more youthful ambience of this area makes it a welcome refuge from the commercial hustle of inner Florence, and although one of the top tourist attractions – the Accademia – draws the coach parties out here, it has a number of sights that are often overlooked.

The Museo di San Marco

One side of the square is taken up by the Dominican convent and church of **San Marco**, recipient of Cosimo il Vecchio's most lavish patronage. In the 1430s he financed Michelozzo's enlargement of the buildings, and went on to establish a vast public library here. Abashed by the wealth he was transferring to them, the friars of San Marco suggested to Cosimo that he need not continue to support them on such a scale – to which he replied "Never shall I be able to give God enough to set him down as my debtor." Ironically, the convent became the centre of resistance to the Medici later in the century – Girolamo Savonarola, leader of the theocratic government of Florence between the expulsion of the Medici in 1494 and his execution four years later, was prior of San Marco from 1491.

As Michelozzo was altering and expanding the convent, its walls were being decorated by one of its friars, **Fra Angelico**, a painter in whom a medieval simplicity of mind was allied to a non-medieval sophistication of manner. Now deconsecrated, the church and convent today house the **Museo di San Marco** (Tues–Sat 9am–2pm, Sun 9am–1pm; L3000), in effect a museum dedicated to the art of Fra Angelico.

The **Ospizio dei Pellegrini** (Pilgrims' Hospice) contains a collection of around twenty paintings by him, a large number of them brought here from other churches in Florence. A *Deposition* and a small *Last Judgment* are outstanding – the former remarkable for its aura of tranquillity, as though the minds of its protagonists were already fixed on the Resurrection.

Across the cloister, in the **Sala Capitolare** (Chapter House), is a powerful fresco of the *Crucifixion*, painted by Angelico and assistants in 1441, but for the drama of its setting and the lucidity of its composition, nothing matches the famous *Annunciation* at the summit of the main staircase. Right round this upper floor are ranged the 44 tiny **dormitory cells**, each frescoed either by Angelico himself or by his assistants. Most of the works in the file of cells on the left are entirely by Angelico – don't miss the *Noli me tangere* (cell 1), the *Annunciation* (cell 3), the *Transfiguration* (cell 6) and the *Coronation of the Virgin* (cell 9). In all likelihood, the marvellous *Madonna Enthroned*, on the facing wall, is by Angelico too. The incongruous monastic onlookers in several of the scenes are Saint Dominic (with the star above his head) and Saint Peter Martyr (with the split skull); the latter zealot, responsible for a massacre of Florentine heretics in the thirteenth century, is the city's home-produced Dominican saint. Michelozzo's **library**, a room that seems to exude an atmosphere of calm study, is off the corridor to the right, at the end of which is the pair of rooms used by Cosimo il Vecchio when he came here on retreat.

San Marco church, greatly altered since Michelozzo's intervention, is worth a visit for two works on the second and third altars on the right: a *Madonna and Saints*, painted in 1509 by Fra Bartolomeo (like Fra Angelico, a friar at the convent), and an eighth-century mosaic of *The Madonna in Prayer*, brought here from Constantinople.

The Galleria dell'Accademia

Florence's first Academy of Drawing – indeed, Europe's first – was founded in the mid-sixteenth century by Bronzino, Ammannati and Vasari. Initially based in Santissima Annunziata, this *Accademia del Disegno* moved in 1764 to Via Ricasoli 66, and soon afterwards was transformed into a general arts academy, the *Accademia di Belle Arti*. Twenty years later the Grand Duke Pietro Leopoldo founded the nearby **Galleria dell'Accademia** (Tues–Sat 9am–2pm, Sun 9am–1pm; L4000), filling its rooms with paintings for the edification of the students. Later augmented with pieces from suppressed religious foundations and other sources, the Accademia has an impressive collection of paintings, especially of Florentine altarpieces from the fourteenth to the early sixteenth centuries (including a brace of Botticellis). But the pictures are not what pull the crowds in numbers equalled only by the Uffizi – the attraction is the sculpture of **Michelangelo**, or rather, the **David**.

Once the emblem of the city's republican pride, and later of the illimitable ambition of the Renaissance artist, Michelangelo's *David* is nowadays the heraldic device of touristic Florence. Seeing it for the first time as a physical object can be something of a shock. Finished in 1504, when Michelangelo was just 29, and carved from a gigantic block of marble whose shallowness posed severe difficulties, it's an incomparable show of technical bravura. But the *David* is a piece of monumental public sculpture (it stood in the Piazza della Signoria until 1873), not a gallery exhibit: closely surveyed in the Accademia's specially built tribune, it is perturbing rather than uplifting. Adolescent in its proportions, the monstrous figure impresses more in the refinement of its details than as a well composed entity.

Michelangelo once described the process of carving as being the liberation of the form from within the stone, a notion that seems to be embodied by the remarkable unfinished **Slaves** nearby. His procedure, clearly demonstrated here, was to cut the figure as if it were a deep relief, and then to free the three-dimensional figure. Carved in the 1520s, they were intended for the tomb of Julius II; in 1564 the artist's nephew gave them to the Medici, who installed them in the grotto of the Bóboli gardens. In their midst is another unfinished work, *St Matthew*, which was started immediately after completion of the *David* as a commission from the Opera del Duomo; they actually requested a full series of Apostles, but this is the only one Michelangelo ever began. The *Pietà*, though labelled as a work by Michelangelo, is no longer thought to be by him.

Piazza Santissima Annunziata and around

Its porticoes and church make **Piazza Santissima Annunziata** the Florentines' favourite square. Until the seventeenth century the Florentine year used to begin on March 25, the Feast of the Annunciation – hence the city's predilection for paintings of the Annunciation, and the fashionableness of the Annunziata church, which is still the place for society weddings. The festival is marked by a huge fair in the square and the streets leading off it. Giambologna's final work, the **equestrian statue of Grand Duke Ferdinando I**, holds the centre of the square; it was cast by his pupil Pietro Tacca, creator of the two bizarre **fountains**, on each of which a pair of aquatic monkeys dribble water at two whiskered sea-slugs.

The Spedale degli Innocenti

The tone of the square is set by Brunelleschi's **Spedale degli Innocenti**, which was opened in 1445 as the first foundlings' hospital in Europe, and still incorporates an orphanage – Luca della Robbia's ceramic tondoes of swaddled babies advertise the building's function. The convent, centred on two beautiful cloisters, now contains the **Museo dello Spedale degli Innocenti** (summer Mon, Tues & Thurs–Sat 9am–2pm, Sun 8am–1pm; winter closes 1pm each day; L3000, last ticket 1hr before closing), a miscellany of Florentine Renaissance art including one of Luca della Robbia's most charming Madonnas and an incident-packed *Adoration of the Magi* by Domenico Ghirlandaio. No collection from this period could be anything other than interesting, but Florence has plenty of museums that you should check out before this one.

Santissima Annunziata

The church of **Santissima Annunziata** is the mother church of the Servite order, founded by seven Florentine aristocrats in 1234. Its dedication to the Virgin Annunciate took place in the fourteenth century, in recognition of its miraculous image of the Virgin: the story goes that the painting, left unfinished by the monastic artist, was completed by an angel. So many pilgrims came to adore the image that the church was rebuilt to accommodate them in the second half of the fifteenth century. The architect was Michelozzo (brother of the prior), the paymasters the Medici. In the **Chiostro dei Voti**, the atrium that Michelozzo built onto the church, are preserved some beautiful frescoes; mainly painted in the 1510s, they include a *Visitation* by Pontormo and a series by Andrea del Sarto, whose *Birth of the Virgin* achieves a perfect balance of spontaneity and geometrical order.

So frequent are masses at Santissima Annunziata that the interior is open to tourists only between 4pm and 5pm from Monday to Saturday. Much of its gilt and stucco fancy dress was perpetrated in the seventeenth and eighteenth centuries, but the ornate **tabernacle** of the miraculous image, cordoned by candles and lanterns to the left of the entrance, was produced by Michelozzo. His patron, Piero di Cosimo de'Medici, made sure that nobody remained unaware of the money he sank into the shrine – an inscription in the floor reads "Costò fior. 4 mila el marmo solo" (The marble alone cost 4000 florins). The painting encased in the marble has been repainted into obscurity, and is rarely shown anyway; far more interesting are the frescoes by **Andrea del Castagno** in the first two chapels on the left – *The Vision of St Jerome* and *The Trinity*. Separated from the nave by a triumphal arch is the unusual **tribune**, begun by Michelozzo but completed to designs by Alberti; the chapel at the furthest point (rarely accessible to visitors) was altered by Giambologna into a monument to himself.

The adjoining **Chiostro dei Morti**, entered from the left transept, is worth visiting for Andrea del Sarto's calculatedly informal *Madonna del Sacco*, painted right over the door.

The Museo Archeologico

A hundred metres from the church, on Via della Colonna, is the **Museo Archeologico** (Tues–Sat 9am–2pm, Sun 9am–1pm; L3000; free guided tours Sat 11am & Sun 10.30am). This is the pre-eminent collection of its kind in north Italy, though at the moment its quality doesn't exactly shine out at you – a modernisation of the displays is in progress, and they are still rectifying damage caused by the flood of 1966, so the museum generally has something of an *ad hoc* air about it.

The museum's special strength is its showing of **Etruscan** finds, many of them part of the Medici bequest. On the ground floor there's a varied and well-labelled display of Etruscan funerary figures and Greek statuary, but pride of place goes to the *François Vase*, an Attic krater from the sixth century BC. It's been restored twice – once after its discovery in 1845, in an Etruscan tomb at Chiusi, and again after a butter-fingered member of staff bounced it off the floor in 1900, converting it into a 638-piece jigsaw. Of comparable importance in the first-floor **Egyptian collection** is a Hittite chariot made of bone and wood and dating from the fourteenth century BC.

The rest of this floor and much of the floor above are given over to the **Etruscan, Greek and Roman collections**, arranged with variable clarity. Outstanding among the Roman pieces is the nude known as the *Idolino*, probably a copy of a fifth-century BC original. The Hellenic head of a horse, in the same room, once adorned the garden of the Palazzo Medici, where it was studied by Donatello and Verrocchio. In the long gallery stand the best of the Etruscan pieces: the *Arringatore* (Orator), the only known Etruscan large bronze from the Hellenistic period; and the *Chimera*, a triple-headed monster of the fifth century BC, much admired by Cosimo I's retinue of Mannerist artists, as well as by all subsequent connoisseurs of the bizarre. The adjoining room is a storehouse of Etruscan funerary caskets, stacked in a way that invites the visitor to pass through quickly.

The Santa Croce district

The 1966 flood changed the character of the area around Santa Croce. Prior to then it had been one of the more densely populated districts of the city, packed with tenements and small workshops. Lying lower than the surrounding area, **Piazza Santa Croce** and the streets around it were devastated when the Arno burst its banks, and many of the residents moved out permanently in the following years. Leather shops and jewellers are still in evidence, but the souvenir stalls are now a more conspicuous presence.

Traditionally this has been one of the city's main arenas for festivities. The Medici used it for self-aggrandising pageants, and during the years of Savonarola's ascendancy, the square was the principal site for the ceremonial execution of heretics. It's still sometimes used as the pitch for the *Gioco di Calcio Storico*, a sort of football tournament between the city's four *quartiere*; the game is held three times in Saint John's week (last week of June), and is characterised by incomprehensible rules and a degree of violence from which the heavy sixteenth-century costumes offer inadequate protection. Tickets for the event are sold at the *Chiosco degli Sportivi* in Via de'Anselmi – by the end of May there are few left.

The Church of Santa Croce

The Franciscan church of Florence, **Santa Croce** (daily 7.15am–12.30pm & 2.30–6.30pm) was begun in 1294, possibly by the architect of the Duomo, Arnolfo di Cambio. Construction was held up by a split in the Franciscan ranks and not resumed until the early fifteenth century, the period when Santa Croce acquired its status as the mausoleum of Florence's eminent citizens. Over 270 tombstones pave the floor of the church, while grander monuments commemorate the likes of Ghiberti, Michelangelo, Machiavelli, Galileo and Dante – though the last of the group is actually buried in Ravenna, where he died in exile.

A lovely relief by Antonio Rossellino surmounts one of the simpler and more eloquent tombs, attached to the first pillar on the right: it's that of **Francesco Nori**, murdered with Giuliano de'Medici by the Pazzi conspirators. Right by this is Vasari's monument to **Michelangelo**, whose body was brought back from Rome to Florence in July 1574, a return marked with a spectacular memorial service in San Lorenzo. On the opposite side of the church is the tomb of **Galileo**, built in 1737, when it was finally agreed to give the great scientist a Christian burial. Back in the right aisle, the Neoclassical cenotaph to **Dante** is immediately after the second altar, while against the third pillar there's a beautiful **pulpit** by Benedetto da Maiano, carved with scenes from the life of Saint Francis. The side door at the end of the aisle is flanked by **Donatello**'s gilded stone relief of *The Annunciation* and Bernardo Rossellino's tomb of the humanist **Leonardo Bruni**, a design which spawned innumerable imitations.

The chapels at the east end of Santa Croce are a compendium of Florentine fourteenth-century art, showing the extent of Giotto's influence and the full diversity of his followers. The **Cappella Castellani**, on the west side of the right transept, was completely frescoed in the 1480s by **Agnolo Gaddi** and his pupils, while the adjoining **Cappella Baroncelli** was decorated by Agnolo's father, **Taddeo**, a long-time assistant to Giotto himself. Taddeo's cycle features the first night scene in Western painting, *The Annunciation to the Shepherds*. A doorway just inside the corridor alongside the Cappella Baroncelli opens into the **sacristy**, where the centrepiece is a *Crucifixion* by Taddeo; the tiny **Cappella Rinuccini**, separated from the sacristy by a grille, is covered with frescoes by the more solemn **Giovanni da Milano**. The corridor ends at the **Cappella Medici**, notable for its large terracotta altarpiece by Andrea della Robbia; like the corridor, the chapel was designed by Michelozzo, the Medici's favourite architect.

Both the **Cappella Peruzzi** and the **Cappella Bardi** (on the right of the chancel) are entirely covered with frescoes by **Giotto**. The former (further from the chancel), shows scenes from the lives of Saint John the Baptist and John the Evangelist; the latter, painted slightly earlier and with some assistance, features the life of Saint Francis. **Agnolo Gaddi** was responsible for all the frescoes round and above the high altar, and for the design of the stained glass in the lancet windows. The *Scenes from the Life of St Sylvester* in the **Cappella Bardi di Vernio** (the fifth after the chancel) were painted in the 1330s by **Maso di Banco**, perhaps the most inventive of Giotto's followers. At the end of the left chancel, the second **Cappella Bardi** houses a wooden *Crucifix* by **Donatello** – supposedly criticised by Brunelleschi as resembling a "peasant on the Cross".

THE CAPPELLA DEI PAZZI, CLOISTERS AND MUSEUM

If one building can be said to typify the spirit of the early Renaissance, it's Brunelleschi's **Cappella dei Pazzi**, which stands at the end of Santa Croce's first cloister (entrance to chapel, cloisters & museum: summer Thurs–Tues 10am–12.30pm & 2.30–6.30pm; winter 10am–12.30pm & 3–5pm; L2000). Designed in the 1430s and completed in the 1470s, several years after the architect's death, the chapel achieves an unprecedented harmony of composition and integration of decorative detail. The polychrome lining of the portico's shallow cupola is by Luca della Robbia, as is the tondo of *St Andrew* over the door; inside, Luca also produced the blue and white tondoes of the *Apostles*. The vividly coloured tondoes of the *Evangelists* were produced in the della Robbia workshop, possibly to designs by Donatello. The spacious **second cloister**, also by Brunelleschi, is probably the most peaceful spot in the centre of Florence.

The **Museo dell'Opera di Santa Croce**, off the first cloister, houses a miscellany of works of art, the best of which are gathered in the refectory. Cimabue's *Crucifixion* has become the emblem of the havoc caused by the 1966 flood, when eighteen feet of filthy water surged into the church, tearing the Crucifix from its mounting and stripping much of its paint away. Also in this room are Taddeo Gaddi's fresco of the *Last Supper and Crucifixion*, fragments of the Orcagna frescoes that covered Santa Croce's nave before Vasari renovated it, and Donatello's enormous gilded *St Louis of Toulouse*, made for Orsanmichele.

Casa Buonarotti

The **Casa Buonarotti** (Wed–Mon 9.30am–1.30pm; L4000), north of Santa Croce at Via Ghibellina 70, is enticing in name but slightly disappointing in substance, in that it contains few items directly connected with the great man. Michelangelo did own this property, but he never actually lived here. He bequeathed it to his nephew, his sole descendant, whose son in turn converted part of the property into a gallery dedicated to his great-uncle. Much of the space is taken up by homages to Michelangelo, copies of works by him and portraits of him, the exciting items being confined to a few rooms on the first floor.

The two main treasures are to be found in the room to the left of the stairs: *The Madonna of the Steps* is Michelangelo's earliest known work, carved when he was no older than sixteen, and the similarly unfinished *Battle of the Centaurs* dates from immediately afterwards, when the boy was living in the Medici household. In the adjacent room you'll find the wooden model for the facade of San Lorenzo, while the room in front of the stairs houses the largest of all the sculptural models on display, the torso of a *River God* intended for the Medici chapel in San Lorenzo. To the right is a room containing a painted wooden *Crucifix* discovered in Santo Spirito in 1963; it's now generally thought to be a Michelangelo sculpture whose existence has long been known through documents, but was feared lost. In addition to these, original architectural drawings and other studies are sometimes on display, and the ground floor is often given over to exhibitions devoted to a specialised aspect of Michelangelo's career.

Oltrarno and San Miniato

Visitors to Florence might perceive the Arno as merely a brief interruption in the urban fabric, but Florentines still talk as though a ravine ran through their city. North of the river is known as *Arno di quà* (over here), while the other side of the river is *Arno di là* (over there) or the *Oltrarno*, a terminology which has its roots in medieval times, when the district to the south was geographically more detached. Though traditionally an artisans' quarter, the Oltrarno has always contained prosperous enclaves, and many of the ruling families choosing to settle in this area. Nowadays some of the city's swankiest shops line Borgo San Jacopo, parallel to the river's southern bank, while the windows of Via Maggio are an amazing display of palatial furnishings.

FROM PONTE VECCHIO TO SANTA FELÌCITA

The direct route from the city centre to the heart of Oltrarno crosses the river on the **Ponte Vecchio**, the only bridge not mined by the retreating Nazis in 1944. Built in 1345 to replace an ancient wooden bridge, the Ponte Vecchio has always been loaded with shops propped over the water, but the monopoly of jewellers dates from 1593, when Ferdinando I ejected the butchers' stalls then in occupation. Crammed with sightseers and high-income shoppers during the day, the bridge remains busy after the shutters come down, when the street traders set out their stalls and the local lads gather round the bust of Cellini, waiting to see what the sky will let fall in the way of company.

The reason for Ferdinando's eviction notice was that the slabs of meat lay directly beneath the corridor that Vasari had constructed between the Palazzo Vecchio and Palazzo Pitti. It was to accommodate this corridor that Vasari stuck a portico onto the nearby **Santa Felìcita**, possibly the oldest church in Florence after San Lorenzo. Remodelled in the sixteenth century – when it became the Medici chapel – and in the eighteenth, the interior is worth a visit for the paintings by **Pontormo** in the Cappella Capponi (on the right, just inside the door). His *Deposition* is one of the masterworks of Florentine Mannerism, in which the lifeless body of Christ is borne up on a swirl of sky-blue and pink draperies.

Palazzo Pitti

Although the Medici later took possession of it, the largest palace in Florence – the **Palazzo Pitti** – still bears the name of the man for whom it was built. Luca Pitti was a prominent rival of Cosimo il Vecchio, and much of the impetus behind the building of his new house came from a desire to trump the Medici. The palace was started in around 1457, possibly using the design by Brunelleschi which the architect had intended for the Palazzo Medici but which had been rejected by Cosimo as being too grand. The central block was continually expanded up to the early seventeenth century, when it finally achieved the gargantuan bulk it has today.

The Palazzo Pitti and its stupendous gardens – the Giardino di Bóboli – contain six separate museums, all of them open Tues–Sat 9am–2pm, Sun 9am–1pm. The standard entrance charge is L4000, but the ticket for the Museo degli Argenti covers admission to the Museo delle Porcellane and Galleria del Costume as well.

THE GALLERIA PALATINA

Many of the paintings gathered by the Medici in the seventeenth century are now arranged in the **Galleria Palatina**, a suite of 26 rooms in one first-floor wing of the palace. After the Uffizi, this is Florence's most extensive public gallery and you'll need the best part of a morning to see it properly. Stacked three deep in places, as they would have been in the days of their acquisition, the pictures conform to no ordering principle except that of making each room as varied as possible – a pleasant alternative to the didactic intent of modern museums.

The art of the sixteenth century is the Palatina's forte – in particular, the art of **Raphael** and **Titian**. There are half a dozen excellent Raphaels here, while the even larger contingent of supreme works by Titian includes a number of his most trenchant portraits – among them *Pietro Aretino*, the preening *Cardinal Ippolito de'Medici*, and the disconcerting *Portrait of an Englishman*, a picture which makes the viewer feel as closely scrutinised as was the subject. **Andrea del Sarto** is represented in strength as well, as is **Rubens**, whose *Consequences of War* packs more of a punch than most other Baroque allegories. Individual works to look out for are Fra Bartolomeo's *Deposition*, a treatment of the same theme by Perugino, a tondo of the *Madonna and Child* by Filippo Lippi, a *Sleeping Cupid* by Caravaggio, and Cristofano Allori's *Judith and Holofernes*, incorporating portraits of the painter, his mistress and his mother.

THE PITTI'S OTHER MUSEUMS

Much of the rest of the first floor comprises the **Appartamenti Monumentali**, the Pitti's state rooms; they were completely renovated by the Dukes of Lorraine in the last century, but at the moment a restoration keeps their handiwork hidden from view.

On the floor above is the **Galleria d'Arte Moderna**, a chronological survey of primarily Tuscan art from the mid-eighteenth century to 1945. Most rewarding are the products of the *Macchiaioli*, the Italian division of the Impressionist movement; most startling, however, are the sublime specimens of sculptural kitsch, such as Antonio Ciseri's *Pregnant Nun*.

The Pitti's **Museo degli Argenti**, entered from the garden courtyard, is not – as its name implies – exclusively a museum of silverware, but a collection of luxury artefacts in general. Lorenzo il Magnifico's trove of **antique vases**, displayed in one of the four splendidly frescoed reception rooms on the ground floor, are most likely to elicit straightforward admiration. The later the date of the exhibits, though, the greater the discordance between the skill of the craftsman and the taste by which it was governed; by the time you reach the end of the jewellery show on the first floor, you'll have lost all capacity to be surprised or revolted.

Visitors without a specialist interest are unlikely to be riveted by the two remaining museums currently open. In the **Galleria del Costume** – housed in the Palazzina della Meridiana, the eighteenth-century southern wing of the Pitti – you can admire the dress that Eleanor of Toledo was buried in, but you can admire it easily enough in Bronzino's portrait of her in the Palazzo Vecchio. The **Museo delle Porcellane**, on the other side of the Giardino di Bóboli, is well displayed and dull.

THE GIARDINO DI BÓBOLI AND THE BELVEDERE

The creation of the Pitti's enormous formal garden, the **Giardino di Bóboli** (daily March, April & Oct 9am–5.30pm; May–Sept 9am–6.30pm; Nov–Feb 9am–4.30pm; free), began when the Medici took possession of the Palazzo Pitti, and continued into the early seventeenth century. It is the only extensive area of greenery in the centre of the city, and thus tends to get crowded in the areas close to the gates; it gets quieter in the heart of the garden, however, as the sharp gradients of its avenues take their toll.

Of all the garden's Mannerist embellishments, the most celebrated is the **Grotta del Buontalenti**, close to the entrance to the left of the palace facade, past the turtle-back figure of Cosimo I's court dwarf (as seen on a thousand post-cards). In amongst the fake stalactites are shepherds and sheep that look like calcified sponges, while embedded in the corners are replicas of Michelangelo's *Slaves*, replacing the originals that were here until 1908. In the deepest recesses of the cave (normally visible only through the railings) stands Giambologna's *Venus*, leered at by attendant imps.

The vast **amphitheatre** facing the palace courtyard was designed in the early seventeenth century as an arena for Medici festivities, the site having already been laid out by Ammannati as a garden in the shape of a Roman circus. A set piece of comparable scale is the fountain island called the **Isolotto**, which is the focal point of the far end of the gardens; it's best approached along the central cypress avenue known as the **Viottolone**, many of whose statues are Roman orig-inals. Carry straight on from here and you'll come to the **Porta Romana** entrance, which takes its name from the fourteenth-century gate in the street outside.

It's usually possible to leave the gardens by the gate which leads to the **Forte di Belvedere** (daily 9am–8pm; free), the star-shaped fortress built on the orders of Ferdinando I in 1590, ostensibly for the city's protection but really to intimidate the Grand-Duke's fellow Florentines. Art exhibitions are sometimes held in the box-like palace in the centre of the fortress, but they rarely offer any inducement to turn away from the incredible urban panorama. The road approach to the fort is from the Costa San Giorgio, which begins at the back of Santa Felicita. East from the Belvedere stretches the best-preserved stretch of Florence's fortified walls – it's followed by Via di Belvedere, an attractive if tiring route to San Miniato (see below).

Santo Spirito and the Carmine

Some indication of the importance of the parish of Santo Spirito is given by the fact that when Florence was divided into four adminstrative *quartieri* in the four-teenth century, the entire area south of the Arno was given its name. The slightly seedy Piazza Santo Spirito, with its market stalls and cafés, and the neighbouring streets, with their furniture workshops and antiques showrooms, together encap-sulate the ambivalent character of Oltrarno, a character not yet compromised by the encroachments of tourism.

Don't be deterred by the vacant facade of **Santo Spirito** church: the interior, one of Brunelleschi's last projects, prompted Bernini to describe it as "the most beautiful church in the world". It's so perfectly proportioned that nothing could seem more artless, yet the plan is extremely sophisticated – a Latin cross with a continuous chain of 38 chapels round the outside and a line of 35 columns running in parallel right round the building. Unfortunately a Baroque baldachin covers the high altar, but this is the sole disruption of Brunelleschi's arrange-ment. The best paintings are in the transepts: in the right there's Filippino Lippi's *Nerli Altarpiece*, and in the left a *St Monica and Augustinian Nuns*, attributed to Verrocchio. Also worth a peep is the sacristy, entered through a vestibule that opens onto the left aisle; both rooms were designed at the end of the fifteenth century by Giuliano da Sangallo.

A fire in 1471 destroyed all the monastery except its refectory, now the home of the **Fondazione Salvatore Romano** (Tues–Sun 9am–1pm; L1000, free on Sun); the collection merits a visit for its assortment of Romanesque carvings and a huge fresco of *The Crucifixion* by Orcagna and his workshop.

SANTA MARIA DEL CARMINE

In 1771 fire wrecked the nearby Carmelite convent and its church of **Santa Maria del Carmine**, but somehow the flames did not damage the Cappella Brancacci's frescoes by **Masaccio**, a cycle of paintings that makes the Carmine one of the essential sights of Florence, and has recently provided the Italian art world with one of its characteristic controversies. A restoration of the Carmine frescoes began in 1981 and was pretty well finished in 1988. At the time of writing, however, they are still under wraps, ostensibly because the authorities can't decide whether to replace a Baroque altar which turned out to be obscuring some fragmentary frescoes. Cynics maintain that somebody somewhere is making a lot of money by protracting the work – the suggestion being that people with influence are profitting from the rental charges for scaffolding and other incidental costs.

The decoration of the **Cappella Brancacci** was begun by Masolino in 1425 or thereabouts, and Masaccio joined him soon after as his assistant. Within a short while the teacher was taking lessons from the pupil, whose grasp of the texture of the real world, of the principles of perspective, of the drama of the Biblical texts they were illustrating, far exceeded that of his precursors. (In places the work of Masolino and Masaccio is accordingly difficult to distinguish – a diagram in the chapel identifies the areas painted by each.) Plenty of artists had depicted the expulsion of Adam and Eve from Eden before, but none had captured the anguished remorse of the sinners so graphically. Three years later Masaccio was dead, aged just 27, but in the words of Bernard Berenson "his frescoes at once became ... the training school of Florentine painters." Michelangelo used to come here to make drawings of Masaccio's scenes, and had his nose broken by an irate young sculptor whom he enraged with his condescending manner. After a hiatus of about sixty years, the cycle was completed by Filippino Lippi, his most distinctive contribution being *The Release of St Peter* on the right-hand side of the entrance arch.

San Miniato al Monte

The brilliant multicoloured facade of **San Miniato al Monte** lures troops of visitors up the hill from the south bank of the Arno, and the church more than fulfills the promise of its distant appearance. The oldest church building in Florence after the Baptistery, San Miniato is also the finest Romanesque church in Tuscany. The church's dedicatee, Saint Minias, belonged to a Christian community which settled in Florence in the third century; according to legend, after his martyrdom his corpse was seen to carry his severed head over the river and up the hill to this spot, where a shrine was subsequently erected to him. Construction of the present building began in 1013, with the foundation of a Cluniac monastery; the gorgeous marble facade – alluding to the Baptistery in its geometrical patterning – was added towards the end of that century, though the mosaic of *Christ between the Virgin and St Minias* dates from the thirteenth.

With its choir raised on a platform above the large crypt, the interior (daily 8am–12.30pm & 2–6.15pm) is like no other in the city, and its general form has changed little since the mid-eleventh century. The main structural addition is the **Cappella del Cardinale del Portogallo**, built onto the left aisle as a memorial to Cardinal James of Lusitania, who died in Florence in 1459. His chapel is a paragon of artistic collaboration – the basic design was by Antonio Manetti (a pupil of Brunelleschi), the tomb itself was carved by Antonio Rossellino, and the terracotta decoration of the ceiling was provided by Luca della Robbia. In the lower part of the church, don't overlook the intricately patterned panels of the pavement, dating from 1207, and the tabernacle between the choir stairs, designed in 1448 by Michelozzo. The majority of the frescoes along the aisle walls were painted in the fifteenth century; the most extensive are the sacristy's *Scenes from the Life of St Benedict*, painted in the 1380s by Spinello Aretino.

Drinking, eating and entertainment

Florentines have always seemed to prefer wine to coffee, and the city can't really claim to have a café tradition like that of Rome or Paris – **bars** are both more plentiful and generally more attractive places to rest your weary limbs. In recent years Florence's gastronomic reputation has suffered under the pressure of mass tourism, and many of the locals swear there's scarcely a single genuine Tuscan **restaurant** left in the city. Certainly there's a dearth of good places to eat if you're operating on a limited budget, but a decent meal isn't hard to come by if you explore the remoter quarters. The university and the annual influx of language students and other young visitors keeps the **nightlife** lively, while **seasonal events** such as the *Maggio Musicale* maintain Florence's standing as the cultural focus of Tuscany.

Cafés, bars, pasticcerie and gelaterie

At the beginning of the century the **cafés** of the Piazza Repubblica were pivotal to high-society and intellectual life in Florence, but nowadays they tend to live on the prestige of the past. The outside tables of the elegant *Caffè* on Piazza Pitti are a fine place from which to observe the spectacle of Florentine life, but you pay a lot for your pleasure. *Caffellatte*, Via degli Alfani 39/r, housed in a former dairy shop, is good for breakfast and brunch – and those allergic to caffeine will welcome their range of teas.

Main tourist streets such as Via de'Panzani, Via de'Cerretani, Via Por Santa Maria or Via Guicciardini are lined with **bars** whose food – sandwiches, slices of pizza or bowls of fruit – offers ample compensation for their lack of character. More authentic places can be found with only a little effort: the university area around Piazza San Marco is a good spot for bars, and you'll come across similar venues over in Oltrarno, around Piazza Santo Spirito or Piazza de'Nerli. (For more, see "Snacks", below.)

After dark there's no shortage of places to drop in on. *Rifrullo*, Via San Niccolò 55/r, situated in the vicinity of a section of the city walls, attracts an affluent young clientele, and shares the building with a small family-run *latteria* which makes ice cream on the premises. *Dolce Vita*, on Piazza del Carmine (10pm–1am; closed Sun), is a trendy bar that's often a venue for small-scale art exhibitions; the nearby *Tiratoio*, on Piazza de'Nerli, is a large easy-going place, with a couple of video jukeboxes and a wide range of food. In the university district, *Video Diva*, Via San Zanobi 114, is always packed with students and serves good cocktails (every night 9.30pm–1.30am). For a quiet drink in a beautifully situated, plain and genuine bar, stroll along Viale Michelangelo to *Fontana* (closed Mon) – quite pricey but worth it.

PASTICCERIE

Although some bars serve a cooked breakfast, the natives tend to start the day at a **café-pasticceria** with a quick coffee and a pastry. Best of the *pasticcerie* are *Zatti*, Borgo Albizi 19, *Ruggini*, Via de'Neri 76, and *Cennini*, Borgo San Jacopo 51. The classiest café is *Rivoire*, at Piazza Signoria 5r; it's popular with tourists and Florentines alike, but be warned that only the wealthy should sit down at the tables.

GELATERIE

For **ice cream**, leader of the pack is *Vivoli*, near Santa Croce at Via Isola delle Stinche 7/r (closed Mon and all Aug). Running it close, and by far the best of the central *gelaterie*, is *Perchè No!*, Via Tavolini 19 (closed Tues). Over the river, try *Ricchi Alfredo*, in Piazza San Spirito.

Snacks

One of the focal points of a Florentine parish is the **vinaio**, a characteristic institution that's part wine cellar, part snack bar and part social centre. The typical customer calls in for a chat, a glass of wine at the bar and a few *crostini* – small pieces of bread, occasionally fried, dressed with chicken liver sauce, or some other savoury topping. The *vinaio* at Via Cimatori 38 (between Piazza della Repubblica and Piazza della Signoria) is a perfect example; equally enjoyable is the place at Via Alfani 70, in the university area, which serves stuffed tomatoes and a range of other vegetables in addition to the traditional *crostini*. At the *Piccolo Vinaio*, Via Castellani 25 (at the back of the Palazzo Vecchio), the only space for tables is on the pavement outside, so if the weather's lousy the bar doesn't open; try their *panzanella*, a sort of salad made with stale bread, onions and parsley. For classier snacks, try the *panini* and pasta at *Fiaschetteria*, Via de'Neri 17, or the similar fare at *Fiaschetteria da 11 Latin*, Via del Palchetti 6/r, behind Palazzo Rucellai.

Another Florentine speciality is the **friggitoria**, an approximate equivalent of the fish and chip shop, serving *polenta*, potatoes and apple croquettes; most are closed on Sundays. The *friggitoria* at Via Sant'Antonio 50 (Mon–Sat 7.30am–7.30pm) also sells slices of pizza, and the one at Volta di San Pietro 5 (8am–9pm) serves hamburgers, sausages and salads, after which you can drink a glass of wine from *All'Antico Noè*, just over the road.

A good alternative to the trattoria is the **rosticceria**, a sort of delicatessen serving first courses and roast meat dishes. Usually these are take-away places, but there are seats at *Mario*, a superb rosticceria-trattoria at Via de'Neri 74, and at *Da Moreno*, in Via Val di Lamona (back of the *Porcellino* market).

Fans of Florentine tripe and lamprey sandwiches extol the virtues of the stall that sets up at the *Porcellino* market in the evenings. The city's best *panini tartufati* (truffled rolls) are sold at the expensive and unwelcoming *Procacci*, Via Tornabuoni 64.

Restaurants and pizzerias

Tuscan cuisine is distinguished by the simplicity of its culinary techniques and the modesty of its raw materials – tripe and calves' feet are typical ingredients, while grilling is a favoured method of preparation for better meat. Unfussy it might be, but quality Tuscan cooking doesn't come cheap in Florence – most of the restaurants that meet with the locals' approval are in the L70,000 category and upwards. Yet there are plenty of decent low-cost places serving food that at least gives some idea of the region's characteristic dishes, and even the simplest trattoria should offer *bistecca alla Fiorentina*, a large steak grilled with salt and pepper. Unless specified otherwise, a full meal in the places listed below shouldn't cost more than L20,000.

STATION AND MARKET AREAS
Palle d'Oro, Via Sant'Antonio 43. Halfway between a rosticceria and a trattoria; besides full meals, they do sandwiches to take away.

Da Mario, Via Rosina 2. Popular with students and market workers – be prepared to queue and share a table. Closed Sun.

Za-Za, Piazza del Mercato 26. A few tables on ground level, but a bigger canteen below – *fettunta con fagioli* (olive oil and white beans on bread) is something of a speciality, but it requires a strong stomach.

Pizza Nuti, Borgo San Lorenzo 39r. Claims to be the oldest trattoria in town, but is now fast and slick. The menu isn't limited to pizzas, and all the food is reasonably cheap. The best of the several large pizzeria-restaurants in this street. Closed Wed.

Mensa Universitaria (student refectory), Via San Gallo 25a. A gourmet delight it isn't, but the L6500 two-course meal plus fruit and drink fills a hole cheaply. Open to all student card holders Mon–Sat noon–2.15pm & 6.45–8.45pm; closed mid-July to mid-Sept.

Nuova Cina, Piazza Santa Maria Novella 9. Friendly, fast and affordable Chinese restaurant, very popular with Florentines.

CITY CENTRE AND SANTA CROCE AREA
Alle Mossacce, Via del Proconsolo 55. Once the haunt of Florence's young artists, who occasionally paid for their meals with a painting or two; the bohemian element has since dispersed, but the food remains excellent. Closed Sat & Sun.

Osteria, Via Matteo Palmieri 37r. Menu from L12,000, with tables out on the square. Closed Tues.

Bar Santa Croce, Borgo Santa Croce 31. A good lunchtime *menu fixe*, and marvellous pasta dishes. Mon–Sat noon–3pm.

Benvenuto, Via de'Neri 47. Looks more like a delicatessen than a trattoria from the street, but the groups waiting for a table give the game away; the *gnocchi* and *arista* are delicious. Closed Wed.

Mezzopepe, Via di Mezzo 26 (near Sant'Ambrogio). Student clientele; excellent salads and pasta at unbeatable prices.

OLTRARNO
Dante, Piazza Nazario Sauro 10. Busy pizzeria with around a dozen types of spaghetti on the menu too. Closed Wed.

Pizzeria i Tarocchi, Via de'Renai 12. Similar food to *Dante*, and just as popular. Closed Wed.

Trattoria i Raddi, Via Ardiglione 47. One of the area's newer places, recommended for its *peposa* – veal casseroled with pepper but no salt.

Cantinone del Gallo Nero, Via Santo Spirito 6. Offers appetisers, first courses and special *crostini*; its main claim to fame, though, is as a stockist of the best Tuscan wines – wine at table is sold only by the bottle, starting at L7500.

Trattoria Casalinga, Via Michelozzi 9r. Just about the best low-cost authentic Tuscan dishes in town, and always crowded; their *lesso con le cipolle* (chopped beef with onions) is marvellous. Closed Sun.

La Taverna, Via Michelozzi 15. Good for a regional first course and a glass of quality wine. Closed Sun.

Trattoria Nello, Borgo Tegolaio 21. Offers both a full lunchtime *menu fixe* and a half-portion one, an option that invariably packs the place out; in the evenings it's possible to get an excellent *à la carte* meal for under L20,000. Closed Sun.

Dei Quattro Leoni, Via Vellutini 1. Rough and ready, and very cheap; as a starter try the *finocchiona*, a type of Tuscan salami. Closed Sun.

Angiolino, Via Santo Spirito 36. The open kitchen allows you to see the Tuscan delicacies being prepared; expect to pay around L25,000 for a full meal with wine.

Trattoria Oreste, Piazza Santo Spirito. Good *menu fixe*, delicious *salsiccia e fagioli* – sausage and beans Tuscan-style – and tables on the square. Closed Sun.

Trattoria le Sorelle, Via San Niccolò 30. Specialises in salami and *penne*; quality meals for around L25,00, salads and pasta for much less.

Ruggero, Via Senese 89r. The magnificent *pappa al pomodoro* and *braciola della casa* more than make up for the slightly frosty staff.

Nightlife

For up-to-date information on all activities in Florence from unofficial politics to after-dark events, call in at *Box Office*, Via della Pergola 10a/r (10am–8pm; ☎242.361), an offshoot of the local *Controradio* FM station; their shop sells fanzines from all over Italy. Listings are featured in magazines such as *Firenze Spettacolo*, *Metró*, and *Time Off*.

Live music

Chiodo fisso, Via Dante Alighieri 16r. A good spot for folk guitar music and occasionally for jazz; open every night.

Pegaso, Via Palazzuolo 82r. Jazz performers 10pm–2.30am; membership is cheap.

Amadeus, Via Alfani 26r. Jazz and rock, plus cabaret acts Thurs and Sun; membership at the door. Closed Mon.

Stonehenge, Via dell' Amorino 16r. Rock venue, operating under the slogan "Do it, then come here". Tues–Sun 10pm–4am.

Genius, Via San Gallo 22r. Jazz sessions organised by the local *Red Bean* jazz group, every night except Saturday from 10pm; serves good food and drink, but the decor is off-puttingly cold.

Jazz Club, Via Nuova de'Caccini 3. Exactly as the name suggests. Closed Mon.

Clubs / music bars / other venues

Liquid, Borgo Albizi 9. Vaguely underground/avant-garde, with constantly changing interior design. Open from 10pm into the small hours every night.

Last Exit, Borgo Pinti 17r. Home of the psychedelic tendency. Tues–Sun 10pm–3am.

Cayenna, Via Carducci 37r. Attracts the city's ecological campaigners; serves beer and wine, and fresh croissants late at night. Wed–Mon 9pm–1am.

Danny Rock, Via Pandolfini 13. Employs a French cook who creates marvellous crêpes, among other things; large suspended screens show concerts and sporting events. Open 7.30pm–1am (2am Sat).

Sfizio, Lungarno Cellini 1r. A new place with a video jukebox inside and an open-air area close to the Arno – a drawback being the traffic between you and the river.

Caffè Voltaire, Via dela Scala 9r. Base of a left-wing association that puts on exhibitions, video shows, readings and other events; annual membership is compulsory but cheap – which is more than can be said for its restaurant.

Discos

Some discos operate as private clubs, but this generally doesn't cause any problems for foreigners; for updated information, ask at *Box Office*, who are in touch with all the venues. As a rule, entry is around L10,000, which usually includes your first drink.

Tenax, Via Pratese 47, Peretola (bus #29). The biggest and most popular disco in Florence, and one of its leading venues for new and established bands. Open Wed–Sun.

Space Electronic, Via Palazzuolo 37. The first place to introduce videos in Florence, and still top of the tree; now fitted out with a glass dance floor and lasers, it's a favourite with young foreigners. Open every night.

Yab Yum, Via de'Sassetti 5r. Right in the centre; has a vast dance floor. Closed Mon.

Tabasco, Piazza Santa Cecilia 3r (closed Mon); **Flamingo**, Via Pandolfini 26. The two principal gay hangouts.

Culture

Florence does its best to live up its exalted history: special art exhibitions are held all through the year, and the cultural calendar is filled out with seasons of opera, theatre, ballet, and music of all varieties. You can usually find information in English about concerts and shows at the city council kiosks in Piazza Repubblica or inside the Palazzo Vecchio; otherwise, check out the tourist offices, advertising posters, and local magazines. Tickets for most events can be bought at *Box Office* (see "Nightlife"), where they also sell tickets for major concerts in other towns.

CLASSICAL MUSIC

The **Maggio Musicale Fiorentino** is one of the most famous festivals of opera and classical music in Italy; confusingly, it isn't limited to May, but lasts from late April to early July. Events are staged at the Teatro Comunale, the Teatro della Pergola, the Palazzo dei Congressi, and occasionally in the Bóboli gardens. Information and tickets – usually expensive – can be obtained from the festival HQ in the Teatro Comunale, Corso Italia 16 (☎277.9236). The Comunale also has a winter concert season from November to mid-December and an opera season from then until mid-January.

　Estate Fiesolana, held in Fiesole every summer, is a slightly less exclusive festival, concentrating more on chamber and symphonic music. Films and theatre groups are also featured, most events being held in the open-air Teatro Romano.

　From October to June concerts are organised by the **Musicus Concentus**, a classical music company that sometimes arranges high-quality jazz events too; discounts for students are common.

THEATRE

Teatro della Pergola, Via della Pergola 12 (☎247.9651), is Florence's main classical theatre, rivalled principally by *Teatro Variety*, Via del Madonnone 47 (☎663.666). *Teatro Niccolini*, Via Ricasoli 3 (☎213.282), is one of the oldest in town, but its repertoire has a decidedly modern look. Shows by the *Teatro Regionale Toscano*, Tuscany's highly-esteemed regional theatre company, are held in various theatres in town.

CINEMA

Florence has a large number of cinemas, but there are only a couple of places to see films undubbed: *Astro*, in Piazza San Simone (near Santa Croce), screens mainly English-language films (Tues–Sun), while *Spazio Uno*, near Santa Maria Novella at Via del Sole 10 has occasional films in English. From June to September there's a season of films on an open-air screen at the *Forte Belvedere*, above the Bóboli gardens; the ambience is beautiful and the films are usually good.

Listings

Airlines *Alitalia*, Lungarno Acciaioli 10–12 (☎263.051/2/3); *British Airways*, Via della Vigna Nuova 36r (☎218.655); *Pan Am*, Lungarno Acciailoi 10 (☎282.716); *TWA*, Piazza Santa Trinita 2 (☎284.691).

Airport enquiries *Aeroporto Galileo Galilei*, Pisa (☎050/40.132); information also from check-in at Santa Maria Novella train station, platform 5 (7am–8pm), or ☎2788.

Books A good general stock of books in English is carried by the *Paperback Exchange*, Via Fiesolana 31r, which operates an exchange scheme for second-hand books, and has informative and very friendly staff. For new Italian books, go to *Seeber*, Via Tornabuoni 68r; for art books, *Salimbeni*, Via M. Palmieri 14–16, and *Centro D*, Piazza dei Mozzi 1.

Bus enquiries For local services: *ATAF*, Piazza Duomo 57r (☎580.528). For routes outside the city: *SITA*, Via Santa Caterina da Siena 15r (☎214.721); *LAZZI*, Piazza Stazione (☎215.154); *CAP*, Via Nazionale 13 (☎214.637); *CAT*, Via Fiume 2 (☎283.400); *COPIT*, Piazza Santa Maria Novella 22 (☎215.451).

Car hire *Avis*, Borgognissanti 128r (☎213.629); *Hertz*, Via Maso Finiguerra 33r (☎298.205); *Maggiore*, Via Maso Finiguerra 11 (☎210.238).

Car parks Only residents are now allowed to park in the very centre of Florence; non-residents must leave their cars at one of the carparks on the periphery. The main car parks near the centre are: in front of and behind the train station; Piazza dell'Unità Italiana; Piazza Vittorio Veneto; Piazza del Carmine; Piazza Mentana; Piazza Piave; Piazza Santa Maria Nuova.

Consulates *UK*, Lungarno Corsini 2 (284.133); *US*, Lungarno Vespucci 38 (298.276). Travellers from Ireland, Australia, New Zealand and Canada should contact their Rome consulates.

Doctors Night service ☎477.891. The *Tourist Medical Service*, Via Lorenzo il Magnifico 59 (☎475.411), has English-speaking doctors on 24hr call.

Exchange Some banks in Florence, such as the *Cassa di Risparmio di Firenze*, are open for a few hours on Saturday in addition to the usual banking hours. Otherwise try *American Express*, Via degli Speziali 7 (Mon–Fri 9am–6pm, Sat 9am–1pm), or the *Esercizio Promozione Turismo*, just north of Piazza Signoria at Via Condotta 42 (Mon–Sat 10am–7pm, Sun 10am–6pm).

First Aid *Misericordia*, Piazza del Duomo 20 (☎212.222).

Football *Fiorentina*'s home ground is at Campo Marte (bus #19 or train). Tickets from L10,000.

Hospital Santa Maria Nuova, Piazza Santa Maria Nuova 1 (☎27.581).

Laundry Lavanderia Manfredi, Via Sant'Antonio 66r, near Mercato Centrale.

Left Luggage Train station left-luggage desk open 24hr; L1500 per item.

Lost property Via Circondaria 19 (Mon–Wed & Fri–Sat 9am–noon; ☎367.943).

Pharmacies All-night pharmacies: at the train station; Molteni, Via Calziuoli 7r; and Paglicci, Via della Scala 49.

Police Emergency ☎113; Urban police ☎352.141. The Questura, for passport problems, reporting thefts and so on, is at Via Zara 2 (☎49.771).

Post office Central post office at Via Pellicceria (Mon–Fri 8.15am–7pm, Sat 8.15am–noon; telegram office open 24hr); Poste restante at counters 23 & 24. Main office at Via Pietrapiana 53–55 (same hours).

Swimming pools Costoli, Viale Paoli, at Campo di Marte; Amici del Nuoto, Via del Romito 38; Tropos, Via Orcagna 20; Le Pavoniere, Viale degli Olmi, at Cascine (open-air); Bellariva, Lungarno Colombo 6 (open-air).

Taxis Main ranks by the train station and in Piazza della Repubblica; radio cabs ☎4798 or ☎4390.

Telephones 24-hr booths at train station, at Via Pellicceria post office, and at SIP office (Via Cavour 21r).

Train enquiries ☎278.785.

Around Florence: Fiesole, the Medici Villas, Prato, Pistoia and Chianti

If you settle into Florence as a base, there's a lot to be said for a couple of days' escape to the environs. Within the area of Greater Florence, city buses run to the hill village of **Fiesole**, and to the various **Medici villas** – originally country retreats, now all but consumed by the suburbs. Further afield, **Prato** and **Pistoia** – respectively 25 and 35 minutes distant by train or bus – each make fine day trips, with their medieval ensembles and Florentine-inspired Renaissance art. And to the south, though requiring your own transport to explore properly, lie the hills and vineyards of **Chianti**, Italy's premier wine region and expatriate settlement.

Fiesole

A long-established Florentine retreat from the summer heat and crowds, **FIESOLE** spreads over a cluster of hilltops above the Mugnone and Arno valleys, some 8km northeast of Florence. First settled in the Bronze Age, then by the Etruscans, then absorbed by the Romans, it rivalled its neighbour until the early twelfth century, when the Florentines overran the town. From that time it became a satellite of Florence, being especially favoured as a semi-rural second home for its wealthier citizens.

The #7 *ATAF* bus runs every quarter of an hour from Florence train station, through San Domenico (see below) to the central square of Fiesole, Piazza Mino da Fiesole; the journey takes around twenty minutes, and costs the standard L800. The town itself is small enough to be explored in a morning, but the country lanes of its surroundings invite a more leisurely tour, and might even tempt you to stay.

Accommodation on a tight budget is a problem, though: *Villa Sorriso*, Via Gramsci 21 (☎59.027), is the cheapest close to the centre, with doubles from L34,000; about a kilometre further out, *Villa Baccano*, Via Bosconi 4 (☎59.341), is in the same price range. Fiesole's **campsite**, *Camping Panoramico* (☎599.069), is 3km out of town in Via Peramonda; the #70 bus goes to the foot of the hill on which it's situated. The Fiesole **AAST** is at Piazza Mino da Fiesole 45.

The Town

Nineteenth-century restoration has ruined the exterior of the **Duomo**, on the central piazza. The interior is something like a bare version of Florence's San Miniato, though there's relief from the overall austerity in the Cappella Salutati, to the right of the choir: it contains two fine pieces carved by Mino da Fiesole in the mid-fifteenth century – an altar frontal of *The Madonna and Saints* and the tomb of Bishop Salutati.

Fiesole's other major churches, **Sant'Alessandro** and **San Francesco**, are reached by the steep Via San Francesco, which just below the churches widens into a terrace giving a remarkable panorama of Florence. Sant'Alessandro (daily 10am–noon & 3–5pm) was founded in the sixth century on the site of Etruscan and Roman temples; recent repairs have rendered the outside a whitewashed nonentity, but the beautiful *marmorino cipollino* (onion marble) columns of the basilical interior make it the most atmospheric building in Fiesole. Again, restoration has not improved the Gothic church of San Francesco (same hours), which occupies the site of the acropolis. Across one of the convent's tiny cloisters there's a chaotic museum of pieces brought back from Egypt and China by missionaries. An alternative descent back to the main square is through the public park, entered by a gate facing San Francesco's facade.

Around the back of the duomo, in Via Marini, is the entrance to the **Teatro Romano** and **Museo Archeologico** (April–Sept Tues–Sun 9am–7pm; Oct–March Tues–Sun 10am–4pm; L3000). Built in the first century BC, the 3000-seater theatre was excavated towards the end of the last century and remains in good enough repair to be used for performances during the *Estate Fiesolana* festival. Most of the museum exhibits were discovered in this area, and encompass pieces from the Bronze Age to the Roman occupation.

San Domenico

If you've time to spare in Fiesole, wander down the narrow Via Vecchia Fiesolana, which goes by the **Villa Medici** (built for Cosimo il Vecchio by Michelozzo) on its way to the hamlet of **SAN DOMENICO**, 1.5km southwest of Fiesole. Fra Angelico was once prior of the Dominican **monastery** here, and the church retains a *Madonna and Angels* by him (first chapel on left); the chapter house also has a Fra Angelico fresco of *The Crucifixion* (ring at no. 4 for entry).

Five minutes' walk northwest from San Domenico brings you to the **Badia Fiesolana**, Fiesole's cathedral from the ninth century to the eleventh. Cosimo il Vecchio had the church altered in the 1460s, a project which left the magnificent Romanesque facade intact while transforming the interior into a superb Renaissance building.

The Medici Villas

The finest country houses of the Florentine hinterland are, predictably enough, those built for the Medici. The earliest of these grand villas were intended as fortified refuges to which the family could withdraw when the political temperature in the city became a little too hot, but by the sixteenth and seventeenth centuries, when they were established as the unchallenged rulers of the city, the villas became more ostentatious, signifying the might of the dynasty through their sheer luxuriousness. They had a financial function too: as Florence's importance as a manufacturing city began to dwindle, the Medici decided to divert some of their resources into agriculture.

Villa Medicea di Careggi

Originally a fortified farmhouse, the **Villa di Careggi** was altered by Michelozzo in the 1430s for Cosimo il Vecchio, but is particularly associated with his grandson Lorenzo il Magnifico, whose academy of Platonic scholars used to meet here. Lorenzo, his father and Cosimo all died here. The best-known of all the Medici villas, it's now a nurse's home, and permission to visit the interior normally has to be obtained in advance (☎277.4329), though a request at the office inside the entrance sometimes succeeds, and the surrounding gardens and woodland can be explored freely. The #14c bus covers the 5km from the train station to the villa, or you can walk from La Petraia (see below).

Villa Medicea della Petraia

The **Villa della Petraia** (bus #28 from the train station; Tues–Sun 9am–2pm; free), now hedged about by the industrial sprawl of Florence's northern edge, was adapted from a medieval castle in the 1570s and 1580s by Buontalenti, working to a commission from the future Grand-Duke Ferdinando I. The interior was altered in turn by Vittorio Emanuele II, who glassed over the interior courtyard to convert it into a ballroom; its walls are covered by a seventeenth-century fresco cycle glorifying the Medici. Giambologna's bronze statue of *Venus*, now transplanted to a small room indoors, used to adorn the marble fountain on the upper terrace of the magnificent garden (Tues–Fri 9am–2pm, Sat & Sun 9am–sunset).

Villa Medicea di Castello

A little over five minutes' walk from La Petraia is the **Villa di Castello**, which was bought in 1477 by Lorenzo and Giovanni de'Medici, second cousins of Lorenzo il Magnifico and the principal patrons of Botticelli. The fame of the villa rests on its spectacular **gardens** (Tues–Sun 9am–sunset; free), which were laid out by Tribolo for Cosimo I and completed by Buontalenti, who also redesigned the house. Delighted by its labyrinths, fountains and myriad Mannerist tricks, Montaigne judged this to be the best garden in Europe. The outstanding eccentricities are Ammannati's shivering figure of *January*, the triple-bowled fountain topped by the same sculptor's *Hercules and Antaeus*, and the *Grotto degli Animali*, a man-made cave against whose walls stands a menagerie of artificial creatures.

Poggio e Caiano

For the most complete image of what life was like in the Medici villas in the family's heyday, make the trip to the **Villa Medicea di Poggio e Caiano** (Tues–Sat 9am–1.30pm, Sun 9am–12.30pm; L3000), 18km northwest of Florence at the foot of Monte Albano. (Take the *COPIT* bus from Piazza Santa Maria Novella; they leave every 30min, and take around 30min to get there.) Lorenzo il Magnifico bought a farmhouse on this site in 1480 and had it rebuilt as a classical rural palace by Giuliano da Sangallo – the only architectural project instigated by Lorenzo that has survived. Additions made by later members of the family fit well within Sangallo's design – the imposing entrance loggia, for instance, was commissioned by Lorenzo's son Giovanni, the future Pope Leo X. Inside, the focal point is the double-height *salone* which the architect made out of the original courtyard; its sixteenth-century frescoes include works by Pontormo and del Sarto. The **gardens** (Mon–Sat 9am–dusk, Sun 9am–12.30pm), modified by the Lorraine princes into an English-style landscape, contain some magnificent old trees.

Villa dell'Artimino

From Poggio e Caiano a bus runs south, past COMEANA, to the walled village of Artimino, site of the **Villa Artimino**, sometimes known as *La Ferdinanda* (summer Tues 8am–noon & 2–6pm; winter Tues 8.30am–noon & 2–4pm; free). Designed by Buontalenti as a hunting lodge for Ferdinando I, the villa has the appearance of a rather dandified fortress, and its most distinctive external feature has earned it the nickname "the villa of the hundred chimneys". The interior is pleasingly unpretentious; in the basement there's a museum of Etruscan finds from the tombs at Comeana, infuriatingly open at different times from the rest of the house (Sat 3.30–6.30pm, Sun 9am–noon, Mon 9am–noon & 3–6pm; L3000).

Pratolino

Nothing remains of Francesco I's favourite villa, the Villa Demidoff at **Pratolino**, except its expansive park, and even this is but a shadow of its earlier self (May 1– Sept 24 Fri–Sun 10am–8pm; L2000, free Fri June–Sept). The mechanical toys, trick fountains and other practical jokes that Buontalenti installed in the grounds of Pratolino were the most ingenious ever seen, and required so much maintenance that there was a house in the grounds for the court plumbers. Only Giambologna's immense *Appennino* – a man-mountain who gushes water – survives from the original garden, but the park is still one of the pleasantest green spaces within a bus-ride of Florence. It's 12km north of the city and is served by the #25 route.

Prato

PRATO is Italy's chief textile city – a position it has occupied since the early Middle Ages. As such, it is not, perhaps, on a top list of Italian towns. However, the city's long-time wealth, and the Florentine influence, has left a fair legacy of buildings and art, including Filippo Lippi's most engaging cycle of frescoes.

The *Centro Storico* remains enclosed within a hexagon of walls, making orientation surprisingly straightforward. Buses from Florence run direct to the Piazza del Duomo. Coming from the train station cross the Ponte della Vittoria, the bridge in front of the square, and Viale Vittorio Veneto leads you to the walls. Directly ahead (past a Henry Moore sculpture) is the Norman-style **Castello d'Imperatore** (Mon, Tues & Thurs–Sat 9am–noon & 4–7pm), built in the thirteenth century for Emperor Frederick II. The castle is heavily restored – concerts are held in the courtyard in summer – but you can wander around the ramparts for views over the old city and the industrial suburbs. Virtually adjacent is Prato's major Renaissance monument, Giuliano Sangallo's church of **Santa Maria delle Carceri** (closed noon–4.30pm). Heavily influenced by Brunelleschi's Strozzi chapel, it makes a decorative gesture towards the Romanesque (and Prato's cathedral) with its bands of green and white marble. The interior is lightened by an Andrea della Robbia frieze. Behind the church, at Via Cairoli, the **AAST** provide maps and details of the many summer cultural events.

The Piazza del Duomo, three or four blocks further in, forms an effective space for the Pisan-Romanesque facade of the **Duomo** (closed noon–4pm), distinguished by another Andrea della Robbia terracotta (over the portal) and, on the corner, an external pulpit designed by Donatello and Michelozzo. The interior has three major frescoes. In the chapel immediately left of the entrance is Agnolo Gaddi's *Legend of the Holy Girdle* (1392–95); the girdle, supposedly given by the Virgin to Thomas (doubting, again, the reality of her Assumption) and brought from the Holy Land to Prato in the twelfth century. Filippo Lippi's frescoes are behind the high altar. Completed over a period of fourteen years (1452–66), they depict the martyrdoms of *Saint John the Baptist* and *Saint Stephen* (bring coins). During the period of his work, Lippi, a Florentine friar from the Carmine, was tried for fraud, and abducted then had a child (Filippino Lippi) by a nun, Lucrezia – said to be the model for the dancing figure of Salome. These cycles are marvellous, sensual paintings, perfectly out of key with their intended theme. The chapel right of the high altar has scenes from *Lives of the Virgin and Saint Stephen*, reputedly begun by Paolo Uccello, though completed in Mannerist style. To see the original panels of Donatello's exterior pulpit, look in at the **Museo dell'Opera del Duomo** (Mon & Wed–Sat 9am–12.30pm & 3–6.30pm, Sun 9.30am–12.30pm; L1000), housed alongside the Duomo in the Bishop's Palace. The sculpted putti are rivalled by those of Maso di Bartolomeo's *Reliquary for the Sacred Girdle*, the museum's other main treasure.

For further art, you could make your way a block south to the **Palazzo Pretorio**, whose **Galleria Comunale** (Mon–Sat 9am–1pm & 3–7pm; L1000) has a good collection of Renaissance Florentine art, including works by both Lippis. But you get more of a feel for Prato, and its former wealth, by following Via Ricasoli down from the Palazzo Pretorio, then turning left at Piazza San Francesco onto the Via Rinaldesca. At the centre of this street is the **Palazzo Datini**, the fourteenth-century home of the merchant and banker Francesco di Marco Datini, whose life is superbly recreated in Iris Origo's classic study, *The Merchant of Prato*. The late Gothic building was completely frescoed inside and out; it is not open to visits, but its decoration can be glimpsed from the street.

Practicalities

Prato is under half an hour from Florence, by bus or train, and it can be an alternative for accommodation when there's nothing available there. Its three one-star **hotels** all charge around L38,000 a double: best of them is the *Centrale*, Via Magnolfi 15, just off Piazza Duomo (☎0574/23.182); others are *La Toscana*, Piazza Ciardi 3 (☎0574/28.096), and *Roma*, Via Carradori 1 (☎0574/31.777). If you can afford L50,000 for a double, try the two-star *Stella d'Italia* in Piazza Duomo (☎0574/27.910) or *Il Giglio* in Piazza San Marco (☎0574/37.049).

The city has plenty of **restaurants** – the *Trattoria Lapo* is a good local place in Piazza Mercatale, and there's a cheap snack bar opposite the Palazzo Datini on Via Mazzi. If you stay, there's also an adventurous **arts cinema**, the *Terminale* at

Via Frascati 36. And, in addition to Florentine connections, keep in mind that Prato itself has its own **transport** routes. A useful local link is bus #1 to Poggio e Caiano (see "The Medici Villas").

Pistoia

The provincial capital of **PISTOIA** is one of the least visited cities in Tuscany: an unjustified ranking for this quiet, well-preserved medieval city at the base of the Apennines. Just 35 minutes by train from Florence (about the same by bus), it is an easy and enjoyable day trip – and also forms the most attractive approach to Lucca and Pisa, with both of which it has strong architectural links.

The city was known through medieval times for its feuds and was pilloried by both Dante and Machiavelli. It was an important metalworking city, too, and left a legacy to the world in the pistol, derived from its name. These days, Pistoia maintains its industrial tradition with a large rail plant, but is better known for the acres of garden nurseries on the slopes around. In terms of art attractions, its appeal lies in a sequence of Romanesque churches and sculpture, and, its most famous image, a superb technicolour della Robbia frieze.

The City
Arriving by train (or by bus from Florence) you are just a couple of hundred metres south of the *Centro Storico*. Viale XX Settembre leads through the walls and into the heart of the city, the superb medieval complex of the **Piazza del Duomo**, where the **EPT** are housed in the Bishop's Palace.

The **Duomo** will be immediately familiar if you have come from Pisa or Lucca, built in the distinctive Pisan-Romanesque style of striped black and white marble and multiple arcades. On the portico is a delicate Andrea della Robbia relief. The interior (closed noon–4pm) has an outstanding array of sculpture, including several tombs by Verocchio, a marvellous font by Andrea da Fiesole, and (on the right-hand wall) a monument to Dante's friend, Cino da Pistoia; the poet is shown lecturing to pupils, among them, so it is said, Petrarch. Just beyond the monument is the *Cappella di San Jacopo*, endowed with one of the richest pieces of silverwork to be seen – an altarpiece begun in 1287 and completed in the fifteenth century, when Brunelleschi cast the two figures on left.

The cathedral's adjacent **Campanile** was a medieval watchtower, rather bizarrely adapted with Romanesque arcades and a Gothic turret. Opposite is the **Baptistery**, a more deliberate Romanesque design by Giovanni Pisano, and next door the old Palazzo del Podestà. The **Palazzo Comunale**, beside the cathedral, houses an unexceptional Museo Civico on its upper floors, and, on the ground floor, a more interesting permanent exhibition of works by the Pistoia-born artist **Marino Marini** (1901–80). Marini found an early influence in the realism of Etruscan sarcophagi, expressed in endless sculptures of horses and riders, a theme that endured through his life; in the 1940s he turned to portraiture – figures here include Thomas Mann, Henry Miller and Marc Chagall. (Tues–Sun 9am–1pm & 4–7pm; free).

From the Piazza del Duomo, you can strike off in any number of directions along lanes that will reveal a Romanesque church facade or medieval palazzo. The three most rewarding churches each date from the twelfth century and are distinguished by a trio of pulpits that show state-of-the-art Tuscan sculpture in the thirteenth. In **San Bartolomeo in Panatano**, west of Piazza Duomo, is the earliest of the pulpits, executed in 1250 by Guido da Como. Off to the south, outside the original circuit of walls is the majestically arcaded **San Giovanni Fuorcivitas**, with a 1270 pulpit by a pupil of Nicolo Pisano and a holy water stoup by his son, Giovanni. Giovanni's own pulpit – the city's masterpiece – is in **San Andrea**; it is based on his father's design for the Pisa baptistery pulpit and only marginally less elaborate than his own later work in Pisa cathedral.

A circuit around the churches will also take you past the **Ospedale del Ceppo**, in a square at the end of Via Pacini, off behind the Palazzo Comunale. Emblazoned along the whole length of the hospital is Giovanni della Robbia's painted enamel frieze of the *Seven Works of Mercy*. Completed in the early sixteenth century, it is a startling, technicolour panoply of Renaissance types and costume: pilgrims, prisoners, the sick, the dead, all committed with a fascinating attention to domestic realism.

Practicalities

Pistoia's low tourist profile is matched by a dearth of **accommodation**. If you plan to stay, phone ahead – the pensions are small and the hotels pricey. Two to try, at around L35,000–40,000 a double, are *Albergo Autisti*, Viale Pacinotti 93 (☎0573/217.71), and *Albergo Firenze*, Via Curtatone e Montanara 42 (☎0573/231.41).

The liveliest time to be in Pistoia is late July, when the *Luglio Pistoiese* – a month-long programme of concerts and events – culminates in the **Giostra dell'Orso**, a medieval joust held in the Piazza del Duomo. Other times of year, the city stirs a little for Wednesday and Saturday **markets** in Piazza della Sala.

Leaving Pistoia, *Lazzi* **buses** (for Florence and Prato) leave from by the train station; *COPIT* buses (for Vinci and Empoli) from Piazza San Francesco. The route to Vinci, Leonardo's birthplace (see p.469), runs over beautiful Monte Albano and allows a loop to Florence or Pisa if you set out early in the day.

Chianti

Ask a sample of wealthy northern Europeans to define their idea of paradise and the odds are that several will come up with something that sounds much like **Chianti**, the territory of vineyards and hill towns that stretches between Florence and Siena. Every aspect of life in Chianti is in perfect balance: the Tuscan landscape is the sort of terrain devised by painters to evoke the Golden Age; one of the most fascinating cities in the world is nearby, but not so close as to make its crowds a nuisance; and, of course, the climate for most of the year is balmy, and even in the pit of winter rarely too grim. And on top of all this, there's the wine, the one Italian vintage everyone knows.

The British and others from similarly ill-favoured zones were long ago alerted to Chianti's charms and the rate of immigration has been so rapid since the 1960s that the region is now generally known as "**Chiantishire**". The effects of this moneyed influx have been all too predictable – an escalation in property prices and the gentrification of some of the more picturesque villages. Yet it would be an exaggeration to say that Chianti is losing its character in the way that many of Italy's coastal towns have lost theirs – the tone of certain parts has been altered, but it's still a largely unspoilt district.

Buses from Florence and Siena connect with the more populous Chianti towns, but the only really feasible way to get to know the region is by car. Your own **transport** allows you to roam into the quieter recesses of the hills, and to stop off at one of the 800-odd farms and **vineyards** to sample the local produce. If you pick up a detailed survey map of the region, you can pick out some of the innumerable miniature **lakes,** too – offering the quietest swimming you'll find anywhere in Tuscany in the summer. The best **road** to follow is the so-called *Chiantigiana* (N222), a route from Florence to Siena that passes through the most beautiful parts of Chianti.

Chianti Towns

The district's heart is formed by the three small towns which constituted the fourteenth-century League of Chianti: **GAIOLE** (2hr by *SITA* bus from Florence), **RADDA IN CHIANTI** (1hr 40min) and **CASTELLINA IN CHIANTI** (1hr 35min). Castellina and Radda (Chianti's unofficial capital) are where the medieval splendour has left its clearest traces; Gaiole has become a modern market town, but its wine co-operative offers splendid tasting opportunities. Perhaps the best target for oenophiles is **GREVE** (1hr by bus from Florence), a town with a wine shop on every street and Chianti's biggest wine fair in September. If you are interested in visiting a classic Chianti *cantina*, perhaps the best to make for is **Castello di Brolio**, just outside the village of **BROLIO**, near Gaiole. The building itself is majestic and tours are generally given without appointment.

Practicalities

Hotel accommodation in Chianti is unremittingly expensive; the only budget options are the **campsites** at Castellina and the fortified town of BARBERINO VAL D'ELSA. Much the same goes for the area's **restaurants**. A pleasant, regular trattoria is the *Trattoria San Sano* in SAN SANO (near Gaiole), a combined restaurant, bar and general store, with tables outside – a good stop if you're driving through. *Il Molino delle Bagnaie* (☎0577/747.062), a very attractive cellar in a small converted mill on the road from Gaiole to Pianella, has music most evenings – part cabaret, part Tuscan folk songs. It's middlingly expensive and, for Chianti, distinctly offbeat.

AREZZO PROVINCE

The Arno valley upstream from Florence is a solidly industrialised district, with warehouses and manufacturing plants enclosing many of the small towns strung along the train line. The villages up on the sides of the valley often retain an appealing medieval square or a cluster of attractive buildings, but there's no very compelling stop before you reach the provincial capital of the upper Arno region, **Arezzo**, one hour's train ride from Florence. Foreign visitors come to Arezzo in their thousands for its paintings by Piero della Francesca (a pleasure temporarily unavailable – see below), while Italians flock there in even greater numbers for its antiques, traded on the town's Piazza Grande in quantities scarcely matched anywhere else in the country.

In the **Casentino**, the stretch of the Arno valley between Arezzo and the source of the river to the north, the character of the region is quite different: small hill towns such as **Poppi** and **Bibbiena** stand above a terrain of vineyards, olive groves and pastures, and business activity tends to be small-scale. For visitors on the trail of the masterpieces of Tuscan art, the essential call in the vicinity of Arezzo is **Sansepolcro**, almost on the Umbrian border to the east – the birthplace of della Francesca, it possesses two magnificent works by him. To the south of Arezzo stretches the plain of the **Valdichiana**, where picturesque if unexceptional little towns punctuate a landscape of farming estates. The ancient hill town of **Cortona** is the major attraction of this part of the province, its steep streets forming a distinctive urban landscape.

Arezzo

Occupying a site that controls the major passes of the central Apennines, **AREZZO** was one of the most important settlements of the Etruscan federation. It maintained its pre-eminence under Roman rule, and was a prosperous independent republic in the Middle Ages, until, in 1289, its Ghibelline loyalties brought about military defeat by the Guelph Florentines. This was a reversal from which it temporarily recovered, but definitive subjugation by Florence came about in 1384. During the Renaissance, Petrarch, Pietro Aretino and Vasari, all native Aretines, brought lasting prestige to the city, yet it was an outsider who gave Arezzo its permanent Renaissance monument – Piero della Francesca, whose fresco cycle for the church of San Francesco belongs in the same category as Masaccio's frescoes in Florence and Michelangelo's in Rome.

Today Arezzo's economy rests on its innumerable jewellers and goldsmiths (the city has the world's largest gold manufacturing plant), and on its antiques industry. In the vicinity of the Piazza Grande there are showrooms filled with the sort of furniture you put in a bank vault rather than in your living room. At noon on the Saturday before the first Sunday of every month a less exclusive *Fiera Antiquaria* (Antiques Fair) pitches camp in the square, pulling in dealers from Rome and further afield. It's fun to look around – the stalls spill out into junk the further you go from the Piazza – though don't expect any bargains.

The Town

There are two distinct parts to Arezzo: the **older quarter**, at the top of the hill, and the businesslike **lower town**, facing you at the exit from the train station. The bus terminal is diagonally opposite the train station. The traffic axis between the upper and lower town is Via Guido Monaco, a street which nobody walks along except to shop on it; the parallel **Corso Italia**, now pedestrianised, is the route to take up the hill, and the place to hang out in the evening.

All the principal sights are in the upper part, with the exception of the **Museo Archeologico** (Tues–Sat 9am–2pm, Sun 9am–1pm; free), which occupies part of a monastery built into the wall of the town's Roman amphitheatre, to the right of the station. The desultory remains of the amphitheatre are part of the museum, but more impressive are the marvellously coloured **coralline vases**; produced here in the first century BC, they show why the Aretines achieved their reputation as consummate craftsmen throughout the Roman world.

San Francesco

Off to the left of the Corso, not far from its summit, stands the building every tourist comes to Arezzo to see – the church of **San Francesco**. Built after 1322, the plain and pleasant basilica earned its renown in the early 1450s, when the Bacci family commissioned **Piero della Francesca** to paint the walls of the choir. The subject chosen was *The Legend of the True Cross*, in which the Cross itself forms the physical link in the cycle of redemption that begins with humanity's original sin. The tree from which the forbidden fruit was taken is shown as the tree from which Christ's Cross was made, the legend continuing with Constantine's conversion after a vision of the Cross, and the Cross's eventual return to Jerusalem. Piero painted the series in narrative sequence, beginning on the right wall, continuing until his visit to Rome in 1459. He painted the left wall on his return, with some assistance, as is evident in the slightly lower quality.

Unfortunately, you can currently see nothing more than postcards of this fabulous series of paintings. The entire choir is **closed for restoration** and is not due to be unveiled until 1992, the five-hundredth anniversary of the artist's death.

Pieve di Santa Maria and the Piazza Grande
Further up the Corso stands the twelfth-century **Pieve di Santa Maria**, one of the finest Romanesque structures in Tuscany. Its arcaded facade, elaborate yet severe, belongs to a type associated more with Pisa and western Tuscany, and is

doubly unusual in presenting its front to a fairly narrow street rather than to the town's main square. Dating from the 1210s, the carvings of the months over the portal are a perfect Romanesque group; the fourteenth-century campanile, known locally as "the tower of the hundred holes", has become the emblem of the town. The oldest section of the irregular interior is the raised sanctuary, where the altarpiece is Pietro Lorenzetti's *Madonna and Saints* polyptych, painted in 1320.

The steeply sloping Piazza Grande, on the other side of the church, is bordered by a diverting assortment of buildings. On the west side is the apse of Santa Maria and the tiered facade of the **Palazzetto della Fraternità dei Laci**, with a Gothic ground floor and fifteenth-century upper storeys, while the northern edge is formed by **Vasari's loggia**, occupied by shops that in some instances still have their original stone counters. Socially, though, it's less than engrossing, only coming alive for the *Fiera Antiquaria*, and – more raucously – for the *Giostra del Saraceno*, a costumed joust held on the first Sunday in September.

The Duomo and around

At the highest point of the town rises the large and unfussy **Duomo**, its harmonious appearance belying its history. Begun in the late thirteenth century, it was virtually finished by the start of the sixteenth, but the campanile comes from the last century and the facade from this.

The stained-glass windows, made around 1520, are by Guillaume de Marcillat; they let in so little light that his other contributions to the interior – the paintings on the first three bays of the nave – are virtually impossible to see. Off the left aisle, separated from the nave by a huge screen, the Cappella della Madonna del Conforto has terracottas by the della Robbia family. Just beyond the organ is the **tomb of Bishop Guido Tarlati**, head of the *comune* during its resurgence in the early fourteenth century; the monument, plated with marble reliefs showing scenes from the militaristic bishop's career, was possibly designed by Giotto. The tiny fresco nestled against the right side of the tomb is **Piero della Francesca's** *Magdalen*, his only work in Arezzo outside San Francesco.

The town's public park, the **Passeggio del Prato**, extends from the east end of the duomo; the **Fortezza Medicea**, at the far end, is a good place to take a picnic and gaze down over the town. Cosimo I's fortress here was demolished in the eighteenth century, leaving only the ramparts.

San Domenico and the northern district

A short distance in the opposite direction from the duomo is the church of **San Domenico**. Constructed mostly in the late thirteenth century (but with a Gothic campanile), it's more striking inside – the high altar has a dolorous *Crucifix* by **Cimabue** (1260), painted when the artist would have been about twenty, and tatters of fifteenth- and sixteenth-century frescoes all round the church create the effect of a gigantic picture album.

Signs point the way to the nearby **Casa di Giorgio Vasari** (Tues–Sat 9am–2pm, Sun 9am–1pm; free), designed by the celebrated biographer-architect-painter for himself. Taking greater pleasure from the products of his imagination than later generations have managed to extract, Vasari coated the walls of his home with frescoes, a decorative scheme that makes this the most lurid domestic interior in Tuscany.

Down the slope, in Via San Lorentino, the fifteenth-century Palazzo Bruni-Ciocchi houses the **Museo Statale d'Arte Medioevale e Moderna** (Tues–Sat

9am–2pm, Sun 9am–1pm; L2000); its collection of paintings by local artists and majolica pieces dating from the thirteenth to the eighteenth centuries, generously spread over three floors of the palazzo, requires severe editorial work from the visitor.

Practicalities

The **EPT** (Mon–Fri 9am–noon & 4–6pm, Sat 9am–noon) is at Piazza Risorgimento 116, first right off Via Guido Monaco; a map and the latest information on accommodation is displayed outside, so you can get the essentials even if you roll into town in the evening.

Rooms are hard to come by on the first weekend of every month (because of the *Fiera*), and at the end of August and beginning of September, when the *Concorso Polifonico Guido d'Arezzo* (an international choral competition) and the *Giostra del Saraceno* follow in quick succession. Best of the one-star **hotels** is the *Milano*, close to the EPT at Via Madonna del Prato 83 (☎0575/26.836), with doubles from L30,000. If that's full, try the similarly priced *Michelangelo*, Viale Michelangelo 26 (☎0575/20.673) – it's on the busy road to the right of the station, but the rooms are all clean and comfortable, and many are well insulated from the traffic noise. Alternatively, there's a **youth hostel**, the predictably-named *Ostello Piero della Francesco*, near the top end of the Piazza Grande at Via Borg'Unto 6 (☎0575/354.546; open 6–11.30pm in summer, 6–10.30pm winter).

For **restaurants**, the best deal is at *La Scaletta*, next to the main post office at Piazza del Popolo 11 (closed Thurs), which offers filling set meals from L11,000. *Da Guido*, at Via Madonna del Prato 85 (closed Sun), is a basic local trattoria; though the portions are smaller than at *La Scaletta*, it compensates in atmosphere. For high-quality Tuscan cuisine (at around L35,000 per head), try *La Buca di San Francesco* (closed Sun & Mon), right by San Francesco church.

Corso Italia is where people gather in the evenings, the *passeggiata* crowds thinning out towards the top of the climb. Most of the popular **bars** are around here, one of the busiest spots being the bar-pizzeria *La Tavernetta* (closed Mon) on the junction with Via Roma. Another excellent place for **pizzas** is *Il Ruspante*, at Via Roma 34; it's not cheap, but the pizzas are the genuine wood-oven article.

East to Sansepolcro

For those who have come to Arezzo for its della Francesca paintings, the next leg of the itinerary is eastwards to Sansepolcro, the artist's birthplace. Just over 15km south of the town lies the village of **MONTERCHI**, normally a crucial station on the della Francesca trail, as the cemetery chapel on the outskirts contains his *Madonna del Parto*, the only representation in Renaissance art of the pregnant Madonna. But, as with the Arezzo cycle, the fresco is now being restored and won't be ready until 1992.

The *CAT* bus from Arezzo, which goes close by Monterchi, takes an hour to get to **SANSEPOLCRO**, an unassuming place which makes its way in the world as a manufacturer of lace and, more lucratively, *Buitoni* pasta. (There's no train link between the two towns, the rail approach to Sansepolcro being the Terni–Perugia line.)

Born here at some time in the 1410s, Piero della Francesca returned in the 1470s, having abandoned painting altogether, and devoted most of his time to working on his treatises *On Perspective in Painting* and *On the Five Regular Bodies*. The greatest treasure of the **Museo Civico** (daily 9.30am–1pm & 2.30–6pm; L3000) is his spectral *Resurrection* – an image which has occasioned more exotic prose than any other of his paintings. Kenneth Clark's fervent description at least has the virtue of being provocative – "This country god, who rises in the grey light while humanity is asleep, has been worshipped ever since man first knew that the seed is not dead in the winter earth, but will force its way upwards through an iron crust." An earlier della Francesca masterpiece, the *Madonna della Misericordia*, epitomises the graceful solemnity of his work. Other pieces that attract attention are by Pontormo and Luca Signorelli, the latter a student of della Francesca.

Lesser art treasures are to be found in the **Duomo**, a Romanesque-Gothic structure, which has two panels by Matteo di Giovanni that used to flank della Francesca's *Baptism*, now in London's National Gallery. And finally, the church of **San Lorenzo** has a *Deposition* by Rosso Fiorentino, painted within half a century of della Francesca's last works, but seeming to belong to another world.

If you need to **stay** in Sansepolcro – and there is little to stay for once you have seen the *Resurrection* – there is usually space in the town's half dozen hotels. Cheapest, with doubles around L22,000, is the one-star *Lisina* (☎0575/735.139) at Via Piero della Francesco 64. The last bus back to Arezzo leaves at 8pm.

The Casentino

The hills and valleys of the **Casentino** stretch north of Arezzo: a lush, wooded area, once it gets clear of Arezzo's textile factories, whose high, often walled towns see few tourists. The best target for a day trip is **Poppi**, which is connected to Arezzo by bus and by a privately run train line. To strike into the hills, to the monasteries of **La Verna** and **Camáldoli**, needs more time – or ideally a car.

Bibbiena and La Verna

The chief town of the Casentino, **BIBBIENA** has an attractive innermost quarter cordoned by a large tobacco factory and straggling development. The main sight is the church of **San Lorenzo**, a fifteenth-century building that contains a fair quantity of terracotta from the della Robbia workshops.

The daily bus from Arezzo continues to the monastery of **La Verna**, 23km east of Bibbiena. Saint Francis came here to meditate and it was here, in 1224, that he received the stigmata. Now a site of pilgrimage, its fifteenth-century Basilica contains works by Andrea della Robbia that are generally considered his masterpieces.

Poppi and Camáldoli

POPPI, 5km to the south of Bibbiena, is sited high above the road and train station. If you emerge at the latter, in the modern lower suburb of Ponte a Poppi, follow Via Dante Alighieri – a cobbled lane, and shortcut, which leads to the upper town in ten minutes' walk. The old town is not much more than a couple of squares and an arcaded main street (Via Cavour) but it is lent a monumental aspect beyond its size by the **Palazzo Pretorio** – built for the Guidi lords in the thirteenth century to a design identical to Florence's Palazzo Vecchio. A superb array of arms covers the walls, fourteenth-century frescoes decorate the grand hall, and there are splendid views from the tower (Mon–Sat 9am–2pm). Via Cavour climaxes in a second piazza and the magnificent twelfth-century church of **San Fedele**; its very dark interior contains a beguiling thirteenth-century painting of the *Madonna and Child*. Opposite the church are a couple of bars and restaurants and the small one-star *Pension Casentino* (☎0575/529.090), with doubles for around L40,000.

Just over 15km northeast of Poppi is **Camáldoli** (infrequent buses from Ponte a Poppi), where, at the start of the eleventh century, Saint Romauld founded an especially ascetic order of the Benedictines. The much rebuilt monastery complex is of little interest except for its sixteenth-century pharmacy, which now sells herbal products. But the countryside is beautiful – thick forests of pine and fir – and an hour's walk up the hill brings you to the **Eremo** and its Baroque church. Only male visitors are allowed to past the gate to see the twenty monastic cells at close range – women have to peer from afar.

The Camáldoli area is an extremely popular holiday district in summer. BADIA PRATAGLIA, 10km east of Camáldoli, is the focus of activity, with marvellous walks in all directions. To the north, determined hikers might consider searching out the source of the Arno, near Monte Falternona.

South to Cortona

Travelling south from Arezzo you enter the **Valdichiana** – former swampland that is now prosperous cattle country, producing the much prized Florentine *bistecca*. If you are heading for Siena, to the west, you'll pass through **MONTE SAN SAVINO**, a hilltop market town with a scattering of Renaissance buildings and sculpture – among them a handful of works by local boy Andrea Sansovino, who later found fame in the court of Lorenzo de'Medici.

Along the road to Cortona, **CASTIGLION FIORENTINO** is in similar vein. It preserves its walls, has a modest Pinacoteca in its Palazzo Communale (a fine Signorelli *Virgin with St Anne*), and centres on an elegant piazza with a loggia, supposedly by Vasari, framing the hills around. South from here, to the left of the Cortona road, the thirteenth-century castle of **Montécchio Vesponi** rears above the hills. Commanding a great sweep of valley, this was the base of the English condottiere Sir John Hawkwood – he of the fresco in Florence's Duomo. It is now a private residence, though open for guided tours on Mondays, on the hour from 9am to noon.

Cortona

Girdled by terraces of vines and olives, the hill town of **CORTONA** feels a very ancient place. From its heights – a five-kilometre road winds up to the city from the plains below – there are views over a vast domain: the Valdichiana stretching out to the west, Lago Trasimeno across the plains to the south. There was already a sizeable settlement here when the Etruscans took over in the eighth century BC, and the town remained a significant Roman centre until its destruction by the Goths around AD 450. Subsequently, it did not really prosper again until the early fifteenth century, when it was appropriated by Florence. A scattering of Etruscan tombs aside, it is the medieval character that dominates today – the town's constricted ridge-site having limited modern expansion and industrialisation to CAMUCIA, down on the floor of the Valdichiana.

The Town

Any approach to the old town takes you into **Piazza della Repubblica**, dominated by the squat, castellated **Palazzo del Comune**. To the right, the square leads into **Piazza Signorelli**, named after the artist Luca Signorelli, Cortona's most famous son, and overshadowed by the precarious sixteenth-century **Duomo** and the **Palazzo Pretorio**.

The latter now houses the **Museo dell'Accademia Etrusca** (summer Tues–Sun 10am–1pm & 4–7pm; winter Tues–Sun 9am–1pm & 3–5pm; L3000), which, despite its name, has only two rooms given over to Etruscan remains. These are the highlights of the museum, though – the major exhibit being an enormous bronze lamp from the fifth century BC, with its alternate male and female squatting figures. The Futurist painter Gino Severini, another native of Cortona, gets a room to himself at the end.

Cortona's other main sight, apart from the steep medieval streets themselves, is the **Museo Diocesano** (summer Tues–Sun 9am–1pm & 3–6.30pm; winter 9am–1pm & 3–5pm; L3000), just beyond the Museo Etrusca in Piazza del Duomo. Tiny though it is, this is one of Tuscany's most entrancing collections of Renaissance art, featuring work by – among others – Signorelli, Sassetta, Lorenzetti and Fra Angelico, whose exquisite *Annunciation* was painted during his ten years at Cortona's monastery of San Domenico.

A further work by Signorelli is to be found in the church of **San Nicolò**, reached by veering right across Piazza della Pescaia, at the end of Via Berrettini. The high altarpiece is a standard which he painted on both sides – an *Entombment* on the front and a *Madonna and Saints* on the back. From this church, a steep path leads past **Santa Margherita** – rebuilt in the nineteenth century, and housing the fine medieval tomb of the ascetic Margaret of Cortona – to the **Fortezza Medicea**, at the summit of the town. The fortress building itself is shut in the middle of the day, but the area around is good ground for a lunchtime picnic, looking down over ruined ancient walls – Etruscan and Roman – and between lines of cypress trees.

Another good walk is to make your way down the hillside from Piazza Garibaldi to the perfectly proportioned, though crumbling, Renaissance church of **Santa Maria del Calcinaio**. Just past the church, signs direct you further down the hill to the Etruscan **Tanella di Pitagora** – a well-preserved fourth century BC chamber tomb, fancifully identified with the Greek mathematician.

Practicalities

Cortona is easily visited as a day trip from Arezzo. There are more or less hourly *LFI* **buses** between the two towns, and stopping **trains** from Arezzo call at Camucia-Cortona station, from where a shuttle runs up to the centre of the old town. If you are moving on outside the province by train, to Rome for example, take the shuttle service to the Teróntola station, 6km south. Heading south for Montepulciano, catch the bus to Chianciano and change.

The bus terminus is in **Piazza Garibaldi**, which gives remarkable views over Lago Trasimeno. From here the only level street in town, **Via Nazionale**, leads to the core of the town, Piazza della Repubblica and Piazza Signorelli. The **AAST**, at

Via Nazionale 72 (Mon–Sat 8.30am–12.30pm & 3–6pm), can provide maps and help out with accommodation.

There are half a dozen **hotels** in the town proper (others are located down at Camucia and Teróntola); the one-star places – *Athens*, Via S. Antonio (☎0575/603.008), and *Italia*, Via Ghibellina 5 (☎0575/603.264) – each have doubles in the L30,000–35,000 range. A good budget alternative, sited right in the heart of the old town, is the IYHF **youth hostel**, *Ostello San Marco*, at Via Maffei 57 (☎0575/601.392).

For **meals**, try the youthful *Pizzeria-Ristorante Zerolandia*, Via Ghibellina 3 (closed Wed), or, a bit pricier but with the best site in town, *La Logetta* on the Piazza della Repubblica (closed Mon). For evening entertainment, the public gardens, where the Cortonese take their *passeggiata*, has a summer open-air **cinema**. There are also a couple of summer **discos**, their attendance boosted by American students on art and language programmes held here by the University of Athens, Georgia.

Lastly, a Saturday **market** is held in Cortona's Piazza della Repubblica, and on Mondays a huge agricultural fair and general market takes place in Camucia.

SIENA AND CENTRAL TUSCANY

Siena is the perfecf antidote to Florence. Self-contained and still rural in parts behind its medieval walls, its great attraction is its own cityscape – a majestic Gothic whole that could be enjoyed without venturing into a single museum. To get the most from it (and, certainly, if you want to take in its art) you'll need to stay. Too many visitors don't, romping through on a day trip that leaves no chance of easing into the life and moods of its quarters.

As a provincial capital, Siena has good transport links with some of the finest sights of Tuscany. The most popular trip is to the multi-towered village of **San Gimignano**, to the northeast; it's worthwhile, though packed out in midsummer. For a little more isolation with your Tuscan architecture and landscape, head south to a pair of monasteries: **Monte Oliveto Maggiore**, on the Montepulciano road, or ruined **San Galgano**, towards Grosseto. To the west, the medieval and ancient Etruscan town of **Volterra** is a rewarding stop en route to Pisa.

Siena

For a hundred or so years, in the twelfth and thirteenth centuries, **SIENA** was one of the major cities of Europe. It was virtually the size of Paris, controlled most of southern Tuscany and its flourishing wool industry, dominated the trade routes from France to Rome, and maintained Italy's richest pre-Medici banks. The city also developed a highly sophisticated civic life, with its own written constitution, a quasi-democratic government, and a council responsible for as wide a range of duties as any modern city.

This era reached something of an apotheosis with the defeat of a much superior Florentine army at the battle of **Montaperto** in 1260. Although the result was reversed nine years later – and from then on the fulcrum of political power turned towards Florence – Siena, governed by its merchants, embarked on an unrivalled urban development. Under the rule of the **Council of Nine**, from 1287 to 1355, the city's hugely rich commerce underwrote first the completion of its cathedral and then the extraordinary shell-like **Campo** – the greatest medieval square in Italy – with its exuberant Gothic **Palazzo Pubblico**.

The prosperity came to an abrupt halt with the **Black Death**, which reached Siena in May 1348. By October, when the disease exhausted its course, the population had dropped from 100,000 to 30,000. The city was never fully to recover (the population today is 60,000) and its politics, always factional, moved into a period of intrigue and chaos. The chief figures of the following century were the city's two nationally renowned saints – **Catherine** and **Bernardino** – whose mysticism exercised an enormous grip on the age, amid two further outbreaks of plague.

A period of autocratic rule under the tyrannical Pandolfo Petrucci brought a further victory over Florence, but ended with the city embroiled in ever-expanding intrigue involving the Borgias, Florentines, Papacy, French, and the empire of **Charles V**. The latter proved too big a figure for the Sienese, imposing a fortress and garrison, and then, after the city had with French assistance expelled his troops, laying siege to it and the Sienese countryside. The effects of the siege (1554–55) proved more terrible even than the Black Death, with the population slumping from 40,000 to as little as 8000. Two years after the siege, Philip II, Charles's successor, gave up Siena to **Cosimo de'Medici** in lieu of war services, and the city subsequently became part of Cosimo's Grand Duchy of Tuscany. This was the real death knell. For sixty years the Sienese were forbidden even to operate banks, while control of what was now an increasingly minor provincial town reverted, under Medici patronage, to the nobles.

The lack of subsequent development, as the city slipped to little more than a market centre, explains Siena's astonishing state of medieval preservation. Little was built and still less demolished, while allotments and vineyards occupied (as they do today) the spaces between the ancient quarters. Since the last war, however, Siena has again become prosperous, partly due to **tourism**, partly to the resurgence of the **Monte dei Paschi di Siena**. This bank, founded in Siena in 1472, is one of the major players in Italian finance and in its home base is by far the largest employer. It today sponsors much of the cultural life of the city, co-existing, apparently easily, with Italy's strongest **communist council**. (Of the 250,000 population of Siena province, 35,000 are card-carrying PCI members.)

The council themselves perceive their major problem as dealing with tourism and its effects. Siena's population is ageing, and there is little in the tourist industry to encourage the young to stay. Building on the existing strengths of the university, the council have plans for a biotechnology park and other high-tech projects – hoping to create, perhaps, a kind of Tuscan equivalent of Cambridge.

The *Contrade*

Alongside the fabric of the medieval city, Siena preserves its ancient division into wards, or *contrade*. These are integral to the competition of the Palio (see box) and they also lend a unique neighbourhood identity, clearly visible as you wander around the streets. Each of the seventeen *contrade* – there were originally sixty, based on military obligations – has its own church, social centre and museum. Each, too, has a heraldic animal motif, displayed in a modern fountain-sculpture in its individual piazza. There were once social distinctions between the *contrade* and although these today are blurred to the point of extinction, allegiance to one's *contrada* – conferred by birth – remains a strong element of social life.

The *contrade* **museums**, with their displays of Palio trophies, are all open to visitors during the build-up to the Palio and at other times by appointment (ask the tourist office to phone). Each *contrada* also has its own annual celebration, accompanied by parades and feasts. At almost any time of year, you will see their groups of *comparse* practising flag-waving and drum-rolling in the streets.

THE PALIO

The **Siena Palio** is the most spectacular festival event in Italy: a bareback horse race around the Campo, preceded by days of preparation, medieval pageantry and intrigue. Only ten of the *contrade* can take part in any one race; these are chosen by lot, and their horses and jockeys (who are not local) are also assigned at random. The only rule is that riders cannot interfere with each others' reins. Everything else is accepted and practised; each *contrada* has a traditional rival, and ensuring it loses is as important as winning oneself. Jockeys may be bribed to throw the race, or whip a rival or his horse; *contrade* have been known to drug horses, and even to ambush a jockey on his way to the race. This is primarily a show that the Sienese put on for themselves. For visitors, in fact, the undercurrent of brutality and rivalry, and the bragging, days-long celebration of victory, can be quite a shock.

The race has been held since at least the beginning of the fourteenth century. Originally it followed a circuit through the town, but it has been focused, since the sixteenth century, on three laps of the **Campo**, around a track covered with sand and padded with mattresses to minimise injury to horses and riders. There are two palios a year, on July 2 and August 16, with the following build-up:

June 29 and August 13: The year's horses are presented in the morning at the town hall and drawn by lot. At 7.15pm the first trial race is held in the Campo.

June 30 and August 14: Further trial races at 9am and 7.45pm.

July 1 and August 15: Two more trial races at 9am and 7.45pm, followed by a street banquet in each of the *contrade*.

July 2 and August 16: The day of the Palio opens with a final trial at 9am. In the early afternoon each *contrada* takes its horse to be blessed in its church (if the horse shits it's a good omen). At around 5pm the town hall bell begins to ring and riders and *comparse* – equerries, ensigns, pages and drummers in medieval costume – proceed to the Campo for a display of flag-twirling and other pageantry.

The race itself begins at 7.45pm in July, 7pm in August, and lasts little more than one incredibly exciting minute. There's no PA system to tell you what's going on. At the start (in the northwest corner of the Campo) all the horses except one are penned between two ropes; the free one charges the group from behind, when his rivals least expect it, and the race is on. It's a hectic and violent spectacle; a horse which throws its rider is still eligible to win. The jockeys don't stop at the finishing line, but keep going at top speed out of the Campo, pursued by a frenzied mass of supporters. The *palio* itself is a silk banner subsequently presented to the winner.

There are viciously expensive stands for dignitaries and the rich (booked months ahead), but most spectators crowd (free) into the centre of the Campo. For the best view, you need to have found a position on the inner rail by 2pm (ideally at the start and finishing line), and to keep it for the next six hours; otherwise, there's no great hurry, as you'll be able to see a certain amount from anywhere within the throng. Toilet and refreshment facilities are minimal, though very little drinking goes on in the crowd. For at least two hours you won't be able to leave the centre.

Rooms are extremely difficult to find at Palio time, and if you haven't booked, either reckon on staying up all night, or commuting in from a neighbouring town. The races are shown live on TV and repeated endlessly all evening.

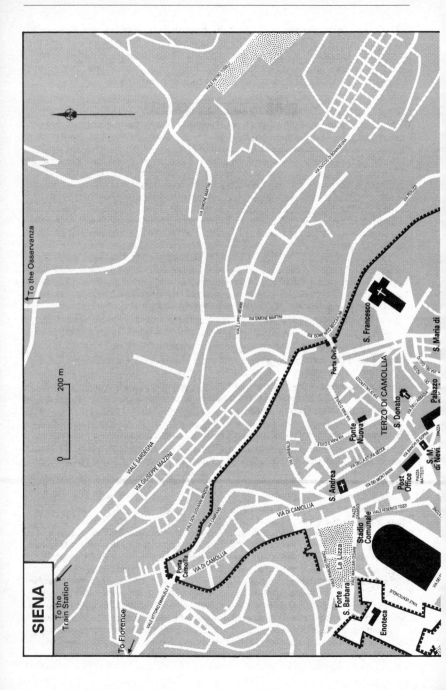

SIENA

To the Train Station

To Florence

To the Osservanza

200 m

VIALE P. TOSELLI

VIA DUCCIO DI BONINSEGNA

VIA SIMONE MARTINI

VIA SIMONE MARTINI

VIALE LIPPO MEMMI

VIA DOMENICO BECCAFUMI

VIA FIORENTINA

VIALE SARDEGNA

VIALE GIUSEPPE MAZZINI

VIA DEL ROMITORIO

VIA DEL COMUNE

VIA PIER ANDREA MATTIOLI

VIA DEI PISPINI

VIA DEL PIGNATTELLO

Porta Ovile

S. Francesco

S. Maria di

S. Donato

Palazzo

TERZO DI CAMOLLIA

VIA DELL'ABBADIA

Fonte
Nuova

VIA PADRE D'OVILE

VIA DELLA STUFA SECCA

S. M.
di Nevi

VIA DEI MONTANINI

Post
Office

PIAZZA
MATTEOTTI

VIA BANCHI DI SOPRA

VIA DEL PARADISO

VIA DI VALLEROZZI

VIA DEI ROSSI

VIALE DON GIOVANNI MINZONI

VIA DEI CAMPANI

VIA DI CAMOLLIA

S. Andrea

VIA DI CAMOLLIA

VIA GARIBALDI

PIAZZA
GRAMSCI

VIALE FEDERICO TOZZI

Stadio
Comunale

La Lizza

Porta
Camollia

VIA VITTORIO EMANUELE II

VIA DI MONTE CESARE

Forte
S. Barbara

Enoteca

VIALE VENTIQUATTRO

VIALE VITTORIO EMANUELE II

Arrival, orientation and accommodation

The centre of Siena is its great square, **Il Campo**, built at the convergence of the city's principal roads, the **Banchi di Sopra**, **Banchi di Sotto** and **Via di Città**. Each of these roads leads out across a ridge, straddled by one of the city's three medieval *terzi*, or quarters: the **Terzo di Città** to the southwest, the **Terzo di San Martino** to the southeast, and the **Terzo di Camollia** to the north. This central core – almost entirely medieval in plan and appearance – has, since the 1960s, been effectively pedestrianised. Finding your way around is therefore simple and enjoyable; everywhere of interest is within easy walking distance.

Arriving by **bus**, you are dropped along Via Curtatone, by the church of San Domenico, from where you can see the city – dominated by the cathedral and town hall belltowers – spread out below. The **train station** is less convenient, 2km to the northeast in the valley below the city; connecting buses shuttle between here and Piazza Matteotti, at the top end of Via Curtatone. **Driving**, follow signs to the *centro* and try to find a parking space around Piazza Gramsci, just north of Piazza Matteotti; an attendant issues tickets by the day or half-day.

Accommodation

Finding a room is less of a struggle than in Florence, though as ever it pays to phone ahead. If you haven't, make your way on arrival either to the **Cooperativa "Hotels Promotion"** booth (☎288.084), opposite San Domenico on Via Curtatone, or to the **AAST** at Via di Citta 43 (☎280.551). The former will book you a room in any of the city's thirty regular hotels or at one of the two *residenze turistico*; the AAST provide lists of rooms in private houses and extremely good (and free) contour **maps** of the city and environs. Some of the **private rooms** are taken by students in term-time and others have a minimum stay of one week – but they're worth at least a try; rates are around L25,000–30,000 a double.

> The Siena area **phone code** is ☎0577.

HOTELS

Locanda Garibaldi, Via Giovanni Dupre 18 (☎284.204). A good, no-nonsense *locanda*, sited above one of the city's cheapest restaurants, just south of the Campo (off to the right hand side of the Palazzo Pubblico). Midnight curfew. Doubles from L30,000.

Tre Donzelle (☎280.358), **Nuove Donzelle** (☎288.088), Via Donzelle 5 and 1–3. The Donzelle and its newer annexe are right in the heart of town, just off Banchi di Sotto, north of the Campo. Good, clean rooms and a cheapish restaurant, too. 12.30am curfew. Doubles from L36,000.

Bernini, Via della Sapienza 15 (☎289.047). Reasonable value but rather pokey rooms on a street running downhill and east from San Domenico. Doubles from L30,000.

Piccolo Hotel Il Palio, Piazza del Sale 19 (☎281.131). Pleasant rooms and a fine location in the earthier quarter of Terzo di Camollia. Doubles from L33,000.

Lea, Viale XXIV Maggio 10 (☎283.207). Modern hotel, a bit of a climb from the centre on the road looping around the Forte di Santa Barbara. Doubles from L35,000.

Cannon d'Oro, Via Montanini 28 (☎44.321). A stylish small hotel tucked down an alleyway east of Piazza Matteotti. Doubles from L38,000.

Centrale, Via Calzoleria 24 (☎280.379). As the name suggests – a block north of the Campo. Large doubles from L44,000.

La Perla, Via delle Terme 25 (☎47.144). Second-floor *pensione* on street two blocks west of Banchi di Sopra. Basic but not cheap as all rooms have baths; doubles from L45,000.

Chiusarelli, Via Curtatone 9 (☎280.562). A nice old villa, with a garden at the back, on a busy street near the bus station. Doubles from L54,000.

Duomo (annexe), Via Stalloreggi 34 (☎289.088). Modest annexe of a pricey three-star hotel two doors up the same street – the westward continuation of Via di Città. Doubles (with bath) from L57,000.

Continentale, Via Banchi di Sopra 85 (☎41.451). Elegant hotel in a sixteenth-century palazzo on the main *passeggiata* route. Most doubles are priced at L77,000 but there are a few tiny, bathless singles and doubles at L33,000 and L58,000 respectively.

HOSTELS AND CAMPING

Ostello della Gioventù "Guidoriccio", Via Fiorentina 17 (☎522.12). The city youth hostel is 2km northwest of the centre; take bus #10 or #15 from Piazza Matteotti or, if you're coming from Florence, ask the bus driver to let you off at "Lo Stellino" (just after the Siena city sign). Dormitory beds and also several doubles for L12,000 per person, including breakfast; restaurant and bar. *IYHF* card required. Curfew 11pm.

Conservatori Femminili Riuniti, Via del Refugio 4 (☎280.376). Women-only hostel, with beds again around L12,000. Off Via Roma in the Terzo di San Martino. Phone in advance to check that it's operating.

Campeggio Siena Colleverde, Strada di Scacciapensieri 37 (☎280.044). Secure, well-maintained campsite, 2km out to the north; take bus #8 from Piazza Matteotti (last one runs at 10pm). Shop, bar and swimming pool. Open late March–late Sept; L9000 per person.

The Campo and southern *terzi*

The Campo, with its amphitheatre curve, seems an almost organic piece of city planning. In fact, when the Council of Nine began its construction in 1347, they were building on the only possible land – the old marketplace, which stood at the convergence of the city quarters but belonged to none.

To build, it was necessary to make an enormous buttress beneath the lower half of the square, where the Palazzo Pubblico, or town hall, was to be built. The square itself the council created in nine segments to commemorate their highly civic rule, adding to the stage-like aspect. It was, from the start, a focus of city life, the scene of executions, bullfights, communal boxing matches, and, of course, the Palio. San Bernardino preached here, too, holding before him the monogram of Christ's name in Greek – IHS – which he urged the nobles to adopt in place of their own vainglorious coats of arms. A few did so (the monogram is to be seen on various palazzi), and it was adopted by the council on the facade of the Palazzo Pubblico, alongside the city's she-wolf symbol, itself a reference to legendary foundation by the sons of Remus.

The **Palazzo Pubblico**, with its 320ft belltower, the **Torre del Mangia**, is in every sense the focus of the Campo, occupying virtually its entire south side. Its lower level of arcading is a characteristic of Sienese Gothic, as are the columns separating the windows. The council were so pleased with this aspect of the design that they ordered its emulation on all other buildings on the square – and it was indeed gracefully adapted on the twelfth-century **Palazzo Sansedoni** across on the north side. The other main exterior feature of the Palazzo Pubblico is the **Cappella di Piazza**, a stone loggia set at the base of the tower, built to celebrate the end of plague in 1348.

At the highest point of the Campo the Renaissance makes a fleeing entry with the **Fonte Gaia** (Gay Fountain), designed and carved by Jacopo della Quercia in the early fifteenth century. Its panels are reproductions; the originals, badly eroded, can be seen on the rear loggia of the Palazzo Pubblico.

The Palazzo Pubblico

The Palazzo Pubblico remains in use as Siena's town hall, but its principal rooms have been converted into a **Museo Civico** (daily 9.30am–7.30pm, 9.30am–5.30pm in winter; L5000), entered through the courtyard to the right of the Cappella di Piazza. Off to the left of the courtyard there is separate access to the **Torre del Mangia** (daily 10am–7pm; L3000), with its fabulous views across town and countryside. The tower takes its name from its first watchman – a glutton (*mangia*), commemorated by a statue in the courtyard.

If you have time or inclination only for one of Siena's museums, it should be the Museo Civico, a series of former public rooms, frescoed with themes integral to the secular life of the medieval city. The visit begins on the first floor, with a rather miscellaneous picture gallery and the **Sala del Risorgimento**, painted with nineteenth-century scenes of Vittorio Emanuele. The medieval interest begins as you reach the **Sala dei Priori**, frescoed by Spinello Aretino in 1407 with episodes from the life of Pope Alexander III and his conflict with Emperor Frederic Barbarossa, and, beyond it, the **Cappella del Consiglio**, frescoed by Taddeo di Bartolo a year later, and with a majestic wrought-iron screen by Jacopo della Quercia.

These are little more than a warm-up, however, to room 10, the **Sala del Mappamondo**, named from its (partial) frescoed cosmology. On one wall of this room is the fabulous *Maestà* (Virgin in Majesty) of Simone Martini, an extraordinary, translucent work, painted in 1315 and touched up by Martini (the site was damp) six years later. The style is distinctively Sienese, heavily influenced by Byzantine paintings which had reached Italy through Pisa, then in allegiance with Siena. It was a symbolic art, laying great stress on spirituality and almost none on such Renaissance concerns as perspective or naturalistic illusion. This painting, with its warmth and handling of space, is one of the acknowledged masterpieces.

The picture on the opposite wall, the *Equestrian Portrait of Guidoriccio da Fogliano*, has also long been credited to Martini – indeed it is almost a symbol of Siena – and accounted as one of the earliest Italian portraits and landscape paintings. It is undoubtedly a marvellous image, with the knight setting forth from his battle camp to besiege a walled hill town, but it is not, as Sienese guides and postcards continue to maintain, by Martini. Art historians had long puzzled over the anachronistic castles in the painting – much later in style than its date of 1328 – and in the mid-1980s conclusive evidence was found when, during restoration, a Renaissance fresco by Sodoma was revealed underneath. A fragment of two figures outside a castle, believed to be an authentic Martini, is to be seen below the main picture and may have provided inspiration for the fake.

The Palazzo Pubblico's most important frescoes are to be seen in room 11, the former **Sale dei Nove**, the "Room of the Nine". These are Ambrogio Lorenzetti's *Allegories of Good and Bad Government*, commissioned in 1377 to remind the councillors of the effects of their duties. Beyond the basic theme they have a complex iconography of allegorical virtues and figures; it is worth catching a lecture from one of the guides.

Some of the finest panel paintings – by Lorenzetti's contemporaries, Guido da Siena and Matteo di Giovanni – are displayed in the **Sala della Pace**, off the Sala dei Novi. Take time, too, for a visit to the rear **loggia**, where, in addition to the original panels of the Fonte Gaia, you can crane your neck to see the current (and again frescoed) council chambers.

Southeast from the Campo: Terzo di San Martino

Walk behind the Palazzo Pubblico and you find yourself several levels below in the **Piazza del Mercato**, now mainly a car park with a belvedere-like platform at the end. You realise here how abruptly the town ends: quarters rise to right and left for a few hundred metres along the *terzi* but in the centre land drops away to a rural valley.

At the top end of the Campo, at the intersection of the principal streets, is the **Loggia di Mercanzia**, built as a tribune house for the merchants to do their deals. It is a fifteenth-century structure, essentially Renaissance but still reluctantly so, with its Gothic niches with saints. Following the Banchi di Sotto from here, you pass the **Palazzo Piccolomini**, a more committed Renaissance building by Bernardo Rossellino – the architect employed by the Sienese pope Pius II (Enea Piccolomini) at Pienza. It now houses the **state archive** (Mon–Fri 9am–1pm; free admission – ask at reception), which displays the painted covers of the *Tavolette di Biccherna*, the city accounts. The earlier paintings depict religious themes, but they soon move towards secular images of the city's life and events – the monks doing the audits, victories against the Florentines, the demolition of the Spanish fortress, the entry of Cosimo I.

Heading south along the parallel Via Salicotto you find yourself in the territory of the **Torre contrada**, with their museum (at no. 76) and their fountain-square a few houses beyond. This street, or Via San Martino, will bring you out towards the end of the Terzo di San Martino and to **Santa Maria dei Servi**, the Servites' massive monastic church. Inside, there are two contrasting frescoes of the *Massacre of the Innocents* – a Gothic version by Lorenzetti, in the second chapel behind the high altar, and a Renaissance treatment by Matteo di Giovani (1492) in the fifth chapel on the right. The church has some fine altarpieces, too, by Lippo Memmi and Taddeo di Bartolo.

Southwest from the Campo

Via di Città cuts across the oldest, cathedral quarter of the city, fronted by some of Siena's finest private palazzi. The **Palazzo Chigi-Saracini** at no. 82 is a Gothic beauty, with its curved facade and back courtyard (wander inside). The actual palace, closed to the public, is home to the Accademia Chigiana, who sponsor music programmes, and houses an art collection (rarely open), including works by Botticelli and Donatello.

Off to the left at the end of the street, Via San Pietro leads to the **Pinacoteca** (Mon 8.30am–2pm, Tues–Sat 8.30am–7pm; L3000), housed in a fourteenth-century palace. The collection is a roll of honour of Sienese Gothic painting, though, individually, few of its works are up to the standards of the Martini and Lorenzetti in the Palazzo Pubblico, or the Duccio in the cathedral museum.

Keeping south from here, you pass **Sant'Agostino**, erratically open, with frescoes by Sodoma and Matteo Giovanni, and beyond it a patch of botanical garden. Looping along the **Via della Cerchia** from here makes a nice walk – and offers some good local restaurants (see "Practicalities") around the church of **Santa Maria del Carmine**, a predominantly student section of the town. If you follow the Via del Fosso di San Ansano, north of the Carmine square, you find yourself on a country lane, with terraced vineyards below, before emerging at the **Selva** (rhinoceros) *contrada*'s square and church of **San Sebastiano**. Climb up the stepped Vicolo di San Girolamo and you reach the Duomo.

The Duomo and around

Few buildings reveal so much of a city's history and aspirations as Siena's **Duomo**. Complete to virtually its present size around 1215, it was subjected to constant plans for expansion throughout Siena's years of medieval prosperity. An initial project, at the beginning of the fourteenth century, attempted to double its extent by building a baptistery on the slope below and using this as a foundation for a rebuilt nave, but the work ground to a halt as the walls and joints gaped under the pressure. For a while, the chapter pondered knocking down the whole building and starting from scratch to the principles of the day, but eventually they hit on a new scheme to re-orientate the cathedral instead, using the existing nave as a transept and building a new nave out towards the Campo. Again, cracks appeared, and then, in 1348, came the Black Death. With the population decimated, and funds suddenly cut off, the plan was abandoned once and for all. The extension still stands at the north end of the square – a vast structure that would have created the largest church in Italy outside Rome.

The Duomo as it stands, however, is a delight. Its style is an amazing conglomeration of Romanesque and Gothic, delineated by bands of black and white marble, an idea adapted from Pisa and Lucca – though here with much bolder and more extravagant effect. The **facade** was in fact designed by the Pisan sculptor Giovanni Pisano, who with his workshop created much of the statuary – philosophers, patriarchs, prophets, now replaced by copies. In the next century a Gothic rose window was added. The mosaics in the gables, however, had to wait until money was found to employ Venetian artists in the nineteenth century.

The use of black and white decoration is continued in the *sgraffito* marble **pavement**, which begins with geometric patterns outside the church and then takes off into a startling sequence of 56 panels within. They were completed between 1349 and 1547, virtually every artist who worked in the city trying his hand on a design. Many are obscure in the extreme, like Pinturicchio's *Allegory of Virtue* (a rocky island of serpents with a nude posed between a boat and the land) in the nave. The finest are reckoned to be Beccafumi's *Moses Striking Water from a Rock* and *Sacrifice of Isaac*, just beyond the dome area. These are kept covered except from August 7–22.

The rest of the **interior** is equally arresting, with its line of popes' heads – many sculpted with an apparent eye to their perversity – set above the multi-striped pillars. Among the greatest individual artistic treasures are **Nicolo Pisano's font** – completed after his commission at Pisa and more elaborate in its high relief details of the *Life of Jesus* and *Last Judgment* – and, in the north transept, a bronze Donatello statue of *Saint John the Baptist*. Midway along the nave, on the left, the entrance to the **Libreria Piccolomini** (daily 9am–7pm, 9am–5pm in winter; L1500) is signalled by Pinturicchio's brilliantly coloured fresco of the *Coronation of Pius II*. Within the library a further ten frescoes by Pinturicchio and his pupils (who included Raphael) illustrate scenes from Pius's life – his travels to Scotland, canonisation of Saint Catherine, and officiation at the marriage of Frederick Barbarossa with Eleonora of Portugal outside Siena's Porta Camollia.

The Piazza and Baptistery

Opposite the cathedral is the medieval **Ospedale di Santa Maria di Scala**, still in use as a hospital, and with fifteenth-century frescoes in its *Sala dei Pelegrini*. The other sides of the square continue the history of Sienese power, with the

Archbiship's Palace, the **Palazzo del Magnifico** built for Petrucci in 1508, and the **Palazzo Granducale** built later in the century for the Medici.

The **Baptistery** (9am–1pm & 3–6pm; free) is reached down a flight of steps behind the cathedral, past an opportunistic Cripta delle Statue "museum". The baptistery is fronted by an unfinished Gothic facade and houses a Renaissance **font** with panels illustrating the Baptist's life by Jacopo della Quercia (*The Angel Announcing the Baptist's Birth*), Lorenzo Ghiberti (*Baptism of Christ* and *John in Prison*) and Donatello (*Herod's Feast*). Take plenty of coins for illumination.

Museo dell'Opera del Duomo

After the Museo Civico, the best art in Siena is to be seen in the **Museo dell'Opera del Duomo** (daily 9am–7.30pm; L4000), which occupies the projected, re-orientated nave. Downstairs are Pisano's original statues from the facade. Upstairs, amid a comprehensive display of cathedral treasures, is a fine array of panels, including works by Simone Martini, Pietro Lorenzetti and Sano di Pietro, and the cathedral's original altarpiece, the stark, haunting Byzantine icon known as the *Madonna dagli Occhi Grossi* (Madonna of the Big Eyes).

The painting that merits the museum admission, however, is the cathedral's second altarpiece, Duccio's *Maestà*. On its completion in 1311 this painting was taken in a ceremony that processed from Duccio's studio, then around the Campo to a special mass in the Duomo; everything in the city was closed and virtually the entire population attended. They can only have been impressed, for this is possibly the climax of the Sienese style of painting – its iconic, Byzantine spirituality accompanied by Duccio's own attention to narrative detail in the panels (originally on the reverse of the altarpiece) of the *Life of Christ and the Virgin*.

An additional bonus to the museum is the chance to climb up onto the top of the "new nave", arguably a better vantage point than the Torre di Mangia.

San Domenico, San Francesco and the Terzo di Camollia

Monasteries were essentially rural until the beginning of the thirteenth century when the idea of an exclusively meditative retreat was displaced by the preaching orders of friars. Suddenly, in the space of a few decades, each of the orders founded monasteries on the periphery of the major Italian cities. In Siena the two greatest orders, the Dominicans and Franciscans, located themselves respectively to the west and east.

San Domenico, founded in 1125, is closely identified with Saint Catherine of Siena. On the right of the entrance is a kind of raised chapel, with a contemporary portrait of her by her friend Andrea Vanni; below are steps and a niche, where she received the stigmata. Her own chapel, on the south side of the church, has frescoes of her in ecstasy, by Sodoma, and a reliquary containing her head.

Saint Catherine's family house, where she lived as a Dominican nun, is a short distance away to the south, near the Fontebranda on Via Santa Caterina. The entrance to the **Casa Sanctuario di Santa Caterina** (daily 9am–12.30pm & 3.30–6.30pm; L1500) is on Via Benincasa, behind. The building has been much adapted, with a Renaissance loggia and a series of oratories – one on the site of her cell – as is only fitting for Italy's patron saint (and the first ever canonised woman). Her career, encompassing innumerable miracles, was pretty extraordinary in secular terms, too, reconciling Tuscan cities to each other, and persuading the pope, Gregory XI, to return to Rome from Avignon.

Catherine died in 1380, the year of the birth of San Bernardino, who began his preaching life at the monastic church of **San Francesco**, across the city to the east. His **Oratorio** (ring for admission), with an upper chapel frescoed by Sodoma, stands beside the main church, which, like that of the Dominicans, is vast, Gothic and austere.

Between these two saintly locales lies the heart of business Siena. Close by Piazza Matteotti, on Banchi di Sopra, is the **Palazzo Salimbeni**, the headquarters throughout its history of the **Monte dei Paschi di Siena**. The building behind the facade is a radical 1980s design by Pierlugi Spadolini, though scarcely visible unless you can convince the doorman of an architectural interest.

North of Piazza Matteotti you enter the less monumental neighbourhood of the **Terzi di Camollia**, with a solid shopping street along **Via Montanini** and largely untouristed bars and restaurants. The church of **San Stefano** fronts one of the nicest *contrade* squares in the city, home of the Istrici or porcupine. Away to the west, the gardens of **La Lizza** lead up to the walls of the **Forte di Santa Barbara**, rebuilt on Charles V's foundations by the Medici, and housing the **Enoteca Italiana** (see below).

Practicalities

Siena feels distinctly provincial after Florence. The main action of an evening is the **passeggiata** from Piazza Matteotti along Banchi di Sopra to the Campo – and there's not much in the way of nightlife to follow. For most visitors, though, the Campo, the city's universal gathering place, provides diversion enough, while the presence of the university ensures a bit of life in the bars, as well as a cluster of cheaper *trattorie* alongside the pricier tourist restaurants.

Posters for city **events** are to be seen around Piazza Matteotti or on the stepped alley leading out of Piazza del Mercato to Via di Salicotto. The local communist party organise a range of concerts (mostly rock and jazz) as part of their local *Festa dell'Unità*, and the *Monte dei Paschi* and *Accademia Chigiana* put on some impressive classical concerts throughout the year.

Eating and drinking
Restaurants cost a bit over the odds in Siena, especially so if you're determined to eat out in the Campo – though a meal in the square, it has to be said, is worth a few thousand extra lire. If you are looking for cheaper meals, you'll do better walking out a little from the centre, west towards Santa Maria del Carmine, for example, or north towards the Porta Camollia. Recommendations below are in ascending order of price:

Mensa Universitaria, Via Sant'Agata 1 (noon–2pm & 6.45–9pm; closed Aug). The university canteen has full meals for L8000, pasta dishes for a lot less. It's a bit hidden away, on the continuation of Via G. Dupre, below San Agostino.

Il Barbero, Piazza Il Campo 80–81 (noon–2.30pm & 7–10pm). Having cautioned against the Campo's prices, this is an honourable exception – an excellent value self-service.

Nuova Donzelle, Via delle Donzelle 1 (closed Sun). Unexciting but solid meals for L14,000 in the restaurant of this backpacker-favoured hotel. Just north of the Campo.

Carlo e Franca, Via di Pantaneto 1216. Unpretentious café-like place with generous pizza and pasta at very regular prices.

San Marco, Via San Marco 48 (closed Sun); **Vecchia Osteria**, Via San Marco 8; **La Mantellina**, Piano dei Montellini 2 (closed Mon). Three local eateries in an untouristed part of the city behind Santa Maria del Carmine. Full meals from L11,000.

Pizzeria Braceria, Piazza del Mercato. Impressive pizzas and great views south over the town and countryside, and up to the back of the Palazzo Pubblico.

Trattoria da Dino, Via Casato di Sopra 71 (near the Pinacoteca; closed Fri). Full meals for L17,000 featuring a few adventurous and traditional specialities.

Alla Speranza, Piazza Il Campo 33–34 (closed Wed). A prime spot for alfresco eating in the Campo, with good quality food; not cheap, but a memorable experience.

Osteria Le Logge, Via del Porrione 33 (by the Logge del Papa, east of the Campo; closed Sun). Very popular and tasteful trattoria, in an old and beautiful *farmacia*. Excellent pasta and some unusual *secondi*. Around L24,000 for a full meal.

Cane e Gatto, Via Pagliaresi 6 (☎220.751; closed Thurs). This can be an expensive restaurant if you go for the full works – seven sublime courses for around L35,000 plus wine – but the quality is high and if you want to pay less, you can discuss dishes and prices before you eat. It's a friendly place, though, disconcertingly, it doesn't have a menu.

Snack alternatives – which still allow a meal in the Campo – include a range of **pizza by weight** at Via delle Terme 10, and an extravagantly-stocked **deli**, the *Pizzicheria Morbidi* at Banchi di Sotto 27. The market building south of the Campo in Piazza del Mercato is also good for picnic lunch provisions, while Wednesday morning sees a full-scale open-air **market** sprawling across La Lizza, below the fortress.

Ice cream is bought by most Sienese at one or other end of the *passeggiata* – either at *Nannini's*, at the Piazza Matteotti end of Banchi di Sopra, or at the *Gelateria Artigiani*, just off the Campo at the corner of Via di Città and Via dei Pellegrini. Siena's own individual speciality is **panforte**, a dense and delicious Christmas-cake-like wedge of nuts, fruit and honey; buy it fresh by the *etto* (or, less good, gift-packaged) in any of the *pasticcerie* along Bianchi di Sopra.

For a **drink**, there are pleasant, neighbourhood bars in most *contrade* – Via del Porrione, southeast of the Campo, has several, as does Via Camollia, north of Piazza Matteotti. If you want to watch the Sunday evening Italian league **football** matches, make your way to *Video Bar* at Via del Pantaneto 85, where you can have beer and pizza in front of the big screen.

Lastly, if you are interested in sampling Italian **wines**, there's the **Enoteca** inside the fortress. This has a cellar exhibiting every single wine produced in the country and a bar – at its best early evening – where you can order up a glass (of any wine under L25,000 a bottle) or bottle from the range.

Transport

Leaving Siena is easiest by **bus**. From the station by San Domenico, *Lazzi and Tra-In* have connections throughout the province – half-hourly to Poggibonsi (for connections to San Gimignano buy a through ticket), and half a dozen times daily to Montalcino and Montepulciano. *Lazzi* services also run throughout the day to Florence (take a *diretto*, which arrives in 1hr; those marked Via Strove take nearly 3hr), and regularly to Massa Maríttima, Volterra and Rome (buy tickets in advance).

Trains are less convenient as they're slower and the station involves a connecting bus (see "Arriving"). However, Siena is linked with the Florence to Pisa line via Empoli, with Grosseto (and thence Rome) to the southwest, and there's a very pretty minor line southeast through Asciano and San Giovanni d'Asso – local stations if you fancy a hike to Monte Oliveto Maggiore (see below).

If you feel the need of your own transport to explore the Sienese countryside – and it has good claim to being Italy's finest – try *Autonoleggi Intercar Eurodrive* at Via San Marco 96 (☎411.48), who hire both **cars** and **scooters**.

Listings

Books and newspapers English-language books – novels plus a fair selection on Siena and Tuscany – at the *Libreria Senese*, Via di Citta 94, and *Feltrinelli*, Banchi di Sopra 66. British newspapers from *Bassi*, Via di Citta 8.

Currency exchange There's a concentration of banks along Banchi di Sopra, with automatic exchange machine and computer currency display in the window of the Monte dei Paschi (no. 92). The *Hotel Coop* opposite San Domenico, and the train station ticket office, also offer cash and traveller's cheque exchange.

Phones International calls from the office at Via dei Termini 40 (Mon–Sat 8am–8.30pm, Sun 9am–12.45pm & 3–7.45pm). Or try *Bar Centrale* (open till midnight) at Via Cecco Angiollieri 37, a block north of the Campo.

Post Office Main post office – with poste restante – is on Piazza Matteotti (Mon–Fri 8.15am–7pm, Sat 8.15am–noon).

Monte Oliveto Maggiore

It takes some effort to visit the **Abbazia di Monte Oliveto Maggiore**, but the rewards are there: Tuscany's grandest monastery is sited in one of the most beautiful tracts of Sienese countryside. Approached from BUONCONVENTO, to the west, you climb quickly into forests of pine, oak and cypress, and then into the olive groves that enclose the monastery. From the east, coming through ASCIANO or SAN GIOVANNI D'ASSO, the road passes through a sparsely populated farming region of forever-shifting colours and cultivation – the beautiful **Crete**, "craters" or moors.

The Monastery

When Pius II visited Monte Oliveto Maggiore in 1463, it was the overall scene that impressed him: the architecture, in honey-coloured Sienese brick, merging into the woods and gardens that the monks had created from the eroded chalk hills around. The monastery had been founded a century and a half earlier, in 1313, by Giovanni (later Bernardo) Tolomei, a Sienese noble. He belonged to one of the wealthiest merchant families of the region, but, in the pattern of monastic legend, was struck blind, saw visions of the Virgin, and renounced worldly life. With two companions, he came to this place – known then as the desert of Accona – and lived the life of a hermit, soon drawing a following. Within six years, the pope recognised his Order – the **Olivetans**, or White Benedictines – and over the following two centuries this, their principal house, was transformed into one of the most powerful monasteries in the land. It was only in 1810, when the monastery was suppressed by Napoleon, that it fell from influence. It is today maintained by a small group of Olivetan monks, who supplement their state income with a very modern centre for the restoration of ancient books.

From the **gateway**, surmounted by a square watchtower and niches containing della Robbia terracottas, an avenue of cypresses leads to the abbey. Off to the right signs direct you along a walk to the **Blessed Bernardo's grotto** – a chapel built on the site where Tolomei settled as a hermit.

The abbey itself is a huge complex, though much of it remains off limits to visitors. The entrance leads past a giftshop, selling herbal cures and liquors, to the

Chiostro Grande, covered by the series of frescoes depicting the *Life of St Bernard*. The cycle begins on the east wall, just on the right of the door into the church. It was begun in 1497 by Signorelli, who painted nine panels (in the middle of the series) before abandoning the work for a more stimulating commission at Orvieto cathedral. His sequence starts with the scene depicting a collapsing house. The colourful, if minor, artist, Antonio Bazzi, known as Il Sodoma, then took over, painting the remaining 27 scenes from 1505 to 1508. He was by all accounts a lively presence in the abbey, bringing with him part of his menagerie of pets – which included badgers, depicted at his feet in a self portrait in the third panel. There's a sensuality in many of the secular figures: the young men especially, as befits his nickname, and the "evil women" (originally nudes, until protests from the abbot) seen tempting the monks.

The **church** was given a Baroque remodelling in the eighteenth century, and some superb stained glass in the present one. Its main treasure are the choir-stalls, inlaid by Giovanni di Verona (1503) with architectural, landscape and domestic scenes (including a nod to Sodoma's pets with a cat in a window). Back in the cloister, stairs lead up to the **library**, again with carving by Giovanni; sadly, it has had to be viewed from the door since the theft of sixteen of its twenty codices in 1975.

Access

The monastery is **open to visits** from 9.15am to 12.30pm and from 3.15 to 6.30pm (5.30pm in winter). At the gatehouse there is a good **café-restaurant**, and also a hostel – as is the Benedictine custom. There is, however, a minimum stay of ten days (most guests stay two to three months) and summer places are almost always taken. If you want to try your luck, phone ☎0577/707.017.

Transport to Monte Oliveto is a little difficult. The nearest village served by bus is CHIUSURE, 2km east: this has a daily departure easier from Siena at 2pm, returning at 7pm (Mon–Sat only). It's considerably easier to get to either Buonconvento, 9km southwest, or Asciano, 9km north, which each have train and bus connections with Siena. If you want to hike the rest of the way, the Asciano road is the prettier; hitching, there's much better chance of a lift from Buonconvento.

Buonconvento and Asciano

BUONCONVENTO is the most obvious place to stay if you are visiting the monastery and travelling on south. The town looks grittily industrial on the approach, but preserves a perfect, walled medieval village at its heart. It's an enjoyable stop, with a single **hotel-restaurant**, the *Albergo Roma* (☎0577/806.021), inside the walls; doubles from L35,000. Along the street, the **Collegiata** has a classic Sienese altarpiece by Matteo Giovanni and there are further Sienese Renaissance paintings in a small **Museo di Arte Sacra** (Tues–Thurs 10am–noon, Sat 10am–noon & 2–4pm, Sun 9am–1pm), opposite.

ASCIANO, too, is partly walled, and shelters a **Museo di Arte Sacra** (its highlight is Ambrogio Lorenzetti's *St Michael and the Dragon*) and tiny **Etruscan museum**. Its **hotel**, *Lo Spiedo* (☎0577/718.755), has doubles at L30,000.

If you are driving, or leave Monte Oliveto early in the day, Montalcino or San Quirico d'Orcia (see below) are alternative bases for **accommodation**. There are regular connections to both places from Buonconvento.

San Gimignano

SAN GIMIGNANO – "delle Belle Torri" – is probably the best known town in Tuscany, after Florence, Pisa and Siena. Its image as a "Medieval Manhattan", with its skyline of towers, has caught the tourist imagination – helped along, no doubt, by its convenience as a day trip from Florence or Siena.

The town is, in fact, all that it's cracked up to be: quietly monumental, very well-preserved, enticingly rural, and with a fine array of religious and secular frescoes. However, from May through to October, San Gimignano has very little life of its own – and a lot of day trippers. If you want to get any feel for the place, beyond the level of art treasures or quaintness, you really need to come well out of season. If you can't, then aim to spend the night here – in the evenings the town takes on a very different pace and atmosphere.

Some history

Founded around the eighth century, San Gimignano was quite a force to be reckoned with by the early Middle Ages. It was controlled by two great families – the Ardinghelli and the Salvucci – and its 15,000 population (twice the present number) prospered on agricultural holdings and its position on the Lombardy to Rome pilgrim route. At its heyday, in the fourteenth century, the town's walls enclosed five monasteries, four hospitals, public baths and a brothel.

Feuds, however, had long wreaked havoc. The first Ardinghelli-Salvucci conflict erupted in 1246, and for the following century there were few years of peace. Guelph-Ghibelline loyalties provided further fuel, and whenever the town itself was united there were wars with Volterra, Poggibonsi and other nearby towns. They came to a halt only through the Black Death, which reached San Gimignano in 1348. It had a devastating effect both on the population and – as the pilgrim trade collapsed – on the economy. The Ardinghelli family, despite opposition from the Salvucci, applied to Florence for the town to become a part of the city's comune: an appeal that was accepted by only one vote – a reflection on medieval wariness of San Gimignano's reputation.

Subjection to Florence broke the power of the nobles and so San Gimignano was unaffected by the struggles between aristocracy and town council which racked other Tuscan towns. The towerhouses, symbolic of real control elsewhere, posed little threat – and so were not torn down; today, fifteen (of an original 72) survive. The town itself, further hit by plague in 1464 and 1631, passed into a rural backwater existence. At the turn of the present century, travellers spoke of it as "miserably poor", a condition that was barely romanticised by E.M. Forster, who took the town (he calls it Monteriano) as the setting for his novel *Where Angels Fear to Tread*. San Gimignano's postwar history has been one of ever-increasing affluence, through tourism and the production of an old established, but recently rejuvenated, white wine, *Vernaccia*.

The Town

San Gimignano is not much more than a village: you could walk from one end to the other in fifteen minutes, or around the walls in an hour. It deserves at least a day, however, both for the frescoes in the churches and museums, and for the countryside – some of the loveliest in Tuscany.

To the Piazza del Duomo and Rocca

The main entrance gate, facing the bus terminal (and carpark), is **Porta San Giovanni**, on the south side of town. From here **Via San Giovanni**, lined with a series of defensive palazzi leads to the town's interlocking main squares, the Piazza della Cisterna and Piazza del Duomo. On the right of the street, about a hundred metres up, is the former church of **San Francisco** – a Romanesque building converted now, like many of the palazzi, to a *Vernaccia* cellar.

You enter the **Piazza della Cisterna** through another majestic gateway, the **Arco dei Becci**, part of the original fortifications before the town expanded in the twelfth century. The square itself is flanked by an anarchic cluster of towers and palazzi, with a thirteenth-century cistern – still functioning – in the centre. It was here, and in other streets within these inner walls, that most of the leading families had their houses. To the left of the square, beside an arch leading through to the Piazza Duomo, is one of the old Ardinghelli towers; a Salvucci rival rears up behind.

The more austere **Piazza Duomo**, off to the left, introduces further towers and civic palazzi. Facing the duomo (more properly the Collegiata, as San Gimignano no longer has a bishop), the crenellated **Palazzo del Popolo**, still the town hall, stands to your left, the older **Palazzo del Podestà**, behind you. The latter's *Torre della Rognosa* was once set as the maximum height – 160ft – for any tower. Looking around the skyline, the rule, clearly, was not much respected.

Just behind the Piazza del Duomo, a signposted lane leads to the **Rocca**, the old fortress, with its one surviving tower and superb views. It was built, at local expense, by the Florentines "in order to remove every cause of evil thinking from the inhabitants" after their union with the comune. Later, its purpose presumably fulfilled, it was dismantled by Cosimo Il Medici. Nowadays it encloses an orchard-like public garden, with figs, olives and a well in the middle.

The Collegiata

The Collegiata's plain facade could hardly provide a greater contrast with the interior: one of the most comprehensively frescoed churches in Tuscany. You need a good pocketful of L100 coins to do justice to the cycles, which fill every available space, their brilliant colours set off by Pisan-Romanesque arcades of black and white striped marble. The church is closed from 12.30 to 3pm.

The principal cycles are scenes of the Old Testament (on the left wall) and the New Testament (on the right); in the lunettes above, scenes of the Creation are paralleled by those of the Nativity. The **Old Testament** scenes were completed by Bartolo di Fredi around 1367. They are full of medieval detail in the costumes, activities (*Abraham and Lot leading their flock towards Canaan*) and interiors (the bedroom of *Joseph's Dream*). They are also quirkily naturalistic – there are few odder frescoes than that of *Noah drunk*, exposing himself in his stupor. The **New Testament** scenes were begun by Barna da Siena (1381) and completed by a pupil after his death – he fell from the scaffold while at work. They are more Renaissance in conception – there is none of Bartolo's delight in genre scenes – and impress most by their portrait narratives: the focus of eyes in *Judas's Betrayal* and *Christ Carrying the Cross*.

An altogether different vision pervades Taddeo di Bartolo's **Last Judgment** (1393) on the inner wall of the facade. This is one of the most gruesome depictions of a customarily lurid subject, with no-holds-bared delineations of the Seven Deadly Sins, including Bosch-like fantasies on lust and gluttony. Below is a

comprehensively punctured *Saint Sebastian* by Benozzo Gozzoli, painted in gratitude at the end of plague in 1464.

The chapels of the cathedral were remodelled in the mid fifteenth century by
Giuliano da Maiano, and San Gimignano made its most important Renaissance
commission – a cycle by Domenico Ghirlandaio – for the **Cappella di Santa
Fina**. This is a superb work, access to which is included on a general tourist
ticket (L4000) that includes entry to the town's museums. The subject is a local
saint, born in 1238, who was struck by a dreadful and incurable disease at the age
of ten. She gave herself immediately to God, repented her sins (the worst seems
to have been accepting an orange from a boy), and spent the five years until her
death – predicted in a vision of Saint Gregory – lying on a plank on the floor.

To the left of the cathedral, an arch surmounted by a statue of San Gimignano
leads into a courtyard, fronted on the near side by a loggia, with an *Annunciation*
by Ghirlandaio. Rather anonymous **Sacred Art** and **Etruscan museums** are
housed in buildings off the court, where musicians often busk in summer.

Palazzo del Popolo

A visit to the **Palazzo del Popolo** (Tues–Sat 9.30am–12.30pm & 3.30–6.30pm;
Oct–March closes at 5.30pm) gives you the chance to climb the **Torre Grossa**,
the highest surviving (160ft) and best preserved of the towers – and the only one
you can ascend. It's an impressively solid structure, with various vaults and a
gallery of spectacular panoramic views .

In the same building, a number of rooms have been given over to the **Museo
Civico**. The first of these, frescoed with hunting scenes, is known as the **Sala di
Dante** – the poet visited as Florence's ambassador to the town in 1300, making a
plea here for Guelph unity. Most of the paintings displayed are fourteenth-
century works, Sienese in origin or inspiration in these years before San
Gimignano passed into the Florentine Renaissance orbit. The highlight in the
Sala di Dante is Lippo Memmi's *Maestà* (1317), his masterpiece, modelled on that
of Simone Martini in Siena. The most fascinating and enjoyable paintings in the
palazzo, however, are hidden away in a small room off the stairs. These are **frescoes of wedding scenes**: a tournament, where the wife rides on her husband's
back, followed by the lovers taking a shared bath and climbing into bed. Unique
in their subject matter, they were completed early in the fourteenth century by
the Sienese painter Memmo di Filipuccio.

The rest of the town: Sant'Agostino

Heading away from the central squares and Via San Giovanni, the crowds quickly
thin away. Following the Via di Castello, east of Piazza della Cisterna, leads you
past Romanesque **San Lorenzo in Ponte** (one of the few other churches kept
open – with dramatic fragments of a frescoed *Last Judgment*) and the attached
Farmacia Preindustriale (Tues–Sun 9.30am–12.30pm & 3.30–6.30pm). This
was part of a medieval hospital, supported by the town council, and has an interesting display of medicines and equipment, as well as the story of San Gimignano
under plague. At the end of the street is **Via del Ponte**, almost a rural lane,
which winds down between vineyards to the walls, a public wellhouse – the **Fonti**
– and open countryside.

North from Piazza Duomo, **Via San Matteo** is one of the grandest and best
preserved of the city streets, with quiet little alleyways again running down to the
walls. The street ends at the **Porta San Matteo**, just inside of which, in a corner

of walls, is the large, hall church of **Sant'Agostino** (8am–noon & 3–7pm; Oct–March closes at 5pm). There are several fine paintings and chapels, including a much-damaged fresco cycle of the *Life of the Virgin* by Bartolo di Fredi. But the great attraction is a cycle of seventeen scenes of the *Life of Saint Augustine* by Benozzo Gozzoli (1465), behind the high altar. The reluctantly celibate saint is depicted studying grammar at Carthage university, being flogged by his teacher (Augustine recalls these punishments in his *Confessions*) and travelling to Milan to teach philosophy.

Practicalities

San Gimignano's three hotels are expensive, with double rooms in the L70,000 range. **Budget accommodation**, however, is provided by the *Ristorante Il Pino* (Via San Matteo 102; ☎0577/940.415) and by twenty or so private houses, most of which have doubles for around L35,000–40,000. There is also a good new **youth hostel** at Via delle Fonti 1 (☎0577/941.991; reception open 7.30–9.30am and 5–11.30pm); no membership required, L12,000 per person including breakfast and shower. Best of all, if you write or phone ahead, the **Convento di Sant'Agostino** (☎0577/940.383) has a dozen or so beautiful doubles at around L30,000.

Out of season, it's easy enough to hunt out a **room** for yourself. Full lists are available from the **tourist office** on Piazza del Duomo. From May through to September, you'll save a lot of frustration by using the *Ufficio Informazioni Turistiche* at Via S. Giovanni 125 (Mon–Sat 9.30am–12.30pm & 2.30–7.30pm, Sun morning only; ☎0577/940.809), who arrange rooms for L2000 commission. If you want to **camp**, the nearest site is *Il Boschetto* (☎0577/940.352; reception closed 1–3pm & 8–9pm), 3km downhill at Santa Lucia. This has sporadic bus connections (L500), a bar and shop; fees are L4000 per person, L2000 per tent.

There are some fairly hefty charges for sitting outside at any of the bars and **restaurants** – so take good stock of menus in advance. One of the most popular choices, a fraction cheaper than most, is *Le Vecchie Mura* on Via Piandornella (follow sign off Via San Giovanni); this offers good value pizzas and set meals. For **snacks**, there is pizza by weight at Via San Giovanni 38, or, if you're in town on Thursday or Saturday morning, a variety of fare (including rolls with roast wild boar – cinghiale) at the open-air **market** in Piazza del Duomo.

The townscape is entertainment enough for most visitors, but from June to October San Gimignano hosts a small **summer festival**. Events include classical concerts, theatre and films in the Rocca.

The most frequent **bus connections** are with Poggibonsi, where you'll need to change coming from (or going to) Siena or Florence. Poggibonsi also has a train station on the Empoli–Siena line. Westward, there are five or so connections a day with Volterra.

Poggibonsi, Colle di Val d'Elsa and Monteriggioni

POGGIBONSI has little more than its transport links and its politics to recommend it. An industrial town – conspicuously ugly alongside its Tuscan neighbours – it is reputed as the home of Italy's reddest council. Travelling by public transport in this region, you are almost bound to have a Poggibonsi halt. The place has bars and cafés to pass the time and a cheapish hotel, but there's not much else to explore.

COLLE DI VAL D'ELSA, with its old upper town, is much more interesting – and again has plentiful connections to Florence and to Siena and its province. Buses stop in the main piazza of the lower town, with a couple of modest **hotels** (cheapest is the *Olimpia*; ☎0577/921.662). **Colle Alta**, the upper town, is a steep climb up – and has a slightly ghost-town atmosphere with its single main street, **Via del Castello**, along a narrow ridge. It is lined with a scattering of medieval palazzi (including a tower-house, at no. 63, where the architect Arnolfo di Cambio was born) and opens out, midway along, to the Piazza del Duomo. The **Palazzo Vescovile** (ring for admission), here, has frescoes of hunting scenes by Bartolo di Fredi and a fair collection of Sienese paintings. At the far end of the street is the **Porta Nuova**, designed by the Renaissance architect Giuliano da Sangallo.

A final, possible stop, if you are heading for Siena, is the tiny fortress-village of **MONTERIGGIONI**, whose towers Dante compared to giants. The village's walls and position are its most imposing aspect: it is visible for miles, high above the Florence–Siena autostrada. There is a good, though rather pricey, restaurant, *Il Pozzo* (closed Sun evening and Mon), in the main square.

Volterra

Built on a high plateau enclosed by volcanic hills, **VOLTERRA** seems a bleak, isolated place – a surprise after the pastoralism of the region around. Etruscan Volterra (*Velathri*) was one of the earliest and most important commercial centres in Italy, flourishing through a combination of mineral resources and impregnable position, attributes which ensured its survival through the Roman and Dark Ages. Its isolation, however, was later its downfall. Under Florentine control from 1360, it proved unable to keep pace with changing and expanding patterns of trade, and the town itself began to subside, its walls and houses slipping away to the east over the *balze* (cliffs), which form a dramatic approach coming in on the Pisa road.

The town occupies less than a third of the ancient extent, essentially medieval in appearance, with cobbled and stone streets, grim palazzi and walled gateways. In summer it lives a little too exclusively on tourism, with every other shop selling alabaster ware (an Etruscan survival), but it's all atmospheric enough – and there are great views, good walks and a major Etruscan museum.

The Town

There is little more to Volterra than its old, walled centre, so orientation is straightforward. Buses arrive on the south side of the town at **Piazza XX Settembre** (car parking, also), from where it's a five-minute walk to the central Piazza dei Priori, with the **tourist office** around the corner at Via G. Turazza 2.

Around Piazza dei Priori

The **Piazza dei Priori** is almost totally medieval. It is flanked by the town hall, the **Palazzo dei Priori**, built in the thirteenth century and said to be the oldest communal palace in Italy. It may have served as the model for Florence's Palazzo Vecchio, though the influences seem largely reversed – the facade is studded with Florentine medallions; its unusual pentagonal tower is popularly known as the **Torre del Porcellino** (Piglet's Tower), from an animal carved on its front.

Inside the palazzo, on the first floor, is a huge, frescoed *Annunciation* by Orcagna.

A block away, the cathedral square seems rather down-at-heel, with the crumbling masonry of the Baptistery (locked for safety) and the unfinished facade of the Duomo. The **Baptistery**, built on the site of a pagan temple, makes a nod towards the Renaissance in its design, executed, like the churches of Pisa, in bands of black and white marble. The **Duomo** is a more ancient conglomerate of styles. The best of its works is a thirteenth-century sculpture of *The Deposition*, in the south chapel, disarmingly repainted in its original bright colours, and a fresco of *The Magi* by Benozzo Gozzoli, in an oratory to the left of the main entrance.

Other works gathered from local churches, including one that was swallowed up by the *Balze*, are displayed in a **Museo di Arte Sacra** housed in the old Bishop's Palace in Via Roma and the **Pinacoteca Communale**, Via dei Sarti 1; both are just off the Piazza dei Priori and open daily 10am to noon and 3 to 6pm (Arte Sacra closed Thurs). Highlight of the former is Andrea della Robbia's ceramic bust of Saint Linus – a Volterran who was Saint Peter's successor as pope. The latter is a good provincial collection, worth the fee for an *Annunciation* by Signorelli and Rosso Fiorentino's agitated *Descent from the Cross*.

Leading away from the Piazza dei Priori, Via Porta dell'Arco runs downhill to the **Arco Etrusco**, an Etruscan gateway, third-century BC in origin, built in Cyclopean blocks of stone; the three blackened and eroded lumps on its outer face are probably images of Etruscan gods. The gate was narrowly saved from German destruction in the last war, during the course of a ten-day battle between the Partisans (Volterra was a stronghold) and Germans.

The Museo Guarnacci

The Etruscan legacy is represented most importantly at the **Museo Guarnacci**, Via Don Minzoni 15 (April–Sept 9am–1pm & 2.30–6pm; Oct–March 10am–2pm; L3000). One of Italy's major archaeological museums, it consists entirely of local finds, including some six hundred **funerary urns**. Carved in alabaster, tufo and terracotta, they date from the fourth to first centuries BC; earlier tombs were lost as the cliffs fell to nothing. On the side of the urns bas reliefs depict domestic events (often boar hunting) or Greek myths (usually a trip to the underworld); on the lid is a bust of the subject, and there are symbolic flowers, too – one for a young person, two for middle-aged, three for elderly. The urns intrigued D.H. Lawrence, who described them as "an open book of life . . . ripe with the phallic knowledge" in his *Etruscan Places*.

Unfortunately the display, grouped according to subject, is stultifyingly old-fashioned and uninstructive, and only a few pieces manage to stand out from the mass-produced ware. The best are mostly on the top floor, where examples from the "golden age" of the third and second centuries BC are gathered. Among them is the much-reproduced **Gli Sposi**, a disturbing portrait scene of (supposedly) a husband and wife – all piercing eyes and dreadful looks. On this floor, too, are a number of small bronze sculptures, including the extraordinary **Ombra della Sera** (Shadow of the Evening), an elongated nude which provided inspiration for the Swiss sculptor Giacometti.

The Rocca and Balze

The Medicean **Rocca** dominates the southern section of town. With its rounded bastions and central tower, it's one of the great examples of Italian military architecture – and perhaps the most overbearing Renaissance palace in the country. For the last century and a half it has been a prison, for lifers and hardcasers – off limits to more casual visitors.

Below the prison stretches a lush area of grass, trees and shade known as the **Parco Archeologico** (daily 10am–noon & 4–7pm; free). There's not much archaeology about the place – a few odd lumps of rock, said to be part of a Roman bathhouse – but it's a beautiful part of the town to lie around for a few hours, and there is a good value café-snackbar in one corner. Rather more evidence of the past remains on the north side of town, where a **Roman theatre and bath complex** have been excavated, the latter with mosiac floors.

To reach the Balze, follow the Via di San Lino northeast from the Piazza dei Priori. This passes the church of **San Francisco**, with fifteenth-century frescoes of the *Legend of the True Cross* (see "Arezzo" for explanation) by Cenni di Cenni, before leaving town through the Porta San Francisco. From here, follow Borgo Santo Stefano and its continuation, Borgo San Giusto, past the Baroque church and former abbey of **San Giusto** – its dilapidated but striking facade framed by an avenue of cypress trees.

At the **Balze** you gain a real sense of the extent of Etruscan Volterra, whose walls drop away into the chasms. Gashes in the slopes and the natural erosion of sand and clay are made more dramatic by alabaster mines, ancient and modern. Below are buried great tracts of the Etruscan and Roman city, and landslips continue – as evidenced by the locked and ruined Camoldesi monastery, ebbing away over the precipice.

Practicalities

Volterra looks thin on accommodation if you judge by the hotel lists, but the local *Cooperativa Nuova SCAP* fill the gaps for most budgets, running a youth hostel, campsite and a couple of villa accommodations just outside the town. There are also plentiful rooms at the **monastery** of San Andrea, on the northeast outskirts of the town; these are generally available if you just turn up – the views are great and charges are a modest L10,000 per person.

Of the *SCAP* accommodation, the **youth hostel**, *Ostello della Gioventù* (✆0588/85.577), is in a converted mansion, close by the Etruscan museum at Via del Poggetto; it's open from 6pm, membership is not required, and the 11.30pm curfew is unlikely to prove a problem given Volterra nightlife. Beds are L12,000 per person in six-person rooms. The **campsite**, *Le Balze* (✆0588/87.880; off season ✆0588/85.132; open April–Sept), is nicely positioned, too – 1km from the city, outside Borgo San Giusto; follow the signs for the Balze.

Charging roughly three-star hotel prices, the two *SCAP* **villas** are both beautiful places to stay: *Villa Giardino* (✆0588/85.634) is at San Girolamo, 500m from town; *Villa Domus Aeoli* (✆0588/86.041) is 1km away at Borgo San Lazzero. There are five other, regular **hotels** – four three-stars and one four-star. Of the three-stars, the *Villa Nencini* (✆0588/86.386) is the most attractive, just outside Porta San Francisco; rooms run around L68,000 but there are a few without bath at L50,000.

As a hunting centre, Volterra's gastronomic efforts are dominated by wild boar (*cinghiale*). You see stuffed heads of the unfortunate beasts throughout town, and the meat is packaged as salamis or hams, as well as roasted in the **restaurants**, alongside *lepre* (hare) and *coniglio* (rabbit). In terms of price, there's little to choose between any of the eating places, and you may as well plump for quality at the locally favoured *Ristorante Beppino*, Via delle Prigioni 15–19 (closed Tues). Cheaper options include a lone self-service at Via Matteotti 19 (the main street) and a few pizzerias – a good one opposite the *Beppino*.

Leaving Volterra is easiest by **bus**. *Bar Jolly* in Piazza Vente Settembre sells tickets and has timetables for *Tra-In* departures to Pisa, San Gimignano, Siena and Florence. The nearest **train station** is at SALINE, 8km away (connecting bus); the rail line links to the busy coastal route between Pisa and Rome.

South to Massa Maríttima

Most travellers take in Volterra from the Florence–San Gimignano–Siena route, heading back east, or striking north to Pisa. The road south, **over the mountains to Massa Maríttima**, is much less explored and scenically magnificent: classic Tuscan countryside which is given an added surreal quality by the presence of *soffioni*, hot steam geysers from which boric acid is extracted.

If you want to break the journey to Massa, **LADERELLO** makes an interesting stop. This is the centre of *soffioni* country and *ENEL*, the electricity company, have set up a small museum tracing the development of power from natural steam. Around the town huge silver pipes run across the fields, with steam and smoke rising intermittently from chimneys amid the dark foliage.

Massa Maríttima

MASSA MARÍTTIMA, like Volterra, has been a wealthy mining town since Roman and Etruscan times. In 1225 it saw Europe's first ever charter for the protection of miners and it still peddles a militant politics – its Communist council is a major link in Italy's red belt. Maríttima (maritime) is a misnomer. It's a long time since the sea lapped the town walls, and the coast is now 19km distant across a silt-filled plain.

Crashing waves would have made the hilltop location that much more impressive. Today the road skirts a small industrial estate before the town comes into view across a whaleback of hills. Blocks of new buildings take an edge off the medieval splendours, yet tourism is now as big a part of the economy as the mines. Menus posted in English are the norm, while the estate agents push their farmhouses in fluent German. There's perhaps rather less than the hype merits, but the Piazza Garibaldi and Duomo are certainly enough to warrant a visit.

The Old Town

The Old Town is divided into two. The lower, walled section, the **Città Vecchia**, is predominantly Romanesque, and has most to see. The Gothic so-called **Città Nuova**, above, is still pretty old but less a place to wander, having been built largely as a residential centre. An immensely steep but picturesque lane, Via Moncini, connects the two. For most of the Middle Ages the lower town was inhabited by a Pisan clan, the Todini, the upper by their Sienese rivals, the Pannochieschi. The Florentines collared the lot in the sixteenth century.

Most of the medieval interest centres on the **Piazza Garibaldi**, a small, eccentric and exquisite example of Tuscan town planning at the heart of the Città Vecchia. The **Duomo** (1228–1304) is the climax of the ensemble, set on broad steps at a dramatically oblique angle to the square, its porticoes, tiny columns and blind arcades adding up to a highly individual Romanesque mix. The adjoining **campanile** is no less unique, its windows duplicating to the apex in mathematical progression. The cathedral has an unusual dedication to the sixth-century Saint Cerbone; his claim to fame was to persuade a flock of geese to follow him when summoned to Rome on heresy charges.

The Duomo's exterior grandeur is matched by an airy internal space, and it's worth lingering over; little else in the town compares with its simple bare stone appeal, nor its handful of artistic offerings. Check in particular the eleventh-century carvings at the rear: the grinning and cross-eyed faces have the power of primitive, almost pagan art, a dramatic contrast to the severe, polished Roman sarcophagus to the right. Take a look, too, at the *Madonna delle Grazie* at the end of the left transept, a damaged but gorgeous Sienese work attributed to Duccio or Simone Martini.

For more art you could head for the **Palazzo del Podestà**, the smaller of the two palaces on the piazza (L2500, tickets from the tourist office opposite the Duomo). The fee is steep but admits you to the presence of the town's undisputed masterpiece, a *Maestà* by Ambrogio Lorenzetti, considered his finest work; San Cerbone and his geese lurk in the right-hand corner.

Inevitably, given Massa's mining heritage, there is also a large – and, if you're into this sort of thing, impressive – **Miniera Museo** (Tues–Sun: April–Sept 10am–12.30pm & 3.30–7pm; Oct–March 9am–1pm & 3–5pm), five minutes from Piazza Garibaldi on Via Corridoni. Sited appropriately enough underground, but in an old air-raid shelter rather than a mine-shaft, the museum boasts 700 metres of galleries, with a chronological display of the area's mining methods and equipment. You might want to couple this with a visit to the **Museo di Arte e Storia delle Miniere**, located on Piazza Matteotti in the Città Nuova, which houses a small collection of fossils and archive photographs of local history.

Practicalities

Getting to Massa is no problem. There are three or four **buses** a day from Volterra (change at Monterotondo), two daily from Florence and Siena, and a connecting shuttle to meet **trains** along the main Pisa–Rome rail line at the station of Massa-Follonica (19km; 40min; tickets at the station bar). Leaving, tickets and schedules for inter-city buses are available from the very helpful *Agenzia Massa Veterensis* at Piazza Garibaldi 18 (☎0566/902.062). Connecting buses to the train station, Piombino and local destinations run to and from the Piazza XXIV Marzo in the upper town. You can pick up a free map and limited information from the **AST**, opposite the *Azienda*.

Given Massa's popularity, there are surprisingly few **places to stay**. The only central hotel is the one-star *Hotel Cris*, Via Roma 9–10 (☎0566/903.830), with doubles around L35,000. The town's other two hotels, the two-star *Duca del Mare* (☎0566/902.284) and *Girifalco* (☎0566/902.177) are down below on the Via Massetana; doubles from L42,000. The only low-budget alternative to the *Cris* is *Pension Massa Vecchia* (☎0566/90.885) at Massa Vecchia 1. The nearest **campsites** are on the coast around the modern town of FOLLONICA: *Tahiti* (☎0566/60.255; open May 15–Sept 30) at Prato Ranieri, and *Pineta del Golfo* (☎0566/53.369; June 1–Sept 30) at Pineta di Levante; both are rated one-star.

For **meals**, settle for Piazza Garibaldi's flytrap restaurants only in desperation; if you want to hang out in the square, the key bar is under the arches in the corner by Via Moncini. Elsewhere in the old town, *Trattoria Roma*, at Via Parenti 19, is something of a tourist trap but with good cooking and a strange local rosé wine from Monte Reggio. For straight, cheap pizza, and a decent bar with outside tables, try the *Pizzeria la Torre* in Piazza Matteotti in the Città Nuova; for a snack, there's a no-nonsense *pizza tagla* at Via Moncini 44.

San Galgano

The **Abbazzia di San Galgano**, midway between Massa and Siena, is perhaps the greatest Gothic building in Italy. It is certainly the most romantic – roofless, with a grass field for a nave, patches of fresco amidst the vegetation, and panoramas of the sky, clouds and hills through a rose window. If you have seen Tarkovsky's film *Nostalgia*, it will be immediately familiar from the finale.

This region south of Siena was one of the heartlands of medieval monasticism: over to the west the Benedictines had their main house at Sant'Ántimo (see "Montalcino"), while the Vallombrosan order maintained theirs a few miles to the north at Torri. In the twelfth and thirteenth centuries, however, Cistercian San Galgano was the leading power in Tuscany. Its abbots ruled over disputes between the cities, and at Siena its monks oversaw the building of the duomo and held posts as *casalinghi*, or accountants, for the *comune*. They were a mix of Italians and French – from the principal house at Cîteaux – and through them the ideas of Gothic building were imported to Italy, along with sophisticated schemes for land drainage and agriculture.

The real appeal of the abbey is its state of ruin – which is owed principally to the papacy. The Cistercians lost much power in the late thirteenth century, during which the English *condottiere* Sir John Hawkwood took the opportunity to sack the abbey, and by 1397 the abbot was the sole occupant. But during the following century it recovered its numbers for a while, until the papacy made over its income to a particularly profligate cardinal. The monks left and the building gradually decayed – the campanile collapsing dramatically during a mass attended by villagers.

On the hill above the monastery, the unusual round Romanesque church of **Monte Siepi** commemorates the spot where San Galgano – a soldier from the nearby village of Chiusdino – had a vision of Saint Michael and began his life as a hermit. The saint's sword-in-the-stone legend is depicted in one of a series of frescoes by Ambrogio Lorenzetti in the adjacent chapel.

Staying – and Torri

Visting San Galgano by public **transport** involves juggling with bus times – there are three services daily between Massa and Siena – or hitching, which shouldn't be too difficult in summer. If you need to stay, the nearest **accommodation** to be found is at the village of PALAZZETTO, 4km back on the road to Massa. The *Bar-Albergo Il Palazzetto* (☎0577/750.160) has doubles from L28,000 and a good restaurant, too.

If you are driving to or from Siena, **TORRI**, 2km east of the road, is a worthwhile stop. The **Monasterio dei Santi Trinità e Mustiola** is less dramatic than San Galgano, but a fine Romanesque building nonetheless, with a triple cloister of black and white marble.

SOUTHERN TUSCANY

The region **south of Siena** is Tuscany at its best: an infinite gradation of hills, trees and cultivation that runs across the *crete* – the Sienese badlands, and through the vineyards of Montepulciano and Montalcino, before climbing into the hills around Monte Ammiata. The towns on the whole live up to the landscape – **Montepulciano**, especially, with its independent hill-town life and (like neighbouring **Pienza**) Renaissance ensemble. **Montalcino** has wine and the superb abbey of **Sant'Antimo**; while further south, there are medieval centres and mountain walking at **Arcidosso** and **Abbadia San Salvatore**, the remarkable sulphur springs of **Saturnia**, and the isolated drama of **Pitigliano** and **Sovana**.

Montepulciano

At nearly 2000ft, **MONTEPULCIANO** is the highest of the Tuscan hill towns. It is built on a narrow ridge, along which runs the **Corso**, flanked by a dark series of alleys, dropping away to the walls. Henry James, who compared it to a ship, spent most of his time here drinking: a good policy, in view of the fine local table wine and (more expensive and mature) *Vino Nobile*. The town remains today one of the most enjoyable places to stay in Tuscany, set in superb walking country and maintaining a refreshingly low-key tourist profile.

Around the Town

Montepulciano's imposing site is complemented by an unusually consistent array of Renaissance palazzi and churches, a reflection of its remarkable development after 1511, when, after intermittent alliance with Siena, the town finally threw in its lot with Florence. In that year Cosimo I de'Medici sent **Antonio Sangallo the Elder** to rebuild the town's gates and walls, which he did so impressively that the local council took him on to work on the town hall and a series of churches, while local nobles hired him, his son, and their Florentine compatriot, Vignola, to work on their own palazzi. The work of this trio and of their contemporary, Michelozzo, totally assured in its conception and execution, makes an interesting comparison with Pienza, completed sixty or so years earlier.

Sangallo's first commission, the main town gate of **Porta al Prato**, stands opposite the carpark and bus stop at the north end of town. Inside the gate the **Corso** begins, the **palazzi** immediately making clear the town's allegiance to Florence. In the first square, beside the *Albergo Marzocco*, is a stone column bearing the heraldic lion (*marzocco*) of Florence, while across the street further lion heads decorate the **Palazzo Avignonesi** (no. 91), probably the work of Vignola. Sangallo makes his first appearance with the **Palazzo Cocconi** (no. 70), opposite the **Palazzo Bucelli** (no. 73), its base inset with Roman and Etruscan reliefs.

Just beyond this crop of palazzi is the church of **Sant'Agostino**, designed by another Medici protegé, Michelozzo. Across the street a medieval towerhouse – a rare survival in Montepulciano – is surmounted by a bizarre Commedia dell'Arte figure of a clown, the **Pulcinella**, who strikes out the hours on the town clock. Characteristically Neapolitan (and most un-Tuscan), it is said to have been put up by an exiled bishop from that city.

About 100m further along you reach a **loggia** and a fork in the roads. The Corso continues to the left, past further palazzi – including Sangallo's **Palazzo Cervini**, now the *Banco Toscana*, with its grand civic gesture of an external court-yard – before eventually looping out of the **town walls**, into a rural area that feels far from the town, and re-entering by the old **Fortezza**, now part occupied by a group of houses. At the end of Via di San Donato, the last loop back into town, you find yourself in the cathedral and town hall square, Piazza Grande.

A quicker approach to Piazza Grande would be to head right at the loggia, then take the first left along Via del Poggio and its continuation (beyond the church of San Francesco) Via Ricci. This is flanked on one side by the Renaissance **Palazzo Ricci** (housing the tourist office), on the other by the Sienese-Gothic **Palazzo Neri-Orselli**. The latter is home to a **Museo Civico** (Tues–Sun 10.30am–12.30pm and 4.30–7pm), an extensive collection with a good deal of small-town Gothic and Renaissance work though few masterpieces. Its most important paint-ing is a twelfth-century *Saint Francis*, painted by his contemporary, Margaritone da Arezzo; its most enjoyable, Jacopo de Mino's lush *Coronation of the Virgin*.

The Piazza Grande

The **Piazza Grande**, a fine but rather empty-seeming main square, is built on the highest point of the ridge. Its most distinctive building is the **Palazzo Communale**, the town hall, a thirteenth-century Gothic palace to which Michelozzo added a tower and rustication in imitation of the Signoria in Florence. You can climb the tower, for a small fee, and on those fabled clear days the view supposedly stretches to Siena, 65km northeast. The other two palazzi on the square were both designed by Sangallo. The **Palazzo Tarugi**, by the lion and grif-fon fountain, is the most innovative, with a public loggia cut through one corner. More tangible pleasures await at the **Palazzo Contucci**, one of several buildings scattered about the town that serve as *cantine* for the **wine trade**, offering *degus-tazione* and sale of bottles of the *Vino Nobile*.

Sangallo never got around to building a facade for the **Duomo**, whose plain brick pales somewhat against the neighbouring palazzi. Its interior, however, is a solid Renaissance design, scattered with sculptures by Michelozzo. These were originally a single work – a tomb for a local papal secretary – the core of which remains by the door, while its statues are dotted about the chapels and its frieze forms the high altar. The church's great treasure, a Taddeo di Bartolo altarpiece of the *Assumption*, belongs to an earlier age when Montepulciano belonged within Siena's orbit.

San Biagio

Sangallo's finest efforts of all are revealed in the temple-church of **San Biagio**, set in classic Renaissance isolation on a slope below town. To reach it, follow Via Ricci back to the Piazza San Francesco and then take Via de Grassi and Via di San Biagio out through the town walls. It's about half an hour's walk.

The church is one of the most harmonious Renaissance creations in Italy. The exterior is perfectly blended into its niche in the landscape, all soft, honey stone and studied proportion. Within, it is spoilt a little by decoration – a Baroque *trompe l'oeil* covers the barrel vault – but makes up for everything with a superb acoustic. Nearby, scarcely less perfect a building, is a **Canonica** (rectory), endowed by Sangallo with a graceful portico and double loggia.

Practicalities

Arriving in Montepulciano by bus (or coming in by car), you will find yourself just outside the town walls, by the **Porta al Prato**. To get an idea of the layout of the town, walk through the gate and take a look at the map displayed in the window of the *Albergo Il Marzocco*, 50m up on the left; it indicates all the hotels and the **tourist office** at Via Ricci 9 (Tues–Sun 10am–noon & 4–6pm), which has maps, booklets, and lists of rooms in private houses.

If they have space, the *Marzocco* (☎0578/757.262) is the **hotel** to make for; an elegant nineteenth-century place with a full-size billiards table, it has doubles from L44,000. Alternatives, at similar prices, are *La Terrazza*, Via Piè al Sasso 16 (☎0578/757.440), off Via di Voltaia, and *Albergo Duomo* (☎0578/757.473), just off the Piazza Grande. Slightly cheaper rooms – around L30,000 a double – are to be found at *Ristorante Cittino* (☎0578/757.335), Vicolo della Via Nuova 2, off Via di Voltaia; or at one of the **private houses**. Among the latter, try phoning *Bellavista* (25 Via Ricci; ☎0578/757348) or *Brilli* (Piazza Minzoni – where the bus arrives; ☎0578/716.972). If you're stuck, get the bus to CHIANCIANO TERME, 8km east, a huge spa resort with over two hundred hotels.

The town has a good spread of **restaurants**, all of them offering local wines. Best, perhaps, is the *Trattoria Diva* (closed Tues), just inside the gate on Via Gracciano; it's moderately priced unless you go for a vintage *vino nobile* from the co-owned *enoteca* next door. Its main rival, a fraction cheaper (a fair bit so if you stick to pizza) is *Ristorante-Pizzeria Il Cantuccio*, on an alley to the right of Via Gracciano (at no. 67). Buying your own food, there's an open-air **market**, held in the gardens outside the Porta al Prato, on Thursday morning; this is also the site of the local **youth bar**, with table football and a jukebox through to midnight.

The main **transport** links are with Chiusi. *LFI* **buses** run more or less every half hour (last at 9.10pm) to Chianciano Terme, Chiusi and Chiusi station. To the west, *Tra-In* has seven buses daily on the Pienza, San Quirico d'Orcia, Torrenieri (change for Montalcino), Buonconvento circuit, with three continuing to Siena. All buses leave from outside Porta al Prato; buy tickets from the bars or shops nearby (not on the bus). If you're making a **train** connection, go to Chiusi; Montepulciano's own station, 10km northeast, is a stop only for local slow-trains.

Chiusi

CHIUSI, 14km east of Montepulciano, is a useful transport hub, with trains and buses south to Orvieto and Rome, and north to Castiglione del Lago, Cortona and Arezzo. It is not really a place to make an excursion to, although, if you're passing through, the Etruscan museum and cathedral are good for an hour or two. They stand more or less opposite each other on Via Porsenna, a short walk up from the bus stop; a tourist office is on the same street at no. 61. The train station is a further 3km east at CHIUSI SCALO, a stop on all the inter-town buses.

The **Museo Etrusco** (Tues–Thurs 9am–2pm, Sat & Sun 9am–1pm) ought to be pretty good, for the region is littered with tombs. Many of the best exhibits, however, have been spirited away to Florence and Rome, and what remains is modest: numerous sarcophagi, a few terracottas with traces of ancient paint, cabinets of pots (one with erotic dancing scenes), and the odd treasure – notably the enigmatic *Gualandi urn*. If you are interested in seeing **Etruscan tombs**, ask one of the museum guards if they'll take you to the *Tombas della Pelegrina e*

Leone, 3km north of the town, for which they hold the keys. Other local tombs (including the more famous, frescoed *Scippia*) have been locked in recent years.

At the Romanesque **Duomo** there is further evidence of Chiusi's ancient past. The building itself consists almost entirely of Etruscan and Roman blocks, while the museum (L1000) gives access to **catacombs** below – used by early Christians in the fifth century. The cathedral interior is a mass of apparent mosaic work, actually painted, in Byzantine style, in 1915.

If you have more time to fill, there's a very trendy **bar-pizzeria**, the *Osteria dei Bonci*, on Via dei Bonci, off Via Porsenna. Alternatively, following Via Porsenna to the square at its end, Piazza Graviano, you reach *Ristorante Zaira*, which serves "Etruscan dishes" – boar, pigeon and the like – for L10,000 and up. Should you want to stay, Chiusi has just one **hotel**, *Albergo La Sfinge* at Via Marconi 2 (☎0578/20.157); doubles from L40,000. Other cheaper hotels are clustered down at Chiusi Scalo, an unattractive modern suburb that makes its living from a very large slaughterhouse and meat storage plant.

Lago di Chiusi

Chiusi's **lake** lies 5km north of the town, reached along the road past the Etruscan tombs. It is served sporadically by bus (4 daily on weekdays) but for anyone driving, or planning to camp for a few days, makes a fine detour. The buses run to the **restaurant-bar-campsite** *Pesce d'Oro* (☎0578/21.403), set amid trees by a small quay for rowing boats; the swimming is warm in summer.

Pienza, Santo Quírico and Bagno Vignoni

The best way to see the countryside **west of Montepulciano** is to walk. Pienza is only around 11km following the old road across country through Monticchiello, while another track from Pienza winds south to the medieval baths at Bagno Vignoni. If you are dependent on buses, which have a lull in the morning along this route, it's certainly worth hiking at least one of these stretches. **MONTICCHIELLO** is a minor attraction in itself: a walled village, with a leaning watchtower, and a **Pieve** (key in house next door) housing fourteenth-century Sienese frescoes and a panel of the *Madonna* by Pietro Lorenzetti.

Pienza

PIENZA, as complete a Renaissance creation as any in Italy, was created as a Utopian "New Town" – and an act of considerable vanity – by **Pope Pius II**. The site was previously a small village, Cortignano, where Pius, son of an exiled Sienese family, was born. Its transformation began just a year after Pius's election, the architect being **Bernardo Rossellino**, who worked on all the major buildings under the guidance of Alberti. The cost was astronomical, but, astonishingly, the cathedral, papal and bishop's palaces, and the core of a town, were completed in just three years.

After consecration of the cathedral in 1462, Pius issued a papal bull changing the name (in his honour) and stipulating that no detail of cathedral or palaces should be changed. Pius established his papal court here, but lived just two more years, and of his successors only Pius III, his nephew, paid Pienza any regard. The city, intended to spread across the hill, never grew beyond a couple of blocks to either side of the Corso, and its population (2500 today) remained scarcely that of a village. Today it still has an air of emptiness and folly: a natural stage set, which was in fact used by Zeffirelli for his film of *Romeo and Juliet*.

There is no difficulty finding your way about. Roads, buses and cars converge on the **Piazza Dante**, just outside the main entrance gate, Porta al Murello, and from here the **Corso** leads to Rossellino's centrepiece, the **Piazza Pio II**. This is enclosed by the Duomo, Palazzo Piccolomini (papal palace), Bishop's Palace, Palazzo Pubblico, and, in the corner, a fourth palace built by one of Pius's more ambitious Vatican followers – Cardinal Borgia, the future Pope Alexander VI. The square makes the usual medieval nod to Florence in its town hall, but it is otherwise entirely Renaissance in conception.

The **Duomo** (closed 1–3pm) has one of the earliest Renaissance facades in Tuscany; the interior, on Pius's orders, took inspiration from the German hall-churches he had seen on his travels, and remains essentially Gothic. The chapels house a rather indifferent series of Sienese altarpieces, commissioned by the pope and his architect from the major painters of the age – Giovanni di Paolo, Matteo di Giovanni, Vecchietta and Sano di Pietro. How long the building itself will remain standing is uncertain, as, to fit the cramped site, Rossellino had to build on sandstone that soon gives way to clay. Even before completion a crack appeared, and after an earthquake this century it has required progressively more buttressing and ties.

Pius's residence, the **Palazzo Piccolomini** was modelled on Alberti's Palazzo Rucellai in Florence, with an imaginative addition of a triple-tiered loggia at the back. You can walk into the courtyard at any time of day. The **apartments** (Tues–Sun 10am–12.30pm & 4–7pm; L2500) include Pius II's bedroom, library and other rooms filled with collections of weapons and medals. Further mementoes of the pope – notably his embroidered cope – are to be seen, along with Sienese panels, across the piazza in the **Museo Civico** (Wed–Sun 10am–1pm & 4–7pm).

From Cortignano, two earlier churches survive. **San Francesco**, adjacent to the Palazzo Piccolomini, has fourteenth-century frescoes, a cloister and panoramic snack bar above the Piccolomini gardens. Down below, ten minutes' walk to the west, is the Romanesque **Pieve** where Pius was baptised. An odd structure, with a cylindrical tower, it has a portal sculpted with knights, fish and mermaids.

Practicalities

There's not much life to Pienza, and it's perhaps easiest seen as a trip out from Montepulciano. If you want to stay, there are **rooms** for L40,000 a double at the *Ristorante Dal Falco* (☎0578/748.551) in Piazza Dante. You're spoilt for choice for picnic **food**, as the town, centre of a region producing *peccorino* sheep's cheese, seems to have gone overboard on delicatessens and "natural food" shops. There are, alternatively, good value beers and *crostini* at the *Birreria Sperone Nudo* in the middle of the town, and a couple of restaurants in Piazza Dante.

San Quírico d'Orcia and Bagno Vignoni

SAN QUÍRICO D'ORCIA, a rambling, part-walled village, stands at a crossroads on the Siena to Bolsena road, and overlooking the Orcia and Asso valleys. It's quiet and rather decayed, with a couple of bars and an exceptionally pretty Romanesque **Collegiata**, with a delicate triptych by Sano di Pietro. The village has a small hotel, *La Patrizia* (☎0577/897.715); doubles from L28,000.

Bagno Vignoni

Six kilometres southeast of San Quírico, **BAGNO VIGNONI** is scarcely a hamlet – just a handful of buildings around a central square. The square, however, is one of Tuscany's most memorable sights, occupied by an arcaded Renaissance **piscina**. This was built by the Medici, who, like Saint Catherine of Siena, took the sulphur cure here. The hot springs still bubble away in the bath (they formed a perfect set in Tarkovsky's film *Nostalgia*), though immersion is nowadays limited to a modern complex behind.

Heading south from here, you enter more sulphur country on the route through Monte Ammiata to Saturnia (see below). If you need to break the journey, Vignoni has two hotels – which could be among the stranger places to stay in the province. The cheaper, with doubles from L48,000 is *Le Terme* (☎0577/ 887.150).

Montalcino

MONTALCINO is another classic Tuscan hill town. Set within a full circuit of walls and watched over by a *rocca*, it looks tremendous from below; and from above the countryside around – all vineyards, orchards and olive groves – looks equally wonderful in turn. In the fifteenth century the town was for a time of great symbolic importance: the last of the Sienese *comunes*, holding out (after Siena itself had capitulated to the Florentines) against Medici, French and Spanish troops. This role is acknowledged at the Siena *Palio*, where the Montalcino contingent – under their medieval banner proclaiming "The Republic of Siena in Montalcino" – still take place of honour.

The town today is a quiet place, affluent in an unshowy way from its tourist trade and the production of *Brunello* wine, reckoned by some the finest in Italy. By bus, you arrive at the north end, in **Piazza Cavour**. From here the main street, Via Mazzini, leads to the **Piazza del Popolo**, an odd little square, set beneath the elongated tower of the town hall, based (in all but its dimensions) on that of Siena. An elegant double loggia, almost a reprimand in proportional architecture, occupies another side, with a wonderful and rather Germanic nineteenth-century café, the *Fiaschetteria Italiana*, opposite.

There is little pressure to do anything cultural in Montalcino and the café is very much the heart of town life – the focus, inevitably, of the evening *passeggiata* along Via Mazzini. Following Via Mazzini's continuation, Via Matteotti, or the upper road, Via Ricasoli (past Romanesque Sant'Agostino, with fourteenth-century frescoes), you emerge at the south end of town by the **Rocca** (Tues–Sun 9am–1pm & 2–8pm). Impressively complete, this encloses a public park and plush **Enoteca** – a good place to sample some of the famed *Brunello*; the *enoteca* also sells tickets giving access to the ramparts (L1200) and a glimpse at the famous banner.

To the east of the Rocca, a lane, Viale Strozzi, runs just inside the walls, past plots and orchards to the distinctive Renaissance **Santuario della Madonna del Soccorso**. It's a short walk from here down to Piazza Cavour where you can look in at the **Museo Civico** and adjacent **Museo Archeologico** (summer 10am–noon & 4–6pm; winter 10am–noon & 3–5pm; L1000 each). Both are rather miscellaneous collections.

Practicalities

Accommodation is sparse. In Piazza Cavour there is the *Albergo Giardino* (☎0577/848.257), with doubles from L44,000, and the *Bar/Camere Prato*, doubles around L30,000, and nearby the *Camere Idolina* (☎0577/846.434) at Via Mazzini 2. The alternative – and first choice hotel – is *Albergo Il Giglio* (☎0577/848.167), with doubles from L32,000, near the Rocca on Via Saloni. If you're stuck, the **tourist office** at Via Mazzini 33 may be able to find you a private room.

The best budget **meals** are at *Trattoria Soiame*, 23 Via Ricasoli, or the *Pizzeria-Enoteca S. Giorgio* on Via Saloni. Resist any temptation to try Montalcino's swanky restaurant, *Eduardo's*, which makes a peculiarly ill-starred attempt at *cucina nuova*.

Buses run more or less hourly to Buonconvento and Siena, most of them via Torrenieri, and five times daily (Mon–Sat) to Monte Ammiata, passing Sant'Antimo (see below). If you're headed elsewhere, TORRENIERI is a more promising junction with six daily buses south to Arcidosso and five east to San Quírico and Montepulciano.

Sant'Antimo

At the hamlèt of CASTELNUOVE DELL'ABATE, 9km south of Montalcino, is the **Abbazia di Sant'Antimo**, a glorious, isolated building in a league with the monasteries of San Galgano and Monte Oliveto. On weekdays there are buses, or alternatively it's a fine country walk. The abbey is open regularly only on Sundays (9am–noon & 2–5pm) but, if you find it locked, the sacristan can usually be found at Castelnuove – ask at the bar-trattoria on the roadside.

Little remains of the monastic buildings – a ruined refectory and chapter house are used as barns – but the **church** remains in good repair. It was built in the twelfth century, in a soft, creamy stone that seems to reflect the season's light. Its proportions are perfect, too, the rounded apse flanked by roofed side chapels, and inside, columns running around both apse and nave. Equally delightful are the details of the **carving and frescoes**. As so often with the Romanesque, these feature animals, and have an earthy sense of humour. One of the capitals depicts *Daniel in the Lions' Den*, aloof while his fellow prisoners are crushed and eaten by romping beasts. In the sacristy, an array of primitive black-and-white frescoes include details like a rat looking up attentively at Saint Benedict, and a pair of copulating pigs. Further frescoes are to be found in some of the rooms built around the **gallery**, approached from the nave by a circular stairway.

Monte Ammiata

The extinct volcano of **Monte Ammiata**, at 1739m, is the highest point in Tuscany. Rising from the comparative desolation of the *crete*; in a succession of hills rather than a peak, it is visible for miles around. The area is basically a winter resort, with snow lingering late into the spring. Its **forests** of chestnut and fir are said, rather fancifully, to delineate the Italian flag – the white of snow, green of pine and (pushing it a bit) red of chestnuts. Around the summit there are numerous marked **hiking trails** and several *rifugi* – though they are all in the L50,000 and upwards range for a double.

Abbadia San Salvatore

The centre of skiing activity is **ABBADIA SAN SALVATORE**, easiest reached from the San Quírico to Bolsena road (and by bus from Chainciano Terme or Siena). The **Abbadia**, which the village grew up around, is Benedictine. Founded under the Lombards and rebuilt in 1036, it was once the richest in Tuscany – exceeding even Monte Oliveto Maggiore. Today only a mere fraction remains of the original establishment, and most of the surviving parts date from the Middle Ages; the highlight is a large and beautiful eighth-century crypt, its columns decorated with crude Lombard motifs.

The town around, though greatly expanded since the war, retains a Gothic and Renaissance aspect with its age-blackened buildings enclosed within castellated walls. It sees plenty of summer visitors, up here for the landscape, cool upland breezes and some good easy walking. There are quite a number of **hotels**, including half a dozen one- and two-star options. About the cheapest, and a good choice, is the small *Hotel Roma* on Via Matteotti 32 (☎0577/778.015); doubles L40,000, closed September. For alternatives, consult the **tourist office** at Via Mentana 77.

Arcidosso and Santa Fiora

ARCIDOSSO is in a similar mould to Abbadia: another summer walking centre, with prosperous new development surrounding a well-preserved medieval quarter of steep narrow streets. The cheapest **place to stay** is the two-star *Hotel Giardino* at Via Risorgimento 4 (☎0564/966.406); doubles around L40,000; closed October to Christmas. An alternative, at similar prices, is the *Park Hotel* (☎0564/967.355), 3km out of the town at CAPERTI on the Santa Fiora road.

Good **walks around the town** could include a ramble to the nearby Romanesque **Abbadia Santa Maria ad Lamulas** and the less interesting Renaissance church of Madonna Incoronata, both passed along the way to the village of MONTELATERONE, 3km to the northwest. More demanding is the hike up **Monte Labbro** (1193m) to the south, though for drivers the summit can be reached by unmetalled road, or the ridges from the hamlet of Zancona. On the summit you can visit the ruins of a church established by Davide Lazzaretti, who claimed to be the Second Christ in the 1870s.

SANTA FIORA, again, is a medieval village and popular summer walking base. Its crop of buildings, flanking the hillside, are slightly more notable: the **Abbadia** and fortified **Palazzo Comunale** each have fine exteriors, and the three churches each house della Robbia terracotta work.

Saturnia, Pitigliano and the southern borders

Heading **south from Arcidosso** on a winding road over the hills, you are suddenly confronted by pillars of white smoke on the hillsides. This is sulphur country, a landscape full of underground springs which are tapped at intervals to provide energy for one of Tuscany's wildest and least populated regions. The route is covered very sporadically by buses (operated by *RAMA*) but it is worth a fair amount of effort to get down to the springs at Saturnia, and, if Tuscany's surplus of tourism is beginning to wear you down, the towns beyond, on the southern borders of the province, should provide an antidote.

Terme di Saturnia

The sulphur springs at **TERME DI SATURNIA** are not that easy to spot. Following the road past the village of SATURNIA, a large **spa complex** (with fierce admission charges and a five-star hotel) is signposted to the right. A couple of hundred metres beyond, a dirt track veers off to the left, unsignposted but usually signalled by a cluster of cars and campervans. This is the site of the **cascate**, sulphur springs which cascade down from the hills, forming natural rock-pool jacuzzis of warm water. Entrance is unrestricted and free.

They are quite a bizarre spectacle – all the more surreal if the weather is overcast and the steam rises overhead – and have a bit of a cult aspect; it's not unusual for parties to come up at night from Rome. The fun, though, is the same at any time of the day: the chance to lie around for hours in the pools submerged up to your neck. There is a small café, but otherwise no commercialisation.

Staying near the springs, you'll need a shower to wash off the sulphur smell, which is not too noticeable when bathing, but lingers for days. There is a campsite 2km to the north, and a small *Albergo-Ristorante* 1km south on the road to Manciano. Saturnia village also has a hotel, the *Saturnia* (☎0564/601.007), rooms to let (☎0564/601.034), and a couple of pizzeria-trattorias. Alternatively, you could head south to MANCIANO, which has a large Sienese castle, and hotels, or, more enticingly, to Pitigliano.

Pitigliano

PITIGLIANO is best approached along the road from Manciano, to the west. As you arrive, the town soars above you on a spectacular outcrop of tufa, its quarters linked by an awesomely imposing aqueduct. The largest settlement in this southern region of Tuscany, it was for centuries known for its flourishing Jewish community – annihilated in the last war. It has today a slightly grim grandeur, the result in part of its mighty fortress – dividing the old upper town from the more modern lower suburb – in part of the tall alleys of the old Jewish district.

With its scattering of Renaissance monuments and the drama of its site, the town makes a good night's stopover. In the Piazza Petruccioli, where you'll arrive by bus or car (parking space), is the town's single **hotel**, the modest two-star *Albergo Guastino* (☎0564/616.065); with doubles from L32,000, they should have space. For **meals**, try the restaurant at the *Guastini*, or the pizzeria-birreria *Chalet Il Noce* on Piazza Garibaldi, through the gateway from Piazza Petruccioli.

Piazza Garibaldi is a good place to begin a wander around the town, flanked by the fortress and aqueduct, and with views across of houses wedged against the cliffside. The **aqueduct** and **fortress** are contemporaries, completed in the mid-sixteenth century under Sangallo the Younger, along with a complex string of fortifications; within the fortress is the Renaissance **Palazzo Orsini**.

Through the piazza you reach Via Romana and the twisting, convoluted sidealleys of the old **ghetto**. Signposts direct you to the ruins of the **synagogue** and **Jewish bakery** – behind the Baroque cathedral. Traces of **Etruscan wall** are to be seen, too, below the Porte Capisotto, on the far west end of the spur.

Sovana

SOVANA, 8km northwest of Pitigliano on a minor but highly picturesque loop road to Saturnia and Arcidosso, was the medieval capital of this southern region. It owed part of this prosperity to the fact that the reforming Pope Gregory VII (1073–85) was born here. His family built the **Rocca**, though this apart there are few reminders of medieval splendour: malaria and susceptibility to Sienese attack brought an all too swift decline. The town today, a cluster of low buildings centred on a Romanesque church, humble Palazzo Pretorio, and small civic palaces, is tumbling down and part abandoned.

The town is even less visited than Pitigliano, but if you have transport it is definitely worthwhile, along with the set of **Etruscan tombs**, their facades carved from the rock, a kilometre and a half to the south. The best is the **Tomba Ildebranda**, built in the form of a temple, with a well-preserved entrance stairway. If you want to stay in Sovana, the *Taverna Etrusca* (☎0567/615.539) has a few **rooms**; L25,000–40,000 according to season.

PISA, LUCCA AND THE COAST

The **Tuscan coast** is a mixed bag. At its best – out of season on the islands of **Elba** or **Giglio** – it's as good as any in Italy. But travelling down the mainland your main impression is of development and sameness: a hundred scrubby strips of hotels and campsites, their sands remorselessly staked out by beach-umbrella operators. And on the islands, in summer, the most talked about topic seems to be the impossibility of finding any kind of accommodation.

Bright spots include the mountain backdrops of the north, shadowed by the **Alpi Apuane**, and the wild peninsula of **Monte Argentario** in the southern Maremma. But for most foreign, as opposed to Italian visitors, it's the region's inland attractions that exercise most pull. **Pisa** needs little introduction; **Lucca** rather more – walled and elegant, this is Tuscany's Romanesque city without rival; and, for anyone who has ever contemplated the origins of Michelangelo's sculptures, there are the marble quarries of **Carrara**, up in the mountains.

Pisa

There's no escaping the Leaning Tower in **PISA**. The medieval belltower is one of the world's most familiar images and yet its beauty still comes as a surprise, set in chessboard formation alongside the Duomo and Baptistery on the manicured grass of the Campo dei Miracoli – the "Field of Miracles".

Each of these buildings on the Campo, and a dozen or so churches and palazzi scattered about the town, belong to Pisa's "Golden Age", the twelfth and thirteenth centuries, when the city, then still a port, was one of the maritime powers of the Mediterranean. The Pisan Romanesque style – distinguished by showy, white and black marble facades – was accompanied by some of the finest medieval sculpture in Italy, from the workshops of Nicola and Giovanni Pisano.

The city's political zenith came in the second half of the eleventh century with a series of victories over the Saracens, whom the Pisans drove out from Corsica, Sardinia and the Balearic islands, and harassed even in Sicily. Decline, however, set in early, with defeat at sea by the Genovese in 1285, followed by a silting up of the harbour. From 1405 the city was governed by Florence, turning its attentions towards intellectual effort as one of the leading universities of the Renaissance; Galileo, Pisa's most famous native, was one of the teachers. Subsequent centuries saw the city fade into provinciality – its state when the Shelleys and Byron took palazzi here, forging what Shelley termed their "paradise of exiles". The modern city has been revitalised by its airport, industrial suburbs, university, and wealth from the reclaimed coastal marshes.

The City

Orientation in Pisa is pretty straightforward. Coming in by **train** you arrive at the **Piazza della Stazione** on the south bank of the Arno; by **bus** at the nearby **Piazza Vittorio Emanuele II** or adjacent **Piazza San Antonio**. From here, the **Campo dei Miracoli** is about twenty minutes' walk, across the Ponte di Mezzo, or a five-minute bus ride (#1) from outside the train station; local bus tickets are sold at a kiosk to the left of the station as you leave.

If you arrive by **car**, follow the signs to the official carpark outside the Porta Nuova, just west of the Campo dei Miracoli. Coming from the **airport** (Galileo Galilei) take the Florence train (leaving at 40min past each hour), which makes its first stop (5min) at Pisa.

The Campo dei Miracoli

Coming upon the **"Field of Miracles"** is startling. Nowhere in Italy are the key buildings of a city – the cathedral, bapistery and belltower – set out with such precision and refinement. Nowhere, either, is there a Leaning Tower quite like Pisa's; others exist (two at Bologna, for example), but none have its exuberance.

Perhaps the strangest fact of the **Leaning Tower**, the Campanile or belltower, is that it has always tilted. It was begun in 1173, but a subsidence in the soil disrupted the foundations when it had reached just three of its eight storeys; for the next 180 years a succession of architects were brought in to try and correct the tilt, until eventually, around 1350, Tomasso di Andrea da Pontedera accepted the angle and completed the tower. Eight centuries on, it is thought to be nearing its limits: the overhang is over 15ft and is increasing each year by around a milli-metre. In October 1989 the Ministry of Public Works (in Rome) actually declared the tower unsafe and suggested its closure to visitors, though, not surprisingly, given that its revenues amount to over £1m a year, the Pisans disagreed. So for the foreseeable future you can still pay L4000 admission (daily 9am–7pm, winter 9am–5pm), wander around the vertigo-inducing open arches of the storeys, and climb to the top – from where Galileo dropped metal balls of different mass to demonstrate his theory of the constancy of gravity.

The **Duomo** (daily 9am–7pm; winter 7.45am–12.45pm and 3–5pm) was built over a similar timespan. Its original doorway, the Portale di San Ranieri, stands opposite the tower; their scenes from the Life of Christ, cast in bronze around 1180 by Bonnano Pisano, show strong Greek and Roman influences. The massive central doors of the main facade are more ambitious, with a panoply of Renaissance detail from the workshop of Giambologna. Even their scale, however, is simply a point of detail in what is a staggering main **facade**. With its delicate balance of black and white marble, tiers of arcades and geometric motifs, and control of light and shadow, this set the model for Pisa's highly distinctive brand of Romanesque.

The **interior** continues the use of black and white marbles, and with its long arcades of columns has an almost oriental aspect – not far in spirit from the Great Mosque of Córdoba, for example. It was redecorated, and some of the chapels remodelled, after a fire in 1596, so most of the paintings and sculpture are Renaissance or later; a notable survivor is Cimabue's mosaic of *Christ in Majesty* in the apse. Its acknowledged highlight, the Gothic **pulpit** sculpted by Giovanni Pisano, was packed away after the fire, its style having fallen from fashion, and was rediscovered only in 1926. An inscription in Latin around the base records that Giovanni had "the art of pure sculpture . . . and would not know how to carve ugly or base things, even if he wished to". It is certainly a work of personal virtuosity, taking inspiration from Classical sculpture but taking it further, into more dramatic and astonishingly detailed (bring L100 coins for the lights) narrative. Lastly, the cathedral has a piece of scientific legend. It is said that the forerunner of the huge bronze incense lamp, swung to fumigate the central aisle, provided the idea for Galileo's theory of the movement of the pendulum.

The third building of the Miracoli ensemble, the circular **Baptistery** (same hours as the Duomo), is a slightly bizarre mix of Romanesque (the three storeys of arcades) and Gothic (an elongated dome). The overall effect is rather like a beached spacecraft. It is contemporary with its neighbours and was embellished with statuary (now displayed inside) by Giovanni Pisano and his father Nicola. The height of the interior is immediately striking, as are the beautiful acoustics – demonstrated at intervals by the custodian. At the centre, continuing the exotic aspect of Pisan Romanesque is a mosaic-inlaid **font** by Guido da Como (1246), raised on stone steps for ease of immersion. To the left is Nicola Pisano's **pulpit**, sculpted in 1260, half a century before his son's work in the cathedral. It was Nicola's first major commission and is regarded as having introduced the Gothic style of sculpture to Italy.

Along the north side of the Campo is the **Camposanto** (daily summer 9am–7pm; winter 9am–5pm; L2000), a cloistered cemetery built towards the end of the thirteenth century. The walls and some of the halls are frescoed and include Old Testament scenes by Benozzo Gozzoli (left of the entrance) and a fascinating Theological Cosmograph (on the north wall). The most important cycle, though, is the fourteenth-century *Triumph of Death* in the Cappella Ammanati: a ruthless catalogue of horrors, painted in the aftermath of the Black Death. There are collections, too, of paintings, a number of sculptures (some by the Pisanos) and numerous Roman sarcophagi – Nicola Pisano's original sources of inspiration.

A vast array of statuary from the cathedral and baptistery, ecclesiastical finery and paintings are displayed in the **Museo dell'Opera del Duomo** (daily summer 9am–7.30pm; winter 9am–5pm; L4000), at the southeast corner of the Campo. This huge collection includes statuary by each of the Pisano family – much of it still polychromed – and, in room 13, remarkable examples of intarsia, the art of inlaid wood, much practised here in the fifteenth century.

Lastly, on the south side of the Campo, behind the kitsch souvenir stalls, there is the **Museo delle Sinopie** (daily summer 9am–7pm; winter 9am–5pm; L2000). This is a new, well-arranged museum, created for the *sinopie* – the reddish-brown sketches made below frescoes – removed from the Camposanto. Specialists only.

Elsewhere in the City

Away from the Campo dei Miracoli, Pisa takes on a very different character, as tourists give way to students at the still-thriving university. It's a quiet place, eerily so at night, set about a series of erratic squares and arcaded streets, and with clusters of Romanesque churches and, along the banks of the Arno, a number of fine palazzi.

The Piazza dei Cavalieri is an obvious first stop from the Campo, a large square that opens unexpectedly from the narrow back streets. It was the central square of medieval Pisa, before being remodelled by Vasari as the headquarters of the Knights of Saint Stephen – a crusading order patronised by Cosimo I. Their palace, the curving **Palazzo dei Cavalieri**, covered in *sgraffiti* and topped with busts of the Medici, faces a statue of Cosimo, and the order's church of **San Stefano**, designed by Vasari and housing banners captured from the Turks. On the other side of the square is the Renaissance-adapted **Palazzo dell'Orologio**, with its archway and clocktower. This was a medieval palace, in whose tower the city's Ugolino dynasty was starved to death in 1208 – an episode described in Dante's *Inferno* and Shelley's *Tower of Famine*.

Heading from here towards the Arno, follow Via Dini into the arcaded **Borgo Stretto**. Off to the right, the city's **market** takes place – on weekday mornings and all day Saturday – with fruit, vegetable, fish, meat, and clothing stalls spilling onto the lanes around Piazza Vettovaglie. Past **San Michele** (with a fine Pisan-Romanesque facade), the Borgo meets the river at Piazza Garibaldi and the Ponte di Mezzo. Crossing the bridge and turning left, you can follow **Lungarno Galilei** past the **Palazzo Lanfranchi**, rented by Byron in 1821–22 and now a school, to the ruined **Palazzo Scotti**, Shelley's home during the same period.

Just across the river from here is the **Museo Nazionale di San Matteo** (Tues–Sat 8.30am–7.30pm, Sun 8.30am–1.30pm; L3000), housed in a twelfth-century former convent. Its collection is currently in the throes of reorganisation, but if the right rooms are open, highlights include fourteenth-century panels by the *Maestro di San Torpè*, a Simon Martini polyptych, and a panel of *San Paolo* by Masaccio. Also housed in the museum is the antique armour and wooden shields (marked with the city quarters) used in the annual *Gioco del Ponte* pageant.

The *lungarni* to the west of the Ponte di Mezzo reveal further palazzi and, on the south bank, the beautiful, turreted oratory of **Santa Maria della Spina**, built in 1323 by a merchant who had acquired one of the thorns (*spine*) of Christ's crown. Originally closer to the river, it was moved here for fear of floods in 1871.

Practicalities

People tend to cover Pisa as a day trip, or stay just a night, so **accommodation** is usually not too hard to find. It is important, though, either to phone ahead or arrive early in the day. To pick up a **map** – and full hotel lists for the city and province – look in at one of the **tourist offices**: to the left of the station (as you leave), or beside the Camposanto (both open Mon–Sat 8.30am–1pm & 3–6pm; plus in summer Sun 10am–3pm).

There are **currency exchange** bureaux at the station, the airport, and in the middle of the row of stalls at the Campo dei Miracoli. The station also has a 24-hour **telephone office** and a **left luggage office**, while the main post office is a hundred metres away in Piazza Vittorio Emanuele.

Hotels and Camping
The most attractive of Pisa's budget hotels are grouped **around the Campo dei Miracoli**. A definite first choice should be the elegant, old *Albergo Gronchi*, just east of the Campo in Piazza Arcivescovado (☎050/23.626); doubles L34,000. Others nearby include the *Locanda Galileo*, Via Santa Maria (☎050/40.621); *Hotel Giardino*, tucked behind a self-service restaurant on Via Cammeo, by the Porta Nova (☎050/56.2101); and *Pensione Helvetia*, Via Don G. Boschi 31, off Piazza Arcivescovado (☎050/41.232). Doubles from L25,000, L30,000 and L25,000, respectively. There are also a couple of places – usually filled by students in term-time – **around Piazza Dante** in the centre of town: *Pensione Rinascente* at Via del Castelletto 28 (☎050/502.436), and *Locanda Serena* at Via D. Cavalca 45

(☎050/24.491); doubles at either from L18,000–35,000. If these are all full, you may as well reconcile yourself to the **station area**. Places here are pretty medio-cre, but there are a lot of them. One of the better ones is the *Albergo Milano*, Via Mascagni 14, off Piazza della Stazione (☎050/23.162); doubles from L34,000. A good **women-only** alternative, five minutes' walk from the station (first right), is the *Casa della Giovane*, Via Corridoni 31 (☎050/22.732); L15,000 per person.

The city **campsite**, *Campeggio Torre Pendente* (☎050/561.704), is 1km west of the Campo dei Miracoli at Viale delle Cascine 86 (signposted from Piazza Manin). It's a large, well maintained site, with a laundry, bar, restaurant and shop; L5000 per person, L5000 per tent and L5000 per car. The nearest **youth hostel** to Pisa is 15km away, on the coast at Tirrenia (*Ostello San Francesco*, Calambrone; ☎050/374.42); take bus #7 from the station.

Restaurants
Restaurants in the environs of the Leaning Tower are not good value, but head a few blocks south, to the area **around Piazza Cavalieri and Piazza Dante**, and you find predominantly local places, many with prices reflecting student custom. One of the most popular is *Trattoria Stelio*, Piazza Dante 11 (closed Sat night and Sun), good for meals around L15,000 and impressive pizzas for a lot less. At Piazza Dante 1 there's a cheaper, unnamed *pizzeria*. Or, over to the west, *Scarpellini Cassio*, Piazza Cavallotti 14 (closed Wed), is a good *tavola calda*.

Also in this area, the modern university building on Via Martiri, off Piazza Cavalieri, houses a student **Mensa** (mid-Sept to mid-July Mon–Fri noon–2.30pm & 7–9pm; Sat & Sun noon–2.30pm). Meals from L8000.

Festivals and Events
The city's big traditional event is the **Gioco del Ponte**, held on June 27, when teams from the north and south banks of the city stage a series of "battles", push-ing a seven-ton carriage over the Ponte di Mezzo. The event has taken place since Medici times and continues in medieval costume. Other celebrations – concerts, regattas, art events – are held around the same time, and the city has a festive feel, for most of the month, with banners, posters and pavement drawings.

Among **regular events**, look out for concerts at the *Teatro Comunale Verdi*, Via Palestro, and for more off-beat and contemporary shows (even the odd rock concert) held in a former church at the end of Via San Zeno. The city also has an adventurous **arts cinema**, *Cinema Nuove*, in Piazza Stazione.

Pisa to Florence

By **train** it's just an hour from **Pisa to Florence** – a pleasant journey, though with no very compelling reason to stop. **Pontedera** and **Empoli** are predomi-nantly industrial towns, the latter of interest mainly for its connections south to Siena (by train or bus) and north to Leonardo's birthplace at Vinci. If you're **driv-ing**, you'll do best on the autostrada, via Lucca, Pistoia and Prato. The direct road (N67) is one of the slowest highways in Italy, rewarding only for its detours.

Certosa di Pisa
The **Certosa di Pisa** (12km east of Pisa) is a fourteenth-century Carthusian monastery, set beautifully at the foot of Monte Pisano, close by the village of

CALCI. It is open for guided visits (May–Sept Tues–Fri 9am–7pm, Sun 9am–4pm; Nov–April Tues–Fri & Sun 9am–4pm; L2000), which in an hour or so give a remarkable sense of how the building related to the lives of this strict order. The monks here could not talk to each other except on a Sunday, nor look at each other; each had his own small chapel; and meals were served through hatches, positioned to minimise the possibility of coming face to face.

The **monks' cells** and undisturbed priory **cloisters** provide a bizarrely extreme contrast with the elaborate doorways and ceilings of the **staterooms**. The decoration of these is mostly original – stunning in the delicate colours, Baroque design and original use of perspective. Some rooms appear to be paved, others to have high-domed ceilings, and everywhere there are illusionistic painted marble pillars.

San Miniato

SAN MINIATO is more or less equidistant from Pisa and Florence: a strategic military position which, along with its hilltop site, made it one of the most important of medieval fortresses. From its castle, on a clear day, you're said to actually be able to see the sea to the west and Fiesole to the east.

If it's the views, though, that are the principal appeal of **San Miniato Alto**, the old Upper Town also has an elegance about its squares: the **Piazza della Repubblica**, with seventeenth-century *sgraffiti* and (restored) fourteenth-century shops, and the **Prato del Duomo**, with its ancient belltower and Lombard palace. The cathedral itself is hacked-about Romanesque, with an enjoyably over-the-top Baroque interior. The best of the churches is **San Domenico**, with a tomb designed by Donatello and carved by Bernardo Rossellino.

If you get a **bus** from San Miniato station, or from Pontedera, it should deposit you by the Duomo (some stop only at the Lower Town – a stiff walk). From here it's a short walk up to the fabled viewpoint of Frederick II's **Rocca**, reconstructed after damage in the last war and now housing a very pricey restaurant.

Empoli and Vinci

The glass manufacturing town of **EMPOLI** is a major junction of road and rail routes. It has at least hourly connections by both bus and train with Florence (35min) and Siena, and buses (every 40min) to Vinci. The **Vinci buses** are run by *COPIT* and leave from outside the *Bar Azzurro* (tickets), across the square from the Pisa/Florence *Lazzi* buses. If you want a quick look around town, head for the central Piazza degli Uberti, where you'll find the **Collegiata**, the bottom half of which is Romanesque, the top nineteenth-century imitation. Adjacent is the **Museo Collegiata** (Tues–Sun 10am–noon), with a good collection of Renaissance sculpture and painting (Masolino, Botticini, Bernardo Rossellino).

VINCI, 11km north, is set in a fine swathe of countryside, all hills and olive groves. The village itself is a bit dull but preserves a thirteenth-century castle, in which a **Museo Vinciana** (daily 9.30am–noon & 2.30–6pm; L3000) has been set up. It doesn't have a single work or memento of the master but compensates with an imaginative display of models – tanks, water cannon, flying machines, gear-boxes, all manner of pulleys – reconstructed from Leonardo's designs. Leonardo's actual **birthplace** (free admission) is further into the hills at the hamlet of ANCHIATA, a lovely walk past fields of poppies.

From Vinci you could make a circuit **north to Pistoia**, along a fine scenic road. Buses from Empoli pass through the village three times daily.

Lucca

LUCCA is as graceful a provincial capital as they come. It is set inside a thick swathe of Renaissance walls, fronted by gardens and huge bastions, and with a quiet, almost entirely medieval streetplan. Palazzi and the odd tower – one capped by a holm oak – dot the streets, and at intervals they open onto a church square, invariably overlooked by a brilliantly decorated Romanesque facade. The city is not exactly undiscovered, but, for once, the number of tourists seems to fit.

The city lies at the heart of one of Italy's richest agricultural regions, renowned above all for the quality of its olive oil, and it has prospered since Roman times. Its heyday, however, was the eleventh to fourteenth century, when the silk trade brought wealth and, for a time, political power. In a brief flurry of military activity, Lucca first lost its independence to Pisa (in 1314), then, under the command of a remarkable adventurer, Castruccio Castracani, itself forged an empire in the west of Tuscany. Pisa and Pistoia both fell, and, but for Castracani's untimely death in 1325, Lucca might well have taken Florence. In subsequent centuries it remained largely independent until falling into the hands of Napoleon, the Bourbons and, just prior to Italian unification, the Grand Duchy of Tuscany.

Around the City

The most enjoyable way to get your bearings on Lucca is to follow the wide path around the top of the **walls**. These are nearly 4km in extent, built with genuine defensive capability – including further rings of moats and earthworks – in the early sixteenth century, before being transformed to their present, garden aspect by the Bourbon ruler, Marie Louise. They had in fact seen their last defensive duty during the reign of Marie's predecessor, Napoleon's sister Elisa Baciocchi, when they prevented flooding from the overflowing River Serchio.

Arriving by **bus**, you'll find yourself just inside the western stretch of walls, in Piazza Verdi; the **train station** is just outside the walls to the south. The centre of town is basically the **Piazza Napoleone**, a broad expanse carved out by the Bourbons to house their administration in the Palazzo Ducale. From here, **Via Fililungo** – the "thread" – heads north through the heart of the medieval city, and past the **EPT** on Piazza Guidiccioni. It's along Fililungo, and in the elegant **Piazza del Giglio** (adjoining Piazza Napoleone), that the *passeggiata* takes place.

Getting around the city, you might want to **hire a bike** – Lucca's major mode of transport. They are available from the **APT** in the city walls at Porta San Donato (April–Sept 10am–7pm; L6000 per day).

The Duomo, San Michele and the centre
It needs a double-take before you realise why the **Duomo of San Martino** (closed 3.30–6.30pm) looks odd. The city's cathedral is fronted by a severely assymetric facade – its right-hand arch and loggias foreshortened by the presence of the belltower. It is also unfinished, lacking the final turreting loggia, while the belltower itself has a makeshift aspect, its upper storeys abruptly switching from brick to stone. Nonetheless, the building sets a tone for Lucca's churches, with its fluent and elaborate version of Pisan Romanesque. Like Pisa's Duomo, it is part sculpted by Nicola Pisano – his portico reliefs include a *Deposition* and *Adoration of the Magi*; other panels (showing the *Life of St Martin*) between the doors are the masterpiece of the facade's architect, Guidetto da Como (1210).

LUCCA

200 m
0

To Pistoia
VIALE CASTRACANI
VIALE GUGLIELMO MARCONI
VIALE A. MITI
VIA DEI BACCHETTONI
PIAZZALE
DON A. MEI
VIALE G. PACINI
Porta
Elisa
S. Francesco
Museo
Guinigi
VIA DELLA QUARQUONIA
VIA DI MEZZO
VIA DEI BACCHETTONI
VIA ELISA
VIA DEL FOSSO
VIA SANTA CROCE
VIA FILLUNGO
VIA S. PAOLINO
Porta S. Maria
PIAZZA
S. FRANCESCO
VIA DELLA ZECCA
VIA S. GEMMA GALGANI
VIA S. PAULO
VIA D. FATINELLI
VIA DEL FOSSO
VIA S. CHIARA
VIA DEL FOSSO
Giardino
Botanico
VIALE GIUSEPPE GIUSTI
VIA SAN NICOLAO
S. Pietro
PIAZZA
S. PIETRO
VIA S. FRATTA
VIA SAN NICOLAO
VIA SAN NICOLAO
Casa
Guinigi
S. Maria
Forisportam
Post
Office
Duomo
Porta S. Pietro
Train
Station
VIA DEL GIARDINO BOTANICO
VIALE REGINA MARGHERITA
VIALE CARLO DEL PRETE
S. Frediano
PIAZZA DEL
COLLEGIO
PIAZZA S.
FREDIANO
PIAZZA DELL'ANFITEATRO
ROMANO
VIA FILLUNGO
VIA S. ANDREA
VIA GUINIGI
EPT
Palazzo
Bernardini
VIA DELL'ANGELO CUSTODE
VIA DELLE SERVE
VIA DEL BATTISTERO
VIA DELLA ROSA
PIAZZA DEI
SERVI
Palazzo
Pfanner
S. Agostino
VIA SAN GIORGIO
PIAZZA S.
AGOSTINO
PIAZZA DEL
SALVATORE
VIA BURLAMACCHI
VIA FILUNGO
S. Cristoforo
VIA BECCHERIA
PIAZZA
S. CROCE
VIA SANTA CROCE
VIA DEL BATTISTERO
PIAZZA S.
GIOVANNI
PIAZZA S.
GIUSTO
Porta S. Donato
PIAZZALE
VERDI
Palazzo
Mansi
VIA GALLI TASSI
VIA S. GIUSTINA
S. Michele
PIAZZA
S. MICHELE
S. Giovanni
VIA ROMA
VIA CENAMI
VIA FILLUNGO
VIA CALDERIA
CORSO GARIBALDI
To Bagni di Lucca
& Youth Hostal
VIA MATTEO RIVELLINO
PIAZZA
S. DONATO
Commune
Tourist Office
(Bike rental)
Bus
Station
S. Paolino
VIA GALLI TASSI
VIA S. PAOLINO
VIA DI POGGIO
Palazzo
Ducale
PIAZZA
NAPOLEONE
PIAZZA
DEL GIGLIO
VIA DEL GIGLIO
VIA S. ANNA
VIA DEL CARMINE
PIAZZA
RISORGIMENTO
VIA CAVOUR
VIALE CAVOUR
To Viareggio
& Genoa
Porta V.
Emmanuele
VIA VITTORIO
EMANUELE
S. Romano
VIA VITTORIO EMANUELE
CORSO GARIBALDI
VIA DELLA CITTADELLA
PIAZZA
INDIPENDENZA
VIALE S. CONCORDIO
To Pisa

N

Sadly, recent years have seen these sculptures covered for **restoration**, along with virtually all the highpoints of the great hall-like interior. These include paintings by Fra Bartolomeo, Tintoretto (*The Last Supper*), Ghirlandaio (*Sacra Conversazione*), the main altarpiece by Filippino Lippi, and Jacopo della Quercia's sculptured *Tomb of Ilaria del Carretto* (1405).

There is more opportunity, however, to appreciate the work of Lucca's finest sculptor, **Matteo Civitali** (1435–1501), represented here by two fonts, the pulpits and various tombs. His greatest work is the *Tempietto* (in the north aisle), which he sculpted to house the city's most famous and lucrative relic, the **Volto Santo** (Holy Face). Legend had it that this "true effigy of Christ" came to Lucca of its own volition from the Holy Land, at first by boat then by oxcart: a story remarkably similar to the ecclesiastical sham of Saint James's bones at Santiago del Compostela in Spain. As at Santiago, the icon provided a focus for international pilgrimage – along with considerable power for the local church. It may be no coincidence that it appeared during the bishopric of Anselmo da Baggio, who later made it to the papacy.

Heading northwest from the Duomo and across Via Fililungo, or more directly north from Piazza Napoleone, brings you to the square surrounding **San Michele in Foro**, which in many respects seems a better candidate for the role of cathedral. It is again unfinished, but this time it was the facade that was completed before money ran out for raising the body of the church to its level. The effect is wonderful, the upper loggias (and the rose windows behind) fronting air, like the figure of the archangel at their summit. In a triumph of eccentricity – mirrored in many of the city's churches – each of the loggia columns is different, some twisted, others sculpted or candystriped. The interior is comparatively plain, though there's a good Andrea della Robbia terracotta, and a painting of Saints Jerome, Sebastian, Roch and Helena by Filippino Lippi.

Giacomo Puccini was born almost opposite San Michele at Via di Poggio 30; his father and grandfather had been organists at the church. Their home, the **Casa di Puccini** (Tues–Sun; April–Sept 10am–6pm; Oct–Mar 10am–4pm), is now a school of music and maintains a small museum, with the Steinway piano on which he composed *Turandot*, along with original scores and photographs from the premieres. Entrance is free and the students take it in turn to show visitors around and put on records.

Just a couple of blocks west is **San Paolino**, where Puccini had his first job as organist. The church, rebuilt during the Renaissance, honours Lucca's first bishop and patron saint, whose remains are kept behind the high altar. At the end of the street, in Via Galli Tassi, is the seventeenth-century **Palazzo Mansi**, which houses a **Pinacoteca Nazionale** (Tues–Sat 9am–7pm, Sun & Mon 2–7pm). This is an indifferent collection of pictures, but the palace itself is a sight – all over-the-top Rococo, which reaches its zenith in a spectacularly gilded bridal suite.

North to San Frediano and the Anfiteatro

North of San Michele, **Via Fililungo** cuts through Lucca's most affluent shopping district, past the **Torre delle Oro**, the city clocktower, the beautiful *Caffè di Simo* (at no. 58), and into a warren of lanes leading to Piazza San Frediano, site of an occasional flower market.

The Basilica of **San Frediano** is, once again, Romanesque – though its facade is quite different from San Michele or the Duomo. In place of the multiple loggias is a brilliant thirteenth-century **mosaic** of *Christ in Majesty*, with his Apostles gathered below. The interior lives up to the facade's promise: a hall-like basilica, delicately lit, with subtly varied columns and capitals – and some fine treasures. Most enjoyable of these is the **font**, carved with Romanesque scenes of Moses, the Good Shepherd and the Apostles; set behind it is a ceramic *Annunciation* by Andrea della Robbia. Equally fine Gothic carving is represented by Jacopo della Quercia's altarpiece and pavement tombs in the **Trenta chapel** (fourth on the right). The best **frescoes** in the city, meanwhile, are to be found in the second chapel of the left aisle: Amico Aspertini's sixteenth-century scenes of the *Arrival of the Volte Santo* (see "The Duomo"), the *Miracles of San Frediano* (saving the city from flooding by the River Serchio) and *Life of St Augustine*.

Close by, at Via degli Asili 33, is the **Palazzo Pfanner** (April–Sept Tues–Sun 10am–5pm). The palace houses a collection of eighteenth- and nineteenth-century costume – not of great general interest. However, its loggia and statued gardens are exquisite. They can be seen to equally good effect from the ramparts.

Also worth looking down upon from the ramparts, as well as exploring at close range, is the remarkable **Piazza Anfiteatro** – a circuit of medieval buildings, whose foundations are the arches of the Roman amphitheatre. The streets around this square are among the oldest and most atmospheric in the city and house the odd antique or craft shop, and a couple of attractive restaurants.

The east of the City: the Gunigi Tower and Museum

The strangest sight of Lucca's cityscape is undoubtedly the **Casa Guinigi**, just southeast of the Piazza Anfiteatro. The fifteenth-century home of Lucca's leading family, its battlemented tower is surmounted by holm oaks whose roots have grown into the room below. The tower has been restored – climb it for one of the best views over the city (April–Sept 9am–7pm; Oct–March 10am–5pm; L3000).

Two blocks south, **Santa Maria Forisportam** ("outside the walls") signals the extent of the Roman and medieval city, before the current ramparts were built. The church is fronted by another, classic Luccan facade – again unfinished. To the east, the **Via del Fosso**, with its shallow canal, cuts off the eastern district of the city. At its midpoint the canal runs briefly under the surface, below the square of **San Francesco**, with its rose window and simple, striking facade. There are fourteenth-century frescoes in the courtyard of the monastery attached.

Beyond San Francesco and across the street is the fifteenth-century **Villa Guinigi**, built to supplement the family's old medieval town house. This is now the home of the city's major **museum** of art and sculpture (Tues–Sun; April–Sept 9am–7pm; Oct–March 10am–4pm; L3000). The collection includes a good deal of lively Romanesque sculpture gathered from throughout the city and province, and some good work by the cathedral's maestro, Matteo Civitali.

Practicalities

Lucca is an excellent base for exploring northwest Tuscany, with Pisa, the coast and the Alpi Apuane just a short bus ride away. However, **accommodation** is a major problem at almost any time of year.

Hotels

The city's dozen one- and two-star **hotels** are often taken up by students or permanent residents, and you'll generally need to phone a number of them before striking lucky. The best plan is to phone ahead – or go straight to – the **accom-**

modation service operated by *Agenzia Civ-Ex* at Via Vittorio Veneto 28, off Piazza Napoleone·(☎0583/56.741).

If you look around on your own, the cheapest hotels **within the walls** are *Albergo Cinzia*, Via della Dogana 9, by the Duomo (☎0583/41.323), and *Albergo l'Orologio*, Via San Pierino 7, near San Paolino (☎0583/53.419); doubles at either from L28,000. Slightly more expensive, with doubles from L40,000 are *Albergo Diana*, Via del Molinetto 11 (☎0583/42.202), and *Hotel Rex* in the train station square (☎0583/47615); or, from around L50,000, there are the nicely situated *Albergo di Poggio*, Via del Poggio (☎0583/55.421) and *Pensione Ilaria*, Via del Fosso 20 (☎0583/47.558).

Two hotels that fill less quickly, two blocks west of Porta Elisa, are *Albergo Melecchi* (☎0583/950.234) and *Albergo Stipino* (☎0583/950.317), Via Romana 37 and 95; doubles from L35,000. Also **outside the walls**, to the north, is the **youth hostel** (☎0583/953.686): leave the city at Porta Santa Maria, turn right at the roundabout onto Viale Batoni, then first left up Viale Civitali and first right onto Via del Brennero – the hostel is on the left. It is open March 1 to October 15; reception 6 to 11pm; curfew midnight; L8000 per person with breakfast.

Food and Festivals

As a gastronomic centre, Lucca is packed full of delicatessens, and quality is reflected, too, in the **restaurants**. The best, as ever, are fiendishly expensive – *Il Buca di Sant'Antonio* on Via della Cervia is rated one of the best in Italy. On a much more realistic level, try: *Trattoria da Leo*, Via Tegrimi 1, near Piazza del Salvatore (closed Sat); *Trattoria da Giulio*, Via San Tommaso 29, by the Palazzo Mansi (closed Sun & Mon); *Trattoria da Guido*, Via Battisti 28; or *Ristorante Sergio*, Via S Croce 44 (closed Mon afternoon & Tues). All have possibilities for full meals around L12,000–20,000. For excellent pizza by weight try *Pizzeria Castagnacci*, Piazza San Michele 25 (closed Sun); for a full pizza meal, with good beer, try *Pizzeria Queens* (Via Cenami 13).

Entertainment centres around classical music and dance. During the summer there are special concerts and events as part of the *Festival di Marlia* (held at the Villa Reale, 8km towards Pistoia), and in September the focus shifts back to the city with the *Settembre Lucchese*. Both feature at least one Puccini opera, staged during the *Settembre* at the intimate, four-tiered **Teatro Comunale** in Piazza del Giglio. Details from the tourist office. An **antiques market** takes place over the third weekend of each month in Piazza San Martino.

Coast and Mountains: Viareggio to Carrara

The **Riviera della Versilia**, the coast between Viareggio and Carrara, is a more or less solid strip of resorts – none of them very attractive. It ought to be otherwise, given the 6000-foot backdrop of the **Alpi Apuane**, but the beaches share the coastal plain with a railway, autostrada and clogged urban roads, and the water, too, is polluted.

If you are passing through the region, en route to greater rewards in Liguria, **Viareggio**, the largest Tuscan resort, provides a bit of life and beach access, and Torre del Lago an opera festival. Otherwise, the only real appeal lies inland, hiking in the Alps above the marble quarrying centres of **Massa** or **Carrara**.

Viareggio and Torre del Lago

VIAREGGIO is the Biarritz of the Riviera della Versilia: a large and once elegant nineteenth-century resort, which continues to aim for a well-heeled clientele. It has its attractions, with a fair amount of nightlife (including big-name concerts) and some neat Art Deco buildings along the boardwalk, Passeggiata Margherita. But the beaches are privatised and expensive, and in season, at least, the hotels tend to be full – and those that aren't often hold out for *pensione completa*. The one time to actively visit is during **carnevale** (Jan 22–Feb 7), one of the liveliest in Italy. Each Sunday there's an amazing parade of floats or *carri* – colossal, lavishly-designed papier-mâché models of politicians and celebrities. Outside carnival time these are displayed in the **Hangar-Carnevale** at the top end of Via Marco Polo (10.30am–noon & 4.30–7pm; free). They're very much an art form (top *carri* designers are famous), highly imaginative, and a lot of fun.

Arriving at the **train station**, 600m back from the seafront, you can pick up a map from the information office. **Buses** (*Lazzi*, *CAT* and *CLAP*) stop nearer the centre, by the Giardini d'Azeglio; turn right along the seafront, past Piazza Mazzini and you'll find the **EPT** at Viale Carducci 10 (8.30am–noon). The biggest concentrations of budget hotels are along Via Carducci and Via Leonardo da Vinci and Via Vespucci (which run from near the train station to the seafront). **Bikes** can be hired at the long city park, Pineta di Ponte.

Equipped with a bike, or your own transport, you could make for the public beaches, past the port area and south along the wooded road to **MARINA DI TORRE DEL LAGO**. The later stretches of sand are undeveloped, while inland, by the lake of Massaciúccoli is the **Villa Puccini** (summer 9am–noon & 3–7pm; winter closes 5.30pm). At the town, **TORRE DEL LAGO PUCCINI**, a summer **Festival Pucciniano** presents the master's works at an open-air theatre. There are several **campsites** around the town and lake.

North to Massa and Carrara

There is little to entice a stop between Viareggio and Carrara. The coast is continuously developed, with the prettiest beaches tightly coralled by **FORTE DEI MARMI**, the Versilia's most upmarket resort.

MASSA and its port, MARINA DI MASSA, are more or less merged in a sprawl of holiday development. It is basically an Italian family resort – not very appealing, with weed-ridden beaches and shallow water a long way out to sea. The Massa **youth hostel**, however, *Ostello Apuano* (☎0585/240.288), might prove useful. It is actually at Viale delle Pinete 89, Località Partaccia, most easily accessible from the Carrara-Avenza train station (take a bus from here for 3km towards Marina di Massa); there's a free beach adjacent.

CARRARA again has its beach strip, MARINA DI CARRARA, which serves also as the port for the town's prodigious quarrying of marble. The **marble** trade has been going here since Roman times, and in earnest since Michelangelo came to find a block for the tomb of Pope Julius II. You can see the slashes of quarries in the mountainside from the town, which itself is dominated by the trade. The Romanesque-Gothic **Duomo** is full of marble statuary, and there's a **Museo del Marmo** (daily May & July–Sept 10am–1pm & 3.30–6.30pm; June 5–8pm) with interesting displays on the history of quarrying and of Carrara sculpture. The most exciting display of contemporary Carrara marble, though, comes with the annual **Scolpire all'Aperto** programme (late July to early Oct), when the local commune invites international sculptors to the town and provides them with marble to carve in the Piazza Alberica.

To get a closer view of the **quarries**, take a bus (hourly from Via Minzoni) towards COLLONICA, twenty minutes' twisting ride into the mountains. Ask to be set down just before the village at the **Cava**, a huge marble basin, its floor and sides perfectly squared by the wire saws used to cut the blocks.

Marble aside, Carrara makes a pleasant stop – an integral, self-sufficient place that comes as a relief after the holiday coast. There's a Monday market, several shops for gathering up a picnic, and a few bars and pizzerias. Most accommodation is down in Marina di Carrara, but there's a good two-star **pension**, *Albergo da Roberto*, just north of Piazza Alberica on Via Apuana (☎0585/54.033).

Walks in the Alpi Apuani

There are mapped-out **paths** throughout the **Alpi Apuani**. They are genuine mountains, though altitudes are relatively low and distances short – you are never very far from a road, *rifugio* or hotel; hikes are quite feasible in trainers. Two **leaflets** are available from the Carrara EPT (Piazza II Giugno 14). One is a disorientated "map" showing paths, refuges, roads and rivers – and nothing else; the second contains "Itineraries for Tourists", of which half a dozen at the back are for walkers. Most are two- to three-hour walks.

The nearest refuge (*Rifugio Carrara*; ☎0585/72.232) and junction of paths to Carrara is at **CAMPO CECINA**, but you'll have to hitch to get there – buses run only on Sundays.

South: Livorno to Piombino

If the Versilian Riviera sounds unappealing, the so-called **Etruscan Riviera**, the coast south from Livorno to Piombino, has even less going for it. The backdrop of the Alpi Apuani is replaced by the drabness of reclaimed swampland, while holiday development is, if anything, more intense. **Livorno** has some interest as a major Mediterranean port, and offers **ferry connections** to the islands of Elba and Capráia. But for itself, the mainland coast only really gets appealing way to the south, around **San Vicenzo**.

Livorno

LIVORNO is, after Florence, Tuscany's largest city. It is not a pretty place – heavily bombed during the last war, it now shelters a large American naval base – but it does have the feel of a real Mediterranean port and city. This can be a welcome change from the tourist focus of so much of Tuscany, and if you are just staying a night here, en route for Elba, there are usually beds to be found.

Around the City

Livorno's origins go back to Roman times but the port was properly developed only under the Medici, who set out to transform it into an ideal city. Their plan is still evident in the old, central grid, enclosed by a ring of the canals (*fossi*) built to link Livorno with Pisa, and guarded by a pair of fortresses. Beyond sprawl the suburbs, developed alongside the postwar container shipping industry.

Buses arrive at the heart of the "old town" in **Piazza Grande**; from the **train station**, 2km east, take a local bus (#1, #2 or #8) to the same square. From here it's a five-minute walk down Via Grande to the Porto Mediceo, where the ferries leave for the islands. The **EPT** is at Piazza Cavour 6 (Mon–Fri 8.30am–12.30pm), four blocks south of Piazza Grande (follow Via Cairoli) by the canal.

The **Porto Mediceo** is the most picturesque area of Livorno, with fishing boats spilling back into the canals, often a liner blocking the view out to sea, and Sangallo's **Fortezza Vecchia**, with its sea wall, flanking the harbour. Further down the quay, at the centre of Piazza Micheli, is a bizarre Renaissance **statue of Ferdinando I** with four "Mori", or slaves, chained to its base. It is said to have marked the arrival of slaves to the port – which was, otherwise, one of the most liberal and cosmopolitan in the Mediterranean. A sixteenth-century **synagogue**, restored after the war, survives on Via Cairoli.

The moated, rather derelict **Fortezza Nuova** (10am–7.30pm; free) signals a second, lively area on the east side of the inner grid. Cross Piazza della Repubblica from here and you reach the **Mercato Americano** (Mon–Sat) in Piazza XX Settembre. The cultural endowment of stationed American troops, the stalls sell army surplus clothing, fishing and camping gear, and flick knives. For produce, the **Mercato Central** is across the canal (in the central grid) on Via Buontalenti. The streets around Piazza XX Settembre – **Via Oberdan**, especially – are good territory for cafés, pizzerias and trattorias.

Rooms and Food

Most **hotels** are cheap and basic – some too much so in the port and train station areas. The best plan is to head for the centre, where you should have no great problems finding a double for L25,000–35,000. Among possibilities in this price range, try: *Albergo Italia*, Corso Mazzini 120 (☎0586/882.020); *Hotel Cremona*, Corso Mazzini 24 (☎0586/23.681); *Hotel Goldini*, Via E Mayer 42 (☎0586/898.705); *Albergo Europa*, Via dell'Angiolo 23 (☎0586/888.561); or the rock bottom *Albergo Ariston*, Piazza della Repubblica 11 (☎0586/880.149). The nearest **campsite** is *Camping Miramare* on Via Aurelia, past Antignano (☎0586/580.402).

For **meals**, seafood is for once affordable. The local speciality is *cacciucco*, a spicy fish stew, traditionally made from the scraps the boats couldn't sell. You can get a good plate of this at *Trattoria Il Sottomarino*, Via dei Terrazini 48, off Piazza dell Repubblica (closed July), or *Trattoria Galileo*, Via delle Campare, nearby. For pizza, try *Pizzeria Umbra*, Via E Mayer 1, or *Rustic Inn*, Via Bosi 16.

Ferries

Two main ferry companies operate car and passenger services to Elba, Capraia, Gorgona, Sardinia and Corsica. All the Tuscan island ferries leave from the Porto Mediceo; some Sardinia and Corsica sailings leave from the Porto Industriale (30min by bus #18, L700; or a L20,000 taxi ride). Beware that ferries are often fully booked through July and August; for the Tuscan islands, Piombino is a cheaper and more reliable point of departure.

TO.RE.MAR, Via Calafati 6 (☎0586/896.372). To Elba (Portoferraio), Gorgona and Capraia; twice daily, extra services July–Aug.

NAV.AR.MA, Via Calafati 4 (☎0586/38.068). To Sardinia (Olbia); three times a week, daily in season. To Corsica (Bastia); daily from end of March to early November. Note: US citizens travelling to Corsica will need to obtain a visa from the French consulate at Via Montegrappa 6 (☎0586/896.368).

Beaches – and south to Piombino

If you just want a quick dip, **ARDENZA** (10-min bus ride from Piazza della Repubblica) is the nearest beach to Livorno – a one-time village that is now essentially a suburb. It is, though, very urban and crowded, with swimming off a paved promenade, or (if you pay), a couple of concrete *bagni*. A rather better alternative is to head north to **TIRRÉNIA** (25min by bus), where there's a real stretch of beach, separated from the main road by pine woods, and windsurfers, and a **youth hostel**, *Ostello San Francesco* (☎050/37.442).

Heading south from Livorno and further afield, there's little to distinguish any of the resorts, with their scrubby beaches and remorseless development. The **CÉCINA** area is like a backyard Benidorm, only a lot more expensive. **SAN VINCENZO** is not a lot better, but at least has the virtue of a broad, sandy beach, fronted by a park of ilex and oak trees. Summer rooms here, though, are at a premium, and if you want to stay on a whim you'll probably have to camp.

Inland, the **WWF reserve of Bolgheri** is a classic wildlife habitat, with thousands of birds spending the winter here. It is open to the public every Friday and every first and third Saturday of the month between October 15 and April 15.

Piombino

PIOMBINO is the nearest port to Elba, to which it has mercifully frequent ferries. The town itself is not a great place to stay – a steelworks centre, rebuilt after almost total destruction during the last war. If you come down by train, get out at **CAMPIGLIA MARÍTTIMA**, from where there's a connecting train to Piombino port (don't get off at Piombino town). At the port you can pick up information and tickets; one-way fares (returns aren't sold) for Elba are L5500 per person, and from L40,000 per car, plus five percent port tax. If you need other information, there's a small **tourist office** in Piazzale Premuda.

The same two companies run **ferries out of Piombino** as from Livorno; both have offices by the port train station:

TO.RE.MAR, Calata Italia 22 (☎0586/918.080). Ferries several times daily (almost hourly in summer) to Cavo and Portoferráio (50min); less often to Rio Marina and Porto Azzurro (2hr). Also summer-only hydrofoil (*aliscafo*) to Portoferráio (25–35min).

NAV.AR.MA, Viale Elba 4 (☎0565/92.133 or 918.101). Daily ferries to Portoferráio, en route to Basta (Corsica).

Elba and its archipelago

Mountainous **ELBA** is the third largest Italian island after Sicily and Sardinia: 29 kilometres long by 19 kilometres wide. It has exceptionally clear water, fine white sand beaches, and a lush, wooded interior, superb for walking. For decades, it had a reputation, too, as a quiet hideaway island – though it's now firmly on the package trail, with an estimated one million tourists in August. If you want to enjoy the place, or even just find a room (or campsite space), come well out of season; the climate is mild year-round and ferries run at least once daily.

Historically, Elba has been well out of the mainstream – rural, agricultural and, of course, place of exile for Napoleon, who could have seen his birthplace on Corsica from the highest point, Monte Capanne. Earlier eras saw the island exploited primarily for its iron ore – fashioned by Greeks, Carthaginians,

Etruscans and Romans alike. Through later centuries control passed from Pisa to Genova and on to the Medici, Spain, Turkey and finally France: a cosmopolitan mix that has left its legacy on both architecture and cultivation.

Today, though the economy revolves almost entirely around tourism, Elba's size and topography have allowed the towns and villages to keep distinct characters. **Portoferráio** is very much the capital; **Marina di Campo**, over on the south coast, has the best beach; **Marciano** and **Poggio**, on the north, are sheltered by lush woods and give access to hikes around **Monte Capanne**. To the east, military history is evident in **Capoliveri's** hill-top position and **Porto Azzurro's** fortifications, the latter still in use to detain Elba's criminal population.

Portoferráio

Unless you're interested solely in beachlife, **Portoferráio** is probably the best place to stay. It is the hub of the island's roads (and transport system), has most of the life, and offers a reasonable chance of accommodation – at least outside of July and August.

Accommodation

On arrival, your first point of call if you haven't fixed a room in advance should be the **tourist office** (☎0565/92.671), across the road from the ferry quay at Calata Italia 26 (Mon–Sat 8am–1pm and 3.30–7.30pm; winter, 9am–1pm and 4–6pm). They will provide a map, bus timetable and lists of all the hotels, *apartamenti* and campsites – and will often phone around to find space. So, too, will the **Associazione Albergatori** at Calata Italia 21 (8.30am–12.30pm & 3–7pm; ☎0565/ 92.754). If these fail to turn up something, tour the bars and ask. In season, you should expect to pay well above officially listed prices.

Among the better value Portoferráio **hotels** are: *Hotel Il Faro*, Via Cairoli 18 (☎0565/92.364); *Hotel Emy*, Via G Carducci 5, just off Piazza A. Citi (☎0565/ 917.661); and *Hotel l'Ape Elbana*, Salita Cosimo de Medici 2 (☎0565/92.245), just off Piazza Repubblica in the old part of town; doubles from L32,000, L38,000 and L44,000 respectively. The largest relatively budget hotel – with 68 rooms, so some chance of space – is the *Hotel Massimo*, Calata Italia 23 (☎0565/92.766); doubles from L70,000. If you can get together a group of people, *apartamenti* may well work out better value; bookable through the tourist office, most have two double rooms with cooking facilities, from L60,000 a day, less by the week.

The nearest **campsites** are *La Sorgente* (☎0565/917.139) and *La Enfola* (☎0565/915.390), 5km and 6km distant, on the road west to Viticcio; and *Rosselba Le Palme* (☎0565/966.101), 8km east at OTTONE. These are all quite accessible. Be warned that some of the others on the island are not, involving infrequent buses and long walks – often followed by further walks to poor beaches.

If you fail to find any accommodation – which may happen in July or August – you can get by for a few days sleeping out on the beaches (though this is officially prohibited). Leave most of your luggage at the *Desposito Bagagli* below the tourist office (L2000 a day), rent a moped (see below) if you can afford it, and set out.

Getting around

Hiring a bike or moped is invaluable for checking out accommodation, finding a better place for the next day, or just for exploring the island. They are available at *Rent Ghiaie*, Via Cairoli 25, Spiaggia delle Ghiaie (☎0565/92.666), and at the

more professional *Brandi Motori*, Via Manganaro 11 (☎0565/92.359), out in the
suburbs. The *Haethaltour* agency on Calata Italia will book ahead for you.
Mopeds run at L38,000 per day, bikes L22,000.

Buses run regularly from Portoferráio to Procchio (21 daily), Marina di
Campo (13 daily) and Porto Azzurro (12 daily). Services elsewhere are sporadic –
and there's little running anywhere after 7 or 8pm. For getting to beaches, **boats**
supplement the bus services; they are well advertised at the ports.

Exploring the Town

Portoferráio consists, essentially, of the "useful" modern part of town (with tourist office, bus stop, ferry terminal and the beach of Le Ghiae), and the old
Medicean port, with its fortifications and fishing harbour, to the east.

The walled **old town** has just two, short tunnelled entrances from the quay.
Just inside is the **Piazza della Repubblica**, where a market (good for beachwear
and leather) is held every Friday. From here, streets climb up the side of the
promontory and to one of Napoleon's exile residences, the **Palazzina dei Mulini**
(Tues–Sat 9am–6.30pm, Sun 9am–1pm; L4000 includes same-day admission to
Napoleon's villa at San Martino). The palace was built specifically for Napoleon –
a well-chosen site, with grand views of the bay – and, though not what the
emperor may have been used to, a fair old building. There's a stunning baroque
bedroom, a library sent over from Fontainebleau, and various items of memorabilia – including the Napoleonic flag of Elba (three golden bees). During his ten-
month exile, Napoleon was technically sovereign of Elba and neighbouring
Pianosa. He established a small court, kept an army of about 1000 men and a navy
with one ship, "The Inconstant".

From the Palazzina, a signposted path leads down to the small, rock-enclosed
beach of **Le Viste**. On the way up to the palace, you pass the **Misericordia**,
housing a not very worthwhile Napoleonic museum.

San Martino

Napoleon's sister, Elisa, bought the **Villa Napoleonica di San Martino** for a
summer residence not long before the emperor left the island. It's located 6km
from Portoferráio on the #1 bus route. On the way is a Museo delle Ceramiche,
where huge walls of ceramic tiles have been landscaped in the countryside.

The villa (same hours as Palazzo dei Mulini) is fronted by a Neoclassical
palazzo, added (with exuberant N motifs) by Prince Demidoff, husband of
Napoleon's niece, who bought up the villa to create a Napoleonic museum. Its
permanent exhibits are no great shakes, though each year exhibitions are held
on a Napoleonic theme. At the back of the palazzo is Napoleon's relatively modest
villa, with its famous graffito – "Napoleon is happy everywhere".

Food and Practicalities

Portoferráio's **restaurants** are expensive, even by Tuscan standards. The
Pizzeria Il Castagnaccaio in Via del Mercato Vecchio (off Piazza della Repubblica
in the old town) is about the cheapest. Better but pricier is *Trattoria La Barca* in
Via Guerrazzi, with a wood-fired oven in view of the street; next door is an excellent wine and *grappa* shop. If you want to put your own meal together, there are
grocers, and a pizza-by-weight place, on Via Carducci, just behind the harbour.

As to other facilities, there's a **post office** (poste restante pick-up) at Piazza
Hutre, off Piazza della Repubblica; a **bookshop** (paperbacks and some British

papers) at Calata Mazzini 9, in the old port; and public **telephones** in *Bar l'Angolo*, Via Cavalieri di Vittorio Veneto (7am–midnight). If you plan to do some **hiking** on the island, the *Communita Montana*, Viale Manzoni 4, provide a contour map of the Monte Capanne area, marking all footpaths.

Leaving Elba by ferry, it's best to book a ticket well in advance in summer – especially if you're taking a car. *TO.RE.MAR* are at Calata Italia 22, *NAV.AR.MA* just round the corner at Viale Elba 4. Both offices are for advance reservations; buying a ticket on the day you leave, go to the kiosks by the quay.

Western Elba

The main road west from Portoferráio runs through **BIÓDOLA**, which, with VITTÍCCIO to the north, has the best beaches on the north coast. It has a couple of discos and a decent **campsite**, *Camping Scaglieri* (☎0565/969.940), where there's usually space for anyone arriving without a car, dog or children.

PROCCHIO, at the junction of the roads south and west, is a small town, enclosed by greenery – oaks, acacias, firs, the odd fig and bamboo. Its beach is fairly concealed by deckchairs but there's fine white sand underneath it all – it's accessible to the non-paying swimmer – and windsurfers for hire. *Calda da Angelo*, near the junction, is a good value **café-restaurant**. There is a cluster of **hotels** (cheapest are the *Pensione da Renzo*, ☎0565/907.504, and *Pensione La Pergola*, ☎0565/907.506; doubles from L30,000), but no campsite.

Staying on the north coast, **MARCIANA MARINA** is unexciting – a small marina and shingly beach, overlooked by a cylindrical tower built by the Pisans in the twelfth century. A short bus ride inland, however, brings you up (past a *grappa* stall, with tasting) into the foothills of Monte Capanne and the villages of **MARCIANA** and **POGGIO**. These have an air of isolation, distinct from other Elban settlements. Marciana has a skeletal fortress; Poggio, the more attractive of the two, bright gardens and decorated doorways. If you want to sample **Monte Capanne** without doing the walking, there's a primitive and very pricey **cable car** (*cabinovia*) to the summit from Marciana. The shortest walk to the summit (marked #2 on the trail map) is from Poggio – about two hours at a leisurely pace.

With your own transport, you can cut across the island from Poggio on a cano-pied road down to the south coast. This runs through **SAN PIERO IN CAMPO**, a village of old stone doorways and a church with Roman mosaics. There's a good value pizzeria, *Al Campanile*.

Emerging at the coast, turn right and you'll reach **SECCHETO**, good for a swim from the rocks at the western end of town, and with a largely nudist stretch further along. Nearby CAVOLI is an awkward and more upmarket layout of beach and hotels, but has windsurfers. There is no campsite (and no shelter); hotels to try are *La Stella* at Seccheto (☎0565/987.013) and *Lorenza* at Cavoli (☎0565/987.054).

Turn left and you come to the long white beach at **MARINA DI CAMPO**. This is very popular – the district has Elba's major concentration of hotels, after Portoferráio – but the water is clear and there's visible sand at the east end, rocks and fewer people at the west. Windsurfers again are for hire. If you arrive early enough in the day, you might find space at one of the four **campsites**; for a **room** it's wise to phone ahead – try *Pensione Elba*, Via Mascagni 43 (☎0565/97.224), or *Orsa Minore*, Viale Etruschi 23 (☎0565/92.027). Intending beach-sleepers beware that the police patrol at intervals through the night. Best deal for a **meal** is *Il*

Golfo at the eastern end of the beach, or the mouthwatering takeaway *rosticceria/ pizzeria* at the west end of the main street. Marina di Campo has perhaps Elba's liveliest nightlife, with late-night samba on the beach at *Bar Tropicana*.

LACONA, midway between Marina and Porto Azzurro, on the south coast, is a pleasant beach but swamped by campsites.

Eastern Elba

The old fishing town of **PORTO AZZURRO**, 14km from Portoferráio, was heavily fortified by Philip III of Spain in 1603, to protect it against continual raids. His fortress is today the town prison, but, delicately signposted as a simple "Fortezza", it does little to deter visitors to the town. A walk around the outer ramparts will bring you to a shop selling pottery and other prison craft goods.

The fort aside, Porto Azzurro has attractive and traditional open-front shops, in the cobbled area near Piazza Matteotti, and fine balconied houses, and swimming from the rocks east of the harbour. Accommodation is predictably tight. Try the *Residence Porto Azzurro*, Via d'Alarcon 58 (☎0565/95.527), with doubles from L40,000; or seek help at the tourist information kiosk at the junction of the Portoferráio and Rio Marina roads (9–12.30am & 4–8pm). A rare self-service restaurant, *Rosticceria d'Alarcon*, and the *Pizzeria Giannini*, both on Via Alarcon, are best bets for budget eating.

North of Porto Azzurro, the road runs below the ruined castle of Volterraio, to the iron ore mining town of **RIO NELL'ELBA** and its port, **RIO MARINA**. Beyond is the isolated and rather shabby, polluted town of **CAVO** – its beach a very un-Elban dirt-grey. A hydrofoil runs from here to Piombino in summer.

Time is much better spent at **CAPOLIVERI**, to the south of Porto Azzurro. This is a naturally fortified town, its peninsula site commanding all possible approaches from the "mainland" part of Elba. It has a busy, prosperous feel and few concessions to tourism in the old, close-knit streets. There are, though, several **restaurants** – *Da Beppe*, Via Roma 25, is modestly priced, *Il Chiasso*, Via Sauro (closed Tues), pricey but superb for fish and seafood – and a one-star **hotel**, *Golfo Azzurro*, Via Appiani 5 (☎0565/968.167).

A much greater concentration of hotels are to be found south again, down on the coast, at MORCONE, PARETI, TRAPPOLA and NAREGNO, each of which have beaches. Two recommendable one-star hotels at Naregno are *Fonte di Rose* (☎0565/96.8788) and *La Voce del Mare* (☎0565/968.455). At Trappola, *The Sugar Reef* has jazz groups every Friday, Saturday and Sunday.

Islands around Elba: Capraia and Montecristo

Of the four islands around Elba, **Gorgona** and **Pianosa** host prisons and are off limits to casual visitors; **Capraia** has a prison, too, but also a few tourists; **Montecristo** is a protected nature reserve, accessible only on day trips. **Boats** run to Capraia from Marciana Marina and Portoferráio and to Montecristo from Porto Azzurro and Marina di Campo.

· Capraia

About 400 people live on **CAPRAIA**, a mountainous and volcanic "island of goats", scattered with Roman ruins and Romanesque churches and fortresses begun by the Pisans and finished by the Genovese. There is an agricultural open prison to the north and on the western side of the island are several large caves – the **Grotto di Parino** was used as a place of meditation by monks in the fifth century and today seals have set up home in the **Grotta della Foca**.

The only built-up area is the town of **CAPRAIA ISOLA**, with the port about half a kilometre down the only hard road. Here there is one **hotel**, the *Milano* (☎0565/95.032), and two **pensioni** – *Il Saracino* (☎0565/95.018) and *Da Beppone* (☎0565/95.001). Your fellow guests are as likely to be visiting inmates at the agricultural open prison to the north as holidaymaking.

Montecristo

MONTECRISTO is a well-protected nature reserve 40km south of Elba: a near-circular, granite island, covered in thick woods. Its somewhat limited fame is due to Alexander Dumas' novel *The Count of Monte Cristo*. A legend that Benedictine monks had buried treasure before abandoning the island had given him the inspiration for the tale, though there is no record of his ever visiting it.

Today, a guard and his family are the only occupants, housed in a once royal villa. Day-trippers are permitted to come ashore at **Cala Maestra** to enjoy a small, sandy bay, but are limited to the beach. It is not possible to explore the woods, nor the ruins of the monastery.

South to Lazio: the Maremma Coast

The term **Maremma** defines the entire coastal strip from Cecina as far south as Civitavecchia, well into Lazio, and extends as far east as Monte Amiata, the highest point in Tuscany. The region was the northern heartland of the Etruscans but became depopulated in the Middle Ages as wars disrupted the drainage schemes and allowed malarial swamps to build up behind the dunes. These became almost synonymous with disease in Italy and nineteenth-century guides devote a lot of space to advising very strongly against a visit. Today, the regional capital of **Grosseto** remains a pretty miserable city, though there are bright patches of scenery – the protected nature reserve of **Monti di Uccellina** – and some attractive (though upmarket) resorts around the peninsula of **Monte Argentario**. Once again, however, hotels along this strip are expensive and full in summer, so without reservations don't expect more than a camping place.

Grosseto and around

Until the mid-nineteenth century, **Grosseto** was a malaria-ridden backwater. The draining of the marshes, however, which was finally effected only under Mussolini, has transformed it into a provincial capital for the Maremma and its prosperous agricultural hinterland. The last thirty years have seen an explosion of population, and the city – heavily damaged in the war – virtually rebuilt.

With its characterless condominiums and commercial buildings, it is – deservedly – undervisited, though it is a major communications centre and you may well find yourself passing through. Most **trains** on the Genova to Rome coastal line stop here and you can change for the line to Siena or *locale* connections to Orbotello and the south, Follonica (for Massa Maríttima) and Cécina (for Volterra). Timetabling always seems to leave about an hour between trains – about all you'd want to see what remains of the old town and pick up information on the region from the **tourist office** at Viale Ximenes 21 (just outside the walls of the old town, to the southeast).

The medieval **centro storico** is, in fact, a compact, quite appealing quarter, planned as a complex hexagon within strong defensive walls, most of which remain intact. You can wander around on top of the defences on a public path (a half-hour circuit), and lounge about in gardens built into the corner strongholds. The fortifications are impressively purposeful. This was the last Sienese city to fall to the Florentines, changing hands only in 1559.

Within the walls, the much restored **Duomo** has a pretty, pink and white marble front – though little within. Above the sacristy, the **Museo Diocesano di Arte Sacra** (closed Tues) contains a handful of Sienese works from local churches. Highlights are Sassetta's *Madonna of the Cherries* and a *Madonna and Child* attributed to Simone Martini. Nearby, a **Museo Archaeologico/ Pinacoteca** (Thurs–Tues 9.30am–12.30pm & 4.30–8.30pm) on Via Mazzini displays finds – coins, urns, bronzes, tufa carvings – from ancient Rusellae and other local Etrusco-Roman sites.

Rusellae and Vetulonia

If you are an enthuisiast, and you're driving, it's easy enough to visit this pair of Etrusco-Roman sites near Grosseto. **RUSELLAE**, modern ROSELLE, lies 10km away to the northeast. It's a mildly interesting detour, with a forum and the odd street discernible.

VETULÓNIA, about 20km northwest of Grosseto, off the road to Follonica, is rather more rewarding. The ancient city was one of the twelve members of the Etruscan Federation and tell-tale blocks have been incorporated into the present village, which has the appearance of a medieval hill town. On the approach road, about 5km northwest, a huge necropolis is currently being excavated. These remains (which also boast the foundations and graffiti of an Etruscan brothel) are unenclosed, except where the archaeologists are digging during the year, and you can wander at will. A **Museo-Antiquario** displays excavated relics and the latest finds. In the village, off the main square, there is a very fine **restaurant** – it looks like an ordinary bar, with the dining room through a bead curtain; the views and food are magnificent.

Marina di Grosseto and Castiglione della Pescaia

MARINA DI GROSSETO and **CASTIGLIONE DELLA PESCAIA**, Grosseto's local resorts, have the mixed blessing of broad, shelving beaches. Each is now conclusively developed, having lost its old identity as a fishing village, though they both preserve walls and towers and a bit of character. Marina is least spoilt, with a good sandy beach and pinewood hinterland, and a small tourist office at Via Piave 10 (☎0564/34.449), who might be able to help with rooms. Otherwise count on camping at one of the six **campsites** in the vicinity. The best are the small three-star *Rosmarina* (☎0564/36.319; open April–Sept), on the outskirts of the town at Via delle Colonie 37, and much larger two-star *Principina* (☎0564/ 35.647), 4km south at PRINCIPINA A MARE. The others are huge complexes.

Short walks along the **Pineta della Tombolo**, the pine woods between the two resorts, brings relative peace – disturbed mainly by the presence of wild boar, which you are almost certain to see. At Castiglione there are **ferries**, in season, across to the island of Giglio.

Monti dell'Eccellina Nature Reserve

The **reserve of Monti dell'Eccellina** comprises a strip of coastal mountains, beginning about a dozen kilometres south of Grosseto. The area is said to be the only virgin piece of coastline in all Italy, and its wildlife includes huge numbers of migratory birds, boars, and semi-wild horses. **Access** is strictly controlled. On Wednesdays and weekends, you can enter the reserve at ALBERESE, where there is a visitors' centre, and follow any of four marked trails into the woods. All other access is restricted except, by special permission, at TALAMONE, where another three trails are marked out.

To get a glimpse of the reserve outside these times, you can take the one regular road around the southernmost tip. This leads from FÓNTEBLANDA to the cape at **TALAMONE**, an attractive (but much frequented) fishing village out on a promontory; at one time the Sienese planned to make this hole-in-the-wall fishing harbour into a port to rival Pisa and Genova.

Orbotello and Monte Argentario

Two pine-clad sandspits (the *tombole*) and an isthmus containing **Orbotello**, tenuously connect **Monte Argentario** to the mainland. Enclosed within the three tongues of land is a lagoon, scenic if you see it from the coast, with the mountainous interior of the Argentario behind. It's the mountains that you want to head for. Though becoming increasingly well known – with two idle rich playgrounds in **Port'Ércole** and especially **Porto San Stéfano** – the peninsula's interior is wild and beautiful. It's something of a birdwatching eldorado, too, with 200 species in evidence over the year.

Orbotello

ORBOTELLO is an inoffensive slip of town, though often a bottleneck of cars as Romans pile in for the weekend. Like most places in this region, it was once Etruscan, though its tangible history – the fortifications – is the result of a Spanish garrison in the sixteenth century. There is a provincial main drag, thronged with the usual evening *passeggiata*, and very little else. If you're very lucky, you might get a **room** at the *Hotel Touring*, close to the centre at Via Mazzini 21 (☎0564/867.151); it's a one-star hotel, rare in these parts, with doubles from L34,000. If you're desperate, quite a few people seem to end up sleeping in the train station, en route to or from Giglio.

If you plan to explore Monte Argentario, you'll probably need to camp. There are fourteen **campsites** in all, most of them concentrated on the Tómbolo della Gianella and the north area of the lagoon. The closest is *Gianella-La Costa* (☎0564/820.049); the most attractive, *Campo Regio* (☎0564/870.163), a one-star site, open all year, up to the north at FONTEBLANDA. Getting around, you ideally need your own **transport**. There are a few bus services between Orbotello, Porto San Stéfano and Port'Ércole, but nothing into the interior. A combination of walking and hitching should work out if you're committed.

Porto San Stéfano and Port'Ércole

PORTO SAN STÉFANO is the more developed of the Argentario resorts. It's also fashionable – which in Italy is a lot worse than being just plain popular. Visitors, Roman and foreign, are rich, and facilities are designed for thick wallets.

The charm that brought people here, though, can still just about be caught around the port's twin harbours; one for the yachts, the other for the few surviving fishing boats. A saving grace is the fish market and, if you can afford them, the fish restaurants. Most budget travellers stay only as long as it takes to get a boat to the island of Giglio (see below).

Old **PORT'ÉRCOLE** was badly bombed in the last war, but is still fronted by a pair of fortresses on either side of the headland. Its chief claim to fame is that the painter **Caravaggio** is buried in the parish church.

Ansedonia

Back on the mainland, **ANSEDONIA**, with another crop of Roman holiday villas, and a rail station, is a last possible stop before Lazio if you're interested in Roman remains. The site of ancient **COSA** spreads over a hill just to the west of the town. Founded in 273 BC, this was one of the most important commercial centres of Roman Tuscany, and according to the historian Rutilius its population was driven out by an army of mice. The Roman walls still stand eight metres high in places, along with remains of a circuit of eighteen defensive towers, a forum, temples, and recently uncovered mosaics and wall paintings.

Isola del Giglio

The island of **GIGLIO** is connected by ferry from Porto San Stéfano (eight times daily in season – four regular and four, more costly, hydrofoil runs). It's a bit out of the way for most foreign tourists, but popular with Romans – rich, yacht-owning ones especially. In high season, there's standing room only on the boats.

A bus meets the **ferry** to shuttle arrivals to the two villages, Campese and Castello. The handful of permanent residents live either here or in scattered red-roofed houses on the hillsides; the land rises straight up out of the sea – there are no beach coves as on Elba. If you want to stay (you could easily see the island in a day), there's a **tourist office**, opposite the ferry ramp, which does its best to try and find accommodation.

There are thirteen **hotels** (six with three stars, the rest with two), a **campsite** (just outside Campese), and a number of rooms to let in private houses (advertised in the windows). Most hotels offer only full board in high season and many only open from June to September. For a room with a difference, try *Pardini's Hermitage Hotel* (☎0564/809.034 or 412.227), built on an isolated part of the coast, accessible only by boat or on foot; cheapest room in high season is .93,000 per day full board. The island's cheapest hotel is *Da Giovani*, Via di Mezzo Franco 10, Campese (☎0564/804.010), with doubles at L45,000 and full board L65,000 per person; *Albergo Meuble Giardino delle Palme* (☎0564/804.037), also at Campese, is only a fraction more. The **campsite**, Baia del Sole (☎0564/804.036; May–Sept) is mostly regular tents; it is located near Campese.

Castello

CASTELLO is hidden away in the hills, just under six hairpin-kilometres from the port. It is a remarkably preserved village, surrounded by thick defensive walls and round towers. The bus stops near a vine-covered patio bar in the large main square; at the first bungalow up a path from the bar is a sign for rooms to let (☎0564/806.074). An open-air disco, *Il Fracco*, opens up for the summer, too.

At the far side of the sunny quadrangle is the entrance to the granite castle town. Granite was quarried here from Roman times on, and Giglio stone was used to construct many medieval churches. Rough paths have been made around the **castle walls** so you can clamber up steps and over rocks for superb views over the island, picking out various ancient remains a very long way below.

Campese

CAMPESE, 4km further along the sole road, has the island's only **beach**, save for a tiny strip near the ferry quay. It is a fine stretch of sand, curving for about a mile from a huge phallic rock that tourist brochures are too modest to photograph, and overlooked by a Medici tower. Around the base of the tower is a modern, turreted apartment complex, which has a couple of restaurants, tennis courts and all manner of watersport facilities – including **diving** gear for hire and lessons to show you how to use it. The Giglio diving club have mapped out the coast around the island for the best places to see rocks, fish, plants and even a shipwrecked Spanish galleon.

Giannutri

The southernmost Tuscan isle, **GIANNUTRI**, is privately owned, and night stays are permitted only by invitation. Ordinary mortals can visit, though the island policeman asks travellers to remove backpacks before setting ashore. Given that – and the island's physical make-up (flat, dull and walkable end-to-end in two hours) – it's one really for island obsessives only. If you're curious, the tiny **boat** *M/S Gabbiano II* leaves Santo Stéfano daily (May 1–Sept 15) at 10.30am, returning at 4.30pm; out of season it runs only on a Wednesday, Saturday and Sunday.

travel details

Trains

From Florence to Rome (hourly; 2hr 15min–3hr 30min); Naples (2 daily; 4hr); Venice-Mestre/ Udine (10 daily; 2hr 45min–3hr 20min/5hr 20min– 6hr); Venice central (hourly; 3hr 25min–4hr 10min); Trieste, usually changing at Venice-Mestre (9 daily; 5hr–6hr 15min); Milan (18 daily; 2hr 50min–4hr 50min); Arezzo (hourly; 1hr); Bologna/Ancona/Rimini (hourly; 1hr 30min/2hr 30min–4hr/3hr 30min–6hr); Bologna direct (2 per hour; 1hr 5min–1hr 40min); Genova (hourly; 3hr 10min–4hr 30min); Pistoia/Lucca/Viareggio (hourly; 30–45min/1hr 5min–1hr 50min/1hr 30min–2hr 25min); Pisa central (2 per hour; 55min); Pisa airport (hourly; 1hr); Empoli (3 per hour; 25min); Prato (every 30min; 20min); Perugia/Assisi/Foligno (11 daily; 2hr 10min/2hr 35min/2hr 55min), plus 1 daily to Perugia only; Verona/Bolzano (14 daily; 2hr 40min–3hr 40min/ 5hr 50min/4hr 10min); Bari (12 daily; 8hr 15min– 9hr), 7 continuing to Lecce (10hr 25min–12hr); Reggio Calabria (from Florence Campo Marte station, 4 direct trains daily; 11hr / from Florence Santa Maria Novella station, changing at Rome, 7 daily; 11hr).

From Pistoia to Florence (hourly; 30-45min); Lucca (hourly; 35min–1hr); Bologna (hourly; 1hr).

From Arezzo to Florence (hourly; 1hr); Rome (hourly; 1hr 40min), most calling at Orvieto (1hr 15min); Chiusi (hourly; 1hr); Assisi (2 daily; 1hr 35min); Perugia/Foligno (every 2hr; 1hr 15min/1hr 50min); Terni (1daily; 2hr 35min); Camucia, for Cortona (hourly; 20min); Verona/Trento/Bolzano (5 daily; 5hr 15min/7hr/7hr 30min); Venice/Udine (5 daily; 5hr 10min/7hr). Plus *LFI* services to Bibbiena & Poppi (every 1–2hr; 50min & 57min).

From Pisa Fto lorence (hourly – all trains start at *Pisa Aeropuerto*; 1hr), via Empoli (35min; change for Volterra and Siena); Lucca (hourly; 30min); Viareggio (half hourly; 20min); Livorno (every 20min; 15–30min).

From Lucca to Pisa (hourly; 30min); Florence (hourly; 1hr 5min–1hr50min), Viareggio (hourly; 35min).

From Viareggio to Pisa (half-hourly; 20min); Livorno (hourly; 40min); Lucca (hourly; 35min).
From Livorno to Rome (half-hourly; 3–4hr); La Spézia (5 daily; 1hr 20min).

Buses

From Florence *SITA* services to Barberino di Mugello (17 daily; 40min); Bibbiena (8 daily; 2hr 15min); Certaldo (4 daily; 2hr 20min); Castellina in Chianti (1 daily; 1hr 35min); Gaiole (2 daily Mon–Fri; 2hr); Greve (around 25 daily; 1hr 5min); Poggibonsi (10 daily; 1hr 20min); Pontassieve (12 daily; 50min); Poppi (9 daily; 2hr 5min); Radda in Chianti (1 daily Mon–Sat; 1hr 40min); San Casciano (14 daily; 40min); Siena (12 express daily; 1hr 15min / plus 9 stopping services); Volterra (6 daily; 2hr 25min).

Other services include:

Lazzi to Empoli, Livorno, Lucca, Montevarchi, Pisa, Pistoia, Prato and Viareggio.

CLAP to Lucca and Lucca province.

CAT to Anghiari, Arezzo and San Sepolcro.

CAP to Borgo San Lorenzo, Impruneta and Prato.

COPIT to Pistoia, Poggio e Caiano and Vinci.

RAMA to Grosseto.

From Arezzo to Sansepolcro (6 daily; 1hr); Bibbiena & La Verna (1 daily – change at Bibbiena for Poppi & Camáldoli); Cortona (hourly Mon–Sat, 3 on Sun; 50min); Siena (1 daily).

From Cortona to Arezzo (hourly; 50min); Castiglion del Lago (7 daily; 1hr); Chianciano (4 daily; 1hr).

From Siena to Arezzo (4 daily; 2hr); Buonconvento (10 daily; 35min); Florence (30 daily, last at 8.15pm; 1hr30–3hr); Grosetto (4 daily; 2hr); Massa Maríttima (4 daily;1hr 40min); Montalcino (3 daily; 1hr); Montepulciano (4 daily; 1hr 20min); Abbadia San Salvatore (3 daily; 1hr 20min); San Galgano (3 daily; 40min); San Gimignano (16 daily via Poggibonsi; 1hr–1hr 30min); Volterra (6 daily; 2hr).

From Volterra to Florence (4 daily; 2hr); Siena (5 daily; 1hr); San Gimignano (4 daily; 25min).

From Massa Maríttima to Follonica (every 45min; 15min; Piombino (2 daily; 25min); Siena (2 daily; 1hr 40min); San Galgano (2 daily; 1hr).
From Montepulciano to Pienza–Santo Quirico–Torrenieri–Buonconvento (7 daily; 20min/40min/50min/1hr; 4 continue to Siena); Chianciano/Chiusi (every 30min; 25min/50min).
From Torrenieri to Montalcino (15 daily; 20min); Buonconvento (6 daily; 25min); Arcidosso (6 daily; 40min); Grosseto (2 daily; 1hr 20min).
From Montalcino to Buonconvento (hourly – change for Siena; 35min); Monte Ammiata (5 daily; 1hr).
From Poggibonsi Innumerable connections, including San Gimignano (17 daily; 35min).
From San Gimignano to Poggibonsi (17 daily; 35min); Florence (10 daily; 2hr 25min); Volterra (5 daily; 25min).
From Chiusi to Chianciano/Montepulciano (14 daily; 30min/45min).
From Lucca to Pisa (hourly; 1hr); Pistoia (hourly; 50min); Prato (6 daily; 1hr10min); Viareggio (hourly; 20min).
From Pisa to Viareggio (hourly; 20min); Florence (hourly; 1hr 10min); Livorno (half-hourly; 20min); La Spezia (7 daily; 1hr 20min).
From Lucca to Viareggio (hourly; 25min); Pisa (hourly; 25min).
From Viareggio to Pisa (half-hourly; 35min); La Spézia (9 daily; 2hr).
From Livorno to Piombino (8 daily; 2hr); Pisa (half-hourly; 20min).

Ferries

From Livorno to Gorgona, Capraia, Portoferráio [Elba] (2 daily; 4hr to Elba); Bastia [Corsica] and Olbia [Sardinia] (daily in season, 3–4 weekly out).
From Piombino to Portoferráio [Elba] (hourly, last at 10pm; 1hr).
From Porto San Stéfano to Giglio (8 daily in season, 4 out; 55min); Giannutri (daily from May–Sept, 3 weekly the rest of the year; 1hr 20).

Flights

From Pisa to Elba (daily in season), Sardinia, Rome, etc.

CHAPTER NINE

UMBRIA

Often referred to as "the green heart of Italy", **Umbria** is a beautiful region of rolling hills, woods, streams and valleys, and despite the growing number of visitors has largely retained an unspoilt air. Within its borders it also contains a dozen or so classic hill towns, each resolutely individual and crammed with artistic and architectural treasures to rival bigger and more famous cities.

Umbria was named by the Romans after the mysterious Umbrii, a tribe cited by Pliny as the oldest in Italy, and one that controlled territory reaching into present-day Tuscany and the Marche. Their influence was mainly confined to the east of the Tiber, the darker and bleaker towns to the west – such as Perugia and Orvieto – being founded by the Etruscans, whose rise forced the Umbrii to retreat into the eastern hills. Roman domination was eventually destroyed by the barbarian invasions, in the face of which the Umbrians withdrew into fortified hill towns, paving the way for a pattern of bloody rivalry between independent city states that continued through the Middle Ages. Weakened by constant warfare, the towns finally fell to the papacy, entering a period of economic and cultural stagnation that has continued almost to the present day.

Historically, however, Umbria is best known as the birthplace of **Saint Francis of Assisi**, and a religious tradition that earned the region such names as *Umbra santa*, *Umbra mistica* and *la terra dei santi* (land of saints). The landscape itself has contributed much to this mystical reputation, and even on a fleeting trip it's impossible to miss the strange quality of the Umbrian light, the silver haze that hangs over the gentle curves of the land.

After years as an impoverished backwater, Umbria has begun to capitalise on its charms. Foreign acquisition of rural property is now as rapid as it was in Tuscany twenty years ago, but the area now projects a renewed sense of identity and a youthful enthusiasm, and artistic initiatives have turned Umbria into one of the most flourishing cultural centres in Italy.

Most visitors head for **Perugia**, **Assisi** – with its extraordinary frescoes by Giotto in the Basilica di San Francesco – or **Orvieto**, where the Duomo is one of the greatest Gothic buildings in the country. For a taste of the region's more understated qualities, it's best to concentrate on lesser-known places such as **Todi**, **Gubbio** – ranked as the most perfect medieval centre in Italy – and **Spoleto**, for many people the outstanding Umbrian town. Although there are few unattractive parts of the Umbrian landscape (the factories of Terni and the Tiber valley being the largest blots), some districts are especially enticing: principally the mountainous **Valderina** and **Lago di Trasimeno**, which is the largest lake in the Italian peninsula, with plenty of opportunities for swimming and watersports.

Getting around the region by public transport presents no problems. Distances between the main sights are short, and there are excellent rail links both within the region and to both Florence and Rome.

PERUGIA AND THE NORTH

Most of what you'll want to see in Umbria is accessible from Perugia. Trains run out to all the major highlights, complemented by fast new roads and an extensive if complicated bus network. The north is bleaker than much of the region, short on towns and communications, but home to **Gubbio**, one of Italy's medieval gems, as well as miles of high, wooded countryside. Out to the west is the placid and low-hilled **Lago Trasimeno**, scenically less spectacular, but preferable to the dreary Tiber valley northwards, and the first chance after Florence to put your feet up on a beach. Perugia's uncharacteristic metropolitan bustle shouldn't deter you from pushing on into Umbria's more rustic and appealing hinterland.

Perugia

Provincial capital, large, central and modern, **PERUGIA** is the most obvious, if not the most picturesque base to kick off a tour of Umbria. As usual the centre of town is still medieval, but it's surrounded by miles of fairly ugly suburbs and not a little industry. *Buitoni*, the pasta people, have a big works, and Italy's best chocolate, Perugini, is made here. Come summer the streets become claustrophobic and exhausting: if your idea of Umbria is rural peace and quiet and lolling around old hill towns – and really that's what the region is about – you probably won't want to spend a lot of time here. On the other hand there's a day's worth of good sightseeing plus some big-city attractions and the chance to catch up with other travellers.

The main draw in the summer is **Umbria Jazz**, Italy's foremost jazz event, whose line-ups may well tempt you into staying – past stars have included Miles Davis, Sting, Stan Getz, Gil Evans and Wynton Marsalis. Information and tickets are best sussed out well in advance from the **AAST**, Corso Vannucci 94a (☎075/23.327).

The presence of the **Università Italiana per Stranieri** (the Italian University for Foreigners) is another plus – set up by Mussolini to improve the image of Italy abroad, it's now run as a private concern and gives the town a welcome dash of style and an unexpectedly cosmopolitan flavour. The big state university also means there's an above-average number of films, concerts and miscellaneous cultural events, stuff you won't get elsewhere in the region.

Arriving and orientation

If you're **arriving** by car be prepared for hassle: all the town's approaches are up steep hills and the signposting leaves plenty to be desired. Parking in the centre is a nightmare (it's closed to traffic at peak times anyway) and you'll do best to leave the car at the main railway station and take a bus. Alternatively you could head towards one of the big peripheral carparks such as Piazza Partigiani (also the **bus terminus** for inter-town buses) and then jump on an escalator (really) through some weird subterranean streets to the centre. Buses #26, #27, #29 and #32–36 all run to Piazza Italia or Piazza Matteotti from the station (15min). Tickets are valid for either forty or seventy minutes, and if the small booth in the forecourt is shut, they are available from the small machine next to the station entrance. The walk from the station to the centre is an ordeal of cars, dust and high-rises – not even to be considered.

Once safely in Piazza Italia, however, **orientation** is straightforward. The town hinges around a stylish single street, the Corso Vannucci, a broad pedestrian thoroughfare constantly buzzing with action and one of the country's best for people-watching or striking up conversations. Bar the odd church, it's also at the heart of everything you'll want to see.

The town centre

At the far end of the Corso Vannucci is the big and austere **Piazza Quattro Novembre** (once a Roman reservoir), backed by the plain-faced **duomo**, recently reopened after damage caused by the 1983 earthquake. You feel maybe they shouldn't have bothered, because while the Baroque interior is big on size, it's pretty small on works of art, and comes as a disappointment after the fifteenth-century facade. As a change from pieces of the True Cross, one of the chapels contains the Virgin's "wedding ring", an unwieldy one-inch-diameter piece of agate that changes colour according to the character of the person wearing it. The Perugians keep it locked up in fifteen boxes fitted into one another like Russian dolls, each opened with a key held by a different person. It's brought out for general public edification once a year on July 30. In one of the transepts there's an urn holding the ashes of Pope Martin IV, who died in the city after eating too many eels. Urban IV's remains are here too – he was reputedly poisoned with "aquetta", an imaginative little brew made by rubbing white arsenic into pork fat and distilling the unpleasantness that oozes out.

Outside in the piazza (which is the town's main hangout), the centrepiece is the **Fontana Maggiore**, designed by Fra Bevignate, the monk who had a hand in the shaping of Orvieto's cathedral, and sculpted by the father and son team, Nicola and Giovanni Pisano. The sculptures and bas-reliefs on the two basins – now decidedly the worse for wear – describe episodes from the the the Old Testament, classical myth, Aesop's fables and the twelve months of the year. By some canny design work they never line up directly, encouraging you to walk round the fountain chasing a point of repose that never comes.

Just opposite rises the gaunt mass of the **Palazzo dei Priori**, hyped by normally reserved Italian guides as one of the greatest public palaces in Italy. Sheer bulk aside, it's certainly impressive – with rows of trefoil windows (from which convicted criminals were thrown to their deaths), majestic Gothic doorway, and business-like Guelph crenellations – but the overall effect is rather grim; its real beauty derives from the overall harmony set up by the medieval buildings around it. The **Sala dei Notari** (the lawyers' meeting hall), at the top of the fan-shaped steps is noted for its frescoes – lots of colour, fancy flags, swirls and no substance – but it's free to get in, so worth a quick glance. (9am–1pm & 3–6pm).

The **Collegio della Mercanzia**, further down the Corso side of the palace and hidden behind an innocuous door, was the seat of the Merchants' Guild, and is a small room covered entirely in intricate fifteenth-century panelling. (9am–12.30pm & 2.30–5.30pm, closed Mon & Sun afternoon; L2000). The admission also gets you into the more impressive **Collegio di Cambio** a few doors down – the town's medieval money exchange – its walls superbly frescoed by Perugino at the height of his powers. They're considered the artist's masterpiece, and in true Renaissance fashion represent an attempt to fuse ancient and Christian culture. Up on the door-side wall there's a famous but unremarkable self-portrait with the artist looking like he had a bad lunch. The small chapel to the right of the Collegio is frescoed by Giannicola di Paolo (1519), the last important Umbrian painter influenced by Perugino.

The **Galleria Nazionale di Umbria** (closed Mon 9am–2pm; L4000) is on the fourth floor of the palace complex, with the entrance through its opulently carved **doorway**. (You have to push past harassed-looking Perugians on their way to do

battle with council bureaucracy on the other floors.) It's one of central Italy's biggest and best – a 33-room romp through the history of Umbrian painting (not all second division religious stuff as some people make out) with one or two stunning Florentine masterpieces (Fra Angelico, Piero della Francesca) and early Sienese works (Duccio) thrown in for good measure. The rooms could do with brightening up, but the entrance is worth every penny if you're the slightest bit interested in early and mid-Renaissance art. Be warned, though, that a major restructuring is under way, and the rooms devoted to Perugino and Pintoricchio – potentially the most appealing – may be closed or missing certain paintings.

There are one or two ritzy **bars** on the Corso, worth at least one pricey cappuccino just for the streetlife. *Cafe'del Cambio* at no. 29 is the trendiest. The easily missed *Pasticceria Sandri* at no. 32 opposite is the most atmospheric – turn-of-the-century Viennese style with lots of brass, wood panels and frescoed ceilings and not the rip-off it appears from outside. At the top left-hand corner of the piazza via delle Volte bear right to Piazza Morlacchi with *Bar Morlacchi* at no. 6. It looks dubiously smart and expensive but it's aimed at students, so not to worry.

North and west of Corso Vannucci

The best streets to wander around for a feel of the old city are right and left of the duomo, **Via dei Priori** being the most characteristic. In the Via della Gabbia part way down there once hung a large iron cage used to imprison thieves and sometimes even clergy. In January 1442, wrote a medieval chronicler, priest Angelo di Ferolo "was put back into the cage at midday, and it was very cold and there was much snow, and he remained there until the first day of February both night and day and that same day he was brought out dead." You can still make out long spikes on some of the lower walls, used as hooks for the heads of executed criminals. Medieval Perugia was evidently a hell of a place to be. "The most warlike of the people of Italy," wrote the historian Sismondi, "who always preferred Mars to the Muse". Male citizens played a game (and this was for pleasure) in which two teams, thickly padded in clothes stuffed with deer hair, and wearing beaked helmets, stoned each other mercilessly until the majority of the other side were dead or wounded. Children were encouraged to join in for the first two hours to promote "application and aggression".

In 1265 Perugia was also the birthplace of the **Flagellants**, who had half of Europe whipping itself into a frenzy before the movement was declared heretical. In addition to some hearty scourging they took to the streets on moonlit nights, groaning and wailing, dancing in white sheets, singing dirges and clattering human bones together, all as expiation for sin and the wrongs of the world. Then there were the infamous **Baglioni**, the medieval family who misruled the city for several generations, their spell-binding history – full of vendetta, incest, mass-slaughter – the stuff of great medieval soap-opera.

Via dei Priori passes **Madonna della Luce** on the right after the medieval Torre degli Scirri, little more than a chapel dominated by an impressive altarpiece (by a follower of Perugino). It takes its name – Madonna of the Light – from the story that in 1513 a young barber swore so profusely on losing at cards that a Madonna in a wayside shrine closed her eyes in horror and kept them closed for four days. The miracle caused celebrations, processions and the building of a new church. Some way beyond is a nice patch of grass perfectly placed for relaxing with the crowd from the art school next door or for admiring Agostino di Duccio's colourful **Oratorio di San Bernardino**, whose richly embellished facade (1461) is far and away the best piece of sculpture in the city. To the right is what's left of San Francesco, once a colossal church, now ruined by centuries of earthquakes and neglect, but with a curiously jumbled and striking facade still just about standing.

From here you can wander round via A. Pascoli, past the hideous university buildings, to the **Università Italiana per Stranieri** in Piazza Fortebraccio. The big patched-up gateway here is the **Arco di Augusto** – its lowest section one of the few remaining monuments of Etruscan Perugia. The upper remnant was added by the Romans when they captured the city in 40 BC. The university bar atmosphere is friendly and cosmopolitan – obviously a good place for contacts – but don't expect much joy out of the (surely ironically titled) Information Desk in the foyer. Posters around the place give details of concerts and English films, (especially in the summer). Terms run from April to December.

About a minute's walk away on Corso Garibaldi is the sadly half-defunct **Sant'Agostino**, once Romanesque, now botched Baroque and filled with wistful signs explaining what paintings used to hang in the church before they were spirited to France by light-fingered Napoleonic troops. The missing pictures have been replaced with some horrendously inappropriate pieces of what someone somewhere obviously considers "modern art" . The church , however, is not entirely ruined: there's a beautiful choir (probably based on a drawing by Perugino) and a couple of patches of fresco on the left-hand wall, giving a tantalising idea of what the place must once have been. Next door to the left is the fifteenth-century **Oratorio di Sant'Agostino**, its ludicrously ornate ceiling looking as if it's about to erupt in an explosion of gilt, stucco and chubby plaster cherubs. Fifteen minutes walk up the street is the fifth-century church of **Sant'Angelo**, situated in a tranquil spot and based on a circular pagan temple. The 24 columns, each made from a different stone, are from the earlier building.

Corso Cavour

The rest of Perugia's highlights are on the other side of town, grouped together on **Corso Cavour**, a busy and dustily unpleasant road in the summer, and just plain unpleasant the rest of the time. On the way over you could join the smooching couples in the small but well-kept **Giardini Carducci** (Piazza Italia) to see why Henry James called Perugia the "little city of the infinite views". When the haze lifts – which except on crisp winter mornings isn't often – half of Umbria is laid out before you, with the mountains of Tuscany in the distance.

Below the Piazza you could take a short walk past the strange octagonal church of **Sant'Ercolano** (rarely open) – built on the site where the head of Perugia's first bishop miraculously reattached itself to his body after the Goths chopped it off – and through the Porta Marzia, where a subterranean road of medieval houses (Via Baglioni Sotteranea) leads under the ruins of the Rocca Paolina (a once-enormous Papal fortress destroyed by the Perugians at Unification). You come eventually to **San Domenico**.

The church, Umbria's biggest, has a desolate and unfinished air from the outside – pigeons nesting where they shouldn't, grass growing from the pinky-orange marble – but it's also pretty in a big and sad sort of way. The original Romanesque interior, however, collapsed in the sixteenth century and the Baroque replacement is vast, cold and bare, something like an EC warehouse waiting for a food-mountain. Like Sant'Agostino, however, it's full of hints as to how beautiful it must have been; nowhere more so than in the fourth chapel on

496/U M B R I A

the right, where a superb **carved arch** by Agostino di Duccio, spoilt only by Victorian Christmas card decorations and a doll-like Madonna. At the top of the church, to the right of the altar, is the **tomb of Benedict XI** (1324), another Pope who died in Perugia, this time from eating poisoned figs. It's an elegant and well-preserved piece by one of the period's three leading sculptors, Pisano, Lorenzo Maitini or Arnolfo di Cambio, no-one knows which. There's also another good choir, and – a welcome splash of colour in the midst of all the mud-coloured paint – some impressive **stained glass** windows, the second biggest in Italy after those in Milan Cathedral.

Housed in the church's cloisters is the **Museo Archeologico Nazionale dell'Umbria** (Tues–Sat 9am–2pm, Sun 9am–1pm; L2000). Before being hammered by Augustus, Perugia was a big-shot in the twelve-strong Etruscan federation of cities, which is why this museum has one of the most extensive Etruscan collections around. There's also a sizeable section devoted to pre-history. If the Etruscans get you going you might try the local tombs, the **Pogeo dei Volumni** (Tues–Sat 9am–5pm, Sun 9am–1pm; L2000), seven kilometres east of the town (bus or train to Ponte San Giovanni and then a short walk). Though the best in Umbria, they're quite small and without any of the usual racy paintings; not a patch on the graves at Tarquinia or Cerveteri (see *Rome and Lazio* chapter).

Further on down the Corso Cavour, advertised by a rocket-shaped bell tower, is the tenth-century basilica of **San Pietro**, the most idiosyncratic of all the town's churches. It's tangled up in a group of buildings belonging to the university's agriculture department, the none too obvious entrance being through a frescoed doorway in the far left-hand corner of the first courtyard off the road. Few churches can be so sumptuously decorated – every inch of available space being covered in gilt, paint or marble. Things appear to have been done with a sense of taste rather than to create some intimidating effect, and in the candle-lit gloom it actually feels like the sacred place it's meant to be. All the woodwork is extraordinary: **the choir** has been called the best in Italy, and there is a host of works by Perugino, Fiorenzo di Lorenzo and others.

Practicalities

The friendly **AAST** is at 94a Corso Vannucci past the big Standa supermarket (☎075/23.327). A second, smaller office opens at the station during the summer. They have a room-finding service and lots of semi-useful bumph, though the maps are fourth-rate. Cheap and central **accommodation** is no problem. The **youth hostel**, two minutes from the duomo, Via Bontempi 13(☎075/22880), is nicely situated, pleasant, and you don't need IYHF membership. It's closed from 9.30am though, and there's a midnight curfew. As for hotel rooms try *Anna*, Via dei Priori 48 (☎075/66.304), *Piccolo*, Via Bonazzi 25, *Etruria*,Via della Luna 21, or *Lory* and *Rosalba* (in that order) at Corso Vannucci 10 (☎075/24.266 and 28.285). *Pensione Paola*, Via della Canapina 25, is hard to find – follow signs for the Hotel Umbria off the Corso and then bear left – but popular, so try and call in advance (☎075/23.816). In the summer it's possible to rent empty university rooms dirt cheap, but they're not central and there's a lot of bureaucratic hassle involved. For info try the **CTGS Student Centre**, Via del Roscetto 21. The *Il Rocco* and *Paradise d'Ete* campsites are five kilometres out of town at Colle della Trinità (#36 bus and a short uphill walk) but you're better off heading to the superior sites on Lago Trasimeno (see below).

On the **food** front, there's a lot of *Perugino* chocolate about, plus the inevitable ice cream – try *Gelateria 2000*, Via L. Bonazzi 3 – and plenty of cheap basic **pizzerias**. The tiny *Da Peppino* (at Via Danzetta 9 – a small alley opposite the *Banco Commerciale Italia* on Corso Vannucci) is highly typical Italian greasy spoon, run by a quiet old couple straight out of Fellini, serving simple, good value food in even more simple surroundings. Otherwise you could try: *La Botte*,Via Volte della Pace 31; *Tavola Calda*, Piazza Dante 16; *Pizza Medioveo*, Via Baldo; *Trattoria Brizi*, Via Fabretti 75 – close to the Università per Stranieri; – or the very large *Pizza Grimana*, Via Scortici 6 – ditto. They're all busy student hangouts. Further afield there's *Cavour*, Via Cavour 28, and *Cantinone*, Via Ritorta 6. Best of the upmarket places is *La Fontenella*, Piazza Piccinino 11, which is cheap if you stick to basics.

Lago Trasimeno

The most tempting option around Perugia – whose surroundings are generally pretty bleak – is **LAGO TRASIMENO**, an ideal spot to hole up for a few days, and particularly recommended if you want to get in some **swimming**. It's the biggest stretch of water on the Italian peninsula, the fourth largest in Italy overall, and, though you wouldn't think so to look at it, never deeper than seven metres – hence bath-like warm water in summer. And because the tourist and fishing industries are the economic bread and butter of the surrounding towns it's also clean. Large banks of weed drift in during the summer, but the council takes care of these, dumping them with little subtlety on the shore.

A winning combination of tree-covered hills to the north, Umbria's subtle light, and miles of placid lapping water produces some magical moments, but on overcast and squally days the mood can turn melancholy. Not all the reed-lined shore is uniformly pretty either; steer clear of the northern coast recently opened up by Perugia's new motorway spur, and head for the stretches south of Magione and Castiglione if you're after relative peace and quiet. Be warned, too, that **unofficial camping** is not as easy as it looks, partly because a lot of the immediate shoreline is marshy, but mainly because many of the good spots have already been grabbed by locals.

Passingnano
PASSINGNANO, a newish town with a medieval heart, strung out along the northern shore, and served by hourly trains from Perugia and Terontola (30min), is the lake's most accessible point. Popular with Italians whose idea of a day out is to spend the whole day in a car, the town in summer often resembles nothing so much as a big traffic jam. In the evenings, however, when people come flooding in from the surrounding campsites, the place is jumping, with bars, discos and fish restaurants aplenty. There are dozens of **rooms**, none of them particularly cheap – the best value are *Aviazione*, Via Roma 54, and *Beaurivage*, Via L. A. Pompili.

Somewhere on the coast towards TUORO, probably at Sanguineto ("the Place of Blood") or Ossaia ("the Place of Bones") is the spot where the Romans suffered their famous clobbering at the hands of **Hannibal** in 217 BC. Hannibal was headed for Rome, having just crossed the Alps, when he was met by a Roman force under the Consul Flaminius. Things might have gone better for Flaminius if he'd heeded the omens that piled up on the morning of battle. First he fell off his horse, next the legionary standards had to be dug out of the mud, then – and this really should have raised suspicions – the sacred chickens refused their breakfast. Poultry accompanied all Roman armies, and by some means presumably known to the legionnaire in charge of chickens, communicated the will of the gods to waiting commanders in the field. With the chickens against him Flaminius didn't stand a chance. Hannibal lured him into a masterful ambush, with the only escape a muddy retreat into the lake. Sixteen thousand Romans, including the hapless commander, were killed.

Tuoro sul Trasimeno
TUORO, three kilometres' walk from the supposed battlefield, is a quieter base from which to explore the switchback mountains north of the lake, the best of the **scenery** within easy reach of Perugia. The area's pretty desolate, but the village of **Castel Rigone** stands out, with some superb views and an outstanding Renaissance church, **Madonna dei Miracoli**.

There's also some good **walking**, with treks possible up Mount Castiglione (802m) on the mule track from the Gosparani Pass (7km north of Tuoro), Mount Acuto (926m) taking Galera or Montacuto as the starting point, or Mount Murlo (818m) reached from PREGGIO, a hill village worth a look in its own right. With a car, this could also be a good time to cross the border into Tuscany to visit CORTONA (26km).

Castiglione del Lago
CASTIGLIONE DEL LAGO is the most appealing town on the lake and cuts a fine silhouette from other points around the shore, jutting out into the water on a fortified promontory. In the event it doesn't live up to its distant promise, but is still a friendly, unpretentious place with enough charm and action to hold anyone's interest for a couple of days – longer if all you want to do is crash out on an (albeit modest) beach. It's easy to reach by rail, though as a lot of the new Inter-City trains on the Rome–Florence run no longer stop here, you'll probably end up taking a slow "locale" either from Chiusi (heading north) or Terontola if you're coming from Arezzo or Perugia.

There's a good **AAST** in the single main square (Piazza Mazzini 10) whose flashiness in such a small town suggests an imminent inundation of tourists. They have a lot of reasonable but characterless **rooms** on their books, and apartments to rent on a weekly basis, usually a cheaper option if you can get a party together and plan on staying. Most of the **campsites** are off the main road some way south of the town. *Lido Trasimeno* on the shore north of the castle has good facilities (swimming, **windsurfing school**, sailing etc.), but it's next to a training school for police alsations. Best **eating**, outside the summer-only restaurants on the promenade, is the excellent *La Cantina*, at the lower end of the old town's single main street. Best **swimming** is at the public lido on the southern side of the promontory.

Regular boats make the trip out to the **Isola Maggiore**, one of the lake's three islands, a fun ride if you don't mind the crowds and some steep prices in the couple of restaurants when you get there. There's a pretty walk round the edge of the island, and you should have no problem pitching a tent when everyone else has packed up and gone home.

Panicale

The surrounding countryside is best appreciated from a reclining position on the beach. The low hills make a good scenic backdrop but they're not worth exploring, though if you have a car **Panicale** to the south has some picture-postcard views of the lake, plus two easily-missed Peruginos tucked away in the church of San Sebastiano (off Piazza Vittoria). During the town's April fiesta, thanks to some miraculous plumbing, the fountains run with wine; well worth checking out.

The Upper Tiber

Rome's great and famously polluted river, the Tiber, actually spends most of its short life in Umbria, rising in the Alpe della Luna (the mountains of the moon) above Sansepolcro. In its rather unexciting upper reaches north of Perugia – largely given over to sheep and fields of tobacco – you're faced with the familiar problem that everything you don't want to see is easily accessible and everything you do is out of reach without a car, bike or lucky hitch. **The Central Umbrian Railway** and fast N3 to Sansepolcro are perfect for Città di Castello, the area's only town of note, after which you'll probably want to strike east on the N257 across the mountains to Urbino (70km). The best reason to follow the Tiber is to stay on the trail of **Piero della Francesca's** mysterious and unsettling masterpieces at Sansepolcro, Arezzo and Monterchi.

The region's best aspect, in fact, is not the valley, but the desolate countryside on either side, regions, which like the Valnerina in the east, give the lie to the notion of Umbria as some sort of pastoral idyll. With few roads and fewer villages, but thousands of hectares of natural woodland and abandoned pasture, it teems with protected wildlife, including many rare species of birds, deer, wild boar and even wolves, now apparently pushing further up the Italian peninsula every year. **Pietralunga** and **Apecchio** to the north are the best exploring bases, with a **campsite** at Candeleto close to the first (*La Pineta*, open from June to mid-Sept), but there's obviously plenty of scope for solo camping if you're geared up.

Umbertide

UMBERTIDE is modern and lightly industrial, having been bombed almost to oblivion in the last war, but it doesn't come over as a place which had much going for it in the first place. It's only useful (and then only if you have transport) for trips into the surrounding hills. The big castle, **Civitella Ranieri**, looms invitingly to the northeast, but it's privately owned, so don't be suckered into the steep climb for a closer look. **Mount Corona** (693m), six kilometres south, has some good views and the reasonably evocative remains of a fifteenth-century monastery. The hill village of MONTONE is the one to see if you're not just passing through, thanks to a surprisingly good collection of paintings in the fifteenth-century Gothic church of San Francesco. Much further south – and with a car you could tackle this from Perugia – is the **Abbazia di Montelabate**. While the immense adjoining church of Santa Maria is second rate, the eleventh-century crypt and fourteenth-century cloisters are medieval perfection.

Città di Castello

The Church's seventh-century nickname for CITTÀ DI CASTELLO was "castrum felicitas" – the castle of happiness – though why, when it had been all but obliterated by Totila, is hard to fathom. Today there's nothing very cheerful about the place – unless you've drunk sufficient qualities of the local Colli Altotiberini **wines**, or you happen to be in town during August for its renowned **Festival of Chamber Music**.

Once an important Roman centre – the grid-iron of streets is the only legacy – today the plain-bound site is drab and preserves only a handful of fairly mediocre medieval monuments. The town's only real merit is its ten-roomed **pinacoteca** (Palazzo della Cannoniera, 22), reckoned one of the region's best after Perugia's. The collection takes in works by **Raphael, Signorelli, Ghirlandaio and Lorenzetti** (plus a wondrous *Maestà*, in Room 1, by the anonymous fourteenth-century Maestro di Città di Castello). There are also several **sculptures**, the most notable by Ghiberti, and a glittering reliquary of Florentine origin (1420).

If you stop off, then the banal reworked **Duomo** warrants a call for its museum, which contains the **treasure of Canoscio**, a precious hoard of sixth-century silver chalices dug up in 1932. The town's other more paltry offerings include a late Renaissance **choir**, located in San Francesco's Cappella Vitelli, and the fourteenth-century **Palazzo Comunale**, an imposing but unfinished work by Angelo da Orvieto, who was responsible for the vastly more impressive palaces in Gubbio.

A far more compelling option than the town itself is the recently opened **folk museum** at GARAVELLE a couple of kilometres north. It's basically an eight-eenth-century farmhouse which has been preserved with all the ordinary accou-trements of daily life – pots, pans, furniture and so forth, plus a range of exhibits covering rural activities from wine-making, weaving, carpentry through to the blacksmith's forge. Totally out of context the museum also has a **model railway collection**. Details of opening times from the **AAST** in Città di Castello at Via Raffaele di Cesare 2/b (☎075/855.4817).

Gubbio

GUBBIO is the most thoroughly medieval of the Umbrian towns, an immediately likeable place that's hanging onto its charm despite an ever-increasing influx of tourists. (It's being hailed – possible kiss of death – as the Umbrian Siena.) The streets are picture-book pretty, with houses of rosy-pink stone, and seas of orange-tiled roofs; only the market in pricey but attractive ceramics suggests seri-ous pandering to the town's sightseers. A broad and largely unspoilt plain stretches out in front (there's the odd quarry and cement works roundabouts, but out of sight), with the first high peaks of the Apennines rising behind, a lovely tree-covered backdrop which gives the place the feel of a mountain outpost – something it's always been in fact.

A powerful medieval commune, and always important as the gateway to Ravenna and the Adriatic (it was a key point on the Roman Via Flaminia), these days it's a town apart, not really part of either Umbria, Tuscany or the Marche – the reason it's been spared the onslaught of the twentieth century and why getting here can be tricky. The best **approach** is by bus from Perugia (ten a day) – with superb countryside en route – or by train from Foligno to FOSSATO DI VICO, 19km away but with an hourly connecting bus service. Coming from Città di Castello or the north (Arezzo, San Sepolcro) means back-peddling to Umbertide to pick an easy hitch over the mountains. The one road, through CAMPO REGIANO is minor but busy.

The town

Centre-stage is the immense and austere **Palazzo dei Consoli** (fourteenth-century), whose crenellated outline and 98-metre campanile command your attention for miles. Probably designed by monumental architect Matteo Gattopone – also responsible for Spoleto's Ponte delle Torri – it took a couple of hundred years to build, and required the levelling of vast tracts of the medieval town, mainly to accommodate the huge and windswept Piazza della Signoria. (The lesser **Palazzo Pretorio** opposite was built to the same architectural plan). Deliberately dominating and humbling, it was what medieval civic pride was all about, an attempt to express power and supremacy in bricks and mortar. Behind a plain square facade (there's a small hole top right where criminals were hung in a cage called *la gogna* – from *vergogna* or "shame") is a cavernous baronial hall, the Salone dell'Arengo, where council officials and leading citizens met to discuss business. The word "harangue" derives from *arengo*, so business obviously got pretty heated. It's base for the town **Museo Civico** (9am–1pm & 3–5pm; L2000), a typical miscellany, unremarkable except for the famous **Eugubine Tablets**, Umbria's most important archaeological find.

Discovered in 1444 by an illiterate shepherd, later conned into swapping priceless treasure trove for a worthless piece of land, the seven bronze tablets are more or less the only extant record of the ancient Umbrian language, a vernacular tongue without written characters. The bastardised Etruscan and Latin of their religious texts was aimed at producing a phonetic translation of the dialect using the main languages of the day. Gubbio was close to the shrine of the so-called Apennine Jove, a major pagan deity visited by pilgrims from all over Italy, so the tablets were probably the work of Roman and Etruscan priests taking advantage of the established order to impose their religious cults in a region where their languages weren't understood. Most importantly, they suggest Romans, Etruscans and Umbrians achieved some sort of co-existence, refuting a long-held belief that succeeding civilisations wiped one another out.

Admission to the museum gets you into the three-roomed **Pinacoteca** upstairs, worth a look for works by the Gubbian School Ottaviano Nelli, Guido Palmerucci – one of central Italy's earliest, and a collection of ponderous fourteenth-century furniture. Try the door at the back for views from the palace's **Loggia**. The palace also boasts 26 medieval toilets; it was the first in Italy with interior piped water.

A couple of steets above the Piazza della Signoria lurks a not very inspiring thirteenth-century **duomo**, partly redeemed by the odd fresco, twelfth-century **stained glass**, and some arches gracefully curved to emulate the meeting of hands in prayer. There are also a pair of carved **organ lofts** that for once don't look as if they'd be more at home in a fairground. The small adjoining museum is worth five minutes, mainly for a florid Flemish cope, presented to the cathedral by Pope Marcellus II, who was born in Gubbio.

The plain-faced Gothic pile is overshadowed by the **Palazzo Ducale** opposite (Tues–Sun 9am–2pm), built over an earlier Lombard palace by the Dukes of Montefeltro as a scaled-down copy of their more famous palace in Urbino. The **courtyard** is particularly good, but most of the interior has been closed for years.

On the hillside above the town stands the **Basilica of Sant'Ubaldo**, a place Gubbians drive to for their Sunday morning walk, but pleasant enough for all that. There's a very handy bar, plenty of shady spots to crash out, and some great views (even better ones if you can be bothered to climb up to the **Rocca**). There's not much to see in the Basilica itself, except the body of the town's patron saint, St.Ubaldo, who's missing three fingers, hacked off by his manservant as a religious keepsake. You can't miss the big wooden pillars (*ceri*) featured in Gubbio's annual **Corsa dei Ceri** (May 15), little known outside Italy, but second only to Siena's Palio in terms of exuberance and bizarre pageantry. The rules and rigmarole of the 900-year-old ceremony are mind-boggling, but boil down to three teams racing from Piazza della Signoria to the Basilica, carrying the *ceri* (each representing a different saint) on wooden stretchers. The *cero* of Sant'Ubaldo always wins, the other teams having to ensure they're in the Basilica before the doors are shut by the leaders. There's hours of involved ritual at either end, vast crowds and plenty of drinking. A scholarly debate rages as to whether the whole thing's intrinsically religious (commemorating the day in 1155 Ubaldo talked Barbarossa out of flattening Gubbio), or a hangover from some pagan fertility rite. Nowadays the Church not suprisingly claims it as its own, but judging by the very phallic *ceri*, and the roar that goes up when they're raised to the vertical, there's something more than religion going on.

There are several ways up to the Basilica, one being via the steep track that strikes off from behind the duomo, but it's quicker and more fun to take the **funicular** from Porta Romana, over on the other side of town. While you're waiting you could take in more of Ottaviano Nelli's paintings, tucked away in the thirteenth-century **Sant'Agostino** and **Santa Maria Nuova** nearby. The unusually lovely *Madonna del Belvedere* (1408) in the latter is a masterpiece of the detailed and highly decorative style for which he was famous. His most majestic efforts – seventeen frescoes on the life of the Virgin – are in **San Francesco**, the big church that dominates the Piazza dei Quaranta Martiri at the foot of the town. The piazza's named in memory of forty citizens shot by the Germans in 1944, a reprisal for partisan attacks in the surrounding hills.

Gubbios's **porte della morte**, the "doors of death", are as controversial as phallic *ceri*. Almost unique to the town (there are a few others in Assisi and southern France), they're narrow, bricked-up doorways wedged into the facades of its medieval townhouses (with the best examples in via dei Consoli). The party line is that they were used to carry a coffin out of a house, and then having been tainted with death, were sealed up out of superstitious fear. Nice theory, and very Italian, but judging by the constricted stairways behind the doors, their purpose was probably defensive – the main door could be barricaded, leaving the more easily defended passageway as the only entrance.

There are dozens of picturesque odds and ends around the streets, which are as wonderfully explorable as any in the region. The **Bargello** in via dei Consoli, the medieval police station, is worth tracking down, and gives you the chance to survey the adjacent **Fontana dei Matti** (the "fountain of the mad"), otherwise undistinguished but for the tradition that anyone walking round it three times (unless being honoured in a special ceremony) will wind up mad. There's usually someone wondering whether to give it a go.

Practicalities

You shouldn't have any problem **staying** in Gubbio, though the place gets busy, and too many of the hotels and restaurants cater to well-heeled Italians. It's a good place to pass a couple of days, and if you have your own transport, perfect for trips into the hills and neighbouring towns. Check for cheap **rooms** with the **AAST**,

Piazza Odersi 6, (☎075/927.3693), or try *Locanda Galletti,*Via Piccadi 3 (☎075/927.4247), *Grotta dell'Angelo*, via Gioia 47 (☎075/927.3438) or, if funds allow, the popular and perfectly placed *Albergo dei Consoli* at Via dei Consoli 59 (☎075/927.3335). There's a good selection of **eateries**, including the upper-bracket *Taverna del Lupo* ,Via Repubblica 41; the touristy *Porta Tessenaca*, Via Piccardi 21 and, if you want to be outdoors, the *Trattoria San Martino*, Via dei Consoli 8. Best cheap **pizzeria** (and there are plenty) is *Il Bargello,*Via dei Consoli 37.

Around Gualdo and Nocera Umbra

GUALDO TADINO, like Gubbio, is distinct from the rest of Umbria, and, similarly mountain-outpost in character. Sprawling over the lower slopes of the Apennines, it has a bleakly medieval centre, hedged about with light industry, and unplanned housing around the station and plain below. It's easy to reach, with frequent **trains** from Foligno and Fabriano, and deserves more attention than it gets. With Umbrian and Roman origins, its single historical claim to fame was as witness to the death of Totila the Hun, who was slain by the Romans under the town walls.

The only remarkable thing about the thirteenth-century Gothic **duomo** is that the facade has two tiers instead of Umbria's usual three; the interior, done to death in the nineteenth century, has absolutely nothing to recommend it. The **Pinacoteca**, housed in the angular San Francesco, is far more interesting, with an impressive collection for so modest a town. Much space is given to local painters such as Matteo da Gualdo (fifteenth-century), but the centrepiece is a polyptych by **Nicolò Alunno**, considered unsurpassed amongst the central Italian artists before Perugino. Without the sugary quality of some Umbrian offerings – all soft-focus saints and dewy-eyed Madonnas – Alunno has a harder edge and a wider and more genuine range of emotion.

Without a lot to see or do, you'll be here for the flavour, which you could easily soak up between trains. Cheapest **rooms** if you need them, are at *Centro Sociale Verde Soggiorno*, Via del Bosco 50 (☎075/916.263), or at the five-roomed *Da Anna* 5km south in BOSCHETTO. (☎075/810.171). The best **food** is at *Gigiotto*, Via Morone, 5. The **AAST** at Via Calai 39 will fill in the gaps.

Whether you make the fifteen-kilometre trip south to **NORCERA UMBRA** depends whether you're sticking with Umbria, or heading to URBINO or FABRIANO in the Marche. The rail links, and the N3 and N76 roads are the major (virtually the only) routes east, making Gualdo an important watershed. Highly accessible, Norcera itself could just as easily be seen from Assisi, 20km away to the southwest. Hitching locally is a doddle, and there are plenty of trains. A place for a flying visit, it's yet another hill town, middling by Umbrian standards, and with a sizeable new town on the valley floor to detract from its medieval charms. It's most famous for its **mineral waters**, exported worldwide, and renowned since the sixteenth century when people came from as far afield as Portugal and Turkey, lured by reputedly miraculous cures. (The biggest public **spa** is at BAGNI DI NOCERA, 4km southeast on the COLFIORITO road).

Attractions are sparse, limited to the usual warren of streets, a nondescript fifteenth-century duomo (ransacked in the eighteenth century), and an extraordinarily good **art gallery** (secreted away in the church of San Francesco). Local artists predominate, as in Gualdo, and there's another big canvas attributed to

Nicolò Alunno. If you've got transport, the villages and hilly countryside to the east repay aimless exploration, and there's a scenic route over to MATELICA (45km) in the Marche.

The mountains

The "mountain resort" of **VALSORDA**, 8km northeast of Gualdo (bus service), is a launching pad for **hill walks**, and at a height of 1000m, a reasonably scenic, if developed spot in its own right. You can tackle the straightforward trek up the **Serra Santa** (1421m), on a track of motorway dimensions, carved out by pilgrims over the years, or press on along the more difficult ridge to Monte Penna (1432m) and Monte Maggio to the north. Base camp in either case could be the **campsite** at Valsorda (May 20–Oct 10; ☎075/913.261), or the one-star pensione *Narciso*, which also doubles as a restaurant (☎075/913.282).

Head north past FOSSATO DI VICO (passable old town on the hill with eleventh-century Romanesque gem, **San Pietro**, and Nelli frescoes in the Cappella della Piaggiola) and you stumble across one of Umbria's bigger surprises, the **Grotta di Mount Cucco**, at 922 metres the fifth deepest cave system in the world, and gradually being opened up to the public. There are buses from Perugia, Fano and Foligno. The best place to go whether you want to get seriously wet and muddy, or just tag along with a tour party, is the **Centro Nazionale di Speleologia** in COSTACCIARO, 17km north of Gualdo on the N3 – you'll find it at Corso Mazzini 9 (☎075/917.0236). As well as the lowdown on caving, they issue a 1:16,000 map of local walks, and have details on a wealth of outdoor pursuits, with a special bias towards **hang gliding**. This is the operations end of the set-up; for more general background you should contact the office in Perugia (Via Fabretti 6; ☎075/28613). If you're not into this sort of thing or scenery for its own sake, the whole area's going to be a bit of a letdown.

There's a **youth hostel** at nearby SIGILLO (*Ostello Villa Scirca* ☎075/917.0307) and a **campsite**, the *Rio Verde*, at FORNACE near Costacciaro (☎075/917.0138 April–Sept). The restaurant *Zio Brando*, 1100m up in the Val di Ranco (road from Sigillo), and the hotel *Da Tobia* (☎075/917.914) are mountaineers' and cavers' hangouts.

Exhilarating roads from Scheggia, Costacciaro and Sigillo lead almost to the summit of Monte Cucco (1565m), Umbria's highest peak; the switchback from Sigillo (9km) is the most direct, and drops you nearest the summit if you want a cushy walk. Pushing on beyond Scheggia the N3 to CAGLI breaks into the beautiful and wooded **Burano gorge**, a popular picnic spot for weekending Italians, but with enough secluded corners to find plenty of privacy. Once embarked on the hairpins, it's almost impossible to leave a car and it becomes increasingly difficult to get down to the river. Therefore try to find a spot early on, and scramble down to one of numerous pools and pebbly beaches.

ASSISI AND
THE VALE OF SPOLETO

The broad southern sweep of the Vale of Spoleto constitutes Umbria's historic and spiritual heartland, boasting three or four of its most archetypal hill towns – with **Assisi** and **Spoleto** the obvious highlights – plus great swathes of the sunny, pastoral countryside for which the region has been traditionally famous. (Though be prepared for the occasional blight of factories and unplanned housing). Everything is accessible from Perugia and within easy reach of the main routes, the railway to Terni and dual carriageway (N75) being particularly useful. Scenically inviting **Norcia** and the **Valnerina** are more tricky to reach, but well worth the effort – the best approach if you don't have transport is by bus from Spoleto.

Assisi

ASSISI is already too well known, thanks to **Saint Francis**, Italy's premier saint and founder of the Franciscan order – with its various splinter groups, the world's biggest. Had the man not been born here in 1182 the town wouldn't be thronged with tourists and pilgrims for ten months of the year, but then neither would it have the **Basilica of Saint Francis**, one of the greatest monuments to thirteenth- and fourteenth-century Italian art. On balance you'll probably feel it's worth putting up with the crowds and commercialism for art's sake, but you may not want to hang around once you've seen all there is to see – something which is going to take well under a day. That said, Assisi quietens down in the evening, and it does retain some medieval hill town charm. Ash trays, key rings and other tacky paraphernalia are off-set by geranium-filled window boxes, tranquil back streets and some lovely buildings in the muted, pinkish stone that softens all towns in this area.

SAINT FRANCIS

Whatever your feelings about religion, Saint Francis comes over as an extraordinary man. Made patron saint of Italy in 1939, he achieved fame throughout Europe – travelling as far afield as Spain and the Holy Land – using nothing more persuasive than preaching and the power of personal example. His message was disarmingly simple – throw out the materialistic trappings of daily life and return to a love of God rooted in poverty, chastity and obedience, and learn to see in the profusion and beauty of the natural world the all-pervasive hand of the Divine – a keystone of humanist thought, and a departure from the doom-laden strictures of the Dark Ages. It had few takers in the corrupt, wealthy and decadent Papacy of the time, though Francis' Messiah-like popularity meant there was little it could do but applaud while he was still alive. After his death the sheer size of his Order brought inevitable splits and divisions. The Papacy moved in to hammer the purist elements (in other words, the true Franciscans) and encouraged the more acceptable and moderate wings, gradually shaping the movement to its own designs and institutionalising Francis' message in the process. The saint's achievement, however, as the first man to fracture the rigid orthodoxy of a hitherto hierarchical church, remains unquestioned.

The background material is copious. If you're interested in knowing more G.K.Chesterton's somewhat anglophile *St.Francis* makes for a lively introduction. *The Little Flowers* is a more extravagant medieval version, probably part-written by the saint himself. Otherwise brochures from the **Tourist Office** (Piazza del Comune 12) contain a standard bread-and-butter life story.

The Basilica di San Francesco

Pilgrims and art lovers alike usually make straight for the **Basilica di San Francesco**, justifiably famed as Umbria's single greatest glory, and one of the most overwhelming collections of art outside a gallery anywhere anywhere in the world. Started in 1228, two years after the saint's death, and financed by donations that flooded in from all over Europe, it's not as grandiose as some religious shrines, though it still strikes you as being a long way from the embodiment of Franciscan principles. If you don't mind compromised ideals, the two churches making up the Basilica – one built on top of the other – are a treat. Most people start with Giotto in the **Upper Church**, mainly because it's the first one they come to, but the sombre **Lower Church** – down the steps to the left – comes earlier, both structurally and artistically. The complicated floor plan and claustrophobic low-lit vaults were intended to create a mood of calm and meditative introspection – an effect added to by brown-robed monks, strict rules on silence and no photographs. Francis lies under the floor in a **crypt** (entrance midway down the nave) only brought to light in 1818 after 52 days of digging. He was hidden after his funeral for safekeeping.

Frescoes cover almost every available space and span a century of continuous artistic development, giving you a sort of do-it-yourself lesson in art history. Stilted early works by anonymous painters influenced by the Byzantines sit alongside Roman painters such as Cavellini, who with Cimabue pioneered the move from mosaic to naturalism and the "new" medium of fresco. They were followed by the best of the Sienese School, **Simone Martini and Pietro Lorenzetti**, whose paintings are the ones to make a real point of seeing.

Martini's frescoes are in the *Cappella di San Martino* (1322–26), the first chapel on the left as you enter the nave. He was given free rein in the chapel and every detail, right down to the floor and stained glass, follows his drawings, adding up to a unified scheme that's unique in Italy. Lorenzetti's works, dominated by a powerful *Crucifixion*, are in the transept and small chapel to the left of the main altar. Vaults above the altar itself contain four magnificent frescoes, complicated but colourful allegories of the virtues on which Francis founded his Order; Poverty, Chastity and Obedience. Once thought to have been the work of Giotto, they're now attributed to one of the church's army of unknown artists. Big feature in the right transept is Cimabue's over-restored *Madonna, Child and Angels with St. Francis*, a painting Ruskin described as the noblest depiction of the Virgin in Christendom.

The more straightforward **Upper Church**, built to a light and airy Gothic plan – that was to be followed by countless Franciscan churches – is a completely different experience. It's less a church than an excuse to show off **Giotto**'s dazzling frescoes on the life of Saint Francis. *Francis Preaching to the Birds* and *Driving the Devils from Arezzo* are just two of the famous scenes reproduced worldwide on cards and posters. The cycle starts on the right-hand wall up by the main altar and continues clockwise. Giotto was still in his twenties when he accepted the commission, having been recommended for the job by Cimabue, whose own frescoes – almost ruined now by the oxidation of badly chosen pigments – fill large parts of the apse and transepts.

If time allows check out the **cloisters,** accessible from the rear right-hand side of the Lower Church, and the **Treasury,** (April–Oct, Tues–Sun; L2000), reached via the apse of the Lower Church. The latter, often passed by, contains a rich collection of paintings, reliquaries and general religious clutter given to the Franciscans over the centuries.

The rest of the town

Via San Francesco – what else – festooned with tourist trash, leads back to the town centre. Halfway down on the right are the remains of the fifteenth-century **Oratorio dei Pellegrini,** frescoed inside and out by local painters Mezzastris and Matteo da Gualdo – modest offerings after the Basilica. The same goes for the fairly nondescript **Museo Civico,** housed in the crypt of the now defunct church of San Nicolo. The collection includes Etruscan fragments and finds from the excavations now in progress to uncover the Roman forum, buried under the tourist-filled Piazza del Comune. The piazza is dominated by the so-called **Tempio di Minerva,** an enticing and perfectly preserved Classical facade from the first century; it was the only thing Goethe was bothered about seeing when he came to Assisi – the Basilica he avoided, calling it a "Babylonian pile." It's great to look at from the outside, but the interior is a seventeenth-century Baroque conversion of no interest whatsoever.

On the other side of the piazza the much-restored Palazzo Comunale contains the town's small **pinocoteca** (Tues–Sun 9am–noon 4–7pm; L2000), whose small Renaissance collection feels like a light snack after your previous artistic gorging. Francis' birthplace is next door, marked by the dull *Chiesa Nuova.*

A short hike up the steep Via di San Rufino brings you to the thirteenth-century **Duomo,** with a typical and very lovely three-tiered Umbrian facade and sumptuously carved central doorway. The only point of interest in a stultifyingly boring interior is the font used to baptise Saint Francis, Saint Clare and – by an historical freak – the future Emperor Frederick II, born prematurely in a field outside the town. The cathedral makes a good point to strike off for the **Rocca Maggiore,** one of the bigger and better-preserved in the region with some all-embracing views after a stiff climb (9am–noon 2–6pm in the summer. Winter opening times are variable. Admission is free).

Below the Duomo is the Piazza Santa Chiara, scene of considerable traffic chaos, but more noted for the **Basilica di Santa Chiara,** burial place of Saint Francis' devoted early companion, who at the age of seventeen founded the Order of the Poor Clares, the female wing of the Franciscans. By some peculiar and not terribly dignified quirk she's also the patron saint of television. The church was consecrated in 1265, and is a virtual facsimile of the Basilica up the road, down to the simple facade and opulent rose window. Its engineering wasn't up to the same standards, however, and arches had to be added in 1351 to prevent the whole thing being undermined by crumbling foundations.

Instead of art, the scantily decorated interior has the once withered and maca-brely blackened body of Chiara herself (now back from a session with a Roman saint-restorer) and a Byzantine crucifix famous for having bowed to Francis and commanded him to embark on his sacred mission to repair God's Church.

You're not long off the Francis trail in Assisi; **San Damiano** (daily 10am–6pm), a peaceful spot of genuine monastic charm, is one of its highlights. It's easily reached by taking the Borgo Aretino beyond the Basilica and following signs from the Porta Nuova, a steep downhill walk of about fifteen minutes. Original home to the Poor Clares, and one of Saint Francis's favourite spots – he is thought to have written his well-known *Canticle to the Sun* here – the church, cloisters and rustic setting preserve a sense of the original Franciscan ideals of humility and simplicity often missing in the rest of the town.

From the railway station you can see the town's other major attraction, the vast and majestically uninspiring **Santa Maria degli Angeli**, built in the seventeenth century and rebuilt after an earthquake in 1832. Somewhere in its Baroque bowels are the remains of the **Porzuincola**, a tiny chapel which was effectively the first Franciscan monastery. Francis lived here after founding the Order in 1208, attracted by its then remote and wooded surroundings, and in time was joined by other monks and hermits who built a series of cells and mud huts in the vicinity. Today the church is crammed full of largely fourth-rate works of art and bears no relation to the Franciscan ideal.

After you've exhausted the myriad Francis connections, Assisi has the usual churches, Roman remains and miscellaneous odds and ends that characterise most Italian towns of similar age. If you have time you could check out the **Roman amphitheatre** near Porta Perlici (east of the duomo) or the Romanesque church of **San Pietro**, brilliantly restored for once, in Piazza San Pietro.

Practical Information

Getting there is easy. **Buses** connect regularly with surrounding towns – especially Perugia – putting down and picking up in Piazza Santa Chiara or Piazza San Pietro, depending on the one-way system of the moment. One bus a day leaves for Rome and two for Florence, all from Piazza San Pietro. There are hourly **rail** links to Foligno (via Spello) and Terontola (via Perugia), with connecting half-hourly bus services from the station to Assisi (which is 5km from its station).

There are plenty of cheap places to **stay** in Assisi, most of them catering to the enormous pilgrim market, which means problems if you're in town at the same time as anything vaguely resembling a religious event. (Easter is especially bad.) With its Franciscan associations and the encouragement of the present Pope, the town has also become a symbolic focus for the Catholic church's efforts to promote world peace – which means extra pressure on accommodation from people up for vigils, demonstrations and the like. In town the functional *La Terrazza*, Piazza A. Luigi 1 (☎ 075/812.368), is the biggest of the cheapies, but before that you might try: *Albergo La Rocca*, Via Porta Perlici 25 (☎ 075/812.284); the five-roomed *Grotta Antica*, Via M.Vecchi 1 (☎075/813.467); *Anfiteatro Romano*, Via Anfiteatro 4 (☎ 075/813.025), or the convenient (and therefore often full) *Properzio*, Via San Francesco 38 (☎ 075/813.188). If you get stuck and go to the tourist office, only let them send you down towards the station in the last resort, and on no account be palmed off with rooms in nearby BASTIA. There's a big **campsite** at Fontemaggio (☎075/813.636) on the road out to the **Eremo di Carceri** (a beautifully situated but only mildly interesting monastery), with an adjoining **youth hostel** run by the campsite management.

Multilingual tourist menus proliferate in the town's restaurants, and prices can be steep. For straight pizzas there's *Il Pozzo Romano* (Via Sant'Agnese – near Santa Chiara) and *Ristorante Pizzeria*, Via Italia 34. *Palotta*, Via San Rufino 4, is near some sticky tourist traps but reasonable and friendly. Moving upmarket *Buca di San Francesco*,Via Brizi 1, is the locals' favourite – medieval and atmospheric, but busy and potentially expensive.

Spello and Bevagna

Ranged on broad terraces above the Vale of Spoleto, medieval and pink-stoned **SPELLO** is the best place for a half-hour taste of small-town Umbria if you haven't time or means to explore further, being easy to reach by road and rail (20min from Assisi or Spoleto). Emperor Augustus gave land in the adjacent valley to faithful legionaries to build themselves retirement homes, turning the town (*Hispellum)* into a sort of Roman Eastbourne in the process, an ambience it still rather retains.

Rooms are a little pricey, but they're usually available when those in Assisi or Spoleto are fully booked. Try *La Bastiglia*, via Salnitraria 15 (☎0742/651.277) or *Julia*, Via Sant'Angelo 22 (☎0742/651.174), both central in what is anyway a compact and small place. There's also a **campsite** at nearby CHIONA, the *Internazionale Umbra* (April–Oct). The **tourist office** is at Via Garibaldi 17.

The walls and three gateways are the most obvious Roman remnants. (Don't bother walking out to the paltry and overgrown remains of the old **amphitheatre** hidden away beyond the main road – you can see all you need to from the top of the town). By far the most distinguished sight are **Pintoricchio's frescoes** in the thirteenth-century church of Santa Maria Maggiore (Piazza G. Matteotti). Number Two Umbrian painter after Perugino, he left other important works in Siena (the duomo), Rome (the Sistine Chapel, Borgia Apartments) and a host of churches scattered over central Italy. The frescoes themselves are fresh and glowing from recent restoration, with Pintoricchio's famous details and colouring brought out to stunning effect. Unfortunately they're behind glass, which also means you can't get a closer look at the chapel's praised but faded fifteenth-century **ceramic pavement**.

Bevagna

BEVAGNA is quieter and less visited than Spello, but a serene backwater if ever there was one, with a windswept **central square** of absolute austere perfection. Flanked by two of Umbria's finest Romanesque churches (both untouched and creaking with age) the Piazza Silvestri dates from around the thirteenth century. The only exception is the fountain, which while blending perfectly, was installed in 1889. Look out particularly for the surreal and demented gargoyles over the doorway of the larger church, San Michele. And if it's open, check out the Palazzo Comunale, which was converted in the nineteenth century into one of Umbria's prettiest provincial theatres.

There's not a lot else to the town, other than the backwoods charm of the streets. You can take a **bus** here from Foligno (8km) or hitch easily on the road that crosses the plain. The **tourist office**, *Pro Mevania*, is in Piazza Silvestri, and there's a three-star **campsite** at Pian di Boccio in the nearby hamlet of CAGLIOLI (Mar 15–Sept 30; ☎0742/62.391).

Foligno and Montefalco

To move on anywhere from Spello means a trip to **FOLIGNO**, and a lull in proceedings, because it's a large modern town and flat in every sense of the word. Its star turns were bombed out of existence in the war, and the place is now a mediocre provincial backwater sprawled over an unattractive plain. However, much of what's left is conveniently grouped together in the central **Piazza della Repubblica**, and as you're likely to be passing through a quick look isn't going to hurt. The town's also brimful of hotels and acts as a nodal point for trains and local village buses.

For the **tourist office** and **bus station** (Porta Romana) follow Viale Mezzetti from the train station, turn right into Piazzale Alunno and the office is in the top-right hand corner. Continue up Corso Cavour and you hit the historic centre two minutes later. The twelfth-century **duomo** has two good Romanesque facades (there's an extra one on the side) but the interior was finished off in the eighteenth century to predictable effect. The nearby **Palazzo Trinci** is the only thing worth making a real effort to see. The Trincis were Foligno's medieval big-shots, with territory and influence extending over great swathes of Umbria, and their palace is an art-filled monument to wealth and power – all frescoed stairways, carved ceilings and general opulence, most of it recently restored. Inside are a small **archaeological museum** and a **pinacoteca** with good frescoes by the fifteenth-century Gubbian painter, Ottaviano Nelli.

The only other monument which hints at Foligno's former glory is **Santa Maria Infraportas** (off Piazza San Domenico), a church of pagan origins in which Saint Peter himself is said to have conducted a Mass. Oldest bit of the current building (eighth-century) is the Cappella dell'Assunta off the left nave, dominated by the town's most precious piece of art, a twelfth-century Byzantine mural.

Montefalco

Short of a lucky hitch (stand at Porta Todi, round Via N. Sauro from Piazza Alunno) a bus is the only way to get from Foligno to **MONTEFALCO**, a faintly forlorn medieval village, but home to a superb collection of paintings that definitely merit a morning. Its name, meaning Falcon's Mount, was glorified with the appendage "la ringhiera dell'Umbria" – the balcony of Umbria, a hyperbolic tribute to its **views**. It was also the birthplace of eight saints, good going even by Italian standards. Nowadays the town's sleepy rather than holy, only a stupendously ugly water tower and very slight urban sprawl to take the edge off its moderate medieval appeal. The strong, blackberry-flavoured **local wine**, *Sangrantino passito*, is well worth a try; there's a good little shop in the main square for this and other liquid purchases.

The lofty location was a godsend to Spoleto's Papal governors, left high, dry and terrified by the fourteenth-century defection of the Popes to Avignon. They took refuge here, and their cowering presence accounts for the rich decoration of the town churches, a richness out of all proportion to the town's size. The cavernous ex-church of **San Francesco** in Via Ringhiera Umbra (off the central Piazza del Comune) houses the town's big feature, Benozzo Gozzoli's sumptuous **fresco cycle** on the life of Saint Francis (9am–noon & 3.30–6.30pm, closed Sun; L2000). With Fra Angelico, Gozzoli was one of the most prolific and influential Florentine painters to come south and show the backward Umbrians what the Renaissance was all about. Resplendent with colour and detail, the cycle copies many of the ideas and episodes from Giotto's Assisi cycle, but with 200 years of artistic know-how to draw on, is more sophisticated and more immediately appealing (if lacking Giotto's austere dignity). Amongst numerous other paintings in the gallery are works by most of the leading Umbrians (**Perugino, Nicolò Alunno, Tiberio d'Assisi**) as well as a host of more minor efforts by local fifteenth-century artists. There are more early frescoes in **Sant'Agostino** across the main piazza in Via Umberto I.

The rest of the town is relatively low key and doesn't take long to see. Probably the most bizarre sight is the mummified body of Saint Clare (Santa Chiara) which languishes in the otherwise dismal church of the same name, five minutes from San Francesco in Via Verdi (this is a second Saint Clare, not to be confused with the one in Assisi). Ring a bell, and if the nuns aren't praying, they'll show you round the adjoining convent. It's a good behind-the-scenes look at monastic life, the sisters showing you the remains of the saint's heart, and the scissors used to hack it out. The story goes that Christ appeared to Clare, saying the burden of carrying the Cross was becoming too heavy; Clare replied she would help by carrying it in her heart. When she was opened up, a cross-shaped piece of tissue was found on her heart. Other exhibits include three of her kidney stones, and a miraculous tree that grew from a staff planted in the garden by Christ, who appeared to her here. Apparently it's the only one of its kind growing wild in Europe; the berries are used to make rosaries, and are said to have powerful medicinal qualities.

Fifty metres beyond the church, preceded by a triple-arched Renaissance porch, is the chapel of **Sant'Illuminata**, comprehensively but not terribly well frescoed by Melanzio in 1510. Keep on heading out of town, turn left at the T-junction, and fifteen minutes of tedious walking brings you to **San Fortunato**, nicely situated amongst ilix woods, and noted for the frescoes by Tiberio d'Assisi (1512), in the Cappella delle Rose (left of the main courtyard). Check out the macabre bundle of blackened bones in the main church, the remains of San Fortunato himself, martyred in 390.

There's no need to spend more than a morning in Montefalco, but if you do decide to **stay**, best bets are the *Ringhiera Umbra*, Via Umberto 1 (☎0742/79.166) – also good for a **meal** – and the five-roomed *Nuovo Mondo*, Via Mameli 67 (☎0742/79.243). Both are one-star jobs, the *Nuovo Mondo*, with its garden and swimming pool, is more ritzy and more expensive.

Trevi and the Fonti di Clitunno

The best way to move southwards from Foligno is by train, which skirts the plain of Spoleto, and whisks past the light industrial sites that blight the whole stretch of the valley to Terni and beyond. Not many people stop before Spoleto itself, giving **TREVI** and its towering position no more than an admiring glance from the train. Its daunting inaccessibility is one of the reasons for its appealing and easy-going charm. The feeling is of a pleasant, ordinary provincial town still stuck somewhere in the Fifties, unvisited and unspoilt. Beyond it lie miles and miles of olive groves, renowned for producing central Italy's finest oil. The town's also apparently famous for its celery.

The medieval centre, looming away high on its hill, is 4km from the station, a dull and exhausting trek – take the connecting bus service instead. The **AAST** in via Roma (off the central Piazza Mazzini) is invaluable for maps to the peripheral churches, which contain a sprinkling of Umbrian paintings. The most noteworthy are in **San Martino** and **Madonna delle Lacrime**, the latter containing excellent and recently restored works by **Perugino** and Lo Spagna. The twelfth-century **Duomo** of Sant'Emiliano at the town's highest point, suffered more than usually violent nineteenth-century butchery of its innards, but is fine from the outside, and conserves a series of sixteenth-century frescoes by Melanzio, a half-decent painter active in several villages locally.

The small **Museo-Pinacoteca** in Piazza Mazzini houses a predictable display of coins, ceramics and Roman trivia, and one genuine masterpiece, a *Coronation of the Virgin* (1522) by Lo Spagna. Trevi's medieval governors commissioned it as a copy of a more famous work by the Florentine, Ghirlandaio, mainly because they couldn't afford the real thing. Todi's comune had the same economical idea, and got Lo Spagna to knock them out another copy. The original is in Terni.

Il Cochetto in Via Dogagli (below and parallel to Via del Duomo), is the best **eating** option, with garden terrace, good views, and half the town in evidence on Sunday lunchtime.

Fonti di Clitunno

A short hop from Trevi on the road south, are the sacred **FONTI DI CLITUNNO**, an unexpected beauty spot, given the pock-marked surroundings. There's a certain amount of commercialised fuss and bother at the entrance, but the springs, streams and willow-shaded lake beyond – painted by Corot and inspiration to poets from Virgil to Byron – are pure, languid romanticism. Faint traffic noise and the occasional mega-coach party are the only intrusions. The spa waters have attracted people since Roman times – the likes of Caligula and Claudius came here to party – but their major curative effect is allegedly the dubious one of completely removing any appetite for alcohol. Earthquakes over the years have upset many of the underground springs, so the waters aren't as plentiful as they were, but they still flow as limpid as they did in Byron's day, the "sweetest wave of the most living crystal . . . the purest god of gentle waters . . . most serene of aspect and most clear . . . a mirror and a bath for Beauty's youngest daughters." The site closes for lunch, but opens again until dusk, with a small admission charge to get in. A mini tourist office doles out background information in the summer.

A few hundred metres north is the so-called **Tempietto di Clitunno**, looking for all the world like a miniature Greek Temple, but actually an eighth-century Christian church, cobbled together with a mixture of idiosyncrasy, wishful thinking and old Roman columns. It's only a small, one-off novelty, but still evocative, and with the bonus inside of some faded frescoes said to be the oldest in Umbria. If it's shut you can try ringing the bell on the small gateway.

Spoleto

SPOLETO is Umbria's most compelling town, and many people's central-Italian favourite. Known mainly for its big **summer festival**, it's remarkable also for its thorough-going medievalism, an extremely pretty position, and several of Italy's most ancient Romanesque churches. Far more graceful and provincial a city than Perugia, nowadays it plays second-fiddle to its long-time historical enemy, though for several centuries it was amongst the most influential of Italian towns. Two kilometres of well-preserved walls stand as testament to the one-time grandeur of its Roman colony, though its real importance dates from the sixth century when the Lombards made it the capital of one of their three Italian dukedoms. The autonomous **Duchy of Spoleto** eventually stretched to Rome, and by 890 its rulers had become powerful enough to lay claim to the Imperial throne itself, making Spoleto, for a short time at least, the capital of the entire Holy Roman Empire. Barbarossa flattened the city in a fit of pique in 1155 and in 1499 the nineteen-year-old Lucrezia Borgia was appointed governer by her father, Pope Alexander VI. After that it was one long decline until about thirty years ago, and the arrival of the festival.

The lower town

The first thing which greets you outside Spoleto's quaint Thirties-style station is a ludicrously out-of-place sculpture heralding the town's delusions of cultural grandeur; a shame, because the overall feel of the place is anything but pretentious. The lower town to which it's a gateway was badly damaged by World War II bombing, and its only real interest lies in a couple of churches, most impressively the fourth-century paleo-Christian **San Salvatore**. If you're not into church excursions a bus runs from the station up to the heart of the medieval town, tempting with a superb skyline of spires, tiled roofs and splashes of craggy countryside.

San Salvatore is on the outskirts of the modern suburb, half-hidden in the **town cemetery**, whose spooky glimpse of the Italian way of death provides a faintly bizarre attraction in itself. The church was built by Christian monks from the Eastern Mediterranean in the fourth century, since when it's hardly been touched. Conceived when the only models for religious buildings were Roman temples, that's pretty much what the monks came up with, the net result leaning more to primitive paganism than Christianity. The walls inside are bare, the floors covered in fallen stone and the dusty gloom is heavy with an almost eerie antiquity. Crumbling Corinthinian columns from different ages are wedged awkwardly alongside one another, and at some point the arches in the nave were filled in to prevent total collapse. Try to visit at dusk to get the full effect

In the vicinity is **San Ponziano**, much praised, but easily ignored if it weren't for a distinctive Romanesque facade. There's also a fascinating tenth-century **crypt** if you can tempt the caretaker out of his cave-like house to show you it. The lower town's other attraction close by is the church of **San Gregorio**, started in 1069, but looking as if it was built yesterday, a result of recent cleaning and restoration. The tower and intriguing portico are made from a patchwork of fragments

---

THE FESTIVAL DEI DUE MONDI

Hosting Italy's leading international arts festival has been a double-edged blessing for Spoleto – crowds and commercialism being the price it has had to pay for culture. Having already rejected thirty other Italian towns, the influential arts guru Giancarlo Menotti plumped for the town in 1958, attracted by its scenery, small venues and general good vibes. The ensuing jamboree is a great attraction if you're into music, dance or theatre, though the place forgoes a good part of its charm as a result. On top of the crowds, ticket prices for top companies and world-class performers can be off-putting, as can the jet-set, well-heeled cut of the audiences. Be warned too that while the Festival's in progress you can expect packed hotels, madness in the restaurants and higher prices all round. At the same time there's an Edinburgh type fringe and plenty of fellow travellers (plus lots of film, jazz, buskers and so on). Organisers, moreover, have recently looked to more avante-garde acts to recover the artistic edge of the Festival's early days. So count on seeing some wacky shows, but be prepared for a possible fleecing in the process. Check out **tickets and information** from the **AAST** (Piazza Libertà) or the Festival's own box office (Piazza del Duomo 9; ☎0743/28.120). Year-round details of future line-ups are available from the Festival Press Agency, Via del Duomo 7 (☎0743/32.141).

clearly pinched from earlier Roman remains, but it's the interior that commands most attention. Stripped back to their Romanesque state, the walls are dotted with substantial patches of fresco, and interrupted by a series of unusual, rather intimidating stone confessionals. The presbytery is raised several metres above the level of the naves to allow for a masterful little **crypt**, supported by dozens of tiny pillars.

Tradition has it that somewhere under the church are the bones of ten thousand Christian martyrs killed by the Romans in the **amphitheatre** close by. There are still traces of the bloodbath visible in the military barracks up the road. No-one seems to mind if you just walk straight in; bear right from the gateway for the best remains, none of which are terribly substantial. The ever-ingenious Romans apparently constructed special gutters to drain blood from the arena into the nearby Torrente Tessino, which ran crimson as a result. Now the river's full of rubbish and a long way from being a puddle, let alone a torrent.

The upper town

There's really no single, central piazza in Spoleto, but the place to head for is **Piazza Libertà**, local **bus terminal** and home to the town's **AAST** (☎0743/28.111). With few obvious reference points, general **orientation** is difficult, but as aimless wandering is one of Spoleto's pleasures this isn't too much of a problem. The much-restored first-century **Roman theatre** opposite the tourist office is used throughout the summer for festival performances, but is singularly unevocative thanks to the gaudily painted buildings on all sides. In 1319 four hundred Guelph supporters of the Pope were rounded up by the Spoletans and dumped on the stage with their throats cut. Not content with the result, Saint Francis' countrymen pushed their victims into a pile and made them into a large bonfire.

Cutting into the adjoining Piazza della Fontana are more Roman remains, all far more humble than the vast wad of tourist blurb leads you to expect. Of the town's many arches from the period, the **Arco di Druso** (AD23) straddling the entrance to the Piazza del Mercato, is the only one not embedded in a wall. It was intended as a triumphal gateway to the old forum, and built to honour what must have been very minor campaign victories on the part of Drusus, son of Tiberius. The patched-up walls behind it are the city's oldest, built in the sixth century BC by the Umbrians, who otherwise are as mysterious and elusive as ever. To the right of the arch is what is described as a Roman **temple**, but unless you've a vivid imagination it's difficult to see it as anything other than a ditch. Pop into the adjacent church of **San Ansano** for a look at more of the temple, and the fresco-covered crypt, originally the home of sixth-century monks.

Nowhere do you get a better sense of Spoleto's market-town roots than in the homely **Piazza del Mercato** beyond, a fine opportunity to take in some colourful streetlife. (Though there are more incongruous sculptures – this time horses with big brass backsides.) Old women wash fruit and vegetables in a fountain, its crown embellished with a highly eccentric clock, the men drink in the bars and swap unintelligible stall-holders' gossip and tourists make barely a dent in the overall proceedings. The *alimentari* on all sides are a cornucopia of goodies, with a definite bias towards truffles and sticky liqueurs (the *Amaro di Tartufo* guarantees a grim morning after).

Turning the corners of the attractive streets roundabouts, it's a short walk to the **duomo**, whose facade of restrained elegance is one of the most memorable in the region. The careful balance of Romanesque and Renaissance elements are framed by a gently sloping piazza and lovely hanging gardens, but the broad background of sky and open countryside is what sets the seal on the whole thing. The church suffered like many in Italy from the desire of rich communities to make their wealth and power conspicuous, a desire usually realised by tearing the guts out of old churches and remodelling them in the latest style. This worked well on the thirteenth-century **facade** which has an arched portico tacked on in 1491, but less well in the interior where Pope Urban VIII's architect, Luigi Arrigucci, applied great dollops of Baroque midway through the seventeenth century. His "improvements", luckily, are eclipsed by the apse's superlative **frescoes** by the great Florentine artisit Fra Lippo Lippi, dominated by his final masterpiece, a *Coronation of the Virgin* (1469).

He died shortly after their completion, the rumour being that he was poisoned for seducing the daughter of a local noble family, his position as a monk having had no bearing on his sexual appetite. The Spoletans, not too bothered by moral laxity, were delighted at having someone famous to put in their cathedral, being, as Vasari put it, "poorly provided with ornaments, above all with distinguished men," and so refused to send the dead artist back to Lorenzo di Medici, his Florentine patron. Interred in a **tomb** designed by his son, Filippino Lippi (now in the right transept) the corpse disappeared during restoration two centuries later, the popular theory being that it was spirited away by descendants of the compromised girl – a sort of vendetta beyond the grave.

You should also make a point of seeing the **Erioli Chapels** at the beginning of the right nave, primarily for a faded *Madonna and Child* (with Lago di Trasimeno in the background) by Pintoricchio (1497), and for the cruder frescoes in the adjoining chapel by the Sicilian artist Jacopo Santori. There's also a good **Cosmati marble floor** and the inevitable **icon**, which Barbarossa gave to the town in 1185 to try and make amends for having flattened it thirty years earlier.

The town's **museums** are minor and motley affairs, difficult to find, and even harder to get into. The **Opera del Duomo** (10am–noon & 3–5pm, closed Mon; L2000) is at Piazza del Duomo 3, round the corner from the tiny and elegant nineteenth-century Teatro Caio Meliss. Amidst a less than absorbing collection of cannon-balls, sarcophagi, chimney breasts and other bits and pieces, only the *Lex Spoletina* merit a special mention, two Roman inscriptions which forbade the chopping down of trees in the sacred woods of **Monteluco**. The injunction must have worked because the forests, home to second-century hermits and later to Saint Francis, are still there, 8km east of the town. Take one of the hourly buses from Piazza di Libertà if you're not into the stiff walk, and head away from the hotel-restaurant complex and accompanying crowds into the footpaths that cross the woods. You don't have to walk far before you're alone. The views are great on a good day, and it's a welcome relief from the summer maelstrom down in Spoleto itself.

The **pinacoteca** is stuck away in the farthest reaches of the Palazza del Municipio, the town's council building (10am–1pm & 3–7pm closed Tues; L2000; check latest times with the AAST). You're sold a ticket by a policeman from a very officious office to the right of the main entrance, and then have to wait for someone to show you reluctantly around the gallery on the upper floor. The half dozen rooms are sumptuously decorated, and many of the paintings outstanding, though most are unlabelled. The best stuff is the early Umbrian work in the last of the rooms, particularly a couple of big canvases by a local follower of Perugino, **Lo Spagna**.

The medieval town's most celebrated **church** is the twelfth-century **Sant'Eufemia**, architecturally unique in Umbria for its *matronei*, high-arched galleries above the side-naves which served the purpose of segregating women from the male congregation in the main body of the church. It was built over the site of the eighth-century Lombard ducal palace, and appears to have been partly constructed from the remains of this and earlier Roman monuments; one or two of the completely mismatched columns are carved with distinctive Lombard motifs. The general dank solemnity of the place clearly points to an early foundation. As one of the region's Romanesque highlights it warrants a few minutes of attention – as long as you're lucky enough to find it open.

The Ponte, Rocca and San Pietro

If you do nothing else in Spoleto you should take the short walk out to the **Ponte delle Torri**, the town's picture-postcard favourite, and an astonishing piece of medieval engineering. It's best taken in as part of a circular walk around the base of the **Rocca** or on the longer trek out to **San Pietro** (see below). Within a minute of leaving shady gardens in Piazza Campello you suddenly find yourself in superb countryside, with a dramatic panorama across the the Tessino gorge and south to the mountains of Castelmonte. (There's an informal little bar to help you enjoy the views).

The bridge is a genuinely impressive affair, with a 240-metre span supported by ten 80-metre arches that have been used as a launching pad by jilted lovers for six centuries. Designed by the Gubbian architect, Gattapone, who was also responsible for Gubbio's Palazzo dei Consoli, it was initially planned as an aqueduct to bring water from Monteluco, replacing an earlier Roman causeway whose design Gattopone probably borrowed and enlarged upon. In time it also became used as an escape from the Rocca when Spoleto was under siege. The remains of what used to be a covered passageway connecting the two are still visible straggling down the hillside .

The **Rocca** itself, everyone's idea of a cartoon castle, with towers, crenallations and sheer walls, was another in the chain of fortresses with which the tireless Cardinal Albornoz hoped to re-establish Church domination in central Italy, a primacy lost during the fourteenth-century Papal exile to Avignon. It served until recently as a high-security prison – testimony to the skill of its medieval builders – and was home to, amongst others, Pope John Paul II's would-be assassin and leading members of the Red Brigade.

Best plan at the Ponte is to cross over – with a giddy pause to look over the edge – and make for the church of **San Pietro**, whose facade beckons from a not-too-distant hillside. If the idea of another church doesn't appeal you can easily double back to town on the circular Via della Rocca.

Though the walk to San Pietro is a longish one (2km), it's pleasantly shady with some good glimpses of Spoleto; and far nicer, in any case, than walking through the streets in the southern part of the town. The only thing to look out for on the country road (no pavements) are crazed Italians taking the bends too fast. The church would be otherwise unremarkable were it not for the splendid **sculptures** adorning its facade. Taken with Maitini's bas-reliefs in Orvieto, they are the best Romanesque carvings in Umbria, partly Lombard in their inspiration, and drawing variously on the Gospels and medieval legend for their complicated narrative and symbolic purpose. A particularly juicy scene to look out for includes the Death of a Sinner (left series, second from the top) where the Archangel Michael abandons the sinner to a couple of demons who bind and torture him before bringing in the burning oil to finish the job. Fourth panel from the top (right series) shows a wolf disguised as a friar before a fleeing ram – a dig at dodgy monastic morals.

Practicalities

Cheap **rooms** are hard to come by when the Festival's in full swing. *Pensione dell'Angelo* is central, Via Arco del Druso 25 (☎0743/32.185) but small. If you can't stay here you could at least eat in the busy **trattoria** downstairs. Otherwise try *Pensione Aurora* off Piazza Libertà, Via dell'Apollinare 4 (☎0743/28.115). The lower town is very much a second choice, but there are more likely to be rooms available, and it's still handy for the medieval highlights. Addresses to try here are *Fracassa*, Via Focaroli 15 (☎0743/21.177), and *Anfiteatro*, Via dell'Anfiteatro 14 (☎0743/49.853).

Campsites are a more promising option. Closest is *Camping Monteluco*, (☎0743/28.158) behind San Pietro and an easy downhill walk from Piazza Libertà; open from May to September, it (officially) only has places for twenty tents. *Il Girasole* (☎0743/51.335) in the village of PETROGNANO (hourly buses from the station) is a bigger and flashier affair, with swimming pool and tennis courts (open all year).

Bargain **meals** of school-dinner quality and quantity are served up in *Ristorante Economico*, courtesy of the town council (Via San Carlo 7 – between Piazza Libertà and San Pietro). There are a couple of cheapies in Piazza Del Mercato, the Trattoria at no. 29 and an unnamed remnant from the nineteenth century at no. 10, both catering mainly to Spoleto's workmen and market traders. The best basic trattoria, always full of locals, is the *Trattoria del Festival* in Piazza Fontana. *Il Panciolle* (Largo Muzio Clemente) is more upmarket, but has a great summer terrace in a lime tree filled piazza.

The Valnerina and Norcia

The **VALNERINA** is the most beautiful part of Umbria, but is hard to get to without your own transport. Strictly translated as the "little valley of the Nera", it effectively refers to the whole eastern part of the region, a self-contained area of high mountains, poor communications, steep wooded valleys, upland villages and vast stretches of barren nothingness. Wolves still roam the summit ridges, and are to be protected by a proposed (but long awaited) regional Nature Reserve. The area is a genuine "forgotten corner", deserted farms everywhere bearing witness to a century of continuous emigration.

Six **buses** daily run from Spoleto station to Norcia (1hr 15min), calling at PIEDIPATERNO (2 daily connections to MONTELEONE), BORGO CERRETO, SERRAVALLE and villages in between (timetables from the tourist office in Spoleto). Because roads are scarce, what few there are tend to be busy, so you shouldn't have too many problems **hitching**.

The beautiful and tortuous N395 road from Spoleto is virtually the only access point until you hit the "main" SS209 and the more pastoral run up the Nera Valley towards NORCIA. **Mountains** roundabout are around 1500m high, with excellent walking, creeping up as you move eastwards to about 2500m in the **Monti Sibillini**. It's difficult to explore with any sort of plan (unless you stick to the Nera), and the best approach is follow your nose, poking into small valleys, tracing high country lanes to remote hamlets.

More deliberately, you could make for VALLO DI NERA, most archetypal of the **fortified villages** that pop up along the lower Nera. Medieval TRIPONZO is a natural focus of communications, little more than a quaint staging post and fortified tower (and a better target than modernish CERRETO nearby). MONTELEONE is the only place of any size for miles, with a fine church, and popular with trippers.

CASCIA figures large on the map, but is disappointing in actuality, only recommendable to pilgrims in search of **Saint Rita**, whose presence (and stupendously ugly twentieth-century **Basilica**) dominate both the new and earthquake-damaged hill town. Rita's cult is enormous in Italy, particularly amongst women, who've virtually adopted her as their (uncrowned) patron saint. There's not much a woman can suffer that Rita didn't come through, which is the main reason for her "Everywoman" appeal and why she's sometimes known as the "saint of the impossible". Apparently you invoke Saint Rita when an "ordinary" miracle isn't enough. A poor child of aged parents, she endured a forced marriage, followed by eighteen years of mistreatment from an alcoholic husband, who died in a brawl weeks after repenting his evil ways. Both sons died trying to avenge their father, leaving Rita alone in the world and, as a widow, unable to become a nun. A relaxation of convent rules did eventually allow her to take holy orders, a turnaround held up as one of her "impossible" miracles.

Norcia

Small, stolid **NORCIA**, a mountain retreat if ever there were one, is the only place of any size or substance in the Valnerina. Noted on one hand as the birthplace of **Saint Benedict** – founder of Western monasticism – and on the other as the producer of Italy's top **salami**, its air of shadowy desolation, and low, sturdy houses (built as protection against earthquakes) are a world away from the pastoral, fairy tale cities to the west. It's friendly and appealing, though, if you don't mind the leaden atmosphere, and if transport allows, it can be the base for some good trips into neighbouring territory, particularly the famed **Piano di Castellucio**. A big new road over the mountains to the Marche looks set to open up the area – good news for local employment, which is scarce, but probable doom for the environment. Hang gliders and winter sports enthusiasts are pouring in, another mixed blessing.

Taking in the town itself doesn't detain you long. Most of the action is in the central **Piazza San Benedetto**, site of the Roman forum, and presided over by a statue of Benedict. The duomo you can largely forget about – its facade aside – destroyed by several earthquakes (the last big one was in 1979), and patched up to look like nothing on earth. The **Castellina** is more captivating: a papal fortress, full of gaunt medieval echoes, it's a strange bedfellow for the church of **San Benedetto**, which supposedly was built over the saint's birthplace, but more likely raised from the ruins of an earlier Roman temple. Inside there are a few paltry frescoes, nothing more. The **tourist office** sits next door to the square's last component, the Palazzo Comunale, a confused but pleasing mixture of architectural styles.

Meat-eaters would be daft not to try the deservedly famous pork products. Anything that can be done to a pig, the Norcians apparently do, and supposedly better than anyone else. Even today you still see butchers in other parts of Italy called "un nurcino", after the town, a measure of its widespread notoriety. If finances stretch you could indulge in the area's prized black **truffle**. Several thousand lire will buy a light dusting over your tagliatelle. The season runs from January to April.

Cheapest **hotels** are the nine-roomed *Da Benito*,Via Marconi 5 (☎0743/816.670) and the bigger (and slightly cheaper) *Monastero S. Antonio*,Via dei Vergini 13 (☎0743/816.657).

The eerie, expansive **Piano di Castellucio**, twenty kilometres to the east, is definitely one of Umbria's sights, an extraordinary prairie ringed by bare, whaleback mountains, and unbroken for miles and miles by tree, hedge or habitation – rather what the Scottish Highlands would look like fertile and four times as big. It's much photographed – especially in spring when its ablaze with poppies – and was used by Zeffirelli as a setting in his Franciscan film *Brother Sun, Sister Moon*. The desperately isolated village of **Castellucio** hangs above it at around 1400m; as the curious trickle in, it's no longer the sole reserve of shepherds, but remains an unspoilt base, and the ideal starting point for any number of **mountain walks**. Rough **camping** is no problem, and there's a one-star hotel-restaurant, *La Sibilla*, in the village itself. If you can't get out here, the smaller **Piano di Santa Scolastica**, due south of Norcia, will give you a watered-down idea of what you're missing.

Other worthwhile trips if you're short of time to spend in aimless exploration, include the road north to **PRECI** and thus to VISSO in the Marche. Walled and castled Preci was known throughout Europe in the sixteenth century as a school for surgeons, their main trade being removal of kidney stones. However, they had a more notorious sideline – castrating young boys who were foolish enough to show operatic potential. A kilometre above nearby PIEDIVALLE is the **Abbey of San of San Eutizio**, one of the cradles of the Benedictine movement. Now only a twelfth-century Romanesque church stands on the site, but in its day the community of monks held sway over more than a hundred castles and local churches.

ORVIETO AND THE SOUTH

Towards its southern edge Umbria loses its pastoral mystical character and begins to feel like a flat foretaste of Rome and Lazio. **Terni**, its main focus, is a grim industrial city, and little more than a watershed for regional transportation, though less than half an hour to the north are the classic hill towns of **Orvieto** and **Todi**, too popular with tourists for their own good, perhaps, but still essential viewing. **Rail** is the key to getting about, with the single-track **FCU** branching off to Todi and thence to Perugia, complementing the **FS** line which runs down from Spoleto to connect with the Rome–Florence route at Orte. Trains from Terni via Rieti are perfect if you intend to head south into the Abruzzi. Good road links follow almost identical routes, and if you're hitching, the big junction with the AI at **Orte** – an obvious gateway in and out of the region – offers great opportunities for lifts in all directions.

Terni and Lago di Piediluco

TERNI was the unlikely birthplace of one of the world's most famous saints, **Saint Valentine**, bishop of the town until his martyrdom in 273. Someone stole his head in 1986, but you can still pay court to the body in the saint's personal basilica at San Valentino, a village two kilometres to the southwest.

A less romantic city, however, would be hard to imagine. Terni's important arms and steel industries made it a natural target for Allied bombing in 1944, and eighty percent of the town was reduced to rubble, including, sadly, the best part of its Roman and medieval heritage. Rebuilding replaced what was lost with a grey grid-iron city straight out of post-war Eastern Europe; it also put the arms industry back on its feet – the gun which shot Kennedy was made here – and though the town no longer lives up to its nineteenth-century nickname of "the Manchester of Italy", high-tech weaponry and the stench of chemicals aren't the most enticing of prospects. The **tourist office**, should you need it, is at Viale Battisti 5. Take Viale della Stazione from the station; Viale Battisti is 300m up, seventh on the right.

The best place to make for locally is the **MARMORE WATERFALL** (train or bus from Terni), created by the Romans in 271 BC when they diverted the River Velino into the Nera during drainage of marshlands to the south. The highest waterfall in Europe (at 165m), it was boosted by the damming of Lake Piediluco in 1930s to satisfy the demands of industry for cheap hydroelectric power. Pictures of the falls in full spate adorn most Umbrian tourist offices, but what they don't tell you is that the water can be turned off at the flick of switch (in favour of electric turbines), leaving a none-too-spectacular trickle for the expectant tourist. No two sources agree on when exactly the water is likely to be switched on, but the best chances of finding it running seem to be weekend lunchtimes and evenings when there's often a *son et lumiére*. From July 15 to August 11 it also does the business on weekdays, between 5–6.30pm. The observation platforms are below on the SS 209 and above in the village of Marmore, with a steep path between the two. The green and luxuriant setting, tumbling water and the acres of gleaming polished marble add up to a spectacular show – shame about the factories round the corner, though. There's a **campsite** at Marmore, open from May to September (☎0744/671.980).

Lago di Piediluco

If you want to carry on up the Velino valley, **Lago di Piediluco** makes an attractive target. Surrounded by steep and thickly wooded hills, it's Umbria's prettiest lake, something like a miniature version of one of the northern Alpine lakes. Very dark and deep, the water's a bit on the cold side for swimming (and in places unsafe), though it's a big sailing and canoeing centre. The **station** is at the western end, some distance from the town of **PIEDILUCO** itself (bus from Terni), but perfect if you want to put up a tent on the southern, less-visited shore, or walk the scenic minor road on this shore to Monte Caperno. There's a quay here with boats to and from Piediluco, as well as a famous four-second **echo**, constantly and enthusiastically being tested out. Piediluco is picturesque – with the lake on its doorstep it doesn't have to try too hard – but is filled by people escaping from Terni at the weekends. This said, if you're a fishing or watersports fan, or just need a quiet spot for your tent, you may want to go to ground for a couple of days.

Accommodation can be tight: try *La Brace* (Via R. Salvati) or the two-star *Lido* (☎0744/68.354) on the lake shore and also a popular restaurant. There's a big and usually packed **campsite** (May 15–Sept 15; ☎0744/68.371). If Piediluco seems too frenetic, you could always push onto neighbouring CORNELLO or CAPOLOZZA.

To the Abbazia di San Pietro in Valle

There are further worthwhile excursions from Terni, particularly if you're making for Norcia and The Valnerina from the south rather than Spoleto. The only route is the SS209, which follows the mountainous Nera valley almost to its head. Buses make the run up to TRIPONZO, but the valley's highlight is **the Abbazia di San Pietro in Valle**, 18km from Terni. You could, if tempted, stop off beforehand at ARRONE and MONTEFRANCO, the first of several spectacularly-sited **fortress villages** lining the valley. The Valnerina, now desolate and sparsely populated, was once the strategic and bustling hub of communications between the Kingdom of Naples and the Dukedom of Spoleto, and later a bone of contention between the Church and Imperial armies – hence the castles.

FERENTILLO, last village before the abbey, sprawls across two barren hillsides, guarded by twin fourteenth-century towers and merits a brief stop only if the idea of **mummies** is appealing. Grotesquely propped up in the crypt of San Stefano, these bizarre figures have been preserved by dry sandy soils and dessicating exposure to wind from south-facing windows. They include two French prisoners hung during the Napoleonic wars, a hapless Chinese couple from the last century who came to Italy for their honeymoon and died of cholera instead, and a pile of cheerfully leering skulls.

Much more enjoyable is to continue five kilometres up the valley to the **Abbazia**, the real point of the exercise if you're not passing through simply for the scenery. Founded by the Lombard Duke Faroaldo II, who retired to the monastic life after being deposed by his son in 720, it was amongst the most powerful religious houses in Umbro-Romano, controlling vast tracts of land and dominating the lives of thousands of people. It's set high on the hillside near a thickly wooded cleft, the first impression being of a dull blockhouse affair, with nothing to hint at the splendour of the Lombard and Byzantine art inside. The **frescoes** (1190) which cover the body of the main church are the first tentative attempts to create a distinctively Italian art and move away from the stylised influence of Byzantine painting, an influence that nonetheless was to prevail until the advent of Pietro Cavellini, Cimabue and Giotto a century later. The **altar**, beautifully set off by the rose-coloured stone and rich Romanesque display all around, is a rare and important example of Lombard sculpture, carved with what look like pagan, almost Celtic figures and motifs. To each side are well-preserved but nondescript Roman sarcophagi, backed by a profusion of gorgeously coloured frescoes. A doorway (not always open) to the left leads to the twelfth-century **campanile**, a Lombard import of a type common in Rome and Lazio, and distinguished by fragments and reliefs salvaged from the eighth-century church. There's also a faultless double-tiered **cloister** from the twelfth century and a pricey restaurant.

By following the SS209 through the walled, medieval village of SCHEGGINO you can pick up the Spoleto road into the Valnerina, a route covered earlier on in the chapter.

Carsulae

The building of the Via Flaminia in 220 BC between Rome and Ancona cemented Umbria's strategic importance as the crossroads of central Italy. Staging-posts and fully fledged colonies sprang up along its route, turning into modern-day Narni, Terni, Spoleto, and Spello. Some settlements, however, such as **CARSULAE** (the largest Roman site in Umbria), were subsequently abandoned in the wake of earthquakes and civil war. In its day this particular pile of stones was known as the Pompeii of central Italy, and both Tacitus and Pliny the Younger praised its beauty.

The surrounding plain, though rustic and peaceful, has little real interest, but the excavated remains are reasonably impressive. The site's dominated by a church, **San Damiano**, made from materials filched from the ruins (other stones and precious marbles went to build local houses), behind which runs a stretch of the original Via Flaminia, complete with grooves made by carts and chariots, part of the arched northern gate, tombs, baths, wells, an amphitheatre and all the other trappings of an ex-Roman town.

Narni, Amelia and Otrícoli

It's an easy half-hour hop on the train from Terni to **Narni**, with a hilltop site jutting into the Nera valley on a majestic spur, and crowned by another of Albornoz's formidable papal fortresses. Commanding one end of a steep gorge (about ten minutes of fairly spectacular rail travel), it was once the gateway into Umbria, the last post before the Tiber Valley and the undefended road to Rome. However, while the town retains a fine medieval character, the views from its heights are marred by steel and chemical works around NARNI SCALO, the new town that's grown up in the valley below. The trick is to keep your gaze firmly fixed on the gorge side of the walls and pretend the factories don't exist.

The heart of the **old town** (bus from the station) has all the standard fittings: the medieval piazzas, the warren of streets, a modest art gallery, the usual crop of Romanesque churches, and a huge *Rocca*, currently being restored. There's a **Roman bridge** on the outskirts, the subject of considerable local hype. Goethe arrived in Narni in the middle of the night and was peeved not to have seen it; he was only missing a solitary arch in the middle of the river – just as easily viewed from the train.

In what's an appealing but relatively low-key centre, things revolve around the narrow **Piazza dei Priori**, (which has the **AAST** at no. 12). Pride of place goes to the fourteenth-century **Palazza dei Priori**, unremarkable except for a fountain and graceful **loggia** designed by the Gubbian architect Gattapone. The gaunt and somewhat eccentric building opposite is the Palazzo del Podestà, cobbled together by amalgamating three town houses and adding some token decoration. The thirteenth-century Romanesque sculptures above the main door are worth a glance, and there's a a small **pinacoteca** on the first floor whose main feature is a superlative and much-copied canvas by Ghirlandaio. The bulk of its paintings are in the process of being moved to the gallery in the ex-church of San Domenico, just a minute away in Via Mazzini, where there are key works by Benozzo Gozzoli and Fiorenzo di Lorenzo, plus fourteen- to sixteenth-century frescoes removed from churches in surrounding villages. The walk down to the gallery offers a chance to look at the tiny and easily overlooked church of **Santa Maria in Pensole**, unaltered since 1175 – you can still see the date above the door – and adorned across the width of its facade with a marvellous carved frieze.

The twelfth-century **Duomo** merits a brief mention, chiefly because its front steps are where the town hangs out. Inside, the Cosmati marble floor and a recently discovered ninth-century mosaic of Christ don't give much cause to linger.

There's no real reason for staying overnight in Narni, but should you want to there's a collection of cheap but uninspiring **rooms** around the station, and a **campsite** out of town at Monte del Sole (April 1–Oct 30; ☎0744/746.3360).

Amelia

Amelia, 11km northwest of Narni, and plonked on top of a sugar-loaf hilltop, is by far the most tempting local excursion if the ruins don't appeal. Though not big on monuments, it's a delightful and unvisited town, noted mainly for its extraordinary **cyclopean walls**, claimed as some of the oldest and mightiest in Italy. Supported by their own weight and comprised of vast polygonal blocks up to seven metres across, they reach a height of over twenty metres in places and date back, according to early Roman historians, to the Umbrian settlement of the eleventh-century BC. Most of the town's churches were ruined in the nineteenth century, and art's thin on the ground – San Giacomo's **double cloister** and a **tomb** by **Agostino di Duccio** are the only highlights – but Amelia's charm is the typically Umbrian mixture of good views, medieval streets and lovely countryside close at hand. The local speciality is a tooth-rotting combination of white figs, chocolate and crushed nuts, but for more substantial fare there are two good **restaurants** – *Anita*, Via Roma 31, and *Le Colonne*, Via Roma 191. Both have **rooms** to rent – *Le Colonne* is smaller and more intimate; *Anita* is cheaper.

If you have wheels, the run on to Orvieto along the backroads is a treat; plenty of oak forests and fine walks, and the chance to catch one of Umbria's Romanesque highlights, the twelfth-century church of **Santa Maria Assunata** at LUGNANO IN TEVERINA.

Otrícoli

OTRÍCOLI, 15km south of Narni, is almost the last town in Umbria, and a reasonable miniature of all the region's hilltowns. Its medieval delights, though, are eclipsed by the remains of Roman **Otriculum**, a ramshackle collection of ruins within easy walking distance of the village. To reach them get on the main road that bypasses the village, head downhill for two hundred metres and take the signposted track that strikes off right towards the Tiber. So far no more than a trickle of tourists visits the colony – still largely unexcavated and evocatively draped in clinging undergrowth – but plans by the state to make them the centre of a big archaeological park mean they're headed for the big-time.

Unusually, the settlement has no walls, mainly because it was more a pleasure garden than a defensive site, built as a sort of holiday village for Rome's hoi polloi, who travelled up from the capital by boat on the then still navigable Tiber. Turner stopped off to paint a picture (now in the Clore gallery), and in the sixteenth century Montaigne described the spot as "infinitely pleasant", though it probably won't stay that way for much longer. You can find **rooms** up in Ortrícoli – itself reasonably charming – at the *Pensione Umbra* (Via Roma 18).

Todi

TODI is one of the emerging Umbrian hilltowns, at heart still a thriving and insular agricultural centre, but recently a favoured trendy retreat for Rome's arts and media types. In the way of these things the tourists can't be far behind, but neither fact should deter you from making a day trip: few places beat it for sheer location and fairy tale medievalism. With a stunning and extremely daunting position, it makes a highly inviting prospect from below, though you'd have to have some sort of death wish to tackle the approaches on foot or on a bike. Once up, it feels as if Todi, high and isolated, cares little for the rest of the twentieth century – at least for the time being.

Getting there, and sussing out how to fit it into an itinerary, are likely to be your biggest problems. Basically you come either from Terni on the *FCU* (40min, trains approximately hourly), or from Perugia, again on the *FCU*. Moving on, in addition to the train, there's the option of a straightforward hitch or a daily bus to Orvieto. Todi's **stations** (there are two) are both in the middle of nowhere, and buses to the centre don't always tie in with the trains. Ponte Naia, 5km distant, is marginally more convenient, but the uphill walk is a bit of a slog, so you're probably better off putting your thumb out.

The Piazza del Popolo

The central **Piazza del Popolo** is why most people come here; just about every guidebook describes it as the most perfect medieval piazza in Italy, and it's every inch what it's claimed to be, though the cars detract and the tone's a bit more gaunt and austere than you're led to expect. The **Duomo** at the far end, atop a broad flight of steps, is the main feature – a meeting point of the last of the Romanesque and the first of the Gothic forms filtering up from France in the early fourteenth century. The square, three-tiered **facade** is inspired simplicity; just a sumptuous rose window (1520) and ornately carved doorway to embellish the pinky weathered marble – the classic example of a form found all over Umbria. Inevitably the interior is less impressive. There's some delicate nineteenth-century stained glass in the arched nave on the right, and a good altarpiece by Giannicolo di Paolo (a follower of Perugino), but an appalling sixteenth-century copy of Michelangelo's "Last Judgement" defaces the back wall, putting everything else in its dismal shadow. The strikingly carved **choir** (1530) – of incredible delicacy and precision – is the region's best, with panels at floor level near the front depicting the tools used to carve the piece.

Back in the piazza, the other key buildings are the three **public palaces**, squared off near the duomo in deliberately provocative fashion as an expression of medieval civic pride – definitely trying to put one over on the Church. The adjoining Palazzo del Capitano and adjacent Palazzo del Popolo are most prominent, thanks mainly to the stone staircase which looks like it's been the scene of a thousand B-movie sword fights. Several films have actually been shot in Todi, lured by its relative proximity to Cinecittà and scenographic "authenticity". Most notable was the doomed *Cleopatra* – hence the yellowing photographs of a pouting Elizabeth Taylor in some of the bars.

The Palazzo del Capitano houses the town's small **art gallery**, but it's been closed for "reordering" since 1977 and shows no signs of reopening. Hard to know why because it only has a couple of dozen paintings. More of a loss is the **Etrusco-Romano** museum in the same building, by all accounts a small but interesting collection, but likewise closed to the public.

The Palazzo dei Priori (1293–1337) is the southernmost building in the square, with all the various crenellations, battlements and mullioned windows of the other palaces, but with the difference they've just been restored. It's been the seat of all the town's various rulers and today is still the town hall; if you can look like you're on council business you should be able to peep inside. Best place to enjoy the streetlife is from the **bar** down on its right-hand side, more of a locals' local than the flashy newcomer halfway down the piazza (but which does do a good line in sandwiches).

The rest of the town

There's not much more to Todi, but what there is is likeable. Streets to the right of the duomo are quiet and dozy, and worth a wander, though the single most celebrated thing in the town after the piazza is a church, **San Fortunato**. Set above some half-hearted gardens a very short stroll from the centre, it's an enormous thing given the size of the town – testimony to Todi's medieval wealth and importance. The squat, messy and clearly unfinished facade, an amalgam of Romanesque and Gothic styles, reflects the time it took to build (1292–1462) and at first glance doesn't exactly raise expectations. A florid **Gothic doorway** of arched swirls and carved craziness, however, is the first of several surprises, second of which is the enormous interior, recently highlighted by cleaning and several dazzling coats of whitewash. For once it's a light airy and pleasing sort of size – a legacy of its Romanesque origins – rather than the aircraft-hangar dimensions that church builders seemed to indulge in for their own sake.

It marks the pinnacle of the Umbrian tradition for large vaulted churches, a style based on the smaller and basic "barn churches" common in Tuscany, which were distinguished by a single, low-pitched roof and naves and aisles of equal height. (San Domenico in Perugia is another example.) Also interesting is the increasing use of side-chapels, a habit picked up from Catalonia and southern France in the thirteenth century, and made necessary by the rising demand for daily Masses as the Franciscans became a more ministering Order.

There's another good **choir,** heavier, and with more hints of the Baroque than the one in the duomo, as well as a few scant patches of Sienese fresco. The fresco by **Masolino di Panicale** in the sixth chapel on the right is supposed to be the best painting in the town, and a good example of this rare painter's work, but these days it's in such a bad state (restoration notwithstanding) that you could easily walk past without noticing it. Some lovely **cloisters** to the rear (outside and to the right) round off a distinctive and worthwhile church.

More than can be said of **Santa Maria della Consolazione**, considered the town's big draw to judge by the way it's plastered over all the tourist literature. Ninety-nine years in the making, it's a late Renaissance effort (finished in 1607) probably built on a plan by Bramante, architect of Saint Peter's, and claimed by some to be the way he would have liked the Rome church to turn out. Victorian writers called it the best Renaissance church in Italy (pretty close to saying the best in the world). Worth a look to judge for yourself, but certainly not a special journey.

Your time could be more enjoyably spent taking a siesta in the rambling **Giardino Pubblico**, full of shady nooks and narrow pathways, and a cut above the normal town plot. There's also a kids' playground and a very small **Rocca**, both far less noteworthy than the views, which are extensive, though usually hazy. The gardens are best tackled via the stony track to the right of San Fortunato, less of a sweat than the path which comes up from Piazza Oberdan.

Todi's tourist offerings are soon exhausted, but if you want to go the whole hog, check the so-called **niches** in Piazza del Vecchio Mercato, all that's left of the Roman colony. The town's proud of them, but they don't amount to much; four big, and slightly overgrown arches of completely unknown purpose. Two minutes' walk down the lane in the lowest corner of the piazza brings you to the tiny **San Carlo** (1020), an ancient Lombard chapel well off the beaten track that's all too often locked to protect a set of frescoes by Lo Spagna. A few metres beyond the church, and next to a crumbling flower-strewn arbour, is the **Fonte Scarnabecco** (1241), an unusual arched fountain that's now all but redundant, but the town's lifeblood and social meeting place before piped water. During your wanderings look out for the **three sets of walls**, concentric rings that mark Todi's Umbrian, Roman and medieval limits. They're seen to best effect on Via Matteotti.

Practicalities

Todi is still not really geared up to dealing with its expected visitors, and the **AAST** under the arched vaulting of the Palazzo del Capitano needs a bit of pestering to get any action. The people in *Retro*, a clothes shop at Via del Duomo 16, are often friendlier and more helpful; they co-publish a free guide to the town and surroundings, with a good map and plenty of addresses.

Rooms are likely to be your biggest problem. *Cavour*, Corso Cavour 12 (☎075/882.417), which almost overlooks the Piazza del Popolo, and less central *Hotel Zodiaco*, Via del Crocefisso 23 (☎075/882.625), are the only cheapies, with booking recommended as a result.

Local and long-haul **buses**, including those for the station, leave from Piazza della Repubblica in front of San Fortunato. Most move off in convoy at 1.30pm Monday to Saturday and ferry schoolkids back to outlying villages – a good way of getting to some obscure places. **Tickets** from the fruitshop next to the (not very good) *Ristorante Jacopone*. For **food**, it's worth putting something aside to blow in the highly recommended *Ristorante Umbra* (behind the AAST), which must have one of the most stunning outside terraces going – views over half of Italy. Cheaper alternatives include the *Ristorante Cavour*, Via Cavour 21, and basic *Pizzeria Rosticceria*, off Corso Cavour in Piazza B. d'Alviano, 100m from Piazza del Popolo (closed Mon and after 8pm).

Deruta and the Tiber valley

North of Todi, the Tiber valley broadens out into a flat plain edged with low hills and dotted with light industry. It's not somewhere you'll want to spend a lot of time, but there are one or two things worth catching if you're in no hurry to get to Perugia (though MARSCIANO, the area's main town, certainly isn't one of them).

Instead try and take in some of the hill villages along the route – almost any you choose will boast a **Romanesque church**. Most are built over the graves of early monks and martyrs, the Tiber and Naia valleys having been amongst the earliest to be colonised by Christians fleeing Roman persecution, and thus the springboard of Umbria's powerful monastic tradition. The most rewarding churches are those you come upon by accident, in crumbling hamlets or in the midst of the ilex woods that blanket surrounding hills, but if you prefer to plan a visit the following are a cut above the rest: Viepri, Villa di San Faustino, Santa Maria in Partano, San Teranzano and the Abbazia di San Fidenzo.

If you don't get to the peripheral villages, **Madonna dei Bagni** is the one church on the main N3 bis that's definitely worth a look. Its walls are covered with hundreds of votive tiles left by pilgrims over 300 years, making a unique social document and occasionally wacky insight into the peculiarities of religious belief. Day-to-day life in the fields, the insides of houses, transport (from horse to carriage to car), clothes and so on are represented almost as cartoons, though the most entertaining tiles are those offered as thanks for "miraculous" escapes from dangerous and not so dangerous corners – a fall from a cow, a bite from a donkey, fire, flood and famine. A hundred tiles were stolen in 1980, so opening times are curtailed as a result. The best time to try is Saturday morning (when it's not unknown for coach parties to show up) otherwise ask at the AAST in Deruta, 2km up the road.

Deruta

The town of **DERUTA** is best known for its **ceramics**, and seems to be devoted to nothing else. Some of the stuff is mass-produced trash, and some pieces so big you'd need a trailer to get them home, but most is beautiful – handmade, hand-painted, and by general consent, Italy's best. The Romans worked local clay, but it was the discovery of distinctive blue and yellow glazes in the fifteenth century, allied with the Moorish-influenced designs of southern Spain, that put the town on the map. Some fifty workshops traded as far afield as Britain, and pieces from the period have found their way into most of the world's major museums. Designs these days are mainly copies, with little original work, though it's still very much the place for browsing and buying if you're serious about this sort of thing. Avoid the roadside stalls and head for the workshops of the new town for best choice and prices.

The **old town** on the hill isn't particularly compelling, but there's a mildly interesting **Museo-Pinocoteca** (9am–1pm, closed Sun; L2000) alongside the AAST in Piazza dei Consoli. Highlights of the three small rooms downstairs are paintings by Nicolò Alunno and Fiorenzo di Lorenzo, but most sections, not surprisingly, are given over to ceramics, largely unremarkable except for a **tiled floor** (1524) lifted wholesale from the town's parish church.

Torgiano

TORGIANO, 8km north, is the last worthwhile stop before Perugia. It's a fairly dull town, but home to Umbria's finest **wines**, all of them produced by Giorgio Lungarotti, one of the new breed of Italian producers. A self-made man, and now something of a national celebrity, he's put together an unexpectedly interesting **wine museum**, a varied and comprehensive look at every aspect of viticulture, and the best non-liquid reason for a visit. (Palazzo Graziani, Via Garibaldi. Daily 9am–noon and 3–7pm; L2000). Wines to look out for (and they're not all cheap) include *Rubesco*, *Torre di Giano*, *Chardonnay* and *Castel Grifone*.

Orvieto

ORVIETO, out on a limb from the rest of Umbria, is perfectly placed between Rome and Florence to serve as an historical picnic for tour operators. Tourists flood into the town in their millions, drawn by the **Duomo** – one of the greatest Gothic buildings in Italy. But once its facade and Signorelli's frescoes have been admired, the town's not as exciting as guides and word of mouth make out. This is partly to do with the gloominess of the dark volcanic rock (tufa) from which it's built, and, more poetically, because it harbours something of the characteristic brooding of Etruscan towns. (It was one of the twelve-strong federation of Etruscan cities.) Two thousand years on, it's not difficult to detect a more laid-back atmosphere in the cities east of the Tiber – sunnier and easier-going chiefly because they were founded by the Umbrians, a sunnier and easier-going people.

All the same Orvieto is likeable, the duomo unmissable, and the rest of the town good for an enjoyable couple of hours. And there's always its renowned white **wine** if you're stuck with time on your hands.

Arriving

First impressions of Orvieto from afar tend to be the ones that linger; its position is almost as remarkable and famous as its cathedral. The town, rising 300m sheer from the valley floor, sits on a table-top plug of volcanic lava, one of four such remnants in the vicinity. It starts to look fairly average again from the dismal town around the station, but hit the twisting three-kilometre road up to the old centre and you begin to get a sense of its drama and one-off weirdness. If you arrive by train the **#1 bus** makes the regular trip from the **station** to Piazza XXIX Marzo (buy two tickets at the platform bar – one for the return leg). Inter-town buses take you directly to Piazza Cahen or Piazza della Repubblica, depending on the service. Outward buses leave from the same places. Plans to resurrect a nineteenth-century water-powered funicular from the station are being considered. The **tourist office** is at Piazza del Duomo 24 (daily 9am–1pm and 3–7pm; ☎0763/41.772).

The Duomo

Burckhardt described Orvieto's duomo as "the greatest and richest polychrome monument in the world," while Pope Leo XIII called it "the Golden Lily of Italian Cathedrals", adding that on the Day of Judgment it would float up to heaven carried by its own beauty.

According to a tradition fostered by the Church it was built to celebrate the so-called **Miracle of Bolsena** (1263), an event centred on a Bohemian priest travelling to Rome to shake off an heretical disbelief in transubstantiation – the idea that the body and blood of Christ are physically present in the Eucharist. While he celebrated Mass in a church near Lago di Bolsena, blood started to drip from the Host onto the *corporale*, the white linen cloth that covered the altar. The stained linen was whisked off to Pope Urban IV, who like many a pope was in Orvieto to escape the heat and political hassle of Rome. He immediately proclaimed a miracle, and a year later Thomas Aquinas, no less, drew up a papal bull instigating the feast of **Corpus Domini**. The Church at the time, however, was in retreat, and the Umbrian towns at the height of their civic expansion. It's likely that the building of an awe-inspiring cathedral in one of the region's most powerful comunes was less to commemorate a miracle than a shrewd piece of political opportunism designed to remind errant citizens of the papacy's power.

It was miraculous that the duomo was built at all. Medieval Orvieto was so violent that at times the population thought about giving up on it altogether. Dante wrote that its family feuds were worse than those between Verona's Montagues and Capulets – the originals for Romeo and Juliet. The building was also dogged by a committee approach to design – even the plans took thirty years to draw up. Yet though construction dragged on for three centuries, and exhausted 33 architects, 152 sculptors, 68 painters, and 90 mosaicists, the final product is a surprisingly unified example of the transitional Romanesque-Gothic style. Credit for guiding the work at its most important stage goes to the Sienese architect **Lorenzo Maitini** (1330–60), with the initial plans probably drawn up by Arnolfo di Cambio (architect of the Duomo and Palazzo Vecchio in Florence).

The facade

The facade is the undoubted star-turn, owing its undeniable impact to a decorative richness just the right side of overkill. It's a riot of columns, spires, bas-reliefs, sculptures, dazzling and almost overpowering use of colour, colossally emphasised doorways and hundreds of capricious details just about held together by four enormous fluted columns.

Stunning from the dwarfed piazza, particularly at sunset or under floodlights, it's not all superficial gloss. The **four pillars** at the base, one of the highlights of fourteenth-century Italian sculpture, are well worth a close look. The work of Maitini and his pupils, they describe episodes from the Old and New Testaments in quite staggering detail: lashings of plague, famine, martyrdoms, grotesque mutilation, mad and emaciated figures, the Flagellation, the Massacre of the Innocents, strange visitations, Cain slaying Abel (particularly juicy), and only the occasional touch of light relief. In its day it was there to point an accusing finger at Orvieto's moral slackers, as the-none-too cheerful final panel makes clear, with the damned packed off to fire, brimstone and eternal misery.

The interior

The inside is a disappointment, at least at first glance, as if the facade either took all the enthusiasm or all the money, and the church was tacked on as an after-thought to prop everything else up. Adorned with the alternating stripes of coloured marble found in the cathedrals of Siena, Florence and Pisa, it's mainly distinguished by **Luca Signorelli's** *Last Judgment* (1499–1504). Many claim it surpasses even Michelangelo's similar cycle in the Sistine Chapel, painted forty years later, and obviously heavily influenced by Signorelli's earlier treatment.

Several painters including Perugino and Fra Angelico (who completed two ceiling panels) tackled the chapel before Signorelli – a free-thinking and singular artist from nearby Cortona – was commissioned to finish it off. All but the lower walls are crowded with the movement of passionate and beautifully observed muscular figures, creating an effect that's realistic and almost grotesquely fantastic at the same time. Draughtsmanship and a delight in the human form are the frescoes' most obvious attributes, but there are plenty of bizarre details to hold the narrative interest. A mass of monstrous lechery and naked writhing flesh fill the *Inferno* panel, including that of the painter's unfaithful mistress, immortalised in hell for all to see. In another an unfortunate is having his ear bitten off by a green-buttocked demon. Signorelli, suitably clad in black, has painted himself with Fra Angelico in the lower left corner of *The Sermon of the Antichrist*, both calmly looking on as someone is garrotted at their feet.

All this overshadows the twin **Cappella del Corporale**, which contains the sacred corporale itself, locked away in a massive, jewel-encrusted casket, (designed as a deliberate copy of the facade), plus some appealing frescoes by local fourteenth-century painter Ugolino di Prete, describing events connected with the Miracle of Bolsena. There's also a valuable free-standing painting, *The Madonna dei Raccomandati* (1339), by the Sienese painter Lippo Memmi.

The entire apse is covered in more frescoes by Ugolino, many of which were partly restored by Pintoricchio, who was eventually kicked off the job for "consuming too much gold, too much azure and too much wine". The **choir** is good, but in Umbria – which is renowned for its medieval carving – similar examples are ten a penny. Also worth a mention are an easily missed *Madonna and Child* by Gentile da Fabriano and a beautifully delicate fifteenth-century font, both near the main doors.

The rest of the town

Next to the duomo on the right as you look at it is the **Museo dell'Opera del Duomo** (9am–1pm & 2–5pm, closed Mon; L2000), more charming for its atmosphere than for what it contains. There's probably no other Italian museum quite as chaotic and badly organised. Imagine opening up an attic that's been sealed for centuries, and you get the idea. Amongst the meaningless stone fragments, rusty keys, motheaten vestments, dusty pottery and woodwormy sculptures (all unlabelled) you'll unearth one or two gems, all the better for requiring a bit of rooting around to find them. There are paintings by Martini and Pastura (an artist from Viterbo influenced by Perugino), several important thirteenth-century sculptures by Arnolfo di Cambio and Andrea Pisano, and a lovely font filled with Escher-like carved fishes.

The **Museo Etrusco** or **Museo Faina**, opposite the cathedral (9am–1pm & 3–7pm, closed Mon; L2000) has a predictable collection of vases and fragments excavated from local tombs. Nothing's been done to cheer up a display that would be dull at the best of times, though a bust known as the *Larth Cupures Aranthia* and a fourth-century sarcophagus are mildly interesting. The sixth-century BC **tombs** (9am–dusk; free) near Piazza Cahen are more worth tracking down – rows of massive and sombre stone graves, though with none of the grandeur or paintings of the more famous necropoli in Tarquinia and Cerveteri.

As far as the town's **churches** go, they all pale besides the duomo, though they've a lot more going for them in terms of humility. The tiny and simple **San Lorenzo di Arari** is the perfect antidote, a Romanesque chapel built in 1291 on the site of a church destroyed by monks from nearby San Francesco because the sound of its bells got on their nerves. Four recently restored frescoes on the left of the nave describe typically traumatic scenes from the life of Saint Lawrence. There's also an Etruscan sacrificial slab which rather oddly serves as the Christian altar (*arari* meaning "altar"). From Piazzale Cacciatore there's a goodish **walk** around the city's southern walls (Via Ripa Medici) with views over to a prominent outcrop of rock in the mid-distance, part of the old volcanic crater.

Ten minutes or so brings you to **San Giovenale**, whose rustic surroundings, on the very western tip of the *rupa*, Orvieto's volcanic plateau, are a far cry from the bustle of the duomo. It's not much to look at from the outside, but the musty **medieval interior** is the best (and oldest) in the town, though virtually no-one makes the trek out to see it. The thirteenth-century Gothic transept, with its two pointed arches, rather oddly stands a metre above the rounded Romanesque nave, making for a hybrid and distinctive church, all of it exhaustively decorated with **thirteenth- and fifteenth-century frescoes**. Check out the *Tree of Life* fresco right of the main door, and the macabre *Calendar of Funeral Anniversaries* partly covered by the side entrance.

From the church back to the centre of town Via Malabranca and Via Filippeschi are the best of the **medieval streets**, all tantalising doorways and tiled roofs, but second-rate by the standards of neighbouring hill towns. **San Andrea** is worth a mention, more for its strange twelve-sided **campanile** than the bits and pieces of the Roman and Etruscan city in the crypt. In the Piazza del Popolo, further up Corso Cavour, (the town's pedestrianised main drag), there's a daily fruit and veg market plus the odd craft stall – all far more fun than the noted but forlorn ruins of the **Palazzo del Popolo**, out of bounds during the inevitable restorations.

Il Pozzo di San Patrizio (daily 9am–7pm; L2000) is the town's novelty act, a huge cylindrical well commissioned in 1527 by Pope Clement VII to guarantee the town's water supply during an expected siege by the Imperial army (which never came). It's a dank but striking piece of engineering, 13m wide and 62m deep, named after its supposed similarity to the Irish cave where Saint Patrick died in 493 aged 133. Water was brought to the surface by donkeys on two broad staircases, cannily designed never to intersect. Apart from a small Etruscan tomb halfway down and the fact it was carved from solid tufa, however, the whole thing's simply an impressive hole in the ground.

Practicalities

The **AAST** is at Piazza del Duomo 24, with a room-finding service and plenty of information, though they often tend to run out of the more useful stuff. Most of the town's **nightlife** and cheap **rooms** are near Piazza Cahen and down in Orvieto Scalo, the unlovely district around the station. Hotels are pricey, the best deals being the two-star *Corso*, Corso Cavour 343 (☎0763/42.020), the four-roomed *Primavera*, Strada dell'Arcone 4/6 (☎0763/47.181) in the old town, or the more expensive but more central *Antico Zoppo*, Via Marrabottini 2 (☎0763/40.370). The nearest **campsite** is 10km away on Lago di Corbora (bus to Baschi/Civitella); it's a three-star job with a swimming pool, but out of the way, and only open Easter to the end of September (☎0744/950.240).

Cheap **restaurants** are grouped together at the bottom of Corso Cavour, though the best-value eating in the town is close to the duomo at the co-operatively run *CRAMST*, Via Maitini 15 (☎0763/43.302; closed Sun). Very popular with locals, it's a 450-seat canteen affair, offering a choice between restaurant and self-service pizzeria. To sit outside, *Da Pepe*, Via Beato Angelico 4 (closed Wed) has a nice garden, and is a safe bet for a quiet unpretentious meal. Others worth a try are *Da Anna*, Piazza Corsica 4–5 (closed Fri), *Della Mezza Luna*, Via Ripa Serancia 3 (closed Sun), and *Ricci*, Via Magalotti 22 (closed Mon). Prices generally are over the odds.

The wine bars around the duomo are an expensive way of sampling the well-known Orvietan white, a better wine before local producers turned to mass-production to satisfy the demands of the American market. Most bizarre place to drink or buy the stuff is in *Il Pozzo della Cave* halfway down the steep Via della Cave. It's located in the cave from which the street gets its name and boasts an odd funnel-shaped well into the bargain; the owner offers the least enticing sales incentive in marketing history – a free postcard of the well with every purchase. There's great **ice cream** at *L'Archetto*, an ivy-covered gelateria to the left of the duomo.

Around Orvieto

Moving on from Orvieto there are plenty of choices of destination. The obvious targets are Rome and Florence, both about ninety minutes away by train, but if you're in no hurry you could just as well head west into Tuscany and Lazio. There are buses from Piazza Cahen to VITERBO and BOLSENA. The road to Bolsena has some of the best **views** of Orvieto: it's where the postcard shots are taken from and was also where Turner set up his easel (the resulting picture's now in the Clore wing of the Tate Gallery).

The wooded pocket of countryside west of Orvieto around CASTEL GIORGIO is pretty enough, but probably only worth bothering with if you're in a car. Depending on the route you've taken so far you could stay in Umbria and take a slow train north through CITTÀ DELLA PIEVE) or follow one of two good routes east to TODI. The first of these runs through Monte Peglia, some of the region's classic hill country.

Monte Peglia

Monte Peglia is the generic name for the triangular expanse of land that rises between the Chiani valley in the west and the Tevere in the east. It's wild, sparse and timeless countryside, with hilltop hamlets, olives, vines, herds of white oxen and miles of deserted roads and tracks – the archetype of the pastoral lowlands you find all over the region. Although the map marks several villages, most turn out to be no more than scattered farms, many of them abandoned. The only realistic way of tackling the remoteness is by your own transport.

You'll get the best quick taste of the area on the circuitous and beautifully deserted N79 bis from Orvieto Scalo to Todi. You might be lucky and get a hitch, though most of the traffic these days takes the newer and infinitely quicker route south of lago di Corbara. Superb initial views of Orvieto peter out as the road climbs through many a hairpin into densely wooded hill country, with occasional glimpses (haze allowing) as far as Perugia.

The best of the scenery is north of the road, where, as its name suggests, the area's woods, rivers and fields are a haven for **wildlife**. It's about the only place in Umbria you'll see otters, for example, and is well known for the variety of its birds, who owe their immunity from the Sunday morning blast-anything-that-flies fraternity to an ancient tract of land – *una bandita demeniale di caccia* – where hunting has traditionally been forbidden.

It's quicker and almost equally scenic to take the new N448 to Todi, which after meandering along the flattish southern shore of Lago di Corbara takes off into an unexpectedly dramatic **gorge** for the rest of the run onto Todi. Nobody seems willing to swim in the lake, it's not used for any sort of watersports – and to be honest it doesn't actually look that inviting. Further on things get better, when the strange purple-red rocks of the gorge, along with sheer cliffs and forested slopes, add up to a more enticing package. The road's pretty quiet, with plenty of **camping** and picnic opportunities as the valley flattens out towards Todi.

Città della Pieve

Città della Pieve is most famous as the birthplace of Perugino (1445–1523), but it has a modicum of charm that merits a short visit in its own right. Again, you're better off in a car, for the station is a long haul from the town, and it's the sort of place that can easily be seen in an hour. From below, in the Tiber valley, the town straggles along a distant ridge to the east, vaguely and mysteriously enticing, but once up in the streets it lacks the impact of other Umbrian towns, the chief appeal being the tiny red-bricked houses (there was no local building stone), old women knitting and a proliferation of geraniums at every window. One of the streets, Via della Baciadonna, claims to be the narrowest in Italy, the width of a "woman's kiss" the translation suggests. If you prefer your poetry liquid, the town's fountains run with wine during its April *festa*.

Otherwise its only real interest lies in the handful of **Perugino's paintings**, which lie scattered around the town's fairly dismal churches. If the small **AAST** is shut, at Piazza Matteotti 4 (☎075/28.031), there's a map of the town's few highlights outside the unremarkable duomo in Piazza Gramsci (or Piazza Plebiscito, depending on your politics).

The cathedral itself has a couple of late works which show the painter in his worst light. Perugino's reputation today, though still very high, is lower than it was in his own time, when contemporaries put him in the same bracket as Leonardo and Michelangelo. He trained with Leonardo da Vinci in Florence but largely remained faithful to the tenets of the Umbrian School – sublime misty landscapes behind ethereal religious subjects. His great facility enabled him to produce vast numbers of dewy-eyed saints and Madonnas, whose occasional absence of genuine religious sentiment horrified those who demanded sincerity above all else in devotional art. What in his youth had been profound and innovative gradually came to seem stilted and repetitive. Accused of merely replicating a successful formula, he also did nothing to discourage pupils finishing his works, adding his signature to some real shockers – especially in old age. He remains, however, one of the leading and most influential of the Renaissance painters. The painting not to miss is *The Adoration of the Magi* in **Santa Maria dei Bianchi**, considered his greatest work still resident in Italy (Napoleon removed many to the Louvre), with lesser paintings in nearby **San Antonio Ababte** and **Santa Maria dei Servi**.

travel details

Trains

From Perugia Very frequent service to Foligno (40min) via Assisi (25min) and Spello (35min). Also frequent – same line, different direction – to Passingnano (30min) and Tero'ntola (40min), with connections to Rome (2hr), Florence (2hr 15min) and Siena (3hr 30min – change at Chiusi). Also 8 hourly connections on *FCU* line to Todi (45min); Terni (1hr 30min) and Sansepolcro (1hr 30min) with stops en route.

From Foligno 10 daily to Perugia and Teróntola. Frequent trains to Rome (2hr 30min) via Spoleto

(25min); Terni (1hr) and Narni (1hr 15min). Also stopping trains. Frequent to Norcera (20min); Gualdo (40min); Fabriano (1hr) and Ancona (2hr 45min).

From Terni Frequent to Rieti (50min). Additional stopping trains via Mamore and Piediluco. Regular *FCU* service to Perugia and San Sepolcro via Todi, Città del Castello and halts en route.

From Orte Frequent services to Rome (45min) and Florence (2hr 15min) via Orvieto, Chiusi, Castiglione del Lago and Arezzo. Change for stopping train to Chiusi via Orvieto (45min) and Città della Pieve. Erratic service to Viterbo (2 trains daily).

From Chiusi Additional stopping trains to Arezzo and Orte. Frequent to Siena (1hr 30min).

Buses

From Perugia Frequent buses to most major Umbrian destinations. Also to Rome, Tuscany and the Marche. 10 daily to Gubbio, plus a network of village buses.

From Orvieto Various destinations. One daily to Todi, 7 to Viterbo.

From Spoleto 7 daily to Foligno via Trevi and Fonti di Clitunno. 2 (early morning) to Perugia. 6 daily to Norcia (change at Piedipaterno for San Anatolia and Monteleone – 3 daily). Daily bus from Rome to Urbino (3hr 30min) calls at 9.30am. Rimini (weekends only).

From Terni buses in all directions, including Rieti (Lazio). One daily to Ascoli Piceno (in the Marche), and to San Elpidio (in the Marche) via Tolentino (2hr 30min) and Marcerata (3hr).

CHAPTER TEN

MARCHE

L ying between the Apennines and the Adriatic, Marche is a varied region, and one you could spend weeks exploring. Its mountains and valleys form a backdrop for historic towns and remote villages, the best-known sights being the Renaissance palace of **Urbino** and the fortress of **San Leo**. Much of the region is unspoilt – particularly in the southwest between **Macerata** and the Sibillini mountains, where crumbling hill villages make atmospheric bases for hikes into the stunning **Monti Sibillini** range. Not that all of Marche is free from tourism – much of its coastline is studded with modern grid-plan resorts, and ranks of sun-umbrellas fill many of its beaches. Marche also has a fair amount of industry, heaviest around the port of **Ancona**, and along the main road and rail route into the region from Umbria.

Of Marche's larger resorts, **Pésaro** is the most appealing, with a Renaissance centre maintaining its dignity behind the package-tour seafront; and to the south of Ancona is the **Cónero Riviera**, a spectacular stretch of coast, with small beaches nestling beneath the dramatic cliffs of Monte Cónero. For an upbeat resort, head south to **San Benedetto del Tronto**, with six kilometres of beach, five thousand palm trees, and numerous discos.

Getting around on public transport is not too much of a problem, though you'll save time in the remotest parts of the region if you're prepared to hitch. Four of the provincial capitals, Urbino, Pésaro, Macerata, and Ascoli Piceno are interesting towns in themselves, as well as being well served by public transport, while the fifth, Ancona, is a place to catch ferries to Greece or Yugoslavia, or buses to the Cónero Riviera. In general, though, you'll get closer to the region and its people if you stay in a smaller centre: for hiking in the Sibillini, **Amandola** has the best bus service, but if you don't mind hitching, or relying on fewer buses, **Montefortino** is a prettier base.

Urbino

During the second half of the fifteenth century, **URBINO** was one of the most prestigious courts in Europe, ruled by the remarkable Federico da Montefeltro, who employed some of the greatest artists and architects of the time to build and decorate his palace in the town. Baldassare Castiglione, whose sixteenth-century handbook of courtly behaviour, *Il Cortegiane* (The Courtier), is set there, reckoned it to be the most beautiful in all Italy, and it does seem from contemporary accounts that fifteenth-century Urbino was an extraordinarily civilised place, a measured and urbane society in which life was lived without indulgence.

Arriving and finding a place to stay

Urbino is notoriously difficult to reach – the best approach is by bus from outside Pésaro's train station. They stop in Borgo Mercatale, at the foot of the Palazzo Ducale, which is reached either by lift or by Francesco di Giorgio Martini's recently restored spiral staircase.

For **accommodation**, the cheapest options are rooms in private houses, most of which are to be found on Via Budassi. To be sure of a place in high season, write ahead to Signora Diottalevi at Via Budassi 55 (☎0722/320.631), or to *Pensione Fosca*, Via Budassi 64 (☎0722/2521) – otherwise ask at the **AAST** on Piazza Rinascimento (June–Sept Mon–Sat 9am–2pm & 3–7pm; Oct–May mornings only). The most convenient **hotels** are the *Italia*, Corso Garibaldi 32 (☎0722/2701), with doubles from L33,000 and the *San Giovanni*, Via Barocci 13 (☎0722/2827), which charges the same in season, but has smaller off-season reductions. The *Pineta* **campsite** (☎0722/4710), beyond San Bernadino, is open from Easter to mid-September – bus #7 (#4 on Sun) drops you close by.

The Palazzo Ducale

The **Palazzo Ducale's Facciata dei Torricini**, overlooking the surrounding countryside, is a fitting monument to Federico – an elegant combination of the aesthetic and the practical, it comprises a triple-decked loggia in the form of a triumphal arch flanked by twin defensive towers. In contrast, the Palazzo's bare

FEDERICO DA MONTEFELTRO

Federico was a formidable soldier, a shrewd and humane ruler, and a genuine intellectual, qualities which were due in part to his education at the Mantua school of the most prestigious Renaissance teacher, Vittorino da Feltre. Poor scholars and young nobles were educated together in Vittorino's classes, and were taught self-discipline and frugal living as well as the more usual Latin, maths, literature and the courtly skills of riding, dancing, and swordsmanship.

As the younger and illegitimate son of the Montefeltro family, Federico only became ruler of Urbino after his tyrannical half-brother Oddantonio was assassinated during a popular rebellion. Federico promptly arrived on the scene – fuelling rumours that he'd engineered the uprising himself – and was elected to office after promising not to punish those responsible for Oddantonio's death, to cut taxes, to provide an educational and medical service, and to allow the people some say in the election of magistrates.

Urbino was a small state with few natural resources, and a long way from any major trading routes, so selling the military services of himself and his army was Federico's only way of keeping Urbino solvent. In high demand because of his exceptional loyalty to his employers, Federico's mercenary activities yielded an annual income equivalent to £7,000,000, a substantial portion of which was used to keep taxes low, thus reducing the likelihood of social discontent during his long absences. When he was at home, he seems to have been a remarkably accessible ruler: he would leave his door open at mealtimes so that any member of his 500-strong court might speak to him between courses, and used to move around his state unarmed (unusual in a time when assassination was common), checking up on the welfare of his people. Stores of grain were bought in from Puglia, to keep prices low when the harvest failed, and "revisers" were dispatched around the villages to investigate grievances.

Between his military and political commitments, Federico found time to devote to the arts – according to his biographer, Vespasiano di Bisticci, "He delighted greatly in music . . . and maintained a fine choir with skilled musicians and many singing boys . . . He preferred delicate to loud instruments, caring little for trombones and the like." But Federico's first love was architecture, which he considered to be the highest form of intellectual and aesthetic activity. He was a friend of the leading architectural theorist, Alberti, and according to Vespasiano his knowledge of the art was unequalled: "Though he had his architects about him, he always first realised the design and then explained the proportions and all else; indeed, to hear him discourse . . . it would seem that his chief talent lay in this art; so well he knew how to expound and carry out its principles." The Dalmation architect Luciano Laurana was scarcely known until taken up by him, and he later employed the more established Francesco di Giorgio Martini and one of the greatest of all painters and theorists of architecture, Piero della Francesca.

brick south facade, forming one side of the long central Piazza Rinascimento, looks rather bleak, and it's only once you get inside that you begin to understand its reputation as one of the finest buildings of the Renaissance. Whereas a tour of most palaces of this size tends to reduce the visitor to a state of crabby exhaustion, the spacious rooms of the Palazzo Ducale instil a sense of calmness. The palazzo now houses the **Galleria Nazionale delle Marche** (Tues–Sat 9am–2pm & 3–7pm, Sun 9am–1pm; L4000) but only the few remaining original Urbino works justify much attention. Until you hit these, it's the building itself that will make the biggest impression.

Just inside the entrance, the **Cortile d'Onore** is your first real taste of what Urbino is about. The courtyard is not immediately striking – in fact if you've spent any amount of time in Italy, you'll have seen a host of similar ones already – but this is a prototype of the genre. Designed by Luciano Laurana – selected by Federico after he'd failed to find a suitably bold artist in Florence – it's at once elegant and restrained. Although each element, from the furling Corinthian capitals to the inscription proclaiming Federico's virtues, is exquisitely crafted, it's the way in which they work together that is Laurana's real achievement. Pilasters on the first floor echo columns on the ground floor, pale stone alternates with dark, and the whole is enhanced by the subtle interplay of light and shadow.

Off the cortile is the room that housed Federico's library, which in its day was more comprehensive than Oxford University's. He spent fourteen years and over thirty thousand ducats gathering books from all over Europe, and employed forty scribes to make illuminated copies on kidskin, which were then covered in crimson and decorated with silver. They disappeared into the vaults of the Vatican after Urbino fell to the Vatican in 1631, and all that's left of the room's former grandeur is one of the more outrageous representations of Federico's power – the Eagle of the Montefeltros surrounded by tongues of fire, symbolising the artistic and spiritual gifts bestowed by Federico.

One of Italy's first monumental staircases takes you up to the first floor. Wandering through the white airy rooms, you'll see doors inlaid with everything from gyroscopes and mandolins to armour, representing the various facets of Federico's personality. On carved fireplaces, sphinxes are juxtaposed with angels and palm trees with dolphins, while ceilings are stuccoed with such symbols of Montefeltro power as ermines, eagles and exploding grenades.

The best-preserved part of the palazzo is the suite of rooms known as the **Appartamento del Duca**, behind the Facciata dei Torricini. Displayed here is **Piero della Francesca**'s uncanny *Flagellation*, whose precise meaning continues to elude art historians. The geometric architecture divides the canvas into two unequal spaces – a slice of a cool courtyard and a perfect cube bathed in crystalline light. At the back of the cubic room Christ is almost languidly beaten, while in the foreground, in the courtyard, stand three figures, a beautiful youth, thought to be Federico's assassinated half-brother, Oddantonio, and two older men, who, if the Oddantonio identification is correct, are evil counsellors. Piero's application of mathematical principles to the representation of architecture and the human form had a profound effect on the architects of the palazzo.

No painting better embodies the notion of perfection held by Urbino's elite than *The Ideal City*, long attributed to Piero, but now thought to be by one of his followers. This famous perspective painting of a perfectly symmetrical and utterly deserted cityscape was probably intended as a design for a stage set, but sums up the desire for a civic order which mirrored that of the heavens.

Paolo Uccello's last work, the six-panelled *Profanation of the Host*, is pervaded by a fairy tale atmosphere, possibly in reaction to the depression of getting old – shortly after completing it, he filled in his tax return with the statement "I am old, infirm and unemployed, and my wife is ill." The story is of a woman who sold a consecrated host to a Jewish merchant. She was hanged, and the merchant and his family were burned at the stake – the angels and devils are arguing over custody of the woman's soul.

In the same room is the most famous portrait of Federico da Montefeltro, by the Spanish artist **Pedro Berruguete**. Painted as ever in profile (having lost his right eye in battle), Federico is shown as warrior, ruler, scholar and dynast – wearing an ermine-fringed gown over his armour, he sits reading a book, with his pale and delicate son, Guidobaldo, standing at his feet. It's in the three most intimate rooms of the palazzo, however, that you get most insight into Federico's personality. A spiral staircase descends to two adjoining chapels, one dedicated to Apollo and the Muses, the other to the Christian God. This dualism typifies a strand of Renaissance thought – thinkers like Federico reconciled mythology and Christianity by positing a universe in which pagan deities were seen as aspects of the omnipotent Christian God.

Back on the main floor you come to the most interesting and best preserved of the palazzo's rooms, Federico's *Studiolo*, a triumph of illusory perspective created not with paint, but with intarsia (inlaid wood). Shelves laden with geometrical instruments appear to protrude from the walls, cupboard doors seem to swing open to reveal lines of books, a letter lies in an apparently half-open drawer. Even more remarkable are the delicately-hued landscapes of Urbino as it might appear from one of the surrounding hills, and the life-like squirrel perching next to an equally realistic bowl of fruit. The upper half of the room is covered with 28 portraits of great men, another indication of Federico's eclecticism, as they range from Homer and Petrarch to Solomon and Saint Ambrose. (Only fourteen are originals, the rest having ended up in the Louvre.)

The Town

Next door to the Palazzo Ducale, the **Duomo** is a pompous Neoclassical replacement for Francesco di Giorgio Martini's Renaissance church, destroyed in an earthquake in 1789. The only reason for going in is to see Barocci's *Last Supper*, with Christ surrounded by the chaos of washers-up, dogs and angels.

Urbino is a lively university town, and its bustling streets – a pleasant jumble of Renaissance and medieval houses – can be a welcome antidote to the rarefied atmosphere of the Palazzo Ducale. You can wind down in one of the many bars and trattorias, or take a picnic up to the gardens within the **Fortezza Albornoz**, from where you'll get great views of the town and the countryside out to **San Bernardino**. A fine Renaissance church atop a hill 2km from Urbino, San Bernardino is the resting place for the Montefeltros, whose black marble memorial stones were placed inside when it was realised that the mausoleum designed for the Palazzo Ducale was never going to get built. It was long thought to have been the work of Bramante but is now attributed to Francesco di Giorgio Martini.

There's a yet more interesting church within Urbino, the **Oratorio di San Giovanni** (daily 10am–noon & 3–5pm; L1000), behind whose unfortunate modern facade is a stunning cycle of early fifteenth-century frescoes, depicting the life of Saint John the Baptist and the Crucifixion. Vividly coloured and full of expressive detail, so different from the cool economy of later Renaissance artists, the frescoes are at their liveliest in such incidental scenes as the boozy picnic in the background of the *Baptism of the Multitude*, or the child trying to escape from its mother in the *Crucifixion*.

A visit to Raphael's birthplace, the **Casa di Raffaello**, is not worth the L3000 entrance fee, unless you're especially interested in fifteenth-century domestic architecture. There's just one example of Raphael's work, an early *Madonna and Child*: otherwise the walls are covered with reproductions and minor works by his contemporaries and his father, Giovanni Santi.

Eating and drinking

There are plenty of places to **eat** in town – the best deal being at the university
Mensa on Piazza San Filippo (open to ISIC card holders only). Otherwise, there
are a number of fast food and self-service outlets – try the *Self Service Franco* on
Via del Poggio (off Piazza Rinascimentale), or, for a take-away, the *rosticceria* off
Via Raffaello. If your budget's not too tight, *Il Girarrosto*, outside the church of
San Francesco at the foot of Via Raffaello, serves good traditional food, and *Le Tre
Piante* on Via Budassi is very pleasant too. For **drinking and snacks**, the best
atmosphere is at the *ARCI* bar, *Pablo Neruda*, on Via Pozzo Nuovo; if you're in
need of British beer, there's a reasonable selection at the *Bosom Pub*, on Via
Budassi.

North of Urbino – Sassocorvaro and San Leo

The villages of northern Marche, though pleasant enough, cannot compete with
the crumbling hill settlements further south, and the rarity of buses makes exploration by public transport something of an ordeal. However, two places within the
region are worth the effort.

Perched above a twee artificial lake some 30km northwest of Urbino by road,
SASSOCORVARO is dominated by one of Francesco di Giorgio Martini's most
ambitious fortresses. Like San Leo (see below) it was built to withstand the
recently invented cannon, but as the site lacked San Leo's natural advantages,
Francesco was forced to find a strictly architectural solution. He did away, as far
as possible, with straight walls, and built a grim and cunning fortress bulging
with hour-glass towers. Inside, it's something of a surprise to find an elegant

Renaissance courtyard and an intimate and frescoed theatre – the fortress was built on the orders of Federico da Montefeltro for one of his *condottieri*, Ottaviano degli Ubaldini.

It's a tribute to the strength of Francesco's architecture that the fortress was selected as a safe house for some of Italy's greatest works of art during World War II, including Piero della Francesca's *Flagellation* and Giorgione's *La Tempesta*, reproductions of which are on show. There's also a good **museum of folk life** (daily 10am–noon & 3–6.30pm; L2000), with displays of traditional weaving, wine-making equipment and a mock-up of an old kitchen.

San Leo

The menacing fortress of **SAN LEO** (daily 9am–noon & 2–7pm; closes at least an hour earlier in winter), clamped to the summit of a dizzy precipice in the northern tip of the Marche, has staggered generations of visitors with its intimidating beauty. Machiavelli praised it, Dante modelled the terrain of his Purgatory on it, and Pietro Bembo considered it Italy's "most beautiful implement of war". In fact it's not as impregnable as it seems, and has fallen to a successsion of powers, most recently to the Fascists in World War II, who used it as an aircraft sighting post. One of the few invaders to have been repelled was Cesare Borgia, who was twice driven out of the citadel, despite having first persuaded a weak-willed retainer to give him the key.

There's been a fortress at San Leo since the Romans founded a city on the rock. Later colonisers added to it as necessary until the fifteenth century, when Federico da Montefeltro realised that it was no match for the new gunpowder-charged weapons, and set his military architect, Francesco di Giorgio Martini, the task of creating a new one. The walls were built on a slight inward slope and backed with earth, thus reducing the impact of cannonballs and providing a rampart. Three large squares were incorporated for the manoeuvring of heavy cannons, and every point was defended with firing posts. San Leo's greatest advantage, however, remained its position, which allows unwelcome visitors to be spotted from a great distance.

From the eighteenth century San Leo was used as a prison for enemies of the Vatican, of whom the most notorious was the womanising Count of Cagliostro, a self-proclaimed alchemist, miracle doctor and necromancer. At first the charismatic heretic was incarcerated in a regular prison, but on the insistence of his guards, who were terrified of his diabolic powers, he was moved to the so-called *Pozetto di Cagliostro* (Cagliostro's Well) now the fortress's most memorable sight. The only entrance was through a trap-door in the ceiling, so that food could be lowered to him without the warden running the risk of engaging Cagliostro's evil eye. There was one window, triple-barred and placed so that the prisoner couldn't avoid seeing San Leo's two churches. Not that this had any effect – Cagliostro died of an apopleptic attack, unrepentant, after four years of being virtually buried alive.

Though the churches had no impact on Cagliostro, they're worth a visit. The **Parrochio** was built in the ninth century, with material salvaged from a Roman temple to Jupiter, by Byzantine-influenced architects from Ravenna. The capitals, dimly lit by the tiny windows, are carved with stylised foliage; also notable is the raised sanctuary, designed to impress upon the common worshippers the elevated position of their social superiors. Sunk beneath the back of the church is a sixth-century chapel founded by and later dedicated to Saint Leo, whose body lay here until 1014 when Henry II, Emperor of Germany, calling in at the town on his way home from defeating the Greeks and Saracens in Rome, decided to remove it to Germany. His plans were thwarted by the horses bearing the saint's body – after a few miles they refused to go any further, so San Leo's body was left in the small village of Voghenza near Ferrara.

The heavy lid of the sarcophagus remains in the twelfth-century **Duomo**, dedicated to the saint. Like the Parrochio it's built of local sandstone and incorporates fragments from the Jupiter temple, on whose site it was raised. The best of these are the Corinthian capitals sitting on the stubby Roman columns in the raised sanctuary. Above them, vaults are supported on the heads of crouching caryatids – which are more aesthetically pleasing than structurally efficient, for the church walls and arches have been distorted by bearing the brunt of the weight. The lid of San Leo's sarcophagus is in the crypt, which is far older than the church, and was perhaps once used for pagan worship, as there are primitive pagan carvings on the wall behind the altar.

Pésaro and around

PÉSARO remains lively, elegant and stylish, despite its growing reputation as an international package-holiday playground, and has subtly adapted its historical core to cope with the demands of being a provincial capital. Its post office is entered through the delicate portal of a Gothic church, for instance, and the bus terminus is overshadowed by an imposing fifteenth-century fort housing a prison. The grid of gleaming stucco hotels and apartments along the long sandy beach is punctuated by a handful of Art Deco villas, including one on Piazzale Libertà whose eaves are supported by white plaster lobsters. Not only are there four kilometres of beach and a wanderable old centre, but, connected by regular buses to Urbino and to lesser-known towns like Gradara and Fano, Pésaro is also an ideal base from which to explore the northern Marche.

The Town

Centre of town is the coolly dignified **Piazza del Popolo**, in which the rituals of the pavement café scene are played out against the bombast of sundry Fascist buildings and the Renaissance restraint of the **Palazzo Ducale**. The most significant relic of Renaissance Pésaro, however, is Giovanni Bellini's magnificent *Coronation of the Virgin* polyptych, now housed in the art gallery of the **Museo Civico** (April–Sept Tues–Sat 9.30am–12.30pm & 4–6.45pm, Sun 9.30–12.30pm; Oct–March Tues–Sat 8.30am–1.30pm, Sun 9.30am–12.30pm; L2000, free on Sun). Painted in the 1470s for the church now known as Madonna delle Grazie (in Via San Francesco), the altarpiece situates the coronation not in some cloudy heaven, but in the countryside around Pésaro, dominated by the castle of Gradara. Fully individualised portraits of saints flank the central scene, ranging from the hesitant Saint Lawrence to the dreamy Saint Anthony. Below is a *Nativity* and scenes from the saints' lives, each set in a landscape evocative of a particular mood. Although none of the gallery's other paintings can compare with the Bellini, don't miss Marco Zoppo's *Pietà*, in which the dead Christ's muscled sensuousness prompts speculation on the artist's necrophiliac tendencies.

Renaissance Pésaro was famed for its ceramics, and the museum houses a fine collection – ranging from a Madonna and Child surrounded by pine cones, lemons and bilberries from the workshop of Andrea della Robbia, to plates decorated with an Arabian bandit and a rape scene. The most striking ceramic, however, stands above the entrance to the museum – a ferocious snake-haired Medusa by the local artist Ferruccio Mengaroni.

A block beyond the museum, the old and narrow Via Castelfidardo leads down to Pésaro's most attractive street, the porticoed Corso XI Settembre. If you want to do more than browse in its shops, take a look inside the church of

Sant'Agostino – the choir stalls are inlaid with landscapes, Renaissance cityscapes, and, displaying a wit to rival the *studiolo* at Urbino, half-open cupboards and protruding stacks of books.

On Via Mazza, the continuation of Via Castelfidardo, is Pésaro's archaelogical museum, the **Museo Oliveriano** (Mon–Sat 9.30am–12.30pm; apply at the adjacent library), with a small but unusual collection of local finds. Among the relics from the Iron Age necropolis at nearby Novilara is a child's tomb filled with miniature domestic utensils, and a tomb slab carved with pear-shaped figures rowing a square-sailed boat into battle. Even more intriguing is the collection of ex-votoes – breasts, feet, heads and even a dog – collected not from an early Catholic church, but from a Roman sacred grove at San Veneranda (3km from Pésaro), consecrated in the second century BC. Pride of place, however, goes to a bronze statue of a Grecian youth, exquisite even though it's a copy of a Roman copy of a fifth-century BC Greek original.

Finally, Pésaro is the birthplace of **Rossini** – the theatre is named after him, and hosts an opera festival in his honour every August. At other times, opera buffs have to content themselves with a visit to his house, now a modest shrine of memorabilia, at Via Rossini 34.

Practicalities

Finding your way around Pésaro is no problem – Viale Risorgimento leads from the **train station** to the town's main axis, Via Branca-Via Rossini-Viale della Repubblica, which cuts straight through the historical town to the beach. Bisecting it at Piazza del Popolo are Corso XI Settembre, scene of the evening *passeggiata*, and Via San Francesco, which leads to the **bus terminus** on Piazza Matteotti.

The main **EPT** (Mon–Fri 8am–2pm) is on the corner of Via Rossini and Via Mazzolari, just beyond Piazza del Popolo; there's an **AAST** (Mon–Fri 8.30am–1.30pm & 3–7.30pm) on Piazzale della Libertà, at the beach end of Viale della Repubblica, and in summer a small office operates at the station (Mon–Fri 9am–noon & 4–7pm). All have good maps of the town, showing all hotels and sights, and have information on the surrounding area; the two AAST's will help you find a room.

Geared as they are to the family holiday, Pésaro's **hotels** are not cheap – the best deal is for people staying a week or longer on half or even full board. One of the most reasonable and convenient is *Villa Olga*, just to the left of Piazzale della Libertà at Viale Colombo 9 (☎0721/62.783), charging L30,000 for a double without bath. The *Alba*, on Viale della Vittoria, opposite the Palazzo dello Sport (☎0721/64.516), is a short walk from the beach, but slightly more expensive – take bus #1 to the Palazzo from the train station or Piazza Matteotti. If you want more comfort, the *Abbazia*, Viale Trento 147 (☎0721/33.694), is a good deal in low season, offering doubles with bath for L30,000 – in high season the price rises to L43,000. It's just off Viale della Repubblica, a couple of minutes' walk from the beach.

There's no problem finding **snack** bars – the stall on Piazza Matteotti has good stuffed vegetables, and *Blitz Dinner* is a *tavola calda* on Piazza Lazzarini, at the beginning of Via Branca. There are also plenty of **pizzerias** – *Da Silva* on Corso XI Settembre is a good deal, as is the takeaway *Falcioni* on the same street. *Cigno Bianco*, on Via Castelfidardo, is a combined restaurant, pizzeria and pub, while *Bibo e Biba*, on Via G. Bruno (off Piazza del Popolo), has reasonably priced pasta. If you want to splash out on a fish meal, *Da Maria*, on Via Mazzini (off Corso XI Settembre) gets good reports.

North of Pésaro

The pleasantest route north from Pésaro is the *Strada Panoramica*, a minor road winding through the coastal hills to GABICCE MARE, a large resort with a fine beach and an expensive clifftop disco.

If you want beaches without crowds, **FIORENZUOLA** and **CASTEL DI MEZZO**, just a few kilometres along the *Strada Panoramica* from Pésaro, are tiny fishing villages, with miniscule beaches reached only by steep narrow tracks. Most people visit them only to eat at their fish restaurants, so you should have the beaches to yourself. En route you'll also pass the *Panoramica* **campsite**, in a beautiful setting some 7km north of Pésaro.

Alternatively, you can escape beaches altogether by taking a trip (organised by Pésaro's tourist office on summer Wednesdays) to the sixteenth-century **Villa Imperiale** (Mon–Sat 9am–2pm, Sun 9am–1pm; L3000), a sumptuous mansion in extensive grounds, with rooms decorated by Bronzino and Genga.

Gradara

To the north and further inland is the castle of **GRADARA** – not a place to go in season if you want to avoid crowds, as it's one of the main package-tour excursions. A fairy tale confection of mellow red brick and swallow-tail turrets, it's said to be the scene of the thirteenth-century scandal involving Francesca da Rimini, who committed adultery with Paolo da Malatesta, her husband's brother. The lovers were killed for their transgression, and later consigned to hell by Dante – he meets their spirits in Canto V of the *Inferno*, where they are caught in a ceaseless whirlwind.

Inside the castle is a room decked out as the scene of the crime, with a sumptuously refurbished four-poster bed, fake wall hangings and an open book – Francesca tells Dante in hell that it was while reading the story of Lancelot and Guinevere that she and Paolo first succumbed to their passion. Further reminders of the story are found in two nineteenth-century paintings – one showing the lovers either dead or in a state of post-coital collapse watched by the crippled husband, the other, less ambiguous, of the naked couple. Other rooms are furnished as a torture chamber, complete with spiked iron ball, handcuffs and lances, and as the guards' room, a strange mixture of tavern and armoury. After touring the castle, it's well worth paying the extra L500 to walk round the walls for the fine views over the surrounding hills. Incidentally, Francesca's unhappy spirit is supposed to wander the castle when the moon is full.

Fano

FANO has changed since Robert Browning came here in 1848, seeking relief from the heat and crowds of Florence. Its beaches remain splendid – the sandy and sheltered Lido and the long, pebbly Sassonia – but it's become one of the Adriatic's most popular resorts. If all you want is an enjoyable beach, better head south to the resorts of TORRETTE and MAROTTA, easily reached by bus. If, on the other hand, you don't plan a session of uninterrupted sun-soaking and swimming, Fano is a pleasant enough place, comfortably combining its role as resort with those of small fishing port and minor historical town.

The Town

Buses into Fano stop outside the crenellated **Porta Maggiore** and the remnants of the medieval defensive walls. Behind them is a Roman gate, the **Arco di Augusto**, impressive despite having been truncated in the fifteenth century when Federico da Montefeltro blasted away its upper storey. You can see what it used to look like in a relief on the facade of the adjacent church of San Michele.

The Roman precursor of Fano, named *Fanum Fortunae* after its Temple of Fortune, stood at the eastern end of the *Via Flaminia*, which cut across the Apennines to Rome. The town is still built around a Roman crossroads plan: Via Arco di Augusto and Corso Matteotti follow the routes of the *cardus* and *decumanus*, and their junction is marked with a copy of a Roman milestone stating its distance from the capital (195.4 Roman miles). There are few other relics of Roman Fano, although the fifteenth-century fountain in the main square, along Via Mazzini, is dedicated to Fortune.

Overlooking it are the reconstructed thirteenth-century Palazzo della Ragione and the fifteenth-century **Corte Malatestiana**, dating from the time Fano was ruled by the Malatesta family. Its most notorious member was Sigismondo, whose disagreements with the pope led to the siege of Fano (when the Arco di Augusto lost its top) and his excommunication. After the death of his first wife – whom he was suspected of having poisoned – Sigismondo remarried in Fano in 1449, holding a three-day banquet in the Corte Malatestiana. Rumours about Sigismondo's sinister interest in his wives' diet revived when, seven years later, this wife also died, leaving him free to marry his long-time mistress, Isotta degli Atti. The Corte is at its best nowadays on summer evenings, when its loggias, turrets and trefoil windows provide a backdrop for concerts. Inside there's a small **museum** (July–Sept Tues–Sat 9am–noon & 5–7pm, Sun 9am–noon; Oct–June Tues–Sun 8.30am–12.30pm; L2000) whose most striking exhibit is a mosaic of a winged figure riding a panther. Upstairs is the **art gallery**, worth visiting for an insight into the Victorian psyche, as it's here that you'll find Guercino's *The Guardian Angel*, a painting which entranced Browning during his stay here, and inspired a poem of the same title. Expressing a wistful desire to take the place of the child depicted here learning how to pray, the gushingly sentimental poem ("And wilt thou bend me low . . . and gently tether me as thy lamb there . . .") became incredibly popular, and Italy was flooded with reproductions of the painting for holidaying Browning fans. The keenest disciples set up a club, membership of which was gained by travelling to Fano and sending the founder a postcard.

Less saccharine paintings are to be found in the Renaissance church of **Santa Maria Nuova** on Via de Pili, off the main square. The two works by Perugino, *Madonna, Child and Saints* and an *Annunciation* are both suffused with a calm luminosity, emanating as much from the figures as from the landscapes behind them.

A less demanding way of punctuating your sessions on the beach would be to browse through the classy shopping arcade tastefully laid out in the cloisters of the ex-convent of San Domenico.

Practicalities

Fano's two **AAST**s, on the Lido and in the centre of Sassonia beach, both have good maps indicating all hotels. The **hotels** tend to be pricey, especially in high season. Two of the cheaper options are *Da Angelo*, at the Lido end of town at Via

Spontini 12 (☎0721/866.233), and *Leila*, on Sassonia beach at Viale Adriatico 164 (☎0721/84.765), both of which charge L30,000 for doubles without bath in season.

Even in high season, accomodation need not be prohibitively expensive, as there are plenty of **campsites** and a **youth hostel** nearby. The campsites *Norina* (☎0721/55.792) and *Marinella* (☎0721/55.795), both open from May to September, are on the coast between Pésaro and Fano, and easily reached by bus. Close by the campsites (look out for the *Campanina* restaurant from the bus), is the *Ardizio* youth hostel (☎0721/55.798), open mid-May to early September. South of Fano, the *Stella Maris* (☎0721/884.464) and *Torette* (☎0721/884.119) campsites are near the small resort of Torette, and many others are strung along the coast in between, all easily accessible by bus from Fano.

For **eating**, apart from numerous pizzerias and snack bars, there's a cheap and earthy fish taverna, *Quinta*, in the fishing harbour – it caters mostly for fishermen and the prices reflect it. Just round the corner from the port is an even cheaper place, *Self Service del Mare* (open May–Sept), specialising in cheaper fish like sardines, anchovies and mackerel.

Senigallia

A typical family resort, with one of the Adriatic's best beaches, **SENIGALLIA** is primarily a place for beach-lazing and swimming. The town centre, with its endless arcades and rickety Neoclassical forum, though cheerful enough in season, is gloomy out. It's a conceivable base for exploring the surrounding area: although you'll have to travel into Falconara or Ancona for bus or train connections, it's far pleasanter than Ancona. The major non-beach activities are shopping and café-hopping, but if you want something slightly more taxing, the imposing **Rocca Roveresca**, built for Federico da Montefeltro's son-in-law by Luciano Laurana, architect of the Palazzo Ducale in Urbino, is worth an hour of your time. Its austere exterior is embellished by white stone brackets, while inside airily elegant Renaissance halls stand above an underground warren of vaulted storage rooms and dungeons. It seems that the Rocca was rarely used as a ducal residence – the fireplaces and beautiful spiral staircase show little sign of use. The cells, though, were a different matter: converted from cannon positions when the region fell to the pope, they were designed with diminutive air-holes to inflict a slow and agonising death on their occupants. Fine views are to be had from the towers, built in the fifteenth century when the Adriatic coast was plagued by Turkish bandits.

The Rocca overlooks Senigallia's scruffy and dilapidated sixteenth-century ducal palace, and, more interesting, the **Palazzo Baviera**. Now the seat of the *comune*, it still contains some original furniture and wall coverings, and its ceilings – stuccoed with scenes from Greek mythology, Roman history and the Old Testament – are, to say the least, sumptuous.

Practicalities
The **AAST** (Oct–April Mon–Sat 8am–2pm & 4–9pm; May–Sept also open Sun 8am–1pm), is behind the train station on Piazzale Morandi, a block from the beach.

Hotel prices are on a par with the rest of the Adriatic resorts, and rooms are hard to come by in July and August. The cheapest hotels are to the south: *Gasthof*, at Via Galilei 24 (☎071/61.629), has doubles at around L29,000; *Simona*, Via Pisa 4 (☎071/60.428), is in the same price range; *Angela*, Via Rieti 65 (☎071/63.521), has doubles with bath for L38,000; while *Del Sole*, Lungomare Dante Alighieri 118 (☎071/62.089), charges L35,000. If you want to stay in the centre, *Bice*, Viale Leopardi 105 (☎071/62.951), reached by bus #2, has doubles from L28,500.

With sixteen **campsites**, Senigallia is ideal if you've got a tent – reckon on paying about L4000 per person and L8000 for your tent. Most of the hotels and all the campsites are along the coast, those to the south reached by bus #2, and those to the north by bus #1, both of which leave from the train station. If you want to be independent, there are **bikes** for hire at the Rotonda in the centre of the beach.

Senigallia's liveliest street, Corso 2 Giugno (behind the Rocca), runs down to the Foro and the grim tunnel of arcades called the Portici Ercolani, which are the best hunting grounds for cheap **snacks** – *Da Memmo*, a self-service with pasta and stuffed vegetables, is one of the best. For more substantial sit-down meals a good deal is *Da Franco*, at Via Fratelli Bandiera 55, specialising in local dishes like *vincisgrassi*, a lasagne of ham, cream and truffles.

Ancona and around

ANCONA is a depressing place. Severely damaged by war and earthquakes, it has a few historical monuments embedded in a squalid tangle of cracked and collapsing buildings, while the modern centre is a bland grid of broad avenues and palm-shaded piazzas. However, as the mid-Adriatic's largest port, with ferries to Greece and Yugoslavia, it's a convenient departure point.

Regular buses run along the seafront from the train station to the port, passing the pentagonal **Lazzaretto**, built within the harbour in the eighteenth century as a quarantine station for immigrants. The port itself is headed by a well-preserved Roman arch, the **Arco di Traiano**, raised in honour of Emperor Trajan, under whose rule Ancona first became a major port. Behind it is the **Arco Clementino**, a piece of architectural self-congratulation by Pope Clement XII, who made Ancona a free port in the eighteenth century, and thus considered himself Trajan's equal.

On a steep hill overlooking the port rises the town's Romanesque duomo. What survives of old Ancona is spread out below it, and a wander up the hill is the pleasantest way of filling in time before your ferry leaves. At the foot of the hill is Piazza della Repubblica, from which Via della Loggia leads past the **Loggia dei Mercanti**, whose Gothic splendours are now barely discernible through layers of grime – though you can just make out the figures of medieval dignitaries and horsemen below its elaborately carved windows.

More appealing is the Romanesque church of **Santa Maria della Piazza**, its facade a fantasia of blind loggias and its portal carved with chunky figures and elegant birds. Behind the church, on Via Pizzecolli, is the town's **art gallery** (Tues–Sat 10am–7pm, Sun 9am–1pm), highlight of which is Titian's *Apparition of the Virgin*, with a display charting the recently completed restoration. It's a sombre yet impassioned work, with the Virgin appearing to a rotund and fluffy-bearded bishop in a stormy sunset sky. There's also a glorious *Sacra Conversazione* by Lotto, a view of sixteenth-century Ancona by Andrea Lilli, and an exquisite yet chilling *Madonna and Child* by Carlo Crivelli, with a mean-looking Mary pinching the toe of a rather pained Christ, incongruously flanked by bunches of apples and a marrow.

Beyond the art gallery is the church of **San Francesco delle Scale**, named for the steps leading up to it. Titian's *Apparition* was painted for here, but today its most remarkable work is an almost orgasmic *Assumption* by Lotto. Further up the hill is the **Museo Nazionale delle Marche**, just reopened for the first time since the 1972 earthquake. It's well worth a visit, both for its frescoed ceilings by Tibaldi, and for a magnificent first-century gilded bronze sculpture of two Roman emperors on horseback.

Passing the remains of the Roman amphitheatre, now capped with graffitied earthquake-shattered buildings, you climb up to the pink and white **Duomo** (or San Ciriaco). Though mostly built in a restrained Romanesque style, there's an outburst of Gothic exuberance in the doorway's cluster of slender columns, some plain, others twisted and carved. The simple and calm interior is built on a Greek-cross plan, enlivened by a cupola that from below resembles an elongated umbrella. The most memorable feature, however, is a screen along the edge of the raised right transept, one section of which is carved with eagles, fantastic birds and storks entwined in a tree, the other with saints.

Ferries and other practicalities

All **ferry** lines charge about the same – tickets are on sale at the Stazione Marittima, as well as at the numerous agencies that line the road to the port. The **AAST**s at the train station and port have details of timetables and prices if you want to make a choice at your leisure. As most departures are at night, you're unlikely to need to stay over in Ancona. If you do, the most convenient **hotels** are those opposite the train station: the *Dorico* (☎071/42.761), *Gino* (☎071/43.333) and *Fiore* (☎071/43.390) all charge around L28,000 for a double without bath. There are also a couple of pensioni in the modern centre – *Centrale*, Via Marsala 10, off Corso Garibaldi (☎071/54.388), and *Astor*, on the corner of Corso Mazzini and Via Marsala (☎071/202.776). However, don't rely on them being open out of season.

Bars and **pizzerias** are plentiful along the port, but for more interesting food go to either *Osteria del Pozzo*, in the old town on Via Bonda (off Via dei Mercanti), or *Trattoria Vittoria*, Corso Mazzini 109, off piazza Cavour. Both charge around L13,000 for a full meal.

Inland: the Esino Valley and Fabriano

Cutting right across the Marche, the **Esino valley** is broad and bland in the east, but narrows to a dramatic limestone gorge – the Gola di Rossa – just before the town of Fabriano and the border with Umbria. Although Fabriano and Jesi are heavily industrialised, most of the valley is given over to agriculture, and is best known for *Verdicchio*, a dry white wine produced in the hill-top villages around Jesi. What most visitors come for, however, are the vast Frassassi caves.

Jesi

Though its industrial development has led to **JESI** being known as "the little Milan of the Marche", the historic centre of the town is well-preserved. Clinging to a long ridge, it's fringed by pale brown medieval walls and retains a scattering of Renaissance and Baroque palaces. One of the most majestic of these, the

Palazzo Pianetti, is home of the **Pinacoteca Comunale** (Tues–Sat 9.30am–12.30pm & 4–7pm, Sun & holidays 10am–1pm). The highlight of its opulent interior is the magnificent 72-metre-long stuccoed, gilded and frescoed gallery – a rococo fantasy of shells, flowers and festoons framing cloud-backed allegorical figures. The picture collection is best known for its late works by Lotto, including the graceful *Annunciation* panels (once part of a triptych), scenes from the refreshingly assertive life of Saint Lucy, and the *Visitation*, set in a simple domestic interior. If you've time, walk to the Gothic **San Marco**, outside the town walls on Viale della Vittoria: it has some wonderful Giottoesque frescoes, including a *Crucifixion* in which every face in the crowd is individually realised and totally absorbing.

Verdicchio country

No wine is produced in Jesi itself – if you want to indulge in some wine sampling, head for the *Colonnara cantina*, at **CUPRAMONTANA**, accessible by bus from Ancona and Jesi. The *cantina* is disappointingly up-to-date, but the wines, including a champagne-like *charmant*, are generally good. The best time to visit is on the first Sunday in October, when there's a parade and dancing, and the village streets are lined with stalls of wine and food for the **grape festival**. The idea is that the harvest should begin the day after, but owing to hangovers, it's usually a couple of days before anyone feels fit enough to start work.

The Frassassi Caves and San Vittore Terme

Further up the Esino valley, just after the Gola di Rossa, a road leads up from GENGA train station to the Frassassi gorge, carved by the River Sentino, which was also responsible for creating the eighteen kilometres of caves beneath it. The largest cave of the **Grotte di Frassassi** (daily 8am–8pm; last tour 6.30pm; L10,000 high season, L8000 low season, students L5000) was discovered only in 1971, and just over a kilometre of its caverns and tunnels are now open to the public. As ever, the most remarkable stalactite and stalagmite formations have been named – there's a petrified Niagara falls, a giant's head with a wonderfully Roman profile, a cave whose floor is covered with candles, complete with holders, and a set of organ pipes. (The sounds of the drips have been electronically processed and marketed as a cassette.) The vast Cave of the Great Wind, at 240m high, is one of the biggest in Europe, and large enough to contain Milan Cathedral. It's been used for a series of experiments, ranging from sensory deprivation (as a possible treatment for drug addicts) to a sociological exploration of the dynamics that developed between a group of people enclosed there for a month.

Fabriano

Famous for two things – paper-making and Gentile da Fabriano, the best of the International Gothic artists – **FABRIANO** is now heavily industrialised, and a dismal town at first sight. You're most likely to pass through on your way on to Umbria and Rome, and frankly there's little reason to stop off unless it's to visit the **Museum of Paper and Watermarks** (Tues–Sat 9am–noon, Sun 10am–12.30pm), housed in the ex-convent of San Domenico. The sort of place kids are dragged to on rainy days, it's owned by the biggest of Fabriano's paper mills, *Miliani*, which produces a staggering 900km of paper each day, including watermarked paper for bank notes of various currencies.

The Cónero Riviera

Just south of Ancona the white cliffs of Monte Cónero plunge straight into the sea, forming the northern Adriatic's most spectacular stretch of coastline. Although the beaches at Sirolo and Numana are developed, you should be able to find a quiet cove or a rocky ledge from which to swim in peace, even in high season.

Portonovo

Closest to Ancona is **PORTONOVO**, nestling beneath Monte Cónero, and undeveloped save for two campsites and three expensive hotels, one of which is sited in the Napoleonic fort which dominates the bay. Although its pebbly beach gets fairly busy in summer, the scenery is unbeatable, and the crowds are as nothing compared to those at Sirolo and Numana. There are also a few tiny beaches to the south, which you can reach if you're prepared to paddle and clamber. There's also a lovely Romanesque church, **Santa Maria**, perched above the beach at the end of an oleander-lined path (key to the grounds from the custodian's house on the right). At present you can see it only from the outside, but this is enough – the clear light reflected from the sea bathes it in a golden glow, the shadows adding to the delicate interplay of arcades and wavily tiled roof.

Portonovo is the starting point for the trail across Monte Cónero to Sirolo, beginning at a stairway to the right of the *Hotel Internazionale*. Though rewarding, it's a steep and tricky hike, so don't attempt it without a map – there's a good plan of all Cónero's paths in Burattini's *Guida del Monte Cónero*, or alternatively get hold of Stefano Ardito's *Backpacking in Italy*.

To Sirolo and Numana

The most stunning stretch of coast, a series of tiny coves at the base of Monte Cónero between Portonovo and Sirolo, is best explored by boat – they leave from both bays. You can go just for the scenery or ask to be dropped off somewhere along the way for a few hours of swimming. Particularly inviting is the small beach close to the jagged mid-sea rocks of the *Due Sorelle*, although you won't have it to yourself in peak season.

SIROLO and **NUMANA** are now almost as crowded in July and August as the rest of the Adriatic resorts, the main difference being that their cliff-backed beaches are more picturesque. The beach of SAN MICHELE, just north of Sirolo, is slightly quieter, with a section to the far end where nudism is tolerated. Numana has the added attraction of a **museum** filled mostly with relics of the Piceni tribe, who occupied the area between Senigallia and Pescara from the seventh century BC; the extent to which they were influenced by the Greeks, who set up a trading post nearby, is clearly visible in the red and black pots decorated with scenes from Greek mythology.

Riviera Practicalities

Portonovo, Sirolo and Numana are all accessible by **bus** from Ancona (Piazza Stamira). In Numana, the **hotel** to go for is the *Morelli* (☎071/936.227), with doubles for a mere L13,000; in Sirolo, the *Valeria* (☎071/936.135) charges L27,350. Portonovo's two **campsites**, *Camping Club Adriatico* and *Camping Communale La Torre*, are both open from June to mid-September and charge about L4000 per person and L6000 per tent. Numana and Sirolo's campsites are outrageously expensive in July and August – it's cheaper to stay in a hotel, although you'll need to book well in advance.

Loreto

One of Italy's most popular sites of pilgrimage, attracting three million visitors every year, **LORETO** owes its existence to one of the Catholic Church's more surreal legends. The story goes that in 1292, when the Muslims kicked the Crusaders out of Palestine, a band of angels flew the **house of Mary** from Nazareth to Dalmatia, and then, a few years later, whisked it across the Adriatic to Loreto. In the face of growing scepticism, the Vatican came up with the more plausible story that the Holy House was transported to Loreto on board a Crusader ship. Not surprisingly, though, this theory has not had the same hold on the Catholic imagination, and the Madonna of Loreto continues to be viewed as the patron of aviators – Lindbergh took an image of the Madonna of Loreto on his Atlantic flight in 1927, and a medallion inscribed with her image also accompanied the Apollo 9 crew. Among the Madonna of Loreto's more unlikely fans were Galileo, later denounced and imprisoned as a heretic, and Descartes, who reckoned she'd helped him refine his philosophical method. For centuries she also had military victories attributed to her – presumably she was thought to have power over projectiles – though the builders of Loreto's Basilica, aware that the site was vulnerable to Turkish pirates, decided not to rely on the Madonna's defensive capabilities, and accordingly constructed a formidable fortified church here.

Loreto's treasures were indeed covetable, the most costly and idiosyncratic being a golden baby donated by Louis XIII of France, weighing the same as his long-tried-for heir, the future Louis XIV. The Basilica was ransacked in 1798 by Napoleonic troops, most of the plunder ending up on the shelves of the Louvre. Following Napoleon's demise, subsequent popes managed to retrieve many of the valuables, but the majority were stolen again in 1974, in what's known as the "holy theft of the century".

Numbering among its contributors such figures as Bramante, Antonio da Sangallo, Sansovino, Lotto and Luca Signorelli, the Basilica is a must for anyone midly interested in the Renaissance. However, for the non-believer the atmosphere of devotional hard-sell can soon become stifling. Loreto can also be a distressing, or a moving place, depending on your attitude to faith – between April and October so-called "white trains" bring the sick and terminally ill on three-day missions of hope, the main event being a mass in Piazza della Madonna, outside the Basilica.

The pilgrimage site

Had it been completed according to Bramante's design, the **Piazza della Madonna** would have been an ideal Renaissance square. It still looks pretty good, although Bramante's **Palazzo Apostolico** has only two of its projected three wings, and his low facade for the basilica, designed to make its elegant dome the piazza's focal point, was never built. Instead, the dome, masked by a fluid late-Renaisance facade, is best seen from the back. Here you can see how Bacio Pontelli, who had a hand in most of the Marche's fifteenth-century military architecture, fortified the church – the loggia that runs along the sides and around the nine apses doubles as a walkway for meditating monks and a battlement, looking down over the sturdy defensive walls.

Inside the Basilica

The church's **interior** (Sat–Thurs 9am–1pm & 3–6pm) is the jumbled result of Bramante's, Sansovino's and Sangallo's attempts to graft Renaissance elements onto the late-Gothic structure. Clashing with the pointed arches of the nave, Loreto's raison d'être, the *Santa Casa* (Holy House), is encased in a marble cuboid designed by Bramante and encrusted with statues and reliefs. With typical Renaissance panache pagan sibyls are juxtaposed with Old Testament prophets, sharing the honour of foreseeing Mary's life, scenes from which decorate the rest of the walls. The best are by Sansovino – a *Nativity* on the south side and an *Annunciation* on the front. Vasari considered the angel in the latter "not to be made out of marble at all, but truly celestial, as though actually speaking the words *Ave Maria*."

The Holy House itself is a primitive stone building, with no foundations and only three walls – proof to believers of its authenticity (the basement and fourth wall were formed by a grotto which can still be seen in Nazareth), but evidence to sceptics of the research undertaken by its fakers. Pride of place is given to a copy of the famous *Black Madonna of Loreto* – the medieval original, once crazily attributed to Saint Luke, was destroyed in a fire in 1921. Madonna and Child are usually to be seen swathed in an ornate but ill-fitting wrap known as a dalmatic – a tradition started by Pope Pius VII in 1801 in celebration of the statue's return from the Louvre. Pope Julius II contributed the cannon shell hanging on the right wall, attributing his escape from being killed by it in the siege of Mirandola to the Madonna of Loreto's missile-deflecting powers.

One of the most recent of the church's twenty-five chapels is the **Capella Americana**, featuring a plane in recognition of the Madonna's role as patron of aviators. Of more artistic interest is the **Capella del Crocifisso** whose wooden Crucifixion is a triumph of baroque ingenuity – viewed from the left, Christ appears to be still alive; from the centre, to be drawing his last agonising breath; and from the right, to be dead. Less theatrical is the **Sagrestia di San Giovanni**, frescoed by Luca Signorelli – most striking is the *Conversion of St Paul*, with its panic-stricken courtiers. The sacristy's inlaid cupboards, featuring a jumble of trompe l'oeil bric-a-brac, are influenced by those in the *studiolo* of Urbino's palace.

Next door, in the **Capella dei Duchi di Urbino**, commissioned by the last Duke, Francesco Maria II della Rovere, is an *Annunciation* Barocci, taking place before an open window through which the Palazzo Ducale can be seen. By far the most entertaining chapel, however, is the **Sagrestia di San Marco**, where vault frescoes feature Prophets who seem to be resolving the knotty problem of the sex of angels by peering up their skirts. Ezekiel looks appalled, Zacharias flushed and embarrassed, Jeremiah delighted, and David completely overwhelmed.

To the left of the Chapel of the Crucifix, a corridor leads to the sumptuously stuccoed atrium and the **Treasury**, its vault frescoed by Pomerancio. The artist won the competition for the commission in 1604 thanks to Vatican manoeuvring, much to the chagrin of the loser, Caravaggio, who hired a cutthroat to slash Pomerancio's face. Surveying the unremarkable work Pomerancio produced, you have to suppress a feeling of regret that Caravaggio didn't select a more competent hitman.

The Museo-Pinacoteca

The items left behind in the treasury after the 1974 burglary are now kept in the **Museo-Pinacoteca** (summer Sat–Thurs 9am–1pm & 4–7pm; winter open mornings only), housed in the west wing of the Palazzo Apostolico. If you've liked what you've seen of **Lorenzo Lotto** elsewhere in the Marche, don't miss it – five of his paintings are here, including his final work, *The Presentation in the Temple*. Plagued by neurosis and lack of money, Lotto finally joined the religious community at Loreto, and died here in 1556. Looking at *The Presentation*, with its rotund, crumbling priest and frail, almost skeletal nun, it would appear that he never found much inner peace. *Christ and the Adulteress* is an even more powerful work, with Christ surrounded by maniacally intense men and a swooning adulteress. For some light relief, take a look at the best of all the depictions of the Holy House's angel-powered flight – a fluffy-clouded fantasy by GB Tiepolo.

Practicalities

Loreto is easily accessible by **train** from Ancona – the train station is some way out of town, but connected with the centre by bus. The busiest periods are December 8–12 (the anniversary of the legendary flight), September 5–10, Easter and from Christmas until January 7; it's also pretty crowded throughout the summer, and finding accommodation can be difficult. All the cheap **hotels** are run by religious orders, the cheapest being *Istituto Orsoline di Gesu* (☎071/970.192), with doubles for L25,000. If that's full, the **AAST** at Via Solari 3 (Mon–Fri 8am–1.30pm & 4–8pm, Sun 9am–noon) has a complete list. Also in Via Solari is the *Ristorante Centrale*, which does good fresh pasta.

Recanati and Porto Recanati

A few kilometres along the Macerata road from Loreto is **RECANATI**, a small town that makes a comfortable living from having been the birthplace of the opera singer Beniamino Gigli, and the nineteenth-century poet Giacomo Leopardi. The visitor can wallow in Gigli memorabilia in the civic art gallery, or visit places that feature in Leopardi's poems, but if such acts of homage don't appeal, there's little point in coming to Recanati. It's attractive in a forgettable sort of way, but the precious provinciality soon becomes stultifying – Leopardi himself, though loving Recanati for its views of sea, hills and mountains, found most of its inhabitants stodgy and narrow-minded.

A tour of Recanati

Recanati's **Pinacoteca Civica** (summer Tues–Sun 10am–1pm & 4–7pm; winter Tues–Sat 10am–1pm & 3.30–6.30pm, Sun 10am–1pm) is housed in the nineteenth-century **Palazzo Comunale**, a fussy mock-Renaissance symbol of Recanatese obtuseness – in order to build it they ripped down a fine medieval palace. All that remains of this is the vast **Torre del Borgo**, glowering down on the municipal architecture that surrounds it.

Once inside the gallery you can forget all this and lose yourself in Gigli's world, evoked by costumes worn by the great tenor, presents received by him (including a walking stick from Verdi and a dagger from D'Annunzio), and, best of all, a replica of his dressing-room. A crackly recording of his voice is often playing on a wind-up gramophone as accompaniment to the exhibits.

The gallery itself has only two paintings worth spending time on, both by **Lotto**. There's a polyptych, complete save for its predella (which somehow ended up in the USSR), and an *Annunciation*, better known as *The Madonna of the Cat* for the cat scuttling between the Madonna and angel – thought by some critics to represent the devil.

Turning left out of the piazza, the main street leads down to the **Palazzo Leopardi**, where the poet was born in 1798. The odd name of the square in front of it, Piazzuola Sabato del Villagio, comes from one of Leopardi's poems, in which he observes a typical Recanati Saturday, with "a swarm of children shouting on the piazzuola". You're almost bound to meet crowds of schoolkids here, but their elation tends to come from relief at finishing the tedious tour of Leopardi's gloomy house. The poet's lack of success with women is the best known fact about him – possibly the result of his smothering mother, who still cut up his meat for him when he was 25. Bits of poetry are affixed to a couple of houses, where women who obsessed him once lived. Leopardi sought solace for the pains of love, or rather the lack of it, in the view from the edge of town – on a good day it extends as far as the Apennines. The lower hills, which seem to roll endlessly towards the mountains, inspired his most famous poem *Colle Infinito* (Infinite Hills), and a plaque with a line from it has been stuck on a wall, above a heap of rocks from Naples, where he died and is buried. As the ultimate irony, the place where he came to forget his failures with women has become a lovers' lane.

Porto Recanati

If you're not familiar with either Gigli or Leopardi, you may as well head straight to **PORTO RECANATI**, the nearest resort to Loreto. With its main street (Corso Matteotti) headed by the turreted tower of a medieval castle, and an old quarter of pale stuccoed fishermans' cottages in the centre of the hotels and apartment buildings, it's one of the Adriatic's pleasanter resorts. Apart from the beach, attractions include a **sailing and windsurfing school** – details from the **AAST** (☎071/979.9084) on the Corso – and five discos.

When you tire of the beach there's an **art gallery** inside the castle, which includes a view of Venice attributed to Turner, and a portrait of a peasant at work by Millet. Even better, the castle courtyard has an **arena** – a wonderfully atmospheric place to see film and theatre. Within Italy Porto Recanati is best known for its *brodetto*, a classy fish soup cooked with nine varieties of fish, spiced with saffron and served with squares of toast. If you want to splash out, the place to go is *Bianchi Nicolo* on the sea front – the chef is justifiably known as the *mago del brodetto* (the brodetto magician), and conjures up other equally delicious dishes, including delicate seafood starters and a superb fish risotto.

There are only two cheap **hotels**, both on Corso Matteotti – *Laura*, at no. 86 (☎071/979.6614), has doubles for L29,000, and *Cacciatore*, at no. 11 (☎071/979.9234), charges a couple of thousand lire more. The *Pineta* campsite to the south, on Viale della Repubblica, is reasonably convenient, and has four-person bungalows as well – they work out at about L10,000 per person in low season, L15,000 in high season.

Macerata

A little-known provincial capital surrounded by some of the Marche's loveliest countryside, **MACERATA** is one of the region's liveliest historical towns, thanks to its ancient university. Easy-paced and unpretentious, it's an ideal place to wind down in the evenings after exploring the province's considerable attractions. For opera and ballet fans, its annual *Stagione Lirica*, held in Italy's best open-air venue outside Verona, is a must – in recent years it has drawn such heavyweights as Placido Domingo, Birgit Nilsson and Nureyev. And if you're the slightest bit interested in contemporary art, Macerata has a gallery that alone is reason enough for visiting the town.

The Town

Macerata's modern periphery is easily bypassed – buses take you straight up from the train station to Piazza della Libertà, heart of the old town. It's an odd square, the disparate buildings vying with each other for supremacy and all of them failing. Amongst their number is the Renaissance **Loggia dei Mercanti**, supplied by Alessandro Farnese, better known as Pope Paul III, instigator of many architectural improvements to sixteenth-century Rome; sadly he did nothing else for the Piazza della Libertà, and the loggia is elbowed out by the bland **Palazzo del Comune** and overlooked by the dull **Torre del Comune**. The dreariest feature, however, is the mournful brick facade of **San Paolo**, a deconsecrated seventeenth-century church now used as an exhibition space.

Things buzz a bit more along the main *passeggiata* route, the boutique- and bar-lined Corso della Repubblica, which ends at Piazza della Vittoria and the **Pinacoteca Civica** (Tues–Sat 9am–1pm & 5–7.30pm, Sun 9am–noon). The collection, ranging from the Renaissance perfectionist Crivelli, to Ancona-born Futurist Cagli, isn't bad, but if you're pressed for time, give it a miss.

Greatly more challenging is the stunning collection of Italian contemporary art in **Palazzo Ricci**, just off the piazza in Via D. Ricci. Both the building and the collection are owned by a local bank, and unless you're in Macerata on a Tuesday afternoon or Saturday morning, you should phone to book a visit in advance (☎0733/4261), a day or two ahead of your arrival if you want to be sure of getting in. There are two thrilling sculptures by Francesco Messina – a nerve-charged nude of a dancer putting on her shoes, and a leaping horse which is surely one of the finest images of the creature ever made. Enrico Baj's *Military Head* depicts a general decorated with assorted fabric on a background of upholstery material, and you might see a similarly satiric intent in Manzu's bronze bas-relief of a clutch of cardinals. Manzu's obsessive interest in the form of the cardinal's dress resulted in his producing over fifty sculptures of the subject; he insisted, though, that he was neither ridiculing nor glorifying the church, but simply regarded the figures as still-lifes, with no more significance than a plate of apples. A good cross-section of Italian Futurists is followed by de Chirico's weird *Worried Muse*, while de Chirico's brother, Alberto Savinio, provides the gallery's jokiest piece of social satire – a richly dressed society woman whose long neck ends in a goose's head.

Seeing the rest of Macerata's sights doesn't take long. Via Padre Matteo Ricci leads along to the bleak and vacuous Piazza Mazzini, below which is the

Neoclassical **Sferisterio**, built in the early nineteenth century as an arena for *sphaera*, a traditional game which involved bashing a ball with an iron spiked glove. It was also used for bullfights, horse racing and mock jousts until, in 1921, the opera festival was inaugurated and the musicians took it over. It's a dismal place, not worth visiting unless to see a performance.

Macerata's **Duomo**, up Via Ciccarelli from Piazza Mazzini, is no architectural triumph either – a workaday chunk of Baroque, it might have looked slightly more appetising had its facade been finished. Inside there's a statue of Macerata's saint, Giuliano, whose path to sainthood sounds like something out of a Sunday tabloid. He arrived home to find two people in his bed, and, thinking they were his wife and her lover, promptly killed them. Discovering he'd murdered his parents, he hacked one of his arms off in remorse – the severed limb is now kept in a church strong room, encased in a sleeve of gold and silver. The relic is displayed on request, but you need to give a day's notice.

Practicalities

Buses #2, #2a, #6 and #8 connect the **train station** with Piazza della Libertà. The **AAST**, on the square, has maps and a good display of local crafts. If it's closed, the **EPT**, at Via Garibaldi 87, works office hours.

There aren't many **hotels** in Macerata, and in the opera season (July 20–Aug 20) it's a good idea to book in advance. *San Giorgio*, Via T. Lauri 6 (☎0733/48.300), and *Pensione Gioberti*, Via Gioberti 5 (☎0733/48.903) are convenient and adequate, and both charge L34,500 for doubles with bath.

You can **eat** fairly cheaply if you stick to takeaways and pizzas. *Pizzeria Scalette*, on the stepped Piaggia delle Torre (between Piazza della Libertà and Piazza Mazzini), is excellent value, and the nearby *Da Silvano* is good if somewhat pricey. There's a fast food outlet on Vicolo Ferrari (off Via Matteotti), and on the same street is *Pizzeria Luciana*. The *Quercia* is a self-service restaurant on the fringe of the old town, at Via Sibillini 37. Finally, if you've got the money to indulge yourself, go to Macerata's best restaurant, *Da Secondo*, on Via Pescheria Vecchio, near the university; they do a superlative *vincisgrassi*, a sinfully rich lasagne – it's usually packed out, so ring ahead (☎0733/44.912).

The town's most likeable **bar** is the *Firenze*, also on Via Pescheria Vecchia, a student hangout that sadly closes at around 8pm. The bars on Piazza della Libertà are open till late – try *Mercurio* under the Loggia dei Mercanti. Trendies make for the *Maracuja Club* on Piazza Vittorio Veneto, a cocktail and ice cream bar open till midnight (later in the summer), and the expensive *Disco Tartaruga*, in Vicolo S. Fiora (off Corso Garibaldi).

Seats for the **opera** are bookable at the *Biglietteria dell'Arena Sferisterio*, Piazza Mazzini 10 (☎0733/40.735 or 49.508); tickets range from L10,000 to L100,000, and tend to sell out well in advance.

East of Macerata

With its hills rising from the coast and rippling towards the Apennines, its medieval villages and scattering of Romanesque abbeys and churches, the area around Macerata is interesting to explore. You can get to most places by bus from Macerata, although if you're wanting to visit some of the more out-of-the-way hill villages, you may find it convenient to sleep over.

The Chienti Valley

From Macerata road and railway run east to the coast through the **Chienti valley**, passing some of the region's most characteristic hill towns and two of its best churches. About 10km from Macerata, close to the turn-off for Morravalle, is the Romanesque church of **San Claudio al Chienti**, approached along a cypress-lined avenue. It's recently been carefully restored after years of use as a farm out-building, and appears to be none the worse for its undignified past – you'd never guess that the two cylindrical towers that flank its facade used to serve as grain silos. The upper storey, intended for church dignitaries, was entered through the elegant marble portal, while lesser mortals were directed to the tunnel-like door on the ground floor. The marble for the portal, like much of the church's fabric, was scavenged from a Roman village, Pausula, which stood on the site of the adjacent field. The interior is atmospheric enough, though there's not much to absorb you for long.

Morravalle

Above San Claudio, the hill village of **MORRAVALLE**, skirted by a stepped street which disappears through arched gates, is worth a visit only if you have your own transport.

The main piazza, tucked away at the top, is a tightly enclosed, even claustrophobic square, which for the past six centuries has been given over to municipal business. Flanked by the eighteenth-century Palazzo del Comune and squat Palazzo del Podestà (where Italy's first pawnshop was set up by Saint Bernadino in 1428), is the Palazzo Lazzarini, built by those members of the Lazzarini family who survived their internecine battle for the privilege of ruling Morravalle. The palazzo, though built in the fourteenth century, incorporates an earlier Romanesque-Gothic portal, possibly taken – somewhat inappropriately, given the family history – from a local church.

Montelupone

The even more remote **MONTELUPONE** is the most memorable of the district's walled hill villages because it appears to be on the point of collapse. The problem is subsidence, and most of its golden stone buildings are held up by medieval-looking wooden scaffolding, which makes the stepped streets and narrow alleys a pleasurable sort of obstacle course. Get there, if you can, in the early evening – the village is liveliest then, and looks particularly good glowing in the late sun. If it's clear, you can also catch a photographer's dream sunset from the belvedere – the view extends from Monte Cónero on the coast and across to the most beautiful of the Appenines, the Monti Sibillini.

You can get to Montelupone by (rare) bus from Macerata; if you're hitching, it's easiest from the Montelupone fork on the SS77 below Recanati. There's a very cheap **hotel**, the *Damiani* (☎0733/586.371), which charges only L24,000 for a double without bath, and also has a restaurant.

Santa Maria a Piè di Chienti

Back in the valley, road and railway pass the ex-monastery of **Santa Maria a Piè di Chienti** just after the fork for MONTECOSARO. It was built by Cluniac monks, who came to the area in the tenth century, draining the flood-prone river into channels, and creating fertile land out of what had been a fever-ridden marsh. Situated close to the coast, the monastery was vulnerable to Saracen invasions, so the monks encircled it with ditches, which could be flooded in the event of a raid. It survived until the early nineteenth century, when it was destroyed by Napoleonic troops – all that remains is the church itself. The facade was rebuilt in the eighteenth century, and the church's best external features are now its apses, decorated with fake pilasters and scalloped arcades. However, it's the interior (key from the adjacent bar) that's really special, its columns and arches bathed in the half-light that falls from the windowpanes of alabaster. After wandering around the vaulted chamber beneath the raised presbytery, and up the stairs to the galleries (narrow to ensure that they were climbed slowly, with a prayer on every step), you'll need to switch the lights on (by the right transept) to see the fifteenth-century frescoes properly. The best-preserved are in the apse, showing New Testament scenes in Renaissance settings, framed by fake mosaics and dominated by a stony-faced Christ.

Civitanova Marche and Civitanova Alta

From Santa Maria it's only a short trip to the coast and **CIVITANOVA MARCHE**, a large and somewhat soulless resort. There's little reason to hang around, although it can be a useful stopover as it's on the main Adriatic road and rail route. You can escape the hordes by heading up to **CIVITANOVA ALTA**, 4km away, which is still partly surrounded by medieval walls and has a small **modern art gallery** with works by Morandi, Carrà and Manzu. If you decide to stay, the hotel *La Lucciola* in Via N. Da Recco, off the main Via Colombo (☎0733/761.039), charges L26,000 for a double.

Tolentino and around

Girded by ugly modern suburbs, **TOLENTINO** improves markedly after its turretted thirteenth-century bridge, a short way beyond which stands the **Basilica di San Nicolo**, the main reason for visiting the town. Its west front is a real feast for the eyes – a curly Baroque facade with a grinning sun instead of a rose window, and a fancily twisting Gothic portal topped by an oriental-style arch enclosing a dragon-killing saint. The interior is nothing special until you hit the **Capellone di San Nicola**, whose Gothic frescoes create a kaleidoscope of colourful scenes of medieval life. In fact, they are episodes from the life of Christ, painted in the fourteenth century by one of Giotto's followers, known only as the *Maestro di Tolentino*. The most striking are *The Marriage at Cana*, with hefty servants carrying massive jugs of wine on their shoulders, *The Slaughter of the Innocents*, and *The Entry into Jerusalem*, in which an attempt at perspective is made by peopling the trees with miniature figures.

Just off the main piazza is the **Museo Internazionale della Cariacatura** (Mon–Sat 9am–12.30pm; also open afternoons in summer), which is filled with some of the world's best satirical cartoons. After this, there's not much else to detain you.

San Severino Marche

Twelve kilometres north of Tolentino lies the old, silvery grey town of **SAN SEVERINO MARCHE**, the centre of which is an unusual elliptical piazza surrounded by porticoes. Here you'll find the **tourist office**, which has rudimentary maps and a guide to the town's art gallery.

Known as the **Pinacoteca Tacchi-Venturi** after a local historian, the gallery is just above the piazza on Via Salimbeni (Tues–Sun 9am–1pm; July–Sept also 4–7pm), and contains a memorable assembly of pieces. A gilded polyptych of saints by Paolo Veneziano is followed by an even more sumptuous altarpiece by Vittore Crivelli, which centres on a china-doll Madonna weighed down in heavy gold embroidery. It's the frame that really catches your eye, though – an opulent confection of scalloped arches topped with urns from which spring gesticulating ecclesiastics. Other highlights are the works by the Salimbeni brothers, who were born and worked in San Severino in the fifteenth century – they are represented by delicate and expressive frescoes detached from local churches and a wooden polyptych of *The Marriage of Saint Catherine*.

In the same building is the **Museo Archaeologico**, with relics from the Roman valley town of Septempeda, whose inhabitants, driven out by barbarian invasions in the sixth century, escaped up the nearest hill, to found the forerunner of San Severino.

Other works by the Salimbeni brothers adorn San Severino's two most interesting churches. One of these, the ancient **San Lorenzo in Doliolo**, at the top of Via Salimbeni, looks slightly odd thanks to a medieval brick tower standing on top of its stone portal. The Salimbeni frescoes, illustrating the story of Saint Andrew, are on the vault of the tenth-century crypt, looking far older and more primitive than they really are, because of their antique surroundings; the back part of the crypt is thought to be a pagan temple dating back to the time of the refugees from Septempeda, and thus San Severino's oldest building.

It's a long and steep walk to the upper part of San Severino, known as *castello*, but there are occasional buses from the main square. A lonely, evocative place, it was here that the Romans from Septempeda came, though as *castello* continued to be the hub of religious and political life until the eighteenth century, any traces of them have long been covered over. Close to its thirteenth-century walls, sheltered by a Gothic portico, is the **Fontana dei Sette Canelle**, a seven-spouted fountain where you'll occasionally see old women doing their washing. Right at the top, dwarfed by the medieval Torre del Comune, is the **Duomo Vecchio**, founded in the tenth century, but with a Romanesque-Gothic facade, simple Gothic cloisters, and a much rebuilt interior. Not surprisingly, it's lost a bit of atmosphere with all these reconstructions, but the baptistery vault still has its Salimbeni frescoes. Also worth a look are the inlaid choir stalls and the tomb of the town's patron, Saint Severinus.

Ússita and hiking territory

On the border with Umbria, close to the Monti Sibillini, is ÚSSITA, a rather anonymous winter sports resort, squeezed into a narrow valley at the foot of Monte Bove. However, it's a good first base for mountain **hikes**, as you can get there by bus from Macerata. From Ússita you can walk up to the *Rifugio Forcella del Fargno* (open all of August, and Sundays from June to November) from which there's a good choice of walks, including the ascent of the three-peaked mountain known as the *Pizzo Tre Vescovi* because it resembles three mitred bishops. The going can be tricky, as the upper peaks are covered in snow for most of the year, so you'll need a good map (*Kompass* 666 is the best), and if you can read Italian the *CAI Guida dei Monti Sibillini* is helpful, being packed with information on flora, fauna and local legends. The cheapest place to stay in Ússita is the *CAI*-owned *Rifugio Città di Macerata*, in the Frontignano district (Dec 15–May 1 & June 15–Sept 15; ☎0737/90.193), where you'll find most of the town's hotels and its sports centre.

If you have your own transport, or don't mind road walking, with the slight possibility of a hitch, you can head up to the **Santuario di Macereto**, set on a wild high plain above Ússita. It's no rustic chapel, but a classy Bramantesque church built in the sixteenth century as a spiritual stopover for shepherds bringing their flocks up from their winter grazing grounds in the south, and is surrounded by arcaded stalls for the animals.

South of Macerata – the road to Sarnano

With the Sibillini mountains on the horizon, snow-capped for most of the year, the route south from Macerata ranks as one of Le Marche's most beautiful. Ten kilometres along the road, on the edge of a dense wood, you reach the Romanesque-Gothic complex of the Cistercian **Abbazia di Fiastra**. More enticing than the abbey and the adjoining eighteenth-century house (in which Wagner once stayed) are the trails through the woods and the **Museo della Civiltà Contadina**, a folk museum laid out in the abbey's low-vaulted outhouses. Among the agricultural and weaving equipment is a decorated wagon such as most farming families owned, until the middle of this century, using it as a manure cart, a wedding carriage, or whatever form of transport was needed. For some insight into the economics of marriage, take a look at the dowry lists, itemising the value of household goods. A small **archaeological museum** contains finds from the nearby Roman town of Urbisaglia.

URBISAGLIA (or URBS SALVIA) was one of the Marche's most important Roman towns until it was sacked by Alaric in AD 409. Its fame continued into the Middle Ages, for Dante invoked it as an example of a city fallen from glory in his *Paradiso*. So far an amphitheatre, theatre, baths and parts of the walls have been excavated, and frescoes of hunting scenes discovered in an underpassage. It should be opening to the public in the early 1990s – ask at Macerata's tourist office or at the souvenir shop at Fiastra for details.

South of Urbisaglia, the hill town of **SAN GINESIO** is justifiably known as the balcony of the Sibillini: the panoramic view from the gardens of the Colle Ascarano, just outside the town walls, stretches from the Adriatic and Monte Cónero to the Sibillini mountains and the highest of the Apennines, the Gran Sasso in Abruzzo. There's a fair amount to see in the town itself, though as it's primarily set up as a summer health resort, you may find its hyper-cleanliness a little unreal. Its central piazza is dominated by one of the Marche's most unusual churches, the **Collegiata della Annunziata**, whose late-Gothic facade is decorated with filigree-like terracotta moulding. Rising above it are two campaniles, one capped by an onion dome, and the other by what looks like a manicured cactus. Gothic frescoes adorn some of the chapels, and the crypt has frescoes by the Salimbeni brothers – including a *Pietà* in which Mary looks completely demented and Christ is so covered with nail-holes that he appears to have chicken pox. Like most of Le Marche's hill towns, San Ginesio has an enticing warren of stepped streets, and as its only **hotel** – *Miramarche*, Via Trensano 25

(☎0733/666.022) – charges just L29,000 for a classy double, you might well want to stay over.

Sarnano

Until a few years ago, **SARNANO**, south of San Ginesio, was a poor and virtually abandoned village. Then the town woke up to the potential of its radioactive springs, known since Roman times to have wide-ranging curative properties, and Sarnano began to develop itself into an exclusive spa resort. The medieval core, coiling in concentric circles around a gentle hill, was subtly restored, and though it's now more of a showpiece than a living village, its narrow interconnecting cobbled streets and picturesque old houses make it an ideal place for a undemanding day's wandering.

It's worth getting a map from the **AAST** just off Piazza della Libertà in the small new town, before heading up through **Porta Brunforte** into old Sarnano. Just inside is the fourteenth-century church of **San Francesco**, decorated with Palestinian plates, thought to have been brought to Sarnano by souvenir-collecting Crusaders. Its convent is now the seat of the *comune*, and houses a small **pinacoteca** (summer daily 9am–1pm & 3–7pm; rest of the year Tues & Wed 3–8pm, Thurs–Sat 3–7pm, plus Tues, Thurs & Sat 9am–1pm), the major item being a *Madonna and Child* by Vittore Crivelli. Plans exist to set up a museum about the area's experiences in World War II – at present there's a room stacked with rusting grenades and boxes of guns.

Continue climbing to the summit of the town and you hit Piazza Alta, once the political and religious centre. When Sarnano fell under papal rule in the sixteenth century, the limitation of local power made participation in public life lose its allure; eventually, in the last century, the underused fourteenth-century **Palazzo del Popolo** was converted into a theatre. It also proved increasingly difficult to ordain priors, as Rome refused to accept those chosen by the people, and the **Palazzo dei Priori** became the prison. These and the square's other medieval buildings are now in the process of restoration, and it's likely that the *comune* will move back here one day.

At present the most interesting of the piazza's buildings is the thirteenth-century church of **Santa Maria di Piazza**, whose fifteenth-century frescoes include a figure known as the *Madonna with Angels*, for the host of celestial musicians and choristers surrounding her. The wooden statue of Christ on the altar has been saddled with one of popular tradition's looniest myths – if it's about to rain, his beard is supposed to grow.

On the second Sunday in August, Santa Maria is the starting point for Sarnano's annual medieval knees-up – though apart from the costumes and processions, it has more in common with a kids' sports day, featuring a tug-of-war, pole climbing, and a race in which the competitors have to balance jugs of water on their heads.

Sarnano's **hotels** are not cheap: best value is the *San Giacomo*, Via Garibaldi 88 (☎0733/667.201), with doubles from L27,000. Otherwise *Ai Pini*, Via F Corridoni 101 (☎0733/667.183), has doubles with bath from L35,000. If you want to **ski** in winter, or to spend a few summer days in the mountains, there's a small resort, SASSOTETTO, 10km away – the cheapest hotel there is *La Sibilla* (Dec–March & June–Sept; ☎0733/665.102), with doubles for L30,000.

The Monti Sibillini

With a mountain lake reddened by the blood of the devil, a narrow pass known as the gorge of hell and a cave reputed to have been the lair of an enchantress, the **Monti Sibillini** not only are the most beautiful of the Apennines, but teem with ancient legends too.

The best way of exploring the Sibillini is on foot – even if you're not a seasoned hiker there are easy but stunning trails, while for diehard backpackers there are challenging long treks. The most agreeable bases are the medieval hill villages which crown the Sibillini foothills, but there are also a number of *rifugi* if you want to be closer to the starting points for walks. Most villages are served by buses, but as they're few and far between, you'll probably find hitching more convenient.

Amándola

The small town of **AMÁNDOLA** is easy to get to on public transport and has an excellent **youth hostel** in a newly converted eighteenth-century palazzo – all rooms have a bathroom, and there are plans to install individual kitchens as well. Though not the prettiest of the Sibillini villages, it's the most forward-looking, holding a week-long international **theatre festival** in the first week of September. Low on pretension and high on participation, the festival overcomes language barriers with mime and movement performances and workshops – the atmosphere is irresistible, and it's well worth sticking around for the whole week.

As for Amándola itself, it's a great place to wind down after a day's hiking, especially if you spend your evenings drinking the local wine at the *osteria* below the youth hostel. Outside festival time, the main sight is the **Museo della Civiltà Contadina** (open summer only), housed in the ex-convent of the church of San Francesco. The collection is fascinating, ranging from wine-making and grappa-distilling apparatus, to a hand-pulled ambulance and carts decorated with Fascist symbols. It's in the kitchen, though, that things really come alive – the clutter includes a jar of roasted barley (a coffee substitute), a sausage-making machine, mosquito spray, and a primitive potty and wooden baby-walker.

Around Amándola

One kilometre outside Amándola is the fifteenth-century church of **Santa Maria a Piè d'Agello** – no architectural masterpiece, but a fine country church, with slots in the window sills for offerings, and a few simple frescoes, though many were destroyed by the lime with which they were covered in the seventeenth century. It was thought, in plague-ridden times, that frescoes were unsanitary.

Further along the Tenna valley road you come to the abbey of **San Ruffino**, a thirteenth-century church built above catacombs. Their frescoes, dating back to the ninth and tenth centuries, indicate how long it was before Christianity was tolerated outside the main towns – in fact, it wasn't until Saint Francis visited the area in the late eleventh century that Christianity took a hold on the popular imagination, and paganism finally began to decline.

Montefortino

For real hiking terrain you'll need to head south, towards the hill village of **MONTEFORTINO**. A prettier base than Amándola, it's touristy in season and dead quiet out – and less well served by buses. The cheapest place to stay is *Del*

Girone, Via Papiri 5 (☎0736/969.128 or 969.219), with doubles at L22,000 in season. Primarily a place to wander and admire the Sibillini views, Montefortino also has a small **art gallery** (Sat & Sun 10am–noon; at other times ask custodian at house no. 1, to the right of the piazza), whose chief attractions are a polyptych by Alemanno – a follower of the Crivelli who took as much delight in painting embroidery as they did – and an arresting twelfth-century portrait of a man with a pipe and candle emerging from the darkness. Appropriately, given the necromantic traditions of the area, there's also an eighteenth-century painting of *Circe* with her occult apparatus.

Into the Gorge of Hell

To the south, just before the hill village of MONTEMONACO, is the starting point for one of the most spectacular (and easiest) walks through the **Gola dell'Infernaccio** (Gorge of Hell). If you go by bus, ask to be dropped at the Infernaccio fork. Even the approach to the gorge, down a narrow valley, is evocative – silent, except for the distant roar of the River Tenna seething through the Gola. Although a straightforward walk in summer, it can be hazardous in winter, as the plaques to dead hikers on the cliffs at the entrance testify. Climbing up beyond the bridge, the path follows the river, squeezing its way under jagged overhanging rocks, accompanied by the deafening sound of raging water. After a second bridge the path forks – the lower leading to the tranquil source of the Tenna, and the upper, more interestingly, in about half an hour, to the **Hermitage of San Leonardo.**

Founded in the ninth century by monks who destroyed the site's pagan temple, it's been rebuilt many times – most recently by a Capuchin hermit, Pietro Lavini, who moved in fifteen years ago. By now he's accustomed to being a tourist attraction and will show you round the bare church and his even barer living quarters. He's virtually self-sufficient, growing fruit and vegetables in his tiny mountain-top garden, and though well-wishers have donated equipment to help his work, the basement is stacked with agricultural machinery rusting and cobwebbed from lack of use.

Montemonaco and the Cave of the Sibyl

MONTEMONACO, a walled medieval village of cobbled streets and honey-gold houses, is not only close to the Gola dell'Infernaccio, but is also the place to stay if you want to visit the **cave of the Sibyl**, whose alleged occupant gave her name to this mountain group.

Most commonly the Sibyl is characterised as a temptress possessed by the devil – a fifteenth-century romance, *Guerrin Meschino*, tells of a Christian knight who spends six months in her pleasure dome of golden palaces, stolidly resisting the seductive advances of the beautiful women who live there. However, feminist historians have shown that in pre-Roman times the Sibyl was a wise woman who gave advice on everything from agriculture to medicine; the Romans, finding it unacceptable that such knowledge should be attributed to a woman, turned her into a passive Mother Earth figure. With the advent of Christianity she became a prophetess who foresaw the birth of Christ – which is why you see Sibyls in churches. Finally, in the war-torn fourteenth century, the notion of the alluring and malevolent Sibyl provided a convenient explanation for military failure. The hold the Sibyl had on the medieval imagination is indicated by the fact that in 1320 an international gathering of churchmen discussed reports from the Sibillini that a group of dissident Ghibellines (pro-emperor) had participated in a black sabbath to shorten the pope's life. Somewhat alarmed, the pope deduced that his diseased liver and disturbed intestine were attributable not to over-eating and drinking, but to the Sibyl's machinations. From the town to the cave is a two-hour walk. Don't be tempted to investigate the cave too thoroughly – a few years ago a couple of Dutch students disappeared in its depths.

Montemonaco's cheapest **hotel** is the *Orsa Maggiore* on Via Roma (☎0736/960.128), but the *Rifugio Monte Sibilla* (information from the *comune* at Montemonaco) is closer to the cave, and the best base for climbing Monte Sibilla – you'll have to hitch or walk the 8km to get there, however. As the path is only barely visible you'd be advised to take the *Monti Sibillini* map by *Kompass*.

Pilate's Lake

To do the best of the Sibillini treks, you need to hitch from Montemonaco to FOCE, where you can stay in the *Rifugio della Montagna* (☎0736/960.327). The hike, through the **Valle del Lago di Pilato** and up to the **Lago di Pilato** and **Pizzo di Diavolo** (Devil's Peak), is fairly tough, and you'll need the *Kompass* map; unless you're an experienced cross-country skier, don't try the trip outside summer, as the snows don't melt until June. If you want to extend the hike, you can camp on the shores of the lake, and the next morning climb the highest of the Sibillini peaks, **Monte Vettore**.

According to the legend of the lake, Pilate's body was dispatched from Rome on a cart pulled by two wild oxen, who climbed up into the Sibillini and ditched the corpse in the water here. In the Middle Ages it became a favourite haunt for necromancers seeking dialogues with the devil – stones inscribed with occult symbols have been found on its shores. Deciding they wanted to be rid of the magicians, the local lords one night put soldiers on guard around its shores. Nothing happened until the morning, when the soldiers discovered that the lake had turned red – assuming it was with the devil's blood, they fled. What in fact turned the water red was a mass of miniscule red *chirocephalus marchesonii*, a species of fish indigenous to Asia; a shoal was left behind here millions of years ago, when the sea receded, and its descendants still thrive here.

East of the Sibillini – Fermo and Porto San Giorgio

East of Amándola, a short distance from the coast, is the attractive old town of **FERMO**. Its web of streets is lined with medieval and Renaissance buildings, erupting out of which is a wooded peak crowned with a Romanesque-Gothic duomo. The town's most spectacular monument, however, is hidden from view – a first-century underground complex of thirty filter beds known as the **Piscina Epurtoria Romana**. Entered from Via Aceti, off the main Piazza del Popolo, it's something akin to a flooded cathedral, with its well-preserved vault and arches subtly lit, and, in the sections which remain in use, reflected in the dark, still water.

From Fermo a road descends to the resort of **PORTO SAN GIORGIO**, with a small fishing and sailing port and a long sandy beach. Its palms, pines and oleanders, and its sprinkling of Art Deco villas, make it a pleasant enough place, though the modern seafront is predictably bland. The best day to visit is on the second Sunday in July, for the *Festa del Mare*, when fish are fried in the open air in a giant frying pan – five metres across, it weighs 10,000 pounds and needs 3310 pounds of oil to fill it.

Áscoli Piceno

ÁSCOLI PICENO owes its existence to a woodpecker that led a band of nomadic shepherds to the wedge of land between two rivers on which the city now stands. At least, that's one of the many legends to have grown up around the origins of Áscoli and the Piceni tribe for whom it is named – other versions replace the woodpecker-guide with Diomedes or the son of Saturn, and the nomadic shepherds with veterans of the Trojan war or Greek traders. Whatever the truth, the Piceni were real enough, and the relics of their civilisation suggests that they were a pretty emotional and impetuous people – writing curses on missiles before firing them, gauging the intensity of grief by measuring the volume of tears, and losing a critical battle against the Romans when they interpreted an earthquake as a sign of divine wrath, and abandoned the fight.

Today the Ascolani seem initially to be reserved, as if in obedience to the aphorisms urging moderation, hard work and reticence that are inscribed on many of their houses. However, one taste of the exuberance of the central piazza in the early evening is enough to dispel such an impression. If you come for Mardi Gras, you'll be able to participate in the Marche's most flamboyant carnival, while on the first Sunday in August there's the *Quintana*, a medieval festival which incorporates a spectacular joust.

The Town

The central Piazza del Popolo, the stage for the evening *passeggiata*, is the place to get the feel of Áscoli. Paved with gleaming travertine and flanked by Renaissance porticoes, it's the setting for two of the city's finest buildings, the pleasantly jumbled **Palazzo dei Capitani del Popolo** and the refined Gothic San Francesco. The former was built in the thirteenth century, when the free commune of Áscoli was at its height. That anything of the building has survived is something of a miracle, for in 1535 a certain Giambattista Quieti, fearing that his rivals might seek refuge there, set fire to it. The interior was gutted but enough remained of the facade for a swift facelift to suffice. Rectangular windows were slotted into medieval arches, and a grand portal affixed, on top of which sits a statue to Pope Paul III, who reintroduced peace by replacing Quieti with a neutral outsider. Not that peace lasted long – a few years after the portal had been completed, the Ascolani, finding themselves under the rule of an overbearing papal representative, solved the problem by murdering him in the sacristy of the duomo. The Palazzo's ground floor is now partly occupied by the **AAST** (April–Oct and carnival period Mon–Fri 9am–12.30pm & 3–7.30pm; other times go to Via Trivio 1 – summer 8.30am–1.30pm & 3–6.30pm; closes 6pm in winter).

When they weren't slaughtering each other, at least some of Áscoli's rulers found time to collect public money in order to finance city improvements. The sixteenth-century **loggias** that enclose the piazza are one of the results – each of a slightly different width, to correspond to the size of the contribution made by the various merchants and shopkeepers who worked there.

The church of **San Francesco**, on the other hand, was financed by the sale of a Franciscan convent outside the city, after Pope Alexander IV had given the Franciscans permission to move within its walls. Construction started in 1262 but wasn't completed until 1549, when the low cupola was added. It's a somewhat restrained church, with little to seize the attention except for the intricate west

ÁSCOLI PICENO

Train Station

River Castellano

River Tronto

River Tronto

CORSO VITTORIO EMANUELE

Palazzo Malaspina (Contemporary Art Gallery)

Duomo

Baptistery

PIAZZA ARRINGO

VIA XX SETTEMBRE

CORSO MAZZINI

CORSO TRENTO E TRIESTE

Palazzo del Comune (Pinacoteca)

S. Gregorio

S. Maria

VIA DEL TRIVIO

PIAZZA DEL POPOLO

AAST

Palazzo dei Capitani del Popolo

S. Francesco

S. Pietro Martire

PIAZZA BASSO

SS. Vincenzo e Anastasio

VIA SOLESTÀ

VIA DELLE TORRI

VIA DINO ANGELINI

Palazzetto Longobardi (Youth Hostel)

Roman Bridge

River Tronto

VIA DELLA CO...

Porta Gemina

Roman Theatre

portal on Via del Trivio. Unless you need to cool and calm down after the heat and bustle of Áscoli's narrow streets, there's little point in going inside. Adjoining the south side of the church is the sixteenth-century **Loggia dei Mercanti**, sometimes attributed to Bramante. It was once the scene of commercial wheeling and dealing – there are still niches cut into the back wall in which bricks could be checked for size before being purchased. Lower-scale commerce now takes place in the cloister to the north of the church, where market stalls fill the area to which the monks would have come to meditate. The church's smaller and older cloister is far prettier and remains tranquil despite forming the garden of an office block.

San Vincenzo and around
Via Trivio continues up towards Piazza Ventidio Basso, the medieval commercial centre of town, now of interest for its two churches. **San Vincenzo e San Anastasio** is Áscoli's most distinctive church, with a fifteenth-century chessboard facade that was once filled out with frescoes. Beneath the mainly eleventh-century body of the building is a primitive crypt erected over a spring which was supposed to have leprosy-curing properties. Although the plunge bath is still there, the spring was diverted elsewhere in the last century.

San Pietro Martire is a far less appealing building, erected by Dominican monks in the thirteenth century in order not to be outdone by their Franciscan rivals down the road. It's as austere and intimidating as Saint Peter Martyr himself, who, between founding Dominican communities like that at Áscoli, gained such a reputation as a persecutor of religious sects that he became the patron of inquisitors after his murder by a couple of so-called heretics.

The dark Via Soderini, leading out of the square, forms the spine of Áscoli's riverside medieval quarter. Lined with buildings out of which the occasional defensive tower sprouts, it's an evocative street, giving you a clear idea of how rigorously the town was defended. Tiny streets fan out from it, many of them spanned by covered passages which in times of siege served as escape routes and as stations from which to pour oil down onto the heads of attackers. Of the defensive tower houses, one of the best preserved is the **Palazzetto Longobardi**, a virtually windowless twelfth-century building; it's been converted into a youth hostel.

After exploring the quarter you can cut through to the river and the thirteenth-century gate, the **Porta Solestà**, from which one of Italy's largest and most impressively preserved **roman bridges** spans the river. An underpassage tunnels through it, and it's worth taking the effort to arrange to have it opened for you at the tourist office, as much for the uncanny experience of walking across an unseen river with traffic crossing just above your head, as for the opportunity to examine colossal Roman masonry at close quarters.

To San Gregorio
There's little else of Roman Áscoli to see, except some sparse remains of a **Roman theatre**, on the southwest edge of town, close to the Roman **Porta Gemina**, or twin gate, at the beginning of the road to Rome. From the theatre a road leads up to the **Parco della Rimembranza**, for a great rooftop view of the town, and on to the steep and picturesque Via Pretoriana, whose small craft shops make it a good hunting ground for gifts. Close by is the fourteenth-century church of **San Gregorio**, ingeniously built around the remains of a Roman temple. Incorporated into the facade are two lofty Corinthian columns, originally

imported by the Romans from Greece, and patches of *opus reticulatum* (diamond brickwork). In the adjoining convent is a tiny revolving door with the inscription *Qui si depositano gli innocenti* (Here you deposit the innocent), designed so that parents could remain anonymous when leaving unwanted children to the care of priests and nuns.

The Duomo, Pinacoteca and Museo Archaeologico

With the pregnant caryatids on the facade of the **Palazzo del Comune** over-looked by the pompous **Duomo**, Piazza Arringo is a testimony to the lack of taste of Áscoli's Baroque architects. However, as the duomo shelters what is reckoned to be Carlo Crivelli's best work, and the Palazzo del Comune one of the Marche's best art galleries, the square's daft flamboyance does have its positive side.

In the duomo's flashy interior chandeliers are suspended on strings of illumi-nated beads, the apse is painted with a fake Persian carpet, the pillar capitals and vault ribs are gaudily gilded, and the cupola is painted with late nineteenth-century frescoes of obscure Ascolani saints against a backdrop of impossibly blue skies and feather-mop palm trees. The **Crivelli polyptych**, in the Cappella del Sacramento, thus comes as a welcome relief. Even if Crivelli's penchant for rare-fied opulence isn't to your taste, it has to be admitted that he did what he did with style, and, in this work, with admirable psychological insight. The most arresting of the ten panels is the central *Pietà*, in which the haggard expression of Mary, the bitter torment that distorts Christ's face, and Magdalene's frozen horror as she examines the wound in his hand are rendered all the more intense by the strict semi-circular formation in which their heads are arranged.

The **Pinacoteca Civica** (due to be reopened this year) contains other pieces by Crivelli, none as sophisticated or as well preserved as the duomo's polyptych, but engaging works nonetheless – one shows the sprawling baby Christ, chin in hand, apparently mesmerised by an apple. Pietro Alemanno, Crivelli's follower, contributes an *Annunciation* featuring a view of medieval Áscoli bristling with towers, and there are also a few foreign works – most notably a *Portrait of a Woman* by Van Dyck, and a *Deposition* by Rogier van der Weyden.

If you want to know more about ancient Áscoli, head for the **Museo Archaeologico** (daily 9.30am–1.30pm, Sat also 3.30–5.30pm), across the square. The collection includes Piceni projectiles inscribed with curses against their Roman enemies, jewellery, heavy bronze rings that were placed on the stomachs of dead women, and small test tube-like containers used to assess the quality of grief by measuring the volume of tears.

Practicalities

Ascoli is a town to explore on foot – you'll only need to use public transport when you arrive or leave. The town is not particularly well-connected, but there are regular buses and trains to San Benedetto al Tronto, on the main east coast rail-way line. You're likely to need to stay over, but the **hotels** are not too promising – the *Nuovo Picchio*, Via C. Battisti 11 (☎0736/51.051) with doubles from L26,000, is usually full, and if you want some comfort at the *Piceno*, at Via Minucia 10 (☎0736/52.553), you'll need to pay upwards of L42,000 for a double with bathroom. More pleasant than either is the **youth hostel**, *Ostello de' Longobardi*, housed in a converted medieval tower at Via Soderini 26 (☎0736/50.007 or 63.788); it's offi-cially open from June 15 to September, but at other times apply to the warden, Guido Biondo at Via Guiderocchi 1, or to Francesço Fratini at Via Guiderocchi 5.

To compensate, food is good value in the town, and there are loads of cheap pizzerias dotted around the centre. More interesting fare is to be had at the *Trattoria da Giovanna* just off Piazza Arringo at Rua dei Marcolini 3, at *Zio Pipo*, Via del Trivio 43, and at *Al Teatro*, Via del Teatro 3, off Via del Trivio behind the main theatre.

The Áscoli Coast

Easily accessible by bus or train from Áscoli Piceno, **SAN BENEDETTO DEL TRONTO** is the most extravagant of the Marche's resorts. Known as the Riviera delle Palme, for the five thousand palms that shade its promenade, and with six kilometres of sandy white beach, it'll give you a hedonistic buzz if you're in the mood for beaches, discos and *passeggiata* posing – if you're not, give it a miss. Of its hundred **hotels**, there are a handful with doubles from around L26,000, details of which are available from the **tourist office** at the beginning of Viale Colombo. As reasonable as any, and not far from the train station, is the *Triestino*, Viale Moretti 21 (☎0735/2004). **GROTTAMARE**, a few minutes further up the coastal rail line, is a lower-key resort on the same model, but without San Benedetto's panache. One factor that makes it worth considering, though, is the extremely cheap *Parco* hotel, at Via Lungomare 28 (☎0735/631.015), with doubles from L15,000.

travel details

Trains

From Pésaro to Ancona (up to 27 daily; 40min–1hr).

From Ancona to Loreto (up to 12 daily; 15–25min).

From Macerata to Tolentino/San Severino (up to 13 daily; 20min/25min).

From Áscoli Piceno to San Benedetto al Tronto (up to 13 daily; 40min).

Buses

From Pésaro to Urbino (up to 20 daily; 50min); Gradara (up to 6 daily); Fano/Torrette/Marotta (up to 7 daily; 10min/15min/20min).

From Ancona to Jesi (up to 8 daily); Senigallia (up to 23 daily); Macerata (up to 9 daily; 1hr 20min).

From Macerata to Fiastra/Sarnano (up to 8 daily; 15min/1hr–1hr 15min); Recanati/Loreto/Portorecanati (up to 8 daily; 30min/50min/1hr); Morrovalle (up to 5 daily; 30min); Sarnano/Amándola (up to 7/5 daily; 55min/1hr 10min).

From Amándola to Áscoli Piceno (up to 3 daily; 1hr 20min); Montefortino/Montemonaco (5 daily Mon–Sat; 10min/20min); Fermo/Porto San Giorgio (up to 4 daily; 1hr/1hr 15min).

From Áscoli Piceno to San Benedetto al Tronto (up to 33 daily; 50min); Amándola/Montefortino/Montemonaco (3 daily Mon–Sat; 1hr 20min/1hr 30min/1hr 45min).

Ferries from Ancona

Minoan Lines (☎071/56.789) to Igoumenitsa and Patras (March–mid-June and mid-Sept–Dec 4 per week; mid-June–mid-Sept 5 weekly; 24hr/32hr). Most services call at Corfu (22hr 30min).

Marlines (☎071/50.062) to Igoumenitsa/Patras/Iraklion/Kusadasi (1 weekly; 24hr/32hr/64hr77hr).

Karageorgis Lines (☎071/201.080) to Patras (Sept–June 2 weekly; July & Aug 3 weekly; 32hr).

Strintzis Lines (☎071/204.247) to Corfu/Igoumenitsa/Patras (Nov–April 2 weekly; March–June & Sept–Oct 4 weekly; July & Aug10 weekly; 23hr/25hr 30min/34hr.); to Split (June & Sept–Oct 2 per week; July & Aug 6 weekly; 8–9 hr); to Dubrovnik (summer 1 weekly; 13 hr).

Jadrolinija (☎071/202.034) to Split/Stari Grad (Hwar)/Vela Luka (Korcula) (July & Aug 1 weekly; 9hr/12hr/14hr 45min).

CHAPTER ELEVEN

ROME AND LAZIO

O f all Italy's historic cities, it's Rome which perhaps exerts the most compelling fascination. There's arguably more to see here than in any other city in the world, with the relics of a constant two thousand-plus years of population packed into its sprawling urban area; and as a contemporary European capital, it has a feel which is quite unique. Even if you don't intend to travel any further south, it would be a great mistake to exclude it from any tour of the north of the country.

Rome is, in many ways, the ideal capital of Italy. Perfectly placed between Italy's warring North and South factions and heartily despised by both, it has long been the country's parasite, under the papacy ruling its dominions with a distant and autocratic hand, overweighted with courtiers and hangers-on, and since Unification spending money that's largely made in the prosperous North on programmes imposed on the poor and helpless South. Romans, the thinking seems to go in other Italian cities, are a lazy bunch, not to be trusted, living very nicely off the fat of the rest of the land. The Romans, for their part, are happy to agree, considering themselves a breed apart from their compatriots, with no particular allegiances, and comfortable in the knowledge that their city is where the things that matter happen. In fact, much of Italy's power-broking goes on else-where, amongst the bosses of Turin and Milan; and the politicians are often manipulated by the country's powerful industrialists. But Rome remains the proud centre of government string-pulling, the wastefulness, inefficiency and corruption of its bloated bureaucracies a national fact of life. In a city of around four million people, there are around 600,000 officeworkers, compared to an industrial workforce of around a sixth of that.

For the traveller, all of this is less evident than the sheer weight of history in the city, its various eras crowding in on each other to an almost breathtaking degree. Nowhere else in the world, perhaps, are you forced to take account of history in such an uncompromising way. There are, of course, the **classical** features, most renownedly the Colosseum, the rubbly Forum and Palatine Hill; and relics from the **early Christian** period in ancient basilicas. And the fountains and churches of the **Baroque** period go a long way to determining the look of the city centre, most notably in the work of Bernini. But these are just a part of the picture, which is an almost continuous one right up to the present day, taking in **Romanesque** churches, **Renaissance** palazzi, **Rococo** fountains, right up to the ponderous buildings of **post-Unification** and the often destructive, self-publicising legacies of **Mussolini** – often all found within a few paces of each other. There are medieval churches atop early Christian basilicas above Roman palaces; houses and apartment blocks incorporate fragments of Roman temples, inscribed in Latin; roads and piazzas follow the lines of classical amphitheatres and stadia.

All of which is to say that Rome is not an easy place to absorb on one visit, and you need to approach things slowly, taking care not to try and see too much too quickly, even if you only have a few days here. Apart from anything, it's hard to get anywhere very fast. Despite regular threats to close the city centre off to motor vehicles altogether, the congestion problem is awful and getting worse; on foot it's easy to lose a sense of direction winding about in the twisting old streets, and in any case you're so likely to see something interesting that detours and stopoffs are almost inevitable. Stout, comfortable shoes and loose, cool clothes – Rome can get very sticky in summer – will be your greatest assets. One further thing: don't come in August, when the city centre is half closed up and the only people in town fellow tourists.

Beyond Rome, the region of **Lazio** inevitably pales in comparison, with rela-tively few centres of note and a landscape that varies from the gently undulating green hills of its northern sector to the more inhospitable mountains south and east of the capital. It's a poor region, its lack of identity the butt of a number of Italian jokes, and the closest you'll get to the feel of the Italian South without catching a train all the way to Naples. Much, however, is easily seen on a day-trip from the capital, not least the ancient sites of **Ostia Antica** and Hadrian's villa at **Tivoli** – two of the Rome area's most important (and intriguing) sights. Further afield, in the north of Lazio the Etruscan sites of **Tarquinia** and **Cerveteri** provide the main and most obvious tourist focus, the rather gloomy town of **Viterbo** the principal regional centre; while Romans head out at weekends to soak up the gentle beauty of lakes **Bracciano**, **Vico** and **Bolsena**. The region east of Rome is sparsely populated and poor, though scenically appealing, its high hills unfolding beyond the main – and dull – regional centre of **Rieti**. The south, on the other hand, is the one part of Lazio where you might want to spend a little longer, especially if you're beating a leisurely path to Naples. You can, of course, see towns like **Anzio** and **Nettuno** as a day-trip too, and they make the best places to swim while based in the capital. But the coast beyond demands more attention, resorts like **Sperlonga** and **Terracina** relatively unknown outside Italy, and islands like **Ponza** one of the most gorgeous spots, at least out of high season, on the entire west coast. Inland, much is mountains and fairly remote but that's part of the appeal, the monasteries at **Subiaco** and **Montecassino** just two worthwhile stops on what might be a rewarding – certainly an original – route south.

ROME

Rome's earliest **history** is caked with legend. Rea Silvia, the daughter of a local king, Numitor, had two twin sons by Mars. They were supposed to be sacrificed to the god but the ritual wasn't carried out, and the two boys were abandoned and found by a she-wolf, who suckled them until their adoption by a shepherd – who named them **Romulus and Remus**. Later they laid out the boundaries of the city on the Palatine Hill, but it soon became apparent that there was only room for one ruler, and, unable to agree on the signs given to them by the gods, they quarrelled, Romulus killing Remus and becoming in 753 BC the city's first monarch.

Such is the legend, though it seems more likely that Rome was simply an obvious spot to build a city: the Tiber could be easily crossed by way of the Isola Tiberina, making the location a key one on the trade routes between Etruria and Campania. Rome as a kingdom lasted until about 507 BC, when the people rose up against the tyrannical King Tarquinius and established a **Republic**, appointing the first two Consuls and instituting a more democratic form of government. Under the Republic the city prospered, growing greatly in size and subduing the various tribes of the surrounding areas – the Etruscans to the north, the Sabines to the east, the Samnites to the south. By the third century BC the city had begun to extend its influence beyond the boundaries of what is now mainland Italy, pushing south into Sicily and across the ocean to Africa and Carthage, soon becoming the dominant power in the Mediterranean. Domestically, however, the history of the Republic is one of internal strife, faction fighting faction among the patrician ruling classes as everyone tried to grab a slice of the riches that were pouring into the city from its plundering expeditions abroad – and the ordinary people, or plebians, enjoying little more justice than they had under the Roman monarchs.

Following the murder of Julius Caesar, a brief period of turmoil gave way, in 27 BC, to the founding of the **Empire** under Augustus, a triumph for the new democrats over the old guard. Augustus heaved Rome into the Imperial era, determined to turn the city – as he claimed – from one of stone to one of marble, building arches, theatres and monuments of a magnificence suited to the capital of an expanding empire. The city swelled to a population of a million or more, its people housed in cramped apartment blocks or *insulae*; crime in the city was rife, and the traffic problem apparently on a par with today's, one contemporary writer complaining that the din on the streets made it impossible to get a good night's sleep. It was, however, a time of peace and prosperity, the Roman upper classes living a life of indolent luxury, in sumptuous residences with proper plumbing and central heating, and the empire's borders being ever more extended, reaching their maximum limits under the emperor Trajan, who died in AD 117.

The **decline** of Rome is hard to date precisely, but it could be said to have started with the emperor Diocletian, who assumed power in 284 and divided the Empire into two parts, East and West. The first Christian emperor, Constantine, shifted the seat of power altogether in 330, and Rome's heady period as capital of the world was over, the wealthier members of the population moving east and a series of invasions by Goths in AD 410 and Vandals about forty years later only serving to quicken the city's ruin. By the sixth century the city was a devastated and infection-ridden shadow of its former self.

It was the **papacy,** under Pope Gregory I ("the Great") in 590, that rescued Rome fom its demise, Gregory sending missions all over Europe to spread the word of the Church and publicise its holy relics, so drawing pilgrims – and their money – back to the city, and in time making the papacy the natural authority in Rome. The pope took the name "Pontifex Maximus" after the title of the high priest of classical times (literally "the keeper of the bridges", which were vital to the city's well-being during the Roman era). The crowning a couple of centuries later of Charlemagne as Holy Roman Emperor, with dominions spread Europe-wide but answerable to the pope, intensified the city's revival, and the pope and city became recognised as head of the Christian world.

There were times over the **next few hundred years** when the power of Rome and the papacy was weakened: Robert Guiscard, the Norman king, sacked the city in 1084; a century later, a dispute between the city and the papacy led to a series of popes relocating in Viterbo; and in 1305 the French born Pope Clemente V temporarily transferred his court to Avignon. But otherwise, aided by Boniface VIII's declaration of Holy Year in 1300, the Papal Court and the city thrived. Power gradually became concentrated in a handful of families, who swapped the top jobs, including the papacy itself, between them. Under the burgeoning power of the Pope, the city began to take on a new aspect: churches were built, the city's pagan monuments rediscovered and preserved, and artists began to arrive in Rome to work on commissions for the latest pope, who would invariably try and outdo his predecessor's efforts with ever more glorious self-aggrandising buildings and works of art. The fragile power structure broke down briefly in the mid-fourteenth century when Cola di Rienzo seized power, setting himself up as the people's saviour from the decadent ways of the city's rulers and forming a new Roman republic. But the increasingly autocratic ways of the new ruler soon lost popularity and di Rienzo was deposed and the papal-nobles alliance reasserted.

Restored to power, the papacy set about the task of beautifying the city with renewed vigour, the **Renaissance** making its presence felt in Rome in the works of Bramante, Raphael and Michelangelo – each of whom worked in the city, on and off, for much of their careers. The reigns of Popes Julius II and Leo X were something of a golden age, the city at the centre of Italian cultural and artistic life, and site of the creation of great works of art like the Sistine Chapel frescoes, Raphael's *Stanze* in the Vatican Palace and fine palaces like the Villa Farnesina,

Palazzo Farnese and Spada, not to mention the commissioning of a new Saint Peter's as well as any number of other churches. In 1527 all was brought abruptly to an end, when the armies of the Bourbon monarch, Charles V, swept into the city, occupying it – and wreaking havoc – for a year while Pope Clement VII cowered in the Castel Sant' Angelo.

The ensuing years were ones of yet more restoration, and because of this it's perhaps the **seventeenth century** which has left the most tangible impression of Rome today. The period saw the completion of Saint Peter's under Paul V, and the ascendancy of Pietro Bernini as the city's principal architect and sculptor under Pope Urban VIII, the vigour of the counter-Reformation throwing up huge sensational monuments like the Gesù church that were designed to confound the scepticism of the new thinking. Many of the city's exotic fountains date from this Baroque era, as do a great many of its churches and palaces.

The **eighteenth century** saw the decline of the papacy as a political force, a phenomenon marked by the occupation of the city in 1798 by Napoleon, Pius VI being unceremoniously sent off to France as a prisoner and Napoleon declaring another Roman republic – something which lasted until 1815, when papal rule was restored. Thirty-four years later a pro-Unification caucus under Mazzini declared the city a republic but was soon chased out, and Rome had to wait until Garibaldi stormed the walls in 1870 to join the **unified country** – the last but symbolically most important part of the Italian peninsula to do so. "Rome o morte" Garibaldi had cried, and he wasted no time in declaring the city the capital of the new kingdom, confining the by now quite powerless pontiff, Pius IX, in the Vatican until agreement was reached on a way to coexist.

The **Concordat of 1929** recognised the Vatican City as sovereign territory, independent of Italy, together with the key basilicas and papal palaces in Rome, which remain technically independent of the Italian state to this day. As capital of a modern European country, Rome was (some would say still is) totally unequipped, and the Piemontese rulers of the new kingdom set about building a city fit to govern from, cutting new streets through Rome's central core (Via Nazionale, Via del Tritone) and constructing self-consciously grandiose buildings like the Altar of the Nation. Fifty years later, Mussolini's motivations weren't dissimilar when he bulldozed his way through parts of the Roman forum and began work on the futuristic, self-publicising planned extension to the city known as EUR.

Since the war Rome's growth has been steadily upwards, its population soaring to close on four million and the city centre becoming ever more snarled up by the increase in traffic. The traffic problems of the *centro storico*, in particular, are notorious, and the effect of the city's poisoned air on the ancient monuments has reached crisis proportions, the authorities swathing the stones and columns with netting and scaffolding but otherwise seemingly paralysed into indecison. Poverty, too, is endemic in parts of the city, the estates on its outskirts finding it hard to swallow the huge upsurge in the city's population without showing the signs of alienation and violence that plague other western capitals. Famous for fifteen minutes in the Sixties as the home of Fellini's *Dolce Vita* and Italy's bright young things, the country's cutting edge has shifted north in the past couple of decades. But with the refurbishment of the city for the 1990 World Cup, recently begun after a long period of squabbling among the city authorities, the capital could be entering a more positive phase in its history.

Arriving, getting around and information

Rome has two **airports**: Leonardo da Vinci (better known simply as Fiumicino), which handles all scheduled flights, and Ciampino, where you'll arrive if you're travelling on a charter. Taxis in from either airport are very expensive – only worth considering if there's four of you – and you're really best off with the public transport links. From **Fiumicino** (☎60.121) it's easy: between 6am and 9pm *ACOTRAL* buses run every fifteen minutes to Stazione Roma Termini (Via Giolitti) – a journey of about 45 minutes; price L5000; at other times they're every half-hour. From **Ciampino** (☎4694) things are more complicated: take an *ACOTRAL* bus from the terminal to the Subaugusta stop of metro line A, from where it's a twenty-minute ride to Termini. (Leaving Rome for Ciampino, be sure to take the yellow bus marked "Aeroporto", *not* the blue bus for Ciampino, which only goes to Ciampino village).

Travelling by **train** from most places in Italy, you also arrive at Stazione Termini (☎4775) – centrally placed for all parts of the city and meeting-point of the two metro lines and many city bus routes. There are other rail stations in Rome: Tiburtina is a stop for some north–south inter-city trains, Ostiense the stop for Ostia Antica and Lido; while selected routes around Lazio are handled by both the Laziali platform of Stazione Termini and the *ACOTRAL* station on Piazzale Flaminio (☎361.0441) – the so-called Roma-Nord line.

Arriving by **bus** could leave you in any one of a number of places around the city. Main stations include Viale Castro Pretorio, five minutes' walk east of Termini, for southern Lazio; Via Gaeta, opposite Termini, for Tivoli and points east of the city; and Via Lepanto, across the Tiber north of the Vatican, for northern Lazio. But there are others spread around the city; phone *ACOTRAL* (☎5798 or 57.005) for full details.

Coming into the city **by road**, the Grande Raccordo Anulare circles the city and is connected with all of the major arteries into of the city centre – the Via Cassia from the north, Via Salaria from the northeast, Via Tiburtina or Via Nomenta from the east, Via Appia Antica or Via Cristoforo Colombo from the south, and Via Aurelia from the west.

City Transport

Like most Italian cities, even the larger ones, the best way to get around Rome is to **walk** – you'll end up seeing more and appreciating the city best. The city wasn't built for motor traffic, and it shows – in the traffic jams, the pollution, and the bad tempers of its drivers. That said, its **bus service**, run by *ATAC*, is a good one – cheap, reliable and as quick as the clogged streets allow. Flat fare **tickets** cost L700 from bars with an *ATAC* sign or booths at major bus stages, and will take you as far as you want to go – cancel it in the machine by the rear doors when you get on. You can make savings by purchasing a block of ten tickets for L6000, or opting for a half-day ticket for L1000, either valid from midnight until 2pm, or from 2pm until midnight. Needless to say, if you're hopping around a lot by bus, two half-day tickets will invariably save money. Other tickets available include a one-day ticket valid for all bus and train services in the city for L2800; a weekly tourist ticket valid on all day and night buses for L10,000; or a monthly pass valid for all ATAC bus lines for L22,000. All are available from the *ATAC* booth on Piazza dei Cinquecento.

Galeria Borghese

To S. Agnese & S. Constanza

Villa Torlonia

PIAZZA BOLOGNA

orghese

VIA NOMENTANA

CORSO D'ITALIA

Aurelian Walls

Pta. Pia

British Embassy

Policlinico

VIA XX SETTEMBRE

VIA TIBURTINA

EPT

Museo Nazionale Romano

Città Università

Verano Cemetery

PIAZZA BARBERINI

Pal. Barberini

PIAZZA D. REPUBBLICA

PIAZZA CINQUECENTO

Stazione Termini

S. Lorenzo Fuori le Mura

QUIRINALE HILL

VIA NAZIONALE

VIA DELLE QUATTRO FONTANE

VIA CAVOUR

Aurelian Walls

VIA CAVOUR

S. Maria Maggiore

Emanuele ument

ESQUILINE HILL

PIAZZA V. EMANUELE II

VIA MERULANA

VIA DEI FORI IMPERIALI

man Forum

Colosseum

VIA LABICANA

PIAZZA DI PORTA MAGGIORE

E HILL

SS. Giovanni e Paolo

S. Croce in Gerusalemme

Pta. S. Giovanni

S. Giovanni in Laterano

Aurelian Walls

S. Gregorio Magno

CELIAN HILL

Baths of Caracalla

VIA APPIA NUOVA

Valls

ma-

Pta. S. Sebastiano

To Eur

To the Catacombs

To sidestep the traffic, Rome also has a **metro**, though it's not as useful as you'd think, its two lines more directed at ferrying commuters out to the suburbs than transporting tourists around the city centre. Nonetheless it's much less crowded (and cooler) than the buses, and there are a few useful city centre stations: Termini is the hub of both lines, and there are stations at the Colosseum, Piazza Barberini and the Spanish Steps. Metro maps are posted up in every station, and the Yellow Pages has a complete list of bus and tram lines, but if you're going to use the system a lot, especially the buses, it's worth investing in a **transport map** – L1000, again from the Piazza dei Cinquecento information booth.

The buses and the metro stop around midnight, after which a network of **night buses** clicks into service, accessing most parts of the city through to about 5am. During the day there are also a few **tram** routes in operation, one of which – the #30 – is a nice leisurely way to see the sights of the city centre, its route taking you on a two-hour circular meander from Piazza del Risorgimento to Piazza San Giovanni di Dio, all for L700. *ATAC* also run a city tour; see "Listings" for details.

USEFUL BUS ROUTES

#23 Termini–Trastevere

#27 Termini–Colosseum–Roman Forum

#64 Termini–Piazza Venezia–Piazza Navona–Saint Peter's

#65 Staz. Tiburtina–Porta Pia–Piazza Venezia–Saint Peter's (Porta Cavallaggeri)

#81 Colosseum–Via Nazionale–Saint Peter's (Piazza del Risorgimento)

#93 Termini–Santa Maria Maggiore– Baths of Caracalla–EUR

#95 Piazza Venezia–Via del Tritone–Via Veneto–Piazzale Flaminio

#118 Colosseum–San Giovanni in Laterano–Via Appia Antica

Taxis aren't really worth taking unless you're in a group or it's late: they're not always very much quicker and they can be costly. If you want a taxi, don't try and hail one but go to a rank – central ones include Termini, Piazza Venezia, Piazza San Silvestro – or call ☎3570, ☎3875 or ☎4994. Only take a licensed yellow cab, and make sure the meter is switched on as you move off (it should start at L2500).

Finally you could also hire a **bike or scooter**. *Scoot-a-long*, Via Cavour 302 (☎678.0206), rents scooters (but not bikes) for around L30,000 a day; *Motonoleggio*, Via della Purificazione 66 (☎465.485), rents out scooters and bikes.

Information

There are **EPT information booths** on arrival at Fiumicino airport and Stazione Termini (daily 8.30am–7pm) – though the heavy queues that often develop at both of these means you're usually better off heading straight for the **main office** at Via Parigi 5 (Mon–Sat 8.30am–7pm; ☎463.748). They have free maps which should – together with our own – be ample for finding your way around. And they can also help with accommodation needs, as well as handing out any amount of bumph on Rome and around; the free booklet *Qui Roma* is useful and available in English. For information on Italy beyond Rome, there's also the national tourist organisation's office, the **ENIT**, to the right of Termini station as you come out, at Via Marghera 2 (Mon–Fri 9am–1pm; ☎497.1282).

Finding a place to stay

In summer Rome is as crowded as you might expect, and although the city's huge number of **hotels and hostels** offers a vast capacity for absorbing visitors painlessly, during the height of the summer it's not unusual to find nearly everywhere full. Book in advance if you can; if you can't, make straight for the EPT office to save your legs. You will almost certainly be offered a hotel room at Stazione Termini, but these are only usually in the middle to upper price bracket; in any case you should only accept if the offerer of the room is carrying proper identification, and make sure you establish the (full) price beforehand, in writing if necessary.

Many of the city's cheaper hotels are handily located close to Stazione Termini, and you could do worse than hole up in one of these: the streets both sides of the station square – Via Amendola, Via Principe Amedeo, Via Marghera, Via Magenta, Via Palestro are just five – are stacked full of cheap hotels, and some buildings have several pensions to choose from. If you want to stay somewhere more central and more picturesque, there are hotels in the *centro storico*, some of them not that expensive, but again be warned that they might be full during the summer – best phone in advance before heading down there. Consider also staying across the river in the Borgo district – a pleasant neighbourhood, nicely distanced from the hubbub of the city centre proper, and handy for the Vatican and Saint Peter's.

> The Rome area telephone code is ☎06

Hostels and student accommodation

Ostello del Foro Italico, Viale delle Olimpiadi 61 (☎396.4709). Rome's official *IYHF* hostel, with dorm beds for around L13,000 a head, including breakfast, if you're a member; membership cards are on sale if you're not. Not particularly central or easy to get to from Termini: take bus #492 or metro line A to Ottaviano, then bus #32. From the city centre take bus #48 from Piazzale Flaminio. Advance bookings through AIG, Via Carlo Poma2, 00195 Roma (Mon–Fri 8am–2pm; ☎385.943).

YWCA, Via C. Balbo 4 (☎460.460). For women only, and much more conveniently situated than the *IYHF* hostel, ten minutes' walk from Termini. But not particularly cheap, at around L30,000 for a single room, L40,000 for a double – no dormitories. Midnight curfew.

Student accommodation. During high season (end July–mid-Sept) the university rents out vacated student accomodation for about L14,000 per person for bed and breakfast in single or double rooms. Sites at Viale Ministero Affari Esteri 6 and Via Cesare de Lollis 20. Either ask at the EPT or contact AIG – address above.

Hotels and *pensioni*

Around Stazione Termini

Capitol, Via G. Amendola 77 (☎462.617). Up a bracket in price from most of the hotels around here, but comfortable. Doubles for around L50,000.

Fiorini, Via P. Amadeo 62 (☎465.065). Recently upgraded to a two-star hotel – doubles around L50,000.

Germano, Via Calatafimi 14 (☎486.919). Friendly and cheap. Double rooms for around L35,000.

Katty, Via Palestro 35 (☎482.7385). One of the cheaper options east of the station. Double rooms for around L30,000.

Perugia, Via del Colosseo 7 (☎679.7200). On a peaceful but central street, with doubles for about L30,000.

Pezzotti, Via P. Amadeo 79 (☎734.633). Amicable *pensione* with flat prices of around L25,000 per person. The same people also own the *Stella Elsa* in the same building – same standards and prices.

Rasella, Via Rasella 127 (☎462.042). A bit more of a walk from Termini, but worth it for the more central location, ten minutes' away from the Spanish Steps. And the prices – around L30,000 for a double – are among Rome's lowest.

Di Rienzo, Via P. Amadeo 79 (☎736.956). In the same building as *Pezzotti* (above); double rooms L44,000.

Romano, Largo C. Ricci 32 (☎679.5851). Well-priced hotel in a central location, with doubles for around L30,000.

Rosetta, Via Cavour 295 (☎461.598). A marginally more upmarket choice but a nice location close to the Colosseum. Doubles L45,000.

Tony, Via P. Amadeo 79 (☎736.994). Pleasant rooms for around L45,000.

Villafranca, Via Villfranca 9 (☎494.0206). Reliable two-star luxury and prices – around L60,000.

Vulcania, Via Cavour 117 (☎485.856). Good value two-star hotel; doubles start at L45,000.

Around the centre

Abruzzi, Piazza della Rotonda 69 (☎679.2021). Bang in front of the Pantheon, and as such you pay for the location. But not that pricey at around L50,000 for a double room.

Della Lunetta, Piazza del Paradiso 68 (☎656.1080). Close to Campo dei Fiori, an unspectacular hotel with doubles for around L40,000.

Navona, Via dei Sediari 8 (☎654.3802). Perfectly placed *pensione* run by an Italian-Australian couple. Doubles around L45,000.

Piccolo, Via dei Chiavari 32 (☎654.2560). Cheap hotel handily located for Piazza Navona. Doubles from around L30,000.

Pomezia, Via dei Chiavari 12 (☎656.1371). Down the street from the *Piccolo*, with slightly cheaper double rooms.

Smeraldo, Via dei Chiodaroli 11 (☎687.5929). Doubles for around L50,000.

Sole, Via del Biscione 76 (☎654.0873). Overlooking Piazza del Campo dei Fiori, one of the nicest city centre locations, with doubles for about L45,000.

Across the river: Borgo and Trastevere

Alimandi, Via Tunisi 8 (☎679.9343). Close to the Vatican, this place has good facilities and double rooms fro about L40,000.

La Rovere, Vicolo San'Onofrio 5 (☎654.0739). Affable small Trastevere *pensione* with doubles for around L45,000.

Manara, Via Luciano Manara 25 (☎589.0713). The place to come if you want to be in the heart of Trastevere. Doubles from L35,000.

Prati, Via Crescenzio 87 (☎687.5357). Two-star hotel with doubles for L45,000 up. Nice, family-run feel.

Camping

All Rome's campsites are some way out of the city, and although easy enough to get to, not especially cheap. Closest is **Camping Flaminio**, 8km north of the centre on Via Flaminia Nuova (☎327.9006); bus #202, #204 or #205 from Piazzale Flaminio, which is connected with Termini by metro line A. In the opposite direction, close to the sea in Ostia, **Camping Capitol**, Via Castelfusano 45 (☎565.0621), is better equipped and actually slightly less expensive, though it's much further out – take a train to Ostia Lido and a #5 bus.

The City

Rome's city centre divides neatly into distinct blocks. The warren of streets that makes up the **centro storico** occupies the hook of land on the left bank of the Tiber, bordered to the east by Via del Corso and to the north and south by water. From here Rome's central core spreads east: across Via del Corso to the major shopping streets and more labyrinthine streets and alleys around the **Spanish Steps** down to **Via Nazionale**; to the major sites of the **ancient city** to the south; to the huge expanse of the **Villa Borghese** park to the north. The left bank of the river is oddly distanced from the main hum of this part of the city, home to the **Vatican and Saint Peter's**, and to the south of these, **Trastevere** – even in ancient times a distinct entity from the city proper and still with a reputation for separatism, as well as the city's liveliest concentration of nightlife.

For most of this, you'd be mad to risk your blood pressure in any kind of vehicle, and really the best way to see the city centre and points east to Termini is to walk. The same goes for the ancient sites, the Vatican and Trastevere. Keep public transport for the longer hops, down to Testaccio, EUR or the catacombs, or other scattered attractions around the centre's outskirts.

Piazza Venezia, the Capitoline Hill and west to the Tiber

Piazza Venezia is not so much a square as a road junction, and a busy one at that. But it's a good central place to start your wanderings, close to both the medieval and Renaissance centre of Rome and the bulk of the ruins of the ancient city. Flanked on all sides by imposing buildings, it's a dignified focal point for the city in spite of the traffic, and a spot you'll find yourself returning to time and again. Forming the western side of the piazza, the **Palazzo di Venezia** was the first large Renaissance palace in the city, built for the Venetian Pope Paul II in the mid-fifteenth century and for a long time the embassy of the Venetian republic. More famously, Mussolini moved in here while in power, occupying the vast *Sala del Mappamundo* and making his declamatory speeches to the huge crowds below from the small balcony facing on to the piazza proper. In those days the palace lights would be left on to give the impression of constant working in what was the centre of the Fascist government and war effort; now it's a much more peripheral building, a venue for the odd temporary exhibition and home to a **museum** of Renaissance arts and crafts (Mon–Sat 9am–1.30pm, Sun 9am–12.30pm; L4000), made up of the magpie-ish collection of Paul II.

Adjacent to the palace on its southern side, the church of **San Marco** (daily 9am–noon), accessible from Piazza San Marco, is a tidy basilica rebuilt in 833 and added to over the years by various Renaissance and eighteenth-century popes. It's a warm, cosy church, restored by Paul II – who added the graceful portico and gilded ceiling – with an apse mosaic dating from the ninth century showing Pope Gregory offering his church to Christ.

But the church, the palace, everything pales into insignificance beside the marble monstrosity that rears up across the street – the **Vittorio Emanuele**

Monument or Altar of the Nation, erected at the turn of the century to commemorate the Unification and about as likeable as most of the other buildings inspired by that event. Romans refer sardonically to it as "the typewriter", American GIs christened it the "Wedding Cake" – and without question it's a pompous, overweening structure, too big, too white (the marble used will never mellow with age), and altogether too boastful. King Vittorio Emanuele II, who it's in part supposed to honour, probably wouldn't have thought much of it either – he was by all acounts a modest man; indeed the only person who seems to have benefited from the building is the Prime Minister at the time, who was (perhaps not entirely coincidentally) deputy for Brescia, from where the marble was supplied. Incidentally, the equestrian statue of the king, behind the Tomb of the Unknown Soldier, is claimed to be the world's largest (its moustache is apparently 3m long) – though perhaps the greatest irony is that all this honours a royal dynasty which produced just four monarchs.

The Capitoline Hill

The real pity about the Altar of the Nation is that it obscures views of the **Capitoline Hill** behind – once, in the days of Imperial Rome, the spiritual and political centre of the Roman empire and still the nominal centre of the city, at least for tourists and bureaucrats. Apart from anything else, this hill has contributed key words to the English language: "Capitol", obviously, derives from this site, as does the word "money", which comes from the temple to Juno Moneta which once stood up here and housed the Roman mint. The Capitoline was also a key point in medieval and Renaissance times: the flamboyant fourteenth-century dictator, Cola di Rienzo, stood in triumph and seven years later was murdered by the mob here – an uncharacteristically humble statue marks the spot where he is said to have died – and, a century after Michelangelo was commissioned to redesign the site as a symbol of Rome's regeneration after the sack of the city.

On the left, the church of **Santa Maria in Aracoeli** (daily 7am–noon & 3.30pm–sunset) crowns the highest point on the hill, built on the site of a temple to Jupiter and reached by a flight of steps erected by Cola di Rienzo in 1348. It's a steep climb to the top of these, and you might find it easier to approach the church via the more gentle ascent to the right; whichever way you go, the church is worth it, one of Rome's most ancient, with some fine, humane frescoes by Pinturicchio recording the life of San Bernadino – realistic tableaux of landscapes and bustling town scenes. The church is also known for its role as keeper of the so-called "Bambino", a small statue of the child Christ, carved from the wood of a Gethsemane olive tree, that is said to have healing powers, and was traditionally called out to the sickbeds of the ill and dying all over the city, its coach commanding instant right of way through the heavy Rome traffic. The bambino is still appealed to from time to time, and still enjoys the privileges normally accorded to foreign statesmen (though he now apparently prefers to travel by taxi); the rest of the time he sits in a chapel at the eastern end of the church, bejewelled and smug and wrapped in luxurious swaddling clothes.

At the top of the shallower right-hand flight of steps or *cordonata*, topped with two Roman statues of Castor and Pollux, the **Piazza Campidoglio** is one of Rome's most elegant squares, designed by Michelangelo in the 1550s for Pope Paul III, who was determined to hammer Rome back into elegant shape for a visit by Charles V – which makes it even odder that the zealots of the Unification should have wanted it hidden behind the hideous white marble typewriter. In the centre of the square Michelangelo placed a statue of Marcus Aurelius on horse-back, which had stood unharmed for years outside San Giovanni in Laterano because it was believed to be of the Emperor Constantine. The statue has been gone for some time, taken away for a thorough cleaning, and sadly only the plinth remains, but otherwise the square is much as Michelangelo planned it, focusing on the **Palazzo Senatorio**, now Rome's town hall, at the far end, and flanked by the two branches of one of the city's most important museums of antique art – the **Capitoline Museums** (Tues–Sat 9am–1.30pm, Tues, Thurs & Sat also 5–8pm, Sun 9am–1pm; L4500, students L2500, free on last Sun of each month).

Of these, it's the **Palazzo del Museo Capitolino**, on the left, which really steals the show, and if you only have time for one of the two you should really make it this. It's much smaller, but on its first floor concentrates some of the best of the city's Roman and Greek sculpture into half a dozen or so rooms and a long gallery crammed with elegant statuary. There's a remarkable, controlled statue of the *Dying Gaul*, a Roman copy of a Hellenistic original; a naturalistic *Boy with Goose* – another copy; an original grappling depiction of *Eros and Psyche*; a *Satyr Resting*, after a piece by Praxiteles, that was the inspiration for Hawthorne's book, the *Marble Faun*; and the red marble *Laughing Silenus*, another Roman copy of a Greek original. Walk through, too, to the so-called *Sala degli Imperatori*, with its busts of Roman emperors and other famous names – a young Augustus, a cruel Caracalla, a portrait of Helena, the mother of Constantine, reclining gracefully. And don't miss the *Capitoline Venus*, housed in a room on its own – headless now, but a coy, delicate piece, again based on a work by Praxiteles.

The same ticket will get you into the **Palazzo dei Conservatori** across the square (though it must be on the same day) – a larger, more varied collection, with more ancient sculpture but later pieces too. Littered around the courtyard are the feet and other fragments of a gigantic statue of Constantine. Inside, in various first floor wings, there are friezes and murals showing events from Roman history, a couple of enormous statues of Popes Innocent X and Urban VIII, the exquisite *Spinario* – a Hellenistic work from the first century BC showing a boy plucking a thorn from his foot – and the sacred Roman statue of the she-wolf suckling the twins, thought to be originally an Etruscan work. Look, too, for the so-called *Esquiline Venus* and *Capitoline Tensa* – the latter a reconstructed chariot in bronze; and the soft *Muse Polymnia* and a gargantuan Roman copy of *Athena*. The second floor holds Renaissance painting – numerous works by Reni and Tintoretto, a vast picture by Guercino that used to hang in Saint Peter's, some nice small-scale work by Carracci, especially an early *Head of a Boy*, Caravaggio's *Gypsy and Fortune Teller* and a handful of Velazquez and Van Dyck portraits.

After seeing the museums walk around behind the Palazzo Senatorio for a view – Rome's best – of the Forum and across to the Colosseum beyond. On the right, Via del Monte Tarpeio follows, as its name suggests, the brink of the old **Tarpeian Rock**, from which traitors would be thrown in ancient times – so-called after Tarpeia, who betrayed the city to the Sabines. To the left, the road skirts the Forum down to the little church of **San Pietro in Carcere** (daily 9am–noon & 2–6.30pm), built above the Mamertine Prison of ancient Roman times where spies, vanquished soldiers and other enemies of the state were incarcerated, and where Saint Peter himself was held. Steps lead down into the murky depths of the gaol, where you can see the bars to which he was chained, along with the spring the saint is said to have created to baptise the other prisoners down here. At the top of the staircase, hollowed out of the honeycomb of stone, is an imprint claimed to be of Saint Peter's head as he was tumbled down the stairs. It's an unappealing place even now, and you won't be sorry to leave – through an exit cunningly placed to lead you through the gift shop.

West from Piazza Venezia
Via del Plebiscito forges west from Piazza Venezia, a dark, rather gloomy thoroughfare that's almost permanently jammed up with traffic. About 300m down, flanking the north side of **Piazza dei Gesù** is the dark-grey decaying bulk of the **Palazzo Altieri**, a monster of a project in its time which people thought – like Nero's Golden House – would consume Rome by its very size. One compassionate act, though, was for the Altieri pope, Clement X, to build around the house of an old woman who refused to make way for the palace: the two spyhole windows that were left can still be seen above the ground floor windows, three windows to the right of the main entrance. Lording it over the piazza proper (said, incidentally, to be the windiest in Rome), the church of **Gesù** (daily 6am–12.30pm & 4–7.30pm) is a typical Baroque church of the Counter-Reformation, and of the Jesuit order: high and wide, with a single-aisled nave and short transepts edging out under a huge dome – ideal for the large and fervid congregations the Jesuits wanted to draw; indeed it has served as the model for Jesuit churches everywhere. The facade is by Giacomo della Porta, the interior the work of Vignola. Today it's still a well patronised church, notable for its size (the left transept is surmounted by the largest piece of stone in existence) and the richness of its interior (sumptuous would be an understatement), especially the paintings of Baciccia in the dome and the ceiling's ingenious trompe l'oeil, which oozes out of its frame in a tangle of writhing bodies, flowing drapery and stucco angels stuck like limpets.

Continuing west, **Corso Vittorio Emanuele** opens out onto **Largo di Torre Argentina**, a good-sized square frantic with traffic circling around the ruins of four (Republican era) temples, now home to a thriving colony of cats and not open to the public. There's not a lot to see here – it's more a place to wait for a bus than to deliberately linger – but on the far side of the square, the **Teatro Argentina** was in 1816 the venue for the first performance of Rossini's *Barber of Seville* – not a success at all on the night, Rossini apparently booed into taking refuge in Bernasconi's pastry shop next door. Built in 1731, it still hosts the greater part of Rome's opera productions.

Campo dei Fiori and around
From Largo Argentina you can either push on down Corso V. Emanuele, or cut left towards the Tiber and right at Piazza Cairoli into the network of streets that centres on Campo dei Fiori. Taking the Corso route, you pass the church of **Sant' Andrea del Valle**, which has the distinction of sporting the city's second tallest dome (after St Peter's), built by Carlo Maderno. A little further down, on the left, the Piccola Farnesina palace, built by Antonio Sangallo the Younger, holds the **Museo Barracco** (temporarily closed), a small but fine quality collection of ancient sculpture that was donated to the city at the turn of the century by one Baron Barracco. The palace itself was actually never anything to do with the Farnese family; it in fact got its name from the lilies on the outside, which were confused with the Farnese heraldic lilies. There's another museum in the eight-

eenth-century Palazzo Braschi opposite, home of the **Museo di Roma**, which displays an assortment of exhibits relating to the history of the city from the Middle Ages to the present day. There are paintings showing the city during different eras, frescoes from demolished palaces and the open railway carriage that the nineteenth-century Pope Pius IX used for journeys out of the city – though this too is for the moment closed for restoration.

Crossing over once again, the grand **Palazzo di Cancelleria** was the seat of the papal government that once ran the city. From behind, the streets tangle down to **Piazza di Campo dei Fiori**, in many ways Rome's most appealing square, home to a morning fruit and veg market and with the restaurants and cafés that flank it on every side busy pretty much all day. No one really knows how the square got its name – "field of flowers". One theory holds that it was derived from the Roman Campo Martius which used to cover most of this part of town; another claims it is after Flora, the mistress of Pompey, whose theatre used to stand on what is now the northeast corner of the square – a huge affair by all accounts, where Julius Caesar was cut down by Brutus (you can still see the foundations in the basement of the *Da Pancrazio* restaurant, on the tiny Piazza del Biscione). Later it was an important point on papal processions between the Vatican and the major basilicas of Rome (notably San Giovanni in Laterano), and a site of public executions. The most notorious killing here is remembered by the statue of **Giordano Bruno** in the middle of the square. Bruno was a late-sixteenth-century rationalist who followed the teachings of Copernicus and was denounced to the Inquisition; his trial lasted for years under a succession of different popes, and finally, when he refused to renounce his philosophical beliefs, he was burned at the stake.

Just south of the Campo, **Piazza Farnese** is a quite different square, with great disc-shaped fountains brought from the Baths of Caracalla and the sober bulk of the **Palazzo Farnese** itself, now the French Embassy, begun in 1514 by Antonio di Sangallo the Younger and finished off after the architect's death by Michelangelo, who added the top tier of windows and cornice. It's a pity you can't get in here: the building holds what has been called the greatest of all baroque ceiling paintings, Caracci's *Loves of the Gods*, finished in 1600. Make do instead with the Palazzo Spada, back towards Via Arenula, and the **Galeria Spada** inside (daily 9am–2pm; L2000; guided tour, in Italian, Sat 11am), though its four rooms, decorated in the manner of a Roman noble family, aren't spectacularly interesting unless you're a connoisseur of seventeenth- and eighteenth-century Italian painting. Best are a couple of portraits by Reni, works by the odd Italian-influenced Dutch artist (Van Scorel, Honthorst) and, among bits and pieces of Roman statuary, a seated philosopher. The building itself is better: its facade is frilled with stucco adornments, and, left off the courtyard, there's a crafty trompe l'oeil by Borromini – basically a tunnel in which the actual length is multiplied about four times through the architect's tricks with perspective.

Behind the Farnese and Spada palaces, **Via Giulia**, which runs parallel with the Tiber, was built by Julius II to connect the Ponte Sisto with the Vatican. The street was conceived as the centre of papal Rome and Julius commissioned Bramante to line it with imposing palaces. Bramante didn't get very far with the plan, as Julius was soon succeeded by Leo X, but the street became a popular residence for wealthier Roman families, and is still packed full with stylish apartment blocks and the like.

The Jewish Quarter and around, and Isola Tiberina

By way of contrast, cross over to the far side of Via Arenula and you're in the old **Jewish Quarter** of the city, a crumbling area of narrow, switchback streets and alleys, easy to lose your way in, and with a strong sense of lingering age. There was a Jewish population in Rome as far back as the early days of the Empire, which with the accruing of Middle Eastern colonies eventually swelled to around 40,000. Revolts in the colonies led to a small tax on Jews and a special census, but they were never an especially persecuted group, and were only effectively ghettoised here in the mid-sixteenth century when Pope Paul IV issued a series of punitive laws that forced them into what was then one of Rome's most squalid districts: a wall was built around the area and all Jews (with chilling echoes of future events) had to wear yellow caps and shawls.

Main artery of the Jewish area is **Via Portico d'Ottavia**, principal thing to see the vast nineteenth-century **Synagogue** on the river, which houses a permanent exhibition on the Roman Jewish community. Take a look, also, at the **Fontana delle Tartarughe** or "tortoise fountain" on the tiny Piazza Mattei, a delightful late-sixteenth-century creation perhaps restored by Bernini.

Via Portico d'Ottavia leads down to the **Portico d'Ottavia**, a not terribly well preserved second-century BC gate, rebuilt by Augustus and dedicated to his sister in 23 BC, that was the entranceway to the adjacent **Teatro di Marcello**. This, now in a state of some decay, has served many purposes over the years: begun by Julius Caesar, finished by Augustus, it was pillaged in the fourth century for the construction of the Ponte Cestio and not properly restored until the Middle Ages, after which it became a formidable fortified palace for a succession of different rulers, including the Orsini family.

Between the theatre and the river lies the broad open space of **Piazza della Bocca della Verità**, home to two of the city's better-preserved Roman temples – the **Temple of Fortuna Virilis** and the circular **Temple of Vesta**, both of which date from the end of the second century BC. You can't get into the temples, and they can't help but look a little neglected in the middle of what is yet another busy traffic spot; but they're fine examples of republican-era places of worship, and the Temple of Vesta is, for what it's worth, the oldest surviving marble structure in Rome. More interesting is the church of **Santa Maria in Cosmedin** on the far side of the square (daily 9am–noon & 3–5pm), a typically Roman medieval basilica with a huge marble altar and surround and a colourful and ingenious Cosmati-work floor – one of the city's finest. Outside in the portico, the **Bocca di Verità** (Mouth of Truth) gives the square its name, an ancient Roman drain cover in the shape of an enormous face that in medieval times would apparently swallow the hand of anyone who hadn't told the truth.

There are more ancient remains opposite the square, out on the Tiber, where the **Ponte Rotto** (Broken Bridge) is all that is left of the first stone bridge to span the river – built between 179 and 142 BC – since its collapse at the end of the sixteenth century.

The **Ponte Fabricio** further down, which links the Tiber bank to **Isola Tiberina**, has fared rather better, built in 62 BC and the only classical bridge to remain intact without help from the restorers (the Ponte Cestio, on the other side of the island, was partially rebuilt in the last century). As for the island, it's a calm escape from the city centre proper, its originally tenth-century church of San Bartolomeo worth a peep on the way across the river to Trastevere.

The *Centro Storico*

You need to walk a little way north from the Capitoline Hill to find the real city centre of Rome, the **centro storico**, which makes up the greater part of the roughly triangular knob of land that bulges into a bend in the Tiber, above Corso Vittorio Emanuele. This area was the old Campus Martius of Roman times, outside the main body of the ancient city, a low-lying area that was mostly given over to barracks and sporting arenas together with the odd temple. Later it became the heart of the Renaissance city, and nowadays it's the part of the town that's densest in interest, an unruly knot of narrow streets and alleys that holds some of the best both of Rome's classical and baroque heritage, and its street-and nightlife.

The boundary of the historic centre to the east, **Via del Corso** is Rome's main street, the old Via Lata of ancient Rome, so-called because of its exceptional width and now holding its principal shops and cutting straight through the heart of the city's centre. On its far side it gives onto the swish shopping streets that lead up to Piazza Spagna; on the western side the web of streets tangles its way right down to the Tiber. Walking north from Piazza Venezia, the first building on the left, the Palazzo Doria Pamphilj, is one of the city's finest rococo palaces, and nowadays holds the **Galeria Doria Pamphilj** (entrance in Piazza Coll. Romano; Tues & Fri–Sun 10am–1pm; L3000). This is one of many galleries open to the public housed in palaces belonging to old Roman patrician families, and is probably the best, at least for the quality of its collection. The Doria-Pamphilj family still lives in part of the building, and you can visit a carefully selected group of private apartments – a cosily furnished library, a couple of salons filled with busts of the family and the ballroom – which takes just half an hour and for an extra L2000 isn't really worth it. As for the paintings, these are only numbered and to know what you're looking at it's necessary to invest in a catalogue (L3000). Among a rich group of works, including Rome's best concentration of Dutch and Flemish paintings, there are canvases by Caravaggio, one catching the bones and skin of the body with a heavy chiaroscuro not unlike Michelangelo (indeed, it's said Caravaggio painted this after seeing the Sistine chapel ceiling). A small room off the main gallery holds Velasquez's painting of the Pamphilj pope, Innocent X, an irritable character regarding the viewer with impatience. Bernini's bust of the same man is quite different, the pope seemingly about to erupt into laughter.

The next left after the palace leads into Piazza **Sant'Ignazio**, an odd little square, laid out like a theatre set and dominated by the facade of the church of **Sant'Ignazio** (daily 8am–12.30pm & 4–7.15pm): a spacious structure with a marvellous Baroque ceiling by Pozzo showing the entry of Saint Ignazio into paradise. The saint isn't actually buried here (he's in the Gesù church a little way south) but it's worth looking in just for the ceiling, a spectacular work employing sledgehammer trompe l'oeil effects, notably in the mock cupola painted into the dome of the crossing. Stand on the disc in the centre of the nave for the truest sense of the ingenious rendering of perspective (directly underneath it just looks wrong): figures in various states of action and repose, conversation and silence fix you with stares from their classical pediment.

Cut through Via di Seminario from here and you're standing right in front of the **Pantheon** (Tues–Sat 9am–2pm, Sun 9am–1pm; free) on Piazza della Rotonda, easily the most complete ancient Roman structure in the city, and with the

CENTRAL ROME

Museo Nazionale Romano
EPT
S. Maria degli Angeli
S. Maria Maggiore
S. Clemente
Domus Aurea

S. Maria in Vittoria
S. Carlo alle Quattro Fontane
S. Pietro in Vincoli
Colosseum

Capuchin Church
Palazzo Barberini
Palazzo del Quirinale
Arch of Constantine
Palatine Hill

Trinità dei Monti
Fontana di Trevi
Palazzo Colonna
Trajan's Forum
Roman Forum

Mausoleo di Augusto
Post Office
Palazzo Montecitorio
S. Ignazio
Palazzo Doria Pamphilj
S. Maria in Aracoeli
Capitoline Museums
Tempio di Fortuna
Tempio di Vesta

Ara Pacis Augustae
Palazzo Montecitorio
Pantheon
S. Maria Sopra Minerva
Gesù
Vittorio Emanuele II Monument
Palazzo Venezia
Santa Maria in Cosmedin

Palazzo di Giustizia
S. Luigi dei Francesi
S. Ivo
S. Andrea di Valle
Largo Argentina
Teatro Marcello

S. Agostino
Museo di Roma
PIAZZA NAVONA
Palazzo Farnese
Palazzo Spada
Isola Tiberina

S. Agnese
Castel Sant'Angelo
Palazzo di Cancelleria
River Tiber
Palazzo Corsini
S. Maria in Trastevere
S. Pietro in Montorio

Vatican Museums
S. Pietro
Villa Farnesina
JANICULUM HILL

S. Onofrio

200 m

Colosseum visually the most impressive. Though originally a temple that formed part of Marcus Agrippa's redesign of the Campus Martius in around 27 BC – hence the inscription – it's since been proved that this building was the work of the Emperor Hadrian, finished around the year AD 125. It's a formidable architectural achievement even now, its dome beaten in span only this century, and still, apart from the Palazzo dello Sport in EUR (built for the 1960 Olympics), the largest in Rome. Like the city's other Roman monuments, it would have been much more sumptuous in its day. Consecrated as a Christian structure in AD 609, and dedicated to Santa Maria ad Martiri in allusion to the Christian bones that were found here, its bronze roof was stripped soon after, and the bronze from the ceiling of the portico removed by Pope Urban VIII for materials for the baldachino in Saint Peter's and the cannons of the Castel Sant'Angelo. (Interestingly some later found its way back here when after the Unification the cannons were melted down to provide materials for the tombs of the new Italian kings, which are in the building). Inside you get the best impression of the engineering expertise of Hadrian: the dimensions of the dome and height are precisely equal, the hole in the centre of the dome – from which shafts of sunlight descend to illuminate the musty interior – a full nine metres across. Most impressively, there are no visible arches or vaults to hold the whole thingup; instead they're sunk into the concrete of the walls of the building. Again, it would have been richly decorated, the coffered ceiling heavily stuccoed and the niches filled with the statues of gods. Now, apart from the sheer size of the place, the main thing of interest is the tomb of Raphael, between the second and third chapel on the left, inscribed by the writer and priest Bembo: "Living, great Nature feared he might outvie Her works, and dying, fears herself may die." The same kind of sentiments might well have been reserved for the Pantheon itself.

There's more artistic splendour on view behind the Pantheon, though Bernini's **Elephant Fountain** doesn't really prepare you for the church of Santa Maria sopra Minerva beyond. The fountain is Bernini's most endearing piece of work, if not his most characteristic: a cheery elephant trumpeting under the weight of the obelisk he carries on his back – a reference to Pope Alexander VII's reign, and supposed to illustrate the fact that intelligence should support wisdom. **Santa Maria sopra Minerva** is Rome's only Gothic church, and worth a look for just that, though its soaring lines have since been heavied by marble and frescoes. Built in the late thirteenth century on the ruins of a temple to Minerva, it is also one of Rome's art-treasure churches, crammed with the tombs and self-indulgences of wealthy Roman families. Of these, the Carafa chapel, in the south transept, is the best known, holding Filippino Lippi's fresco of *The Assumption*, a bright effervescent piece of work, below which one painting shows a hopeful Carafa (the religious zealot, Pope Paul IV) being presented to the Virgin Mary by Thomas Aquinas; another depicts Aquinas confounding the heretics in the sight of two beautiful young boys – the future Medici popes Leo X and Clement VII (the equestrian statue of Marcus Aurelius, still not in place on the Capitoline Hill, is just visible in the background). You should look too at the figure of *Christ bearing the Cross*, on the left-hand side of the main altar, a proud serene work that Michelangelo completed in 1521 specially for the church.

Cut through fom here towards Piazza Navona, passing on the way the church of **Sant'Ivo**, accessible from the courtyard of the Palazzo della Sapienza and, from the outside at least, one of Rome's most impressive churches, with a playful facade designed by Borromini. Built for probably the most famous Barberini pope, Urban VIII, each of the two small towers is topped with weird, blancmange-like groupings, and the central cupola spirals helter-skelter-fashion to its zenith, which is crowned with flames – the whole thing supposed to represent the sting of the Barberini bee, the family's symbol. Entry, however, is difficult: you need to find a porter to let you in.

Just beyond, **Piazza Navona** is in many ways the central square of Rome, an almost entirely enclosed, and pedestrianised, sausage-shaped space fringed with cafés and restaurants, that through most of the year is thronged with tourists, street artists and pigeons. It's a place that more or less everyone sees at some point on a visit to Rome, a focus both for political demonstrations and some of the city's most expensive food – and, in *Tre Scalini* on the western side, some of the city's most delicious chocolate ice cream. Really, the best time to come is at night, when the inevitably tourist-geared flavour of the place is at its most vibrant, crowds hanging out around the fountains or clocking the scene while nursing a pricey drink on the terrace of one of the chi-chi bars. But there's plenty to see by day too. The space actually follows the lines of the Emperor Domitian's arena, principal home to the sports and chariot races that took place in the Campus Martius. Until the mid-fifteenth century the ruins of the arena were still here, overgrown and disused, but the square was given a facelift in the mid-seventeenth century by Pope Innocent X, building most of the grandiose palaces that surround and commissioning Borromini to design the church of Sant'Agnese on the west side – not one of Rome's most interesting churches perhaps, but certainly one of its most visited. The story goes that Saint Agnes was exposed naked to the public in the stadium, whereupon she miraculously grew hair to cover herself: this church, typically squeezed into the tightest of spaces by Borromini, is supposedly on the spot where it all happened.

The **Fontana dei Fiumi** opposite, one of three that punctuate the square, is by Borromini's arch-rival, Bernini, and it's no coincidence that all the figures are shielding their eyes in horror from the church – Bernini was an arrogant man who never had time for the work of the less successful Borromini. The fountain itself, however, is no mean creation, each figure supposed to represent one of the four great rivers of the world – the Nile, the Danube, Ganges and Plate – though only the horse, symbolising the Danube, was actually carved by Bernini himself. The grand complexity of rock is topped with an obelisk brought here from the Circus of Maxentius by Innocent X – which explains the ancient Roman inscriptions.

Bernini also had a hand in the fountain at the southern end of the square, designing the central figure of the "Moro" or Moor. Just west of here, the small space of **Piazza Pasquino** isn't quite what you'd expect from the scene of centuries of satire, but the battered torso of Pasquino itself, anonymous poker of fun at the rich and famous during the Middle Ages, still stands in the corner, the most famous among a number of so-called "talking statues" of Rome, on which anonymous comments on the affairs of the day would be attached – comments which had a serious as well as a humorous intent. Pasquino gave us our word "pasquinade" but hasn't seen much use for over a century, the last and most famous outburst occuring after the Unification when it was hung with the words S.P.Q.R. – Sanctus Pater Quondam Rex, or "The Holy Father Once a King". "The finest piece of ancient sculpture in Rome", Bernini called it, though now Pasquino is so knocked about it's hard to tell what he meant.

Beyond are some of Rome's liveliest streets, narrow and noisy at night, holding some of the city's most vigorous restaurants and bars. Thread your way through to **Via dei Coronari**, home to a sizeable few of Rome's antique dealers, and back east across the northern end of Piazza Navona (where, glassed-in in the foyer of a building, there are the only visible remains of Domitian's arena). Beyond here, the Renaissance facade of the church of **Sant'Agostino** takes up one side of a drab piazza of the same name: not much to look at from the outside but with a handful of art treasures that might draw you in – among them Raphael's vibrant *Isaiah*, on the third pillar on the left, Sansovino's craggy *Saint Anne, Virgin and Child*, and, in the first chapel on the left, a *Madonna and Pilgrims* by Caravaggio, though this is so dark you might well be better off buying a postcard to appreciate it best. There's more work by Caravaggio down Via della Scrofa, in the French national church of **San Luigi dei Francesi** (daily 7.30am–12.30pm & 3.30–7pm; L200 to illuminate the paintings), in the last chapel on the left: early works, describing the life and martyrdom of Saint Matthew, best of which is the *Calling of Saint Matthew* on the left wall – Matthew the dissolute-looking youth on the far left, illuminated by a shaft of sunlight. Caravaggio's first public commission, these paintings were actually rejected at first, partly on grounds of indecorum, and it took considerable reworking by the artist before they were finally accepted.

From the church cut back to Piazza della Rotonda and beyond to Piazza Montecitorio and the **Palazzo di Montecitorio**, home since 1871 of the Italian parliament – though the building itself is another Bernini creation. The obelisk in the centre of the square was brought to Rome by Augustus and set up in the Campus Martius, where it formed the hand of a giant sundial. Just beyond, the **Palazzo Chigi** flanks the north side of **Piazza Colonna**, official residence of the Prime Minister. The **Column of Marcus Aurelius** that gives the square its name has recently been unveiled following repairs, originally erected in AD 180–190 to commemorate military victories in northern Europe, and decorated with reliefs depicting the aspects of the campaigns. There are actually steps up to the top but you need to get permission to climb them.

Three hundred metres or so further on down Via del Corso and left, **Via della Ripetta** was laid out by Leo X to provide a straight route out of the city centre from the old river port area here. A little way up, the **Mausoleum of Augustus** was the burial place of the Emperor and his family, now closed to the public and these days no more than a peaceful ring of cypresses, circled by paths and flowering shrubs. On the far side, enclosed in a glass box between the river and the mausoleum, the **Ara Pacis Augustae** (summer Tues–Sat 9am–1.30pm, Tues, Thurs & Sat also 4–7pm, Sun 9am–1pm; winter Tues–Sat 9am–1.30pm, Sun 9am–1pm; L2000) or "Altar of Augustan Peace" is a more substantial – and recognisable – Roman remain, built in 13 BC to celebrate Augustus's victory over Spain and Gaul and the subsequent peace it established. Much of this had been dug up piecemeal over the years, but the bulk of it was found during the middle half of the last century. It was no easy task to put it back together: excavation involved digging down to a depth of 10m and freezing the water table, after which many other parts had to be retrieved from museums the world over. But it's a superb example of Imperial Roman sculpture, and holds on its fragmented frieze the portraits of many familiar names, most shown in the victory procession itself, which is best preserved on the eastern side. The first part is almost completely gone, but the shape of Augustus is a little more complete, as are the figures that follow – first Tiberius, then the priests with their skull-cap headgear, then Agrippa. The women are, respectively, Augustus's wife Livia, daughter Julia, and niece Antonia, the latter caught simply and realistically turning to her husband.

Around their feet run various children clutching the togas of the elders, the last of whom is said to be the young Claudius.

The oval-shaped space at the far end of Via della Ripetta is **Piazza del Popolo**, a dignified square and meeting of roads designed by Valadier in 1814 that provides an impressive – and very French – entrance to the city, all symmetry and grand vistas. Out of siesta time at least it's an undisciplined free-for-all of cars and people competing for space to cross; during summer the steps around the obelisk, and (if you're trendy or wealthy enough) the bars on either side, are popular hangouts. But the square's real attraction is the unbroken view it gives all the way back down Via del Corso through the centre of Rome to glimpse the central columns of the vulgar Vittorio Emanuele Monument.

On the far side of the piazza, hard against the city walls, the church of **Santa Maria del Popolo** holds some of the best Renaissance art of any Roman church. The church was originally erected here in 1099 over the burial place of Nero, in order to sanctify what was believed to be an evil place, and rebuilt for the last time during the fifteenth century. Inside it holds frescoes by Pinturicchio in the south aisle and the Bramante-designed apse which in turn boast two fine tombs by Andrea Sansovino. The penultimate chapel in the northern aisle, the Chiga chapel, was designed by Raphael for Antonio Chiga in 1516 – though most of the work was accomplished by other artists and not finished until the seventeenth century. Michelangelo's protege, Sebastiano del Piombo, was responsible for the altarpiece, and two of the sculptures in the corner niches, of Daniel and Habakkuk, are by Bernini. But it's two pictures by Caravaggio which get the most attention, in the left-hand chapel of the north transept. These are dramatic works, typically Caravaggio in style – one, the *Conversion of Saint Paul*, showing Paul and horse bathed in a beatific radiance, the other, the *Crucifixion of Saint Peter*, showing Peter as an aged but strong figure, dominated by the muscley figures hoisting him up. Like the same artist's paintings in the church of San Luigi dei Francesci (see above), both works were considered extremely adventurous in their time, their heavy chiaroscuro and deliberate realism too much for the church authorities, who rejected them out of hand.

East of Via del Corso

The area immediately southeast of Piazza del Popolo, fast under the heights of the Villa Borghese gardens and stretching down as far as the Spanish Steps and around, is travellers' Rome, historically the artistic quarter of the city, for which eighteenth- and nineteenth-century Grand Tourists would make in search of the colourful, exotic city, lending the area a distinctly cosmopolitan air. Keats and Giorgio de Chirico are just two people who used to live on Piazza di Spagna, Goethe had lodgings in nearby Via Condotti; and institutions like *Caffè Greco* and *Babington's Tea Rooms* were the meeting-places of a local artistic and ex-pat community for close on a couple of centuries. Today these institutions are gradually giving ground to more latter-day traps for the tourist dollar: *American Express* and *McDonalds* have a high profile in the area, Via Condotti and around is these days strictly international designer territory, with some of Rome's fanciest stores, and the local residents are more likely to be investment bankers than artists or poets. But the air of a Rome being discovered, even colonised, by foreigners remains, even if most of them are more likely to be flying-visit InterRailers than short-term residents.

Piazza di Spagna and around

Via del Babuino, which leads south from Piazza del Popolo, sets the tone for the area, in the Sixties the core of a thriving art community and home to the city's best galleries and a fair number of its artists, until high rents forced out all but the most successful. Now it supports a prosperous trade in antiques. At its southern end is **Piazza di Spagna**, a long thin straggle of a square almost entirely enclosed by buildings and centring on the distinctive boat-shaped **Barcaccia** fountain, the last work of Bernini's father. Recently restored, this remembers the great flood of Christmas Day 1598, when a barge from the Tiber was washed up on the slopes of Pincio hill close by. At the southern end of the square, a **column** commemorates Pius IX's nineteenth-century official announcement of the dogma of the Immaculate Conception – more controversially so than ever these days, since an *American Express* scheme to donate L200 or so from every card used in Rome towards its restoration raised the heckles of Protestant visitors. The **McDonalds** restaurant, opposite, provoked similar reactions a few years back, this time from Romans, when plans were unveiled to open another branch of the world's most ubiquitous fast-food chain on one of Rome's most historic squares. That *McDonalds* is here now is proof that the American multinational won, but it's to the city's credit that it's one of the most discreet examples you'll ever see.

Facing directly onto the square, opposite the fountain, the **Keats-Shelley Memorial House** (Mon–Fri 9am–1pm & 3–6pm; L3500), where the poet John Keats died in 1821, now serves as an archive of English-language literary and historical works and a museum of manuscripts and literary mementoes relating to the Keats circle of the early nineteenth century – namely Keats himself, Shelley, Mary Shelley and Byron (who at one time lived across the square). Among many bits of manuscript, letters and the like, there's a silver scallop shell reliquary containing locks of Milton's and Elizabeth Barrett Browning's hair, while the poet's death mask, stored in the room where he died, catches him in resigned grimace. Keats didn't really enjoy his time in Rome, referring to it as his "posthumous life": he was tormented by his love for Fanny Browne, and he spent months in pain before he finally died, confined to the rooming house with his artist friend Joseph Severn, to whom he remarked that he could already feel "the flowers growing over him".

As for the **Spanish Steps**, which sweep down in a cascade of balustrades and balconies beside the house, the only thing that is Spanish about them is the fact that their architect, Alessandro Specchi, was also responsible for the facade of the nearby Spanish Embassy, which gave the square and steps their name. In the last century they were the hangout of young hopefuls waiting to be chosen as artists' models; nowadays the scene is not much changed, as the venue for international posing and fast pick-ups late into the summer nights. At the top, the **Trinità dei Monti** adds to the international flavour of the square, a largely sixteenth-century church designed by Carlo Maderno and paid for by the French king. Its rose-coloured Baroque facade overlooks the rest of Rome from its hilltop site and it's worth clambering up just for the views. But while here you may as well pop your head around the door for a couple of works by Daniel da Volterra, notably a soft flowing fresco of *The Assumption* in the third chapel on the right, which includes a portrait of his teacher Michelangelo. His *Deposition*, across the nave, is also worth a glance, though it's hard to see under the current dim lighting. Poussin considered it the world's third greatest painting (Raphael's *Transfiguration* was, he thought, the best), painted from a series of cartoons by Michelangelo.

South of Piazza di Spagna

From the church you can either continue left along past the French Academy to the Pincio terrace and the gardens of the Villa Borghese (see below), or head south down Via Sistina to **Piazza Barberini**, a busy traffic junction at the top end of the shopping street of Via del Tritone – named after Bernini's **Fontane del Tritone**, which gushes a high jet of water in the centre of the square. The fountain lends a unity to the square in more ways than one: traditionally this is the Barberini quarter of the city, a family who were the greatest patrons of Gian Lorenzo Bernini, and the sculptor's works in their honour are thick on the ground around here. He finished the Tritone fountain in 1644, going on shortly after to design the **Fontane delle Api** (Fountain of the Bees) at the bottom end of Via Veneto. Unlike the Tritone fountain you could walk right by this, a smaller, quirkier work, its broad scallop shell studded with the bees that were the symbol of the Barberinis.

A little way up Via Veneto, the Capuchin **Church of the Immaculate Conception** was another sponsored creation of the Barberini, though it's not a particularly significant building in itself, only numbering Reni's *Saint Michael Trampling on the Devil* among its treasures – apparently a portrait of Innocent X, whom the artist despised and who was apparently a sworn enemy of the Barberini family. But the Capuchin cemetery (daily 9am–noon & 3–6.30pm), on the right of the church, is one of the more macabre – and bizarre – sights of Rome. In this the bones of 4000 monks coat the walls of a series of chapels, a monument to "Our Sister of Bodily Death", in the words of Saint Francis, that was erected in 1793. The bones cover the walls in abstract patterns or as fully clothed skeletons, their faces peering out of their cowls in various twisted expressions of agony – somewhere between the chilling and the ludicrous.

Via Veneto itself, which bends north from here up to the southern edge of the Borghese gardens, is a cool, materialistic antidote to the murky atmosphere of the Capuchin grotto, its pricey bars and restaurants, once the haunt of Rome's Beautiful People, made famous by Fellini's *La Dolce Vita* but now the home of high-class tack and overpriced sleaze, not to mention the fortified bulk of the US Embassy on the right. Anita Ekberg probably wouldn't be seen dead here these days, Piazza del Popolo being a more likely target for the fashion brigade, and you'd really do better to retrace your steps back to Piazza Barberini and push on up Via delle Quattro Fontane. Just off to the right of here, **Via Rasella** was the scene of an ambush of a Nazi military patrol in 1944 that led to one of the worst Italian wartime atrocities – the reprisal massacre of 300 Romans in the catacombs outside the city. The bullet-holes in the house on the corner of Via Bocaccio remain as a kind of memorial. Oddly enough, Mussolini had a flat on Via Rasella in which he would entertain his mistresses.

On the other side of the road, the **Palazzo Barberini** is home to the **Galeria di Arte Antica** (Tues–Sat 9am–2pm, Sun 9am–1pm; L3000), which displays a rich patchwork of mainly Italian art from the early Renaissance to late Baroque period in the palace's converted rooms. In addition to canvases by Tintoretto, Titian and El Greco, highlights include Fra Filippo Lippi's warmly maternal *Madonna and Child*, painted in 1437 and introducing background details, notably architecture, into Italian religious painting for the first time; and Raphael's beguiling *Fornarina*, a disputed painting in fact, claimed by some experts to be the work of a pupil, though Raphael's name appears clearly on the woman's bracelet.

But perhaps the most impressive feature of the gallery is the building itself, worked on at different times by the most favoured architects of the day – Bernini, Borromini, Maderno – and the epitome of Baroque grandeur. The *Salone*, certainly, is guaranteed to impress, its ceiling frescoed by Pietro da Cortona in one of the best examples of exuberant Baroque trompe l'oeil work there is, a manic rendering of *The Triumph of Divine Providence* that almost crawls down the walls to meet you.

Continue on up Via delle Quatro Fontane and you're at another famous seventeenth-century landmark, the church of **San Carlo alle Quattro Fontane** (daily 10am–12.30pm). This was Borromini's first real design commission, and in it he displays all the ingenuity he became known for, cramming the church elegantly into a tiny and awkwardly shaped site that apparently covers roughly the same surface area as one of the main columns inside Saint Peter's. Outside the church are the four **fountains** that give the street and church their name, each cut into a niche in a corner of the crossroads that marks this, the highest point on the Quirinal hill. Walk west from here and you're passing the blank featureless wall of the **Palazzo Quirinale**, a sixteenth-century structure that was the official residence of the popes until the Unification, when it became the royal palace. It's now the home of Italy's president and not open to the public, but you can appreciate its exceptional siting from the **Piazza del Quirinale** at the far end on the right, from which views stretch right across the centre of Rome.

Hidden among the tight web of narrow, apparently aimless streets below is one of Rome's more surprising sights, easy to stumble upon by accident – the **Fontane di Trevi**, a huge, very baroque gush of water over statues and rocks built onto the backside of a Renaissance palace that's fed by the same source that surfaces at the Barcaccia fountain in Piazza di Spagna. There was a Trevi fountain around the corner in Via dei Crociferi, a smaller more modest affair by all accounts, but Urban VIII decided to upgrade it in line with his other grandiose schemes of the time and employed Bernini to design an alternative. This wasn't carried out until Niccolo Salvi started work on the fountain in 1723, and even then it took 39 years to finish the project. Salvi died in the process, his lungs shot by the time spent in the dank waterworks of the fountain.

The Trevi fountain is now, of course, the place you come to chuck in a coin if you want to guarantee your return to Rome (though you might remember Anita Ekberg throwing herself into it in *La Dolce Vita*), and it's one of the city's most vigorous outdoor spots to hang out of an evening. Opposite, the grubby little church of **Santi Vicenzo ed Anastasio** is the parish church of the Quirinal Palace and, bizarrely, holds in marble urns the hearts and viscera of the 22 popes who used the palace as a papal residence. A short stroll directly south from here brings you to the **Galeria Colonna**, Via del Pilotta 17 (Sat only 9am–1pm; L5000), part of the Palazzo Colonna complex and, although outranked by many of the other Roman palatial collections, worth forty minutes or so if only for the chandelier-decked Great Hall, where most of the paintings are displayed. Best on the whole is the gallery's collection of Dughet landscapes (Poussin's brother-in-law), but other works which stand out are Carracci's early – and unusually spontaneous – *Bean Eater* (though this attribution has since been questioned), a *Narcissus* by Tintoretto, and a *Portrait of a Venetian Gentleman* caught in supremely confident pose by Veronese.

Via Nazionale and east

Five minutes from the gallery, **Via Nazionale** begins its long straight route east, connecting Piazza Venezia and the centre of town with Stazione Termini and the districts beyond. This in a sense is Rome's main shopping street, and a focus for much development after Unification, its heavy, overbearing buildings, like those on Via XX Settembre contructed to give Rome some semblance of modern sophistication when it became capital of the new country, now occupied by department stores and boutiques. At the top end, **Piazza della Repubblicca**, formerly Piazza d'Esedra, is typical of this nineteenth-century regeneration, a stern, once dignified but now rather tawdry semi-circle of buildings given over to cheap hotels and travel agents.

The square actually occupies part of the site of Diocletian's Baths, the scanty remains of which lie across the square in the church of **Santa Maria degli Angeli** – not Rome's most welcoming church but giving the best impression of the size and grandeur of Diocletian's bath complex. It's a huge, open building, used these days for official occasions, state visits and the like, with an interior standardised after a couple of centuries of piecemeal adaptation (started by an aged Michelangelo) by Vanvitelli in a rich eighteenth-century confection. The pink granite pillars are, however, original, and the main transept formed the main hall of the baths; only the crescent shape of the facade remains from the original caldarium (it had previously been hidden by a newer facing), the vestibule (the tepidarium) and main transept. The meridian which strikes diagonally across the floor here was, until 1846, the regulator of time for Romans (now a cannon shot is fired daily from the Janiculum Hill).

Michelangelo is also said to have had a hand in modifying another part of the baths, the courtyard which makes up part of the **Museo Nazionale Romano** behind the church (Tues–Sat 9am–2pm, Sun 9am–1pm; L1000) – entrance off Piazza dei Cinquecento. This could be a very good museum – its collection of Greek and Roman antiquities is superb and second only to the Vatican – but like many Roman museums it suffers from under-funding; whenever you're here, expect to find major parts closed – and be sure to enquire what's open *before* you cough up the admission fee. Of the items worth paying for, the courtyard contains various Roman sarcophagi, statues and mosaic fragments; the first floor holds some good mosaics at the top of the stairs – though a paltry collection compared to Naples – and stucco work from the ruins of an Augustan-era villa discovered in the grounds of the Villa Farnesina; and in a separate room there's an almost entirely complete set of frescoes from the Villa Livia on the Palatine Hill, representing an orchard dense with fruit and flowers and patrolled by partridges, doves and other birds. The museum is also home of the so-called Ludovisi Throne, a fifth-century BC Greek work embellished with reliefs depicting, among other things, the birth of Aphrodite.

Through the trees of the museum garden, you can faintly discern the low white shape of **Stazione Termini** and the bus-crammed hubbub that is **Piazza dei Cinquecento** in front. The latter is probably the city's biggest open space, and the focal point for all kinds of traffic – most buses pass through here, the two metro lines converge at Termini and it's a good place to find taxis. As for the station itself, it's an ambitious piece of modern architectural design that works very well, completed in 1950 and entirely dominating the streets around with its low-slung self-consciously modern lines – a fine place to arrive.

Beyond Termini, heading east past the buildings of the Policlinico and the university, the neighbourhood of **SAN LORENZO** spreads from the far side of Via Tiburtina to the railway tracks, a solidly working-class district that retains something of its local air. The area takes its name from the church of **San Lorenzo fuori le Mura** (daily 3.30–6.30pm; tours every half-hour), further up Via Tiburtina, one of the seven great pilgrimage churches of Rome, oddly sited to the side of the main road in front of the enormous **Campo Verano** cemetery – since 1830 the burial-place of all Catholics in Rome, and in itself worth a visit for the grandiose tombs in which many of them are laid. The church is a typically Roman basilica, fronted by a columned portico and with a lovely twelfth-century cloister to its side. The original church here was built over the site of Saint Lawrence's martyrdom by Constantine – the saint was reputedly burned to death on a gridiron, halfway through his ordeal apparently uttering the immortal words, "turn me, I am done on this side". Where the church of San Lorenzo differs is that it is actually the combination of three churches built at different periods – one a sixth-century reconstruction of Constantine's church by Pelagius II, which now forms the chancel, another a fifth-century church from the time of Sixtus III, both joined by a basilica from the thirteenth century by Honorius II. Inside there are features from all periods, though inevitably heavier on the later one – a Cosmati floor, thirteenth-century pulpits and a paschal candlestick. The mosaic on the triumphal arch is a sixth-century depiction of Pelagius offering his church to Christ; while below stairs, catacombs lead a dank path from the pillars of Constantine's original structure to the Romanesque cloister and its well-tended garden.

North of Termini

A short walk north of Piazza della Repubblica, the church of **Santa Maria della Vittoria** on Via XX Settembre was built by Carlo Maderno and has an interior that is one of the most elaborate examples of Baroque decoration in Rome – almost shockingly excessive to modern eyes, its ceiling and walls pitted with carving, statues crammed into remote corners like an over-stuffed attic. The church's best-known feature, Bernini's carving of *Ecstasy of Saint Theresa*, the centrepiece of the sepulchral chapel of Cardinal Cornaro, continues the histrionics – a deliberately melodramatic work which features a theatrically posed Saint Theresa against a backdrop of theatre-boxes on each side of the chapel, from which the Cornaro cardinals murmur and nudge each other as they watch the spectacle. The semi-visible figure on the left may well be a portrait of Bernini; whether it is or not, there's no question that the sculptor considered this his most beautiful piece of work, and many have since agreed with him.

Beyond the church **Via XX Settembre** spears out towards the Aurelian Wall – not Rome's most appealing thoroughfare by any means, flanked by the deliberately faceless bureaucracies of the national government, erected after Unification in pompous anticipation of Rome's ascension as a new world capital. The street itself was the route by which Garibaldi's troops entered the city on September 20 1870, and the place where they breached the wall is marked with a column. At the end of XX Settembre, the **Porta Pia** was one of the last works of Michelangelo, erected under Pope Pius IV in 1561. The other side of busy Corso d'Italia (in effect forming part of the central ringroad which girdles the city centre), the luxury villas which line the wide boulevard of **Via Nomentana** have long been home to some of the city's more illustrious names, not least the nineteenth-century **Villa Torlonia** on the right, which was in 1925 donated by its owner, the banker Prince Giovanni Torlonia, to Mussolini to use as long as he needed it. You can't visit the house but the grounds are open to the public.

Further up Via Nomentana is the church of **Sant'Agnese fuori le Mura**, dedicated to the same saint who was martyred in Domitian's Circus in AD 303 (see "Piazza Navona"). To get into the church, walk through the adjacent building and down the long staircase to the narthex of the building, which apart from some very out-of-place later fixtures is much as it was built by Honorius I in the seventh century, when he reworked Constantine's original structure. The apse mosaic is Byzantine in style and contemporary with Honorius's building, showing Agnes next to the pope, who holds a model of his church. Out of the narthex the custodian will lead you down into the **catacombs** that sprawl below the church, which are among the best preserved and most crowd-free of all the city's catacombs. Indeed if you only have time for one set of catacombs during your stay in Rome (and they really are all very much alike), these are among the best.

After the catacombs the guide will show you a further part of what is really a small complex of early Christian structures, the church of **Santa Constanza**, which more than any other building in Rome, perhaps, illustrates the transition from the pagan to Christian city in its decorative and architectural features. Built in AD 350 as a mausoleum for Constantia and Helena, the daughters of the Emperor Constantine, it's a round structure which follows the traditional shape of the great pagan tombs (consider those of Hadrian and Augustus elsewhere in the city), and the mosaics on the vaulting of its circular ambulatory – fourth-century depictions of vines, leaves and birds – would have been as at home in a Roman *domus* as they were in a Christian church.

South of Piazza Venezia

From Piazza Venezia **Via dei Fori Imperiali** cuts south through the heart of Rome's ancient sites, a somewhat soulless boulevard imposed on the area by Mussolini in 1932. Before then this was a warren of medieval streets that wound around the ruins of the ancient city centre, but as with the Via della Conciliazione up to Saint Peter's, the Duce preferred to build something to his own glory rather than preserve that of another era. The plan was to create a huge archaeological park which stretched right down to the catacombs on the Via Appia Antica, but this was never carried out; the scheme was revived a few years back but half-heartedly, and for the moment much of the ancient city remains unexcavated, buried beneath the road.

Via dei Fori Imperiali is used for the odd military parade, and it's a useful link for traffic between the Colosseum and Piazza Venezia. But its main pedestrians are tourists, rooting about among the ancient sites. Of these, the main section of the Forum and the Palatine hill beyond, and of course the Colosseum, are the principal things to see, all off to the right of the main road. In addition to these, though, scattered along on either side of Via dei Fori Imperiali, are the remains of various imperial forums, built during the closing days of the Republic after the forum proper had become too small to accommodate the needs of the ever-expanding city.

One of the major victims of Mussolini's redesign was the **Forum of Trajan** on the left side of the road, in its day the most sumptuous of the imperial forums but now fairly unrecognisable. The main section is no more than a sunken area of scattered columns to the left of the road, fronting the semi-circle of **Trajan's Markets**, a tiered ancient Roman shopping centre that's accessible from Via IV Novembre and is used for temporary exhibitions. Behind, the **Torre delle Milizie** is better preserved, said to be the tower from which Nero watched Rome burning, though the most prominent – and intact – relic is nearer Piazza Venezia. This is **Trajan's Column**, erected to celebrate the emperor's colonisation of Dacia (modern-day Romania) and nowadays carefully shrouded, in a seemingly permanent state of restoration. Though for the moment you can't actually see them, the column's reliefs illustrate the highlights of the Dacian campaign.

The Roman Forum and Palatine Hill
Summer Mon & Wed–Sat 9am–7pm, Sun & Tues 9am–1pm; winter daily 9am–3pm; L5000.

Cross the road from here and you're outside the very partially excavated remains of the **Forum of Caesar** – just a few piles of broken columns really – and the entrance to the main part of the **Roman Forum** and the **Palatine**. These are very near the top of most visitors' things to see in Rome, and it's rare that you'll be alone; but for many it's also one of the city's most disappointing sites, and you need an imagination and some small grasp of history to really appreciate the place at all.

Certainly both sites hold some of the most ruined Roman ruins you'll see: the area was abandoned for so long that there's very little that remains anything like intact. But this five or so acres was the heart of the Mediterranean world, and is a very real and potent testament to a power which ruled a large chunk of the earth for close on five centuries, and whose influence reverberates right up to the present day – in language, in architecture, in political terms and systems, even in the romance that the last couple of hundred years have lent to its ruins. Even in ancient times Rome was a very large city, stretching out as far as the Aurelian Wall in a sprawl of apartment blocks or *insulae*. But the Forum was its centre, home to its political and religious institutions, its shops and market stalls, and a meeting-place for all and sundry – which it remained until the Imperial era, when Rome's increased importance as a world power led to extensions being built nearby. The Forum never really recovered from this: neglect set in, a fire in the third century AD decimated many of the buildings, and although the damage was repaired, Rome was by this time in a general state of decay, the coming of Christianity only serving to accelerate the process, particularly with regard to its pagan temples and institutions. After the later downfall of the city to various barbarian invaders, the area was left in ruin, its relics quarried for the construction in other parts of Rome during medieval and Renaissance times and the odd church or tower being constructed out of the more viable piles. But excavation of the site didn't start until the beginning of the nineteenth century, since when it has continued pretty much without stoppage: you'll notice a fair part of the site closed off for further digs.

THE FORUM
Running directly through the core of the Forum, from below the Capitoline Hill in the west to the far eastern extent of the site and the Arch of Constantine (where there's a handy exit for the Colosseum), the **Via Sacra** was the best-known street of ancient Rome, along which victorious emperors and generals would ride in procession to give thanks at the Capitoline's Temple of Jupiter. At the bottom of

the hill, the scattered rows of towering columns mark an array of temples dedicated to various gods and emperors, though there's precious little left of any other part of the buildings. Better preserved, just in front, the **Arch of Septimus Severus** was constructed in the early second century AD to commemorate the emperor's tenth anniversary in power. You can't get very close, and in any case the arch is masked in netting, but it's the most impressive of the triumphal arches that adorn the site. The friezes on it recall not only Severus but his son, Caracalla, who ruled Rome with a reign of undisciplined terror for seven years; there's a space, too, where Severus's other son Geta was commemorated: he was joint-ruler of the empire after his father's death but Caracalla soon had him murdered and removed his name from the arch altogether.

Next to the arch, the **Rostra** faces the grassy, wide-open scatter of paving, dumped stones and beached columns that makes up the central portion of the Forum, the place where most of the life of the city was carried on, and in ancient times usually crowded with politicians, tribunes and traders. Nearby, the black, fenced-off paving of the **Lapis Niger** marks the traditional site of the tomb of Romulus, the steps beneath leading down to a monument that was considered sacred ground during Classical times. Behind, the **Curia** is one of the few whole structures in the forum, a huge barnlike building with a plain pediment that was begun in 80 BC, restored by Julius Caesar soon after and rebuilt by Diocletian in the third century AD. The Senate met here during the Republican period, and augurs would come to announce the wishes of the gods. For years the Curia served as a church, only reverting to its original form earlier this century.

More columns and stones mark more temples and basilicas along the northern side of the Forum, notably the **Basilica Emilia**, from which you can easily discern the original shape of the building, and the **Basilica Julia** on the other side of the forum. Next to the Basilica Julia, the columns of the **Temple of Castor and Pollux**, cocooned in scaffold and netting, is one of the site's oldest remains, dating back to 430 BC and dedicated to the divine twins who appeared miraculously to ensure victory for the Romans in a key battle. Just behind, the church of **Santa Maria Antiqua** formed the vestibule to the emperor Domitian's palace on the Palatine hill, and was the first ancient building to be converted for Christian worship. The church is now normally kept closed, but you can glimpse its seventh- and eighth-century frescoes through a grate on the Capitol side of the building.

Beyond here, crouching under the brow of the Palatine Hill, huge monolithic remains are still being excavated; better to turn in the opposite direction for the **House of the Vestal Virgins**, a second century AD reconstruction of a building originally built by Nero. The cult of the Vestal Virgins was an important one in ancient Rome: the six women who lived here were charged with the responsibility of keeping the sacred flame of Vesta alight always; if it should go out, the woman responsible was scourged; if she should lose her chastity, she was scourged and then buried alive (the man was merely flogged). Not surprisingly, it wasn't a job too many young girls were eager to take up, although the Vestals enjoyed many privileges and the palace was very comfortable: four floors of rooms around a central courtyard, with the round **Temple of Vesta** at the near end. The rooms are mainly ruin now, though they're fairly recognisable on the Palatine side, and you can get a good sense of the shape of the place from the remains of the courtyard, still with its pool in the centre and fringed by the statues or inscribed pedestals of the women themselves.

Opposite the Vestals' house, the neat round **Temple of Romulus**, from the fourth century AD, has also been sanctified and serves as vestibule for the church of **Santi Cosma e Damiano** behind, which sports a wide and majestic sixth-century apse mosaic showing Christ and the Apostles (entrance on Via dei Fori Imperiali). Just past the temple, a short arcade leads round to the **Basilica of Constantine and Maxentius**, a joint effort of the two emperors, which rises up towards the main road – in terms of size and ingenuity probably the forum's most impressive remains. It's said that Michelangelo studied the hexagonal coffered arches here when grappling with the dome of Saint Peter's, and Renaissance architects in general apparently used its apse and arches as a frequent model.

From the basilica the Via Sacra climbs more steeply, past a series of ruins no one has been able to positively identify to the **Arch of Titus**, which stands commandingly on a low arm of the Palatine Hill, looking one way down the remainder of the Via Sacra to the Colosseum, and back over the forum proper. This is the only arch you can currently get close to, unencumbered by scaffolding and with inside reliefs showing the spoils of the sacking of Jerusalem being carried off by eager Romans.

THE PALATINE HILL

Turning right at the Arch of Titus takes you up to the **Palatine Hill**, supposedly where the city of Rome was founded and holding some of its most ancient ruins. It's a pleasanter site to tour than the forum, larger, greener and more of a park – a good place to have lunch and relax after the rigours of the stones below. In the days of the Republic, the Palatine was the most desirable address in Rome (from it is derived our word "palace"), and the big names continued to colonise it during the Imperial era, trying to outdo each other with ever larger and more magnificent dwellings.

Following the main path up from the forum, the **Domus Flavia** was one of the most splendid residences, and although it's now almost completely ruined, the peristyle is easy enough to identify, with its fountain and hexagonal brick arrangement in the centre. To the left, the top level of the gargantuan **Domus Augustana** spreads to the far brink of the hill – not the home of Augustus as its name suggests, but the private house of any emperor (or "Augustus"). You can look down from here on its vast central courtyard with mazelike fountain, and wander through a handful of its bare rooms, afterwards inspecting the deep trench of the **Stadium** – though this is often off-limits to the public. On the far side of the stadium, the ruins of the **Baths of Septimus Severus** cling to the side of the hill, the terrace giving good views over the Colosseum and the churches of the Celian hill opposite; down below is another entrance/exit to the site.

Walking in the opposite direction from the Domus Flavia, steps lead down to the **Cryptoporticus**, a long thin passage built by Nero to link his Domus Aurea on the far side of the Colosseum (see below) with the Domus Augustana and other Palatine palaces, and decorated along part of its length with well-preserved Roman stucco-work. You can go either way along the passage: a left turn leads to the **House of Livia**, originally believed to have been the residence of Livia, the wife of Augustus, though now identified as simply another part of Augustus's palace (the set of ruins beyond). Its courtyard and some of the inner rooms are decorated with scanty frescoes, though the best of them are in the Museo Nazionale Romano.

Turn right down the passage and up some steps on the left, and you're in the **Farnese Gardens**, among the first botanical gardens in Europe, laid out by Alessandro Farnese in the mid-sixteenth century and now a tidily planted, shady retreat from the exposed heat of the ruins. The terrace here looks back over the forum, while the terrace at the opposite end looks down on the church of San Teodoro, across to Saint Peter's, and down on the new excavations immediately below. This is the real centre of Rome's ancient beginnings: the Iron Age hut, known as the **House of Romulus**, is just the best preserved of a ninth-century Iron Age village discovered here; and the so-called **Lupercal**, beyond, is traditionally believed to be the cave where Romulus and Remus were suckled by the she-wolf.

The Colosseum, the Celian Hill and east to San Giovanni in Laterano

Immediately outside the Forum site, the fourth-century **Arch of Constantine** marks the end of the Via Sacra, the friezes on its inside pillaged from other, earlier monuments. Across the way from here, the **Colosseum** (Mon, Tues & Thurs–Sat 9am–7pm, Sun & Wed 9am–1pm; free) is easily Rome's most awe-inspiring ancient monument, and one which – unlike the Forum – needs little historical knowledge or imagination to deduce its function. Originally known as the Flavian Amphitheatre, it was begun by the emperor Vespasian around AD 72 and finished by his son Titus about eight years later – an event celebrated by 100 days of continuous games. The Romans flocked here for many things: gladiatorial contests were the big attraction, designed to prime soldiers for real combat, but there were other, equally cruel spectacles, pitting man against animal, animal against animal, even staging mock sea battles in an arena which could be flooded within minutes. The unifying factor was violence: the slaughter, of animals especially, was huge, leading to the extinction of entire species in Africa; and although gladiators earned big money – and great fame – by fighting in the Colosseum, the tussles were often to the death.

The games were eventually outlawed in the fifth century and, pillaged over the centuries for stone to build some of Rome's grandest palaces (the Barberini and Cancelleria palaces, even St Peter's, all used stone from here), the Colosseum is not much more than a shell now. The floor of the arena has gone entirely, exposing the labyrinth of tunnels beneath, from which the animals would be hoisted into view; around the outside, the arches would originally have held statues, and there are gaping holes where metal brackets linked the great blocks together. But the basic structure of the place is easy to see, and has served as a model for stadiums around the world ever since. You'll not be alone in appreciating it, and during summer the combination of people and scaffolding can make a visit more like touring a contemporary building-site than an ancient monument. But visit late in the evening or early morning before the tour buses have arrived, travel up a level to get a real sense of the size of the building, and the arena can seem more like the marvel it really is.

The animals that did time in the Colosseum were kept in a zoo up on the **Celian Hill**, just behind the arena, the furthest south of Rome's seven hills and probably its most peaceful, clothed almost entirely in woodland and with the gorgeous park of **Villa Celimontana** at its heart. You can get in here by way of the entrance on Piazza di Navicella, a little way down Via Claudia, and you could do worse than take a stroll through. But if you're in more of a hurry follow Clivo di Scauro from the square, around the edge of the park up to the summit of the hill and the church of **Santi Giovanni e Paolo** (daily 8am–noon & 3.30pm–5.30pm), marked by its colourful campanile and set in a peaceful square that's a neat bubble of medieval facades. Originally founded by a Roman senator called Pammachius, this is in a way a memorial to conscientous objection, dedicated to two dignitaries in the court of Constantine who were beheaded here in AD 361 after refusing military service. The relics of their house are downstairs (ask the sacristan for the key) – around twenty rooms in all, frescoed with pagan and Christian subjects – and the railed-off square in mid-nave marks the supposed place of martyrdom.

From the church the road descends under a succession of brick arches to the church of **San Gregorio Magno** on the left, in a commanding position above the traffic drone of the the road below, and looking over to the lollipop pines of the Palatine hill opposite. Again, it's the story behind the place that's most interesting. It was from here that Saint Gregory dispatched Saint Augustine in the early seventh century to convert England to Christianity, and though the rather ordinary Baroque interior shows little evidence of it now the chapel of the saint does have a beautifully carved altar showing scenes from his life, and there's a room which contains his marble throne.

Back at the Colosseum, it's a short walk east down Via San Giovanni in Laterano to the church of **San Clemente** – a light, white twelfth-century basilica that encapsulates better than any other the continuity of history in the city. It's in fact a conglomeration of three places of worship. The ground floor church is a superb example of a medieval basilica: its facade and courtyard face east in the archaic fashion and there are some fine, warm mosaics in the apse. Downstairs (daily 9am–12.30pm & 3.30pm–6.30pm; L1000), there's the nave of an earlier church, dated back to AD 392, with a frescoed narthex showing, among other things, the *Miracle of San Clemente*, one of the first popes, believed to have been ordained by Saint Peter. And at the eastern end of this church, there are the remains of a Roman house – a labyrinthine set of rooms including a Mithraic temple of the late second century, drippy and dank and centring on an altar of Mithras.

Continuing down the same street brings you out eventually at the Basilica of **San Giovanni in Laterano**, officially Rome's cathedral and the former seat of the pope until Unifications – after which the pope took refuge in the Vatican and only emerged when the Lateran Treaty of 1929 accorded this and the other patriarchal basilicas extra-territorial status. There has been a church on this site since the fourth century, the first established by Constantine, and the present building, reworked by Borromini in the mid-seventeenth century, evokes – like San Clemente – Rome's staggering wealth of history, with a host of features from different periods. The doors to the church, oddly enough, were taken from the Curia or Senate House of the Roman Forum. Inside, the first pillar on the left of the right-hand aisle shows a fragment of Giotto's fresco of Boniface VIII, proclaiming the first Holy Year in 1300, while further on, a more recent monument commemorates Sylvester I – "the magician pope", bishop of Rome during much of Constantine's reign – and incorporates part of his original tomb, said to sweat and rattle its bones when a pope is about to die. Kept secure behind the papal altar are the heads of Saint Peter and Saint Paul, the church's prize relics. Outside, the cloisters (L1000), are one of the most pleasing parts of the complex, decorated with early-thirteenth-century Cosmati work and with fragments of the original basilica arranged around in no particular order, including a remarkable papal throne assembly and various papal artefacts (not least the vestments of Boniface VIII) in a room off to the side.

Adjoining the basilica is the **Lateran Palace**, home of the popes in the Middle Ages and also formally part of Vatican territory. Next door, the **Baptistery** is the oldest surviving baptistery in the Christian world, an octagonal structure built during the fifth century that has been the model for many such buildings since. There are more ancient remains on the other side of the church, on Piazza di Porta San Giovanni, foremost among which is the **Scala Santa**, claimed to be the staircase from Pontius Pilate's house down which Christ walked after his trial. The 28 steps are protected by boards, and the only way you're allowed to climb them is on your knees – which pilgrims do regularly. At the top, the chapel of **San Lorenzo** holds an ancient (sixth–seventh century) painting of Christ said to be the work of an angel, hence its name – *archeiropoeton*, or "not done by human hands".

Across the the far side of the square, the **Porta San Giovanni** marks the Aurelian Wall, one of the city's grander gateways. Follow the wall on the city side by way of Viale Carlo Felice to another key Roman church, **Santa Croce in Gerusalemme**, one of the seven pilgrimage churches of Rome, built on the site of the palace of Constantine's mother Saint Helena to house the relics of the true cross she had brought back from Jerusalem. The building is mainly Baroque in style following an eighteenth-century renovation, but the relics of the cross are stored in a chapel at the end of the left aisle, and the Renaissance apse mosaics, recording the discovery of the fragments, are very fine indeed. North of here towards the railway tracks, the **Porta Maggiore** is probably the most impressive of all the city gates, built in the first century AD to carry water into Rome from the aqueducts outside.

The Esquiline Hill and north to Termini

On the far side of the main road from the Colosseum, the **Esquiline Hill** is the highest and largest of the city's seven hills and was one of the most fashionable residential quarters of ancient Rome. After the fire of AD 64, Nero began to build a huge palace here, the **Domus Aurea** or "Golden House", the like of which Rome had never seen before. The facade was supposed to have been coated in solid gold, there was hot and cold running water in the baths, one of the dining rooms was rigged up to shower flowers and natural scent on guests, and the grounds – which covered a full square mile – held vineyards and game. Nero didn't get to enjoy his new home for very long, however – he died a couple of years after it was finished, and his successor, Vespasian, tore it down in disgust, building the Colosseum on one of its lakes. Later Trajan built his baths on top of the rest of the complex, and it was pretty much forgotten about until the wall paintings were discovered by Renaissance artists, including Raphael, who apparently used them as models for his work in the Vatican palace.

The ruins of Nero's Golden House are only partially excavated, and there's not really much to detain you for long; indeed it's hard to make out much shape to the place at all. The rest of this part of the Esquiline Hill has never been built upon since, and is still a refuge for a good-sized cat population and those just wanting to laze around. On the far northern side, the one feature of interest is the church of **San Pietro in Vincoli** (daily 6.30am–12.30pm & 3.30–7pm), one of Rome's most delightfully plain churches, nestled in its own tranquil square. As its name suggests, San Pietro was built to house an important relic, the chains of

Saint Peter from his imprisonment in Jerusalem, to which were added those that bound him when a prisoner in Rome. These can still be seen under the canopy in the apse. But most people come for tomb of Pope Julius II in the southern aisle, which occupied Michelangelo on and off for much of his career and was the cause of many a dispute with Julius and his successors. Michelangelo reluctantly gave it up to paint the Sistine Chapel, and never again found the time to return to it for very long, being always at the beck and call of the latest pope, who had little interest in promoting the glory of one his predecessors. He never finished the tomb, but the figure of Moses, pictured as descended from Sinai to find the Israelites worshipping the golden calf, and flanked by the gentle figures of Leah and Rachel, is one of the artist's most captivating works, the rest of the composition – completed by later artists – dull and static by comparison.

Steps lead down from San Pietro to **Via Cavour**, a busy central thoroughfare which carves a route between the Colosseum and Termini station. It's a good place to eat cheaply, especially up near the station, though the quality of the food is nothing special. After about half a kilometre the street widens to reveal the basilica of **Santa Maria Maggiore** (daily 9am–6.30pm), one of the city's four great basilicas, and inside one of Byzantine Rome's best preserved relics – a fact belied by the eighteenth-century casing that encloses it. Unlike the other great places of pilgrimage in Rome, Santa Maria Maggiore was not built on any special Constantinian site, but instead went up during the fifth century after the Council of Ephesus recognised the cult of the Virgin and churches venerating Our Lady began to spring up all over the Christian world. Inside, the basilica survives intact, its broad nave fringed on both sides with strikingly well-kept mosaics, most of which date from the church's construction and tell, in comic strip form, of incidents from the Old Testament. The Sistine chapel, on the right, holds the elaborate tomb of Sixtus V, while the equally fancy Pauline chapel has a venerated twelfth-century Madonna topped with a sculpted panel showing the legendary tracing of the church's plan after a snowfall – an event celebrated every August 5 with a pontifical mass.

There are two other, smaller churches worth seeing in the neighbourhood. Behind Santa Maria, off Via Merulana, the ninth-century church of **Santa Prassede** occupies an ancient site, where Santa Prassede harboured Christians on the run during the Roman persecutions. She apparently collected their blood and placed it in a well where she was later buried; a slab in the floor of the nave marks the spot. In the southern aisle, the Chapel of Saint Zeno was built by Pope Paschal I as a mausoleum for his mother, Theodora, and is decorated with marvellous ninth-century mosaics.

On the other side of Via Cavour, the church of **Santa Pudenziana** on Via Urbana has equally ancient origins, dedicated to Santa Prassede's sister (who was equally active in the early Christian movement) and for many years believed to have been built on the site where Saint Peter lived and worshipped – though this has since been entirely discredited. There were for years two relics in the church, the chair which Saint Peter used as his throne and the table at which he said mass, though both have long gone – to the Vatican and Saint John Lateran respectively. But the church still has one feature of ancient origin, the superbly stylised fifth-century apse mosaics – apparently the oldest in Rome.

Having seen this group of churches you can either push on up to Termini station or make a left down Via Carlo Alberto to **Piazza Vittorio Emanule II**, centre of a district which became known as the "quartiere piemontese" when the government located many of its major ministeries here after Unification. The arcades of the square, certainly, recall central Turin, as do the heavy palatial buildings which surround it. But otherwise it's hard to imagine the area as a centre of the nation's government: the palaces are dilapidated and converted to cheap apartments, and around the square and the streets beyond there's a **market** that is one of the city's cheapest, stalls clog the pavements all the way around, selling food, cheap clothes and secondhand furniture.

Villa Borghese and north

Immediately above the Piazza del Popolo, the Pincio Hill marks the edge of the city's core and the beginning of a collection of parks and gardens that forms Rome's largest central open space – the **Villa Borghese**, made up of the grounds of the seventeenth-century palace of Scipione Borghese, which were bought by the city at the turn of the century. It's a vast area, and its woods, lakes and grass criss-crossed by roads are about as near as you can get to peace in Rome without making too much effort. There are any number of attractions for those who want to do more than just stroll or sunbathe: a boating lake, a zoo – a cruel affair well worth avoiding – and some of the city's finest museums.

The **Pincio Hill** isn't formally part of the Villa Borghese, but its terrace and gardens, laid out by Valadier in the early nineteenth century and fringed with increasingly decrepit looking classical statues (pinching bits is a major Roman sport), give fine views over the roofs, domes and TV antennae of central Rome, right across to Saint Peter's. Walking south from here, there are more gardens in the grounds of the **Villa Medici**, though as the villa is home to the French Academy these days, they can only be visited on selected days.

The Galeria Borghese
Mon–Sat 9am–1.30pm, Sun 9am–1pm; free
The Villa Borghese proper lies across the far side of the Aurelian wall and the sunken road that follows it. The best place to make for first, if you want some focus to your wanderings, is the **Casino Borghese** itself, on the far eastern side, which was built in the early seventeenth century and turned over to the state when the gardens became city property in 1902 as the **Galeria Borghese**. Made up of an assortment of works collected by Cardinal Scipione Borghese, this has been in restoration for as long as most people can remember, and the work looks like going on for some time. But the ground floor of the villa remains open and is free, and contains the very best of the museum's sculpture collection, made up of a mixture of ancient Roman items and seventeenth-century works. Not surprisingly, Bernini, a protege of Borghese's, dominates, his work the essence of Italian Baroque, not least in the bust of his patron, which typically brings its subject to life. Other rooms house more dramatic works. There's an *Aeneas and Anchises*, carved with his father when he was fifteen; an ingenious *Rape of Proserpine*, in a room surrounded by busts of Roman emperors; and best of all his *Apollo and Daphne*, a dramatic, poised work that captures the split second when Daphne is transformed into a laurel tree, her fingers becoming leaves, her legs tree trunks, while Apollo looks on helplessly. In the next room, Bernini's *David* is a self-portrait of the sculptor aged 25, said to have been carved from a mirror held for him by Scipione Borghese himself; while the centrepiece of the following gallery remembers another member of the family, *Pauline Borghese*, whose daring

portrait by Canova depicts her reclining as Venus on a couch, the thin drapery leaving little to the imagination. Pauline Borghese was the sister of Napoleon, and a shocking woman in her day, with grand habits. There are tales of her jewels and clothes, of the negro who used to carry her from her bath, of the servants she used as footstools, and of course her long line of lovers. The statue was considered outrageous by everyone but herself: when asked how she could have posed almost naked she simply replied: "Oh, there was a stove in the studio".

The Villa Borghese's other museums

The Villa Borghese's two other major museums are situated across the other side of the park, along the Viale delle Belle Arti. Of these, the **Galeria Nazionale d'Arte Moderne** (Tues–Sat 9am–2pm, Sun 9am–1pm; L4000) is probably the least compulsory, its huge lumbering Neoclassical building housing a collection that isn't really as grand as you might expect – a wide selection of nineteenth- and twentieth-century Italian names, of which most are undistinguished. Be selective. Broadly speaking, of the permanent collection, nineteenth-century works are displayed on the left side, twentieth-century on the right: names you might recognise include Modigliani, De Chirico, Giacomo Balla, Boccione and other futurists, along with the odd Cezanne, Mondrian and Klimt.

The **Villa Giulia**, ten minutes' walk away in the direction of Via Flaminia, is more of an essential stop, a harmonious collection of courtyards, loggias, gardens and temples put together in a playful Mannerist style for Pope Julius III in the mid-sixteenth century that is worth a visit for itself. But most people come for the **Museo Nazionale di Villa Giulia** (Tues–Sat 9am–7pm, Sun 9am–1pm; L4000) – Rome's, indeed the world's, primary collection of Etruscan treasures, and a good introduction (or conclusion) to the Etruscan sites in Lazio, which between them contributed most of the artefacts on display here. It's not an especially large collection, and as such it's worth taking the trouble to see the whole. It splits roughly in two, the left side holding artefacts from the sites north of Rome – Tarquinia, Cerveteri, Veio – and the right those from the south – Nemi, Praeneste (Palestrina). The sculpture is a must: strong, dignified, highly personalised works, best among which is the group of *Apollo and Herakles*, from Veio, and the remarkable *Sarcophagus of a Married Couple* from Cerveteri – on which the figures' features are sharply rendered as portraiture. Other highlights include the *Cistae* recovered from tombs around Praeneste – drumlike objects, engraved and adorned with figures, that were supposed to hold all the things needed for the care of the body after death. In the same room, look too at the marvellously intricate pieces of gold jewellery, delicately worked into tiny horses, birds, camels and other animals.

North of the Villa Borghese

The area north of Villa Borghese is the posh **PARIOLI** district – one of Rome's wealthiest neighbourhoods though of little interest to anyone who doesn't live there. Immediately east stretches the enormous expanse of the **Villa Ada**, connected with Villa Borghese by Via Salaria – the old trading route between the Romans and Sabines, so called because the main product transported along here was salt. The Villa Ada was once the estate of King Vittorio Emanuele III and is about as interesting as any park – a bucolic enough place to while away an afternoon but otherwise not really worth the special journey from the centre of town. The **Catacombe di Priscilla** (Tues–Sun 8.30am–noon & 2.30–5pm; L2000), which you can reach from Via Salaria, are the only real thing to see, the (obligatory) guided tours taking you through a frescoed labyrinth of tunnels to see the earliest known painting of the *Virgin and Child*, believed to date from the latter part of the second century.

On the far side of the Parioli district the Tiber sweeps around in a wide hook-shaped bend. These northern outskirts of Rome aren't particularly enticing, though the **Ponte Milvio**, the old originally Roman footbridge where the Emperor Constantine defeated Maxentius in AD 312, still stands and provides wonderful views of the meandering Tiber, the city springing up green on the hills to both sides, the river running fast and silty below. On the northern side of the river, **Piazzale di Milvio** sports a market and a handful of cheap birrerias and restaurants, and is just ten minutes' walk – past the huge Foreign Ministry building – from the **Foro Italico** sports centre, one of the few parts of Rome to survive intact pretty much the way Mussolini planned it. This is still used as a sports centre, and has facilities for numerous activities, but it's worth visiting as much for its period value as anything else. At the centre, there's a fountain surrounded by mosaics of muscle-bound figures indulging in healthful sporting activities, which gives onto an avenue, past the ski slope, patched with more mosaics revering the Duce. Either side of the fountain are the two main stadiums: the larger of the two, on the left, was used for the Olympic Games in 1960 and is still the venue for Rome's two soccer teams on alternate Sundays; the smaller, the *Stadio dei Marmi* ("stadium of marbles"), is a typically fascist monument, ringed by sixty great male statues, groins modestly hidden by fig leafs, in a variety of elegantly macho poses.

The South of the City

On its southern side, the Palatine Hill drops suddenly down to the **Circo Massimo**, a long thin green expanse that was the ancient city's main venue for chariot races. The arena could apparently hold a crowd of around 200,000 betting punters, and if it was still even half intact could no doubt have matched the Colosseum for grandeur. As it is, a litter of stones at the Viale Aventino end is all that remains.

Across the far side of Piazza di Porta Capena, on the right on the corner of Via Antonina, the **Baths of Caracalla** (daily 9am–6pm; L3000) are rather better preserved, and they give a much better sense of the scale and monumentality of Roman architecture than most of the extant ruins in the city; looking at what's left of this huge complex, there's no doubt that the Romans believed in building *big*. The baths are no more than a shell now, but the walls still rise to very nearly their original height. There are many fragments of mosaics – none spectacular, but quite a few bright and well-preserved – and it's easy to discern a floor plan. As for Caracalla, he was one of Rome's worst and shortest-lived rulers, and it's no wonder there's nothing else in the city built by him. The baths are still used for opera performances during the summer, which is a good, if pricey, way to see them at their most evocative.

The Aventine Hill, Testaccio and the Protestant Cemetery

Otherwise, if you're here during the day, it's a good idea to cross back over Viale Aventino after seeing the baths and scale the **Aventine Hill** – the southernmost of the city's seven hills and the heart of plebian Rome in ancient times. These days the working-class quarters of the city are further south, and the Aventine is in fact one of the city's posher residential areas. A short way up Via Santa Sabina, the church of **Santa Sabina** (daily 6.30am–12.45pm & 3.30–7pm) is a strong contender for Rome's most beautiful basilical church: high and wide, its fifth-century nave and portico left mercifully free from the tampering of centuries. Look especially at the main doors, which are contemporary with the church and boast eighteen panels carved with Christian scenes, forming a complete illustrated Bible, which includes one of the oldest representations of the Crucifixion in existence. Santa Sabina is also the principal church of the Dominicans, and it's claimed that the orange trees in the garden outside are descendants of those planted by Saint Dominic himself. Whatever the truth of this, the views from the gardens are splendid – right across the Tiber to the centre of Rome and Saint Peter's.

There are other churches on the Aventine, and in any case it's a nice place to wander, following the road south past the **Priorato di Malta**, one of the city's several buildings belonging to the Knights of Malta, which has a celebrated view of the dome of Saint Peter's through its main gate keyhole. On the far side of the road below, the solid working-class neighbourhood of **TESTACCIO** groups around a couple of main squares, a tight-knit community with a market and a handful of bars and small trattorias that was for many years synonymous with the **Mattatoio** or slaughterhouse that sprawls down to the Tiber just beyond. Not surprisingly perhaps, the area's restaurants are known for their adroitness in cooking offal, and it's still a good place to come and eat. But the slaughterhouse is disused now, a large complex that for the moment hosts the occasional offbeat art exhibition and is utilised by the Roman *cavallari* to stable their horses. There's talk of sprucing up the buildings in a Covent Garden-like affair of new shops and restaurants – something which would change the neighbourhood irreparably – but nothing has yet happened and the Mattatoio is likely to remain largely disused for some time to come.

Opposite the slaughterhouse, **Monte Testaccio** gives the area its name, a 35m-high mound created out of the shards of Roman amphorae that were dumped here over some six hundred years. It's an odd sight, the ceramic curls clearly visible through the tufts of grass that crown its higher reaches, the bottom layers hollowed out by the workshops of car and bike mechanics. But you can climb to the top for some excellent views over the river and beyond; a path leads off Via Zabaglia on the far side.

On the opposite side of Via Zabaglia, Via Caio Cestio leads up to the entrance of the **Protestant Cemetery** (daily 8.30am–11.30am & 3.30–5.30pm; free), one of the shrines to the English in Rome, and a fitting conclusion to a visit to the Keats-Shelley house on Piazza Spagna, since it is here that both poets are buried, along with a handful of other well-known names. It's a small and surprisingly tranquil enclave, crouched behind the mossy pyramidal tomb of one Caius Cestius – a local landmark and haunt of several families of cats. Keats lies next to his friend the painter, Joseph Severn, in a corner of the old part of the cemetery near the pyramid, his stone inscribed as he wished with the words "whose name was writ in water". Severn died much, much later than Keats but asked to be laid here nonetheless, with brushes and palette. As for Shelley, his ashes were brought here at Mary Shelley's request and interred after much obstruction by the papal authorities in the newer part of the cemetery, at the opposite end. Edward Trelawney lies next door, Gramsci on the far right-hand side in the middle – though if you're at all interested in star spotting you should either borrow or buy (L4000) the booklet from the entrance.

From here it's a longish walk or short bus ride back into the centre of town. With energy to spare, you could make a long detour back following the length of the **Aurelian Wall**, built by the emperor Aurelia in AD 275 to enclose Rome's seven hills, the best-preserved stretch of which runs between Porta San Paolo and Porta San Giovanni – a fairly lengthy hike, but it leaves you about a kilometre from the Colosseum. Failing that, there are a number of specific attractions which might draw you further south, though they really all demand at least a bus ride.

Further South: San Paolo fuori le Mura, EUR and Tre Fontane

Two kilometres or so south of the Porta San Paolo, the basilica of **San Paolo fuori le Mura** is one of the four patriarchal basilicas of Rome, occupying the supposed site of Saint Paul's tomb, where he was laid to rest after being beheaded at Tre Fontane (see below). Of the four, this basilica has probably fared the least well over the years. It was apparently once the grandest of them all, connected to the Aurelian Wall by a mile-long colonnade made up of 800 marble columns, but a ninth-century sacking by the Saracens and a devastating fire in 1823, which left it almost entirely destroyed, means that the church you see now is largely a nineteenth-century reconstruction, sited in what is these days an unenticing neighbourhood of apartment blocks and factories.

For all that, it's a very successful rehash of the former church, succeeding where Saint Peter's tries but ultimately fails by impressing with sheer size and grandeur: whether you enter by way of the cloisters or the west door, it's impossible not to be awed by the space of the building inside, its crowds of columns topped by round-arched arcading. Some parts of the building did survive the fire. In the south transept, the Paschal Candlestick is a remarkable piece of Romanesque carving, supported by half-human beasts and rising through entwined tendrils and strangely human limbs and bodies to scenes from Christ's life, the figures crowding in together as if for a photocall. The bronze doors were also rescued from the old basilica and date from 1070, as was the thirteenth-century baldachino, under which Saint Paul's remains are supposed to lie. The arch across the apse is original too, embellished with mosaics; and the Cosmatesque cloister, just behind here, is probably Rome's finest, its spiralling, mosaic-encrusted columns enclosing a peaceful rose garden. Just off here, the Relics Chapel houses a dustily kept set of semi-august relics and the Pinacoteca shows engravings depicting San Paolo before and after the fire.

From San Paolo, Via Ostiense leads south to join up with Via Cristoforo Colombo which in turn runs down to **EUR** (pronounced "Ai-oor") – the acronymic label for the district known as the "Esposizione Universale Roma", reachable on bus #93 from Termini or on metro line B. This is not so much a neighbourhood as a statement in stone: planned by Mussolini for the aborted 1942 World's Fair and not finished until well after the war, it's a cold, soulless grid of square, buildings, long vistas and wide processional boulevards linked tenuously to the rest of Rome by a train but light years away from the city in feel. Come here for its numerous museums, some of which *are* worth the trip, or if you're interested in modern city architecture and planning; otherwise stay well clear.

The great mistake about EUR is that it's not built for people: the streets are wide thoroughfares designed for easy traffic-flow and fast driving, shops and restaurants are easily outnumbered by offices and museums, and those that there are – along the main drags of Viale Beethoven and Viale Europa – are high-priced clothes stores and upscale eateries. Of the buildings, the postwar development of the area threw up bland office blocks for the most part, and it's the prewar fascist-style constructions that are of most interest. The **Palazzo di Civiltà di Lavoro** in the north west corner stands out, Mussolini-inspired architecture at its most assured – the "square Colosseum" some have called it, which sums up its mixing of modern and classical styles perfectly. To the south, **Piazza Marconi** is the nominal centre of EUR, where the wide, classically inspired boulevards intersect to swerve around an obelisk in the centre.

All the museums are within easy reach of here. On the square itself, the **Folk Art Museum** (Mon–Sat 9am–2pm, Sun 9am–1pm; free) is a thoughtful run-through of applied arts, costumes and religious artefacts from the Italian regions – though, as ever, all is labelled in Italian; bring a dictionary. The **Prehistoric and Ethnographic Museum** (Mon–Sat same times as above; L3000) is unquestionably complete, and arranged in manageable and easily assimilable order, but its prehistoric section is mind-numbingly exhaustive; the ethnographic collection does something to relieve things, with artefacts from South America, the Pacific and Africa, and much is well worth skimming. The **Museum of the Early Middle Ages** in the same building (Tues–Sat 9am–2pm, Sun 9am–1pm; free) concentrates on artefacts from the fifth century to the tenth century – local finds mainly, including some beautiful jewellery from the seventh century and a delicate fifth-century gold fibula found on the Palatine Hill. But of all the museums, of most interest is the **Museo della Civiltà Romana** (Mon–Sat 9am–1.30pm, Sun 9am–1pm; L4500), which has among numerous ancient Roman finds a large scale model of the fourth-century city – perfect for setting the rest of the city in context.

The perfect antidote to the sense of alienation induced by EUR is just a short walk away, at the **Abbazia delle Tre Fontane**, a complex of churches founded on the spot where Saint Paul was martyred; it's said that when the saint was beheaded three springs erupted where his head touched the ground, and the churches were sited at these spots. In those days it was a malarial area, and was soon abandoned, but in the second half of the last century Trappist monks drained the swamp and planted eucalyptus trees in the vicinity; they still distill a eucalyptus chest remedy here, sold at the small shop by the entrance.

As for the churches, they were rebuilt in the sixteenth century and restored by the Trappists. They're not particularly outstanding buildings, appealing more for their peaceful location, which is relatively undisturbed by visitors, than any architectural distinction. On the right, the church of **Santa Maria Scala Coeli** owes its name to a vision Saint Bernard had here: he saw the soul he was praying for ascend to heaven; the Cosmatesque altar where this is supposed to have happened is in the crypt. Beyond, the church of **San Paolo alle Tre Fontane** holds the pillar to which Saint Paul was tied, and a couple of mosaic pavements from Ostia Antica.

Via Appia Antica: the catacombs

During classical times the **Via Appia** was the most important of all the Roman trade routes, the so-called "Queen of Roads", carrying supplies right down through Campania to the port of Brindisi. It's no longer the main route south out of the city – that's Via Appia Nuova from Porta San Giovanni – but it remains an important part of early Christian Rome, its sides lined with the underground burial cemeteries or **catacombs** of the first Christians.

Laws in ancient Rome forbade burial within the city walls – most Romans were cremated – and there are catacombs in other parts of the city. But this is by far the largest concentration, around five complexes in all, dating from the first century to the fourth century, almost entirely emptied of bodies now but still decorated with the primitive signs and frescoes that were the hallmark of the then-burgeoning Christian movement. Despite much speculation, no one really knows why the Christians decided to bury their dead in these tunnels: the rock here, tufa, is soft and easy to hollow out, but the digging involved must still have been phenomenal, and there is no real reason to suppose that the burial places had to be secret – they continued to bury their dead like this long after Christianity became the established religion. Whatever the reasons, they make intriguing viewing now. You can get to the main grouping on bus #118 from the Colosseum (Via San Giovanni in Laterano): the three principal complexes are within walking distance of each other, though it's not really worth trying to see them all – the layers of shelves and drawers aren't particularly gripping after a while.

Via Appia Antica begins at the **Porta San Sebastiano**, built in the fifth century, a little way on from which the church of **Domine Quo Vadis** signals the start of the catacomb stretch of road. Legend has this as the place where Saint Peter saw Christ while fleeing from certain death in Rome and asked "Where goest thou, Lord ?", to which Christ replied that he was going to be crucified once more, leading Peter to turn around and accept his fate. Continuing on for a kilometre or so you reach **San Callisto** (Thurs–Tues 8.30am–noon & 2.30–5pm; L3000), the first catacombs of any significance, burial place of all the third-century popes (of whom San Callisto was one), whose tombs are preserved in the papal crypt, and the site of some well-preserved seventh- and eighth-century frescoes. A little way west from here, the catacombs of **Domitilla** (Wed–Mon 8.30am–noon & 2.30-5pm; L3000), are quieter than those of San Callisto, and adjoin the remains of a fourth-century basilica erected here to the martyrs Achilleus and Nereus. The labyrinth itself is Rome's largest, stretching for around 17km in all, and contains more frescoes and early wall etchings.

The catacombs of **San Sebastiano** (Fri–Wed 9am–noon & 2.30–5pm; L3000), five hundred metres further on, are probably best for a visit, situated under a (much-renovated) basilica that was originally built by Constantine on the spot where the bodies of the apostles Peter and Paul are said to have been laid for a time. Downstairs, half-hour tours wind around dark corridors showing signs of early Christian worship – paintings of doves and fish, a contemporary carved oil lamp and inscriptions dating the tombs themselves. The most striking features, however, are not Christian at all, but three pagan tombs (one painted, two stuccoed) discovered when archaeologists were burrowing beneath the floor of the basilica upstairs. Just above here, Constantine is said to have raised his chapel to Peter and Paul, and although Saint Peter was later removed to the Vatican, Saint Paul to San Paolo fuori le Mura, the graffiti collected above records the fact that this was indeed, albeit temporarily, where the Apostles rested.

Trastevere and the Janiculum Hill

Across the river from the centre of town, on the right bank of the Tiber, the district of **TRASTEVERE**, a small, tightly-knit neighbourhood sheltered under the heights of the Janiculum Hill, was the artisan area of the city in classical times, neatly placed for the traded goods that came upriver from Ostia and were unloaded nearby. Later, during the Middle Ages and the Renaissance period, it became Rome's main immigrant quarter, first for Jews (who later migrated across the river to the Ghetto) and after that for other migrants to the city. Today the percentage of immigrants here is much less – they're more likely to be holed up in the poor suburbs on the city's outskirts – but Trastevere still sees itself as a place apart from the rest of the city. The Roman dialect is at its most exaggerated here, with many distinctive vernacular words – there was even a nineteenth-century school of dialect poets based in Trastevere. And the neighbourhood celebrates its independence from Rome proper every year with its *Festa Noiantri* ("We Others"), which takes place in July.

Actually, Trastevere is becoming more and more absorbed into the city of Rome. As a traditionally dissenting voice, the district has been exploited over the last few decades as the city's alternative focus, home to much of its most vibrant and youthful nightlife. Newcomers have moved in, encouraged by the cheap rents, and new bars, restaurants and nightclubs are continually opening up, all helping to make the typical Trasteverini increasingly hard to find; indeed many simply can't afford to live here anymore. Nonetheless it still feels distinctly distanced from the city across the water, its narrow streets and closeted squares peaceful in the morning and vigorous by night; and it still hosts Rome's most intriguing market by far, and some of its best (and, if you know where to look, cheapest) restaurants.

The obvious way to approach Trastevere is to cross over from Isola Tiberina, which leaves you five minutes from the heart of the neighbourhood's life. But on a Sunday it's worth walking over the Ponte Subiaco to Porta Portese, from which the **Porta Portese** fleamarket stretches down Via Portuense to the Trastevere railway station in a congested medley of antiques, old motor spares, cheap clothing, trendy clothing and assorted junk. Come early if you want to buy, or even move – most of the bargains have gone by 10am, by which time the pack of people can be intense – and afterwards stroll north a little way up Via Anicia to the church of **Santa Cecilia in Trastevere**, a cream, rather sterile church (apart from a pretty front courtyard) whose antiseptic eighteenth-century appearance belies its historical associations. A church was originally built here over the site of the second-century home of Saint Cecilia, whose husband Valerian was executed for refusing to worship Roman gods, and who herself was subsequently persecuted for Christian beliefs. The story has it that Cecilia was locked in the caldarium of her own baths for several days but refused to die, singing her way through the ordeal (Cecilia is patron saint of music). Her head was finally half hacked off with an axe, though it took several blows before she finally died. Below the high altar, Stefano Maderna's limp, almost modern statue of the saint shows her incorruptible body as it was found in 1599, swathed in a golden robe, with three deep cuts in her neck, a fragile, intensely human piece of work which has helped to make Cecilia one of the most revered of Roman saints. To the side, you can descend to the excavations of the baths (make a small offering for the light), though hints at restoration have robbed these of any atmosphere and there's little to mark out what's what. Only the caldarium itself, on the other side of the church down a small passageway off the right aisle, is clearly marked.

Santa Cecilia is situated in the quieter part of Trastevere, on the southern side of **Viale Trastevere** – the wide boulevard which cuts through the centre of the district. There's more life on the far side of here, centred – during the day at least – around two main squares. The first, **Piazza San Cosimato**, holds a lively produce market every morning except Sunday, after which the action transfers to **Piazza Santa Maria in Trastevere**, a short walk north – the heart of old Trastevere, named after the church in its northwest corner. The church of **Santa Maria in Trastevere** (daily 9.30am–12.30pm & 4–7pm) is held to be the first Christian place of worship in Rome, built on a site where a fountain of oil is said to have sprung on the day of Christ's birth. The greater part of the structure now dates from 1140, after a rebuilding by a Trastevere pope, Innocent II. These days people come here for two things. The church's mosaics are among the city's most impressive: those on the portico were completed a century or so after the rebuilding, and show the Madonna surrounded by ten female figures with lamps – once thought to represent the Wise and Foolish Virgins. Inside, there's a Cosmatesque pavement of spirals and circles, and apse mosaics contemporary with the building of the church – Byzantine-inspired works depicting a solemn yet very sensitive parade of saints centring on Christ and Mary. The other reason you'll see people flocking here is to queue for free samples of a mysterious drug, as yet not sanctioned by the Italian health authorities, said to cure cancer. Because it is technically illegal, the compound is handed out to anxious sufferers from the portico, which is Vatican territory, and on any given day the lines can stretch way out into the piazza.

You may recognise the square from Fellini's film *Roma*, although the traffic and general sleaze of the place have changed it irredeemably over the last decade or so. Trastevere is these days a prime tourist attraction, and the coachloads regularly disgorge into the piazza. You'd do well to avoid the rip-off restaurants here and dive into the streets behind, where both the prices and the level of traffic are more manageable.

Cutting north through the back streets towards the Tiber, the **Palazzo Corsini** is an unexpected cultural attraction on this side of the river, built orignally for Cardinal Riario in the fifteenth century, rebuilt in the eighteenth century, and nowadays housing the other half of the *Galeria Nazionale di Arte Antica* (which it shares with the Palazzo Barberini) – though it's in fact a much less essential stop than the Barberini collection, including paintings by Caravaggio, Reni, Flemish artists, and Pozzo's designs for the trompe l'oeil ceiling of Sant'Ignazio, which you may have seen across the river.

More interesting is the **Villa Farnesina** across the road, built during the early sixteenth century by Baldassare Peruzzi for the Renaissance banker, Agostino Chigi, and known for its Renaissance murals. Inside you can view the Raphael-designed painting of *Cupid and Psyche* in the now glassed-in loggia, completed in 1517 by the artist's assistants, Guilio Romano, Francesco Penne and Giovanni da Udine. Vasari claims Raphael didn't complete the work because his infatuation with his mistress was making it impossible to concentrate, and says that Chigi arranged for her to live with the painter in the palace while he worked on the loggia. More likely he was simply so overloaded with commissions that he couldn't possibly finish them all. He did, however, manage to finish the *Galatea* next door, which he fitted in between his Vatican commissions for Julius II; "the greatest evocation of paganism of the Renaissance", Kenneth Clark called it. The other paintings in the room are by Sebastiano del Piombo and the architect of the building, Peruzzi, who also decorated the upstairs *Salone delle Prospettive*, which shows trompe l'oeil views of Rome – one of the earliest examples of the technique.

The Janiculum Hill

From the Villa Farnesina, it's about a fifteen-minute walk up Via Garibaldi (or take bus #41 from Piazza Santa Maria in Trastevere) to the summit of the **Janiculum Hill** – not one of the original seven hills of Rome but one of the highest in the city, with easily the best and most accessible views over the centre. About halfway up, on the right of Via Garibaldi, you pass the church of **San Pietro in Montorio**, built on a site once – now, it's thought, wrongly – believed to have been the place of the saint's crucifixion. The church itself isn't of much interest and in any case is often closed (its one draw, Raphael's *Transfiguration* which used to hang in the apse, was removed to the Vatican in 1809). But the little **Tempietto** in the courtyard on the right is one of the Renaissance's seminal works, built by Bramante at the turn of the fifteenth century and one of his earliest creations in Rome. Built on the supposed precise spot of Saint Peter's martyrdom, the small circular building – it holds a maximum of ten people – is like a classical temple in miniature, perfectly proportioned and neatly executed. The courtyard that surrounds was supposed to have been remodelled on circular lines to complete the effect but this was never carried out.

The Janiculum was the scene of a fierce 1849 set-to between Garibaldi's troops and the French, and the white marble **memorial** opposite the church remembers all those who died in the battle. A little further up the hill, the **Fontane di Paolo** gushes water at a bend in the road, constructed for Paul V with marble from the Roman Forum. At the top, the **Porta di San Pancrazio** was built during the reign of Urban VIII, and today it marks the turnoff for the grounds of the **Villa Doria Pamphilj**, which stretch across the back side of the Janiculum Hill. This is the largest and most recent of Rome's parks, laid out in 1650 and acquired for the city in the Seventies. It's a good place for a picnic, but most people continue straight on up the hill along the **Passeggieta del Gianicolo** – which is itself now a park – to the peak of the hill. At the top, on Piazzale Garibaldi itself, the equestrian monument to Garibaldi is an ostentatious work from 1895 and marks the spot, just below, from which a cannon is fired at noon each day for Romans to check their watches. Further on, the fiery statue of Anita Garibaldi recalls the important part she played in the 1849 battle and marks her grave; just opposite are some of the best of the vistas over the city, its brown and orange roofs punctured by the blue-grey of domes and green splashes of its hills.

Descending from here towards the Vatican and Saint Peter's, follow some steps off to the right and, next to a small amphitheatre, you'll find the gnarled old oak tree where the sixteenth-century Italian poet **Tasso** whiled away his last days. Further down the hill, past the Jesuit children's hospital, the church of **Sant'Onofrio** (open mornings only) sits on the road's hairpin, its L-shaped portico fronting the church where Tasso is buried and, on the right, the city's plainest but most delightful small cloister, above which are ranged the rooms of the Fransiscan cloister where he died. You can visit the poet's cell, which holds some manuscripts, his chair, his death mask and personal effects.

Across to the Vatican: Castel Sant'Angelo, Saint Peter's and the Vatican Museums

On the right bank of the Tiber, directly across from Rome's historic centre, the **VATICAN CITY** was established as an independent sovereign state in 1929, a tiny territory surrounded by high walls on its far, western side and on the near side opening its doors to the rest of the city and its pilgrims in the form of Saint Peter's and its colonnaded piazza. Saint Peter's and the part of the palace kept up as the Vatican Museums are open to the public, and you don't need to pass through any entrance formalities to visit them.

In addition to these it's also possible to visit the **Vatican Gardens,** though only on organised tours. There are tours between November and February every Tuesday, Thursday and Saturday at 10am (Price L8000); the rest of the year, between March and October, you must visit the gardens with either the Sistine Chapel (Tues & Thurs at 10am; L16,000) or Saint Peter's (Tues & Sat at 10am; L8000). The **Vatican Information Office** (daily except Sun 9am–noon & 2–5pm; ☎698.4466)) is the place to find out about these, and pick up bumph, detailed guides and postcards, which you can post from one of a couple of portacabins in the square if you want a Vatican postmark – and, it's reckoned, speedier delivery than the notoriously bad Italian service. Finally, you can also, if you wish, attend a **papal audience**: these happen once a week, usually on Wednesday at 11am in the Audiences Room, and are by no means one-to-one affairs. But you can often get a place on one if you apply not more than a month and not less than two days in advance to the Prefettura della Casa Pontifica, 00120 Citta del Vaticano (☎6982).

Crossing the river: Castel Sant'Angelo and Piazza San Pietro

The best route to the Vatican and Saint Peter's is across **Ponte Sant'Angelo**, flanked by angels carved to designs by Bernini (his so-called "breezy maniacs") and home to a procession of secondhand bookstalls. On the far side is the great circular hulk of the **Castel Sant'Angelo** (Mon–Sat 9am–2pm, Sun 9am–1pm; L3000), burial place of the Emperor Hadrian, and in later times the papal city's main fortified defence. Designed by Hadrian himself, the mausoleum was a grand monument, faced with white marble, surrounded with statues and topped with cypresses, designed "to form a black pyramid high in the sky". It was renamed in the sixth century, when Pope Gregory the Great witnessed a vision of Saint Michael here that ended a terrible plague. Later the castle's impressive fortifications and position were not lost on the papal authorities, who converted the building for use as a fortress and built a passageway to link it with the Vatican as a refuge in times of siege or invasion – a route utilised on a number of occasions, most notably when Clement VII sheltered here for several months during the Sack of Rome in 1527. Even now a papal suite is still kept furnished in case of need. Inside, rooms hold swords, armour, guns and the like, others are lavishly decorated with grotesques and paintings, while below dungeons and storerooms are testament to the castle's grisly past as the city's most notorious Renaissance prison – Benvenuto Cellini and Cesare Borgia are just two famous names to have been held here. Upstairs the official papal apartments, accessible from the terrace, are extravagantly decorated with frescoes depicting Michael sheafing his sword and lewd friezes crammed with naked bodies in various poses of revelry, amid paintings by Poussin, Jordaens and others.

The military still lays claim to the Castel Sant'Angelo, and would like to turn it into a museum of post-Unification history, but for the moment it remains papal property. The surrounding neighbourhood, too, the **BORGO**, which stretches up towards Monte Mario, was once all the pope's land, though it was incorporated into the city of Rome at the end of the sixteenth century. The names of many of the streets still have the "Borgo" prefix, which stemmed from the fact that the area's one-time colonisation by Saxon pilgrims – the word "Borgo" is a mutation of their word "burh" – and they are remembered by the old hospital and church of **Santo Spirito in Sassia** on Via di Penitenzieri. The church was founded in 726 by the resident Saxon population and rebuilt in the sixteenth century by Antonio di Sangallo the Younger.

Beyond here, the approach to Saint Peter's – **Via della Conciliazione** – is disappointing: typically, Mussolini swept away the houses of the previously narrow street and replaced them with this wide sweeping avenue, and nowadays Saint Peter's somehow looks too near, the vast space of Bernini's **Piazza San Pietro** not really becoming apparent until you're on top of it – the people sitting on the steps of the basilica (moved at intervals by keen attendants) not much more than dots in the distance. In tune with the spirit of the Baroque, the church was supposed to be even better hidden than it is now: Bernini planned to complete the colonnade with a triumphal arch linking the two arms, so obscuring the view until you were well inside the square, but this was never carried out and the arms of the piazza remain open, symbolically welcoming the world into the lap of the Catholic church. The obelisk in the centre was originally brought to Rome by Caligula in AD 36, and it stood for many years in the centre of Nero's Circus on the Vatican Hill (to the left of the church); according to some theories it marked the site of Saint Peter's martyrdom. It was moved here in 1586, when Sixtus V ordered it be erected in front of the basilica – a task which took four months and was done in silence, on pain of death. Either side, the two fountains are the work of Carlo Maderno (on the right) and Bernini; in between, the exact centres of the two ellipses which make up the piazza's oval shape give ingenious views of the four-rowed colonnade as a single line of columns.

Saint Peter's Basilica

The piazza is so impressive, you can't help but feel a little let down by the basilica of **Saint Peter's** (daily 7am–7pm; free), its facade – by no means the church's best feature – obscuring the dome that signals the building from just about everywhere else in the city. Built to a plan initially conceived at the turn of the fifteenth century by Bramante and finished off, heavily modified, over a century later by Carlo Maderno, Saint Peter's is a strange hotchpotch of styles, bridging the gap between the Renaissance and Baroque eras with varying levels of success. It is, however, the principal shrine of the Catholic church, built as a replacement for the rundown structure erected here by Constantine in the early fourth century on the site of Saint Peter's tomb, and as such can't help but impress, worked on by the greatest Italian architects of the sixteenth and seventeenth century and occupying a site rich with historical significance.

In size, certainly, Saint Peter's beats most other churches hands down. Unlike most other Christian structures (though like a number in Rome), Saint Peter's actually faces west rather than east, since this was the way pagan basilicas, which the first Christian churches followed, were orientated. Bramante had originally conceived a Greek cross plan rising to a high central dome, but this plan was altered after his death and only revived with the (by then) very elderly Michelangelo's accession as chief architect. Michelangelo was largely responsible for the dome, but he too died shortly afterwards and, under orders from Pope Paul V, Carlo Maderno took over changing the church quite radically by again exchanging the Greek Cross for a Latin Cross, which had the advantage of being more practical for large congregations. Nor did it have the pagan associations of the original shape and followed more directly the plan of Constantine's original basilica. But it completely unbalanced all the previous designs, not least in the way it obscured the dome (which he also modified) from view in the piazza. The inside, too, is very much of the Baroque era, largely the work of Bernini, who created many of the most important fixtures.

INSIDE SAINT PETER'S

You need to be properly dressed to enter Saint Peter's, which means no shorts, miniskirts or short sleeves – a rule that is very strictly enforced. Inside on the right is Michelangelo's other legacy to the church, his **Pietà**, completed at the opposite end of his career – when he was just 24 – and now, following an attack by a vandal a few years back, strangely removed from the life of the rest of the building behind glass. Looking at the piece, its fame comes as no surprise: it's a staggeringly sensitive and individual work, and an adept one too, placing the limp body of a grown man across the legs of a woman with grace and ease. Etched into the strap across Mary's chest are words proclaiming Michelangelo's authorship – uncharacteristic of the sculptor and apparently done after he heard his work, which had been placed in Constantine's basilica, misattributed by passers-by.

Walking down the nave, the size of the building becomes more apparent – and not just because of the shrill bronze comparisons with the sizes of other churches alongside. The **dome** is breathtakingly imposing, no question, rising high above the supposed site of Saint Peter's tomb and with balconies decorated with reliefs depicting the basilica's so-called "major relics" – Saint Veronica's handkerchief, adorned with a miraculous image of Christ, the lance of Saint Longinus which pierced Christ's side and a piece of the True Cross – which are displayed here at Easter. Close by, on the right side of the nave, the bronze statue of **Saint Peter** is another of the most venerated monuments in the basilica, carved in the thirteenth century by Arnolfo di Cambio and with its right foot polished smooth by the attentions of pilgrims. Bronze was also the material used in Bernini's **baldachino**, the centrepiece of the sculptor's baroque embellishment of the interior, a massive 85 feet high (the height, apparently, of the Palazzo Farnese), cast out of metal pillaged from the Pantheon roof in 1633. It's an almost grotesque piece of work actually, at least to modern eyes, its wild spiralling columns unwittingly copied from the original canopy. But it has the odd personal touch, not least in the female faces and beaming baby carved on the plinths – said to be done for a niece of Bernini's patron, Urban VIII, who gave birth at the same time as the sculptor was finishing the piece. *

Bernini's feverish sculpting decorates the apse, too, his **cattedra** enclosing the supposed (though doubtful) chair of Saint Peter in a curvy marble and stucco throne, surrounded by the doctors of the church and puffs of cloud ascending into the heavens. To the right, the tomb of Urban VIII is less grand but more dignified, though more interesting is Bernini's monument to **Alexander VII** in the south transept, with its skeleton struggling underneath the heavy marble drapes and significantly clutching an egg-timer. This is Baroque at its most melo-

---

* The Baldachino and confessio just in front are supposed to mark the exact spot of the **tomb of Saint Peter**, and excavations earlier this century did indeed turn up – directly beneath the baldachino and the remains of Constantine's basilica – a street of Roman tombs, with inscriptions confirming that the Vatican Hill was a well-known burial ground in classical times. Whether the tomb of Saint Peter was found or not is less clear: a shrine was discovered, badly damaged, that agrees with some historical descriptions of the saint's marker, with a space in it through which ancient pilgrims placed their heads in prayer. Close by, the bones were discovered of an elderly but physically fit man, and although these have never been claimed as the relics of the apostle, speculation that they are has always been strong. It is possible to visit the Vatican necropolis but you must get official permission; contact the office on Piazza San Pietro (see above) for details.

dramatic, even most political. On the left sits Mercy, on the right, Justice, the foot of which rests on a globe and specifically on England – where, according to Bernini, justice was most needed at the time.

There are innumerable other tombs and works of art in the basilica, and you could spend hours inspecting each one. But you'd do better to be more selective. An entrance off the aisle leads to the **treasury** (daily 9am–6pm; L2000), which along with more recent additions holds those artefacts left from the earlier church – a spiral column (the other survivors form part of the colonnade around the interior of the dome), a wall-mounted tabernacle by Donatello, a rich blue and gold dalmatic that is said once to have belonged to Charlemagne (though this has since been proved doubtful) and the massive, though fairly ghastly, late-fifteenth-century bronze tomb of Sixtus IV by Pollaiolo – which as a portrait is said to be very accurate. There's also, for those frustrated by glass and distance, a plaster copy of Michelangelo's *Pietà*. Back at the central crossing, steps lead down under Bernini's statue of Saint Longinus to the **Crypt**, where a good number of popes are buried in grandiose tombs – in the main those not distinguished enough to be buried up above. None are particularly interesting and you can't turn back, so leave this for your route out. Far better to cross over to the opposite side of the church for the **ascent to the roof and dome** (without lift L2000, with lift L2500) – though you'll probably need to queue. You can ascend to the vertiginous gallery around the interior of the dome, and afterwards go out onto the roof to look down from behind the huge statues on the grasp of Bernini's piazza below. From the inner balcony a series of steps and ramps lead eventually to the lantern at the top of the dome, from which the views over the city are as glorious as you'd expect.

The Vatican Museums
Summer daily 9am–2pm, last tickets 4pm; L8000, students L4000, last Sun of each month admission free; buses leave Pizza di San Pietro 9am–2pm at regular intervals, back 10.30am–2.10pm; guidebook L7500.

A five-minute walk out of the northern side of the piazza takes you up to the only part of the Vatican Palace you can visit independently, the **VATICAN MUSEUMS** – quite simply, the largest, richest and most compelling museum complex in the world. If you found any of Rome's other museums disappointing, the Vatican is probably the reason why: so much booty from the city's history has ended up here, from both classical and later times, and so many of the Renaissance's finest artists were in the employ of the pope, that not surprisingly the result is a set of museums so stuffed with antiquities as to put most other European collections to shame.

As its name suggests, the Vatican Palace actually holds a collection of museums on very diverse subjects – displays of classical statuary, Renaissance painting, archaeological and Egyptian sections, not to mention displays of books, old maps and the furnishings and decorations themselves. There's no point in trying to see them all, at least not on one visit, there's simply too much; just seeing one tenth of the total exhibits could take you half a day. You'd do far better to select what you want to see and aim to return another time if you can. It's worth also taking account of the official, colour-coded routes through the museums, which are constructed for varying amounts of time and interest and can take you anything from 45 minutes to the best part of a day. Above all, be conservative – the distances between different sections alone can be vast and very tiring.

THE RAPHAEL STANZE

There are obvious – and deserved – highlights. First major stop should perhaps be the **Raphael Stanze**, at the opposite end of the building to the entrance and reached by way of a long hike through the west wing. This route in itself takes in a fair quantity of interest: for example, the Gallery of Candelabra, with a marvellous collection of Roman sculptures that includes the candelabra that gives the gallery its name; three rooms of tapestries, woven in Brussels after designs by Raphael's pupils; and, most engagingly, a Map Gallery with sixteenth-century wall maps showing cities and reliefs of Italy and the islands of the Mediterranean. But it's the Raphael Rooms themselves which are the real prize, though only two – the *Stanza Eliodoro* and *Stanza della Segnatura* were actually decorated by Raphael himself.

The **Stanza Eliodoro** was painted by Raphael for Pope Julius II, and its principal painting, the *Expulsion of Heliodorus from the Temple*, is an exciting piece of work packed with action, in which the figures on the right seem ready to jump into the room; it's also an allusion to the military success of Julius II, captured on the left in portrait. Not to be outdone, Leo X, Julius's successor, in the *Meeting of Atilla and Saint Leo* opposite, ordered Raphael to substitute his head for that of Julius II, turning the painting into an allegory of the Battle of Ravenna at which he was present; thus he appears twice, as pope and (confusingly) as the equally portly Medici cardinal just behind. The *Deliverance of Saint Peter* is an undisguised reference to the captivity of Leo after the same battle, portraying him as both victim and martyr in the same room, but is most impressive for its radiant lights over the slumbering Peter, and contrasting soft glows on the armour. Opposite, over the inner window (and using the window shape to heighten the effect of a flight of steps), the *Mass at Bolsena* shows Julius again on the right, pictured in attendance at a famous thirteenth-century miracle in Orvieto where real blood issued during a mass said by a doubting priest: the composition is neat, the colouring rich, the onlookers kneeling, turning, gasping, as the miracle is realised.

The next room, the **Stanza della Segnatura** or Pope's study, is probably the best-known – and with good reason. Raphael decorated this between 1512 and 1514, the subjects again the choice of Julius II, and it comes close to the peak of the painter's art composed with careful balance and harmony. The *School of Athens*, on the near wall as you come in, steals the show, a representation of the "Triumph of Scientific Truth" (to pair with the *Disputation of the Sacrament* opposite, which is a reassertion of religious truth) in which all the great minds from antiquity are represented. Plato and Aristotle discuss philosophy in the background, spread across the steps is Diogenes, lazily ignorant of all that is happening around him, while to the right Raphael cheekily added a solitary, sullen portrait of his rival Michelangelo, who was working on the Sistine Chapel at the time, almost next door.

The last room, the **Stanza Incendio**, was the last to be decorated, and in a sense it brings together three generations of work. The ceiling was painted by Perugino, Raphael's teacher, and the frescoes were completed to Raphael's designs by his pupils (notably Giulio Romano), most striking of which is the *Fire in the Borgo*, facing the main window – an oblique reference to Leo X restoring peace to Italy after Julius II's reign.

THE SISTINE CHAPEL

Steps lead down from here to the **Sistine Chapel**, a huge barnlike structure, built for Pope Sixtus IV in 1481, which serves as the pope's official private chapel and the scene of the conclaves of cardinals for the election of each new pontiff. The **wall paintings** down each side wall are contemporary with the building, depictions of scenes from the lives of Moses and Christ by – among others – Perugino (the *Keys to St Peter* and the *Calling of Peter and Andrew*), Botticelli (*Cleansing of the Leper*) and Ghirlandaio (*Resurrection*), and in any other church they would be pored over very closely indeed. But it's the ceiling frescoes of Ghirlandaio's pupil, Michelangelo, depicting the **Creation**, that everyone comes to see: as famous a work of art as there is on earth, executed almost singlehanded (though there have been recent disputes about this) in a sustained burst of creative energy over a period of about four years. It depicts scenes from the Old Testament, starting with the *Drunkenness of Noah* at the eastern end and working back to *Creation of Light* above the altar wall – the sides decorated with figures from Christian and pagan theology. Oddly enough Michelangelo hadn't wanted to do the work at all: he considered himself a sculptor, not a painter, and was more eager to get on with carving Julius II's tomb (now in San Pietro in Vincoli) than the ceiling, which he regarded as a chore. Julius, however, had other plans, drawing up a design of the twelve apostles for the vault and hiring Bramante to design a scaffold for the artist from which to work. Michelangelo was apparently an awkward, solitary character: before he had barely begun painting, he had rejected Bramante's scaffold as unusable, fired all his staff and dumped the pope's scheme for the ceiling in favour of his own. But the pope was easily his match: there are all kinds of tales of the two men clashing while the work was going on – Michelangelo would lock the doors at crucial points, ignoring the pope's protestations to see how it was progressing; and legend has the two men at loggerheads at the top of the scaffold one day, resulting in the pope striking the artist in impatience.

Julius II lived only a few months after the Sistine Chapel ceiling was finished, but the fame of the work he had commissioned soon spread far and wide. Certainly, it's staggeringly impressive, all the more so for its recent restoration (financed by a Japanese TV company to the tune of $3 million in return for world TV rights), which has lifted centuries accumulated soot and candle grime off the paintings to reveal a much brighter, more vivid painting than anyone thought existed. The restorers have also been able to chart the progress of Michelangelo as he moved across the vault. Images on fresco must be completed before the plaster dries, and each day a fresh layer of plaster would have been laid, on which Michelangelo would have had around eight hours or so before having to finish for the day. Comparing the different areas of plaster, it seems the figure of Adam, in the key *Creation of Adam* scene, took just four days; God, in the same fresco, three days.

Restoration work is now underway on the fresco of the **Last Judgement**, on the west wall of the chapel, painted by Michelangelo over twenty years later, and it will be interesting to see how its murky colours come up afterwards. Michelangelo wasn't especially keen to work on this either – he was still engaged on Julius II's tomb, under threat of legal action from the late pope's family – but Pope Paul III was keen to complete the decoration of the chapel. It was another five years' work, again alone, but the painting is probably the most spirited, most inspired and most homogeneous large-scale painting you're ever likely to see, the technical virtuosity of Michelangelo taking a back seat to the sheer exuberance of the work, fashioning the human body into a finely-captured set of exquisite poses: even the damned, even the aged prophets, appear as a celebration of the human form. Perhaps unsurprisingly the painting offended some and even before it was complete Rome was divided as to its merits, especially regarding the etiquette of introducing such a display of nudity into the pope's private chapel. But Michelangelo's response to this was unequivocal, lampooning one of his fiercer critics with ass's ears and an entwined serpent in the bottom right hand corner of the picture. Later the pope's zealous successor, Pius IV, objected to the painting and would have had it removed entirely had not Michelangelo's pupil, Daniele da Volterra, appeased him by carefully – and selectively – adding coverings to some of the more obvious nude figures, earning himself forever the nickname of the "breeches-maker". Whether the renovation will restore the painting's full nudity has yet to be decided.

THE REST OF THE PALACE

Having seen the Raphael rooms and the Sistine Chapel you've barely scratched the surface of the Vatican. From hereon you need to be choosy about what you devote most time to. Moving to the upper level, the **Appartamento Borgia** – small draughty rooms that have little hint of papal luxury about them – sport a patchy collection of modern religious art, though the ceiling frescoes in the *Salla dei Santi*, by Pinturrichio, are worth seeing, typically rich in colour and detail and dominated by a large portrait of Lucrezia Borgia as Saint Catherine.

At the opposite end of the Vatican Palace are grouped most of the other museums, best of which is the small **Museo Pio-Clementino**. Here you'll find the Cortile di Belvedere, a small courtyard which holds some of the best of the Vatican's classical statuary, including the serene *Apollo Belvedere*, a Roman copy of a fourth-century BC original, and the second-century BC *Laocoon* – two statues which influenced Renaissance artists more than any others. The *Laocoon* especially, which was discovered under Nero's Golden House in 1506 and depicts the treacherous priest of Apollo being crushed with his sons by serpents, lays claim to be the most famous classical statue ever, referred to by Pliny and written about by Byron – who described its contorted realism as "dignifying pain".

Near the Pio-Clementino museum, the **Museo Chiaramonti** and **Braccio Nuovo** hold more classical sculpture, though they are the Vatican at its most overwhelming – close on a thousand statues crammed into two long galleries that you need a keen eye to sort through meaningfully. Better to head straight for the **Museo Egizio**, founded in the nineteenth century by Gregory XVI, and the **Museo Gregoriano Etrusco** above, which holds sculpture, funerary art and applied art from the sites of southern Etruria – a good complement to the Villa Giulia.

Failing that, you could miss these out entirely and make straight for the **Pinacoteca**, housed in a separate building on the far side of the Vatican's main spine – possibly Rome's best picture gallery, with works from the early to High Renaissance. Among early work , there are pieces by Crivelli, Lippi and Giotto – best a triptych of the *Martyrdom of SS Peter and Paul* which captures everyone's attention. There are the rich backdrops and elegantly clad figures of the Umbrian School painters, Perugino and Pinturrichio. And Raphael has a room to himself, including the unfinished *Transfiguration*, painted at the end of his life, that hung above the artist as he lay in state. Leonardo's *Saint Jerome*, in the next room, is unfinished too, but it's a remarkable piece of work, Jerome a rake-like ascetic torn between suffering and a good meal. Caravaggio's *Descent from the Cross* however gets more attention, a warts'n'all canvas that is imitated successfully by Reni's *Crucifixion of Saint Peter* in the same room.

Leaving the Pinacoteca leaves you well placed for the grouping of further museums in the modern buildings around. The **Museo Gregoriano Profano** holds more classical sculpture, mounted on scaffolds for all-round viewing, including Roman funerary work, notably the *Hatieri tomb friezes*, which show backdrops of ancient Rome and realistic portrayals of contemporary life. The adjacent **Museo Pio Cristiano** has intricate early Christian sarcophagi, and, most famously, an expressive third-century AD statue of the *Good Shepherd*. And the **Museo Missionario Etnologico** displays art and artefacts from all over the world, collected by Catholic missionaries.

Drinking and eating

Drinking is not something Romans do a lot of – at least not in public. **Eating out** is a different matter, and in a city of comparatively scarce nightlife is one of the things you'll spend a lot of time doing – mainly in Italian restaurants, though we've included some brief listings of non-Italian eateries too, some varieties of which (notably Chinese) have been booming of late. We've also listed a handful of places serving **snacks** – though most bars serve *panini* and *tramezzini* – and the best of the city's **gelaterie** and **pasticcerie**, together with a checklist of **late and all-night drinking** places. For **gay** and **women's** drinking and nightlife, see the *Nightlife* heading.

Bars

You'll find a **bar** on every corner in Rome, but as with the rest of Italy most are functional daytime haunts, not at all the kinds of places you'd want to spend an evening. To get around the licensing laws, many of Rome's evening drinking places are run as private clubs (usually known as *centri culturali*), a device which means you may be stung for a membership fee – particularly where there's music – though as a one-off visitor some places will let you in without formalities.

Many drinking spots are slick and expensive excuses for people to sit and pose, but all have the advantage of staying open late – up until 4am in summer. **Prices** generally are over the odds – reckon on about L6000 (and upwards) for a medium (50cl) beer, more for anything really fancy. The only slightly cheaper places you'll find are the odd **birreria** or a handful of relaxed and reasonably-priced **wine bars**.

Central

Caffè Greco, Via Condotti 86. Founded in 1742 and patronised by, among others, Casanova, Byron, Goethe and Stendhal. Today it's a tourist joint of dubious cleanliness and quality. Curiosity value only.

Bar della Pace, Via della Pace 5. Just off Piazza Navona, this is *the* summer bar, with outside tables full of Rome's self-consciously beautiful people. Quieter (but still pricey) during the day, when you can enjoy the nineteenth-century interior – marble, mirrors, mahogany and plants – in peace.

Camilloni, Piazza Sant'Eustacchio 54. One of three or four bars to claim the best coffee in Rome (*Eustacchio* across the street is another). Busy until late but otherwise unexceptional. A few tables on a quiet but not particularly scenic piazza.

Cul de Sac, Piazza del Pasquino 73. Bustling and atmospheric wine bar in two narrow rooms, both invariably packed. Wines from every Italian region at surprisingly low prices, and good snacks served from antique marble bar at the front. Open lunchtime and 8pm until midnight.

Del Fico, Piazza del Fico. Standard bar, but a cheaper and less self-conscious alternative to Bar della Pace round the corner. Tables outside to take in streetlife.

Enoteca Piccolo, Via del Governo Vecchio 75. Intimate candlelit wine bar with a dozen wines by the glass and many more by the bottle. Open 5pm–2am, closed Tues.

The Fox, Via Monterone 19. Small, boozy birreria behind Largo Argentina with "as much as you can drink for L10,000" on Tuesday nights. Some ex-pats and a high-volume jukebox. Open 9pm–2am, closed Mon.

Gelocremeria, Via della Pigna 58. A quiet, no-frills bar still with Fifties fittings. Good for a sit-down during the day without being ripped off, and a welcome refuge from the Pantheon's nearby tourist traps.

La Tazza d'Oro, Via degli Orfani. Straight off Piazza del Pantheon. Drab, but by common consent Rome's best cup of coffee.

Trastevere

Bar della Malva, Piazza della Malva 14. Day and night bar for Trastevere's dodgier types. Summer tables usually full of foreign students. Dingy TV/games room at the back.

Bar San Calisto, Piazza di San Callisto 4. Ordinary bar off Piazza Santa Maria. Attracts an eclectic bunch of late drinkers. Outside tables in summer and smoky side room full of card-playing old men and their dogs. Closed Sun.

La Scala, Piazza della Scala. The most popular Trastevere birreria – big, bustling and crowded. Pub food, cheap beer and occasional (dire) music. Closed Wed. Recommended.

Melvyn's, Via della Politeama 8. Big, noisy and slightly tatty bar that packs in the punters for videos and live music. A good place to start an evening, but can get slightly dodgy later on. Open 9pm–3am.

Pub-Birreria, Vicolo del Cinque 31a. Exactly what it says, an easy-going birreria that's worth a visit for the frescoed ceilings alone. Some pub food.

Trastè, Via della Lungheretta 76. Refined meeting-place for the young and cultured Trastevere crowd. Emphasis more on fancy teas than getting well-oiled. Good for informal eating. Open 5–11pm.

Colosseum and around

Druid's, Via San Martino ai Monti 28. Appealing Irish pub with a genuine Irish feel (and Irish owners). Mixed ex-pat/Italian clientele, but not just for the homesick. Cheap and lively, with occasional impromptu music – good for an evening out in its own right. Open 8pm–1am.

Enoteca Cavour, Via Cavour 313. At the forum end of Via Cavour, a handy retreat that's little-known to tourists. Easy-going studenty feel, lots of wine and bottled beers, and (slightly over-priced) snacks. Closed Sun.

Fiddler's Elbow, Via dell'Omarta 43. Another Irish bar but roomier than *Druid's* and with a decidedly more Latin feel. Open 5pm–1am. Closed Mon.

Tempera, Via di San Marcello 19. Centrally situated behind Piazza Venezia, this is potentially Rome's best birreria, with cheap beer, good pub-type food and a convivial atmosphere. Open 12.30–3pm & 7–11pm. Closed Sun.

Venice LA, Via del Boschetto 132. One of Rome's rare alternative-styled bars. High-fashion punk, with videos, occasional invites to parties and info on some of the city's more out-to-lunch events.

Gelaterie and *Pasticcerie*

Alberto Pica, Via della Seggiola 12 (between Ponte Garibaldi and Piazza Arenula). Fresh fruit sorbets are the house speciality, with a hundred-flavour assortment. Open 8am–1am. Closed Sun.

Bernasconi, Largo Argentina 1. One of the oldest and busiest *pasticcerie* in town. Also a central day-time bar.

Dagnino, in an arcade off Via E.Orlando, near Piazza Repubblica. Wonderful Forties bar/pasticceria with Sicilian specialities and wide range of general goodies.

Gelateria della Palma, Via della Maddalena 20. Designer ice cream in suitably stylish surroundings. 104 flavours including fig, pomegranate, avocado, After Eight and muesli. Currently Rome's best. Open 8am–2am. Closed Wed.

Giolitti, Via del Vicaro 40. An Italian institution which once had a reputation – now lost – for the country's top ice cream. Still pretty good, however, with a choice of 70 flavours. Open 7am–2am. Closed Mon.

Tre Scalini, Piazza Navona. Renowned for its absolutely remarkable *tartufo* – death by chocolate.

Valzani, Via del Moro 37. One of the oldest of the city's pastry shops, still keeping up the traditions.

Snacks and self-service

Bibo, Via Ripetta 15. Smarmy black marble interior, but plenty of tables to eat at without the expense of a cover charge.

Caffe Capranica, Piazza Capranica 104. Down-at-heel environment but a cheap place to eat in an otherwise expensive area.

Corso Chianti, Via del Gesù 88. Sit-down snacks or full meals. Small, friendly and popular. Arrive early.

Il Delfino, Corso V. Emanuele 67. Central and very busy caféteria with huge choice of snacks and full meals. Good for a fast fill-up between sights.

Only One, Piazza della Maddalena. Very conveniently located birreria, which is rather nicer at lunchtimes than evenings, and makes an ideal stop-off for either snacks or light meals between sights.

L'Orologio, Via Firenze 57. Rather charmless self-service restaurant quite close to Termini. Main advantage is the very low prices.

Paneformaggio, Via Ripetta 7–8. Some hot dishes, filled croissants and huge range of rolls and pastries. Takeaway or small space at the bar.

Pino's, Via delle Quattro Fontane 27. Well-placed snack and fast-meal joint just off Via Nazionale.

Restaurants

Rome's culinary specialities are pretty unappetising – tripe, brain, veal, offal – but if you want them they crop up on even the cheapest menus. Prices in all but the really flash places are remarkably uniform: L20,000 should buy you a full meal with wine in most central Rome restaurants, and the quality, even in the well-touristed centre, remains of a reasonable standard. You'll find a good array of places in the **centro storico**, not all of them tourist traps by any means, and **Via Cavour** and up to and around **Stazione Termini** is a good source of cheaply-priced restaurants – though the area isn't renowned for its food quality rating. Similarly you can eat reasonably and cheaply in the **Borgo** district around the Vatican. **Trastevere** is Rome's traditional restaurant ghetto – touristy now, inevitably, but still the home of some fine and not over-priced eateries.

Central

Al Leoncino, Via del Leoncino 28. Cheap and genuine pizzeria, little known to out-of-towners.

Baffetto, Via Governo Vecchio 114. A tiny, highly authentic pizzeria that has long been a Rome institution, though it now tends to be swamped by tourists. Amazingly it's still good value, and has tables outside in summer, though you'll always have to queue. Open 6pm–1am. Closed Sun.

Bibliotechina, Via dei Redentoristi, behind Largo Argentina. Not to be confused with the adjoining *Bibliotecha*. Cheap pizza and beer in pleasant bierkeller atmosphere.

Chianti Corsi, Via del Gesù 88. Old world wine shop with a few tables at the back. The good food, cheap prices and friendly service mean it's always busy. Come at noon for lunch. Recommended.

Da Mario, Piazza del Coppelle 51. Good simple Roman restaurant, close to the Pantheon but undiscovered by most tourists.

Da Loreto, Corso V. Emanuele. Rather average food but low prices and a good central location. Open lunchtimes.

Da Settimo, Via dell'Arancio 50. Excellent and innovative food that merits the higher prices charged. Informal, with amiable service but a slightly self-conscious, arty feel. Closed Sun.

Filetti di Baccala, Largo dei Librari 88. A fish and chip shop without the chips. Paper-covered Formica tables, cheap wine and beer, fried cod for L3000. Recommended. Closed Sun.

Grappola d'Oro, Piazza della Cancelleria 80. Curiously untouched by the hordes in Campo dei Fiori. Genuine Roman cuisine and traditional trattoria feel. Has featured in a *New Yorker* article as the epitome of Rome. Prices in upper bracket. Closed Sun.

Il Corallo, Via del Corallo 10. Modern, friendly restaurant which attracts a lively mixed crowd and serves a choice and quality of food – especially pizzas – that's way above average. Trendy and consequently not especially cheap, but recommended nonetheless. Closed Mon.

L'Insalata Ricca, Largo di Chiavari 85. Anglo-American presence in a relaxed and slightly out of the ordinary place. Interesting salads, as name suggests, some wholefood options and reasonably priced Italian fare. Closed Wed.

Le Coppelle, Via delle Coppelle 39. Small, cosy and tastefully decorated restaurant behind the Pantheon. Situated in the heart of night-time Rome, so it can get busy.

Romanesca, Piazza di Campo dei Fiori 23. On the Campo, so inevitably it attracts some tourists, but it's used by market traders too and retains a thoroughly Roman atmosphere. Closed Mon. You could also try the better-known *La Carbonara* across the square, which is more frequented by tourists but has plenty of outdoor seating and an excellent selection of antipasti.

Trattoria, Via del Governo Vecchio 18. Utterly plain, quiet, cheap and straightforward – a rare survivor of Rome as it was. Completely untouched by tourists or the city's gilded youth.

Trattoria da Luigi, Piazza Sforza Cesarini 23. Pleasant no-nonsense restaurant off Corso V. Emanuele. Good for lunch with tables on a shady piazza. Closed Mon.

Trattoria Polese, Piazza Sforza Cesarini 39. Plainer and smaller than *Da Luigi* across the square, but equally good value and also with tables outside. Closed Tues.

Trastevere

Ivo, Via di San Francesco a Ripa 157. *The* Trastevere pizzeria. Arrive early to avoid a chaotic queue. Recommended, but in danger of becoming a caricature. Open 6–11pm. Closed Mon.

La Fraschetta, Via di San Francesco di Ripa 134. The calmer alternative to *Ivo*, less well-known, with good pizzas and above-average desserts. Closed Mon.

Mario's, Via del Moro 53. Well-known and much-frequented cheapie now given over almost exclusively to foreigners. Atmospheric in its own way, and a genuine bargain, but service can be excruciatingly slow. Closed Sun.

Popi-Popi, Via delle Fratte di Trastevere. Good place to eat in summer, when there's a good quantity of tables outside. Not expensive either.

Trattoria G.Ficini, Via Natale del Grande 10. Slightly plastic but serving good cheap pizzas cooked in a big wood-fired oven. Another alternative to *Ivo* round the corner.

Trattoria Il Generale, Via del Moro 1a. Opposite *Mario's*, and often empty as a result, but food is good and cheap. Atmosphere Roman and relaxed. Cheap Castelli wine.

Trattoria, Piazza de Renzi 15. Relaxed and genuine restaurant in a quiet piazza off the tourist beat. Recommended.

Around Termini

La Diligenza Rossa, Via Merulana 271. Low-priced, convivial eatery full of locals.

Da Dino, Via Rattazzi 16a. Almost identical to *L'Archetto*, but a touch more upmarket (nicer tablecloths). No tourist menu which in this area is generally a good sign.

Dal Matriciana, Via Milazzo 8b. One to make for if you're lugging a pack – only 100m from the station, but clear of the hassle. No-frills canteen atmosphere, good for a beer and a snack. Room to the rear for more substantial meals. Closed Mon.

Da Pino, Via Catalafima 12. Cheap traditional Roman. One of two or three acceptable eateries on this street (including a Chinese at no. 29 and good Pizzeria-Birreria *Da Adorno* at no. 30).

Hosteria Angelo, Via Principe Amedeo 104. Appealing atmosphere (rare around here). Below average prices and above average menu. Probably best choice this side of the tracks. Closed Wed.

Hosteria L'Archetto, Via F. Turati 106. Clean, small and straightforward, with big choice (including pizzas) and a touch cheaper than its neighbours.

Hosteria da Bruno, Via Varese 29. Shade more pricey than others in the area, but quieter and – tellingly – with no English menu. One to think about if you're staying nearby. Closed Sun.

Hosteria Veneta, Two doors from *Dal Matriciano*, but decked out as more of restaurant should you want to linger. Standard menu.

Pizza Economica, Via Tiburtina 44. This well-named restaurant is a legend among the cheaper Rome eateries. The cheapest pizza in town.

Pizzeria-Steak House, Via Montebello 77. The Steak House bit sounds ominous, but the place is okay. Clean white interior with fresh flowers on the tables. Clear menu, with choice of four "tourist meals" which for once are worth thinking about. Pizzas, otherwise, are the best bet. Closed Sun.

Elsewhere

Federico, Via di Portacastello 12. Very cheap prices, very close to Saint Peter's.

Il Cantinone, Piazza Testaccio. Typical Testaccio neighbourhood restaurant – raucous and cheap, and serving excellent food. Bus #27 or tram #30.

Il Pozzetto, Borgo Pio 168. Pasta for around L5000 a plate, spitting distance from the Vatican and Saint Peter's. Borgo Pio is lined with other, fairly cheap restaurants, not all of them solely aimed at tourists.

Trattoria/Pizzeria, Via Michele di Lando 32. Just off Piazza Bologna, this is a fair way out from the centre, but it's worth the effort for the excellent inexpensive pizzas and warm, neighbourhood atmosphere. Tables outside in summer. Bus #65.

Non-Italian restaurants

Centro Macrobiotico Italiano, Via delle Vite 14. Predictable vegetarian with a L5000 membership charge. Cheap after that, with relaxed but somewhat soulless air. Weekdays 10am–7.30pm.

Dragon Garden, Via del Boschetto 41. Run by an Italo/Chinese couple, and probably the best-value Chinese in the city. Slow service but worth waiting for. Closed Tues.

Hosteria Africa, Via Gaeta 28. Arguably the city's most interesting food, and the first culinary sign of Rome's new Ethiopian and Somalian population.

Lotus, Via Vespasiano 25. Out of the way, extra-cheap Sri Lankan restaurant.

Margutta, Via Margutta 119. Upmarket, super-tasteful vegetarian that serves generous helpings at OK prices. Recommended, despite the rather precious atmosphere. Closed Sun.

Namaskar, Via della Penitenza 7. For a long time Italy's only Indian restaurant, and as such not a cheap place to eat at all. Seating only by reservation (☎654-7053). Closed Sun.

La Pasta Vitale, Vicolo del Bologna 9. Worthy vegan restaurant – ridiculously cheap but sometimes inedibly bland. Also includes a wholefood shop and Green information/meeting place (☎581-7404).

Nightlife: music, clubs, the performing arts and film

Roman **nightlife** still retains some of the smart ethos satirised in Fellini's *Dolce Vita*, with dressing up normal for most outings and prices above what you might pay in other European capitals. But if you're here in summer, you'll find the city quieter than you might be expecting: nightlife here suffers as much from the July/August exodus as any Italian city, leaving only the centre's core of jazz bars and Latin American clubs for rollicking nights out. **Live music** is less affected by the summer lay-off. Most name **rock and pop** artists come to Rome (the bigger ones playing the tents dotted around the city) and **classical music**, **theatre** and **film** are well-served by the summer *L'Estate Romana* and *L'Estate Tiberina* festivals – though much of the latter two is inevitably inaccessible for non-Italian speakers.

Information and tickets

For **what's on information** the city's best source of listings is *Trovaroma*, a free supplement published with the Saturday edition of *La Repubblica*. It's in Italian, but it's easy to make sense of what's happening. The daily arts pages of the main Rome newspapers – *La Repubblica* and *Il Messagero* – can also be useful references. English-language listings magazines are limited to the fortnightly *Wanted in Rome*, free from the EPT office – though this has very limited information – and the more comprehensive booklet, *This Week in Rome* (L4000, only available monthly from newsstands) is rather bland in approach.

First stop for **tickets** should be *Orbis* at Piazza Esquilino 37 (☎475.1403), though you'll also find box offices at the following shops or bars: *Babilonia* (Via del Corso 85), *Rinascita* (Via delle Botteghe Oscure 1), and *Venice LA* (Via del Boschetto 132).

Discos and clubs

Rome's **discos and clubs** cover the range. There are vast glitter palaces with stunning lights and sound systems, predictable dance music and an over-dressed, over-made-up clientele – good if you can afford it and just want to dance (and observe a good proportion of Romans in their natural Saturday night element). But there are also places that are not much more than upmarket bars with music, and other, more down-to-earth places to dance, playing a more interesting selection of music to a younger, more cautious-spending crowd. There is, too, a small group of clubs which cater specifically for gay or lesbian customers. Whichever you prefer, all tend to open and close late, and some charge a heavy entrance fee, the more spectacular places as much as L30,000.

Clubs

Acropolis, Via Luciana 52 (☎870.504). Standard disco catering to a fairly youthful crowd. Restaurant and garden bar that's nice on a summer night. Closed Mon. Open 10pm until dawn.

Black Out, Via Saturnia 18 (☎759.6791). One of the better cheapies, with occasional live music, oddball exhibitions and alternative fashion shows. Sounds sometimes by DJs from one of the city's more go-ahead radio stations, *Cittàuno*.

Gilda, Via Mario de'Fiori 97 (☎678.4838). Currently the city's hippest club – slick, stylish, the focus for the city's minor (and would-be) celebs.

Hysteria, Via Giovannelli 3 (☎864.587). Enjoyed brief notoriety when it opened in 1983 as the most extravagant of the city's discos. Now slightly dated, but still popular. Music has a funk/soul edge. Fri–Sat 11pm–late.

Piper, Via Tagliamento 9 (☎854.459). One of the oldest discos in Rome, with live music, videos and different nightly events. Closed Mon.

Le Stelle, Via Beccaria 22 (☎361.1240). At time of writing one of the emerging favourites with Rome's smart crowd. Well up on the latest musical trends.

Lesbian and gay clubs

Angelo Azzurro, Via Cardinale Merry del Val (☎580.0472). Relaxed gay club with music, small rooms and discreet lighting. Young, highly camp crowd. Closed Mon.

Easy Going, Via della Purificazione 9 (☎474.5578). Aggressively gay disco, with big transvestite element. Free Mon–Fri. Door policy in force. Closed Sun.

Hanger, Via in Selci 69 (☎461.397). Popular video bar near Santa Maria Maggiore. Closed Tues.

L'Alibi, Via Monte Testaccio 44 (☎578.2343). Predominantly but not exclusively male venue that's one of Rome's best gay clubs. Downstairs cellar disco and upstairs open-air bar. Closed Mon.

St James, Via Campania 37a (☎493.706). Long established and traditional to the point of compulsory jacket and tie.

Live music

Rome's **rock scene** is a fairly limp affair, focusing mainly on imported product and the big venues. Summer sees local bands giving irregular free concerts in the piazzas, but the city is much more in its element with **jazz**, with lots of venues and a wide choice of styles performed by a healthy array of local talent. There's a burgeoning **Latin music** scene too. Sadly most clubs close during July and August, sometimes longer; bear in mind, too, that you may have to pay a membership fee on top of the admission price. Drinks, though, are generally no more expensive than you'd pay in the average bar. As for other kinds of music, **opera** here has long been overshadowed by Milan but is improving, while **classical music** can be heard at a number of venues all over the city, most atmospherically in concert series organised in its churches.

Rock and pop

Caffè Latino, Via Monte Testaccio 96. Multi-event club in the newly hip area near the Protestant cemetery. Film, cartoons and cabaret, with varied live music. Best at weekends when it's crowded and more atmospheric.

Folkstudio, Via G. Sacchi 3 (☎589.2374). Inexpensive Trastevere club, given over largely to folk/blues. Closed July–Sept.

Forte Prenestino, Via Delpino 14. Squatted anarchist club way out in eastern suburbs. Rock, cinema and alternative events, most of them free. Look out for posters. Buses #14, #19, #516.

Grigio Notte, Via dei Fienaroli 30b (☎581.3249). Hi-tech club with live jazz, salsa, poetry readings and a games room.

Melvyn's, Via Politeama 8 (☎581.3300). Roman bands of every musical shade play nightly at this popular Trastevere bar. Open until 4am. Closed Sun.

Palaeur. Immense sports arena out in EUR that's the automatic choice for visiting megastars. Appalling acoustics and usually packed. Metro Line B or bus #93 from Termini.

Tenda Pianeta, Viale de Coubertin. One of Rome's two permanent tent venues, hosting mainly semi-famous Italian groups, and the odd ethnic show or festival. Bus #95 from Piazza Venezia, or tram #19.

Tenda Strisce, Via Cristofo Colombo 393 (☎541.0196). The other tent, a middle-sized stage for non-mainstream bands, both foreign and Italian. Bus #93.

Uonna Club, Via Cassia 871. Well out of town, but one of the most adventurous rock venues, with a punk/Gothic slant. Foreign cult groups, and if not the best of the Roman bands, certainly the most original.

Jazz and Latin

Alexanderplatz, Via Ostia 9 (☎359.9398). Reliable club/restaurant with free entry except when there's star-billing. Three-month membership L3000. Closed Mon.

Big Mama's, Vicolo San Francesco a Ripa 18 (☎582.551). Trastevere-based jazz/blues club of long-standing hosting nightly acts. Membership L5000; admission L10–20,000. Closed July–Oct.

Billie Holiday, Small club with interesting local or lesser-known foreign musicians. Jam sessions on Sunday afternoons. Membership L2000; admission L10–20,000 with first drink free. Open Thurs–Sun late. Closed July to Sept.

Blatumba, Piazza in Piscinula 20 (☎605.4810). Small, inviting club that stages authentic Latin American acts. Very busy Fri and weekends. Open 10pm until late. Closed Mon. Admission L10,000, including first drink.

El Charango, Via Sant'Onofrio 28 (☎687.9908). Currently best of the Latin clubs and heavily patronised by the city's South American population.

Fonclea, Via Crescenzio 82a (☎653.0302). Long running jazz/salsa outfit, with live music most nights.

Lune, Via dei Salumi 3 (☎581.7332). Hit-and-miss mixture of Afro-Latin music, "happenings", cabaret and films, Usually full of ex-punks and posers in bow ties.

Music Inn, Largo dei Fiorentini 3 (☎654.4934). Legendary Rome club – the city's oldest – in the smoky den mould. Music still lives up to past reputation and prices are reasonable. Membership L5000; admission L10–20,000. Open Thurs–Sun. Closed July to Sept.

Saint Louis, Via del Cardello 13a (☎474.5076). Modern club known for serious, high-quality music. Admission free, but cover charge of L3000 on the first drink. Closed Tues and July–mid-Sept.

Saxophone, Via Germanico 26 (☎380.047). Pub atmosphere and prices, with live jazz from 8pm every Wed, Fri & Sun.

Tusitala Jazz Club, Vicolo dei Neofiti 13a (☎678.3237). Intimate, friendly and multi-cultural, with jazz, blues, poetry, traditional and ethnic music – and sometimes ethnic food. Recommended. Membership L2000; admission L10,000.

Yes! Brazil, Via San Francesco a Ripa 103 (☎581.7332). Brazilian-staffed bar with live Latin music nightly.

Classical and opera

During the summer there are quite a few places you can hear **classical music**. Apart from the performances on offer as part of the *L'Estate Romana* summer festival, the city's **churches** host a wide range of choral, chamber and organ recitals, all widely advertised and many of them free. In addition there are sponsored **Sunday morning concert cycles**, best known of which are the *Alitalia* at the *Teatro Brancaccio*, Via Merulana 244 and *Italcable* at the *Teatro Sistina*, Via Sistina 129 (☎475.6841). Ideally you should pick tickets up during the week, but there are usually people unloading spare seats on the morning. In a similar vein the city authorities organise an **autumn season** of music at the Villa Doria Pamphilj, Via Aurelia Antica 183 and the RAI opens the doors at concerts broadcast from the Foro Italico.

Year-round, the **Accademia di Santa Cecilia** (☎654.1044) is at the hub of the city's classical music, responsible for staging concerts by its own or by visiting orchestras. These are usually in winter at least, held at Via dei Greci 18 (☎678.3996), but there are also summer recitals, often with world-class performers, staged outdoors in the Piazza del Campidoglio. The city's other orchestras include the **Accademia Filarmonica**, Via Flaminia 118 (☎393.304); **Arcum**, Piazza Epiro 12 (☎759.6361); **Auditorio del Gonfalone**, Via del Gonfalone 321a (☎687.5952); and the **Instituzione Universitaria dei Concerti**, Via Fracassini (☎361.0051) – all of whom stage concert series.

Rome's **opera** scene bases around the **Teatro dell'Opera** on the corner of Via Torino and Piazza Beniamino Gigli (☎461.755), between November and May. Tickets, priced from L5000, go on sale two days before the performance at 10am–1pm and 5–7pm. In summer the season moves outdoors to the remains of the Roman baths at **Terme di Caracalla**, a beautiful and suitably spectacular location for what are usually productions on an epic and madly lavish scale – *Aida* is the repertoire's mainstay. Purists should be prepared for a carnival atmosphere and plenty of unscheduled intervals.

Film

Rome's only English-language cinema is the **Pasquino** in Trastevere, a homely affair on Vicolo del Piede (☎580.3632). It shows recent general releases, with a programme which changes every few days, and a popular late-night screening that goes out around 10.30pm. Tickets are currently L4000. The only alternative to this is films dubbed into Italian, many of which, if you can cope with the language, come out several months ahead of their British release. Ticket prices for first runs are about L8000. You'll find major listings in all the newspapers, which also include a section on film clubs, where – very occasionally – English language films go out as matinee; look out for the words *lingua originale*. Best bets for these are the **Labirinto**, Pompeo Magno 27 (☎312.283,) and the excellent **Grauco Cineclub**, Via Perugia 34 (☎755.1785).

Listings

Airlines *Alitalia*, Via Bissolati 13 (☎5454); *British Airways*, Via Bissolati 48 (☎479.991); *Pan Am*, Via Bissolati 46 (☎4773); *TWA*, Via Barberini 67 (☎4721). Note that most other airlines are in one of these two streets, or very close by.

Airports Fiumicino (☎6012); Ciampino (☎4694). Ways of getting to Rome's two airports are detailed under "Arrival"; if time's tight or there's four of you, it's worth considering a limousine service – a flat fare of L50,000 gets you a silver Mercedes. Information from the offices in the termini.

American Express Travel office and exchange facilities at Piazza di Spagna 38 (☎67.641). Open Mon–Fri 9am–5pm, Sat 9am–noon.

Baths Hot baths, sauna and steam baths at *Casa del Passeggero*, Via del Viminale 1a.

Beaches Rome's nearest beach is at Lido di Ostia, half an hour away by train, and this is where the tourist board will try and point you. Don't listen to them, and make instead for either Anzio or Nettuno an hour to the south of the city by frequent (hourly) train from Termini. Clean, if fairly crowded beaches, and at Anzio especially, excellent seafood. See "Rome".

Books The *Lion Bookshop*, Via del Babuino 181 (☎360.5837) is the city's biggest and best-stocked English-language bookstore, and has an English-speaking staff for enquiries. Try also the *Economy Book Center*, Via Torino 136, which has a good stock of new and used English-language paperbacks.

Bus enquiries *ATAC* (☎46.951); *ACOTRAL* (☎5798 or 57.005).

Camera repair *Vasari*, Piazza della Repubblica 61 ☎475.4505) is a centrally-placed store that repairs most makes of camera.

Car hire *Avis*, Piazza Esquilino 1 (☎4701); *Hertz*, Via Sallustiana 28 (☎51712); *Maggiore*, Piazza della Repubblica (☎463.715).

Car repair ☎116 for emergency breakdown service. Otherwise consult the telephone directory for specialised repair shops.

Dentist The *Ospedale di Odontoiatria G. Eastman*, Viale Regina Elena 287b (☎491.195) has a 24-hour emergency service.

Embassies *Australia*, Via Alessandria 215 (☎841.241); *Canada*, Via G.B. de Rossi 27 (☎855.341); *New Zealand*, Via Zara 2 (☎851.225); *United Kingdom*, Via XX Settembre 80 (☎475.5441); *USA*, Via V. Veneto 119 (☎4674).

Emergencies ☎113. The central police station is at Via San Vitale 15 (☎4686).

Exchange For exchanging currency and travellers' cheques out of banking hours, there are two offices at Termini station, one on the upper level, another down below. Otherwise try *Frama*, Via Torino 21/b or Corso Rinascimento 73–75 (Mon–Fri 9am–1.30pm & 3–5pm, Sat 9am–1.30pm), friendly and rarely with large queues.

Football Rome's two teams are *Roma* and *Lazio*, who play at the Stadio Olimpico, Via del Foro Italico (☎36.851) on alternate Sundays. Unsurprisingly feelings run high between the two teams, and derby games have in the past been noted for violence and – although this seems endemic in Italian football generally – a certain amount of corruption. Until recently, *Roma* (supporters middle-class, establishment) were clearly the better side, but *Lazio* (supporters poorer, more working-class) have recently been promoted to Division A and are going some way to challenging the long-established supremacy of *Roma*. Tickets for matches cost from L10,000 from either *Societá Roma*, Via del Circo Massimo 7, or *Societá Lazio*, Via Col di Lana 3, or from the stadium direct. The stadium is reachable by way of metro line A to Ottaviano, then bus #32.

Hospital In case of emergency ☎462.371 or ☎113. Otherwise the most central hospital is the Policlinico Umberto I, Viale del Policlinico (☎490.771).

Laundry Coin-operated laundrette at Via Montebello 11.

Left-luggage At Stazione Termini 7am–9pm; L1000 per item per day.

Libraries The British Council, Via della Quattro Fontane 20, has a lending library and mounts film-showings and other events in English. The library is, however, closed during summer and you must produce proof of residence to join. There's also a library at the English church of Santa Susanna, Via XX Settembre 14 (Sun & Thurs mornings, Wed afternoons), with a good noticeboard for finding work, accommodation, etc.

Lost property For property lost on a train ☎4730.6682.

Newspapers You can normally buy English newspapers the same day of publication from newsstands at Termini, or Piazza Colonna and on Piazza Barberini.

Ostia Antica Boats leave Ponte Marconi, in the south of the city close to San Paolo fuori le mura, every day at 9.30am and 3.30pm for the ruins of Ostia Antica – a much pleasanter way to get to the site, though at L25,000 a head a great deal more expensive too. Information on ☎495.0284.

Pharmacies ☎1921 for a list of late-opening pharmacies in central Rome. Or check the newspapers.

Post Office The main post office is on Piazza San Silvestro (☎6771); post and telegraphic enquiries on ☎160. Opening times Mon–Fri 8.30am–9pm, Sat 8.30am–noon. Telegrams can be sent at any time, day or night, on ☎679.5530.

Radio *CittàUno*, 98.0 FM, plays better music than most of the local radio stations.

Swimming pools There are two public pools at Foro Italico, one indoor one outdoor, the latter only open June–September. The only other public pool is *Piscina delle Rose*, Viale America 20 in EUR (metro line B to EUR-Marconi), or *Piscina Foro Italico* (bus #32).

Telephones You can make international calls and pay afterwards at the following places: Stazione Termini (7am–midnight); main post office, Piazza San Silvestro (8.30am–8pm); SIP, Via Santa Maria in Via (8am–9.45pm). At all expect long queues, especially in the evening.

Touring Club Italiano Head office at Via Ovidio 7 (☎388.602).

Tours A number of companies run organised trips around the city centre, though these are, for the most part, over-priced. For general orientation and a glance at the main sights, you can either take tram #30, which passes most places of interest on its route, or join the daily *ATAC*-run bus tour, which (between April and September) leaves Termini at 3.30pm and costs L6000 per person.

Train enquiries Stazione Termini (☎4775); Stazione Tiburtina (☎423.972); Stazione Ostiense (☎575.8748); Stazione di San Pietro (☎631.391); Stazione Trastevere (☎585.155); Roma-Nord line (☎361.0441). The information booth at Termini is open daily 7am–11.30pm.

Travel agencies *CIT*, Piazza della Repubblica 68 (☎475.1909); *CTS*, Via Genova 16 (☎446.791).

Women's Rome The women's bookshop on Piazza Farnese is the best place to go for contacts and to find out what's happening from its noticeboard. *Fruellandia*, Vicolo del Piede 18 in Trastevere, is a friendly women-only bar. The *Surreal Bar*, Vicolo del Leopardo 39/a, near Corso V. Emanuele, is a disco with a women-only night on Thursday, though it closes down during summer.

Out from the city: Tivoli and Ostia

You may find there's quite enough of interest in Rome to keep you occupied during your stay. But Rome can be a hot oppressive city, its surfeit of churches and museums intensely wearying, and if you're around long enough you really shouldn't feel any guilt about freeing yourself from its weighty history to see something of the countryside around. Two of the main attractions visitable on a day-trip are, it's true, Roman sites, but just the process of getting to them can be energising. **Tivoli**, about an hour by bus east of Rome, is a small provincial town famous for the Travertine quarries nearby, and its fine ancient Roman villa and landscaped gardens and parks. **Ostia**, in the opposite direction from the city near the sea, and similarly easy to reach on public transport, is the city's main seaside resort (though one worth avoiding) and home of the port of Rome in classical times, the site of which is well preserved and worth seeing. Bear in mind, too, that a number of **other places in Lazio** – Lake Bracciano and the Etruscan sites north of Rome, the Castelli Romani, Palestrina and Subiaco, and parts of the southern coast – are close enough to the city to make a feasible day-trip, especially if you have access to a car. See the relevant headings for details.

Tivoli

Just 40km from Rome, perched high on a hill and looking back over the plain, **TIVOLI** has always been something of a retreat from the city. In classical days it was a retirement town for wealthy Romans; later, during Renaissance times, it again became the playground of the monied classes, attracting some of the city's most well-to-do families out here to build villas. Nowadays the leisured classes have mostly gone, but Tivoli does very nicely on the fruits of its still-thriving travertine business, exporting the precious stone worldwide (the quarries line the main road into town from Rome), and supports a small airy centre that preserves a number of relics from its ritzier days.

The Town

Most people head first for the **Villa d'Este** (summer daily 9am–7pm, winter daily 9am–4pm; L5000), across the main square of Largo Garibaldi – the country villa of Cardinal Ippolito d'Este that was transformed from a convent by Pirro Ligorio in 1550 and is now often thronged with visitors even outside peak season. It's the gardens rather than the villa itself – a parade of dim, scruffy rooms decorated with faded Mannerist murals – that they come to see, peeling away down the hill in a succession of terraces: probably the most contrived garden in Italy, but also the most ingenious, almost entirely symmetrical, its carefully tended lawns, shrubs and hedges interrupted at decent intervals by one playful fountain after another. In their day some of these were quite ingenious – one played the organ, another imitated the call of birds – though nowadays the emphasis is on the quieter creations. There's the central, almost Gaudi-like *Fontana di Bicchierone* by Bernini, one of the simplest and most elegant; on the far left, the *Rometta* or "Little Rome" has reproductions of the major buildings of the city and a boat holding an obelisk; while perhaps the best is the *Fontana del Ovato* on the opposite side of the garden, fringed with statues, behind which is an arcade, rather dank, in which you can walk.

The Villa d'Este is an expensive way to spend an hour, and if you're short of time or money, you may prefer to visit the **Villa Gregoriana** (daily 9am–7pm; L1500), a park with waterfalls created when Pope Gregory XVI diverted the flow of the river here to ease the periodic flooding of the town in 1831. It's less well-known and less touristed than the d'Este estate, with none of the latter's conceits, its vegetation lush and overgrown, descending into a gashed-out gorge over 60m deep. There are two main waterfalls – the larger *Grande Cascata* on the far side, and a small Bernini-designed one at the neck of the gorge. The path winds down to the bottom of the canyon and the water, scaling the drop on the other side past two grottoes, where you can get right up close to the pounding water, the dark, torn shapes of the rock glowering overhead. It's harder work than the Villa d'Este – don't go lightly down to the bottom of the gorge, it's a long way back up the other side – but in many ways more rewarding; the path leads up on the far side to an exit and the substantial remains of a **Temple of Vesta**, which you'll have seen clinging to the side of the hill. This is now incorporated into the gardens of a restaurant, but it's alright to walk through and take a look, and the view is probably Tivoli's best – down into the chasm and across to the high green hills that ring the town.

The Villa Adriana
Summer daily 9am–7pm; winter daily 9am–4pm; L4000

Once you've seen these two sights you've really seen Tivoli – the rest of the town is nice enough but there's not that much to it. But just outside at the bottom of the hill, fifteen minutes' walk off the main Rome road (ask the Rome–Tivoli bus to drop you or take the local *CAT* #4 from Largo Garibaldi), the **Villa Adriana** casts the invention of the Tivoli popes and cardinals very much into the shade. This was probably the largest and most sumptuous villa in the Roman empire, the retirement home of the emperor Hadrian for a short while between AD 135 and his death three years later, and it occupies an enormous site. You need time to see it all; there's no point in doing it at a gallop, and with the rest of Tivoli it makes for a long day's sightseeing – set out *early*.

The site is one of the most soothing spots around Rome, its stones almost the epitome of romantic, civilised ruins. The imperial palace buildings proper are in fact one of the least well-preserved parts of the complex, but much else is clearly recognisable. Hadrian was a great traveller, and a keen architect, and parts of the villa were inspired by buildings he had seen around the world. The massive *Pecile* for instance, through which you enter, is a reproduction of a building in Athens. And the *Canopus*, on the opposite side of the site, is a liberal copy of the sanctuary of Serapis near Alexandria, its long, elegant channel of water fringed by sporadic columns and statues leading up to a *Temple of Serapis* at the far end. Nearby, a museum displays the latest finds from the usually ongoing excavations, though most of the extensive original discoveries have found their way back to Rome. Walking back towards the entrance, make your way across the upper storey of the so-called *Pretorio*, a former warehouse, and down to the remains of two bath complexes. Beyond is a fishpond with a *cryptoporticus* winding around underneath and behind that the relics of the emperor's imperial apartments. The *Teatro Marittimo*, adjacent, with its island in the middle of a circular pond, was the place to which it's believed Hadrian would retire at siesta time to be sure of being alone.

Tivoli practicals
Buses leave Rome for Tivoli every half an hour from the western end of Via Gaeta, just off Piazza Cinquecento; tickets cost L3400 return from the office on the right; journey-time 45 minutes. In Tivoli they both stop and leave from the main Largo Garibaldi, opposite the **AAST** (Mon–Sat 9am–2pm) – which has information on the town's sights, and on accommodation if you're planning to stay over.

Ostia

There are two Ostias: one an over-visited seaside resort, the so-called Lido di Ostia, which is well worth avoiding; the other, one of the finest ancient Roman sites – the excavations of the port of Ostia Antica – which are on a par with anything you'll see in Rome itself and easily merit a half-day journey out.

Lido di Ostia
The **LIDO DI OSTIA**, reachable by train in thirty minutes from Stazione Ostiense at Porta San Paolo, has for many years been the number one seaside

resort for Romans and has suffered accordingly. The beaches here are notorious: dangerously filthy and bordering some equally murky water, and mostly sectioned off as private stretches stacked with over-priced bars that you have to pay to enter.

As for the town, it's on the whole a poor outpost of the city with little, if anything, to recommend it. All in all, even if you're desperate for a swim you'd really be better off travelling further afield to, say, ANZIO or NETTUNO – both of which are only an extra half an hour by train away from the city.

Ostia Antica

The stop before Lido di Ostia on the train from Rome, the site of **OSTIA ANTICA** marked the coastline in classical times, and the town which grew up here was the port of ancient Rome, a thriving place whose commercial activities were vital to the city further upstream. The excavations (daily 9am–6pm; L4000) remain relatively unvisited; indeed until the 1970s the site was only open one day a week and few people knew – or even cared – that the port had been quite well-preserved by the Tiber's mud. But it's an evocative site, still free of the bustle of tourists, from which it's much easier to reconstruct a Roman town than any amount of pottering around the Forum.

It's also very spread out, so be prepared for a fair amount of walking. From the entrance, the **Decumanus Maximus**, the main street of Ostia, leads west, past the **Baths of Neptune** on the right (where there's an interesting mosaic) to the town's commercial centre, otherwise known as the **Piazzale di Corporazione** for the remains of shops and trading offices that still fringe the central square. These represented commercial enterprises from all over the ancient world, and the mosaics just in front denote their trade – grain merchants, ship fitters, rope-makers and the like.

Flanking one side of the square, the **theatre** has been much restored but is nonetheless impressive, enlarged by Septimus Severus in the second century AD to hold up to 4000 people. On the left of the square, the **House of Apulius** preserves mosaic floors and, beyond, a dark aisled *mithraeum* with more mosaics illustrating the cult. Behind here – past the substantial remains of the *horrea* or warehouses that once stood all over the city – the **Casa di Diana** is probably the best preserved private house in Ostia, with a dark, mysterious set of rooms around a central courtyard, and again with a *mithraeum* at the back. You can climb up to its roof for a fine view of the rest of the site, afterwards crossing the road to the **Thermopolium** – an ancient Roman café, complete with seats outside, a high counter, display shelves and even wall paintings of parts of the menu.

North of the Casa di Diana, the **Museum** (daily 9am–1pm & 2–6pm) holds a variety of articles from the site, including wall paintings depicting domestic life in Ostia and some fine sarcophagi and statuary. Left from here, the **Forum** centres on the **Capitol** building, reached by a wide flight of steps, and is fringed by the remains of baths and a basilica. Continuing on down the main street, more **Horrea** superbly preserved and complete with pediment and names inscribed on the marble merit a detour off to the right; although you can't enter, you can look into the courtyard. Beyond, the **House of Cupid and Psyche** has a courtyard you can walk into, its rooms clearly discernible on one side, a colourful marbled floor on the other.

NORTHERN LAZIO

Northern Lazio is a quite different entity from the region south of the capital. Green and wooded in its central areas, its steadily more undulating hills hint at the landscapes of Tuscany and Umbria further north. There are few large centres, though, and interest is sparse: with determination (and, in some cases, a car), you can see much of it on day-trips from Rome. Foremost among the area's attractions is the legacy of the **Etruscans**, some of whose most important sites, scattered along the southern stretch of coast, are readily accessible by road or rail – necropoli mainly, but the only remains of a civilisation which ruled the area for close on a thousand years. The **coast** itself is of very little appeal until you get close to the Tuscan border, and if you want to swim you'd be better off doing so inland, around lakes **Bracciano**, **Vico** or **Bolsena** – happy hunting-grounds for hot and bothered Romans on summer weekends. Between these, **Viterbo** is the main centre, a dour provincial town that can make a good base for visiting both the lakes and the region's **Mannerist villas and gardens**, though all over this central area bear in mind that touring without your own transport can be a full-time job. Over to the east, **Rieti** is the big centre, a rather bland and deservedly unvisited town on the way to Abruzzo. Beyond it lie the **lakes and mountains** of Terminillo and Amatrice, scenically spectacular, but again virtually out of reach unless you have your own transport.

Etruria and the coast

D.H. Lawrence had pretty much the last word on the plain and low hills stretching north from Rome towards the Tuscan border: "A peculiarly forlorn coast," he lamented, "the sea peculiarly flat and sunken, lifeless looking, the land as if it had given up its last gasp and was now forever inert." His *Etruscan Places*, published in 1932, is one of the best introductions to both the Etruscans and their cities, which, one or two beaches excepted, are the only good reasons for venturing out here.

Fregene and Ladispoli

For a so-called resort, **FREGENE** is one of the grimmest places imaginable. First main stop on the train out of Rome, its 4km of **beaches** – twenty years ago Lazio's trendiest – are plagued by mosquitos, blighted by the usual commercial tat, and only very slightly redeemed by huge stands of umbrella pines. Romans pile out here mainly for the fish restaurants. The sand's marginally cleaner and less crowded than Ostia, but the gravy-coloured water fails every health and safety test going. Sunbathing slumbers are also disturbed by jets flying out of Fiumincino down the coast, and for decent, almost deserted beaches, you'd do better to stay on the train.

Neighbouring **LADISPOLI** is even worse, summed up by Lawrence in a thumbnail sketch that's still spot-on sixty years later: "Ladispoli is one of those ugly little places on the Roman coast," he wrote, "consisting of new concrete villas, new concrete hotels, kiosks and bathing establishments; bareness and non-existence for ten months in the year, seething solid with fleshy bathers in July and August . . . desecration put upon desolation."

Cerveteri

The station at Ladispoli also serves **CERVETERI**, which provides the most convenient first taste of the Etruscans if you're commuting from Rome. Buses also run to the town from Via Lepanto. Once at the station be warned that it's a 7km hike to the centre, and buses timetabled to shuttle passengers into town don't always materialise.

There's been a settlement here since the tenth century BC, when it was already known to the Greeks as an important trading centre. Cerveteri, the Roman *Caere*, was among the top three cities in the twelve-strong Etruscan federation, its wealth derived largely from the mineral riches of the **Tolfa hills** to the northeast – a gentle range which give the plain a much-needed touch of scenic colour. In its heyday the town spread over 8km (something like thirty times its present size), controlling territory that stretched for 50km up the coast. The rot set in from 351 BC, when it became a dependency of Rome, having failed, like most of Etruria, to maintain a neutrality with the new power.

The present town is a thirteenth-century creation, dismissed by Lawrence – and you can't blame him – as "forlorn beyond words". On arrival, make straight for the Etruscan **necropoli**, just a kilometre away, and signposted from the central piazza (May–Sept 9am–7pm; Oct–April 10am–4pm; L3000). The Etruscans constructed a literal **city of the dead** here, weird and fantastically well-preserved, with complete streets and houses, some formed as strange round pill-boxes carved from the living rock – almost Egyptian in feel – others still covered in earth to create the tumuli effect that ripples over the surrounding plateau. The general span of the graves is seventh to first century BC: as far as anyone can make out, women were buried in separate small chambers within the "house" – easy to distinguish – while the men were laid on death beds (occasionally in sarcophaghi) hewn directly from the stone. Slaves were cremated, and their ashes placed in urns alongside their masters – civilised by comparison with the Romans, who simply threw their slaves into mass burial pits.

The twelve or so show-tombs – lying between the two roads that bisect the city – are grouped together beyond the entrance; they close in random rotation, so it's difficult to know in advance which ones are going to be open. If possible don't miss the **Tomba Bella** (Tomb of the Bas-Reliefs); **Tomba dei Letti Funebri** (Tomb of the Funeral Beds) and the **Tomba dei Capitalli**. **Maps** of the cemetery are on sale at the entrance, as is a good local guide (in English) with the unlikely title of *Let's Meet the Etruscans* (L6000).

If the tombs whet your appetite (and you could spend an hour or so wandering about), you might head back to town and take in the **Museo Nazionale Cerite**, at the top of the old quarter in the sixteenth-century Castello Orsini (Tues–Sun 9am–1pm & 4–7pm). Two large rooms contain a fraction of the huge wealth that was buried with the dead – vases, sarcophaghi, terracottas and a dull run of miscellaneous day-to-day objects; most of the best stuff has been whisked away to Rome.

Civitavecchia: on to Sardinia

The only reason to break a journey in **CIVITIVECCHIA**, 30km north, is to change trains, or to pick up a **ferry to Sardinia**. It's an ugly and forgettable port that is otherwise best avoided. The **docks** are at the end of Viale Garibaldi, a right turn out of the station, with an **EPT** midway along at Viale Garibaldi 42. Night crossings are best, since they save the dubious pleasure of spending a night in the town. Cheapest rides come with *FS*, who run ferries that in theory coincide with the main train connections from Rome and Genova. There are two crossings daily (morning and evening) to Golfo Aranci (9hr), and one each to Olbia (7hr) and Cagliari (13hr). *Tirrenia* operate bigger and pricier boats to Arbatax and Cagliari. In the summer when half of Italy wants to get to the island, you should make car bookings several months in advance; in August even deck-class is a bit of a squeeze. Extra sailings are laid on but don't make much impression.

The tourist office sell **tickets** for both lines, but you can book ahead from many travel agents, buy direct from booths at Rome Termini (for *FS* crossings) or go to the *Tirrenia* office in Rome at Via Bissolati 41 (☎474.2041). Should you get stuck, there's plenty of functional **accommodation**. Try *Locanda Moderna*, second right turn off Viale Garibaldi, at Via A. Cialdi 2 (☎0766/20.902), or *Albergo Miramore*, Viale della Repubblica 6 (☎0766/ 26.167), almost immediately outside the station on the right. If you've an hour to kill there are plenty of cheap pizzerias, and a small **archaeological museum** on the corner of Largo Plebiscito (off Via Garibaldi).

Tarquinia

TARQUINIA is the most touted of the Etruscan necropoli, and as such it can't help but come as a disappointment. The town itself, though partly walled, with an evocative crop of medieval towers, is an unappealing place by any standards. The museum is rather overrated. And the site is spread out and large parts of it often closed. If you've only got the chance to see one Etruscan site, Cerveteri is probably a safer bet.

The town ... and the Museo Nazionale

There's very little in Tarquinia that merits any degree of attention. It's a gloomy, derelict place for the most part, and easily discarded. Its **castle** commanded the town approaches for several centuries, and holds within its walls a twelfth-century Romanesque church, **Santa Maria di Castello** – notable for its rib vaulting, the first known example in Italy. But besides that it's the **Museo Nazionale** (Tues–Sat 9am–2pm, Sun 9am–1pm; L4000) that draws the crowds, tickets to which also admit you to the tombs outside town. Actually, the museum is not all it's cracked up to be. The lower floor has been closed for years, and judging by the builder's rubble, looks set to stay that way. In the half-dozen rooms upstairs, there are some genuinely lovely things, making up in quality what they lack in quantity, including the renowned **terracotta horses** (fourth-century BC), probably from a temple frieze and a striking example of the Etruscans' skill in decorative carving. There are also funeral urns, some superb pieces of jewellry, the usual painted vases and terracotta heads, and several very bizarre, three-legged candle sticks.

The site

Tues–Sun 9am–7pm; L4000

It's the **necropolis** itself, though, which really makes the journey worthwhile, a warren of graves spread across a plateau southeast of the town – all that's left of a city that was once the artistic, cultural and probably political capital of Etruria. Founded in the tenth century BC, its population has been estimated at 100,000, declining gradually from the fourth century BC with the growing influence of Rome. Etruscan cities were built almost entirely of wood, so most vanished quickly – and those that didn't were redeveloped by the Romans, making this one of the few extant remnants of a culture that was around for something like 1000 years.

Excavations started in 1489, the first recorded in modern times, since when 6000 tombs have been uncovered (900 in 1958 alone), with many more apparently still to be unearthed. Grave-robbing is common (thieves are known as *i tombaroli*), and there are patrols. Also, the recent increase in the number of visitors means that only five or so tombs are open at any time – a list of which is posted up at the national museum's ticket office. As for getting there, you could walk – the first of the tombs are about fifteen minutes' walk from the museum, but they're ranged over an 8km stretch and it can be a long round-trip. There are about four buses a day, though at pretty unhelpful times, or you could take a taxi. Whichever way you decide to go, take Via Umberto I from the museum, pass through the Porta Romana, skip the roundabout (Piazza Europa) and follow Via IV Novembre/Via delle Croci until you find the custodian.

Etruscan burial places were often straight copies of houses (here less literally so than at Cerveteri) and filled with the clutter of daily life to provide the dead with all they would need in the afterlife. But the Tarquinia tombs have something else besides – **wall paintings**, the oldest of which date from about the seventh century or eighth century BC. There's been much speculation on the purpose and style of these. The earliest paintings emphasise mythical and ritualistic scenes, but later works from the fourth century to sixth century – in the Orco, Auguri, Della Caccia and Della Pescia tombs – show greater social realism, giving an insight into the habits, customs and scenes from the life of the deceased. The style of theses later works is a mixture of Greek, indigenous Etruscan and even Eastern influences, their ease and fluidity pointing to a civilization that was at the pinnacle of its development. The Greek aspects are particularly important, representing the only allusions to Hellenistic monumental painting, a form which otherwise has vanished largely without trace. From the fourth century BC decadence sets in, with the appearance of increasingly morbid and purely necromantic drawings.

Practical details ... and Tarquinia Lido

Train is the best way of **getting here from Rome** – about fifty minutes' journey if you manage to take a *diretto*; there are also eight buses a day from Rome's Via Lepanto, though it's debatable whether the town is worth the two-hour trip each way. Regular buses connect the station to the 2km-distant town (tickets on the bus), dropping you in Barriera San Giusto. The **AAST** is just over the road and doles out maps and addresses if you make a point of asking.

There are few places to **eat** and even fewer places to **stay** in town. The two main hotels are the *Croce* and the pricier *San Marco* (☎0766/857.190), both on Piazza Cavour. For beer and pizza, there's the oddly-named *Der Etrusker* on Via Mazzini (avoid the grubby *Cucina Casarecchia* over the road), and for pasta and nightlife too there's *Il Bucchero*, Via XX Settembre 27. The most atmospheric place to drink is *Osterina il Grottina*, a rather dingy cavelike bar at Dante Aligheri 8 that serves wine siphoned out of barrels piled in the corner.

Most of Tarquinia's real action happens down at **Tarquinia Lido**, reachable by hourly bus from Barriera San Giusto via the *FS* station. Three huge **campsites** here and at Riva di Tarquinia to the north deal with great herds of holidaymakers, and beaches are inevitably heavily developed, with restaurants, discos, sports facilities, "pubs", even cinemas. Best bet if you want to avoid the crowds is to round off a day-trip with a quick dip and head back to the station.

North to the Tuscan border

Continuing north offers more peaceful opportunities for camping, though you'll probably want to skip **MONTALTO DI CASTRO**, a quiet but unexciting hilltop village famous throughout Italy for its huge, half-built nuclear power station. The plant became a *cause célèbre* for the country's emergent Green Party, and was at the heart of the 1987 referendum which voted against the country's nuclear power programme. After much government double-dealing it's now – at vast cost – going to be converted to either oil or natural gas. If you really want to sleep in the eerie shadow of nuclear reactors, there are seafront **campsites** at Montalto Marina and Pescia Romana.

VULCI, some 11km inland, is another **Etruscan site**, but despite the presence of an estimated 15,000 tombs, has next to nothing to see. Many of the tumuli have been ransacked and left to decay, though there's ample scope for scrambling around what's left. North of the remains is the **Ponte d'Abbadia**, a single arched Roman-Etruscan bridge over a pretty ravine and next to a ninth-century abbey that houses a small collection of finds from the local necropoli.

The best and quietest of the **beaches** on this coast are at **CHIARONE**, singled out in a report as enjoying the first unpolluted water north of Rome. Fifteen kilometres of unbroken sand stretch emptily towards the Argentario peninsula, with a **lagoon** midway down at Burano, and plenty of opportunities for camping in the dunes. Things get grubby on-shore as the summer wears on, but the gentle shelving seabed makes for good swimming, and all it takes for complete solitude on the sand is a few minutes' walk. A handful of Grosseto-bound trains stop nearby (90min from Rome), where you'll find a shop and a couple of bars. The beach lies fifteen minutes' walk from the station, with an obvious **bar and campsite** at the end of the road.

With a car from Chiarone it's possible to visit one of Italy's oddest and increasingly well-known works of modern art, **Il Giardino dei Tarocchi** or the Tarot Garden – a huge set of monumental sculptures by Niki de Saint Phalle, most famous for the "Fontaine Stravinsky" (with Jean Tinguely) in Paris. Ten years in the making, it's a whimsical mixture of Gaudi and sheer fun, is loved by children and admired by grown-ups, and is definitely worth the detour. The brightly coloured, mirror-covered pieces are clearly visible inland from the Via Aurelia: to reach them it's a 5km drive on the road from Chiarone to Pescia Fiorentina. Still only a cult attraction, opening times are restricted to summer weekends.

Lago di Bracciano and around

The closest of northern Lazio's lakes to Rome, **Lago di Bracciano** fills an enormous volcanic crater, a smooth, roughly circular expanse of water that's popular – but not too popular – with Romans keen to escape the summer heat of the city. It's nothing spectacular, with few real sights and a landscape that verges on the dull, but its shores are fairly peaceful even on summer Sundays, and you can eat excellent lake fish in its restaurants. You can also combine a visit with a sidetrip to the Etruscan site of Veio on the way – though you'd need a a car and a full day to do justice to both.

The lake's main settlement is the town of **BRACCIANO** on the western shore, about half an hour by train from Rome San Pietro (direction Viterbo). It's a small town, dominated by the imposing **Castello Orsini-Odelscalchi** (guided tours summer daily 9am–noon & 3–8pm, winter daily 10am–noon & 3–5pm; L5000), a late-fifteenth-century structure now privately owned by the Odelscalchi family, whose outer walls, now mostly disappeared, contained the rectangular piazza of the medieval town. Nowadays it's rather rundown, the interior home to rusting suits of armour and faded frescoes, but the view from the ramparts is worth the admission price alone.

The best place to **swim** in the lake is from the sandy **Lido di Bracciano**, below Bracciano town. For about L10,000 you can hire a boat and picnic offshore; and the nearby trattorias are good and inexpensive. There are also good restaurants at Trevignano and Anguillara, best the *Belvedere* just beyond the Piazza del Commune in Anguillara, which has a large terrace that gives magnificent views over the village.

Veio

Midway between Lake Bracciano and Rome, 2km beyond the turnoff for Bracciano, **Veio** (summer daily 9am–7pm, winter Tues–Sun 9am–2pm; L2000) was the largest of the twelve cities of the Etruscan League, at its height between the eighth century and sixth century BC. Nowadays, however, it's one of the least appealing of the Etruscan sites – spread over a wide area and not at all well-preserved. Captured by the Romans in 396 BC, its chief attraction is its *Sanctuary of Apollo*, the remains of which constitute the most important example of an Etruscan temple yet found – although its terracotta roof decorations and the statue of Apollo itself have long since been removed to the Villa Giulia in Rome. A good sign board explains things (in Italian), and a map helps you make out what's what. But it's a bleak site and for the most part hard work for all but the most dedicated lovers of the Etruscans.

Lago di Vico and around

The smallest but most appealing of north Lazio's lakes, and the only one deemed worthy of declaring a nature reserve, **Lago di Vico** is another former volcanic crater, ringed by appreciable mountains, the highest of which – Monte Fogliano – rises to 963m on the western shore. The **Via Ciminia** traverses the summit ridges, and is a popular scenic drive – dotted with restaurants, but there's a quieter road lower down (closed to cars) which skirts closer to the shoreline. The flatter northern edge, marshy in places, is a spot for discreet unofficial **camping**.

Getting around this part of Lazio is a sweat, and in an ideal world you'd have your own transport, but at a push and with patience you can get by with trains and the occasional bus. Two rickety **branch lines** spear around the lake from ORTE, and with careful scrutiny of the timetables these can just about be made to work for you. One ties in to the Rome–Viterbo line at CAPRANICA, with halts at Ronciglione and Caprarola, the other winds up to Viterbo via Bomarzo and Montefiascone.

Caprarola: the Palazzo Farnese

Over and above the lake's sheer prettiness, there's not much besides the odd attractive village and a scattering of Roman and Etruscan remains – none terribly interesting in their own right, but worthwhile if you can string several together. More properly deserving of individual attention is the **Palazzo Farnese** (summer daily 9am–7pm; winter 9am–4pm; spring 9am–6.30pm; L2000) at **CAPRAROLA**, which (like the villas at Bagnaia and Bomarzo; see below) counts among the highpoints of seventeenth-century Italian Mannerism. There's a **bus** from Viterbo, and a very infrequent **train** from Orte (35min – connections to Rome), but bear in mind the Caprarola rail station is a stiff forty-minute walk from the town. (For the centre bear left from the station, turn right at the T-junction and keep walking straight ahead).

The town is pleasant enough, owing its present prosperity to vast hazlenut groves which blanket the surrounding countryside, though you can't help feeling the place is simply an excuse for the **palace**, which stands huge and imposing at the top of the steep main street. If you're keen on the period, the building is clearly a masterpiece – Stendhal described it as a building where "architecture married Nature". Begun by Antonio di Sangallo the Younger for Pierluigi Farnese in the early 1520s, it was originally more a castle than a palace, situated at the centre of the lands belonging to the Farnese family. Later, Cardinal Alessandro Farnese took up residence here, in 1559 hiring Vignola to modify the building while retaining the peculiar pentagonal floor-plan. Vignola was an inspired choice. Apprenticed at Fontainbleau, responsible for crucial advances in sixteenth-century garden design, he was among the most accomplished architects of the late Renaissance, and exemplifies the Mannerist style at its best in his creation at Caprarola, which celebrates the period's values of superiority of art over nature, style over substance, together with a self-satisfied, almost gloating eulogising of the patron's virtues.

Most of the palace's five floors are closed to the public, and there's no escaping a certain seediness which seems to have overtaken the place of late, both in the fag-ends and graffiti in the curving forecourt, and in the state rooms themselves, which have lost all their furniture, suffering a cold unlived-in feel as a result. There are frescoes from 1560 by the brothers Zuccaro chronicling the Farnese family's greatness, much lauded as the building's highlight, though some are embarrassingly crude and others terribly knocked about; and a monumental spiral staircase up to the first floor, huge and heavy with its thirty pairs of Doric columns, that is considered one of Vignola's best moments. About the only place not given over to glorifying the Farnese clan is the *Sala del Mappomondo*, actually the most beautiful room in the palace, decorated with huge painted maps of the known world and a wonderful ceiling fresco of the constellations.

Outside there are twin **gardens**, divided into a south-facing summer terrace, and an east facing winter-terrace, with plants and design appropriate to each. Look out for the man-made grotto and the stalactites, brought from a real cave and stuck on. Beyond is a **park**, some of it open four times daily, the rest a summer hideaway for the Italian president.

Practicalities

Caprarola only has one **hotel**, the *Farnese*, a modern building in modern surroundings that should be kept for emergencies only. For **food** there's a trattoria midway down the main street at Via F. Nicolai 44, and a pizzeria off Piazza Romei in front of the palace.

South of the lake

South of Caprarola lies a trio of towns, each good for about half an hour if you've got your own transport. **RONCIGLIONE** is closest, its old quarter nicely situated over one of the small east-running **ravines** that cut through the area. Turner thought it picturesque enough to paint, though Dickens later described it as "a little town like a large pig-sty". These days it's the self-styled "Gateway to Etruria" and claims to be the birthplace of Pontius Pilate, though a couple of churches aside there's little to see (the **AAST** at Corso Umberto 22 can fill you in further).

SUTRI, 6km south, has more solid attractions, enclosed by part medieval, part Etruscan walls, with odd traces of cyclopean gateways. The site itself – on a rocky tufa outcrop between valleys – is one typically chosen by the Etruscans, and it's an Etruscan site that provides the town's one real draw: an **amphitheatre** south of the town off the main Via Cassia, carved completely from the solid rock. Later adapted by the Romans, it had seating for 6000, and though now overgrown is a neat antidote to over-restored theatres elsewhere in Italy. Back along the Cassia towards the old town a left-hand track across the river takes you to **Madonna del Parto** – rarely open, but an extremely ancient church, again carved from the rock, and probably converted first from old Etruscan tombs and subsequently from a Mithraic temple.

NEPI is another outcrop village, perched over three valleys on the road to CIVITA CASTELLANA. Principal attraction is the eleventh-century Romanesque **Basilica of Sant'Elia**, 2km away to the east, a pleasant cypress-surrounded spot, with traces of an eighth-century church and twelfth-century frescoes in the apse.

Back up the Cassia to VETRALLA, and there are a couple of good **walks** nearby. If you feel ambitious, one follows an old railway from Capranica to Civitavecchia, cutting through the **Tolfa hills**, a two to three day excursion. The others – more of a doddle – leave from the medieval village of BLERA (bus from Viterbo or Tarquinia): one takes in the **Etruscan necropoli** to the north (2hr), the other is a more scenic wander through the wooded ravine to BARBARANO ROMANO (3hr).

Viterbo and around

Capital of its province, and indeed of northern Lazio as a whole, **VITERBO** is easily the region's most historic centre, a medieval town that during the thirteenth century was once something of a rival to Rome. It was, for a time, the residence of popes, a succession of whom relocated here after friction in the capital. Today there are some vestiges of its vanquished prestige – a handful of grand palaces and churches, an intact set of medieval walls – but the town is a rather shabby place, refreshingly untouched by much tourist traffic but only really worth staying in if you're keen to visit the surrounding area. If you don't, it's worth knowing that trains run frequently from Rome and you can comfortably see the town in a day.

The Town

If there is a centre to Viterbo it's **Piazza del Plebiscito**, an appropriately named square girdled almost entirely by the fifteenth- and sixteenth-century buildings that make up the town's council offices. The lions that echo each other across the square are Viterbo's symbol, and you'll see them repeated, in grandiose echoes of Venice, all over town. You can look in on the fine Renaissance courtyard of the main, arcaded building of the town hall, and climb the stairs from here to view a *Pietà* by Sebastiano del Piombo. You can also view the council chamber itself (accessible through the modern extension, by the door under the bridge), decorated with a series of murals depicting Viterbo's history from Etruscan times in a weird mixture of pagan and Christian motifs – a mixture continued across the square in the church of **Sant'Angelo**, which holds a Roman sarcophagus on its facade.

There are a number of directions you can walk from the piazza. Most interesting is to take a left off the square down Via San Lorenzo, which leads past the pretty Piazza di Gesù, where there's a small market, to the macabrely named Piazza del Morte. Left from here takes you through Viterbo's oldest quarter, the **Quartiere Pellegrino** – a tight mess of hilly streets hinged onto the arched axis of Via San Pellegrino. It's a nice neighbourhood, home to a number of art and antique shops, but half an hour should be more than enough time to see it all. In the opposite direction, Piazza San Lorenzo is flanked by the town's most historic group of buildings, most notably the **Papal Palace** itself, a thirteenth-century structure whose impressive site, looking over the green gorge that cuts into central Viterbo, is best appreciated from its open Gothic loggia. You can peep into the Great Hall, venue of the election of half a dozen or so popes, but otherwise the palace is closed to the public, and you have to content yourself with a wander into the **Duomo** opposite – a plain Romanesque church that has an understated beauty unusual among Italian churches.

Walking east from Piazza del Plebiscito, Via Roma soon becomes **Corso Italia**, Viterbo's main shopping street. At its far end, steps lead up from Piazza Verdi to the nineteenth-century church of **Santa Rosa**, which holds the saint's corpse in a chapel in the south aisle – a faintly grotesque, doll-like figure with a forced grin, dressed up in a nun's habit; for a close-up view ring the bell on the right-hand side of the church entrance and someone will let you into the chapel itself. After this, the rest of Viterbo can't help but seem a bit sinister, and in any case you've seen it all except for one quarter. This is at the top of the hill above Piazza Verdi. Follow Via Matteotti up to **Piazza della Rocca**, a large square dominated by the fierce-looking home of a small **archaeological museum** of Etruscan artefacts.

Practical details

Viterbo's **FS railway station** is situated just outside the Porta Romana to the south of the town centre, around ten minutes' walk from Piazza del Plebiscito. The private **Roma-Nord line station**, also connected with Rome, is on the other side of town, just off the main ringroad, Viale R. Capocci, on Viale Trieste. There's an **EPT** office (Mon–Sat 8am–2pm) on Pizza Caduti, two minutes down Via F. Ascenzi from Piazza del Plebiscito, which has free maps of Viterbo and the surrounding area, and information on **accommodation**. Via della Cava and Via Cairoli, which both wind up to Piazza della Rocca, have a number of inexpensive hotels: the *Milano*, Via della Cava 54 (☎0761/30.705), is one, with rooms for around L30,000 a double; the *Tuscia*, Via Cairoli 41 (☎0761/223.377), is another – doubles for about the same. **Eating** places are fairly thin on the ground. For a light lunch, the *Birreria Bevilacqua*, at Corso Italia 69, is a safe bet for panini and pizza. For more elaborate fare, try *Tre Re*, Via Marcel Gattesco, off Piazza dell'Erbe.

Around Viterbo: Bagnaia, Bomarzo and Tuscania

Viterbo makes by far the best base besides Rome for seeing much of northern Lazio, especially the places that aren't really feasible on a day-trip from the capital. The Mannerist villas of Caprarola (see above) and Bagnaia are a short distance away and relatively easily reached on public transport, as are – from the same era – the bizarre gardens of Bomarzo, and the shores of Lake Bolsena. Less excitingly, Viterbo is also connected by regular bus with Tuscania, the dull centre of a very dull locality.

Bagnaia
BAGNAIA, about 5km east of Viterbo, isn't much of a town, but like Caprarola further south it's completely dominated by a sixteenth-century palace, the **Villa Lante**, whose small but superb **gardens** are considered Vignola's masterpiece, and one of the supreme creations of Renaissance garden art – "the most lovely place of the physical beauty of nature in all Italy or in all the world", according to Sachaverell Sitwell. They're a bit of a grind to reach directly from Rome (three hours on the Roma-Nord line), but from Viterbo there are hourly **buses** from Piazza Verdi, or less frequent trains on the Roma-Nord line.

The **villa** is actually two villas, built for a pair of cardinals twenty years apart, but symmetrically opposed as part of the same architectural plan. Only open on the big public holidays, they're nothing much to write home about, and in contrast to Caprarola it's the **gardens** that take pride of place – some of the best preserved from the period, and a summing up of Mannerist aspirations. The main group lie behind the villas, ranged over five gently sloping terraces, and are only open in the company of a guide (Tues–Sun 9am–noon; L2000). An attempt at a stylised interpretation of the natural world, they were an ambitious project, even by the standards of the time, depicting the progress of a river from its source in the hills to its outlet in the sea – represented here by a large *parterre*. The route takes in various watery adventures – waterfalls, lakes and the like – and among numerous fountains and low hedges there are plenty of humorous (or plain silly) touches, such as a cascade designed as an elongated crayfish, and the so-called "wetting sports" – hidden sprays of water that drenched unsuspecting onlookers and were a big favourite of Mannerist funsters. Only the guide gets to play with these.

The adjoining **park**, through which you're free to wander, has an even more ambitious narrative, attempting to describe, through horticulture, the progress of civilisation from primitive times to the glories of the sixteenth century. In true Mannerist style almost as much weight is given to allegory as to architecture,

For **accommodation** you're better off in Viterbo; for **food** try *Checcarello*, Piazza XX Settembre 26 – smartish but with local specialities (closed Wed).

both here and on the villas. The various square motifs that appear around the buildings, for example, were supposed to represent the perfection of Heaven brought to earth.

Bomarzo

Twelve kilometres northeast of Bagnaia, the village of **BOMARZO** is home to another Mannerist creation, the **Parco dei Mostri** (daily dawn–dusk; L6500, students L4000) – and a greater contrast to the former's restrained elegance would be hard to find. It's still ostensibly a garden, but one look at the tangled wood and its huge, completely crazed sculptures, is enough to see that this is Mannerism gone mad. Salvador Dali loved the surreal flavour of the place, even making a film here, and its strange other-worldly qualities – like a sixteenth-century theme park of fantasy and horror – have made it one of northern Lazio's primary tourist attractions.

Built in 1552 by the hunch-backed Duke of Orsini, the *Sacro Bosco* or "Sacred Wood", as he called it, set out to parody Mannerist self-glorification by deliberate vulgarity. It knocked the intellectual pretentions of the day by mocking idealised Arcadian retreats from society and Art's supposed "triumph" over nature, while retaining typically Mannerist calculated attempts at sensationalism. Apparently built by Turkish prisoners captured at the Battle of Lepanto (though this seems a doubtful Christian rationalisation of the park's "heretical" features), there's an Etruscan influence too, manifest in the plentiful urns and pine cones, and its madder moments are said to have been induced by a popular epic of the time, Ariosto's *Orlando Furioso*, a tale of lost sanity. The giant warrior at the entrance tearing apart a woodcutter comes from the story, a symbol of Orlando's madness, and deeper into the park an English prince pours Orlando's brains down an elephant's trunk – another symbol apparently, this time of the restoration of sanity. There are many other dank, mossy sculptures – tortoises, elephants, Moby Dick, a mad laughing mask, dragons, nymphs, butterflies and plenty of things you couldn't put a name to. And there's a Doric temple which makes a deliberate dog's dinner of all Classical conventions. Legend has it that the Duke's wife took one look and dropped dead of heart failure.

Only four **buses** a day run from Viterbo to Bomarzo, from where the Parco dei Mostri is a signposted ten-minute walk. You can also get here by **train** – the nearest station is Attigliano-Bomarzo, on the Orte-Montefiascone-Viterbo link, but this is a 5km walk from the park.

Tuscania

Sheep and then more sheep are the only thing to break the monotony of the wide, desolate country between Viterbo and Tarquinia. The only thing, that is, apart from **TUSCANIA**, a strange, open-plan town announced by a fine avenue of cypresses and distinguished by a long-ranging spread of medieval walls and some well-preserved towers. Its largely Renaissance centre is attractive and almost unvisited, and it's a charming town in its way. But the real point of a visit lies in the two justly celebrated **Romanesque chuches** on the eastern edge of the town, close to the rocky outcrop of the old Etruscan settlement.

From the central Piazza Basile take the Via Clodia until the unmistakable bulk of **San Pietro** looms into view. Considered one of the gems of the Italian

Romanesque, it's an essentially thirteenth-century construction with eighth-century fragments of Lombard origin. Fronted by a threadbare grass piazza – giving an odd courtyard effect – it's also flanked by the remains of a Bishop's Palace, and two sturdy towers, the whole church having once been fortified as part of the town's defensive scheme. The facade's marble embellishments – look out for the dancer and a man being strangled by a snake – may well come from an Etruscan temple. The interior is solemn and airy, with huge blunt pillars supporting curious notched arches, a feature known in Italian as *dentati* (literally "toothed"), and early twelfth-century frescoes in the transept, somewhat the worse for wear after an earthquake in 1971.

The town's other focal point, **Santa Maria Maggiore**, is a stone's throw away down the hill, a less gracious affair than San Pietro, despite the fact that it deliberately repeats some of its features and was built over the same period. The arched marble doorway is a carbon copy, probably added by Pisan sculptors in the twelfth century; the rest of the ruddy stone facade is largely Gothic, only the left portal preserving the zigzags of Norman motif. Inside is the usual bare simplicity of the Romanesque – stone walls, the odd fresco, and most remarkably, a font designed for total immersion.

The rest of the town is decidedly less impressive, boasting only a small **archaeological museum**, housed in the cloisters of Santa Maria di Rosa on Via XX Settembre. In addition to the predictable Etruscan display, there's a collection of twelfth- to seventeenth-century ceramics, many taken from the walls of local houses.

Lago di Bolsena and around

Heading north from Viterbo by road, there's little choice but to take the Via Cassia to **MONTEFIASCONE**, an ugly journey, not improved by opting for the **railway**, which runs alongside. If you're **hitching** and want to move out of the area fast, there's a new dual carriageway (not marked on all maps) from just north of Viterbo, linking up with the *Autostrada del Sole* (A1) at Orte.

Montefiascone itself rears up high, perched on the rim of an old volcanic crater, an Etruscan city and possibly the site of a huge temple to Voltumna – a sort of Houses of Parliament for the heads of the twelve-city Etruscan Federation. The seventeenth-century **Duomo** is immediately striking, a huge octagonal pile that totally dominates the skyline, though it's less interesting than the twelfth-century church of **San Flaviano** a little way out of town on the road to Orvieto. An extraordinary Romanesque work, consisting of two interconnected but opposite-facing basilicas, the lower church contains several fourteenth- and fifteenth-century frescoes, as well as the tomb of Bishop Giovanni Fugger, who reputedly died from knocking back too much of the local wine, *Est!Est!Est!*. Bumph from the **AAST**, Via Verentana 4, regales you with other unlikely legends surrounding the brew, and has details of a **campsite** – *Amulasanta*, Via del Lago 77 (☎85.294) – out on the MARTA road at PRATO RONCONE.

Buses run from Montefiascone to ORVIETO, and to most points on **Lago di Bolsena** – a popular destination whose hotels and restaurants tend to make their pitch in German and English, though it rarely gets overcrowded. If you want to be away from the crowds and plan on spending some time here, head for the less-visited western shore – better for camping rough, and more picturesque into the bargain. The lake, Lazio's biggest, occupies the remains of a broad volcanic crater. The surrounding soil is immensely fertile, and there's a super-mild micro climate, with most of the shores intensely cultivated as a result. Dante praised the quality of its eels, though fishermen today are hampered by the so-called *sesse* – odd tide-like variations in the lake's level.

CAPODIMONTE, on the southern shore, is one of the more developed spots, an attractive town which pushes into the lake on a half-wooded peninsula. The only sight worth a mention is the sixteenth-century **Castello Farnese**, an octagonal tower commanding the tip of the promontory, but there's good **swimming** from a tree-lined shore, and boat-trips run out to the **Isola Bisentina**, which sports Etruscan tombs, five frescoed chapels, and another Farnese villa – the summer retreat of several popes. The nearest **campsite** is 1.5km away at SAN LAZZARO (open May–Sept; ☎88.102).

On the opposite shore, **BOLSENA** is the lake's main focus, a relaxed and likeable place that's worth a stop even if you don't intend to hang around. Medieval nooks and alleyways run off the single main drag, with a well-preserved fourteenth-century **castle** perched over the western end. The thirteenth-century church of **San Francesco** adds character to the town's main Piazza Matteotti, and occasionally hosts concerts and small exhibitions, and the eleventh-century **Santa Cristina** conceals a good Romanesque interior behind a wide Renaissance facade added in 1494. Santa Cristina was the daughter of the town's third-century Roman prefect, who tortured her as a Christian, eventually throwing her into the lake with a stone round her ankles. Miraculously the stone floated and saved her life, becoming marked with the imprint of her feet – though she died from further mistreatment aged just 12. The stone makes up the altar of the *Cappella del Miracolo*, off the left-hand aisle – an altar which also starred in the Miracle of Bolsena (see "Vatican Museums", earlier in this chapter), when a sceptical priest was assured of the mystery of transubstantiation by real blood. Adjoining the chapel is the Grotta di San Cristina, once part of early Christian catacombs.

Set back a kilometre from the lake, the town itself tends to shut down come nightfall, when the **bars and restaurants** on the shore get into full swing. Closest of the **campsites**, most of which are out of town, is the *Lago*, open all year round, at Viale Cadorna 6 (☎98.191); *La Pineta*, open May to September, is a kilometre away at Viale Diaz 48 (☎989.801); and nearby there's a **youth hostel**, *La Colonia*, at Viale Diaz 10 (☎98.001), open all year. For full details call in at the **AAST** office on Piazza Matteotti.

To the east of Bolsena stretches an extraordinary, almost lunar landscape, pitted with deeply eroded **canyons**, some wooded but most just bare, wasted slopes. At its heart lies the tiny village of **CIVITA**, known as "la città che muore" – the city which is dying – due to the erosion of the rock below it. People have been emigrating from here since the sixteenth century, leaving a population today of around seven, and a strange eerily deserted village that's slowly becoming a tourist attraction in its own right. Apparently an Italian computer company has plans to buy up the place wholesale, but for the moment it's worth a visit just for its very weirdness. Stranded evocatively on an isolated rocky outcrop, the only access is from the nearby village of BAGNOREGIO.

Due north of the lake, **SAN LORENZO NUOVO** is just one of many villages you'll pass through if you're continuing up by road to SIENA. It's not a town of monuments, but it does come as a pleasant surprise if you are passing through. A planned settlement, centred on an octagonal piazza, it was constructed in 1774 to house the inhabitants of the village of San Lorenzo, who had been forced to move by the malaria that once ravaged the entire lake-shore. By some architectural freak the design was copied from a suburb of Copenhagen. If you have time and transport, hilltop **GRADOLI**, a few kilometres west, is at the heart of a big wine area, and has another palace built by the Farnese family. A rough road just beyond, from LATERA, leads to the **Lago di Mezzano**, a beautiful and highly recommended spot if you're travelling with a tent.

Rieti and around

Pleasantly situated, but thoroughly dull, **RIETI** is capital of Lazio's largest province, occupying the plumb geographical centre of Italy – and with a plaque in Piazza di San Rufo to prove it. In the days of the Romans this was a key region – the so-called *Umbilicus Italiae* – with the Via Salaria or "Salt Road" forming an essential route for trading salt (extracted at Ostia) with the Sabines who lived up in these hills. But nowadays it's on its last legs, with the second lowest population density in the country (after Aosta), and a drift from the land that's more often associated with the South. Three-quarters of the rural population has moved from the countryside since 1950, most of them to Rome, and it doesn't look like changing: poor communications have deterred any sort of industrial initiative – something which is to the visitors' if not the locals' advantage, leaving Rieti's mountain-ringed plain almost entirely unscarred by factories or housing.

The town

At best Rieti is somewhere to while away an hour waiting for a bus, so don't be fooled by the tourist office's artful pictures of medieval walls and arches – the only traces of the medieval town you'll find are the **Duomo** and the **Palazzo Vescovile** off the main street, and a short stretch of twelfth-century wall to the north of the centre. For those planning serious walking or camping trips it's worth visiting the main **EPT**, 50m from the duomo at Via Cintia 87, who have maps of the town and, more importantly, detailed routes for **high level walks** around Terminillo. With their help you also shouldn't have problems planning a tour of the four **Franciscan monasteries** around Rieti, all connected one way or another with important episodes in the saint's life. They're all scenic enough, though without a special interest in Saint Francis you may not find them terribly exciting. The most famous is at **GRECCIO**, where Francis created the first ever Christmas crib, a real life nativity with cows and all, for the benefit of local peasants.

Practical details

Rieti's train and bus **station** is just north of the town centre on the far side of Viale L. Morroni. By **train** from Rome it's around three hours to Rieti: there's no direct link and you have to change at Terni (and sometimes Orte) for a line that eventually continues to L'Aquila and Sulmona. Several **buses** a day ply back and forth to Rome, though they tend to take around the same amount of time. You can **eat** cheaply without straying far from the station at the bar/pizzeria *Al*

Girarrosto in Piazza Mazzini. On the other side of town there's *Il Pappomondo*, Piazza Cavour 63, a cheap pizzeria close to the river and local bus terminal. Best of a handful of more upmarket restaurants is *Tito Brucchietti* at Via San Rufo 5 (off Via Roma). If you need to stay, the *Moderno*, Via Tullio Crispolti 36 (☎0746/44.784), is a rock-bottom hotel; the *Stella*, in the same street, at the end of Via San Rufo, is just a touch more expensive (☎0746/44.164).

Around Terminillo

Less than 20km from Rieti, reachable by way of a heart-stopping bus ride, **TERMINILLO** lies amidst 2000m-high mountains and scenery of almost Alpine splendour, a winter ski-resort that likes to think of itself as something of an elite tourist centre. As such it's dominated by clusters of big modern hotels, ski-lifts and associated winter sports paraphernalia. Terminillo's not an especially attractive place, more a string of ski-centres than a town, with facilities that seem rather out of place and redundant in summer, but there's plenty of off-season scope for walking and climbing in the hills around, including a series of refuges if you want to do more than stroll.

The **Club Alpino Italiano**, Via Garibaldi 264b in Rieti, has advance details of some of the most challenging hikes. Once here, there's an **AAST** office in Via Covemese at Terminillo/Pian de Valli (☎0746/61.121), which can also advise on **accommodation**. There's a **youth hostel** (*Ostello della Neve*) at Terminillo/ Campoforogna (☎0746/61.169). **Hotels** – busy in season – start in the two-star bracket: go for *Il Ghiacciolo* in Campoforogna (☎0746/61.240) or the *Regina* in Pian de Valli (☎0746/61.375).

If you've just turned up on the off-chance, one tremendous and manageable low-level hike you can make is by way of **La Valle Scura**, 12km across country to SIGILLO. If you plan on trekking off into the wilderness, bear in mind that many slopes away from the ski-runs are thickly wooded, especially in the Vallonina towards Leonessa, and you often have to get quite high before finding open country. Another good base for hikes is **AMATRICE**, easily hitchable from Terminillo, a rather drab grid-iron town laid out in 1529, famous only for having given birth to a pasta dish, the spicy *spaghetti all'amatriciana*. Behind, the Monti della Laga rise to seriously high peaks – 2400m up – which continue on into Abruzzo's Gran Sasso D'Italia. The **AAST** at Via Madonna della Porta 19 issue a detailed map with several marked paths, most of which start from rough roads above the hamlets of SAN MARTINO and CAPPRICCHIA. If you're staying, the cheapest **hotel** is *La Conca* on Via della Madonnella (☎0746/85.267).

The Sabine Hills

THE SABINE HILLS, south of Rieti, are an altogether softer option than the mountains to the east. For an area so close to Rome they suffer only a trickle of tourism – partly because there are no big sights, and partly because it's difficult to get around in what is an area of small villages and secondary roads. If you decide to bother with the region it'll be for the scenery, the best of which is east of the Via Salaria around **Lago del Turano** and **Lago del Salto**, where the village of **ROCCA SINIBALDA** provides a focus – though it's not really more than a fortified castle, surrounded by high wooded hills. Northeast of here, a great swathe of desolate country centres around Monte Nuria (1888m) and Monte Moro (1524m)

– walking and backpacking territory mostly, with the small **Lago Rascino** providing a wild and unspoilt target, particularly if you're camping.

On the other side of the Via Salaria, many of the villages have been doubly destroyed, first in the Fifties by people emigrating to Rome, and then more recently – ironically – by richer Romans returning to buy up holiday homes. They still look much as they've always done – small self-contained nuclei on the tops of low hills – but varying degrees of medieval character are about all they've got going for them. The rolling countryside in between – looking like a higher version of the Cotswolds – is still moderately pretty. One undoubted highlight in a lacklustre area is the old Benedictine abbey at **FARFA**, situated in fine olive-covered countryside 6km from FARO – to which it's connected by an *ACOTRAL* bus service. Founded in the fifth century and endowed by Charlemagne, it was one of the single most powerful abbeys in Europe for a while, with a huge economic base, a merchant fleet, even its own army, and rights to Aquila, Molise, Viterbo, Spoleto, Tarquinia and Civitavecchia – central Italy in effect. By the end of the Middle Ages, however, it was in decline, and most of its early medieval splendour has since been submerged under fifteenth- and sixteenth-century additions. The **Abbey Church** is stacked with various treasures, and a few eleventh-century frescoes survive in the bell-tower, but the new **museum** is the main focus, collecting together parts of the Abbey's heritage as well as local archaeological fragments. Most fascinating is the **Cures Pillar**, a sixth-century BC Sabine inscription found in a local river bed in 1982. It's the only example known, and, still undeciphered, it remains an emblem for studies of the previously ignored Sabine culture.

SOUTHERN LAZIO

The saying goes that the Italian South begins with the first petrol station south of Rome, and certainly there's a radically different feel to the **southern part of Lazio**, the green wooded hills north of the city having given way to a mix of flat marshy land and harsh unyielding mountains that has a poor, desperate look in places. Many skate straight through the area on their way south to Naples and you may want to do the same. But if you've time, the **coast** is worth taking in on a more unhurried route south: its resorts – **Anzio**, **Terracina**, **Sperlonga** – are fine places to take it easy after the rigours of the capital, and the **Pontine Islands**, a couple of hours offshore, are (out of high season at least) among Italy's most undiscovered treasures. **Inland**, too, the landscape can be rewarding: the towns of the **Castelli Romani** are the most accessible taste of the region, easily assimiliated on a day-trip from Rome; **Subiaco** and the **Ciocaria** region to the south are more remote, but hold some of Lazio's most inspiring scenery – broad tree-clad hills and valleys sheltering small towns unknown to many tourists.

The Castelli Romani and Alban Hills

Just free of the sprawling southern suburbs of Rome, the thirteen towns that make up the **Castelli Romani** date back to medieval times, since when these hills – the **Colli Albani** – have served as an escape for the rich and powerful from the summer heat of the city. It's a wine-growing area (the vines grow easily on the volcanic soil), and is now pretty heavily built-up, most of the towns ringed by unprepossessing new suburbs; and summer weekends can see Romans trooping out in huge numbers for lunch at local trattorias. But if you avoid the rush hour times and peak season holidays, the region is still worth the journey, either as a day-trip from Rome or on the way south through Lazio. By car, there are two obvious routes, both starting with Frascati and Grottaferrata and then spearing off at Marino along either the eastern or western side of Lago Albano. On public transport, buses for the area leave from the terminus opposite the Metro station Subaugusta (line A).

Frascati, and east of Lago Albano

At just 20km from Rome, **FRASCATI** is the nearest of the Castelli towns and also the most striking, dominated by the majestic **Villa Aldobrandi** built by Giacomo della Porta in 1598 for one Cardinal Aldobrandi. Since it still belongs to the family you can't actually get inside, but the **gardens** are open to the public on application to the AAST on Piazza Marconi. These are somewhat neglected these days, and sadly the potentially spectacular water garden at the rear of the villa is often switched off. But the view from the terrace in front of the house is superb, with Rome clearly visible on a clear day. Frascati is also about the most famous of the Colli Albani wine towns: ask at the AAST for details of local wine producers that run tours and tastings; or have lunch at the *Spartaco* restaurant on Viale L. Bonaparte, where you can eat outside in summer.

The tourist office will also tell you about **Tusculum**, beautifully sited on a hilltop just outside Frascati, which was a favourite retreat of Roman patricians. Cicero had a villa here, but the resort was destroyed in 1191 by Pope Celestine III, the inhabitants moving down the hill to modern-day Frascati, and most of the Roman remains seem to have disappeared forever beneath the undergrowth. There's a small theatre, and the views, again, are fine.

Three kilometres or so down the road, **GROTTAFERRATA** is also known for its wines, and the eleventh-century **Abbey** – a fortified Basilian (Greek Orthodox) monastery surrounded by high defensive walls and a now empty moat. It's a timeless spot, the little church of Santa Maria inside with a Byzantine-style interior decorated with thirteenth-century mosaics and, in the chapel of Saint Nilus off the right aisle, frescoes by Domenchino. Through the inner courtyard there's a small museum (9am–12.30pm & 4–7pm) displaying classical and medieval sculptures.

MARINO, another four kilometres further on, isn't a particularly attractive place, though its wine is perhaps the region's best after Frascati, and is distributed free on the first Sunday of October during its *Sagra dell'Uva* festival. From here, the scenic Via dei Laghi skirts the eastern rim of **Lago Albano** before reaching the turn-off for **NEMI**, built high above the tiny crater **lake** of the same name. The village itself isn't much to write home about, but a cobbled road leads down to fields of strawberries which lie between the steep walls of the crater and the shores of the lake and make a good place to picnic. The town is known for its strawberries in fact and celebrates this each June in the *Sagra delle Fragole*. On the northern shore of the lake you'll notice a large hangar-like building, which contains the scanty remains of two Roman ships said to have been built by Caligula. Signs at nearby GENZANO would have you believe there's something exciting to see; in fact the museum there has been closed indefinitely for some time.

Before you reach Nemi, a winding road leads up from Via dei Laghi to **Monte Cavo**, at 949m the second highest of the Colli Albani, and topped with the masts and satellite dishes of the Italian military – who operate from nearby Ciampino airport. There used to be a hotel here, a former Passionist convent, but the building is now derelict, and the summit is much less of a tourist attraction than it used to be. A temple to Jupiter once stood here, but now the only extant antiquity is the Via Sacra, which, about 1000m from the top, emerges from dense undergrowth, snaking down through the woods for a kilometre or so before disappearing again into thick bush.

On the far side of Monte Cavo, the road bears right for **ROCCA DI PAPA**, at 680m the highest of the Castelli Romani towns, and one of its most picturesque, with a medieval quarter tumbling down the hill in haphazard terraces, and motor traffic at a (forced) minimum. The large main square, Piazza Repubblicca, is modern and dull; instead, make for the small Piazza Garibaldi, a lively place in summer with a bar and restaurant, and soak up the views.

West of Lago Albano

Leaving Marino, the road joins up with the old Roman Via Appia, which travels straight as an arrow down the west side of Lago Albano. **CASTEL GANDOLFO** is the first significant stop, named after the castle owned by the powerful twelfth-century Genevose Gandolfi family and now best known as the summer retreat of the pope – though John Paul II is said to prefer visiting the mountains further north during the summer months, much to the digruntlement of the town. At over 400m above the rim of Lago Albano, it's a pleasantly airy place, but inevitably papal business predominates, especially on Sundays when the pope traditionally gives a midday address between July and September from the courtyard of the Papal Palace. Unless you want to see the pope, it's best to avoid this. You can visit the **palace** and its gardens, originally built by Carlo Maderno in 1624, but you need a special permit from the director. Better, if it's hot, to take advantage of the lake: there's a pleasant **Lido** just below the town, from where, if you've the energy, you can make an on-foot circuit of the whole lake in about two hours.

From Castel Gandolfo a panoramic road leads to **ALBANO LAZIALE**, probably the most appealing of the towns along the Via Appia, its large Piazza Mazzini looking south to the lovely Villa Communale park, with sketchy remains of a villa that once belonged to Pompey. The town also has other Roman remains. Along the high street, Corso Matteotti, the church of **San Pietro** was built over the foundations of the baths of a Roman garrison, which you can see built into the walls. Opposite, the **Palazzo del Comune** (daily 9.30am–1.30pm & 4.30–7.30pm) houses a small but quality archaeological collection including Roman artefacts found locally. Walk out also to the **Tomb of Horatii and the Curiatii**, just outside town on the Ariccia road, whose strange "chimneys" date from the Republican era. There's an **amphitheatre** too, on the hill above – in heavy ruin now, and currently closed, but once with room for 15000 spectators.

The Via Appia continues on to **ARICCIA** across the nineteenth-century **Ponte di Ariccia** – from where you can see the arches of the old Roman viaduct just below – into the central piazza of the town, a well-proportioned square embellished with Bernini's round church of **Santa Maria dell'Assunzione**. **GENZANO**, 2km further on, also has a pleasant medieval centre, built around Piazza Frasconi, from where a road leads to the edge of Lake Albano's crater and sweeps down to the shore through dense woods. The town is the scene of the yearly *Infiorata* in May, when Via Italo Belardi, which scales the hill from the piazza, is carpeted with flowers. **VELLETRI**, though larger, is scarcely more interesting, its largely modern centre rebuilt after extensive war damage and with a Baroque cathedral, the fourteenth-century Torre del Trivio and a small archaeological museum among its scant sights.

Palestrina, Subiaco and the Ciociaria

Considering its proximity to the capital, it's a surprise that the southeastern rim of Lazio isn't more discovered; in fact it's one of Italy's least-known areas to tourists, for the most part a poor region of low hills edging into the mountains of the Abruzzi which is bypassed by those heading south on the fast *Autostrada del Sole*.

Palestrina

PALESTRINA was built on the site of the ancient *Praeneste*, originally an Etruscan settlement and later a favoured resort for patrician Romans. "Cool Praeneste", as Horace called it, was the site of an enormous Roman Temple of Fortune, whose foundations more or less determine the extent of the modern town centre, which is stepped up the hillside in a series of terraces constructed on the different levels of the once vast edifice – the ruins of which you can see at every turn.

Buses run to Palestrina about every 30–45 minutes from Rome and take about an hour, dropping you on Via degli Arcioni, from where you have to walk up to the steep town centre. You can see this in no time. There's a much-changed **Duomo** with fragments of a Roman road at the top end of the right aisle and a copy of Michelangelo's *Pietà di Palestrina* – the original, sadly, is now in Florence. And the stepped streets of the place are appealing enough for some casual strolling. But you have to climb to the top of the town for the real attraction – the **Palazzo Colonna-Barberini**, which houses the **Museo Nazionale Archaeologico Prenestino** (Tues–Sun 9am–2pm, closed Mon; L3000). Originally built in the eleventh century and greatly modified by Taddeo Barberini in 1640, this occupies the uppermost level of the Temple of Fortune, now largely modernised inside and containing a slightly faded display of artefacts. Among a number of Roman pieces, there's a torso of a statue of Fortune in slate-grey marble, other bits from the temple and funerary *cistae* much like those displayed at the Villa Giulia in Rome.

At the top, the museum's prize exhibit is the marvellous first-century BC *Mosaic of the Nile*, which depicts the flooding of the river with a number of Egyptian scenes of life along the waterway from the source to the delta. Look closely and you'll notice a wealth of detail: there's a banquet going on under the vines on the left, soldiers and priests are grouped in front of the Serepaeum on the right, while the source of the river among the mountains is pictured at the top of the mosaic, where hunters and wild animals, labelled with Greek lettering, congregate. Outside the museum, your ticket admits you to the top **terrace** of the temple, the ruins of which command fine views over the surrounding countryside.

Subiaco

Around 15km northeast of Palestrina, **SUBIACO** (accessible by bus from Tivoli or direct from Rome's Viale Castro Pretorio in about two hours), is beautifully set, pyramided around a hill topped by the Rocca Abbazia castle, close to Mount Liviato – Lazio's premier ski resort. It grew up originally as a purpose-built settlement to accommodate workmen building Nero's grand villa nearby (very thin traces of which survive), and later, during the fifth century, became the chosen contemplative base of Saint Benedict, who lived a life of seclusion and prayer in a cave on the slopes of a nearby mountain. Saint Benedict left after three years to found the monastery at Montecassino (see below), but his legacy lives on in the town, in the shape of two monastic complexes just outside.

The **Convento di Santa Scolastica** (9am–12.30pm & 4–7pm) is the closer (and larger) of the two, about 25 minutes' walk out of town following the Ienne road from the main bus stop and following the signs off to the left before the bridge. Dedicated to Benedict's sister, it's been heavily restored over the years: the facade, with the Benedictine motto *Ora et Labore* over the entrance, isn't original and the only features of any real age in the church inside are two cipolino marble pillars from Nero's villa. The two cloisters, though, are delightful, the first one of the oldest Gothic works in Italy, lushly planted and fragrant, the second a Cosmati work with lovely arcades of pillars.

Continuing up the same road, the landscape grows more dramatic, after about fifteen minutes reaching the **Convento di San Benedetto** (daily 9am–12.30pm & 3–6pm) – a complex of two churches, chapels and other buildings clasping the rocky hillside on the precise site of Saint Benedict's cave. This is much the more interesting of the two monasteries: its church divides into several levels, the upper part decorated with fourteenth-century frescoes of the Schools of Siena and Perugino, the lower leading into the *Sacro Speco* – the actual cave where Saint Benedict lived, now left in its natural condition but for a serene statue by Raggi, a disciple of Bernini. From here a spiral staircase leads up to the chapel of San Gregorio – often closed, but containing a thirteenth-century picture of Saint Francis that's reckoned to be one of the oldest ever portraits. In the other direction, stairs lead down to another chapel, from which Benedict would preach to shepherds, and a terrace which looks out on to the so-called "Holy Rose Tree" – actually a three-aisled bush that's said to have been created by Saint Francis from a bramble.

Practicalities

You can comfortably see Subiaco and its monasteries on a **day-trip** from Rome: the bus journey takes around two hours and you can arrive in the town by lunchtime, eat, visit the monasteries in the afternoon and take an evening bus back to Rome (the last one leaves at 7.30pm).

The town's location may, however, make you want to linger: there's a reasonable **hotel** in the centre of town, the *Aniene* (doubles around L25,000; ☎85.565), which also has an adequate **restaurant**. And if you're **heading south** there's an early bus out to FROSINONE – from where you can get train or bus connections on to other points in Lazio and Campania. The **AAST** office at Via Cadorna 57 (Mon 8am–2pm, Tues–Sat 8am–2pm & 3.30–7.30pm, Sun 9am–noon) has full details.

The Ciociaria

From Subiaco the road heads south into a region known as the **Ciociaria**, a relatively remote corner of Lazio that takes its name from the sandals – *ciocie* – worn here in days gone by. It's hilly country, and historic too, settled several centuries before the Romans by the Hernici tribe who built inaccessible and heavily fortified towns, the remains of which – due to the shrewd Hernici policy of allying themselves with Rome – can still be seen today in the form of extraordinary "cyclopean" walls of their citadels, that are quite unlike anything else in Italy.

The first town you come to, **FIUGGI**, is a spa resort whose bottled mineral water you will probably have already noticed in supermarkets, and which attracts health-conscious Italian tourists throughout the summer. For all that it's not an especially appealing place, its spa facilities, gardens and sports halls chic and pricey places that are either overflowing with crowds or (in winter) entirely dead.

From Fiuggi there's a choice of two routes, either west to **ANAGNI** or south to ALATRI. Anagni, a former Hernici stronghold, is a well-preserved old place that produced a number of medieval popes from its powerful local Segni family, including Boniface VIII, whose **palace** here was invaded in 1303 by representatives of Philip IV of France when he attempted to assert the absolute authority of the papacy. There's not much left of the palace, which is now mostly modern, but a statue of Boniface stands on the outside of Anagni's **Duomo**, an imposing Romanesque basilica dating from the eleventh century. Inside there's a fine Cosmatesque pavement, a thirteenth-century baldachino, some thirteenth-century frescos in the crypt and a treasury containing some of the pontifical effects of Pope Boniface.

In the opposite direction, **ALATRI** – the Hernici *Aletrium* – preserves its "cyclopean" walls from the sixth century BC, massive fortifications, still very much intact, and built long before the more sophisticated stone-cutting techniques of the Romans. The town's streets wind around the citadel at the top, cut by two square gateways (the arch hadn't yet been invented when this was built), inside of which the cathedral and Episcopal Palace stand on the site of the Hernici's ancient temples, since lost. The views, incidentally, are terrific.

FERENTINO, 10km west, also sports a good set of walls, though a hybrid one, modified by the Romans. You can get up to the old citadel here too, though it's some way from the modern town's station, and the Roman temples and cathedral there are seldom open. **FROSINONE**, 10km or so further south is the main town of the Ciociaria, but is of little interest, a bland sprawling place with no obvious centre and barely any remains of the Hernici settlement. But it's a good place to pick up bus and train connections on to other points in Lazio and Campania: buses run west to Priverno from here, near to which you can pick up trains south or north and see Fossanova Abbey; and trains connect Frosinone's *FS* station (way out of town but connected by bus), with Naples, Cassino and Caserta.

Buses reach **PRIVERNO** in about fifty minutes, another hilltop town with a pretty main square flanked by a Gothic town hall and a duomo from 1283 which apparently holds the relics of Saint Thomas Aquinas. About 5km outside the town, an hour or so's walk or reachable by regular bus from Piazza XX Settembre, the **Abbey of Fossanova** (summer daily 8am–noon & 4–7.30pm, winter daily 3.30–5.30pm) was where Aquinas died in 1274, en route between Naples and Lyon – a monastery of the Cistercian order that may tempt you off the road if you're waiting for a train at the nearby Priverno-Fossanova railway station, 2km beyond. It's a fairly tame complex on the whole, much restored, but its thirteenth-century Burgundian Gothic church is a refreshingly plain affair after the gaudiness of most Italian churches. A door leads from here out to a plain Romanesque cloister, with a garden in the centre and a chapter house off to one side, with wide windows through which lay brothers could watch the services (the corridor on the far side of the cloisters was for their use). A door to the left leads through a small separate courtyard to the guest wing where, at the northern end, Saint Thomas is supposed to have breathed his last.

Further south: Cassino and the Abbey of Montecassino

The town of **CASSINO**, fifty minutes down the railway line from Frosinone, is the site of another important monastery, the **Abbey of Montecassino** (daily 8am–noon & 3.30–6pm; free), founded in 529 by Saint Benedict after he left Subiaco (see above), on a spot to which he was guided by three ravens. This was for many years one of the most important and influential monastic complexes in the Christian world, its monks spreading the word as far away as Britain and Scandinavia and developing the tradition of culture and learning that was at the core of the Benedictine order. Over the years it has been repeatedly destroyed: its strategically vital position perched high on a mountaintop between Rome and Naples has been fought over by a succession of invaders, culminating in 1944 when Allied troops clashed with German forces in a battle that lasted nearly six months. The abbey was the key to the German presence in this part of Italy, and the Allies eventually bombed it to ruins in May 1944, losing over 1000 Polish lives in the process. It was rebuilt soon after, and the austere medieval style of its buildings has been followed faithfully, but it's really more impressive for its siting than for itself: much of the complex is not open to the public, and its sterile white central courtyard is engaging only for the views it gives over the surrounding hills and the Polish war cemetery below. The church, off here, in a hideously ornate Baroque style, has a small museum containing incunabula, old manuscripts and suchlike. But otherwise you really feel that Montecassino's glory days firmly ended with the war.

The **town** below was fairly comprehensively destroyed too, and has very little appeal. There's an **AAST** on Via Condotti (Mon–Sat 9am–2pm), on the opposite side of the centre to the train and bus station, and buses scale the mountain to the abbey at 9.45am and 3.45pm each day – though if you miss one it's fairly easy to hitch. If you need to stay, hotels are at least cheap – pick up a list from the AAST.

The Southern Lazio Coast

The Lazio **coast** to the south of Rome is a much more attractive proposition than that to the north. Its towns are more attractive, the water is less polluted, and in the further reaches, beyond the dreary flats of the Pontine Marshes and Monte Circeo, the shoreline begins to pucker into cliffs and coves that hint gently at the glories that await in Campania further south. All good either for day-trips and overnight outings from the city, or for a pleasant wayward route to Naples.

Anzio and Nettuno

About 40km south of Rome, and easily seen on a day-trip, **ANZIO** is the first town of any note, centre of a lengthy spread of settlement that focuses on a lively central square and a busy fishing industry. Much of the town was damaged during a difficult Allied landing here on January 22, 1944, to which two military cemeteries (one British, one, at nearby Nettuno, American), bear testimony. But despite a pretty thorough rebuilding it's a likeable resort, still depending as much on fish as tourists for its liveliehood. The town's seafood **restaurants** are reason enough to come, crowding together along the harbour and not unreasonably priced, and the **beaches**, which edge the coast on either side, don't get unbearably stuffed outside of August. Anzio is also a possible route on to the islands of Ponza or Ischia, or Naples, for which **hydrofoils** leave daily in summer – ask for timings at the tourist office in the harbour (daily 9am–12.30pm & 5–8pm).

NETTUNO, a couple of kilometres down the coast (and walkable by the coast road), is more of the same, but with slightly less beach space and water that's not so clear and calm. Again it's a mostly modern town, but there's a well-preserved old quarter, still walled, with a couple of trattorias on the main square – information from the office on the right as you walk down to the seafront from the station.

The Pontine Marshes, Monte Circeo and San Felice

Beyond Anzio and Nettuno lie the **Pontine Marshes**, until sixty years ago a boggy plain prone to malaria that was populated by few except water buffalo. Julius Caesar had planned to drain the area but was assassinated before he could carry out his plan, and it was left to Mussolini to reclaim the region in 1928 – in a scheme that built a series of spanking new towns and provided acres of fertile, fresh farmland.

LATINA lies at the centre of the development, the provincial capital, founded in 1932, and centre of the thriving local agricultural economy, though of little interest now save for its transport connections. If you do end up here, it's instructive to at least have a brief walk around the town centre, which is something of a monument to fascism, large open squares and sturdy-looking buildings interrupting broad avenues radiating out with classical uniformity from the central Piazza del Popolo.

The area around **SABAUDIA**, another new town 20km away on the coast, gives some impression of what the marshes were like before they were drained, poised between two lagoons that make up the coastal Lago di Sabaudia. A large area to the north of the town, the Salve del Circeo, four coastal lakes, the huge bulk of Monte Circeo to the south and the offshore island of Zannone together form the **Parco Nazional del Circeo**, set up in 1934 to preserve something of the marshes' wildlife and almost sinister natural beauty. It's a fine spot for birds: all kinds of water species can be seen here – herons, buzzards, storks, fish hawks, and rare species like the peregrine falcon and Cavaliere d'Italia; and the flora includes eucalyptus groves, oaks, elms, ash and wild flowers in spring.

Monte Circeo itself lies to the south of Sabaudia across several kilometres of gleaming water, the sandy beach coming to an end at the sixteenth-century **Torre Paola**, set at the entrance of a canal linking Lago di Sabaudia to the sea. There's a little pier usually manned by a group of fishermen, from where the road turns inland and skirts the northern slopes of the mountain, passing through splendid woods. After about 4km a road branches off to the right and rounds the mountain to emerge at **SAN FELICE CIRCEO**, a picturesque village of pretty stone houses bleached yellow by the sun, that can be a fairly trendy spot in summer, its marina choc-a-bloc with fancy motor launches and yachts and its sandy beaches crowded with glistening oiled bodies. The small **Piazza Municipio** has a tourist office and a local museum, open in July and August, from behind which a road winds its way up to the summit of the **mountain** and the site of an ancient **temple**. Not surprisingly, the views are marvellous. There's a large carpark at the top, with a bar open in summer, near to which is the entrance to the sparse relics of a Roman town – *Circeii* – and its rather better preserved cyclopean walls, not unlike the constructions in the Ciociaria (see above).

Back in the village you can rest up on the beaches or hire a boat out to the famous **Grotta della Magna Circe** – though this is only possible in season. For quieter swimming-spots, take the road towards the lighthouse, the "Faro di Torre Cervia", which after a couple of kilometres reaches a secluded rocky spot – great for snorkelling. It's handy, too, for the *Il Faro* hotel a little further on, which has a **restaurant** serving good seafood on its sea-facing terrace.

Terracina

A further 15km down the coast from San Felice (buses half-hourly) or, if you're coming from Rome, a short train ride on the local line from Priverno – **TERRACINA** is an immediately likeable little town, divided between a tumble-down old quarter high on the hill above and a lively newer area by the sea. During classical times it was an important staging-post on the Appian Way, which reaches the sea here; nowadays it's primarily a seaside resort, and one of the nicest along this stretch of coast, with good, ample beaches, and frequent connections on to the other points of interest around.

Practical details: accommodation, food, beaches

If you're staying, there are a number of reasonably-priced **hotels**, among them the *Astoria*, Via Roma 38 (☎0773/727.157), centrally-placed with doubles for L24,000, and *For You*, right next to the beach at Viale Circe 116 (☎0773/730.914), doubles L25,000, and *Vittoria*, Piazza Mazzini 1 (☎0773/727.603) – doubles around L30,000. The nearest **campsite** is the *Costazzurra*, a fifteen-minute walk south along the coast road – though at L17,000 for two with tent it's not a great saving on a hotel bed.

The **AAST**, just off Piazza Mazzini (July–Aug 9am–noon & 5–6pm; rest of the year 9am–noon), has more information, hotel lists and a map of the town. **Bikes** are for hire at *Caccia e Pesca*, Via Roma 9, for around L8000 a day. For **eating** you could do worse than stop in at *Pizzeria Marino* on Piazza Repubbicca, whose low-priced pizzas are very popular locally; if you don't fancy pizza, the *Miramare*, Viale Circe 32, at the end of Viale Vittoria, is also cheap and has a convivial terrace. As for the **beaches**, apart from a scrubby oval of beach in the centre of town, they stretch north pretty much indefinitely from beyond the main town harbour, and are large enough not to get overcrowded.

The Town

Terracina splits into two distinct parts, the old town on the hill and the new town below, whose main street, Via Roma, is a continuation of Via Appia, cutting through the town to the sea. Centre of the old quarter is **Piazza Municipio**, which occupies the site of the old Roman forum and now focuses on the colonnade of the town's **Duomo**, with its elegant mossy campanile. It's an endearing little church with a fine mosaic floor and a beautiful mosaic-studded pulpit, built over the remains of a Roman temple, some of which are visible inside. Also on the square, there's a small **Museo Archaeologico** (May–Sept Tues–Sat 9am–1pm & 5–7pm, Sun 9am–1pm; rest of the year Mon–Sat 8am–2pm; free), which has Greek and Roman finds from the locality, including a well-preserved statue of Zeus after a Hellenistic model.

Terracina's main attraction, and rightly so, is the **Temple of Jupiter Anxurus**, which crowns the hill above the town. Take the steps up from Piazza Municipio onto Via Anxur and follow this for 200m, from where you can either follow the winding road to the top (forty minutes) or, 100m after the sign to the temple, turn off right and climb up by way of a rocky path – which takes half as long. There's a bar at the top with erratic opening times but you should really bring supplies of your own. The temple is believed to date back to the first century BC and was connected to Terracina by some lengthy walls, though all that's now visible is the base of the structure, in the form of an arched terrace from which the views are stupendous – Terracina boxed neatly below and the bay curving round on either side.

The coast to Campania: Sperlonga, Gaeta, Formia, Minturno

The coast south of Terracina is probably Lazio's prettiest stretch, the cliff punctured by tiny beaches signposted enticingly from the road. **SPERLONGA**, built high on a rocky promontory, is a fashionable spot locally, its whitewashed houses and narrow streets more Greek than Italian in feel, and sadly given over entirely to tourists during summer (though cars are not allowed into the centre). There are some excellent restaurants specialising in seafood, and a few pricey *pensioni*, but these are often full and you might find it easier to hole up in Terracina and come to Sperlonga for the day (half-hourly buses). The beach, certainly, is worth stopping for, a lengthy stretch of sand to the south with the town as backdrop and abundant space.

Between Sperlonga and Gaeta the coast steepens markedly, with yet more appealing beaches, and, if you're camping, any number of handy campsites. A couple of kilometres from Sperlonga, there's a small museum and the remains of the **Villa of Tiberius** (open year-round; sunrise–sunset) – worth a stop if you're independently mobile. The house was built around a large ornamental pool which extends into a large grotto in the cliff face. The museum holds finds from the villa, centrepiece of which is a large complex group of statues in the style of the Vatican's *Laocoon* (see "Rome"), possibly by the same sculptors.

Some 10km further on, **GAETA** signals the beginning of its broad bay from its high castle-topped headland, an appealing place at first sight (especially from the southern side), piled up untidily onto the head of its defensive rock. The fortress here was impregnable: it resisted Gothic and Saracen invaders and the town flourished under the Normans, some of its architecture dating back to that time – and earlier. The tiny church of **San Giovanni al Mare**, by the water, hails from the tenth century; and on the summit of Monte Orlando, now a park, there's the classical tomb of one **Munatius Plancus**, the founder of Lyons, decorated with a frieze showing scenes of battle. Close by, a **terrace** gives fine views over the Serapo bay below, next to which the small church of **Santuario del Crocifisso** is built on a boulder breaching the chasm of Montagna Spaccata, literally suspended a few hundred feet above the sea.

But for all this, it's Gaeta's modern-day role as a naval port that colours the place most significantly. Much of the old town is closed off to the public (parts of the port and the castle itself) and the quayside bars advertise "burgers and chips" to visiting American servicemen off the warships often docked in the harbour. The main square, **Piazza del Municipio**, flanks the portside, and is a lively enough spot, with a small market; and there's an **AAST** office (for maps) on Piazza XIX Maggio. But you'd do best to visit Gaeta for the **beaches** north of the headland – though be warned that these, especially the closest *Spiaggia di Serapo*, can get quite packed and have been bought up almost exclusively by restaurants.

Around the bay, hard under the glowering backdrop of the Monti Aurunci, **FORMIA** is not much better, a largely modern town that was an important resort during Roman times. Cicero had a villa here, at which he was murdered by Mark Antony's soldiers in AD 44 after opposing the triumvirate that had succeeded Caesar. There are **beaches** to the north of the town centre, and an **AAST** office just behind the central Piazza Mattei (Mon–Fri 8am–1.30pm, Sat 9am–noon). But otherwise Formia is more a stopover than a stop in itself, with plentiful connections on to Naples, Rome and inland to CASSINO, and regular ferries and hydofoils to PONZA. If you're taking an early boat, the *Hotel Ariston* is the most convenient **hotel** to the harbour, but it costs L50,000 a night; the *Marino* on the corner of the central Piazza Vittoria is cheaper, with rooms for about L30,000. For **food**, try *Muro di Nerva* a little way north of the Ariston hotel on the right of the main Viale dell'Unità d'Italia – friendly and with excellent food.

A few kilometres south of Formia – and the next stop on the train – **MINTURNO** is the last town before the Campania border, a maze of tiny lanes and vaulted streets oddly reminiscent of an Arab *medina*. Its massive crumbling **castle**, on the main square, was owned until the middle of this century by the Carraciolo-Carafa dynasty; a plaque on the west wall recalls a visit by Saint Thomas Aquinas in 1272. Behind, the town's **Duomo** is a Norman structure not unlike that of nearby Sessa Arunca or Ravello, with a similar colourfully mosaiced pulpit. About 4km south of town are the ruins of the ancient Roman port of **Minturnae** (daily 9am–6pm; L2500), a once flourishing town that became depopulated as this low-lying area grew more malarial. Most striking among the rubble are the remains of a large amphitheatre, below which there's a small antiquarium containing finds from around the site and a broken-down aqueduct that runs for 2km southwest. A worthy stop if you're travelling south by car; otherwise stay on the train for Naples.

The Pontine Islands

Scattered across the sea between Rome and Naples, the **Pontine Islands** are one of Italy's least well-known island groupings, relatively unvisited by all except Italians. Volcanic in origin, only two are inhabited, **Ponza** and **Ventotene**, of which only Ponza supports any kind of tourist industry. Visit in July and especially August and you'll find this fairly well-developed, many people coming here as an alternative to crowded Capri; at any other time the island is yours for the asking.

Ponza

Even **PONZA**, the main island of the Pontine group, is manageably small, a sharp, rocky hunk of land just five miles end to end and at its widest point a mile across. Ferries sail to **PONZA TOWN**, one of the most beautiful small towns along this coast, which is heaped around its bay in a series of neat pastel-coloured pyramids, its flat-roofed houses focusing on the pink semi-circle that curls around the fishing harbour. It's a marvellous place to rest up for a while: designer boutiques and souvenir shops are still thin on the ground, and although there's not a lot specifically to see on the island, the town is a fun place to wander through, particularly at *passeggiata* time, when the crowds turn out to parade along the yellow-painted **Municipio** arcade of shops and cafés. To laze and swim, there's a small **beach** in the town, which is clean, and it's a ten-minute walk to the other side of the island to the **Chiaia di Luna** beach: a sheer sickle of cliff lined by a slender rim of sand – though be warned that the waves here are much choppier than those on the mainland-facing side of the island.

The only other real settlement on the island is **LA FORNA**, a wide green bay dotted with huddles of houses. There's a beach here, but a small dirty one, and you'd be better off following the path down from the road around the bay to the rocks and swimming from there: the water is lovely and clear, and, with the so-called **Piscina Naturale**, perfect for sheltered swimming when the fishing boats have finished for the day. For really secluded swimming, you can also take a boat from here (L7000 per person return) around the headland to **Spiaggia Santa Lucia**, where you're likely to have the beach to yourself.

Settlement straggles on from La Forna towards the sharp northern end of the island, where the road ends abruptly and a steep stony path (to the right) leads down to more rocks from which you can swim.

PRACTICAL DETAILS

The **Pro Loco** in Ponza Town (daily 9am–1pm & 4–8pm), up the hill from the Banco di Napoli on the right side of the harbour, has maps and accommodation lists. You may well be accosted with offers of **rooms** as you get off the ferry: if so, L25,000 a double is a fair price; if not, the woman at Via Chiaia di Luna 8 (☎0771/80.043) takes in visitors for a negotiable fee. Of the island's **hotels**, cheapest in Ponza Town is the *Luisa*, on Via Chiaia di Luna (☎0771/80.075), with rooms for a little under L30,000; *Gennarino al Mare*, next to the town beach (☎0771/80.071), is more expensive at around L50,000 a double but worth the splurge. In La Forna, the *Ortensia* charges around L30,000. **Getting around**, there's an island bus service connecting Ponza Town with other points on the island, including La Forna, roughly hourly. Or you can hire scooters from *Ciccio Nero*, left of the main harbour, for L60,000 a day (L10,000 per hour). Motorboats, too, are a good (sometimes the only) way of seeing the most dramatic parts of the island: L50,000 a day from a number of outlets around the harbour.

For **food** you're spoilt for choice: there are plenty of restaurants in Ponza Town and most are good, albeit expensive. Try *Al Delfino Blu* in the harbour, which serves the local speciality of *zuppa di lenticchie* (lentil soup); the *Ippocampo*, in the Municipio above, does good pasta and fish; or the *Gennarino al Mare* hotel has an excellent restaurant.

Ventotene

The only other inhabited Pontine island, **VENTOTENE** is quite separate from Ponza, situated a fair way south, flatter and much less lush and green. It's much smaller, too, and although it makes a nice stop on a leisurely route to Naples, it's unlikely to detain you for long – though if you do want to stay, there are a couple of hotels. The single town – village really – has a population of around 500, its dusty piazza home to a museum displaying finds from an imperial era villa, remains of which you can see spread over the headland to the left of the village. On the other side, there's a small beach of grey volcanic sand.

travel details

Trains

From Rome (Termini) to Cerveteri (11 daily; 45min); Civitavecchia (8 daily; 45min); Tarquinia (5 daily; 3hr 30min); Anzio/Nettuno (hourly; 1hr); Latina (hourly; 35min); Priverno-Fossanova (hourly; 1hr); Formia (hourly; 1hr 25min); Naples (hourly; 2hr 30min); Florence (hourly; 2–3hr 30min); Bologna (12 daily; 3hr 20min); Milan (12 daily; 3hr–5hr 40min); Ancona (8 daily; 3hr 15min–6hr); Pescara (4 daily; 3hr 40min); L'Aquila (5 daily, change at Terni; 4hr 40min).

From Rome (Laziale) to Palestrina (5 daily; 35min); Anagni (14 daily; 55min).

From Rome (Ostiense) to Ostia Lido (every 20min; 30min).

From Rome (San Pietro) to Bracciano (8 daily; 40min); Viterbo (6 daily; 1hr 45min).

From Priverno-Fossanova to Terracina (10 daily; 40min).

From Frosinone to Cassino (12 daily; 1hr 10min); Caserta (8 daily; 1hr 10min); Naples (6 daily; 1hr 55min).

Buses

From Rome (Viale Castro Pretorio) to Subiaco (hourly; 2hr).

From Rome (Via Gaeta) to Tivoli (every half-hour; 45min).

From Rome (Piazza dei Cinquecento) to Palestrina (every 30–45min; 1hr).

From Rome (Via Lepanto) to Cerveteri (8 daily; 1hr); Civitavecchia (8 daily; 1hr 30min); Tarquinia (8 daily; 2hr).

From Terracina to Cassino (1 daily; 2hr 30min); Sperlonga (every half-hour; 30min); Formia (every half-hour; 1hr); Sabaudia (hourly; 1hr); San Felice Circeo (every half-hour; 30min).

From Viterbo to Bagnaia (hourly; 20min); Bomarzo (4 daily; 40min).

From Subiaco to Frosinone (3 daily; 2hr).

From Frosinone to Priverno (hourly; 50min).

Ferries

From Formia to Ponza (1 daily; 2hr 30min); Ventotene (1 daily; 2hr 10min).

From Terracina to Ponza (1–2 daily; 1hr).

From Civitavecchia to Golfoaranci (2 daily; 9hr); Olbia (1 daily; 7hr); Calgliari (1 daily; 13hr).

Hydrofoils

From Formia to Ponza (1 daily; 1hr 15min).

From Anzio to Ponza (3 daily; 1hr 10min); Ischia (1 daily; 3hr); Naples (1 daily; 4hr).

From Formia to Ventotene (1 daily; 1hr 15min).

From Pomza to Ventotene (Mon–Sat 1 daily; 30min).

CHAPTER TWELVE

ABRUZZO AND MOLISE

O ne region until 1963, **Abruzzo** and **Molise** – previously just plain Abruzzi – together make Italy's transition from North to South. Both are sparsely populated mountainous regions prone to earthquakes, and both have always been outside the mainstream of Italian affairs. You could spend a whole, and very varied holiday in Abruzzo. Bordered by the Appenines, it holds some of Italy's wildest terrain: silent valleys, vast untamed mountain plains and abandoned hill villages, as well as some great historic towns, many of them rarely visited by outsiders. But this is only half the story: the Abruzzese have done much to pull their region out of the poverty trap, developing resorts on the long, sandy Adriatic coastline, and exploiting the tourist potential of the large, mountainous National Park. Actions you may baulk at, until you see the poverty and neglect of Molise.

Molise is still manifestly a part of the south, its countryside is gentler than Abruzzo, its mountains less forbidding, and its villages and towns less appealing – either modern and functional to withstand the shock of earthquakes, or rotting into quiet ruin due to lack of funds and organisation. The lasting impression is one of despair, and of a people unused to outsiders, let alone foreigners. You may, however, pass through on your way south to Puglia, and it's feasible to stop off for a few days in the seaside town of Térmoli, visit one of Italy's least-visited Roman sites, Saepinum, or go hiking in the Matese mountains on the border with Campania. Don't expect to rush through, though – getting around in both regions on public transport demands patience, and the careful studying of bus and train timetables.

ABRUZZO

Abruzzo, over the last century or so, has become better known for its emigrants than for itself. These number Dante Gabriele Rossetti, film star Alan Ladd, and, most recently Madonna, whose ancestors left Abruzzo to seek their fortunes in Britain and America. They left behind them hilltop villages and medieval towns overlooked by mountain ranges in which wolves, bears and chamois roamed, and legends of witches and werewolves persisted.

Abruzzo has now entered the twentieth century, but although its coast is lined by a string of lucrative resorts, and its wolves, rounded up, enclosed and demystified, have become a major tourist attraction in its **National Park**, there are still vast tracts of unspoilt countryside, and villages (like Pacentro, which Madonna's grandparents left) where life is hard and strangers a novelty. There's a strong, unshakeable sense of the provincial here, and although the region's costumes, crafts and festivals are now popular tourist attractions, there is little hype, and you could almost believe that the traditions are perpetuated as much for the locals as for their power to attract revenue.

L'Aquila, at the foot of Gran Sasso, and **Sulmona** just to its south, are the most visited of Abruzzo's historic towns. Both are good bases: Sulmona is convenient if you're coming by train from Rome, L'Aquila if you're approaching from Umbria. The hill villages around L'Aquila are worth visiting if you're based here for any length of time: those below the **Gran Sasso**, the Appenines' highest peak, are deeply rural places, where time can seem to have stopped in the fifteenth century; **Bominaco**, to the east, has two impressive churches, one a perfect and pristine example of the Romanesque, the other covered with Byzantine-style frescoes. The rail route from the Marche runs down the coast, through Abruzzo's numerous grid-plan resorts – none of them anything special, but adequate sun-and-sand stopovers. A good first stop on the coast is **Pineto**, with a pine-fringed beach and bus connections inland to the sleepy old town of **Atri**, whose cathedral holds a stunning cycle of frescoes.

South of Sulmona, Abruzzo is more traditional. In **Scanno** the women wear costumes that – like the Scannese – originated in Asia Minor, and make intricate lace on cylindrical cushions known as *tómbole*. Just down the road, **Cocullo** is a scruffy hill village that on the first Thursday in May hosts one of Europe's most bizarre religious festivals – draping a statue of the local saint with live snakes, and parading it through the streets.

L'Aquila

At first sight **L'AQUILA** seems a severe city. Overlooked by the bulk of the Gran Sasso, which cuts it off from the coastal province of Téramo, its sombre grey stone resists even the strongest of sunlight, creating an atmosphere of almost Teutonic austerity. Founded by a German emperor, its brooding northern air is apt, while the story of its foundation is worthy of a Grimm fairy tale. In 1242 Frederick II drew together the populations from 99 Abruzzo villages to form a new city. Each village built its own church, piazza and quarter: there's a medieval fountain with 99 spouts; and the town hall clock still chimes 99 times every night.

L'Aquila may no longer be the city of 99 churches, most of them having been destroyed in earthquakes, but two magnificent ones remain. And the city itself is a brighter place than you might expect – an appealing blend of ancient and modern, with smart shops, bustling streets and a daily market where you can buy anything from black-market cassettes to traditional Abruzzese craftwork.

Arrival, information and accommodation

L'Aquila's **train station** is some way out of the centre, connected with the main part of town by regular buses. Long-distance **buses** stop on Piazza Battaglione Alpini, at the beginning of the main street, Corso Vittorio Emanuele. The **information booth** there has bus timetables covering L'Aquila province. There are two **tourist offices**, the AAST at Via XX Settembre 8, and the EPT, more conveniently placed on Piazza Santa Maria Paganica (daily 8.30am–1.30pm & 4–6pm).

There are a handful of cheap **hotels** scattered around the centre. The *Italia*, Corso Vittorio Emanuele 79, (☎0862/20.566) has doubles at L26,000, and, housed in a rambling and decaying palazzo, has the most character. The *Centrale*, on Via Simonetto (☎0862/64.211) and *Aurora*, Via Cimino 21 (☎0862/22.053) both off the main Corso, are cheaper and seedier, with doubles from around L21,000, while the cheapest, *Orazi*, Via Roma 175 (☎0862/69.545), with doubles for L19,500, is further out – a longish walk from Piazza Annunziata.

The City

L'Aquila's **centre** is relatively compact, and best seen on foot. Of its sights, only two are outside the central core – the 99-spouted fountain, a short walk from the railway station, and the church of Santa Maria di Collemaggio, which is a stroll away from the Porta Bazzano below the main piazza.

Marking the northeastern entrance to the city centre is **Piazza Battaglione Alpini**, overlooked by a formidable castle built by the Spanish in the sixteenth century to keep the citizens of L'Aquila in order after an uprising. The Spanish forced the L'Aquilans to pay for the castle by imposing an annual tax and heavy fines. In the Fascist period the castle's surroundings were landscaped as a park, and, following the devastation wreaked by the Nazis in 1943, the building was renovated and the museum established. Today the armament and gunpowder stores are used for temporary art and photography exhibitions, and the barracks house the **Museo Nazionale d'Abruzzo** (Tues–Sun 9am–2pm; L3000). The most popular exhibit here is the skeleton of a mammoth, found about 14km from L'Aquila in the 1950s, but the collection of works of art rescued from abandoned and earthquake-ravaged churches is also worth a brief visit. Among the clumsily-painted wooden Madonnas, those by Silvestro d'Aquila stand out, spare, ascetic and nerved with inner strength, while the best of the paintings are the dreamy and mystical works attributed to Andrea Delitio, a fifteenth-century Abruzzo artist responsible for the region's best fresco cycle – in the cathedral at Atri (p.689). The exhibit with the most sensational history is an elaborate silver crucifix by Nicola da Guardiagrele: after being stolen from L'Aquila's duomo and auctioned at Sotheby's, it's now kept for safety in the museum.

From Piazza Battaglione Alpini, arcaded **Corso Vittorio Emanuele** is L'Aquila's main street, lined with upmarket clothes shops, jewellers and cafés and liveliest in the evenings when L'Aquila's youth turn out for the *passegiata*. To the left down Via San Bernadino, the church of **San Bernadino** has a sumptuous facade: three magnificent white tiers bedecked with classical columns, pediments, friezes and inscriptions. Inside, its ceiling is luxuriously gilded and skilfully carved – in some places bold and chunky, in others as complex and sinuous as oriental embroidery. The glazed blue and white terracotta altarpiece by Andrea della Robbia is very fine, as is San Bernadino's mausoleum, sculpted by Silvestro d'Aquila, known as the Michelangelo of Abruzzo – to see why, look at the mausoleum's lively high-relief figures. As for San Bernadino, he was originally from Siena but died in L'Aquila, where his relics remain – ritually visited every year on his feast day by Sienese bearing gifts of Tuscan oil.

Corso Vittorio Emanuele leads on to the central **Piazza del Duomo**, more remarkable for its daily **market** than for its architecture. The duomo, having been destroyed on several occasions by earthquakes, now boasts a tedious Neoclassical front. More striking is the facade of the eighteenth-century **Sanctuario del Suffragio**, a voluptuous combination of curves, topped by a flamboyant honeycombed alcove.

Tumbling down the hill below the piazza, steep stepped streets of ancient houses lead down to **Porta Bazzano**, one of the old city gates. Rather than heading straight there, take time to wander the abutting streets, lined with Renaissance and Baroque palaces. Some of these are still opulent, others decaying, providing an evocative backdrop for the church of **Santa Giusta**, whose rose-window is decorated with twelve figures representing the various craftsmen and women who contributed to the building.

From Porta Bazzano, Via Porta Bazzano leads up to the church of **Santa Maria di Collemaggio**. One of Abruzzo's most distinctive churches, its massive rectangular bulk is faced with a geometric jigsaw of pink and white stone, more redolent of a mosque than a church, pierced by delicate lacy rose-windows and entered through a fancy Romanesque arch. It was founded in the thirteenth century by Peter of Morrone, a hermit unwillingly dragged from his mountain retreat to be made Pope by power-hungry cardinals who reckoned he would be easy to manipulate. When he turned out to be too naive even for the uses of the cardinals he was forced to resign, and posthumously compensated for the ordeal by being canonised. Thieves stole his relics in April 1988, intending to hold them to ransom, but they were soon safely retrieved, and returned to their grandiose Palladian-style sarcophagus. One of the few things Peter managed to do during his short reign was to install a Holy Door in the church – opened every year on August 28, when sinners pass through it to procure absolution.

Finally there's L'Aquila's best-known sight, the unique 99-spouted fountain, **Fontana delle 99 Cannelle**, outside the town centre close to the railway station, tucked behind the medieval Porta Riviera. Set around three sides of a sunken piazza, overlooked by abandoned houses and the tiny church of San Vito, the water pours from an unknown source through 93 toby-jug gargoyles (six are undecorated), each a symbol for one of the villages that formed the city. This constant supply of fresh water sustained the L'Aquilans through the plagues, earthquakes and sieges to which the city was subjected, and was used for washing clothes until after the war. The fountain is now frequented mostly on summer evenings, when it serves as the backdrop for a series of classical concerts (details from the tourist office).

Eating and drinking . . . and local crafts

L'Aquila's **restaurants** and **trattorias** are reasonably-priced and numerous, with good hearty traditional Abruzzese fare on offer at *Trattoria del Giaguaro*, Piazza Santa Maria Paganica, and *Alpina* on Via Crispomonti, off the main Corso (where there's also a *spaghetteria*). For more exotic – and expensive – dishes, flavoured with local saffron and black truffles, there's *La Mimosa* on Via Navelli. If your budget is really tight, you can rough it at the formica-topped tables of the *Il Gatto* pizzeria on Via Gatto, or get **takeaway** pizza and hot stuffed vegetables from the outlet at the beginning of Corso Vittorio Emanuele.

L'Aquila is full of **craft shops**, some with workshops where you can watch the craftsmen and women at work. The best ceramics workshop is housed in the ex-convent of San Bernadino on Via V. Veneto. For traditional Abruzzese lace formed on a cylindrical cushion, the *tómbola*, head for *Nuvoloni Genoveffa* on Via dei Sali off the Corso, just below the castle; while at *Arduini Doroa* on Corso Federico II, beyond Piazza del Duomo, you'll find copper and wrought-iron work.

The Gran Sasso and Campo Imperatore plain

Whether you approach Abruzzo from the Marche in the north or Rome in the west, your arrival will be signalled by the spectacular bulk of the **Gran Sasso** massif, containing by far the highest of the Appenine peaks. If you come by motorway from the Marche, you'll actually travel underneath, through a recently constructed 10km tunnel, passing the entrance to the area's worst-kept secret – an atomic research laboratory bored into the very heart of the mountain range.

The massif itself consists of two parallel chains, flanking the vast **Campo Imperatore** plain which stretches for 27km at over 2000m above sea-level. It's a bleak but atmospheric place, overlooked by abandoned and semi-abandoned hill villages, its rolling grasslands in places laid bare to reveal rocks, carved into moonscape ripples by the wind.

The itinerary below is an easy day's drive from L'Aquila, but if you're travelling by bus you'll need at least two days to see everything, and will need to study the timetables carefully. Hitching across Campo Imperatore is virtually impossible outside the summer months, and even then it's not easy – if you're without your own transport you may have to content yourself with viewing the plain by *funivia* (cable car), and taking buses up to the hill villages from L'Aquila via the less interesting southern route.

Fonte Cerreto and the Corno Grande

The first leg, however, is easy. Bus #6 from L'Aquila's Corso Vittorio Emanuele runs regularly up to **FONTE CERRETO**, the gateway to Campo Imperatore: basically two hotels, a restaurant and a campsite clustered around a funivia station. Most of these were built in the Thirties as part of Mussolini's scheme to keep Italians fit by encouraging them to take exercise in the mountains. Ironically he was imprisoned here in 1943, first at the *Villetta* inn in Fonte Cerreto, and then at the *Albergo-Rifugio Campo Imperatore*, a grim hotel at the top of the funivia. Apparently it was with some trepidation that Mussolini stepped into the cable car, enquiring whether it was safe and then hastily covering his cowardice by adding, "Not for my sake, you understand, because my life is over. But for those who accompany me." Mussolini's cable car has recently been replaced, but still ends up at the Albergo-Rifugio, where *Il Duce* spent his days on a diet of eggs, rice, boiled onions and grapes, contemplating suicide. Hitler came to his rescue, dispatching an ace-pilot to airlift him out in a tiny aeroplane, which is supposed to have terrified Mussolini almost as much as the cable car.

Mussolini's prison-hotel is now the most popular starting-point for assaults on the Gran Sasso's highest peak, the **Corno Grande** (2912m). A cheaper place to sleep is the *Duca degli Abruzzi Rifugio* (2388m) (☎06/654.3424) a short walk beyond. It's only open from July to mid-September, and outside these months the ascent, which at all times includes some fairly killing scree climbing and alarming descents, should only be attempted by experienced climbers. Perhaps the most challenging route is the tough trek from the *Albergo Campo Imperatore* right across the mountain range, taking in the Corno Grande, sleeping over at the *Rifugio Franchetti* (☎0861/95.642) also open June to mid-September, and then walking across to the Arapietra ridge. From here a ski-lift will take you down to the ugly ski resort of PRATI DI TIVO – which nevertheless offers some of the best views of Gran Sasso – from where you can get a bus to the town of Teramo. If you're going to do any of the Gran Sasso trails, you'll need the CAI Gran Sasso d'Italia map, and should check out weather conditions from the *CAI* office in L'Aquila, via XX Settembre 15 (☎0862/24.342), usually open only 6–7pm.

The Campo Imperatore plain

For non-hikers the road continues from Fonte Cerreto across **Campo Imperatore**, whose weird rock formations have been prime fodder for film-makers over the years, masquerading as everything from the surface of Mars to a remote region of Tibet. Film crews and the occasional hiker apart, the only people you're likely to meet here are nomadic shepherds, who bring their flocks up to the plain for summer grazing after wintering in the south – a practice that has been going on since Roman times. Although the sheep are now transported by lorry rather than on foot, a peep in one of the shepherd's shacks sprinkled across the plain, suggests that their living standards have changed very little.

The plain is fringed with hilltop villages, some with a few hotels and villas, others virtually abandoned. If you want to stay over, the best bet is the **youth hostel** at **CASTEL DEL MONTE** (apply at the Comune on the village square for access), a medieval village, heavily fortified and crowned with a ruined castle and church, that is now a minor tourist attraction. It was the scene of a chilling incident early this century when workmen discovered caves underneath them, filled with clothed skeletons seated on cane chairs. This was the traditional way of burying the village's dead until 1860, when an outbreak of cholera alerted the inhabitants to the health hazard. All the skeletons that could be found were burned; those that weren't were lost forever when the cave was set alight and later filled in. As for the rest of the village, the steep streets and dark tunnels were designed to slow down invaders; windows, strategically placed high up, enabled the inhabitants to chuck hot oil down on the heads of unwelcome visitors. It's still not a particularly welcoming place. Visitors are viewed as a useful source of revenue, but be prepared, especially out of season, to be stared at; and women can expect to feel uncomfortable when they enter the bars.

If you can't cope with suspicious stares, head instead to **ROCCA CALASCIO**, a honey-pale castle crumbling above a completely abandoned village. The bus from L'Aquila passes by, dropping you at the bottom of the hill, and there's no reason why you shouldn't camp out in one of the deserted houses. You can catch a bus in the morning back to L'Aquila, or on to **SAN STEFANO DI SASSANIO** – a Medici stronghold in the fifteenth century, still with Tuscan-style loggias and Medici coats of arms stuck on the dilapidating and semi-abandoned houses.

North of L'Aquila: Amiternum and San Vittorino

The countryside to the north of L'Aquila is undistinguished. **Lago di Campotosto**, encircled by bland hills smeared with small tourist resorts, is one of the town's most popular nearby attractions, but is really just an uninteresting artificial lake, regularly restocked with fish to keep the anglers happy. Closer to L'Aquila, and accessible by bus, are the theatre and amphitheatre surviving from the Sabine, and later Roman, city of **Amiternum**, (Tues–Sun 9am–1pm) now used for concerts and plays in the summer. Above Amiternum, **SAN VITTORINO** is hardly one of Abruzzo's more appealing villages, but it has a series of **catacombs** underneath its church that make for a dank and spooky way to pass an hour, with skulls and bones spilling out of coffin-shelves and the remains of S.Vittorino stuffed underneath an altar. Someone called Buci has the key to these – he lives in a brown house with a glass porch opposite three shacks near the entrance of the village. Get here on the last Sunday in May and you can join in an underground procession through the passages.

South to Sulmona: Bominaco

From L'Aquila, the SS17 follows the ancient route of the local shepherds across the saffron fields south to Sulmona. If you have your own transport, it's worth making a short diversion *en route* to see two of Abruzzo's most beautiful churches at **BOMINACO** (also accessible by bus from L'Aquila). The village itself is an inauspicious knot of grubby houses, but the endearingly skew-whiff and lichen-mottled facade of **San Pellegrino** conceals floor-to-ceiling frescoes in vivid hues reminiscent of a peacock's plume. There's also an intriguing thirteenth-century calendar, with the signs of the zodiac looking down over lists of religious festivals and miniatures of men engaged in supposedly typical activities for the time of year – boozing in January, chopping wood in February, sleeping in March . . .

Santa Maria dell'Assunta, just beyond, has a more coolly refined exterior, but its aloofness is tempered by monsters carved at the bases of the windows – notably a chimera with the face of a diabolic lion, flexing its talons and flicking its serpentine tail. Inside, the creamy-white carvings are so exquisitely precise that it seems the mason has only just put down his chisel. In fact they're 800 years old. There's been some restoration, but this is scarcely discernible, and the lack of the usual cracks and crumblings is uncanny. This is particularly striking in the extraordinary free-standing column, consisting of two entwined rolls of stone so supple and sensuous that you expect them to dimple to the touch. To get the keys, you'll need to search out the custodian. His house is tucked behind a garage bearing the number two on the left of the main street; if he's out, try the village's bars.

Sulmona

Flanked by bleak mountains, and bristling with legends about its most famous son, Ovid, **SULMONA** is a rich and comfortable provincial town which owes its wealth to gold jewellery and sugar almonds. An atmospheric little place, with a dark tangle of a historical centre lined with imposing palazzi, its sights can be seen in a day, but the town makes a good base for exploring the surroundings, and you may want to stay longer.

Arrival and accommodation

Arrive in Sulmona **by bus** and you'll be dropped outside the park at the western end of Corso Ovidio; **long-distance buses** also leave from the park (timetable posted at the end of the Corso). **By train**, regular buses connect the station with the centre – get off at Piazza XX Settembre. halfway along Corso Ovidio. The **AAST** (Mon–Sat 9am–1pm), with maps and leaflets on the town, is at Via Roma 21.

The best of the town's affordable **hotels** is the *Italia* (☎0864/52.308) just behind Piazza XX Settembre – comfortable, clean, convenient, and numbering Puccini among its first guests. A double room costs L25,000, the same as at the less characterful *Nuova Madrigale* on Via Paolina, off Corso Ovidio by the Annunciata (☎0864/51.785). *Stella*, on Via Mazzara, off Corso Ovidio (☎0864/52.653) and *Di Giovanni*, on Via Peligna, off Via Mazzara (☎0864/51.397) both charge around L22,500 for doubles.

The Town

Corso Ovidio, Sulmona's main street, cuts through the centre from the park-side bus terminus, leading up to Piazza XX Settembre, an intimate square that's home to the art nouveau **Gran Caffè**. Nowadays the elegant twists and curlicues of the wrought-iron lamps on its terrace have a soundtrack of blipping video games, but it makes a nice spot for sipping a drink. A couple of minutes back up Corso Ovidio, the **Annunziata** is Sulmona's architectural showpiece, a Gothic-Renaissance palazzo adjoining a flamboyant Baroque church. Its steps are these days a hangout for the town's lads during the evening *passegiata*, but once they would have been crowded with Sulmona's ill and destitute: the Annunziata housed a hospital, a pharmacy and a store of grain, donated by the rich and shared out to the needy. It was established by a confraternity to take care of the citizens from birth until death, and most of the external decoration is designed to remind onlookers of the life-process: around the first door is a tree of life; a frieze with scenes of birth, marriage and death stretches right across the facade; a wheel of life stands above an ornate window; and statues of saints gaze piously down from pedestals, firmly placing the symbolism in a Christian context. The most intriguing statue, however, is just inside the entrance: Ovid, metamorphosised from pagan poet of love into an ascetic friar. Inside the Annunciata is a small **museum** (Mon–Sat 10am–12.30pm & 4.30–7pm, Sun 9am–12.30pm), with examples of work by Sulmona's Renaissance goldsmiths – a tradition which continues here today, as evidenced by the number of jewellers' shops along the Corso.

The Corso's **shops** are also full of Sulmona's other great product – *confetti*, a confection of sugar almonds twisted with wire and ribbons into elaborate flowers. Through ingenious marketing the Sulmonese confetti barons have made gifts of their sugar almond sculpture *de rigueur* at christenings and confirmations throughout Catholic Europe. At Abruzzese weddings bride and groom are painfully pelted with loose white confetti. Most apparent in the Corso's shops, however, are the brashly coloured giant daisies designed to tempt kids and tourists.

Beyond Piazza XX Settembre, the weighty Romanesque portal of **San Francesco delle Scarpe** was the only part of the church solid enough to withstand the 1703 earthquake. The church gets its name – delle Scarpe means "with the shoes" – from the fact that Franciscans wore shoes instead of sandals like other orders of monks. Opposite, the impressive Gothic aqueduct, built to supply water to the town and power to its wool mills, ends at a fifteenth-century fountain, the **Fontana del Vecchio**, named for the chubby-cheeked old man on top. On the other side of the aqueduct is **Piazza Garibaldi**, a vast square dominated by the austere slopes of Monte Morrone, on which the hermit, Pietro Morrone, lived until he was dragged away to be made Pope (see L'Aquila). The former nunnery in the corner is being renovated as a museum of Abruzzo's nomadic shepherds – take a look at the courtyard, where there's a tiny door outside which unmarried mothers were permitted to abandon their babies.

For centuries, women suffering from the opposite problem – infertility – would visit a Roman ruin outside the town known as **Ovid's Villa**, where they would pray to the poet, who was seen as some kind of fertility god. A stone phallus then lay upon the steps, and although archaeologists have now put paid to the myth by identifying the ruin as a temple of Hercules, the site is still evocative – beneath a rocky crag topped by a monastery, with fine views over the valley to the Maiella massif; and there's a well-preserved mosaic pavement decorated with leaping dolphins. To get there, take a bus to Bagnatura/Badia, get off after the prison and walk up the hill. The Ovid connection continues behind the prison, in the **Fonte d'Amore** where – the Sulmonese claim – Ovid was caught making love to a fairy or (for sceptics) to the Emperor Augustus' granddaughter.

Eating

Sulmona has some excellent **restaurants**, even the finest of which – the *Italia* on Piazza XX Settembre – is very reasonably priced; count on L25,000 for a full meal, less than half that for a large dish of pasta with salad and wine. The chef, Nicola, bases his dishes on traditional Abruzzese fare, but is ever inventing new variations – try his fresh cannelloni stuffed with ricotta and various secret ingredients. *Al Quadrivio*, Vico Odorisio, off Via Mazzara, is good too, but slightly more expensive. Other options are the *Trattoria Nafalda* on Via Solimo, where you can eat outside in a pretty walled garden, the *trattoria* on Piazza Garibaldi, also with outdoor seating, and gaze at Monte Morrone, and *Ristorante Cesidio* on Via Gramsci, which does full meals for L16,000. If you want fast food or pizza, wander along to the west end of Corso Ovidio.

Around Sulmona: the western slopes of Maiella

The beautiful **Maiella** mountain range rises high above Sulmona, its steep wooded slopes and red and gold cliffs giving way to an upland plain as smooth as a cricket field. If you have your own transport you could explore it in a day; by bus, you either have to make a very early start, or sleep over in one of the many villages with facilities for tourists. There are regular buses to some villages, and if you're stuck it's easy enough to hitch.

One of the easiest places to reach is **PACENTRO**, a pretty village topped by the three towers of its castello, though most famous these days for the fact that the grandparents of pop star Madonna emigrated from here. The village has become used to being invaded by the world's tabloid hacks, and there are controversial plans afoot to erect a bustiered bronze monument in her honour.

If this is not your scene, head instead to the mountain-top forest of **Bosca Sant'Antonio** on the bus route to Pescocostanzo. As well as walking and picnicking, you can also hire horses, and if you want to stay over the *Hotel Sant'Antonio* (☎0864/67.101) has doubles for L30,000. Alternatively, after a morning in the woods you could move on to **PESCOCOSTANZO**, a well-preserved village with steep grey and white stone streets lined with craft workshops selling lace, gold filigree, wrought-iron work and woven rugs and bedspreads. As the sprawl of Swiss-style apartments on the periphery might have warned you, it's also an extremely popular winter and summer resort. The best of the local crafts are to be found in the **Collegiata** a fifteenth-century church at the head of the main street, with a magnificently carved and gilded Baroque ceiling and some superb wrought-iron work – lifelike putti and curling, delicate flowers incorporated into the iron chapel screen and the lampholders. The **AAST** (open in season only) is on the main square, next to a café. The only two **hotels** are three-star, but the *Eden* (☎0864/641.414) in the new quarter, has some doubles without baths for around L30,000.

There's little reason for visiting the other villages, now suffocated by purpose-built resorts, unless you're going **skiing** or want somewhere cheaper to stay. The major centres for skiing are **CAMPO DI GIOVE**, **RIVISONDOLI** and **ROCCARASO**. These are connected to Sulmona by (admittedly few) trains as well as by bus, and accommodation prices are not high. At Campo di Giove *Del Lago* (☎0864/40.107), *Fonte Romana* (☎0864/40.111) and *Locanda D'Amico* (☎0864/40.120) have doubles for around L25,000, at Rivisondoli the *Monte Pratello* (☎0864/69226) and *La Botte* (☎0864/69129) have doubles for around L21,000, as do Roccaraso's *Italia* (☎0864/62174) and the *Locanda Duca Degli Abruzzi* (☎0864/62176). And there's a **youth hostel** in Roccaraso at Via Roma 23 (☎0864/639.247) with beds for around L10,000.

South of Sulmona: Cocullo and Scanno

A tatty hill village, connected by rare trains and even rarer buses with Sulmona, **COCULLO** is understandably neglected by outsiders for 364 days of the year. However, on the first Thursday in May it's invaded by TV crews, journalists, deformed beggars, buskers, street-vendors and what seems like half the population of Central Italy. Market stalls sell everything from digital watches to spit-roast pork, and the roads – and on occasions even the nearby motorway – are crammed with parked cars and flustered traffic police. The reason for all this activity is Cocullo's weird **festival of snakes**, an annual event celebrated in memory of San Domenico, the patron saint of the village, who allegedly rid the area of venomous snakes back in the eleventh century.

It's an odd affair, a mixture of the modern and archaic. Everyone pours into the main square, while a wailing mass is relayed from the church over aged tannoys, competing with pulsing ghetto-blasters and the cries of the beggars. After the service a number of snake-charmers in the crowd drape a wooden statue of Domenico with a writhing mass of live but harmless snakes, which is then paraded through the streets in a bizarre celebration of the saint's unique powers (he was apparently good at curing snake-bites too). Actually, it is thought that Cocullo's preoccupation with snakes dates back to before the advent of Domenico. In the pre-Christian era, local tribes worshipped their goddess Angitia with offerings of snakes, and it seems too much of a coincidence that Domenico's powers also related to the creatures. Scholars have attempted to rationalise the festival by drawing a parallel between snakes shedding their skins and the ancient Cocullans shedding their paganism for Christianity – but whatever the origins, Cocullo's festival is today is more than anything a celebration of Domenico's power to attract enough tourist lucre in a day to keep the village going for a year. Incidentally, if you're suffering from toothache, Domenico is also reckoned to have the power to cure it, the only snag being that you have to ring the church bell with the rope in your teeth.

Lago di Scanno . . . and Scanno

Twenty kilometres down the road, but most easily reached by bus from Sulmona, **SCANNO** is another popular tourist destination, reached by passing through the narrow and rocky Saggitario Gorge, past the glassy green **Lago di Scanno**. There's a **campsite** here, *Il Lupo* (☎0864/740.100), with boats and horses for hire, and a good restaurant, the *Trattoria del Lago*. Perched over the lake is a church, **Madonna del Lago**, encrusted with ex-votives and with the cliff as its back wall. If you're planning on staying over, be warned that it's packed out in summer, especially August.

A couple of kilometres beyond, Scanno itself is a well-preserved medieval **village** encircled by mountains. At most times of the year, although especially in the summer season, women can be seen wearing their local costume – long pleated skirts, either heavy and dark or richly brocaded, a black velvet bodice and an embroidered fez with coils of cord looped behind to conceal the hair. The hat, and the fact that at Scannese weddings the women squat on the floor of the church, has led scholars to believe that the Scannese originated in Asia Minor; Scannese jewellery also has something of the Orient about it – large, delicately filigreed earrings, and a star, known as a *presuntuosa*, given to fianceés to ward off other men. If you want to watch a goldsmith at work, go to the jewellers round the corner from the tourist office on the main square. There's a shop on Via Roma selling Scannese costumes, and if this doesn't tempt you, the mountain cheeses, hams and salami and the sticky Scannese cakes on sale in the main café probably will. Scanno is also linked by chair lift to a small **ski-resort** – worth going up just for the view of lake and mountains, especially at sunset.

Every August Scanno holds a **classical music festival**, and on January 17 a **lasagne festival** – more properly called the *Festa di San Antonio Abate*, involving the cooking of a great cauldron of lasagne and beans outside the door of the church, which is then blessed and doled out with a somewhat unholy amount of pushing, shoving and squabbling. For the rest of the year you'll have to make do with the **restaurants**, best of which is *Gli Archetti* on Via Silla. If you're **staying over** the cheapest options are the *Eden* (☎0864/74.328) or the *Pensione Nilde* (☎0864/74.359).

Southwest Abruzzo and the National Park

Heading west towards Rome from Sulmona, road and railway skirt the **Fucino Plain**, an endless, unreal and utterly flat expanse of agricultural land whose only landmarks are the satellite dishes of *Telespazio*, Italy's biggest telecommunications complex. The Fucino was once Italy's third largest lake, and is the largest lake in the world to have been artificially drained. Attempts to empty it began nearly two thousand years ago. The *Marsi* tribe who lived on its shores, fed up with the fact that it flooded every time the mountain snows melted, managed to persuade Emperor Claudius to build a 6km-long outlet tunnel, designed to transfer the water from the lake into a nearby valley. On the day of the draining, the shores and surrounding mountains were packed with spectators: the proceedings were inaugurated by a mechanical Triton who rose up from the lake blowing a trumpet, whence a mock battle ensued, with warships manned by condemned criminals, after which Claudius gave the signal for the outlet gates to be opened. Unfortunately, the tunnel couldn't cope with the vast volume of water, and thousands of spectators, including members of the Imperial party, only narrowly escaped being washed away. Frederick II attempted to open up the tunnel in 1240, but the lake was only finally drained in 1875, as much to gain agricultural land as to solve the flooding problem – though it has brought associated problems. The climate has grown humid, misty and mosquito-ridden, and it's clear that that lakeside tourist developments would have been far more profitable than agriculture.

Avezzano, Alba Fucens and Tagliacozzo

Fringing the plain are **CELANO**, a pretty village crowned by a turreted toytown castle, and **AVEZZANO**, an unfortunate city that was destroyed – along with 10,000 inhabitants – by an earthquake in 1915. It was rebuilt, but flattened again by World War II bombings. It's since been reconstructed, but is a bland garden city, and the only reason for a visit is to get a bus out to the substantial ruins of a Roman colony at *Alba Fucens* , or south to the National Park (see below).

Buses to **Alba Fucens** leave from outside the railway station; three early in the morning, and four between 11am and 2.50pm (make sure that your bus goes right on to Alba Fucens and not just to Massa d'Albe), dropping you at the far end of the village of **ALBE** a straggle of prefabs, from where you can either wander around the site alone or be shown round by a guide, who will give you a down-to-earth (Italian) commentary.

Alba Fucens

Alba Fucens was a garrison town of about 30,000 inhabitants, founded by the Romans in 304 BC to keep the surrounding tribes in check. Aerial photographs have identified remains spreading over three square kilometres, but only the area nearest to Albe has been excavated. The main street of the town, Via Valeria, originally ran to Rome, 68 Roman miles away, according to a milestone on the town's edge. Walking down the parallel street, you reach the market place, still with the walls and arches of the small shops that used to surround it. Beyond is a bar, consisting of a sink with pipes through which hot wine with honey and pine-resin was dispensed; behind are the steam baths – you can see the holes in the raised pavement through which the steam rose. A good many statues, most notably a gargantuan marble Hercules, were also found, but these are now kept at Chieti's archaeology museum (see below). Further on, above the amphitheatre, the beautiful Romanesque church of San Pietro has some excellent Cosmatesque inlaid and twisted marble decoration.

Tagliacozzo

Twenty minutes beyond Avezzano by train is **TAGLIACOZZO**, a picturesque town with an unspoilt Renaissance core, nestling beneath a pine-wooded cliff. There's not a lot to see here, but it's a much pleasanter base for Alba Fucens than Avezzano, with some gorgeous small squares enclosed by fourteenth- and fifteenth-century houses, a tangle of narrow streets and alleys, and the church of San Francesco, with its paper doily rose window and column capitals carved with twisting flowers and leaves. Above the church is the impenetrable **Palazzo Ducale**, and the small **Teatro Thalia** – named, like Tagliacozzo itself, after the Greek muse of theatre. The story goes that the town was founded by Greeks from Mount Parnassus: next to San Francesco is a church dedicated to two Greek saints, Cosmo and Damiano, and there are supposedly still traces of Greek in Tagliacozzo's dialect.

There's an **AAST** on Piazza Argoli which has leaflets and a map of the town; if you want to stay overnight, there's a small **hotel** on Via Transimele, just behind Via Duca degli Abruzzi, near the *Blue Moon* nightclub. You'll have no problem finding **somewhere to eat**: *Petit Restaurant chez Nunzia* on Via XXIV Maggio, parallel with Viale Aldo Moro, is good, friendly, and family-run, and serves a type of pasta known as *strozza preti* which means "priest-strangler".

The Abruzzo National Park

At four hundred square kilometres, the **Parco Nazionale dell'Abruzzo** is Italy's third largest national park, and holds some of its wildest mountain land, providing a hunter-free haven for wolves, brown bears, chamois and a pair of royal eagles. This in mind, the over-enthusiastic development of the park for tourists is a shame. **CIVITELLA ALFEDENA**, on the shores of the artificial Lake Barrea, has its wolves, stripped of the mystery that made stories of werewolves so prevalent around these parts, lazing placidly behind barbed wire, less forbidding than Alsatian dogs; everywhere you'll see the park's cute logo – a brown bear looking as daft and cuddly as Winnie the Pooh; and the central village, **PESCASSÉROLI**, is surrounded by campsites and fake Tyrolean holiday flats and hotels, mainly full of coachloads of schoolkids and German pensioners.

You can get away from all this if you're prepared to hike; if you're not, there's little point in coming to the park at all. There's no free camping, just certain fields laid aside for anyone who can cope without facilities, and between April and September the numbers coming here can be immense. If you want more comfort, you'll have to put up with everything-but-the-kitchen-sink car campers, or with their heartier but less hardy compatriots in a hotel. The trick is to treat the twee tourism as a joke, take advantage of the comprehensive information service, and get walking as quickly as possible: as soon as you get away from the tourist villages, and their nearby short tracks that would be negotiable in stilettos, the wild Appenine beauty really makes itself felt.

Information and walking routes

There are **information offices** in PESCASSÉROLI, as well as OPI, VILETTA BARREA, BARREA and CIVITELLA ALFADENA. All are open daily 9am–1pm and 4.30–7.30pm in summer and 9am–1pm and 4.30–6.30pm in winter, and have leaflets outlining specific walks. All of these take less than an hour, and are very easy and very popular. More usefully, there's a map (currently L6000) marked with *all* routes along with an indication of difficulty (F=easy, M=moderate, D=difficult), the time needed, and the flora and fauna you're likely to see on the way. There are getting on for a hundred **walking routes**, starting from 26 letter-coded points, so making a choice can be difficult. The following are just suggestions, taking into account the ease of reaching the starting point by bus.

From point #F, near Opi, there's a two-hour walk through the **Valle Fondillo** – one of the loveliest parts of the park but best done very early morning, to avoid other hikers and have a small chance of seeing bears. If you do see a bear, take care, keep quiet and don't panic – they've never harmed a tourist but are nevertheless extremely strong, and will attack if under threat. Alternatively, from the same point you can climb **Mont'Amaro** (1862m) for great views over to Lake Barrea. Another good climb is up **Monte Tranquillo** (route #C3 from point #C) about a kilometre out of Pescasséroli, taking the road to the left on entering the village, past the *Hotel Ivy*. The mountain (1841m) is crowned by a small sanctuary, dedicated to the black Madonna of Tranquillo. From the summit you can either retrace your steps or take path #Q3 into the **next valley**, where's there's a campsite, and tracks leading into the remoter reaches of the park. Your best chance of seeing some of the park's chamois is to take path #I1, turning left just before the youth hostel at Civitella Alfedena, and through the forested **Valle de Rosa**, until the forest gives way to the grassy slopes where the chamois graze. A path zigzags from here up the slope to **Passo Cavuto**, and beyond to the *Rifugio Forca Resuni* (see below for information on *rifugi*). From here a path (#K6) descends into the **Valle Iannanghera** – where you may see bears – and back to Civitella Alfedena. This circuit should take 5–6 hours.

Accommodation and practicalities

PESCASSÉROLI is the least pleasant of the park's villages but is fairly well served by buses (from Avezzano, and from Castel di Sangro on the border with Molise) so you may find it convenient to stay. In high season, there's little chance of finding a **room** on arrival – you'll need to book at least a month in advance. The cheapest place is *Al Castello* (☎0863/91.357) on Via Gabriele d'Annunzio off the main piazza, with doubles at L22,000; otherwise it's a steep L34,000 at *Peppe di Sora* (☎0863/91.908), across the river on Viale B. Croce. Campers should manage to find space on one of the four **campsites**. The simplest to reach is *dell' Orso* (☎0863/91.955) on the main approach road (SS83), which also has a hostel, open all year, but again, you'll need to book well in advance. Of the other sites, *Marsicano* (☎0863/912.356) is closer to the village on the SS83; *Sant'Andrea* (☎0863/912.173) is to the left off the SS83; and *Panoramica* (☎0863/912.257) is out of the village at the foot of the funivia up to M.Vitelle. If you plan on staying for a week or more, the **AAST** (daily 9am–noon & 3–7pm) on Via Piave, a right turn off the main street, has a list of families who rent out rooms: again, in the summer, contact the tourist office about a month before you plan to come.

Among the other villages, CIVITELLA ALFADENA has a **youth hostel**, *La Torre* (☎0864/89.166), and a camping area, *Valiuni sotto i cerri* (☎0864/89.336). VILLETTA BARREA also has a **hostel** (☎0864/89134), and BARREA, at the far end of the lake, has a hostel *Le Vicenne* (☎0864/88.348), and two campsites – *Colle Ciglio*, (☎0864/88.348) half a kilometre along the road to Alfedena, and *La Genziana* (☎0864/88.101), convenient for walk-point #K up to the tiny mountain Lago Vivo or the larger Lago Montana Spaccata. The quietest village to stay in is hilltop OPI, near the starting point for the Valle Fondillo walk – and worth considering if you don't mind the steep twenty-minute climb from the main road (buses are infrequent). There's a **hostel** here (☎0863/91.622), in the same building as the **Pro Loco** on the approach road, or alternatively there's the *Pensione All' Aragnino* (☎0863/91.352) in the centre of the village.

The best of the park's **restaurants** are expensive, and it's often a better bet to picnic, though in most villages you'll find fairly cheap pizza and pasta. If you can afford to splash out a bit, *Boselli*, on Via B. Croce in Pescasséroli, serves traditional food and isn't too pricey. For splurges, try *Il Pescatore* in Villetta Barrea; or, slightly cheaper, *Alle Vecchie Arcate* in Pescasséroli.

Northeast Abruzzo: Téramo and around

Rising from the Adriatic and rolling towards the eastern slopes of the Gran Sasso, the landscape of northeast Abruzzo is gentle, and its inland towns are usually ignored in favour of its long, sandy and highly popular coastline. TÉRAMO, capital of the province of the same name, is a modern town with an elegant centre harbouring a couple of Roman ruins and a treasure-filled cathedral. Not much to draw you, but Teramo does have good bus and train connections with the northern Abruzzo coast, and if you're heading for the sea you may well pass through.

Buses stop at **Piazza Garibaldi**, to which the **train station** is linked by regular city buses. Just off the piazza, on Via del Castello is the **AAST** and Téramo's cheapest **locanda** the *Castello* (☎0861/321.117).

Even if you're just passing through, it's worth looking in on Téramo's main attraction, the **Duomo**, at the top of Corso San Giorgio, behind whose patchy facade lies a remarkable silver altarfront. It's worth squatting down for a good look at this (ask the sacristan to switch the lights on). Crafted by the fifteenth-century Abruzzese silversmith Nicola da Guardiagrele – also responsible for the statues of Mary and Gabriel that flank the church doorway – there are 35 panels with lively reliefs of religious scenes, starting with the *Annunciation*, and moving through the New Testament, punctuating the narrative with portraits of various saints. Nicola was famous enough to feature in a sumptuous **polyptych** by a Venetian artist, Jacobello del Fiore, in a Baroque chapel to the left. Set into an ornate gilded frame are static portraits of saints, in rich blue, red and gold gowns, flanking the *Coronation of the Virgin*, and beneath it a model of Téramo, set against a gilded sky, with Nicolo wearing a monk's habit on the left, Jacobello in the red gown on the right.

To the right of the duomo, Via Irelli leads to the heart of Roman Téramo, with fragments of the **amphitheatre**, and the more substantial walls of the **theatre**, where two of the original twenty entrance arches remain. Just behind Piazza Garibaldi, is the town's modest **museum** (Tues–Sat 9.30am–1.30pm; summer also 4.30–7.30pm), whose collection of local art over the centuries includes two appealing works – a lovely almond-eyed Madonna by a local fifteenth-century artist, Giacomo da Campli, and Campli's *Madonna Enthroned with Saints* – a polyptych in which the colours are lucid, and the forms almost sculpted.

The Northern Abruzzo coast: Alba Adriatica to Pescara

The northern Abruzzo coastline isn't at first sight the region's most appealing stretch, its ribbon of sand hugged for most of its considerable length by road and railway, studded with grids of beach umbrellas and flimsy cabins and lined with concrete-box apartment blocks and hotels. However, the beaches are good and frequently palm-fringed, there are plenty of campsites, and though the resorts may look bland they can be fun – especially if you're weary of travel or culture.

The coastal railway line ensures that access to the resorts couldn't be easier, though finding a hotel can be a problem, as the cheaper ones tend to be closed out of season, and they get booked up in advance for most of the summer – your best bet at most of the coastal towns is to head straight for the tourist office on arrival.

ALBA ADRIATICA, is the most northerly of the Abruzzo resorts – a good place to stop off if you're heading on to Marche. **GIULIANOVA** has a best-avoided flea-bitten old town perched above its resort quarter, though its five campsites (bus #1 or #4 from opposite the railway station) and connections with Téramo make it a useful stop-off if you want a last swim before heading inland. Ten kilometres further south, **ROSETO DEGLI ABRUZZO** is modern and undistinguished, but has views up the Vomano valley towards the Gran Sasso.

PINETO is probably the most attractive option, a well-organised resort with a palm-lined beach and every hotel clearly signposted from the railway station. It's also a good base for visiting Atri (see below). Of the many hotels *Azzura al Mare* (☎085/949.1462) has doubles without bath for around L26,000; *Mare Blu* (☎085/949.0545), *Maria* (☎085/085.2065), and *Oasi* (☎085/949.1564) all have doubles with bath for between L28,000 and L31,000.

Atri

The approach to **ATRI**, about 10km inland from Pineto, is like travelling through the background of a Renaissance painting – with gently undulating hills planted with orderly olive groves giving way to a surrealist landscape of sleek clay gullies known as *calanchi*, water-eroded into smooth ripples, wrinkles and folds. Regular buses make the trip from Pescara and Téramo as well as Pineto, and it's a journey that's undeniably worth making. Atri's duomo contains Abruzzo's greatest cycle of frescoes, and the town itself, with its narrow stepped and bridged streets, is one you're likely to be reluctant to leave.

Buses drop you near **Porta San Domenico**, the town's only surviving defensive gate. To get to the centre, walk through the gate and cut down one of the narrow sidestreets to the main street which leads up to the central piazza, dominated by the thirteenth-century **Duomo**. Its facade is understated, pierced by a rose-window and perforated by the holes in which scaffolding beams were slotted during construction. The inside is similarly simple, with patches of frescoes on the brick columns and – visible through glass set into the floor of the apse – an octagonal mosaic pavement decorated with sea-horses, dolphins and fish, from the Roman baths over which the church was built. The duomo's highlight, however, is the cycle of **fifteenth-century frescoes** by Andrea Delitio on the apse walls. Delitio has been called the Piero della Francesca of Abruzzo for his sophisticated use of architecture and landscape; but in contrast to Piero's cool intellectualism and obscure symbolism, Delitio places the religious scenes in realistic contexts. *The Birth of Mary*, for example, has servants giving the newly-born baby a bath; in the vault the four Evangelists are placed in natural settings, the animals that are the emblems of the saints behaving as domestic pets; and back on the walls, the lives of the rich – especially in the *Dinner at Cana* and *Presentation in the Temple* – contrast with the lives of the poor, notably Mary, Joseph and the shepherds in the *Nativity*. The most emotionally-charged scene is the *Slaughter of the Innocents*, in which the horror is intensified by the refined Renaissance architectural setting, and the fact that the massacre is coolly observed from a balcony by Herod's party of civic bigwigs. One opulently dressed slaughterer slices a child with chill, technical accuracy as if it were a joint of meat; another holds a child upside down by the ankles, while the mothers weep wretchedly over the tiny corpses.

For a touch of light relief, head back up the right-hand aisle to see a piece of Renaissance kitsch – a font with four oversized frogs clinging to the basin. In the cloisters is the entrance to a cavernous Roman cistern, and there are more Roman relics outside the cathedral – the foundations of what was possibly a dyeworks, complete with a vat. By 1990 the **archaeological museum** should be open, with further finds from Roman Atri. Though really the best thing to do in Atri is just wander around, strolling out to the belvedere for views, nosing into the many churches, or simply sitting in a café and watching the small-town life around you.

You may well want to stay over in Atri, and there's a great **hotel** – three-star quality at one-star prices – the *San Francesco* (☎085/87.287), housed in an ex-convent next to the church of San Francesco on Corso Adriano. The best **restaurant** is *Alla Campana d'Oro*, on Piazza del Duomo, and there are a couple of **pizzerias**, one on the piazza, the other a takeaway on the main street near the post office.

Pescara

Abruzzo's main seaside resort is **PESCARA**, also a port and bureaucratic centre that's probably Abruzzo's busiest, most commercial and expensive city. Beach-seeking or not, you could well end up here: it's at the centre of eastern Abruzzo's bus network and has ferries to Yugoslavia and flights to England in the summer. The beach development stretches for an unrelenting 16km, and there are more relaxed places to sunbathe and swim, but it's a convenient spot, and it perks up in July for its one-week **jazz festival**.

Architecturally, Pescara isn't a distinguished town. In fact, it's the **central railway station** which makes the city's most impressive sight, strangely enough the most up-to-date in Italy, with a slick network of slinky escalators, smoked glass screens and non-slip black rubber pavements. Opposite, the main street, **Corso Umberto**, is lined with designer boutiques and packed with the label-conscious Pescarese, who also hang out in the elegant cafés on **Piazza Rinascita**, known as Pescara's *salone*. More usefully, its porticoes also shelter the **AAST** (daily 8.30am–1.30pm & 4.30–8.30pm). If you've time to kill, the **beach** is obviously first choice; otherwise **Gabriele d'Annunzio**, poet and mentor of Mussolini, was born nearby on Corso Manthone, and you can visit his birthplace (summer daily 9am–1pm & 6–8pm; winter Tues–Sun 9am–1pm). If you're seriously bored there's also a **museum of fish** on Lungofiume Paolucci (summer daily 8.30am–1.30pm & 3.30–7.30pm; winter Mon–Sat 8am–2pm).

Practical details

Pescara has two **railway stations**: *Stazione Centrale* is most convenient for the town centre, *Stazione Porta Nuova* for ferries. **Buses** to Rome (quicker than the train), Naples and local towns leave from outside the central railway station. **Ferries** to Split, Yugoslavia, leave from the Stazione Marittima (☎085/65.247) at the mouth of the river.

If you do stay, the only **campsite** (June–Sept) is on Lungomare Colombo, south of the centre. Most of the **hotels** are on the beach front north of the river, though cheaper and more central is the *Corso* (☎085/21.210) opposite the railway station. Alternatively, in the streets to the south of Corso Umberto you'll find the *Bristol* (☎085/374.126) on Via Trento, the *Centrale* (☎085/421.1772) on Via Firenze and the *Igea* (☎085/421.1348) on Via Milano.

This area is also the best bet for **eating**. *Oca Bianca* is a good and fairly cheap restaurant off Via Roma, and there are a number of well-priced pizzerias. If you want to picnic, *Casa del Formaggio* on Via Roma has a vast selection of cheeses. Draught beer and cheap pasta can be had at the *Birreria Adriatica*, near the central railway station, and the *Happy Time* club, off the Corso, sometimes has good **live jazz** to accompany your boozing.

Chieti, Guardiagrele and Lanciano

Just twenty minutes by train from Pescara, **CHIETI** is a pleasanter place to stop over between trains or before catching a ferry. It holds Abruzzo's best museum by far, with an extensive collection of finds from the region, and the town itself, though not particularly attractive, has a relaxed and appealing provincial air. Give it a night at most – then move on.

Coming by train you arrive at CHIETI SCALO, from where it's a short bus journey (#1) up the hill to Chieti proper, which spreads over a curving ridge and has great views of the Maiella and Gran Sasso – and, when it's clear, out to sea. Buses arrive at Piazza Vittorio Emanuele alongside the ugly and much-reconstructed cathedral, from where Corso Marrucini cuts through the town centre to Piazza Trento e Trieste. **Maps** are available at the **EPT** on Via Spaventa, just off the Corso, and behind the post office opposite are the remains of three little Roman temples. But it's the **Museo Nazionale Archaeologico di Antichitá** (Tues–Sat 9am–2pm, Sun 9am–1pm) which is of most interest, laid out in a dignified villa encircled by a park beyond Piazza Trento e Trieste. It holds finds from Abruzzo's major sites: there's a Roman portrait-bust of an old man, in which the stone appears as soft, wrinkled and flaccid as real skin; a massive and muscley white marble Hercules from the temple at Alba Fucens (see above); and a metal and uncomfortably narrow bedstead from a tomb at Amiternum. If you've seen Amiternum, look also at the frieze showing how its amphitheatre would have looked in the first century, packed with bloodthirsty spectators at the gladiatorial games. Upstairs, don't miss the *Capestrano Warrior*, a statue of a Bronze Age soldier with a body so curvaceous that there's a question mark over its gender. There's no doubt about the sexes of the occupants of Bronze Age tombs, as you'll see in the adjacent rooms – the men were buried with armour and weapons, the women with jewellery, kitchen utensils, spindles, and in one case even a nail-brush. For more insight into prehistoric hygiene, head for the extraordinary exhibition about palaeolithic dental health, conclusions about diet being drawn from the state of the palaeolithic teeth.

If you're not bothered about your own teeth, sample Chieti's sweet and gooey speciality, *Torrone di Fichi Secchi*, (nougat with dried figs) before you leave. More practically, there are good-value full **meals** at the *Trattoria Dante* on Piazza Trento e Trieste, and, somewhat livelier, fairly cheap pizzas at the *Magico Alvermann Video Pub* on the Corso. For **sleeping**, there's a reasonable hotel a few minutes walk from Piazza Vittorio Emanuele – the *Marrucino* (☎0871/2647) on Via dei Veneziani, off Corso Marrucini.

Near Chieti: Guardiagrele and Lanciano

From Chieti, most people head south to the lovely historical town of LANCIANO, taking in the smaller town of **GUARDIAGRELE** on the way if they have a car. The town enjoyed a literal golden age in the fifteenth century, when it was home to Nicola da Guardiagrele, a gold and silversmith whose ornate crucifixes and altar-fronts can be seen in churches and museums throughout Abruzzo. Guardiagrele itself, however, has only one piece by Nicola – a silver processional crucifix in the church of **Santa Maria Maggiore**. The church's external fresco of St Christopher, by another great fifteenth-century Abruzzo artist, Andrea Delitio, (see Atri) was supposed to bring travellers good fortune. It had its own share of luck in 1943 when it escaped being destroyed by the German soldiers who smashed the church's portico.

LANCIANO, some 18km east of Guardiagrele, holds one of Abruzzo's most enticing and best preserved historical quarters and is well worth the onward journey. Indeed, its handful of cheap hotels make it a feasible alternative base for this part of the region.

As Italy's main producer of needles and host of an important wool and cloth fair, Lanciano was a major commercial centre during the Middle Ages, and the main **Piazza Plebiscito**, in the words of a contemporary, was invariably crowded with "peasants in red and blue jackets, Jews in yellow sashes, Albanians, Greeks, Dalmatians and Tuscans: there was an assortment of languages, it was a muddle, a nightmare . . ." The square is not much quieter now, a chaotic junction where the cathedral balances on a reconstructed **Roman bridge** – a testament of even earlier prosperity, built in the time of Emperor Vespasian to give easy access to the merchants of the Roman era.

Corso Roma leads out of the piazza and up to the church of **San Francesco**. Behind its austere rectangular facade are the relics of one of the more improbable miracles of the Catholic church, the *Miracolo Eucaristico*. Contained in two reliquaries are five coagulated globules of blood and a fragment of muscular heart tissue, both 1200 years old. The story goes that during a communion service in the eighth century the bread became flesh and the wine blood in order to prove Christ's presence to a doubting monk. The relics have been forensically analysed by the Vatican's scientists, right down to their trace minerals, and the findings are presented in an exhibition, in which it is verified that the relics are indeed human blood and flesh, and that they both have the same blood group (AB) as that traced on the now discredited Turin shroud.

From the church, Via Fieramosca and Via Finamore climb up to the **Torri Montanare**, a bulwarked, multi-towered and crenellated stronghold as grim and impenetrable as when it was built in the eleventh century to protect the town's newly built residential quarters. You can walk along the walls, for great views of the Maiella mountain range, or descend to Via Santa Maria Maggiore to explore the appealingly crumbling houses of the medieval quarter, **Civitanova**, and Lanciano's best church, **Santa Maria Maggiore**. Its Gothic portal, surrounded by a series of columns carved into twists, zigzags and tiny leaves and flowers as elaborate as piped icing, is slightly crumbled, while inside there's a silver processional cross by Nicola da Guardiagrele, delicately decorated with biblical reliefs and hanging with silver incense baubles.

A few streets further on, a long flight of steps decends towards the centre. This marks the boundary of **Ripa Sacca**, the medieval Jewish ghetto – a series of the narrowest of stepped streets spanning out like ribs from a barely wider central spine. Here eighty Jewish families lived, obliged to observe a strict curfew, allowed to follow only certain professions, and forced to identify themselves by wearing a yellow sash at all times. A handful of the original houses remain on Via and Vico Santa Maria Maggiore, but even the later houses are in character. Below is the large and scruffy Piazza Garibaldi, and from there a flight of steps climbs up to Via degli Agorai, which was named after its fifteenth-century needlemakers. The same street skirts another wanderable quarter, **Lancianovecchia**, not as old as its name suggests, but still something of a centre for the town's artisans.

Lanciano practicalities

The **railway station**, where **buses** also stop, is at the head of a broad avenue, off which Corso Trento e Trieste runs down to Piazza Plebiscito. There's a rarely open **AAST** here; if it's closed, **maps** are available at the Comune opposite, open weekday mornings until 2pm. If you're **staying overnight**, Lanciano's cheapest and most convenient hotel is the *Allegria* (☎0872/24.154) on Via Fieramosca. Doubles cost L26,000 and it's also a good bet for a reasonable meal. Otherwise, the *Rimembranza* (☎0872/25.130), on Piazza Vittoria behind Via V. Veneto, which runs parallel to Corso Trento e Trieste, has rooms for about the same price, while the *Alba* (☎0872/35.740), just off Viale del Mare, is slightly more expensive – take bus #1 from Piazza Plebiscito and get off after the FINA garage. There are no meals at the hotel, but the pizzeria *Riviera* nearby is adequate.

The Southern Abruzzo coast

The coast south of Pescara is less developed than the northern stretch; the long ribbon of sand continues, followed by the railway line and punctuated with mostly small resorts. The largest, **FRANCAVILLA AL MARE**, is a characterless place, basically a continuation of Pescara. **ORTONA**, further along, is of most interest for the daily summer ferries to the Tremiti Islands (see *Chapter Fourteen*, Puglia), its mainly reconstructed centre dominated by the shell of a castle and the massive dome of its cathedral. The town was at the centre of a six-week battle in 1943, fought over the territory between the Sangro and Mora rivers, which ended in the German occupation of Ortona and the deaths of thousands of British soldiers; there's a military cemetery 3km south of Ortona on the banks of the Moro.

On the other side of the river lies **SAN VITO**, a small resort and fishing centre, with a pebbly beach and rocky coast. From here you can take a bus or – more fun – the gradient-scaling small-gauge railway inland to Lanciano (see above), or continue down the coast to the equally small resort of **FOSSACESIA**. There's only one, rather expensive, hotel here, but a 2km-walk inland is a campsite, *Shanty Boy* (☎0872/60135), open year round. Just before you reach the site is the creamy-gold Romanesque church of **San Giovanni in Venere**, which owes its name to the fact that it was built over a Roman temple dedicated to Venus the conciliator and is visited by anyone seeking the return of peace within their family. The church, with its finely carved sandstone door and triple apse is superbly sited among the undulating fields above the coast and is still a favourite outing for Abruzzo families – harmony now being sought by the treat of a slap-up meal in the swanky restaurant outside the church. If you're visiting at the weekend or during holidays and want the church to yourself, aim to get there at lunchtime, while everyone else is safely esconced behind plates of pasta.

Vasto

VASTO, further south, close to the border with Molise, is a fine old city, overlooking the resort of **VASTO MARINA**. There are boats in the summer to the Tremiti Islands, plenty of campsites, and a handful of reasonable hotels along the broad sandy beach – palm-lined and beach-hutted in the centre, wilder and rockier to the north.

Though its sights are pretty run-of-the-mill, Vasto is a nice place to hang out for a while. Buses from the railway station run along the seafront and to the upper town, its rooftops and campanili rising above palms and olive groves. Centre of town is Piazza Rossetti, its gardens dominated by the chunky **Castello Calderesco**. The piazza is named after Gabriele Rossetti, a local eighteenth-century poet who is better known as the father of the Pre-Raphaelite poet, Dante Gabriele Rossetti.

Just off the piazza, next to the small Duomo, the **Palazzo d'Avalos** has a Renaissance splendour still perceivable through its scruffiness. Once the home of the poetess and friend of Michelangelo, Vittoria Colonna, famous in her time for the bleak sonnets she wrote after her husband's death, it now houses Vasto's **museum** (Mon–Sat 8am–2pm), best of whose exhibits are some bellicose second-century bronzes, a third-century warrior with an arm missing, and a collection of Greek coins – evidence of Vasto's early importance as an international trading city.

Alongside the palazzo, **Piazza del Popolo** is home to the **AAST**, which works short hours, but has lists of hotels and campsites in the window. The piazza opens onto a panoramic promenade, which takes you to Vasto's most memorable sight, the door of the church of **San Pietro**, surrounded by Romanesque twists and zigzags, standing isolated against a backdrop of sky, sea and trees, the rest of the church having been destroyed in a landslide.

Pleasant as the upper town is, most of the action is down by the **beach** in **VASTO MARINA**, and it's here that you're more likely to want to stay. There's another **AAST** on the seafront, open summer only, numerous **campsites** along the coast: *Sea Garden* (0873/801.097) is the most central. The cheapest of the many **hotels** here are the *Cigno Bianco* (☎0873/801.753) on Via Donizetti, above the railway station, and *La Bitta* (☎0873/801.979), close to the beach on Lungomare Cordella – both have doubles for L29,000. If you do want to stay in the upper town, *Dei 7* (☎0873/609.23) on Via San Michele, to the left of the centre by the public gardens, has doubles for L34,000, and *Palizzi* on the busy Corso Mazzini (☎0873/2361) has doubles for a rock-bottom L23,000. As for **eating and drinking**, there are loads of pizzerias and "pubs" in Vasto Marina.

MOLISE

Molise is the most recently created and least-known of Italy's regions. Gentler, less rugged and much poorer than Abruzzo, it has more in common with southern than central Italy. Much of the region still seems to be struggling out of its past, its towns and villages victims of either neglect or over-development. The old hill villages, which look so enticing from a distance, are on closer inspection either collapsing and rotting, or suffocated by bland housing estates. And the cities, **Isernia** and **Campobasso**, are large and bland, fringed with factories erected by northern money that has been lured here by the low price of land and labour.

But Molise has its compensations. Just as the twentieth-century industrial tycoons have invaded Molise, scattering it with formula-built Anytowns, so, over 2000 years ago, the Romans charged into the region, forcing the native Italic Samnite tribes to leave their small villages and live in equally formula-built settlements. Molise still has a scattering of low-key Roman ruins – most interestingly at **Saepinum**, Italy's most complete example of a Roman provincial town, and a site that's still well off the beaten tourist track. Wandering among the ruins, and looking out over the green fields to the mountains beyond, you get some inkling of what it must have been like for Italy's first Grand Tourists.

It's a region of contrasts, too. Traditions that would have been ancient two hundred years ago persist even in the boom-towns. In many a new apartment block, Benetton-clad girls will be making lace alongside their grandmothers and in the village of **Ururi**, settled by Albanian refugees in the fourteenth century, there's an annual chariot race, as barbaric as anything the Romans dreamed up.

Finally there's the sheer physical aspect of the place. Forty percent of Molise is covered by **mountains**, and although they are less dramatic than Abruzzo's there are masses of possibilities for hiking. A must is the trail up **Monte La Gallinola** in the **Matese** mountains, from where on a clear day the whole of the peninsula, from the Bay of Naples to the Adriatic, stretches out before you.

Isernia and around

An air of tragedy hangs over **ISERNIA**. Severely damaged for the eighth time by an earthquake in 1984, the few remaining streets of its old town are scarcely visible behind the tunnels of scaffolding that support them. They cluster round a desperate square, Piazza X Settembre, where the skeletons of houses destroyed in a bombing raid on September 10 1943, overlook a monument to the 4000 who were killed – an anguished nude ankle-deep in fractured tiles, bricks and gutters. Abutting all this is the new town, a soulless grid of apartment blocks built more to last than to charm.

Isernia's one attraction is the **Museo Nazionale della Pentria e Isernia** (Tues–Sun 9am–1pm & 3–7pm), in the heart of the old town. In 1979 local road-builders unearthed traces of a million-year-old village here, the most ancient signs of human life yet found in Europe. The exhibits are backed up by computer programmes in four languages, including English, which reconstruct the village and put the ancient civilisation in context. Contrary to the misleading publicity, there were no human remains found, just weapons, traps, traces of pigment thought to have been used as body paint, and animal bones, laid out to create a solid platform on the marshy land for the village.

Though unattractive in itself, Isernia can be a useful starting-point for exploring the rest of Molise: **buses** to local villages leave from Via XXIV Maggio, parallel with Corso Garibaldi, and longer distance buses, including those to Rome and Naples, from outside the railway station. Avoid sleeping over, though, as the cheapest **hotel**, the *Sayonara*, Via G. Berti 132 (☎0865/50.992), the second street parallel to Corso Garibaldi, charges L35,000 for a double. The **eating** prospects are better: there's a good traditional restaurant, *Taverna Maresca*, in the old town on Corso Marcelli. If you're on a budget, their pasta, bean or polenta-based first courses are filling and cheap; if you're not, you can then gorge yourself on roast kid or lamb cooked in various mysterious but delicious ways.

Around Isernia

The countryside **around Isernia** is lush and gentle, at its best in spring, when the meadows are sprinkled with wild flowers. The valleys are headed by hill villages, most of them rundown places ringed with new housing estates, and the rewards of exploring are principally those of being the first foreigner to have visited in ages. This is not always the most comfortable of experiences, and women can expect to be stared at, cat-called or even kerb-crawled – there's no chance of anonymity in a village where everyone knows everyone else. Getting around, too, isn't easy: buses are organised around the school day, which means you'll have to leave either very early in the morning or at around 2pm – after that there may be no other bus until the next day.

Just outside **PIETRABBONDANTE**, northeast of Isernia, are the remains of a pre-Roman Samnite village, notably a well-preserved theatre set in a green field at the foot of Monte Caraceno. Further along the road, **AGNONE** is best known for the fact that it produces, as it has for the last thousand years, church bells. The **Marinelli Pontifical Foundry** still makes bells in the traditional way, using a priest to bless the molten bronze as it's poured into the mould, which supposedly ensures that the bell's tones will be pure. If you're into metalwork, Agnone is also famous for its coppersmiths, most of whom work on the main street.

To the west of Isernia, the bus calls at **CERRO AL VOLTURNO**, crowned by one of Molise's more spectacular castles, almost growing out of the grey rock on which it is perched. A few kilometres further on is **CASTEL SAN VINCENZO**, another pretty-from-a-distance hill village: get off the bus below the village at the *Cartiera* (paper mill) and walk along the road to the left for about one kilometre, until you come to the abbey of **S. Vincenzo al Volturno** – a much-reconstructed complex, with a crypt covered by a complete cycle of ninth-century frescoes in rich Byzantine colours, the only surviving example of ninth-century Benedictine art. **Be warned**, though, that the abbey is very rarely open – so check at Isernia's tourist office before leaving.

South of the abbey, but most easily accessible by train from Isernia, is the village of **VENAFRO**, topped by a derelict castle, and with a Roman amphitheatre (just by the railway station) that was converted into an oval piazza in the Middle Ages. The piazza, dry and dusty, is less startling for its architecture than for its squalor and neglect – the Roman arcades now lead into dilapidated shacks, and, usually deserted, it resembles more a pre-gunfight western movie set than an ancient site. For real spaghetti-western action, however, you need to be in Molise at the beginning of August, when the village of **MONTENERO VAL COCCHIARA**, north of Cerro al Volturno, holds an annual **rodeo**.

Campobasso, Saepinum and the Matese

Home of a top security prison and the National Caribinieri School, **CAMPOBASSO**, the regional capital, is about as appealing as you'd expect – a modern, rather faceless town that was once known for its cutlery industry. It's a good base, though, for the remarkable ruins at **Saepinum**, and if you're around in early June, its Corpus Christi **Sagra dei Misteri** procession is a spectacular event. Citizens are dressed as saints, angels and devils, inserted into Heath-Robinsonish contraptions and transported, seemingly suspended in mid-air, through the streets.

But at any other time of the year there really isn't much to see. There is supposed to be a museum of Samnite antiquities opening soon, but until then, the steep alleys of the small, old upper town are a mild diversion, and lead up to a couple of Romanesque churches – **San Bartolomeo**, which has eerily contorted figures carved around its main door, and **San Giorgio**, whose entrance displays a dragon surrounded by stylised flowers. The views at least are extensive, though they consist mostly of Campobasso's suburban sprawl. And there's little point carrying on up the hill to the monastery and sixteenth-century castle: the monastery is modern, and the castle now a weather station.

Should you need to sleep over, both the cheap **hotels** are outside the centre on the road to Térmoli: the *Tricolore* (☎0874/63.190) has doubles for L22,000, and the *Locanda Morana* (☎0874/65.839), charges L13,500 per person. The **EPT** on Piazza Vittoria in the new town has details of local events and bus routes to elsewhere in the province.

Saepinum

It's **SAEPINUM**, a ruined Roman town to the south, close to the border with Puglia, that makes the stopover in Campobasso worthwhile. Three kilometres from the nearest village, surrounded by a lush plain fringed with the foothills of the Matese mountains, it's the best example in Italy of a provincial Roman town – and is refreshingly tourist-free.

The main reason Saepinum is so intact is that it was never very important: nothing much ever happened here, and after the fall of the Roman Empire it carried on as the sleepy backwater it had always been – until the ninth century when it was sacked by Saracens. Over the centuries its inhabitants added only a handful of farms and cottages, incorporating the odd Roman column or architrave, and eventually moved south to the more secure hilltop site of present day Sepino. Some have now moved back, and have rebuilt the farms and cottages on Saepinum's peripheries, contributing if anything to the site's appeal. Their sheep graze below an ancient mausoleum, chickens scratch around the walls, and the only sounds are from the geese and white peacocks in their tiny smallholdings.

To get to Saepinum from Campobasso, try to take a bus that stops at **ALTILIA**, right outside the site. Unfortunately there are only a couple a day, and you may have to go to SEPINO, and walk the 3km to Saepinum, unless you can persuade the driver to detour to the "zona monumentale" – they sometimes will.

The site
Entrance to Saepinum is through the **Porta Terravecchia**, one of the town's four gates, from which you can follow the *cardus maximus*, still paved with the original flags, to the crossing with the *decumanus* – centre of town and home to the public buildings and trading quarters. On the left, grass spills through the cracks in the pavement of the **forum**, now used by the few local kids as a football pitch, bordered by the foundations of various municipal bulidings: the *comitium*, the *curia*, a temple, baths, and in the centre a fountain with a relief of a griffin. Beyond the forum, on the left of the *decumanus*, the **Casa Impluvio Sannitico** contains a vat to collect rain water, from the Samnite town that stood on the site before the Romans sacked it in 293 BC. Beyond lies the **Porta Benevento**, adjoining which is one of the two **museums** (both Tues–Sun 9am–1pm) documenting the process of excavation, and with a section on more recent rural traditions. Until quite recently the village was passed through, as it had been for over 2000 years, by nomadic shepherds, moving their flocks between their winter grazing lands in the south and summer pastures in Abruzzo. The *trattura*, as it's called, still takes place, but by lorry and motorway. Further along the road is what

must have been a welcome, if bizarre, landmark for generations of shepherds – an enormous stone cylinder resembling a modern water tower that is in fact the mausoleum of one of Saepinum's Roman citizens.

Back down the *decumanus* on the other side of the crossroads, is the well-preserved **Basilica** that served as the main courthouse. Beyond is the most interesting part of the town – the octagonal *macellum* (market place), with its small stone stalls and central rain-collecting dish, and a series of houses fronted by workshops, with the small living quarters behind. This leads down to the best-preserved gate, the **Porta Boiano**, flanked by cylindrical towers and statues of prisoners celebrating some victory over barbarian invaders. Following the walls around, you reach the **theatre** and the second **museum**, which contains fragments of sculpture.

The Matese

One of Italy's least visited mountain ranges, scattered with high plains, forests and lakes, the **Matese** stretches between Molise and Campania. Wolves still wander its woods, and the peaks are home to eagles, falcons and hawks. The streams are well-stocked with fish, and the valleys full of the much-coveted *porcini* mushrooms.

Trains running between Isernia and Campobasso stop at **BOIANO**, a pleasant town overlooked by a densely wooded hill crowned with the remains of a castle. The town is a good starting-point for the hike (around two hours) up **Monte Gallinola**: best done on a clear day when the views take in Italy's eastern and western coastlines. The road leads from beyond the central Piazza Pasquino up to a *rifugio*; from here a steep road, later a footpath, climbs through a forest to the Costa Alta, a mile-high pass whose views are good – though nothing compared to what you'll see when you get to the summit. The path then leads across ski-slopes to the base of Monte la Gallinola, where a track leads up to the top, from which you look down over the Lago del Matese, and, if weather permits, get the much-touted panoramic view.

You can, of course, see something of the Matese in more comfort, taking a bus to the winter sports centre of **CAMPITELLO MATESE** from either Boiano or Campobasso. But Campitello's hotels are pricey: the cheapest, *Lo Sciatore* (☎0874/784.137), charges L43,000 for a double with bath. Instead, try the *Matese* (☎0874/780.378) at **SAN MASSIMO**, northwest of Boiano, which has doubles with bath for L30,000. From Boiano, take the road marked Castellone and San Massimo and, coming down from the mountains, take the left branch when the road forks.

Towards the coast: Larino and the Albanian villages

Halfway between Campobasso and Térmoli, **LARINO** is considerably more attractive than most Molise towns, its medieval centre clasped in the valley, relatively untouched by the concrete and pace of the modern industrial town that supports it. The highlight is its cathedral, but there are also some minor Roman relics in its small museum and a neglected amphitheatre in the modern town.

To the left of the **railway station**, Via Gramsci leads down to old Larino. The main street widens out at Piazza Vittorio Emanuele and the old town's one **hotel**, the *Albergo Moderno* (☎0874/822.895), which has doubles at L24,000. Backing onto it is the **Palazzo Comunale**, whose **museum** (mornings only) contains the *Ara Frentana*, a pre-Roman sacrificial altar, large Roman mosaics and a hoard of coins. Close by is the **Duomo**, built in the early fourteenth century just after the town had been flattened by an earthquake and sacked by the Saracens, with an intricately carved Gothic portal. The interior is unremarkable, but the rickety steps and precarious ladders up the sixteenth-century campanile give good views.

The oldest part of the town starts beyond the duomo – but appealing as the houses and steep alleys are, it is the glimpses of centuries-old streetlife which are more memorable – women making lace and preparing vegetables outside their houses, while the kids play at their feet and the men do absolutely nothing unless they're boozing in the bar.

If you take a bus from Piazza Vittorio Emanuele to the upper city, you'll jump a couple of centuries in five minutes. Modern Larino is a bustling place, built on the site of the original Samnite/Roman town. The large and overgrown **amphitheatre** (off Via Viadotto Frentano) gives some idea of the importance of early second century BC *Larinum*, though apart from this the mosaic pavement off Viale Molise and a few fragments of walls, behind the Scuola Materna off Viale Giulio Cesare, are hardly sufficient clues to how Larino once looked.

The Albanian Villages

URURI, 12km from Larino, and **PORTOCANNONE** closer to the coast, are isolated villages, most easily reached by bus from Térmoli (although you could hitch from Larino). Their isolation is such that 600 years after their ancestors emigrated from Albania, the locals still speak an Albanian-Italian dialect incomprehensible to outsiders. Portocannone's Romanesque church contains an icon of the Madonna of Constantinople, brought over by the original emigrés, and in Ururi, at the beginning of May, a **festival** is staged: a fierce and furious race through the village streets on gladiator-style carts, pulled by bulls and pushed by men on horseback with spiked poles. It's a ruthless business: the horses are fed beer before the race to excite them, and although the riders are supposed to push only the back of the carts, they are not averse to prodding the flanks of the bulls – who have already been given electric shocks to liven them up. The race itself is terrifying, but unforgettable, with bulls, carts and spikes hurtling past the frenzied crowds. There are almost inevitably injuries, and at least one person has been killed. If you want to go, the tourist offices at Campobasso or Térmoli will have the precise date.

The Molise coast

The brief stretch of the Molise **coast** is less developed than Abruzzo's. Its only real town, **TÉRMOLI**, a fishing port and smart, attractive resort, makes for a relaxing place to spend a few days. The beach is long and sandy, the modern town has browsable shops, and the old town, walled and guarded by a castle, has an interesting cathedral. It's also departure point for ferries (all year) to the Tremiti Islands and, in summer, to Vasto in Abruzzo and Gargano in Puglia.

Térmoli is the place where Italian and Central European time is set – from the observatory inside the stark castle built above the beach in 1247 by Frederick II. Beyond the castle the road follows the old walls around the headland, holding what's left of the old town, focus of which is the **Duomo**. This is most notable for its Romanesque exterior, decorated all the way round with a series of blind arcades and windows – a feature introduced by Frederick II's Norman-influenced architects. Inside are the relics of Saint Timothy, best known for the letters he received from Saint Paul, who advised him on how to go about converting the Greeks. That he ended up in Térmoli is thanks to Térmolese crusaders, who brought his bones back from Constantinople as a souvenir. The Térmolese hid them, fearing that if the Turks ever succeeded in penetrating the city they would seize and destroy them. In fact the relics were hidden so well they weren't discovered until 1945, during restoration work to repair bomb damage (the sacristan will show you them now).

However, the main reason for being in Térmoli is for sun, sea and sand, and, if you can afford it, a splurge in one of its seafood **restaurants**. One of the best places for seafood is *Da Pasquale*, on Via Fratelli Brigada, where a full meal will cost around L17,000. The prices at *Blutuff*, on Lungomare Columbo, are about the same; if you want somewhere cheaper try *Gatto Verde*, Corso Nazionale 59, *Il Padrino*, Corso Umberto 85, or *L'Opera* at Via Adriatica 32. In addition there are plenty of **pizzerias** and **trattorias** on Via Fratelli Brigada, along the seafront and on the parallel Via Vittorio Emanuele III.

Térmoli's **AAST** (July & Aug 7am–1pm & 5–9pm; rest of the year 8am–1pm & 5–6.15pm) is beside the **bus station**, through the gallery at the beginning of Corso Umberto, and has lists of hotels, bus timetables and ferry times posted in the window. The cheapest **hotel** is *Al Caminetto* (☎0875/52.139) on the coast road, SS Europa 2, served by hourly buses from the railway station, with doubles for L21,000. On the same route is the **campsite**, *Cala Saracena* (☎0875/52.113). If you want to be closer to the railway station, *Villa Ida* (☎0875/2666), on Via M. Milano, has doubles for L33,500.

An alternative resort, if you're heading south, is **CAMPOMARINO**, a short train or bus ride from Termoli. It's less attractive, with high-rise developments along the beach, but is worth considering if you're on a tight budget as there are two amazingly cheap **hotels**: *Avia* (☎0875/539.084) and *De Risio* (☎0875/539.088) – both with doubles without bath for L10,000 (with bath L12,000).

travel details

Trains
From L'Aquila to Terni (up to 13 daily; 2hr 10min); Sulmona (up to 11 daily; 1hr 10min).
From Sulmona to Isernia (up to 4 daily; 2hr 30min–2hr 50min); Avezzano (up to 15 daily; 1hr–1hr 30min); Campo di Giove/Rivisondoli/Castel di Sangro (7 daily; 40min/1hr/1hr 10min).
From Téramo to Giulianova (up to 7 daily; 25min).
From San Vito to Lanciano (up to 8 daily; 20–30min).

From Pescara to Sulmona (17 daily; 1hr–1hr 20min); Rome (10 daily; 3hr–3hr 30min); Térmoli (up to 14 daily; 1hr 5min–1hr 50min); Ancona (up to 29 daily; 1hr 30min–2hr 20min); Pineto (up to 11 daily; 15min); Giulianova (up to 24 daily; 15–35min); Vasto (up to 16 daily; 50min–1hr 15min).
From Avezzano to Tagliacozzo (up to 16 daily; 10–20min); Rome (up to 18 daily; 1hr 30min–2hr 30min).
From Campobasso to Térmoli (up to 8 daily; 1hr 40min–2hr).

From Térmoli to Foggia (up to 21 daily; 50min–1hr).

Buses
From L'Aquila to Téramo (up to 7 daily; 1hr 20min); Castel del Monte (5 daily, Mon–Fri only; 1hr); Bominaco (4 daily, Mon–Fri only; 30min); Sulmona (6 daily, Mon–Fri only; 1hr).
From Sulmona to Scanno (up to 8 daily; 50min); Cocullo (2 daily; 30min); Pescasséroli (up to 2 daily; 1hr 30min).
From Avezzano to Albe (9 daily; 30min); Pescasséroli (up to 10 daily; 1hr 30min).

From Pescara to Chieti (approx every 20min; 40min); Atri (up to 13 daily; 35–55min); Lanciano (up to 15 daily; 55min–1hr 25min); Áscoli Piceno (up to 6 daily; 2hr 20min–2hr 45min).
From Téramo to Atri (3 daily; 1hr).
From Atri to Pineto (up to 12 daily; 25min); Pescara (up to 12 daily; 55min).

International Ferry
From Pescara to Split (July–mid-Sept 5 weekly; April–June & mid-Sept–mid-Nov 3 weekly; 8hr).

CHAPTER THIRTEEN

CAMPANIA

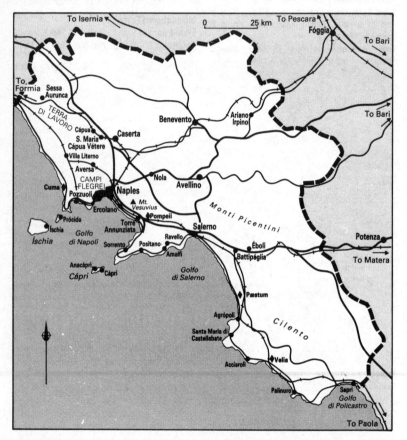

The region immediately south of Lazio, **Campania**, marks the real beginning of the Italian South or *mezzogiorno*. It's the part of the South too – inevitably – that most people see, easily accessible from Rome and home to some of the area's (indeed Italy's) most notable features – Roman sites, spectacular stretches of coast, tiny islands. It's always been a sought-after region, first named by the Romans, who tagged it the *campania felix* or "happy land" (to distinguish it from the rather dull *campagna* further north), settling down here in villas and palatial estates that stretched right around the Bay.

You might, of course, find this hard to believe now, and anyone coming in search of the glories of the Bay of Naples is likely to be disappointed. Industry has eaten into the land around the city as to render it almost unrecognisable, and even in the city the once-grand vistas are often hindered by cranes and smoke-belching chimneys. Most people take one look and skate right out again, disappointed at such a grimy welcome.

But give the area time. **Naples** is the obvious focus, an utterly compelling city (to say the least) and dominating the region in every way. At just two and a half hours by train from the capital, there's no excuse for not seeing at least this part of Campania, though of course you need a fair few days to absorb the city properly, and once established it's a base for some remarkable attractions. The **Bay of Naples**, certainly, is dense enough in interest to occupy you for a good week: there are the ancient sites of Pompeii and Herculaneum, just half an hour outside – probably Italy's best preserved and most revealing Roman remains; there is the odd, volcanic **Campi Flegrei** area to the north of the city; and of course there are the islands, **Cápri**, **Ischia** and **Prócida** – swarmed over by tourists these days, but Cápri, at least, so beautiful that a day there is by no means time squandered.

Inland Campania is by contrast a poor, unknown region for the most part, but the nearby towns of **Cápua** and **Caserta** repay visits, and are easily seen on day-trips. Similarly **Benevento**, an old stop on the Roman route to Bríndisi, has its moments, though you might want to make this part of a wider trip through Campania's interior (or on to Puglia), bearing in mind that it's a difficult and not obviously rewarding area to travel through. The area **south of Naples** has more immediate appeal – beach bum territory on the whole, though certainly not to be avoided. **Sorrento**, at the far east end of the Bay, has all the beer 'n' chips trappings you'd expect from a major Brit package destination, but is a likeable place for all that; and the **Amalfi Coast**, across the peninsula, is probably Europe's most dramatic stretch of coastline, harbouring some enticing – if crowded – beach resorts. Further south, **Salerno** is an inviting place, and gives access to the Hellenistic site of **Paestum**, and the more undiscovered coastline of the **Cilento** just beyond.

NAPLES

Whatever your real interest is in Campania, the chances are that you'll wind up in **NAPLES** – capital of the region and, indeed, of the whole Italian South. It's the kind of city people visit with preconceptions, and it rarely disappoints: it is filthy, it is very large and overbearing, it is crime-infested, and it is most definitely like nowhere else in Italy – something the inhabitants will be keener than anyone to tell you. In all these things lie the city's charm. Perhaps the feeling that you're somewhere unique makes it possible to endure the noise and constant harassment, perhaps it's the feeling that you've travelled from an ordinary part of Europe to somewhere that feels like an Arab bazaar in less than three hours. One thing, though, is certain: a couple of days here and you're likely to be as staunch a defender of the place as its most devoted inhabitants. No city on earth, except perhaps New York, excites fiercer loyalties.

In Naples, all the pride and resentment of the Italian South, all the historical differences between the two wildly disparate halves of Italy, draw into focus. This is the true heart of the *mezzogiorno*, a lawless, petulant city that has its own way of doing things. It's a city of extremes, fiercely Catholic, its streets punctuated by bright neon Madonnas cut into niches, its miraculous cults regulating the lives of the people as they have always done. Football, too, is a religion here: the celebrations went on for weeks after Napoli wrested the Italian championship from the despised North in 1987, and "Grazie Napoli" graffiti is still a prime feature of the urban landscape. Music, also, has played a key part in the city's identity: there's long been a Naples style, bound up with the city's strange, harsh dialect – and, to some extent, the long-established presence of the US military: American jazz lent a flavour to Neapolitan traditional songs in the Fifties; and the Seventies saw one of Italy's most concentrated musical movements in the urban blues scene of Pino Daniele, and the music around the radical *Alfa Romeo* factory out at Pomigliano.

Some history

There was a settlement here, *Parthenope*, as early as the ninth century BC, but it was superceded by a colony formed by the Greek settlers at nearby Cumae, who established an outpost here in 750 BC, giving it the name *Neapolis*. It prospered during Greek and later Roman times, escaping the disasters that befell the cities around and eventually declaring itself independent in 763 – which it remained for close on 400 years, until the Normans took the city in 1139. The Normans weren't here for long: like the rest of this region, the city soon came under the rule of the Hohenstaufen dynasty, who stayed rather half-heartedly until 1269, when their last king, Conradin, was beheaded in what's now Piazza del Mercato, and the Angevins took over the city. With one exception, Robert the Wise, who was a gentle and enlightened ruler, and made the city a great centre for the arts, the Angevin kings ruled badly, in the end losing Naples to Alfonso I of Aragon in 1422, thus establishing a Spanish connection for the city for the next 300 years, until Charles of Bourbon arrived in 1734. Neither the Spanish nor the French were very good for the city, like all great colonialists taking much and contributing little. But it's they who have left most mark on the city today, both in their grand architecture and the history that goes with it. Under the French the city became one of the most populated in Europe, and one of the most iniquitous, setting a trend which still holds good today. For the rest of Europe, Naples was the requisite final stop on the Grand Tour, a position it enjoyed not so much for its proximity to the major classical sites as for the ready availability of sex. Naples was for a long time the prostitution capital of the continent, and its reputation drew people from far and wide, giving new meaning (in the days when syphilis was rife) to the phrase "See Naples and die".

More recently, Naples and its surrounding area has been the recipient of much of the money that has poured into the South under the *Cassa per il Mezzogiorno* scheme and its industry is spreading, if not exactly booming. But the real power in the area is still in the hands of organised crime or the Camorra: much of the coastline west of the city – to Bagnoli – was built by Camorra money, and, though it's not at all publicised, little happens that matters here without the nod of the larger families. Not surprisingly, much government money has found its way into their hands too, with the result that there's been little real improvement in the living standards of the average Neapolitan: a very high percentage remain unemployed, and a disgraceful number still inhabit the typically Neapolitan one-room *bassi* – slums really, letting in no light and housing many in appallingly overcrowded conditions. Only ten years ago there was a cholera outbreak in part of the city, and it is perhaps only a matter of time before the same thing happens again: Naples produces more rubbish than any other city in the world, and yet its refuse-collecting is abysmally inefficient. The notorious city government has long been too at odds with itself to do anything about all this, and even if it tried would probably be thwarted by the interests of the Camorra. For how much longer the city can limp on is anybody's guess, and for the moment Naples is either romanticised by its aficianados or vilified by its oppponents – neither of these standpoints likely to much help the people who live here.

Arrival, information and getting around

Naples' **Capodochino Airport** is a little way northwest of the city centre at Viale Umberto Maddalena (☎780.5763), connected with Piazza Garibaldi by bus #14 about every fifteen minutes; buy tickets (L700) from the tobacconist in the departures hall. The journey takes 20–30 minutes – not much more than a taxi, for which you'll pay at least L20,000.

By train, Napoli Centrale (☎264.644) is at one end of Piazza Garibaldi, leaving you at the main hub of city (and suburban) transport services. City and some local **buses** stop on the square itself; others (*SITA* to Salerno, for example) pull up and leave from Corso Arnaldo Lucci, beside the station; *CTP* buses to outlying towns like Cápua and Caserta stop on Piazza Capuana, just north of the Piazza Garibaldi.

Information

There's an **EPT** office (Mon–Sat 8.30am–8pm, Sun 8.30am–2pm) in Stazione Centrale, though its opening times are a little unreliable and queues can be long and slow-moving. If they are, there is another office at Via Partenope 10a (Mon–Sat 8.30am–2pm, Sun 8.30am–noon; ☎406.289), on the seafront near Villa Communale. Both have free maps of the city and information on accommodation and attractions in and around the city. There are also two **AAST** offices: one in the old part of the city Piazza Gesù Nuovo (Mon–Sat 9am–3pm), another across the main courtyard of the Palazzo Reale (Mon–Fri 9am–2.30pm; take the lift up), which are generally less helpful but do give out copies of the free monthly booklet *Qui Napoli* – very handy for current events and exhibitions, listings of ferry and bus connections, opening times and useful telephone numbers.

> The Naples area telephone code is ☎081

Getting around the city

The only way to really get around Naples and stay sane is to **walk**. Having a car would be a nightmare, similarly taxis can be interminably slow (if you do take one be sure the driver switches on the meter), and to negotiate the narrow streets, hectic squares and racetrack boulevards on a moped or scooter takes years of training. In any case, *not* to walk would mean you'd miss a lot – Naples is the kind of place best appreciated from street level.

NAPLES

0   500 m

TANGENZIALE OVEST DI NAPOLI

PIAZZA
MAZZINI

PIAZZA
MEDAGLIE
D'ORO

Stazione F.S.
Napoli Montesanto

Funicolare di Montesanto

VÓMERO

Castel
Sant'Elmo

VIA BERNINI

PIAZZA
MANTELLI

VIA CIMAROSA

Certosa
San Martino

Funicolare Centrale

QUARTIERE
SPAGNOLI

Funicolare di Chiaia

Villa
Floridiana

Ferrovia Cumana
Stazione Corso
Vitt. Emanuele

Stazione F.S. Napoli
Piazza Amedeo

CORSO VITTORIO EMANUELE

VIA DEI MILLE

PIAZZA
TRIESTE E
TRENTO

VIA FRANCESCO CRISPI

Villa
Pignatelli

LARGO VASTRO A CHIAIA

CHIAIA

VIA CHIAIA

PIAZZA DI
PLEBISCITI

Virgil's
Tomb

Villa
Communale

Aquarium

PIAZZA
DEI MARTIRI

Stazione FS
Naples Mergellina

PIAZZA DELLA
REPUBBLICA

RIVIERA DI CHIAIA

VIA CARACCIOLO

PIAZZA
VITTORIA

EPT

VIA PARTENOPE

PIAZZA
SANNAZZARO

MERGELLINA

Marina

Castel
dell'Ovo

Funicolare di Mergellina

→ Hydrofoils to Cápri,
Ischia & Prócida

Museo Nazionale
di Capodimonte

TANGENZIALE OVEST DI NAPOLI

VIA DON BOSCO

CORSO AMEDEO DI SAVOIA

VIA FORIA

CORSO NOVARA

VIA TERESA DEGLI SCALZI

Museo
Nazionale
PIAZZA
CAVOUR

Stazione FS
Piazza Cavour

VIA S. GIOVANNI A CARBONARA

Duomo

PIAZZA
CAPUANA

PIAZZA
PRINCIPE UMBERTO

VIA ALESSANDRO POERIO

Train Station:
Napoli Centrale

VIA PESSINA

VIA SAPIENZA

VIA DEI TRIBUNALI

FORCELLA

PIAZZA GARIBALDI

VIA PORT'ALBA

VIA DUOMO

PIAZZA
DANTE

San Domenico
Maggiore

CORSO UMBERTO I

VIA S. BIAGIO DEI LIBRAI

PIAZZA
NOLANA

sù Nuovo

VIA B. CROCE

CORSO GARIBALDI

CORSO ARNALDO LUCCI

Santa Chiara   AAST

PIAZZA
NICOLA AMORE

Stazione
Circumvesuvian

PIAZZA
CARITÀ

VIA MEZZOCANNONE

CORSO UMBERTO I

PIAZZA
MERCATO

st Office

VIA ARMANDO DIAZ

PIAZZA BOVIO

VIA NUOVA MARINA

PORT AREA

VIA AGOSTINO DEPRETIS

VIA CRISTOFORO COLOMBO

Castel
Nuovo

PIAZZA
MUNICIPIO

Palazzo
Reale

Molo
Beverello

Passenger ferries
to Sardinia & Sicily

Ferries to Cápri,
Ischia & Prócidia

SANTA LUCIA

For longer journeys – and Naples is a big, spread-out city – there are a number of alternatives, both for the city itself and the Bay as a whole. City **buses** are efficient though crowded and slow, but are much the best way of making short hops across the city centre: fares are a flat L600 per journey; buy tickets in advance from tobacconists or the booth on Piazza Garibaldi (the latter is less likely to rip you off) half-day tickets are also available for L1000. The bus system is supplemented by the **metropolitana**, a small-scale underground network which crosses the city centre, stopping at about four stops between Piazza Garibaldi and Mergellina – perfect for long, quick jumps across the congested city centre – and runs eventually out to Pozzuoli and Solfatara in about half an hour. In addition, three **funiculars** scale the hill of the Vomero from stations at Piazzas Montesanto, Amadeo and Augusto (see map), another runs up the hill above Mergellina from Via Mergellina; same ticketing as for buses.

For solely **out-of-town trips** – around the bay in either direction – there are three more railway systems. The **Circumvesuviana** runs from its station on Corso Garibaldi right round the Bay of Naples about every half-hour, stopping everywhere, as far as Sorrento, which it reaches in about an hour. The **Ferrovia Cumana** operates every twenty minutes from its terminus station in Piazza Montesanto west to Pozzuoli and Baia. And the **Circumflegrea** line runs, again from Piazza Montesanto, west to Cuma – again about every twenty minutes. Ticketing for all these depends on where you're going, but as a rough guide, expect to pay around L600 to Ercolano on the Circumvesuviana, around the same to Pozzuoli in the other direction.

USEFUL BUS ROUTES

#CA Piazza Garibaldi–Piazza Bovio–Via Toledo–Piazza Trieste e Trento–Pizza Garibaldi

#CD Piazza Garibaldi–Piazza Dante–Piazza Carlo III–Piazza Garibaldi

#CS Piazza Garibaldi–Piazza Carlo III–Piazza Dante–Piazza Garibaldi

#140 Piazza Gesù–Piazza Plebiscito–Piazza Vittoria–Mergellina–Posillipo

#150 Piazza Garibaldi–Corso Garibaldi–Via Colombo–Via Partenope–Riviera di Chiaia–Via Mergellina–Pozzuoli

For details on the frequency of the rail lines, see "Travel Details"

Finding a place to stay

Accommodation prices in Naples may come as a refreshing change after the north of Italy, but they're still not cheap, and the city being the kind of place it is you need to choose carefully between the cheaper dives. A good many of these are conveniently situated around Piazza Garibaldi, spitting distance from the railway station and not badly placed for the rest of town; others group on the far side of the *centro storico*, near the university. The station EPT may point you somewhere good (certainly it's worth enquiring); if not, just follow the listings below – and don't, whatever you do, go with one of the touts outside the station. It's unlikely you'll be getting into anything dangerous but it *is* a possibility and in any case the hotel room probably won't be up to much. Incidentally, if you can, try and book somewhere in advance, especially in high season, when the city – like everywhere else in Italy – gets crowded.

Hotels and hostels

Ambra, Via Mezzacanone 109 (☎206.896). Handy for the university and consequently cheap and often full. If you can get in, L20,000 for doubles.

Ausonia, Via Caracciolo 11 (☎682.278). Neatly placed on the far side of town. Doubles L45,000 upwards, including breakfast. Bus #C4 or #106.

Corso, Corso Umberto I 377 (☎283.201). A short walk down Corso Umberto on the left, close to the *Trentino* (below) if that's full. Doubles from L30,000.

Crispi, Via F. Giordani 2 (☎664.804). Well-established budget hotel close to the Mergellina metropolitana stop. Doubles L30,000 plus.

Fiore, Via Milano 109 (☎338.798). Very cheap hotel off to the right of Piazza Garibaldi. Nothing special but with doubles for L25,000.

Odeon, Via Silvio Spaventa (☎285.656). Two-star hotel just two minutes from the station, off Piazza Garibaldi. Doubles from L35,000.

Ostello Mergellina, Salita della Grotta 23 (☎761.2346). Nice location, if somewhat removed from the life of the city centre, offering two-, four- and six-bedded rooms for around L12,000 for members, non-members a little more. The drawbacks are an 11.30am curfew and a three-day maximum stay during July and August. Metropolitana to Mergellina or bus #152 from Piazza Garibaldi.

Trentino, Corso Umberto I 311 (☎220.397). Well-placed for both the station and old part of the city, a little way down Corso Umberto on the left. Doubles from around L30,000.

San Pietro, San Pietro ad Aram (☎260.313). Just off Corso Umberto on the right. Clean though characterless rooms from L35,000 for a double.

Campsites

There are a number of **campsites** within a feasible distance of Naples. The closest is the *Vulcano Solfatara* site in Pozzuoli at Via Solfatara 161 (☎ 867.3413), open between April and October. Bus #152 runs right there from Piazza Garibaldi, or take the metropolitana to Pozzuoli and walk ten minutes up the hill. Out of these months, you're probably best off going to one of the other sites around the Bay – perhaps at Pompeii or, rather nicer, Sorrento, neither of which are more than an hour out from the city. See the relevant headings for details.

The City

Naples is a surprisingly large city, and a sprawling one, with a centre that has many different focuses. The area between Piazza Garibaldi and Via Toledo, roughly corresponding to the old Roman *Neapolis* (much of which is still unexcavated below the ground), makes up the old part of the city – the **centro storico** – the main streets still following the path of the old Roman roads. This is much the liveliest, most teeming part of town, an open-air casbah of hawking, yelling humanity that makes up in energy what it lacks in grace. Buildings rise high on either side of the narrow, crowded streets, cobwebbed with washing; there's little light, not even much sense of the rest of the city outside – certainly not of the proximity of the sea.

But the insularity of the *centro storico* is deceptive, and in reality there's another, quite different side to Naples, one that's much more like the sunwashed Bay of Naples murals you've seen in cheap restaurants back home. **Via Toledo**, the main street of the city, edges the old centre from the **Palazzo Reale** up to the **Archaeological Museum** and the heights of **Capodimonte**; to the left rises the

Vómero, with its fancy housing and museums, and the smug neighbourhood of Chiaia – beyond which lies the long green boulevard of **Villa Comunale**, stretching around to the district of **Mergellina**: all neighbourhoods which exert quite a different kind of pull – that of an airy waterfront city, with views, seafood eaten *al fresco* and peace and quiet.

Piazza Garibaldi to Via Toledo: the *centro storico*

However you actually get to Naples, there's a good chance that the first place you'll see is **Piazza Garibaldi**, a long, wide square criss-crossed by traffic lanes that cuts into the city centre from the modern railway station. It's the city's transport hub – most of the city buses leave from here, as do the Metropolitana and Circumvesuviana lines – and one of its most hectic junctions; indeed it's Piazza Garibaldi, perhaps more so than any other part of the city, that puts people off Naples. The buildings aren't particularly distinguished, you're likely to be accosted on all sides by street hawkers selling a dubious array of pirate cassettes and cigarettes, underwear and sunglasses, and you need to have all your wits about you to successfully negotiate the traffic – which is as congested as any part of the city and comes from all sides.

Forcella and around

Piazza Garibaldi is good preparation for the noise, confusion, even menace that make up the rest of the city centre – especially in the streets around, which are sleazy and some of them best avoided at night if you're alone. The other side of the square, the *centro storico* spreads west as far as Via Toledo – the tangled heart of Naples, and its most characteristic quarter. Off the right corner of the square, the **Porta Capuana** is one of several relics from the Aragonese city walls, a sturdy defensive gate dating from 1490, delicately decorated on one side in Florentine Renaissance style. Across the road, the white and much renovated **Castel Capuano** was the residence of the Norman king William I, and later, under the Spanish, became a courthouse, which it still is.

Behind here, the **FORCELLA** quarter, which spreads down to Corso Umberto I, is the main city centre stronghold of the Camorra and home to its most important families. It's also the city's open-air **market**, stamping-ground of yet more contraband tobacco dealers, cassette and sunglasses hawkers, and a quantity of food stalls – chickens sit in boxes waiting for the chop, after which they'll be plucked and cleaned up while you wait. As you might fast become aware, the trade in black market ciggies is an old-established one, and takes place throughout the city. It is, like just about every criminal activity in Naples, run by the Camorra, and used to be a high earner for them. Nowadays, though, the big money is in drugs, and the only people you'll see touting cigarettes are little old ladies in need of a few bob.

The two main streets of the *centro storico* are **Via dei Tribunali** and **Via San Biagio dei Librai** – two narrow streets, lined with old arcaded buildings, which lead due west on the path of the *decumanus maximus* and *ducumanus inferiore* of Roman times, both charged with atmosphere throughout the day, a maelstrom of hurrying pedestrians, revving cars and buzzing, dodging scooters. Via dei Tribunali cuts up to **Via Duomo**, which ploughs straight through the old town to meet Corso Umberto I and Piazza Nicola Amore, laid out after a cholera epidemic in 1884 decimated this part of the city.

CENTRAL NAPLES

The Duomo

The **Duomo**, sharp on the right, is tucked away unassumingly from the main street, a Gothic building from the early thirteenth century (though with a late-nineteenth-century neo-Gothic facade) dedicated to the patron saint of the city, San Gennaro. The church – and saint – are key reference points for Neapolitans: San Gennaro was martyred at Pozzuoli, just outside Naples, in 305 under the purges of Diocletian. When his body was transferred here, tradition has it that two phials of his blood liquefied in the bishop's hands, since which time the "miracle" has continued to repeat itself no less than three times a year – on the first Saturday in May (when a procession leads from the church of Santa Chiara to the cathedral) and on September 19 and December 16. There is still much superstition surrounding this event: San Gennaro is seen as the saviour and protector of Naples, and if the blood refuses to liquefy – which luckily is rare – disaster is supposed to befall the city, and many still wait with bated breath to see if the miracle has occurred. Interestingly, one of the few times this century Gennaro's blood hasn't turned was in 1941, an event followed by Vesuvius's last eruption. The last time was in May 1988, the day after which Naples lost an important football match to their intense rivals, Milan.

The miraculous liquefaction takes place during a special mass in full view of the congregation – a service it's perfectly possible to attend (see below for a note on procedure), though the church authorities have yet to allow any close scientific examination of the blood or the "miraculous" process. Whatever the truth of the miracle, there's no question it's still a significant event in the Neapolitan calendar, and one of the more bizarre of the city's institutions.

The first chapel on the right as you walk into the cathedral is dedicated to San Gennaro and holds the precious phials of the saint's blood and his skull in a silver bust-reliquary from 1305. On the other side of the church, the basilica of Santa Restituta is almost a church in its own right, officially the oldest structure in Naples, erected by Constantine in 324 and supported by columns that were taken from a temple to Apollo on this site. The baptistery, too, contains relics from very early Christian times, including a late-fifth-century structure preserving fragments of contemporary mosaics and a font believed to have been taken from a temple to Dionysos. Downstairs, the crypt of San Gennaro is one of the finest examples of Renaissance art in Naples, founded by Cardinal Carafa and holding the tombs of both San Gennaro and Pope Innocent IV.

Spaccanapoli

Across Via Duomo, Via Tribunali continues on past **Piazza Girolimini**, on which a plaque marks the house where, in 1668, Giambattista Vico was born – now ironically the home of a well-known Camorra family. Vico was a late-Renaissance Neapolitan philosopher who advanced theories of cyclical history which were far ahead of their time and still echo through twentieth-century thinking: James Joyce's *Finnegans Wake* was based on his writings. Vico lived all his life in this district and was buried in the church of **Girolimini** (entrance on Via Duomo).

Further on down Via Tribunali, on the left, the church of **San Lorenzo Maggiore** is a light, spacious Gothic church, unspoiled by later additions and with a soaring Gothic ambulatory at its apse – unusual in Italy, even more so in Naples, where garishly embellished church interiors are the order of the day. It's a mainly fourteenth-century building, though with a much later facade, built during the reign of the Angevin king Robert the Wise on the site of a Roman basilica – remains of which are in the cloisters. In a way it was at the centre of the golden age that Naples enjoyed under Robert, the focus of its cultural activity. Petrarch stayed for a while in the adjacent convent, and Boccaccio is said to have

THE MIRACLE OF SAN GENNARO

If you're in Naples at the right time it's possible to attend the service to witness the **liquefaction of San Gennaro's blood**, but you must be sure to arrive at the cathedral early. The mass starts at 9am and queues begin to form two hours before that; arrive much after 7am and there's a chance you won't get in. Once the line of carabinieri have opened up the church everyone one will make a dash for the front; for a good view of the proceedings you'll have to join them – and pushing and shoving is, incidentally, very much part of the procedure. The atmosphere in the church throughout the service is a boisterous one. The preliminary mass goes on for some time, the chancel of the church ringed by armed policemen and flanked by a determined press and photographic corps, until a procession leads out of the saint's chapel holding the (still solid) phial of the blood aloft, to much applause and neck-craning, and cries of "Viva San Gennaro". After ten minutes or so of emotional imprecations the reliquary is taken down from its holder and inspected – at which point, hopefully, it is declared to tumultous applause and cheering that the saint's blood is indeed now liquid, and the phial is shaken to prove the point. Afterwards the atmosphere is a festive one, stallholders setting up outside the church and the devout queueing up to kiss the phial containing the liquefied blood – a process which goes on for a week.

met the model for his Fiammetta, believed to be Robert's daughter, during mass here.

You're now in the city's busiest and most architecturally rich quarter, the so-called **SPACCANAPOLI** or "split-Naples" that's the real heart of the old city. Cut down to its other main axis, **Via San Biagio dei Libra** by way of **Via San Gregorio Armeno**, a street specialising in the making of *presepi* or Christmas cribs. This is a Neapolitan tradition, kept up to this day, and the workshops along here start turning out the often-inventive creations well before Christmas. The church of **San Gregorio in Armeno** on the same street is also worth a quick look, frescoed by the late-seventeenth-century Neapolitan artist Luca Giordano.

There's more work by Giordano back on Via Duomo, in the **Museo Filangieri** (Mon–Fri 9am–1pm, Sat & Sun 9am–2pm; L2000), housed in the knobbly fifteenth-century Palazzo Cuomo and made up of the collection of Prince Gaetano Filangieri, reassembled after the original collection was burned by the Nazis in 1943. Giordano was easily the most prolific of all the Neapolitan painters, known as *Luca fa presto* or "Luca paint quickly" for his astonishing output. He was the pupil of another well known Neapolitan painter, Jose Ribera (otherwise known as "Il Spagnoletto"), whose work is also here, alongside the canvases of his contemporary and similar stylist Mattia Preti, and an assortment of porcelain, old manuscripts and other bits and pieces.

More compellingly, west down Via San Biagio leads to the **Largo di Corpo di Nilo**, where a Roman statue of a reclining old man is a representation of the Nile, sculpted in Nero's time, and has a habit, it's claimed, of whispering to women as they walk by. The church nearby, **Sant'Angelo a Nilo**, has sculpture by Michelozzo and Donatello, the first Renaissance work to be seen in Naples, but it's often closed; try your luck early morning. Further on, **Piazza San Domenico Maggiore** is marked by the **Guglia di San Domenico** – one of the whimsical Baroque obelisks that pop up all over the city, built in 1737. The **church** of the same name flanks the north side of the square, an originally – though much messed about – Gothic building from 1289, one of whose chapels holds a miraculous painting of the *Crucifixion* which is said to have spoken to Saint Thomas Aquinas during his time at the adjacent monastery.

North of here, Via de Sanctis leads off right to one of the city's odder monuments, the **Capella Sansevero** (Mon–Fri 10am–1pm & 5–7pm, Sat & Sun 10am–1pm; L2000), the tomb-chapel of the di Sangro family decorated by the sculptor Guiseppe Sammartino in the mid-eighteenth century. The decoration, at least, is unique, the centrepiece a carving of a dead *Christ*, laid out flat and covered with a veil of stark and remarkable realism, not least because it was carved out of a single piece of marble. Even more accomplished is the veiled figure of *Modesty* on the left, and, on the right, its twin *Disillusionment*, in the form of a woeful figure struggling with the marble netting of his own disenchantment. Look, too, at the effusive Deposition on the high altar, and the memorial above the doorway which shows one Cecco di Sangro climbing out of his tomb, sword in hand. You might also want to take a look downstairs. The man responsible for the chapel, Prince Raimondo, was a well-known eighteenth-century alchemist, and down here are the results of some of his experiments: two bodies under glass, their capillaries and most of their organs preserved by a mysterious liquid developed by the prince – who, incidentally, was excommunicated by the pope for such practices. Even now they make for gruesome sights – not for the queasy.

Continuing west, Via San Biagio becomes Via San Benedetto Croce, named after the twentieth-century philosopher who spent much of his life in this neighbourhood, living in the palace at no. 12. A little way down, the street broadens out at Piazza del Gesù Nuovo, centring on another ornate **Guglia**, this one from 1750. On the right, the **Gesù Nuovo** church is most notable for its lava-stone facade, originally part of a fifteenth-century palace which stood here, prickled with pyramids that give it an impregnable, prison-like air. The inside is as gaudy as you might expect, in part decorated by the Neapolitan-Spanish painter Ribera.

Facing the Gesù church, the church of **Santa Chiara** is quite different, a Provençal-Gothic structure built in 1328 that was completely gutted by the last war and rebuilt with a bare Gothic austerity that's pleasing after the excesses opposite. There's not very much to see inside, only the tombs of the Angevin monarchs, including Robert the Wise at the altar, showing the king in a monk's habit. But the attached convent, established by Robert's wife, Sancia, has a cloister (entrance to the left of the church) that is truly one of the gems of the city, a shady haven lushly planted and furnished with benches and low walls covered with colourful majolica tiles depicting bucolic scenes of life outside.

Corso Umberto I, Piazza Municipio and the Palazzo Reale

Off the far left corner of Piazza Garibaldi, **Corso Garibaldi** runs down to the sea, past the main Circumvesuviana terminal and, on the right, the **Porta Nolana**, a solid-looking Aragonese gateway that signals the entrance to Naples' main fish market – a grouping of streets lined with a wonderful array of stalls piled high with wriggling displays of fish and seafood. Behind, towards the water, the church of **Santa Maria del Carmine** dates back to the thirteenth century and is traditionally the church of the poor in Naples, particularly fishermen and mariners – the main port area is close by. Axel Munthe, the Swedish writer and resident of Cápri, used to sleep here after tending to victims of the 1884 cholera outbreak.

Just west, the still war-damaged **Piazza del Mercato** was for centuries home to the city's scaffold, and is a bleak, dusty square even now. There's little to detain you in this part of town, and you may as well cut back up to **Corso Umberto I**, which spears through the old part of the city, a long straight journey from the seedy gatherings of prostitutes and kerb-crawlers at its Piazza Garibaldi end, past many of the city's more mainstream shops, to the symmetrical **Piazza Bovio** and its elegant seventeenth-century Fontana del Nettuno.

From Piazza Bovio it's a short walk down to **Piazza del Municipio**, a busy traffic junction that stretches from the ferry terminal on the water up to the Palazzo Municipale at the top, dominated by the brooding hulk of the **Castel Nuovo** opposite, erected in 1282 by the Angevins and later converted as the royal residence of the Aragon monarchs. These days it's used by the Naples and Campania councils and entry is sometimes restricted, but saunter up to the entrance for a look at the triumphal arch that it incorporates – built in 1454 to commemorate the taking of the city by Alfonso I, the first Aragon ruler, and showing details of his triumph topped by a rousing statue of Saint Michael.

Just beyond the castle, on the left, the **Teatro San Carlo** is open for tours daily from 9am to noon, though you'll need to hang around and join a group. It's an oddly unimpressive building from the outside, but once inside you can see why this theatre was the envy of Europe when it opened in 1737 in time for Charles of Bourbon's birthday, for whom it was built. It's still the largest opera house in Italy, and one of the most distinguished in the world. Opposite, the **Galleria Umberto I** has fared less well over the years, its high arcades, erected in 1887, remarkably empty of the teeming life that characterises the rest of Naples, and in the evening even something of a danger spot. Its rather downbeat collection of shops can't compete with those of, say, Milan's Galleria, built ten years earlier – though you'll still pay way over the odds in its rather grotty cafés.

Come out of the Galleria and you're on **Piazza Trieste e Trento**, more a roundabout than a piazza, whose life you can watch while sipping a pricey drink on the terrace of the sleek **Caffè Gambrinus**. To the left, **Piazza del Plebiscito** is another attempt at civic grandeur gone badly wrong, its curve of columns – modelled on Bernini's piazza for St Peter's in Rome – shabby and belittled by the expanse of cars which use the square as a parking space, not to mention the buses which line up in front. The church of **San Francescó di Paola** in the centre is no great success either, a copy of the Pantheon in Rome, whose attempts at classical majesty are thwarted by the traffic and graffiti – and only really work once you're standing under the impressively enormous dome.

Opposite, the **Palazzo Reale** (Mon–Sat 9am–2pm, Sun 9am–1pm; L3000) manages better than most of the buildings around here to retain some semblance of its former glories, though it's a bland, derivative building for the most part and even a bit of a fake, thrown up hurriedly in 1602 to accommodate Philip II on a visit here and never actually occupied by a monarch long-term. Indeed it's more of a monument to monarchies than monarchs, the various dynasties that ruled Naples by proxy for so long represented in the niches of the facade, from Roger the Norman to Vittorio Emanuele II, taking in among others Alfonso I and a slightly comic Murat on the way. Upstairs, the palace's first-floor rooms are decorated with fine Baroque excesses of gilded furniture, tromp l'oeil ceilings, great overbearing tapestries and lots and lots of undistinguished seventeenth- and eighteenth-century paintings. Best bits are the chapel, on the far side of the central square (you may have to ask someone to open this for you), with its finely worked altarpiece; the little theatre – the first room on the right – which is refreshingly restrained after the rest of the palace; and the terrace, which gives good views over the port and the forbidding Castel Nuovo. Look also at the original bronze doors of the palace at the bottom of the dwarfing main staircase, cast in 1468 and showing scenes from Ferdinand of Aragon's struggle against the local barons. The cannonball wedged in the bottom left-hand panel dates from a naval battle between the French and the Genovese that took place while the former were pillaging the doors from the palace.

Just south of Piazza del Plebiscito, Via Santa Lucia curves around towards the sea, the main artery of the **SANTA LUCIA** district – for years the city's most famed and characteristic neighbourhood, site of a lively fish market and source of most of the *O Sole Mio*-type cliches about Naples you've ever heard. It's a much less neighbourly place now, home to most of the city's poshest hotels on the streets around and along the seafront Via Partenope, though one or two decent restaurants make it a better than average place to come and eat. Down on the waterfront, a grouping of seafood restaurants cluster around the grey mass of the **Castel dell'Ovo** or "egg-castle" – so named because of the story that it was built over an egg placed here by Virgil in Roman times: Colosseum-like, if the egg breaks then Naples will fall. Actually it was built by the Hohenstaufen king Frederick II and extended by the Angevins, and nowadays belongs to the military and is off-limits to ordinary visitors. But you can walk over the short causeway that connects its small island to the mainland and eat at one of the surrounding restaurants – which make an atmospheric if not always culinarily memorable place to spend the evening; *La Bersagliera* on the landward side is best.

From Piazza Trieste e Trento to Capodimonte

Piazza Trieste e Trento marks the beginning of the city's main shopping street, **Via Toledo** – or, to give it its official name, Via Roma – which leads north in a dead straight line, climbing the hill up to the National Archaeological Museum and separating two very different parts of Naples. To its right, across as far as Piazza Gesù Nuovo, the streets and buildings are modern and spacious, centring on the unmistakable mass of the central **Post Office**. The streets to the left, on the other hand, scaling the footslopes of the Vómero, are some of the city's most narrow and crowded, a grid of alleys that was laid out to house Spanish troops during the seventeenth century and is hence known now as the **Quartiere Spagnoli**. It's an enticing area, at least for visitors, in that it's what you expect to find when you come to Naples, with the buildings so close together as to barely admit any sunlight. But it's as poor a part of Italy as you'll find, home to the notorious Neapolitan *bassi* – one-room windowless dwellings that open directly onto the street – and as such a national disgrace.

Further up Via Toledo, just north of Piazza Carità on the edge of the old part of the city, the church of **Monteoliveto** was rebuilt after a sound wartime bombing but it holds some of the city's finest Renaissance art, including a sacristry frescoed by Vasari, a rather startling almost life-size *pietà* of eight figures by Guido Mazzoni (the faces are said to be portraits) and two sculptural works by Antonio Rossellino – a nativity scene and the tomb of Mary of Aragon, daughter of Ferdinand I.

Continuing on up the hill, **Piazza Dante** is another Neapolitan square which looks as if it has seen better days, designed by Luigi Vanvitelli during the eighteenth century and cutting an elegant semi-circle off to the right of the main road that focuses on the pumps of a small, grimy petrol station and a statue of Dante splotched with graffiti. There are a couple of restaurants here, and it's a turnaround point for buses, but otherwise – unless you want to cut through the seventeenth-century **Port'Alba** into the old part of the city – you may as well push on up the street to the Archaeological Museum, housed in a grandiose late-sixteenth-century army barracks on the corner of Piazza Cavour.

The Museo Archaeologico Nazionale

Mon–Sat 9am–2pm, Sun 9am–1pm; L4000; bus #110 from Piazza Garibaldi

Naples isn't really a city of museums – there's more on the streets that's worth observing on the whole, and most displays of interest are kept *in situ* in churches, palaces and the like. But the **Museo Archeologico Nazionale** is an exception, home to the Farnese collection of antiquities from Lazio and Campania, and the best of the finds from the nearby Roman sites of Pompeii and Herculaneum. Sadly, some parts of the museum are often closed "for restoration" and there's a good chance you won't be able to see it all; plus none of the exhibits are labelled, making identification at best difficult. But the most impressive sections are usually open, and it would be a shame to miss them, especially if you intend visiting the sites themselves.

The ground floor of the museum concentrates on sculpture from the **Farnese collection**, displayed at its best in the mighty Great Hall, which holds Imperial-era figures like the *Farnese Bull* and *Farnese Hercules* from the Baths of Caracalla in Rome – the former the largest piece of classical sculpture ever found. The mezzanine floor at the back holds the museum's collection of **mosaics** – remarkably preserved works all, giving a superb insight into ordinary Roman customs, beliefs and humour. All are worth looking at – images of fish, crustacea, wildlife on the banks of the Nile, a cheeky cat and quail with still-life beneath, masks and simple abstract decoration. But some highlights to look out for include a realistic *Battle Scene* (no. 10020), the *Three Musicians with Dwarf* (9985), an urbane meeting of the *Platonic Academy* (124545), and a marvellously captured *Group of Soothsayers* (124666) giving a dour and doomy consultation.

Upstairs through the *Salone della Meridiana*, which holds a sparse but fine assortment of Roman figures (notably a wonderfully strained *Atlas* and some demure female figures – Roman replicas of Greek originals), a series of rooms holds the **Campanian Wall Paintings** that are the museum's other major draw after the mosaics – lifted from the villas of Pompeii and Herculaneum, and rich in colour and invention. There are plenty here, and it's worth devoting some time to this section – some of the smallest and most easily missed works are among the most exquisite. Among those to look out for are a paternal *Achilles and Chirone* (9109); the *Sacrifice of Iphiginia* (9112) in the next room, one of the best preserved of all the murals; the dignified *Perseus Frees Andromeda* (8998); and *Theseus Victorious over the Minotaur* (9043), showing the strong figure of Theseus the subject of much wonder and admiration. Look out too for the group of four small pictures in the first main room, best of which is a depiction of a woman gathering flowers entitled *Primavera* – a fluid, impressionistic piece of work capturing both the gentleness of spring and the graceful beauty of the woman.

Beyond the murals are the actual **finds from the Campanian cities** – everyday items like glass, silver, ceramics, charred pieces of rope, even foodstuffs (petrified cakes, figs, fruit and nuts), together with a model layout of Pompeii in cork. On the other side of the first floor, there are finds from one particular house, the **Villa dei Papiri** in Herculaneum – sculptures in bronze mainly. The *Hermes at Rest* in the centre of the second room is perhaps the most arresting item, rapt with exhaustion, but around are other adept statues – of athletes, suffused with movement, a languid *Resting Satyr*, the convincingly woozy *Drunken Silenus*, and, in the final room, portrait busts of soldiers and various local big cheeses.

Around the museum ... and up to Capodimonte

To the left of the Archaeological Museum as you come out, **Piazza Cavour** is a busy traffic junction and bus stop. Beyond, Via Foria leads off east past the **Orto Botanico** (Wed & Thurs 9am–2pm or by request; ☎449.759) – founded in 1807 and a detour worth making if you're interested in such things. Perhaps more intriguing is the enormously long facade of the **Albergo dei Poveri** alongside, a workhouse built in 1751 that has been empty for years, and forms a vast, oddly derelict landmark along the top side of Piazza Carlo III.

Back in the other direction, you can either take a bus up to Capodimonte from Piazza Cavour or make the lengthy stroll via the **Catacombe di San Gennaro** (tours Fri, Sat & Sun 9.30am, 10.15am, 11am & 11.45am; L3000), on the left just before the road sweeps around to climb the steep hill, behind the huge Madre del Buon Consiglio church. These were only discovered recently, next to the originally eighth-century church of San Gennaro in Moenia, and hold early Christian frescoes and mosaics, newly restored and amazingly bright.

The Palazzo Reale di Capodimonte

Tues–Sat 9am–2pm, Sun 9am–1pm; L3000; buses #110 or #127 from Piazza Garibaldi, #160 or #161 from Piazza Dante

At the top of the hill, the **Palazzo Reale di Capidomonte** – and its extensive grounds – was the royal residence of the Bourbon King Charles III, built in 1738 and now housing the picture gallery of the Naples museum, the **Museo Nazionale di Capodimonte**. The royal apartments, on the first floor, are smaller and more downbeat than those at Caserta (see "Inland Campania"), and in many ways more enjoyable, not least because you can actually walk through the rooms freely. That said, you'll need a keen interest in the Bourbon dynasty to want to linger: highspots are the ballroom, lined with portraits of various Bourbon monarchs and other European despots, and a number of rooms of porcelain, some painted with local scenes and one in particular a sticky confection of Chinese scenes, monkeys and fruit and flowers from the Capodimonte factory here.

Upstairs, the picture gallery holds a superb collection of Renaissance paintings, though once again parts sporadically close down for restoration. Assuming all is open, there is a good group of Flemish works, including a couple of Bruegels – *The Misanthrope* and *The Blind* – and two triptychs by Joos van Cleve. Early Italian rooms take in canvases by Perugino and Pinturicchio, an elegant *Madonna and Child with Angels* by Botticelli and Lippi's soft, sensitive *Annunciation*. Later paintings include a room full of Titians, with a number of paintings of the shrewd Farnese Pope Paul III in various states of ageing and the lascivious *Danae*; Raphael's austere portrait of *Leo X* and a worldly *Clement VII* by Sebastiano del Piombo; and Bellini's impressively coloured and composed *Transfiguration*.

Chiaia, Villa Communale, Mergellina and Posillipo

Via Chiaia leads west from Piazza Trieste e Trento into a quite different Naples from the congested *vicoli* of the *centro storico* or Quartiere Spagnoli, lined with the city's fanciest shops and bending down to the **Piazza dei Martiri** – named after the column in the centre, which remembers the martyrs of various nine-teenth-century revolutions. This part of town – the **CHIAJA** neighbourhood, which spreads up the hill towards Vomero – displays a sense of order and classical elegance which is quite absent from the rest of the city centre, its buildings well preserved, the people noticeably better-heeled. From the square, you can stroll down to the waterfront and **Villa Communale** – Naples' most central city park and the place from where it's possible to appreciate the city best as a port and seafront city, the views stretching right around the Bay from the long lizard of its northern side, rising up on the right, to the gloomy shape of Vesuvius in the east – godlike behind the cranes and far-off apartment blocks of the sprawling industrial suburbs.

The park is girdled by the hum of the omnipresent Naples traffic but it makes a nice way to walk around the bay to Mergellina, particularly in the early evening when the lights of the city enhance the views. On the way you might want to take in the century-old **Aquarium** (Tues–Sat 9am–5pm, Sun 10am–7pm; L1000), though its rather glum collection of tanks containing fish, turtles, eels, octopuses and rays, together with a revolting array of pickled marine life, may put you off your dinner. Across from here, on the other side of Riviera di Chiaia, the gardens of the **Villa Pignatelli** (Tues–Sat 9am–2pm, Sun 9am–1pm; L2000) are a peaceful alternative to the Villa Communale, and the house itself, now a museum, is kept in much the same way as when it was the home of a prominent Naples family and a turn-of-the-century meeting place for the city's elite. It's tastefully furnished and by Naples standards low-key, its handful of rooms holding books, porcelain, the odd painting and a set of photos signed by various aristocrats and royal personages.

Villa Communale stretches around the bay for a good mile, at the far end of which lie the harbour and main square – Piazza Sannazzaro – of the **MERGELLINA** district, a good place to come and eat at night and a terminus for hydrofoils to the Bay's islands. There's not a lot else here, only the dense **Parco Virgiliano** (9am–1pm) north of Piazza Sannazzaro, which holds the spot where the Roman poet Virgil is supposed to be buried, marked by a Roman monument. Of the other neighbourhoods nearby, the **FUORIGROTTA** district, the other side of the Mergellina hill, is not of interest unless you're going to a football match, since it's home to Napoli's San Paolo Stadium (see "Listings" for details). Ditto **POSILLIPO**, further along the shore, which is an upmarket suburb of the city stacked with fat villas and pockets – though, again, people do come out here to eat.

The hills above: Vómero

Like Chiaia below, and Mergellina to the west, **VÓMERO** – the district topping the hill immediately above the old city – is one of Naples' modern additions, a light, airy and relatively peaceful quarter connected most directly with the teeming morass below by funicular railway. It's a large area but mostly residential, and you're unlikely to want to stray beyond the streets which fan out from each of the three funicular stations, centering on **Piazza Vanvitelli**.

Come up on the Montesanto funicular (see map) and you're well placed for a visit to two of the buildings which dominate Naples, way above the old city. Five minutes' walk away, the **Castel Sant'Elmo** occupies Naples' highest point and is an impressive fortification, a fourteenth-century structure once used for incarcerating political prisoners and now lording it grandly over the streets below. But it's the same story with this as so many other historical structures in Naples: you can't get in, and no one quite seems to know why, though the military have sole use.

Beyond the castle, the fourteenth-century **Certosa San Martino** has the best views over the bay, and is also accessible, now being home to the **Museo Nazionale di San Martino** (Tues–Sat 9am–2pm, Sun 9am–1pm; L3000). Much of this, too, often appears to be under restoration, but the monastery itself, throughly Baroqued in the seventeenth century, and the views from its cunningly constructed terrace, are well worth the entrance fee – short of climbing Vesuvius as good a vista of the entire Bay of Naples as you'll get. The church, on the left of the entrance, is typically garish Baroque, with a colourful pavement and an *Adoration of the Shepherds* by Reni above the altar. In the museum proper, there are paintings by Neapolitan masters – Ribera, Stanzione, Vaccaro – and other rather dusty bits and pieces rescued from churches and the odd minor aristocrat, as well as historical and maritime sections displaying models of ships, and documents, coins and costumes recording the era of the Kingdom of Naples. The Baroque cloisters are lovely, though again rather gone to seed. The display of *presepi* or Christmas cribs is probably the most remarkable – and unique – aspect of the museum, the craft of which is peculiar to the city and continued avidly today (see above).

There's another museum up here, ten minutes' walk away in the Neoclassical **Villa Floridiana**, close to the Chiaia funicular, whose lush grounds (daily 9am–7.30pm) might make a good place for a picnic. The **Museo Duca di Martino** (Tues–Sat 9am–2pm, Sun 9am–1pm; L2000) is, however, of fairly specialist interest, a porcelain collection such as you've never seen before, varying from the beautifully simple to the outrageously kitsch – hideous teapots, ceramic asparagus sticks and the like. There are examples (of course) of Capodimonte and Meissen, and eighteenth-century English, French, German and Viennese work – as well as a handful of pieces of Qing dynasty Chinese porcelain and Murano glass, and exquisite non-ceramic items like inlaid ivory boxes and panels. On the whole, a small museum that's worth taking in before salivating over yet another view, this time from just below the villa.

Eating, drinking and nightlife

It's arguable that **Neapolitan cuisine** is Italy's best – simple dishes cooked with fresh, healthy ingredients that have none of the richness or pretentions of the north. Also, as a not primarily tourist-geared city, most restaurants are family-run places used by locals and as such generally serve good food at reasonable prices. Seafood is good, as is all pasta (Naples is the home of spaghetti), and specialities include *spaghetti alle vongole*, *zuppa di cozze* (steamed mussels served with hot pepper sauce) and *pasta e fagiole* – frugal dishes originally but nowadays firmly in the mainstream. Naples is also the home of the pizza, and there's no better place in Italy to eat it, at a solid core of almost obsessively unchanged places that still only serve the (very few) traditional varieties. Eating on your feet, too, is nowhere difficult. Or you can pick something up from the city's streetmarkets – La Forcella or the fish market at Porta Nolana.

Cafés and snacks

Attanasio, Vico Ferrovia, off Via Milano. Bakery that specialises in *sfoglia tella* (ricotta-stuffed pastries).

Gambrinus, Via Chiaia 1–2. The oldest and best-known of Neapolitan cafés, founded in 1861. Not cheap, but its aura of peeling gentility may appeal.

Motta, Via Toledo 152. Large and basic café serving both sit-down and take-away food and drink.

Scaturchio, Piazza San Domenico. Another elegant old Naples standard, it's been serving coffee and pastries in the heart of Spaccanapoli for decades.

Restaurants and pizzerias

Alle Brace, Via S. Spaventa 14–16. Good cheap alternative just off Piazza Garibaldi.

Bellini, Via Santa Maria di Constantinopoli 80. One of the city's most famous and longest established restaurants. Great pizza, and with a very good selection of other dishes – though more expensive than some of the more basic pizzerias.

Bersagliera, Borgo Marinaro. Fine food, though inevitably you pay for the location, slap next to the Castel dell'Ovo, and the *"O Sole Mio"* minstrels who wander between the tables.

Brandi, Salita Sant'Anna di Palazzo 1–2, off Via Chiaia. Possibly Naples' most famous pizzeria, said to be where they invented the *pizza margherita* in 1889 in honour of the visiting Queen Margherita of Savoy. Very friendly, serving pasta and (excellent) pizzas from L3000.

California, Via Santa Lucia 101. Another Naples institution, though a rather different one, serving a menu that's an odd hybrid of American and Italian specialities. Best for its full American breakfasts.

Da Gennarino, Via Capuana alla Medelena 1–2. Again one of the best pizzerias in the city, well situated (opposite the Porta Capuana) for hungry arrivals by train. Very cheap; outside seating only.

Gloria, Piazza Sannazzaro 70. Good-value Mergellina restaurant with tables outside and a wide choice of seafood dishes.

Gorizia, Via Bernini 29. Excellent pizza and pasta dishes in this Vomero restaurant.

Leone d'Oro, Piazza Dante. Pleasant centrally placed restaurant with outdoor seating and excellent food. Try the *pasta e fagiole*.

Lombardi, Via B. Croce 59. Another well-known and well-respected pizza restaurant, and with a varied menu besides pizza.

O Marenaro, Via Casanova. Around the corner from Piazza Garibaldi, opposite the *CTP* bus station, a great place to try *zuppe di cozze*, with tables outside.

Di Matteo, Via dei Tribunali 94. Unpretentious and cheap *centro storico* pizzeria.

Da Michele, Via Cesare Sersale 1–3. The most determinedly traditional of all the Naples pizzerias and possibly the best, offering just two varieties – *marinara* (with tomato, garlic and oil) or *margherita* (with tomato and cheese). Tucked away off Corso Umberto I in the Forcella district.

Da Pasqualino, Piazza Sannazzaro 79. Inexpensive Mergellina restaurant with outdoor seating and great seafood and pizzas.

Da Peppino Avellinese, Via S. Spaventa 31. The most welcoming and best value restaurant of the many options on and around Piazza Garibaldi. Used by tourists and locals alike.

Port'Alba, Via Port'Alba 18. Old-established pizzeria just off Piazza Dante that has a wide menu besides pizza. Said to be the oldest pizzeria in Italy.

Spaghetteria, Via G. Paladino 7. Inexpensive plates of pasta in a youthful restaurant patronised by students from the nearby university.

Trianon (da Ciro), Via Colletta 46. Nearby rival to *Da Michele* (above), but serving a wider range. From L3000.

Nightlife and culture

The ease of accessibility on public transport, and the fact that much of Naples' youth lives out in the suburbs anyway, means that the Naples **nightlife** scene stretches right around the Bay, with some of the best of the area's clubs and discos situated in the beach areas north or south of the city. The *Mito* and *Music on the Rocks*, both in Positano, draw crowds in summer, as does the *Blu Club* in Sorrento – a large outdoor disco with two bars and a big dancefloor. The *Metropolis*, in Ischitella, north of Cuma on the road to Formia, is also popular, though difficult to get to without your own transport.

In the city proper, some people like to start their evening at the bars of Borgo Marinaro, near the Castel dell'Ovo, munching on *code d'aragosta* (special cakes shaped like lobster tails) before moving on to the *Virgilio* open-air disco in Posillipo, just below the Parco della Rimembranza (admission L7000, open until 4am). There are other clubs in Posillipo, a number along Via Manzoni, try *Jimmy Club*, Via Manzoni 28, or *Zeppelin Club*, Via Manzoni 176.

Other clubs are more down-to-earth, attracting a crowd more into posing than dancing – punks and goths and the like. The area behind Villa Communale is a popular area for bars, which group along the streets leading up to Piazza Amedeo. For drinking and music, try the *Chiatamoon Sax Café* on Via Chiatamone, *Café della Luna* just off Via Bisignano, or *Chez Moi*, Parco Margherita 13. For something a little different, there's *Riot*, housed in an old palazzo on Via San Biagio dei Librai, close to Via Duomo, which is popular with a self-consciously alternative crowd. Or, if you're more into serious **culture** than late-night dancing, there's always the *Teatro San Carlo*, whose opera season runs from Decmber to May; ticket information on ☎797.2370.

Listings

Airlines *Alitalia*, Via Medina 41–42 (☎542.5111); *British Airways*, Piazza Municipio 2 (☎400.144); *Pan Am*, Via Cervantes 55 (☎209.456); *TWA*, Via Partenope 23 (☎412.834).

Airport enquiries ☎780.5763.

Books English-language books from *Universal*, Rione Sirignano 1.

Bus enquiries *CTP* station, Piazza Porta Capuana, for Caserta, Cápua, etc. (☎554.0507); Piazza Garibaldi, for Benevento, Avellino, etc (☎334.677); *SITA*, for Salerno (☎552.2176).

Car hire Most of the larger car-hire firms group along along the seafront near the Castel dell'Ovo. *Avis*, Via Partenope 32 (☎407.333); *Europcar*, Via Partenope 38 (☎401.454); *Hertz*, Via Partenope 29 (☎400.400); *Maggiore*, Via Cervantes 92 (☎321.900); *InterRent*, Via Partenope 14 (☎422.332).

Consulates *UK*, Via Crispi 122 (☎ 663.511); *USA*, Piazza della Repubblica (☎660.966).

Emergencies ☎113. The main police station is at Via Medina 75 (☎794.1111).

Exchange Outside normal banking hours you can change money and travellers cheques at the booth inside Stazione Centrale (daily 7am–9pm).

Football The Stadio di San Paolo in Fuorigrotta is the home of the championship-winning *Napoli* side, one of Italy's best and most consistent teams, with Diego Maradona as their (now rather overweight) star player. Matches take place on Sundays; ☎615.623 for details; tickets cost upwards of L15,000. To get to the ground, take the Ferrovia Cumana from Montesanto to Campi Flegrei and walk five minutes to Piazzale Vincenzo Tecchio.

Funerals Death is big business in Naples, and if you're lucky you can still see the incredibly ornate traditional black hearses pulled by teams of horses on the streets of the city – the preferred way to go of Neapolitan fat cats and higher-ranking Camorra members. There are other, equally bizarre Neapolitan customs regarding death: a white hearse, for example, means a child or virgin has died; and despite official discouragement some corpses are still dug up by their families after burial, in a bizarre celebration of the dead centring on All Souls Day – November 2.

Hospital ☎751.3177 or go to the Guardia Medica Permanente in the Palazzo Municipio, open 24 hr.

Left luggage At Stazione Centrale, on the right as you come out.

Lottery Along with San Gennaro and Diego Maradona, the Lottery is a fanatically observed institution in Naples. Winning the lottery is seen, in a way, as the ultimate triumph over the system, and superstitions around it are rife – to the extent that there's even a book, *La Smorfia*, which interprets the meaning behind each lottery number. There are also people, called *assisti* (literally "guided ones"), who claim to have supernatural access to knowledge of what the winning numbers are to be. If you're keen to see the lottery draw, it's made every Saturday noon at the Ufficio Lotto on Via San Biagio dei Librai, to the accompaniment of much noise and hysteria.

Pharmacy Late-night pharmacies work on a rotation system. ☎192 for addresses of current ones. There's also a pharmacy at Stazione Centrale open Mon–Sat 8am–8pm.

Post office The main post office is in the enormous building on Piazza Matteotti, just off Via Toledo. Open Mon–Fri 8am–7.40pm, Sat 8.30am–noon.

Taxis Ranks at the railway station, on Piazza Trieste e Trento, or ☎364.444 or ☎364.340.

Telephones *ASST* at Stazione Centrale, open 24hr, though large queues early evening. The *ASST* at Via Depretis 40, also open 24hr, is quieter. *SIP* in Galleria Umberto (Mon–Sat 8am–9.30pm) is usually chaos.

Tours The Naples ASST run guided tours of various parts of the city every Sunday morning beginning at 10.30 (details on ☎418.744). Between June and September you can also cruise Naples harbour by night on the *Love Boat*, which leaves from the Via Caracciolo harbour, near the US Consulate, several times each evening for an hour or so's run out past Posillipo. Price L3500 per person;

details on ☎575.1532. Finally a number of companies also offer guided tours of places of interest outside the city – Pompeii, Cápri, Ischia and suchlike – for anything between L25,000 and L50,000 and lasting either a half or full day. Try *CIT*, Piazza Municipio 70 (☎552.5426), or *Aritur*, Piazza Trieste e Trento 7–8 (☎400.487).

Train enquiries Phone ☎ 264.644. Or go to the information booths at the station and be prepared to queue (daily 7.30am–10pm).

Travel agents *CTS*, Via A. de Gasperi 25 (☎552.0074), for discount tickets, budget flights, etc.

THE BAY OF NAPLES

For the Romans, Campania and particularly the **Bay of Naples** was the land of plenty, a blessed region of mild climate, gorgeous scenery and an accessible location that made it a favourite vacation and retirement area for the city's nobility. Patrician Rome built villas here by the score – Hadrian had a house at Baia, for example – and towns like **Pompeii** and **Herculaneum** were among the richest in the Imperial era: the "Bay of Luxury" Cicero called it. Later, when Naples became the final stop on northerners' Grand Tours, the Bay became no less fabled, the relics of its heady Roman period only adding to the charm for most travellers.

And it's a charm which is easy to detect – the landscape is still there and still as impressive, and the offshore islands of **Cápri**, **Ischia** and **Prócida** are no less enticing than they ever were, if immeasurably more crowded. But the fact is that these days it's hard to tell where Naples ends and the countryside begins. Northern money and Camorra speculation mean that the city now sprawls around the Bay in an industrial and residential mess that is quite at odds with the region's popular image, and whatever it was once like, the environment close to the city is pretty much beyond recall. You need to head some way out of the city before reaching anywhere you might want to stay for longer than an afternoon, especially if you want to swim. Even if the water is clean, the proximity of the Bay's industry will make you think it isn't; and it's only when you reach **Sorrento** in the east, **Pozzuoli** in the west, or any of the islands, that you really feel free of it all. Luckily this is easy by way of the extra-urban train services out of Naples (see "Getting Around", above), or one of the Bay's plentiful ferry connections: most of the places mentioned below are convenient for day-trips – though many obviously demand longer.

West from Naples: Pozzuoli and the Campi Flegrei

The area around Naples is one of the most unstable in the world. Vesuvius is only the best known of the many and varied examples of volcanic activity in the province, the most concentrated instances – volcanic craters, hot springs, *fumaroles* – being northwest of the city in the region known as the **Campi Flegrei** (Fiery Fields). This is the *Phlegrean Fields* of classical times, a mysterious place in turn

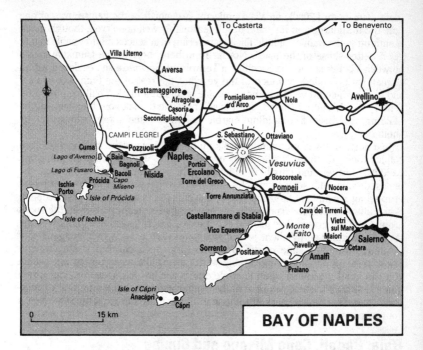

To Caserta   To Benevento

Villa Literno

Aversa

Frattamaggiore
Afragola
Casoria
Secondigliano

Pomigliano
d'Arco   Nola   Avellino

CAMPI FLEGREI   S. Sebastiano   Ottaviano

Cuma   Pozzuoli
Lago d'Averno   Baia   Bagnoli   Naples   Vesuvius
Lago di Fusaro   Bacoli   Nisida   Portici
Ischia   Prócida   Capo   Ercolano
Porto   Miseno   Torre del Greco   Boscoreale
Isle of Prócida   Pompeii   Nocera

Torre Annunziata

Isle of Ischia   Cava dei Tirreni
Castellammare di Stabia   Vietri
Monte   sul Mare
Vico Equense   Faito   Maiori   Salerno
Ravello   Cetara
Sorrento   Positano   Amalfi
Praiano

Isle of Cápri
Anacápri   Cápri

0   15 km

BAY OF NAPLES

mythologised by Homer and Virgil as the entrance to Hades and eulogised as the Elysian Fields for its beauty. These days most of the mystery is gone – like most of the Bay, the presence of Naples dominates in the form of new building and suburbs – and much of the volcanic activity is extinct. But parts of the area still retain some of the doomy associations that first drew the ancients here, and there are some substantial remains of their presence – not to mention some of the best and most accessible of Naples' nearby beaches.

Pozzuoli and the Solfatara

The first town that can really be considered free of Naples' sprawl is **POZZUOLI**, which sits on a stout promontory jutting out from the slender crescent of volcanic hills behind. It's a workaday little place, nothing special but likeable enough, with ferry connections to the islands of Prócida and Ischia. And although you wouldn't want to stay here (unless you're a camper; see "Finding a place to stay" above), it's a good first stop before travelling on to the rest of the Campi Flegrei.

Pozzuoli has suffered more than most of the towns around here from the area's volcanic activity. Twenty years ago a minor tremor caused a number of buildings to collapse, and subsidence is still a major – and carefully monitored – problem. Best time to come is on Sunday, when the whole town turns out for the morning fish market, afterwards eating lunch in one of the many waterfront restaurants – *Del Capitano*, *Grottino d'Amara* and *Lampadara* are all good. In town there are a number of relics of the Romans' liking for the place. The **Amphitheatre Flavio** (daily 9am–5pm; L2000), on Via Domiziana just north of the centre, was at one time the third largest in Italy and is still reasonably well preserved, though much is shut off to the public – a little illicit clambering over fences might enable you to get a better sense of the place. Not far from here, beyond the Cumana station between Via Roma and Via Sacchini, a **Temple of Serapide** sits enclosed within a small park, flooded for much of the year but the rest of the time accessible – and in fact since proved to be not a temple at all but a market hall from the first century AD. It's pretty ruined, but it is still possible to make out the shape of the building, its three freestanding marble columns eaten away halfway up by shellfish.

Just north of town, ten minutes' walk up the hill beyond the main station from Naples (bus #152 from Naples stops outside), the **Solfatara** (daily 8.30am–7pm; L2000) is further, and tangible, evidence of the volcanic nature of the area, the exposed crater of a semi-extinct volcano – into which you can walk – that hasn't erupted for a couple of thousand years; in fact, it was a major tourist attraction in Roman times too. Not surprisingly, it's a weird place: steam rises from the rocks around and the grey-yellow ground is hot to the touch (and sounds hollow to the stamp), emitting eerily silent jets or *fumaroles* that leave the air pungent with sulphurous fumes. Some of the *fumaroles* have been covered artificially with brick, creating an almost unbearably warm, sauna-like environment into which you can bend if you can stand it, while others are just left open. You can hire a guide (L12,000) to steer you clear of the dangerous parts, but it's not really necessary – there's a clearly marked route and it's far more fun exploring the site on your own.

Baia, Bacoli, Capo Miseno and Cumae

The next town along from Pozzuoli, reached in fifteen minutes by train from the Cumana station, is **BAIA**, a small port with a tiny, rather unattractive bit of beach and a set of Imperial-era Roman ruins piling up on the hill above. This was one of the Bay's most favoured spots in Roman times, a trendy resort at which all the most fashionable of the city's patricians had villas: the emperor Hadrian died here in AD 138 and Nero was rumoured to have murdered his mother in Baia.

Immediately behind the station, remains of some enormous Roman baths leave you in no doubt of the town's function in ancient times. Steps lead up from the station square to the entrance to the **excavations** (Tues–Sun 9am–sunset; L2000) of a Roman palace of the first to the fourth century AD, which are structured across several levels. It's hard to tell what's what here – the site is very ruined and there's little or no labelling – but it's an evocative location, and can afford a happy hour of stumbling around among the stones and passages. Follow the steps down from the entrance level to the first terrace of the palace: the rooms on the right contain patches of Roman stucco-work depicting birds and mythical creatures, and a statue of Mercury, beheaded by vandals a decade ago. Below are the remains of a small theatre, and an open space – a former *piscina* – bordered on one side by a pretty loggia and now used for summer drama performances.

There are more ruins inland from Baia at **Lago d'Averno**, where Agrippa constructed a military harbour in 37 BC. The lake itself is the *Lake Avernus* of antiquity, a volcanic crater that the Greeks believed – and Virgil later wrote – was the entrance to Hades: birds flying over were said to suffocate with the toxic fumes that rose from the lake's murky waters, and sacrifices were regularly made here to the dark deities that lurked beneath the gloomy surface. These days it's a more cheerful place, no longer surrounded by thick forest (this was cut down by Agrippa), although there's not really any other reason to come – the water of the nearby sea is much more enticing for swimming.

A few kilometres down the coast from Baia, **BACOLI** has more Roman remains (a Roman swimming pool, the *piscina mirabile*) and a small stretch of beach – more appealing than Baia's; though if it's **beaches** you're after you'd be well advised to stay on the bus until **MISENO**, where, just beyond the lake of the same name, there's a very broad strand. You'll not find it empty by any means, but it's large enough to find yourself a space – and beach bars and restaurants abound.

If you've the energy, you can make the stiff climb to **Capo Miseno** from here, an almost level-topped hump at the furthest tip of the Campi Flegrei, though it's only really worth it if the weather's clear – the views back to Naples and up the coast to Gaeta are the main attraction. Otherwise push up to **CUMAE**, home to one of the most lauded of the ancient sites hereabouts.

The town of **Cumae** was the first Greek colony on the Italian mainland, a source of settlers for other colonies (Naples was originally settled by Greeks from Cumae) and a centre of Hellenistic civilisation. Later it was home to the so-called Cumaean Sibyl, from whom Tarquinius purchased the Sibylline Books that laid down the laws for the Republic. The **site** (Tues–Sun 9am–sunset; L2000), a short walk from the bus stop, is spread over a large area and not at all comprehensively excavated. But the only part you're likely to want to see forms a tight nucleus close to the entrance. The best known feature is the *Cave of the Sibyl*, a long dark corridor that was home to the most famous of the ancient oracles. Rectangular in shape, with light admitted from a series of niches in the western wall, the Sibyl used to dispense her wisdom from the three large chambers at the far end of the forty-foot passageway, the most famous occasion being when Aeneas came here to consult her – an event recorded by the lines of Virgil posted up either side of the entrance.

But the best of Cumae is still to come. Climb up the steps to the right of the cave entrance and follow the winding Via Sacra past a constructed belvedere on the left and the fairly scanty remains of a temple on the right to the Acropolis. Here you'll find the remains of a temple to Jupiter, but it's the views that you really come for: from the far side of the temple way south across the shellfish-filled **Lago Fusaro** and the bottom corner of the coast; and, if you clamber down from the other side of the temple, north up the curving coast to the Gulf of Gaeta.

The coast north of Cumae

The coast north of Cumae up to the Lazio border is known as the **Costa Domiziana**, after the Roman road that leads north from here to join up with the Via Appia, and looks, at least from the heights of Cumae itself, enticingly empty – which it can be if you've a car to reach its more isolated spots. But most of the resorts along this stretch of coast are polluted and over-developed and hard to recommend for any kind of visit. **PINETA A MARE** is the closest resort to Cumae and fairly typical – tacky, rather dirty and, according to local newspaper reports, something of a haunt of warring drug dealers. **BAIA DOMIZIA**, further north, close to the Lazio border, is much the same.

East from Naples: Ercolano to Sorrento

The coast **east from Naples** is no better, perhaps even a little worse than the coast west of the city – the Circumvesuviana train edging out through derelict industrial buildings and dense housing that squeezes ever closer to the track. Most people come here for the ancient sights of Herculaneum and Pompeii, or to scale Vesuvius – or they skip the lot for the resort town of Sorrento. All are easy day-trips, though Sorrento is worth a little more time, and is a good base for seeing some of the Amalfi coast.

Ercolano: Vesuvius and the site of Herculaneum

The first real point of any interest is the town of **ERCOLANO**, the modern offshoot of the ancient site of *Herculaneum*, which was destroyed by the eruption of Vesuvius on August 2, AD 79. It's worth stopping here for two reasons: to see the excavations of the site and to climb to the summit of Vesuvius – to which buses run from outside the railway station. A word of warning, though: if you're planning to visit both Herculaneum and scale Vesuvius in one day (and it is possible), be sure to see Vesuvius first, and set off reasonably early – buses stop running up the mountain at lunchtime, leaving you the afternoon free to wander around the site.

Herculaneum: the site

Daily 9am–1hr before sunset; L4000

Situated at the seaward end of Ercolano's main street, the **site** of *Herculaneum* was discovered in 1709, when a well-digger accidentally struck the stage of the buried theatre. Excavations were undertaken throughout the eighteenth and nineteenth centuries, during which period much of the marble and bronze from the site was carted off to Naples to decorate the city's palaces, and it wasn't until 1927 that digging and preservation began in earnest. Herculaneum was a residential town, much smaller than Pompeii, and as such it makes a more manageable site, less architecturally impressive and less outside the modern mainstream (Ercolano virtually abuts the site), but better preserved and more easily taken in on a single visit. Archaeologists held for a long time that unlike Pompeii, on the other side of the volcano, most of the inhabitants of Herculaneum managed to escape. However, recent discoveries of skeletons in various poses of horror suggests otherwise, and it's now believed that most of the town's population were buried by huge avalanches of volcanic mud, which later hardened into the tufa-type rock that preserved much of the town.

Many of the houses on the site are kept locked, and you may have to ask one of the many attendants to open them up for you (in return for a tip). There are always plenty of guides hanging around, some English-speaking: if you feel you can afford it, they'll take you around the whole site; if you can't, tag along discreetly with an English-speaking group.

Because Herculaneum wasn't a commercial town, there was no central open space or forum, just streets of villas and shops, cut as usual by two very straight main streets which cross in the centre. A set itinerary is a bad idea: it's a fairly small site and most is worth seeing. But there are some buildings that you shouldn't miss. The **House of the Mosaic Atrium**, at the bottom end of the main street, Cardo IV, was a grand villa in its day and retains its mosaic-laid courtyard, corrugated by the force of the tufa. Behind here, the **House of the Deer** was another luxury villa, its two storeys built around a central courtyard and containing corridors decorated with richly coloured still-lifes, and, as the centre-piece of one of its rooms, a bawdy statue of a drunken Hercules seemingly about to piss all over the visitors. Further up Cardo IV, on the left, the **House of the Wooden Partition** preserves its original partition doors under glass – evidence that it was the home of a poorer class of person than many of the buildings here. The next-door **House of Opus Craticium** was a plebian dwelling too, divided into flats and with a workshop out the back.

There are more impressive houses on the far side of the Decumanus Inferiore, but it's the large **Thermae** or bath complex which dominates, the domed *frigidarium* of its mens' section decorated with frescoes of fish, its *caldarium* containing a plunge bath at one end and a scallop-shell apse complete with washbasin and water pipes. The women's section has a well preserved mosaic of Neptune and glass shards in its window that are original. Across the street, in the **House of the Carbonised Furniture**, there's a room with the marital bed still intact and portraits of the gent and lady of the house nearby – the former, in the room to the right, marked by a satyr, the latter voluptuously posed on the left-hand wall of an alcove. Close by, the dining room has pictures of Roman dishes – chicken, mush-rooms and the like – while on the left as you enter there's a kitchen with an oven in the corner, and a toilet on the other side. Next door, the **House of the Neptune Mosaic** holds another sparklingly preserved mosaic floor, again includ-ing portraits of the owners of the household, and flower and vegetable frescoes which served in lieu of a garden; the concrete hatch to the right was a *vomitarium*, which allowed guests to relieve themselves of excess food before proceed-ing to the next course of their meal. Under the house is a **wine shop**, stocked with amphorae and with a coiled rope left as it stood when disaster struck. Most of the rest of the town's **shops** were on the street behind here – a variety of places including a baker's, complete with ovens and grinding mills, a weaver's, with loom and bones, and a dyer's, with a huge pot for dyes. Retracing your steps from here, there's another **baths** building – more intact than the other but subject to flooding and often out of bounds.

Mount Vesuvius

Since its first eruption in AD 79, when it buried the towns and inhabitants of Pompeii and Herculaneum, **Mount Vesuvius** has dominated the lives of those who live on the Bay of Naples, its brooding bulk forming a stately backdrop to the ever-growing settlements that group around its lower slopes. It's a still active volcano, the only one on mainland Europe. There have been more than a hundred eruptions over the years, but only two of real significance – one in December 1631 that engulfed many nearby towns and killed 3000 people; and the last, in March 1944, which caused widespread devastation in the towns around, though no one was actually killed. The people who live here still fear the reawak-ening of the volcano, and with good reason – scientists calculate it should erupt every thirty years or so, and it hasn't since 1944. It's carefully monitored, of course, and there is apparently no reason to expect any movement for some time. But the subsidence in towns like Ercolano below is a continuing reminder of the instability of the area, incidentally one of southern Italy's most densely populated; and it's odd that there are no emergency plans as to what to do in case of an eruption.

There are two ways of making the **ascent**. *SITA* run bus services from Ercolano railway station to a car park and huddle of souvenir shops and cafés close to the crater throughout the morning (currently at 7.30am, 9.30am and 1.30pm) – much the easiest way of working things. If you've more energy, or have missed the bus, you can also take a local bus (#5) from the roundabout near the railway station to the end of the line and walk from there – a good couple of hours to the crater. One way of doing it might be to walk up and take the bus back down (the last one descends at 6pm). The walk is certainly a pleasant one, winding through the fertile lower slopes of the volcano, covered with vines and olives, past the main lava flows of the 1944 eruption as far as the carpark, which sits just above the greenery among the bare cinders of Vesuvius's main summit.

The walk up to the crater from here takes about half an hour, a stony stroll across reddened, barren gravel and rock on marked-out paths, though with nothing on your right to prevent you falling down the smooth side of the mountain – take care. At the top (admission L3000), the crater is a deep, wide, jagged ashtray of red rock swirled over by midges and emitting the odd plume of smoke, though since the last eruption effectively sealed up the main crevice this is much less evident than it once was. You can walk most of the way round, but again take it easy – the fences are old and rickety, and not to be relied upon.

The Bay to Sorrento

Beyond Ercolano the Bay doesn't really pick up: it's still hard to distinguish much countryside between the towns – most of which sadly seem more in tune with their proximity to the city than to the sea. **TORRE DEL GRECO**, the first place you reach, is famous for its coral industry, and you can still buy coral jewellery here, but the business is threatened by the polluted nature of the waters of the Bay.

Further along, **TORRE ANNUNZIATA** is no more appealing at first sight, though about half a kilometre from the railway station there's a recently excavated **Roman villa** that was covered, and preserved, by the AD 79 eruption. It was sumptuous residence in its time, part of a suburb of Pompeii known as *Oplontis*, with elegant loggias, murals and graceful gardens, which have been reconstructed in the style of their day.

By the time you reach **CASTELLAMMARE DI STABIA**, a few kilometres further round the Bay, the houses have begun to thin out a little. But the town isn't any more appetising for all that, dominated by the ships and gantries of the Italian navy's military harbour here. Oddly enough, Castellammare is the kind of place people still come for a holiday, or at least for a cure: its spas are well known hereabouts and draw many for their healing properties. From the station you can take the funicular up to the top of **Monte Faito** (1100m), though really you'd do better not to tarry here at all, instead hurrying on south to Salerno or west to Sorrento – both feasible jumping-off points for the Amalfi coast.

Pompeii

The other Roman town to be destroyed by Vesuvius – **Pompeii** – was a much larger affair than Herculaneum, and one of Campania's most important commercial centres in its day. After a spell as a Greek colony, Pompeii came under the sway of the Romans in 200 BC, later functioning as both a monied resort for wealthy patricians and a trading town that exported wine and fish products, notably its own brand of fish sauce. A severe earthquake destroyed much of the city in AD 63, and the eruption of Vesuvius sixteen years later only served to exacerbate what was already a desperate situation.

Vesuvius had been spouting smoke and ash for several days before the eruption and in fact most of the town had already been evacuated when disaster struck: out of a total population of 20,000 it's thought that only 2000 actually perished, asphyxiated by the toxic fumes of the volcanic debris, their homes buried in several metres of volcanic ash and pumice. Pliny, the Roman naturalist, was one of the casualties – he died at nearby Stabiae (now Castellammare) of a heart attack. But his nephew described the full horror of the scene soon after in two vivid letters to the historian Tacitus, who was compiling a history of the disaster, describing the sky as turning dark "as a sealed room".

In effect the eruption froze the way of life in Pompeii as it stood at the time – a way of life that subsequent excavations have revealed in precise and remarkable detail; indeed Pompeii has probably yielded more information about the ordinary life of Roman citizens during the Imperial era than any other site: its social conventions, class structure, domestic arrangements and its (actually very high) standard of living. Some of the buildings are even covered with ancient graffiti, either referring to contemporary political events or simply to the romantic entanglements of the inhabitants; and the full horror of their way of death is apparent in plaster casts made from the shapes their bodies left in the volcanic ash – faces tortured with agony, or shielding themselves from the dust and ashes.

The first parts of the town were discovered in 1600, but it wasn't until 1748 that excavations began, continuing more or less without interruption – after 1860 under the auspices of the Italian government – until the present day. Most of the site has now been uncovered, and much is very complete, though bear in mind that most of the best mosaics and murals (from Herculaneum too) have found their way into the Archaeological Museum in Naples, and that as you can only see a small proportion of those found *in situ*, visits to both sites really need to be supplemented by an additional one to the museum.

Pompeii practicals

To **reach Pompeii from Naples**, take the Circumvesuviana to Pompeii-Scavi-Villa dei Misteri – about thirty minutes; this leaves you right outside the western entrance to the site. The Circumvesuviana also runs to Pompeii-Santuario, outside the site's eastern entrance, or you can take the roughly hourly mainline train (direction Salerno) to the main Pompeii *FS* station, on the south side of the fairly characterless modern town, which stretches east from the amphitheatre entrance.

It makes most sense to see the site from Naples, and there's really no need to stay overnight, though if you get stuck or are planning to move on south after seeing Pompeii, there are plenty of **hotels** in the modern town, and a large and well-equipped **campsite** – *Zeus*, right outside the Pompeii-Villa dei Misteri station. Talk to modern Pompeii's **AAST** at Via Sacra 1, just off the main square, for more details. There's also an **AAST** office outside the site on Piazza Esedra (turn right outside Pompeii-Villa dei Misteri station), which has a plan of the site and other information.

Pompeii: the site

Daily 9am–1 hour before sunset; L5000

The site of Pompeii covers a wide area, and seeing it properly takes half a day at the very least; probably you should devote most of a day to it and take plenty of breaks – unlike Herculaneum there's little shade, and the distances involved quite large: flat comfortable shoes are a must.

All of this makes Pompeii sound a bit of a chore – which it isn't. But there is a lot to see, and you should be reasonably selective: many of the streets aren't lined by much more than foundations, and after a while one ruin begins to look much like another. Again, many of the most interesting structures are kept locked and only opened when a large group forms or a tip is handed over to one of the many custodians. To be sure of seeing everything you could take a tour, but as large groups are one of the main features of Pompeii this will probably be the least of your problems.

Entering the site from the Pompeii-Villa dei Misteri side, the **Forum** is the first real feature of significance, a long, slim open space surrounded by the ruins of what would have been some of the town's most important official buildings – a basilica, temples to Apollo and Jupiter, and a market hall. Walking north from here, up the so-called Via di Mercurio, takes you towards some of the town's more luxurious houses. On the left, the **House of the Tragic Poet** is named for its mosaics of a theatrical production and a poet inside, though the "Cave Canem" (Beware of the Dog) mosaic by the main entrance is more eye-catching. Close by, the residents of the **House of the Faun** must have been a friendlier lot, its "Ave" (Welcome) mosaic outside beckoning you in to view the atrium and the copy of a tiny bronze dancing faun (the original is in Naples) that gives the villa its name.

On the street behind, the **House of the Vettii** is one of the most delightful houses in Pompeii, and one of the best maintained, a merchant villa ranged around a lovely central peristyle that gives the best possible impression of the domestic environment of the city's upper middle classes. The first room on the right off the peristyle holds the best of Pompeii's murals actually viewable on site: the one on the left shows the young Hercules struggling with serpents; another, in the corner, depicts Ixion tied to a wheel after offending Zeus, while a third shows Dirce being dragged to her death by the bull set on her by the song of Antiope. There are more paintings beyond here, through the villa's kitchen in a small room that's normally kept locked – erotic works showing various techniques of lovemaking (Greek-style, woman on top; Roman-style, man on top) together with an absurdly potent-looking statue of Priapus from which women were supposed to drink to be fertile; phallic symbols were also, it's reckoned, believed to ward off the evil eye.

Cross over to the other side of the site for the so-called **new excavations**, which began in 1911 and actually uncovered some of the town's most important quarters, stretching along the main Via dell'Abbondanza. The **Grand Theatre**, for one, is very well preserved and is still used for performances, overlooking the small grassy, column-fringed square of the **Gladiators' Barracks** – not in fact a barracks at all but a refectory and meeting-place for spectators from the nearby amphitheatre. Walk around to the far left side of the Grand Theatre, down the steps and up again, and you're in front of the **Little Theatre** – a smaller, more intimate venue also still used for summer performances, and with a better kept corridor behind the stage space. As for the **Amphitheatre**, it's one of Italy's most intact and accessible, and also its oldest, dating from 80 BC. It's pleasantly overgrown now but once had room for a crowd of some 12,000 – well over half the town's population. Next door, the **Palestra** is a vast parade ground that was used by Pompeii's youth for sport and exercise – overgrown too now, but still with its square of swimming pool in the centre. It must have been in use when the eruption struck Pompeii, since its southeast corner was found littered with the skeletons of young men trying to flee the disaster.

One last place you shouldn't miss at Pompeii is the **Villa dei Misteri**, outside the main site, a short walk from the Porta Ercolano and accessible on the same ticket. This is probably the best preserved of all Pompeii's palatial houses, an originally third-century BC structure with a warren of rooms and courtyards that derives its name from a series of paintings in one of its larger chambers: depictions of the initiation rites of a young woman into the Dionysiac Mysteries, an outlawed cult of the early Imperial era. Not much is known about the cult itself, but the paintings are marvellously clear, remarkable for the surety of their execution and the brightness of their tones and colours. They follow an obvious narrative, starting with the left-hand wall and continuing around the room with a series of freeze-frames showing sacrifice, flagellation, dancing and other rituals, all under the serene gaze of the mistress of the house.

Sorrento

Topping the rocky cliffs close to the end of its peninsula, the last town of significance on this side of the bay, **SORRENTO** is solely and unashamedly a resort, its inspired location and mild climate drawing foreigners from all over Europe for close on 200 years. Ibsen wrote part of *Peer Gynt* in Sorrento, Wagner and Nietzsche had a well-publicised row here, and Maxim Gorky lived for over a decade in the town. Nowadays it's strictly package-tour territory, but really none the worse for it, with little of the brashness of its Spanish and Greek equivalents but all of their vigour, a bright, lively place that retains its southern Italian roots. Cheap restaurants aren't hard to find; neither – if you know where to look – is reasonably priced accommodation; and there's really no better place outside Naples itself from which to explore the rugged Amalfi shore and the islands of the Bay.

Sorrento's centre is **Piazza Tasso**, five minutes from the railway station along the busy Corso Italia, named after the wayward sixteenth-century Italian poet to whom the town was home and with a bust of him in rememberance. There's nothing much to see in the town itself – only the slightly garish *intarsio* inlaid-wood craft shops and the local **Museo Correale** on Via Correale (Mon–Sat 9.30am–12.30pm & 5–7pm, Sun 9.30am–12.30pm), which has a small collection of crafts, archaeological finds and odds and ends pertaining to Tasso. But it's nice to wander through the streets which feed into the square, some of which are pedestrianised for the lively evening *passeggiata*.

Otherwise the town is entirely given over to pleasure. Strange as it may seem, Sorrento isn't particularly well provided with **beaches**: most people make do with the rocks and tiny, crowded strip of sand at **Marina Grande** – fifteen minutes' walk or a short regular bus ride from Piazza Tasso – or invest in an umbrella and bathing hut on one of the wooden jetties. If you do come down here, it's a good idea, for a while at least, to hire a pedal-boat (L6000 an hour) and get free of the shore; if you don't fancy this, try the beaches further along, like the tiny **Regina Giovanna** at Punta del Capo, again connected by bus from Piazza Tasso, where the ruins of the Roman Villa Pollio Felix make a unique place to bathe. Or dispense with Sorrento altogether and take the bus from the railway station to Positano (45min) or Amalfi (1hr 30min) – both of which have larger expanses of beach.

Practical details: information, sleeping and eating

Sorrento's **train station** is located in the centre of town, five minutes from the main Piazza Tasso. There's an **AAST** in the large yellow *Circolo dei Foresteri* on Via de Maio, just off Piazza San Antonino (Mon–Sat 8.30am–2.30pm & 4.30–7.30pm), which has maps and details on accommodation and camping; otherwise the travel offices on Piazza San Antonino can deal with bus and ferry enquiries and reserve tickets. Incidentally, if you don't want to rely on public transport, a number of firms hire **scooters**: try *Ciro's*, Via degli Aranci 138, or *Thomas*, Piazza San Antonino 4, who both rent machines for around L30,000 a day; *Ciro's* also rent ordinary bikes as well. *Coltur*, in neighbouring Sant'Agnello, hire out all manner of **seafaring equipment** – canoes, windsurfers, waterskis and the like.

    Sleeping cheaply in Sorrento isn't really a problem, though during peak season you should probably book in advance. There's a **youth hostel** close to the railway station at Via Capasso 5 (☎081/878.1783); right out of the station and it's on your left. And there are a number of centrally placed **hotels**, one of the cheapest of which is the *Rivoli*, just off Piazza San Antonino at Via Santa Maria delle Grazie 14–16 (☎081/878.1709), with doubles for L25,000; if this is full, try the *Astoria* (☎081/878.1405) in the same street, *Il Pozzo*, nearby at Via Tasso 8 (☎081/878.3502), or the *City*, Corso Italia 221 (☎081/878.1883) – all of which have rooms for similar prices. The *Savoia*, near the railway station at Via Fuorimura 48 (☎878.2511) is good too, only slightly more expensive, and the bordering township of Sant'Agnello has a couple of low-priced hotels and numerous **campsites**. For campers wanting to stay in Sorrento, the cheapest and closest site is *Nube d'Argento*, ten minutes' walk from Piazza Tasso in the direction of Marina Grande at Via del Capo 12 (☎081/878.1344).

    For **eating**, keep away from Piazza Tasso and you should be OK. The *Gioiello*, Via S. Cesereo 39, just off the main square, serves good food very cheaply, as does the *Ristorante San Antonino*, off Piazza Antonino, which has a garden as well. For unadulterated splurges, the *Parruchiano* at Corso Italia 71 serves marvellous and not overly expensive food in a wonderful setting. If you just want a snack, *Bar Rita* on Corso Italia can't be bettered; and for people-watching and sipping, *Bar Ercolano* on Piazza Tasso isn't as pricey as you'd think and is vibrantly sited. For late-night boozing and **nightlife**, there are of course the town's English-style pubs: the *Rover's Return*, off Piazza Tasso on Via Correale, and the *Brittania*, near the station on Corso Italia, are just two places for good-natured revelry – and, if you can stomach it, live music; and Sorrento also has a number of discos which people come from as far away as Naples to sample. *2001* on Piazza San Antonino, and *Blu Club*, are just two. Rather more genteel, the *Circolo dei Foresteri* has a nice terrace and live music of an evening.

The Islands

Guarding each prong of the Bay of Naples, the islands of Cápri, Ischia and Prócida between them make up the best known group of Italian islands. Each is a

GETTING TO THE ISLANDS

Ferries and **hydrofoils** are run by three companies: *Carremar*, who operate from the main harbour at the bottom of Piazza Municipio, *SNAV*, who run hydrofoils from Mergellina, and *Linee Lauro*, who operate from both places. Between them, they depart for all of the islands from Naples, Pozzuoli and Sorrento, with some connections from Salerno, Amalfi and Positano. Whichever you take, day-trips are quite feasible; usually the last connection delivers you back on the mainland in time for dinner. The following is to give a rough idea of frequencies during the summer, and you should either check with the local tourist office or buy a copy of *Il Mattino* for specific timings. Or phone the companies direct: *Carremar* (☎551.3882); *Linee Lauro* (ferries ☎551.3236, hydrofoils ☎761.1004); *SNAV* (☎761.2348).

HYDROFOILS

Naples (Molo Beverello)–Cápri (6 daily; 40min).

Naples (Molo Beverello–Ischia (6 daily; 50min).

Naples (Molo Beverello)–Prócida (6 daily; 35min).

Naples (Megellina)–Cápri (12 daily; 40min).

Naples (Mergellina)–Ischia (12 daily; 45min).

Naples (Mergellina)–Forio (Ischia) (6 daily; 55min).

Naples (Mergellina)–Casamicciola (Ischia) (4 daily; 55min).

Naples (Mergellina)–Prócida (4 daily; 35min).

Salerno–Cápri (via Amalfi and Positano) (3 daily; 1hr).

Sorrento–Ischia (via Naples) (2 daily; 1hr).

Sorrento–Cápri (6 daily; 20min).

Casamicciola (Ischia)–Prócida (4 daily; 30min).

FERRIES

Naples (Molo Beverello)–Cápri (6 daily; 1hr 15min).

Naples (Molo Beverello)–Ischia (12 daily; 1hr 20min).

Naples (Molo Beverello)–Prócida (5 daily; 1hr).

Pozzuoli–Ischia (4 daily; 1hr 40min).

Pozzuoli–Casamicciola (Ischia) (5 daily; 1hr 50min).

Pozzuoli–Prócida (4 daily; 1hr 10min)

Ischia–Prócida (4 daily; 40min).

Sorrento–Cápri (5 daily; 50min).

Salerno–Cápri (via Amalfi) (1 daily; 2hr).

Salerno–Ischia (via Amalfi and Positano) (1 daily; 2hr 30min).

very different creature though. **Cápri** is a place of legend, home to the mythical Sirens, and a much-eulogised playground of the super-rich in the years since – though now settled down to a lucrative existence as a target for day-trippers from the mainland. Visit by all means, but bear in mind that you have to hunt hard these days to detect the origins of much of the purple prose. Similarly with **Ischia**, predominantly package-tour territory now and just as crowded, primarily with German sunseekers who colonise the place during the summer months. Only **Prócida** remains reasonably untouched by the high season, the smallest of the islands and probably the least interesting – though the best venue for fairly peaceful lazing.

Cápri

Sheering out of the sea just off the far end of the Sorrentine peninsula, the island of **Cápri** has long been the most sought-after part of the Bay of Naples. During Roman times Augustus retreated to the island's gorgeous cliffbound scenery to escape the cares of office; later Tiberius moved the Imperial capital here, indulging himself in legendarily debauched antics until his death in AD 37. After the Romans left, Cápri was rather neglected until the early nineteenth century, when the discovery of the Blue Grotto the and island's remarkable natural landscape coincided nicely with the rise of tourism, and the island has never looked back, attracting a steady flow of artists and writers and, more recently, inquisitive tourists, ever since. The English especially have always flocked here: D.H. Lawrence and George Bernard Shaw were among more illustrious visitors, Graham Greene and Gracie Fields have (or had) houses here; and even Lenin visited for a time after the failure of the 1905 uprising.

Cápri tends to get a mixed press these days, the concensus being that while it might have been an attractive place once, it's been pretty much ruined by the crowds and the prices. And Cápri *is* crowded these days, mainly with Germans and Americans (though the Brits continue to hold their own), and in July and August it would be sensible to give it a miss. But reports that the island has been irreparably spoilt are way overstated. Ischia is just as busy, Prócida isn't nearly as interesting – or beautiful – and it would be hard to find a place with more inspiring views. It's expensive, too, especially if you sit and drink on its main squares. But prices aren't really any higher than other major Italian resorts, and you can cut out the inflated expense of accommodation by visiting on a day-trip; indeed a couple of these and you can see all of the island comfortably.

Around the island

Ferries and hydrofoils dock at **MARINA GRANDE**, the waterside extension of the island's main town, which perches on the hill above. You can take boats to the Blue Grotto from here (about L6000 a head return, then more to actually enter), and there's an **AAST** office (Mon–Sat 9am–1pm & 3.30–6.45pm) which doles out maps and other information. But beyond that you may as well take the **funicular** (L1300 one-way) up the steep hill to **CÁPRI** itself – the main town of the island, nestled between its two mountains, its houses connected by winding, hilly alleyways that give onto the dinky (almost toytown) main square of **Piazza Umberto**, crowded with café tables and, invariably, a lot of people. Sit on the steps and eat your lunch and watch the drinkers and diners digging deep for the (undeniable) ambience.

Of things to see in or near Cápri, the **Certosa San Giacomo** on the far side of the town is a rundown old monastery with a handful of paintings, a couple of shapeless Roman statues dredged up from the deep and an odd, overgrown cloister given over in part to a music school. To the right of the monastery, the **Giardini Augustos** give tremendous views of the coast below and the towering jagged cliffs above, and from there you can wind down to either the beach below (rocks really) or, beyond, to **MARINA PICCOLA** – a small huddle of houses and restaurants around a few patches of pebble beach: pleasantly uncrowded out of season, though in July or August you might as well forget it.

You can also reach the ruins of Tiberius's villa, the **Villa Jovis** (daily 9am–6pm; L2000), from Cápri town, a steep thirty-minute hike from Piazza Umberto following Via Botteghe out of the square and Via Tiberio up the hill. It was here that Tiberius retired in AD 27 to lead a life of vice and debauchery, and to take revenge on his enemies, many of whom he apparently had thrown off the cliff-face. You can see why he chose the site: it's among Cápri's most exhilarating, with incredible vistas of Ischia, Prócida and the Bay; on a clear day you can even see Salerno and beyond. There's not much left of the villa, but you can get a good sense of the shape and design of its various parts from the arched halls and narrow passageways that remain. Below, there's another, more recent **villa**, that of one Count Fersen-Adelsward, a gay Swedish millionaire who built the house early this century apparently to entertain pick-ups from the town. Its gates are locked, the building in a sad state of disrepair, but the adventurous may want to clamber in for a hunt around.

The island's other main settlement, **ANACÁPRI**, is more sprawling than Cápri itself, less obviously picturesque, its tacky main square, **Piazza Vittoria**, flanked by souvenir shops, bland fashion boutiques and restaurants decked with tourist menus: Cápri without the chic. During the season, a chairlift operates from Piazza Vittoria up to **Monte Solaro** (9am–sunset), shifting you up to the summit of the 596m-high mountain, the island's highest point, in about twelve minutes. At the top there's only a ruined castle and café that is no longer in use, but the views are marvellous.

A short walk away from Piazza Vittoria down Via G. Orlandi, the church of **San Michele** is the village's principal sight, its tiled floor painted with an eighteenth-century depiction of the Fall that you view from an upstairs balcony – a lush work after a drawing by the Neapolitan painter Solimena, in rich blues and yellows, showing cats, unicorns and other creatures. Continuing in the same direction, a good 45-minute hike away starting off down Via Lo Pozzo (or reachable by bus every twenty minutes from Piazza Vittoria), the **Blue Grotto** (Grotta Azzura) is probably the island's best-known feature – though also its most exploitative, the boatmen here whisking visitors onto boats and in and out of the grotto in about five minutes flat. The grotto is quietly impressive, the blue of its innards caused by the sun entering the cave through the water, but it's rather overrated, and the process is all over so quickly as to be barely worth the trip down here, let alone the extortionate L6750 fee. Technically, you can swim into the cave – it's not the exclusive preserve of the boatmen, though they'll try and persuade you otherwise – but the route through is so busy that unless you're a strong swimmer it's not advisable to try. Incidentally, it's also possible to take a boat trip to the Grotto direct from Marina Grande (see above), though at L6000 a head it's an expensive way to get here, and doesn't include the price you pay to the boatmen who take you inside.

Time is much better spent walking in the opposite direction from Piazza Vittoria, past a long gauntlet of souvenir stalls to Axel Munthe's **Villa San Michele** (daily 9am–6pm; L3000), a light, airy house with lush and fragrant gardens that is one of the real highlights of the island. The Swedish writer Munthe lived here for a number of years, and it's filled with his furniture and knick-knacks, as well as Roman artefacts ingeniously incorporated into the villa's rooms and gardens. Busts and bronzes abound: one statue of Hermes was given to Munthe by the city of Naples in thanks for his work in the city during the cholera epidemic of 1884 (see *Naples*); Corinthian capitals are converted as coffee tables, other surfaces topped with intricate Cosmati mosaic-work.

Practical details

There are **AAST** offices in Marina Grande, on Piazza Umberto in Cápri town, and in Anacapri on Via G. Orlandi. **Getting around** the island, there is a decent bus service between all the main centres – Marina Grande, Cápri, Marina Piccola, Anacapri and buses also run regularly down to the Blue Grotto.

You'd be well advised not to **stay overnight** on Cápri: in peak season space is extremely limited, and the prices through the roof; day trips here from Naples or Sorrento are easy. If you are keen to stay, however – and the island certainly is a lot quieter after the day-tripping crowds have gone home – you could try the *Quattro Stagioni*, Via Marina Piccola 1 (✆081/837.0041) or *Stella Maris*, Via Roma 27 (✆081/837. 0452) – both centrally placed and with doubles for around L50,000. Even if you don't stay, **eating** can be an expense, and you might prefer to knock yourself up a picnic lunch: in Cápri town there is a supermarket and a bakery a little way down Via Botteghe off Piazza Umberto, and well-stocked *salumerie* at Via Roma 13 and 30. For sit-down food, *Moscardino* on Via Roma is an inexpensive restaurant in a good location, as is *Di Giorgio* in the same street.

Ischia

Largest of the islands in the Bay of Naples, **ISCHIA** rises out of the sea in a series of pointy green hummocks, downbeat sister to more glamorous Cápri and these days the favoured playground of German and Scandinavian tourists, who flock in increasingly huge numbers during peak season to its beach resorts, thermal springs and therapeutic sands. It's not hard to see why its reputation has always been poorer than Cápri's: it's not nearly so beautiful, and there's not a lot here that's all that historic. But you can at least be sure of being alone in exploring parts of its mountainous interior; and if you're after a straight bit of beach lounging and don't want to stray too far from Naples, it might just be the place.

Around the island

Main town of Ischia is **ISCHIA PORTO**, where most of the ferries dock, a long straggle of hotels, boutiques and beach shops, fronted by patches of beach and punctuated by cafés serving *wurst* and hamburgers to the large crowds of young Germans. The main stretch of beach is **Spiaggia dei Pescatori**, beyond which **ISCHIA PONTE**, which adjoins the port, is a quieter and less commercialised centre, with a focus in its **Castello Aragonese** (daily 10am–5pm; L4000, plus L1000 for the lift to the top) – crowning an offshore rock and accessible from a short causeway. The Renaissance poet and close friend of Michelangelo, Vittoria Colonna, spent much of her life here, following the seizure of her family's land by Alexander VI. The citadel itself where she lived is rather tumbledown now and closed to the public, but below is a complex of buildings, almost a separate village really, around which you can stroll. There's the weird open shell of a cathedral destroyed by the British in 1804, a prison that once held political prisoners during the upheavals of the Unification, and the macabre remnants of a convent, in which a couple of dark rooms ringed with a set of commode-like seats served as a cemetery for the dead sisters – placed here to putrefy in front of the living members of the community.

The island is at its most developed along its northern and western shores – heading west from Ischia Porto. The first village you reach, **CASAMICCIOLA**

TERME, is a bland spa centre with many hotels and a crowded central beach – though you can find a quieter one on the far side of the village. Ibsen spent a summer here, and the waters are said to be full of iodine, but otherwise you may as well push on to **LACCO AMENO**, a brighter little town, again with a beach, and spa-waters that are said to be the most radioactive in Italy. **FORIO** sprawls around its bay, another growing resort with a long stretch of (dirty) beach to the right of its harbour – though it's quite pretty behind its tawdry seafront of bars and pizzerias.

Ischia is much more pleasant on its southern side, the landscape steeper and greener, with fewer people to enjoy it. **SANT'ANGELO** is probably its loveliest spot, a tiny fishing village crowded around a narrow isthmus linking with a humpy islet that's out of bounds to buses, who drop right outside. There's a good beach nearby, **Spiaggia dei Maronti**, about a kilometre east (walkable or reached by taxi boat – L2500), and after a swim you're well poised for an assault on the craggy summit of Ischia's now dormant volcano, **Monte Epomeo**, which you can walk up to from **FONTANA**, high above Sant'Angelo and connected by bus. Even if you don't fancy the volcano, the bus ride to Fontana is superb, and from the village buses run frequently back east to Ischia Porto.

Practical details

Buses run around the island, stopping just about everywhere, leaving every half-hour from Ischia Porto on two circular routes – one in each direction; tickets are valid for half an hour. Alternatively, you can rent **mopeds** opposite the ferry terminal for around L20,000 a day. If you're planning on **staying**, accommodation is at least cheaper than Cápri (though again I'd recommend a day-trip from Naples): in Ischia Ponte, the *Monastero*, near the Castello (☎081/992.435), offers rooms for a little over L20,000 a double; the *Del Mare*, Via Jasolino 80 (☎081/991.508), has the advantage of being close to the port, with doubles for around 35,000, likewise the *Rosita*, Via Quercia 38 (☎081/993.875). For **eating**, the *Mastu Peppe*, down by the ferry quay in Ischia Porto, is cheap and quite good.

Prócida

A serrated hunk of volcanic rock that's the smallest and nearest island to Naples, **PRÓCIDA** has managed to fend off the kind of tourist numbers that have flooded into Cápri and Ischia – and arriving here it's easy to see why. It lacks the spectacle, or variety, of both islands, though it more than compensates with the extra room and extra peace. With a population of just 10,000, there are few real population centres, its main town, **MARINA GRANDE** – where you arrive by ferry – an oddly rundown conglomeration of houses rising from a pastel-painted waterfront to a network of steep streets winding up to the fortified tip of the island. Part of this is given over to a rather forbidding prison, but it's worth walking up anyway, both for the views and the abbey church of **San Michele**, whose domes are decorated with a stirring painting by Giordano of Saint Michael beating back the Turks from Prócida's shore.

For the rest, Prócida's appeal lies in its opportunities to swim and eat in relative peace. There are **beaches** in Marina Grande itself, on the far side of the jetty and in the opposite direction, beyond the fishing harbour, though both are fairly grubby. Similarly, **Spiaggia Chiaia** in nearby CORICELLA comes touted as a bathing beach but isn't very large and can get crowded. Better to make the fifteen-minute bus journey to **CHIAIOELLA**, where there's a long stretch of uncrowded and clean sand together with a handful of bars and restaurants. From here you can also follow the beach road over the bridge onto the islet of **Vivara** – very peaceful and overgrown, though the cliffs are very steep and offer no chance for bathing.

Practical details

There's an **AAST** office by the water (daily 9.30am–1pm & 5–9pm) with free maps and advice on accommodation. For getting around, a bus service connects Marina Grande with Chiaioella, coinciding with ferries. There's not much choice if you want to **stay**: of five hotels, the *Riviera* in Chiaioella (☎081/896.7197) is the least expensive, but even this will set you back over L40,000 for a double room – and you'll obviously need to book. There are also a couple of *pensioni*, which may be cheaper: try *La Rosa dei Venti*, Via V. Rinaldi 32 (☎081/896.8385), who rent out self-catering cottages around the island for between two and six people. **Eating** is rather easier. Restaurants line Via Roma, main street of Marina Grande: *La Medusa*, opposite the ferry terminal, is expensive but very good; cheaper alternatives include *Ipanema*, a little further down past the tourist office, or *L'Affrodo*, almost next door.

INLAND AND SOUTHERN CAMPANIA

Away from the coast Campania's appeal fades. The **interior** is a poor and remote region that few tourists visit – quite different from the populous and much-lauded coast. Large towns are few, travel can be slow and unless you're spending a long time in the area, or are an enthusiast for obscure ancient sites, there's not much of interest anyway. What places there are that might appeal – the royal palace at **Caserta**, the Roman amphitheatre at **Cápua**, the ancient town of **Benevento** – are best seen on a day-trip from Naples.

The south of the region, on the other hand, holds some of Campania's real gems. The **Amalfi coast** is as spectacular a bit of shoreline as Italy has to offer, and worth a visit for just that, though you may find the tourist presence in high season a bit offputting. **Salerno**, at the far end of this stretch, is a genial working port, and a jumping-off spot for the less-developed **Cilento** coast that stretches all the way to the Basilicata border. Inland from here is also very undeveloped, and difficult to reach without your own car. But it can be a rewarding area, its high hills and valleys sheltering some supremely unspoilt routes and villages.

North from Naples: Caserta and Cápua

There's not much to draw you to the territory immediately north of Naples. The towns just outside the city – Casoria, Afragola, Acerra – are collectively known as the "**Triangle of Death**" for their Camorra connections and make up a bleak conurbation of poor housing and industrial messiness.

Caserta

Further inland, a short train- or bus-ride direct from Naples, **CASERTA**, incongruously surrounded by a sprawl of industrial complexes and warehouses that stretches all the way back to Naples, is known as the "Versailles of Naples" for its vast eighteenth-century royal palace, which utterly dominates the town. There's not much point in coming here if you don't want to see this; if you do, be sure to also see the old village of **Caserta Vecchia**, 10km north of the modern town, where the population lived before the building of the palace. It's now almost entirely deserted but is a bucolic antidote to Caserta's soulless streets, and has a twelfth-century cathedral that is a fine example of southern Norman architecture.

The Palazzo Reale

The palace and its grounds are royal creations on the grandest of scales, and made a fitting setting for the signing of the German-Italian armistice in 1945. Begun in 1752 for the Bourbon King Charles III, to plans drawn up by Vanvitelli, and completed a little over twenty years later, it's an awesomely large complex, built around four courtyards, with a facade 245m long, nestling between two curving brick arms and overlooking a massive, classically ordered square. However it's ultimately a dull structure that substitutes size for inspiration. Only the majestic central staircases up to the **royal apartments** (daily 9am–1.30pm; L3000) hit the right note. And the apartments themselves are a grand parade of heavily painted and stuccoed rooms, sparsely furnished in Empire style, some with great, overbearing classical statues, and all, in their brazen, overstated display of wealth, pretty disgusting – not least in the smug portraits of the Bourbon dynasty, especially the one of the podgy Francis I with his brat-like children. There's little point in singling out anything of special significance: there isn't anything really, and it's the feel of the building and its pitiless overstatement that are the real attractions.

Behind the palace, the **gardens** too are classically ordered, and on no less huge a scale, stretching out behind, along one central 3km-long axis, and punctured by myth-inspired fountains. The main promenade is longer than it looks from the palace (it's a good half an hour's walk or a free bicycle ride), and regular buses make the round-trip, dropping you off at selected intervals along the way and turning round by the main cascade at the top, which depicts Diana turning Actaeon into a stag. Walk to the top, look back at the palace, hop on a bus . . . and depart.

Santa Maria Cápua Vetere, Cápua and the Terra di Lavoro

Regular buses run from Caserta, either from the bus/train station or the stop just to the left as you exit the palace, down to **SANTA MARIA CÁPUA VETERE** – a not especially pleasant journey past jutting signs, petrol stations and rundown housing. There's not a blade of grass in sight, and the feeling is one of grinding, hapless urban poverty. There's not much to Santa Maria itself either, but in its day this originally Etruscan, later Samnite, city, then known as *Cápua*, was the second city of Italy, centre of the rich and important region of Campania and famous for its skill in working bronze. Its first century AD **amphitheatre** was once the largest in Italy after the Colosseum, and parts of it remain on the far side of town, a right-turn shortly after Piazza San Francesco d'Assisi. In its day this held a reputed Roman gladiator school and barracks, and it was here that the gladiators' revolt, led by Spartacus, broke out in 73 BC – a revolt that was only put down after two years and four lost battles. The amphitheatre now is less well preserved than the Colosseum (though better than Pozzuoli's), having lost most of the surrounding tiers – and many of the remaining ones have been concreted over. But the network of tunnels underneath survives reasonably intact, and is accessible. You can also ask for the keys to a nearby **Mithraeum** across the road, down Via Antifeatro and then left down Via Morelli – one of the best-preserved in the country, and redolent with the bizarre, bloodletting rites that accompanied the cult of Mithraism.

There are heaps of rubble and a handful of artefacts dotted around the amphitheatre, not least a large piece of mosaic, but most of the finds have found their way to the **Museo Campano** in **CÁPUA**, 4km down the road (Tues–Sat 9am–2pm, Sun 9am–1pm; L2000) – a smaller town than Santa Maria, settled by refugees when the original city was plundered in 856 by Saracens. Sited on the broad curve of the Volturno river, it's a marginally more attractive place than Santa Maria, but it's not really worth the trek (or even bus ride) if you're without a car.

The area northwest of Cápua, the **Terra di Lavoro**, is a flat fertile plain that's one of Campania's prime agricultural regions, yielding a healthy array of fruit and supporting plentiful herds of mozzarella-producing buffalo. The main town, **SESSA ARUNCA**, has a pleasant centre of narrow arched streets, and a Romanesque cathedral which has a pulpit similar to those at Salerno and Ravello. But otherwise there's not a lot to persuade travellers to stop, and most push straight on to Formia or Rome.

Benevento

BENEVENTO, further inland than Cápua or Caserta and reachable in about an hour and half from Naples by bus, was another important Roman settlement, a key point on the Via Appia between Rome and Brindisi and as such a thriving trading town. Founded in 278 BC, it was at the time the farthest point from Rome to be colonised, and even now it has a remote air about it, circled by hills and with a centre that was (pointlessly) bombed to smithereens in the last war and even now seems only half-rebuilt. Its climate also ranks among southern Italy's most extreme.

Buses from Naples drop you on the main square, where the **Duomo** is an almost total reconstruction of its thirteenth-century Romanesque original; what's left of its famous bronze doors, believed to be Byzantine, is now stashed inside. Left from here, the main street, **Corso Garibaldi**, leads up the hill, a once elegant thoroughfare lined with ancient palaces. Off to the left about halfway up, the **Arch of Trajan** is the major remnant of the Roman era, a marvellously preserved triumphal arch that is refreshing after the scaffolding and netting of Rome's arches, since you can get close enough to study its friezes. Built to guard the entrance to Benevento from the Appian Way, it's actually as heavy-handed a piece of self-acclaim as there ever was, showing the emperor Trajan in various scenes of triumph, power and generosity. Further up Corso Garibaldi, the **Museo Sannio**, in the cloister behind the eighth-century church of Santa Sofia (Mon–Sat

9am–1pm; free), holds a selection of Roman finds from the local area, including a number of artefacts from a temple of Isis – various sphinxes, bulls and a headless statue of Isis herself. There are also terracotta votive figurines from the fifth century BC, and the cloister itself has capitals carved with energetic scenes of animals, humans and strange beasts – hunting, riding and attacking.

There are more bits and pieces from Roman times scattered around the rather battered old quarter of town, the **Triggio** – reached by following Via Carlo Torre off to the left of the main road beyond the cathedral. The **Bue Apis**, at the far end of Corso Dante, is another relic from the temple of Isis, a first-century BC sculpture of a bull. And in the heart of the old quarter there are the substantial remains of a **Roman Theatre** built during the reign of Hadrian – though it's been a little over-restored for modern use. In Hadrian's time it seated 20,000 people, rather less today as the upper level remains mossily decrepit, but it's still an atmospheric sight – like most of Benevento, relatively unvisited by tourists and looking out over the green rolling countryside of the province beyond.

Practical details

Benevento is roughly 60km from Naples and **buses** run roughly every two hours from Piazza Garibaldi – an hour and a half's trip. **Trains** stop down the hill from the centre and are in any case slower and more infrequent. Benevento is easily seen on a day-excursion and there's no need **to stay**, but if you're pushing on east to Foggia and Puglia (to which there are regular train connections), or if you get stuck, the *Genova*, at Viale Principe di Napoli 130 (☎0824/42.926), has rooms for under L30,000. For **food**, if you're just here for the day you're likely to be content with the snacks, pizza and *tavola calda*-style dishes at *Pizzeria Romana*, next door to the cathedral on the corner of Via Carlo Torre. For evening eating there are adequate restaurants dotted on and around the main Corso Garibaldi.

The Amalfi Coast

Occupying the southern side of Sorrento's peninsula, the **Costiera Amalfitana** lays claim to being Europe's most beautiful stretch of coast, its corniche road winding around the towering cliffs that slip almost sheer into the sea. By car or bus, it's an incredible ride, and if you're staying in Sorrento shouldn't be missed on any account; in any case the towns along here hold the beaches that Sorrento lacks. The coast as a whole has become rather developed, and these days it's in fact one of Italy's ritzier bits of shoreline, villas atop its precarious slopes fetching a bomb in both cash and kudos. But the cliffs are so steep, and the towns' growth so inevitably constrained, that it seems unlikely that the Amalfi coast can ever become completely spoilt.

Positano and Praiano

There's not much to **POSITANO**, only a couple of decent beaches and a handful of clothing and souvenir shops. But its location, heaped up in a pyramid high above the water, has inspired a thousand picture postcards, and helped to make it a monied resort that runs a close second to Cápri in the celebrity stakes. Since John Steinbeck wrote up the place in glowing terms back in 1953, the village has enjoyed a fame quite out of proportion to its tiny size. Franco Zefferelli is just one of many famous names who have villas nearby, and the people who come here to lie on the beach consider themselves a cut above your average sun-worshipper.

All this means it's expensive, and an overnight stay isn't recommended. But its beaches – a small one to the right of the pyramid, a larger one to the left, ringed with overpriced bars and restaurants – are rarely unpleasantly crammed. And if you can't bring yourself to get back on the bus, there are summer hydrofoil connections with Cápri, Amalfi and Salerno. For food, try the *salumeria* next to the *tabacchi* where you buy the hydrofoil tickets.

PRAIANO, a little further along, is smaller than Positano, but no less congested, and becoming more so as its status as fashionable hangout increases. There is a small patch of beach, but food and rooms are again pricey.

Amalfi

For affordable food and accommodation, you'd do better to push on to **AMALFI**, set in a wide cleft in the cliffs – the largest town along this coast, and an established seaside resort since Edwardian times, when the British upper classes found the town a pleasant place to spend their winters. Actually Amalfi's credentials go back much further: it was an independent republic during Byzantine times, and one of the great naval powers, with a population of some 70,000; Webster's *Duchess of Malfi* was set here, and the city's traders established outposts all over the Mediterranean, setting up the Order of the Knights of Saint John of Jerusalem. Amalfi was finally vanquished by the Normans in 1131, and the town devastated by an earthquake in 1343, but there is still the odd remnant of Amalfi's past glories around today, and the town has a crumbly attractiveness to its whitewashed courtyards and alleys that makes it fun to wander through.

The **Duomo**, at the top of a steep flight of steps, utterly dominates the town's main piazza, its decorated, almost gaudy facade topped by a glazed tiled cupola that's typical of the area. The bronze doors of the church came from Constantinople and date from 1066. Inside it's a mixture of Saracen and Romanesque styles, though now heavily restored, with a major relic in the body of Saint Andrew buried in its crypt, though the cloister is the most appealing part of the building – oddly Arabic in feel, with its whitewashed arches and palms.

Close to the duomo, the **Museo Civico** displays the original *Tavoliere Amalfitane* – the book of maritime laws which governed the republic, and the rest of the Mediterranean, until 1570. Amalfi is now better for its high-quality paper industry, and you can visit a functioning **paper mill** just outside the town, where there's a museum with paper-making tools, manuscripts and other such artefacts.

Practical details

Beyond these, the focus is along the seafront, a humming, cheerfully vigorous strand given over to street stalls, a carpark for the town's considerable tourist traffic – and an acceptably crowded **beach**. There's an **AAST** office (daily 8am–2pm & 4.30–7pm), next door to the post office, which has maps of the town and information on accommodation. If you do want to stay – and Amalfi is the best place along this coast (aside from Sorrento and Salerno) to find accommodation – there are a couple of fair-priced **hotels**: the *Proto*, off Via Genova (☎089/871.003), has double rooms for just over L20,000, the *Vittoria*, Salita Truglio 5, also off Via Genova (☎089/871.057), for upwards of L30,000. As for **eating**, the *Green Bar*, a little way up the main street on the right, has pizza slices, *calzone* and the like, and a prodigious choice of beer. For something more substantial, try *Trattoria Vincola*, further up, where you can sit outside; *Trattoria Gemma*, back towards the sea on the opposite side, has a lovely terrace overlooking the street; or there's *Il Tari*, also on the left side of the street, which is also inexpensive.

Ravello

The best views of the coast can be had inland from Amalfi, in **RAVELLO**: another renowned spot, "closer to the sky than the seashore" wrote Andre Gide – with some justification. Ravello was also an independent republic for a while, and for a time an outpost of the Amalfi city-state; now it's not much more than a large village, but its unrivalled location, spread across the top of one of the coast's mountains, 1100 feet up, makes it more than worth the thirty-minute bus ride up from Amalfi – although, like most of this coast, the charms of Ravello haven't been recently discovered. Wagner based part of *Parsifal*, one of his last operas, on the place; John Huston filmed his languid movie *Beat the Devil* in the town (a film in which the locations easily outshine the plot) and Gore Vidal is just one of the best known of many celebrities who spend at least part of the year here.

Buses drop off on the main **Piazza Vescovado**, outside the **Duomo**: a bright eleventh-century church, renovated in 1786, that's dedicated to Sant Pantaleone, a fourth-century saint whose blood – kept in a chapel on the left-hand side – is supposed to liquefy like Naples' San Gennaro twice a year on May 19 and August 27. It's a richly decorated church, with a pair of bronze doors, twelfth-century, cast with 54 scenes of the Passion; inside, attention focuses on a monumental *ambo* of 1272, adorned with mosaics of dragons and birds on spiral columns supported by roaring lions, and with the coat of arms and the vivacious profiles of the Rufolo family, the donors, on each side. The superb bust, downstairs in the crypt, is also said to be a portrait of Sig. Rufolo, alongside a collection of mosaics and reliquaries from the same era.

The Rufolos figure again on the other side of the square, where various leftovers of their **Villa Rufolo** (daily 9.30am–1pm & 3–7pm; L1000) scatter among rich gardens overlooking the precipitous coastline. If the crowds put you off – and you certainly won't be alone here – turn left by the entrance and walk up the steps over the tunnel for the best (free) view over the shore, from where it's a pleasant stroll through the back end of Ravello to the main square. Failing that, walk in the opposite direction to the **Villa Cimbrone** (daily 9am–sunset; L2000), ten minutes away, whose gardens, laid out by an obscure Yorkshire aristocrat earlier this century, spread across the furthest tip of Ravello's ridge. Most of the villa itself is not open to visitors, though it's worth peeking into the crumbly, flower-hung cloister as you go in, and the open crypt down the steps from here – probably the only crypt with views over cliffs and open sea. But the gardens are entirely accessible, dotted with statues and leading down to what must be the most gorgeous spot in Ravello – a belvedere that looks down to Alatri below and the sea beyond.

Practical details

Buses run up to Ravello from Amalfi roughly hourly from the seafront carpark. It's not really worth staying – accommodation is much cheaper in Amalfi – but if you can't tear yourself away the **AAST** on Piazza Vescovado (Mon–Sat 9am–8pm, Sun 8am–1pm) has information on rooms. There are some marvellous places **to eat**, all doing their best to exploit the location, one of the best of which is the

Giardino restaurant, on the way to the Villa Cimbrone – though this isn't at all cheap and tends to be snooty. For more down-to-earth food and service, but equally spectacular views, the *Garden* restaurant, through the tunnel off the main piazza on Via Boccaccio, should more than suffice.

Amalfi to Salerno

The coast road maintains the attack on the senses beyond Amalfi, though the resorts grow less exclusive and for the most part less appealing. **ALATRI** is an extension of Amalfi really, and was indeed another part of the maritime republic, with a similarly styled church sporting another set of bronze doors from Constantinople, manufactured in 1086. **MINORI**, further along, is a pretty village with the ruins of a Roman villa and a small beach. **MAIORI**, next, has a longer but rather ugly stretch of beach and is a much louder, brasher place than anywhere else along here – not at all the coast's most enticing spot. Stay on the bus as far as **CETARA**, a tiny fishing village clasped tightly at the end of its narrow valley that has another very small beach, three restaurants and hotel – the *Cetus* – which has rooms for around L50,000 a double but a lovely location perched on top of its own sandy cove. **VIETRI SUL MARE** is larger and livelier, and the location of a small ceramics industry. Most of the town's shops sell ceramic wares, and you can visit a factory where they make the goods, not to mention the town's long broad beach.

Salerno and south

Capital of Campania's southernmost province, **SALERNO** has much of the scruffy, disorganised charm of Naples: a busy, dirty port city that's well off most travellers' itineraries, and so holds a good supply of cheap accommodation – making it a good base for both the Amalfi coast and the ancient site of Paestum further south. During medieval times the town's medical school was the most eminent in Europe. More recently, it was the site of the Allied landing of September 9, 1943 – a landing which reduced much of the centre to rubble. The subsequent rebuilding has restored neither charm nor efficiency to the town centre, which is an odd mixture of wide, rather characterless boulevards and a small medieval core full of intriguingly dark corners and alleys. But the town's siting, strung along the top of its gulf and looking across to the sheer wall of the Amalfi coast, is fine.

Arriving and staying
Salerno's **railway station** lies at the southern end of the town centre on Piazza Vittorio Veneto. City and local **buses** pull up here; those from Paestum and further south arrive and leave from Piazza Della Concordia, down by the waterside nearby; buses from Amalfi or Naples use the *SITA* bus station at Corso Garibaldi 119.

For information, there's an **EPT** office outside the station (Mon–Fri 9am–8pm, Sat 9am–noon), which has free maps, hotel lists and information on the Salerno area, and an **AAST** at the other end of town on Piazza Amendola. There's a **youth hostel** about ten minutes' walk south from the station (☎089/237.234), next to a mucky beach, but it's small and often welcomes members only. Alternatively, most of the town's cheaper **hotels** are handily placed along (or just off) Corso V. Emanuele, which leads north into the town centre from the station. The *Italia*, about 150m down on the right (☎089/226.653), is about the cheapest, with doubles for L20,000; others include the *Santa Rosa*, at no. 16 (☎089/225.346), for L26,000, the *Corso*, at no. 66 (☎089/232.163), for around L22,000, and the *Cinzia*, at no. 74 (☎089/232.773), for L22,000 – though this last is rather uninviting.

The Town

There isn't a great deal to see in Salerno, but it's pleasant to wander through the vibrant streets of the centre, especially the old medieval quarter at the far end of Corso V. Emanuele, where **Via dei Mercanti** is the main axis. To the right up Via Duomo, the **Duomo** squeezes into the congested streets, an enormous church built originally in 1076 by Robert Guiscard. Like the cathedrals of the Amalfi coast, the main features are yet another set of bronze doors from Constantinople and, inside, two elegant mosaic pulpits dating from 1173 and a similarly decorated paschal candlestick. Outside, the courtyard is cool and shady, its columns plundered from Paestum, centring on a gently gurgling fountain.

Outside, the opening times of the **Museo Duomo** are erratic but it's worth a hammer on the door to see its large altar-front, embellished with ivory panels in the late eleventh century and the largest work of its kind in the world. Failing that, turn right out of the courtyard, left at the bottom of the steps, then first right, and 50m or so further on is the **Museo Provinciale** (daily 9am–1pm & 5–7.30pm) – a fairly dull museum occupying two floors of a much-restored Romanesque monastery and displaying a deadening array of fossils and fragments of ancient sculpture from the surrounding area.

Eating and swimming

Salerno isn't a tourist town and it shows in the choice of **restaurants**. Again there's a dense concentration of cheap eateries around the railway station, including – for those on the tightest of budgets – takeaway pizza places on Piazza Mazzini and around the corner on Corso Garibaldi, and a good *tavola calda* at Corso V. Emanuele 15. The fruit and veg market at the far end of Corso V. Emanuele is a good source for picnics. Among sit-down options, the nearby *Trattoria Rosalia*, tucked away off Corso V. Emanuele at Via degli Orti 22, is a reliable and inexpensive restaurant, used by locals, serving decent fish and seafood – as is *La Trappola*, among another grouping of restaurants at the other end of town at Via Roma 170. Incidentally, if you want to **swim**, there is a small scrap of beach in the town at the northern end of Lungomare Trieste, but you'd really do better to either take a bus north to one of the towns along the Amalfi shore or south to Paestum and the northern Cilento (see below).

Paestum

Site and museum 9am–1 hour before sunset; L3000

About an hour's bus ride south of Salerno, the ancient site of **PAESTUM** spreads across a large area at the bottom end of the **Piana del Sele** – a wide flat plain grazed by buffalo that produce a good quantity of southern Italy's mozzarella cheese. Paestum, or *Poseidonia* as it was known, was founded by Greeks from Sybaris in the sixth century BC, and later, in 273 BC, colonised by the Romans, who latinised the name. But by the ninth century a combination of malaria and

Saracen raids had decimated the population and left the buildings deserted and gradually overtaken by thick forest, and the site wasn't rediscovered until the eighteenth century during the building of a road through here. It's a desolate, open place even now ("inexpressibly grand" Shelley called it), mostly unrecognisable ruin but with three golden-stoned **temples** that are among the best preserved Doric temples in Europe. Of these, the Temple of Neptune, dating from about 450 BC, is the most complete, with only its roof and parts of the inner walls missing. The Basilica of Hera, built a century or so earlier, retains its double rows of columns, while the Temple of Ceres at the northern end of the site was used as a Christian church for a time – though it's now sectioned off from the public. In between, the forum is little more than an open space, and the buildings around pure rubble. But the **museum**, across the road, holds finds from the site and around, including a set of archaic period Greek metopes from another temple at the mouth of the Sele River, a few miles north – brutish, rather crude scenes of fighting and hunting mainly. Much else is dull stuff, but you should see the fourth-century ceramics and tomb paintings at the back of the building, possibly the only extant examples of Greek wall painting – most again rather crude except for those from the so-called "Tomb of the Diver", which are graceful and expressively naturalistic pieces of work.

Paestum practicals

It's perfectly feasible to see Paestum on a day-trip from either Salerno to the north or Agrópoli to the south (see below) – to which it's much nearer. However, you can also stay in one of the many **hotels** or **campsites** that are strewn along the sandy shore beyond the site. The **AAST** on the main road close to the site entrance (Mon–Sat 8am–2pm) has details. Or just walk down to the beach (about fifteen minutes) and take your pick: the *Santa Lucia* (☎0828/811.133) and *Poseidonia* (☎0828/811.066) are among the cheaper hotels, close by the site to the left of where the main road hits the beach, with double rooms for L25,000–35,000. Most of the campsites are much of a muchness: the *Apollo* (☎0828/811.178) and *Mare Pineta* (☎0828/811.086) are two of the most central, to the right of the main beach road and well signposted. As for the **beach** itself, the development behind it is fairly tacky, and it's a bit grimy in places. But space, even in peak season, is rarely too much of a problem.

The Cilento

Immediately south of Paestum, the coastline bulges out into a broad mountainous hump of territory known as the **Cilento** – one of the remotest parts of Campania, thickly wooded with olives and chestnuts. The region divides into two distinct parts: inland, which is still wedded to a fairly traditional way of life, and the coast, which is where tourists go – although even in the main resorts you'll find far fewer people than further north.

The Cilento coast

After the sands of the Piana del Sele, the Cilento coast is fairly rocky territory, more suited to scuba-diving than sunbathing, though it does have sandy moments. **AGRÓPOLI**, the first town you reach, fifteen minutes out from

Paestum, is a good base for the ruins (buses every hour), and its blend of the peaceful old quarter, heaped on a headland, and the new modern centre down below, makes for a nice place to spend a few days, with a vivacious main street *passeggiata*. The beaches aren't great – dirty on the north side of town, crowded to the south in the Lido di Trentova – but you can swim from the flat rocks in the harbour and the water's perfectly clean. For **accommodation**, the *Hotel Carola* (☎0974/823.005) in the harbour is central and has double rooms for a little over L40,000, or there's the *La Lanterna* (☎0974/838.003), which has rooms for around L25,000. Agrópoli is also on the main Salerno–Reggio railway line.

Buses from Salerno run down the coast as far as the next town of Santa Maria di Castellebate, 8km south, but if you've time and energy it's preferable to walk, taking the **dirt road** from behind the Lido di Trentova's tennis courts, which skirts the hillsides past abandoned farmhouses, above rocky bays, eventually becoming a fairly good-quality track a little way before **SANTA MARIA DI CASTELLEBATE**. This is another small resort, with a small harbour and bus connections south, along one of the most isolated stretches of the Cilento coast. There's a long **beach** of clean, golden sand just north of the town, the so-called "Lago" area, close to where the path from Agrópoli comes out, with a number of inexpensive **hotels and campsites**. The *Pizzeria Zia Rosa* (☎0974/961.506) is the cheapest place to stay, letting out rooms in summer for L30,000–40,000; *La Duna* and *Trezene* are the best value of several campsites.

SAN MARCO, three kilometres or so further along from Santa Maria, is a picturesque, very active fishing village which supplies fish to most of the villages along this part of the coast, though its tiny centre can get very crowded in summer. A narrow track leads from here down to **PUNTA LICOSA**, where there's a small harbour fringed by rocks from which you can swim. The offshore reef that's topped by a lighthouse is inhabited by lizards said to be of a unique species. From here you can either return to San Marco or follow the track around to **OGLIASTRO MARINA**, an attractive little village with a hotel and cheap *pensione* (*Da Carmine*) and some indifferent restaurants – and a long, rather dirty beach that in summer attracts a good number of holidaymakers.

The facilities, and the beaches, improve the closer you get to **ACCIAROLI**, about 10km further south – one of the Cilento's larger resorts, and a port for the hydrofoils which ply the coast during summer. The railway joins the shoreline again at **MARINA D'ASCEA**, a fairly indifferent resort but surrounded by hotels and campsites, especially along the lengthy sand beach which stretches north to Marina del Casalvelino.

Close by, **MARINA DI VELIA** gives access to the site of **Velia** (daily 9am–1 hour before sunset; L3000) – comprising the ruins of the Hellenistic town of *Elea*, founded around 540 BC and an important port and cultural centre, home to its own school of philosophy. Later it became a favourite holiday resort for wealthy Romans, Horace just one of many who came here on the advice of his doctor. The decline of Velia parallels that of Paestum – malarial swamp rendering much of the area uninhabitable – though the upper reaches were lived in until the fifteenth century. There, however, the comparison ends: the remains of Velia are considerably more decimated than those of Paestum and the town was never as crucial a centre, with nothing like as many temples. At the centre of the ruins the "Porta Rosa", named after the wife of the archaeologist who conducted the first investigations, is one of the earliest arches ever found – and the first indication to experts that the Greeks knew how to construct such things. Up from here, the

Acropolis has relics of an amphitheatre and a temple, together with a massive Norman tower – visible for some distance around.

Outside the site there's a restaurant, the *Casa Bianca*, and beyond here a small beach – though this can get crowded in summer. The beaches further down the coast near **PISCIOTTA** are better, and the town itself is a lively place of an evening. **PALINURO**, too, further south, is worth a stop, named after the legendary pilot of the *Aeneid*, who is supposed to have been buried here. It's a more cosmopolitan spot than anywhere else on the Cilento coast, and so can be packed out. But the harbour area retains a certain fishing port authenticity, and it's a good alternative to Agrópoli, both as a base for the site of Velia and a beach-bumming spot. There are a number of **campsites** and **hotels** around – the *Sant'Anna* (☎0974/931.150) and *Parigino* (☎ 0974/931.027) start at about L30,000 for a double – though bear in mind that in August at least it can be a good idea to book in advance. For **food**, you can either eat adequately in two restaurants in the upper part of town – the *Corniglia* or *La Carminella*, on Capo Palinuro overlooking the sea. Or blow your last few lire at the *Da Carmelo* restaurant, 2km south of town, whose fish and seafood is said to be the best for miles around.

The last real resort, **MARINA DI CAMEROTA**, is less busy than Palinuro, and has a shingly beach, three campsites and a couple of hotels – the *Pollina* (☎0974/932.051) offers doubles for L30,000. **POLICASTRO BUSSENTINO**, too, is a quiet resort, with a crumbly *centro storico* and a shingle beach in a majestic setting, clasped by the high walls of the Golfo di Policastro. Or you can push straight on to **SAPRI** – not much of a place in itself, but with an outstanding restaurant in *A Cantina I Mustazz* on the main town square, Piazza Plebiscito, at which you can sample traditional Cilento cooking at its best, and at very reasonable prices.

Inland Cilento

Inland the Cilento is lonely and often inaccessible, especially if you don't have your own transport. The train cuts through part of the region but doesn't stop, buses are few and far between and in any case there's only a couple of proper roads winding across the rocky mountainsides. There are also few large settlements, and little in the way of accommodation – although the countryside can be gorgeous, offering some splendidly panoramic routes, fine mountain walks and spectacular gorges and caves.

There are a number of villages you might structure a long day's car journey around. In the north, the caves of **CASTELCIVITA** (L4000) form just one of several systems that riddle the Cilento, discovered by two brothers who got lost here in 1889 – one of whom died as a result, while the other was found to have gone totally insane. Guided tours every half-hour wind past intricate stalactites and under clusters of bats; whatever the weather outside, bring a jumper – it can get cold.

About 10km further south (though much longer by road), the village of **ROSCIGNO VECCHIO** is an example of a typical Cilento village from the turn of the century, deserted now following a landslip but with a small museum of Cilento rural life in its old church. Back towards the coast, **VALLO DELLA LUCANIA**, a little way inland from Velia, is an example of the more prosperous recent years here, the largest town inland and a lively place with a busy *passeggiata* of an evening. Three kilometres outside, **NOVA VELIA** is a tiny village overshadowed by 1705m-high **Monte Sacro**, at the top of which is a **sanctuary** which has been a place of pilgrimage since 1323 – an odd, very remote complex of dormitories and churches and even a small post office that's open from the end of May until the beginning of October. With luck and L15,000 you should be able to stay the night.

travel details

Naples And The Bay
Metropolitana
Connects Naples Centrale, and a number of other stops within the city centre, with Mergellina, Fuorigrotta, Bagnoli and Pozzuoli.
Circumflegrea
Connects Naples Montesanto with Cuma, Lido Fusaro, Torregaveta. departures every 20min.
Circumvesuviana (information ☎779.2444)
This line runs between Naples and Sorrento, with many stops around the southern part of the Bay, roughly every 20min.
Ferrovia Cumana (information ☎551.3328)
Connects Naples Montesanto with Fuorigrotta, Agnana, Bangoli, Pozzuoli, Baia, Fusaro, etc. Departures every 20min.

Trains
From Naples to Salerno (hourly; 45min); Agrópoli-Castellebate (around 10 daily; 1hr 15min); Sapri (12 daily; 2hr); Paola (Calabria) (every 2hr; 3hr); Avellino/Benevento (5 daily; 1hr 20min/2hr); Caserta (every 30min; 40min); Santa Maria Cápua Vetere/Cassino (8 daily; 30min/1hr 30min); Formia (hourly; 1hr); Rome (hourly; 2hr 30min); Foggia (4 daily; 3hr).
From Benevento to Foggia (8 daily; 1hr 20min).
From Salerno to Paestum/Agrópoli-Castellebate/Ascea Marina/Sapri (around 6 daily; 40min/50min/1hr 40min/2hr 30min).

Buses
From Naples to Caserta (every 20min; 1hr); Cápua (hourly; 1hr 15min); Benevento (every 2hr; 1hr 30min); Salerno (every 30min).
From Sorrento to Positano (hourly; 40min); Amalfi (hourly; 1hr 40min); Salerno (every 1–2hr; 2hr 45min).
From Salerno to Naples (every 15–30min; 1hr); Vietri (every 20min; 20min); Amalfi (hourly; 1hr 10min); Positano (every 1–2hr; 2hr); Sorrento (every 1–2hr; 2hr 45min); Paestum (hourly; 1hr); Agrópoli (hourly; 1hr 15min).
From Agrópoli to Salerno (hourly; 1hr 15min); Paestum (hourly; 15min); Santa Maria di Castellebate (hourly; 30min); Acciaroli (6 daily; 55min); Sapri (1 daily; 3hr 30min).

Ferries
From Naples to Sorrento (3 daily ferries/6 daily hydrofoils; 1hr 15min/40min); Palermo (1 daily at 8.30pm; 10hr 30min); Cagliari (every Sun & Wed at 5.30pm; 15hr 30min); Aeolian Islands/Milazzo (every Wed & Sat at 9pm; 12hr); Reggio/Catania/Siracusa/Malta (every Thurs at 8.30pm; 7hr/24hr).

For details of ferry and hydrofoil connections between Naples, the Amalfi coast and Salerno and the islands, see p.735.

CHAPTER FOURTEEN

PUGLIA

P uglia is the long strip of land, 400km from north to south, which makes up the "heel" of Italy. It was for centuries a strategic province, colonised, invaded and conquered (like its near neighbours, Calabria and Sicily), by just about every major power of the day; from the Greeks through to the Spanish. As elsewhere in the south, each ruling dynasty left its own distinctive mark on the landscape and architecture, often changing the face of the province completely – as with the surviving traces of Roman agricultural schemes and the fortified medieval towns. There's no escaping some of the historical influences in Puglia, paramount the Saracenic casbah-like quarters of many towns and cities, the one at **Bari** the biggest and most atmospheric. The Normans covered Puglia with splendidly ornate cathedrals; there's one at **Trani** which skilfully blends many strands of craftsmanship, from north and south. And the Baroque exuberance of towns like **Lecce** and **Martina Franca** are evidence of the Spanish legacy. But if there's one symbol of Puglia that stands out, it's the imposing castles built by the Swabian, Frederick II, all over the province – foremost of which are the **Castel del Monte** and the remnants of the palace at **Lucera**.

Despite these attractions, Puglia is still very much a province through which you pass on the way elsewhere, an echo of the Middle Ages when crusading knights stopped off en route to the Holy Land. Today, the cities, including Bari, have little that's characteristic enough to warrant long stays: **Táranto** and its surroundings have fought a losing battle with the local steel industry, while **Bríndisi** is known and visited only for its ferry connections with Greece. Nevertheless, there's a geographical diversity to Puglia which can be very attractive, given the time to get away from the main train routes. The very southern tip, the **Salentine peninsula** is rocky and dry, more Greek than Italian, while there's plenty of barren mountain scenery in the undulating plateau of **Le Murge**, in the centre of the province. Best escape, though, is to the north and to the mountains, forests and beaches of the **Gárgano promontory**, slowly opening up to holidaymakers seeking some of the finest unpolluted sand and sea to be found anywhere on the Adriatic.

Getting around Puglia by public transport is fairly easy, at least as far as the main towns and cities go. *FS* **trains** connect nearly all the major places, while small, private lines head into previously remote areas – in the Gárgano and on the edges of Le Murge. Most other places can be reached by **bus**, though as ever services are often infrequent or inconveniently early – a problem which can only really be solved by taking, or hiring, your own **car**. Incidentally, if you're on your way **to Greece**, it's worth noting that you don't have to leave from Bríndisi: there are year-round departures from Bari (to Yugoslavia too) and seasonal ferries from **Otranto**, south of Lecce.

Foggia and the Tavoliere

The broad sweep of the **Tavoliere plain** stretches from the Basilicata border to the edge of the Gargano massif – flat, fertile lands that are southern Italy's wheat bowl – and source of much of the country's pasta. It was the Romans who attempted the first intense cultivation of the area, parcelling the land up into neat squares for distribution to its pensionable centurions. This lent the land its chessboard appearance, from which the Tavoliere takes its name, but for the centurions the gift was a mixed blessing. Foggia province proved to be an unhealthy place, an earthquake-prone swampland rife with malarial mosquitos, and settlements here suffered from disease and disaster in fairly equal proportions. It wasn't until the advent of irrigation schemes in the 1920s that the mosquitos lost their malarial bite, and the area began to take on its present rich appearance.

Foggia

The Tavoliere's main town, **FOGGIA**, looms out of the plain without warning, a fine starting-point for exploring northern Puglia and the Gárgano promontory though in itself itself not that encouraging a stop. Although Foggia flourished under Frederick II, who declared it an Imperial residence and built a palace here, the town was devastated in turn by the French in 1528, an earthquake in 1731, and Allied bombs during the World War II. Today the city's streets are all reassuringly earthquake-proof, wide and low-built, a modern layout which is handsome enough but doesn't make for a lot of investigative interest. You're going to have to search hard in between the tree-lined boulevards for what little is left of the old town.

What there is scatters around the **Duomo**, left off Corso Vittorio Emanuele, the main drag that runs down from the central, fountained Piazza Cavour. The cathedral is an odd Romanesque-Baroque sandwich, the top part tacked on in the eighteenth century after the earthquake. Much of what was once notable about it was lost in the 'quake – particularly the tomb of Charles I of Anjou and a receptacle said to contain Frederick II's heart – but the crypt survived, and it features some finely decorated Romanesque capitals. A Byzantine icon, housed in a chapel next to the presbytery, was reputedly discovered in a pond by eleventh-century shepherds, upon which burned three flames – now the symbol of the city.

While you're here, take a look at the nearby **Museo Civico** (Tues–Sun 9am–1pm; free), reached by walking on down the Corso to Via Arpi and turning right; the museum is on Piazza Nigri. Incorporated into the side of the building are three portals, one of which – the Porta Grande, with the thoughtful-looking eagles – is all that remains of Frederick II's Imperial palace. Duck inside and there's the usual regional archaeological finds, but also an interesting section on local life and folklore.

That really is it, as far as Foggia's sights go, though there are enough green spaces and shopping streets up in the new town to occupy any remaining time – something you might well have, as Foggia is an important rail junction, on the main Bologna–Lecce and Naples–Bari lines.

Practical details

The **railway station** is on the northern edge of town, a short walk from Piazza Cavour and the centre. Local **buses** (for Lucera and Troia) arrive at and depart from just outside. The **EPT** (Mon–Fri 8.30am–1pm, Sat 8.30–11am), bad on Foggia, good on the Gárgano promontory, is well out of the centre a long slog away at Via Senatore E. Perrone 17, off Piazza Puglia – probably not worth the bother if you're just passing through.

Staying in Foggia is possible though not a desperately attractive option; Lucera is a better bet if you're not in a hurry. There are several rather rundown *pensioni* near the station, but most are uninspiring and not particularly cheap. Better bets are the *Hotel Bologna*, Via Monfalcone 53 (☎0881/21.341), down Viale XXIV Maggio from the station then second right, and *Hotel Venezia*, Via Piave 40 (☎0881/26.711), the third right – both of which have doubles for L30,000. The only time that bed space will be short is at the beginning of May, during the **Fiera di Foggia**, one of Italy's oldest fairs (though what was once a medieval fair is, today, a huge international agricultural affair held on the outskirts of the town).

Lucera

Just eighteen kilometres west, within easy reach of Foggia (hourly buses), **LUCERA** is a far better introduction to Puglia, a small town with a bright and bustling centre in the process of being carefully restored. Once the capital of the Tavoliere, it has a distinct charm, its vast castle dominating the landscape for miles around. It was once a thriving Saracen city: Frederick II, having forced the Arabs out of Sicily, resettled 20,000 of them here, on the site of an abandoned Roman town, allowing them complete freedom of religious worship – an almost unheard of act of liberalism for the early thirteenth century.

Buses arrive in Piazza del Popolo, from where it's only a short walk up Via Gramsci to the **Duomo**, which marks the centre of the medieval walled town. It's a dark, rather miserable building built on the site of a mosque that was destroyed by the Angevins, who massacred the Arabic inhabitants of Lucera in the early fourteenth century. At the end of Angevin rule, little remained of the Islamic-influenced buildings which once adorned the town. However, though the buildings may have been destroyed, the Angevins didn't alter the Arabic layout of Lucera and there's a powerful atmosphere here – best appreciated by wandering the narrow streets of the old town, peering into the lived-in courtyards and alleyways. Close to the cathedral, a little way down Via de Nicastri, is the **Museo Civico** (Tues–Fri 9am–2pm, Wed & Fri also 5–7pm, Sat & Sun 9am–1pm; L1000), well stocked with Greek pottery and their Puglian copies. There are some fine mosaics and terracotta heads too, and the bust of a Greek youth said (rather optimistically) to be that of Alexander the Great.

Other sights are all outside the old centre, most notably the **Castello** (sunrise–sunset; free), built by Frederick and designed to house a lavish court which included an exotic collection of wild beasts. To get there from Piazza Duomo, follow Via Bovio and Via Federico II to Piazza Matteotti and look for the signs. The largest in southern Italy after Largopescole in Basilicata, the castle commands spectacular views over the Tavoliere, stretching across to the foothills of the Appenines to the west and the mountains of Gárgano to the east. Contained within the walls and towers, a kilometre long, are the suggestive remains of Frederick's great palace, fragments of mosaic work and fallen columns peering out of a dense undergrowth of wild flowers.

Stopping over in Lucera wouldn't be a bad thing. There's an excellent **hotel**, the *Albergo Al Passeto*, at Piazza del Popolo 30 (☎0881/941.124) – L35,000 with bath. Built into the old walls of Lucera, it has a fine **restaurant** too.

Troia

Frequent buses also make the short ride (from either Lucera or Foggia) to **TROIA**, 18km due south of Lucera. The locals seem curiously blasé as to the origin of their village's name (it means "bitch" in Italian), and no one is able to offer a reasonable explanation. Whatever the reason, the Troiani atone for the name by having five patron saints, whose statues are paraded around town in procession every July 9.

At all other times of the year the highlight in Troia – an otherwise quiet, dusty village – is the excellent **Duomo**, an intriguing eleventh-century blend of Byzantine and Apulian-Romanesque styles, with a generous hint of Saracen influence, too. The great bronze doors are covered with reliefs of animals and biblical figures, while above, surrounded by a frenzy of carved lions frozen in stone, is an extraordinary rose window. Distinctly Saracen in flavour, it resembles a finely carved piece of oriental ivory made up of eleven stone panels, each one delicately carved. There's more exact detail inside too, including a curiously decorated pulpit and some ornate capitals.

West and south of Foggia

Well off the beaten track in Foggia province are some of the most handsome hill-top villages in this part of Italy. Most are little visited and requests for information about them are likely to be met with a blank gaze at the tourist office. Indeed, although the area is slowly beginning to open up to vistors, it's still very much a quiet backwater of forests and hills.

Most remote is the scattering of settlements which lies to the **west of Lucera**, in the gentle **Monti di Daunia**. The inhabitants are Albanian in origin, first arriving in the fifteenth century to help fight the French, and later as refugees fleeing from the Turks, though nowadays it's hard to get here without your own wheels, and there's not a lot here if you do.

South of Foggia is more interesting. **BOVINO** near the Campanian border is a small and distinctly medieval village, with fragments of Roman fortifications and a thirteenth-century cathedral looking out over a fine landscape of undulating wooded slopes. The snag is that Bovino is an alarmingly steep seven-kilometre climb away from its railway station, and if you're travelling by train **ORDONA**, over to the east, is probably an easier target. Sited on the banks of the river Carapelle, the ancient Daunic people of the Tavoliere once had a town here, destroyed by Pyrrhus (who used elephants) in the third century BC. Over what was left the Romans built *Herdonia*, large parts of which still survive. The **site** (open at all times; free) is a short walk south from the present village of Ordona, and there are the obvious remains of a forum and a small amphitheatre, as well as scantier pieces of a small basilica and two temples.

Manfredonia

By Puglian standards, **MANFREDONIA** is a new town, a mere 600 years old, founded – as the name suggests – by Manfred, illegitimate son of Frederick II. The Austrians struck the first blow of World War I on Italian soil here, by bombing the town railway station in 1915, but this is really – apart from recent demonstrations against chemical waste dumping in the port – Manfredonia's only claim to fame. The town is seen more as the gateway to the Gárgano promontory and most people pass quickly through. Still, what the town lacks in historical sights is more than made up for by its sandy beaches, which stretch for miles down the coast.

The easiest way to reach Manfredonia is by train from Foggia: from the **railway station**, turn right and it's a short walk along Viale Aldo Moro to Piazza Marconi. Just across the square Corso Manfredi leads down to the **AAST** (Mon–Sat 8am–2pm), good for maps and information on the Gárgano area. Further down Corso Manfredi, the **Castello** was started by Manfred and extended by the Angevins. Its huge bastions were added in 1607 by the Spanish to stave off a Turkish attack: they failed to do so, the Turks landing in 1620, ravaging the hapless inhabitants and destroying much of the town – though most of the protective walls still survive.

The castle now houses the **Museo Nazionale** (Tues–Sun 9am–1.30pm & 4–7.30pm; L2000), largely devoted to Daunic finds from the seventh and sixth centuries BC, particularly several stone slabs or *stelae*, thought to be tombstones, richly carved with images of armoured warriors, female figures and scenes from daily life.

Practical details: sleeping and eating

If you're going to use Manfredonia as a base, there's no shortage of **accommodation**. Most reasonable in town is the *Albergo San Michele*, Via degli Orti 10 (☎0884/21.953), with rooms for L25,000. If this is full, the nearby *Albergo Santa Maria Grazie*, Piazza San Nacquisto 5 (☎0884/22.465), has similarly priced though shabbier rooms.

There are plenty of places **to eat** too, best of which is the *Trattoria Il Baracchio*, Corso Roma 38 – traditional Puglian dishes and a cheapish *pranzo turistico*. Otherwise, try the *Al Fuego*, Via G. di Palma 13, signposted down a side street off Corso Manfredi, a little way down on the right from the AAST.

The beach: Siponto

SIPONTO, 3km south down the coast from Manfredonia, was once a thriving medieval port. But constant malarial attacks and damaging earthquakes have left it with little beyond its good sandy **beaches** to draw you – all an easy ten-minute walk from the railway station. They're signposted from town and in summer you can expect them to be packed to the gills.

Siponto is also a fairly useful place **to stay** if you don't fancy Manfredonia: the cheapest choice is the *Ninfa Marina* on the Lungomare del Sole (☎0884/541.551), which offers rooms for L22,000. There are **campsites** strung out south along the coast, the nearest 4km from town, but unless things have changed recently, you'll probably have to walk there; check with the AAST in Manfredonia.

The Gárgano Promontory

The **Gárgano Promontory** rises like an island from the flat plains of the Tavoliere, geographically and culturally different from the rest of Puglia. Its landscape is remarkably diverse: beaches and lagoons to the north, a rocky, indented eastern coast and a mountainous, green heartland of oaks and beech trees – reminiscent of a Germanic forest rather than a corner of southern Italy. For centuries the promontory was extremely isolated, visited only by pilgrims making their way along the valley to Monte Sant'Angelo and its shrine. Nowadays tourism has taken off in a big way, especially on the coast around Vieste, though much of the interior remains supremely unspoiled and quiet. Plans are underway to turn the whole peninsula into a national park, something that would help protect Gárgano from overbearing development.

Approaches to the promontory are pretty straightforward. *FS* trains run from Foggia to Manfredonia on the southeast side of Gárgano, from where it's only 16km by bus to Monte Sant'Angelo, and there are buses straight up the coast as well. Alternatively, in the north of the region, *Ferrovia del Gárgano (FG)* operates **trains** between San Severo and Peschici-Calanelle, from where a bus connects with Peschici. Note that most *FG* stations are quite a distance from the towns and villages they serve, so always go for the connecting bus if there is one.

Getting around can be a little more tortuous. **Buses** are run by three companies: *SITA* serves the inland towns and operates the inland route to Vieste; *ATAF* runs a coastal route to Vieste; while *FG* runs the trains and connecting buses in northern Gárgano, roughly between San Severo and Peschici. See "Travel Details" for more information.

Monte Sant'Angelo and the pilgrim route

Just to the north of Manfredonia, perched almost 800m up in the hills, **MONTE SANT'ANGELO** is the highest – and coldest – settlement in the Gárgano. Pilgrims have trudged up the switchback paths and roads for centuries to visit the spot where the archangel Michael is said to have made four separate appearances, mostly at the end of the fifth century – making the sanctuary here one of the earliest Christian shrines in Europe, and one of the most important in Italy. Today, the pilgrims come by coach, and the major festivals on May 8 and September 29 every year attract locals from miles around who turn up in traditional dress.

The **bus** from Manfredonia drops you in Piazza Duca d'Aosta, from where you should follow the road uphill to the edge of the old town and the Via Reale Basilica, where you'll find the **Santuario di San Michele** itself (daily 10am– dusk). Apart from a lean octagonal thirteenth-century campanile, the sanctuary seems rather plain on the outside, but from the small courtyard on the right a flight of stone steps leads down to the grotto – heralded by a magnificent pair of eleventh-century bronze doors, made in Constantinople, that form the entrance to the church built on the site of the cave in which the archangel first appeared (in 490). Opposite the campanile, another set of steps leads down to the nearby ruins of the **Chiesa di San Pietro**, behind which is the so-called **Tomba di Rotari** – an imposing domed tower once thought to be the tomb of Rothari, a seventh-century Lombard chieftain who was converted to Christianity. More prosaically,

THE GARGANO
PROMONTORY

it's more likely to have been a twelfth-century baptistry, the large baptismal font just on the right as you enter the tower. Little remains of the church itself, wrecked by an earthquake, but look out for the rose-window – a catherine wheel of entwined mermaids.

Back on Via Reale Basilica, it's an easy clamber up to the ruined Norman **Castello**, for good views over the town and valley. From here, you can cut down through the narrow whitewashed streets of the old town to Piazza San Francesco d'Assisi, and the **Museo Tancredi** (Tues–Sun 10am–12.30pm & 3.30–7pm; L1000), an arts and crafts museum housed in a fine, old vaulted building.

Some practicalities

Information can be had from the **Pro Loco** (Mon–Sat 9am–1pm & 4–6pm), just off Piazza Duca d'Aosta at Via C. Durazzo 2. They have a glossy booklet on the town which includes a useful map. If you're going to stay overnight (though don't count on available beds at the main pilgrimage times), best bet for **accommodation** is the spotlessly clean *Albergo Moderno*, Via Leone Garganico 34 (☎0884/61.331), which has double beds for L30,000; bear right at the Pro Loco and walk downhill – the hotel is on your left. Otherwise, there's **hostel** accommodation at the well sited *Casa del Pellegrino* on Via Carlo d'Angio (☎0884/62.396) – L11,000 a head out of season, a rip-off L22,500 July to Sept). **Eating** is straightforward at a number of places along Via Reale Basilica: *Trattoria Paradise* has an outdoor garden, while for pizzas *Sixty Seven* is the local choice.

The pilgrim route: San Giovanni Rotondo

The ancient **pilgrim route** weaved its way along the Stignano valley between San Severo in the west and Monte Sant'Angelo and until comparatively recently was the only road that linked the villages of the Gárgano interior. With your own transport, it's still a good route to explore a couple of the region's most important religious centres. By public transport, though, the service and connections from San Severo eastwards are sketchy. With this in mind, if you want to follow the pilgrim route by bus, you'll probably have to do it *returning* from Monte Sant'Angelo.

Direct bus services between Monte Sant'Angelo and the first village on the route, San Giovanni Rotondo, are inconveniently early and infrequent, and the village is actually better connected by bus with Manfredonia, a *SITA* service from there making around fourteen trips a day. Nestling under the highest peak hereabouts, Monte Calvo, **SAN GIOVANNI ROTONDO** is no mean religious centre itself, the burial place of Padre Pio, a local priest who died in the 1960s. At a time of reform for the Catholic church, Padre Pio caused consternation in the Vatican with his apparently effortless ability to appear before cardinals in Rome while asleep in San Giovanni Rotondo: there's no escaping his frail portrait throughout the Gárgano peninsula, but it's especially prominent here. The town takes its name from the **Rotonda di San Giovanni**, a building of indeterminate origin or purpose at the edge of the old town – like the Tomba di Rotari, it's thought to have been a baptistry, built on the site of an earlier pagan temple.

Nine kilometres further west, and looking splendidly out over the Tavoliere plain, **SAN MARCO IN LAMIS**, though considerably smaller than San Giovanni, is dominated by a huge sixteenth-century monastery. Every Good Friday the town holds a noisy and lively affair, of pagan origin, called the **fracchie**, when huge bundles of burning wood are hauled through the streets.

Vieste and the Costa Garganico

About 15km north of Manfredonia, the road tunnels under a mountain to emerge in a softer, greener landscape. **MATTINATA**, a small but popular resort with good campsites, sits back from the coast, overlooking olive groves and pine trees which drop down gently to a magnificent stretch of beach. Beyond Mattinata the road splits: one branch (which the *SITA* bus takes) winds its way through the eastern part of the Foresta Umbra (see below) to Vieste; the coastal route (and the *ATAF* bus) runs up to **PUGNOCHIUSO**, a panoramic bay dominated by a vast *Club Med* holiday village. If you're interested, one of the easiest of the local **hiking trails** starts close by. The path is clearly marked off the Mattinata–Pugnochiuso road, about 3km north of BAIA DI ZAGARE, and the trail (around 3km each way) runs sharply down to a beach, the *Spiaggia di Vignanotica*. To reach the start of the trail, take the *ATAF* bus for Pugnochiuso/Vieste and ask to be let off at Localita Megoli.

Vieste

VIESTE juts out into the Adriatic on two promontories, the most easterly point of the Gárgano peninsula. Fifty years ago there wasn't even a proper road here, but today Vieste, with its excellent beaches, is the holiday capital of Gárgano (and Puglia), particularly popular with German tourists who pack the streets and sand in the summer months. Despite this it has managed to survive as a lively and inviting town with, in addition to its active nightlife, enough of historical interest around to warrant at least a short stop – certainly if you're killing time before taking the ferry from here to the offshore Tremiti Islands.

The **old town** sits on the easternmost of the two promontories, at the tip of which stands the **Chiesa di San Francesco**, once a thriving monastery, and a **trabucco** – a mass of beams, winches and ropes still used by fishermen to catch mullet. Made of wood, these structures are a feature peculiar to the rocky Gárgano coast, probably Phoenician in origin, and the principle at least is straightforward. As mullet swim head to tail, a live mullet is attached to a line and used to entice others to swim over a net suspended below, which is then hoisted up to the platform.

From the church, climb up Via Mafrolla, walking into the old town to Piazza Seggio. Straight ahead, Via Duomo is site of the so-called **Chianca Amara**, the "bitter stone", where as many as 5000 local people were beheaded when the Turks sacked the town in 1554. Further down, beyond the stone, the **Cattedrale**, eleventh-century in origin but tampered with in the eighteenth century, is a cool retreat from the fierce glare of the sun in the whitewashed streets; and beyond here the **Castello** is another of Frederick II's installations – owned by the military now and not open to the public, but giving good views over the beaches and town.

You'll **arrive** by bus at Piazza Mazzoni, to the west of town; bear right from here along Viale XXIV Maggio, which becomes Corso Lorenzo Fazzini – the main street. On Piazza Vittorio Emanuele II, at the edge of the old town, there's an **AAST** office (Mon–Fri 9am–12.30pm & 5.30–7pm). Though there's no shortage of accommodation, **staying over** in Vieste, at least in the summer, can be very expensive. Try and avoid August if you can, when prices increase threefold. Best deals you'll find are *Pensione al Centro Storico*, Via Mafrolla 32 (☎0884/77.030), and *Albergo Vela Velo*, Lungomare Europa 19 (☎0884/76.303), around 500m north of the castle along the shore, both of which charge around L25,000 for a single room.

Around Vieste

There are a number of day trips worth making **around Vieste**. The most obvious move is to the **beaches** – a small one between the promontories, a second (*San Lorenzo*) to the north, and a third just to the south of town – the latter much the nicest. Best of all, though, and certainly less crowded, is the marvellous *Scialmarino* beach, 4km up the coast towards Peschici, walkable if you don't have transport.

Otherwise, Vieste is an excellent base for seeing the **Tremiti Islands** (see below) or for visiting the grotto-ridden **coastline** around the Testa del Gárgano, south of town. For **ferry tickets**, go to *Gárgano Viaggi*, Piazza Roma 7; the daily departures (currently at 9.05am) in the summer cost around L8600 one-way. Excursion boats for the grottoes leave from next to San Francesco church at 8.30am and 2.30pm, a three-hour trip; tickets, around L12,000, also available from *Gárgano Viaggi*.

Peschici and northern Gárgano

Atop its rocky vantage point overlooking a beautiful sandy bay, **PESCHICI** is without doubt the pick of all the towns and villages in the Gárgano – less touristy, less expensive and more attractive than Vieste, and well worth visiting while it remains that way. Though originally built in 970 as a buffer against Saracen incursions, its labyrinth of tiny streets and houses sporting domed roofs has a distinctly Arabic tinge. There's nothing to do beyond beach-lazing, though the town does make a good base for exploring parts of the coastline nearby – an interesting mixture of caves and defensive medieval towers. The easiest trips are to the grotto at **San Nicola**, 3km east of town (some buses), or 5km west to the **Torre di Monte Pucci** for some fine coastal views.

The *FG* **train** line ends at Calanelle, a few kilometres west of Peschici but connected to town by a bus. This, and other **buses**, drops you in the newer part of Peschici from where it's a short walk down to Corso Garibaldi, the main street. For information there's a **Pro Loco** (Mon–Sat 9am–noon & 4.30–8pm) just off the Corso, on Via XXIV Maggio. For **accommodation**, head for the *Locanda Al Castello*, Via Castello 29 (☎0884/94.038), which charges L40,000 for a double with bath. The Pro Loco also has lists of **private rooms** available in town, and there's a **campsite**, *Camping di Monte* (☎0884-91.717), west along the coast, about 1km from the *FG* station at San Menaio. **Eating**, there's an expensive but excellent restaurant in the *Locanda Al Castello*, with good home cooking; or, more cheaply, try *Fra Stefano* at Via Forno 8.

The **ferry** from Manfredonia to the Tremiti Islands makes a stop at Peschici's tiny port, down below the old town. Buy **tickets** at Corso Garibaldi 49; daily departures in summer, currently at 10.05am, L6800 one-way.

West along the coast

Sticking with the coast, there's a mass of white sandy beaches stretching from San Menaio to **RODI GARGANIGO** – originally a Greek settlement ("Rodi" is derived from Rhodes), and nowadays – with its beaches and fast hydrofoil links with the Tremiti Islands – a highly popular resort in summer. Again, it's full and expensive in August, but come a couple of months either side and it can be delightful. From here road and railway then skirt the large **Lago di Varano**, a once-malarial swamp which swallowed the ancient Athenian town of Uria in the fourth century BC. The region around the lake, its villages traditionally poor and backward, is probably the least visited part of the Gárgano peninsula – though the lake itself is full of eels and attracts a great variety of birdlife, particularly curlews and warblers. Further west, the thin **Lago di Lésina** is a highly saline shallow lagoon, cut off from the sea by a 27km stretch of sand dunes. It's still mercifully free from development – unlike the northern spit of Varano which is slowly beginning to fill with campsites.

Alternatively, from Cagnano Varano the *FG* train line cuts southwest, skirting the promontory, to **SAN SEVERO**, a small market town known for its wines but otherwise not a place you'll want to do much more than change transport. The *FG* line ends in San Severo, from where you can pick up mainline trains down to Bari, and the occasional bus to San Marco in Lamis in Gárgano 's interior.

Inland Gárgano: Vico del Gárgano and the Foresta Umbra

The **interior** of the Gárgano peninsula can make a cool break from the promontory's busy coast, though it's not possible to see much of it without your own transport. **VICO DEL GARGANO** is the nicest of the villages, and firmly off the beaten track, sited on a hill surrounded by citrus groves and with a creakingly ancient centre full of steep, tangled streets. It's also right on the edge of the **Foresta Umbra** (or "Forest of Shadows") which stretches right across the centre of the Gárgano massif – 11,000 hectares of pines, oaks and beeches, hiding a rich variety of wildlife, roe deer especially. It's the last remnant of an ancient forest which once covered most of Puglia. There are numerous marked **walks** through the forest and a **Centro di Visita** in the middle which doles out advice and information. **Public transport** is a bit thin on the ground. During July and August, a twice-daily bus runs from Rodi Garganigo to the Centro da Visita, leaving Rodi in the morning and returning in the afternoon. There's also a daily *SITA* bus (Mon–Sat) between Vico del Gárgano and Manfredonia, passing through the forest. If you do get stranded in the forest, hitch towards Vico Gárgano or Monte Sant'Angelo, as the Vieste road is pretty dead.

The Tremiti Islands

A small group of islands 40km off the Gárgano coast, the **Tremiti Islands** (Isole Tremiti) are almost entirely given over to tourism in the summer, when the tiny population is swamped by visitors. Despite this, the islands remain relatively unspoilt, the sea is crystal clear, the beaches some of the best in Puglia.

Oddly enough, the islands were traditionally a place of exile and punishment in the past. Augustus banished his granddaughter Julia to the islands, while Charlemagne packed his father-in-law off here (minus eyes and limbs) in the eighth century. Monks from Montecassino, on the mainland, first set about building a formidable fortress-abbey on one of the islands in the eleventh century, which managed to withstand frequent assault by the Turks. Later, during the eighteenth century, the islands returned to their old role as a place of confinement for political prisoners, though the Bourbons, concerned at the decline in the local population, shipped in 200 women from the Neapolitan taverns to encourage a recovery.

The 7am **ferry** (mid-April–Sept) from Manfredonia calls at Vieste, Peschici and Rodi Garganigo, before reaching the islands at San Nicola; the full one-way trip costs L15,000, though from Rodi Garganigo it's only L5500. There are also services from Vasto and Ortona (see *Abruzzo and Molise*, chapter 12) and out of season an infrequent service from Térmoli. See "Travel Details".

The Islands

The main Tremiti group consists of three islands – San Nicola, San Domino – the biggest – and Capraia, of which only the first two are inhabited. **Ferries** all arrive at **SAN NICOLA**, where you wander around the monastic fortress and the tiny church of **Santa Maria a Mare**, built by the monks in the eleventh century on the site of an earlier ninth-century hermitage. San Nicola is rugged and rocky with no beaches, although there is nude bathing on its east side, and there's good swimming to be had off the whole island.

Ignore the offers of pricey boat-trips to the other islands and instead take the ferry to **SAN DOMINO** for just L3000. It's a greener island than its neighbour, its pines offering a welcome shade from the heat. Although there is a sandy **beach** (*Cala delle Arene*) on the northeast side of the island, it's packed in the summer. Your best bet is to follow the signs for the *Villagio TCI*, and make for the west of the island and its quieter coves. You can buy **maps** from souvenir shops. **Accommodation** on the islands is limited to San Domino and is largely full-board only, especially in high season (July & August). Prices for this are as high as you might expect: count on L60,000 a night per person. The Municipio holds a list of **private rooms**; or you could try the small *Albergo La Nassa* (☎0882/663.075) or *Albergo Gabbiano* (☎0882/663.044), which charge L30,000 a head – though it's essential to book ahead for these. A cheaper alternative is to **camp** at the *Villagio TCI*, open all year: you can rent tents if you haven't brought your own, for around L12,000 a night. Bear in mind, too, that provisions have to be brought in from the mainland, so **eating out** can be a costly exercise – bring a picnic.

Along the coast to Bari

The first part of the coastal route south from Manfredonia is unremarkable, flat lands given up to saline extraction. You won't, anyway, be able to come this way by train or bus – though there is a direct coastal road for drivers. First stop, by rail at least, isn't until **MARGHERITA DI SAVOIA**, at the edge of the Tavoliere, a small town producing ninety percent of the country's salt. Beyond here, though, the rest of the coastline is easily accessible by public transport, all the towns covered below on the main Bologna–Lecce railway line. It's a varied stretch and there are two enjoyable stops, at Trani and Molfetta.

Barletta

The first place that's really worth a stop is **BARLETTA**, nearly 60km from Manfredonia – an indifferent and rather shabby town really, but worth a stop if you happen to be passing on the last Sunday in July, when it's the venue of one of Puglia's largest medieval pageants, the **disfida**. The event re-enacts an occasion in 1503 when thirteen Italian knights challenged thirteen French knights to a duel for control of the besieged town. They had been drinking together and following a brawl the Italians won and the siege was lifted.

For the rest, Barletta's dowdy atmosphere says little about its former importance as a medieval Crusader port, the only relic of its earlier days a five-metre high statue in the town centre known as the **Colosso** – said to be the largest Roman bronze in existence, and a relic from the Venetian sacking of Constantinople in 1204. Towering dourly over pedestrians on Corso Vittorio Emanuele, its identity is a mystery although most money is on Marcian, one of the last Eastern Roman emperors. Over the way from here, the thirteenth-century **Basilica di San Sepolcro** has been restored to its original thirteenth-century simplicity, though the only other place of real interest is the **Museo Civico de Nittis** (Tues–Sat 9am–1pm; free) at Via Cavour 8. This houses the usual regional archaeological finds and, as a bonus, displays a large collection of paintings by the nineteenth-century artist Giuseppe de Nittis, a local lad who spent most of his short but prolific life in Paris, painting under the influence of the Impressionists.

Practical details

Information can be gleaned from the **AAST** at Via Gabbia 4 (Mon–Fri 8am–1pm & 4–6pm, Sat 8am–1pm). You can **eat** at the reasonable *Bella Napoli*, Corso Garibaldi 127, near the museum, and **sleep** at the *Pensione Prezioso*, Via Teatini 11 (☎0883/32.006), which has rooms for L36,000.

Trani

Thirteen kilometres down the coast from Barletta, **TRANI** is a very different kind of place, with a cosmopolitan air not found in any of the other towns nearby. One of the most important medieval Italian ports, it was a prosperous trading centre with a large mercantile and Jewish community, during the Middle Ages rivalling Bari as a commercial port and in the fourteenth century powerful enough to take on the domineering Venetians.

Twentieth-century Trani is still a prosperous town, its elegant buildings spruce and smart. Centrepiece of the town is the cream-coloured eleventh-century **Duomo**, overlooking the sea on a large open piazza at the edge of the old town. Dedicated to San Nicola Pellegrino, it consists of no less than three churches, stacked on top of each other like an inverted wedding cake – the facade austere, but lightened by a pretty rose window. Inside it has been restored to its original Norman state, the stark nave displaying a timbered ceiling, while near the presbytery fragments of a twelfth-century mosaic have been uncovered. Below the vaulted crypt is the earlier church of Santa Maria della Scala whose marble columns are Roman, while further down the *Ipogea di San Leucio* is an early Christian underground chamber dating from the sixth century. Back outside, the **Castello** is visible from Piazza Duomo, currently under restoration after years of service as a prison. A wander through the adjacent streets gives an impression of the medieval city, not least in the names which echo the town's mercantile and Jewish origins – Via Sinagoga, Via Doge Vecchia and Via Cambio ("Street of the Moneylenders"). The **Palazzo Cacetta** on Via Ognissanti is a rare example of fifteenth-century Gothic architecture; the **Chiesa di Ognissanti**, close by, was a twelfth-century chapel of the Knights Templar, once part of a hospital for injured Crusaders. Sadly, it's unlikely to be open but hang around and someone may appear with a key.

Practical details

If you're going to stick around in Trani, the **AAST** is at Via Cavour 83 (Mon–Fri 8.30am–1pm, Sat 8.30–11am), just down the road from the **railway station**. Further along, opposite the public gardens, the *Albergo Lucy* on Piazza Plebiscito (☎0883/41.022) has **rooms** for L35,000. Do your **eating** in *La Darsena*, right on the harbour near Piazza Quercia, at Via Statuti Marittimi 98 – great fresh fish – or get pizzas in the *Antica Cattedrale*, just behind the duomo, tables outside in the piazza in summer.

Molfetta

The last stop worth making on this stretch of coast is at **MOLFETTA**, a working port, unashamedly non-touristy and all the better for it, with a twelfth-century **Duomo** that's a mishmash of styles from the Romanesque and Byzantine eras and a tiny alleywayed old centre – once an island – that's home to one of the biggest fishing fleets on the southern Adriatic. There are no beaches as such, but it's a busy, evocative place, its waterfront active with visiting Russian, Yugoslav and Albanian ships and thronged by an evening *passeggiata* that sweeps down to the docks to watch the gorgeous sunsets over the Adriatic. You probably won't want to stay, but if you do there's one central **hotel**, the *Tritone* on Lungomare M. Colonna (☎080/911.069), though at L45,000 a double it's not particularly cheap. If you need to **eat** and are feeling flush, try the *Bistrot*, Corso Dante 33 – around L20,000 a head but worth it. For **snacks** the *Al Duomo*, next to the duomo, has outdoor tables, ideal for watching Molfetta amble by.

Bari

Commercial and administrative capital of Puglia, a university town and the Mezzogiorno's second city, **BARI** has its fair share of interest. But although an economically vibrant place, it harbours no pretensions about being a major tourist attraction. Primarily people come here to work, or to leave for Yugoslavia and Greece on its many ferries.

Bari was already a thriving centre when the Romans arrived. Later the city was the seat of the Byzantine governor of southern Italy, while under the Normans Bari rivalled Venice, both as a maritime centre and, following the seizure of the remains of Saint Nicholas, as a place of pilgrimage. Since those heady days Bari has declined considerably. Its fortunes revived briefly in 1813 when the King of Naples foisted a planned expansion upon the city – giving the city its contemporary gridded street pattern, wide avenues and piazzas. And Mussolini instituted a university and built numerous examples of strident fascist architecture. But the city was heavily bombed during the last war, and today its vigorous centre is more a symbol of the South than much of tourist centre.

Orientation and information

Bari is a fairly compact city, running from the railway station in the gridded new city, down to the bulging old centre, the *citta vecchia*, in just ten blocks. **Orientation** is straightforward, more so than ever if you go first to the **EPT** (Mon–Fri 8.30am–1pm, Sat 8.30–11am) on Piazza Aldo Moro, in front of the main

railway station, and grab a map; ask for the monthly magazine *Ecobari* which has the only decent plan of the old city. A **word of warning**: the Barese take a positive delight in portraying the old city as a den of thieves and, certainly, stalking around the narrow alleys with your camera in full view isn't particularly wise. Bag snatching by young kids on mopeds (the *topini*, or "little mice") isn't as rife as it once was, but neither is it extinct. Keep your wits about you.

Arriving and getting around

There are several **railway stations** in Bari. The main *FS* station is in Piazza Aldo Moro, and serves both regular *FS* trains and those of the private *Ferrovia del Sud-Est* (*FSE*) line. Nearby, there's a separate station for trains on another private line, the *Ferrovia Bari-Nord* (*BN*), while *Ferrovia Calabro-Lucane* (*FCL*) trains leave from a station on Corso Italia; see "Listings", below, for destinations. **Buses** complicate the issue even further: from the coastal towns north of Bari you'll arrive at Piazza Eroi del Mare; *SITA* buses from inland and southern towns pull up in Piazza Aldo Moro; while the private railways' bus services – *FCL* and *FSE* – leave respectively from stations on Corso Italia and Largo Ciaia. Again, see "Listings".

Ferries all use the Stazione Marittima, next to the old city: there are services to Dubrovnik, Split and Bar (Yugoslavia) and Igoumenitsa, Corfu and Patras (Greece); take bus #20 from outside to the main *FS* railway station. The **airport** is about 9km out of the city, an *Alitalia* bus connecting with arrivals and dropping at Via Calefati 3.

Getting around, you're best advised to walk – not a bad option in such a small city. **Buses** are bright orange and run from 5.30am until around midnight, mostly focusing on Piazza Aldo Moro. Tickets cost L600 for each trip, though under-30s can ride for free in summer.

Around the city: new and old

There's not a lot to the **new city**, bar a good museum or two. Its straight streets are lined with shops and offices, rarely relieved by the odd piazza and bit of greenery, best of which is the start-point of the evening *passegiata*, **Piazza Umberto I** – usually full of stalls selling jewellery, books and prints. Off the piazza, the university building holds an excellent **Museo Archaeologico** (Mon–Sat 9am–2pm; L3000, free Mon and for students/under-30s), with a good selection of Greek and Puglian ceramics, and a solid collection of artefacts from the Daunic, Messapian and Peucetic peoples – Puglia's earliest inhabitants. Afterwards, cut to the right for tree-lined **Corso Cavour**, Bari's main commercial street, which leads down to the waterfront. Right along here, in the Palazzo della Provincia, the **Pianoteca Provinciale** (Tues–Sun 9am–1pm; free) is a local art collection of mainly southern Italian stuff, twelfth- to nineteenth-century, with strong work by the fifteenth-century Vivarini family.

The old city

Quite clearly it's the **old city** which is Bari's more entrancing quarter, a jumble of streets at the far end of Corso Cavour that's possibly the most confusing place to walk around in southern Italy. Its labyrinth of seemingly endless passages weaving through courtyards and under arches was originally designed to spare the inhabitants from the wind and throw invaders into a state of confusion. This it still does admirably, and even with the best of maps you're going to get lost.

Of specific sights there are few. The **Basilica di San Nicola** (daily 9am–1pm & 5–7pm), in the heart of the old city, was consecrated in 1197, as an inscription at the side of the main door testifies, to house the relics of the saint plundered a century earlier from southern Turkey. From the outside it all looks thoroughly Norman, especially the twin fortress-like towers, but it's a misleading impression: the right-hand tower predates the church, the other was added later for balance, and even the simple nave is shattered by three great arches and an ornate seventeenth-century ceiling. The real beauty of the church lies in its stonework: the twelfth-century altar canopy is one of the finest in Italy, the motifs around the capitals the work of stonemasons from Como; and the twelfth-century carved doorway and the simple, striking mosaic floor of the choir are lovely, prey to a very heavy Saracen influence. Best of all is the twelfth-century episcopal throne behind the altar, a superb piece of work suported by small figures wheezing beneath its weight. Down in the **crypt** are the remains of the saint, patron of pawnbrokers and sailors (and of Russians, who made the pilgrimage here until 1917). Behind the tomb-altar, the richly decorated fourteenth-century icon of the saint was a present of the King of Serbia.

It's not far from the basilica to Bari's other important church, the **Cattedrale di San Sabino** (daily 8.30am–1pm & 5–7pm), off Piazza Odegitria, dedicated to the original patron saint of Bari, before he was usurped by Nicholas, and built at the end of the twelfth century. It's well worth coming just for the contrast: uncluttered by arches, it retains its original medieval atmosphere, and – unlike the basilica – a timbered roof. The cathedral houses an icon, too, an eighth-century work known as the *Madonna Odegitria*, brought here for safety from Constantinople by Byzantine monks. It's said to be the most authentic likeness of the Madonna in existence, having been taken from an original sketch by Luke the Apostle, and it's paraded around the city at religious festivals.

Across the piazza the **Castello Normanno-Svevo** (Mon–Sat 8.30am–1pm & 3–7pm, Sun 8.30am–1pm; L3000) sits on the site of an earlier Roman fort. Built by Frederick II, much of it is closed to the public, but it has a vaulted hall that provides a cool escape from the afternoon sun. You can also see a gathering of some of the best of past Puglian craftsmanship, in a display of plaster-cast reproductions from churches and buildings throughout the region – specifically from the Castel del Monte, the cathedral at Altamura, and an animated frieze of griffons devouring serpents from the church of San Leonardo at Siponto.

Sleeping, eating and other practicalities

Though Bari has its share of crummy hotels, finding somewhere cheap **to sleep** can be tricky: start looking in the streets around the station and the university, especially on Via Crisanzio and Via Calefati. A couple you might try straight-off are the *Hotel Bristol*, Via Calefati 15 (☎080/211.503), which has doubles for L35,000, and the *Pensione Darinka* in the same building (☎080/235.049), which is a little cheaper. There's also the *Pensione Giulia*, Via Crisanzio 12 (☎080/216.630), though this charges L40,000, and – swankier still – the *Grand Hotel Moderno*, Via Crisanzio 60 (☎080/213.313) where doubles cost L50,000.

If these prices are beyond you, the EPT have a list of available **private rooms**. Or if you're under 30, *CTS* (address below) sometimes offer special cut-rate package deals during summer, including accommodation, meals, even free public transport; contact them direct for details. In any case you can **camp** for free between June and September if you're under 30 at *Pineta San Francesco*, on the outskirts of the city – reachable on bus #5 from the main railway station, bus #1 from Corso Cavour. Out of season, the nearest campsite is 6km south of the city on the SS16 – *Camping San Giorgio* (☎080/491.202); bus #12 from Teatro Petruzzelli.

Eating out, for snacks and sandwiches try the *Caffe del Levante* at the corner of Via Sparano, across from the station, or the *Bar Oceano*, Corso Cavour 49. Two **cheap restaurants** in the old city are *Le Travi*, on Largo Chiurlia, and *Da Nicola*, Piazza del Ferrarese. The *Trattoria al Pescatore*, Via Frederico II di Sveia 8, just east of the castle, does marvellous fish, though it can cost anything up to L40,000 a head.

Onwards . . . to Yugoslavia and Greece

Ferry services to Dubrovnik and Split in **Yugoslavia** are operated by *Adriatica*; the cheapest one-way summer ticket is L67,000. To **Greece** the lines is *Ventouris*, which runs services to Corfu, Igoumenitsa and Patras. Prices range from L30,000 one-way to Igoumenitsa/Corfu to L35,000 one-way to Patras. See below for ferry company addresses. Travel agents around town often have a wide variety of offers on **tickets**, including *CTS*, who give a ten percent discount on student/youth fares. *InterRail* pass holders get discounts too; see *Basics*. Once you've got your ticket, you must report to the relevant desk at the Stazione Marittima at least two hours before departure.

Listings

Beach Nearest is north of the city, bus #1 from Teatro Petruzzelli to Palese/ Santo Spirito.

Buses *FCL* to Basilicata (from Corso Italia 6); *FSE* to Bríndisi (from Largo Ciaia); Marozzi to Rome (from Corso Italia 3).

Exchange Outside banking hours at the information desk in the main railway station.

Ferry companies *Adriatica*, Via Roberto da Bari 133 (☎080/330.360) and Stazione Marittima (☎080/235.825); *Ventouris*, c/o *Pan Travel*, Via 24 Maggio 40 (☎080/521.0504) and Stazione Marittima (☎080/218.493).

Post office Main office is behind the university in Piazza Battisti.

Telephone International calls from SIP (8am–9pm), Via Oriani, near the castle.

Trains Of the three private lines operating out of Bari, *FSE* run to Castellana Grotte, Martina Franca and Alberobello; *BN* connect Bari with Bitonto, Andria and Barletta; the *FCL* line goes to Altamura, Gravina, and Matera and Potenza in Basilicata.

Travel Agent *CTS*, Via Dante 111, Corso Italia 3.

Le Murge

Rising gently from the Adriatic coast, **Le Murge** – a low limestone plateau – dominates the landscape to the south and west of Bari. Around 50km wide, 150km long, it's generally divided into "Low" and "High" Murge: the further away from the coast you are, the higher and more barren it gets. The towns in the region are not natural holiday destinations: the area is sparsely populated, especially further inland, and the small settlements that there are, rural backwaters with a slow pace of life. But they do make an interesting day out from the more popular coastal towns, or a good stopover if you're heading for Basilicata province. There are some buses and trains from Bari, but, as always, without your own car travelling very extensively can be difficult.

The Low Murge

Andria and the Castel del Monte

Main town of the Low Murge is **ANDRIA**, a large agricultural centre easily reached from Barletta or Bari that's at its best on market day (Monday) – though it otherwise has little to hold you. It was, though, a favourite haunt of Frederick II, who was responsible for the main local attraction these days, the **Castel del Monte**, 17km south – the most extraordinary of all Puglia's castles and one of the finest surviving examples of Swabian architecture. Frederick began this place in the 1240s, a high, isolated fortress precisely built around an octagonal courtyard in two storeys of eight rooms. A mystery surrounds its intended purpose. Although there was once an iron gate which could be lowered over the main entrance (as tell-tale grooves in the portal show), there are no other visible signs of fortification, and the castle may have served as a mere hunting lodge. Nonetheless the mathematical precision involved in its construction, and the preoccupation with the number eight, have excited writers for centuries. It's argued the castle is in fact an enormous astrological calendar, also that Frederick may have had the octagonal Omar mosque in Jerusalem in mind when he designed it; but despite his recorded fascination with the sciences, no one really knows. There is only one record of its use. The defeat of Manfred, Frederick's illegitimate son, at the battle of Benevento in 1266, signalled the end of Swabian power in Puglia; and Manfred's sons and heirs were imprisoned in the castle for over thirty years – a lonely place to be incarcerated.

Sadly the castle is only open on Sunday mornings, which if you haven't got a car means you have to time your visit carefully and get up early. Short of hitching, there is only one bus a day from Andria (at 8.10am, for Spinazzola), stopping at Castel del Monte and returning to Andria at 12.25pm.

The rest of the Low Murge

West of Andria, on the edge of the Low Murge, **CANOSA DI PUGLIA** used to be a thriving commercial centre but has never really recovered from its destruction by the Saracens, and today it's an aged, broken-down old place, only worth a stop for its **Duomo** – uninteresting from the outside but with a wealth of treasures in its beautiful eleventh-century interior. The bishop's throne behind the altar, carved with plants and animals, and supported by a couple of rather fed-up looking elephants, dates from 1079. Adjacent is a tomb with a solid bronze door, richly engraved in an Arab fashion, its occupant Bohemond – the son of the Norman, Robert Giuscard.

About the same distance east of Andria (but best reached by hourly bus from Molfetta), the old centre of **RUVO DI PUGLIA** is a more attractive stop, with a quiet, timeless atmosphere. In the autumn, the pavements of the old town are strewn with almonds, spread out to dry in the sun as they have been for centuries. The town was also famous once for its pottery, the locals strong on copying Greek designs to great effect. Just across from the **Pro Loco** (Mon–Fri 9am–1pm), the **Museo Jatta** (Mon–Fri 9am–noon & 5.30–7pm, Sat 9am–noon; L3000), in Piazza Bovio, houses a dusty collection of the homemade stuff as well as some beautiful Greek originals – like a fifth-century BC *krater* depicting the death of Talos. Ruvo's thirteenth-century **Duomo**, tucked into the tightly packed streets of the town's old quarter, is well worth time, too. Its beautiful portal is guarded by animated griffons balancing on fragile columns, while recent work has restored the interior to its original state – exposing some of the sixteenth-century frescoes which used to cover the walls. What distinguishes Ruvo's cathedral, though, is the sheer amount of decoration that survives on the outer walls, like the rose window, and the arches tapering off into human and animal heads.

There's a similar cathedral in **BITONTO**, just a few kilometres out of Bari (20min by train), again with fiercely animated portals and a thirteenth-century pulpit with a bas-relief depicting Frederick and his family. Bitonto is also the centre of olive oil production in Puglia, and is a fairly attractive place to visit anyway, pottering around the mazey medieval centre making for a pleasant afternoon's escape from the city noise of Bari.

The High Murge

Around 45km south of Bari (and reachable by train), **ALTAMURA** is the largest town in the High Murge, an originally fifth-century BC settlement fortified by the Peucetians – parts of whose town still remain. You'll see bits of the walls as you come in from the station, over 4m thick in places. Destroyed by the Saracens, the ancient town lay abandoned until the thirteenth century when Frederick restocked a new settlement with Greeks, and built the high walls from which the town derives its name.

Altamura's most interesting feature is its **Duomo**, a mixture of styles varying from Apulian-Romanesque to Gothic and Baroque. The original thirteenth-century structure was badly damaged by an earthquake and suffered further in the sixteenth century when it was restyled: the portal and rose window were moved round to what had been the apse, and a couple of campaniles were tacked on – the pinnacles added later when Baroque was all the rage. Thankfully, the intricately carved medieval portal survived the switch, while the interior is still suitably austere. Take a look, too, at the tiny church of **San Nicolo dei Greci**, built by the Greek colonists in the thirteenth century, and in which they celebrated their Orthodox religion for over 400 years. It's on Corso Frederico di Svevia.

Twelve kilometres west, not far from the border with Basilicata, lies **GRAVINA IN PUGLIA** – a castle-protected town which clings to the edge of a deep ravine. During the early Barbarian invasions the locals took refuge in the caves along the sides of the ravine, a move which seems to have paid off until the arrival of the Saracens, who promptly massacred every cave-dwelling inhabitant. Under the

Normans, though, the shattered town settled down to a quieter life as a fiefdom of the wealthy Pope-producing Orsini family, whose mark – an enormous spreadeagle – is all over town. In the dilapidated old quarter, the cave-church of **San Michele dei Groti**, a dark, dank affair hewn out of the rock, holds bones that are said to be the remains of victims of the last Saracen attack, almost a thousand years old. (The church is currently closed but the caretaker, Signora Cascarano, lives nearby.) The **museo** (Mon–Sat 9am–2pm) in Piazza Santomasi contains some artefacts from the excavations of the ancient town abandoned to the invaders. But more engaging, certainly if you couldn't get into San Michele, is the reconstruction of San Vito Vecchio, another cave-church, set up on the ground floor with some remarkable tenth-century Byzantine frescoes.

Down the coast from Bari: to Monópoli and the Ruins of Egnazia

The coast south of Bari is a rocky stretch, rock-built villages perching above tiny sandy coves. Just ten minutes by *FS* train from Bari (or bus #12 from Piazza Aldo Moro), **TORRE A MARE** provides one of the easiest escapes from the city, situated on a rocky crag high above two large caves, though its ease of access from Bari means it can get quite crowded. There'll be less people around another twenty minutes on, at **POLIGNANO A MARE**, which, despite some newfound tourists, remains fairly low-key. It's a small port, with a tiny medieval centre perching on the edge of the limestone cliffs here. Polignano is best reached by train, although there is a bus service, run by *FSE*, from Largo Ciaia in Bari.

MONÓPOLI, 8km further down the coast, was, like Polignano, once controlled by the Venetians, a trading centre originally populated by the ancient Egnazians, whose maritime know-how lives on in what is still a large commercial port. Other than the goings-on at the dockside, there's not a lot to see, though the old town is worth wandering through, its steep narrow streets revealing fragments of its Venetian past. A brief scout around might take in the **Museo della Cattedrale** on Largo Cattedrale (daily 8am–noon & 4–7pm; L2000), which contains some beautiful examples of religious art, including a tenth-century Byzantine reliquary, and the tiny chapel of **Santa Maria Amalfitana**, tucked away on Largo Plebiscito – built in the twelfth century by wealthy merchants from Amalfi on the site of an earlier cave-church, which is now the crypt.

The ancient city of Egnázia

There's more of interest south of the town, at the site of the ancient city of **Egnázia**, or *Gnathia* (daily 8.30am–sunset; free), easily reached by bus from Monópoli's Villa Communale (direction "Torre Canne"). Egnazia was an important Messapanic centre during the fifth century BC, fortified with over 2km of walls, large parts of which still stand in the northern corner of the ruined town – up to 7m high. It was later colonised by the Greeks and then the Romans (in 244 BC), who built a forum, amphitheatre, a colonnaded public hall and temples: one was dedicated to Syria, a goddess popular with the early Romans who – according to Lucian – was worshipped by men dressed as women. Horace is known to have dropped by here to see the city's famous altar, which ignited wood without a flame.

At the turn of the first century AD, the **Via Egnatia** was constructed by the Emperor Trajan, a road which ran down to Bríndisi and continued from what is now Durres in Albania, via Thessaloniki, right the way to Constantinople, marking Egnázia's importance as a military and commercial centre. Parts of the road survive, running alongside the Roman public buildings. With the collapse of the Roman Empire, however, the city fell to subsequent Barbarian invasions, and was almost completely destroyed by the Gothic king Totila in AD 545. A community struggled on here, seeking refuge in the Messapian tombs, until the tenth century when the settlement was finally abandoned. There's a new **museum** (Mon–Sat 8.30am–1.30pm; L2000) on the site housing a fascinating array of artefacts, including examples of the distinctive earthenware for which the ancient town was prized, uncovered during excavations that are still underway.

The *FSE* Line: Castellana Grotte to Martina Franca

Meandering lazily down towards the **Valle d'Itria** and – finally – to TÁRANTO, the *Ferrovia Sud-Est* passes through some of the prettiest of Puglia's landscapes. The olive gradually loses ground to vineyards, cherry and peach orchards, neatly partitioned off by dry stone walls. About 40km out of Bari are the **Grotte di Castellana** (daily; mid-March–Oct 8.30am–1pm & 2.30–7pm; rest of the year 9am–noon; L20,000, students L15,000), a spectacular set of underground caves. The barren limestone terrain of Le Murge, which touches the region, swallows rivers whole (south of the Ofanto, near Barletta, few rivers make it to the sea), producing a landscape cut by deep ravines and pitted with caverns and grottoes. At Castellana, a lift takes you down to the largest of the caverns, *La Grave*, 60m below ground, which was used as the local rubbish dump until its accidental discovery in 1938. From here, there's over a kilometre of strangely formed caves to explore, variously named according to shape, ending in the most impressive of them all, the *Caverna Bianca* – a shimmering sea of stalagmites and stalagtites.

To **get to the caves**, simply follow the signs from the station; the grotto is about two kilometres southwest of town. **Tours** leave roughly every hour and take around an hour and three quarters. There are also cheaper, one-hour trips and evening tours at 9pm in August.

PUTIGNANO, next stop down the line, marks the beginning of the Valle d'Itria. It's really only worth a call if you happen to be in the area when its riotous carnival explodes at the beginning of February. But there is a grotto here, too, if you haven't already had your fill – this one of shimmering pink alabaster, about 1km north of town, signposted *Grotta di Putignano*.

After Putignano the natural gives way to the man-made, and **trulli** come to dominate the landscape: cylindrical, whitewashed buildings with grey conical roofs which taper out to a point or sphere, often adorned with painted symbols. Confined to this part of Puglia, their ancient origins are obscure, though few today date back more than a couple of hundred years. Apart from their intrinsic beauty, there seems no special reason for building houses like this, and certainly no reason for them popping up here – though many theories abound, one claiming that the dome-shaped houses are much cooler in the baking Puglian summers. Certainly they make full use of local building materials and are remarkably easy to adapt: when you need more room, you simply knock a hole in the wall and build another next door. (See *Contexts* for more.)

If you want to take a closer look, **ALBEROBELLO** is the best place to get off, where there's a large local concentration of *trulli* – around 1500 cluttering Alberobello's narrow streets. Most are south of the town centre, on and around Largo Martellotta, past the Pro Loco from the station. Just a few kilometres south, **LOCOROTONDO**, which owes its name to its circular layout, gives good views over the whole area, speckled with red- and grey-roofed *trulli* in a sea of olives, vines and almond trees.

Martina Franca

The *trulli* are still plentiful by the time you reach **MARTINA FRANCA**, a surprising town with a tangible Moorish flavour. Reputed to have been founded by Tarentine settlers fed up with constant Saracen attacks during the tenth century, it was the Angevin prince of Táranto who bolstered the community in the early fourteenth century by granting it certain tax privileges. The town derives its name from this – *franca* meaning duty or stamp. Today its centre shelters within an unprepossessing approach of tower blocks, a medieval core adorned with some of the most subtle and least overbearing examples of architecture from the baroque period you'll find.

There's a spasmodic bus service from the **railway station** up to the centre of town, otherwise you'll have to walk – left out of the station and up Viale della Liberta to Corso Italia, which leads to the old town centre, marked by the so-called **Porta di Santo Stefano**. Through here, Piazza Roma is dominated by the vast **Palazzo Ducale**, dating from 1688 and now housing the town hall, but with a handful of rooms open to the public most mornings – most of them smothered in classically eighteenth-century Arcadian murals by a local artist. Just across the square the **AAST** (Mon–Fri 9.30am–1pm & 4.30–7.30pm, Sat 9.30am–1pm) has good maps of the town. From here narrow Via Vittorio Emanuele leads right into the old town and Piazza Plebiscito, fronted by the vast Baroque facade of the **Chiesa di San Martino**, an eighteenth-century church built on the site of an earlier Romanesque structure, of which only the campanile survives. From adjacent Piazza Immacolata you can either bear left down Via Cavour, with its Baroque palazzi and balconied streets, or wander further into the old town, the roads running around the edge of the surviving fourteenth-century town walls offering an excellent panorama of the Valle d'Itria, with its neatly ordered fields dotted with *trulli*.*

Visits to Martina Franca are best if they coincide with the **Festivale della Valle d'Itria**, held from the end of July until the first week in August, one of the most important events on the Italian musical calendar, with opera, classical, jazz music and the like. Although tickets aren't cheap, it's a congenial and unpretentious event. Information from the festival office in the Palazzo Ducale.

The cheapest **hotel** in town is the *Hotel da Luigi* on Via Táranto (☎080/ 901.324), which charges L44,000 for a double with shower – though at festival time you won't even get a room here. If your budget is tighter than this, it'll have to be the **youth hostel**, the *Ostello Papa Martino*, 6km south of town on the Táranto road at SAN PAOLO (☎080/700.052). Beds cost L10,000 a head; take the

---

* If you're further interested in finding out about life in the *trulli*, there's a **Museo della Civilta dei Trulli**, 7km from Martina Franca on the road to Ceglie Messapico.

FSE bus for Táranto from Piazza Crispi, off Corso Italia. **Eating**, you'll get an excellent meal at *La Tavernetta*, Corso Vittorio Emanuele 30, though the food is cheaper down Corso dei Mille (off Corso Italia) – try the *Scacco Matto*, at no. 26, for pizzas. Or head straight for the town's best pizzas at *La Panca*, 14 Via Spirito Santo, off Via Bellini.

Táranto

There are numerous legends connected with the origins of **TÁRANTO**. It was variously founded by the Spartan deity Phalanthus, Taras, the son of Neptune, or – perhaps more likely – illegitimate Spartans born while their fathers were away fighting. Whatever the truth is, Taras, as it was known to the Greeks, was a well-chosen site and soon became the first city of Magna Graecia, renowned for its wool, its oysters and mussels, and its dyes – the imperial purple was the product of decayed Tarentine molluscs. Resplendent with temples, its acropolis harboured a vast bronze of Poseidon that was one of the wonders of the ancient world. Sadly, little remains of ancient Taras or even of later Roman Tarentum, their monuments and relics confined to the great museum in the modern city. After being destroyed by the Romans, Táranto was for years little more than a small fishing port, its strategic position on the sea only being recognised in Napoleonic times. It was home to the Italian fleet after Unification, and consequently heavily bombed during the last war, since when attempts to rejuvenate the town have left its medieval heart girdled by heavy industry, including the vast *Italsider* steel plant which throws its flames and lights into the skies above.

Finding your way around shouldn't cause too many problems. The city divides neatly into three distinct parts: the northern spur is the industrial part of town, home of the steel works and railway station. Cross the Ponte di Porta Napoli and you're on the central island containing the old town. And the southern spur contains the modern city centre (the *Borgo Nuovo*), the administrative and commercial hub of Táranto, linked to the old town by a swing-bridge.

The City

In Greek times the island holding the **old town** wasn't an island at all but part of the southern peninsula, connected by an isthmus to the southern spur. Here the Greeks raised temples and the acropolis, while further south lay the residential districts. There's one extant fragment of ancient Táranto – the Doric **columns**, re-erected in a corner of Piazza Castello, which once adorned a temple of Poseidon. The rest of the tiny island is a mass of poky streets and alleyways, buttressed by scaffolding seemingly to prevent the whole place from falling down. The Aragonese **Castello** (now owned by the navy and closed to the public) at the southern end surveys the comings and goings of warships and fishing boats. The narrow canal they slide through, between the city's two inland "seas", was built in the late nineteenth century, on the site of the castle's old moat. "Seas" is a bit of a misnomer: the *Mare Piccolo* is really a large lagoon, home to Táranto's famous oysters and the Italian navy; and the *Mare Grande* is really a vast bay, protected by sea walls and the offshore fortified island of San Pietro.

At the heart of the old town lies the eleventh-century **Cattedrale**, which once did duty as a mosque – dedicated to Táranto's patron saint, Cataldo (Cathal), a

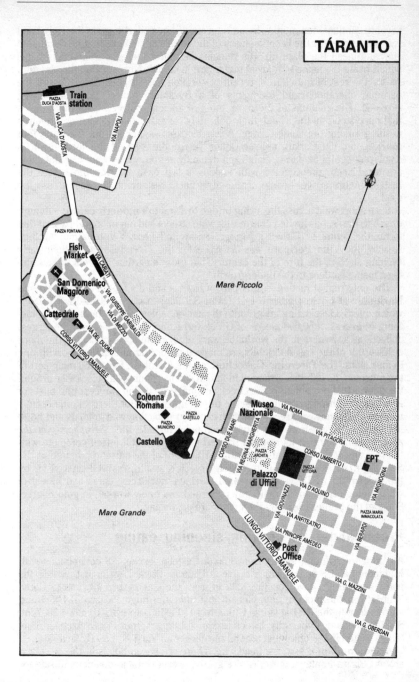

TÁRANTO

Train station
PIAZZA DUCA D'AOSTA

VIA DUCA D'AOSTA

VIA NAPOLI

PIAZZA FONTANA

Fish Market

VIA CARIATI

San Domenico Maggiore

VIA GIUSEPPE GARIBALDI

VIA D. MEZZO

Cattedrale

VIA DEL DUOMO

CORSO VITTORIO EMANUELE

Mare Piccolo

Colonna Romana

PIAZZA CASTELLO

PIAZZA MUNICIPIO

Castello

CORSO DUE MARI

VIA REGINA MARGHERITA

Museo Nazionale

VIA ROMA

PIAZZA ARCHITA

VIA PITAGORA

CORSO UMBERTO I

PIAZZA VITTORIA

EPT

Palazzo di Uffici

VIA D'AQUINO

VIA GIOVINAZZI

VIA ANFITEATRO

VIA MIGNOGNA

PIAZZA MARIA IMMACOLATA

VIA BETARDI

Mare Grande

VIA PRINCIPE AMEDEO

Post Office

LUNGO VITTORIO EMANUELE

VIA G. MAZZINI

VIA G. OBERDAN

seventh-century Irish monk who on returning from a pilgrimage to the Holy Land was so shocked by the licentiousness of the town's inhabitants that he decided to stay and clean the place up. His remains lie under the altar of a small chapel which bears his name – "a jovial nightmare in stone", Norman Douglas thought. As for the rest of the church, recent restoration has stripped away most of the baroque alterations and fragments of a Byzantine mosaic floor have been revealed. The columns of the nave, too, are ancient, pillaged from the temples that once stood on the island, their delicately carved capitals depicting tiny birds nestling among the stone foliage. A few blocks away, check out the city's **fish market**, on Via Cariati, a lively affair where the best of the local catch is displayed: octopi lie dazed, clams spit defiantly at you, while other less definable creatures seem preoccupied with making a last dash for freedom before the restauranteurs arrive – some of the city's finest restaurants are just across the road.

It's a short walk across the swing-bridge to Táranto's **modern centre** – though this, like Bari's, has limited charms, its wide streets laid out on a grid pattern that forms the centre of Táranto's *passeggiata*, around Piazzas Vittoria and Archita. Nearby, the **Villa Peripato** was *the* place for the Tarentini to take their early evening stroll at the turn of the century, but today's gardeners seem to be fighting a losing battle with the undergrowth.

The only real attraction in this part of town – and it's a gem – is the **Museo Nazionale** at Corso Umberto I 41 (Mon–Sat 9am–2pm, Sun 9am–1pm; L3000), which offers a fascinating insight into the ancient splendour of Taras. With something in excess of 50,000 pieces of Greek terracotta alone, it's one of the largest collections anywhere in the world; be wary of trying to see too much – the more noteworthy of the cased exhibits are marked according to importance, with one to four stars. The **Tarentine Collection**, on the first floor, forms the main part of the museum, its exhibits arranged in fifteen rooms running anti-clockwise around the floor. Most prominent is the Greek sculpture, including two beautiful busts of Apollo and Aphrodite dating from the fifth century BC. But there's Roman sculpture, too, and mosaics (second- to fifth-century) depicting wild animals and hunting scenes. Finds from the city's necropolis include the *Sarcophagus of the Athlete*, from 500 BC, its original painted decorations still intact, complete with the remains of the young athlete within. Highlight of the museum, though, is the *Sala degli Ori* (Room of Gold). Magna Graecia's wealth was well catered for by the goldsmiths of Taras, who created earrings, necklaces, tiaras and bracelets with minute precision, all delicately patterned and finely worked in gold filigree. Some of the best examples of their work are on display.

Practical details: arriving, sleeping, eating

All **buses** arrive and depart from Piazza Castello, except *FS* connections with Metaponto and Potenza, which arrive at Piazzale Duca d'Aosta, just outside the **train station**. To save you the walk in from the station, bus #8 runs to Corso Umberto in the modern city. Get off just after the huge Palazzo di Uffici and you're close to the **EPT** at Corso Umberto I 113 (Mon–Fri 9am–1pm & 4.30–7pm, Sat 10am–noon). Other **city buses** arrive and depart from Piazza Archita: timetables posted in the office just around the corner on Via d'Aquino (L500 a ride).

Accommodation is a real headache. There are cheap hotels in the old town, around Piazza Fontana, but most are grotty, overpriced and distinctly unsafe for women. Best bet instead is to make for the modern city. The *Bella Táranto*, Via Principe Amadeo 60 (☎099/22.505), is safe and popular so ring ahead, and has rooms for L20,000. Otherwise, there's the *Albergo Aquila d'Oro*, Via Regina Margherita 8 (☎099/20.472), for L26,000, and a few doors down – the more expensive *Hotel Bologna* (☎099/26.071/2).

There's also a **youth hostel** near Martina Franca, quite easily reached by bus from Piazza Castello; get off at San Paolo. For **camping**, you have to head 10km south of the city, to Lido Bruno near CAPO SAN VITO: the *Sun Bay* (☎099/532.172; open all year) is right on the beach. Get there on the *Circola Rossa* and *Circola Nera* buses from Via d'Aquino, off Piazza Archita.

For **eating**, *La Nuova Grande Birreria*, Via Regina Margherita 43, is all things to all people – a restaurant, self-service joint, tavola calda and pizzeria. Or check out the tourist menu at the *Ristorante Basile*, Via Pitagora, and the good local specialities at *Da Mimmo*, around the corner from the museum.

Around Táranto

With some form of transport it's fairly easy to get away quickly from the city. One of the best targets, and only 13km to the southeast, is the coast beyond the adjacent small towns of **LEPORANO** and **PULSANO**, taken up by white sandy beaches flanked by pine woods. If you want to swim, consider the other direction too, west of the city, where a series of empty beaches stretches right along the Golfo di Táranto into Basilicata, pine woods again providing a cool escape from the August sun. The train stops at several small stations along this coast if you want to explore it further.

Inland from Táranto, due east of the city, the mildly undulating lands were once known as as "Albania Salentina", after the large numbers of Albanian refugees who settled here during the late fifteenth century, following the forced conversion of the Albanian population to Islam by the Turks. One of these Albanian settlements is **GROTTAGLIE**, only fifteen minutes by train from Táranto, honeycombed with caves, the *grotte* from which the town takes its name. It's been a centre of earthenware production since the tenth century and tucked away in the potters' quarter, under the shadow of Grottaglie's massive fourteenth-century castle, they're still making convincing replicas of ancient Greek ceramics. The town's roofs, walls and pavements – in fact any part of the town with a flat surface – are covered with stacks of earthenware pots, plates and amphorae.

Northwest of Táranto: ravines and cave-churches

Inland and **northwest** of the city, the scenery changes dramatically, gorges and ravines marking a landscape that's closer to that of Basilicata than Puglia. **MASSAFRA**, about 15km from Táranto (regular trains), is split in two by a ravine, the *Gravina di San Marco*, lined with grottoes dating mainly from the ninth to the fourteenth century. Many contain cave-churches, hewn out of the rock by Greek monks and decorated with lavish frescoes. Unfortunately, many are difficult to get to and badly signposted, but there are some that are relatively easily accessible, on the edge (quite literally) of the old town on Via del Santuario. A Baroque staircase runs down to the eighteenth-century **Santuario della Madonna della Scala**, built onto an earlier cave-church, which features a beautiful fresco of a Madonna and Child, dating from the twelfth to the thirteenth century – beyond which more steps lead down to an eighth-century crypt. The nearby **Cripta della Buona Nuova** houses a thirteenth-century fresco of the Madonna and a striking painting of Christ Pantocrator. About 200m away, at the bottom of the ravine, is a mass of interconnected caves known as the **Farmacia del Mago Greguro**, now in a pretty pitiful state but once used by the medieval monks as a herbalist's workshop.

Fifteen minutes further west by train, **CASTELLANETA** clings to the edge of another ravine, 145m deep and 350m wide, commanding some spectacular views over the Golfo di Táranto and the mountains of Basilicata. It, too, has a sprinkling of cave-churches, though it's better known as the birthplace of Rudolph Valentino – to whom the locals have erected a statue on the windy town square.

Easily the most spectacular of the ravine towns is **LATERZA**, close to the border of Basilicata. You can reach the town by *FSE* bus from Táranto's Piazza Castello. It's situated on the edge of one of the largest gorges in Puglia, 10km long, 200m deep and 500m wide in places – an Apulian "Grand Canyon", complete with buzzards and kites. Like the other ravine towns, the walls are scoured with cave-churches, over 180 of them dating from the eleventh century, of which about thirty can be visited. Contact the *Vigili Urbani* in town for information.

Bríndisi . . . and on to Greece

Switching seas (Ionian to Adriatic), **BRÍNDISI** lies 60km east of Táranto, once a bridging point for crusading knights and still strictly a place for passing through. The natural harbour here, the safest on the Adriatic coast, made Bríndisi an ideal choice for early settlers. In Roman times, the port became the main crossing point between eastern and western empires, and later, under the Normans, there came a steady stream of pilgrims heading east towards the Holy Land. The route is still open, and now Bríndisi – primarily – is where you come if you're heading for Greece from Italy. First impression on arriving is that the entire town is full of shipping agents. This, when all is said and done, is the town's main business. But even if you're leaving the same night you'll almost certainly end up with time on your hands. You could just while away time in a bar or restaurant down the main Corso Garibaldi but the old town is pretty compact, and although it isn't brimming with ancient monuments, has a pleasant, almost oriental, flavour about it and a few things to see tucked down its narrow streets. And the town's *passeggiata* is one of the South's best.

The town and around

Just around the corner from the helpful **EPT** on Viale Regina Margherita (Mon–Sat 8.30am–12.30pm & 4.30–7.30pm) is the nineteen-metre-high **Colonna Romana** which dates back to the first century BC. It's at the top of a broad flight of steps known as the *Scalinata Virgiliana* (Virgil's Steps) and marked the end of the ancient Via Appia, which ran all the way from the Porta Capena in Rome. A marble tablet in the corner of the piazza marks the supposed site of the house in which Virgil died, in 19 BC. Via Colonne, with its seventeenth- and eighteenth-century palazzi, runs up to the **Duomo** – remarkable, if only for the fact that it's survived seven earthquakes since its construction in the eleventh century. Just outside the cathedral, the **Museo Archaeologico Provinciale** (Mon–Sat 9am–1pm; L3000, free Tues & Fri) stores ornaments and statues from the necropoli

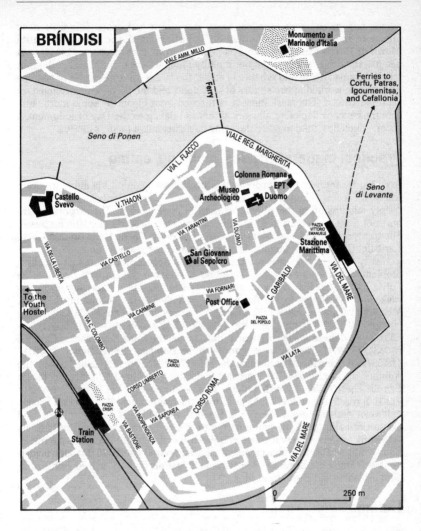

that lined the Via Appia in Roman times, as well as finds from the excavations at Egnazia. Follow Via Tarentini from here and bear left for the tiny round church of **San Giovanni al Sepolcro**, an eleventh-century baptistry. It's a little dark and decrepit inside, but you can just make out some of the original thirteenth-century frescoes. And there are more frescoes, this time a century earlier, in the **Chiesa di Santa Lucia**, just off Piazza del Popolo.

If you've got the time, take the little **ferry** which runs from Viale Regina Margherita, the *Seno di Ponente* (tickets L1000 from the *Casalmare* office on the harbour), over the water to the **Monumento al Marinaio d'Italia**, erected in the 1930s as a memorial to Italian sailors. A lift runs up the 52-metre-high rudder-like edifice and gives some excellent views over town and coast. Bríndisi's most important medieval monument, though, is further afield, the **Chiesa di Santa Maria di Borgo Casale** – a 3km bus-ride from town; take bus #3 (for the airport) and ask the driver when to get off. Built by Philip of Anjou at the end of the thirteenth century, it's an odd mixture of styles, the facade an Arabic mass of geometric patterns, worked in two shades of sandstone, and the portal with an almost art deco touch to it. The stark interior is rescued from gloom by some fourteenth-century frescoes depicting allegorical scenes relating to the Day of Judgment, a vision of hell designed to scare the living daylights out of the less devout.

Practical matters: arriving, sleeping, eating

Arriving by ferry at the **Stazione Marittima** leaves you on Via del Mare, from where it's a few minutes' walk to the bottom of Corso Garibaldi, and another twenty minutes up to the **railway station** in Piazza Crispi. The **airport** is 5km north of town and connected with the railway station by regular *Alitalia* buses. For transport around town, lots of **buses** run down Corso Umberto and Corso Garibaldi (L500 a ride); **taxis** sit in ranks outside the railway station.

Nearly all the ferries leave in the evening so **accommodation** isn't usually a problem. If you need to stay, the rock-bottom option is the *Locanda Doria* on Via Fulvia (☎0831/26.453), where a room costs L12,000, but it's way out of town – walk down Via Appia to Via Arione and Via Fulvia is the second on the right. More central are the *Hotel Villa Bianca*, Via Armengoli 23 (☎0831/25.438), which charges L27,000 a double, and the *Venezia*, Via Pisanelli 6 (☎0831/25.411), for L30,000. And there are fairly cheap rooms, too, at the *Hotel Roial*, Piazza Cairoli 5 (☎0831/28.547). The nearest **campsite** is *Camping Materdomini* (☎0831/418.537), 5km northeast of town on the PUNTA PENNE road, reached during the summer by local buses for the coast – details from the *STP* office on Piazza Cairoli. There's also a **youth hostel**, 2km out of town at Via Brandi 2 (☎0831/413.100) reachable on bus #3, #4 or #5 from the train station. Beds around L8000.

It's not difficult to **eat** cheaply in Bríndisi, the whole of Corso Umberto and Corso Garibaldi (particularly the port end) is smothered in bars and restaurants staffed by waiters who will chase you down the street with copies of the menu. You should be able to grab a complete meal for around L8000–10,000. One favourite is the *Pizzeria L'Angoletto*, Via Pergola 3, just off Corso Garibaldi, which has outdoor tables and cheap local wine.

Listings

Bus to Rome There's a twice daily service to Rome, which departs from *Il Globo*, Corso Garibaldi 97.

Exchanging To buy/sell Greek drachmas, avoid the numerous exchange offices in town and stick to the banks, who shouldn't clobber you with exorbitant charges – though they might need persuading to deal with you. *Banco di Napoli* and *Credito Italiano* are both on Corso Garibaldi; the *Cambio* at the Stazione Marittima is open on Saturdays until 9pm.

Hitching To get out of the city, ask around at the harbour as there's a steady stream of traffic, particularly around 10am and again at 4–5pm when the ferries arrive.

Showers Public showers (L4000) signposted from the EPT.

Telephone calls Make them from Via XX Settembre 6 or at the Stazione Marittima (9am–1pm & 3–6pm).

ONWARDS TO GREECE: FERRIES, TICKETS AND SOME TIPS

Agents

There is a staggering array of **agents** selling ferry tickets to Greece and you must take care to avoid getting ripped off. Ignore the touts clustered around the railway station, who specialise in selling imaginary places on non-existent boats, and *always* buy your ticket direct from the company's office or an approved agent. The **most reliable agencies** are *Hellitalia*, Via del Mare 6 (☎0831/222.988) and *UTAC Viaggi*, Corso Garibaldi 27 (☎0831/24.921). The *Agenzia Marittima Angelo TITI*, Corso Garibaldi 73/75 (☎0831/23.514/5), can also handle bookings through to Turkey, Israel, Egypt and Yugoslavia, and give advice on the more seaworthy seasonal offers which crop up. **Peak period** (roughly mid-July to mid-August) is calamitous, and less reputable agents make crass overbookings: book well in advance or travel a month either side of these dates, when things are appreciably better.

Ferry Companies

Ferry companies can't always be trusted either. Many appear overnight in July and August operating craft of questionable seaworthiness. A rough guide (though there are honourable exceptions) is that nearly all the reliable companies' ferries sail at night (between 9 and 10.30pm); only the pirates depart during the day. The companies listed below are not necessarily the cheapest, but their ferries will at least get you there: *Adriatica*, on the first floor of the Stazione Marittima (☎0831/23.825), to Corfu, Igoumenitsa and Patras; *Hellenic Mediterranean Lines*, Corso Garibaldi 8 (☎0831/28.531), destinations as above, and to Cefalonia; *Fragline*, Corso Garibaldi 88 (☎0831/21.589), to Corfu, Igoumenitsa and Patras; *Hellenic Coastal Lines*, Corso Garibaldi 97 (☎0831/27.684), destinations as above, but also for Cefalonia, Paxi and Itaca with connections for Lefkada and Zakynthos included in the price. For full **schedules** get a timetable from the companies concerned, and see "Travel Details" at the end of this chapter. Roughly, though, *Adriatica* run virtually daily throughout the year, the others operate daily services between March and October.

Prices and Other Things

Prices vary considerably according to season. On the whole, *Adriatica* are the most expensive, *Fragline* the cheapest – you're looking at around L35,000–45,000 one-way in low/middle season to Corfu/Igoumenitsa or Patras, though less than double that for returns. *InterRail Boat/EurRail* pass holders go free, *InterRail* pass holders get a thirty percent discount; motorbikes go free in low season with *Fragline*. Everyone pays an **embarkation tax** – currently L6000.

  Leaving Italy, you must present your boarding card to the authorities at the Stazione Marittima (first floor); do it as soon as you have your ticket to avoid the crowds. Then, you should go to the terminal **at least two hours** before ship's departure, and make sure that any stop-over you are making on the way to Patras is clearly marked on your ticket. Don't forget to **stock up on food and drink** in Bríndisi's supermarkets, as there are some serious mark-ups once on board.

East of Brìndisi: Ostuni

If you're stuck in Brìndisi for long enough, **OSTUNI**, 40km north of the town, represents a much better way of passing the time than moping around the centre, and, just 35 minutes away by train, is one of the most stunning small towns of southern Italy. Situated on three hills at the southernmost edge of Le Murge, and an important Greco-Roman city in the first century AD, its old centre spreads across the highest of the hills, a gleaming white splash of sun-bleached streets and cobbled alleyways, dominating the plains below. The maze of streets makes for a fascinating amble and there are some exceptional views – particularly from Largo Castello over the woods to the north. Bits of cavorting rococo twist out of unexpected places, a reminder of Ostuni's erstwhile Spanish rulers – including an ornamented eighteenth-century obelisk, 21m high, dedicated to Saint Oronzo, which stands on the southern edge of the old town. Here, in Piazza Liberta, the **AAST** dish out a useful map with suggested walks through the medieval maze of the old town.

Ostuni's proximity to a popular sandy coastline, 9km away, makes budget **accommodation** tricky to find. The AAST can help with private rooms in town, or you can go for one of two rather pricey hotels: the *Hotel Orchidea Nera* on Corso Mazzini (☎0831/971.366), which has rooms for L45,000, or the *Rex*, at Via G. di Vittorio 12 (☎0831/972.143), for much the same price. For **eating**, there are a number of excellent restaurants in Ostuni, both higher up in the old town, and in the new part where *El Dorado*, Via F. Ayroldi 2, comes particularly recommended.

Of the **coastal resorts** accessible from Ostuni, there's more happening at **OSTUNI VILLANOVA** than OSTUNI MARINA: if you wanted to stay here, go for the *Baia del Re* at Villanova (☎0831/970.144) – doubles L40,000 a night.

Lecce and the Salentine Peninsula

A fast 40km south from Brìndisi, Baroque **Lecce** is a place to linger, with some diverting Roman remains and a wealth of fine architecture scattered about an appealing old town area. It's also a good starting point for excursions further into the **Salentine Peninsula**, which begins south of the city. Following its long association with traders and settlers, the landscape here begins to take on a distinctive Greek flavour, a mildly undulating region planted with carob, prickly pear and tobacco. The Adriatic coast is pitted with cliffs, topped with ruined watchtowers, with rugged coves and caves right the way down to the **southern cape**. The hinterland, by comparison, is more barren, although there's again a Greek element to it, with its tiny, sun-blasted villages growing out of the dry stony red earth, the flat-roofed houses painted in bright pastel colours.

Lecce

Whether or not you like the Baroque style, you can't fail to be impressed by the exuberant building styles on display in **LECCE**. Previously prey to opportunist attack, the defeat of the Turkish fleet at Lepanto in 1571 signalled a settled era for the city. The subsequent arrival of religious orders (Jesuits, the Teatini and Franciscans) brought an influx of wealth which was reflected in the building of opulent churches and palazzi, and it's this architectural extravagance that still

pervades today's city. The flowery style of "Leccese Baroque" owed as much to the materials to hand as to the skills of the architects: the soft local sandstone could be intricately carved, and then hardened with age. Unfortunately, modern pollution is in danger of ruining many of the buildings, keeping the mass of stonemasons and carpenters who still work in Lecce well occupied.

Around the city

Start in **Piazza Sant'Oronzo**, the hub of the old town, named after the first-century bishop of Lecce who went to the lions under Nero. His bronze statue lurches unsteadily from the top of the **Colonna di Sant'Oronzo** which once stood at the end of the Via Appia in Bríndisi. It resurfaced here in 1666 to honour Oronzo, who was credited with having spared the town from plague ten years earlier. The south side of the piazza is taken up by the weighty remains of the **Anfiteatro Romano**, which probably dates from the time of Hadrian. In its heyday it seated 20,000 spectators, and it's still used in summer for concerts and plays. Sadly, though, most of its decorative bas-reliefs, of fighting gladiators and wild beasts, have been removed to the town's museum for safekeeping, and nowadays it looks rather depleted.

The best of Lecce's Baroque churches are all a short distance from Piazza Sant'Oronzo. The finest, certainly the most ornate, is the **Basilica di Santa Croce**, just to the north, whose florid facade, the work of the local architect Antonio Zimbalo, took around 150 years to complete, its upper half a riot of decorative garlands and flowers around a central rose-window. The **Church of Santa Chiara**, in the opposite direction on Piazza V. Emanuele, is similarly loaded down with ornament, its interior full of little chapels groaning with garlands and gilt. There's more baroque extravagance on offer on Via Vittorio Emanuele, where the **Church of Sant'Irene** houses the most sumptuous of Lecce's Baroque altars – lavishly frosted and gilded, and smothered with decoration. Nearby, facing onto Piazza del Duomo, the **Seminario** holds an impressively ornate well, carved stone masquerading as delicately wrought iron. Next door, the balconied **Palazzo Vescovile** adjoins the **Duomo** itself, twelfth-century in origin but rebuilt entirely in the mid-seventeenth century by Zimbalo. He tacked on two ornate facades and an enormous five-storeyed campanile that towers 70m above the square; you'll need to track down the sacristan to be let in.

There's further work by Zimbalo in the **Church of San Giovanni Battista** (or del Rosario), by the Porta Rudiae in the southwest corner of town – the ornate facade and twisting columns fronting some extremely odd altars, dumpy cherubim diving for cover amid scenes resembling an exploding fruitbowl. But if the baroque trappings of the town are beginning to pall, there's the odd relic from other eras too, not least a well-preserved **Teatro Romano** near the church of Santa Chiara, the only one of its kind to be found in Puglia, with its rows of seats and orchestra floor still remarkably intact. There's also the fine Romanesque church of **Santi Nicola e Cataldo**, built by the Normans in 1190, with a cool interior that reveals a generous hint of Saracen influence in the arches and the octagonal rounded dome. Little remains of the frescoes that once covered its walls, though an image of San Nicola can be found on the south side, together with a delicately carved portal. One more stop you should make, near the railway station on the other side of town, is the **Museo Provinciale** (Mon–Fri 9am–1pm & 3.30–5.30pm, Sun 9am–1pm; free) which has finds from the old Roman town, including decorative panels from the amphitheatre, as well as some striking religious gold and silverwork.

Practical details

Regional **buses** arrive at the Porta Napoli, or at the *FSE* bus station on Via Adua. **Trains**, both *FS* and *FSE*, use the same station, a kilometre south of the centre, at the end of Via Oronzio Quarta. The sixteenth-century **Palazzo Sedile**, on Piazza Sant'Oronzio, holds the **EPT** (Mon–Fri 9am–1pm & 4–7pm, Sat 9am–1pm).

There's plenty of good **accommodation** around. Cheapest is the *Albergo Faggiano*, near the castle at Via Cavour 4 (☎0832/42.854), which charges L22,000 for a double room; or try the *Locanda Carmen*, Via V. Morelli 13 (☎0832/46.408) – L29,000 with bath. Otherwise, the EPT can help you find a private room in someone's home. The nearest **youth hostel** is the *Ostello per la Gioventu Adriatico*, on the beach in Marina di San Cataldo (☎0832/650.026). It's open May to September and buses run from Viale Bríndisi. The closest **campsite** is at MARINA DI TORRE CHIANCA, 10km north of Lecce and open all year round; buses from the Villa Communale to *Solicara Camping Club* (☎0832/656.064).

For cheap **eats**, the *Ristorante da Claudio*, Via Cavour 11 does a good value tourist menu; and the food's good, too, at the *Trattoria Gambero Rosso*, Via Marino Brancaccio 16. For quick **snacks**, *La Rusticana* on Via Vittorio Emanuele (at the side of Santa Irene) sells excellent pasties and olive-stuffed bread.

The Eastern Peninsula: Otranto and the Southern Cape

The quickest escape from Lecce, to the coast, is to **SAN CATALDO**, popular with the locals, and with sandy beaches served by frequent buses from Lecce's Villa Communale. Without your own transport, though, you won't be able to see anything else of the coast south of San Cataldo until Otranto. If you have, it's a pleasant route south, along a rocky shoreline littered with ruined towers, a legacy of the defences erected against Turkish incursions. You'll pass several low-key resorts. Just south of **SAN FOCA** there's a spectacular rockpool, the *Grotta della Poesia*, big enough to swim in; while **ROCA VECCHIA** still displays traces of its ancient Messapic walls. **TORRE DELL'ORSO**, a couple of kilometres beyond, takes its name from the tower which stands on a stony promontory, the surrounding coves pockmarked by the remains of houses and tombs cut out of the rock. If you're looking to stay, the *Casa del Turista* at San Foca (☎0832/841.006) has rooms for L21,000, right on the coastal road. Between Torre dell'Orso and Otranto lie the **Lagi di Alimini**, two lakes surrounded by extensive pine woods, another popular green stop on this otherwise barren coast; there's **camping** here at *Camping Frassanito* (☎0833/85.005; May–Sept).

Otranto

OTRANTO, a miniscule town nestling around its harbour, makes an ideal base for exploring this part of the Adriatic. It's only an hour by train from Lecce (change at MAGLIE) and still very much a quiet Puglian backwater – though a summer ferry service to Greece and a new *Club Med* affair nearby are beginning to attract the crowds. Its history, however, is decidedly grim. One of the last Byzantine towns to fall to the Normans, in 1070, Otranto remained a thriving port for crusaders, pilgrims and traders. But in 1480 a Turkish fleet layed siege to the town, which held out for fifteen days before capitulating. It's said that as a punishment the archbishop, upon capture, suffered the indignity of being sawn in half, a popular Turkish spectacle. Nearly 12,000 people lost their lives and the 800 survivors, refusing to convert, were taken up a nearby hill and beheaded. Otranto never really recovered, though the town does feature one glorious survivor of the Turkish attack inside its cathedral.

This, the **Cattedrale di Santa Maria Annunziata**, lies down a small alleyway just to the left of the castle, a Romanesque structure with a rose-window added in the fifteenth century, and a marble-columned nave adorned by an extraordinary **mosaic floor**, a multicoloured tapestry in stone. Composed in three distinct but interconnecting parts, the mosaic stretches the length of the nave, centring on its main theme of the "Tree of Life", adorned with zodiacal signs and scenes from the medieval calendar, and flanked by two smaller trees in the aisles depicting biblical scenes. Historical and animal figures are shown as a mix of myth and reality – Alexander the Great, King Arthur, the Queen of Sheba, crabs, fish, serpents and mermaids. The work of a twelfth-century monk, for all its rough simplicity the mosaic provides a captivating picture, empowered by a delightful child-like innocence.

Not far from the cathedral, the town's Aragonese **Castello** juts out into the bay, defending the harbour. Recently restored, its walls incorporate fragments of Roman and medieval inscriptions, while Charles V's coat-of-arms looms from its portal. Outside on a dusty square, old men still play a highly animated form of *boules*, impervious to passers-by. Out on the southern edge of town is the hill, covered with cypress trees, where the survivors of the Turkish siege were beheaded. At the top of the hill, the sixteenth-century **Chiesa di San Francesco di Paola** holds inscriptions of the names of the victims, together with a vivid description of the terrible events of July 1480.

If you want **to stay** in Otranto, your best bet is the *Pensione Bellavista*, Via Vittorio Emanuele 16 (☎0836-86.359), with rooms for L30,000. The nearest **campsite** is signposted from the port, *Campeggio Hydrusa* (☎0836/81.255), open May to August. There are some excellent **fish restaurants** in town, like *Il Gambero* at the Porta Terra. Also, there's a variety of musical and theatrical events in Otranto throughout summer, usually centred around the castle, and an annual **festival** commemorating the "800 Martyrs" – August 13–15. Details of this and other information from the **AAST**, Lungomare Kennedy 2 (Mon–Fri 9am–1pm & 4.30–6pm).

If you're heading **to Greece**, *R Line* operates a ferry to Corfu and Igoumenitsa between June and late September, Monday to Friday at 10.30pm – L60,000 oneway: buy tickets from the office at the port.

To the southern cape

From Otranto, all the way down to the cape at Santa Maria di Leuca, the coastline is steep and rugged. **CAPO D'OTRANTO**, five kilometres south of Otranto, is the most easterly point on the Italian peninsula, topped by a lighthouse and the rather desolate ruins of a seventh-century abbey. On a clear day there's a commanding view across the Straits, the mountains of Albania visible, about 80km away. (On seriously clear days they say you can even see Corfu, 100km away.) **CASTRO**, about 30km down the coast, is the nicest of the towns around here. Fortified by the Aragonese in the twelfth century, it lies slightly inland, 100m above the small fishing hamlet of Castro Marina, the rocky creek serving as a harbour – and reputedly the landing place of the Trojan hero Aeneas. The area hereabouts is full of grottoes, the most spectacular and easiest to reach the **Grotta Zinzulusa**, a little way north of Castro Marina. An irridescent mass of stalactites and stalagmites, its dark waters are home to a rather odd species of blind fish. If you feel confident enough to explore a grotto by swimming, ask around in **MARINA D'ANDRANO** (about 6km down the coast from Castro Marina) for the un-signposted **Grotta Verde**, which is splendidly phosphorescent.

There isn't really much to draw you down as far as **SANTA MARIA DI LEUCA**, a somewhat barren spot that's a fitting "land's end", with a scattering of Neolithic remains and an uninspiring marina. The once-supposed "end of the world" is marked by the tiny church of **Santa Maria Finnibus Terrae**, built on the site of an ancient temple dedicated to Minerva, which stands perched on the white limestone cliffs. But it's all a bit of an anticlimax: even the cape isn't really the southernmost point, that distinction going to the Punta Ristola, a little to the west. You can get down this far, or at least as far as GAGLIANO DEL CAPO, by train: it's at the end of the *FSE* rail line, just 5km from the cape, and hitching the rest should be possible in the summer months.

The Western Peninsula: Galatina, Nardo and Gallipoli

About half an hour down the rail line from Lecce, **GALATINA** is one of the most intriguing of the Salentine towns. It remained a key Greek colony well into medieval times, while retaining Greek customs and language up until the present century. Today, it's an important centre of the Italian tobacco industry, with much of the weed grown in the fields around, as well as being famed for its excellent local wine.

Most interestingly, Galatina is the only place in the Salentine where the phenomenon of **tarantulism** still survives. Once a year, on the feast day of Saints Peter and Paul (June 28/29), the devout gather at the church dedicated to the saints to perform a ritual – the origins of which go back to the outbursts of mass hysteria that swept Europe in the wake of frequent plagues from the fourteenth century onwards. Victims of the dreaded tarantula bite would come here to give thanks for their survival from the spider's venom. Actually, the tarantula itself wasn't the culprit, but another smaller spider. In any case, the bite induced hallucinogenic symptoms, vomiting and paranoia, and those bitten believed that the only way to survive was to sweat the poison out of the system. This gave rise to a frenzied dance, which could last for days. During the nineteenth century the tarantella, as it was known, was modified into the colourful, popular dance that you see here today.

Fifteen kilometres west of Galatina, reachable by train, **NARDO** is a busy little town with a long and turbulent history of sackings, rebellions and occupations. Despite that, the centre of town, based around Piazza Antonio Salandra and Piazza San Domenico, retains some fine buildings in a more or less preserved state: there's an odd amalgam of ornately sculpted palazzi and bold facades, an fortified town hall and an eighteenth-century *guglia*, or obelisk, similar to the one in Ostuni.

By way of contrast, first impressions of **GALLIPOLI** are fairly uninspiring. The new town sprouted on the mainland once the population outgrew its original island site in the eighteenth century, and all that remains of the once-beautiful city (the *Kalli-pollis*) of the Greeks is a rather weatherbeaten fountain, which sits in the new town near the bridge. Over the bridge, the old town itself is a maze of meandering and twisting whitewashed streets, tiny tomatoes hanging on the walls to dry, providing a sudden blaze of colour alongside the fishing nets. Only the familiar Aragonese castle, which squats in one corner of the island, serves as a reminder that this is still Italy.

The beaches

There are some excellent **beaches** along this part of the coast, all fairly accessible by bus from Gallipoli. The *Baia Verde*, just to the south of the town, is highly popular in summer, though the beaches to the north, near the tiny villages of **SANTA CATERINA** and **SANTA MARIA AL BAGNO**, are better. Although there's been a spate of hotel building in recent years, this stretch remains one of the quietest spots in southern Italy, making it a good place to rest up for a while and see the coast. For **accommodation in Gallipoli**, try the *Pensione Gambero* on Lungomare Gondar (☎0883/22.532); and there are a couple of good **camp-sites** nearby, both 3km from town at TORRE SABEA.

travel details

Trains

From Foggia to Manfredonia (9 daily; 30min); Barletta/Trani/Molfetta/Bari (hourly; 40min/50min/1hr 5min/1hr 30min); San Severo/Peschici (5 daily; 40min/2hr 15min).

From San Severo to Peschici (7 daily; 1hr 40min).

From Barletta to Canosa di Puglia (9 daily; 1hr).

From Bari to Bríndisi (hourly; 2hr); Táranto (hourly; 2hr); Lecce (hourly; 2hr 45min); Molfetta/Trani/Barletta (14 daily; 25min/40min/50min); Bitonto/Ruvo di Puglia/Andria/Barletta (hourly; 20min/40min/1hr/1hr 10min); Altamura (13 daily; 1hr 10min); Gravina in Puglia/Spinazzola (3 daily; 1hr 15min/1hr 45min); Castellana Grotte/Putignano/Alberobello/Locorotondo/Martina Franca (hourly; 50min/1hr/1hr 30min/1hr 40min/1hr 50min); Torre a Mare/Polignano a Mare/Monopoli (hourly; 10min/30min/35min); Ostuni (hourly; 1hr); Naples/Rome (4–6 daily; 4hr 30min/6hr).

From Altamura to Gravina in Puglia (13 daily; 12min).

From Martina Franca to Táranto (8 daily; 40min).

From Táranto to Bari (16 daily; 2hr 20min); Oria/Bríndisi (12 daily; 40min/1hr 30min); Grottaglie (11 daily; 15min); Massafra/Castellaneta (12 daily; 15min/30min); Metaponto/Reggio di Calabria (3 daily; 50min/6hr).

From Bríndisi to Lecce (hourly; 50min); Ostuni (hourly; 35min).

From Lecce to Bari (hourly; 2hr); Gallipoli (9 daily; 1hr); Otranto (7 daily; 1hr); Gagliano del Capo (10 daily; 1hr 30min); Rome (1 daily; 9hr 30min).

Buses

From Foggia to Manfredonia (8–10 daily; 50min); Vieste (5 daily; 2hr 45min).

From Manfredonia to Monte Sant'Angelo (every 2hr; 55min); San Giovanni Rotondo (14 daily; 40min); San Marco in Lamis (10 daily; 1hr); Vico del Gárgano via Foresta Umbra (Mon–Sat 2 daily; 2hr 15min); Vieste (2 daily; 1hr 40min); Bari (1; 2hr 20min).

From Vieste to Manfredonia (3 daily; 1hr 40min); Foggia (2 daily; 2hr 45min); Peschici (9 daily; 45min).

From Peschici to Rodi Garganigo (3 daily; 35min); Vico del Gárgano (1 daily; 45min); San Severo (1 daily; 3hr).

From Vico del Gárgano to Ischitella (9 daily; 15min).

From Rodi Garganigo to Vico del Gárgano/Foresta Umbra (July to Sept 2 daily; 40min/1hr 5min).

From Bari to Molfetta/Trani/Barletta (3–4 hourly; 40min/1hr 5min/1hr 25min); Margherita di Savoia (8 daily; 1hr 45min); Andria (7 daily; 1hr 30min); Canosa di Puglia (11 daily; 2hr 10min).

From Molfetta to Ruvo di Puglia (hourly; 30min).

Ferries

From Manfredonia to the Tremiti Islands via Vieste/Peschici/Rodi Garganigo (1 daily mid-June to mid-Sept, 4 weekly for the two weeks either side, 2 weekly April to mid-May; 2hr/3hr/3hr 40min/5hr 20min).

International Ferries

There's usually at least one daily service from Bríndisi to the Greek ports throughout the year;

services increase between April and September; and mid-June to August is peak season with several sailings a day to most destinations.

From Bríndisi to Corfu (9hr 30min); Igoumenitsa (11hr); Patras (21hr); Paxi (13hr); Itaca (17hr); Cefalonia (18hr).

From Bari to Dubrovnik (5 weekly June to Sept, 3 monthly otherwise; 8hr); Split (3 monthly Oct to May only; 10hr); Corfu/Igoumenitsa/Patras (1 daily June to Sept, otherwise 3 weekly; 12hr/13hr/26hr).

From Otranto to Corfu/Igoumenitsa (5 weekly June to Sept; 9hr 30min/13hr).

CHAPTER FIFTEEN

CALABRIA AND BASILICATA

M ore than any other of the regions of the Italian South, **Basilicata** and **Calabria** represent the quintessence of the *mezzogiorno*. Culturally impoverished, underdeveloped and – owing to emigration – sparsely populated, these rural regions were long considered only good for taxation, and even then they were mismanaged. The feudal era didn't really die here until the Bourbons were ejected at Unification, and remnants of the older society persist in the exaggerated use of titles and the widespread system of patronage. Respect for authority co-exists with a deep scepticism, an apathy and inertia vividly described by Carlo Levi in his *Christ Stopped at Eboli* – a book that for many Italians was the first introduction to the very deep problems besetting the *mezzogiorno*.

Indeed, this area is if anything even more marginalised than it was before Unification, when it was at least the geographical centre of the Bourbon state, and today talk of the Two Nations of Italy is most strikingly manifest in what can seem a very distant region from the emphatically European north – to which its people provide a reluctant supply of cheap labour. But despite the lingering of attitudes on both sides that perpetuate this gulf, much has changed in the South, to the extent that the picture drawn in Levi's book would hardly be recognised today, thanks largely to a massive channelling of funds since the war to finance huge irrigation and land-reclamation schemes, industrial development and a modern system of communications, all helping to set the southern economy on its feet. Unemployment remains the highest in the country, and emigration is still very much a reality, but malaria has been eradicated, previously unproductive land made fertile, and construction is underway everywhere – though often hand-in-hand with the forces of organised crime and with frequently dire consequences for the physical aspect of the land.

On the whole it is the landscape that's the main reason for coming to Basilicata and Calabria. Artistically they are the most barren regions in Italy, but the combination of mountain grandeur and a relatively unspoilt coastline, often in close proximity, are a unique attraction, and one only beginning to be exploited by the tourist industry. The **main cities** – Reggio, Catanzaro, Potenza – are useful as transport hubs only, though **Matera**, the second city of Basilicata, holds a distinctive feature in its Sassi – cavelike dwellings in the heart of the town that were until relatively recently occupied by the poorest of its townspeople. And **Cosenza**, halfway down the Tyrrhenian coast, has a charm of a kind, and can make a vibrant stop-off if you're beach-bumming. Of the coasts, it's the **Tyrrhenian** that is the more obviously appealing, spots like **Maratea**, **Tropea** and **Scilla** well on their way to becoming discovered. The **Ionian** coast, on the other hand, can be

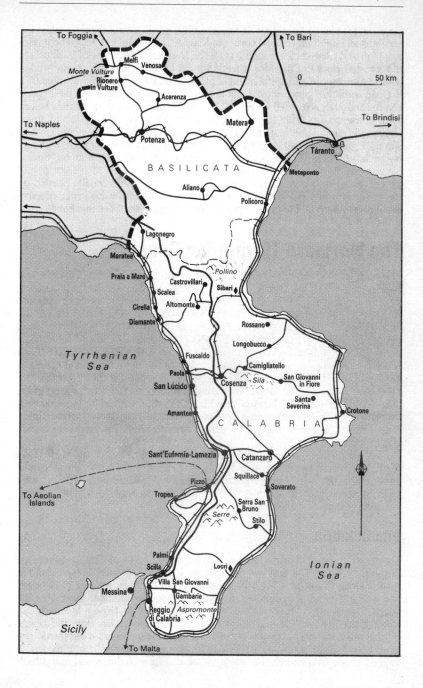

bleak, and is visited mainly for its **ancient sites** – relics from the days when the area was an important colonial corner of Magna Graecia. Inland, Italy's boot rises to a high and rugged core, ranging from the Norman strongholds of Basilicata to the forested slopes of the **Sila massif** around Cosenza, and the craggy wilderness of **Aspromonte**, long the haunt of brigands and their *mafiosi* descendants.

Good **transport** services exist, but in hilly and coastal areas, where the historic centres are often separated by several kilometres from their train stations below, a car is useful, especially to penetrate some of the more far-flung inland areas. Hitching is possible but not always easy: suspicion and fear of strangers is widespread, especially in Calabria, where the crime rate is notoriously high. It should be added, though, that violence against strangers is very uncommon. Sexual harassment, however, is not. The South is still very much a man's world, and women travelling alone will invariably be stared at and occasionally hassled on the street or when entering bars or restaurants. See *Basics* for some effective expletives to ward off the more persistent specimens of southern manhood.

The Northern Tyrrhenian Coast

The northern stretch of the Tyrrhenian coast takes in both Calabria and Basilicata, of which the former – a brief mountainous slice – is the most inspiring stretch, and probably the most visited part of the entire region, its sheer cliffs and rocky coves refreshingly unspoilt by the holiday industry. The main – indeed the only – town on Basilicata's Tyrrhenian seaboard, **MARATEA**, is a pretty place, divided into the districts of **MARATEA PORTO**, a quaint huddle of fishermen's houses and expensive restaurants, and the larger **MARATEA INFERIORE**, to which it's linked by hourly bus. Maratea Inferiore has more hotels and bars, and nestles below **MARATEA SUPERIORE** – starting-point for the climb (a steep kilometre) to the peak of **Monte San Biagio**, passing on the way the straggling, long-abandoned ruins of **Maratea Vecchia**. It's worth the effort for the wide view over the Golfo di Policastro and a close-up of Maratea's enormous marble Christ, arms akimbo, frozen in the act of setting forth to crush the Santuario di San Biagio opposite.

Five kilometres further down, there's a **railway station** at **MARATEA MARINA**, where you'll also find **hotels** – cheapest of which is the *Marisdea* (☎0973/879.003), with doubles starting at L22,000 – and a couple of **campsites** near the sea. The area is well endowed with sandy **beaches** – well signposted, but don't hesitate to explore the less obvious ones.

Into Calabria

Shortly after, the road drops to reveal the flat coast of Calabria, on the other side of the river Noce. The first town you reach, **PRAIA A MARE**, is typical of the resorts along this coast – lively in the summer, rather dead the rest of the time, and with a handful of **campsites**, **hotels** and **pizzerias** to choose from. On the beach, a sixteenth-century castle faces the rocky **Isola di Dino** a little way out, where there are caves and grottoes visitable by hiring a boat from the beach. Behind the town another **grotto** is the home of a widely venerated Madonna. The story goes that the people of nearby AIETA attempted repeatedly to remove this image to their own church, but each time she disappeared and was found back here, where they were eventually forced to let her be. Recently the image disappeared forever, though a replacement was quickly and pragmatically installed.

Beyond Praia, the pretty village of **SAN NICOLA ARCELLA** has a lovely wide **beach**, from which – through a series of passages and a tunnel – you can get to other, emptier beaches. There is a good **pizzeria** here and a hotel, the *Villa Principe* (☎0985 3125), which has doubles for L45,000. The next town south, **SCALEA**, is quite different – Calabria at its worst, the natural beauty of the location overwhelmed by an avalanche of unchecked development encircling a largely abandoned old quarter. Stop here to visit the ruins of the Norman/ Aragonese castle and a frescoed eleventh-century Byzantine chapel, bombed by both sides during the war (the *famiglia* Grisolia holds the key). Then move on.

South of Scalea, excavations are under way on the banks of the River Lao that may bring to light the remains of ancient **Laos**, colonised by the Sybarites following the destruction of their city (see p.818). The seaside town of **CIRELLA** was also a Sybarite colony, devastated by Hannibal, then Romanised, though the theatrical ruins of **Cirella Vecchia**, overlooking the SS18, are of a later date, the result of a French bombardment in 1806 (though local lore attributes other, more sinister explanations, most notably a plague of ants). From behind the ruins a road leads to the hilltop villages of GRISOLIA and MAIERA, close together on the map but actually divided by a gully, across which you may hear conversations being conducted from one village to the other.

Five kilometres down the coast, **DIAMANTE** glistens on its small promontory – a chic seaside town, rather arty, its narrow whitewashed lanes adorned with vast and striking modern murals. A brief walk away from the seafront and over a bridge, *Il Giardino* is an averagely priced **restaurant** where you can sit outside and eat good seafood.

BELVEDERE MARITTIMO, some 10km down the coast, overlooks its unexceptional marina from a spur a little way inland, an imposing and elegant town, full of greenery and having little of the air of neglect typical of Calabria's older centres. Eat at the *Perrera Trattoria* (well marked), and visit its impressive **castle**, originally a Norman construction but rebuilt under the Aragonese, whose coat-of-arms can be seen above the main gate. Its restoration is being planned, and for the moment you can only get in between 5pm and 9pm daily.

CITTADELLA has good **beaches**, and the grand *San Michele* hotel just beyond – one of the last of an Edwardian generation of hotels, with a golf course and a lift down to the beach at the base of the cliff. GUARDIA PIEMONTESE was once the home of a community of Protestant refugees from the north of Italy who were brutally suppressed by the Inquisition in 1560, as the name of one of the gates round the still partly intact city walls recalls: *Porta della Strage*, "Gate of the Slaughter". With the wind blowing in the right direction you can't fail to notice the musty odours emitted from nearby TERME LUIGIANE, the popular hot springs. On the beach at **FUSCALDO**, the *Pepper Pot* is a good place to stop for a bite to eat, run by a friendly Irish-Italian couple.

Paola . . . and south

Next down the coast, **PAOLA**'s size and importance is partly due to its function as the main rail and road junction for COSENZA, partly to its **Santuario di San Francesco di Paola**, in a ravine above the town. San Francesco spent most of his life in the town, and as Calabria's principal saint is venerated throughout the south. People visit the shrine at all times in the year, but particularly during the week leading up to the May 4 **festa** – when a fair occupies the town, with daily festivities culminating in the carrying of his statue into the sea and a grand display of fireworks on the beach at midnight. There are several **hotels** and **trattorias** around the station by the sea, and a good pizzeria near the central piazza above – *Renato*, in via del Cannone – though if you want to stay over, **SAN LÚCIDO**, 6km south, is more attractive. Its *Hotel Irma* (☎0984 81330), near the seafront, has doubles for L30,000, and close by there's one of the best **trattorias** in the region, *La Rupe* – on the cliff in the old centre.

The series of small towns and villages that follow are all split between the original centres located higher up from the shore and more modern marinas – good for beaches but visually uninteresting. The older villages are difficult to get to but, if you can manage it, are worth the hike. **FIUMEFREDDO** has cobbled streets leading to a pleasant lookout perched above a sheer drop and a strange and dilapidated **castle** – a good place for picnics. **BELMONTE**, just beyond, has a mausoleum – easily visible as you pass below – dedicated to its greatest son, **Michele Bianchi**, one of the *quadrumvirate* of Fascists who marched on Rome in 1922, and for a while Mussolini's deputy. **AMANTEA** is the largest and liveliest of the chain, with beaches (either in the town itself or 3km south) and a wide choice of **eating places**; try the rough-and-ready *Trattoria Cavalla* on the main shopping street of the lower part of town, Via Margherita. If you feel like staying, the *Pensione Margherita* is on the same street. As for things to see, there's the fifteenth-century church and convent of **San Barnardino di Siena**, with majolica decoration and a sculpture by Gagini, up towards the old town. And there's one of the best fairy tale **castles** in Calabria nearby; take the turning at CÁMPORA SAN GIOVANNI for CLETO, close to the Savuto River.

Cosenza and around

COSENZA, Calabria's first town of any size if you're travelling from the north, is also the region's most interesting, and makes a useful base to explore the surrounding area – particularly the **Sila** mountains. Historically it has always played an important role in the commercial and intellectual life of Calabria (Norman Douglas wrote, with characteristic hyperbole, "for acute and original thought this town can hardly be surpassed by any other of its size on earth"), and recently the town has generated a degree of wealth which – while still some way below most of Italy – has in the last twenty years or so literally transformed the landscape. New construction, much of it featureless and ugly, has sprouted everywhere, while its recently established university is expanding fast, helping to create a new and strong regional awareness and self-confidence.

Completely enclosed by mountains – the Sila on the east, the Catena Costiera separating it from the sea to the west – Cosenza is the meeting point of two rivers, the Crati and the Busento. Somewhere beneath the latter, tradition has the burial place of **Alaric the Goth**, the barbarian who gave the western world a jolt when he finally managed to prise open the gates of Rome in AD 410. Struck down for his sins by malaria while on his way south, he was interred here along with his booty, and the course of the river deviated to cover the traces, lending Cosenza a place in history and giving rise to countless (and fruitless) projects to discover the tomb's whereabouts.

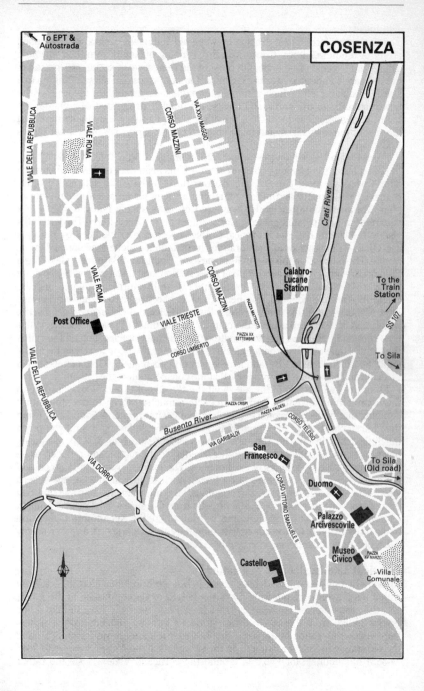

The town

The two rivers form a neat division between old and new Cosenza, with the main artery of the newer town, **Corso Mazzini**, running off south from their junction. This is the liveliest place to be, but most of the things worth seeing are located in the old part, the **centro storico**, a compact knot of steps and alleys rising up to a sturdy Swabian castle. Much of the old town has been abandoned in favour of the newer suburbs to the north, and the area is unfairly denigrated as a ghetto, the haunt of *mafiosi*, delinquents and prostitutes. But there's a tranquillity here that the rest of the town lacks, and more character and charm than most other places in Calabria.

From Piazza Valdesi on the far side of the bridge, Corso Telesio leads off into the old quarter's confusion of narrow streets. This main road of the area is named after Cosenza's most famous son, **Bernardino Telesio**, the sixteenth-century humanist philosopher and major influence on the other great Calabrian philosopher, Tommaso Campanella. Halfway up, Cosenza's stately **Duomo** stands in a square of tall dilapidated palaces. Consecrated on the occasion of Frederick II's visit to the city in 1222, its Provençal Gothic style was later modified by Baroque accretions – though sporadic restorations have undone much of the damage to the facade. The interior – a mixture of Romanesque, Gothic and Baroque styles – has a Roman sarcophagus in a good state of preservation, and a stone carving depicting Isabelle of Aragon, who died in Cosenza in 1271 while returning with her husband Philip III – seen kneeling beside her – from an abortive crusade in Tunisia. Also here is a copy of a thirteenth-century Byzantine icon, the *Madonna del Pilerio*, which was once carried around the country during times of plague; the original is now kept in the **Palazzo Arcivescovile** or Archbishop's Palace, behind the cathedral. This is eventually to be a museum, but ring at the door to see some of the exhibits, which include a Byzantine reliquary crucifix made by Greek craftsmen in Palermo and presented by Frederick II at the consecration of the cathedral.

From the Duomo any of the alleys on the far side of Corso Telesio lead up to the church and convent of **San Francesco**, a much-restored thirteenth-century complex that holds occasional exhibitions (daily 9am–1pm & 4–6pm; free). From the church climb up to the Corso Vittorio Emanuele, following it until you reach the little track leading to the formidable **castle** (9am–1pm & 3.30pm–sunset; mornings only in winter; free), another Frederick II construction reduced to its present condition by a series of earthquakes. The inside is bare and in process of restoration, but it's a good place for a breath of clean air and to enjoy the superb view over Cosenza and its surroundings. If you want to skip seeing San Francesco, you can reach the castle directly from Cosenza's most elegant square, **Piazza XV Marzo**, at the top of Corso Telesio, where the **Accademia Cosentina** houses the **Museo Civico** (daily 9am–noon; free), which sports a rather scanty collection of prehistoric and classical bric-a-brac.

Practical details: sleeping and eating

Arriving by bus you will be deposited at the **bus station** below Piazza Fera, from which it's a twenty-minute walk down the length of Corso Mazzini to the hotels and the *centro storico*. Arriving by train from Paola, you will have to take a bus (every 20min) from the new **railway station** a little way outside town – tickets from inside the station at the bar. Most of Cosenza's **accommodation** is around the old station in Piazza Matteotti: on the square itself the *Hotel Excelsior* (☎0984/74.383) has doubles for L36,000; around the corner in Viale Trieste the rather dingy *Locanda Santelli* (☎0984/73.263) charges L20,000 a double; nearby at Corso Mazzini 27, the *Bruno* (☎0984/73.889) has doubles at L24,000.

There is a wide choice of **eating places** at this end of town: the *Pizza d'Oro* on Via 24 Maggio has a long menu and a garden, but the best deal is to be had at the small **trattoria** on Piazza Crispi, where you can have a complete meal for L10,000. On summer evenings the most congenial place to be is the **birreria** at the old aqueduct, at the end of the winding Via Arnone off Viale della Repubblica, with great views over the valley.

The **EPT** (daily 9am–1pm & 4–7pm) is on Via Pasquale Rossi – below the roundabout for the autostrada – but is of very little help.

Around Cosenza

People spending any time in Cosenza will be mostly interested in excursions into the **Sila** (see below), but some of the villages dotted around the surrounding hills shouldn't be ignored. Especially in summer, when the heat and humidity settle on the town, the focus tends to move out of the city and into the hills, where most of the Cosentine population have their roots and family homes. With the village population swollen too by emigrants back for the summer, the streets are thronged until late, and at night the view over the bowl of the valley is magnificent, a glittering theatre with even Cosenza managing to look romantic. It is also in the summer that the village **festas** normally take place, with each *comune*, or municipal administration, trying to outdo the others in terms of spectacle and expense.

The villages of the **Presila**, on the eastern slope of the valley, have a reputation for late-night revelry and some good **pizzerias** (the best is in PEDACE, *U'Fuccularu*) and **birrerias** (try *Le Demon Rouge* in SPEZZANO DELLA SILA, with quite respectable food). On the other side of the valley the hilltop village of **RENDE** holds the prize for the tidiest village in the region, and it has good views, a **birreria** and a **ristorante**. Opposite Montalto, on the other side of the autostrada and the Crati River, five kilometres above LUZZI, stands the **Abbazia di Sambucina** – a Cistercian abbey founded in the twelfth century and long the centre of this order of monks throughout the South. It has a good portal (rebuilt in the fifteenth century) and the original presbytery.

There are buses to all of these places from the **bus station** in Cosenza below Piazza Fera, though they normally stop at nightfall. Another interesting (but slow) way to get to the Presila during the day (and beyond, into the Sila) is by the **trenino** of the Calabro–Lucane (*FCL*) line, which you can take from a small (unmarked) station behind Cosenza's old station three times a day, offering some marvellous glimpses over the Cosenza Valley, as the train twists and grinds up the mountain through woods and over rivers. It completes the 76km journey to SAN GIOVANNI IN FIORE in just over two hours, twice the time it would take by road, with return tickets at L3900, last departure at 2pm. Make sure of the return times, though, if you don't want to get stranded.

The Sila

Covering the widest part of the Calabrian peninsula, the **Sila** massif is more of an extensive plateau than a mountain range, though the peaks on its western flank reach heights of nearly 2000m. It's divided into three main groups, the *Sila Greca*, *Sila Grande* and *Sila Piccola*, the last two of which are little more than an

administrative division, while the former – although the least entrancing scenically – is distinguished by the Albanian villages from which it takes its name.

At one time the Sila was one huge forest, and was exploited from earliest times
to provide fuel and material for the construction of fleets, fortresses and even for
church-building in Rome, resulting in a deforestation that helped bring about the
malarial conditions that for centuries laid much of Calabria low. The cutting of
trees is now strictly controlled, and since the regional government recognised the
potential of the area and imposed restrictions on building and hunting, there is
plenty here for the outdoors enthusiast, in summer as a relief from the heat of the
towns or coasts and in winter for downhill or cross-country skiing. The other
seasons have their own charms: spring, when the woods are a riot of wild flowers,
and autumn, for the full gamut of decaying colour and – a local speciality – wild
mushrooms.

The Sila Greca

Deforestation has had the most devastating effect on the *Sila Greca*, most northerly part of the massif, leaving mainly cultivated rolling highlands in place of the
dense woods. But the area is easily accessible from the Ionian coast or the autostrada inland, and if you have a car is worth the detour to investigate some of the
Albanian villages scattered around these hills. These mountain communities
have their origin in the fifteenth century, when colonies of Albanians in flight
from Muslim invasions were allowed to settle in some of the poorest areas of the
peninsula by Irene, princess of Bisignano and daughter of **Skanderbeg** – the
Albanian warrior-king, whose fiery image adorns many a main square in these
parts. The villages retain to this day the shabby, untended look of straitened
circumstances, visually unexciting and with few buildings or treasures of great
artistic merit. **SAN DEMETRIO CORONE** is the most interesting, containing
an Italo-Albanian *Collegio* charged with the task of guarding what remains of the
Albanian heritage. Annexed to this is the church of **Sant'Adriano**, a structure
that still shows elements of its Byzantine and Norman origins, including some
Norman paving depicting the various animals which roamed the woods that once
covered these hills – lions, serpents and panthers. Really, though, it's the annual
festivals that show these villages at their best, and you should try and coincide
your visit with one. Along with the opportunity to see their elaborate costumes
and hear some gutsy singing, it may be the only chance of hearing the authentic
language – a fifteenth-century version of modern Albanian – that has only
recently been replaced by *calabrese* dialect as the everyday language in these
parts. Festivals take place in the villages of Santa Sofia (July 15 & 16), San Cosmo
(September 26 & 27), Vaccarizzo (March 31–April 2), and San Giorgio (April 2).

The Sila Grande

Densely forested, and the highest, most extensive part of the Sila range, the *Sila
Grande* has Calabria's main **ski slopes**, as well as the region's three principal
lakes – all artificial (for hydroelectric purposes) and much loved by fishing fanat-
ics who come out in force at weekends. The best base for day trips is Cosenza,
but if you want to spend any time up here it would be advisable either to camp in
the Sila or stay in one of the small towns there. These vary greatly. **SAN**

GIOVANNI IN FIORE, in the heart of the Sila, is the biggest town in the area, but also the dreariest. More interesting is **LONGOBUCCO**, atmospherically enclosed at the bottom of a narrow valley directly below the national park of La Fossiata (see below). There is one **hotel** here, the *Stella* (☎71.074), which has doubles starting at L30,000. For winter-sports enthusiasts and summer trekkers alike, **CAMIGLIATELLO**, well connected by bus with Cosenza, is the best known of the resorts, a tidy little town wholly given over to tourism, with three ski slopes of its own and another at nearby Moccone, facilities for hiring equipment and tuition, and a confusion of hotels, restaurants and souvenir shops. In season there is an abundance of **hotels**, but they can be expensive – for more moderate rates try the *Miramonti* (☎0984/978.343) or the *Tana del Lupo* (☎0984/978.317). For a good **trattoria**, the aptly named *Si Mangia Bene e Si Spende Poco* in Moccone has a well-deserved reputation. For hiking information, the **EPT** is on Via Roma.

From Camigliatello, walk or hitch the 15km to **Lago Cecita**, best starting-place for expeditions to **La Fossiata**, a conservation area that resembles a national park on the American model, with tidy wooden fences along the roads and numerous picnic spots. It is always possible to find your own space, but it's a good idea, too, to follow the planned routes set out by the *Forestale* – paths can run out on you when you least expect it. Camping in the area is forbidden except in the **campsite** near Lake Cecita, but there are many opportunities to hide away undiscovered if you pitch your tent after dark; the foresters are primarily concerned about littering and the danger of fires (a real risk in the summer).

Get hold of a brochure with map and explanations of the area from one of the bars around here, or from the **EPT** in Camigliatello, Cosenza or – if all else fails – the offices of the *Corpo Forestale* in Cosenza (Viale della Repubblica 26). You need to understand Italian to read the route descriptions, and the map is useless for discovering where to find the paths, but it can be helpful as a broad guide to their relative lengths and for switching from one to another.

Camigliatello is also a useful starting point for a ramble that takes in the area's highest peaks, following the *strada delle vette*, snowbound in the winter months, for 13km through pine and beech woods before forking off and up to the three peaks of Monte Botte Donato (1928m). The road continues on down to Lake Arvo and the resort of **LORICA**, from which it is a shorter distance to Botte Donato. Or you can save the sweat and take the chair lift from the *località* Cavaliere, a little outside the main town. Lorica, like Camigliatello, is dedicated to tourism in the height of the winter and summer seasons, but its lakeside location makes it a more relaxed spot, with lots of places for picnicking under the pines and observing the antics of the curious black squirrels that inhabit them. The town is connected by **bus** from Cosenza, arriving in the morning and going back in the afternoon, and there are two **campsites** (one inside, the other just outside the town), and several **hotels** – though only one, the *Belvedere* (☎0984/997.016), is open all year round.

The Sila Piccola

Bounded by Lago Ampollino in the north, Catanzaro and the Ionian coast in the south, the *Sila Piccola* is the region's most densely forested section, centring on the **Foresta di Gariglione** – much reduced from its extent at the turn of the century but still impressively thick, with fir, beech and the gigantic turkey oak from which it derives its name. Its designation as national park protects it from further plundering, though it is not so well adapted for walking as La Fossiata. Apart from the odd resort, it's a sparsely populated area, and most of its villages are in any case unattractive. Only **SANTA SEVERINA**, on the eastern fringes, is worth a stop – an originally Byzantine fortified town built on a hilltop and dominated by a Norman castle. The **Cattedrale** here has an eighth-century Byzantine **baptistery** off its left aisle, with an original font. On the other side of the main piazza the **castle** was rebuilt by Robert Guiscard on the ruins of a Byzantine stronghold. Now occupied by an infants' school but open to visitors, its well-preserved battlements look out over the district known as the *Marchesato*, a former vast feudal domain surrounding Crotone and belonging to the Ruffo family, one of the main landowning dynasties in Calabria.

Further south, **BELCASTRO** – also watched over by a Norman castle – claims to be the birthplace of Saint Thomas Aquinas, whose family once held the town in fief. Further down the SS109, the mountain village of **TAVERNA** has long historical associations, but is best known today as the home of Calabria's foremost seventeenth-century painter, **Mattia Preti**, whose Spanish-looking paintings can be seen in four of the local churches, particularly **San Domenico** – in which, in a corner of his portrait of *St John the Baptist* is a self-portrait of the artist himself. From here it's 25km down a winding road to the regional capital of CATANZARO.

The Southern Tyrrhenian Coast

The province of Catanzaro begins at the Savuto River, and from here down to Reggio the SS18, autostrada and main railway line all run parallel, tracing the coast together apart from the stretch of the Tropea promontory. Immediately after the river, a few kilometres inland from the resort of LIDO DI FALERNA, the hill-village of **NOCERA TIRINESE** (hitch or bus from the station on the coast) is famed for the flagellants that paint the streets red every Easter – a religious festival, not at all laid on for tourists, that grips the whole village with fervour. Wailing processions sway through the streets, and teams of two sprint between churches, one holding a cross, the other slapping himself systematically with a spiked brush, after which his blood is splashed over the doors of the houses to protect those within – not to be washed off until it happens naturally with the rain. It is one of the few cases of this kind of ritual bloodletting still to be found in the South, worth catching if you're around here at the right time.

Further down the coast, between Capo Su'vero (marked by its lighthouse) and LIDO DI GIZZERIA, is a fine **swimming spot**, a sandy spit with a freshwater lake close by, surrounded by palms and bamboo – though it can only be a matter of time before the site is earmarked for development. The plain that stretches east from here, the **Piana di Sant'Eufemia**, is the narrowest part of the Calabrian peninsula, much of it reclaimed only in the last hundred years from malarial swamp: the mosquitos remain but they no longer carry the disease. SANT' EUFEMIA-LAMEZIA is the **rail and road junction** for CATANZARO and the Ionian coast. Heading south on the motorway you begin a slow ascent on the long viaduct that is one of the engineering feats of the *Autostrada del Sole*, the views growing more inspiring as it rises above the coast to the high tableland of the Tropea promontory.

Pizzo and the Tropea Promontory

Following the railway or the SS18, the picturesque little town of **PIZZO** is a good place to spend some time, neatly placed for the **beaches** around Tropea and with a clifftop **youth hostel** (*pizzo* in dialect means rock) converted from a castle built in 1486 by Ferdinand I of Aragon – inside which you can see the room in which the French general **Murat** was imprisoned, and the yard where he was shot in October 1815. Murat, one of Napoleon's ablest generals, met his ignominious end here after attempting to rouse the people against the Bourbons and reclaim the throne of Naples given to him by Napoleon; the people of Pizzo ignored his haughty entreaties and he was arrested and court-martialled.

If you intend staying at the hostel it's a good idea to phone first to check on vacancies (☎0963/231.551); if it's full, the *Hotel Murat* overlooking the main square (☎0963/231.006) is an inexpensive alternative, with double rooms at L35,000 (with bath). There are numerous **places to eat**, including a couple of pizzerias in the main square (*Il Porticato* is one) and in Piazzetta Garibaldi the trattoria *Il Ritrovo* (closed Wednesday), along the main shopping street, Corso Garibaldi – as well as several other places in the port below. Between April and July try the tuna or swordfish, for which Pizzo is a fishing centre.

The Tropea Promontory

Pizzo is also a starting-point for the coastal railway line that rings the **Tropea promontory**; trains run from a separate **station** near the port. The first stop, **VIBO MARINA**, is the major port and industrial centre of this stretch of coast, with a regular peak-season boat service to the Aeolian Islands (see *Sicily*, Chapter 16). Some 10km above the port and served by the mainline station of Pizzo-Vibo Valentia, the larger town of **VIBO VALENTIA** has a history that goes back to Greek times, when it was known as **Hipponion** (fragments of whose walls are still standing 2km north of town). Because of its strategic importance, Vibo has always held a prominent position in Calabria's history: under Murat it was a provincial capital with a flourishing cultural life, inhabited by grandees whose memory survives in the street-names and in the many surviving palaces – all now in a state of decay that doesn't help the town's rather shabby aspect. It's a place to be passed through rather than stopped at, with a small **Museo Archaeologico** in Piazza Garibaldi (summer daily 9am–1pm & 5–7pm; winter Tues–Sat 9am–2pm, Sun 9am–1pm; free), soon to be enlarged but currently containing items from the Greek and Roman sites in the area, and a Norman **castle** reachable on a path which winds up behind – under restoration, but you may be able to enter and admire from its massive walls the view over the coast and the rolling countryside behind.

Inland from here (connected by frequent buses), the village of **SORIANO** is dominated by the ruins of the **church and monastery of San Domenico** – one of the largest and richest houses of the Dominican Order in Europe until it was wrecked by earthquakes in 1659 and 1783. The monastery produced four popes, two of whom can be seen on canvas in the modern adjoining church, along with a miraculous portrait of Saint Dominic said to be painted by no human hand. The majestic ruins still manage to render an idea of the size and wealth of the complex, which must have once striven to out-dazzle the nearby Carthusian monastery at SERRA SAN BRUNO (see p.823).

On the other side of Vibo the golden sands of Tropea stretch invitingly into the Tyrrhenian Sea – one of the least spoilt and most picturesque parts of Calabria. Take your choice among the numerous **campsites** and **beaches**, mostly clean and sandy, though relatively crowded at the height of the season. Try *La Rocchetta* at BRIATICO, with its ruined watchtower and scattered fishing boats, or those around SANTA DOMENICA.

TROPEA itself can claim to be the prettiest town on the whole of the Tyrrhenian coast, and the most fashionable, with a seaside charm missing from many of the other Calabrian resorts, and one which is not yet entirely eroded by the annual influx of tourists. The buildings have character without being twee – see particularly the lovely Norman **cathedral** at the bottom of Via Roma, whose interior harbours a couple of unexploded American bombs from the last war (each accompanied by a grateful prayer to the Madonna), a Renaissance ciborium and a statue of the Madonna and Child from the same period. The views from the upper town over the sea and the church of **Santa Maria dell'Isola** on its rock are superb, and on a clear day you will see the cone of Stromboli and perhaps some of the other Aeolian Islands looming out of the horizon. There are good beaches all around and more trattorias per square metre than in any other town in Calabria, and in season at least plenty of choice of **accommodation** – though it may be wise to book all the same. Try the *Hotel Miramare* on the road heading south out of town (☎0963/61.570), which charges L40,000 for a double though is closed in winter. Open all year round is the *Virgilio* (☎0963/61.978; L48,000) in Viale Tondo.

Further around the promontory, **CAPO VATICANO** is a complex of some of the most popular beaches, including **Grotticelle** – spacious enough to get away from the bustle and with a **campsite** immediately above and a clean hotel (*Grotticelle*; ☎0963/63.157) with rooms for L35,000. To the south of here, the road teeters high above the sea before reaching **NICOTERA**, built in its present position by Robert Guiscard. It has a couple of small **museums**, a **cathedral** with work by Antonello Gagini, and a **marina** below – a pleasant place to eat outside in the summer. There are wide beaches too, with a couple of **campsites** at their southern end.

South to Reggio

From Nicotera there are some long views to be had over the **Piana** stretching south, Calabria's second plain of any size and dedicated to olive cultivation. The towns here are mostly new and unattractive, partly due to the fact that the area is one of the most seismically active in Italy – the epicentre of the notorious 1783 earthquake was at nearby Oppido. The small Tropea railway line connects with the main line at ROSARNO, beyond which **PALMI** holds an interesting **museum complex** in *La Casa della Cultura Leonida Repaci*: a newly-built cultural centre and exhibition hall a little way above the town (take Via San Giorgio, close to the exit onto the SS18). It includes the best collection of folklore items in Calabria, and a museum of art and sculpture with work by Modigliani, De Chirico, Guttuso and Carlo Levi (Mon–Sat 8am–2pm; free).

From Palmi the tall TV mast on the northern tip of Sicily is already visible, but the best view of Sicily and the Calabrian coast (thought by Leslie Gardiner in his *South to Calabria* to be "perhaps the finest viewpoint in southern Italy") is some 5km down the road, at **Monte Sant'Elia**, the first elevation of the Aspromonte massif. From this balcony, perched on cliffs that plunge vertically down to the sea, you can see the two volcanoes of Etna and Strómboli on a clear day; there is a **campsite** behind, and a tourist village. The spot is believed to have been named after Sant'Elia Spelaeotes, who lived in these parts (in a cave, which can be visited on the road leading into Aspromonte from Melicucca) and whose body, when he died aged 94, proved unburnable by the Saracens. Earlier, when his body was washed, the water was used for curing another holy man's toothache – though "Virtues," he said, "are better than miracles".

From here south, the proximity of Sicily becomes the dominant feature looking out to sea, and the stretch of the autostrada that dives down to Villa San Giovanni can claim to be one of the most panoramic in Italy, burrowing high up through mountains with the Straits of Messina glittering below. By train or following the old road, you skirt the so-called *Costa Viola*, passing through BAGNARA, famous for its swordfish, and **SCILLA**, ancient Scylla, with a fine sandy **beach** and lots of action in the summer. This was the location of one of the two dreaded monsters (possibly whirlpools) mentioned as a threat to mariners in the **Odyssey**, the other being Charybdis, corresponding to the modern Cariddi located 6km away on the other side of the Strait. Unquestionably the best place to stay in Scilla is the **youth hostel**, located in the castle that separates the beautiful people on the main beach from the fishing village to the north. Open from April to the end of September, it is likely to be full at the height of the season so phone first to check on availability (☎0965/75.4033). The best alternative is the *Pensione Le Sirene* (phoning also advisable in summer: ☎0965/75.4121) with doubles at L35,000. Otherwise, a blind eye is turned on those who want to sleep on the beach (the southern end).

From Scilla it's just 9km to **VILLA SAN GIOVANNI** (frequent buses), worth stopping at only as a point of embarcation for Sicily. The state-run *FS* **ferries** leave from directly behind the station and arrive at Messina **railway station** in about forty minutes. More frequent are the private *Caronte* ferries (right out of the station and under the rails), leaving approximately every fifteen minutes and pulling in closer to the entrance of the *autostrada*. This is the one the lorry-drivers take, so it's also useful if you're hitching. There's also a hydrofoil service from Villa to the Aeolian Islands (twice a day). If you're heading for REGGIO, take a train or one of the hourly *Salzone* **buses** from outside the station.

Reggio and around

The southernmost province of Calabria – **Reggio** – is, in some ways, the apotheosis of all that makes the Italian South so distinctive. Encapsulating many of the problems to be found throughout the region, it is the place, as Joan Didion once said about California, where hope runs out. But, unlike the American West, the response here is despair. Significantly, emigration from this part of Italy has long been the highest, and continues to be high, though with the narrowing of the international job market the number of escape routes is constantly diminishing. At the same time the land itself, once the heart and soul of the southern peasant culture and economy, is increasingly being abandoned in the face of low returns and high expectations – no-one expects to share in the get-rich-quick society by tilling fields. Misery and delinquency are more evident here than in other parts of the South, earthquakes more frequent, the landscape more extreme in all ways, with dilapidated villages lying stranded among mountains, which are themselves torn apart by wide *fiumare*, or riverbeds – empty or reduced to a trickle for nine-tenths of the year, but swelling with the melting of the winter snows to destructive torrents.

Reggio di Calabria

REGGIO DI CALABRIA, the provincial capital, was originally the first of the ancient Greek settlements on the Italian mainland, and today, with a population of over 170,000, is the town in the region that most resembles a city. It also has all the drawbacks of an urban centre: heavy industry, slum housing, and streets that are in a more ramshackle state than anywhere else in Calabria. Traces of elegance survive – not least in the superb seafront that faces Messina across the Straits, while its main street, Corso Garibaldi, stretching for two kilometres across the centre of town, has one of the most animated *passeggiatas* in Calabria. But the absence of any buildings of historical note testifies to the violence of the earthquakes that have repeatedly devastated the area, the most recent (and most destructive) of which flattened the city in 1908.

Much of Reggio's air of shabby neglect has its roots in deep-seated social problems, specifically the stranglehold that the Calabrian Mafia, or **'ndrangheta**, continues to have on the town. Locally this phenomenon is referred to as the *piovra*, or octopus, whose tentacles penetrate all aspects of the city's life (*tangente*, or protection money, is tacitly understood to be paid by all shopkeepers and businessmen in most parts of the town). For the last three years Reggio has been suffering more than usual from its activities, the result of a bloody *faida* (feud) between rival families over control of the drugs trade, which during 1987 resulted in over 150 killings in the town (compared with 88 in the whole of Northern Ireland during the same period).

Closely linked to the *'ndrangheta*'s hold on the city is the high rate of unemployment in the province (25 percent), which has provoked large demonstrations in recent years attracting a wide spectrum of support. The demonstrations have the dual aim of drawing attention to Reggio's worsening economic situation and demanding a common front against the influence of the criminal bosses, though the prevailing attitude is a general scepticism towards any attempt to improve the situation. A recently elected left-wing council – a rare thing in Reggio – is not expected to make a lot of difference: politicians of all persuasions are held to be intrinsically corrupt, and *clientelismo*, the complicated network of political favours and obligations, is – like the *'ndrangheta* itself – too entrenched.

The Town

Most visitors to Reggio, however, will see little of the state of war that exists here. There are few, in any case, who choose to spend much time here: the city is not exactly bulging with unmissable attractions, though it does possess, in the **Museo Nazionale** in Corso Garibaldi (Tues–Sat 9am–1.30pm & 3.30–7.30pm, Mon 9am–1.30pm, Sun 9am–12.30pm; L4000), the most important collection of archaeological finds in Calabria. Most of the items inside date from the Hellenic period, with examples from all the major Greek sites in Calabria, including the famous *pinakes* or carved tablets from the sanctuary of Persephone at Locri. The most renowned exhibits in the museum are the **Bronzi di Riace**: two bronze statues dragged out of the Ionian Sea in 1972 near the village of Riace. They are

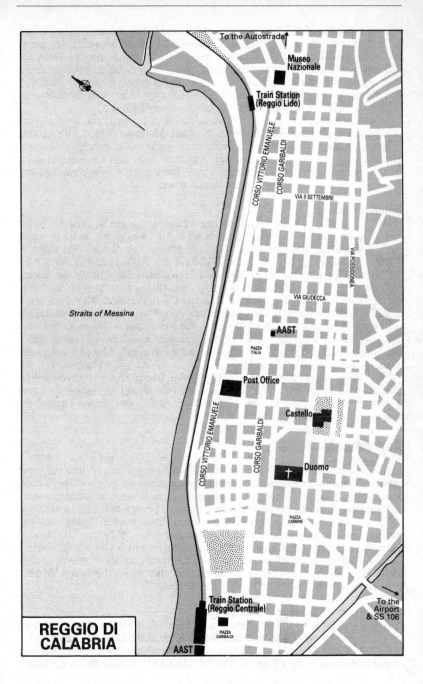

To the Autostrada

Museo
Nazionale

Train Station
(Reggio Lido)

CORSO VITTORIO EMANUELE

CORSO GARIBALDI

VIA II SETTEMBRE

VIA POSSIDONEA

VIA GIUDECCA

Straits of Messina

AAST

PIAZZA
ITALIA

Post Office

Castello

CORSO VITTORIO EMANUELE

CORSO GARIBALDI

Duomo

PIAZZA
CARMINE

Train Station
(Reggio Centrale)

To the
Airport
& SS 106

**REGGIO DI
CALABRIA**

PIAZZA
GARIBALDI

AAST

shapely examples of the highest period of Greek art (fifth century BC), attributed to Phidias or followers of his school, and especially prized because there are so few finds from this period in such a good state of repair. Around them are detailed explanations of the recovery and cleaning-up of the statues that preceded their tour around the country, when they caused a minor sensation. Now they seem almost forgotten in the well-lit basement they share with another prize exhibit – a philosopher's head from the fourth century BC.

As you gaze over the Straits of Messina, you probably won't catch sight of the semi-mythical phenomenon known as the **Fata Morgana**, which appears as a shimmering, magical city of turrets and towers – quite unlike the city of Messina. The legend is said to be connected with Arthurian myths and was brought south by the Normans. But it's an extremely rare occurrence – best conditions are apparently an absolute stillness of the air and water.

Practical details

If you're travelling by train, get off at **Reggio Lido** for the port or museum. Buses end up at the **Reggio Centrale** station a kilometre or so down, which is where you'll find most of the hotels, including the *Albergo San Giorgio* (Via Gaeta 9; ☎0965/99.464), which has rooms for L35,000. A little further out, but worth it for the price, is the *Locanda degli Ulivi* at Via Eremo Botte 30, with beds at around L11,000; ring first (☎0965/90.133) in case it's full. On the same street is the campsite: for both take bus #7 or #8 from Piazza or Corso Garibaldi. There is a youth hostel at Scilla (see p.805), for which buses from Piazza Garibaldi leave hourly until 8pm. There is a small **AAST** office in the bus station, a larger one at Corso Garibaldi 329 (Sun–Fri 8am–1pm & 2–8pm, Sat 8am–noon). Several eating places can be found around Piazza Carmine (behind the Duomo), best of which is the *Trattoria Toscano* in Via Muratori.

From Reggio's port you can reach MESSINA in fifteen minutes by hydrofoil; by car you have to go from Villa San Giovanni (see above). A regular hydrofoil service also leaves daily for the AEOLIAN ISLANDS; see "Travel Details" for frequencies and journey times.

Aspromonte

Most visitors to Reggio province leave without having ventured into the great massif of **Aspromonte**, the last spur of the Appennines on the tip of Italy's boot, and displaying an even more pronounced dialogue between mountain scenery and seascape than elsewhere in Calabria. You can be on a beach and a ski slope within the same hour, passing from the brilliant almost tropical vegetation of the coast to dense forests of beech and pine that rise to nearly 2000m. The physical aspect of the range varies enormously, depending on which side you enter from: coming up from the Tyrrhenian coast you pass through endless groves of olive that are the thickest and tallest in the region, whereas on the Ionian side the mountains have the empty, arid look of desert peaks.

Santo Stefano: Giuseppe Musolino

Access is easiest from the Tyrrhenian side, from BAGNARA or GALLICO, from which frequent buses leave for DELIANUOVA or GAMBARIE. The most scenic route is the SS184 from Gallico, which winds through profusely terraced groves of vine and citrus to the village of **SANTO STEFANO**, famous as the birthplace and resting-place of the last of the great brigands that roamed these parts, **Giuseppe Musolino**. Occupying a sort of Robin Hood role in the popular imagination, Musolino was a legend in his own lifetime, the last thirty years of which he spent in gaol and, finally, a lunatic asylum – the penalty for having led the Carabinieri on a long and humiliating dance up and down the slopes of Aspromonte during his profitable career. While he was alive, he was warmly regarded by all who might otherwise have paled at the mention of brigandage, and even now he is seen as a local hero. A policeman in the village described him to me as "una persona onestissima" – the most honest of people. Musolino's victims were rich, or corrupt, or informers, and he was never known to refuse a plea for help from those in need. It is hard to know how much is myth, but the romantic aura that surrounds him is partly due to the fact that brigandage, with which the region was rife during the Bourbon period, and for which the tormented mountainscape of Aspromonte provided a natural refuge, was also a political gesture of rebellion, and little to do with the organised crime that has succeeded it. Just above the village, in the cemetery, you can see Musolino's grave, now renovated but until recently daubed with the signatures of people come to pay their respects.

Gambarie: skiing and walking

GAMBARIE, a little further up amid thick woods, is a fully-fledged holiday town, used as a skiing resort in the winter and a cooling-off place for over-heated *reggini* (from Reggio) in the summer. There is a **ski slope** from the top of Monte Scirocco (1660m), connected by a sporadically working chair lift, and a small choice of **hotels**, cheapest of which is the *Romeo* (half-board at L35,000 a person). Ask here about hiring facilities for skiing equipment. When the mountain is not snowbound, Gambarie is also a good base for walks in the area: for Aspromonte's highest peak, **Montalto** (1955m), start down along the SS183 towards Melito, turning off left after three or four kilometres onto a broken road, after which it's another 16km to the top, marked by a bronze statue of Christ gazing steadily out over the Straits of Messina – a memorable view. If you still have any energy there is another track that descends steeply to the *santuario* of **Madonna di Polsi**, inhabited only by the monks of the monastery there. A large **fair** takes place here every year on the first two days of September – an unashamedly pagan event that involves the slaughter and sale of large numbers of goats. The monastery can put you up, or else camp in the area.

Delianuova and the coastal route

Continuing on down along the SS183 will bring you eventually to the Ionian coast at MELITO DI PORTO SALVO, a tortuous but highly scenic route with views over towards Sicily. Going up the same road from Gambarie (in the opposite direction) leads along a plain and through more forest to **DELIANUOVA**, another resort, though not as busy as Gambarie, with a trattoria, a birreria and one **hotel**, the *Aspromonte 2001* (☎0966/963.012), with rooms for L45,000. Another path from here leads up to Montalto (about a five-hour hike). Halfway between Gambarie and Delianuova, a turn-off on the right will take you to the **Cippo Garibaldi**, a modern monument in the woods commemorating the spot where the hero, having emerged from his retirement in the summer of 1862 with the intention of marching on Rome, was ignominiously captured by the troops of King Vittorio Emanuele, in whose name he had raised the banner.

The **coastal route** along Italy's toe-tip also offers some interesting excursions into Aspromonte, road and railway running south out of Reggio through the series of small nondescript towns adorned by a profusion of cactus, agave, banana trees and date palms, and surrounded by the extensive plantations of citrus that are a feature of the Reggio area. Look out in particular for the *bergamot*, a fruit resembling a yellow orange whose essence is used as a base for expensive perfumes – one of the principal exports of this area, and until recently, because of the precise conditions required for its cultivation, not found anywhere else in the world.

Campsites abound along this coast, attached to sandy beaches in varying states of cleanliness. Immediately after the *La Tegara* site, the village of **PENTEDATTILO** owes its name to the Greek meaning "five-fingered", on account of the curiously shaped rock on which it stands. Norman Douglas likened it more to an upturned molar, and Edward Lear, travelling through the area in 1848, thought it "perfectly magical" – though its old Byzantine centre has recently been abandoned in favour of a new and ugly town just below.

You are now in the *Zona Grecanica*, named after the villages on these southern slopes of Aspromonte that were settled by Greeks some two thousand years ago, and still retain some traces of the Greek language in the local dialect. One such village is **BOVA**, perched on a crag 15km inland from its seaside satellite, BOVA MARINA – a remote place, with a view justifiably described by Lear as "truly magnificent", though the thick oak forests he saw then no longer exist. From the remains of the **castle** at the top, you can map out some alluring excursions into the wild country around: there are no hotels here but the countryside is perhaps the loveliest and most isolated part of Aspromonte, with plenty of opportunity for camping. Around the corner of the coast, another route into Aspromonte takes you by way of the village of **SAN LUCA**, known to *calabresi* as the home of the writer **Corrado Alvaro,** whose novels (*Gente di Aspromonte* is one) describe the lives of the people living in these mountains. It's also known for its reputation as a *'ndrangheta* stronghold: the triangle of land between the villages of San Luca, Plati and Cimina is a favourite area for holding kidnap victims, often for months at a time, and was recently – following accusations of apathy on the part of the government – the target for a massive army operation to root out the hiding-places. From San Luca a road continues up, leading after 20km to the Santuario della Madonna di Polsi (see above) and from there to the peak of Montalto. The road is asphalted for only half the way and careers up some pretty hairy mountainsides, but is worth the sweat for the truly Himalayan landscape and the numerous possibilities for picnicking and walking. Local people will warn you against travelling alone in these parts . . .

Potenza and around

Basilicata's regional capital, **POTENZA**, has suffered more than most southern towns from the effects of earthquake and war, which have robbed it of much of its historical heritage. There is still considerable restoration work continuing after the last 'quake, in November 1980, adding to the dust and commotion that fill the town's centre and it's not the most pleasant place to be during the heat of summer. The mainland's highest provincial capital, built on a spur between two valleys, it's also rather spread out, with most of the modern districts at the bottom of the hill, a brisk walk down rickety stairways or a short ride on one of the city's frequent buses (pay on board), and most of what's worth seeing in the old town above. The narrow and animated **Via Pretoria** is the main street, partly pedestrianised and at its best during the nightly *passeggiata*. Beyond that Potenza's interests don't amount to much. The church of **San Francesco** contains a Byzantine-style icon of the *Madonna del Terremoto* – though even this is sometimes locked up – and the modern quarter of *Rione Santa Maria*, north of the centre, is home to the **Museo Archaeologico Provinciale**, which holds the region's most important collection of finds from the prehistory of Lucania – though it's been closed for some time and nobody seems to know when it will re-open.

Practical details

Potenza has three **railway stations**, all connected but not all serving the same routes. The central Potenza Città station isn't of very much use at all; the Stazione Superiore in *Rione Santa Maria* serves stops to Foggia; the independent *FCL* line, across the tracks from here, serves Bari and places around Potenza; the Stazione Inferiore, on the other side of town, has less frequent trains to Metaponto and Taranto. Most **buses** leaving for destinations within Basilicata leave from Piazza Crispi; buses for Salerno, Naples and Rome from Piazza Bologna.

Potenza's cheapest **place to sleep** is *La Casa dello Studente* in Piazza Don Bosco (☎0971/37.508), with beds at around L13,000. Closer to the centre is the *Albergo Miramonti* (☎0971/22.987), Via Caserma Lucania 30, with doubles at L35,000. If you want **to eat**, you can do so well and cheaply in the *Trattoria Satriano*, a dark and airless basement frequented by students, just off Piazza Matteotti.

Around Potenza

The best reason for coming to Potenza is to see some of the smaller towns and villages of inland Basilicata, most of which are conveniently situated on the main routes to – or from – the outside world.

South: Grumentum and Moliterno

To the south, just inside the border with Campania and close to a lake formed by the damming of the River Agri, lies ancient **GRUMENTUM**, one of the principal cities of Roman Lucania and the site of two victories over the Carthaginians, most memorably that of 207 BC when the army of Hannibal suffered a defeat in which he lost 8000 of his men and four elephants. At two spots along a narrow country lane (well signposted) are the remains of a theatre, a basilica, baths and an amphitheatre, with fragments of mosaics among the ruins of the houses. A large **museum** is shortly to be opened, but it will probably not contain the most famous finds discovered at this site, the so-called *Siri bronzes*, which have been in the British Museum since 1833.

Following the destruction of the town by the Saracens between 872 and 975, many of Grumentum's inhabitants fled to the nearby town of **MOLITERNO**, a few kilometres up the road, later a Norman stronghold that guarded the western approaches into Basilicata. The birthplace of a clutch of *literati*, it possesses the remains of the **castle** and several mediocre churches.

Acerenza

It's the region to the north of Potenza which is the most interesting historically, with several towns from the Norman era and some good examples of their brand of hybrid architecture. All are connected by bus with Potenza, and most are on the main Potenza–Foggia railway line. The venerable stronghold of **ACERENZA** is the one exception, with a station on the Bari line a few kilometres below the town itself, connected by a regular bus service to the top. It's worth the effort for the grand panoramas and its famous **Cattedrale**, from which it is thought the name of Basilicata derives (it was the bishop of this *basilica* who exercised jurisdiction over the territory around). Constructed in the eleventh century but rebuilt in its present Romanesque form in 1281, probably by French architects, the cathedral has an interesting exterior, though the cylindrical cupola at the top is a recent addition, following the earthquake of 1930. Inside, its crypt is a rare example of the impact of the Renaissance in Basilicata.

Castel Lagopesole and Monte Vulture

Back on the main road out of Potenza, the massive castle of **Castel Lagopesole** is visible long before you reach it, dominating the surrounding country and dwarfing the village at its base. This was the last and greatest of Frederick II's castles, and was said to be his favourite for the rich hunting-grounds in the woods around (now farmland), though the building itself was still unfinished by the time of the emperor's death in 1250. Open every day until sunset (free), you can visit the chapel and some of the royal apartments. Note the two sculpted heads on the outside of the keep, one representing Beatrice, Frederick Barbarossa's second wife, the other Barbarossa himself (Frederick II's grandfather), on whom you may just distinguish the ass's ears for which he was famous.

Proceeding north, the truncated cone of **Monte Vulture** becomes increasingly evident – the only volcano east of the Appenines and now a national park with a large range of fauna and flora. A road leads up through thick woodland to two lakes that occupy the former crater – **lago grande** and **lago piccolo** – separated by a thin strip of land entirely given over to bars, pizzerias and souvenir shops, the area being a favourite for weekend trippers from Naples and Foggia. Signs exhort visitors to be tidy to no avail, ruining what is a genuine beauty spot. If you want to stay over, there are several **hotels** and two **campsites**, one right on the shore of the lago piccolo.

Melfi

From the lakes a road runs down to the historical town of **MELFI**, long a centre of strategic importance, taken by the Normans in 1041 and their first capital in the south of Italy. It was in the formidable **castle** at the top of the town that Pope Nicholas II formally recognised the conquests of **Robert Guiscard** over the Byzantines and Saracens, thereby legitimising the piratical Normans and confirming their place in the embattled history of the South. It was here also that Guiscard imprisoned his first wife Alberada, and from where, in 1231, Frederick II issued his *Constitutiones Augustales*, reckoned to be the most comprehensive body of legislation promulgated since the time of Charlemagne. Repeatedly damaged by earthquake, the castle is currently undergoing restoration work but is normally the home of a **museum** (daily 9am–2pm; free) housing prehistoric finds and objects from the Greek, Roman and Byzantine eras. Most celebrated item is a Roman sarcophagus from the second century, the so-called *sarcofago di Rapolla*, on which are carved five statuettes of gods and heroes and the image of the dead girl, reclining on cushions.

Just off via Vittorio Emanuele, near the centre of town, is the **Duomo**, twelfth-century but rebuilt following earthquakes. After the 1930 'quake, a Byzantine-style fresco of a Madonna and Child was brought to light, which you can see in a chapel to the right of the altar. The cathedral's campanile has miraculously survived the various cataclysms: the two black stone griffons symbolised the Norman hegemony in the south and are now visible everywhere in Melfi, having been adopted as the town's emblem.

On the other side of Piazza Municipio there is a decent **pizzeria**, *La Tavernetta*, in Via Nitti. By turning right at the *Municipio* you can find a cheap **hotel** – *Il Barbato* (☎0972/24.477) which has doubles at L23,500.

Venosa

If Melfi preserves the appearance of a dark medieval town, **VENOSA** has an attractive airiness. It's the survivals of different eras combining to form a harmonious whole, rich with historial associations. Known in antiquity as *Venusia*, it was in its time the largest colony in the Roman world, and much is made of the fact that it was the birthplace of Quintus Horatius Flaccus, known to Italians as *Orazio* and to the English as **Horace** (65–8 BC); his supposed house lies past the cathedral on the right. Venosa's web of narrow streets is full of reminders of the town's long past. The tomb of the Roman general Marcellus, ambushed and killed by Hannibal here in 208 BC, is off Via Melfi. Five minutes' walk away, the formidable **castello** dominates the spacious and arcaded Piazza Umberto, from which the main street – Via V. Emanuele – leads to a small **archaeological zone** holding the sketchy remains of some Roman baths and a palaeochristian baptistery. But Venosa's real attraction is the **Abbazia della Trinità**, a complex of churches begun in the mid-eleventh century that was the resting place of a number of Norman bigwigs, including Robert Guiscard, who is buried along with four of his brothers and his divorced first wife Alberada in the oldest part of the abbey, the *Chiesa Vecchia*, dating from 1059. Alberada's tomb is the only one that has survived. Backing on to the older church, the *Chiesa Nuova* was begun fifty years later, a gigantic construction that was too ambitious to ever properly finish – only the lower part of the walls and the apse were completed.

There are numerous places to eat at Venosa, and a good, cheap **hotel** on the main street between Piazza Orazio and the cathedral, the *Albergo Orazio* (☎0972/31.135), which has rooms for L20,000.

Matera and around

The interior of the **province of Matera** has a great deal in common with Potenza province – a wide, empty terrain, much of it given over to agriculture and pasture, much of it good for nothing in particular. Rundown, depopulated, its bare clay hills appear, in Levi's words, "a sea of white, monotonous and treeless", dotted with solitary villages that are cut off from each other and the rest of the world. Little to recommend for an action-packed tour, then, but plenty of the timeless atmosphere portrayed by film-makers like Rosi and Bertolucci.

Matera

The town of **MATERA** itself is unique, with a degree of culture and elegance unusual by southern standards and, in its **Sassi** – dwellings dug out of the ravine in tiers – one of the country's oddest urban features. The *Sassi* are abandoned now, an eerie troglodyte enclave occupying the lower regions of the city. But until thirty years ago this part of the city was still populated by the poorest of the *materani*.

During the 1950s and 1960s, fifteen thousand people were forcibly removed from the Sassi and rehoused in modern districts on the outskirts of town. Since then the area has been officially cleaned up (some *Sassi* have been sealed with cement to prevent their former inhabitants from returning), and although a certain squalor still hangs about some parts, it's a far cry from the dense malaria-ridden area of thirty years previous. Levi's sister, in *Christ Stopped at Eboli*, compared the Sassi to Dante's *Inferno*, horrified by their disease-ridden inhabitants. "Never before have I seen such a spectacle of misery," she said. They had "the wrinkled faces of old men, emaciated by hunger, with hair crawling with lice and encrusted with scabs. Most of them had swollen bellies and faces yellowed and stricken with malaria." Pursuing her, they begged not for coins but for quinine.

Divided into two sections – the *Sasso Caveoso* and *Sasso Barisano* – you can enter the *Sassi* district from a number of different points around the centre of town, some signposted, some not. The **Strada Panoramica dei Sassi**, newly built with an eye to tourism, skirts through both zones and is a useful reference point, but you need to leave this to penetrate the warren and its *chiese rupestri* or **rock-hewn churches**. One, **Santa Maria de Idris**, perched on the conical Monte Errone that rises in the midst of the *sassi*, has frescoes dating from the fourteenth century, Another, the tenth-century **Santa Lucia alle Malve** in the so-called Albanian quarter (settled by refugees in the fifteenth century), has Byzantine-style frescoes dating from 1250. Others are on the far side of the ravine – detailed itineraries can be obtained at the EPT office.

The more animated face of the old town has its centre at **Piazza Vittorio Veneto**, a large and stately square which in the evening clears of traffic and is given over to a long procession of shuffling promenaders. The *materani* take their evening *passegiata* seriously, and the din of the crowds rising up out of this square can be like the noise from a stadium. Matera's modern quarters stretch out to the north and west of here, but most of the things worth seeing are along the Via San Biagio and Via del Corso.

Winding off from the bottom end of the piazza, the narrow Via del Corso leads down to the seventeenth-century church of **San Francesco d'Assisi**, whose ornate Baroque style was superimposed on two older churches, traces of which, including some eleventh-century frescoes, can be visited through a passage in the third chapel on the left. In the main church there are eight panels of a polyptych by Bartolomeo Vivarini, set above the altar. Behind San Francesco, on Piazza Sedile, the imposing structure on the right was formerly a convent, then the town hall, and is now a conservatory dedicated to the eighteenth-century composer Egidio Duni, a native of Matera who settled in Paris, where he was largely responsible for popularising Neapolitan comic opera among the pre-revolutionary aristocracy. Via Duomo leads off to the right, a good place to view the sprawling *Sassi* below. The **Duomo**, which effectively divides this area into two, was built in the late thirteenth century and retains a strong Apulian-Romanesque flavour. Between the figures of Peter and Paul on the facade is a sculpture of the patroness of Matera, Madonna della Bruna. Her feast day, the *Sagra di Santa Bruna*, is celebrated on July 2, when her statue is carried in procession three times round the piazza before being stormed by the onlookers, who are allowed to break up the papier-mâché float and carry off bits as mementoes.

From Piazza San Francesco, continue down into Via Ridola to admire the elliptical facade of the **chiesa del Purgatorio**, gruesomely decorated with skulls. A little further on is the **Museo Ridola**, housed in the ex-monastery of Santa Chiara and containing an extensive selection of prehistoric and classical finds from the Matera area (Tues–Sat 9am–2pm & 4–7pm, Sun 9am–1pm; free).

Practical details

Matera is on the *FCL* line, the **station** for which is on Piazza Matteotti, where buses also stop. The **EPT** is in Piazza V. Veneto, under the clock (Mon–Fri 8am–2pm & 3–8pm, Sat 8am–2pm). The **SIP** telephone office and the **main post office** are in Via del Corso.

The most convenient **place to stay** in Matera is the *Albergo Roma*, at Via Roma 62 (☎0835/212.701), which has doubles for L19,000, as does the *Moderno* at Via de Sariis 11 (☎0835/ 212.336). The more elegant *Albergo Italia* in Via Ridola has rooms at L36,000 (☎0835/211.195).

Matera's **restaurants** tend to be expensive, but the food is good. Try the *Trattoria Lucana* in Via Lucana for a quality meal. There is a pizzeria in Piazza Sedile, and a much rowdier affair, *La Panca*, a bit further out from the centre, in Via Giolitti (ten minutes' walk up Via Annunziatella). For a snack and a bit of atmosphere, the basement cavern, *La Grottina*, in Via San Biagio, does food and local wine. There's also a pizzeria, *Il Castello*, below the Angevin castle, where you can eat outside.

Around Matera

A short distance from Matera and connected by rail, the hilltop town of **MONTESCAGLIOSO** was once a Greek settlement and is now the site of a magnificent ruined eleventh-century Benedictine abbey, the **Abbazia di Sant'Angelo**. There are good views from here over the Bradano valley, and a **hotel**, the *Venezia* (☎0835/207.412), with doubles at L19,000. On the same line is the lively medieval town of **MIGLIONICO**, with a finely preserved bastion at one end, fifteenth-century, with views all around. It was here in 1481 that the *congiura dei baroni* was held, a meeting of rebellious barons who formed a league in opposition to Ferdinand II of Aragon, from which the castle assumed the name, *Castello del Malconsiglio*.

The SS7, which heads west from here, is the old Via Appia, and a far preferable route to the newer road which runs parallel. Tracing the ridge between the Bradano and Basento valleys, it takes in a number of good stopoffs. **TRICARICO** is another old hilltop village, quite important in its time, with a **duomo** originally constructed by Robert Guiscard. Further south, **ALIANO** is the village in which Carlo Levi set *Christ Stopped at Eboli*; called Gagliano by Levi, it's reachable by bus from PISTICCI, on the Matera line. Apart from the yellow "welcome" sign on the outskirts of the village, and a general air of well-being, the place has not significantly changed since he was there. Nothing is missing: the church, the piazza where the fascist mayor gave his regular addresses to the impassive peasants, which gives onto the steep drop of the *fossa del bersagliere* and a striking view over the Agri and the "endless sweep of clay, with the white dots of villages, stretching out as far as the invisible sea" that Levi knew so well. You can see the rather grand house where he stayed at the bottom of the village ("away from the gaze of the mayor and his acolytes"), nearby which is a **museum** (Mon–Sat 10.30am–12.30pm & 5–7pm, Sun 9.30am–12.30pm) housing some personal items of Levi's and articles of folkloric interest.

The Northern Ionian Coast

From Táranto to Reggio, the **Ionian coast** is a mainly flat sandy strip, sometimes monotonous but less developed than the Tyrrhenian side of the peninsula, and with cleaner water. The **northern** section, from **Metaponto** to **Capo Colonna**, consists of a mountainous interior backing onto an empty seaboard, punctuated only by holiday resorts, a plethora of campsites (overflowing, in the summer months, with legions of Italians from all parts and of all ages) and some notable historical sites. Of these, the most significant are connected with the periods of Greek occupation, the most recent of which was that of the Byzantines, who administered the area on and off for 500 years, leaving their traces most strikingly in the hilltop town of **Rossano**. But a thousand years earlier, the clutch of Greek colonies collectively known as *Magna Graecia* rose and fell, of which **Metapontion**, **Sybaris** and **Croton**, all on this stretch of the Ionian coast, were some of the greatest. Although only the first of these has been properly excavated, there are museums in all, describing an era that was – culturally and intellectually – the brightest moment in the history of Basilicata and Calabria.

The Basilicata coast

The most extensively excavated of the Greek sites, and the only place of any real significance on the Ionian coast of Basilicata, is at **METAPONTO**, an important road and rail junction connecting the coastal routes between Taranto and Reggio with the interior of Basilicata – Potenza by train and Matera by bus. *Metapontion* was settled in the eighth century BC and owed its subsequent prosperity to the fertility of the surrounding land – perfect for cereal production (symbolised by the ear of corn stamped on its coinage) and its position as a commercial centre. **Pythagoras**, banished from Croton, established a school here in about 510 BC that contributed to an enduring philosophical tradition. The city's downfall came as a result of a series of catastrophes: absorbed by Rome, embroiled in the Punic Wars, sacked by the slave-rebel **Spartacus**, and later desolated by a combination of malaria and Saracen raids.

Lido di Metaponto – and the site

Metaponto today is a straggling, amorphous place, comprising railway station, beaches and ruins. Arriving at the station, you're three kilometres from the **LIDO DI METAPONTO**, where there are sandy, well equipped **beaches** and **campsites**. For those who don't want to sleep under canvas, three of these – the *Lido*, *Magna Grecia* and *San Marco* – also have bungalows available; all have their own beaches and the bigger ones have tennis, discos and other facilities. Otherwise the only moderately priced **hotel** is the *Oasi* (☎0835/741.930), in Viale Olimpia, one kilometre from the station off the Lido road: open June to September, a double with bath will cost you L25,000.

For the first batch of **ruins**, take the next turning on the right after the Lido junction (coming from the station), and follow the narrow country lane down to the wide site – signposted *Zona Archaeologica* – which has the remains of a theatre and a Temple of Apollo Licius. This latter, a sixth-century BC construction in the Doric style, once possessed 32 columns, but you need some imagination to picture its original appearance. In a better state of preservation is the Temple of Hera, or *Tavole Palatine*, two or three kilometres further north (where the main SS106 crosses the Bradano River – take one of the buses to Táranto from Metaponto station). With fifteen of its columns remaining it is the most suggestive remnant of this once mighty state. A good selection of other survivals can be seen at the **Antiquarium** just in front (April–Sept 9am–1pm & 3.30–6.30pm; Oct–March daily 9am–noon & 2–5pm; L2000), whose items are displayed on a rotating basis, but should include numerous examples of fourth- and fifth-century statuary and ceramics. The aerial photographs with accounts of the excavations are interesting, and look out for examples of the famous coins.

Policoro

There's a more extensive collection of antiquities at the **Museo Nazionale della Siritide**, 25km down the coast, just behind the village of **POLICORO**. The museum (daily 9am–1pm & 3–7pm, winter until 6pm; L2000) contains some fascinating material taken from the zone between the Sinni and Agri rivers, in its time one of the richest areas on this coast and site of the two Greek colonies of **Siris** and **Heraclea**. The first of these, after which the museum is named, reached such a position of wealth and eminence that the other colonies were persuaded to gang together in the middle of the sixth century BC to put an end to Sirian ambitions, with devastating consequences. Heraclea was founded on the same spot by Tarentines in 432 BC with the aim of driving a wedge between the Achaean cities of Metapontion and Sybaris to the north and south. It was here that **Pyrrhus**, king of Epirus, first introduced elephants to the Romans, and though winning the first of two battles in 280 BC, suffered such high losses that he declared another such victory would cost him the war – so bequeathing to posterity the term "Pyrrhic victory".

Into Calabria: Sibari and Rossano

Shortly after crossing the Sinni River you enter Calabria, skirting the base of the lofty Monte Pollino. Look out for the **castle** at **ROCCA IMPERIALE**, built by Frederick II in the style of Lagopesole and Lucera. Imposing from a distance, its state of abandon becomes more obvious as you approach, but the views from its crumbling walls are impressive. Further inland, at the medieval village of **ORIOLO**, is another **castle**, this one fifteenth-century, and in a better state of preservation, from which you can continue inland into Basilicata and the woods around SENISE, or loop back to the coast at ROSETO, the site of another of Frederick II's castles, prominent at the side of the road. In Norman times this spot marked the boundaries between the territories controlled by Robert Guiscard and his brother Roger.

Sibari

The mountainous slopes soon give way to the wide **Piana di Sibari**, most extensive of the Calabrian coastal plains, bounded by Pollino to the north, the Sila Greca to the west and the Sila Grande in the south. The rivers flowing off these mountains which for centuries kept the land well watered and rich also helped to transform it into a stagnant and malarial mire, and although land reclamation has restored the area's fertility, without visiting the museum and excavations at **SIBARI** you could pass through the area with no inkling of the civilisation that once flourished on these shores.

For long one of the great archaeological mysteries tantalising generations of scholars, the site of ancient **Sybaris** was only definitely identified in the late 1960s, when aerial and X-ray photography confirmed that the site previously known to be that of Roman Thurium was also that of Sybaris. There are in fact three separate levels of construction unearthed here, one Greek and two Roman, each on top of the other. However, the great riches that the excavations were expected to yield have never been found – there have been too many other settlements on this same spot, not to mention the marauders who made regular visits through the centuries. The wealth of the city – said to number 100,000 in population and have dominion over half a million – was only one factor in its fame, around which myth and documentary evidence have combined to produce a colourful muddle of anecdotes. The city's laws and institutions were apparently made to ensure the greatest comfort and wellbeing of its citizens, including the banning from the city of all noisy traders, such as metalworkers, and the planting of trees along every street for shade. Cooks were so highly prized that they were apparently bought and sold in the marketplace for great sums and were allowed to patent their recipes, while inventions ascribed to the Sybarites include pasta and the chamberpot. This was all too much for the Crotonians, who, under their general Milo (more famous as a much-garlanded Olympic athlete) attacked, sacked and destroyed the city in 510 BC, diverting the waters of the river over the site to complete the job. Most of the excavations here belong to the Roman period, but something of the earlier site might still be turned up – the silt and sand of the river bed has yet to be explored properly, work having been effectively halted for the last fifteen years due to shortage of funds. Of the Roman city, the remains are at least impressively displayed and maintained, including baths, a patrician's house with mosaics, and a *decumanus* (claimed to be the widest in existence). Just off the site a small room contains individual finds including some Greek exhibits, mainly ceramic shards, though nothing that would have raised much excitement in the imaginations of the numerous enthusiasts who passed this way.

The excavations lie across the lines some 4km down the new (coastal) SS106. On the left stands the new museum destined to house all finds from each of the local sites, but until that time they live in a low shack (daily 8.30am–12.30pm & 3pm–1hr before sunset; free) across the road, on the banks of the river Crati.

Byzantine Calabria: Pathirion and Rossano

There are remnants from more recent times further south, near the village of **SANTA MARIA DEL PATIRE**, where the **Monastery of Pathirion** sits among groves of olive and holm-oak at the end of a road built by Austrian prisoners during World War I. Its well-preserved church – a simple basilica – has sweeping views over the Sibari plain and the mountains around, but is the only intact relic of the monastery, which lies in ruins below – an extensive complex that had its centre at nearby Rossano, and rivalled the holy mountain of Athos as a centre of monastic learning.

Twelve kilometres away, the resort of ROSSANO SCALO has far outstripped its parent-town of **ROSSANO** in terms of size and bustle, and most of the holiday-makers who frequent its **beach** and **campsite** never even get round to visiting the hilltop town, 7km up an awkward winding road – something which has helped to preserve the old centre from excessive development. The foremost Byzantine centre in the south, Rossano was the focus of a veritable renaissance of literature, theology and art between the eighth century and eleventh century, a period to which the town's greatest treasures belong. Its majolica-tiled **Cattedrale** is an Angevin construction largely rebuilt after the 1836 earthquake, but has a much-venerated ninth-century Byzantine fresco, *Madonna Achiropita*, whose Greek epithet, meaning "not painted by hand", refers to its divine author-ship (there are several of these in Italy). Behind the cathedral, the **Museo Diocesano** (Mon–Sat 10am–noon & 5–7pm, Sun 10am–noon; L1500), contains the famed *codex purpureus Rossanensis*, or **Purple Codex**, a unique sixth-century manuscript on reddish-purple parchment illustrating the life of Christ. The book, that was brought from Palestine by monks fleeing the Muslim invasions, is open at one page, but you can leaf through a good copy and see, among other things, how the Last Supper was originally depicted, with Christ and his disciples not seated but reclining on cushions round the table, and all eating from the same plate. Other items in this tiny museum include a fifteenth-century icon painted on both sides and formerly at Pathirion, and several pieces of silverware of superb craftsmanship. Walk out, also, to the little church of **San Marco**, at the end of Corso Garibaldi on the edge of town, a tenth- or eleventh-century construction with a strong Middle Eastern flavour, its five cupolas surrounded by palms and giving way to a terrace that's a fine lookout over the gorge below. For the key, apply to the *famiglia* Federico at Via Vallone S. Marco 37.

The *Associazione Ruscianum* in Piazza Anargiri has more information on Rossano and around. Just off the square is a reasonable **pizzeria/trattoria** at Via Martucci 4. Another one, *La Botte*, is in Via San Nilo off the higher end of the square. For **hotels**, you've got to go back to the lower town, but they aren't cheap. Try the *Scigliano* (☎0983/21.848), 50m up from the level crossing, which has rooms for L40,000. Or the *Murano* (☎0983/21.788), in Lido Sant'Angelo by the sea. There's also a **campsite** in town.

Crotone and around

Down from Rossano is an empty stretch of beaches; inland, the vineyards of Ciro, the source of Calabria's best-known **wine**. Crossing the River Neto into the fertile **Marchesato** region, the approach to **CROTONE** (the ancient Greek *Croton*) is signalled by a smoky industrial zone – not the most alluring entry into a city but a rare thing in Calabria, and testimony to the town's continuing significance in the region's economy.

Crotone

The site of ancient Croton has been entirely lost, but in its day this was among the most important colonial settlements of Magna Graecia, overshadowed by its more powerful neighbour Sybaris but with a school of medicine that was famous throughout the classical world, and closely linked with the prowess of the city's athletes, who regularly scooped all the honours at the Olympic Games back in Greece. In 530 BC the mathematician and metaphysician **Pythagoras** took up residence in Croton and established an aristocratic party based on his ideas which eventually gained control here, though the political turmoil that resulted from the sack of Sybaris led to their banishment from the city. Croton continued to be the first of the Greek cities in Calabria but was increasingly destabilised by internal conflicts and the external threat of the encroaching barbarians, eventually being destroyed by the Romans. A resurgence of sorts occurred in the thirteenth century when it was made the main town of the Marchesato region, a vast agricultural territory – extending from the Neto to the Simeri rivers – held by the powerful Ruffo family of Catanzaro, but its prosperity was always hindered by the scourge of malaria which poisoned every initiative and debilitated its people.

George Gissing, visiting in 1897, called Crotone "a squalid little town", and it's not much better now, most of its seafront given over to industry – though the view isn't so bad once you get past the port, and it's a good base for the beaches that spread to the south and for the Greek ruins at Capo Colonna. Arriving by **train** you will need to take either a taxi or bus the 3km to the centre of town, Piazza Pitagora, and most of the **hotels**. The small and clean *Pensione Ruffo* in Via Ruffo has doubles for L30,000, the *Albergo Pace*, on Via Cutro, for L20,000. There is no shortage of **pizzerias** in this part of town: opposite the *Pace* the pizzeria *Mery* has a woodfired oven, while the area around Via Nicoletta has dozens of places, of varying standards and prices. For something more than a pizza, try the *Ristorante Da Peppino* in Largo Umberto (especially good for seafood) at one end of Corso Vittorio Emanuele, the main street in the older part of town.

There's not a lot to see in Crotone itself. The cathedral's Black Madonna is paraded through the town out to Capo Colonna at midnight on the third Sunday in May (it's transported back by sea the following night). And at the other end of the Corso, the church of the **Immacolata** has a good ossiary in its crypt, containing hundreds of neatly piled skulls grinning under electric candle-light. Continuing up Via Risorgimento, the modern **Museo Archaeologico Statale** (summer Tues–Sat 9am–1pm & 3.30–7pm, Sun 9am–1pm; free) displays fragments from the excavations at Crotone and its various colonies, and items from Capo Colonna. Further up from the museum is the **castello** (closed), locally called Charles V's but actually constructed by the Spanish viceroy Don Pedro di Toledo in 1541, and today still surrounded by various palazzi of the Spanish nobility.

On from Crotone: Capo Colonna, Capo Rizzuto and La Castella

From the bus office in Via Ruffo, there is one morning departure a day to SANTA SEVERINA, but to get to the famed column at **CAPO COLONNA** on Calabria's extreme eastern point, you have to walk the 11km along the coast to see this solitary remnant of the vast structure that served as the temple for all the Greeks in Calabria. Dedicated to Hera Lacinia, it originally possessed 48 of these Doric columns and was the repository of immense wealth before being repeatedly sacked as Magna Graecia and Hellenism itself declined. The object of Gissing's pilgrimage to Crotone, and a feature of his fevered visions as he lay on his sick bed, he eventually left without seeing it, and it remained forever a mirage for him as he strained his eyes on the Crotone seafront, as unattainable as his attempts to recapture the glories of ancient Greece.

There are some excellent **bathing spots** not far south of here. **CAPO RIZZUTO** is a spit of land, not excessively developed and with plenty of sandy or rocky inlets to swim from. In winter it is dead, but it can get quite feverish in the height of summer and difficult to find space in the **pensiones** or **rooms to rent**. The area has been designated the home of 72 American nuclear missile-carrying F-16s that the Spanish refused to have, the object of much protest coordinated by local and national pacifist groups. Nearby **LE CASTELLA** is another busy holiday spot, but not yet strangled by tourism. It would be hard to spoil the beautifully sited Aragonese **castle** on an islet just off the main town. Open daily from 8am to 8pm (free), you can climb up its restored tower or swim off the rocks around it. A good beach stretches out to the right, with places allocated for tents. The **hotels** tend to be expensive, but there's an official **campsite**, and it's worth asking around for **rooms**.

The Southern Ionian Coast

The southern part of Calabria's Ionian seaboard is less developed than the rest of the region, though it's also less interesting scenically, and most of the seaside towns and villages strung along it unappealing. If you like sandy **beaches**, though, this is where to find them – wild and unpopulated, or, if you prefer, glitzy and brochure-style, as at **Soverato**. At **Locri** there is the best collection of Greek ruins in the region, and, overlooking the coast a short way inland, the craggy medieval strongholds of **Squillace**, **Gerace**, and **Stilo**, with its jewel of Byzantine church-building, the **Cattolica**. Further inland, solace from the hard road may be found in the hills and cool forests of the **Serre**.

Catanzaro

One of the more major resorts is **CATANZARO LIDO**, a bustling, rather overworked place with a variety of **hotels** and eating-places. It's not a place to hang around in, but you might want to push up to **CATANZARO**, perched on a hilltop just out of sight of the coast. Regular buses leave from outside the main station every twenty minutes or so, and trains on the Calabro-Lucane line operate hourly from an anonymous white building up the road.

Despite its fine position, the appeal of Calabria's regional capital is hard to grasp. A crowded, overdeveloped, traffic-ridden city, it's a useful base for the Sila Piccola and is within a short ride of some five-star beaches, but is otherwise best avoided. It has much in common with its northern neighbour, Cosenza, and perhaps for this reason they share an implacable rivalry. Both are inland mountain towns within sight of the Sila range, though Catanzaro also has a view over the sea, from which frequent strong winds keep the town relatively free of the sticky heat that can clog Cosenza during the summer months. Both towns have also been subject to repeated devastations of human and natural causes, though Catanzaro has suffered the most, being almost entirely demolished by a 1783 earthquake and robbed of any residual character by postwar property speculation.

Piazza Matteotti separates the older from the newer end of the city, and is terminus for most of the buses from outside town. Corso Mazzini leads off from the square, an animated stream of cars and people around which is almost everything that is worth seeing in Catanzaro – though, to be frank, it doesn't amount to much. Step into the huge eighteenth-century Baroque church of the **Immacolata**, to see four of the few remaining examples of the work of the Neapolitan Caterina de Iuliani: biblical scenes modelled in wax, rather difficult to make out clearly because they need to be kept away from excessive heat and light. Behind the town hall, **Villa Trieste** is a tranquil public garden on the edge of the ravine, the haunt of card-players and couples in clinches, and with views over one of the two viaducts that tether Catanzaro to the surrounding hills – much used for suicides, they say, before the higher *viadotto* was built on the other side. The nearby **Museo Provinciale** (Thurs & Fri 10am–noon; free) is just three rooms containing a good coin collection, various artefacts from local digs and some paintings.

Sleeping and eating

An **overnight stay** in Catanzaro isn't recommended, but if you get stuck there are a couple of basic *locandas* – the *Locanda Pompea*, Via Poerio 32, behind the *Upim* supermarket, and *Locanda Mario*, on Piazza Galluppi – both of which have beds at L10,000–15,000. Or, more comfortably, there's the *Belvedere* in Via Italia (☎0961/29812), which has doubles for L30,000. An interesting place **to eat**, or just sit for a quick snack or glass of wine, is the old *bettola*, or wine shop, in Vicolo San Rocchello. Recently converted to suit modern tastes without altogether sacrificing its old character, you can sample a variety of local specialities and cheap wine here, and a complete meal shouldn't cost more than L10,000.

Squillace and around

Continuing on down the Ionian coast, the **Roccelletta del Vescovo di Squillace** lies some hundred metres up the side-road signposted San Floro and Borgia – a rather grand name for a shell of an old basilica, partly restored, situated in an olive grove on the left of the road. Once the second largest church in Calabria (after Gerace), it still has a mighty impact on the unsuspecting viewer for its sheer size. It is of uncertain date, though probably Norman in origin, founded by Basilian monks. Much of the building material used in its construction came from the remains of the Roman town of Scolacium, the excavations of which (theatre, amphitheatre and some baths) are not yet open to the public but may be spied by walking on through the olive grove. A museum is also planned.

Five kilometres further, at LIDO DI SQUILLACE, is the turnoff for the old town of **SQUILLACE**, 8km up in the hills, once an important centre but now just a mountain village, rather isolated on its high crag from the currents of Calabrian life. There are lofty views to be enjoyed over the Gulf and beyond Catanzaro as far as the Sila Piccola, and the **castle** (open only in the summer months) is one of the most romantic collections of ruins in Calabria. But the place is probably most renowned for its associations with **Cassiodorus**, whose monastery was located in the vicinity – though all trace of it has long since disappeared. Cassiodorus (480–570) was learned secretary to the Ostrogoth, Theodoric, and used his position to preserve much of Italy's classical heritage against the onset of the Dark Ages, and the book-burning propensities of the Christians. Retiring to spend the last thirty years of his life in seclusion here, Cassiodorus composed histories and collections of documents which have been of invaluable use to historians.

Inland to the Serre

South of Squillace, the golden sands of the resorts of **COPANELLO** and **SOVERATO** beckon, two resort towns which are increasingly attracting the international market. The private lidos hold sway here, charging L2000–5000 for a day under a parasol on a clean **beach** with access to a bar; there are no cheap **hotels**, but plenty of swimming, dancing, and summer madness. From Soverato, buses leave for the leafy uplands of the **Serre**, a little-known area that's well worth a visit for its lush green slopes and shady glens. In its thick beech and oak forest it's still possible to see black-faced *carbonari* making charcoal in the traditional way, cooking the wood in conical ovens resembling dozens of miniature smoking volcanoes.

As far as **hotels** are concerned, you won't find any outside **SERRA SAN BRUNO**, a secluded village in the heart of the Serre where the Soverato bus stops. This is the most visited place in the area, mainly because of the famous Carthusian abbey twenty minutes' walk south of town. The **Certosa di Santo Stefano del Bosco** was built on land granted by the Norman Count Roger in 1090 to Saint Bruno, the founder of the strict Carthusian order who lent his name to the village. The abbey grew in wealth and influence, accumulating vast portions of land in Calabria and Sicily, but was almost completely destroyed by a series of earthquakes in 1783. Rebuilt, it is still going strong, though much reduced from its former glory; one of the monks – who recently died – was rumoured to be one of the American airmen who flew on the atomic-bomb missions to Japan. Men only can visit the ruins of the old monastery inside (ring the bell) from 11am to noon and 4 to 5pm every day except Sunday.

A couple of kilometres further down the road, the little church of **Santa Maria del Bosco** stands on the site of the first church founded here by Saint Bruno. You can see the cave where the saint is said to have prayed, and a pond with his statue kneeling in the middle. Legend has it that when the saint died in 1101 he was buried on this spot, the spring gushing forth when his bones were later dug up to be transferred to the abbey. The water is prized by devotees (and reputed to be especially effective for exorcisms) who gather to bathe here on Whit Monday, when a statue of Saint Bruno is brought from the abbey.

The Coast to Locri

South of the developed lidos around Soverato, the coast assumes a bare, empty look that it keeps until the outskirts of Reggio, though with views of the distant mountains of the Serre and Aspromonte to stave off the monotony. On the far side of Monasterace a turnoff (where the bus stops) leads up to **STILO**, 11km up on the side of the rugged Consolino mountain. An influential centre at different periods, Stilo is best known for the tiny tenth-century Byzantine temple, the **Cattolica** (daily 9am–8pm, or until sunset in winter; free, but tip), which can be reached by car by taking the first hairpin bend on the right at the end of the village, or on foot by climbing up a series of alleys from the village's main street, Via Tommaso Campanella. Once a base for hermits and Basilian monks in the south of Calabria, this perfectly proportioned temple has little remaining inside of its former glory, apart from some damaged frescoes and four slim, upturned columns originally taken from an older temple. The name of **Tommaso**

Campanella occurs everywhere in Stilo, a reminder of the village's close link with this Dominican friar and utopian philosopher. Campanella was hounded by the Inquisition principally for his support of the Copernican model of the solar system, though his idealistic views didn't endear him to the champions of orthodoxy either. The shell of the church of **San Domenico**, that formed part of the convent where he lived, can be seen by following Via Campanella to the Porta Stefanina at the end of the village. Halfway along the road, look into the **Duomo**, thirteenth-century, its ogival Gothic portal the only part remaining from the original construction. Note, too, along with other Byzantine and Norman reliefs, the surreal pair of feet stuck onto the wall on the left of the door, taken from a pagan temple and symbolising the triumph of the Church.

There is one **hotel** in Stilo, the *San Giorgio* at Via Citarelli 8 (☎0964/731153), just off the main Via Campanella. Occupying a seventeenth-century cardinal's palace and furnished in period style, it looks expensive, but at L38,000 for a double room is excellent value, equipped with a swimming pool and with wide views over the Ionian from its spacious terrace. Run by a Milanese acting company who stage performances on the premises, it's unarguably the most unusual hotel in Calabria.

Continuing south, you pass the seaside resort of **RIACE**, where the Bronzi di Riace were found (see "Reggio"), though the most famous classical ruins on this coast are at **Locri Epizefiri**, some 3km beyond the town of **LOCRI**. Founded at some time in the seventh century BC, the city of **Locris** was responsible for the first written code of law throughout the Hellenic world. Its moment of glory came in the second half of the sixth century when, assisted by the Dioscuri (Castor and Pollux) – sent to them by their Spartan allies – 10,000 Locrians defeated 130,000 Crotonians on the banks of the river Sagra, 25km north. Founding colonies, gathering fame in the spheres of horse rearing and music, the city was an ally of Syracuse but eventually declined during Roman times. The walls of the city, traces of which can still be seen, measured some five miles in circumference, and the excavations within are now interspersed over a wide area among farms and orchards. Transport would be useful for some of the more far-flung features, though a lot can be visited on foot without too much effort, including a fifth-century BC Ionic temple, a Roman necropolis and a Graeco-Roman theatre in a good state of preservation. In any case make a stop at the **museum** (daily 9am–1pm & 4–6pm; free) to consult the plan of the site. Inside you can examine the most recent finds, including a good collection of **pinakes**, or votive ceramics – though some of the best items have been appropriated by the Museo Nazionale at Reggio.

When the Saracens devastated Locri in the seventh century AD, the survivors fled inland to found **GERACE**, on an impregnable site which was later occupied and strengthened by the Normans. At the end of a steep and tortuous road 10km up from modern Locri, its ruined **castle** stands at one end of the town on a sheer cliff, as inaccessible now as it ever was. Easier to visit is the **Duomo**, founded in 1045 by Robert Guiscard, enlarged by Frederick II in 1222 and today still the biggest church in Calabria. Its simple and well-preserved interior has twenty columns of granite and marble, each different and with various capitals; the tenth on the right in *verde antico* changes tone according to the weather. Two other churches from the same period that are worth a look are **San Francesco** and **San Giovanello**, at the end of Via Cavour (to the left of the Duomo's main entrance), both showing an interesting mix of Norman, Byzantine and Saracenic influences.

travel details

Trains

From Potenza (Citta) to Bari (6 daily; 2–3hr); (Inferiore) to Naples (14 daily; 2hr 30min); to Rome (3 daily; 5hr); to Foggia (10 daily; 2hr 30min).

From Matera (Calabro–Lucane line) to Bari (12 daily; 1hr 30min).

From Cosenza to Rome (10 daily; 7hr); to Naples (10 daily; 5hr); to Paola (hourly; 30min).

From Reggio to Naples and Rome (15 daily; 8hr).

Buses

From Potenza to Naples (4 daily; 2hr); to Rome (1 daily; 3hr 30min); to Matera (1 daily; 1hr).

From Matera to Potenza (1 daily; 1hr).

From Cosenza to Catanzaro (6 daily; 1hr); to Reggio (6 daily; 2hr).

Ferries and hydrofoils

From Vibo Porto hydrofoil departures for Stromboli mid-June–mid-September only, Tues–Sat 9am.

From Villa San Giovanni daily ferries every 30min to Messina, *FS* or *Caronte* line; daily hydrofoil departures for the Aeolian Islands at 10am.

From Reggio twice daily hydrofoils to the Aeolian Islands, less in winter; hourly or two-hourly hydrofoils to Messina. Boat services to Catania, Siracusa and Malta three times a week on the *Tirrenia* line.

CHAPTER SIXTEEN

SICILY

I like Sicily extremely – a good on-the-brink feeling – one hop and you're out of Europe . . .

D.H. Lawrence in a letter to Lady Cynthia Asquith, 1920.

The Sicilians aren't the only people to consider themselves, and their island, a separate entity. Coming from the Italian mainland, it's easy to spot that **Sicily** (Sicilia) has a different feel, that socially and culturally you *are* all but out of Europe. Occupying a strategically vital position, and as largest island in the Mediterranean, Sicily's history and outlook is not that of its modern parent but of its erstwhile foreign rulers – from the Greeks who first settled the east coast in the eighth century BC, through a dazzling array of Romans, Arabs, Normans, French and Spanish, to the Bourbons seen off by Garibaldi in 1860. Substantial relics of these ages remain: temples, theatres and churches are scattered about the whole island. But there are other, more immediate hints of Sicily's unique past. A hybrid Sicilian language, for a start, is still widely spoken in the countryside; the food is noticeably different, spicier and with more emphasis on fish and vegetables; even the flora echoes the change of temperament – oranges, lemons, olives and palms are ubiquitous.

Sicily also still promotes a real sense of **arrival**. The standard approach for those heading south from the mainland is to cross the Straits of Messina, from Villa San Giovanni or Reggio di Calabria: this way, the train-ferry pilots a course between *Scylla* and *Charybdis*, the twin hazards of rock and whirlpool that were a legendary threat to sailors. Coming in by plane, too, there are spectacular approaches to either of the coastal airports at Palermo and Catania.

Once on land, deciding **where to go** is largely a matter of time. Inevitably, most points of interest are on the coast: the interior of the island is often mountainous, always sparsely populated and relatively inaccessible. The capital **Palermo** is a memorable first stop, a bustling, noisy city with an unrivalled display of Norman art and architecture and Baroque churches, combined with a warren of medieval streets and markets. From modern and earthquake ravaged **Messina**, the most obvious trips are to the chic resort of **Taormina** and the lava-built second city of **Catania**. A skirt around the foothills, and even up to the craters of **Mount Etna** shouldn't be missed on any visit to the island; while to the south sit **Siracusa**, once the most important city of the Greek world, and a baroque group of towns centring on **Ragusa**. The south coast's greatest draw is the Greek temples at **Agrigento**, while inland, **Enna** is typical of the mountain towns that provided defence for a succession of the island's rulers. Close by is **Piazza Armerina** and its Roman mosaics, and to the west, most of Sicily's fishing industry – and much of the continuing Mafia activity – focuses on the area around **Trápani**. To see all these places, you'll need at least a couple of weeks; more like a month if you want to travel extensively inland, a slower and more traditional experience altogether.

The Mafia

Whatever else the **Mafia** is, it isn't an organisation which impinges upon the lives of tourists, and it's unlikely you'll come into contact with Mafia activity of any kind. That said, the Mafia does exist – and for very real historical and social reasons. But what began as an early medieval conspiracy, to protect the family from oppressive intrusions of the state, has developed along predictable lines. Throughout the twentieth century, alongside the endemic poverty, Sicily has endured a system of allegiance, preferrment and patronage of massive self-perpetuating proportions, from which few local people profit. Most of the towns and villages of western Sicily are tainted, and Palermo and Trápani have been noted Mafia centres for decades. There was recently a particularly vicious round of bloodletting in both cities – directed against the judiciary, internal enemies and those brave, or foolish, enough to speak out against the Mafia. But, even with sixteen people gunned down in three days in October 1988, travellers won't be much aware of the problem, due to the power of *omerta*, the law of silence that operates. All this is not to say that **petty crime** won't make itself felt. Take all the usual precautions concerning your money and valuables, and have extra care in the cities – certain parts of Palermo and Catania have deserved reputations it's as well not to test.

A few travel notes

Getting around Sicily can be a protracted business. **Trains** along the northern and eastern coasts (Messina–Palermo and Messina–Siracusa) are extensions of – or connected with – the "express" trains from Rome/Naples, which means that they are invariably delayed. At least an hour late is normal. Also, Sicily's geographical oddities often conspire to place railway stations miles away from the relevant town – check the text for details, and don't expect your rail passes to be as much use as on the mainland. **Buses**, as usual, are generally quicker though more expensive. There's no single bus company – *SAIS* and *AST* are the main two – but the local tourist office can point out where to catch what. Pick up timetables wherever you go and, despite the assertions to the contrary, expect there to be little (if any) service anywhere on a Sunday.

PALERMO AND AROUND

Unmistakably the capital of Sicily, **Palermo** is fast, brash, loud and exciting. Here the Sicilian fusion of all things foreign – art, architecture, culture and lifestyle – exists at its most extreme: elegant Baroque cheek by jowl with Arabic cupolas, Byzantine street markets swamping medieval warrens, Vespas parked against Spanish palazzi. It's a fascinating place to be, as much for just strolling and consuming as for its specific attractions. But Palermo's monuments, when you can get to them through the tight streets and swirling traffic, are the equal of anything on the mainland: the city's unique series of Baroque and Arabo-Norman churches, the unparalleled mosaic work and excellent museums all stand much wider comparison.

You could easily spend a week in Palermo, without ever leaving the city's limits. But make time for at least one day trip: the capital has several traditional bolt-holes if you want a break from the bustle, most obviously the heights of **Monte Pellegrino** and the fine beach at **Mondello**. If your interest has been fired by the

city's great Norman heritage, you won't want to miss the famous medieval cathedral of **Monreale**, just a few kilometres west. Or year-round ferries and hydrofoils
run to **Ústica**, 60km northwest of Palermo – a tiny volcanic island with enough
impressive grottoes and coastal walks to occupy any remaining time.

Palermo

In its own wide bay underneath the limestone bulk of Monte Pellegrino, and
fronting the broad, fertile *Conca d'Oro* ("Golden Shell") valley, **PALERMO** is
stupendously sited. Originally a Phoenician, then a Carthaginian colony, this
remarkable city was long considered a prize worth capturing. Named *Panormus*
("All Harbour"), its mercantile attractions were obvious, and under Saracen and
Norman rule in the ninth to twelfth centuries Palermo became the greatest city in
Europe – famed for the wealth of its court, and peerless as a centre of learning.
There are plenty of relics from this era, but it's the rebuilding of the sixteenth and
seventeenth centuries that shaped the city as you see it today.
    It's worth making Palermo your first stop in Sicily. It's the island's main trans-
port centre, and it boasts Sicily's greatest concentration of sights. Quite apart
from the Arab influence in its finest churches, there's more than a hint of the
city's eastern past in its undisciplined centre, a sprawling, almost anarchic mass
with no real focus: great pockets of medieval alleys, munificent nineteenth-
century piazzas, twentieth-century bombsites and contemporary office blocks
conspire to confuse what is essentially a straightforward street grid. Money from
Rome and from the European Community has been earmarked for a redevelopment of the city centre but it's difficult to see that ever happening: this is partly
due to the age-old system of kick-backs for contracts and tenders to bent politicians and the Mafia, which would cream off much of the money. One of the few to
stand up against this state of affairs has been Palermo's mayor, Leoluca Orlandi,
appointed in 1986 – and knowledgeable sources say he's in line for Mafia elimina-
tion if he keeps up his attacks on the organisation.
    Essential city stops are all pretty central, and if you are disciplined enough you
could get around them in a couple of days. Paramount are the hybrid **Cattedrale**
and nearby **Palazzo dei Normanni** or Royal Palace, with its superb, mosaic-
decorated chapel, the **Capella Palatina**; the glorious Norman churches of **La
Martorana** and **San Giovanni degli Eremeti**; the Baroque opulence of **San
Giuseppe dei Teatini** and **Santa Caterina**; and three magnificent **museums** –
inspiring collections of art, archaeology and ethnography.
    This historical jumble of treasures has its downside. Many people have contin-
ued to live in their medieval ghettoes, unemployment is endemic, the old port
largely idle and petty crime commonplace. Some areas can be positively dangerous if you're not careful, and every *pensione* owner will warn you to watch your
money and camera. There are no Third World extremes here but – like parts of
the southern mainland – plenty of glaring contrasts with the wealthy north of Italy.

Arriving and surviving

All planes use the **airport** at Punta Raisi, 31km west of the city, from where fairly
regular buses (fifteen daily) run into the centre, stopping behind the Politeama
Garibaldi theatre on Via I. La Lumia; first bus at 5.40am, last bus 9.30pm, journey

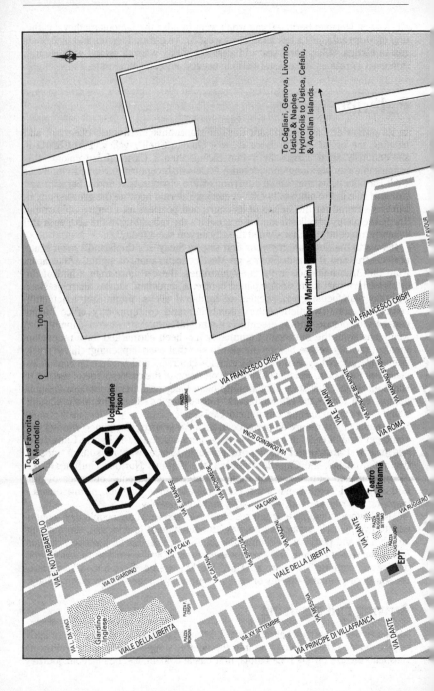

To Cágliari, Genova, Livorno,
Ústica & Naples
Hydrofoils to Ústica, Cefalù,
& Aeolian Islands.

Stazione Maríttima

VIA FRANCESCO CRISPI

VIA FRANCESCO CRISPI

Ucciardone
Prison

To La Favorita
& Mondello

100 m

0

PIAZZA
UCCIARDONE

VIA DOMENICO SCINA

VIA E. AMARI

VIA PRINCIPE BELMONTE

VIA MARIANO STABILE

VIA ROMA

VIA CAVOUR

VIA ALBANESE

VIA ARCHIMEDE

VIA CARINI

VIA MAZZINI

VIA SIRACUSA

VIA CATANIA

Teatro
Politeama

VIA DANTE

PIAZZA
RUGGERO
SETTIMO

VIA RUGGERO

PIAZZA
CASTELNUOVO

EPT

VIA P. CALVI

VIALE E. NOTARBARTOLO

VIA DI GIARDINO

VIA L. DA VINCI

Giardino
Inglese

VIALE DELLA LIBERTA

PIAZZA
F. CRISPI

PIAZZA
MORDINI

VIALE DELLA LIBERTA

VIA MESSINA

VIA XX SETTEMBRE

VIA PRINCIPE DI VILLAFRANCA

VIA DANTE

CENTRAL PALERMO

time 45 minutes (L3300). Taxi fares for the same trip run to around L45,000 per car (though you might be able to negotiate a lower price), so night flight arrivals may prefer to wait for the first bus of the day.

Trains all pull in at the Stazione Centrale, at the southern end of Via Roma, close to the cheap accommodation; buses #14, #15, #16 and #19, from outside the station, connect with the modern city. Other country- and island-wide **buses** operate from terminals all over Palermo; full details in the "Listings" section. All **ferry and hydrofoil** services dock at the Stazione Marittima, just off Via Francesco Crispi, from where it's a ten-minute walk up Via E. Amari to Piazza Castelnuovo.

Information
Palermo's main **EPT** (Mon–Fri 8am–8pm, Sat 8am–2pm; ☎586.122 or 583.847) is at Piazza Castelnuovo 34 – pretty useless as an information office (few of the staff speak English) but with big free maps of the city and province, and a booklet (*Palermo Hotels*) containing full accommodation lists. There are other tourist information offices, which can at least provide maps: on arrival, at the airport (Mon–Sat 8am–8pm), Stazione Centrale (Mon–Fri 8am–8pm, Sat 8am–2pm) and Stazione Marittima (Mon–Sat 9am–1.30pm); and in the city, in Piazza Sepolcro (Mon–Sat 8am–2pm), below the church of San Cataldo. For more complete **city listings** and a rundown of what's on, pick up a copy of *Un Mese a Palermo*, a free arts and entertainment guide issued monthly and available from the EPT offices – in Italian but fairly easy to decipher.

Getting around
Palermo is very much a city in which to **walk**, but you'll find getting around exclusively on foot exhausting and impractical. The **city buses** (run by *AMAT*) are easy to use, covering every corner of Palermo and stretching out to Monreale and Mondello. There's a flat fare of L600 and you buy tickets from the glass booths outside Stazione Centrale or at the southern end of Viale della Liberta, in *tabacchi* and wherever else you see the sign *AMAT* sign; validate one in the machine at the back of the bus every time you ride. There's a discount if you buy twenty tickets at once (L10,000). Buses run up until around 11pm, when night-services take over on all the main routes – generally once an hour. Main city **bus ranks** are outside Stazione Centrale, in Piazza Castelnuovo/Piazza Ruggero Settimo, along Corso Vittorio Emanuele and along the southern stretch of Viale della Liberta. Otherwise, don't be afraid of jumping into a **taxi** (ranks outside the railway station and in other main piazzas), a cheap and safe way to get around at night – just make sure the meter is switched on.

Finding somewhere to stay

Nearly all the reasonable budget **hotel accommodation** in Palermo is on and around the southern ends of Via Maqueda and Via Roma, roughly in the area between Stazione Centrale and Corso Vittorio Emanuele. Here there are often several places in the same block, usually cheaper the higher the floor. Beyond the Corso the streets begin to widen out and the hotels get more expensive, though there are some notable exceptions.

The Palermo area telephone code is ☎091

Some good choices along **Via Roma** include the *Albergo Concordia* (☎617.1514; L29,000) and the dirt cheap *Locanda d'Ignoti* at no. 188 (☎331.282; L18,000), though the latter is fairly grotty. *Locanda Marchese Maria*, Vicolo Mezzani 4 (☎321.9091; L15,000, showers L2000 extra), right down Corso Vittorio Emanuele at the junction with Via Roma, is clean, if spartan. The *Albergo Olimpia* (☎616.1276; L22,000) has rooms overlooking Piazza Cassa di Risparmio (at no. 18), which is off to the right just before Corso Vittorio Emanuele.

On **Via Maqueda**, the large block at no. 8 conceals the *Locanda Eden* (☎237.455l; L15,000, showers L2000 extra) and two hotels, the *Sud* (☎283.681; L24,000) and the *Vittoria* (☎616.2437; L27,000). One of the most atmospheric hotels in Palermo is the *Orientale* at no. 26 (☎616.5727; L28,000), a few cavernous rooms in a marble-studded palazzo; and there are similar prices, though more modern rooms and facilities, at the *Alessandra*, Via Divisi 99 (☎616.7009; L30,000), at the corner with Via Maqueda.

In the newer parts of Palermo, there are several more options – all more expensive but handy if you arrive by ferry or airport bus. The *Castelnuovo* (☎334.072; L30,000) is right on Piazza Castelnuovo (no. 50, under the *Cambridge Academy*), a good location. If there's room try the *Albergo Odeon*, Via E. Amari 140 (☎332.778; L30,000 with bath), opposite the Politeama theatre.

If you're **camping** you'll have to take bus #28 (from the Politeama theatre) out to SFERRACAVALLO, 13km northwest of the city, where there are two sites: the *Trinacria* (☎530.590) on Via Barcarello, open all year and with four-bedded **cabins** for rent (L45,000), and the cheaper *Ulivo* (☎584.392), May to October only, on Via Pegaso. Don't even think of **sleeping rough** in the centre of the city – if the thieves don't get you, the police will.

The City

Historical Palermo sits compactly around one central crossroads, the **Quattro Canti**, and within the four quarters that it delineates: southwest and the **Albergheria**, northwest and the **Capo** quarter beyond the cathedral, northeast and the **Vucciria** and old harbour, and southeast and **La Kalsa**. In these areas you'll find virtually all the surviving ancient monuments and buildings of the city, a confusing chronological jumble. Each quarter, too, retains something of its medieval character in a system of rundown labyrinthine streets and alleys which speak volumes about the quality of life behind the rich churches and sights. Don't be unnecessarily wary though – most areas are never anything less than perfectly safe in the daytime.

Around the Quattro Canti

Heart of the old city is the **Quattro Canti**, or "Four Corners", erected in 1611: not so much a piazza as a dingy Baroque crossroads that divides old Palermo into its quadrants. You'll pass this junction many times, awash with traffic, newspaper vendors sitting under the ugly fountain water spouts, and it's worth one turn around to check the tiered statues – respectively a season, a king of Sicily and a patron of the city – in each concave "corner".

On the southwest corner (entrance on Corso Vittorio Emanuele), **San Giuseppe dei Teatini**, begun in 1612, is the most harmonious of the city's Baroque churches. Inside there's a wealth of detail – especially in the lavish side chapels – given plenty of contrasting space by 22 enormous supporting columns in nave and dome. Outside, across Via Maqueda, is **Piazza Pretoria**, floodlit at night to highlight the nude figures of its great central fountain, a racy sixteenth-century Florentine design since protected by railings to ward off excitable vandals. The piazza also holds the restored Municipio, plaque-studded and pristine, while towering above both square and fountain is the masssive flank of **Santa Caterina** (open at 10am for short visits, Sun only) Sicilian Baroque at its most exuberant, every inch of the enormous interior covered in a wildly decorative, pustular relief-work, deep reds and yellows filling in between sculpted cherubs, Madonnas, lions and eagles.

You enter Santa Caterina from **Piazza Bellini**, just around the corner, the site of two more wildly contrasting churches. The little Saracenic red golfball domes belong to **San Cataldo**, a squat twelfth-century chapel on a palm-planted bank above the piazza. Never decorated, it retains a good mosaic floor in an otherwise bare and peaceful interior. The understatement of this little chapel is more than offset by the splendid interior of **La Martorana** opposite (daily 8.30am–1pm & 3.30–7.30pm; closes 5.30pm in winter and Sun afternoon all year) – one of the finest survivors of the medieval city. A Norman foundation, the church received a Baroque going-over – and its curving northern facade—in 1588. Both, happily, don't detract from the power of the interior, entered through the slim twelfth-century campanile, which retains its ribbed arches and slender columns. Inside, on and around the columns supporting the main cupola, is a series of spectacular **mosaics**, animated twelfth-century Greek works. A gentle Christ dominates the dome, surrounded by angels, the Apostles and the Madonna to the sides. The colours are still strong, the admirable craftsmanship picked out by the sun streaming in through the high windows. Two more original mosaic panels have been set in frames on the walls just inside the entrance to the church: a kneeling George of Antioch (the church's founder) dedicating La Martorana to the Virgin and King Roger being crowned by Christ – the diamond-studded monarch contrasting with a larger, more dignified Christ.

The Albergheria ... and the Palazzo dei Normanni

The district just to the northwest of the railway station – the **ALBERGHERIA** – can't have changed substantially for several hundred years. A warren of tiny streets and tall leaning buildings it's an engaging place to wander in, much of the central area taken up by a street market which conceals several fine churches too. Via Ponticello leads down past the Baroque church of **Il Gesu** (daily 7–10.30am & 5–6.30pm), first Jesuit foundation in Sicily and gloriously decorated inside, to **Piazza Ballaro** – along with adjacent **Piazza del Carmine** the focus of a raucous daily market, with bulging vegetable stalls, unmarked drinking shops and some very basic snack stalls.

At the westernmost edge of the quarter, over Via Benedettini, is the Albergheria's quietest haven, the deconsecrated church of **San Giovanni degli Eremeti** (Mon–Sat 9am–2pm, Tues, Wed & Fri also 3–5pm, Sun 8.30am–1pm) – St John of the Hermits. Built in 1132, it's the most obviously Arabic of the city's Norman relics, with five ochre domes topping a small church that was built upon the remains of an earlier mosque. A path leads up through citrus trees to the church, behind which lie its celebrated late-thirteenth-century cloisters – perfect twin columns enclosing a wild garden.

From San Giovanni it's a few paces to the main road, where, if you turn right and then veer left up the steps, you'll climb out of the fast traffic to gaze on the vast length of the **Palazzo dei Normanni** or Palazzo Reale (Mon & Fri–Sat 9am–12.30pm; free). A royal palace has always occupied the high ground here, above medieval Palermo. Originally built by the Saracens, the palace was enlarged considerably by the Normans, under whom it housed the most magnificent of medieval European courts – a noted centre of poetic and artistic achievement. Sadly, there's little left from those times in the current structure. The long front was added by the Spanish in the seventeenth century and most of the interior is now taken up by the Sicilian regional Parliament (which explains the security guards and the limited opening hours).

To see anything of the interior you have to take a **tour**. Present yourself at the gate (for times, see above) and a guide steers you through the **Royal Apartments**, two flights up, including the so-called *Sala di Ruggero*, decorated with lively twelfth-century mosaics of hunting scenes. You then descend a floor to the beautiful **Cappella Palatina** (Mon–Sat 9am–1pm & 3–5pm, Sun 9–10am, 11–11.30am & 12.15–1pm, closed Wed afternoon), central Palermo's undisputed artistic gem. The private royal chapel of Roger II, built between 1132 and 1143, its interior is immediately overwhelming – cupola, three apses and nave entirely covered in twelfth-century **mosaics** of outstanding quality. As usual, it's the powerful representation of Christ as Pantocrator which dominates the senses, bolstered here by other secondary images – Christ blessing, open book in hand, and Christ enthroned, between Peter (to whom the chapel is dedicated) and Paul. Unlike the bright pictures of La Martorana the mosaics here give a single, effective impression, expressing a feeling of the faith that inspired their creation and more than a hint of the mastery of the work.

The Cattedrale, the Capo and the modern city

Spanning Corso Vittorio Emanuele, on the far side of the Royal Palace, the early sixteenth-century **Porta Nuova** commemorates Charles V's Tunisian exploits, suitably grim and turbanned figures adorning the western entrance. This gate marked the extent of the late medieval city, and the long road beyond heads to Monreale.

The Corso runs back towards the centre, past the huge bulk of the **Cattedrale** (daily 7am–noon & 4.30–6.30pm; free) – a more substantial Norman relic than the palace. It's an odd building in many ways, due to the less than subtle alterations of the late eighteenth century which added the dome – completely out of character – and spoiled the fine lines of the tawny stone. Still, the triple-apsed eastern end and the lovely matching towers are all original, dating from 1185. And despite the Catalan-Gothic facade and arches, there's enough Norman carving and detail to rescue the exterior from mere curiosity value. The same is not true, however, of the inside: grand enough but cold and Neoclassical, the only items of interest the fine portal and wooden doors (both fifteenth-century) and the royal **tombs**, containing the mortal remains of some of Sicily's most famous monarchs – among others, Frederick II and his wife Constance. There's also a **treasury** (L1000), to the right of the choir: a sumptuous collection which includes a jewel- and pearl-encrusted skull cap and three simple, precious rings, all enterprisingly removed from the tomb of Constance of Aragon in the sixteenth century.

From the cathedral you can bear left, around the apses, and up into the **CAPO** quarter, one of the oldest areas of Palermo and another tight web of poor streets, unrelieved by space or greenery. Just around the corner from Piazza del Monte is the fine **Chiesa di Sant'Agostino** (Mon–Sat 7am–noon & 4–6pm, Sun 7am–

noon), built in the thirteenth century. Above the main door (on Via Raimondo) there's a gorgeous lattice work rose window, inside, some calm sixteenth-century cloisters and – along Via Sant'Agostino, behind the market stalls – a sculpted fifteenth-century doorway attributed to Domenico Gagini.

The stalls of the market (mostly clothes) along **Via Sant'Agostino** run all the way down to Via Maqueda, the streets off to the left gradually becoming wider and more nondescript as they broach the area around the late nineteenth-century **Teatro Massimo**. Strictly Neoclassical in style, this is a monumental structure, supposedly the largest theatre in Italy. But it's impossible to judge, since it remains closed indefinitely for restoration.

The theatre marks the dividing line between old and new Palermo and beyond here there's little that's vital, though plenty that is grand and modern. Via Maqueda becomes **Via Ruggero Settimo**, which cuts up through the gridded shopping streets to the huge double square made up of **Piazza Castelnuovo** and **Piazza Ruggero Settimo**. Dominating the whole lot is Palermo's other massive theatre, the **Politeama Garibaldi**, which houses the city's **Galleria d'Arte Moderna** (Tues–Sat 9am–1pm, Tues & Thurs 4–8pm; L500) – a collection of Sicilian art and sculpture.

The Vucciria, archaeological museum and old harbour

Via Roma, running from Stazione Centrale, is a fairly modern addition to the city, all clothes and shoe shops: parallel to Via Maqueda it offers a second chance for orientation if you get lost in the narrow alleys between the two. It's nothing like as interesting as Via Maqueda, its buildings mostly tall apartment blocks concealing hotels, but stick with it as far as the church of Sant'Antonio. Behind here – down the steps – is the sprawling **market** of the **VUCCIRIA**: winding streets radiating out from a small enclosed piazza, wet from the ice and waste of the groaning fish stalls. There's a couple of excellent restaurants, some very basic bars and all manner of food and junk on sale. Other than early morning when the action is at its most frenzied, lunchtime is a good time to stroll around here – the stallholders take a break at card schools set up around packing cases and trestle tables, or simply fall asleep amongst their produce.

The northern limit of the market is marked by the distinctive church of **San Domenico** (daily 7.30–11.30am, Sat & Sun also 5–6.30pm), with a fine eighteenth-century facade that's lit at night to great effect, and an interior of tombs containing a horde of famous Sicilians. Parliamentarians, poets and painters, they're of little interest to foreigners except to explain the finer points behind Palermitan street naming. The **oratory** behind the church (*Oratorio del Rosario*; ring for entry at Via dei Bambinai 16) contains stucco work by Serpotta and a masterful Van Dyck altarpiece, painted in 1628 before the artist fled Palermo for Genova to escape the plague.

From Piazza San Domenico, Via Roma continues north, passing (on the left) Palermo's main post office, the gargantuan **Palazzo delle Poste**. Built by the Fascists in 1933, it's a monstrous concrete block, a wide swathe of steps running up to ten unfluted columns which run the length and height of the building itself. The empty pretension of the post office is put to shame by the sixteenth-century convent behind, which now houses the **Museo Archaeologico Nazionale** (Mon–Sat 9am–2pm, Tues & Fri also 3–6pm, Sun 9am–1pm; L2000 includes free illustrated booklet): a magnificent collection of artefacts, mainly from the western half of the island, displayed on two main floors.

Two cloisters hold anchors and other retrieved hardware from the sea off the Sicilian coast, Egyptian and Punic remains in rooms to either side, and Roman sculpture – notably a giant enthroned Zeus. In rooms at the far end of the cloisters are numerous carved *stelai* and other inscribed tablets, and reconstructions of the assembled stone **lion's head water spouts** from the so-called "Victory Temple" at Himera (fifth century BC), the fierce animal faces tempered by braided fur and a grooved tongue which channelled the water. There are also finds from the temple site of Selinunte, on the southwest coast of the island, highpoint of which – indeed of the museum – is the **Salone di Selinunte**, a room which gathers together the rich stone carvings (or metopes) from the various known temples. Sculpted panels from the friezes which adorned the temples, the metopes are appealing works of art depicting lively mythological scenes: earliest, sixth-century BC, are ones representing the gods of Delphi, the Sphinx, the rape of Europa, and Herakles and the Bull. But it's the friezes from Temples C and F which really catch the eye, vivid fifth-century BC works – like Perseus beheading the Medusa with a short sword. Upstairs has plenty to occupy a lengthy dawdle too: lead water pipes with stop-cock retrieved from a site at Termini Imerese, some 12,000 votive terracotta figures, and two bronze sculptures – the believable figure of an alert ram (third century BC), once one of a pair, and the glistening, muscular study of Hercules subduing a stag, found at Pompeii.

The contrasts in style and surroundings begin again in earnest if you cross back over Via Roma and head towards the water. The church of **Santa Zita**, on quiet Via Squarcialupo, suffered gravely during the war, though it has since been restored, and is justly known for its marvellous **oratory** (ring the bell 11am–noon, or ask in the church in front, San Mamiliano, 8–11am & 4–5.30pm): repository of one of Serpotta's finest works – the Battle of Lepanto – and some rich mother-of-pearl benches. Striking wealth indeed when you step back outside and consider the neighbourhood, the depressed inertia of whose streets spreads to the thumb-shaped inlet of the old harbour, **La Cala**. Once the main port of Palermo, stretching as far inland as Via Roma, the rot set in during the sixteenth century when silting caused the water to recede to its current position. All the heavy work eventually moved northwards to docks off the remodelled post-war streets and La Cala has been left to the few fishing boats that still work out of Palermo.

La Kalsa: churches, gardens and museums

There's a markedly different character to the southeastern quarter of old Palermo. Worst hit by the war and allowed to decay since, these are some of the poorest streets in the city, within some of the most desolate urban landscapes imaginable. But, alongside the bombsites, you'll find a number of Palermo's most remarkable buildings and churches – and a surprising amount of greenery.

Indeed, Palermo's only central park, **Villa Giulia**, is just a few minutes' walk along Via Lincoln from the railway station: an eighteenth-century garden that provides a welcome escape from the traffic. Attractions include planned, aromatic gardens, a kiddies' train, bandstand, deer and ducks and a botanical garden (Mon–Fri 9am–noon, Sat 9–11am).

Cut back to Piazza Garibaldi and walk north, turning off down Via Magione for the church of **La Magione** (Mon–Sat 7–11am & 4–6pm, Sun 7.30am–12.30pm), one of the city's more graceful spots, approached through a palm-lined drive. Built in 1151, the simple Norman church was subsequently given to the Teutonic knights as their headquarters by Henry VI. Today, it's strikingly sparse, inside and out, the reason clear as you step around the back to look at the finely worked apse: you're standing on the very edge of **LA KALSA**, an area subjected to saturation bombing during the World War II (due to its proximity to the port). Planned by the Saracens, the quarter (its name is from the Arabic, *khalisa*, meaning pure) looks old, shattered and – even in daylight – vaguely threatening, parts no more than a huge bombsite, scarred and gutted buildings on all sides. On maps, it just appears as a blank space. It goes without saying that this is one of Palermo's more notorious areas, young pickpockets on speeding Vespas adding to the thrills.

Beyond Piazza della Kalsa is Via Alloro with, at its seaward end, the **Palazzo Abatellis**, a fifteenth-century palace revamped since the war to house Sicily's **Galleria Nazionale** (Mon–Sat 9am–1.30pm, Sun 9am–12.30pm; L2000), a stunning medieval art collection. Inside, there's a simple split – sculpture downstairs, paintings upstairs, the one exception to which, a magnificent fifteenth-century fresco of the *Triumph of Death*, is displayed in the former chapel, coating an entire wall. It's a chilling study by an unknown (possibly Flemish) painter, Death cast as a skeletal archer astride a galloping, spindly horse, trampling bodies planted by his arrows. The other masterpiece on the ground floor is among the works of fifteenth-century sculptor Francesco Laurana (room 4), whose white marble bust of *Eleonora d'Aragona* is a calm, perfectly studied portrait.

Upstairs there's no shortage of excellent Sicilian work, including a fourteenth-century Byzantine mosaic of the Madonna and Child, and paintings and frescoes from the fifteenth century vivid in their portrayal of the coronation of the Virgin, a favourite theme. This floor, too, contains a collection of works by Antonello da Messina (1430–79), including three small portraits of Saints Gregory, Jerome and Augustine and the indisputably powerful *Annunciation*, a placid depiction of Mary, head and shoulders covered, right hand slightly raised.

Via Paternostro, which runs west off Via Alloro, curves north passing the striking thirteenth-century church of **San Francesco d'Assisi** (daily 7–11am), whose portal, picked out with a zigzagged decoration, is topped by a wonderful rose window. The harmonious design is, for once, continued inside too: all the Baroque trappings have been stripped away to reveal a pleasing stone interior, some of the chapels showing excellently worked arches. To the side of the church (at Via Immacolatella 5) is the renowned **Oratorio di San Lorenzo**, harbouring stucco scenes from the lives of Saint Lawrence and Saint Francis by Serpotta. Sadly it's likely to remain closed for some drastic restoration work in the forseeable future.

Nearby, Corso Vittorio Emanuele runs straight down to the water, ending in the Baroque gate, **Porta Felice**, begun in 1582 as a balance to the Porta Nuova to the west. The whole area beyond the gate was flattened in 1943, and has since been rebuilt as the ugly **Foro Italico** promenade, from where you can look back over the harbour to Monte Pellegrino. Back beyond the Porta Felice, around the corner from the large **Palazzo Chiaramonte**, second largest of Palermo's palaces and ex-headquarters of the Inquisition, is the engaging **Museo delle Marionette** at Via Butera 1 (daily 10am–1pm & 5–7pm, Sun 10am–1pm; free), the definitive collection of puppets, screens and painted scenery in Palermo. Come on Saturdays in the summer and there's a free traditional puppet show (*Spettacolo dei pupi*) at 5pm. Like all Sicilian puppet displays, it's great fun – plenty of action, clashing armies and buckets of blood as Roland (Orlando), Rinaldo and friends fight off the Saracen hordes.

The city's outskirts

Even if you don't have the time to see everything in the old centre there are several targets beyond – on the outskirts of the modern city – which warrant investigation. Some, in fact, shouldn't be missed on any visit to Palermo; others have a low-key interest for fans of the Norman period – while one is decidedly ghoulish, for the strong of stomach only.

The third of Palermo's showpiece museums lies on the edge of **La Favorita**, a large park around 3km from Piazza Castelnuovo (bus #14 or #15 from Viale della Libertà). The **Museo Etnografico Pitre** (Sat–Thurs 9am–1pm; L1000) is *the* vital exhibition of Sicilian folklore and culture on the island. There's all the work traditionally associated with Sicily – a wealth of carts painted with bright scenes from the story of the Paladins, a reconstructed puppet theatre (with performances in the summer; ask at the EPT), and dozens of the expressive puppets, scenery backdrops and handbills lining the walls. Fascinating, too, are the other Sicilian artefacts, including a whole series of intricately worked terracotta figures, dolls and games, bicycles, painted masks, even a great, flowery iron bedstead.

To be thorough in tracking down the rest of central Palermo's **Norman relics** entails a lot of fairly fruitless scurrying around the southern and western parts of the city. Most of what survives is often locked or under restoration. Bus #24 runs west to **La Zisa** (from the Arabic, *el aziz*, "magnificent"), a huge palace begun by William I in 1160, and although the exterior is fine, the marvellously rich Islamic interior is out of bounds. Closer to the centre (about 1km beyond Porta Nuova at Corso Calatafimi 100) is **La Cuba** (Wed & Sun 9am–noon), the remains of a slightly later Norman pavilion that formed part of the same royal park as La Zisa, now tucked inside an army barracks. Best excursion, though, is south to the eleventh-century church of **San Giovanni dei Lebbrosi** (Mon–Sat 4.30–6.30pm, Sun 8–11.30am), reachable on bus #11, #26 or #31 from the northern end of Corso dei Mille. Just off the Corso, at Via Cappello 38, it's one of the oldest Norman churches in Sicily, reputedly founded in 1070 by Roger I – its squat tower topped by a red dome, a second dome beyond over the apse, the windows just narrow slits.

For real attention-grabbing stuff, take bus #27 (from Corso Vittorio Emanuele) southwest to Via Pindemonte. Close by, in Piazza Cappuccini, the **Convento dei Cappuccini** (Mon–Sat 9am–noon & 3–5pm; donation expected) retained its own burial ground for several hundred years, placing its dead in catacombs under the church. Later, others were also interred here, right up until 1881. The bodies (some 8000 of them) were preserved by various chemical and drying processes – including the use of vinegar and arsenic baths – and then placed in niches along corridors, dressed in the suit of clothes that they provided for the purpose. Descending into the catacombs is like having a walk-on part in your own horror film. The rough-cut stone corridors are divided according to sex and status, different caverns reserved for men, women, the clergy, doctors, lawyers and surgeons. Suspended in individual niches the bodies are vile, contorted, grinning figures – some decomposed beyond recognition, others complete with skin, hair and eyes fixing you with a steely stare. Those that aren't lined along the walls lie in stacked glass coffins, and – to say the least – it's an unnerving experience to walk among them. Follow the signs for the sealed-off cave which contains the coffin of two-year-old Rosalia Lombardo, who died in 1920. A new process, a series of injections, preserved her to the extent that she looks like she's simply asleep – after nearly seventy years.

Eating and drinking

For **breakfast and snacks**, best stops are at the *Extra Bar* (Via Ruggero Settimo 107), the *Ferrara* (Piazza Giulio Cesare), just to the left of the railway station, and the *Bar Self Service*, Corso Vittoria Emanuele 244 – the latter two also offering complete lunches (L6500–7000). For authentic Sicilian fast food, *Antica Foccacceria San Francesco*, Via A. Paternostro 58 (off Corso Vittorio Emanuele), is an old-time pizzeria with marble-topped tables and fresh pizza slices at around L1200 a go. **Markets** all offer a variety of typically Sicilian takeaway food – boiled octopus, liver-filled bread rolls and cooked artichokes – as well as fruit and vegetables. Best is the Vucciria, off Via Roma between Corso Vittorio Emanuele and the San Domenico church. And there's a *Standa* **supermarket** at the junction of Via Roma and Via Divisi.

The most popular **pizza** restaurants get packed at the weekends, full of young people intent upon a night out rather than just a meal. Easily best is the *Pizzeria Italia*, Via Orologio 54 (off Via Maqueda), where large queues develop quickly. Or try the slightly fancier *Trattoria dal Pompiere* at Via Bara 107, the next parallel street north. More expensive, with a full restaurant menu, is *Peppino* (Piazza Castelnuovo 49), whose management also runs *Bellini* in Piazza Bellini – pricey, but with outdoor tables underneath La Martorana church.

For full blown **meals**, the city's best bargain is *Trattoria-Pizzeria Enzo*, Via Maurolico 17/19, close to the railway station – excellent food, hefty portions and daft prices. A good second choice, the small *Trattoria Azzurra*, Via dei Bottai 54 (off Corso Vittorio Emanuele), has a long list of pasta dishes and healthy fish portions; while the nearby *Shanghai* (not Chinese but Italian) has a restaurant terrace overlooking the Vucciria market at Vicolo dei Mezzani 34. **Non-Italian food** is all but impossible to find in Palermo, but try the *Al Duar*, Via E. Amari 92 – couscous and the like for L11,000.

Bars and nightlife

The strangest thing about Palermo's fast lifestyle is that it stops at 8pm. Apart from a perfunctory *passeggiata* between the Teatro Massimo and Piazza Castelnuovo, everything is quiet outside after dark. In summer, most young people head for Mondello (see below) and buses run there and back all night. Still, for an outdoor, early evening **drink**, **Via Principe di Belmonte** is a good spot, closed to traffic, and with several popular places, including *Brinkhoff's* for crepes and beers. There are a couple of other central options too, notably the *Pinguino* (Via Ruggero Settimo 86), which has excellent ice cream, famous milkshakes and a rank of non-alcoholic cocktails. Or try *Liberty*, a spaghetteria on Via Cerda, off Via Maqueda, which serves food and is open until late.

If it's **discos** and **video bars** you're after, what exists is all in the new, northern section of the city, along Viale Strasburgo, or along Via Generale Arimondi (beyond the Giardino Inglese). Otherwise, there are **cinemas** on Via Cavour and Via E. Amari, and an English Film Club which shows new releases at the *Metropolitan Cinema*, Viale Strasburgo 356 (☎502.278; L5000 entry, 50 percent *ISIC* discount).

Listings

Airport bus Fifteen daily departures to Punta Raisi airport from the terminal at Via I. Lumia, behind the Politeama theatre; first bus at 5.30am, last bus at 9.15pm; L3300, 45min. Enquiries on ☎240.111.

American Express Via E. Amari 40 (☎587.144); Mon–Fri 9am–1pm & 4–7pm, Sat 9am–1pm.

Bookshops Large selection of English books from *Feltrinelli*, Via Maqueda 457, opposite Teatro Massimo; closed Mon mornings.

Bus terminals *AST*, Piazza Lolli/Piazza Marina (for Bagheria, Ragusa, Comiso, Corleone, Modica, Termini Imerese); *Camillieri*, Via P. Balsamo 32 and *Cuffaro*, Via Lincoln 42 (both for Agrigento); *SAIS*, Via P. Balsamo 16 (for Rome, Caltanissetta, Catania, Enna, Piazza Armerina, Gela, Messina, Siracusa, Noto, Cefalù, Termini Imerese); *Segesta*, Via P. Balsamo 26 (for Rome, Trápani).

Car hire *Avis*, Via Principe di Scordia 12/14 (☎333.806); *Europcar*, Via Francesco Crispi 94 (☎329.035); *Hertz*, Via Messina 7 (☎331.668); *Interrent*, Via Cavour 61 (☎328.631); *Maggiore*, Via Agrigento 27/33 (☎297.128).

Chemist All-night service at Via Roma 1, Via Roma 207 and Via Principe di Belmonte 110.

Consulates You'll find your nearest consulates in Naples or Rome.

Exchange For changing money or travellers cheques outside normal banking hours, there's an exchange office at Stazione Centrale (daily 8am–1pm & 4–8pm).

Ferry companies *Grandi Traghetti* to Genova and Livorno (Via M. Stabile 179; ☎587.832); *Siremar* to Ùstica (Via Francesco Crispi 120; ☎582.403); *Tirrenia* to Naples and Cagliari (Via Roma 385; ☎585.733).

Gay information Contact *ARCI Gay* (☎324.917/8), at the cultural wing of the Communist Party's youth section. An information centre is planned at Vicolo Istituto Pignatelli 6 (behind the Politeama theatre), open 5pm–late.

Hospital *Civico Regionale Generale*, Via Carrabia (☎592.122). For emergency first aid ☎321.860.

Left luggage Stazione Centrale (open daily 24hr; L1000 a day); Stazione Marittima (daily 7–9.30am, 10am–4.30pm & 5.30–8.30pm; L800 a day).

Newspapers English newspapers and magazines from the newsagents at the (southern) corner of Via Ruggero Settimo and Piazza Castelnuovo.

Police Tourist police at Piazza S. Sepolcro 1 (☎616.1361); for emergencies, ☎112.

Post office Main post office is the Palazzo delle Poste on via Roma; Mon–Fri 8.10am–7.30pm, Sat 8.10am–1.30pm.

Taxis To call a cab ☎513.311. Otherwise ranks in all the main squares.

Telephones Offices at Via Lincoln, directly opposite the railway station (open daily 24hr) Piazza Ungheria (daily 8am–9.15pm), off Via Ruggero Settimo; and Via Principe di Belmonte 92 (daily 8am–8pm). Reverse charge calls from the first office only.

Train enquiries ☎656.293.

Travel agents *CTS*, Via Sammartino 79 (☎332.209), Mon–Fri 9am–1pm & 4–7.30pm.

Women's movement Contact *ARCI Donna*, Via Dante 44 (☎588.994) or *Unione delle Donne Italiane*, Via Siracusa 16 (☎329.604).

Around Palermo: Monte Pellegrino, Mondello, Monreale and Ùstica

Palermo is a busy city with few quiet spaces and fewer parks, so any respite is welcome. Even on just a short visit to the city, try not to miss any of the trips below – all easy day (or half-day) excursions.

Monte Pellegrino and Mondello

Splitting the city from the bay at MONDELLO (see below) is **Monte Pellegrino**, to which the ride itself is as good a reason as any to go (bus #12 from Via Filipo Turati, opposite the Politeama theatre) – an impressive route through a green belt of trees, cacti and scrub, and with views over Palermo and its plain. The bus drops you at the **Santuario di Santa Rosalia**, a cave in the hillside where the bones of the city's patroness were discovered. A chapel was promptly built over the entrance in 1625: supposedly miraculous water trickles down the walls, channelled and collected by steel plates, and fancy lighting illuminates a bier containing a statue of the saint, around which there's invariably a scrum. A small road to the right of the chapel leads to the summit, a half-hour's walk, affording more splendid views, while paths and trails cover the rest of the mountain top.

If this isn't your bag, the other obvious trip from central Palermo is the short (11km) run to **MONDELLO**, a small seaside resort tucked under the northern bluff of Monte Pellegrino. It features one of Sicily's best stretches of sand (as opposed to the more usual stones), the two-kilometre beach curving round to a tiny working harbour and the remnants of a medieval tower. There's a line of restaurants overlooking the water and the fish, naturally, is temptingly fresh. Alternatively, grab some of the excellent snack food from the waterfront stalls and hit the beach. It's often crowded, but summer nights at Mondello are fun, the real scene of Palermo's *passeggiata*. In winter it's more laid-back, and rarely busy, but the restaurants and snack stalls are still open and it's usually warm enough to swim. To get to Mondello, take buses #3, #14 or #15 (or, summer only, bus #6) from Stazione Centrale or Viale della Liberta – a half-hour ride.

Monreale

Whether or not you get to mountain or beach, there's no excuse for missing Sicily's most extraordinary medieval mosaics in the cathedral at **MONREALE** (Royal Mountain). This small hill-town, 8km southwest of Palermo, commands unsurpassed views down the *Conca d'Oro* valley, the capital shimmering in the distant bay. Bus #9 or #8/9 runs frequently from Piazza dell'Indipendenza, the journey up the valley taking twenty minutes. From the bus stop follow Via Roma up to Piazza Vittorio Emanuele, where Monreale's Norman **Duomo** (daily 8am–12.30pm & 3.30–7pm) flanks one side. The rather severe, square-towered exterior – though handsome enough – is no preparation for what's inside; the most impressive and extensive area of Christian medieval mosaic work in the world, the apex of Sicilian-Norman art.

The cathedral, and the town that grew up around it in the twelfth century, both owe their existence to young King William II's rivalry with his powerful Palermitan archbishop, the Englishman Walter of the Mill. William endowed a new monastery in his royal grounds in 1174; the abbey church – this cathedral – was thrown up in a matter of years. This unseemly haste assisted the splendid uniformity of the cathedral's most famous relic, its interior art a galaxy of coloured mosaic pictures bathed in a golden background.

The **mosaics** were almost certainly executed by Greek and Byzantine crafts-men, and they reveal a unitary plan and inspiration. Once inside, your eyes are drawn immediately over the wooden ceiling to the all-embracing half-figure of Christ in benediction in the central apse: an awesome and pivotal mosaic, the head and shoulders alone almost twenty metres high. Underneath sit an enthroned Virgin and Child, attendant angels and, below, ranks of saints, each individually and subtly coloured and identified by name. Interesting here is the figure of Thomas à Becket (marked *SCS Thomas Cantb*), canonised in 1173, just before the mosaics were begun, and presumably included as a political show of support by William for the Papacy. The nave mosaics are no less remarkable, an animated series that starts with the Creation (to the right of the altar) and runs around the whole church. Most scenes are instantly recognisable: Adam and Eve, Abraham on the point of sacrificing his son, a positively jaunty Noah's ark; even the Creation, shown in a set of glorious, simplistic panels portraying God filling his world with animals, water, light . . . and Man.

Ask at the desk by the entrance to climb the **tower** (L2000) in the southwest corner of the cathedral – an especially attractive idea as the steps give access to the roof, leaving you standing right above the central apse – an unusual and precarious vantage point. It's also worth visiting the **cloisters** (Mon–Sat 9am–7pm, Sun 9am–1pm; L2000), part of William's original Benedictine monastery. The formal garden is surrounded by an elegant arcaded quadrangle, 216 twin columns supporting slightly pointed arches – a legacy of the Arab influence in Sicilian art. No two capitals are the same, each a riot of detail and imagination: armed hunters doing battle with winged beasts; flowers, birds, snakes and foli-age. Entrance to the cloisters (*Chiostro dei Benedettini*) is from Piazza Guglielmo, in the corner by the right-hand tower of the cathedral.

Ùstica

A volcanic, turtle-shaped island 60km north west of Palermo, ÙSTICA is one of the more appealing destinations for a quick trip away from the city. Colonised originally by the Phoenicians, the island took its name from the Latin *ustum*, or "burnt", a reference to its blackened, lavial appearance. Exposed and isolated, it had a rough time throughout the Middle Ages, its scant population repeatedly harried by pirates who used the island as a base. Even as late as the 1890s the few inhabitants were nearly all exiled prisoners. Today, Ùstica's fertile uplands are just right for a day's ambling, while the rough coastline is touted as a skin diver's paradise, the clear water bursting with fish, sponges, weed and coral. Easy, too, is to take a boat trip through Ùstica's rugged grottoes and lava outcrops. The little port of ÙSTICA TOWN, where the boats dock, features a museum devoted to underwater finds from the area, a bank, a dozen restaurants and a handful of places to stay.

Ferries and **hydrofoils** operate roughly once daily from Palermo (from the Stazione Marittima), the cheapest passage around L11,000 one-way by ferry, hydrofoils twice the price in less than half the time. Tickets from *Siremar*, Via Francesco Crispi 120 or *SNAV*, Via Principe Belmonte 51. If you want to **stay**

overnight on Ùstica, ask the Pro Loco, Piazza Vito Longo (daily 9am–1pm & 6–8pm) about private rooms or check on space at one of two cheap places: the *Clelia*, Via Magazzino 7 (☎844.9039) or the less expensive *Locanda Castelli*, Via San Francesco 16 (☎844.9007).

THE TYRRHENIAN COAST

From Palermo, the whole of the rugged **Tyrrhenian coast** is accessible by rail and road, at times a spectacular ride past deserted coves and rocky beaches. Aside from spots of interest at and around **Bagheria** and **Termini Imerese**, the first real attraction is **Cefalù**, a beach resort and cathedral town. Vital stops beyond are few, though the quiet seaside towns further east are all nice enough for a short break. Also, buses run inland from the larger resorts, providing access to the northern **mountain chains**, the Madonie and the Nebrodi. Most of the hill-towns here, especially **Caccamo** and **Castroreale**, are worth time, quiet airy places with castles and good hiking at hand. Sadly, the easternmost part of the coast, around **Milazzo** – Sicily's second largest port – is fairly grim and industrial. However, there's an easy escape to the desolate **Aeolian Islands**, easily visible from much of the Tyrrhenian coast, reached by ferries and hydrofoils from Milazzo.

Out from Palermo: Bagheria, Solunto, Termini Imerese and Caccamo

Although it's tempting to head straight for Cefalù, there are some enticing stops before that – all easily seen on day trips from Palermo if that's where you're based. Road and railway cut eastwards, across Capo Zafferano, to reach the rural town of **BAGHERIA**, a ten-minute ride by train. A seventeenth- and eighteenth-century summer retreat, the city's nobility stamped their mark on a series of (largely neglected) Baroque country villas scattered across town. Most are privately owned, and closed, but you can get into the **Villa Palagonia** (Mon–Fri 9am–12.30pm & 5pm–1hr before sunset, Sat & Sun 11am–12.30pm & 4pm–1hr before sunset; L1000) on Piazza Garibaldi, noted for its menagerie of eccentric gargoyles. The villa is ten minutes' walk from the railway station. You may as well combine a trip to Bagheria with a tour around the Greco-Roman town at **SOLUNTO** (the ancient *Solus*), one stop further on the train (the station is called SANTA FLAVIA-SOLUNTO-PORTICELLO). The **site** (daily 9am–1hr before sunset; L2000) is about half-an-hour's walk from the station, beautifully stranded on top of Monte Catalfano. There's a **museum** at the entrance, as well as the impressive remains of Roman houses (some with mosaics) and shops, a well preserved *agora* and a fragmentary theatre – all looking down on the small bay below, guarded by the medieval **Castello di Solanto**.

Another twenty minutes on, **TERMINI IMERESE** has an upper town whose cliff-edge belvedere is another excellent vantage point for views of the curving shore. The grand piazza holds a seventeenth-century cathedral studded with four sixteenth-century statues, and take a look in the **Museo Civico** (Tues–Sun 9am–2pm; L2000), over the other side of the piazza, which gathers together remains from the ancient Greek site of Himera, 20km to the east. Termini, after a prosperous Greek and Carthaginian period, was also a Roman spa, and in the shaded, congested lower town are the remains of the former baths, covered now by a modern hotel, the *Albergo delle Terme*, close to the little port. Termini would be a fair place to spend the night: there's a scrappy beach and a couple of cheap **places to stay** – most basic, the *Locanda Roma* (**☎**091/814.1566) at Vicolo di Stefano 12, which has doubles for just L14,000. The nearest **campsite**, *Torre Battilamano* (**☎**091/940.044), is at BUONFORNELLO, 15km east of town; take the bus from outside the railway station.

Buses from Termini's railway station also run regularly to **CACCAMO**, 10km south. The small town, a jumble of little houses astride a rocky hill, is dominated by a sturdy, battlemented twelfth-century **fortress**, its sheer walls built on a crag which falls away down into the valley below. Though it's propped up by scaffolding, you should at least be able to climb up to the gates of the castle for views over the steeply stepped streets: for entrance, try ringing at the door of the custodian at Corso Umberto 6.

Cefalù

Despite the recent attentions of *Club Med* and a barrage of modern building outside town, **CEFALÙ** remains a fairly small-scale fishing port, partly by virtue of its geographical position – tucked onto every available inch of a shelf of land underneath a fearsome crag, the *Rocca*. Roger II founded a mighty cathedral here in 1131 and, as befitting one of the most influential early European rulers, his church dominates the skyline, the great twin towers of the facade rearing up above the flat roofs of the medieval quarter. Naturally, it's the major attraction in town, but most visitors are as tempted by Cefalù's fine curving sands – the main reason why the holiday companies have moved in in such great numbers in recent years. Still, it's a pleasant town, nothing like as developed as Sicily's other package resort, Taormina.

The **Duomo** (9am–noon & 3.30–7pm; free) was built – partly at least – as thanks by Roger for fetching up at Cefalù's safe beach in a violent storm. Inside, covering the apse and presbytery, are the earliest and best preserved of the Sicilian church mosaics, dating from 114, though the church is undergoing long-term restoration and only the choir and apses are currently visible. The **mosaics** follow a familiar pattern. Christ Pantocrator dominates the central apse, underneath is the Madonna flanked by archangels, and then the Apostles. Although miniscule in comparison with Monreale, these mosaics are equally effective and, most interestingly, display a quite marked artistic tradition. Forty years earlier than those in William's cathedral, they are thoroughly Byzantine in concept: Christ's face is elongated, the powerful eyes set close together, the outstretched hand flexed and calming.

In high season, when Cefalù's tangibly Arabic, central grid of streets is crowded with tourists, you'd do best to visit the cathedral early in the morning to find it empty. The rest of the time, the long sandy **beach** beyond the harbour beckons. Of a couple of places worth venturing to, the small **museum** (daily 9am–12.30pm & 3.30–6pm; L1500), at Via Mandralisca 13 (across from Piazza Duomo), has a wry *Portrait of an Unknown Man* by the fifteenth-century Sicilian Master Antonello da Messina; and **the mountain** above the town – a steep twenty-minute climb from Piazza Garibaldi – holds the megalithic so-called *Tempio di Diana*. Paths continue right around the crag, inside medieval walls, to the sketchy fortifications at the very top.

If you want to **stay over**, easy and pleasant outside peak season, the *Locanda Cangelosi*, Via Umberto I 26 (☎0921/21.591) has rooms for only L16,000. Best place to **eat** is the *Arkade Grill*, Via Vanni 9 (off Corso Ruggero), which has a small Tunisian menu as well as cheapish pasta and good local wine. The **AAST** (Mon–Fri 8am–2pm & 4.30–7.30pm, Sat 8am–2pm) is at Corso Ruggero 77, the main street, and has free maps and accommodation lists.

The coast to Milazzo ... and inland routes

The best stretches of the Tyrrhenian coast all lie east of Cefalù: clean stony beaches backed for the most part by extensive orange and lemon groves. The train stops at several small, attractive seaside resorts, where there's often cheap accommodation, and there are buses south, into the hills, from various points on the coast.

Frequent trains stop at **SANTO STEFANO DI CAMASTRA**, a ceramics town and small-time resort, where there's a cheap *locanda* (the *U Cucinu*; ☎0921/31.106). Another 30km east, **SANT'AGATA DI MILITELLO** has a small working fishing fleet, which means excellent fish in the local restaurants. The busy summer resort has a long pebbled beach and you can stay here for L16,000 at the *Locanda Miramare* (☎0941/701.773), next to the railway station.

Further down the coast, rounding the cape, there are good **beaches** at CAPO D'ORLANDO itself, and from PATTI's main square you can catch a bus (3 daily) to **TINDARI** and the ruins of ancient **Tyndaris** (daily 9am–1hr before sunset; free). Originally founded in 396 BC, it was one of the last Greek settlements in Sicily and retains its Greek walls. Most of the remains, though, are Roman, including some house ruins and a theatre with splendid views over the sea, together with finds collected in a museum (daily 9am–2pm; free).

There's not much else to stop for before Milazzo; indeed the better destinations are all south and inland, away from the increasingly built-up coast. The SS185 cuts one of the grandest routes on the island, climbing gently into the hills to **NOVARA DI SICILIA**. Creakingly medieval, there are terrific views from the small town and a certain fascination in just wandering the decrepit streets and alleys. A closer target is the hill town of **CASTROREALE**, to the north east, just 8km south of BARCELLONA railway station on the coast – to which it's connected by seven daily buses. This is another extraordinarily sited town, defended in past days by the fourteenth-century castle of Frederick of Aragon, the tower of which survives on top of the pile. It does duty these days as an official *IYHF* **youth hostel** (☎090/905.247), though it's been under restoration recently and may still be closed. Even if you can't stay the night, Castroreale is well worth seeing and provides aimless wandering through the stepped streets, past badly restored sixteenth-century churches and fine nobles' houses.

Milazzo

At the base of a thin spit of land poking into the Tyrrhenian Sea, **MILAZZO** is not the sort of place you're likely to make a beeline for. Disfigured by a giant oil refinery, the coast around is noisy and smelly. But it's the main port of departure for the Aeolian Islands, which means, at best, a couple of hours in town awaiting the ferry/hydrofoil – at worst a night in one of the numerous cheap hotels. Try the *Cosenz* in Via Cosenz (☎090/928.2996), which has rooms for L30,000; or, nearer the port, the *Capital*, Via G. Rizzo 23 (☎090/928.3289) – L35,000.

If there's time to kill, you can poke around the restored **castle** (guided tours roughly hourly; free) which sits inside a much larger and older walled city, complete with its own cathedral. Ticket offices, opposite the docks, have all the information on departures to the islands: hydrofoils are more frequent, twice as quick and twice as expensive as the ferries; in winter, rough weather can disrupt the schedules – be prepared for cancellations. The **railway station** is a ten-minute (signposted) walk from the port, and **buses** from Messina stop right on the harbour front.

The Aeolian Islands

Volcanic in origin, the **Aeolian Islands** lead a precarious existence in the buffeted waters off the northern Sicilian coast. They are named after Aeolus, the Greek god, who kept the winds he controlled shut tight in one of the islands' many caves. According to Homer, Odysseus put into the Aeolians and was given a bag of wind to help him home, but his sailors opened it too soon and the ship was blown straight back to port. More verifiably, the islands were coveted for their mineral wealth, the mining of obsidian (hard glass-like lava) providing the basis for early prosperity. Later their strategic importance attracted the Greeks, who settled on Lípari in 580 BC. Their powerful fleet kept rivals at bay until the islands fell to the Carthaginians, who in turn were pushed out by the Romans in 252 BC. Thereafter began a period of decline: the islands became a haven for pirates and a place of exile, a state of affairs that continued right into the twentieth century with the Fascists exiling their political opponents to Lípari.

It's only comparatively recently that the islanders stopped scratching a subsistence living and started welcoming tourists. Emigration had virtually depopulated some of the islands, and even now the more remote ones are sorely stretched to maintain a decent living. That said, you'll not be alone if you come to the islands during the summer months, the central group – Vulcano, Lípari and Salina – pretty well known to a gradually increasing crowd of devotees. Lípari, particularly, is expensive in high season, rapidly becoming rather a hip resort. But get out to the minor isles or come in blustery winter for a taste of what it was like twenty – or a hundred – years ago: unsophisticated, rough and beautiful.

Getting there is easiest from Milazzo (see above), year-round ferries and hydrofoils connecting the port with all the islands. There are summer services, too, from Naples, Vibo Valentia, Reggio di Calabria and Messina, and from Palermo and (sometimes) Cefalù. **Getting around** in summer is easy as ferries and hydrofoils link all the islands. In winter, services are reduced and in rough weather cancelled altogether, particularly on the routes out to Alicudi and Filicudi. You can take cars to Lípari and Salina but bikes are better, something that's true for all the islands. Most islands have plenty of **accommodation**, though you'll often pay over the odds for a room, but note that the only **campsites** are on Lípari, Vulcano and Salina – and that camping rough elsewhere is illegal. **Food** prices, too, verge on the exclusive, so if you're only going for a short visit, take your own and avoid the pricey restaurants.

Vulcano

Closest to the Sicilian mainland, **VULCANO** is the first port of call for ferries and hydrofoils – around an hour and a half on the slowest crossing. The last volcanic explosion here was in 1890 and you can walk up to the main crater from the harbour, **PORTO DI LEVANTE**, in around an hour. A second hike is to **Vulcanello**, the volcanic pimple just to the north of the port, thrown up out of the sea in 183 BC, and there's good walking to be had around the rest of the island, too. Less energetically, just fifteen minutes' walk from Porto di Levante, across the neck of land separating it from Porto di Ponente, there's an excellent black-sand **beach**. On the way you'll pass Vulcano's sulpherous mud baths and the hot springs which bubble into (and warm) the sea. There are cheapish **rooms** at Porto di Levante: popular places are *Casa Fioritan* on Via Levante (☎090/985.2006) and *Casa Sipione* (☎090/985.2034) at the end of a path beside the church – try and ring before you arrive. The **campsite** (*Sicilia*; ☎090/985.2164), near the port, is only open from June to September.

Lípari

There are regular daily hydrofoil services from Vulcano on to **LÍPARI**, by far the most popular of the islands – and the most diverse. The group's main port and capital, **LÍPARI TOWN** is a thriving little place prettily bunched between two harbours, **arrival** at which is one of *the* island experiences: hydrofoils dock at the Marina Corta, a tiny harbour formed by a church-topped mole and dwarfed by the castle that crowns the hill above; ferries steam straight past, around the mighty sixteenth-century walls of the fort, to dock at the Marina Lunga, a deep water harbour which curves around to the north as a long beach.

It's the upper town within the fortress walls, the **castello**, which is the main focus of interest. Continuously occupied since Neolithic times, finds from the site have enabled archaeologists to date other Mediterranean cultures. Alongside the well-marked **excavations**, there's a tangle of dilapidated churches flanking the main cobbled street, and several buildings (including the seventeenth-century bishop's palace) which make up the separate arms of the **Museo Eoliano** (Mon–Sat 9am–2pm, Sun 9am–1pm; free) – a lavish collection of Neolithic pottery, late Bronze Age artefacts, and Greek and Roman vases and statues, most of it dug up outside. Down below, the streets wind around the base of the fortified hill and down to the harbours. The town is reliant upon tourism these days – as the restaurants and craft shops testify – but it's all fairly small-scale, even now. There's plenty of **accommodation**, though the cheap hotels – like the *Locanda Salina*, Via Garibaldi 12 (☎090/981.2332), and the *Europeo*, Via Vittorio Emanuele 98 (☎090/981.1589) – tend to fill early in the day in high season. Ask around in the harbour bars for **rooms**; you should get something with a shower and a kitchen – from L35,000 a double, but worth it given the price of restaurant food here. *Residence Fiorentino* (☎090/981.2136) is good, a friendly, family-run place at Via Giuseppe Franza 9. There's also a **youth hostel** (☎090/981.1540; March–Oct) in the castle, though it's busy in July and August. If you're **camping**, Lípari's only site (*Baia Unci*; ☎090/981.1909; April–Sept) is at CANNETO, 3km away – connected by at least nine buses daily from the **bus terminal** at Marina Lunga. The **AAST** (Mon–Sat 8am–2pm & 4.30–7.30pm), at Corso Vittorio Emanuele 253, has free maps and accommodation lists.

The **rest of the island** is easy to reach on a network of regular **buses**. **CANNETO** is good excursion, a fishing village with a long pebbled beach and a couple of hotels. From here the road climbs north, passing an excellent sandy beach (the *Spiaggia Bianca*) a couple of kilometres out of Canneto, before reaching the stony beach at **PORTICELLO**.

West of Lípari, the road clambers up the hill to **QUATTROCCHI** ("Four Eyes"), a three-kilometre hike which ends in glorious (and much photographed) views over Vulcano and the spikey *Faraglioni* rocks which puncture the sea between the two islands. Keep on the road to **PIANOCONTE**, which has a couple of popular pizza restaurants, good in the evening, and just before the village, a side road slinks off down to the old Roman thermal baths at **SAN CALOGERO**. This is a particularly fine walk, across a valley and skirting some impressive cliffs.

Salina and Panarea

North of Lípari, **SALINA's** two volcanic cones (both extinct) rise out of a fertile land which produces capers and white *malvasia* wine by the bucketload. Again, it's excellent walking country (though there are bus services between the main villages) and you get some marvellous vantage points over the other islands. Boats arrive either at the main port, **SANTA MARINA DI SALINA** – hotels and **rooms** – or on the south coast at **RINELLA**, a little fishing village. There's **accommodation** here too, and a **campsite** (*Tre Pini*; ☎090/984.2155; June–Sept), as well as boat trips to the most interesting of Salina's grottoes, ranged along the southern coast.

PANAREA, to the east, is the smallest of the Aeolians but easily the most scenic. Only 3km by 1.5km, it packs plenty of small, fairly cheap hotels into **SAN PIETRO**, one of the three settlements, though it's wise to ring ahead in summer; try the *Locanda Stella Maris* (☎090/983.042) or the *Locanda Roda* (☎090/983.006) – both of which have rooms for under L20,000. Half an hour's walk south of San Pietro is the island's one sandy **beach** and, high above here on the other side, **Punta Milazzese**, where a Bronze Age village of 23 huts was discovered in 1948. The site is thought to have been inhabited since the fourteenth century BC and pottery found here (displayed in Lípari's museum) shows a distinct Minoan influence. Elsewhere, there are hot springs at San Pietro and, at **CALCARA** to the north, a beach and sea that sometimes steam – one effect of the island's *fumarole*.

Strómboli

Despite the regularity of the volcanic explosions which throw up noise and flashes – and occasionally chunks of rock – throughout the day, people have always lived on **STRÓMBOLI**. It's a famous phenomenon, but not as frightening as it sounds. All the action is limited to one volcanic trail (the *Sciara del Fuoco*), on the northwest side of the volcano, and the eastern villages – white houses standing out against the green slopes – are safely settled. Most of the many hotels and rooms to let on Strómboli are here, in the adjacent parishes of San Vincenzo, San Bartolo and Piscita, often grouped together as **STRÓMBOLI TOWN** and these days something of a chic resort. Just to the north, beyond Piscita, is the island's main beach, of jet black sand. Boats dock a short distance from San Vincenzo, while an island service also calls at **GINOSTRA** on the southwestern side of Strómboli: a tiny hamlet closer to the craters, with one *locanda* (the *Petrusa*; ☎090/981.2305) and a few rooms to let.

A footpath from Piscita leads to an **observatory**, far enough if all you want is a view of the volcano. Otherwise, it's another three or four hours' climb (following the marks on the rocks) to the **summit** (924m), from where the nightly natural fireworks show is seen to best effect. Guides are available, though there's no reason why you shouldn't do it alone: it's not dangerous and it's easy enough to find your way. Do, though, take warm clothes and a torch, and a sleeping bag if you're going to stay until dawn – well worth it on the less blustery days.

THE IONIAN COAST:
MESSINA TO SIRACUSA

It's Sicily's eastern **Ionian coast** which draws most visitors, the summer mob attention merited by some of the island's most exciting sights – natural and man-made. Likely arrival point is **Messina**, the north–south Italian trains crossing the Straits from Calabria on a constant stream of ferries. **Taormina**, most chic of the island's resorts and famed for its remarkable Greco-Roman theatre, is an hour's train ride south, lava-built **Catania**, Sicily's second city, another hour beyond – both places (indeed the whole of this part of the coast) dominated by the massive presence of **Mount Etna**, Europe's highest volcano. A road and a narrow gauge single-track railway circumnavigate the lower slopes of Etna, passing through a series of hardy towns surrounded by swirls of black rock spewed from the volcano. Further south, out of the lee of Etna, lie traces of the ancient Greek cities which once lined the southeastern coast. **Megara Hyblaea** has the most extensive remains, and the route concludes in **Siracusa** – formerly the most important and beautiful city in the Hellenistic world.

Messina and south

MESSINA may well be your first sight of Sicily; and – from the ferry – it's a fine one, the glittering town spread up the hillside beyond the sickle-shaped harbour. Sadly, the image is shattered almost as soon as you step into the city, bombed and shaken to a shadow of its former self by a record number of disasters. Plague, cholera and earthquakes all struck throughout the eighteenth and nine-teenth centuries, culminating with the great earthquake of 1908 which killed 84,000 people, levelled the city and made the shore sink by half a metre over-night. Allied bombing raids in 1943 didn't help, undoing much of the post-earthquake restoration.

Today, the remodelled city guards against future natural disasters, wide streets and low, reinforced concrete buildings marching off in all directions. Not surpris-ingly, it is a pretty dull spectacle, and most of what interest there is resides in Messina's active port area. Take time at least to walk up Via I Settembre from the railway station to Piazza del Duomo. The traffic-strewn paved square was laid out in the eighteenth century, while the **Duomo** itself is an elegant reconstruction of the medieval cathedral built by Roger II. The facade retains its grand doorways and some original sculpture: inside, most of what you see – from the marble floor to the painted wooden ceiling – has been retouched and rebuilt. The detached **campanile** reputedly contains the largest astronomical clock in the world. Be there at noon and you get the full show, a visually impressive panoply of moving gilt figures including a crowing cock, roaring lion and a succession of doves and angels accompanying the Madonna.

Much of what was saved from the various disasters now resides in the **Museo Regionale** (Mon–Sat 9am–1.30pm, Tues, Thurs & Sat also 4–7pm, Sun 9am–1pm; L2000), 3km out of town – a 45-minute walk along Via della Liberta or a #8, #27 or #28 bus from the railway station. A great deal has been painstakingly stuck and plastered back together in this beautifully laid-out museum, including a couple of Caravaggios, commissioned by the city in 1604. There are also damaged works by Antonello da Messina, a few good Flemish pieces and the city's rescued archaeological remains as well.

Practical details

Trains all use the **Stazione Centrale** by the harbour, adjacent to the **Stazione Marittima** – where the train-ferries from Calabria dock. Other **ferries** and **hydrofoils** (to/from Villa San Giovanni/Reggio di Calabria, the Aeolian Islands and Naples) dock at quays further to the north, around the port and along Via Vittorio Emanuele and Via della Liberta. SAIS **buses** for Taormina and Catania leave from outside the railway station, while those for Milazzo (for boat services to the Aeolian Islands) depart from the nearby *Giuntabus* office at Via Terranova 8 (at the corner of Viale San Martino). The **EPT** (Mon–Sat 9am–1pm) is just outside the railway station, on Piazza della Repubblica, good for free maps and Aeolian Island ferry timetables.

Unless you arrive late in the day, it's hardly necessary to **stay over** in Messina. Still, there are several cheap options, including one, the *Roma* (☎090/775.566), right on Piazza del Duomo and charging only L15,000. Other budget hotels are all close to the railway station, two on Via N. Scotto, an alley to the left of Piazza della Repubblica. There's a **campsite**, *Il Peloritano* (☎090/844.057; May–Oct), out beyond Punta del Faro on the northern coast; bus #28 to RODIA from the railway station. For **eating**, the *Trattoria Firenze* is good value, close to the station, on Via del Vespro, across Piazza della Repubblica.

The coastal route south … and some hill villages

Try and take the train, rather than the slower bus, **south from Messina**, since the line follows the rough, stony shore pretty much all the way: on a clear day there are spanking views back over to Calabria.

SANTA TERESA DI RIVA is the first recognisable resort, with an oversized beach, though it's nothing to shout about. The straggling village is more attractive as a jumping-off point for the foothills of the **Monti Peloritani**, the long mountain range that cuts south from Messina. Buses from Santa Teresa twist the 4km up to **SAVOCA**, a peaceful hill village, evocatively sited up in the clouds. Houses and three churches perch precariously on the cliff sides in clumps, a tattered castle topping the pile. Signs in the village point you to the **Cappuccini monastery** whose catacombs (*catacombe*; April–Sept daily 9am–1pm & 4–7pm; Oct–March Tues–Sun 9am–noon & 3–5pm; free) maintain a selection of mummified bodies, two to three hundred years old, in niches, dressed in their eighteenth-century finery, the skulls of less complete colleagues lining the walls above. More offbeat delight is at hand in the village's *Bar Vitelli*, used as the scene of Michael Corleone's wedding breakfast in Coppola's film of *The Godfather*; there's a still of Marlon Brando inside, terrace tables outside. Two kilometres on, **CASALVECCHIO SICULO** has even better valley views from its terraces, and is the nearest village to the Norman monastery of **San Pietro e Paolo**, a twenty-minute hike away. Built in the twelfth century, its battlemented facade and double domes are visible from quite a distance, and the church betrays a strong Arabic influence.

Taormina

TAORMINA, high on Monte Tauro and dominating two grand sweeping bays below, is Sicily's best-known resort. The outstanding remains of its classical theatre, with Mount Etna as an unparalleled backdrop, arrested passing travellers when Taormina was no more than a medieval hill village: Goethe and D.H. Lawrence are the two big names touted by the tourist office, Lawrence so enthusiastic that he lived here (1920–23) in a house at the top of the valley cleft behind the theatre. Although international tourism has taken its toll over recent years, Taormina still retains much of its small town charm. The one main traffic free street is an unbroken line of fifteenth- to nineteenth-century palazzi and small, intimate piazzas, and there's an agreeably crumbly castle, and lines of flower-filled balconies. The downside is that between June and August it's virtually impossible to find anywhere to stay, and the narrow alleys are filled shoulder-to-shoulder with tourists. April, May or September are slightly better, but to avoid the crowds completely come between October and March, when it's often still warm enough to swim.

In summer, you could see the whole of town and the theatre in a short afternoon. **Trains** pull up at Taormina-Giardini station (left-luggage office) on the water's edge, way below town. It's a very steep thirty-minute walk up to Taormina (turn right out of the station and then, after 200m, left through a gap in the buildings, marked *Centro*). Much better (certainly if you have luggage) is to arrive by bus or take one of the fairly frequent local buses that pick up outside the railway station. The **bus terminal**, where they all stop, is on Via Pirandello in Taormina itself: bear left up the road from the terminal, turn through the Porta Messina, and the main street, **Corso Umberto I**, lies before you. The useful **AAST** (Mon–Fri 8am–2pm & 2.30–7.30pm, Sat 8am–noon) is in the fourteenth-century Palazzo Corvaja, off Piazza Vittorio Emanuele, the first square you come to. Pick up a free map, accommodation listings and bus timetables, and programmes for summer events in the theatre.

It's the **Teatro Greco** (daily 9am–1hr before sunset; L2000) – signposted from just about everywhere – that you should make your way to first, if only to acquaint yourself with Taormina's remarkable siting: southern Calabria, the Sicilian coastline and snow-capped Etna are all visible. That it was founded by Greeks in the third century BC is the extent of the theatre's Hellenistic connections, for the existing remains are almost entirely Roman. It was rebuilt at the end of the first century AD, when Taormina thrived under Imperial Roman rule, and the reconstruction changed the theatre's character entirely. The impressive Roman scene building, for example, is Sicily's only surviving example but can only have obscured the views of Etna – presumably a major reason for the theatre's original siting. Likewise, the stage and lower seats were cut back to provide more room and a deep trench dug in the orchestra to accommodate the animals and fighters used in Roman gladiatorial contests. In July and August the theatre hosts an international film festival and various concerts; tickets and information from the tourist office.

There are a few other Roman vestiges around town, including a much smaller **Odeion** (originally used for musical recitations) next to the AAST. Really, though, Taormina's attractions are all to do with strolling the flower-decked streets and alleys, and window shopping in the converted ground floors of the mansions along the Corso. Centre of town is Piazza IX Aprile, with its restored twelfth-century **Torre dell'Orologio** and terrace overlooking Etna and the bay – though don't sit down at the inviting outdoor cafés unless you have a substantial bankroll. Give yourself time to hike up to the **Castello** by way of a stepped path which leads up from the main road behind the AAST, from where you can continue on to **CASTELMOLA**, 5km above and seemingly growing out of its severe crag. It's about an hour's climb to the village (though there are buses), while another couple of hours beyond are the heights of **Monte Venere** (885m) – take the path behind Castelmola's cemetery – for the last word in local panoramas.

Sleeping and eating

Finding a **bed** in summer is a time-consuming business without a reservation. Only a handful will be both available and affordable, so start looking early. Good possibilities are along **Via Bagnoli Croce** (alongside the public gardens): cheap rooms at no. 66 (L12,000 each; very small but with incredible roof-terrace views), nos. 124–126 (☎0942/23.878; L22,000), above the pizzeria, and no. 88 (*Villa Pompei*, ☎0942/23.812; L22,000). A big step up in price gets you a room at the pleasant *Pensione Elios* at no. 98 (☎0942/23.431; L49,000). Other options are *Villa Liliana*, Via Dietro Cappuccini 4 (☎0942/24.373; L22,000), close to the AAST; and, more expensive but with excellent views, the *Pensione Svizzera*, at Via Pirandello 26 (☎0942/23.790; L37,000 with bath), just up from the bus terminal.

If everywhere is full, you'll have to try nearby Giardini-Naxos (also a good place to eat, see below) or **camp**. The campsite, *San Leo* (☎0942/24.658), is open all year, on the cape below town (next to the *Grande Albergo Capo Taormina*): take any bus running between Taormina and the railway station.

Eating in Taormina can also be terribly expensive. If money is tight, make do with the couple of unspectacular pizzerias outside Porta Messina. The only vaguely cheap trattoria is the basic but good *Trattoria da Nino*, Via Pirandello 37, while *Il Baccanale* in Piazza Filea (end of Via Bagnoli Croce) has outdoor tables and similar prices. Otherwise, there's a daily indoor **market** (mornings only, not Sunday) off Via Dietro Cappuccini and a *Standa* supermarket outside the Porta Catania.

Taormina's beaches ... and Naxos

The **coastline** below town is appealing, no question – a mixture of grottoes and rocky coves – but too many of its beaches are either private lidos (which you have to pay to use) or simply too packed in summer to be much fun.

Closest beach to town is at **MAZZARO** with its much-photographed islet. There's a **cable car** (*funivia*; L1000) service which runs every fifteen minutes from Via Pirandello, and a steep path which starts just below the cable car station. If you're still searching for a bed there's a dozen small **hotels** here, though get the AAST to ring for you first. The beach-bars and restaurants at **SPISONE**, north again, are also reachable by path from Taormina, this time from below the cemetery in town. From Spisone, the coast opens out and the beach gets wider.

With more time, **LETOJANNI** is a little resort in its own right, with rather more ordinary bars and shops, a few fishing boats on a sand beach, two campsites and regular buses and trains back to Taormina.

Roomier and better for swimming are the sands south of Taormina at **GIARDINI-NAXOS**, and to a lesser extent at the holiday village of RECANATI, beyond. Be prepared to pay to use the beach, a few hundred lire for access, a couple of thousand for a sunbed. The wide curving bay of Giardini – easily seen from Taormina's terraces – was the launching-point of Garibaldi's attack on the Bourbon troops in Calabria (1860) and, as significantly, the site of the first Greek colony in Sicily. An obvious stop for ships running between Greece and southern Italy, there was a settlement here by 734 BC, named *Naxos* after the Naxian colonists. It was never very important, and the **excavations** (daily 9am–1hr before sunset; free) are very low-key – a long section of ancient, lava-built city wall, two covered kilns and a sketchy temple. But it's a pleasant walk there through the lemon groves (bus from Taormina to Naxos/Recanati and follow the signs, *Scavi*). Right on the cape, Capo Schiso, in between two restaurants, is an inconspicuous **museo archaeologico** (Mon–Sat 9am–2pm, Sun 9am–1pm; free) housing some of the finds.

Giardini itself, the long town backing the good beach, is an excellent alternative source of accommodation and food. Prices tend to be a good bit cheaper than in Taormina and in high season, if you arrive by train, it's probably worth trying here first. Recommended **places to stay** are the *Locanda Roma*, Via Roma 21 (✆0942/52.137), left from the station and just before the railway bridge, for L17,000, and the *Moderno* (L20,000) right opposite the station. For **eating**, the best and the cheapest is the restaurant/pizzeria attached to the seafront *Lido Europa* (opposite the Chiesa Immacolata); good pizzas and fresh pasta are also to be had at *Fratelli Marano*, Via Naxos 181. **Buses** run half-hourly to Giardini, the last one at 9.30pm; last one back to Taormina at 9pm from the stop outside the *Lido Europa*.

Around Mount Etna: coastal and inland routes, and up the volcano

Mount Etna's massive bulk looms over much of the coastal route south from Taormina. One of the world's largest volcanoes, it really demands a separate visit, but if you're pushed for time you'll have to content yourself with the ever more imminent views of its eastern flank as you head along the coast to Catania. With time, you can make the circular route to Catania on the slow train around the volcano, the **Circumetnea** – one of Sicily's most interesting rides – and stop off on the **volcano** itself. Reaching the lower craters below the summit is eminently possible, on foot or by mountain-bus – either way a thrilling experience.

South down the coast: Acireale, Aci Trezza and Aci Castello

The train is best if you're travelling directly to Catania, a fast route which hugs the coast. The only major town on the way is **ACIREALE**, 35km south of

Taormina. Well sited a couple of kilometres above the rocky shore, and a noted spa centre, Acireale was rebuilt directly over the old lava streams after the 1693 earthquake. Aside from the views along the coast from its pretty public garden, the town's worth a stop for its several striking examples of Sicilian Baroque in the crowded central streets. A good time to come is at *Carnevale* (February/March), when Acireale hosts one of Sicily's best festivals, flower decked floats and fancy dress parades clogging the streets for five noisy days.

Acireale takes its name from the local river Aci, in Homeric myth said to have appeared following the death of the shepherd Acis at the hands of the giant, one-eyed cyclops Polyphemus. Other nearby villages take the name too, like **ACI TREZZA** and **ACI CASTELLO**, a few kilometres south (both reachable on the Messina–Catania bus route). Between the two, just offshore, the jagged points of the **Scogli dei Cicopli** stand: Homer wrote that the now blinded Polyphemus slung these rocks, broken from Etna, at Ulysses as he and his men escaped from the cyclops in their ships. The three main sharp-edged islets present an odd sight and it's a good half day's entertainment to get off the bus at Aci Trezza and walk the couple of kilometres south along the rough coast to Aci Castello. The **Castello** itself (Tues–Sun 9am–1pm & 3–5pm, summer 5–7.30pm; free) is a terrific thirteenth-century building that rises above the sea in splinters from a volcanic rock crag. In summer the rough, lava-scattered coastline around town is popular for sunbathing and swimming, while Aci Castello has a couple of small restaurants, handy for lunch. Very frequent buses connect the two villages with Catania.

The Circumetnea railway: Giarre-Riposto to Catania

If you don't have the time to reach the summit of Etna, then the **Circumetnea** railway provides some alternative volcanic thrills. A private line, 114km long, it runs around the base of the volcano through fertile vegetation and the strewn lava from more recent eruptions, a marvellous ride. The line begins in the twin town of **GIARRE-RIPOSTO**, thirty minutes by train or bus from Taormina; main-line *FS* trains will drop you in Giarre, from where it's a short walk down Corso Italia to the station of Riposto, where the Circumetnea line starts. *InterRail* passes are not valid on this route, and if you make the entire trip, to Catania, allow five hours; tickets L4600 one-way, L8600 return.

The closest town to the summit is **RANDAZZO**, a dark medieval town built entirely of lava. Although dangerously near Etna, Randazzo has never been engulfed; when the 1981 eruption saw it on the point of evacuation, the lava-flow finally stopped just outside town – and easily visible. Poke around the gloomy streets – dingily authentic despite the fact that much of the town has been heavily restored, bombed to bits in 1943 when it figured as the last Sicilian stronghold of the Axis forces.

If you want to break the journey around Etna then Randazzo is probably the place to stay, despite the fact that the only **accommodation** is uninspiring; the tatty *Motel Scrivano* (☎095/921.126), behind the *Agip* petrol station on Via Regina Margherita, with rooms for L35,000. You could, anyway, give Randazzo a couple of hours and pick up the next Circumetnea train for Catania – or the regular branch line (rail passes valid) to Taormina-Giardini.

Mount Etna: the ascent

Fine though the journey and views are, circling **Etna** by road or rail can only be second best to an ascent, a spectacular trip worth every effort to make – though without your own transport that effort can be considerable. At 3323m, Etna is a fairly substantial mountain, the fact that it's also one of the world's biggest volcanoes (and still active) only adding to the draw. Some of the eruptions have been disastrous: in 1169, 1329 and 1381 the lava reached the sea; in 1669 Catania was wrecked and its castle surrounded by molten rock; while this century the Circumetnea railway line has been repeatedly ruptured by lava flows, and, in 1979 nine people killed on the edge of the main crater.

This unpredictability means that it's no longer possible to get close to the main crater. An eruption in 1971 destroyed the observatory supposed to give warning of such an event; another in 1983 brought down the cable car which provided access to the crater. The cable car may have reopened by now, but at the time of writing access was by 10km of rough track. All this is not to say you'll be in any danger, provided you heed the warnings as you get closer to the top.

There are several **approaches** to the volcano and, with a car, some of the best scenery is on the north side of the volcano, taking the road that leads up from Linguaglossa. On **public transport**, though, you'll need to come via **NICOLOSI**, on the southern side of Etna and a hour from Catania by bus. A winter ski resort and last main stop before the steeper slopes begin, it's a good place to pick up information. The small town **information office** is at Via Etnea 65 (daily 8.30am–1pm, summer also 4–7.30pm), the main road that runs through Nicolosi. There are several **hotels** too, a couple in town, the rest on the road out, as well as a **campsite** – all signposted and detailed on full lists available from the information office.

Although there are frequent buses to Nicolosi from Catania, only one (8.05am from outside Catania railway station) continues to **Rifugio Sapienza**, the mountain refuge/hotel that marks the end of the negotiable road up the south side of Etna. Everywhere here the slopes are dotted with earlier, spent craters, grass covered on the lower reaches, like black pimples further up. At the carpark beyond the road there's a line of souvenir shops, a couple of restaurants and the *Rifugio Sapienza* (☎095/911.062) itself, where rooms cost L35,000. Arriving on the early morning bus, you'll have enough time to make the top and get back for the return bus to Catania – it leaves around 4pm from the refuge. Failing that, cadging a lift down with someone isn't impossible.

There are two ways **up the volcano** from the refuge. You can either take one of the tough-looking *SITAS* **minibuses** from outside the old cable car station (L28,500 each; April to Oct/Nov only), a two-hour return-trip which gives you half an hour clambering around just below the main crater. Or you can **walk**, following the rough minibus track. Really it all depends on finances and time: walking up will take between three and four hours, the return obviously a little less. However you go, take warm clothes, good shoes or boots and (especially if you wear contact lenses) glasses to keep the flying grit out of your eyes.

As you climb, the ground under your feet is alternately black, grey or red depending on the age of the lava. The more recent stuff lies in great folds, earlier minor craters signposted as you climb. The highest you're allowed to get (on foot or in the bus) is 2900m, and though there's only a rope across the ground to prevent you from climbing further, it would be foolish to presume that nothing serious would happen to you if you did – gaseous explosions and molten rock are common this far up. From the turn-around point for the minibus you look up to the summit, smoke puffing from the southeast crater immediately above. Higher still is the main crater: depending on the weather conditions you'll see smoke from here too and, if you're lucky, spitting explosions. If you've walked, you'll be glad of the **bar** set up in a wooden hut here, one of the odder places in the world to get a cappuccino.

Catania

First impressions don't do much at all for **CATANIA**, on an initial encounter possibly the island's gloomiest spot. Built from black-grey volcanic stone, its central streets can feel suffocating, dark with the shadows of grimy, high Baroque churches and palazzi; and the presence of Etna dominates everywhere, in the buildings, in the brooding vistas you get of the mountain at the end of Catania's streets – even the city's main street is named after the volcano.

Yet fight the urge to change buses and run: Catania is one of the most intriguing, and historic, of Sicily's cities. Some of the island's first Greek colonists settled the site as early as 729 BC, becoming so influential that their laws were eventually adopted by all the Ionian colonies of Magna Graecia. Later, a series of natural disasters helped shape the city as it appears today: Etna erupted in 1669, engulfing the city, the lava swamping the harbour, which was then topped by an earthquake in 1693 that devastated the whole of southeastern Sicily. The swift rebuilding was on a grand scale, and making full use of the local building material, Giovanni Vaccarini, the eighteenth-century architect, gave the city a lofty, noble air. Despite the neglect of many of the churches and the disintegrating, grey mansions, there's still interest in what, at first, might seem intimidating. Delving about throws up lava-encrusted Roman relics, surviving alongside some of the finest Baroque work on the island.

Arriving and getting around

The **railway station**, for all mainline train arrivals, is in Piazza Giovanni XXIII, northeast of the centre. If you're changing on to the round-Etna train, the **Circumetnea terminus** is on Corso delle Province, just off Corso Italia. The **airport**, Fontanarossa, is 5km south of the city, entry-point of most charter flights to Sicily; if you're not on a package and don't have a bus to meet you, bus #24 leaves from right outside for Piazza del Duomo and the railway station. **Regional buses** to and from Acireale, Nicolosi, Etna (Rifugio Sapienza) and Lentini all park on the other side of Piazza Giovanni XXIII; buses to and from Piazza Armerina stop on Via Luigi Sturzo, just to the left of the square; most other regional and **island-wide buses** stop in Piazza Bellini, a few minutes' walk from Piazza del Duomo.

Immediately outside the railway station you'll find ranks of **city buses**: #27, #29, #33, #36 and #42 run into the centre at Piazza del Duomo. **Tickets** are valid for one journey (L700), two hours (L900) or nine hours (L1200), bought from the booth by the ranks.

There's an **EPT** (summer daily 8.30am–8.30pm; winter Mon–Fri 9am–1pm & 4–7pm) inside the railway station, with accommodation listings, maps and English speaking staff; and there's also an information office at the airport (Mon–Fri 9am–noon & 1–8pm).

CATANIA

To Randazzo

To Mount Etna

CORSO DELLE PROVINCE

VIALE VITTORIO VENETO

Botanical Gardens

Palazzo di Giustizia

CORSO ITALIA

Stazione Circumetnea

PIAZZA TRENTO

VIA XX SETTEMBRE

PIAZZA G. VERGA

VIA PANTANO

VIALE REGINA MARGHERITE

VIA MOROSOLI

VIA A. LONGO

VIA ETNEA

VIA SALVATORE TOMASELLI

VIA ANDRONE

Villa Bellini

VIA G. DE FELICE

VIA UMBERTO I
PIAZZA VITT.
EMANUELE I

VIA DELLA LIBERTA

VIA G. VERDI

Post Office

VIA PACINI

VIA PACINI

PIAZZA CARLO ALBERTO

EPT

VIA S. GAETANO ALLA GROTTA

PIAZZA GRENOBLE

PIAZZA DELLA REPUBLICA

VIA ARCHIMEDE

Anfiteatro

PIAZZA STESICORO

CORSO SICILIA

Santo Carcere

VIA MONTESANO

PIAZZA SPIRITO SANTO

VIA G. DI PRIMA

PIAZZA CAPPELLINI

To Taormina and Messina

VIA MARCH. DI CASALOTTO

VIA CROCIFERI

VIA ETNEA

Stazione Centrale

San Nicolò

PIAZZA DANTE

San Giuliano

VIA ANTONIO DI SANGIULIANO

VIA VI APRILE

VIA GESUITI

Collegiata University

PIAZZA BELLINI

VIA TEATRO MASSIMO

PIAZZA DEI MARTIRI

San Benedetto

VIA ROTONDA

Teatro Bellini

Collegio Cutelli

VIA TEATRO GRECO

Municipio

PIAZZA CUTELLI

VIA VITTORIO EMANUELE

PIAZZA DEL DUOMO

VIA VITTORIO EMANUELE

Museo Belliniano

Duomo

VIA BISCARI

Odeion
Teatro Romano

VIA DUSMET

PIAZZA DUCA DI GENOVA

VIA GARIBALDI

VIA AUTERI

VIA TRANSITO

PIAZZA FEDERICO DI SVEVA

Castello Ursino

VIA PLEBISCITO

VIA CRISTOFORO COLOMBO

0   100 m

To the Airport Beaches & Campsites

Molo Vecchio

To Naples, Réggio di Calabria and Malta

The City

Catania's main square, **Piazza del Duomo**, is a handy orientation point, and stop for most city buses: Via Etnea steams off north, lined with the city's most fashionable shops and cafés; fish market and port lie behind to the south; railway station to the east; the best of the baroque quarter to the west.

It's also one of Sicily's most attractive city squares, rebuilt completely in the first half of the eighteenth century by Vaccarini, and surrounded with fine Baroque structures. Most striking of these is the **Municipio** on the northern side of the piazza, finished in 1741, though to admire it properly you'll have to gain the central reserve of the piazza. Here, the **elephant fountain** is the city's symbol, the eighteenth-century lava elephant supporting an Egyptian obelisk on its back.

Cross back for the **Duomo** (closed noon–5pm) on the piazza's eastern flank. Apart from the marvellous volcanic-rock medieval apses (seen through the gate at Via Vittorio Emanuele 159), this was pretty much entirely remodelled by Vaccarini, whose heavy baroque touch is readily apparent from the imposing facade on which he tagged granite columns from Catania's Roman amphitheatre (see below). The interior is no less grand: adorned by a rich series of chapels, notably the Capella di Sant'Agata to the right of the choir, which conceals the relics paraded through the city on the saint's festival days.

Nearby is Catania's open-air **market**, a noisome affair with slabs and buckets full of twitching fish, eels and shellfish and endless lanes full of vegetable and fruit stalls, as well as one or two excellent lunchtime trattorias. The roads wind through a pretty dilapidated neighbourhood, to an open space punctured by the **Castello Ursino**, once the proud fortress of Frederick II. Originally the castle stood on a rocky cliff, over the beach, but following the 1669 eruption, which reclaimed this entire area from the sea, all that remains is the blackened keep – desperately neglected and surrounded by a low moat filled with all kinds of dumped junk. The local museum, the Museo Civico, is housed inside but it's being rearranged and no one expects it, or the castle, to be open for years.

Back towards the centre, dingy **Piazza Mazzini** heralds perhaps the most interesting section of the city. Everything close by is big and Baroque, and **Via Crociferi** – which strikes north from the main road, under an arch – is lined with some of the most arresting religious and secular examples, best seen on a slow amble, peering in the eighteenth-century courtyards and churches. At the bottom of the narrow street, the house where the composer Vincenzo Bellini was born in 1801 now houses the **Museo Belliniano** (Mon–Fri 8.30am–1.30pm, Sun 8.30am–12.30pm; free), an agreeable collection of photographs, original scores and other memorabilia. A local boy, Bellini notches up several tributes around the city, including a piazza, theatre and park named after him, a berth in the duomo and the ultimate accolade, *spaghetti Norma*. Cooked with tomato and aubergine sauce, and named after one of Bellini's operas, it's a Catanian speciality.

West from here, the **Teatro Romano** (Tues–Sun 9am–1hr before sunset; free) was built of lava in the second century AD, on the site of an earlier Greek theatre, and much of the seating and the underground passageways are preserved, though all the marble which originally covered it has disappeared. Further west, down Via Teatro Greco, the pretty crescent of Piazza Dante stares out over the unfinished facade of **San Nicolo**, the biggest church in Sicily, stark and empty of detail both outside and in following its partial eighteenth-century restoration. The builders are in again now, but there's usually someone around in the early morning to show you the echoing interior – virtually undecorated save for a meridian line drawn across the floor of the transept. The church is part of the adjoining **convent**, also under restoration and (statistically at least) equally impressive – the second largest convent in Europe after Mafra in Portugal.

Nearby, a few minutes' walk north, the little twelfth-century church of **Santo Carcere** (Mon–Fri 8–11am & 4–7pm, Sat & Sun 8am–noon), with its strong defensive walls, couldn't be less roomy. It was built on the site of the prison where Saint Agatha was confined before her martyrdom, and a custodian lets you in to the third-century crypt now appealingly bright and cosy with electric candles and velvet chairs. From here, you drop down into **Piazza Stesicoro**, the enormous square that marks the modern centre of Catania, one half of which is almost entirely occupied by the closed-off, sunken, black remains of Catania's **Anfiteatro Romano**, dating back to the second or third century AD. The amphitheatre could hold around 16,000 spectators, and from the church steps above you can see the seating quite clearly, supported by long vaults.

Staying on in Catania: hotels, restaurants and bars

There are lots of **places to stay** in Catania, and some real bargains if you hunt around. *Pensione Gresi*, Via Pacini 28 (☎095/322.709), is one of the nicest, with rooms for L22,000 including showers; the *Pensione Centrale* at no. 17 on the same street (☎095/310.983) is also good for around the same price. Best of the rest is the *Corona*, Via Crociferi 81 (☎095/327.708), though it fills quickly, or, if you want to stay around Piazza del Duomo, the *Savona*, Via Vittorio Emanuele 210 (☎095/326.982) at L25,000. **Camping**, there are three sites (with lidos and cabins available) a short way south of the city on Lungomare Kennedy; take bus #24, #27 or #D (the latter summer only) from the railway station or Via Etnea.

You'll rarely do better for **eating** than in Catania, fresh fish a speciality. The *Ristorante Rapido*, Via Corridoni 17, off Via Pacini, is probably Catania's best – great at lunch, with an L8000 *pranzo completo*. Worth trying too is the *Trattoria Calabrese*, on Via Penninello, down the steps at the end of Via Crociferi. Of the **bars**, handiest is the *Bar Universita* in Piazza dell'Universita, which sells good milkshakes and fresh fruit drinks; the *Centrale*, Via Etnea 123, is a busy tavola calda with a full range of snacks.

Listings

Airport Tickets for bus #24 into the centre from the airport *tabacchi*; note that buses from Catania to Agrigento and Enna make a stop at the airport. Direct services, too, from the airport to Taormina/Messina and Milazzo (for the Aeolian Islands).

American Express c/o *La Duca & C.*, Via Etnea 63.

Car hire *Hertz* and *Holiday Car Rental* at the airport; *Avis*, Via San Giuseppe La Rena 87 (☎095/347.116); *InterRent*, Via Firenze 104 (☎095/444.063).

Chemists Night chemists at Via Etnea 274, Via Vittorio Emanuale 54 and Corso Italia 105.

Emergencies ☎095/375.050 for an ambulance.

Ferry tickets *Tirrenia Società Navigazione*, Piazza Grenoble 26 (☎095/316.394) for services to Naples, Reggio di Calabria, Siracusa and Malta.

Hospital First aid at the following hospitals: *Garibaldi*, Piazza S. Maria di Gesu (☎095/333.617); *Santa Marta*, Via Clementi 36 (☎095/310.433); *S. Tomaselli*, Via Passo Gravina 185 (☎095/330.333).

Left luggage At the railway station, open 24hr, L1000 per day.

Post office Via Etnea 215, close to the Villa Bellini; Mon–Sat 8am–8pm.

Telephones *SIP* at Via S. Euplio 118; daily 8am–10pm.

Travel agency *CTS*, Viale Regina Margherita 4c.

Across the plain of Catania: Lentini, Augusta and Megara Hyblaea

Compared to the interest further north, there's a real paucity of places if you're looking for another halt before Siracusa. Trains and buses cut right across the **Piana di Catania**, known to the Greeks as the Laestrygonian Fields after the cannibal Laestrygones who was reputed to live there: a pretty ride but with absolutely no reason to get off until **LENTINI**, half an hour or so out of Catania. Lentini was founded in 728 BC, probably to restrict any further northward expansion by the Corinthians in Siracusa. Built far inland, unusual for a Greek colony, it prospered before succumbing to the Romans under Marcellus, who slaughtered some 2000 of the inhabitants in 214 BC. The ancient city – some defences, a necropolis and part of a main gate – lies between Lentini and nearby CARLENTINI, a twenty-minute walk north from the centre, or take bus #1 or #2 from Lentini's railway station. The local **Museo Archaeologico** (Mon–Sat 9am–2pm, Sun 9am–1pm; free) in Lentini, in Piazza del Liceo, holds the finds and a reconstruction of the gate, a necessary first stop before seeking out the remains on the ground.

If this doesn't grab you then trains and direct buses from Catania run around the southern spur of the Golfo di Catania to **AUGUSTA**, oil port and naval base. It's more pleasant than it sounds, built (like Siracusa) on a small islet connected to the mainland, and there are beach resorts to the north, one at BRUCOLI together with a fifteenth-century castle. But the real reason to stay would be as a base for visiting the nearby site of **MEGARA HYBLAEA**, around 10km south, across the bay. Founded by Greeks a few years before Siracusa, the city enjoyed a fair living from sea-trade and pottery until destroyed by first Gelon in 483 BC and later the Romans. The large **site** (always open) shows a Doric temple, some tombs and houses, an eighth-century BC *agora*, as well as a small **museum** (Mon–Sat 9am–2pm, Sun 9am–1pm; free) with plans, photos and some finds. Unfortunately, it's not easy to get to without your own transport: the only possibility is to take a local train from Augusta to MEGARA-GIANNALENA, from where it's a fair hike, though you could reduce it to a kilometre by walking along the rails and climbing up at the road bridge.

The last stretch of the journey to Siracusa, by train especially, is a nightmare of **rampant industrialisation**. As far as PRIOLO, the track skirts the largest concentration of chemical plants in Europe, a stinking, Meccano-built mesh of pipes and tanks that has irreversibly polluted the local sea and air. People living in the coastal villages have had to be evacuated and their houses destroyed, the environment deemed unfit for human habitation.

Siracusa

An easily defendable offshore island, fertile plains across on the mainland, two natural harbours – it's hardly surprising that **SIRACUSA** (ancient Syracuse) should attract the early Greek colonists, in this case Corinthians who settled the site in 733 BC. Within a hundred years, the city was so powerful that it was sending out its own colonists to the south and west; and later Siracusa was the island's main power base – indeed, the city's history reads as a list of Sicily's most famous and effective rulers.

Some history

Syracuse first assumed its almost mythic eminence under **Gelon**, the tyrant of Gela, who moved his rule to the city in 485 BC to increase his power: it was he who began work on the city's Temple of Athena, later to become the Christian cathedral of Syracuse. It was an unparalleled period of Greek prosperity in Sicily, while the extent of a wider Siracusean influence was indicated by the defeat of the Etruscans (474 BC), who had been causing trouble for Greek towns on mainland Italy. It was a growing influence which troubled Athens and in 415 BC a fleet of 134 triremes was dispatched to take Syracuse – only to be blockaded and the fleet destroyed. Those who weren't slaughtered as they ran were imprisoned in the city's stone quarries.

Under **Dionysius the Elder**, the city became a great military base, the tyrant building the first of the Euryalus forts and erecting strong city walls. As the leading European power, Syracuse more or less retained its prime position for two hundred years until it was attacked by the Romans in 215 BC. The subsequent two-year siege was made long and hazardous for the attackers by the mechanical devices contrived by **Archimedes** – who, as the Romans finally forced victory, was killed by a foot soldier.

From this time, Syracuse withered in importance. It became, briefly, an important religious centre in the early Christian period, but for the most part its days as a power were done: sacked by the Saracens, most of its later Norman buildings fell in the 1693 earthquake. Passed by until this century, World War II then brought a double blow, the city bombed by the Allies and then, after its capture, by the Luftwaffe in 1943. Luckily, the extensive ancient remains were little damaged, although decay and new development have reduced the attractions of the modern city. It's an essential stop on any tour of the island, but it's getting daily more difficult to picture the beautiful city which Plutarch wept over when he heard of its fall to the Romans.

Some **orientation** pointers are useful. The original Greek settlement was on the fortified island of **Ortygia**, compact enough to see in a good half-day's stroll, and almost completely late medieval in character. The Greek city spread onto the mainland in four distinct areas: **Achradina**, over the water from Ortygia, was the city's commercial and administrative centre, and today encompasses the new streets which radiate out from the railway station; **Tyche**, to the northeast, was residential and now holds the archaeological museum and the city's extensive catacombs; **Neapolis**, to the west, is the site of the fascinating archaeological park based on ancient Syracuse's public and social amenities; while **Epipolae** stretched way to the northwest, to the city's outer defensive walls and the Euryalus fort.

SIRACUSA

Arriving and surviving

You'll **arrive** in Siracusa in any one of a number of places. The **railway station** is on the mainland, about a twenty-minute walk from either Ortygia or Neapolis. If you're not staying, then dump your bags in the **left luggage office** in the station (open 24hr; L1000 a day) and strike off for one or the other. *AST* **buses** arrive in Piazza della Poste, just over the bridge on Ortygia, where there's also an office doling out timetables for regional and city bus services. *SAIS* buses stop just around the corner, in Via Trieste. **Ferries**, from Naples, Reggio di Calabria and Catania, and for Malta, dock right on the Foro Vittorio Emanuele; tickets and info from *Tirrenia-Adriatica*, Viale Mazzini 4 (☎0931/65.684).

The main **city bus** stops are in Piazza Archimede and Largo XXV Luglio on Ortygia, and along Corso Umberto on the mainland. One ride will cost you L600. For free maps, accommodation listings, details about the performances in the Greek theatre, and other **information**, visit the **AAST** (Tues–Sun 9am–2pm) at Via Maestranza 33, or inside the railway station (Mon–Sat 9am–1pm and 3–7pm). The main **post office** is in Piazza delle Poste; **telephones** (8am–8pm) at Via Brenta 35, close to the railway station.

Central Siracusa: Ortygia and Achradina

A fist of land with the thumb downturned, **ORTYGIA** stuffs more than 2700 years of history into a space barely one kilometre long and half a kilometre across. The island was connected to the mainland at different times by causeway or by bridge: today you approach over the wide Ponte Nuovo to Piazza Pancali, where the sandstone remnants of the **Tempio di Apollo** sit in a little green park surrounded by railings. Erected around 570 BC in the colony's early years, it was the first grand Doric temple to be built in Sicily, though there's not much left to provoke the senses: a few column stumps, part of the inner sanctuary wall and the stereobate can be made out.

Follow Via Savoia towards the water and you fetch up on the harbour front, an active place overlooking the main harbour, the Porto Grande. Set back from the water, a curlicued fifteenth-century limestone gateway, the **Porta Marina**, provides one entrance into the webbed streets of the old town. The walk uphill ends on a terrace looking over the harbour, from where you slip down to a piazza encircling the **Fonte Aretusa**, probably the most enduring of Siracusa's romantic locations. The freshwater spring – incidentally now neither fresh nor a spring – fuelled an attractive Greek myth: the nymph Arethusa, chased by the river god Alpheus, was changed into a spring by the goddess Artemis and, jumping into the sea off the Peloponnese, reappeared as a fountain in Siracusa. Actually, there are natural freshwater springs all over Ortygia, but the landscaped, papyrus-covered fountain – complete with fish and ducks – is undeniably pretty. Admiral Nelson took on water supplies here before the Battle of the Nile, though you'd be better advised to sip a coffee in one of the cafés nearby.

The old town's roads lead on, down the "thumb" of Ortygia, as far as the **Castello Maniace** on the island's southern tip. Thrown up by Frederick II in 1239, the solid square keep is now a barracks, and is off-limits to visitors. Back on the main chunk of Ortygia, the severe thirteenth-century Palazzo Bellomo houses the **Museo Regionale d'Arte Medioevale e Moderna** (Tues–Sat 9am–2pm, Sun 9am–1pm; L2000), an outstanding collection of medieval art. There are some wonderful pieces in here, including notable works by the omnipresent Gagini family and a damaged fifteenth-century *Annunciation* by Antonello da Messina, the museum's most famous exhibit.

Ortygia's most obvious attractions, though, surround the **Piazza del Duomo**, the island's most appealing spot. An elongated space, impressive buildings radiate out up either flank, including the seventeenth-century **Municipio** with the remains of an early Ionic temple in its basement. This was abandoned when work began on the most ambitious of all Siracusa's temples, the **Tempio di Atena**, which was raised in the fifth century BC and now forms the basis of the duomo. In the normal run of things it might be expected to have suffered the eventual ruination that befell most of the Greek temples in Sicily. Yet much of it survives, thanks to the foundation in the seventh century AD of a Christian church which incorporated the temple in its structure – thus keeping the masonry scavengers at bay. The **Duomo** itself (closed noon–4pm) makes the grandest statement about Ortygia's continuous settlement, with twelve of the temple's fluted columns, and their architrave, embedded in its battlemented Norman wall. Inside, the nave of the Christian church was formed by hacking eight arches in the *cella* walls.

Buses run from Largo XXV Luglio over Ponte Nuovo and into **ACHRADINA**, the important commercial centre of ancient Syracuse. Although nowadays there's little of interest here, you may find yourself staying in one of the hotels scattered around its modern streets. The **Foro Siracusano** was the site of the *agora*, the market place and public square, and there are a few remains still to be seen – though the dominant feature is the war memorial in its garden, a Fascist monument of 1936. The only other ancient attraction left in the area is the **Ginnasio Romano**, off Via Elorina behind the railway station: not a gymnasium at all, but a small first-century AD Roman theatre – partly sunken under moss-covered water – and a few pieces of a temple and altar.

Tyche and Neapolis: archaeological museum and park

TYCHE, north of the railway station is mainly new and commercial, and if you want to see the best of Siracusa's archaeological delights you might as well take the bus straight from Ortygia and save your legs. Numbers #1, #4, #6, and #12 (not Sun) leave from Piazza XXV Luglio, #11 from Corso Umberto – all running up Corso Gelone. Get off at Viale Teocrito and signposts point you east for the archaeological museum and west for Neapolis. It's best to take the museum first: it's good for putting the site into perspective and is unlikely to be packed first thing in the morning.

The **Museo Archaeologico** (Tues–Sun 9am–2pm, last entry 1pm; L2000) is Sicily's newest and most spectacular archaeological museum. There is almost indescribable wealth here, starting with geological and prehistoric finds, moving through entire rooms devoted to the Chalcidesian colonies (Naxos, Lentini, Zancle) and to Megara Hyblaea, and finally to the main body of the collection: an immensely detailed catalogue of life in ancient Syracuse and its sub-colonies. Most famous exhibit is the *Venus*, at the entrance to the Syracuse section, a headless figure arising from the sea, the clear white marble almost palpably dripping. Attempt also to track down the section dealing with the temples of Syracuse, fragments from each (like the seven lion-gargoyles from the Tempio di Atena) are displayed alongside model and video reconstructions. There's an explanatory diagram at the entrance to the circular building and everything is colour coded: pick the sector you're interested in and follow the arrows, prehistory starting just to the left of the entrance.

NEAPOLIS, to the west, is now contained within a large **Parco Archaeologico** (Tues–Sun 9am–2hr before sunset), reachable on buses #4, #5 or #6 from Largo XXV Luglio. Although you don't pay for the initial excavations, seeing the Greek theatre and quarries – easily the most interesting parts – costs L2000, paid at a separate entrance. The **Ara di Ierone II**, an enormous altar of the third century BC on a solid white plinth, is the first thing you see, across the way from which is the entrance to the theatre and quarries. The **Teatro Greco** is very prettily sited, cut out of the rock and looking down into trees below. It's much bigger than the one at Taormina, capable of holding around 15,000 people, though less impressive on the whole. But the theatre's pedigree is impeccable: Aeschylus put on works here, and around the top of the middle gangway are a set of carved names which marked the various seat blocks occupied by the royal family. Greek dramas are still played here in even-numbered years, as wooden planking over the surviving seats testifies.

Walk back through the theatre and another path leads down into a leafy quarry, the **Latomia del Paradiso**, best known for its unusually shaped cavern that Dionysius is supposed to have used as a prison. This, the **Orecchio di Dionigi** (or "Ear of Dionysius") is a high, S-shaped cave 65m long: Caravaggio, a visitor in 1586, coined the name after the shape of the entrance, but the acoustic properties are such that it's not impossible to imagine Dionysius eavesdropping on his prisoners from a vantage point above. A second cave, the **Grotta dei Cordari**, used by the ancient city's ropemakers, is shored up at present.

Keep your ticket from the theatre and Latomia del Paradiso, as it will also get you into the elliptical **Anfiteatro Romano**, back up the main path past the altar and through a gate on your right; you have to see this last. A late building, dating from the third century AD, it's a substantial relic with the tunnels for animals and gladiators clearly visible. Again, some of the seats are inscribed with the owner's names.

Out of Siracusa: the Castello Eurialo

If it's hot and crowded, better targets are a few kilometres to the west of the city – the military and defensive works begun under Dionysius the Elder, designed to defend ancient Syracuse from land attack. Added to and adapted over a couple of centuries, they basically consisted of a great wall which defended the ridge of **Epipolae** (the city's western limit), and the massive **Castello Eurialo** (Mon–Sat 9am–6pm, Sun 9am–1pm; free) – *the* major Greek fortification in the Mediterranean still standing.

There are three defensive trenches, the innermost leading off into a system of tunnels and passages. Climb up to the castle proper, its long keep and the lower walls and towers providing hearty views over the oil refineries and tankers of the coast north of the city, and over Siracusa itself. Clambering around the castle and the defensive walls is good fun, and the **youth hostel** (see below) just up the road from the castello is a fine alternative to staying in the packed central city.

Buses #9, #10 or #11 run from the Corso Gelone, outside the archaeological park to the village of BELVEDERE; the site is just before the village, on the right, a fifteen-minute ride.

Sleeping and eating

Accommodation choices aren't spectacular and in high season you must make an advance reservation. A popular choice on Ortygia is the *Gran Bretagna*, Via Savoia 21 (☎0931/68.765) – L38,000 including breakfast. Or ask around the several cheaper hotels on the way in from the railway station: try the *Pensione Gelone*, Via Epicarmo 36 (☎0931/60.004) or the *Hotel Milano*, Corso Umberto 10 (☎0931/66.981), both of which cost between L25,000 and L35,000. The private **youth hostel** out at Belvedere, Via Epipoli 45 (☎0931/711.118), is open all year round, has beds for L10,000 per person and serves meals. The nearest **campsite**, *Agriturist* (☎0931/721.224), open all year, is 5km away; bus #34 or #35 from Corso Umberto.

Eating, too, is not brilliant. Most of the restaurants and trattorias are over-priced but there's a basic **pizzeria** at Via Savoia 12, and one over the road at no. 17 (the *Pizzeria Savoia*; closed Mon). Good **bars** and cafés are easier to come by, two of the best the outdoor *Porta Marina*, on the Foro Vittorio Emanuele, and the *Bar Del Ponte*, right at the end of the Ponte Nuovo on Ortygia – a good breakfast stop.

THE SOUTHERN COAST AND THE INTERIOR

It's tempting to give Sicily's long **southern coast** a miss, especially if you're short on time. But to do so would be to ignore some of the most appealing places on the island. The whole region, coast and hinterland, marks a welcome break from the volcanic fixation of the blacker lands to the north: here the towns are largely spacious and bright, strung across a gentler, unscarred landscape that rolls and pitches down to the sea.

Sicily's **southeastern bulge** was devastated by a calamitous seventeenth-century earthquake and the inland rebuilding, over the next century, was almost entirely Baroque in concept and execution. **Ragusa** dominates, a splendid town on two levels, the older lower town much abandoned but still with its share of grandiose buildings. Elsewhere, similar vigorous baroque towns mushroomed, like little **Modica** to the south and – the undisputed gem – **Noto**, to the east.

Down on the **coast** itself there's a line of small-town resorts which stretches from the southeastern cape, **Capo Passero**. There are good beaches but often the coastline is marred by industrial development and pollution; the only place that's not a resort and worth a stop is **Gela**, which retains its extensive Greek fortifications. More vital, further west, is **Agrigento**, sitting on a rise overlooking the sea above its famed series of Greek temples.

Slow cross-country trains and limited exit motorways do little to encourage stopping in the island's **interior**, but it's only here that you really begin to get off the tourist trail. Much of the land is burned dry during the long summer months, sometimes a dreary picture, but in compensation the region boasts some of Sicily's most curious towns. **Enna** is the obvious target, as central as you can get, the blustery mountain town a pace apart from the dry hills below. There are easy trips to be made from here, north into the hills, and south to **Piazza Armerina** and the fabulous Roman mosaics, and to airy, ceramic-studded **Caltagirone**.

Ragusa and the southeast

The **earthquake of 1693**, which destroyed utterly the towns and villages of southeastern Sicily, had one positive and lasting effect. Where there were ruins, a new generation of confident architects raised planned new towns in an opulent Baroque style. All were harmonious creations, Catania the grandest, Noto the most eagerly promoted by the tourist board. But there is a bagful of other towns too, less visited but all providing surprising pockets of grandeur amid the bare hills and deep valleys of the region.

Ragusa

Best base for any exploration of the area is **RAGUSA**, a busy and likeable provincial capital with an encouraging, friendly atmosphere. The destructive earthquake split the city in two: the old town of Ragusa Ibla, on a jut of land above its valley, was comprehensively flattened, and within a few years a new town emerged, on the higher ridge to the west. Ibla was stubbornly rebuilt around its medieval ruins, while its new rival developed along grander, planned lines. All the business and industry relocated in the prosperous upper town, where oil is the latest venture – derricks scattered around modern Ragusa's higher reaches.

It's here, in the **upper town**, that you'll arrive. All **buses** stop outside the **railway station** and a left turn takes you along the main road and over the exposed Ponte Nuovo. Before you reach it, the **EPT** (Mon–Sat 8.30am–2pm) is at Via Natalelli 131, over Piazza della Liberta. Further on, the bridge spans a huge cleft in the ridge: all the interest in modern Ragusa is on the other side, the gridded Baroque town slipping off to right and left on either side of the steeply sloping Corso Italia. To the right, down the Corso on a wide terrace above Piazza San Giovanni, stands the **Duomo**, conceived on a grand, symmetrical scale. Finished in 1774, its tapered columns and fine doorways are a fairly sombre background to the vigorous small-town atmosphere around. Back towards the railway station, underneath the *Standa* supermarket, there's an important **Museo Archaeologico** (Mon–Sat 9am–2pm, Sun 9am–1pm; free) dealing mainly with finds from the archaeological site of Kamarina (sixth century BC) on the coast to the southwest.

But it's **RAGUSA IBLA**, the original **lower town**, where you'll probably while away much of the day, its weatherbeaten roofs straddling the outcrop of rock about twenty minutes' walk away. Main attraction, the church of **San Giorgio**, stridently placed at the top of Piazza Duomo, is one of the masterpieces of Sicilian Baroque, built by Rosario Gagliardi and finished in 1784. The glorious three-tiered facade, sets of triple columns climbing up the wedding cake exterior to a balconied belfry, is an imaginative work, though typically not much enhanced by venturing inside. As with Gagliardi's other important church in Modica (see below), all the beauty is in the immediacy of the powerful exterior.

The whole town – deathly quiet at lunchtime – is ripe for aimless wandering. Gagliardi gets another credit for the elegant rounded facade of **San Giuseppe** in Piazza Pola, a few steps below the duomo, while Corso XXV Aprile continues down past abandoned palazzi to the **Giardino Ibleo** (daily 8am–8pm) – gardens which mark the very edge of the spur on which the town is built. If you can't face the walk back to the upper town, bus #1 or #3 makes the trip, hourly, from Piazza Pola.

Sleeping and eating

Sadly, there's nowhere to stay in Ragusa Ibla, and even up in the main part of town **accommodation** is limited to a very few fairly expensive hotels. The cheapest, *San Giovanni*, Via Traspontino 3 (☎0932/21.013), has rooms for L30,000, at the railway station end of the lower Ponte dei Cappuccini; the other good-value choice, the *Mediterraneo* (☎0932/21.944), just over the main Ponte Nuovo, costs L42,000. There's a good, basic **trattoria**, the *Trattoria Ragusana*, in Via San Sebastiano which has set meals, including wine, for around L12,000.

Three Baroque towns: Comiso, Módica and Noto

The best of the rest of the Baroque southeast can be seen in easy trips from Ragusa. If you came from the west you might already have passed through **COMISO**, its green centre dominated by the twin domes of two impressive churches. If you didn't, the journey in itself is worth making, up over a barren 600m high plateau looking away to the distant sea. The wild countryside hearabouts continues to impress as you head beyond Ragusa, the route to **MÓDICA**, half an hour to the south, a case in point. As the bus swirls down past Ragusa Ibla and climbs through some rugged hills, all the vegetation seems to have been pulled into the valleys below, the tiered slopes bare and rocky. Modica itself is an enjoyable place to spend half a day. A powerful medieval base of the Chiaramonte, the upper town is watched over by the magnificent eighteenth-century facade of **San Giorgio**, a worthy rival to the church of the same name in Ragusa Ibla. It's thought that Gagliardi was responsible for this too: the elliptical facade is topped by a belfry, the church approached by a symmetrical double staircase which switchbacks up across the upper roads of the town.

But the real highlight of any tour of the Baroque southeast is further afield. **NOTO** is easily the most harmonious post-earthquake creation, and for a time, in the mid-nineteenth century, replaced Siracusa as that region's provincial capital. Indeed, despite its architectural identification with the Baroque towns around Ragusa, Noto is best reached **from Siracusa** – around half an hour's journey by bus or train. Planned and laid out by Giovanni Battista Landolina, adorned by Gagliardi, there's not a town to touch Noto for uniform excellence in design and execution. Its main Corso is lined with some of Sicily's most captivating buildings, all a rich honey colour – from the flat-fronted church of **San Francesco**, on the right, along as far as Piazza XVI Maggio and the graceful, curving church of **San Domenico**. And Piazza Municipio is arguably Sicily's finest piazza: perfectly proportioned, tree-planted expanses flank the raised, twin-towered **Duomo**, finished in 1770, itself hemmed in by two palaces of remarkable decorative quality. Opposite, the **Municipio** (or Palazzo Ducezio) is flanked by its own green spaces, the arcaded building presenting a lovely, simple facade of columns and long stone balconies. Head up the steep **Via Corrado Nicolaci**, an eighteenth-century street which contains the extraordinary **Palazzo Villadorata** (no. 18) on the left. The six balconies facing the street are supported by the last word in sculpted buttresses, a panoply of griffons, galloping horses and fat-cheeked cherubs.

Staying in Noto wouldn't be a bad alternative to Siracusa, though you'll have to move sharp to get a room at the *Albergo Stella*, Via F. Maiore 44 (☎0931/835.695), on the corner of Via Napoli, which has doubles for L32,000. Get free maps and information from the **EPT** in Piazza XVI Maggio (April–Oct daily 9am–8pm; rest of the year 8am–2pm & 4–6pm).

West to Gela

Most of the coastal section west of Capo Passero is pretty inaccessible without your own transport. Even then, to be frank, there's not a lot worth stopping for, the odd seaside town awash with new holiday apartments but little individual character. The railway line touches down at POZZALLO and trains then loop north, through Modica, Ragusa and Comiso before cutting back down to the coast at Gela.

GELA couldn't present a worse aspect as the train edges into town, through a petrochemical mess of futuristic steel bubbles and pipes. There are fine dune-backed beaches in the vicinity but there must be serious doubts about the cleanliness of the water. Once, though, Gela was one of the most important of the island's Hellenic cities, founded in 688 BC, and under Hippocrates and Gelon rivalled even Siracusa as the island's political hub. But, smashed by the Carthaginians, ancient Gela was abandoned to the encroaching sands. Modern Gela was the first Sicilian town to be liberated in 1943, but otherwise – beyond an excellent archaeological museum and a fine set of defensive walls – is almost entirely without interest.

If you want to see these, best leave your bags at the railway station left luggage office – there's really no need to stay longer than half a day. Outside the station (also where buses pull up) turn right down the main road and, at the junction, bear right for the town centre and the main Corso Vittorio Emanuele, at either end of which are Gela's two sights. To the left, a twenty-minute walk, Gela's **Museo Archaeologico** (daily 9am–1.30pm; free) is notable largely for its excellent collection of painted vases: mainly seventh- to fifth-century BC, the black-and-red jugs and beakers were Greek Gela's speciality. Outside the museum a small acropolis has been uncovered, a few walls and a single temple column from the fifth century BC. There are more archaeological remains at the other end of town – along the Corso and then a left fork (Via Manzoni), which runs parallel to the sea as far as the red gates of the site, a hefty three- to four-kilometre walk. Here, at **Capo Soprano**, is a remarkable series of **Greek fortifications** (daily 9am–1hr before sunset; free) dating from the fourth century BC. Preserved by the sand, the walls stand nearly eight metres high in parts, made up of perfectly fitted stone blocks topped by a storey of brick – now covered in protective glass panels. It's a beautiful site, waves crashing onto a particularly fine duned stretch below.

Agrigento

Though handsome, well sited and awash with medieval atmosphere, no-one comes to **AGRIGENTO** for the town. The interest instead focuses on the substantial remains of Pindar's "most beautiful city of mortals", a couple of kilometres below. Here, strung out along a ridge facing the sea, is a series of Doric temples – the most captivating of Sicilian Greek remains and a grouping unique outside Greece.

The site

In 581 BC colonists from nearby Gela and from Rhodes founded the city of Akragas between the rivers of Hypsas and Akragas. They surrounded it with a mighty wall, formed in part by a higher ridge on which stood the acropolis (and, today, the modern town). The southern limit of the ancient city was a second, lower ridge and it was here, in the so-called "Valley of the Temples", that the city architects erected their sacred buildings during the fifth century BC.

A road winds down from the modern city to the **VALLE DEI TEMPLI**, buses dropping you at a carpark between the two separate sections of archaeological remains, the eastern and western zones. The **eastern zone** is unenclosed, and is at its crowd-free best early morning or late evening. A path climbs up to the oldest of Akragas's temples, the **Tempio di Ercole** (Herakles). Probably begun in the last decades of the sixth century BC, nine of the original 38 columns have been re-erected, everything else scattered around like a waiting jigsaw puzzle. Retrace your steps back to the path which leads to the glorious **Tempio della Concordia**, dated to around 430 BC: perfectly preserved and beautifully sited, with fine views to the city and the sea, the tawny stone lending the structure warmth and strength. That it's still so complete is explained by its conversion (in the sixth century AD) to a Christian church. Restored to its (more or less) original layout in the eighteenth century, it's kept its lines and slightly tapering columns, although – sadly – it's fenced off to keep the crowds at bay. The path continues, following the line of the ancient city walls, to the **Tempio di Giunone** (or Hera), an engaging half-ruin standing at the very edge of the ridge. The patches of red visible here and there on the masonry denote fire damage, probably from the sack of Akragas by the Carthaginians in 406 BC.

The **western zone** (daily 9am–1hr before sunset; free), back along the path and beyond the carpark, is less impressive, a vast tangle of stone and fallen masonry from a variety of temples. Most notable is the mammoth construction that was the **Tempio di Giove**, or Temple of Olympian Zeus. The largest Doric temple ever known, it was never completed, left in ruins by the Carthaginians and further damaged by earthquakes. Still, the stereobate remains, while on the ground, face to the sky, lies an eight-metre-high *telamone*: a supporting column sculpted as a male figure, arms raised and bent to bear the temple's weight. Other scattered remains litter the area, including the so-called **Tempio dei Dioscuri** (Castor and Pollux), rebuilt in 1832 and actually made up of unrelated pieces from the confused rubble on the ground.

Via dei Templi leads back to the town from the carpark via the excellent **Museo Nazionale Archaeologico** (Tues–Fri 9am–1.30pm & 3–5pm, Sat & Sun 9am–12.30pm; free) – the bus passes by outside. The extraordinarily rich collection is devoted to finds from the city and the surrounding area, best displays are the cases of vases (sixth to third century BC) and a reassembled *telamone* stacked against one wall. Nip over the road on the way out for the **Hellenistic-Roman quarter** (daily 9am–1hr before sunset; free), which contains lines of houses, inhabited (on and off) until the fifth century AD, many with mosaic designs still discernible.

The modern city and some practicalities

It would be a mistake not to scout round modern Agrigento, modern only in comparison with the temples. Thoroughly medieval at its heart, its tiny stepped streets and fine churches look down over the Valle dei Templi and beyond to the sea. The main street, **Via Atenea**, starts at the eastern edge of the old town, above the railway station, the streets off to the right harbouring ramshackle palazzi and the church of **Santa Maria dei Greci**. Built over a Greek temple of the fifth century BC, the flattened columns are visible in the nave, while an underground tunnel reveals the stylobate and column stumps, all part of the church's foundations.

Trains arrive at the edge of the old town and city buses leave from outside in Piazza Marconi to the temples, the campsite and Porto Empedocle (for ferries to the Pelagie islands). **Buses** from elsewhere in Sicily will drop you at the terminal in Piazza Roselli, near the post office. The **AAST** (Mon–Sat 8am–2pm & 5–7pm) is in the *Banco di Sicilia* building on Piazza Marconi and has hotel listings and maps.

Finding **somewhere to stay** in Agrigento shouldn't be a problem, except perhaps in peak season. Cheapest is the *Albergo Gorizia*, Via Boccerie 39 (☎0922/20.105), off Via Atenea, which charges L18,000, and there are a few rooms for rent at Via di Vela 6, also off Via Atenea – L10,000 per person. If you can afford it, it's probably worth moving up a class: the *Concordia*, Piazza San Francesco 11 (☎0922/56.266), has some smart doubles for L30,000. You can **camp** 5km away at the coastal resort of SAN LEONE, at *Internazionale San Leone* (☎0922/77.625 or 24.140; April to Sept); bus #10 from outside the railway station. For **eating**, the food and local wine is excellent at *La Forchetta*, next door to the *Concordia* hotel, but not particularly cheap. If you're budgeting, you can't beat the L10,000 pasta, pizza and drink combination at *La Corte degli Sfizzi*, a trendy little eaterie on Cortile Contarini, an alleyway above Via Atenea.

West to Eraclea Minoa

From Agrigento you're well poised for moving on into western Sicily, and frequent buses get you to Sciacca in around two and a half hours. If you can, though, first drop in on the other Greek site of importance on this stretch, **ERACLEA MINOA**: originally named *Minoa* after the Cretan king Minos, who chased Daedalus from Crete to Sicily and founded a city where he landed. The Greeks settled here in the sixth century, later adding the tag *Heraklea*. A buffer between the two great cities at *Akragas*, 40km to the east, and *Selinus*, 60km west, Eraclea Minoa was dragged into endless border disputes, but in spite of this it flourished. Most of the remains date from the fourth century BC, Eraclea Minoa's most important period, three hundred years or so before the town declined.

The **site** (daily 9am–1hr before sunset) is finely sited right on the coast, at the mouth of the river Platani. Apart from the good **walls**, once 6km long, which survive in interrupted sections, the main attraction is the sandstone **theatre**, and certain of the finds are held in a small on-site **museum**. It's all well worth the trip, and there's a **beach** and **campsite** (*Camping Eraclea*; ☎0922/847.310; May to Oct) near the ruins. But, without wheels of some description you're going to have to do some tough walking to get here. Take any bus running between Agrigento and Sciacca and ask the driver to let you off at the turning; it's 5km west of MONTALLEGRO, on the SS115, the site another 4km from there. Heading on, west from the site turning, you should be able to flag down a bus going to Sciacca.

The Pelagie Islands

The remote and barren **PELAGIE ISLANDS** (Isole Pelagie) are simply that – dry rocks, south even of Malta and bang in the middle of the Mediterranean. Throughout history they've been neglected, often abandoned, their only days of importance destructive ones: in 1943 the Allies bombed the main island, Lampedusa, prior to springing into Sicily; and Colonel Quadhafi of Libya provided a repeat performance in 1987 when he retaliated against the American bombing of Tripoli by despatching missiles (off-target it turned out) at Lampedusa's US base. That said, the only danger you're likely to face now is a rough sea crossing from Porto Empedocle.

Most travellers will **get to the islands** by ferry from **PORTO EMPEDOCLE**, the indescribably ugly port town 6km south of Agrigento: buses run there hourly (#8, #9 or #10 from outside Agrigento's railway station). It costs around L27,000 one-way to Linosa, L34,000 to Lampedusa (returns double that), and the journey takes six to eight hours; tickets from the harbour-side *Siremar* office and travel agents in Agrigento. The only way to cut this time would be to **fly** from Palermo to the airport on Lampedusa; around L70,000 one-way and an hour's flight.

Ferries call first at **LINOSA**, a volcanic islet, a pretty and a quiet place with four extinct craters, some lavial beaches and not much else in the way of sights. The only village has a few hundred inhabitants, rather fewer cars and a minimal road system. There is one **hotel**, the *Algusa* (☎0922/972.052) – L67,000 with bath – at which you should really make a reservation in advance if you want to stay, and an unofficial **campsite**. The other ferry stop is at **LAMPEDUSA**, 50km south and much bigger. Around 4000 people live here, mostly in the town of the same name, most making their living from fishing, though more and more tourists are arriving every year. It's a flat, dry island with more in common with Africa than Europe, the main attraction the beaches and the sea around the island – bitingly clean and offering easily the best swimming and skin-diving in the Mediterranean. You should have no trouble finding somewhere to stay on Lampedusa either: most of the many **hotels** are a few minutes' walk from the port, and many have double rooms for under L30,000. There's an official **campsite**, too, *La Roccia* (☎0922/970.055), open all year, at Cala Greca.

The interior: inland to Palermo and Enna

The most scenically rewarding parts of Sicily's **interior** are in the east, primarily the hill towns and villages that lie in a wide half-circle to the north of Enna – which is where you should head if you want to see the region by public transport.

Coming from Agrigento, however, there are several worthwhile routes – most only practicable for mobile travellers. One route goes by way of **SANT'ANGELO MUXARO** (daily buses from Agrigento), beyond which begins the most convoluted **approach to Palermo**, the twisting road climbing up to 1000m at PRIZZI, from where there are occasional bus services down to **CORLEONE**. A fairly large town for these parts, it lent Mario Puzo's fictional Godfather, Don Corleone, his adopted family name. There is a bus from Corleone to Palermo, another 60km, though drivers won't want to miss the diversion into the higher hills around **PIANA DEGLI ALBANESI**: one of the most interesting of Sicilian towns, a fifteenth-century Albanian colony whose Greek Orthodox inhabitants still wear the costume and speak the tongue of their ancestors. Any celebration brings out the festive garb, but the best time to visit is at Easter when the local ceremonies form a marked contrast to the island's Catholic rites. Only 25km from Palermo, Piana degli Albanesi could also be seen on a day trip from the capital; regular buses leave from outside the railway station.

The other option from Agrigento, better if you want to head on to the most appealing parts of the interior, is the **route to Enna**. There's a local bus service which connects up the nearer places, while trains make the journey too, up through gentle, tree-planted slopes and then across the hilltops. At **CANICATTI** the line splits, trains running south to Licata, on the coast. Better to keep on to **CALTANISSETTA**, capital of its province and a brisk modern town, which (with its couple of hotels) is a possibility for day-tripping to Enna and Piazza Armerina (see below); the bus timetables, for once, are kindly disposed. Caltanissetta's only tangible attraction is the worthy **Museo Civico** (Mon–Fri 9am–1.30pm, Sat 9am–noon), on Via Napoleone Colajanni, close to the railway station, which contains some of the earliest of Sicilian finds, including vases and Bronze Age sculpted figures. From Caltanissetta it's a short bus ride to Enna – don't take the train as Enna's railway station is way outside town.

Enna

From a bulging V-shaped ridge almost 1000m up **ENNA** lords it over the surrounding hills of central Sicily. The approach to this doughty mountain stronghold is still as formidable as ever, the bus climbing slowly out of the valley and looping across the solid crag to the summit, and the town. For obvious strategic reasons, Enna was a magnet for successive hostile armies, who in turn besieged and fortified the town, each doing their damnedest to disprove Livy's description of Enna as *inexpugnabilis*.

Despite the destructive attention, most of Enna's remains are medieval and in good nick, prize exhibit the thirteenth-century **Castello di Lombardia** (daily 9am–1pm & 3–7pm; free), dominating the easternmost spur of town. A mighty construction with its strong walls complete, it guards the steep slopes on either side of Enna, six surviving towers (out of an original twenty) providing lookouts. From the tallest, the Torre Pisana, the magnificent views take in Enna itself, some rugged countryside in all directions and, if you're lucky, Mount Etna.

In the centre of town virtually all the accredited sights lie stretched out along and around **Via Roma**, which descends from the castle. It's a narrow street, broken by small piazzas – one of which fronts the hemmed-in **Duomo**, dating in part from 1307. The spacious sixteenth-century interior (usually open afternoons) features huge supporting alabaster columns, the bases and capitals of which are covered with an amorphous, writhing mass of carved figures. Outside, behind the apses, the **Museo Alessi** (Mon–Sat 9am–1pm; free) fields a rich collection of local church art, old coins and the impressive contents of the cathedral's own treasury. There's a second museum too, equally good, the **Museo Archaeologico** (Mon–Sat 9am–1.30pm, Sun 9.30am–1pm; free), just over the way in Piazza Mazzini: covering Neolithic to Roman times and including a fine series of painted Greek vases.

Via Roma slopes down to the rectangular **Piazza Vittorio Emanuele**, focal point of the evening *passeggiata*. Off here, there's a long cliff-edge belvedere, while the bottom of the piazza is marked by the plain, high wall of the **Chiesa di San Francesco**, whose massive sixteenth-century tower previously formed part of the town's system of watchtowers. This linked the castle with the **Torre di Frederico**, which stands in isolation in its little park in the largely modern south of the town. An octagonal tower 24m high, it's a survivor of the alterations to the city made by Frederick of Aragon who added a (now hidden) underground passage linking it to the castello.

Practicalities

Overnight stays in Enna are at either the *Belvedere* (☎0935-21.020), for L31,000, on the terraced promenade off Piazza Vittorio Emanuele, or the *Grande Albergo Sicilia* in Piazza Colaianni (☎0935/21.127), below the duomo off Via Roma – L43,000 with bath. Alternatively, you can take a bus (hourly, from San Francesco church) 9km south to **PERGUSA**, supposedly the site of Pluto's carrying off of Persephone to the Underworld. These days the famed Lago di Pergusa is encircled by a motor racing track, alongside which are several new hotels, the two cheapest on the Enna road: the blue *Miralago* (☎0935/36.272) or *La Pergola* (☎0935/36.017) further up – both around L30,000. There's a **campsite** here too, just off the race track. (The last bus from Enna to Pergusa is at 8.30pm; from Pergusa to Enna at 9pm.)

As for **eating**, back in Enna the *Ristorante Familiare*, Via S. Agata 123 (near San Francesco), is recommended and cheap; the *Grotta Azzurra*, Via Colajianni (between Piazza Matteoti and Piazza Vittorio Emanuele), is more adventurous but still reasonably priced.

All long distance **bus services** use the bus terminal in the new town; to get into the centre, turn right and follow Corso Sicilia around until the road forks, then bear right into Piazza Vittorio Emanuele. Enna's **railway station** is an unfortunate 5km below town, an impossibly long and steep walk, though a bus connects roughly hourly with the town centre. Information, as well as a good free map of Enna, is available at the **EPT** in Piazza Garibaldi (Mon–Sat 8.30am–1.30pm).

North of Enna . . . into the hills

Some of the most fascinating, unsung towns of the Sicilian interior are within easy reach of Enna: to the north, along roads which either wind over mountain ranges to the Tyrrhenian coast, or en route to the foothills of Mount Etna. Both directions provide spectacular rides, and unlike destinations further west are feasible by bus.

Closest to Enna, across the valley and accessible by regular buses from Enna's bus and railway stations, is medieval **CALASCIBETTA**, its tightly packed buildings perched above a sheer drop on the eastern side. Buses run further east from Enna, too, to **AGIRA**, again well sited with sparkling views down over the surrounding hills. The bus route continues through REGALBUTO and, eventually, to Catania, a journey that strikes through land that was fiercely contested during the short Sicilian campaign of the World War II.

If you can time it right, three *SAIS* buses a day link Agira with **TROINA**, a tortuous thirty-kilometre ride to Sicily's highest town (1120m). Hardly surprisingly, the journey there is the real event. Without a car you'll probably have to retrace your steps as the two onward routes – east to Cesaro and west to **NICOSIA** – are long, mountainous hauls, not to be hitched lightly. Nicosia, though, can be reached by bus from Enna, changing at Leonforte (as well as directly from Palermo), another momentous ride rewarded by an ancient medieval town of cracked palazzi and the remains of a Norman castle. It's an evocative little place, worth an **overnight stop** if you can: there's an extremely cheap *locanda*, at Via della Pace 6 (☎0935/648.258), with its own good restaurant, off the main street.

South: Piazza Armerina and around

To the south, less than an hour by bus from Enna, **PIAZZA ARMERINA** lies amid thick tree-planted hills, a quiet, unassuming place mainly seventeenth- and eighteenth-century in appearance, its skyline pierced by towers, the houses huddled together under the joint protection of castle and cathedral. All in all, a thoroughly pleasant place to idle around, though the real local draw is an Imperial Roman **villa** which stands in rugged countryside at Casale, 5km south-west of Piazza Armerina. Hidden under mud for 700 years, the excavated remains reveal a rich villa, probably a hunting lodge and summer home, decorated with polychromatic mosaic floors that are unique in the Roman world for their unrivalled quality and extent.

To **get to the villa** from Piazza Armerina, there's a minibus service from Piazza Generale Marescalchi, daily (except Sun) at 1.30pm, which passes the turnoff for the villa, 1km beyond. Otherwise you'll have to walk or hitch, usually an easy enough proposition. (Coming **from Caltanissetta**, currently the daily 8.30am bus gets to Piazza Armerina at 9.50am; return at 4.05pm.) Note that the return bus from Mazzarino passes the turnoff at around 3.30pm.

The Villa Imperiale

The **VILLA IMPERIALE** (daily 9am–1hr before sunset; L2000) dates from the early fourth century BC and was used right up until the twelfth century when a mudslide kept it largely covered until comprehensive excavations in the 1950s. It's been covered again since to protect the mosaics, a hard plastic and metal roof and walls designed to indicate the original size and shape, while walkways lead visitors through the rooms in as logical an order as possible. The mosaics themselves are identifiable as fourth-century Roman-African school, which explains many of the more exotic scenes and animals portrayed; they also point to the villa having had an important owner, possibly Maximianus Herculeus, co-emperor with Diocletian.

The **main entrance** leads into a wide courtyard with fountains, where the **thermae** (baths) group around an octagonal *frigidarium* and a central mosaic showing a lively marine scene. A walkway leads out of the baths and into the villa proper, to the massive central court or **peristyle**, whose surrounding corridors are decorated with animal head mosaics. From here, a balcony looks down upon one of the villa's most interesting pictures, a boisterous **circus scene** showing a chariot race. Small rooms beyond, on either side of the peristyle, reveal only fragmentary geometric patterns, although one contains probably the villa's most famous image, a two-tiered scene of **ten girls**, realistically muscular figures in Roman "bikinis" taking part in various gymnastic and athletic activities.

Beyond the peristyle, a long, covered corridor contains the most extraordinary of the mosaics: the **great hunting scene**, which sets armed and shield bearing hunters against a panoply of wild animals. Along the entire sixty-metre length of the mosaic are tigers, ostriches, elephants, even a rhino, being trapped, bundled up and down gangplanks and into cages, destined for the Games back in Rome. The square-hatted figure overseeing the operation is probably Maximianus himself: his personal area of responsibility in the Imperial Tetrarchy was North Africa, where much of the scene is set.

Other rooms beyond are nearly all on a grand scale. The **triclinium**, a dining room with three apses, features the labours of Hercules, and a path leads around the back to the **private apartments**, based around a large basilica. Best mosaics here are a **children's circus**, where tiny chariots are drawn by colourful birds, and a **children's hunt**, the kids chased and pecked by the hares and peacocks they're supposed to snare.

Piazza Armerina: practical details

Seeing the villa and mosaics might well entail spending the night in Piazza Armerina, but neither of the two places to **sleep** are cheap: the *Selene* at Viale Generale Gaeta 30 (☎0935/80.254) in the lower new town, is friendlier and more central for L45,000 than the similarly priced *Park Hotel Paradiso* (☎0935/680.841 or 85.700), 2km west of Piazza Armerina, beyond the Norman church of Sant'Andrea. The **AAST** (Tues–Fri 8am–2pm & 4.30–7.30pm, Mon & Sat 8am–2pm) is at Via Cavour 15, just off central Piazza Garibaldi, and they can provide a map.

Around Piazza Armerina: Caltagirone

CALTAGIRONE is an hour's ride southeast from Piazza Armerina, one of the least known of Sicily's inland towns, with a fine central body of monumental buildings that dates from the rebuilding after the 1693 earthquake. A noted centre of ceramics, the effect is lightened by tiled decoration found all over Caltagirone, most effectively as flowers and emblems flanking both sides of a bridge (the Ponte San Francesco) on the way into the centre. The grandest statement, though, is made by the 142 steps of **La Scala**, which cut right up one of Caltagirone's hills to a church at the top, the "risers" in between each step covered with a ceramic pattern, no two the same. There's a good value **place to stay** in the *Casa Donata*, Via Portosalvo 22b (☎0933/25.684), close to the hospital in the new town – L30,000 with bath.

TRÁPANI AND THE WEST

The **west** of Sicily is a land apart. Skirting around the coast from **Trápani** – easily the largest town in the region – it looks immediately different: the cubic white-washed houses, palm trees, active fishing harbours and sunburned lowlands seem more akin to Africa than Europe; and historically, the west of the island has always looked south. The earliest of all Sicilian sites, the mountain haunt of **Érice**, was dominated by Punic influence, the Carthaginians themselves entrenched in **Marsala**, at Sicily's westernmost point, for several hundred years; while the Saracen invaders took their first steps on the island at **Mazara del Vallo**, a town still strongly Arabic at heart. The Greeks never secured the same foothold in Sicily's west as elsewhere, although the remains at **Segesta** and **Selinunte** count among the island's best.

Trápani

Out on something of a limb, **TRÁPANI** is not the most enticing of Sicilian cities, more a port of call than a stop in itself. Today, the obvious move is to jump a hydrofoil to the offshore Égadi Islands (see below), or a ferry on to Tunisia. But throughout the early Middle Ages Trápani was a rich trading centre, halfway point for Tunis and Africa. However, all the medieval activity counts for nothing today, and despite the recent revitalisation of the huge salt pans to the south of town, Trápani is in firm decline: the old centre of town has been depopulated, most people moving to the gridded hinterland of modern Trápani. But you might end up spending time here if you're on your way either to Érice or Segesta and there's enough left of the old town to occupy the hours waiting for a bus or ferry.

The Town

Trápani's **old town**, broadly speaking the area west of the railway station, sports a mix of often incongruous architectural styles, something that harks back to Trápani's past as a complex medieval Mediterranean trading centre. It's particularly true of the medieval Jewish quarter, a wedge of hairline streets and alleys that holds one of the city's most characteristic buildings, the **Palazzo della Giudecca** on Via Giudecca – sixteenth-century, with a stone-studded tower and finely wrought Spanish-style Plateresque windows. Just up from here, Trápani is at its most engaging, Corso Italia preceding a confused set of three piazzas, enlivened by their surrounding churches: one doorway of the sixteenth-century **Chiesa di Santa Maria di Gesu** (Via San Pietro) is defiantly Renaissance in execution, and further up, on Piazzetta Saturno, the church of **Sant'Agostino** is even earlier, fourteenth-century and retaining a Gothic portal and delicate rose window – and doing service during the day as a local art gallery.

Off the Piazzetta, Via Torrearsa neatly splits the old town. West of here Trápani's layout becomes more regularly planned, while the main drag and shopping street, the elegant **Corso Vittorio Emanuele**, changes name a couple of times as it runs towards the **Torre di Ligny** – utmost point of the scimitar of land that holds the old town. The squat tower hides Trápani's only other museum, an archaeological collection of fairly dull content, but the water here is clean enough should you to want to swim off the rocks. Finish off your circuit at the daily **market**, at the northern end of Via Torrearsa – fish, fruit and veg sold from the arcaded Piazza Mercato di Pesce, and with several lively bars in the area.

Celebrations and processions at Easter in Trápani are given added piquancy by the carriage around town on Good Friday of the **Misteri**, a group of life-sized eighteenth-century wooden figures representing scenes from the Passion. At other times they are on display in town, though you'll have to ask at the EPT for their current whereabouts: their usual home, the exuberantly sculpted **Chiesa del Purgatorio**, is under restoration and the figures have been stored for the time being in the seventeenth-century **Chiesa di San Domenico** (daily 9–11.30am & 4–5.30pm), up a flight of steps off Via Garibaldi.

Other than arriving, you hardly need to set foot in the newer parts of the city. The only incentive is the interesting **Museo Nazionale Pepoli** (Tues–Sat 9am–1.30pm, Tues & Thurs also 4–6.30pm, Sun 9am–12.30pm; L2000), a good three-kilometre bus ride away in the drab heart of modern Trápani: take buses #1, #10 or #11 from Corso Vittorio Emanuele, Via Libertà or Via Garibaldi, and get off at the garden outside the Santuario Santissima Annunziata, the fourteenth-century convent which houses the museum. Approached through bird-filled cloisters, the collection includes a bit of everything, from Gagini statuary and local archaeological finds, to delicate seventeenth-century coral craftwork and some nice prints and drawings. Most striking exhibit, easily, is a grim wooden guillotine of 1789, awful in its simplicity.

Practical details

Come to Trápani by land from the east of the island and you'll arrive in the modern part of town: most **buses** (including those to and from Érice) pull up at the terminal in Piazza Malta, **trains** stop just around the corner off Piazza Umberto I. Exceptions to the rule are the fast **buses for Palermo and Agrigento**, which leave from Piazza Garibaldi. **Ferries/hydrofoils** for the Égadi Islands, Pantelleria, Cagliari and Tunis dock at the adjacent Molo di Sanita. For information, accommodation listings and free maps, visit the **EPT** offices in the railway station (Mon–Sat 8am–8pm), at the harbour (Mon–Sat 8–9am & 6–8pm), or in Piazzetta Saturno (Mon–Sat 9am–1pm & 2–8pm, Sun 9am–1pm).

Finding **somewhere to stay** at Easter will be tricky, unless you book well in advance, but at other times rooms are easy to come by. Best of the cheaper hotels is the *Messina*, Corso Vittorio Emanuele 71 (☎0923/21.198), where rooms cost L20,000 but are often fully booked; if it's full try the *Maccotta* on Via degli Argentieri (☎0923/28.418), which costs only slightly more. The nearest **camp-site** is a twenty-minute bus ride away at LIDO VALDÉRICE (☎0923/73.086; April to Sept) – five to seven buses daily from the bus terminal.

Eating is particularly good in Trápani. You can get fresh fish in the couple of trattorias along the harbour front, though you pay for location. The *Trattoria Safina*, opposite the railway station at Piazza Umberto I, is both cheap and excellent; for pizzas seek out *Pizzeria Mediterranea*, Corso Vittorio Emanuele 195, opposite Piazza Jolanda – a takeaway joint with a couple of tables at the back.

Out from Trápani: Érice and Segesta

The nearest and most exhilarating ride from Trápani is to ÉRICE, forty minutes away by bus. It's a mountain town with powerful associations: creeping hillside alleys, stone buildings and silent charm. Founded by Elymnians, who claimed descent from the Trojans, the original city was known to the ancient world as *Eryx*, and a magnificent temple, dedicated to Venus Erycina, Mediterranean goddess of fertility, once topped the mountain. Though the city was considered impregnable, Carthaginian, Roman, Arab and Norman forces all forced entry over the centuries. But all respected the sanctity of Érice: the Romans rebuilt the temple and set 200 soldiers to serve as guardians of the shrine; while the Arabs renamed the town *Gebel-Hamed*, or Mohammed's mountain.

If it's fine, the views from the terraces of Érice are stupendous – over Trápani, the slumbering whales of the Égadi Islands and on clear days as far as Cape Bon in Tunisia. Scout around the town at random: the most convoluted of routes is only going to take you a couple of hours and every street and piazza is a delight. You enter through the Norman **Porta Trápani**, just inside which the battle-mented fourteenth-century campanile of the **Chiesa Matrice** did service as a lookout tower for Frederick III of Aragon. From here there's no set route, though passing through pretty **Piazza Umberto** with its couple of outdoor bars is a good idea; and a natural start or finish could be made at the ivy-clad Norman **Castello** at the far end of town. This was built on the site of the famed ancient temple, chunks of which are incorporated in the walls.

Hardly surprisingly, **staying** in Érice means paying through the nose and booking in advance. The one relatively cheap choice, the *Edelweiss*, Cortile Padre Vincenzo (☎0923/869.158), on a cobbled alley off Piazzetta San Domenico, for L42,000. More economical, though usually open July and August only, is the **youth hostel** (☎0923/869.144), outside the town walls on Viale delle Pinete. Check with the helpful **AAST** (daily 8.30am–2pm & 4.30–7pm) on Viale Conte Pepoli, who also dish out maps. **Buses from Trápani** pull up on the same road. If you're coming for the day bring a picnic as there is nowhere to eat worthy of Érice's vastly inflated prices.

The Temple of Segesta

If time is limited, it's hard to know which to recommend most: the heights of Érice or Trápani's other local draw, the temple at **Segesta**. A Greek construction of 424 BC, though unfinished it's one of the most inspiring of Doric temples anywhere and, along with a brilliantly-sited theatre, virtually the only relic of an ancient city whose roots – like Érice – lie back in the twelfth century BC. Unlike Érice, though, ancient Segesta was eventually Hellenised and spent most of the later period disputing its borders with Selinus to the south. The temple dates from a time of prosperous alliance with Athens, the building abandoned when a new dispute broke out with Selinus in 416 BC.

The site is unenclosed, steps rising past a café and carpark to the **temple** itself, crowning a low hill. From a distance you could be forgiven for thinking that it's complete: the 36 regular white stone columns, entablature and pediment are all intact, and all it lacks is a roof. However, get closer and you see just how unfinished the building is: stone studs, always removed on completion, still line the stylobate, the tall columns are unfluted and the *cella* walls are missing. Below the carpark, a road (open to cars; daily 9am–1hr before sunset) winds up through slopes of wild fennel and marigolds to the small **theatre** on a higher hill beyond. The view from the top is justly lauded, across green slopes and the plain to the sea, the deep blue of the bay a lovely contrast to the theatre's white stone – not much damaged by the stilted motorway snaking away below.

Without your own transport **getting to Segesta** involves some walking, though nothing too offputting. The two daily **trains** from Trápani to Alcamo/Palermo make a stop at SEGESTA-TEMPIO, from where it's a twenty-minute walk uphill. To return, unless you make the 11.57am back from Segesta-Tempio, you'll have to walk from the site carpark to **CALATAFIMI**, a signposted 4km away, from where more frequent trains connect with Trápani. There's also a cheap **hotel**, the *Mille Pini* (☎0924/951.260), if you wanted to stay the night in the quiet surroundings.

The Égadi Islands

Of the various islands, islets and rock stacks that fan out from the west coast of Sicily, the three **Égadi Islands** (Isole Égadi) are best for a quick jaunt – connected by ferry and hydrofoil with Trápani. Saved from depopulation by tourism, in season at least you're not going to be alone, certainly on the main island,

Favignana. But a tour of the islands is worthwhile, not least for the caves that perforate the splintered coastlines. Out of season things are noticeably quieter: come between April and July and you may witness the bloody *Mattanza*, an age-old slaughter in this noted centre of tuna fishing.

All **transport** (ferries and hydrofoils several times daily in summer) to the islands departs from Trápani's Molo di Sanita; tickets from the office on Via Ammiraglio Staiti or hydrofoil tickets only from the booth on the dockside. Though less frequent, ferries are, as always, much cheaper.

FAVIGNANA, island and port town, is first stop for the boats from Trápani, a good base since it has virtually all the accommodation and the Égadi's only camp-sites. Only 25 minutes by hydrofoil from the mainland, the island attracts a lot of day-trippers, keen to get onto its few rocky beaches. But get out of the main port and it's easy enough to escape the crowds, even easier if you've brought a bike. (There's a bike rental shop, *Isidoro*, at Via Mozzini 40; around L5000 a day.) Caves all over the island bear prehistoric traces and many are accessible if you're determined enough. Otherwise, the two wings of the island invite separate walks, best the stroll around the eastern part, past the bizarre ancient quarries at Cala Rossa and taking in Lido Burrone, the island's best beach, only 3km from the port. Cheapest **hotel** is the *Egadi*, Via C. Colombo 17 (☎0923/921.232), right in the centre of Favignana town, and there are two **campsites** to the east of town – an easy walk and both well signposted.

LEVANZO, to the north, looks immediately inviting, its white houses against the turquoise sea reminiscent of the Greek islands. The steep coast is full of inlets and, again, is riddled with caves. One, the **Grotta del Genovese**, was discovered in 1949 and contains some remarkable Paleolithic incised drawings, 6000 years old, as well as later Neolithic pictures. To arrange to see the cave you'll have to contact the guardian, who lives at Via Calvario 11 (Signor Giusepe Castiglione; ☎0923/921.704), near the hydrofoil quay, and it's about an hour's walk from the village. There's one **hotel** on Levanzo, the *Paradiso* (☎0923/924.080), though in summer you have to pay half- or full-board. However, you should be able to get rooms in private houses if you ask around the port.

MARÉTTIMO, furthest out of the Égadi Islands, is the place to come for soli-tude. Very much off the beaten track, only a few tourists make it. More white houses scatter across the rocky island, while there's a bar in the main piazza and two restaurants. The spectacular fragmented coastline is pitted with rocky coves sheltering hideaway **beaches**, and there are numerous gentle **walks** which will take you all over the island. Again, although there are no hotels on Maréttimo you should be able to rent a room by asking at the café in the main square.

North: the coastal route to Palermo

Frequent buses run the first section of the route from Trápani, cutting away from the coast until reaching **SAN VITO LO CAPO** at the very nib of the northwest-ern headland. There are some good sands nearby, while the cape itself is only a stride away; and there are three **campsites** too – best value are *La Fata* (☎0923/972.133) and *Soleado* (☎0923/972.166), both open June to September. San Vito is a popular local holiday spot and you don't have to camp – there are several fairly cheap *pensioni* in the village too, as well as trattorias and bars catering to the summer crowds.

You'll have to return to Trápani for onward transport. Buses or, more frequently, **trains** cut across the headland to **CASTELLAMMARE DEL GOLFO**, another popular resort. There are a couple of upmarket hotels here if you want to stay, but a more attractive option is to catch the twice-daily bus (or walk/hitch the 10km) north to **SCOPELLO**. A tuna fishing centre, Gavin Maxwell lived here for several months in the early 1950s, an experience he recorded in his classic account of Sicilian life, *The Ten Pains of Death*. Scopello is still a fairly unspoiled fishing village, prettily sited, with more campsites around and – 3km inland at Scopello di Sopra – a choice of cheap **hotels**.

East of here (and the train from Trápani stops at every town before Palermo) it's a strange – often unpleasant – coastal mixture of industrialisation and tourist development. The wide and fertile gulf provides some good views though, and there's the occasional beach that beckons. The last few towns that line the gulf, **BALESTRATE**, **TRAPPETO** and, inland, **PARTINICO** are more interesting for what they were, and to some extent still are – infamous centres of Mafia influence and social and political neglect. **Daniel Dolci**, a social reformer of remarkable persistence, first came to Trappeto in 1952 from wealthy northern Italy. He was appalled. "Looking all around me, I saw no streets, just mud and dust. Not a single drugstore – or sewer. The dialect didn't even have a word for sewer." Dolci inaugurated a programme of self-help among the local people, building community and cultural centres, promoting local education – things that cut right across the traditional areas of influence in the Mafia-ridden west of Sicily. It's a story told in the words of the local people in Dolci's extraordinary book *Sicilian Lives*: vital reading if you intend to pass this way.

South: Marsala and Mazara del Vallo

Another section of the western rail loop runs south from Trápani down the coast, pretty much within sight of the sea all the way, trains ploughing across the cultivated plain, past white, squat houses and distant burned hills. The region flaunts its tangible non-Greek heritage even more in **MARSALA**, 10km on, which takes its name from the Arab *Marsah-el-Allah*, the port of Allah. Once the main Saracenic base in Sicily, since the late eighteenth century Marsala has been better known for the dessert wine that carries its name, something every bar and restaurant will sell you.

The centre of Marsala is extremely attractive, a clean sixteenth-century layout that's free of traffic and littered with high, ageing buildings and arcaded courtyards. But – pleasant as the town is – save your exploratory legs for two excellent museums. The most central, behind the cathedral at Via Garraffa 57, is the **Museo degli Arazzi** (daily 9am–1pm & 4–6pm; L1000) whose sole display is a series of eight enormous handstitched wool and silk tapestries depicting the capture of Jerusalem – sixteenth-century and beautifully rich, in burnished red, gold and green. Afterwards, walk out to the cape (follow the main Via XI Maggio to Piazza della Vittoria and bear left towards the water) and one of the stone-vaulted warehouses that line the promenade holds the equally impressive **Museo Marsala** (Mon–Sat 9am–2pm, Wed, Sat & Sun 3–6pm; free). An archaeological museum of quality, its major exhibit is a reconstructed Punic warship rowed by 68 oarsmen, probably sunk during the First Punic War and found in 1971. Finds from the ship are on display in the hall while other bits and pieces are from the excavated site (mostly Roman) of *Lilybaeum* (daily 9am–1hr before sunset), around the corner from the museum.

Half an hour further on, **MAZARA DEL VALLO** is one of the most powerfully atmospheric of Sicilian towns, Italy's most important fishing port and a place of equal distinction for the Arabs and Normans who dominated the island a thousand years ago. The first Saracen gain in Sicily, Mazara was Arabic for 250 years until captured by Count Roger in 1075: the island's first Norman parliament met in the town 22 years later, a relic of that period the tiny pink-domed Norman chapel of **San Nicolo**, a little way upriver from the harbour. All around, though, the atmosphere is pungently Arabic, North Africans crewing the colourful fishing boats which block the harbour and river, the old city *casbah* revitalised and a *hamman* advertised in Piazza Bagno. Wandering around the harbour area is easily the most rewarding thing to do in Mazara although you can spend an enjoyable hour or so as well on the seafront promenade, and poking around the **Museo Civico** (Mon–Sat 9am–1pm) in Piazza del Plebiscito, just off Mazara's main square.

East to Sciacca: bandits, Greek temples and thermal baths

There's very little else to stop for around the western coast; even less inland, which is crossed by only one major road, the SS188 running from Marsala to SALEMI. But the southernmost chunk of Sicily's western bulge is easily reached – again by train – and has several places worth more than a cursory glance.

CASTELVETRANO isn't necessarily one of them. If anyone stops at all, it's to take in the nearby Greek ruins at Selinunte (see below), though this can be much better done from the coastal fishing village next to the site. But the centre of Castelvetrano is handsome and you may be intrigued enough by the story of Sicily's most famous bandit, **Salvatore Giuliano**, to want to stop. Less a Robin Hood figure than a political pawn caught between the regrouping Mafia and the Sicilian separatists after the World War II, Giuliano got a sympathetic press – and much covert support – from the local people hereabouts. But like all true folk heroes he was eventually betrayed, his bullet-riddled body found in one of Castelvetrano's courtyards in 1950.

If you're **staying overnight** to see Selinunte, the *Hotel Ideal* (☎0924/44.299), Via Partanna 26, has rooms for L25,000. To get to the site, take a bus from the station down to Marinella on the coast – seven daily, a twenty-minute ride.

Selinunte

The Greek city of Selinus (Selinunte in modern Italian), most westerly of the Hellenic colonies, reached its peak in the fifth century BC when a series of mighty temples were erected. A bitter rival of Segesta, whose lands lay adjacent to the north, the powerful city and its fertile plain attracted enemies hand over fist, and it was only a matter of time before Selinus caught the eye of Segesta's ally, Carthage. Geographically vulnerable, the city was sacked by Carthaginians, any recovery forestalled by earthquakes which later razed the city. Despite the destruction, which left the site completely abandoned until it was rediscovered in the sixteenth century, the ruins of Selinus have exerted a romantic hold ever since.

The site is just west of the village of **MARINELLA**, a better place to stay than Castelvetrano: there are several **hotels**, the ones overlooking the excellent beach expensive, but the *Pensione Costa D'Avorio* (☎0924/46.011), at Via Stazione 5, has rooms for L26,000. There are two **campsites** on the main Castelvetrano road (the bus passes them both), though no one minds if you camp out at the *Mare Pineta*; left from the station and follow the signs to the tree-backed **beach**.

The **site** of Selinus is back behind the main part of the village, split into two parts, with temples in each, known only as Temples A–G. The first stop is at the **East Group**, just over the railway line, the entrance through a carpark and open all the time. Shrouded in the wild celery which gave the ancient city its name, the temples are in various stages of reconstructed ruin: the most complete the one nearest the sea (Temple E), the northernmost (Temple G) a tangle of columned wreckage six metres high in places. The road leads down from here, across the (now buried) site of the old harbour to the second part of excavated Selinus, the **acropolis** (daily 9am–1hr before sunset; L2000), a site containing what remains of the other temples (five in all), as well as the well preserved city streets and massive, stepped walls which rise above the duned beach below. Temple C stands on the highest point of the acropolis, and there are glorious views from its stones out over the sparkling sea: from this temple were removed some of the best metopes (decorative panels), now on show in Palermo's archaeological museum.

To Sciacca

FS **buses** leave from outside Castelvetrano railway station six times daily for Sciacca, picking up at Selinunte station in Marinella village. **SCIACCA**'s upper town is skirted by good medieval walls which form high sides to the steep streets, rising to a ruined Spanish castle. Below, the lower town sits on a clifftop terrace overlooking the harbour, a place where it's easy to while away time drinking in the coastal views. Hot springs 8km from town (at Monte San Calogero) kept the Romans healthy and are still in use. Get there on bus #5 every hour and a half from Sciacca; check on details in the **AAST**, Corso Vittorio Emanuele 84.

Sciacca would be a nice place to stop over – there's an active harbour here and some good beaches close by – and the *Pensione Buenos Aires*, on Via Triolo (☎0925/21.837), has rooms for L20,000. There are also a couple of **campsites** 4km west of town (direct bus June to Sept) at Contrada Foggia, off the SS115.

Pantelleria

Forty kilometres nearer to Tunisia than to Sicily, **PANTELLERIA** is the most singular of Sicily's outlying islands. Volcanic, it has been settled since Neolithic times and later supported a Phoenician colony in the seventh century BC. Its strategic position kept it in the mainstream of Sicilian history for years: developed as one of the main Mediterranean bases by the Fascists during World War II, Pantelleria was bombed without mercy by the Allies in May 1943 as they advanced from North Africa. In part, this explains the morose appearance of the island's main town (also called Pantelleria) – thrown up in unedifying concrete.

There's more than enough that's attractive on the rest of the island, though, to compensate. You're going to have to walk to most places, not something you should tire of through a fertile countryside covered in vineyards and the traditional houses or *dammuso*. Skirted by dry stone walls, they are domed, a throw-back to the buildings of Neolithic times. Major landmark on the island – visible from the ships heading for Malta – is the spent volcano, **Montagna Grande** (836m), to the summit of which there's a track from the old town of Siba. At some stage refresh yourself with the local wine: the island's myriad vineyards produce *Tanit*, a rightly appreciated raisin wine.

Practical details

You **arrive** in the main town and port of Pantelleria. Ferries from Trápani do the journey in five hours for around L23,000 one-way and there's generally one a day in summer; hydrofoils run three times weekly in summer, taking two to three hours and costing around L30,000 one-way. There are also daily flights from Trápani and Palermo, which tourist discounts can make a viable option; a bus connects arrivals with Pantelleria town.

Accommodation is fairly expensive; best budget choice is the *Miryam* on Corso Umberto I (☎0923/911.374) for L36,000, with the *Agadir*, on Via Catania (☎0923/911.100) a good second. There's no **campsite** on the island and camping rough is impractical given the terrain and the lack of water. Better to contact an agency dealing in stays in the *dammuso* houses around the island: try *Dammuso* on Cotrada San Vito (☎0923/911.827). Don't expect **food** to be cheap either, though you should try the local speciality, a sort of fish couscous.

travel details

Trains

From Palermo to Milazzo/Messina (up to 16 daily; 3hr/3hr 30min–6hr); Enna/Catania (5 daily; 2hr/3hr 10min); Agrigento (11 daily; 2hr 30min); Trápani (10 daily; 2hr); Castelvetrano/Mazara del Vallo/Marsala/Trápani (10 daily; 2hr/2hr 30min/3hr/4hr); Términi Imerese (hourly; 35min).

From Términi Imerese to Cefalù (hourly; 30min).

From Messina to Taormina/Catania (approx every 40min; 1hr/1hr 30min); Cefalù/Palermo (up to 16 daily; 2hr 45min/3hr 30min–6hr).

From Taormina to Messina (approx half-hourly; 1hr); Catania/Siracusa (13 daily; 45min/2hr 15min); Randazzo (3–5 daily; 1hr).

From Catania to Siracusa (hourly; 1hr 30min); Taormina/Messina (every 40min; 1hr/1hr 30min); Enna (9 daily; 1hr 30min); Palermo (4 daily; 3hr 15min); Caltagirone/Gela (9 daily; 2hr/2hr 40min).

From Siracusa to Catania (18 daily; 1hr 30min); Messina (14 daily; 3hr); Noto (11 daily; 40min); Ragusa (6 daily; 2hr 20min); Gela (3; 4hr).

From Ragusa to Gela (7 daily; 1hr 20min); Módica (12 daily; 25min).

From Enna to Catania (9 daily; 1hr 20min).

From Trápani to Segesta-Tempio (3 daily; 30min); Marsala/Mazara del Vallo/Castelvetrano (10 daily; 25min/50min/1hr 10min).

Circumetnea trains

From Catania to Randazzo (11 daily; 2hr 10min).

From Randazzo to Riposto (8 daily; 1hr 15min).

Buses

From Palermo to Catania (hourly; 2hr 40min); Messina (1 daily; 4hr 30min); Trápani (hourly; 1hr 45min); Siracusa (4 daily Mon–Sat; 4hr 45min); Agrigento (3–4; 2hr 15min); Enna (2–4; 1hr 50min); Bagheria (hourly; 20min); Términi Imerese (5 daily Mon–Sat; 40min); Piana degli Albanesi (9 daily Mon–Sat; 2 Sun; 30min); Cefalù (Mon–Sat 2 daily; 1hr).

From Términi Imerese to Cefalù (Mon–Sat 1 daily ; 30min).

From Milazzo to Messina (hourly; 40min).

From Messina to Taormina (Mon–Sat half-hourly, Sun 6 daily; 1hr 30min); Catania (Mon–Sat 11 daily, Sun 5; 3hr); Giardini-Naxos/Randazzo (Mon–Sat 4 daily; 55min/2hr 15min).

From Taormina to Castelmola (5–6 daily; 20min).

From Santa Teresa di Riva to Sávoca/Casalvécchio Sículo (Mon–Sat 5 daily, 3 Sun; 20min/30min).

From Catania to Nicolosi (hourly; 40min); Messina (6–12 daily; 3hr 10min); Agrigento (2–4 daily; 2hr 50min); Siracusa (Mon–Sat 7 daily, Sun 1; 1hr 15min); Noto (Mon–Sat 5 daily, Sun 1; 2hr

15min); Caltagirone (Mon–Sat 7 daily; 1hr 30min); Piazza Armerina (Mon–Sat 5 daily, Sun 2; 2hr); Gela (Mon–Sat 7 daily, Sun 2; 2hr); Ragusa (4–8 daily; 3hr).

From Siracusa to Catania (Mon–Sat 7 daily, Sun 1; 1hr 15min); Ragusa (Mon–Sat 8 daily, Sun 1; 1hr 30min); Noto (half-hourly; 40min); Caltagirone/Piazza Armerina (Mon–Sat 1 daily; 2hr/2hr 30min).

From Ragusa to Módica (half-hourly, Sun 6; 20min).

From Siracusa to Ragusa (Mon–Sat 8 daily, Sun 1; 1hr 30min); Noto (half-hourly; 40min); Caltagirone/Piazza Armerina (Mon–Sat 1 daily; 2hr/2hr 30min).

From Ragusa to Módica (half-hourly, Sun 6; 20min).

From Enna to Catania (3–7 daily; 1hr 20min); Piazza Armerina/Gela (1–2 daily; 45min/1hr 40min).

From Agrigento to Porto Empédocle (half-hourly until 8.30pm; 20min); Trápani (Mon–Sat 2 daily; 3hr 30min).

From Trápani to Érice (Mon–Sat 11 daily, Sun 5; 40min).

From Castelvetrano to Marinella (for Selinunte, Mon–Sat 7 daily; 20min); Mazara del Vallo/ Marsala/Trápani (7 daily; 20min/40min/1hr 30min).

Ferries

Most of the services detailed below refer to the June to September period; expect greatly reduced frequencies outside these months, especially to the Aeolian Islands..

From Messina to Villa San Giovanni (*FS* every 45min, *Caronte* every 20min, less at night; 35min); Réggio di Calabria (*FS* 10 daily; 50min).

From Messina to Réggio di Calabria (Mon–Fri every 40min, Sat hourly; 15min); Vulcano/Lípari (4 daily in summer, 2 in winter; 1hr 45min–3hr); Naples (1 daily in summer; 6hr).

From Palermo to Ústica (6–7 weekly; 2hr 45min); Livorno (3 weekly; 18hr); Genova (4 weekly; 23hr); Naples (1 daily; 11hr); Cágliari (1 weekly; 12hr 30min).

From Milazzo to Vulcano/Lípari/Salina/Panarea/ Strómboli/Naples (5 weekly; 16hr 30min); Vulcano/Lípari (2 daily; 1hr 30min/2hr 15min); Salina (2; 3hr 30min); Filicudi/Alicudi (4 weekly, 4hr 30min/6hr).

From Lípari to Milazzo (4 daily; 2hr); Vulcano (4; 30min); Salina/Panarea/Strómboli/Naples (5

weekly; 14hr); Salina (1–2 daily; 50min); Filicudi/ Alicudi (5 weekly; 2hr 25min/3hr 45min).

From Catania to Siracusa (3 weekly; 2hr 15min); Réggio di Calabria (3 weekly; 3hr 15min); Naples (1 weekly; 15hr).

From Porto Empédocle to Linosa/Lampedusa (June to Sept 1 daily at midnight; 6hr/8hr 15min; rest of the year 1 daily Mon–Sat at midnight).

From Lampedusa to Pantelleria (1 weekly on Thurs at 8am; 6hr); Trápani (2 weekly, on Tues at noon, Sun at 8am; 10hr).

From Trápani to Favignana/Lévanzo/Maréttimo (6–7 weekly; 55min/1hr 40min/2hr 50min); Pantelleria (6–7 weekly; 5hr); Lampedusa (2 weekly; 10hr 30min); Cagliari (1 weekly; 11hr).

Hydrofoils

Again, bear in mind that most of the services below are greatly reduced outside summer.

From Palermo to Ústica (1–2 daily; 1hr 15min); Naples (3 weekly; 5hr 20min); summer services to Cefalù (3 weekly; 1hr 10min) and the Aeolian Islands (1–2 daily; 3hr 30min to Lipari).

From Ústica to Naples/Capri (3 weekly; 4hr/5hr 30min); Favignana/Trápani (3 weekly; 2hr/2hr 30min).

From Cefalù to Palermo (3 weekly; 1hr 10min); Vulcano/Lípari (3 weekly; 1hr 50min/2hr 10min).

From Milazzo to Vulcano/Lípari (half-hourly; 40min/55min); Salina (8 daily; 1hr 25min); Panarea/Strómboli (6 daily; 2hr 30min/3hr); Filicudi/Alicudi (1 daily; 2hr/2hr 30min); Naples (1; 4–6hr).

From Lípari to Palermo (2 daily; 3hr 30min); Cefalù (3 weekly; 2hr 10min); Capo d'Orlando/ Sant'Agata (3 daily; 1hr/1hr 30min); Mílazzo (half-hourly; 55min); Messina/Réggio di Calabria (4 daily; 1hr 30min/2hr); Vibo Valentia (Wed–Sun 1 daily; 3hr); Naples (1 daily; 5hr 30min); Vulcano (every 45min; 10min); Salina (12 daily; 15min); Panarea/Strómboli (10 daily; 30min/1hr); Filicudi/ Alicudi (4 daily; 1hr/1hr 30min).

From Trápani to Favignana/Lévanzo/Maréttimo (10 daily; 20min/35min/1hr 5min); Pantelleria (3 weekly; 2hr 15min); Ústica (3 weekly; 2hr 30min); Naples (3 weekly; 6hr 45min).

From Pantelleria to Trápani (3 weekly; 2hr 15min).

Planes

From Palermo to Lampedusa (2 daily; 45min); Pantelleria (1 daily; 35min)

From Trápani to Pantelleria (2–3 daily; 30min).

PART THREE

THE
CONTEXTS

HISTORICAL FRAMEWORK

A specific Italian history is hard to iden-tify. Italy wasn't formally a united country until 1861, and the history of the peninsula after the Romans is more one of warring city states and colonisation and annexa-tion by foreign powers. It's inconceivable now that Italy should fragment once again, although the regional differences do to some extent remain.

EARLY TIMES

A smattering of remains exist from the Neanderthals who occupied the Italian penin-sula half a million years ago, but the main period of colonisation began after the last Ice Age. Evidence of **Paleolithic** settlements dates from this time, around 20,000 BC, the next development being the spread of **Neolithic** tribes across the peninsula, between 5000 and 6000 years ago. More sophisticated tribes developed towards the end of the prehistoric period, beteen 2400 and 1800 BC – those which left the most visible traces were the **Ligurians** (who inhabited a much greater area than modern Liguria), the **Siculi** of southern Italy and Latium, and the **Sards**, who farmed and raised livestock on Sardinia. More advanced still were migrant groups from the eastern Mediterranean, who introduced the techniques of working copper. Later, various **Bronze Age** societies (1600–1000 BC) built a network of farms and villages in the Apennines, and on the Sicilian and southern coasts, the latter population trading with Mycenaeans in Greece.

Other tribes brought Indo-European languages into Italy. The Veneti, Latins and Umbrii moved down the peninsula from the north, whilst the Piceni and the Messapians in Apulia crossed the Adriatic from modern-day Yugoslavia. The artificial line between prehis-tory and history is drawn around the eighth century BC, with the arrival of the **Phoenician** alphabet and writing system. Sailing west along the African coast, the Phoenicians estab-lished colonies in Sicily and Sardinia, going on to build trade links between Carthage and southern Italy. These soon encouraged the arri-val of the **Carthaginians**, who set themselves up on Sicily, Sardinia and the Latium coast, at the same time as both **Greeks** and **Etruscans** were gaining influence.

ETRUSCANS AND GREEKS

Greek settlers colonised parts of the Tuscan coast, and the Bay of Naples in the eighth century BC, moving on to **Naxos**, on Sicily's Ionian coast, and founding the city of Syracuse in the year 736 BC. The colonies they estab-lished in Sicily and southern Italy came to be know as **Magna Graecia**. Along with Etruscan cities to the north they are the earliest Italian civilisations leaving substantial buildings and written records.

The Greek settlements were hugely success-ful, introducing the vine and the olive to Italy, and establishing a high-yielding agricultural system. Cities like **Syracuse** and **Tarentum** were wealthier and more sophisticated than those on mainland Greece, dominating trade in the central Mediterranean, despite competition from Carthage. Ruins such as the temples of **Agrigento** and **Selinunte**, the fortified walls around **Gela**, and the theatres at Syracuse and Taormina on Sicily attest to a great prosperity, and *Magna Graecia* became an enriching influ-ence on the culture of the Greek homeland – Archimedes, Aeschylus and Empedocles were all from Sicily. Yet these colonies suffered from the same factionalism as the Greek states, and the cities of Tarentum, Metapontum, Sybaris and Croton were united only when faced with the threat of outside invasion. From 400 BC, after Sybaris was razed to the ground, the other colonies went into irreversible economic decline, to become satellite states of Rome.

The **Etruscans** were the other major civilisation of the period, mostly living in the area between the **Tiber** and **Arno** rivers. Their language, known mostly from funerary texts, is one of the last relics of an ancient language common to the Mediterranean. Some say they arrived in Italy around the ninth century BC from western Anatolia, others that they came from the north, and a third hypothesis places their origins in Etruria. Whatever the case, they set up a cluster of **twelve city states** in northern Italy, traded with Greek colonies to the south and were the most powerful people in northern Italy by the sixth century BC, edging out the indigenous population of Ligurians, Latins and Sabines. Tomb frescoes in Umbria depict a refined and luxurious culture with highly developed systems of divination, based on the reading of animal entrails and the flight of birds. Herodotus wrote that the Etruscans recorded their ancestry along the female line, and tomb excavations last century revealed that women were buried in special sarcophagi carved with their names. Well preserved chamber tombs with wall paintings exist at **Cerveteri** and **Tarquinia**, the two major sites in Italy. The Etruscans were technically advanced, creating new agricultural land through irrigation and building their cities on ramparted hill tops – a pattern of settlement that has left a permanent mark on central Italy. Their kingdom contracted, however, after invasions by the **Cumans**, **Syracusans** and **Gauls**, and was eventually forced into alliance with the embryonic Roman state.

ROMAN ITALY

The growth of **Rome**, a border town between the Etruscans and the Latins, gained impetus around 600 BC from a coalition of Latin and Sabine communities. The **Tarquins**, an Etruscan dynasty, oversaw the early expansion, but in 509 BC the Romans ejected the Etruscan royal family and became a **republic**, with power shared jointly between two consuls, both elected for one year. Further changes came half a century later, after a protracted class struggle that resulted in the **Law of the Twelve Tables**, which made patricians and plebeians equal. Now stabilised, the Romans

set out to systematically conquer the northern peninsula, and after the fall of **Veii** in 396 BC, succeeded in capturing **Sutri** and **Nepi**, towns which Livy considered the "barriers and gateways of Etruria". Various wars and truces with other cities brought about agreements to pay harsh tributes.

The **Gauls** captured Rome in 390, refusing to leave until they had received a vast payment, but this proved a temporary reversal. The Romans took **Campania** and the fertile land of **Apulia** after defeating the **Samnites** in battles over a period of 35 years. They then set their sights on the wealthy Greek colonies to the south, including Tarentum, whose inhabitants turned to the Greek king, **Pyrrhus of Epirus** for military support. He initially repelled the Roman invaders, but lost his advantage and was defeated at **Beneventum** in 275 BC. The Romans had by then established their rule in most of southern Italy, and now became a threat to Carthage. In 264 they had the chance of obtaining **Sicily**, when the Mamertines, a mercenary army in control of Messina, appealed to them for help against the Carthaginians. The Romans obliged – sparking off the **First Punic War** – and took most of the island, together with Sardinia and Corsica. With their victory in 222 BC over the Gauls in the Po valley, all Italy was now under Roman control.

They also turned a subsequent military threat to their advantage, in what came to be known as the **Second Punic War**. The Carthaginians had watched the spread of Roman power across the Mediterranean with some alarm, and at the end of the third century BC allowed **Hannibal** to make an Alpine crossing into Italy with his army of infantry, horsemen and elephants. Hannibal crushed the Roman legions at Lago Trasimeno and Cannae (216 BC), and then halted at Capua. With remarkable cool, considering Hannibal's proximity, **Scipio** set sail on a retaliatory mission to the Carthaginian territory of **Spain**, taking Cartagena, and continuing his journey into **Africa**. The Carthaginians recalled Hannibal, who was finally defeated by Roman troops at **Zama** in 202 BC. It was another fifty years before Carthage was taken, closely followed by all of Spain, but the Romans were busy in the meantime adding **Macedonian Greece** to their territory.

These conquests gave Roman citizens a tax-free existence subsidised by captured treasure, but society was sharply divided into those enjoying the benefits, and those who were not. The former belonged mostly to the **senatorial party**, who ignored demands for reform by their opposition, the **popular party**. The radical reforms sponsored by the tribune **Gaius Gracchus** came too close to democracy for the senatorial party, whose declaration of martial law was followed by the assassination of Gracchus. The majority of people realised that the only hope of gaining influence was through the army, but **General Gaius Marius**, put into power, was ineffective against the senatorial clique, who systematically picked off the new regime.

The first century BC saw **civil strife** on an unprecedented scale. Although Marius was still in power, another general, **Sulla**, was in the ascendancy, leading military campaigns against northern invaders and rebellious subjects in the south. Sulla subsequently took power and established his dictatorship in Rome, throwing out a populist government which had formed while he was away on a campaign in the east. Murder and exile were common, and cities which had sided with Marius during their struggle for power were punished with massacres and destruction. Thousands of Sulla's war veterans were given confiscated land, but much of it was laid to waste. In 73 BC a gladiator named **Spartacus** led 70,000 dispossessed farmers and escaped slaves in a revolt, which lasted for two years before they were defeated by the legions.

JULIUS CAESAR AND AUGUSTUS

Rome became calmer only after Sulla's death, when **Pompey**, another general, and **Licinus Crassus**, a rich builder, became masters of Rome. Pompey's interest lay in lucrative wars elsewhere, so his absence from the capital gave **Julius Caesar** the chance to make a name for himself as an orator and raiser of finance. When Pompey returned in 60 BC, he made himself, Crassus and Caesar rulers of the **first Triumvirate**.

Caesar bought himself the post of consul in 59 BC, then spent the next eight years on campaigns againt the **Gauls**. His military success needled Pompey, and trouble began. Pompey eventually turned against his

colleague, giving Caesar the chance to hit back. In 49 BC he crossed the river **Rubicon**, committing the offence of entering Roman territory with an army without first informing the Senate, but when he reached the city there was no resistance – everyone had fled, and Caesar became absolute ruler of Rome. He spent the next four years on civil reforms, writing his history of the Gallic wars, and chasing Pompey and his followers through Spain, Greece and Egypt. A group of enemies within the Senate, including his adopted son **Brutus**, conspired to murder him in 44 BC, a few months after he had been appointed ruler for life. **Octavian**, Caesar's nephew and heir, Lepidus, and Marcus Antonius (**Mark Anthony**) formed the **second Triumvirate** the following year. Again, the arrangement was fraught with tensions, the battle for power this time being between Anthony and Octavian. While Anthony was with **Cleopatra**, Octavian spent his time developing his military strength and the final, decisive battle took place at **Actium** in 31 BC, where Anthony committed suicide.

As sole ruler of the new regime, Octavian, renaming himself **Augustus Caesar**, embarked on a series of reforms and public works, giving himself complete powers despite his unassuming official title of "First Citizen".

THE EMPERORS

Tiberius (AD 14–37), the successor to Augustus, ruled wisely, but thereafter began a period of decadence. During the psychopathic reign of **Caligula** (37–41) the civil service kept the empire running; **Claudius** (41–54) conquered southern Britain, and was succeeded by his stepson **Nero** (54–68), who murdered his mother Agrippina and his wife Octavia, moving on to violent persecution of the **Christians**. Nero committed suicide when threatened by a coup, leading to a rapid succession of four emperors in the year 68. The period of prosperity during the rule of the **Flavian** Emperors (Vespasian and his sons Titus and Domitian) was a forerunner for the **Century of the Antonines**, a period named after the successful reigns of Nerva, Trajan, Hadrian, Antonius and **Marcus Aurelius**. These generals consolidated the empire's infrastructure, and created an encouraging environment for artistic achievement. A prime example is the formidable bronze equestrian statue of Marcus Aurelius in Rome – a work not equalled in sophistication until the Renaissance.

A troubled period followed under the rule of Marcus Aurelius' son **Commodus** (180–93) and his successors, none of whom were wholly in control of the legions. Artistic, intellectual and religious life stagnated, and the balance of economic development tilted in favour of the north, while the agricultural south grew ever more impoverished.

BARBARIANS AND BYZANTINES

In the middle of the third century, incursions by **Goths** in Greece, the Balkans and Asia, and the **Franks** and **Alamanni** in Gaul foreshadowed the collapse of the empire. **Aurelian** (270–75) re-established some order after terrible civil wars, to be followed by **Diocletian** (284–305), whose persecution of Christians produced many of the Church's present-day saints. **Plagues** had decimated the population, but problems of a huge but static economy were compounded by the doubling in size of the army at this time to about half a million men. To ease administration, Diocletian **divided the empire** into two halves, east and west, basing himself as ruler of the western empire in Mediolanum (Milan). This measure brought about a relative recovery, coinciding with the rise of **Christianity**, declared the state religion during the reign of **Constantine** (306–337). **Constantinople**, capital of the eastern empire, became a thriving trading and manufacturing city, while Rome itself went into decline, as the enlargement of the senatorial estates and the impoverishment of the lower classes gave rise to something comparable to a primitive feudal system.

Barbarians (meaning outsiders, or foreigners) had been crossing the border into the empire since 376 AD, when the **Ostrogoths** were driven from their kingdom in southern Russia by the **Huns**, a tribe of ferocious horsemen. The Huns went on to attack the **Visigoths**, 70,000 of whom crossed the border and settled inside the empire. When the Roman aristocracy saw that the empire was no longer a shield against barbarian raids, they were less inclined to pay for its support, seeing that a more comfortable future lay in being on good terms with the barbarian successor states.

By the fifth century, many legions were made up of troops from conquered territories, and several posts of high command were held by outsiders. With little will or loyalty behind it, the empire floundered, and on New Year's Eve of 406, Vandals, Alans and Sueves crossed the frozen Rhine into Gaul, chased by the Huns from their kingdoms in what are now Hungary and Austria. Once this had happened, there was no effective frontier. A contemporary writer lamented that "the whole of Gaul is smoking like an enormous funeral pyre". Despite this shock, worse was to come. By 408, the imperial government in **Ravenna** could no longer hold off **Alaric** (commander of Illyricum – modern Yugoslavia), and he went on to **sack Rome** in 410, causing a crisis of morale in the west. "When the whole world perished in one city," wrote Saint Jerome, "then I was dumb with silence."

The bitter **end of the Roman Empire** in the west came after **Valentinian III**'s assassination in 455. His eight successors over the next twenty years were finally ignored by the Germanic troops in the army, who elected their general **Odoacer** as king. The remaining Roman aristocracy hated him, and the eastern emperor, **Zeno**, who in theory now ruled the whole empire, refused to recognise him. In 488, Zeno rid himself of the Ostrogoth leader **Theodoric** by persuading him to march on Odoacer in Italy. By 493, Theodoric had succeeded, becoming ruler of the western territories.

A lull followed. The Senate in Rome and the civil service continued to function, and the remains of the empire were still administered under Roman law. Ostrogothic rule of the west continued after Theodoric's death, but in the 530s the eastern emperor, **Justinian**, began to plan the reunification of the Roman Empire "up to the two oceans". In 536 his general **Belisarius** landed in Sicily and moved north through Rome to Ravenna; complete reconquest was achieved in 552, after which the empire remained virtually intact for 500 years.

During this time the **Christian Church** developed as a more or less independent authority, since the Emperor was at a safe distance in Constantinople. Continual invasions had led to an uncertain political scene in which the **bishops of Rome** emerged with the strongest voice – justification of their primacy having already been given by Pope Leo I (440–461), who spoke his right to "rule all who are ruled in the first instance by Christ". A confused period of rule followed, as armies from northern Europe tried to take more territory from the old empire.

LOMBARDS AND FRANKS

During the chaotic sixth century, the **Lombards**, a Germanic tribe, were driven southwest into Italy. Rome was successfully defended against them, but by the eighth century the Lombards were extending their power throughout the peninsula. In the middle of that century the **Franks** arrived from Gaul. They were orthodox Christians, and therefore acceptable to Gallo-Roman nobility, integrating quickly and taking over much of the provincial administration. The Franks were ruled by the Merovingian royal family, but the mayors of the palace – the Carolingians – began to take power in real terms. Led by **Pepin the Short**, they saw an advantage in supporting the papacy, giving Rome large endowments and forcibly converting pagans in areas they conquered. When Pepin wanted to oust the Merovingians, and become King of the Franks, he appealed to the pope in Rome for his blessing, who was happy to agree, anointing the new Frankish king with holy oil.

This alliance was useful to both parties. In 755 the pope called on the Frankish army to confront the Lombards. The Franks forced them to hand over treasure and 22 cities and castles, which then became the northern part of the **papal states**. Pepin died in 768, with the Church indebted to him. According to custom, he divided the kingdom between his two sons, one of whom died within three years. The other was Charles the Great, or **Charlemagne**.

An intelligent and innovative leader, Charlemagne was proclaimed King of the Franks and of the Lombards, and patrician of the Romans, after a decisive war against the Lombards in 774. On Christmas Day of the year 800, Pope Leo III expressed his gratitude for Charlemagne's political support by crowning him **Emperor of the Holy Roman Empire**, an investiture that forged an enduring link between the fortunes of Italy and those of northern Europe. By the time Charlemagne died, all of Italy from south of Rome to Lombardy, including Sardinia, was part of the

huge **Carolingian empire**. The parts which didn't come under his domain were Sicily and the southern coast, which were gradually being reconquered by Arabs from Tunisia, and Apulia and Calabria, colonised by Byzantines and Greeks.

The task of holding these gains was beyond Charlemagne's successors, and by the beginning of the tenth century the family was extinct and the rival Italian states had become prizes for which the western (French) and eastern (German) Frankish kingdoms competed. Power switched in 936 to **Otto**, king of the eastern Franks. Political disunity in Italy invited him to intervene, and in 962 he was crowned emperor; Otto's son and grandson (Ottos II and III) set the seal on the renewal of the Holy Roman Empire.

POPES AND EMPERORS

On the death of **Otto III** in 1002, Italy was again without a recognised ruler. In the north, noblemen jockeyed for power, and the papacy was manipulated by rival Roman families. The most decisive events were in the south, where Sicily, Calabria and Apulia were captured by the **Normans**, who proved effective administrators and synthesised their own culture with the existing half-Arabic, half-Italian south. At **Palermo** in the eleventh century they created the most dynamic culture of the Mediterranean world.

Meanwhile in Rome, a series of reforming popes began to strengthen the church. **Gregory VII**, elected in 1073, was the most radical, demanding the right to depose emperors if he so wished. **Emperor Henry IV** was equally determined for this not to happen. The inevitable quarrel broke out, over a key appointment to the archbishopric of Milan. Henry denounced Gregory as "now not pope, but false monk", the pope responded by excommunicating him, thereby freeing his subjects from their allegiance. By 1077 Henry was aware of his tactical error and tried to make amends by visiting the pope at **Canossa**, where the emperor, barefoot and penitent, was kept waiting outside for three days. The formal reconciliation thus did nothing to heal the rift, and Henry's son, **Henry V**, continued the feud, eventually coming to a compromise in which the emperor kept control of bishops' land-ownership, while giving up rights over their investiture.

After this symbolic victory, the papacy developed into the most comprehensive and advanced centralised government in Europe in the realms of law and finance, but it wasn't long before unity came under attack again. This time, the threat came from **Emperor Frederick I** (Barbarossa), who besieged many northern Italian cities from his base in Germany from 1154. **Pope Alexander III** responded with ambiguous pronouncements about the imperial crown being a "benefice" which the pope conferred, implying that the emperor was the pope's vassal. The issue of papal or imperial supremacy was to polarise the country for the next two hundred years, almost every part of Italy being torn by struggles between **Guelphs** (supporting the pope) and **Ghibellines** (the emperor).

Henry's son, **Frederick II**, assumed the imperial throne at the age of three and a half, inheriting the Norman **Kingdom of Sicily**. Later linked by marriage to the great **Hohenstaufen** dynasty in Germany, he inevitably turned his attentions to northern Italy. However, his power-base was small, and opposition from Italian comunes and the papacy snowballed into **civil war**. His sudden death in 1250 marked a major downturn in imperial fortunes.

THE EMERGENCE OF CITY STATES

Charles of Anjou, brother of King Louis IX of France, defeated Frederick II's heirs in southern Italy, and received **Naples** and **Sicily** as reward from the pope. His oppressive government finally provoked an uprising on Easter Monday 1282, a revolt that came to be known as the **Sicilian Vespers**, as some 2000 occupying soldiers were murdered in Palermo at the sound of the bell for vespers. For the next twenty years the French were at war with **Peter of Aragon**, who took Sicily and then tried for the southern mainland.

If imperial power was on the defensive, the papacy was in even worse shape. Knowing that the pontiff had little military backing or financial strength left, **Philip of France** sent his men to the pope's summer residence in 1303, subjecting the old man to a degrading attack. Boniface died within a few weeks; his French successor, Clement V, promptly moved the papacy to **Avignon**.

The declining political power of the major rulers was countered by the growing autonomy of the cities. By 1300, a broad belt of some three hundred virtually **independent city states** stretched from central Italy to the northernmost edge of the peninsula. In the middle of the century the population of Europe was savagely depleted by the **Black Death** – brought into Europe by a Genovese ship returning from the Black Sea – but the city states survived, developing a concept of citizenship quite different from the feudal lord-and-vassal relationship. By the end of the fourteenth century the richer and more influential states had swallowed up the smaller comunes, leaving four as clear political front runners. These were **Genova** (controlling the Ligurian coast), **Florence** (ruling Tuscany), **Milan**, whose sphere of influence included Lombardy and much of central Italy, and **Venice**. Smaller principalities, such as Mantua and Ferrara, supported armies of mercenaries, ensuring their security by building impregnable fortress-palaces.

Perpetual vendettas between the propertied classes often induced the citizens to accept the overall rule of one *signore* in preference to the bloodshed of warring clans. A despotic form of government evolved, sanctioned by official titles from the emperor or pope, and by the fifteenth century most city states were under princely rather than republican rule. In the south of the fragmented peninsula was the **Kingdom of Naples**; the **States of the Church** stretched up from Rome through modern-day Marche, Umbria and the Romagna; **Siena**, **Florence**, **Modena**, **Mantua** and **Ferrara** were independent states, as were the **Duchy of Milan**, and the maritime republics of **Venice** and **Genova**, with a few odd pockets of independence like Lucca, for example, and Rimini.

The commercial and secular city states of late-medieval times were the seed bed for the **Renaissance**, when urban businessmen (such as the Medici) and autocratic rulers (such as Federico da Montefeltro) enhanced their status through the financing of architectural projects, paintings and sculpture. It was also at this time that the Tuscan dialect – the language of Dante, Petrarch and Boccaccio – became established as Italy's literary language; it later became the nation's official spoken language.

By the mid-fifteenth century the five most powerful states – Naples, the papacy, Milan, and the republics of Venice and Florence – reached a tacit agreement to maintain the new balance of power. Yet though there was a balance of power at home, the history of each of the independent Italian states became inextricably bound up with the power politics of other European countries.

FRENCH AND SPANISH INTERVENTION

The inevitable finally happened when an Italian state invited a larger power in to defeat one of its rivals. In 1494, at the request of the Duke of Milan, **Charles VIII of France** marched south to renew the Angevin claim to the Kingdom of Naples. After the accomplishment of his mission, Charles stayed for three months in Naples, before heading back to France; the kingdom was then acquired by **Ferdinand II of Aragon**, subsequently ruler of all Spain.

The person who really established the Spanish in Italy was the Habsburg **Charles V** (1500–1558), who within three years of inheriting both the Austrian and Spanish thrones bribed his way to being elected Holy Roman Emperor. In 1527 the imperial troops sacked **Rome**, a calamity widely interpreted at the time as God's punishment to the disorganised and dissolute Italians. The French remained troublesome opposition, but they were defeated at Pavia in 1526 and Naples in 1529. With the treaty of Cateau-Cambresis in 1559, Spain held Sicily, Naples, Sardinia, the Duchy of Milan and some Tuscan fortresses, and they were to exert a stranglehold on Italian political life for the next 150 years. The remaining smaller states became satellites of either Spanish or French rule; only the papacy and Venice remained independent.

Social and economic troubles were as severe as the political upheavals. While the papacy combatted the spread of the **Reformation** in northern Europe, the major manufacturing and trading centres were coming to terms with the opening up of the Atlantic and Indian Ocean trade routes – discoveries that meant that northern Italy would increasingly be bypassed. Mid-sixteenth-century **economic recession** prompted wealthy Venetian and Florentine merchants to invest in land rather than business, while in the south high taxes and repressive feudal regimes produced an upsurge of banditry and even the raising of peasant militias – resistance that was ultimately suppressed brutally by the Spanish.

The seventeenth century was a low point in Italian political life, with little room for manoeuvre between the papacy and colonial powers. The Spanish eventually lost control of Italy at the start of the eighteenth century, when as a result of the War of the Spanish Succession, Lombardy, Mantua, Naples and Sardinia all came under Austrian control. The machinations of the major powers led to frequent realignments in the first half of the century. Piedmont, ruled by the Duke of Savoy, Victor Amadeus II, was forced in 1720 to surrender Sicily to the Austrians in return for Sardinia. In 1734 Naples and Sicily passed to the Spanish Bourbons, and three years later the House of Lorraine acquired Tuscany on the extinction of the Medici.

Relatively enlightened Bourbon rule in the south did little to arrest the economic polarisation of society, but the northern states advanced under the intelligent if autocratic rule of Austria's **Maria Theresa** (1740–80) and her son **Joseph II** (1780–92) who prepared the way for early industrialisation. Lightning changes came in April 1796, when the French armies of **Napoleon** invaded northern Italy. Within a few years the French had been driven out again, but by 1810 Napoleon was in command of the whole peninsula, and his puppet regimes remained in charge until Waterloo. Napoleonic rule had profound effects, reducing the power of the papacy, reforming feudal land rights and introducing representative government to Italy. Elected assemblies were provided on the French model, giving the emerging middle class a chance for political discussion and action.

UNIFICATION

The fall of Napoleon led to the Vienna Settlement of 1815, by which the Austrians effectively restored the old ruling class. **Metternich**, the Austrian Chancellor, did all he could to foster any local loyalties that might weaken the appeal of unity, yet the years between 1820 and 1849 became years of revolution. Uprisings began in Sicily, Naples and Piedmont, when **King Ferdinand** introduced measures that restricted personal freedom and destroyed many farmers' livelihoods. A makeshift army quickly gained popular support in Sicily, and forced some concessions, before Ferdinand invited the Austrians in to help him crush the revolution. In the north, the oppressive laws enacted by **Vittorio Emanuele I** in the Kingdom of Piedmont sparked off student protests and army mutinies in Turin. Vittorio Emanuele abdicated in favour of his brother, Carlo Felice, and his son, **Carlo Alberto**; the latter initially gave some support to the radicals, but Carlo Felice then called in the Austrians, and thousands of revolutionaries were forced into exile. Carlo Alberto became King of Piedmont in 1831. A secretive, excessively devout and devious character, he did a major volte-face when he assumed the throne by forming an alliance with the Austrians.

In 1831 further uprisings occurred in Parma, Modena, the Papal States, Sicily and Naples. Their lack of coordination, and the readiness with which Austrian and papal troops intervened, ensured that revolution was shortlived but even if these actions were unsustained, their influence grew.

One person profoundly influenced by these insurgencies was **Giuseppe Mazzini**. Arrested as Secretary of the Genovese branch of the *Carbonari* (a secret radical society) in 1827 and jailed for three months in 1830, he formulated his political ideology and set up **"Young Italy"** on his release. Among the many to whom the ideals of "Young Italy" appealed was **Giuseppe Garibaldi**, soon to play a central role in the **Risorgimento**, as the movement to reform and unite the country was known.

Crop failures in 1846 and 1847 produced widespread **famine** and **cholera outbreaks**. In Sicily an army of peasants marched on the capital, burning debt collection records, destroying property and freeing prisoners. Middle- and upper-class moderates were worried, and formed a government to control the uprising, but Sicilian **separatist** aims were realised in 1848. Fighting spread to Naples, where **Ferdinand II** made some temporary concessions, but nonetheless he retook Sicily the following year. At the same time as the southern revolution, serious disturbances took place in Tuscany, Piedmont and the Papal States. Rulers fled their duchies, and Carlo

Alberto altered course again, prompted by Metternich's fall from power in Vienna – he granted his subjects a constitution and declared war on Austria. In Rome, the pope fled from rioting and Mazzini became a member of the city's republican triumvirate in 1849, with Garibaldi organising the defences.

None of the uprisings lasted long. Twenty thousand revolutionaries were expelled from Rome, Carlo Alberto abdicated in favour of his son Vittorio Emanuele II after military defeats at the hands of the Austrians, and the Dukes returned to Tuscany, Modena and Parma. One thing which did survive was Piedmont's constitution, which throughout the 1850s attracted political refugees to this cosmopolitan state.

CAVOUR AND GARIBALDI

Nine years of radical change began when **Count Camillo Cavour** became Prime Minister of Piedmont in 1852. The involvement of Piedmontese troops in the Crimean War brought Cavour into contact with Napoleon III at the Congress of Paris, at which the hostilities were ended, and in July 1858 the two men had secret talks on the "Italian question". Napoleon III had decided to support Italy in its fight against the Austrians – the only realistic way of achieving unification – as long as resistance was non-revolutionary. Having bargained over the division of territory, they waited for a chance to provoke Austria into war. This came in 1859, when Cavour wrote an emotive antiAustrian speech for Vittorio Emanuele at the opening of Parliament. His battle cry for an end to the *grido di dolore* (cry of pain) was taken up over Italy. The Austrians ordered demobilisation by the Piedmontese, who did the reverse.

The war was disastrous from the start, and thousands died at Magenta and Solferino. In July 1859, Napoleon made a truce with the Austrians without consulting Cavour, who resigned in fury. Provisional governments remained in power in Tuscany, Modena and the Romagna. Cavour returned to government in 1860, and soon France, Piemonte and the papacy agreed to a series of plebiscites, a move which ensured that by mid-March of 1860, **Tuscany** and the new state of **Emilia** (Duchies of Modena and Parma plus the Romagna) had voted for **union with Piedmont**. A secret treaty between Vittorio Emanuele and Napoleon III ceded Savoy and

Nice to France, subject to plebiscites. The result was as planned, no doubt due in part to the presence of the French army during voting.

Garibaldi promptly set off for Nice with the aim of blowing up the ballot boxes, only to be diverted when he reached Genova, where he heard of an **uprising in Sicily**. Commandeering two old paddle steamers and obtaining just enough rifles for his thousand Red Shirts, he headed south. More support came when they landed in Sicily, and Garibaldi's army outflanked the 12,000 Neapolitan troops to take the island. After that, they crossed to the mainland, easily occupied Naples, then struck out for Rome. Cavour, anxious that he might lose the initiative, hastily dispatched a Piedmontese army to **annexe the Papal States**, except for the Patrimony around Rome. Worried by the possibility that the anti-church revolutionaries who made up the Red Shirt army might stir up trouble, Cavour and Vittorio Emanuele travelled south to Rome, accompanied by their army, and arranged plebiscites in Sicily, Naples, Umbria and the Papal Marches that offered little alternative but to vote for annexation by Piedmont. After their triumphal parade through Naples, they thanked Garibaldi for his trouble, took command of all territories and held elections to a new parliament. In February 1861, the members formally announced the **Kingdom of Italy**.

Cavour died the same year, before the country was completely unified, since Rome and Venice were still outside the kingdom. Garibaldi marched unsuccessfully on the city in 1862, and again five years later, by which time Venice had been subsumed. It wasn't until Napoleon III was defeated by Prussia in 1870 that the French troops were ousted from Rome. Thus by 1871 **unification** was complete.

THE WORLD WARS

After the *Risorgimento*, some things still hadn't changed. The ruling class were slow to move towards a broader based political system, while living standards actually worsened in some areas, particularly in Sicily. When Sicilian peasant farmers organised into *fasci* – forerunners of trade unions – the prime minister responded by sending in 30,000 soldiers, closing down newspapers and interning suspected troublemakers without trial. In the 1890s capitalist methods and modern machinery in the Po Valley created a new social structure, with rich *agrari* at the top of the pile, a mass of farm labourers at the bottom, and an intervening layer of estate managers.

In the 1880s Italy's **colonial expansion** began, initially concentrated in bloody – and ultimately disastrous – campaigns in Abyssinia and Eritrea in 1886. In 1912 Italy wrested the Dodecanese islands and Libya from Turkey, a development deplored by many, including **Benito Mussolini**, who during this war was the radical secretary of the *PSI* (Partito Socialista Italiano) in Forlì.

WORLD WAR I AND THE RISE OF MUSSOLINI

Italy entered **World War I** in 1915 with the chief aims of settling old scores with Austria and furthering its colonial ambitions through French and British support. A badly equipped, poorly commanded army took three years to force Austria into defeat, finally achieved in the last month of the war at Vittorio Veneto. Some territory was gained – Trieste, Gorizia, and what became Trentino-Alto Adige – but at the cost of over half a million dead, many more wounded, and a mountainous war debt.

The middle classes, disillusioned with the war's outcome and alarmed by inflation and social unrest, turned to Mussolini, now a figurehead of the right. In 1921, recently elected to parliament, Mussolini formed the *Partito Nazionale Fascisti*, whose *squadre* terrorised their opponents by direct personal attacks and the destruction of newspaper offices, printing shops, and socialist and trade union premises. By 1922 the party was in a position to carry out an insurrectionary "March on Rome". Plans for the march were leaked to Prime Minister Facta, who needed the king's signature on a martial law decree if the army were to meet the march. Fears of civil war led to the king's refusal. Facta resigned, Mussolini made it clear that he would not join any government he did not lead, and on October 29 was **awarded the premiership**. Only then did the march take place.

Zealous *squadristi* now urged Mussolini towards **dictatorship**, which he announced early in 1925. Political opposition and trade unions were outlawed, the free press disintegrated under censorship and Fascist takeovers, elected local governments were replaced by appointed officials, powers of arrest and detention were increased, and special courts were established for political crimes. In 1929, Mussolini ended a sixty-year feud between Church and State, by creating the **Vatican** – an autonomous church state within the Kingdom of Italy. (As late as 1904, anyone involved in the new regime, even as a voter, had been automatically excommunicated.) By 1939, the motto "Everything within the State. Nothing outside the State. Nothing against the State" had become fact, with the government controlling the larger part of Italy's steel, iron and ship building industries, as well as every aspect of political life.

WORLD WAR II

Mussolini's involvement in the **Spanish Civil War** in 1936 brought about the formation of the **"Axis"** with Nazi Germany. Italy entered **World War II** totally unprepared and with outdated equipment, but in 1941 invaded Yugoslavia to gain control of the Adriatic coast. Before long, though, Mussolini was on the defensive. Tens of thousands of Italian troops were killed on the Russian front in the winter of 1942, and in July 1943 the Allied forces gained a first foothold in Europe, when Patton's American Seventh Army and the British Eighth Army under Montgomery landed in Sicily. A month later they controlled the island.

In the face of these and other reversals Mussolini was overthrown by his own Grand Council, who bundled him away to the isolated mountain resort of Gran Sasso, and replaced him with the perplexed **Marshal Badoglio**. The Allies wanted Italy's surrender, for which they secretly offered amnesty to the king, Vittorio Emanuele III, who had coexisted with the Fascist regime for 21 years. On September 8 a radio broadcast announced that an **armistice** had been signed, and on the following day the Allies crossed onto the mainland. As the Anglo-American army moved up through the peninsula, German divisions moved south to meet them, springing Mussolini from jail to set up the **republic of Salò** on Lake Garda. It was a total failure, and increasing numbers of men and women from Communist, Socialist or Catholic parties swelled the opposing partisan forces to 450,000. In April 1945 Mussolini fled for his life, but was caught by partisans before reaching Switzerland. He and his lover, Claretta

Petacci, were shot and strung upside down from a petrol station roof in Milan's Piazzale Loreto.

MODERN TIMES

A popular mandate declared Italy a **republic** in 1946, and Alcide de Gasperi's **Democrazia Cristiana** (DC) party formed a government. He remained in power until 1953, sustained by a succession of coalitions. Ever since then, the regular formation and disintegration of governments has been the norm, a political volatility that reflects the sharp divisions between rural and urban Italy, and between the north and the south (or *mezzogiorno*). A strong manufacturing base and large-scale agriculture have given most people in the north a better material standard of living than previous generations, but the south still lags far behind, despite such measures as the establishment in 1950 of the *Cassa del Mezzogiorno* development agency, which has pumped much-needed funds into the region.

During the 1950s Italy became a front-rank industrial nation, massive firms such as *Fiat* and *Olivetti* helping to double the Gross Domestic Product and triple industrial production. American financial aid was an important factor in this expansion, as was the availability of a large and compliant workforce, a substantial proportion of which was drawn from the villages of the south.

The DC at first operated in alliance with other right-wing parties, but in **1963**, in a move precipitated by the increased politicisation of the blue-collar workers, they were obliged to share government for the first time with the **Partito Socialista Italiano** (PSI). The DC politician who was largely responsible for sounding out the socialists was **Aldo Moro**, the dominant figure of Italian politics in the 1960s. Moro was prime minister from 1963 to 1968, a period in which the economy was disturbed by inflation and the removal of vast sums of money by wealthy citizens alarmed by the arrival in power of the PSI. The decade ended with the "autunno caldo" (hot autumn) of 1969, when strikes, occupations and demonstrations paralysed the country.

In the 1970s the situation worsened even further: bankruptcies increased, inflation hit twenty percent, and unemployment rocketed – a particularly intense hardship in a country with no social security system. More extreme forms of unrest broke out, instigated in the first instance by the far right, who were almost certainly behind a bomb which killed sixteen people in Milan in 1969. **Neo-fascist terrorism** continued throughout the next decade, reaching its hideous climax in 1980, when 84 people were killed in a bomb blast at Bologna train station. At the same time, a plethora of left-wing terrorist groups sprang up, many of them led by disaffected intellectuals at the northern universities. The most active of these were the **Brigate Rosse** (Red Brigades). Founded in Milan in 1970, they reached the peak of their notoriety eight years later, when they kidnapped and killed Aldo Moro himself. A major police offensive in the early 1980s nullified most of the *Brigate Rosse*, but a number of hardline splinter groups are still in existence, as was proved in 1988 by the murder of an aide of the prime minister.

Yet the DC government survived, sustained by the so-called "historic compromise" negotiated in 1976 with **Enrico Berlinguer**, leader of the **Partito Comunista Italiano** (PCI). By this arrangement the PCI – polling 34 percent of the national vote, just three points less than the DC – agreed to abstain from voting in parliament in order to maintain a government of national unity. The pact was rescinded in 1979, and after Berlinguer's death in 1984 the PCI's share of the vote dropped to around 27 percent – though it is still the second largest party in Italy, and seems to be reviving under the new leadership of **Achille Occhetto**. To the present day the PCI has never been a partner in any national administration, yet it controls several town halls and exerts a constant influence on national politics.*

In its efforts to exclude the PCI from power, the DC has been obliged to accede to demands from minor parties such as the **Radical Party**, which gained eighteen seats in the 1979 election – one of them going to the ex-porn star *La Cicciolina*. Furthermore, the DC's reputation was severely damaged in the early 1980s by a series of scandals, notably the furore surround-

ing the activities of the **P2** masonic lodge, when links were discovered between corrupt bankers, senior DC members, and fanatical right-wing groups. As its popularity fell, the DC was forced to offer the premiership to politicians from other parties. In 1981 Giovanni Spadolini of the Republicans became the first non-DC prime minister since the war, and in 1983 **Bettino Craxi** was installed as the first premier from the **Partito Socialista Italiano** (PSI). Though Craxi resigned in 1987 after four years in power, and the government is now headed by the veteran **Giulio Andreotti** (prime minister twice in the 1970s), he is still the single most powerful party leader, both revered and reviled as the Mr Fixit of Italian politics. Under his leadership the PSI has steadily increased its share of the vote to its current standing of around fifteen percent.

Even through the upheavals of the 1970s the national income of Italy continued to grow, and there is now a national obsession with **Il Sorpasso**, a term that signifies the country's overtaking of France and Britain in the economic league table. Experts disagree as to whether *Il Sorpasso* has actually happened (most think it hasn't), and calculations are complicated by the huge scale of tax evasion and other illicit financial dealings in Italy. All strata of society are involved in the withholding of money from central government, but the ruling power in this **economia sommersa** (submerged economy) is the **Mafia**. Despite the Mafia's interference, though, Italy is now permanently established as an economic superpower.

---

*Part of the PCI's revival under Occhetto has been to decide to discard the "communist" label and reform itself as a democratic socialist grouping along the lines of left-leaning parties in West Germany or Sweden, with a view to bringing the party closer to the Italian Socialists and wresting power from the Right for the first time since the war. At time of writing a name had yet to be decided (though "Partito Laburista" was one contender), but it seems clear that the decision could lead to a complete realignment of the Italian Left.

ITALIAN PAINTING AND SCULPTURE

Italy's contribution to the arts of painting and sculpture far surpasses that of any other nation in the world. This is in part due to the triumph of the Renaissance period, but Italy can also boast many more remarkable artistic achievements, ranging from the seventh century BC to modern times. The country's fragmented political history has led to strong regional characteristics in Italian art: Rome, Pisa, Siena, Florence, Milan, Venice, Bologna and Naples all have distinctive and recognisable traditions, and each has taken turns at the artistic helm of the nation. As one city showed signs of artistic decline, there was almost invariably another on hand to assume its mantle.

THE ETRUSCANS

Italian artistic history begins with the **Etruscans**, whose culture spanned the seventh to the first centuries BC, and whose art still arouses dispute as to its merits. Certainly Etruscan art was distinct from that of Greece, then the dominant nation both politically and artistically, drawing on elements of oriental art and showing a predilection for linear forms.

They used bronze and terracotta as materials in contrast to the marble favoured by the Greeks, though in many other respects Etruscan art consistently shows the impact of contemporary trends in Greece.

Many of the finest Etruscan **sculptures** date from the sixth century BC. Among the best examples, both now in the Villa Giulia in Rome, are the *Apollo and Herakles* from Veio, and the *Sarcophagus of a Married Couple* from Cerveteri, the reclining figures of the latter a typical motif of Etruscan art – the faces realistic and expressive, with prominent eyes and enigmatic smiles, but otherwise little attention paid to human anatomy. Depictions of animals, both real and imaginary, were also common, most famous among which are the *Chimera* from Arezzo, now in the Museo Archeologico in Florence, and Rome's own emblem, the *She-Wolf* in the Palazzo dei Conservatori – both from the fifth century BC.

Surviving Etruscan **wall paintings** are surprisingly numerous, especially considering that (apart from a few at Paestum) all of their Greek counterparts in Italy have vanished. The most outstanding array is in Tarquinia, which preserves examples ranging from the sixth to the first century BC; another fine group is at Chiusi. These paintings were at first of a religious or magic nature, initially intending to provide an amenable environment for the dead man. Later, visionary views of the afterlife were attempted. With their bold drawing, bright colours and lively details, they have an immediate visual appeal.

THE ROMANS

Like the Etruscans, the **Romans** were heavily indebted to the Greeks for their art forms, happily adapting Greek models to suit their own purpose, though they had little taste for the aesthetic values which had played such a key role in Greek art. Admittedly, the great heroic statues of the Greeks were highly prized. Many were brought to Rome, while others were extensively imitated and copied, and some of the most famous pieces of Roman **sculpture** – the *Apollo Belvedere* and the *Venus of Cnidos* in the Vatican, the *Medici Venus* in the Uffizi – are actually Roman copies of lost Greek originals, though they are successful pieces of work in their own right, and the equal of anything produced in Greece itself.

Yet to a great extent this Roman reverence for Greece was based on pure snobbery, and the empire's own contribution to artistic development was to take very different forms. Roman **portraiture**, for example, usually eschewed both characterisation and idealisation in favour of an objective representation of the physical features, typically showing a bony facial structure, bare forehead, pursed lips and large eyes. Only occasionally, as in the reigns of Augustus and Hadrian, was this image softened. Marble portrait busts have survived in vast quantities, but the bronze equestrian statues – a particularly effective means of stressing the power and aura of the emperor – were later melted down. Only that of Marcus Aurelius in Rome (currently being restored) survives.

The Romans also made full and varied use of relief sculpture, not least in the carvings used to adorn the front of **sarcophagi**, their main form of funerary art, and on the **triumphal arches** and **columns** erected to celebrate military victories. Some of these, like Trajan's Column in Rome, which dates from the second century AD, display a virtuoso skill and attention to detail in their depiction of great deeds and battles.

In the domestic environment, **wall paintings** were an essential feature, though relatively few survive. In Rome itself, there are the *Esquiline Landscapes* and *Aldobrandini Wedding* and the frescoes from the Villa Livia, while the best examples are those preserved in the towns of Pompeii and Herculaneum after their submersion by the eruption of Mount Vesuvius in 79 AD. Some of these remain *in situ*, notably the spectacular paintings in the Villa dei Misteri; others have been moved to the Museo Nazionale in Naples. In general, a huge range of subject matter was tackled – landscapes, portraits, still lifes, mythologies and genre scenes – while both realistic and stylised approaches to the depiction of nature were attempted.

EARLY CHRISTIAN ART

The **early Christian** period saw an almost total rejection of sculpture, other than for sarcophagi, though the remarkable wooden doors of Santa Sabina in Rome are a notable exception. The earliest murals were created in the Roman catacombs, and show no great stylistic innovation, but increasingly Christian painters began to render a sense of expression to the facial features, in order that the emotions of pain, sorrow and ecstasy could be depicted, along with a richly symbolic pictorial vocabulary. But the early Christians favoured **mosaics** rather than frescoes as a medium. This painstaking art form had hitherto been associated with floor decoration, but it proved ideal for the decoration of the early churches, its inappropriateness for the depiction of movement in many ways responsible for the rigid artistic forms which took an increasing grip. The earliest surviving cycle, in Santa Maria Maggiore in **Rome**, dates from the second quarter of the fifth century, and is fairly small-scale. The slightly later group in the Mausoleo di Galla Placidia in **Ravenna**, the city which had by then assumed the status of capital of the western empire, are more monumental, their daring geometric patterns, elaborate imagery and sublime colouring representing perhaps the first great milestone of Christian art.

Ravenna continued as a centre of artistic innovation when a century later it became in effect the Italian capital of **Byzantine** culture and politics. Many magnificent mosaic cycles were created, and three sets in particular far surpass in quality anything produced in Constantinople itself, or indeed anywhere else in its empire: the church of San Vitale, where the mosaics are the central focus of the architecture itself; Sant'Apollinare Nuovo, whose two frieze processions were quite unlike anything previously seen in Italian art; and the church of Sant'Apollinare in Classe, whose apse mosaics exude a matchless sense of peace and mystery.

THE MIDDLE AGES

Italy at first played a rather subsidiary role in the Europe-wide re-emergence from the Dark Ages. The **Byzantine tradition** proved surprisingly durable, particularly in Venice and Sicily, which both retained strong trading links with Constantinople. Throughout the twelfth century, Byzantine craftsmen proved that the art of mosaic was far from exhausted, providing works that are worthy successors to those at Ravenna in the Cappella Palatina of Palermo and the duomos of Cefalù and Monreale, and of course the Basilica of San Marco in Venice.

Many Italian **fresco cycles** of the period still show traces of Byzantine influence, and the style was also a feature of the great eleventh-century Benedictine art movement fostered by the abbey of Montecassino. Sadly, nearly all the products of this school have vanished, though the murals in Sant'Angelo in Formis near Capua give an approximate idea of what they must have looked like.

Because of the cost of frescoes, from the second quarter of the twelfth century **panel paintings** became increasingly important, particularly in Tuscany. Subjects fell into three main categories: the Madonna and Child with saints; the portrait of a saint surrounded by scenes from his life; or the *Christus Triumphans*, a large painted crucifix showing an open-eyed Christ with outstretched hands.

The art of **sculpture** was initially slow to revive after its long period in the doldrums, but it came to occupy a crucial role throughout Europe during the Romanesque period, with Lombard and Emilian masons playing a key role in its dissemination. Just after the turn of the twelfth century, a master by the name of **Wiligelmo** carved at Modena what may well be the earliest of the great cathedral porches – a form that was to become one of the outstanding features of European medieval art. His bas-reliefs feature expressive figures grouped with considerable narrative skill, and they suggest at least some familiarity with classical works. The same sculptor may also have carved the magnificent episcopal throne in San Nicolò in Bari. **Nicolò**, a pupil of Wiligelmo, seems to have been responsible for most of the other great portals of northern Italy – those of the Sacra di San Michele, San Zeno in Verona, and the cathedrals of Verona, Ferrara, Piacenza and Cremona. Towards the end of the century, this style was developed in and around Parma by **Benedetto Antelami**, who created the graceful *Deposition* relief in the cathedral, the profuse and lively decoration of the baptistery.

THE PRECURSORS OF THE RENAISSANCE

The distinction between **Gothic** and **Renaissance**, so marked in the painting and sculpture of other countries, is very blurred in Italy. In the mid-thirteenth century, what is normally considered one of the key planks of the Renaissance – the rediscovery of the full sense of form, beauty and modelling characteristic of classical art – had already occurred with the statues of the Porta Romana in **Capua**, fragments of which are preserved in the town's museum. These were commissioned by Emperor Frederick II, who wished to revive memories of the grandeur that was Rome. Increasingly, Italians came to believe that it was northern barbarians who had destroyed the arts, which it was now their own duty to revive.

A sculptor of south Italian origin who was doubtless familiar with the work at Capua, **Nicola Pisano** (c.1220–84), developed this style, in four major surviving works – the pulpits of the Pisa Baptistery and the Duomo in Siena, the Arca San Domenico in Bologna and the Fonte Gaia in Perugia. His figures have a sure sense of volume, with varying levels of relief used to create an illusion of space. **Arnolfo di Cambio** (c.1245–1310), his assistant on some of these projects, developed the mix of classical and Gothic features in his own works, which include the famous bronze *St Peter* in Rome, and the *Tomb of Cardinal de Braye* in San Domenico in Orvieto. The latter defined the format of wall tombs for the next century, showing the deceased lying on a coffin below the Madonna and Child, all set within an elaborate architectural framework.

Of even greater long-term significance was the achievement of **Giovanni Pisano** (c.1248–1314), who abandoned his father's penchant for paganism, adopting instead new and dramatic postures for his figures which were quite unlike anything in the previous history of sculpture. This is nowhere more evident than in the statues he created for the facade of the Duomo in Siena, which are placed high up rather than round the portals, and are a world away from their static counterparts on French cathedrals.

It was only in the last three decades of the thirteenth century that Italian painters finally began to break away from the time-honoured Byzantine formulas, a new sense of freedom initiated by **Pietro Cavallini** in Rome and developed by the Florentine **Cimabue** (c.1240–1302), who introduced rounded forms to his fresco of *The Madonna of St Francis* in the lower church at Assisi. His masterpiece, the Passion cycle in the church above, is sadly ruined, but enough remains to give evidence of the overwhelming tragic grandeur it must once have possessed.

Whereas Cimabue's works are still rooted in the Byzantine tradition, and make no attempt to break away from a flat surface effect, a huge quantum leap was made by his pupil and fellow Florentine, **Giotto di Bondone** (1266–1337), whose innovations were to define the entire subsequent course of Western art. Giotto decisively threw off the two-dimensional restrictions of painting, managing to give his pictures an illusion of depth. Thanks to having better materials at his disposal than Cimabue, his *Life of St Francis* in the upper church at Assisi has survived in good condition, as has his decoration of the Scrovegni Chapel in Padua. These two great cycles are the best examples of Giotto's genius in all its many facets. Among these are such basic principles as a sense for the significant, unencumbered by surplus detail; the convincing treatment of action, movement, gesture and emotion; and total command over technical matters like figure modelling, foreshortening, and effects of light and shade.

THE 14TH AND EARLY 15TH CENTURIES

In spite of these momentous developments, the path towards the Renaissance was not to follow a continuous or consistent course. Indeed, the leading local school of painters in the fourteenth century was not that of Florence, but of neighbouring **Siena**, which had very different preoccupations. This had a great deal to do with the father figure, **Duccio di Buoninsegna** (c.1255–1318), who did not go along the revolutionary path of Giotto, but instead breathed a whole new life into the Byzantine tradition. Duccio's sense of grandeur is well conveyed by the central panel of his masterpiece, the *Maestà* in the Museo dell'Opera del Duomo of his native city. However, it is the small scenes of this vast altarpiece which bring out his best quality: that of a masterful storyteller, adept at arrangement, grouping and the depiction of expression, feeling and movement. Colour, which in Giotto is merely used to bring out the forms, becomes a leading component in its own right.

In spite of the presence in the city of the vibrant statues of Giovanni Pisano, subsequent Sienese painters found Duccio's narrative art the more potent model. **Simone Martini** (c.1284–1344) began his career by painting a fresco counterpart of Duccio's *Maestà* in the Palazzo Pubblico, though his most celebrated work in this building, the commemorative *Equestrian Portrait of Guidoriccio da Fogliano*, is now widely regarded as a fake. His refined, graceful style depended above all on line, colour and decorative effects – seen to best effect in the cycle of *The Life of St Martin* in the lower church in Assisi and in the sumptuous, cunningly designed *Annunciation* in the Uffizi. The latter was painted in collaboration with his brother-in-law **Lippo Memmi** (d.1357), who independently painted the *Maestà* in the Palazzo Pubblico in San Gimignano, and may also have been responsible for the dramatic New Testament frescoes in the Collegiata of the same town, traditionally ascribed to the otherwise unknown **Barna**.

Another Sienese painter who worked at Assisi was **Pietro Lorenzetti** (active 1306–45); his frescoes there show the impact of Giotto, and have a sense of pathos which is uncharacteristic of Sienese painting. His brother **Ambrogio Lorenzetti** (active 1319–47) was a more original artist, whose main achievement was the idiosyncratic *Allegory of Good and Bad Government* in the Palazzo Pubblico, which shows painting being used for a secular, didactic purpose for the first time and raises the landscape background to a new, higher status, with an awareness of perspective uncommon for this date. The other notable Sienese sculptor of the period was the mysterious **Lorenzo Maitani** (c.1270–1330), who is associated with one work only – the wonderfully lyrical reliefs on the most sumptuous facade in Italy, that of the Duomo in Orvieto.

In **Florence**, meanwhile, a whole group of painters consciously followed Giotto's style, without materially adding to it. The most talented was **Maso di Banco**, who was particularly skilled at conveying the master's sense of plastic form, while the most faithful was **Taddeo Gaddi** (d.1366), whose son **Agnolo Gaddi** (d.1396) carried the Giottesque tradition on to nearly the end of the century. **Bernardo Daddi** (c.1290–1349), on the other hand, combined this tradition with aspects of the Sienese style. The sculptor **Andrea Pisano** (c.1290–1348) succeeded Giotto as master mason of the Campanile. The reliefs he executed for it, plus the bronze door he made for the Baptistery, translate Giotto's pictorial language back into a three-dimensional format.

A reaction against the hegemony of the Giottesque style came with **Andrea Orcagna** (c.1308–68) who was equally prominent as a painter and sculptor, developing a flowery, decorative idiom seen to best effect in the tabernacle in Orsanmichele. The paintings of Orcagna and his school re-established the hierarchical tradition of the Byzantines, and rejected the importance of spatial depth.

At the very end of the fourteenth century, the **International Gothic** style, originating in the Burgundian courts, swept across Europe. This introduced a new sense of realism in such matters as the depiction of landscape, animals and costume, though it was unconcerned with intellectual matters. Its dissemination in Italy was largely due to **Gentile da Fabriano** (c.1370–1427), whose *Adoration of the Magi* in the Uffizi (one of his relatively few surviving compositions) shows the gorgeously opulent surface effects of this style at its best. Another leading practitioner was **Masolino da Panicale** (1383–1447), who is best known for having begun the famous fresco cycle in Santa Maria del Carmine in Florence. In the same city, the new movement influenced **Lorenzo Monaco** (1372–1425), whose work bridges the Florentine and Siense traditions.

International Gothic took a particularly firm grip in Verona, chiefly through **Antonio Pisanello** (1395–1455). The latter's fame rests partly on his prowess as a medallist, and only a tantalising handful of his paintings remain, notably the frescoes in the Veronese churches of Sant'Anastasia and San Fermo, and the Palazzo Ducale in Mantua, which magically evoke the idealised courtly world of fairy tales. Numerous drawings prove these were based on patient observations of nature – something that was to be a key element in the unfolding of the Renaissance.

THE FLORENTINE RENAISSANCE

A date often given for the start of the **Renaissance** is 1401, when the Florentine authorities announced a public competition for the right to make a second door for the Baptistery. Candidates had to submit a trial piece of *The Sacrifice of Isaac*, a stiff test presenting problems of narrative, expression, movement and spatial arrangement, in which scenery, animals and both nude and draped figures had to be adequately depicted. The most audacious solution, which can be seen in the Bargello, was provided by **Filippo Brunelleschi** (1377–1446), who in the process fully mastered the science of perspective. He failed to win, and in disgust gave up sculpture in favour of architecture, but the new possibilities opened up by his command over visuals, and the impetus they provided for other artists to experiment and discover, mark the transition from medieval art to modern.

Brunelleschi's mantle was taken over by **Donatello** (c.1386–1466), who began his long career by creating a new kind of freestanding statue to adorn Florence's churches, which became the artistic symbol of the city. These heroic, larger-than-life figures are shown with their feet planted firmly on the ground, displaying facial expressions of great energy and concentration. A typical example is the *St George* made for Orsanmichele, below which was placed an extraordinary carving of the saint slaying the dragon which uses the art of perspective for the first time in stone sculpture, as well as pioneering the technique of very low relief. With the bronze *David*, now in the Bargello, Donatello helped bring the nude – the ultimate figurative challenge – back into the mainstream of art; and he also revived another lost art, the bronze equestrian statue, with the *Monument to Gattamelata* in Padua.

The victor of the Baptistery door competition was **Lorenzo Ghiberti** (1378–1455), who thereafter devoted almost his whole life to the project. Ghiberti initially showed no interest in perspective, and remained loyal to most of the old Gothic formulas, his first set of doors merely refining Andrea Pisano's techniques. However, his second set of doors, nicknamed the *Gates of Paradise*, show how his style evolved under the influence of classical antecedents, creating a sense of space and illusion, and imbuing the grouping and characterisation of the figures with a gently lyrical touch.

Donatello's collaborator **Nanni di Banco** (c.1384–1421) was another to achieve an individual mix of the Gothic and Renaissance idioms, notably in *The Four Saints* on Orsanmichele. Another architect-sculptor, **Bernardo Rossellino** (1409–64), created in the *Monument to Leonardo Bruni* in Santa Croce the prototype of the sort of niche tomb that was to prevail for the rest of the century.

Luca della Robbia (1400–82) began his career as a sculptor of marble and bronze, working in a classically derived style, but a very different one from the essentially serious approach of his contemporaries. However, after Luca invented the art of glazed terracotta, he abandoned other forms of sculpture, laying the foundation for a highly lucrative family business which was continued by his nephew **Andrea della Robbia** (1435–1525).

The painter **Masaccio** (1401–28) belongs with Brunelleschi and Donatello as a key figure of the early Renaissance. His *Trinity* fresco in Santa Maria Novella must have startled his contemporaries, its perfect sense of depth and perspective giving the illusion of peering into the solid wall on which it was painted. Masaccio collaborated with Masolino, most notably in the fresco cycle in Santa Maria del Carmine. In this, the scenes are pared down to the essentials; the figures have a heroic quality and dignity, with their gestures depicted at the moment of maximum intensity. A single source of light is used, with shadows cast accurately.

Fra Angelico (1387/1400–55), like Ghiberti in sculpture, combined new techniques with the Gothic tradition. A devout Dominican monk, his pictures show a rapt, heavenly vision. Colour is a telling ingredient: Angelico's ethereal blue was inimitable, the rest of his palette hardly less fetching. Frescoes in the cells of his own monastery of San Marco, intended as aids to contemplation, rank as his most important body of work. Late in his career, Angelico was called to the Vatican, where he frescoed the Cappella Niccolina, employing a style which had by then lost all Gothic traces.

Fra Filippo Lippi (c.1406–69) gradually moved away from the style of his master Masaccio to develop a greater sense of drama and emotion, seen to best effect in the frescoes in the cathedral at Prato. His later panels show a highly personal, mystical vision, characterised by wistful Madonnas, playful children and poetic landscapes. Fra Angelico's only follower of note was **Benozzo Gozzoli** (c.1421–97), whose work lacks any sense of profundity, but possesses undeniable decorative charm, best seen in the frescoes in the Palazzo Medici-Ricardi, which offer a vivid panorama of contemporary Florentine life.

The city's most eccentric painter was **Paolo Uccello** (1396–1475), who was obsessed by the problems of perspective and foreshortening. His *Sir John Hawkwood* in the Duomo was a deliberate piece of *trompe l'oeil*, though its effect is marred by the use of different vantage points, a characteristic common to his paintings, in which he tried to find as many lines as possible to lead the eye inwards. **Domenico Veneziano** (1406–61) was one of the most admired artists of the day, but only a few works by him survive, notably the serene *St Lucy Altar* in the Uffizi, which shows his talent for spatial arrangement and gentle, pastel-like colouring. **Andrea del Castagno** (c.1421–57), in contrast, favoured harsh, strong colours, and an exaggerated dramatic pose for his figures, as can be seen in *The Last Supper* in Sant'Apollonia. In the series of *Famous Men* in the Uffizi he initiated a Florentine trend by vividly translating on to canvas the late sculptural types of Donatello.

Halfway through the century, a new versatility was brought to Florentine art by **Antonio Pollaiuolo** (c.1432–98), who was active as a painter, sculptor, engraver, goldsmith and embroidery designer. Pollaiuolo was renowned for the advances he made in the depiction of anatomy and movement; he was also one of the first to grapple with the next great challenge facing Renaissance painters, namely how to move beyond making all parts of a picture accurate and realistic, while at the same time creating a satisfying compositional whole. Another painter-sculptor was **Andrea del Verrocchio** (c.1435–88), whose fame as a teacher has unfairly drawn attention away from his own wide-ranging achievements. His *Christ and St Thomas* on Orsanmichele shows crafty compositional skills in fitting two statues into a space intended for one, and marks a move away from classicism, as does his equestrian *Monument to Bartolommeo Colleoni* outside San Zanipolo in Venice. Other Florentine sculptors of this period preferred a much softer approach. **Desiderio da Settignano** (1428–64) made sensitive busts of women and children, and used Donatello's technique of low relief to create scenes of the utmost delicacy. **Mino da Fiesole** (1429–84), **Antonio Rossellino** (1427–79) and **Benedetto da Maiano** (1442–97) showed broadly similar preoccupations, all concentrating on grace and beauty of line.

Subjects drawn from classical mythology became an increasingly important part of the repertoire of Florentine painters in the second half of the fifteenth century, in large part due to the humanist culture fostered at the court. One of Italy's most distinctive artists, **Sandro Botticelli** (c.1445–1510), created the most famous and haunting images in this field, notably *The Birth of Venus* and *Primavera*, both now in the Uffizi. His late work shows a deliberate archaism, perhaps as a result of the religious fanaticism of the time.

Filippino Lippi (1457/8–1504), the result of Fra Filippo's affair with a nun, came to fame with his completion of Masaccio's frescoes in Santa Maria del Carmine. He developed a style based on that of Botticelli, though with a more consciously antique feeling. Another painter with pagan tastes was the reclusive **Pietro di Cosimo** (c.1462–1521), who was at his best in enigmatic mythological scenes. Meanwhile, vivid new frescoes were created for Florence's churches by **Domenico Ghirlandaio** (1449–94), whose works are now chiefly remembered for their documentary interest, being filled with portraits of contemporary notables and vivid anecdotal details.

THE 15TH CENTURY ELSEWHERE IN ITALY

Although the fifteenth century brought a rich crop of artists working throughout Italy – including many places which previously had little tradition of their own to draw on – no other city came near to matching the depth and consistency of the fifteenth-century Florentine school.

However, although the technical innovations pioneered in Florence were to have an enormous influence, they were by no means slavishly followed. Sienese painters proved the continuing vitality of the colourful narrative approach of the previous century, modified by the impact of International Gothic. The works of **Sassetta** (c.1392–1450), which are often impregnated by a sense of mysticism, do make some concessions to the new theories of spatial composition, but this is an essentially subordinate feature. The finest Sienese artist of the century was the sculptor **Jacopo della Quercia** (1374–1438), whose style is essentially linear, though with classical tendencies modified by knowledge of the most advanced northern European art of the day. He was given important public commissions in his native city,

such as the overall supervision of the Baptistery font and the Fonte Gaia. However, his masterpiece is his last work, the reliefs on the facade of San Petronio in Bologna, which show a vigorous approach fully comparable with those of the great Florentines. His main follower was the Florentine-born **Agostino di Duccio** (1418–81), another sculptor heavily dependent on line, whose work abounds with nervous energy. His masterpiece, executed in collaboration with **Matteo de'Pasti** (c.1420–67), is the joyous series of low reliefs in the Tempio Malatestiano in Rimini.

Another artist associated with the Rimini project was the Umbrian **Piero della Francesca** (1410/20–92), who cast an overwhelming influence over the development of painting in central Italy. A painstaking worker, Piero was also active as a mathematician, which helps to explain the importance of perspective and symmetry in his compositions. His figures are painted with a cool sense of detachment yet have a grave, monumental beauty. Piero was also one of the great painters of light, in the blue skies which illuminate his gentle landscapes, and in more dramatic effects, such as in *The Dream of Constantine*, part of his most substantial commission – the fresco cycle in San Francesco, Arezzo.

Melozzo da Forlí (1438–94) was the closest follower of Piero della Francesca, showing a similar interest in perspective, and apparently inventing a favourite Renaissance trick device called *sotto in su* an extreme form of illusion in which figures painted on a ceiling appear to float in space. Another inventive pupil of the same master was **Luca Signorelli** (1450–1523), who developed the ideas of dramatic movement pioneered by Pollaiuolo. In spite of obvious defects, such as harsh colours, stiff drawing and a tendency to overcrowd his compositions, Signorelli was responsible for some of the most heroic paintings of the day. His profound knowledge of anatomy was to be an enormous influence on the succeeding generation, and he used the nude to achieve the most spectacular effects, notably in the frescoes in Orvieto's Duomo.

Pietro Perugino (1445–1523), probably yet another pupil of Piero, developed in a quite different way from Signorelli, producing calm altarpieces featuring soft and beautifully rounded figures set against serene Umbrian landscapes. His collaborator **Bernardino Pintoricchio** (c.1454–1513) was a purely decorative artist whose work has no pretensions to depth, but which is nearly always fresh and pleasing, particularly in his larger schemes such as the Libreria Piccolomini in the Duomo in Siena.

The first important Renaissance painter in northern Italy was **Andrea Mantegna** (c.1431–1506), who represents the apogee of classical influence. Steeped from an early age in the art of the Romans, Mantegna's ideal vision of the antique world permeates nearly all his work, even becoming the predominant element in many of his sacred compositions, together with a phenomenal technical skill, and daring use of unorthodox vantage points – best seen in the grief-laden *Dead Christ* in the Brera, Milan. In total contrast is the exuberant decoration for the *Camera degli Sposi* in Mantua, one of the artist's few works based on direct observation rather than classical inspiration.

Padua in the mid-fifteenth century became an important training ground for artists, thanks to the early successes of Mantegna, and the ten-year stay of Donatello. One of its offshoots was the group of painters active in Ferrara – **Cosmè Tura** (c.1431–95), **Francesco del Cossa** (1435/6–77) and **Ercole de'Roberti** (1448/55–98). Tura's figures are highly charged, with mannered poses and claw-like hands, typically set against fanciful architecture very different from the idealised townscapes painted by other Renaissance artists. Cossa's outline is sharper, his figures energetic rather than theatrical, his colours more resplendent; he too favoured architectural backgrounds, particularly of ruins. Roberti's essentially small-scale style combines something of the pathos of Tura with Cossa's emphasis on colour and line.

Also trained in Padua was the Brescian **Vincenzo Foppa** (1427/30–1515/6), who subsequently became the leader of the Milanese school. His best works have a certain grandeur of conception, and a subdued sense of colouring. His main follower was **Ambrogio Bergognone** (1450/60–1523), who is particularly associated with the Certosa di Pavia. This great building project was also the main outlet for the talents of the leading Lombard sculptors of the day, notably **Giovanni**

Antonio Amadeo (1447–1522), whose other main work is the decoration of the Cappella Colleoni in Bergamo.

Venice, as always, remained something of a law unto itself. Even in mid-century, the sculptures of **Bartolomeo Buon** (c.1374–1464/7) and the crowded panels of **Michele Giambono** (active 1420–62) showed the city's continuing preference for late-Gothic forms. Something of a transition can be seen with the **Vivarini** family – **Antonio** (c.1419–80), his brother **Bartolomeo** (c.1430–91) and his son **Alvise** (c.1445–1505) – who gradually introduced a sense of spatial perspective and an increased attempt at characterisation. **Carlo Crivelli** (c.1430–95) was also associated with them. One of the most inventive and idiosyncratic artists of the day, Crivelli abandoned Venice, preferring commissions from churches in small towns in Marche, which he executed in a deliberately archaic style. His altarpieces are positively opulent, characterised by strong drawing, rich colours, elaborate detail and a superfluity of decoration, with incidental still lifes a common ingredient.

Another, and far more influential, artistic dynasty was that of the **Bellini** family – **Jacopo** (c.1400–70) and his sons **Gentile** (c.1429–1507) and **Giovanni** (c.1430–1516). The last-named was the most significant, standing as a major influence on Venetian painters to come. Though influenced by his brother-in-law Mantegna, Bellini's overall effect is very different, with a soft beauty of both colour and outline. He painted a seemingly endless series of variations on subjects such as the *Madonna and Child* and *Pietà*, yet always managed to make each very different. His larger altarpieces concentrate attention on the foreground, and arrange the figures in such a way that there is a parallel plane behind, rather than the more usual receding landscape. Gentile Bellini was essentially a history painter who popularised the penchant for highly detailed depictions of Venetian life.

Vittore Carpaccio (1460–1523) continued this narrative tradition, and two complete cycles by him can still be seen in the city: that of *St Ursula* in the Accademia, and of *St George and St Jerome* in the Scuola di San Giorgio degli Schiavoni. A love of the picturesque also pervades his altarpieces, which generally give due prominence to fantastic landscapes and resplendent Renaissance buildings.

Venetian Renaissance sculpture was dominated by yet another dynasty, the **Lombardo** family: **Pietro** (c.1438–1515) and his sons **Antonio** (c.1458–1516) and **Tullio** (c.1460–1532). Their strongly classical style was particularly suited to funerary monuments, the best of which are in San Zanipolo. They were also talented decorative carvers, as can be seen in the interior scheme for their own church of Santa Maria dei Miracoli.

Closely associated with the Venetian school was the only important southern Italian painter of the Renaissance, **Antonello da Messina** (c.1430–79), who spent the last years of his life in the city. Antonello's style is derived in large part from fifteenth-century Flemish artists, and it was through contact with their work that he introduced oil painting to Italy. His pictures have a strong sense of pathos, and some of his most arresting images are simple devotional pictures, which follow the same format he favoured for his secular portraits.

THE RENAISSANCE

Just as the beginning of the Renaissance is linked to the specific circumstances of the competition for the Florence Baptistery doors, so the climactic part of the era, known as the High Renaissance, is sometimes considered to have started with the mural of *The Last Supper* in Santa Maria delle Grazie in Milan, painted in the last years of the fifteenth century by **Leonardo da Vinci** (1452–1519). Apart from its magnificent spatial and illusive qualities, this painting endowed each of the characters with identifiable psychological traits, and successfully froze the action to capture the mood of a precise moment. His use of *sfumato*, a blurred outline whereby tones gradually but imperceptibly changed from light to dark, was of crucial importance to his ability to make his figures appear as living beings with a soul – a technique best seen in his portraits.

In Florence, the most original painter of the generation after Leonardo was **Fra Bartolommeo della Porta** (c.1474–1517), who was caught up in the religious fanaticism which also influenced Botticelli. As a device to stress the otherness of the divine, he clad the figures in his religious compositions in plain drapery, rather than the colourful contemporary costumes which had hitherto been fashionable. He also did away with elaborate backgrounds and anecdotal detail, concentrating instead on expression and gesture. **Mariotto Albertinelli** (1474–1515), who worked with him in the same workshop in San Marco that had once been run by Fra Angelico, painted in a broadly similar but less austere manner. **Andrea del Sarto** (1486–1530), on the other hand, was the one Florentine artist who shared the Venetian precept of colour and shade as being the most important ingredients of a picture. His figures are classical in outline, aiming at a balance of nuance, proportion and monumentality.

These Florentines, however, stood very much in the shadow of **Michelangelo Buonarroti** (1475–1564), with whom the Renaissance period reaches its climax. Michelangelo's first love was the creation of marble statues. He had little interest in relief, and none at all in bronze or clay, believing that the slow building up of forms was too simple a task for a great artist. His technique is illustrated most graphically in the unfinished *Slaves* in Florence's Accademia, who seem to be pushing their way out of the stone. The colossal early *David*, also in the Accademia, shows his mastery of the nude, which thereafter became the key focus of his art. In spite of claiming to be a reluctant painter, Michelangelo's single greatest accomplishment was the frescoing of the ceiling of the Sistine Chapel, one of the world's most awe-inspiring acts of individual human achievement. Its confident and elated mood is offset by the overpowering despondency of *The Last Judgment* on the end wall, painted three decades later. His later works are more abstract, as seen in the *Pietàs* in the Museo dell'Opera in Florence and the Milan Castello, which contrast sharply with the formal beauty of his youthful interpretation of the scene in St Peter's.

Raphael (1483–1520) stands in almost complete antithesis to his rival Michelangelo, though the personal friendships he forged with his powerful patrons were as significant in raising the status of the artist as was the latter's less compromising approach. A pupil of Perugino, he quickly surpassed his teacher's style, going to Florence where he became chiefly renowned for numerous variants of *The*

Madonna and Child and *The Holy Family*. Raphael also developed into a supreme portraitist, skilled at both the psychological and physical attributes of his sitters. His greatest works, however, are the frescoes of his Roman period, notably those in the *Stanze della Segnatura* in the Vatican and the Villa Farnesina. Raphael's late works show him moving towards a large-scale, more dramatic and mannered style, but his early death meant that the continuation of this trend was left to his pupils.

Closely related to the classicising tendency of Raphael is that of the Florentine-born sculptor **Andrea Sansovino** (c.1467–1529), whose grandiose tombs in Santa Maria del Popolo in Rome, with standing effigies of the Virtues, set the tone for sixteenth-century funerary monuments. His pupil **Jacopo Sansovino** (1486–1570) took his name and carried on his tradition, spending the latter part of his career in Venice, where although principally active as an architect, he also made monumental sculptures which are inseparable from the buildings they adorn. **Sebastiano del Piombo** (c.1485–1547), on the other hand, stood as a direct rival to Raphael in Rome, striving to transfer Michelangelo's heroic manner to panel painting. In this, he was only variably successful, though he was a highly sensitive portraitist.

Meanwhile **Antonio Correggio** (1489/94–1534) managed to carve out a brilliant career for himself in Parma. His three ceiling frescoes there develop the illusionistic devices of Mantegna, marking Correggio out as a precursor of the Baroque. One of the great painters of mythological scenes, he was also a relentless explorer of the dramatic possibilities of light and shade. Another fine exponent of the contrasts of light was the Ferrarese **Dosso Dossi** (1479/90–1542), a romantic spirit who created fantastic landscapes peopled with gorgeously dressed figures.

The golden period of Venetian painting, ushered in by Bellini, continued with his elusive pupil, **Giorgione** (1475–1510), whose short life is shrouded in mystery. One of the few paintings certainly by him is *The Tempest* in the Venice Accademia, whose true subject matter baffled even his contemporaries. In it, the figures are, for the first time in Italian art, completely subsidiary to the lush landscape

illuminated by menacing shafts of light. The haunting altarpiece in the Duomo of his native town of Castelfranco Veneto is also almost certainly his, but many other paintings attributed to him may actually be by one of many painters who maintained something of his poetic, colourful style. Some of these, notably **Vincenzo Catena** (c.1480–1531) and **Palma il Vecchio** (c.1480–1528), developed recognisable artistic personalities of their own. **Lorenzo Lotto** (c.1480–1556) was the most distinctive of this circle, travelling widely throughout his career, assimilating an astonishing variety of influences.

Giorgione's influence is also marked in the early works of **Titian** (c.1485–1576), the dominant personality of the Venetian school and one of the most versatile painters of all time. His art embraced with equal skill all the subjects that were required by the Renaissance – altarpieces, mythologies, allegories and portraits. Even more than Michelangelo, he was able to pick and choose his patrons, and was the first artist to build up a truly international clientele. As a portraitist of men of power, Titian was unrivalled, setting the vocabulary for official images which was to prevail until well into the seventeenth century. His complete technical and compositional mastery is already apparent in relatively early works such as the *Assumption* in I Frari, the first example of what was to become a Venetian speciality: a panel painting specially designed to fit an architectural space. Towards the end of his life, Titian abandoned his bravura and brilliant palette in favour of a very free style, stretching the possibilities of oil paint to their very limits.

Giovanni Antonio Pordenone (1483/4–1539) was a provincial north Italian painter strongly influenced by Giorgione and Titian. More obviously in direct descent from the Venetian masters was the school of Brescia. **Giovanni Girolamo Savoldo** (active 1508–48) showed particular adeptness at light effects, and was a pioneer of night scenes, while **Alessandro Moretto** (c.1498–1554) was one of the most incisive portraitists of the Renaissance, and seems to have been responsible for introducing the full-length form to Italy. His altarpieces are more variable, but often have a suitably grand manner.

THE HIGH RENAISSANCE

The perfection of form achieved in the late Renaissance was the culmination of centuries of striving. As artists could not hope to improve on the achievements of Michelangelo and Raphael at their peak, they had to find new approaches. As a result, **Mannerism** was born. This was a deliberately intellectual approach, aimed at flouting the accepted rules, notably by distorting the senses of scale and perspective, exaggerating anatomical details, adopting unlikely poses for the figures, and using unnaturally harsh colours.

One artist commonly labelled a Mannerist is **Giulio Romano** (c.1492–1546), one of the most gifted of Raphael's assistants, whose frescoes in the Palazzo del Te in Mantua, which he himself built, show the style at its most bravura, notably in *The Fall of the Giants*, occupying a room to itself. A leading light in the adoption of Mannerism in Florence was **Rosso Fiorentino** (1494–1540), together with **Jacopo Pontormo** (1494–1556) and **Agnolo Bronzino** (1503–72). Pontormo, a brilliant draughtsman, was the most talented of this group, an able decorator and an inquiring if understated portraitist. Bronzino was highly prolific, but only his portraits of royal and noble personages have much appeal today, their detachment, concentrating more on the beauty of their clothing, casting an enormous influence on official portraitists down the centuries. **Giorgio Vasari** (1511–74), originally from Arezzo, was responsible for many of the frescoes in the Palazzo Vecchio, although he is now chiefly famous for his series of biographies of artists, which marked the birth of art history as a discipline.

Another Florentine Mannerist whose writings have helped secure his fame is the sculptor **Benvenuto Cellini** (1500–71), the author of a racy *Autobiography* which offers a fascinating insight into the artistic world of the time. Though he was successful in finding favour at courts all over Europe, only a few of his sculptures, all of a very high quality, survive. The *Bust of Cosimo I*, in the Bargello, marks the departure of the portrait from realism, creating instead a new heroic image. His *Perseus*, in the Loggia dei Lanzi, forms a fitting counterpart to Donatello's late *Judith*, and completely outclasses the *Hercules and Cacus* in the square outside by his rival **Baccio Bandinelli** (1493–1560).

By far the most influential Florentine Mannerist, however, was **Giambologna** (1529–1608), a sculptor of French origin. His favourite medium was bronze, and he established a large workshop which churned out miniature replicas of his most important compositions. These typically show figures in combat, and are designed for the spectator to walk around, rather than examine from only one viewpoint. His most famous image is the typically androgynous *Mercury*; in a conscious rebuttal of the approaches of both Donatello and Michelangelo, this figure appears to float in the air, in the boldest attempt ever made by a sculptor to defy the laws of gravity.

One of the most individualistic Mannerists was **Domenico Beccafumi** (1484/6–1551), who provided a somewhat unusual end to the long line of Sienese painters, though his emphasis on colour was utterly typical of that city. He was a master of decorative effect, as witnessed by his illusionist frescoes in the Palazzo Pubblico, and his large altarpieces for Sienese churches, which show a particular concern for light and shade, perspective effects, and deep emotions. In Parma, **Francesco Parmigianino** (1503–40) retained something of the consciously refined approach of Correggio, but his figures, often shown with an exaggerated emphasis on the hands and neck, reveal considerable spiritual insight. His decorative scheme for Santa Maria della Steccata typifies the Mannerist penchant for surplus ornament and proves the fertility of his imagination.

Venice, as ever, followed its own distinctive late-Renaissance path, having no taste for the sort of Mannerism practised elsewhere in Italy. **Jacopo Tintoretto** (1518–94) aimed at an ideal based on the drawing of Michelangelo and the colour of Titian, though in fact the heroic style he forged had only superficial resemblances to his mentors. To heighten the sense of drama, he used a battery of other methods: unorthodox vantage points, elongated figures, and unexpected positioning of the main subject on the canvas. He also employed contemporary settings and costumes in his religious works, so deepening their spiritual impact.

In strong contrast to Tintoretto, the other leading Venetian painter of the day, **Paolo Veronese** (1528–88), was a supreme decorator on a grand scale. Indeed, some of his best work was conceived for architectural settings, such as San Sebastiano in Venice and the Villa Barbara in Masèr. Veronese's love of pomp and splendour, however, is carried over into his easel paintings, which revel in warm, glowing colours and monumental figures, with little sense of gravitas. The artist fell foul of the Inquisition as a result of the inclusion of German soldiers (which put him under suspicion of Protestant sympathies) and other anachronistic and surplus detail in a huge banquet scene (now in the Venice Accademia) which purported to represent *The Last Supper.* His response was to change the title to *A Feast in the House of Levi.*

Alessandro Vittoria (1525–1608), a pupil of Jacopo Sansovino, embellished Venice's churches with sculptures that have much in common with Mannerist productions elsewhere in Italy, but are more classically modelled. **Jacopo Bassano** (1510/19–92) was trained in the city, but preferred to work in the provincial town after which he takes his name, where he was by far the most remarkable of a dynasty of painters. As a setting for his religious panels, he painted the small town and country life of his day as it really was. He also popularised the inclusion of animals and heaped piles of fruit and vegetables – features eagerly taken up by later northern European artists – and was a superb painter of light and shade, using heavy dabs of colour and strong chiaroscuro.

Another remarkable artist working well away from the main centres was **Federico Barocci** (1535–1612) of Urbino. His paintings were painstakingly executed, their soft rounded forms mirroring the comforting religious image propagated by the Counter-Reformation, and with an emphasis on light and movement that was to some extent anticipatory of the Baroque to come.

THE BAROQUE AGE

The leadership of Italian art away from the sterility of late Mannerism came initially from cities which had hitherto played a minor role in its development. Bologna was the first to come to prominence, through the academy founded there in 1585 by members of the **Carracci** family – **Ludovico** (1555–1619), **Agostino** (1557–1602) and **Annibale** (1560–1609). This was by no means the first attempt to set up a training school for artists, a concept rendered

necessary by the blow the Renaissance had dealt to the old workshop tradition, but it was far more successful than any previous venture. Annibale was easily the greatest and most versatile artist of the three, breathing a whole new life into the classical tradition. His frescoes in the Palazzo Farnese in Rome offer a fresh and highly imaginative approach to mythological scenes, as well as being brilliant examples of illusionism. A more serious intent is noticeable in the artist's canvases, which introduce an emotional yet untheatrical content to well-ordered religious subjects. He was also a major landscape painter, pioneering the sort of luscious scene with a subsidiary subject from the Bible or classical literature which was later to be developed in Rome by the great French painters, Claude and Poussin.

An entirely different but equally novel approach was taken by **Michelangelo da Caravaggio** (1573–1610), whose violent and wayward life led him from Milan to Rome, Naples, Malta, Sicily and most of the way back again. Caravaggio was the great master of chiaroscuro effects, which he used to even more dramatic purpose than Tintoretto. He also used what seemed like shock tactics to his patrons in the Church, stripping away centuries of idealised tradition to present biblical stories as they might have seemed at the time. Real-life peasants, beggars, ruffians and prostitutes were all used as models for the figures, in a bid to enhance the realistic impact. In his commissions for Roman churches such as San Luigi dei Francesi and Santa Maria del Popolo he sometimes had his original canvases rejected, though he always managed to find a private buyer for them. Caravaggio's impact on the great European Golden Age of seventeenth-century painting was immense, spawning whole schools of Dutch and French derivatives, along with Rubens, Rembrandt, and most of the great Spanish masters.

In Italy, Caravaggio's art had an immediate impact on the older **Orazio Gentileschi** (1563–1639), who was particularly keen on its tenebrist effects. The Mantuan **Bartolomeo Manfredi** (c.1580–1620/1) extended the master's style to such genre subjects as card games and soldiers in guardrooms. And Caravaggio's style was brought to Naples by **Giovanni Battista Caracciolo** (c.1570–1637), inspiring the city's painters to raise Naples from its traditionally marginal position in Italian art to a place, throughout the seventeenth century, at the very forefront.

The first important follower of the Carracci in Bologna was **Guido Reni** (1575–1642). In the nineteenth century, Reni was ranked as one of the supreme artists of all time, but suffered a slump in reputation when a reaction against artistic sentimentality set in; it is only very recently that his genuine gifts for the expression of feeling have been given their proper due. Among other Carracci pupils, **Domenichino** (1581–1641) was a faithful follower of the style, extending its hold on Rome, though he was better at its more decorative and idealised aspects. **Guercino** (1591–1666) merged the classical and realistic styles, imbuing chiaroscuro effects with a subtlety very different to that favoured by Caravaggio and his followers.

Giovanni Lanfranco (1582–1647), originally from Parma, combined the Carracci style with elements borrowed from Correggio. His frescoes in Rome and Naples have a greater sense of movement and technical trickery than those Domenichino was painting at the same time, and mark the beginnings of High Baroque painting. In turn, his own work was made to seem out-of-date by **Pietro da Cortona** (1596–1669), who introduced a sense of fantasy and freedom that was far more ambitious than anything previously attempted. His ceiling in the Palazzo Barberini presented the illusion of opening on to the heavily populated heavens above, with figures seen *sotto in su* – apparently teeming down into the hall below. For a century, this was to be the sort of monumental painting favoured in Rome; it was also spread to Florence by Cortona himself, by means of a series of frescoes in the Palazzo Pitti.

The High Baroque style was essentially a Roman phenomenon, born out of the superconfident mood in the world capital of Catholicism as a result of the success of the Counter-Reformation. Its overwhelmingly dominant personality was **Gianlorenzo Bernini** (1598–1680), a youthful prodigy who had created a wholly new sculptural language while still in his early twenties. Such works as *David* and *Apollo and Daphne*, both in the Villa Borghese, were the first great marble statues since Michelangelo, yet in their independence of form showed a decisive rejection of the concept of belonging to the block from which

they were carved, drawing the spectator into the scene and asserting the primacy of the emotions – a key concept of the Baroque. Though only an occasional painter (he in fact spent more time as an architect), Bernini adopted painterly techniques for his work, using different materials for contrast, exploiting sources of light, and using illusionist techniques, producing a drama best seen in *The Ecstasy of St Theresa* in Rome's Santa Maria della Victoria, which goes so far as to recreate the atmosphere of a theatre by the inclusion of a gallery of onlookers.

So overwhelming was the impact of Bernini's art, that most other sculpture of the period is but a pale imitation of it. One of the few sculptors not to be overawed was the Tuscan **Francesco Mochi** (1580–1654), who made two magnificent equestrian monuments in Piacenza. **Alessandro Algardi** (1595–1654) of Bologna managed a brilliant career in Rome as a bitter rival of Bernini, promoting a sculptural version of the Carracci style.

In Venice, the versatile Genovese **Bernardo Strozzi** (1581–1644) tried to revive memories of the great sixteenth-century masters. His exuberant early works are generally more successful, showing the influence of Rubens: they typically have very free brushwork, luminous colours and pronounced modelling. In Naples, **Massimo Stanzione** (1585–1656) combined something of the approaches of Carracci and Caravaggio, though his most original works are his detailed, colourful portraits. A much more aggressively Caravaggesque idiom is apparent in the work of **Artemesia Gentileschi** (c.1597–1651), daughter of Orazio, who was particularly adept at lurid subjects. She enjoyed a remarkable degree of independence and status for a woman of her day, and has attracted a great deal of attention from modern feminists, having a fair claim to the title of "the greatest ever female painter". **Salvator Rosa** (1615–73) painted landscapes that have a wild, mystical quality very different from those of the classical painters of Bologna and Rome. Characteristically, they are populated by bandits or witches, or have an allegorical theme. **Mattia Preti** (1613–99), who originally hailed from the artistic backwater of Calabria, painted some of the most effective canvases in Caravaggio's idiom, excelling at its tenebrist aspects. His later work is more influenced by Roman Baroque, using brighter colours and pronounced spatial effects. In these, he resembles **Luca Giordano** (1632–1705), the main Neapolitan painter of the second half of the century. Giordano was renowned for his ability to paint quickly, and he ranks among the most prolific artists of all time. His output employs a whole variety of styles and is uneven in quality, but shows remarkable technical facility. The last major Baroque painter active in Naples was **Francesco Solimena** (1657–1747), whose large crowded compositions show the full theatricality of the style.

Meanwhile, the Roman vogue for spectacular illusionistic ceilings was continued by **Giovanni Battista Baciccia** (1639–1709), who was warmer in colour and even more audacious in approach than Pietro da Cortona. His most famous decoration is that in the Gesù, which boldly mixes painted and stucco figures. An even greater command of pyrotechnics, however, was displayed by the Jesuit **Andrea Pozzo** (1642–1709) on the ceiling of Sant'Ignazio, whose illusion is designed to be seen from only one specific point.

THE 18TH CENTURY

The decline of Italian art in many of its most celebrated strongholds gathered pace in the eighteenth century, a slump from which only Venice and Rome stood apart. In the case of the former, its pre-eminence was due to a revival of its grand decorative tradition after a century's gap. This gave it a leading position in European **Rococo**, the ornate derivative of late Baroque.

An updated version of the style of Veronese was first fostered by **Sebastiano Ricci** (1659–1734), whose work is superficially similar to Veronese's, but has an airier, lighter feel. A more individual approach is apparent in the work of **Giovanni Battista Piazzetta** (1683–1754), an outstanding draughtsman whose joyful and harmonious paintings give the impression of a free and easy approach, yet which were actually the result of meticulous planning. Venice also boasted a notable female portraitist in **Rosalba Carriera** (1675–1757), who was the first artist to use pastel as an independent medium.

By far the most accomplished exponent of Venetian Rococo, and one of the greatest decorative artists of all time, was **Giovanni Battista Tiepolo** (1696–1770). His work is best seen in an architectural setting, where his illusionistic approach compares favourably with those of the earlier Roman artists in its colour, handling, spatial awareness, sense of fantasy and depth of feeling. The finest schemes were made for foreign patrons (in Würzburg and Madrid), but there are some excellent examples in Udine, Vicenza and Stra, and several in Venice itself, notably the Palazzo Labia and Ca'Rezzonico.

His son, **Giovanni Domenico Tiepolo** (1727–1804), aided him on many projects and painted in a broadly similar style, though he had a more obvious eye for satire. Also active in Venice were a number of painters who specialised in painting views of the city as mementos for its aristoctatic visitors. The best known of these was **Antonio Canaletto** (1697–1738), whose images, often painted on the spot and with the use of a camera obscura, have defined the popular conception of the buildings and lifestyle of Venice ever since. However, they are an idealised representation, with spatial arrangements and even individual buildings altered. Canaletto's nephew, **Bernardo Bellotto** (1721–80), closely followed his style and applied it to cities all over Europe, but took a more literal approach, stressing topographical exactness. A more sombre, musing mood is present in the Venetian views of **Francesco Guardi** (1712–93), who used a darker palette. His emphasis on transitory light effects foreshadowed the French Impressionists, while his figures have a greater vivacity than those of Canaletto. Genre scenes were also much in demand with visiting tourists, and **Pietro Longhi** (1702–85), who had a limited technique but ready sense of humour, vividly characterised the Venetian life of his day for the benefit of this market.

Among non-Venetian painters, the Genovese **Alessandro Magnasco** (1677–1749) is particularly distinctive, often combining into one picture his two favourite themes of mannered landscapes ravaged by the elements and ecstatic monks at prayer. In Rome, the tourist demand for views was met by **Giovanni Paolo Panini** (c.1692–1765/8), who painted both the ruins of the classical period and the modern buildings of the day. These are surpassed, however, by the grandiose large-scale etchings of **Giovanni Battista Piranesi** (1720–78), which fully exploit the dramatic contrasts of light and shade possible in the black-and-white medium.

The latter can be seen as an early manifestation of **Neoclassicism**, a movement which began in the middle of the century, inspired partly by a reaction against Baroque excesses, and partly by the excitement caused by the discovery of Pompeii and Herculaneum, though many of its leading exponents were foreigners resident in Rome. Neoclassicism aimed at the complete revival of the arts of the ancients, a trend that was particularly marked in sculpture, which had a far larger legacy to borrow on than painting. It is best seen in the works of **Antonio Canova** (1757–1822), which show great beauty in modelling, though a certain frigidity in the depiction of emotions. His statues are often highly erotic in effect: the several monuments he made in honour of Napoleon include life-sized nude depictions, one of which is now in the Brera, Milan.

THE 19TH AND 20TH CENTURIES

If the eighteenth century was a lean time for Italian art, the nineteenth century was even worse, Paris becoming the overwhelmingly dominant European trendsetter. **Francesco Hayez** (1791–1882) was just about the only native painter of note at work in the first half of the century, continuing the Neoclassical manner in his history scenes and highly finished portraits. The Europe-wide Romantic movement made little impact on the Italian imagination, although the country's scenery was to be a potent source of inspiration for visiting foreigners.

Just after the middle of the century, there arose a group of Italian painters based in Florence, known as the **Macchiaioli**, who held more modern and definable aims. Their name derives from the Italian word for a blot, as they made extensive use of individual patches of light and dark colour, which was used to define form, in opposition to the supersmooth Neoclassical approach then in vogue. The guiding spirit of the movement was **Giovanni Fattori** (1825–1908), who painted scenes of military life (based on his experiences fighting in the Wars of Independence of 1848–9) and broad landscapes using very free

brushwork and compositional techniques. The group's chief theorist, **Telemaco Signorini** (1835–1901), came to be influenced by the painting of Corot and the Barbizon School, and later followers moved to Paris, to become accepted as peripheral members of the Impressionist circle.

These painters are overshadowed by **Amadeo Modigliani** (1884–1920), the only Italian artist born in the last two hundred years to have gained truly universal recognition. Although most of his adult life was spent in Paris, Modigliani's work is recognisably Italian, being rooted in the tradition of the Renaissance and Mannerist masters. Primitive African art, then being appreciated in Europe for the first time, was the other main influence on his highly distinctive and essentially linear style. His output consists almost entirely of sensuous reclining female nudes, and strongly drawn, psychologically penetrating portraits.

In 1909 an attempt to break France's artistic monopoly was launched – ironically enough, in Paris – by the **Futurists**, who aimed to glorify the dynamism of the modern world, including the key role of warfare. Their approach was similar to the recently-founded Cubist movement in aiming to reproduce several sides of an object at the same time, but differed in wanting to convey movement as well. **Umberto Boccioni** (1882–1916) was the most resourceful member of the group, which never recovered from his death in World War I – for which, true to his principles, he had volunteered. His erstwhile colleagues later developed in different directions. **Giacomo Balla** (1871–1958) painted in a variety of styles, ranging from the academic to the abstract. **Gino Severini** (1883–1966) joined the Cubists after the latter had become more interested in colour, but then turned to mural and mosaic decorations before reverting towards the end of his life to a sense of fantasy characteristic of his Futurist phase. **Carlo Carrà** (1881–1966) did a complete about-face from his Futurist origins, aiming to revive the representationalism of the old Italian masters.

Carrà teamed up in 1917 with **Giorgio de'Chirico** (1888–1978) to form **Pittura Metafisica**, which reacted against both the mechanical approach of Cubism and Futurism's infatuation with the modern world, cultivating instead a nostalgia for antiquity. The movement, which established a school in Ferrara, was influenced by Surrealism, and in particular a penchant for the presence of unexpected, out-of-place objects. De'Chirico's *Metaphysical Interiors* show rooms littered with all the fetishes of modern civilisation; architectural forms of a strange and rigid nature are another recurring theme in his work of this period, though like Carrà he later abandoned this in favour of a consciously archaic approach.

Among other Italian painters of the twentieth century to have gained an international reputation, **Giorgio Morandi** (1890–1964), who was strongly influenced by de'Chirico, specialised in haunting still lifes – very precisely drawn and often in monochrome. Also touched by the Metaphysical tradition was **Filippo de Pisis** (1896–1956). His huge output is experimental in nature, often exploring sensation and the unexpected; consequently, it is highly uneven in quality. The Sicilian **Renato Guttoso** (1912–87) also focused on dramatic subjects, this time with political intent. His early works expressed his opposition to Fascism; in 1947, he helped to found *Fronte Nuovo delle Arti*, which aimed to link art to revolution. Italy's leading practitioner of abstraction is **Alberto Burri** (b.1915), best known for his collages of waste materials with a thick blob of red or black paint.

Modern Italian sculptors have been more successful than painters in reinterpreting Italy's heritage in a novel way. **Giacomo Manzú** (b.1908) has aimed to revive the Italian religious tradition, in a highly personal manner reminiscent of Donatello, whose technique of very low relief he has used extensively. His best known work is the bronze door of St Peter's on the theme of Death, a commission awarded following a highly contentious competition in 1949. **Marino Marini** (1901–80) specialised in another great theme of Italian art, that of the equestrian monument – examples of his work are now displayed in a museum specially devoted to Marini in Florence – while the portraits and female nudes of **Emilio Greco** (b.1913) stand as an updated form of Mannerism.

Gordon McLachlan

ITALIAN ARCHITECTURE

Even if Italy's architecture has not been so consistently influential as her painting and sculpture, the country still boasts a remarkable legacy of historic buildings, an almost unbroken tradition stretching back over more than 2500 years. As in the other arts, strong regional distinctions are evident in most of the main architectural periods.

THE GREEKS AND ETRUSCANS

The earliest important structures still standing in Italy were built by the peninsula's **Greek** colonisers of the sixth century BC. These exhibit the same qualities characteristic of the classical architecture of Greece itself: a strong but simple outline, a rigorous adherence to balanced proportions, a total unity of design featuring a logical system of horizontals and verticals, and extensive use of decoration to emphasise the structure. This architecture, which principally made use of marble, was based on three great **classical orders**, each of which consisted of an upright column, sometimes resting on a base, topped by a capital and an entablature of architrave, cornice and frieze.

Doric, the grandest and plainest of these orders, was used for the **temples** which are the chief glory of the Greek style, dedicated to gods yet always human in scale, never rising

very high, nor appearing in any way overblown. A fine group can be seen on the Italian mainland at **Paestum**; the others – at Agrigento, Selinunte, Segesta and Syracuse – are in **Sicily**. They are older and less refined than the Parthenon in Athens, but their state of preservation compares favourably with any of their counterparts in Greece. Significantly, the Temple of Concord in Agrigento, the most complete of all, was saved by being transformed into a Christian church, while the Temple of Athena in Syracuse was incorporated into the Duomo, where it still remains.

The Greeks were also inveterate builders of open-air **theatres** – generally set against hillsides, with seats for the spectators hollowed out of the rock. Syracuse's Greek theatre is one of the best preserved of its period; that of Taormina, with the peerless backdrop of Mount Etna, also dates back to the Greeks, but was extensively remodelled by the Romans.

A very different form of architecture was practised during the same period in central Italy by the **Etruscans**, who favoured the use of huge, cyclopean stone blocks. Unfortunately, little Etruscan architecture remains above ground, as their Roman conquerors engaged in a deliberate programme of obliteration. The few surviving examples include the city walls of Volterra and Cortona, from the sixth century BC, and the gateways at Volterra and Perugia, from about three centuries later. However, Etruscan **tombs** survive in abundance, mainly at Cerveteri and Tarquinia in northern Lazio.

THE ROMAN PERIOD

In architecture, as in many other fields, the **Romans** borrowed from and adapted Greek models. Just as was the case with other art forms, however, their approach to building shows marked differences, particularly in their preference for order and usefulness above beauty. Functional building materials were favoured, and only from the time of Augustus, which marked the softening of the Roman image, are marble and stucco much in evidence, and then usually for facing purposes only. Furthermore, towns were laid out wherever possible in a regular planned grid format, to the model of a military camp.

Although they used the three Greek orders (preferring the Corinthian, with its elaborate acanthus leaf capital), and invented two more of their own, the Romans relegated the column from the essential structural role it had performed under the Greeks to one that was merely decorative. Instead, they concentrated on solid constructions, employing the rounded forms of the arch and dome, and focusing attention on the end walls. **Vaulting** was the Romans' major contribution to architectural development. Their use of concrete rather than timber frames enabled them to span much larger spaces, and build much higher, than the Greeks had ever done; indeed, their achievements were unequalled until the nineteenth century. Accordingly, they were able to create an architecture which perfectly expressed their own preoccupations of power and glory.

Roman architecture once dominated Europe, showing no appreciable regional variations, and many of the most impressive individual monuments still standing lie outside Italy. However, the most important ensembles are to be found in **Rome** itself, its original seaport of **Ostia**, and the residential towns of **Pompeii** and **Herculaneum** (which were both submerged by the massive eruption of Mount Vesuvius). The heart of a Roman city was its **forum**, a square usually set at the intersection of the two main streets. Its buildings were the focus of all the main aspects of public life: worship, politics, law, finance, trading, shopping and meeting. In time, it often became too small for all these functions: the Roman Forum itself, which largely dates from the days of the Republic, is an extreme case in point, and successive emperors found it necessary to lay out separate new forums in the city.

Each forum usually contained several **temples**, of which notable examples survive in Palestrina, Tivoli, Assisi and Brescia. At first, these tended to follow the Greek model, with the front entrance given due prominence, and often preceded by a flight of steps. Later, circular designs were increasingly favoured, as with the Temples of Vesta in Rome. A circular design was also chosen for the **Pantheon** in Rome, which is not only the greatest temple of all, and the only complete building to have survived from the days of Imperial Rome, but is also one of the all-time masterpieces of both engineering and architecture, its dome still one of the largest in the world.

The main public building in Roman towns was the **basilica**, which was used for meet-ings and administration. In many respects, it was rather like a Greek temple turned inside out, consisting of a large hall terminating in an apse, with aisles to the side, often bearing galleries and with a sloping vault which was lower than that of the main section. No complete examples survive in Italy, but some idea of the development of this type of building can be had by comparing the fragments of the basilicas of Trajan and Maxentius in Rome, which are nearly two centuries apart in date. The former was colonnaded, and had a flat wooden roof, while the latter (as can clearly be seen in the surviving aisle) had a sturdy concrete vault borne by five massive piers.

In the field of leisure, the **thermae** played a key role. These vast edifices had hot, warm and cold baths, as well as halls for all kinds of other activities, those of the Emperors Caracalla and Diocletian, both in Rome, from the third and fourth centuries AD, providing the most potent reminder of their splendour. Roman **theatres** differed from those of the Greeks in being constructed above ground, and in having a semicircular *orchestra*. The Teatro de Marcello, completed under Augustus, is the only survivor in Rome itself; it is also notable for marking the use of superimposed orders in architecture for the first time. However, the Romans as a rule much preferred the atmosphere of their **amphitheatres**, which were used to stage gladiatorial contests and other public spectaculars. These were elliptical in shape, and of very solid construction, using a variety of materials. The outer wall, pierced by rows of arches, had a massive effect; inside, the seats were grouped in tiers. Rome's so-called Colosseum is the best-preserved; others are to be found in Verona, Cápua, Pozzuoli and Pompeii. Proof of the durability of these monuments is provided by the fact that they are still in use.

Roman **houses** fall into three main categories. The *domus* or town dwelling was grouped symmetrically around an atrium and one or more peristyle courts. A more rambling plan characterises the *villa*, a patrician country residence, which tended to be decorated with porticoes and colonnades, and to have rooms specially aligned to catch both the sun and the shade. Poorer Romans lived in *insulae*, tenement-type constructions with several floors, which were often vaulted throughout and grouped symmetrically in streets and squares. Few Roman **palaces** remain. The most important is the misleadingly named Villa Adriana in Tivoli, replete with fantastical recreations of buildings the Emperor Hadrian had seen on his travels, along with grottoes, terraces and fountains. From a century earlier, Nero's fabled Domus Aurea in Rome survives only in part.

Roman law forbade burial inside the city walls, and the Via Appia became the favoured site, lined by cylindrical, tower-like **mausoleums**, the finest being that of Cecilia Metella. A similar but larger structure, of the Emperor Augustus, was the first to be built in the city centre. Another in honour of Hadrian was far the most spectacular funerary monument built by the Romans, but was later converted into the Castel Sant'Angelo.

The **triumphal arch** was a specifically Roman creation, usually erected to celebrate military victories and richly adorned with bas-reliefs, the whole surmounted by a large sculptural group, usually of a horse-drawn triumphal chariot. Several of these arches can be seen in Rome; others are in Ancona, Aosta, Benevento, Rimini and Susa.

Another Roman invention was the **aqueduct**, which was built to transport water to the towns. These were undecorated and purely functional, with the water running down a very gentle gradient along a channel at the top. Nonetheless, they often have a majestic sweep, particularly when the lie of the land dictated the building of several tiers. Traces of aqueducts can be seen south of Rome, though the most impressive surviving examples are in other countries. The Romans also excelled at building **bridges**. There were eleven spanning the Tiber in the capital in imperial times; these have mostly been replaced or altered, but the Pons Fabricius remains substantially intact. Other bridges which have changed little are the graceful Ponte di Solesta in Ascoli Piceno, which is of a single arch only, and the five-arched Ponte di Tiberio in Rimini.

EARLY CHRISTIAN AND BYZANTINE

The **early Christians** in Italy initially had to practise their religion underground in **catacombs** hollowed out of the living rock. Those in Rome are the most famous, but other impressive groups can be seen in Naples and Syracuse. When Christianity was legalised and officially adopted by the Roman Empire, it was hardly surprising that its architecture should base itself very directly on secular imperial models. In particular, **churches** adopted a basilican format. They were generally raised over the graves of martyrs, whose tombs were kept in the crypt, directly below the high altar. In time, they would invariably be orientated towards the east, though in the early churches it was quite normal to face exactly the opposite way. For the interior, columns were often taken from demolished secular buildings.

In **Rome** itself, much the best-preserved church of this time is Santa Sabina, which dates from the fifth century. Its exterior is of a stark simplicity, the plain brick walls pierced only by large windows; the interior shows the move towards regular columns. The larger contemporary basilicas of Santa Maria Maggiore and San Paolo fuori le Mura, though both much altered down the centuries, still clearly show the variations in the basilican plan. **Transepts** were introduced, as a result of a conscious desire to simulate the shape of the Cross; double aisles were also employed, except at Santa Maria Maggiore. Also of this period is San Giovanni in Laterano, which pioneers the Italian preference for a separate, octagonal **baptistery**.

The basic basilican style flourished in the city for centuries, and little in the way of development is discernible between the seventh-century Sant'Agnese and the ninth-century Santa Maria in Cosmedin, or even the twelfth-century San Clemente, though the last is unusually archaic.

The next significant buildings are those of the subsequent imperial capital, **Ravenna**. These are understandably more famous for the resplendent mosaics which adorn their interiors, but they are also of major architectural significance, marking the appearance in Italy of the **Byzantine** style, whose most distinctive characteristic was the development of the dome. Under the Romans, this by necessity had to rest on a circular base; by the use of pendentives, the Byzantines were able to erect a dome on square foundations. The earliest of the surviving Ravenna monuments, the Mausoleum of Galla Placida, dating from about 430, provides a good illustration of this. The church of San Vitale, an ingenious design of an octagon within an octagon, is also remarkable. The other churches here are basilican in form; a curiosity is that the apse is semicircular inside, but has a polygonal exterior. Their cylindrical **campaniles** were added later, probably in the ninth century. These are the earliest freestanding bell towers – from then on, a popular characteristic of Italian churches – to have survived, though the form was actually pioneered in Rome.

Italy's most purely Byzantine buildings are to be found in the Venetian lagoon, whose prosperity was dependent on its eastern trade. The Duomo of **Torcello**, originally seventh-century but extensively remodelled in the early eleventh century, is the oldest of these; Santa Fosca on the same island is in the same style. However, the Byzantine heritage is seen to best effect in the basilica of San Marco in **Venice** itself. This was also much altered in the eleventh century, but the basic layout of the original ninth-century building, modelled on the Church of the Holy Apostles in Constantinople, was preserved. With its five bulbous domes, its Greek-cross plan and sumptuous mosaic decoration it stands as the supreme Byzantine monument of its time.

ROMANESQUE

The European emergence from the Dark Ages in the tenth and eleventh centuries is associated in architecture with the **Romanesque** style, which in Italy draws heavily on the country's own heritage. Features not commonly found in other countries include a continued attachment to the basilical plan, and to cupolas raised on domes, the use of marble for facing, the presence of separate baptisteries and campaniles, and the employment of the arch for decorative rather than purely structural reasons.

Strong regional variations are apparent. The churches of the **Lombard plain** most resemble those of northern Europe, and were among the most internationally influential. Their most dominant features are their tall, stately towers, which are unbuttressed and adorned with pilaster strips. They usually have a projecting vaulted porch on the facade, resting on a base of lions, above which a wheel window serves as the principal source of light for the nave. Decoration is otherwise concentrated in the apse, which often has an open dwarf gallery and corbels delicately carved with grotesque heads. Rib vaulting – revolutionary in its day – was sometimes used inside. The Duomo in **Modena** is particularly outstanding, as are the characteristic trios of duomo, campanile and baptistery at **Parma** and **Cremona**.

All these are surpassed by the highly distinctive style of **Pişa**, which can be seen all over the city but is particularly associated with the Piazza del Duomo, which adds a burial ground (the Camposanto) to the normal group of three, and has the rare advantage of a spacious verdant setting away from the commercial centre. Although the ensemble was begun in the mid-eleventh century and only finished 300 years later, it shows a remarkable sense of unity. The buildings all have marble facing, and their exteriors, in a design conducive to catching wonderful light effects, have open arcaded galleries, which rise all the way to the facade gable – and all the way round the building. A broadly similar approach was adopted in the neighbouring cities of **Lucca** and **Pistoia**.

An even more idiosyncratic Romanesque style was fostered in the earliest surviving buildings of **Florence** – the Baptistery, San Miniato and Santi Apostoli, plus the Badia in Fiesole. The overall layout of these buildings is typical enough of the time, but the continued use of mosaics and marble panelling in the interiors is suggestive of the Byzantine era, while the overall elegance of form shows a debt to Roman models.

In **southern Italy** there was a marriage of Byzantine and Romanesque styles, as can be seen at San Nicola in Bari and the duomos of Salerno, Amalfi, Troia, Trani, Molfetta and Bitonto. An even more intoxicating mix is found in **Sicily**, where the island's traditions were freely welded into an exotic confection which is wholly unique. Sturdy Norman towers are often found in concert with Byzantine domes and mosaics and Saracenic horeshoe arches and stalactite vaulting. The Duomo of **Monreale** – and in particular its fabulous cloister with dazzling mosaics and richly carved capitals – is particularly outstanding. Those of **Cefalù** and **Palermo** are also notable, as are three surprising parish churches, all in the capital – La Martorana, San Cataldo and San Giovanni degli Eremiti. The same city also has two outstanding palaces which show the same mix of styles: the Palazzo dei Normanni and La Zisa.

THE GOTHIC PERIOD

The **Gothic** style, which placed great emphasis on light and verticality, and was associated with the pointed arch, rib vault, flying buttress and large traceried windows, progressed from its mid-twelfth-century French origins to become the dominant architectural force of medieval Europe. But although it was used in Italy from the early thirteenth century to the early fifteenth century, its lifespan here was far shorter than elsewhere, and the forms it took quite different from those of other countries. In many ways, Italy was wholly unsuited to the Gothic, which remained essentially a northern European creation. The pointed arch was foreign to a country steeped in classicism, while the hot climate meant that only small windows were required, or interiors would become stifling. For the same reason, the giant portals of northern Gothic were unwanted; moreover, the large numbers of statues in the round they required were anathema to a nation reared on relief carvings.

In Italian Gothic architecture the emphasis is still on the **horizontal**: buildings seldom rise very high, and often have wooden roofs rather than stone vaults. **Colour** plays a far more important role than in any other country, walls covered with marble facing, mosaics and frescoes. A great deal of attention was lavished on **facades**, but these were again often purely decorative, with no architectural relationship to the structure behind. Many of the most characteristic features of Gothic, such as soaring steeples and graceful pinnacles, flying buttresses and elaborate vaults, are hardly to be found in Italy at all.

As elsewhere in Europe, the spread of the plain early-Gothic style in Italy is associated with the reforming Cistercian order of monks. The abbey of **Fossanova**, which was complete by the first decade of the thirteenth century, is an outstanding example of their architecture, as well as an unusually complete example of a medieval monastic complex. In a similar manner are the monasteries of San Galgano near Siena (now in ruins) and the collegiate church of Sant'Andrea in Vercelli. However, the most outstanding early-Gothic church in Italy is the basilica of San Francesco in **Assisi**, which was built in the wake of the saint's death in 1226. It is a wholly original, symbolical design, with the lower church dark and mysterious, the upper light and airy, each provided with ample wall space which in time was duly filled with appropriate fresco cycles.

Nothing quite like San Francesco was ever built again, but the churches of the Franciscan and Dominican orders became a dominant feature of many cities. In accordance with the emphasis placed on preaching, these were typically barn-like structures, intended to hold a large congregation. They were invariably of brick, but differed considerably in plan. The most imposing are the late-thirteenth-century Santa Croce and Santa Maria Novella in **Florence**, and their fourteenth-century counterparts in **Venice** – I Frari and San Zanipolo.

Only one modest Gothic church (Santa Maria sopra Minerva) was ever built in Rome. Nonetheless, the relatively few important building projects of the period generally took on a spectacular nature. The Duomo in **Siena** is arguably the most sumptuous Gothic cathedral ever built, and boasts a resplendent facade in which sculptures were used in a wholly unorthodox and challenging way. **Florence**'s Duomo has gained world fame through its Renaissance dome, but in essentials it is a highly inventive Gothic design, whose final shape had already been determined by the mid-fourteenth century. Its detached campanile, unbuttressed and faced with coloured marbles and reliefs illustrates the continuing Italian preference for this form. **Orvieto** shows the tendencies of Italian Gothic at its most extreme: the interior architecture is plain, and remarkably close in spirit to an early Christian basilica, whereas the facade surpasses even Siena's for ornateness, with its narrative bas-reliefs, brightly coloured marbles and mosaics. Only the Duomo of **Milan**, begun in the late fourteenth century but only finally completed in the nineteenth century, uses much of the stock vocabulary of northern European cathedral architecture, no doubt due to the fact that German masons were partly responsible for its construction. Yet even here the gleaming white marble and pronounced geometric nature of the design are wholly Italianate.

The scale of this project seems to have inspired that of the nearby Certosa of **Pavia**, the most extensive monastic complex in the country. Here, however, notice was paid to changing artistic tastes, with the result that it progressively moved away from its Gothic origins. San Petronio in **Bologna**, which was started around the same time, was a parish church intended to rival any cathedral, and to surpass them all in length. Work, however, was abandoned on the belated completion of the nave. From a century earlier, another idiosyncratic design worthy of mention is the pilgrimage church of Il Santo in **Padua**. This has an essentially Gothic plan, even including a French-style chevet with radiating chapels. However, the facade is derived from the Lombard Romanesque, while the seven large domes are evidence of the continued attraction of Byzantinism.

In the field of military architecture, the most imposing thirteenth-century **castles** were built in southern Italy by Emperor Frederick II, most impressive of which is the celebrated **Castel del Monte**, which combined classical and Gothic elements in a plan of monotonous regularity, with an octagonal shape used for towers, perimeter walls and courtyard. Frederick's castle at **Lucera** was transformed later in the century by the Angevins, who also built the Castel Nuovo in **Naples** – later altered to serve as a palace in succeeding centuries.

Among fourteenth-century constructions, the Fortezza at **Volterra** is an archetypal medieval castle set high on a hill, with cylindrical keep, round towers, massive outer walls and machicolations. Of the palatial fortresses begun around this time, those of **Mantua**, **Ferrara** and **Verona** are particularly outstanding, the last guarded by a strongly fortified **bridge** over the Adige. Italy's other famous Gothic bridge, the Ponte Vecchio in Florence, presents a total contrast, with jewellers' shops along its length.

In the late thirteenth century, the rise of civic pride led to a passion for building majestic **town halls**, often crowned by a slender tower. The most imposing are the Palazzo Pubblico in Siena and the Palazzo Vecchio in Florence. These same cities, along with many more in central Italy, are rich in Gothic **mansions** of the patrician class. However, the most distinctive residences in the country were built in **Venice**. The Ca' d'Oro is the most refined, whereas the Ca' Foscari and Palazzi Giustinian have a compensating monumental grandeur. All were modelled on Italy's most famous **palace**, the Palazzo Ducale. This is arguably the greatest secular European building of its time, ingeniously combining Gothic and Islamic styles on its exterior walls, with evidence of the classical influence in its courtyards and interiors.

THE EARLY RENAISSANCE

The Gothic style maintained a firm hold over northern European architecture until well into the sixteenth century. In **Florence**, however, it had been supplanted by the second decade of the fifteenth century by the new, classically derived **Renaissance** style, which soon spread throughout Italy. Its conquest of the rest of Europe, if belated, was absolute, establishing an architectural vocabulary which remained unchallenged until the nineteenth century, and still maintains a footing even today. From here on, the history of architecture becomes a history of architects. Previously, major buildings had been designed and built by lodges under masons whose fame was seldom wide or long lasting. To some extent this had been modified in Italy by the appointment of famous painters and sculptors for the most prestigious commissions. This trend continued in the Renaissance period – and was undoubtedly a factor in ensuring that all major buildings were aesthetically pleasing, a casual relationship which was lost in later centuries. However, architecture shed its dilettante connotations, and was henceforth professional in outlook, with full-time practitioners emerging for the first time.

Both the format of modern architecture and the profession of architect were in many respects the single-handed creation of **Filippo Brunelleschi** (1377–1446). Having been unsuccessful in the competition for the Florence Baptistery doors, he turned away from his original training as a sculptor, devoting himself to a careful study of the building practices and techniques of the ancients. He subsequently won another major local competition, that for the Duomo's dome. It was only by reviving Roman methods of herringbone brickwork, and by inventing suitable hoisting machinery, that Brunelleschi· was able to give the final shape to this otherwise Gothic construction, which ever since has served as the focal point of the city, and provided a model for all subsequent domes. In his key original buildings – the Ospedale degli Innocenti, the churches of San Lorenzo and Santo Spirito and the Cappella Pazzi – Brunelleschi seems to have been inspired as much by the distinctive Romanesque legacy of his native city as by ancient Rome. His designs are majestic but uncomplicated; they are entirely original, and in no sense an archaeological revival of any previous style.

Two more Brunelleschi innovations – a new type of urban palace, and a central plan for church design – are best illustrated in buildings by **Michelozzo di Bartolommeo** (1396–1472). The Palazzo Medici-Riccardi established the form of Florentine mansions for the rest of the century – a severe facade with rusticated stonework in the basement and smooth ashlar upstairs, an overhanging cornice, and a compensatingly light inner courtyard. In the church of Santi Annunziata, Michelozzo modelled the tribune on a circular Roman temple in the first centrally planned church design to be built in the Renaissance period; with Santa Maria delle Grazie in **Pistoia** he extended this concept to the entire building. His light and airy library in San Marco is a mould-breaker in its own right; its format of a central nave flanked by aisles was used throughout the Renaissance.

Even more influential was **Leone Battista Alberti** (1404–72). One of the most complete personifications of Renaissance Man, Alberti was above all a writer and theorist, the author of the first architectural treatise since Roman times; he designed buildings, but always relied on other architects to build them. Far more archaeological in taste than Brunelleschi, he set out to give new life to such Roman forms as triumphal arches and pedimented temple fronts. He also articulated the theory of harmonic proportions, which, in emulation of musical intervals, adopted certain ratios of measurement – first put into practice in the facade of Santa Maria Novella. With the Palazzo Rucellai, he solved the problem of how to make the facades of Florentine palaces seem less austere and Gothic in feel by the simple expedient of introducing thin pilaster strips. Alberti's most original creations, however, are outside Florence. Although unfinished, his design for the Tempio Malatestiano in **Rimini** is a magnificent fragment, cloaking the old Franciscan church with a covering inspired by the same town's great Roman monuments. An even more resplendent facade was designed for Sant'Andrea in **Mantua**. Its elements are carefully repeated in the interior, a vast space which daringly omits aisles in favour of a single nave with side chapels.

Bernardo Rossellino (1409–64), who was the builder of the Palazzo Rucellai, used its basic form again in the Palazzo Piccolomini in **Pienza**, where he was also responsible for the duomo. This was part of the most ambitious planning scheme of the day, the laying out of a complete new papal town. Like many subsequent Renaissance projects, it remains incomplete, available funds so often failing to match the grandeur of inspiration. The creation of ideal towns was the main preoccupation of **Antonio Averlino Filarete** (c.1400–69), the second main architectural theorist of the day. He himself built very little, other than part of the Castello Sforzesco and the huge, symmetrical Ospedale Maggiore, both in **Milan**.

Of the next generation of Florentine architects, **Giuliano da Maiano** (1432–90) introduced the Renaissance style to Siena with the Palazzo Spannochi, and also built the duomo in **Faenza**. The last phase of his career was spent in **Naples**, where he was responsible for the Porta Capuana and chapels in the church of Monteoliveto. **Giuliano da Sangallo** (1445–1516) was the first to apply Renaissance principles to the layout of villas, and his work in Florence includes the Palazzo Strozzi, the most ambitious palace of the century, and the heavily antique cloister of Santa Maria Maddalena dei Pazzi, in which Ionic columns boldly take the place of arches.

The most complete and refined early-Renaissance palace was built in the comparative obscurity of **Urbino**, where a cultivated humanist court flourished. **Luciano Laurana** (c.1420–79), an obscure architect of Dalmatian origin, is credited with the overall plan, as well as the building of the elegant courtyard, and the ornate chimneypieces and doorways which are key features of the interior. Also attached to Urbino was the Sienese **Francesco di Giorgio Martini** (1439–1501/2), who is thought to have built the exquisite loggia overlooking the hills, as well as two domed churches: San Bernardino in Urbino itself and Santa Maria del Calcinaio in Cortona. Like many other Renaissance architects, he worked extensively on military projects, specialising in hilltop castles with pioneering defences against artillery. **Ferrara** was another small court where the Renaissance prospered, thanks in large part to an ambitious extension to the town designed by **Biagio Rossetti** (1447–1516), which included numerous churches and palaces, the most original of which is the Palazzo dei Diamanti, named after the diamond shapes used on its facade. **Venice** remained attached to the Gothic style until the 1460s. When the Renaissance finally took root, it was given a pronounced local accent, with hangovers from Byzantinism in the preference for rich surfaces and mystical spatial effects. Architects still enjoyed nothing like the prestige they had gained in Florence, and it was only as a result of nineteenth-century research that **Mauro Coducci** (c.1440–1504) emerged from obscurity to be identified as the builder of many of the city's best buildings of this time – the churches of San Michele in Isola, San Giovanni Crisostomo and Santa Maria Formosa. His rival **Pietro Lombardo** (c.1435–1515) was less concerned with the central tenets of the Florentine Renaissance than with using them to update the Venetian-Byzantine tradition. The tiny church of Santa Maria dei Miracoli, for which he and his sons also made the decoration, shows his highly ornate style at its best.

THE HIGH RENAISSANCE AND MANNERISM

The ornate facades characteristic of the Venetian Renaissance were to some extent repeated all across northern Italy, notably in the early buildings of **Donato Bramante** (1444–1514) in **Milan**. These include the church of San Satiro, which ingeniously incorporates a ninth-century chapel and makes up for the lack of space to build an apse by including a convincing *trompe l'oeil* of one; the centrally planned east end of Santa Maria delle Grazie, which completely outclasses the Gothic nave; and a series of cloisters for Sant'Ambrogio.

With the French invasion of the city in 1499, Bramante fled to **Rome**, where his enthusiasm coincided nicely with the papal authorities' desire to rebuild the city in a manner worthy of its imperial heyday, and the **High Renaissance** in architecture was born. This centred on the demolition of the fourth-century basilica of

St Peter's, and its replacement by a vast new church. Bramante provided a design that was the ultimate in central planning, a Greek cross with four smaller Greek crosses in its arms. This project took well over a century to complete, by which time Bramante's plan had been altered out of all recognition, with only the piers of the dome surviving. Bramante's surviving masterpiece in Rome is the tiny Tempietto of San Pietro in Montorio, whose grandeur is out of all proportion to its size.

Bramante's position as leading architect in Rome was taken over by **Raphael** (1483–1520). His painting activities left him little time for this, but his few buildings were enormously influential. The Chigi chapel in the church of Santa Maria del Popolo brought to fruition the interest in centralised temples first evident in his early panel of *The Marriage of the Virgin* (now in the Brera). It is deliberately set apart from the rest of the church, and opulently adorned with statues, bronze reliefs, paintings, marbles and mosaics, its richness reflecting that of the patron, the papal banker. His pupil **Giulio Romano** (c.1492–1546) was active mainly in **Mantua**, where he consciously distorted the elements of classical architecture, thus beginning the Mannerist style. The Palazzo del Te establishes an organic unity between house and garden, as well as between architecture and interior decoration. The artist's own house in the same city is very different but equally inventive, while his design for the Duomo is an early example of a building concerned above all with effect, the intention being to "suck" the viewer towards the high altar.

Baldassare Peruzzi (1481–1536), originally from Siena, built the most graceful of Rome's High Renaissance palaces, the Villa Farnesina, which is arguably the outstanding secular monument of the time, featuring an unusual U-shaped plan with two superbly frescoed ground floor loggias and an upstairs hall with illusionistic architectural perspectives. The Palazzo Massimo alle Colonne from late in his career successfully overcomes its difficult sloping site by means of a highly original convex facade. Peruzzi also built the pentagonal Villa Farnese in Caprarola in collaboration with **Antonio da Sangallo the Younger** (1485–1546), with whom he also worked on St Peter's. Sangallo's most important independent work, however, is the strongly classical Palazzo Farnese, the most spectacular Roman palace of its time.

Michelangelo Buonarroti (1475–1564) only took up architecture in middle age. His approach was in direct contrast to Alberti's, using plans only as a rough guide, and making constant changes throughout the period of execution. None of his major buildings were finished in his lifetime: his earliest commissions in **Florence** – San Lorenzo's Sagrestia Nuova (which forms a piece with his own sculptures) and the Biblioteca Laurenziana (where every element of the decoration is closely tied to the architecture) – already show an original approach to building. Like Giulio Romano, he adopted an entirely new attitude to space, and turned the vocabulary of classicism to suit his own ends. In **Rome**, he invented the giant order – columns and pilasters rising through two or more storeys – for his palaces on the Piazza dei Campidoglio. Other major projects were the conversion of the central hall of the Baths of Diocletian into the church of Santa Maria degli Angeli, and the work on St Peter's.

The High Renaissance was introduced to **Venice** by **Jacopo Sansovino** (1486–1570), who fled from Rome after its sacking by French troops in 1527. Sansovino quickly became the leading architect in the city, and erected a series of public edifices – the Zecca, the Loggetta and the Libreria Sansoviniana – which transformed the area around San Marco. The last-named is one of the most joyous, festive designs of the Renaissance, a highly successful compromise between classical precision and Venetian love of surface ornament.

Michele Sanmicheli (c.1484–1559) spent much of his career on military projects, building the fortifications of his native **Verona**, including three dignified gateways, and the Fortezza at the entrance to Venice's Lido. He also built very grandiose palaces in both cities, which are especially notable for their facades of richly detailed stonework: the Palazzo Grimani on the Canal Grande and the Palazzo Bevilacqua in Verona are among the finest. The Cappella Pellegrini in San Bernardino, Verona, develops the idea of Raphael's Cappella Chigi, while the later pilgrimage church of Madonna di Campagna in the same city is one of the most ambitious centrally planned churches of the sixteenth century.

Italy's most erudite and internationally influential architect was the Paduan **Andrea Palladio** (1508–80), who distilled features from all his great predecessors, welding them into a distinctive personal style. Palladio is associated above all with the city of **Vicenza**, which he adorned with a magnificent series of palaces, beginning with the so-called Basilica. In a spectacular piece of conjectural archaeology in the same city, he built the Teatro Olympico, the first permanent theatre since the days of antiquity. The villas he created for aristocratic clients in the surrounding countryside were much imitated elsewhere; indeed, they served as the model for British country houses until well into the nineteenth century. In the most famous, La Rotonda, Palladio put the architect's ideal of a central plan to secular use for the first time, and introduced identical temple-like fronts on all four sides of the building.

Genova developed a distinctive architectural character of its own during the High Renaissance thanks to **Galeazzo Alessi** (1512–72), who made the most of the sloping sites common to this hilly city. His huge palaces typically feature monumental staircases and courtyards set on different levels. He also designed the commanding hilltop church of Santa Maria di Carignano, which borrows Bramante's plan for St Peter's.

In **Florence**, the Mannerist style took firm root in the wake of Michelangelo. **Bartolomeo Ammannati** (1511–92) is best known for his additions and amendments to the Palazzo Pitti, which more or less determined its final form, and for the graceful Ponte San Trinità. **Bernardo Buontalenti** (c.1536–1608) was the city's quirkiest architect, celebrated mainly for the grottoes in the Bóboli Gardens and his designs for court spectaculars. Yet he also worked in a conventional idiom, as witnessed by the Fortezza del Belvedere, the Tribuna of the Uffizi and the facade of San Trinità.

Both Ammannati and Vasari also worked in Rome in collaboration with **Giacomo Barozzi da Vignola** (1507–73) on the Villa Giulia, the city's finest expression of the Mannerist delight in architecture mingled with landscape gardening. Vignola also succeeded Michelangelo as architect of St Peter's, but his chief importance lies in the way he prepared the ground for the new Baroque style. The Gesù, mother church of the Jesuits, the order on whom the Counter-Reformation was to depend so much, was Vignola's most important commission, and one which was imitated all round the world. His design was based on Alberti's Sant'Andrea in Mantua, eliminating the aisles and using the nave pilasters and lighting effects to draw the eye towards the high altar.

Vignola died before the Gesù was complete, leaving the facade to be built by **Giacomo della Porta** (c.1537–1602). This imperious front places emphasis on the portal, and presents a highly unified design in which every component plays an essential role. Della Porta was also responsible for the construction and final shape of the dome of St Peter's, making it more ornate than Michelangelo had intended.

While Rome moved confidently into a new era, the High Renaissance was kept alive in northern Italy by Palladio's most faithful follower, **Vincenzo Scamozzi** (1552–1616). He completed many of Palladio's unfinished designs, and added the brilliant perspective stage set to the Teatro Olympico. Many of his original works imitate Palladio's most famous buildings: he built a broadly similar theatre at Sabbioneta, and modelled San Nicola da Tolentino in Venice on Il Redentore.

THE BAROQUE

The **Baroque** was once regarded merely as a late phase of the Renaissance, whose classically inspired architectural forms it continued to use. However, although it may be difficult to pinpoint the exact period when Baroque began, it is recognisably a distinctive style in its own right. Politically, its birth is inexorably linked to **Rome**, a city which needed to reflect in a wealth of new buildings the brash, self-confident mood it had acquired as a result of the Counter-Reformation, its architecture expressing both the pomp and mystery of the religious approach then being propagated. Architects became concerned with daring spatial effects, with rendering movement by the use of curvaceous lines and dazzling tricks of light, and with rich decoration of which painting and sculpture were integral components.

The first architect to build wholly within the new idiom was **Carlo Maderno** (1556–1629). Maderno's reputation has been sullied by his association with a major architectural failure, the completion of St Peter's by the addition of a nave and facade, which destroyed the balance of the Greek-cross plan and masked the view of the dome. Yet Maderno was really only marginally at fault: the clergy had always disliked the democratic nature of centrally planned churches, and it was the new hieratic spirit of the age which prompted the need for the extensions. The highly original facade of Santa Susanna and the dome of Sant'Andrea della Valle prove that Maderno was actually a highly capable designer. He also started Rome's most important seventeenth-century palace, the Palazzo Barberini, though this was much altered by later hands.

The overall appearance of Baroque Rome is due above all to **Gianlorenzo Bernini** (1598–1680). Like Michelangelo, Bernini only took up architecture in mid-career, by which time he had established his reputation as the leading sculptor of the day. His fusion of the arts was to be one of the keynotes of the Baroque. His principal architectural achievements were in the field of town planning: he laid out the Piazza Novona and the Piazza Barberini, in the centre of which he placed a monumental fountain to his own design. Most brilliant of all was his surprisingly simple rearrangement of the square in front of St Peter's into an oval shape, with two sets of colonnades grouped to symbolise the embracing arms of the Church. The nearby Scala Regia is an equally clever design, with the steps, columns and vault all diminishing in size towards the summit to give a far greater feeling of grandeur than the restricted space would seem to allow.

Francesco Borromini (1599–1667), at first Bernini's assistant, but later his bitter rival, was the most daring and inventive Baroque architect. His attitude to decoration was very different to Bernini's, whose sculptural training he did not share. To him, architecture was sculpture in its own right, and he treated the entire wall surface plastically, favouring monochromal effects instead of colours. Even in his first commission, San Carlo alle Quattro Fontane, Borromini showed his total disregard for convention, creating a stunning spatial design based on a complex series of shapes, with two equilateral triangles resolved into an oval at the level of the dome, and a circle in the lantern above. The facade, added later, was highly influential in its mixed use of concave and convex effects. Most of Borromini's subsequent buildings suffered from the handicap of having been begun by other architects. Nevertheless, he achieved many highly unusual effects, notably in Sant'Ivo della Sapienza, and in the seemingly independent towers flanking the dome of Sant'Agnese, a motif that was subsequently much imitated. Borromini's most prestigious commission was the internal remodelling of San Giovanni in Laterano, which transformed the early Christian basilica into a vast Baroque temple.

The third main architect of Baroque Rome was **Pietro da Cortona** (1596–1669). Surprisingly, Cortona desisted from the union of the arts beloved of Bernini, preferring instead whitewashed interior walls. Nonetheless, his mature work combines elements from both Borromini and Bernini: the facade of Santa Maria della Pace, for example, makes considerable play with concave and convex shapes, yet takes this further by rearranging the square in which it is set to form an appropriate backdrop.

Elsewhere in Italy, only a handful of seventeenth-century architects stand comparison with their Roman contemporaries. One of these was **Francesco Maria Ricchino** (1583–1658), whose buildings in **Milan** bear direct comparison with the most progressive designs in Rome. **Bartolommeo Bianco** (c.1590–1657) adorned **Genova** with some of the century's finest palaces, proving a worthy successor to Alessi in the way he turned the sloping ground to advantage.

The leading Baroque architect in **Naples** was the Lombard **Cosimo Fanzago** (1591–1678), whose early buildings, notably the cloisters of the Certosa di San Martino, are restrained and classically inspired. Another south Italian centre for a distinctively exuberant, wilful form of Baroque was the little town of **Lecce**, which was adorned with a series of churches and public buildings by a group of architects whose leading light was **Guiseppe Zimbalo** (active 1659–86).

The only major Baroque architect in **Venice** was **Baldassare Longhena** (1598–1682). His fame rests chiefly on the votive church of Santa Maria della Salute, whose distinctive domed silhouette makes the most of its prominent site. Longhena also built two of the Canal Grande's finest palaces, the Ca' Pésaro and the

Ca' Rezzonico, though here he did little more than update Sansovino's forms.

Turin, which had previously played no significant part in Italian art and architecture, progressively took over from Rome as the leading centre of the Baroque. **Carlo di Castellamonte** (1560–1641) drew up an ambitious plan of the city, and built the Piazza San Carlo as its centrepiece. Even more significant was the arrival of the monk **Guarino Guarini** (1624–83), who was a brilliant mathematician as well as architect. Guarini was unusual among Italians in his interest in both Gothic and Islamic styles of building, but the prime influence on his development was Borromini. He used his mathematical skills to inflate the Roman architect's essentially small-scale approach into the grand manner in such commissions as the Collegio dei Nobili and the Palazzo Carignano. Both San Sidone, built at the east end of the Duomo to house the Turin Shroud, and San Lorenzo feature fantastic conical domes and pyrotechnic spatial effects using a wide variety of shapes.

After a gap of a generation, Turin attracted another remarkable architect, the Roman-trained Sicilian **Filipp Juvarra** (1678–1736). In a twenty-year sojourn in the city, he was responsible for a wealth of buildings, including the planning of new districts, churches, palaces and countryside villas. His imposingly sited Superga basilica combines the pilgrimage church and monastery in a single unit, and is by far the finest of its type in Italy, fully worthy of comparison with its central European counterparts. However, Juvarra's masterpiece is the Palazzina di Stupinigi, an extravagantly decorous villa which uses a triaxial hexagonal design instead of the conventional rectangle.

In **Sicily**, the disastrous earthquake of 1693 led to a wholesale demand for new buildings. Accordingly, the island is richly endowed with flowery late-Baroque creations which are the nearest Italian equivalents to French and German Rococo. Essentially, they are derivative in nature, paying a heavy debt to Borromini as well as to the Churrigueresque style of Spain. The most individual architect was **Giovan Battista Vaccarini** (1702–68), who was particularly associated with the laying out of **Catania**. However, the much smaller planned town of **Noto** provides an even more visually satisfying ensemble.

NEOCLASSICISM

The **Neoclassical** style, which reacted against the sumptuousness of late Baroque by returning to the most basic principles of classicism, is generally considered to have begun in **Rome** in the mid-eighteenth century. Yet long before that, while the century was still young, a number of architects in **Venice** had decisively moved against Baroque excesses, notably **Giovanni Scalfarotto** (1690–1764), whose San Simone Piccolo is demonstrably derived from the Pantheon.

Giovanni Battista Piranesi (1720–78) did more than anyone to popularise the Neoclassical approach in Rome. His inspired large-scale engravings of the city's ruins rank among the all-time masterpieces of graphic art, and were to have a wide circulation. His theoretical writings asserted the superiority of the architecture of Classical Rome over Greece, and advocated a re-interpretation of its forms as the basis for a new style. As a practising architect, Piranesi is known only for Santa Maria del Priorato, a heavily symbolical church for the Knights of Malta, set in a pentagonal square.

A remarkable synthesis of late Baroque and Neoclassicism was achieved by **Luigi Vanvitelli** (1700–73) in the colossal royal palace of **Caserta**, whose ornate apartments with their long vistas show all the swagger of the old style, whereas the exterior has all the calm restraint of the new. His pupil **Giuseppe Piermarini** (1734–1808) became the leading Neoclassical architect in **Milan**, where he designed several severe palaces with long, unadorned facades, along with what became Italy's most prestigious opera house, La Scala.

Another celebrated theatre, La Fenice in **Venice**, is the best-known building by the city's most committed exponent of Neoclassicism, **Giannantonio Selva** (1751–1819). A certain French influence pervades the work of **Giuseppe Valadier** (1762–1839), who was given responsibility for remodelling the interiors of the cathedrals of Spoleto and Urbino while still in his twenties. Later he was based in Rome, where his commissions included the triumphal arch on the Ponte Milvio and the laying out of the Piazza del Popolo.

As with the other visual arts, architecture in Italy was in the doldrums for most of the nineteenth century. Because of the all-

pervasiveness of the classical tradition, there was little of the confident modern reinterpretation of other styles which characterises northern European building of this period. Only **Luigi Japelli** (1783–1852) stands as an exception to this. His masterpiece, the Caffè Pedrocchi in **Padua**, is admittedly firmly Neoclassical, but its extension is neo-Gothic, while his Teatro Verdi in the same city is based on Rococo, and his villas are modelled on Palladio.

The nineteenth century also saw some impressive examples of town planning. One of these was in **Trieste**, where the waterfront area was re-designed. In **Turin**, the work of the previous century was continued by the laying out of the Piazza Vittorio Veneto and Piazza Carlo Felice at opposite ends of the city. Later, **Alessandro Antonelli** (1798–1888) adorned the city with a huge iron supported tower, the Mole Antonelliana, originally intended as a synagogue, but converted into a museum.

The most original piece of planning was in **Milan**, whose status as the commercial hub of the emergent nation-state is symbolised by the construction of the Galleria Vittorio Emanuele II by **Giuseppe Mengoni** (1829–77) – Italy's first important example of design in iron and glass, and the initiator of a trend for covered shopping areas throughout Europe.

With the accomplishment of complete Italian unification in 1870, **Rome** had to be supplied with new streets and buildings worthy of a great modern capital; inevitably, the most monumental classical style possible was chosen, and it was only a partial success. The most strikingly visible – if not the most aesthetically pleasing – late-Neoclassical addition to the city's patrimony is the huge white marble Monument to Vittorio Emanuele II by **Giuseppe Sacconi** (1853–1905).

THE 20TH CENTURY

A reaction against the nineteenth-century infatuation with the past came with the unashamedly modernist **Art Nouveau** movement, whose glittering, sinewy forms dominated European architecture and design in the early years of the new century. In Italy, where it was known as **Lo Stilo Liberty**, its impact was less extensive than in most other countries, and also more restrained, deriving above all from the Viennese Secession. **Giuseppe Sommaruga** (1867–1917) was the most talented exponent; his surviving buildings include the Casa Castiglione and Clinica Colombo in **Milan**, and the Hotel Tre Croci near **Varese**.

Of far more long-lasting significance to the overall direction of Italian architecture were the visionary **Futurist** designs of **Antonio Sant'Elia** (1888–1916), especially his *Città Nuova*, which envisaged a vibrant high-rise metropolis of the future dominated by technological commercial activities and rapid transport systems operating on several levels. Sant'Elia's death in World War I meant that none of this was ever built, save for the posthumously erected and much simplified War Memorial in **Como**. The executant architect for this was **Giuseppe Terragini** (1904–43), a member of the *Gruppo Sette*, which comprised seven of Italy's most progressive inter-war architects, all strongly influenced by the ideas promulgated by the Bauhaus in Germany and Frank Lloyd Wright in America. Terragini built several other buildings in Como, the most original of which was the Casa dei Fascisti, the local Fascist Party headquarters.

In spite of its unpleasant associations, **Fascist** architecture is sometimes of good quality. The status of **Rome** as the national capital meant that it again became the centre of the most ambitious projects, including some appalling examples of planning, the worst of which was the opening up of the Via della Conciliazione linking St Peter's to the Tiber. This exacerbated the flaws caused by the previous failure to build the third wing of Bernini's Piazza, and has spoiled its element of surprise ever since.

New prestige schemes were generally supervised by Mussolini's favourite architect, **Marcello Piacentini** (1881–1960). When left to his own devices – as in the Stadio dei Marmi, with its coarse echoes of Imperial Rome – Piacentini produced the most distasteful monuments of the period. His EUR project, south of the city, was interrupted by World War II, and completed after the fall of Fascism in a modernised Neoclassical manner.

The most internationally celebrated Italian architect of the twentieth century was **Pier Luigi Nervi** (1891–1979). He popularised the use of reinforced concrete, which enabled a greater variety of design than was possible with the steel leads favoured in so many other countries. His celebrated aircraft hangars were destroyed during the war, but the Municipal Stadium in **Florence**, with its helical staircase, survives as an example of his early work. Among his prestigious postwar commissions are exhibition halls in **Turin**, whose amazing wide-span vaults recall the lost hangars; the buildings for the 1960 Olympic Games in **Rome**; and the Papal Audience Chamber in the Vatican.

Nervi also provided the engineering core of Italy's most famous skyscraper, the Torre Pirelli in Milan by **Gio Ponti** (1891–1979), a prolific and versatile designer. **Giovanni Michelucci** (b.1891), who built the Instituto di Mineraolgia in the same complex, was shortly afterwards responsible for the highly stylised train station in **Florence**. In the 1960s, he built just outside the same city one of the century's most striking churches, the expressionistic San Giovanni sull'Autostrada del Sol, dedicated to the men who had died constructing the motorway. Two more impressive examples of railway architecture, both designed by several hands, are the grandiosely Neoclassical station in **Milan**, dating from the Fascist epoch, and its modernist, utopian counterpart in **Rome**, which ranked as the most prestigious architectural project in the aftermath of World War II.

Gordon McLachlan

ITALIAN VERNACULAR ARCHITECTURE

Architecture isn't just about palaces and churches, and it's interesting to see how domestic architecture has developed, especially with regard to the siting and layout of small towns and farming settlements, both of which have had at least as much impact on the landscape of Italy as the country's better-known monumental architecture.

HILL TOWNS

Throughout the Middle Ages in Italy, the countryside was unsafe and unhealthy and the land in many places remained uncultivated, either swamp or barren. As late as the fifteenth century, wolves still prowled within a few miles of Florence, in a landscape populated largely by brigands and deer. The topography of the countryside, with its abundance of hills and mountains rising steeply from fertile plains provided natural sites for fortified settlements which could both remove the population from the malarial swamps and bandits and preserve the limited fertile land for cultivation.

In the period of their greatest expansion – between the twelfth and fourteenth centuries – **hill towns** sprang up all over. Many were superimposed on early Etruscan cities – **Chiusi** and **Cortona** – or cave dwellings, as in **Sorano**. **Matera**, Basilicata, grew from a very early settlement of grottoes formed by the natural erosion of volcanic rock (tufa) along the side of a high ravine. The houses that evolved from these caves (called I Sassi – literally "rocks") remained in use until 1952 when they were condemned. Though most hill towns were built within high and sometimes battlemented perimeter walls, the fortress aspects of many sites obviated the need for additional protection. Houses in **Pitigliano** (in Tuscany), for example, rise like a natural extension of the rock outcropping on which they sit. The sheer drop afforded by these sites (often extended by the use of towers) enabled inhabitants to make good use of gravity to drop a crushing blow onto the heads of enemies attempting to scale the walls.

It also facilitated a precipitate (if practical) dispatch of the dead as well as a simple form of rubbish disposal. After the revolution in fortifications between the thirteenth and fifteenth centuries, and the introduction of gunpowder and cannon reduced the need for enormous vertical drops, towers grew shorter and were adapted to newer methods of warfare.

Although many hill towns were genuinely self-contained communities, the countryside remained under the political and economic control of the cities and of the Comunes, Grand Dukes and Church officials who ran them, particularly in North and Central Italy. Each city-state set up satellite towns of its own, to protect trade routes (whether at sea or on land), or to operate as garrisons for soldiers, weaponry and food in case of war (or civil insurrection). Siena established the fortified hill town of **Monteriggioni** in the early thirteenth century along an important route from Rome into France which also passed through **San Gimignano**. **San Miniato** was also set up as a fortified town by Emperor Frederick II (still quarrelling with the papacy) to take advantage of and protect this same route. At roughly the same time, Florence founded similar frontier outposts, setting up **San Giovanni Valdarno**, **Scarperia** and **Firenzuolo**, all within ten years. Fewer towns emerged in the South during this period, partly because there were fewer cities: of the 26 Italian towns with populations of more than 20,000 in the thirteenth century, only three were in the South.

Hill towns share many features, whatever the impetus for their original development. They are almost always densely built settlements, constructed with materials found on or near their site, helping to give the impression of arising naturally from their geological foundations. They usually rely on just one or two simple dwelling types endlessly repeated. **Strómboli**, off the north coast of Sicily, is an example of the rich effects created by repetition of a single, very basic dwelling type, in this case a simple cube. In most hill towns, houses are built right up to the edge of – and often open out directly onto – the narrow passageways and streets. This reflects the more integral links between the productive activities of the medieval household (carried out on the ground floor) and the street immediately outside which not only became an extension of the works inside but also served as a kind of shop, linked to a wider network of merchants, traders and exchange. Altogether, many more functions were carried out publicly in the streets, traces of which are still visible in the surviving evidence of public fountains and wash-houses, wells, and communal ovens. Streets in medieval hill towns were even more crowded than they are today; houses had over-hanging wooden balconies, used to dry and store a variety of foods. Supports for these balconies (or the holes which held them) can still be seen on the fronts of many houses.

Taken together, hill towns still preserve a great deal of their medieval character. The very characteristics which made them useful for purposes of defence and isolation made them unsuitable for later growth and redevelopment in response to changing circumstances. There are exceptions – in the late-fifteenth century the village of Corsignano near Montepulciano was transformed into the little Renaissance town of **Pienza** to commemorate the birthplace of Pope Pius II. But in general, there is much less evidence of urban planning, or the country's more recent economic history, in hill towns.

SETTLEMENTS ON THE PLAINS

Though variations abound, the basic types of settlements in the plains and coastal areas reveal a great deal about the impact of urban political and economic activity on the development of the countryside. Distinct waves of development correspond to changes in the fortunes of city merchants and in the accumulation of capital required for agricultural investment. Accumulation, in turn, depended on economic prosperity and on relatively long and uninterrupted periods of peace.

Just as the economic incentive for rural development derived from the towns, so did the house types used by the first intrepid petty noblemen in setting up agricultural holdings after centuries of disuse and stagnation. The **house-tower** (la casa-torre), which spread first through the Mugello, Chianti and Casentino districts between the thirteenth and fifteenth centuries, was really a transplanted version of the tall, square, fortified city house, using construction techniques borrowed from urban models, particularly from the fortified towns of Bologna, Perugia, and Siena. The

defensive character of the house-tower can be read from the thickness of its walls, from its restricted openings high off the ground and from its height.

Over successive centuries, the house-tower gradually lost its defensive character, re-emerging as a **dove tower** (la torre colum-baia), protruding from the centre of a new form of extended dwelling which had been wrapped around it. Doves and pigeons were not only adept at killing snakes and consuming weeds but also provided valuable meat for the table and dung for agricultural use. Though this func-tional role gradually fell away, the dove tower became a ubiquitous feature of domestic archi-tecture across almost all of Central and Southern Italy, and still remains an important decorative element in contemporary villas.

The house to which the dove tower belongs is the **casa della mezzadria**, the classic Renaissance country villa, widespread across Tuscany, Umbria and the Marche as well as other areas in central and northern Italy. Usually square in plan, it was built using a combination of brick, stone and terracotta under a tent-like roof with the dove tower at its apex. Depending on its location and the urban models to which it harks back, it might boast a portico at ground level (typically Florentine), and a loggia at first-floor level (typically Arentine), or neither a portico nor loggia but a flat wall on the front facade (more common in the area around Siena).

The house derives its name from the system of sharecropping by which most of the land was farmed. Under this system, la mezzadria (based on the word mezza – "half"), the peas-ant farmer, in exchange for half the seed, yielded up half the annual produce to his land-owner. This gave the landlord no incentive either to invest in stock or to introduce new agricultural methods. At the same time, it impoverished the labour force, compelled by increasing debt to supply free labour – which was used, among other things, to build the main house. Used only occasionally by the landlord, the house was the primary residence of the estate manager (il fattore), who was the agent and overseer of urban capital invested in the countryside. Because this system paid workers in kind rather than in cash, it inevitably tied agriculture to the limited production of subsistence goods and so failed to encourage specialisation (based on natural advantages) and the commercial innovations that modern agriculture required.

By contrast, the alluvial plain across north and central Italy encouraged specialisation very early on. To be made arable, it required large-scale investment in the reclamation and irrigation of land, something that was first undertaken by the Benedictines and Cistercians in the eleventh to thirteenth centuries. The enormous commercial enterprises which subsequently appeared to cater for commercial markets in rice, silk and dairy products, bore some resemblance to the monasteries whose functions they replaced and extended. Square in plan and built around a massive enclosed courtyard which could extend to 150 metres or more on a side, the architecture of the farming complex (*la casa della Pianura Padana*) was often stark with high rectangular porticoes supported by square columns sometimes running along three sides of the enclosed interior space.

Normally, the estate accommodated four basic elements which were architecturally distinct: the owner-manager's house which was more elaborate in design and often taller than the other buildings; housing for workers, tenement-like in character, with external balconies running along the upper floors used to dry and store crops like rice; stables for cows and other animals; and stables for horses with haylofts above. This last is a feature easily recognisable at great distances because of the often striking patterns of brickwork used to create large grates for the ventilation of hay. The overall operation of this kind of enterprise was convincingly portrayed in the film *Tree of the Wooden Clogs*, set in nineteenth-century Lombardy. Today many of these courtyards are inhabited by independent small farmers, each cultivating their own smallholding. Others are abandoned. On the eastern side of the plain, around the Ferrara district, where agriculture has become most mechanised, the stables and storage areas of enclosed-court complexes have become truly vast.

In central and southern Italy (particularly Campania and Puglia), the **masseria** is a more common type of farming settlement. Dominating vast tracts of land which were derived from feudal estates and ultimately from the landed properties of the Roman emperors (*latifondia*), these complex structures are massive in bulk and set in isolated countryside where they are entirely closed to the outside world. Consisting of a dense cluster of separate building elements which were often vertically prominent, *masserie* were sometimes enclosed by a high perimeter stone wall with round turrets built in for defense purposes. They could, however, also consist of a lower grouping of buildings more loosely bound within a larger area. At its largest a *masseria* virtually operated as a self-contained village incorporating church, school, medical clinic and shop within its precinct, in addition to accommodating the full range of agricultural requirements for stabling, housing (of day labourers called *braccianti*) and a wide variety of storage. In their purest, least-altered form, village *masserie* are still visible on the mountain slopes of Sicily. A later parallel to these large farms are the eighteenth- and nineteenth-century worker villages like **San Leucio** near Caserta, set up by the Bourbon Ferdinand IV at the end of the eighteenth century to promote silk weaving; and **Crespi**, built on the Adda in Lombardy by Critoforo Crespi and devoted to the cotton industry.

Trulli, found along the coast of Puglia and inland, form one of the most remote, curious and ancient types of farm settlement in Italy. Of uncertain origin that might be Cretan or North African, appearing in Italy some time between 2000 and 1000 BC, *trulli* consist of clusters of single circular rooms, each covered by a conical roof made of overlapping rough stone tiles and topped by decorative symbolic pinnacles. Built as primitive agricultural communities, the profusion of conical roofs (each dwelling contributing two or three) produces a startling effect on the landscape.

At the more modest end of the spectrum, the house of the **independent farmer** (*la casa colonica*) is to be found all over Italy, adapted to local materials and customs. Of simpler construction, it often consists of a kitchen and bedrooms sitting on top of animal sheds and agricultural stores (common in Central and North Italy), but equally, the barn and house might form separate wings or entirely separate buildings, as is typically found along the slopes of the Appenines running the entire length of the country.

Ellen Leopold

MAFIA, 'NDRANGHETA, CAMORRA: SOCIALISED CRIME IN SOUTHERN ITALY

"And the Mafia – what's this Mafia that the news-papers are always talking about?'

"Yeah, what is the Mafia, after all?" Brescianelli chimed in.

"It's a very complicated thing to explain", Bellodi said, "It's . . . incredible, that's what it is"

Leonardo Sciascia, *The Day of the Owl*

Few modern social phenomena have been more misinterpreted and misunderstood than the **Mafia**, **'ndrangheta** and **camorra**, the three names designating organised criminal activity in **Sicily**, **Calabria** and **Naples**. In some sense it is no surprise that there should be misunderstandings. Numerous hindrances lie in wait for the would-be Mafia observer. Most important of these may be the secrecy in which the Mafia shrouds itself, a secrecy the Mafia ensures through the vow of silence known as *omerta*, which surrounds all those who, however unwillingly, come into contact with it.

An example. At 2am, July 10, 1988, three associates of the Camorra boss Antonio Bardellino were gunned down on the streets of his hometown of Aversa, just outside Naples, by members of a rival clan. The gunfight lasted thirty minutes. A few minutes after the last shots were fired, the police arrived. While they removed one of the corpses from the street, a man in a nearby apartment opened his window to ask in a derisory tone – "anything happen down there?" As Leonardo Sciascia shows in his penetrating portrait of the Mafia world cited above, one knows better than to be a witness to a Mafia crime.

Another, less dramatic, hindrance to making sense of the Mafia, 'ndrangheta and camorra is the complexity of these phenomena. They *are* distinct organisations, based in particular terri-tories, but they also have numerous common characteristics, not to mention continuous deal-ings with one another. The Mafia and 'ndrangheta especially have similar, inter-woven, histories – unless otherwise specified, in this article the term Mafia will be used to indicate them both. The Neapolitan camorra, for all its similarities, is something of a case unto itself, and will be considered separately below.

Until recently organised crime was mostly viewed as a *southern* problem, an issue of "special" interest to those with a criminal curi-osity. But in recent years it has become clear that these organisations are thoroughly enmeshed in the fibre of Italian society as a whole, and that understanding Italy is hardly possible without reference to them. Certainly they are not something that can be eradicated with one trial, defeated in one year or even in ten; indeed to move beyond the Mafia will require the total transformation of Italian soci-ety, politics and economic life. Those that ask what shape Italy will have in the twenty-first century will therefore also need to ask what role the Mafia, 'ndrangheta and camorra will play in it.

MAFIA AND 'NDRANGHETA

The one thing most mafiologues agree on is that the Mafia as a thing, as a noun, *does not exist*. When a defendant in a 1960s Mafia trial was asked if he belonged to the Mafia he responded, "I don't know what the word means". This criminal was not so much evading the question as confessing a real perplexity. Mafiosi never call themselves, or one another, mafiosi, but rather *amici* (friends) or *uomini d'onore* (men of honour). In the words of one noted mafiologue, the defendant above "knew individuals who are called mafiosi, not because they belong to a secret sect but rather because they behave in a particular fashion, that is in a Mafia-like fashion".

What does it mean to behave in a Mafia-like fashion? "It means *to make oneself respected, to be a man of honour*, capable of vindicating by force any offence against his enemy," writes another Mafia expert, Pino Arlacchi. Honour and respect clearly have rather different meanings here than what most people are accustomed to. A man is an *uomo d'onore* when he acts according to the prevailing codes of courage, cleverness and ferocity, never hesitating to resort to violence and trickery in imposing his will upon others.

What gradually emerges from this portrait, however, is a sort of confusion between the Mafia as a "state of mind, a philosophy of life, a moral code, prevailing among all Sicilians" (Luigi Barzini), and organised criminal activity, delinquency and social deviance. In southern Italy, the border between the two is often unclear.

Two aspects of southern Italian culture in particular seem to have contributed to the birth and development of the Mafia as a criminal organisation. The first is the generally positive value which this culture has attributed to assertiveness, aggression and the ability to impose one's will on others. The meek, mild and naive may be saints in their afterlives, but in this life they are, quite simply, fools. The fundamental Neapolitan phrase, *ca'nisciun e'fesso* (I'm no fool – you won't get the best of me), sums up the constant awareness of dominance and submission in which the southern Italian lives.

A second, related aspect is the southern Italian attitude towards the state. Even today, the relationship of the southern Italian (and of many northern Italians as well) to the state is one of profound distrust. The state, its institution and laws, are not something in which one participates as a citizen but are rather things which challenge the citizen's independence, interfering with his family's sacred autonomy. This attitude towards the state may have its origins in the long succession of invading powers that ruled southern Italy over the centuries (Norman, French, Catalan, etc). And also in the distance that separated the mass of peasant-farmers (*contadini*) working on huge estates (*latifondi*) from their absentee landlords residing in Naples or Palermo. Certainly Unification did little to help matters in the South, transferring as it did the capital from Naples to Rome and replacing the Bourbon monarchy with the Turin-based House of Savoy. Whatever the case, the space of distrust between citizen and State is the space in which the Mafia has prospered.

ORIGINS AND DEVELOPMENT

However, there is much more to the Mafia than this, and a look at more recent history shows that Mafia criminality is no longer what it used to be. The Mafia has come a long way from the traditional, feudal ways of the nineteenth century to become an entrepreneurial Mafia moving in the circles of international finance, and of drugs and arms dealing. With this transformation has come a change in the Mafia's relationship to society at large, from one of widespread sympathy and support to that of dismay and alienation.

The word "Mafia" first appears in written documents around the time of Italian Unification, and, although its etymological origins are debatable, many speculate that it derives from the arabic word *mu'afah* meaning "protection". In 1863 a play entitled *I Mafiusi della Vicaria*, based on the life of a Palermo prison, was a roaring success among the high society of Sicily's capital, giving the word its first extensive usage: when the city rose against its new Italian rulers three years later, the British consul described a situation where secret societies were all-powerful: "*Camorre* and *maffie* elected *juntas* share the earnings of the workmen, keep up intercourse with outcasts, and take malefactors under their wing and protection."

The Mafia's appearance at this time is historically significant, its rise paralleling that of the young Italian state. Indeed, in the words of Leonardo Sciascia: "a history of the Mafia would be none other than the history of the State's complicity – from the Bourbons to the Savoys to the Republic – in forming and encouraging this unproductive and parasitic class of power."

Which isn't to say it hadn't existed before in a different form. Early versions of the Mafia were to be found in the Sicilian countryside during the long centuries of foreign rule. This vast, mountainous island was virtually impenetrable to the distant authorities in Naples, Madrid or elsewhere, and "law and order" had to be maintained by local, semi-official authorities. The Bourbons, for example, in the early nineteenth century entrusted their campaign against brigands and bandits to "companions at arms", which consisted of ex-brigands who would be pardoned in return for assistance in helping to catch and prosecute their old friends, the brigands at large. Usually, however, these "companions", instead of catching the brigands would negotiate a kind of peaceful settlement between the bandit who had committed some theft and the offended party. In this way local social harmony was maintained without the direct intervention of central government.

Another early Mafia activity was that of a certain type of rural "middleman" who handled negotiations between property owners, landlords, sharecroppers and dayworkers. During the first half of the nineteenth century, the great estates were divided up numerous times in the crown's attempt to challenge the power of local barons and proprietors. The early mafiosi grew fat off the tensions that these social changes generated, intimidating sharecroppers into accepting unfavourable contracts and dayworkers into accepting low wages, while persuading proprietors and landlords to cede control over their land to them, so fulfilling the important social function of mediation. As E.J. Hobsbawm noted: "we can't say that the Mafia was imposed upon the Sicilians by someone. In a certain sense it expressed the needs of all the rural classes and served their interests in varying ways."

The main characteristic of the traditional, rural Mafia, then, is that of the mediation of social conflict. And by the late nineteenth century these mediators had turned into true mafiosi with well-established codes of honour and a semi-formal, though unwritten, form of organisation. Though much has changed in the Mafia world, its organisation, based on the family, is much the same today as it was one hundred years ago.

The Mafia *family*, however, is not really a domestic unit at all, but a conglomeration of people, some blood-relations and others not, who gather together in the pursuit of illicit aims. Each family takes on the name of the village it comes from (Corleone, for example) or the quarter of a city which it controls (in Palermo — Ciaculli, Santa Maria di Gesù, Porta Nova, etc). Above the families is something called the *commission*, a kind of governing body made up of representatives from all the major groupings. In each family there is a body of "soldiers", presided over by lieutenants, who are in turn presided over by the *capo* or *padrino*

("godfather") and his assistants. Families, in turn, ally themselves in *cosche*, meaning the crown of the artichoke (symbolising the solidarity of many), which act in coordination with other *cosche*, all of which together form the *onorata societa*, the totality of organised crime in Sicily.

All this sounds much neater than in fact it is. Periods of peace, when everyone feels comfortable in their place, when territories are respected and pacts observed, are relatively rare. More often there are wars between and within families, and between and within *cosche*.

There is little or no documentary proof of the "Honoured Society's" rise to power, but most writers agree that between the 1890s and 1920s its undisputed boss was **Don Vito Cascio Ferro**, who presided over a period of unprecedented Mafia peace. Don Vito generated such fear and respect (virtual synonyms in the world of the Mafia) that no theft occurred in Palermo of which he did not receive a substantial cut. Already at this time the Sicilian underworld and its younger cousin in America, the "Black Hand", or *Cosa Nostra* (meaning literally "our thing"), were well coordinated. When Joe Petrosino, head of the Italian squad of the New York Police Department, secretly arrived in Palermo to study the relations between the *onorate societa* and the Black Hand, Don Vito was there at the waterfront to shoot him down. Don Vito later declared, "in all my life I've only killed one person, and I did it selflessly . . . Petrosino was a courageous adversary — he deserved to die in dignity, not by the hand of just any old assassin".

The rise to power of the American Mafia at this time was no accident. Mafia-style groupings and loyalties flourished among the hundreds of thousands of Sicilians who emigrated to America in the early decades of this century, emigrants who had need of their own forms of social and economic security in a country where they lacked the full franchise. In addition to this the Sicilian Mafia had suffered considerable (if temporary) setbacks at the hands of the Fascist authorities and many mafiosi fled to the US for safer operations.

Ferro's career ended with Mussolini's anti-Mafia purges, instigated to clear the ground for the establishment of a vigorous Fascist structure in Sicily. Il Duce sent the legendary prefect, **Cesare Mori**, to Sicily, granting him almost limitless powers to suppress the Mafia. Most importantly, Mori understood that the only way to beat the Mafia was on its own terms: "if the Sicilians are afraid of the mafiosi, I'll show them that I'm the meanest mafiosi of them all." He had understood that in the Sicily of the time it was indeed necessary to fight fear with fear.

This brief, Fascist chapter in the campaign against the Mafia foreshadows certain aspects of the debate over what legal and governmental forms the fight against the Mafia should take today. In particular it raises the question of how much the law should be circumvented by authorities in the attempt to wage an effective fight against the Mafia, and to what extent "extraordinary powers" should be granted to combat this "extraordinary" form of criminality. While opponents of the more "repressive" approach exemplified by Mori agree that the Mafia can be more effectively fought with the tools of repression, they ask at what cost to society as a whole? The fight against terrorism in the late 1970s and early 1980s is a dark example of a fight that was won at the cost of civil liberties, when hundreds of innocent men and women were put in jail.

If Mori, the Fascist, on the one hand, did much to reduce the powers of the Mafia, the Americans, on the other, did a good deal to restore them. When the Allies prepared for their landing in Sicily in 1943, they relied on the Mafia for crucial intelligence information and logistical support for the execution of Operation Husky. One of these informers was **Lucky Luciano**, with whom the US Navy consulted frequently while he was serving his thirty- to fifty-year prison sentence. Luciano not only provided them with important information and connections for the American landing in southwest Sicily but helped them to catch a group of Nazi saboteurs who were operating in New York. After the war the US expressed their gratitude by letting him go free, sending him to the home country where, in Naples, he would play a key role in developing links between the Sicilian, Neapolitan and American underworld.

The most important connection with which Luciano provided the allies was that of **Don Calógero Vizzini**, head of the Mafia of all Sicily during and immediately after the war.

Don Caló was instrumental in clearing the way for the American landing and, afterwards, in helping the Allied Military Government establish itself in Sicily. In order to maintain political control of the island the Allies relied heavily on the Mafia: of the 66 cities on the island, 62 were entrusted either to mafiosi or men connected with the Mafia. **Don Vito Genovese**, the figure on which Mario Puzo modelled Don Corleone in *The Godfather*, was one of these men. After helping the Americans, and the Mafia, consolidate their power in Sicily, Genovese returned to the US to become head of the American Cosa Nostra.

The Mafia was left in a good position to take advantage of the extraordinary economic growth which Italy underwent in the first two postwar decades. Moreover, in the South there was a key novelty which helped the Mafia secure its economic and political base: billions of dollars of government funding were sent here for an "extraordinary intervention" designed to modernise the region and bring it up to par with the wealthy North. The Mafia exploited the situation with ruthless efficiency, landing crucial and lucrative government contracts by intimidating all competitors into not even tendering bids. Needless to say, the Mafia-firm bid would be two to three times the appropriate amount necessary to complete the job.

THE NEW MAFIA

It was during these years that the Mafia underwent a fundamental transformation, from a predominantly rural organisation with a role of mediation, to an active criminal society, with its powerbase in the cities, and interests in construction, real estate and drugs smuggling. The modern Mafia may keep up a "clean and legal" front, but the economic basis for their civilised decorum is predominantly drugs and, to a lesser extent, the arms trade, kidnapping and extortion. In the 1950s the Mafia helped to found and develop an international drug market which extended its influence to all four corners of the globe. Experts estimate that more than half of the world's heroin trade is controlled in Palermo. The dizzying profits are "laundered" – invested in legal activities, all traces of their illicit origin having vanished.

Part of the Mafia's postwar success, then, can be traced to the ability to become "entrepreneurs" in high-risk, high-profit international trade while maintaining a respectable social front as businessmen in both the local and national economy. The strength of the Mafia organisation would not make sense, however, without the presence of another factor which explains its ability to continue to recruit *new* mafiosi. The chronic unemployment which has plagued southern Italy in recent decades has ensured that there will always be a reserve army of idle, able-bodied men who have been denied access to legal employment. And to these unemployed men, an invitation to work for the Mafia is often an offer they simply can't refuse. *

In almost complete symbiosis with the culture and economy of southern Italy, the Mafia has thus established itself in every area of politics and society, obtaining a more modern form of bourgeois respect, based not on fear but economic power. It is a form of economic power, however, whose costs to society are high, which diverts human energy, initiatives and funds from the public sphere where they can be more democratically managed and accounted for. Also, the plague of drug addiction on which the Mafia grows fat, and its perennial family wars, have thoroughly traumatised both Sicilian and Italian society. The death-count has grown too high for the people to remain sympathetic with

---

* One other crucial element of the Mafia's strength and longevity is the role of **women**, who play as important a part in the Mafia as in any family-based institution. All that is really known of Mafia women is that they attend the funerals of their husbands, sons and fathers, dressed in black and lamenting. The handful of women who have actually gone to trial as *mafiose* do little to clear up matters, begging the question of how membership in a criminal family constitutes criminal complicity. Some argue that women should be viewed as fully responsible protagonists of Mafia crime, others as victims; and the Eighties have seen a number of women in Sicily and Calabria, both in and outside Mafia circles, standing up to the culture of "male violence and female submissiveness". Whatever the case, women's relationship to the Mafia, an up to now neglected area of research, may well provide some of the answers to the question of the Mafia's staying power in southern Italy.

these mafiosi who, stripped of all folklore and Hollywood hype, reveal themselves for what they are: rapacious criminals bent on personal accumulation at all costs.

The state responded to the growing power of the Mafia with a **Parliamentary Commission** that sat between 1963 and 1976, which posed enough of a threat to the underworld to provoke a change of tactics by the Mafia, who began to target state officials in a sustained campaign of terror which continues to this day. In 1971 Palermo's chief public prosecutor, Pietro Scaglione, became the first in a long line of **illustrious corpses** – *cadaveri eccellenti* – which has included journalists, judges, lawyers, left-wing politicians and police chiefs. A new peak of violence was reached in 1982 with the ambush and murder in Palermo's city centre of **Pio La Torre**, regional secretary of the Communist Party in Sicily, who had proposed a special government dispensation to allow lawyers access to private bank accounts.

One of the people attending La Torre's funeral was the new Sicilian prefect of police, **General dalla Chiesa**, a veteran in the state's fight against the Red Brigade, and whose dispatch promised new action against the Mafia. He began investigating Sicily's lucrative construction industry, which proved an effective means of investing drug profits. His scrutiny of public records and business dealings threatened to expose one of the most enigmatic issues in the Mafia's organisation: the extent of corruption and protection in high-ranking political circles, the so-called **Third Level**. But exactly one hundred days after La Torre's death, dalla Chiesa was gunned down, together with his wife, in Palermo. The whole country was shocked, and the murder revived questions about the depth of government commitment to the fight. In his engagement with the Mafia, dalla Chiesa had met with little local cooperation, and had received next to no support from Rome, to the extent that his son had accused the politicians of isolating his father. The Italian president and senior cabinet ministers were present at the prefect's funeral, and were pelted with coins by an angry Sicilian crowd – an expression of disgust which has since been repeated at the funerals of other prominent anti-Mafia fighters.

THE MAXI-TRIALS ... AND THE OUTLOOK

This new, more critical attitude to the Mafia is emerging throughout Italian society. A scandal in 1981, surrounding the so-called "Propaganda Due" (P2) masonic lodge, also helped to mobilise public opinion against the Mafia when it was discovered that numerous high-ranking politicians, bankers, military men and even members of the Vatican were involved in a secret masonic organisation with Mafia connections. A year later, the first anti-Mafia law in history was passed by the Italian parliament.

Of equal import has been the recent wave of *pentitismo*, of "repentance" or confession, in which, for the first time, the age-old code of *omerta* has been broken. For the first time mafiosi are revealing the secrets of their organisation, breaking the promise they make during their initiation as mafiosi, when they declare, "may my flesh burn if I do not maintain this promise". **Tommaso Buscetta**, a high-ranking Mafia member, was one of the first to break with *omerta*, setting in motion the Palermo "maxi-trials" or *maxiprocessi* in 1986, the largest ever held against the Mafia. Never before had so high-ranking a member of the *commission* turned on his "friends". His revelations about the most intimate high-level dealings of the *onorata societa* were a breakthrough for the campaign against the Mafia both in Italy and in the US, and led to important prosecutions against members of the massive heroin and cocaine network between Palermo and New York known as the "pizza connection".

The decisions taken by the "maxi-trial" court in Palermo in December of 1987 were hailed as a substantial, if partial, victory of the forces of law and order in Italy. The fears of most seasoned Mafia fighters, however, were soon confirmed: as soon as the media-hype surrounding the "maxi-trial" ended, and the public – and government – turned its attention to other matters, the Mafia went back to business as usual. The Mafia fighters (judges, special investigators, police, parliamentary commissions), deprived of all-important media attention and government support, once again were engaged in a losing battle.

For the first seven months of 1988 the Mafia problem seemed, indeed, to fade out of sight. But in mid-summer something quite unexpected happened which thrust the issue back

on the front pages. Giovanni Falcone, a bright, young member of the special anti-Mafia "pool" of judges in Palermo, issued an accusation against the government's handling of the fight against the Mafia, and against the head of the pool, Antonino Meli. Falcone maintained that the government and anti-Mafia organisations had become lax, returning, he implied, to a form of complicity with the Mafia.

What was at stake in Falcone's accusation, and in the debate which immediately grew around it, were two approaches to the campaign: that of the veteran Antonino Meli, who proposed to conduct investigations through the normal bureaucratic channels, without making waves; and that of Falcone himself, who proposed to take chances, legal and otherwise, asking for a staff of crime-fighters exclusively trained in Mafia affairs, for special measures, special funds.

This local debate soon became a national polemic, involving parliament and the Supreme Court. And during the same period the Mafia itself further awakened the public to the debate's urgency, carrying out a series of ruthless killings of both Mafia members and public officials. In the autumn of 1988 this clamorous situation resulted in a new, stepped-up government commitment to the fight against the Mafia. Parliament granted vast, unprecedented powers to the High Commissioner for the Fight Against the Mafia, Domenico Sica, making him the most powerful anti-Mafia commissioner in postwar history: the use of a branch of the Italian Secret Service, legal clearance to perform wire-tappings, to spy on individuals suspected of Mafia activity, to confiscate funds of suspected mafiosi, and access to information on all citizens in the files of public offices and banks.

Certainly Domenico Sica is not another Prefect Mori, but it's clear that, at the risk of threatening individual liberties, extraordinary measures will need to be taken in any attempt to continue to destabilise the Mafia. Recent tales of the expansion of the Mafia's drug operations into the cocaine as well as heroin trade suggest that the recent onslaught hasn't been as successful as was hoped in destroying the Mafia's power. The fight, however, is ongoing. How successful it will be is open to debate, but it does seem that the notion of Cosa Nostra as being unbeatable is a thing of the past.

THE CAMORRA

Though in recent years the Neapolitan **Camorra** has in many ways become indistinguishable from the Mafia and 'ndrangheta, executing similar illicit activities in the drug trade, extortion, building speculation and suchlike, and often working in collaboration with them, its origins are quite distinct from its southern cousins. While the Mafia and 'ndrangheta were predominantly rural phenomena until World War II, the camorra has always been an urban animal, a secret underworld organisation of gambling and gaming. Today, a main camorra activity is that of the clandestine lottery, which shadows the official one run by the state. Instead of buying an official ticket you buy one printed by the camorra. The winning numbers are those drawn by the official lottery, only the camorra version has a number of advantages: if you win you're paid immediately (instead of waiting a year or two); and, clearly, you pay no taxes.

Though the Mafia has outshone, or outshot, the camorra over the past century, the camorra is much older and was already a well-established and ill-reputed criminal society at the beginning of the nineteenth century. In the bustling Bourbon capital there were great sums of wealth to be controlled by aspiring men of the underworld, and there were few commercial transactions in the city of which the camorrista did not get a substantial cut, known as the *taglio* or *tangente*. Even today, a great number of Neapolitan businesses pay a monthly sum to the camorra for "protection" – which of course means protection from the camorra itself.

Until World War II the camorra was a relatively traditional organisation, performing the familiar social functions of mediation and the maintenance of a kind of social harmony, by whatever violent and parasitic means. With the profound transformations in postwar Naples, and the arrival of the American-trained gangster **Lucky Luciano**, the camorra turned to the traffic in contraband cigarettes and drugs. Like the Mafia, the camorra has become entrepreneurial, and the name of the clan which commanded Naples until recently, the New Organised Camorra, suggests that the new Neapolitan underworld is structured more like a commercial firm than a family.

Still, at the same time as the camorra rule is to retain its business in all corners of the globe, its cardinal rule is to maintain its connection to the culture of the region, to the popular quarters of Naples. Such is the case of the Giuliano family, the clan based in Forcella, the district near the railway station, which controls the centre of Naples. Though members of the family have become millionaires many times over, comfortably moving in the international circles of high society, the family still lives in the centre of one of Naples' most degraded quarters, in a *basso*, or one-room, groundfloor apartment whose name is synonymous with poverty. A friend from Forcella once explained it like this: "These camorristi, for however powerful they become, realise that outside of their quarter, their territory, they're nobodies, provincial hoods. They stay here because this is where they count, this is where their respect and control is beyond dispute."

The "traditional", neighbourhood character of such a camorra clan as the Giuliano family raises a paradox, however, a kind of clash between good neighbourliness and delinquency. By producing and dealing heroin, the camorra, Giulianos included, have brought upon Naples (as elsewhere in Italy) one of the great social tragedies in contemporary Italy. The used needles that litter the streets of Naples are the unnerving, unmistakable proof of this epidemic.

This paradox came home to the Giuliano family in the autumn of 1987 when one of their own, seventeen-year-old Ciro, died of a heroin overdose. What followed was unprecedented: the grandfather/godfather of the family forbade the funeral to take place in his native quarter, making it pass through a street behind Forcella. He wanted to signal to his "people" that something was wrong, that something had to change. This strange admonition, however, did not deter the thousands of mourners from following the funeral cortege, and the 25 limousines bearing flowers from "friends" made clear that it wasn't just any seventeen-year-old who had died.

The other unprecedented aspect of this incident was the reaction of Nunzio Giuliano, the boy's father. Soon after his son's death, Nunzio began a campaign (in the papers, in public gatherings) against the heroin trade and the camorra's perpetration of it – in general terms, taking care not to incriminate any kin. Many see this as a possible turning point in the camorra's operations in Naples, while others, less optimistic, view it as little more than an act of showmanship, a piece of theatre, to divert attention from the real workings of the camorra and an embarrassing family tragedy.

Relatively cut off from the reintensification of Mafia and 'ndrangheta violence in 1988, the camorra has, thus far, also been spared the stepped-up investigations of the anti-Mafia commission. While the various anti-Mafia parliamentary laws and measures include the camorra in their jurisdiction, in recent years the camorra has taken a lower profile in the Naples area, falling short of some of the bolder acts of violence committed by the Mafia and 'ndrangheta. Far from being cause for relief, however, this may well mean that the camorra is finding new, more "acceptable" ways of inserting its illicit activities into the social and economic life of Naples.

Nelson Moe

ITALIAN CINEMA

From the earliest days of the cinema, the Italians have always been passionate movie-lovers and movie-makers. But it was with their films of the postwar period, and the shift from studio-based films to the use of the country's actual town and landscapes – that Italy came to the forefront of world cinema. Their style and technique were ground-breaking, and the use of real locations added a dimension, a mood, which made Italian cinema linger longer in the memory. The endless expanse of the Po Valley plain in *Obsession*, the steaming sulphur springs outside Naples in *Voyage to Italy*, the deserted, off-season seaside resort of Rimini in *I Vitelloni*, created an atmosphere that could never have been achieved in a studio.

THE BACKGROUND

The Italians were once famous for their silent costume epics, pre-World War I dramas that had monumental backdrops and crowd scenes – a leftover from the Italian grand opera tradition. They were often set in the period of the Roman Empire, anticipating the Fascist nostalgia for ancient Rome by at least a decade. **Giovani Pastrone**'s *Cabiria* (1913), set in Babylon, was the most sophisticated and innovative of these, with spectacular sets and lighting effects that the American director D.W. Griffiths imitated in his masterpiece

Intolerance (1916). This borrowing of Italian expertise by Hollywood gave the Taviani brothers the story for their *Good Morning Babylon* (1984).

But even in its early stages the Italian cinema was handicapped by the economic problems that would always keep it lagging behind its rivals, the Americans. The reason for this was not simply lack of funds, but also an inability on the part of the government to realise what a moneyspinner the indigenous film-making talent could be, and what the unregulated influx of foreign films into Italy would mean for the home market.

In addition to this, the Americans themselves began making films in Italy, attracted by the cheap labour, the locations, and the quality of Italian light, so gutting the already fragile indigenous industry. An American film team arrived in 1923 to make an epic version of *Ben Hur*. Three years previous to this, 220 films were made in Italy; by 1927 the number had dropped to around a dozen a year.

The Fascist regime (1922–43) was surprisingly slow to recognise the potential, both economic and propagandist, of the cinema. But in 1934 Mussolini did begin to support it financially. He also limited the number of foreign imports, had film added to the arts festival in Venice, and in 1937 inaugurated "Cinecitta", the film studio complex just outside Rome. From 1938 to 1944 the proportion of Italian productions against imports rose rapidly, though home-produced films would never account for more than a third of the total number of films distributed in the country.

Films made during the Fascist period featured glorious victories from the past (the Romans again), and from the present – the war in Ethiopia, for example. During this time, not all movies were vehicles for propaganda, though no films could be made that were overtly critical of the regime. Most popular at the time were the escapist, sentimental, "white telephone" films, so-called because the heroine would have a gleaming white telephone in her boudoir, Hollywood-style – a touch of the exotic for the average Italian at the time, who never even saw such a thing, let alone owned one, in real life.

Italians were not, however, cut off from what was going on in world cinema between the wars, and the ideas and techniques of

Eisenstein and, even more so, of French directors, particularly Renoir, Pagnol and Carne, began to filter through. Likewise with literature. Probably the biggest single influence on the emerging generation of Italian film-makers was the American novel. Hemingway, Faulkner and Steinbeck spoke directly to the young generation: their subjects were realistic, their stylistic approach was fresh, even raw, the emotion seemed genuine.

It was not surprising, then, that the late 1930s and early 1940s should see an element of documentary-style realism creep into film-making. Contemporary social themes were addressed; non-professional actors were sometimes used. Directors – even those with the official stamp of approval – made the occasional realistic documentary, with none of the bombast or gloss of the typical Fascist film. It was on films such as these that future neorealist directors such as Visconti, Rossellini and De Sica, and the writer Zavattini, did their apprenticeships, learning techniques that they would draw on a few years later when they would be allowed to unleash their creative imaginations.

A film made in 1943 caused a considerable stir. When it was first shown, Mussolini's son, Vittorio, walked out exclaiming "This is not Italy!". But Mussolini allowed it to be distributed anyway, probably because there was nothing politically controversial in it. This was **Luchino Visconti's** *Obsession*, an unauthorised adaptation of the American novel *The Postman Always Rings Twice* by James M. Cain. Visconti transposed this low-life story of adultery and murder to Northern Italy, the characters playing out their seedy tragedy in the relentlessly flat landscape of the Po Valley and among the surreal carnival floats in Ferrara (a favourite town of the surrealist painter Giorgio de Chirico). It showed two ordinary people in the grip of a violent passion, so obsessed with each other that they bring about their own destruction. The original negative was deliberately destroyed when the official film industry was moved north to Mussolini's Saló Republic on Lake Garda.

Obsession was something new in the Italian cinema. It had an honesty and intensity, and a realistic lack of glamour, that pointed the way to the "neo-realist" films of the immediate postwar period.

THE NEO-REALISTS

The end of the war meant the end of Fascist domination of everything, including the film industry. But Italy was left emotionally as well as physically shattered. It now seemed important to film-makers to make sense of the intense experience the Italian people had undergone, to rebuild in some way what had been destroyed.

As the tanks were rolling out of Rome in 1945, **Roberto Rossellini** cobbled together the bare minimum of finances, crew and equipment and started shooting *Rome, Open City*. He used real locations, documentary footage, and low-grade film, and came up with a grainy, idiosyncratic style that influenced not only his Italian contemporaries, but also the American *film noirs* of the late 1940s, and the grittily realistic films of the early 1950s – as well as the French New Wave of the 1960s.

Neo-realism had no manifesto, but its main exponents – Rossellini, De Sica and Visconti – had the following aims, even if they didn't always stick to them: to show real people rather than conventional heroes (using non-actors), real time, real light, real places (shooting on location, not in studios). Their intention was to present the everyday stuff of life and not romantic dreams.

Unusually for an "art" film, *Rome, Open City* was a box office hit. It had a good emotional, even melodramatic, story, with touches of humour, and packed a terrific moral punch. Set in a downbeat quarter of occupied Rome, it is about a partisan priest and a communist who join forces to help the resistance; a collaborator betrays them, and he is taken off to a labour camp by the Nazis while his fiancée (Anna Magnani) is shot down while running after him. The Nazis are depicted as effeminate and depraved, while the partisans – including a band of children – are the true heroes, though taken as a whole the film's impact is ambiguous, and Rossellini seems to pursue immediacy at the expense of making political statements.

This was the first in Rossellini's so-called "war trilogy". It was followed by *Paisa* (1946), which traced the Allied Occupation north from Sicily to the Po Valley, in six self-contained episodes, and the desolate *Germany, Year Zero* (1947) – set in the ruins of postwar Berlin, about a child whom circumstances push to suicide.

In these, as in other neo-realist films, children are seen as the innocent victims of adult corruption. **Vittorio De Sica**'s *Shoeshine* (1946) is an anatomy of a friendship between two Roman boys, destroyed first by blackmarketeers, then by the police. A young boy is also the witness to his father's humiliation in De Sica's *Bicycle Thieves* (1948) – also set in the poorer quarters of Rome – when he sees him steal a bicycle out of desperation (a bicycle means getting his job back) and immediately get caught. The child's illusions are dashed, and it's society's fault for not providing the basic human requirements. At the time *Bicycle Thieves* was called the only truly Communist film of the postwar decade, but in retrospect the message, as in *Rome, Open City*, seems politically ambiguous. Crowds are seen as hostile and claustrophobic, and the only hope seems to lie in the family unit, which the hero falls thankfully back on at the end.

This conflict between Catholic and Marxist ideology is a recurrent theme in Italian cinema, from Rossellini through to Pasolini, and the Taviani brothers in the 1980s, and it's often this that gives their films their necessary tension. More than anyone, Visconti exemplifies this dichotomy. Born an aristocrat in the famous Milanese family, and sentenced to death for being an anti-Fascist in 1944, he was influenced by the writings of Antonio Gramsci, and right up until his death in 1976 veered between two milieux for his films – the honest, suffering sub-proletariat, and the decadent, suffering upper classes.

In 1948 Rossellini made a version of the nineteenth-century Sicilian author Giovanni Verga's novel about a family of fishermen who are destroyed through a series of circumstances, *The House by the Medlar Tree*, which he called *The Earth Trembles*. It was shot on location on the stark Sicilian coast, using an entire village as cast, speaking in their native Sicilian (with an Italian voice-over and subtitles). He adapted the story to incorporate a Marxist perspective, but this fades from view in the pervading atmosphere of stoic fatalism, closer to Greek tragedy than to the party line.

Something else that detracted from the intended message was the sophisticated visual style. Stunning tableaux such as the one where the wives, dressed in black, stand waiting for their husbands on the skyline, looking out to sea, prompted Orson Welles to remark that Visconti shot fishermen as if they were Vogue models. Indeed, style constantly threatened to overtake content in Visconti's work, culminating in the emotionally slick *Death In Venice* (1971).

THE END OF NEO-REALISM

By the early 1950s, neo-realism was all but dead. Social problems no longer occupied centre stage, and film-makers now concentrated on the psychological, the historical, even the magical side of life. There were several reasons for this, not least that the trauma of World War II had receded, and cities (and lives) were being rebuilt. As Rossellini said in 1954, "you can't go on making films about heroism among the rubble for ever". Directors wanted to move on to new themes. Another reason for the break was government intervention. The cinema industry was in the doldrums, and the Christian Democrat minister Giulio Andreotti had banned any more neo-realist films from being made on the grounds that social criticism equalled Communism. The Cold War was just beginning.

Neo-realist films had in any case, with one or two exceptions, rarely been good box office. Of Italian-made films, the general public tended to prefer farces, historical dramas, or comedies. The Neapolitan comic actor **Toto** – who had a colossal career spanning scores of films and several decades – was a particular favourite. In *Toto looks for a Home* (1949), he and his family search for somewhere to live in the postwar ruins of Rome, in a comic variation on a neo-realist theme. It was a sign of the times that people preferred to laugh at their problems rather than confront them.

De Sica meanwhile had moved on from the unremitting pessimism of *Bicycle Thieves*, to a fantastic fable set in Milan, *Miracle in Milan* (1950), about a young man who is given a white dove which can grant the wishes of everyone living in his slummy suburb. Surreal special effects are used to good effect, for example in a shot of the hero and heroine flying high above the pinnacles of Milan cathedral on a broomstick. The moral is still a neo-realist one, but with a change of emphasis: art and imagination can help your problems disappear for a while, but won't solve them.

In 1954 **Visconti** made *Senso*, another adaptation of a nineteenth-century novel but worlds away from *The Earth Trembles*. It opens to strains of Verdi, in the Venice opera house, the Fenice, one night in 1866, and is Visconti's view of the politically controversial Unification, portrayed through the lives of a few aristocratic individuals. It was a theme he would explore again in *The Leopard* (1963). *Senso* was the first of Visconti's historical spectaculars, and the first major Italian film to be made in colour.

THE FIFTIES AND AFTER

Neo-realism was dead, but the next generation of film-makers — Fellini, Pasolini, Bertolucci, Antonioni, Rosi — could not help but be influenced at first by its ideals and techniques, though the style each of them went on to evolve was highly personal.

Federico Fellini, for one, saw neo-realism as more a world-view than a "school". His early films, such as *La Strada* (1954), follow a recognisably realistic storyline (unlike his later movies), but the whole feeling is different to the films of the 1940s. His characters are motivated by human values rather than social ones — searching for love rather than solidarity.

All through his long career Fellini used films as a kind of personal notebook in which to hark back to his youth. *I Vitelloni* (1953) is set in an unrecognisable Rimini, his birthplace, before the days of mass tourism; *Amarcord* (1974) is again set in Rimini, this time under Fascism. He also explores his own personal sexual fantasies and insecurities, as in *Casanova* (1976), and *The City of Women* (1980).

But Fellini isn't all nostalgia and sex. There are philosophical themes that run right through his work, not least the gap between reality and illusion. The heroine of *The White Sheikh* (1952) falls in love with the Valentino-type actor playing the romantic lead for "photo romance" comics (being shot on the coast outside Rome), and has her illusions dashed when reality intervenes and he makes a bungling attempt to seduce her. *Casanova* too is an oddly (and deliberately) artificial-looking film. It wasn't shot in the real Venice, and the water in the lagoon is in fact a shaken plastic sheet — an odd backlash against the real landscapes of the neo-realists.

Religion is also a theme in Fellini's work, and he's at his best when satirising the Roman Catholic church, as in the grotesque clerical fashion parade in *Roma* (1971), or the malicious episode in *La Dolce Vita* (1960) where a couple of children claim to have had a vision of the Virgin Mary, and create the press event of the month.

Pier Paolo Pasolini, murdered under mysterious circumstances in 1975, was a practising Catholic, a homosexual and a Marxist, as well as a poet and novelist. His films reflected this cocktail of ideological and sexual tendencies, though in a less autobiographical way than Fellini. They're also far more disturbing and challenging: *Theorem* (1968) intercuts shots of a spiritually empty middle-class Milanese family, which the mysterious young stranger insinuates himself into, with desolate scenes of a volcanic wasteland. *The Gospel According to Matthew* (1963) is a radical interpretation of a familiar story (and an excellent antidote to Zeffirelli's syrupy late-Seventies *Jesus of Nazareth*) in which Jesus is not a man of peace but the champion of the sub-proletariat and the enemy of hypocrisy. It was filmed in the surprisingly biblical-looking landscape of the poorer regions of southern Italy — Puglia and Calabria — and used the peasants of the area in the cast. Pasolini's *Decameron* (1971) was a record hit at the box office because of its explicit sex scenes, though the director's intention had been political rather than salacious, with Boccaccio's fourteenth-century tales transposed from their original middle-class Florentine setting to the Naples of the sub-proletariat.

Otherwise, the real box-office earners in the 1960s and 1970s were the so-called "spaghetti westerns", shot in the Arizona-look-alike interior of Sardinia, the best of which were directed by **Sergio Leone**. Equally popular were detective stories, and soft porn.

Bernardo Bertolucci started out as Pasolini's assistant, and shared his politics, though his own films are more straightforward and more accessible. *The Spider's Strategem* (1969), filmed in the strange, star-shaped Renaissance town of Sabbioneta near Mantua, was the first of many feature films sponsored by RAI, the Italian state TV network, the anatomy of a destructive father-son ·relationship with constant flashbacks between the Fascist era and the present day. Another early film, *The Conformist* (1970), adapted from the novel by Moravia, had the spiritually empty hero (or rather, anti-hero) search for father-substitutes in Fascist Rome, again a dream-like jumble of flashbacks.

In *The Conformist* Bertolucci used a mixture of Italian and non-Italian actors. It was the first step on the path to a world recognition, and from *Last Tango in Paris* (1971), through *1900* (1976) and *La Luna* (1979), became more commercially as well as critically successful, culminating in the Oscar-winning *The Last Emperor* (1988).

Michelangelo Antonioni again had a neo-realist background, but in the films he made in the 1960s and 1970s shifted the emphasis from outward action and social realism to internal and psychological anguish. The locations he chose – the volcanic landscape of Sicily for *L'Avventura* (1964), the bleak townscape of industrial Milan in *La Notta* (1961), the impersonal Stock Exchange building in Rome for *The Eclipse* (1962), the alienating oil refineries and power plants at Ravenna for *The Red Desert* (1964) – were perfect settings for his almost cinematic equivalents of existential novels.

The Neapolitan director **Francesco Rosi** made a series of semi-documentary "inquiry" films attacking various aspects of the Italian establishment – the Sicilian mafia in *Salvatore Giuliano* (1962), the building mafia in Naples in *Hands Over the City* (1963), the army in *Just Another War* (1970), and vested interests of all kinds in *The Mattei Affair* (1972). Not that these are dry analyses of Italian society: the viewer has to sort through the pieces of evidence – the newsreel footage, the half-heard comments, the absence of comment – to come to their own conclusions about the truth, in kind of do-it-yourself mystery stories.

Later on, in the late 1970s and 1980s Rosi went on in a more personal direction. *Christ Stopped at Eboli* (1979) is a surprisingly un-incisive critique of "the problem of the South", set in a poverty-stricken mountain village in Basilicata. *Three Brothers* (1980) looks at three different political attitudes, as the brothers of the title, reunited for their mother's funeral back home in Puglia, argue, reminisce and dream. Oddly enough, in 1983 Rosi made a completely apolitical film of the opera *Carmen*.

This was a national trend. Hardly any of the major films of the last twenty years have attacked political targets, even after the explosion of the P2 scandal in the early 1980s. Instead there has been a looking back to their recent past. Italian cinema of the last two decades has been dominated by foreign co-productions and TV-sponsored films, which has inevitably led to a loss of national identity – though Italy does remain a cinema-going nation, its audiences less eroded by the successive onslaughts of television, video and TV deregulation than elsewhere. **Ermanno Olmi**'s *Tree of the Wooden Clogs* (1978) has a Bergamasque cast speaking dialect with Italian subtitles, and did well at the box office world-wide. Also prominent among current Italian directors are the **Taviani brothers**, whose *Padre Padrone* (1977), set in Sardinia, and *Kaos* (1984), an adapation of Pirandello stories shot in scenic Sicily, are loving of the Italian land-scape and redolent of a time past. Both films, together with the later *Good Morning Babylon*, have put the brothers' work centre-stage internationally.

Sheila Brownlee

ITALIAN POPULAR MUSIC: GREATEST HITS

At the beginning of this century, Italy had one of the richest and most diverse traditions of folk music of any European country. Nearly a century of industrial, mass-market life and entertainment have done much to level this tradition, and it takes the keenness of the folklorist or anthropologist to find live folk music in Italy today, and determination to locate available recordings in record shops. When you do find it, however, live or recorded, it is always worth the effort.

What *has* happened musically during these years, in particular after World War II, is the cultural colonisation of Italy by the US and UK. And yet however strong these influences have been, the Italians have tended to make their own styles, often creating striking fusions. What follows is an extremely partial listing of Italian music since the war, a listing of those artists which have been popular in Italy *and* which have offered some special, Italian contribution to the pop music genre.

NAPLES AFTER THE WAR

The history of postwar Italian popular music may well begin in Naples in 1944, with the arrival of the Allies. Here the occupying Americans created a kind of Dixieland in exile with their officers' clubs and cafés. For at least a century before Naples had been a goldmine of popular music, providing the nation with such favourites as *O sole mio* and *Funicule Funicula*, and a long line of some of Italy's most distinctive and passionate singer-songwriters which continues to this day. The meeting of these two traditions, the Black American and Neapolitan, is perhaps the single most important factor in the making of contemporary Italian pop music. One man in particular, the pianist and singer-songwriter **Renato Carosone**, played a key role in this fusion. Carosone did much to import the Dixieland-swing sound into Italy during the 1950s. But he always did so with an ironic twist, ridiculing the Italian mania for America even as he fuelled it. In one of Carosone's best-known songs he chides his compatriots, "you want to play the American, but tough luck, kid, you were born in Italy".

THE FIFTIES

During the Fifties, another kind of song was taking form across the rest of the country, one vaguely reminiscent of the cabarets, but with a more sweetened, romantic sound. It was a style that took much from the singing of Peggy Lee, Frank Sinatra, and other American singers of the era. **Ornella Vanoni** and **Gino Paoli**, often singing together, are the best example of this kind of music, whose hits have become a part of the Italian collective musical memory. Together with Paoli and Vanoni, the sound of singers **Domenico Modugno** (of *Volare* fame), **Peppino di Capri** and **Mina**, has come to be associated with a particular moment in Italian history: the economic boom of the late 1950s and early 1960s.

This style of music, it might be added, though usually in watered-down form, was the music of "San Remo", the annual popular Italian music festival. To trace the popular musical consciousness of Italy you need only listen to the hits that came out of that festival.

THE SIXTIES

A spirit of restlessness, of rock, swept over the music scene of the 1960s, an international phenomenon but with a local, Italian accent. A specifically Italian kind of folk-rock is one of the most successful expressions of the decade.

The songs of **Luigi Tenco** mark a kind of fusion between the San Remo sound and that of the new folk-rock. **Fabrizio De André, Francesco Guccini**, and, a little later, **Francesco De Gregori** are all noted for their combination of fine folk guitar music with poetic, and often political, lyrics. At the same time **Gabriella Ferri** mixed the tradition of Roman folk songs and cabaret in her spirited singing.

Out of the late Sixties emerged one of Italy's most original and popular singer-songwriters, **Lucio Dalla**. For twenty years, his songs, teeming with the sounds of every pop genre, have cast a humorous and ironic gaze at Italian society. The Italians appreciate Dalla's playful self-portraits and love him like few other performers. In 1988, Dalla and **Gianni Morandi**, a more romantic singer from the ranks of San Remo, joined forces to take Italian audiences on a nostalgic tour through two decades of their hits.

THE SEVENTIES

During the 1970s the sounds of heavy-metal rock erupted onto the Italian music scene (continuing to this day in the punkified versions played by unknown groups in various "dark" nightclubs in major Italian cities). These were the "anni di piombo", the "years of lead" or "hot" years terrorism and social unrest, and the popularity of certain of these bands, like **Area** and **Stormy Six**, was tied to the radical politics of their music. Area in particular were a rallying point for young activists and intellectuals. Their legacy, however, is as much musical as it is political. With its Greek leader, Demetrios Stratos, Area sought to elaborate a musical style that was not limited to an Italian/US-UK fusion, but which opened itself to the various musical traditions of the Mediterranean, in particular those of the Balkan and the Arab countries.

At the same time that Area was looking to the Mediterranean to create a new form of hard rock, two groups based in Naples, **La Nuova Compagnia di Canto Popolare** and **Musica Nova**, were looking in that direction in an effort to revive long-forgotten traditions of southern Italian folk music. For the past ten years the group, **Operaio é zezi**, composed of workers at the Alfa Sud auto plant outside Naples, has given a political accent to this folk

revival, setting contemporary political lyrics to ancient folk songs which they perform at rallies.

Out of the two dominant tendencies in Naples during the 1970s – the Mediterranean folk revival on the one hand, and American blues and rock on the other – came some of the most interesting musicians on the scene today. Though these performers have come to be grouped together by the label, "new Neopolitan sound", theirs is not one sound but many. **Pino Daniele** is certainly the foremost of these, fusing American rock, blues and funk with Neapolitan lyricism, American slang and Neapolitan dialect. Saxophonist **James Senese**, while collaborating with Daniele, is also a fine jazz musician in his own right. The music of **Tullio De Piscopo**, **Eduardo** and **Eugenio Bennato**, and **Teresa De Sio** are all marked in different ways by a mingling of folk and pop styles.

THE EIGHTIES

The most distinctive performers of the 1980s offer a sampling of many of the styles mentioned above, often carrying them to new heights of sophistication and self-consciousness. **Gianna Nanini**'s rock songs tend to be musically rather traditional, but her husky voice and risqué lyrics have earned her a wide following. **Franco Battiato** bases his music on an unmistakeable personal style: aloof, slick and synthesised. Recently he too has turned to the folk heritage, writing songs in his Sicilian dialect which make use of various elements of Sicilian folk music.

The most innovative group of "ethno-rock" today is the Florence-based **Litfiba**. Seeking to create a new musical language based on Mediterranean traditions, Litfiba blend together Italian, Arab, Latin, Balkan and "dark" sounds in their striking compositions.

As if to turn back the clock to the immediate postwar years, piano man **Paolo Conte** takes the traditions of American swing and French cabaret as his chief inspirations. Decidedly retro, his clever, moody songs have attained considerable international success. The work of TV showman and clarinetist, **Renzo Arbore**, trained in the Neapolitan school of the postwar years, is also nostalgic, displaying that mixture of American musical style and lyrical irony so common to Italian music. But most importantly,

Arbore has shown that Italy, and Italian music, has entered the age of mass media. As the creator of smash hit "variety" shows *Quelli della Notte* and *Indietro Tutta*, he reminds us that music in Italy has become in large part a video phenomenon, and that here, perhaps even more than in other countries, those that successfully make music are usually those that also make the best show of it.

More recent musical output has been less Italian, more international, with bands like **Black Box** and **Starlight** specialising in dance music that could have come from just about any country, their clever synthesis of smooth production, soul-roots and hypnotic rhythms bringing success to Italian music worldwide.

Nelson Moe

MODERN ITALIAN LITERATURE

Modern Italian literature tells the traveller a part of a story which we might call the "making of modern Italy", the transformation of a traditional, rural society into a modern, industrialised nation. One of the keys to appreciating the country's literature is to understand the interplay of regionalism, nationalism and internationalism which to this day has been a dynamic force in Italian social and cultural life – though, for the Anglo-American reader, one of the main expressions of this interplay, the tension between local dialect and standard Italian, is caught imperfectly in translation. For a complete rundown on what *is* available in translation, see "Books", which follows.

TOWARDS A NATIONAL LITERATURE

Italian modern literature arguably begins around the time of Unification (1861), although to start here would be to ignore two writers who in some way inaugurated the literature of the new Italy some decades before, **Giacomo Leopardi** (1798–1837) and **Alessandro Manzoni** (1785–1873).

A poet and philosopher from the Marche, Giacomo Leopardi's obsession with fading youth has earned him the title of pessimist. But if, for Leopardi, "all is vanity", then human imagination is infinitely precious, for through it people create the illusions which allow them to live from day to day. To the suffering poet who sees through these illusions, the poetic imagination offers, if not happiness, at least the comfort that from these worldly sufferings he has created a kind of eternal music. Leopardi published many of his finest poems in the volume, *Canti*.

Through the diversity and force of Alessandro Manzoni's writings, and his long career spanning more than half a century, this Milanese writer has profoundly shaped the Italian reading public's sense of literature and language. His magnum opus, *The Betrothed*, is

no summertime thriller – indeed Italian high school students, who spend a full year reading it, cringe at its mention – but it masterfully weaves together a romance of young lovers and a vast panorama of historical drama, all suffused by a deep religious sense of human destiny.

Most significantly, Manzoni's novel is the key literary intervention in the much-debated *questione della lingua*, the question over what kind of language would be Italy's national language. As only two to four percent of the total population could speak Italian in 1861 (the rest spoke regional dialects), this issue was in the forefront of all writers' minds. The two editions of *The Betrothed* mark the country's contorted attempt to move from linguistic regionalism to nationalism: the 1827 edition was written in a rather thick Milanese dialect, but in 1841 he published an edition which he had "rinsed in the Arno"; that is to say, he had rewritten the novel employing contemporary Florentine, the language which he and many others deemed the most appropriate for the young nation. Manzoni's view, in fact, became the dominant one, and the Italian taught in schools today is still modelled in part on Florentine.

THE SICILIAN EPIC OF GIOVANNI VERGA

The tension between regional and national language is also a prominent feature of the work of Italy's other great nineteenth-century novelist, **Giovanni Verga** (1840–1922). Again, the literary culture and language of Florence and Milan exert an irresistible influence on this writer – it was to these two cities that the young author went to seek his literary fortune – but it is Verga's native Sicily which becomes the scene for his most powerful novels and short stories; and it is, moreover, his fusion of the Sicilian dialect and Milanese-Florentine literary idiom which remains one of his most notable achievements.

Many of Verga's works – *Life in the Fields and Rustic Stories*, for instance – focus on the life of Sicilian peasants and artisans, acutely representing the world-view of that traditional society. *The House of the Medlar Tree* and *Master Don Gesualdo* are, however, in Verga's own words ". . . the sincere and dispassionate study of how the first restlessness for affluence in the poorest, most humble conditions is probably born and develops". In these two grand novels, Verga examines the turmoil which takes place in late-nineteenth-century Sicilian society as it gradually finds itself more and more part of a modern European state and the international capitalist system.

Verga has been an important mentor for later generations of Italian writers, and his success in writing about the poor, marginal elements of Italian society, as well as his particular form of realism, *verismo*, were to be a model for the movement known as neo-realism between 1930 and 1950.

19TH-CENTURY POETRY IN DIALECT

One of the things that distinguishes Italian poetry from Italian prose writing, and, above all, from the poetry of all other European literatures is the large portion of it which is written in dialect. In other words, a great part of "Italian" poetry is not, in fact, in Italian. This creates peculiar difficulties for both poets and readers, and tends to restrict a dialect poet's readership and reputation to his native city and region, or at best to certain Italian cognoscenti. Three of the greatest poets of nineteenth-century Italy are relatively unknown outside of the country: **Carlo Porta** (Milan, 1775–1821), **G.C. Belli** (Rome, 1793–1863) and **Salvatore Di Giacomo** (Naples, 1860–1934), each of whom provide powerful evocations of the spirit and life of their cities. Today, after half a century of relative dormancy, Italian dialect poetry is alive and well again in the verses of Albino Pierro, Tonino Guerra, Franco Loi, Ignazio Butita, and others.

19TH-CENTURY WOMEN'S WRITING

If dialect poets have existed somewhat on the margins of "official" Italian literary culture, they certainly have not been alone. Women writers too have been largely ignored over the years by the Italian cultural establishment, even though some of the most successful writers during the late nineteenth century in Italy were women. Publishing serially in newspapers, **Carolina Invernizio** (1858–1916) thrilled her petit-bourgeois north Italian readers with such tales as *The Bastard*, *The Infamous*,

Dreams of Adultery, and *The Train of Death*. **Matilde Serao** (1856–1927) was another popular writer who wrote stories varying between impassioned and astute social observation, and baroque melodrama based on the tumultuous, desperate life of late-nineteenth-century Naples. **Grazia Deledda** (1871–1936), one of the few female recipients of the Nobel Prize for Literature (1926), wrote most of her numerous novels about her native Sardinia. Her prose style, which owes much to Verga and the French realists but exhibits a heightened interest in her characters' state of mind, make her a kind of link between the literature of nineteenth- and twentieth-century Italy.

SVEVO AND THE DRAMA OF THE MIND

A detailed examination of human psychology marks much of the prose writing of the early 1900s. Italy's great turn-of-the-century master of the tragi-comic machinations of the human psyche, **Ettore Schmitz** (1861–1928), went by the name of **Italo Svevo**, and his choice of a pseudonym reveals a good deal about his own mind's make-up. Italo Svevo means "the Italian-Swabian", that is "the Italian-German". Svevo spent most of his life in his native Trieste, a city which, until the end of World War II, had been the main port of the Habsburg Austrian Empire. Trieste, with its mixed population of Italians, "Swabians", Slavs and Jews, was a city whose ethnic and political identity was in flux, and this instability comes out in profoundly personal, psychological terms in Svevo's writing. With irony and humour Svevo achieves an incisive analysis of the middle-class, middle-European mind. Indeed, Svevo was one of the first writers to incorporate the insights of psychoanalysis into the novel. For those who have ever struggled to give up smoking, the opening of *The Confessions of Zeno* is not to be missed.

PROPHETS OF DECADENCE

The critique of realism implicit in the writings of Italo Svevo becomes bold and explicit in the work of Nobel Prize-winning dramatist **Luigi Pirandello** (1867–1936). Part and parcel of this was Pirandello's critique of positivism, the dominant cultural ideology of late-nineteenth-century Italy. Pirandello opposed the positivist faith in the ability to analyse "reality" scientifically and objectively (which lay behind much of realist writing, such as Verga), showing instead the subjective qualities of human experience, and the way in which "reality" is determined in fact by social convention.

Whether in such grand plays as *Six Characters in Search of an Author*, or *Henry IV*, in the novels *The Late Mattia Pascal* and *The Old and Young*, or his numerous short stories, Pirandello's writing expresses a crisis which is at once cultural and political. Pirandello's works investigate the psychology both of his native, rural Sicily and of metropolitan Rome, and he is a striking example of how the different cultural layerings of region, nation and the world can come together to produce a literature of both local and global resonance.

Behind Pirandello's challenge to the stable appearances of bourgeois reality, its conventions and hypocrisies, lies his affirmation of the dynamism of human existence, of the crucial role that the will, or will power, plays in determining the shape of the world – a world that in the early twentieth century was undergoing a radical transformation.

Will power was also a philosophical trademark of that most flamboyant of Italian intellectuals, **Gabriele D'Annunzio** (1863–1938) – writer, playboy and rabble-rouser. His artistic, amorous and political activities found a kind of dramatic unity as, at every turn, he attempted to embody the Nietzschean "Superman". Like his colleague Giovanni Pascoli – and, in England, Oscar Wilde and Arthur Symons – D'Annunzio explored the aesthetic dissolution of Western European Civilisation, breaking down "sense" into sonorous sensuality in his poetry.

D'Annunzio was, moreover, one of the first Italian writers to appreciate the effects that industrialisation and the mass media had on the writer's role in society. In this he found the company of **Filippo Tommaso Marinetti** (1876–1944), the founder of the Futurist Movement in 1909. Marinetti took things a step further, however, proposing to destroy art and literature as we know it, replacing it with the aesthetics of modern technology and machinery. For Marinetti and the Futurists the beauty of a sonata or poem was far surpassed by that of a machine gun. Indeed they were not so much interested in beauty as in speed, power and violence.

WRITERS IN OPPOSITION

Such prominent cultural figures as Pirandello, D'Annunzio and Marinetti reached the height of their careers during the early years of Fascism in Italy. In different ways, their ideas and actions entwined with the development of Fascism.

At the same time, a generation of younger writers grew up through Fascism, acquiring a new sense of the social function of culture in opposition to it. For some, like **Ignazio Silone** (1900–1978) and **Carlo Levi** (1902–1975), their exile at the hands of Fascist authorities drew their attention to the poorest, marginal areas of Italy. From his exile in Switzerland, Silone wrote about his native Abruzzo, and about the struggle to bring social justice to this mountain area, in such books as *Bread and Wine* and *Fontamara*. Levi was from Turin, raised in the same industrial and metropolitan milieu in which Antonio Gramsci was politically active. Levi's exile in a small village in Basilicata opened his eyes to the existence of a world which, he wrote, "had been denied History and Government", where "the peasant lives out the immobility of his existence in misery and solitude". It was in fact Levi's *Christ Stopped at Eboli*, published in 1946, which awakened the Italian people to the problem of the underdeveloped South, *la questione meridionale*.

Conversation in Sicily, the masterpiece of yet another fine Sicilian writer, **Elio Vittorini** (1908–1966), expresses a more oblique critique of Fascism. The voyage of the novel's alienated young protagonist from the northern industrial city where he works to his island home (and mother) becomes a search for the authenticity of personal memory and communal tradition which stands in clear contrast to the pretence of the Fascist present.

Vittorini is often associated with the Piemontese writer **Cesare Pavese** (1908–1950): both wrote narratives about their native regions in a deeply lyrical and personal-mythical style; both were avid readers of American literature and changed the Italian literary landscape with their translations of it; and both came to be seen as the precursors of the literary "tendency" known as neo-realism.

In a hybrid style of myth and realism, Pavese's novels (as well as an unusual volume of poetry, *Working Tired*) dramatise the trauma of an Italian society in transition from the slow, steady rhythms of an agrarian existence to the shock and speed of the urban, technological age – a trauma which Pavese experienced first-hand in his frequent passage between Turin and the outlying countryside, Le Langhe, where he was born. This trauma, and that of Fascism, proved too much for Pavese, who took his own life in 1950.

NEO-REALISM

The term neo-realism was first used in 1931 to describe the "new" style of Moravia's *The Time of Indifference* and Alvaro's *People of Aspromonte*. A novelist and Communist intellectual from Calabria, the work of **Corrado Alvaro**(1895–1956) has yet to be adequately presented to the English-speaking public. **Alberto Moravia** (born 1907), on the other hand, is one of the best-known Italian writers in the UK and US. He burst onto the scene with *The Time of Indifference* at the age of 22 in 1929 and, with *Agostino* in 1944, *Two Women* in 1957, and numerous recent works, he has been the most prolific and constant presence on the Italian literary scene.

The term neo-realism was applied to Moravia's and Alvaro's novels as an indication of a new interest in social content and history, an interest that seemed to go against the prevailing mood of "decadent" formalism of the early 1930s.

Neo-realism, however, only became a dominant trend in the decade following World War II. As a cultural tendency or "state of mind", neo-realism arose out of the need to make sense of the social and economic ruins in which Italy found itself at the end of the war, and out of the intellectuals' desire for social commitment and civic purpose. Neo-realist writers tended to focus on the life of the provincial, lower classes, of peasants and farmers especially from the South, making frequent use of local dialect and idioms in their prose. In different ways, the works of Alberto Moravia, Elio Vittorini, Cesare Pavese, Vasco Pratolini, Carlo Levi and Corrado Alvaro, manifest neo-realist characteristics. However, it was in Italian cinema, with the films of Rossellini, De Sica, Visconti, et al, that neo-realism achieved greatest artistic success and international acclaim (see "Italian Cinema").

HERMETIC POEMS AND OTHERS

Neo-realists, in different ways, attempted to confront society and politics directly in their writings, to break open what they viewed to be the dense, obscure literary productions that had proliferated under Fascism. The prime polemical target of the neo-realists was that of **Hermeticism**, a term that came to be associated with the poetry of **Giusepe Ungaretti** (1888–1970), **Eugenio Montale** (1896–1981) and **Salvatore Quasimodo** (1901–1968), the latter two Nobel Prize winners. If these three poets were "guilty" of a difficult, oblique style, they also lay claim to having written some of the finest Italian lyrics in this century. Ungaretti's verses pare down the sufferings of World War I trench warfare, and of life's daily vicissitudes, into brilliant, imagistic compositions. Montale evokes a world of metaphysical breakdown, where man stands godless and alone in the storm of existence (*The Storm and Other Poems* is the title of one of Montale's collections of poetry). Quasimodo, at first the most "hermetic" of the three, later converted to a more overtly social kind of poetry. Today, **Andrea Zanzotto** (born 1921) is probably the most articulate descendant of the Hermetic lineage. In striking contrast with the Hermetic tendency, **Umberto Saba** (1883–1957), the Jewish bard of Trieste, offers a rare example of simplicity and directness in Italian poetry.

LATER FICTION: C.E. GADDA

ne prose writer in particular stands out for his intelligent opposition to the neo-realist aesthetic, **Carlo Emilio Gadda** (1893–1973) of Milan. Gadda objected to the seriousness and moral rigidity of the neo-realists, and to their attempt to grasp reality "as it is". He instead saw the world as a welter of sexual energy in which humans, caught between the forces of desire and repression, try desperately to get some satisfaction. In *Acquainted with Grief* and *That Awful Mess on Via Merulana*, Gadda brilliantly demonstrates his conviction that the only way to represent such a world is through parody and pastiche, through a baroque profusion of styles which does not so much grasp reality as show how people "deform" reality according to their own desires.

REWRITING HISTORY

While the debate over neo-realism raged during the first postwar decade, **Giuseppe Tomasi Di Lampedusa** (1896–1957), far removed from the fray, set to meditating on the effects of the Unification in his native Sicily, meditations which would take the form of his novel, *The Leopard*. Published posthumously in 1958, *The Leopard*'s preoccupation with social immobility and its critique of the concept of progress underlying the Unification provoked the "committed" intellectuals of the day into heated debate over its significance. Its publication and ensuing debate in some sense mark the end of the neo-realist aesthetic.

Around the same time, **Elsa Morante** (1918–1986) was writing another kind of history, the history of a child's awakening to adulthood on the island of Prócida in *The Island of Arthur*, though in later years she too turned to an overt reflection on Italian history in *History: A Novel*. Like *The Leopard*, *History* provoked heated discussion of the question of historical interpretation, and of the relationship between literary representation and historical events. *History* also marks a significant moment in the history of Italian publishing: it is the first Italian book to have been published (by Einaudi) in coordination with a widespread publicity campaign. Within a few months of its appearance in 1974 it sold 600,000 copies.

Another history, one commonly viewed as marginal to mainstream Italian history, is that of the Italian Jews. Giorgio Bassani, Primo Levi and Natalia Ginzburg all explore, in different contexts and from different perspectives, the experience of being an Italian Jew. For **Giorgio Bassani** (born 1916), in *The Garden of the Finzi-Contini*, this context is the bourgeois milieu of Ferrara under Fascism. **Primo Levi**'s (1919–1987) writings focus primarily on his experience of the Nazi concentration camps, of which *If This Is A Man*, his first book, is perhaps the most powerful example. And **Natalia Ginzburg** (born 1916), in *Family Sayings*, turns her attention, instead, to the daily experience of home and family.

CONTEMPORARY WRITING

The two Italian writers with the keenest sense of the passage of Italian society into the contemporary world of consumerism and the mass media are **Pier Paolo Pasolini** (1922–1975) and **Italo Calvino** (1923–1985), and the contrast between them is illuminating. Pasolini, who had one of the most refined sensibilities for the "poetry" of rural, peasant society, especially for its dialects (he wrote exquisite poems in his native dialect of Friuli), also experienced the impact of the modern age in the most violent, traumatic fashion.

So much of Pasolini's writing can be read as his attempt to come to terms with the positive and negative aspects of the rapid progress towards modernisation which was bringing an end to the local, dialect-based cultures of agrarian Italy. In the novels *The Ragazzi* and *A Violent Life*, Pasolini grapples with this process in the underworld of the Roman suburbs; his long poem, *The Ashes of Gramsci*, is a more meditative treatment of the same Roman theme. Following Gramsci's footsteps, Pasolini explored the historical necessity of forming a *national* culture, at the same time lamenting the homogenisation of Italy's regions which accompanied this formation. The Italy which took form during these years was a nation in which the majority could speak a standard Italian, light years away from the fragmented, dialect-speaking country at the time of Unification.

Though Pasolini, as a film director, lived out of the realisation that the new Italy would be a predominantly audio-visual (and not literary) society, it was Italo Calvino who displayed the sharpest awareness of the necessity, and possible benefits, of these changes. In books like *Marcovaldo*, *Invisible Cities* and others, Calvino expresses some of the possibilities inherent in the contemporary moment of the metropolis and mass media. While never detached from a critique of capitalism's nefarious effects on human life, Calvino's writing (such as his experimentations with science fiction in *Cosmicomics*) works out new ways of humanely and humorously coping with the modern world. His constructive and pragmatic vision contrasts neatly with Pasolini's tragic and elegiac one.

Umberto Eco (born 1932) is another writer who has reflected upon the role of literature in the age of telecommunications: Eco's insightful observations on these phenomena are found in his various essays on the semiotics of everyday life (on Snoopy, James Bond, television quiz shows, etc). It was by writing the international bestseller, *The Name of the Rose*, however, that he best demonstrated his understanding of the tastes and tendencies of the present moment, not only in Italy but worldwide.

One of Italy's finest living novelists, **Leonardo Sciascia** (born 1912), takes another, more logical, approach to the contemporary moment. Writing again and again about his native Sicily, Sciascia has made of that island what he calls "a metaphor of the modern world". Whether writing on the mafia, reflecting on obscure events in Sicilian history or investigating the assassination of prime minister Aldo Moro, Sciascia displays refined literary talents and historical acumen, and in doing so has redefined the "historical" novel. He is one of the most striking examples of how passionate attention to a local, "provincial" reality can have international significance.

Among younger Italian writers today, a certain excess of rhetoric, an inclination to crowd the text with images, places, styles, seems to be a common characteristic. Though it is just now becoming known abroad, the work of writers like Antonio Tabucchi, Fabrizia Ramondino, Aldo Busi and Daniele Del Giudice suggests promising new directions for Italian literature – and new articulations of an "Italianicity" poised between region, nation and the world on the verge of the twenty-first century.

Nelson Moe

BOOKS

TRAVEL AND GENERAL

Charles Dickens *Pictures from Italy* (Granville £3.95). The classic mid-nineteenth-century Grand Tour, taking in the sights of Emilia, of Tuscany and Rome, and of Naples, in elegant, measured and incisive prose.

Wolfgang Goethe *Italian Journey* (Penguin £5.95). Revealing for what it says about the tastes of the time – Roman antiquities taking precedence over the Renaissance.

Henry James *Italian Hours* (Century £5.95). Urbane travel pieces from the young James; perceptive about particular monuments and works of art, superb on the different atmospheres of Italy.

D.H. Lawrence *D.H. Lawrence and Italy* (Penguin £4.95). Lawrence's three Italian travelogues collected into one volume. *Sea and Sardinia* and *Twilight in Italy* combine the author's seemingly natural ill-temper when travelling with a genuine sense of regret for a way of life almost visibly passing away – classic travel writing, supremely evocative of the spirit of place. *Etruscan Places*, published posthumously, consists of his more philosophical musings on Etruscan art and civilisation, and remains much the most illuminating thing to read on the period.

H.V. Morton *A Traveller in Italy, A Traveller in Rome* and *A Traveller in Southern Italy* (Methuen £8.95, £6.50 & £7.50). Morton's leisurely and amiable books were written in the 1930s, long before modern tourism got into its stride, and their nostalgic charm has a lot to do with their enduring popularity. But they are also packed with learned details and marvellously evocative descriptions.

William Murray *Italy: the Fatal Gift* (Dodd, Mead & Co. $9.95). Murray spent several years in Italy shortly after the last war, and this is a collection of essays inspired by his time there, and many return visits since. Skilfully combining personal anecdote and contemporary Italian history and politics, it's perhaps the most insightful and immediate introduction to the country and its people you can buy – though sadly it's for the moment only available in North America.

Eric Newby *Love and War in the Apennines* (Picador £3.99). Anecdotal, oddly nostalgic account of the sheltering of the author by local people in the mountains of Emilia-Romagna in the closing months of World War II.

Fiona Pitt-Kethley *Journeys to the Underworld* (Chatto & Windus £10). English poet searches Italy for the sibylline sites, a good third of her time spent in Sicily – though Pitt-Kethley's salacious appetite for sexual adventure often distracts from the real interest.

Tobias Smollett *Travels through France and Italy* (OUP £3.95). One of the funniest travel journals ever written – the apotheosis of Little Englandism, calling on an unmatched vocabulary of disgust at all things foreign.

Mary McCarthy *The Stones of Florence/ Venice Observed* (Penguin £4.95). A mixture of high-class reporting on the contemporary cities and anecdotal detail on their histories; one of the few accounts of these two cities that doesn't read as if it's been written in a library.

James Morris *Venice* (Faber £4.95). Some people think this is the most acute modern book written about any Italian city, while others find it unbearably fey. At least give it a look.

Norman Lewis *Naples '44* (Eland £5.95). Lewis was among the first Allied troops to move into Naples following the Italian surrender in the last war, and this is his diary of his experiences there. Part travelogue, part straight journalism, this is without question the finest thing you can read on World War II in Italy – and, despite its often bleak subject matter, among the most entertaining.

Norman Douglas *Old Calabria* (Penguin £2.95). The chronicle of Douglas's travels around the South in the early part of this century. Evocative and descriptive, though riven with digressions. See also the slightly earlier

Siren Land (Penguin £2.95), which focuses on Cápri and Sorrento; and *South Wind* (Penguin £3.95), a comic, if now rather dated novel set very obviously on Cápri, which the author knew well.

Vincent Cronin *The Golden Honeycomb* (Granada £6.95). Disguised as a quest for the mythical golden honeycomb of Daedalus, this is a searching account of a sojourn in Sicily in the 1950s. Although overwritten in parts, it has colourful descriptions of Sicily's art, architecture and folklore.

HISTORY, POLITICS AND SOCIETY

The Longman History of Italy (Longman £9.95–18.95, depending on availability in paperback). When completed, this eight-volume series will cover the history of Italy from the end of the Roman Empire to the present, each instalment comprising a range of essays on all aspects of political, social, economic and cultural history. Invaluable if you've developed a special interest in a particular period.

Giuliano Procacci *History of the Italian People* (Penguin £5.99). A comprehensive history of the peninsula, charting the development of Italy as a nation-state.

Valerio Lintner *A Traveller's History of Italy* (Windrush Press £7.95). Brief history of the country, from the Etruscans right up to the present day. Well written and sensibly concise, it could be just the thing for the dilettante historian of the country. Lots of tables and chronologies for easy reference.

Edward Gibbon *The History of the Decline and Fall of the Roman Empire.* Awe-inspiring in its erudition and magisterial in its analysis, Gibbon's masterpiece is one of the greatest histories ever written, and one of the finest compositions of English prose. The full work is published by Dent in six volumes (£54), but Penguin issue a decent abridgement (£4.95).

Michael Grant *A History of Rome* (Faber £6.95). Straightforward and reliable summary of an impossibly complicated story.

Jerome Carcopino *Daily Life in Ancient Rome* (Peregrine £5.95). Detailed but never dull, this is a seminal work of Roman social history.

Christopher Hibbert *Rome: Biography of a City* (Penguin £8.95). The history of Italy's capital made easy. As ever, Hibbert is readable and entertaining, but never superficial, providing by far the most comprehensive brief account of the city through the ages yet published.

John Julius Norwich *The Normans in the South* (o/p). Accessible, well-researched story of the Normans' explosive entry into the south of Italy. His *Kingdom in the Sun* (o/p) deals with their creation in Sicily of one of the most brilliant medieval European civilisations. Just as stimulating is his *A History of Venice* (Penguin £11.95), the fullest treatment of the subject that's readily available.

Denis Mack Smith *The Making of Italy 1796–1866* (Macmillan £9.95). Admirably lucid explanation of the various forces at work in the unification of Italy. The same author has also written two excellent biographies of Cavour (Methuen £6.95) and Mussolini (Grafton £4.95).

Dennis Mack Smith *Italy and its Monarchy* (Yale £16.95). Learned and entertaining account of Italy's short-lived monarchy, whose kings ruled the country for less than a century. Reveals (truthfully) Vittorio Emanuelle II and co. as a bunch of irresponsible and rather dim buffoons that the country was glad to be rid of.

Christopher Hibbert *Garibaldi and his Enemies* (Penguin £5.99). A popular treatment of the life and revolutionary works of Giuseppe Garibaldi, thrillingly detailing the exploits of "The Thousand" in their lightning campaign from Marsala to Milazzo.

Christopher Hibbert *Benito Mussolini* (Penguin £4.95). Informed and accessible biography of *Il Duce*, with much insight into the politics of the Fascist era.

Luigi Barzini *The Italians* (Hamish Hamilton £7.95). Long the most respected work on the Italian nation, and rightly so. Barzini leaves no stone unturned in his quest to pinpoint the real Italy.

John Haycraft *Italian Labyrinth: Italy in the 1980s* (Penguin £3.95). Rambling study of modern Italy, its customs, politics, social problems, economy and arts. Useful background, though at times a laborious read.

Donald Sassoon *Contemporary Italy* (Longman £9.95). Slightly academic background on the country and its institutions.

Alan Friedman *Agnelli and the Network of Italian Power* (Harrap £12.95). Agnelli publicly didn't like this when it came out, and no wonder. Friedman's book is the first piece of journalism to properly pull no punches on the dynastic and anti-democratic power network that is at the heart of Italian society. If you're intrigued by the inertia of Italian postwar politics, a must.

Daniel Dolci *Sicilian Lives* (Writers and Readers £4.95). Dolci's formidable record of the lives of the Sicilians he met when he moved to Trappeto in the early 1950s. Short accounts told in their own words, it's at once a moving and depressing document.

CRIME

Pino Arlacchi *Mafia Business* (OUP £4.95). Dry and academic account of how the Mafia moved into big business, legal and illegal, its argument contained in the book's subtitle *The Mafia Ethic and the Spirit of Capitalism*. The author has served on the Italian government's Anti-Mafia Commission, which makes him supremely qualified to judge accurately the Mafia's cutting edge.

Norman Lewis *The Honoured Society* (Eland Books £4.95). Famous account of the Mafia, its origins, personalities and customs. Certainly the most enjoyable introduction to the subject available, though much of it is taken up with the story of banditry – really a separate issue – and his lack of accredited sources leaves you wondering how much is conjecture.

Christopher Duggan *Fascism and the Mafia* (Yale £19.95). Well-researched study of how Mussolini put the Mafia in their place. Duggan uses this account for his thesis that there's no such thing as the Mafia, that it was simply dreamed up by Italians seeking a scapegoat for their inability to control the delinquent society.

Tim Shawcross and Martin Young *Mafia Wars* (Fontana £4.50). An account of the Sicilian and American Mafia's move into the international narcotics trade, based around the evidence of a former Godfather, Tommaso Buscetta.

Claire Sterling *The Mafia* (Hamish Hamilton £16.95). The most recently published piece of Mafia scholarship, showing to a disturbing degree just how little Mafia power has been eroded by the state's onslaught of recent years.

ART, ARCHITECTURE AND ARCHAEOLOGY

Henri Focillon *The Art of the West in the Middle Ages* (Phaidon, 2 vols, £5.95 each). Concise overview of the art of pre-Renaissance Europe.

Giorgio Vasari *Lives of the Artists* (Penguin £3.50). One-volume abridgement of the sixteenth-century artist's classic work on his predecessors and contemporaries. Includes essays on Giotto, Brunelleschi, Mantegna, Leonardo, Michelangelo, Raphael, and more. The first real work of art history, and still among the most penetrating books you can read on Italian Renaissance art.

Michael Levey *Early Renaissance* (Penguin £5.95). Precise and fluently written account, and well illustrated; probably the best introduction to the subject. Levey's *High Renaissance* (Penguin £5.95) continues the story in the same style.

Michael Baxandall *Painting and Experience in Fifteenth-Century Italy* (OUP £4.95). Invaluable analysis, concentrating on the way in which the art of the period would have been perceived at the time.

Jacob Burckhardt *Civilisation of the Renaissance in Italy* (Phaidon £7.50). Nineteenth-century classic of Renaissance scholarship.

J.R. Hale (ed.) *Concise Encyclopaedia of the Italian Renaissance* (Thames & Hudson £5.95). Exemplary reference book, many of whose summaries are as informative as essays twice their length; covers individual artists, movements, cities, philosophical concepts, the lot.

Anthony Blunt *Artistic Theory in Italy 1450–1600* (OUP £5.95). Cogent summary of the aesthetic ground-rules of Renaissance art, but – contrary to the impression given by the writer's patrician tone – far from the last word.

Frederick Hartt *History of Italian Renaissance Art* (Thames & Hudson £30). If one book on this vast subject can be said to be indispensable, this is it. The price might seem daunting, but in view of its comprehensiveness and acuity, and the range of its illustrations, it's actually something of a bargain.

Cyril Mango *Byzantine Architecture* (Faber £12.95) **Hans Erich Kubach** *Romanesque Architecture* (£14.95), **Louis Grodecki** *Gothic*

Architecture (£12.95), and **Christian Norberg-Schulz** *Baroque Architecture* and *Late Baroque and Rococo Architecture* (both £12.95). Each of these is part of Faber's solidly-written *History of World Architecture* series. Though they don't deal exclusively with Italian architecture, all these books provide a full context within which to place Italy's contribution to the movements.

Peter Murray *The Architecture of the Italian Renaissance* (Thames & Hudson £4.95). Begins with Romanesque buildings and finishes with Palladio – valuable both as a gazetteer of the main monuments and as a synopsis of the underlying concepts. For a more detailed discussion of those ideas, the standard work is Rudolf Wittkower's *Architectural Principles in the Age of Humanism* (Academy £12.95).

Peter and Linda Murray *Art of the Renaissance* (Thames & Hudson £4.95). Serviceable thumbnail sketch, useful to prepare the ground before a trip to Italy.

John Shearman *Mannerism* (Penguin £4.95). The self-conscious art of sixteenth-century Mannerism is one of the most complex topics of Renaissance studies; Shearman's brief discussion analyses the main currents, yet never over-simplifies nor becomes pedantic.

T.W.Potter *Roman Italy* (British Museum Publications £15). Learned illustrated survey of Roman society based on archaeological sources. Essential reading if you're interested in the period.

Frank Sear *Roman Architecture* (Batsford £12.95). As thorough an account as the lay reader could want.

Rudolf Wittkower *Art and Architecture in Italy 1600–1750* (Penguin £16.95). Exhaustive and sometimes laborious survey of the period; best borrowed from a library.

SPECIFIC GUIDES

Burton Anderson *Vino* (Papermac £8.95). Comprehensive guide to the regional wines and winemaking techniques of Italy.

Stefano Ardito *Backpacking and Walking in Italy* (Bradt £6.95). Skimpy in places, but, in English at least, it doesn't have much competition.

Tim Jepson *Wild Italy* (Ebury £9.95). Recently published guide to the flora and fauna of the Italian peninsula.

(ed.) Stefano Ardito *A Piedi in Piemonte / Lombardia / Emilia-Romagna / Toscana / Abruzzo / Lazio* (Edizione Iter L16,500 each). Available in Italy and not in English, but, with a basic grasp of the language, easy enough to follow, and with lots of very detailed hiking routes of varying standards of difficulty. Worth the price alone for the detailed route-maps and useful addresses.

ANCIENT LITERATURE

Catullus *Poems* (Penguin £3.95). Although his name is associated primarily with the tortured love poems addressed to Lesbia, Catullus also produced some acerbic satirical verse; this collection does full justice to his range.

Cicero *Selected Works* (Penguin £2.95). The rhetorical prose of Cicero was for many Renaissance scholars the paragon of literary style, and his political ideas provided similarly fertile material for discussion. Penguin publish half a dozen volumes of his work.

Livy *Early History of Rome* (Penguin £3.95). Lively chronicle of the city's evolution from the days of Romulus and Remus; Penguin also publish later instalments of those parts of Livy's history that have survived, including the gripping *War with Hannibal*.

Marcus Aurelius *Meditations* (Penguin £2.95). The classic text of Stoic thought, written by one of the few Roman Emperors it's easy to admire.

Ovid *Metamorphoses* and *Erotic Poems* (both Penguin £3.95). The mythical tales of the *Metamorphoses* have been so frequently quarried by artists that they can be enjoyed both as literature and as a key to some of the master-works of Renaissance and later art. His elegiac love poems have a sexual candour that makes them seem almost modern.

Petronius *Satyricon* (Penguin £3.95). Fragmentary, spicy narrative written by one of Nero's inner circle; Fellini's film of the same name gives a pretty accurate idea of the tone.

Plautus *Pot of Gold, and other plays* (Penguin £3.95). The most popular playwright of his time, whose complicated plots provided a model for Renaissance comedies such as *The Comedy of Errors*.

Seneca *Four Tragedies and Octavia* (Penguin £3.95). Violent, fast-paced drama from Nero's one-time tutor; the only plays to have survived from the Roman Empire.

Suetonius *The Twelve Caesars* (Penguin £2.95). The inside story on such vile specimens as Caligula, Nero and Domitian; elegantly written and appalling.

Tacitus *Annals of Imperial Rome* (Penguin £3.95). Covers much of the terrain dealt with by Suetonius, but from the stance of the diligent historian and serious moralist.

Virgil *The Aeneid* (Penguin £5.95). The central work of Latin literature, depicting the adventures of Aeneas after the fall of Troy, and thus celebrating Rome's heroic lineage.

ITALIAN CLASSICS

Ludovico Ariosto *Orlando Furioso* (Penguin, two volumes, £6 & £7.95). Italy's chivalrous epic, set in Charlemagne's Europe; has its exciting moments, but most readers would be grateful for an abridged version.

Giovanni Boccaccio *The Decameron* (Penguin £4.95). Set in the plague-racked Florence of 1348, Boccaccio's assembly of one hundred short stories is a fascinating social record as well as a constantly diverting comic sequence.

Baldassare Castiglione *The Book of the Courtier* (Penguin £3.50). Written in the form of a series of dialogues held in the court of Urbino, this subtle and entertaining book defines all the qualities essential in the perfect gentleman; the idealistic converse of Machiavelli.

Benvenuto Cellini *Autobiography* (Penguin £3.95). Shamelessly egocentric record of the travails and triumphs of the sculptor and goldsmith's career; one of the freshest literary productions of its time.

Dante Alighieri *The Divine Comedy* (OUP, three volumes, £6.95 each). No work in any other language bears comparison with Dante's poetic exegesis of the moral scheme of God's creation – in late medieval Italy it was venerated both as a book of almost scriptural authority and as the ultimate refinement of the vernacular Tuscan language. Numerous translations have been attempted – the OUP edition is clear, and has the original text facing the English version. One of the better translations, Laurence Binyon's, is printed in full in the *Portable Dante* (Penguin £4.95).

Leonardo da Vinci *Notebooks* (OUP £2.95). Miscellany of speculation and observation from the universal genius of Renaissance Italy; essential to any understanding of the man.

Niccolo Machiavelli *The Prince* (Penguin £1.50). A treatise on statecraft which actually did less to form the political thought of Italy than it did to form foreigners' perceptions of the country; there was far more to Machiavelli than the *realpolitik* of the *The Prince*, as is shown by the selection of writings included in Penguin's anthology *The Portable Machiavelli* (£5.95).

Alessandro Manzoni *The Betrothed* (Penguin £5.95). The classic nineteenth-century Italian novel, focussing on the collisions of love and class. First published in 1823, it was reissued in 1840 after Manzoni had improved its diction through the study of the Tuscan dialect.

Petrarch (Francesco Petrarca) *Selections from the Canzoniere* (OUP £2.95). Often described as the first modern poet, by virtue of his preoccupation with worldly fame and secular love, Petrarch wrote some of the Italian language's greatest lyrics. This slim selection at least hints at what is lost in translation.

Marco Polo *Travels* (Penguin £3.50). Buttonholing account of Polo's journey to the court of Kublai Khan, and his seventeen-year stay there; engaging even when the stories are clearly fanciful.

MODERN LITERATURE

Giorgio Bassani *The Garden of the Finzi Continis* (Quarter £6.95). Gentle, elegiac novel, set in the Jewish community of Ferrara during the Fascist period, on the eve of the mass deportations to Germany. Infused with a sense of regret for a Europe that died with the war.

Italo Calvino *If on a Winter's Night a Traveller* (Picador £3.50). Calvino's fiction became increasingly concerned with the nature of fiction itself, and this involuted, witty novel marks the culmination of the process. His first three anti-realistic novels are published in one volume by Picador, under the title *Our Ancestors* (£4.95). Others include *Castle of Crossed Destinies* and *Invisible Cities* (both Picador, £3.95 & £2.95). Picador also publish a volume of Calvino's early short stories, *Difficult Loves* (£3.95).

Gianni Celati *Voices from the Plains* (Serpent's Tail £6.95). Chance encounters on a walk down the Po provide the focus for these atmospheric tales.

Luciano de Crescenzo *Thus Spake Bellavista* (Picador £10.95). Not really classifiable as straight fiction, more a collection of short tales and rambling discussions on Naples, the north-south divide, and the meaning of liberty. As a commentary on the Southern question, it's a useful supplement, but de Crescenzo has a tendency to romanticise rather than analyse his native city.

Gabriele D'Annunzio *Halcyon* (Carcanet £6.95). Self-regarding dandy, war hero and worshipper of Mussolini, D'Annunzio was perhaps the most complex figure of twentieth-century Italian literature; this extended lyric sequence – a troubled idyll set on the Tuscan coast – contains much of his finest poetry.

Umberto Eco *The Name of the Rose* (Picador £4.95). Allusive, tightly plotted monastic detective story. Perhaps the best-selling (if not the best-read) highbrow novel of the Eighties. See also his latest, equally hyped work, *Foucault's Pendulum* (Secker & Warburg £12.95).

Carlo Emilio Gadda *That Awful Mess on Via Merulana* (Quartet £7.95). Superficially a detective story, Gadda's celebrated modernist novel is so dense a weave of physical reality and literary diversions that the reader is led away from a solution rather than towards it; it has the sort of status in Italian fiction that *Ulysses* has in English.

Natalia Ginzburg *Family Sayings* (Grafton £3.50). The constraints of family life are a dominant theme in Ginsburg's writing, and her own upbringing is the source material for this characteristically rigorous yet lyrical work. A radical politician who sits in the Senate in Rome, Ginsburg is Italy's best-known woman writer, and most of her books are available in translation from Carcanet.

Giuseppe di Lampedusa *The Leopard* (Collins 1961 £4.95). The most famous Sicilian novel, written after the war but recounting the dramatic nineteenth-century transition from Bourbon to Piedmontese rule from a aristo-crat's point of view. A good character-study and rich with incidental detail, including some nice description of the Sicilian landscape.

Carlo Levi *Christ Stopped at Eboli* (Penguin £3.95). First published in 1945, this novel, set in a remote region of Basilicata, to which Levi was exiled under the Fascists, was the first to awake modern Italy to the plight of its southern regions.

Primo Levi *If This is a Man/The Truce; The Periodic Table* (Sphere £3.99). Levi's training as a chemist saved his life in Auschwitz, and the first two books here – his first – record the horrors he experienced both in captivity and after the war. The anti-morality of the Third Reich and its repercussions are the recurrent subjects of Levi's later works, every one of which is distinguished by an unwavering exactitude of recollection and judgment.

Eugenio Montale *Selected Poems* (Manchester University Press £5.25). Montale's carefully structured and linguistically rich verse presents formidable problems for the translator; this selection is as good as one could hope for.

Elsa Morante *History* (Penguin £4.95). Capturing the experience of daily Roman life during the last war, this is probably the most vivid fictional picture of the conflict as seen from the city.

Alberto Moravia *Roman Tales* (OUP £3.95). Collection of stories, first published in the Fifties, which attempt to show the underbelly of a city rapidly changing. Evocative both of the city and its people. *The Conformist* (o/p) is a psychological novel about a man sucked into the amorality of Fascism by his desperation to conform; *The Woman of Rome* (o/p) is an earlier work, a teeming and sensual novel, centred on the activities of a Roman prostitute, that is relatively untouched by the bleakness that runs through much of his later writing.

Pier Paolo Pasolini *A Violent Life* (Carcanet £4.95). This super-naturalistic evocation of life in the slums areas of Rome caused a scandal when it was published in 1959. The critics have got used to it now, and the late author's novel is considered one of the classics of Italian post-war fiction. See also the collection of short stories, *Roman Nights and Other Stories* (Marlborough Press £6.95), and *A Dream of Something* (Quartet £5.95) – Pasolini's pastoral tale of growing up in Friuli in the late Forties.

Cesare Pavese *The Moon and the Bonfire* (Quartet £3.50). Exploring the difficulties of achieving an acceptance of one's past, this novel was written shortly before Pavese's suicide at the age of 42; most of his other novels are published only in hardback, by Peter Owen.

Luigi Pirandello *Six Characters in Search of an Author* (Methuen £3.95), *The Late Mattia Pascal* (Dedalus £4.95), *Short Stories* (Quartet £5.95). His most famous and accomplished work, *Six Characters...*, written in 1921, contains many of the themes that dogged Pirandello throughout his writing career – the idea of a multiple personality and the quality of reality. *The Late Mattia Pascal* is an early novel (1904), entertainingly written despite its stylistic shortcomings; while the collection of short stories is perhaps the best introduction to Pirandello's work you can buy: abrasive stuff, the dialogue showing an assured comic touch superbly adapted in the Taviani brothers' movie, *Kaos* (see "Italian Cinema").

Umberto Saba *Ernesto* (Grafton £3.99). Lyrical autobiographical novel by the Triestine poet, recollecting youth and homosexuality. Marvellous translation.

Leonardo Sciascia *Sicilian Uncles* (Carcanet £8.95), *The Wine Dark Sea* (Paladin £3.95), *Candido* (Carcanet £3.95), *The Day of the Owl & Equal Danger* (Paladin £3.95). A Sicilian, Sciascia is the best writer working in Italy today. Economically written, his short stories are packed with incisive insights into the island's quirky ways, and infused with the author's humane and sympathetic views of its people. Recently published in hardback is his *1912 + 1* (Carcanet £10.95), which is a fictionalised attack on the work of Gabriele D'Annunzio.

Ignazio Silone *Fontamara* (Dent £4.50). The tale of a small village driven to revolt against its landlords and the Fascist thugs sent to enforce

their harsh reign. See also *Bread and Wine* (Dent £4.95), first published in Switzerland where Silone fled to escape Mussolini.

Italo Svevo *Confessions of Zeno* (Penguin £5.95). Complete critical indifference to his early efforts so discouraged Svevo that he gave up writing altogether, until encouraged by James Joyce, who taught him English in Trieste. The resultant novel, *The Confessions*, is a unique creation, a comic portrait of a character at once wistful, helpless and irrepressible.

Roger Vailland *The Law* (Eland £5.95). Not an Italian novel but a French one, but worth of inclusion here for its sheer authenticity. Its evocation of life in a small Pugliese town, of its people, etiquette and harsh tradition, is tight, considered and totally convincing.

Giovanni Verga *Short Sicilian Novels* (Dedalus £3.95), *Cavalleria Rusticana* (Dedalus £4.95) and *I Malavoglia* or "The House by the Medlar Tree" (Dedalus £4.95). Verga, born in the nineteenth century in Catania, spent several years in various European salons before coming home to write his best work. Much of it is a reaction against the pseudo-sophistication of society circles, stressing the simple lives of ordinary people, though they're occasionally drawn with a heavy smattering of "peasant passion", with much emotion, wounded honour and feuds to the death.

Elio Vittorini *Conversation in Sicily* (Quartet £5.95). A Sicilian emigrant returns from the north of Italy after fifteen years to see his mother on her birthday. The conversations of the title are with the people he meets on the way, local villagers and his mother, and reveal a poverty- and disease-ridden Sicily, though the scenes are affectionately drawn.

LANGUAGE

The ability to speak English confers prestige in Italy, and there's often no shortage of people willing to show off their knowledge, particularly returned *emigrati*. However, even in the main cities and resorts you'll need to use at least some Italian, and in more remote areas you may find no one speaks English at all.

PRONUNCIATION

Wherever you are, it's a good idea to master at least a little **Italian**, a task made easier by the fact that your halting efforts will often be rewarded by smiles and genuine surprise. In any case, it's one of the easiest European languages to learn, especially if you already have a smattering of French or Spanish, both of which are extremely similar grammatically.

Easiest of all is the **pronunciation**, since every word is spoken exactly as it's written, and usually enunciated with exaggerated, open-mouthed clarity. The only difficulties you're likely to encounter are the few **consonants** that are different from English:

c before e or i is pronounced as in **ch**urch, while **ch** before the same vowel is hard, as in **c**at.

sci or **sce** are pronouced as in **sh**eet and **sh**elter respectively. The same goes with **g** – soft before e or i, as in **g**eranium; hard when followed by h, as in **g**arlic.

gn has the ni sound of our o**ni**on.

gl in Italian is softened to something like li in English, as in sta**lli**on.

h is not aspirated, as in **h**onour.

When **speaking** to strangers, the third person is the polite form (ie *Lei* instead of *Tu* for "you"); using the second person is a mark of disrespect or stupidity. It's also worth remembering that Italians don't use "please" and "thank you" half as much as we do: it's all implied in the tone, though if you're in any doubt, err on the polite side.

All Italian words are **stressed** on the penultimate syllable unless an **accent** (´ or `) denotes otherwise, although accents are often left out in practice. Note that the ending *-ia* or *-ie* counts as two syllables, hence *trattoria* is stressed on the *I*. Generally, in the text we've put accents in whenever it isn't immediately obvious how a word should be pronounced – though you shouldn't assume that this is how you'll see the words written in Italian: for example, in *Maríttima*, the accent is on the first *I*; conversely *Catania* theoretically should have an accent on the first *A*.

You'll find variations in **dialect** all over the country. Neapolitan especially can be difficult to understand, and the Sicilian dialect is different enough from conventional Italian as to be an almost separate language. But everywhere people will slip into more orthodox Italian if they see you're a foreigner.

	ITALIAN NUMBERS						
1	uno	9	nove	17	diciassette	50	cinquanta	200	duecento
2	due	10	dieci	18	diciotto	60	sessanta	500	cinquecento
3	tre	11	undici	19	diciannove	70	settanta	1000	mille
4	quattro	12	dodici	20	venti	80	ottanta	5000	cinquemila
5	cinque	13	tredici	21	ventuno	90	novanta	10,000	diecimila
6	sei	14	quattordici	22	ventidue	100	cento	50,000	cinquanta mila
7	sette	15	quindici	30	trenta	101	centuno		
8	otto	16	sedici	40	quaranta	110	centodieci		

BASICS

Good morning	Buon giorno	Tomorrow	Domani
Good afternoon/ evening	Buona sera	Day after tomorrow	Dopodomani
		Yesterday	Ieri
Good night	Buona notte	Now	Adesso
Hello/goodbye	Ciao (informal; to strangers use phrases above)	Later	Più tardi
		Wait a minute!	Aspetta!
Goodbye	Arrivederci (formal)	In the morning	di mattina
Yes	Sì	In the afternoon	nel pomeriggio
No	No	In the evening	di sera
Please	Per favore	Here (there)	Qui/La
Thank you (very much)	Grázie (molte/mille grazie)	Good/bad	Buono/Cattivo
		Big/small	Grande/Píccolo
You're welcome	Prego	Cheap/expensive	Económico/Caro
Alright/that's OK	Va bene	Early/late	Presto/Ritardo
How are you?	Come stai/sta? (informal/formal)	Hot/cold	Caldo/Freddo
		Near/far	Vicino/Lontano
I'm fine	Bene	Vacant/occupied	Líbero/Occupato
Do you speak English?	Parla inglese?	Quickly/slowly	Velocemente/ Lentamente
I don't understand	Non ho capito		
I don't know	Non lo so	Slowly/quietly	Piano
Excuse me	Mi scusi/Prego	With/without	Con/Senza
Excuse me (in a crowd)	Permesso	More/less	Più/Meno
I'm sorry	Mi dispiace	Enough, no more	Basta
I'm here on holiday	Sono qui in vacanza	Mr . . .	Signor . . .
I'm English/Scottish/ Welsh/Irish	Sono inglese/scozzese/ gallese/irlandese	Mrs . . .	Signora . . .
		Miss . . .	Signorina . . .
I live in . . .	Abito a . . .	(il Signor, la Signora, la Signorina when speaking about someone else)	
Today	Oggi		

DRIVING

Left/right	Sinistro/Destro	No entry	Senso vietato
Go straight ahead	Sempre diritto	Slow down	Rallentare
Turn to the right/left	Gira a destra/sinistra	Road closed/up	Strada chiusa/guasta
Parking	Parcheggio	No through road	Vietato il transito
No parking	Divieto di sosta/Sosta vietata	No overtaking	Vietato il sorpasso
		Crossroads	Incrocio
One way street	Senso único	Speed limit	Limite di Velocità

SOME SIGNS

Entrance/exit	Entrata/Uscita	To let	Affítasi
Free entrance	Ingresso líbero	Platform	Binario
Gentlemen/ladies	Signori/Signore	Cash desk	Cassa
WC	Gabinetto	Go/walk	Avanti
Vacant/engaged	Líbero/Occupato	Stop/halt	Alt
Open/closed	Aperto/Chiuso	Customs	Dogana
Arrivals/departures	Arrivi/Partenze	Do not touch	Non toccare
Closed for restoration	Chiuso per restauro	Danger	Perícolo
Closed for holidays	Chiuso per ferie	Beware	Attenzione
Pull/push	Tirare/Spingere	First aid	Pronto soccorso
Out of order	Guasto	Ring the bell	Suonare il campanello
Drinking water	Acqua potabile	No smoking	Vietato fumare

ACCOMMODATION

Hotel	*Albergo*	Do you have anything cheaper?	*Ha niente che costa di meno?*
Is there a hotel nearby?	*C'è un albergo qui vicino?*	Full/half board	*Pensione completa/ mezza pensione*
Do you have a room . . .	*Ha una ca'mera . . .*	Can I see the room?	*Posso vedere la cámera?*
for one/two/three people	*per una/due/tre person(a/e)*	I'll take it	*La prendo*
for one/two/three nights	*per una/due/tre nott(e/i)*	I'd like to book a room	*Vorrei prenotare una cámera*
for one/two weeks	*per una/due settiman(a/e)*	I have a booking	*Ho una prenotazione*
with a double bed	*con un letto matrimoniale*	Can we camp here?	*Possiamo fare il campeggio qui?*
with a shower/bath	*con una doccia/un bagno*		
with a balcony	*con una terrazza*	Is there a campsite nearby?	*C'è un camping qui vicino?*
hot/cold water	*acqua calda/freddo*		
How much is it?	*Quanto costa?*	Tent	*Tenda*
It's expensive	*È caro*	Cabin	*Cabina*
Is breakfast included?	*È compresa la prima colazione?*	Youth hostel	*Ostello per la gioventù*

QUESTIONS AND DIRECTIONS

Where? (where is/are . . . ?)	*Dove? (Dov'è/Dove sono)*	Can you give me a lift to . . . ?	*Mi può dare un passaggio a . . . ?*
When?	*Quando?*	Can you tell me when to get off?	*Mi può dire scendere alla fermata giusta?*
What? (what is it?)	*Cosa? (Cos'è?)*		
How much/many?	*Quanto/Quanti?*	What time does it open?	*A che ora apre?*
Why?	*Perche'?*	What time does it close?	*A che ora chiude?*
It is/there is (is it/is there . . . ?)	*È/C'è (È/C'è . . . ?)*	How much does it cost (. . . do they cost?)	*Quanto costa? (Quanto costano?)*
What time is it?	*Che ora è/Che ore sono?*		
How do I get to . . . ?	*Come arrivo a . . . ?*	What's it called in Italian?	*Comè si chiama in italiano?*
How far is it to . . . ?	*Cuant'è lontano a . . . ?*		

TRAVELLING

Aeroplane	*Aeroplano*	Bicycle	*Bicicletta*	On foot	*A piedi*
Bus	*Autobus/pullman*	Ferry	*Traghetto*	Bus station	*Autostazione*
Train	*Treno*	Ship	*Nave*	Railway station	*Stazione ferroviaria*
Car	*Macchina*	Hydrofoil	*Aliscafo*	Ferry terminal	*Stazione maríttima*
Taxi	*Taxi*	Hitch-hiking	*Autostop*	Port	*Porto*

A ticket to . . .	*Un biglietto a . . .*	Where does it leave from?	*Da dove parte?*
One-way/return	*Solo andata/andata e ritorno*	What platform does it leave from?	*Da quale binario parte?*
Can I book a seat?	*Posso prenotare un posto?*	How many kilometres is it?	*Quanti chilo'metri sono?*
What time does it leave?	*A che ora parte?*	How long does it take?	*Quanto ci vuole?*
When is the next bus/ train/ferry to . . . ?	*Quando parte il prossimo pullman/treno/ traghetto per . . . ?*	What number bus is it to . . . ?	*Que número di autobus per . . . ?*
		Where's the road to . . . ?	*Dov'è la strada a . . .*
Do I have to change?	*Devo cambiare?*	Next stop please	*La pro'ssima fermata, per favore*

PHRASEBOOKS

Best of the **phrasebooks** is *Harrap's Italian Phrase Book* (Harrap £1.75), which has useful vocabulary sections and menu readers. Harrap also publish a *Mini Dictionary* (£2.50), which is an excellent pocket reference. If you're more serious about **learning the language**, *Teach Yourself Italian* (Hodder & Stoughton £3.95) is a good starting point.

GLOSSARY OF ARTISTIC AND ARCHITECTURAL TERMS

AGORA Square or market place in an ancient Greek city.

AMBO A kind of simple pulpit, popular in Italian medieval churches.

APSE Semi-circular recess at the altar, usually eastern, end of a church.

ARCHITRAVE The lowest part of the entablature.

ATRIUM Inner courtyard, usually of a Roman house.

BALDACHINO A canopy on columns, usually placed over the altar in a church.

BELVEDERE A terrace or lookout point.

CALDARIUM The steam room of a Roman bath.

CAMPANILE Bell tower, sometimes detached, usually of a church.

CAPITAL Top of a column.

CATALAN-GOTHIC Hybrid form of architecture, mixing elements of fifteenth-century Spanish and Northern European styles.

CHIAROSCURO The balance of light and shade in a painting, and the skill of the artist in depicting the contrast between the two.

CELLA Sanctuary of a temple.

CHANCEL Part of a church containing the altar.

CIBORIUM Another word for *Baldachino*, see above.

CORTILE Galleried courtyard or cloisters.

CORNICE The top section of a classical facade.

COSMATI WORK Decorative mosaic work on marble, usually highly coloured, found in early Christian Italian churches, especially in Rome. Derives from the name Cosma, a common name among families of marble workers at the time.

CRYPT Burial place in a church, usually under the choir.

CUPOLA Dome.

CYCLOPEAN WALLS Fortifications built of huge, rough stone blocks, common in the pre-Roman settlements of Lazío.

DECUMANUS MAXIMUS The main street of a Roman town. The second cross-street was known as the *Decumanus Inferiore*.

ENTABLATURE The section above the capital on a classical building, below the cornice.

EX-VOTO Artefact designed in thanksgiving to a saint. The adjective is *ex-votive*.

FRESCO Wall-painting technique in which the artist applies paint to wet plaster for a more permanent finish.

LOGGIA Roofed gallery or balcony.

METOPE A panel on the frieze of a Greek temple.

MITHRAISM Pre-Christian cult associated with the Persian god of Light, who slew a bull and fertilised the world with its blood.

NAVE Central space in a church, usually flanked by aisles.

PANTOCRATOR Usually refers to an image of Christ, portrayed with outstretched arms.

PIANO NOBILE Main floor of a palace, usually the first.

POLYPTYCH Painting on several joined wooden panels.

PORTICO Covered entrance to a building.

PRESEPIO A Christmas crib

PUTTI Cherubs.

RELIQUARY Receptacle for a saint's relics, usually bones. Often highly decorated.

SGRAFFITO Decorative technique whereby one layer of plaster is scratched to form a pattern. Popular in sixteenth-century Italy.

STEREOBATE Visible base of any building, usually a Greek temple.

STUCCO Plaster made from water, lime, sand and powdered marble, used for decorative work.

THERMAE Baths, usually elaborate buildings in Roman villas.

TROMPE L'OEIL Work of art that deceives the viewer by means of tricks with perspective.

TRYPTYCH Painting on three joined wooden panels.

GLOSSARY OF ITALIAN WORDS AND ACRONYMS

ITALIAN WORDS

ALISCAFO Hydrofoil.

ANTIFEATRO Amphitheatre.

AUTSTAZIONE Bus station.

AUTOSRADA Motorway.

CAPPELLA Chapel

CASTELLO Castle.

CENTRO Centre.

CHIESA Church.

COMUNE An administrative area; also the local council or town hall.

CORSO Avenue or boulevard.

DUOMO/CATTEDRAL Cathedral.

ENTRATA Entrance.

FESTA Festival, holiday.

FIUME River.

FUMAROLA Volcanic vapour emission from the ground.

GOLFO Gulf.

LAGO Lake.

LARGO Square.

LUNGOMARE Seafront road or promenade.

MARE Sea.

MERCATO Market.

MUNICIPIO Town hall.

PAESE Place, area, or village.

PALAZZO Palace, mansion, or block of flats.

PARCO Park.

PASSEGGIATA The customary early evening walk.

PIANO Plain.

PIAZZA Square.

SANTUARIO Sanctuary.

SENSO UNICO One-way street.

SOTTOPASSAGIO Subway.

SPIAGGIA Beach.

STAZIONE Station.

STRADA Road.

TEATRO Theatre.

TEMPIO Temple.

TORRE Tower.

TRAGHETTO Ferry.

USCITA Exit.

VIA Road (always used with name, eg Via Roma).

ACRONYMS

AAST Azienda Autonoma di Soggiorno e Turismo.

ACI Autombole Club d'Italia.

DC Democrazia Cristiana; the Christian Democrat party.

EPT Ente Provinciale di Turismo (provincial tourist office); see also *APT* and *IAT*.

FS Italian State Railways.

IVA Imposta Valore Aggiunto (VAT).

MSI Moveimento Sociale Italiano; the Italian Fascist party.

PCI Patito Comunista Italiano; the Italian Communist party.

PSI Partito Socialista Italiano; the Italian Socialist party.

RAI The Italian state TV and radio network.

SIP Italian state telephone company.

SS Strada Statale; equivalent to a British "A" road, eg SS18.

GLOSSARY OF ITALIAN STREET NAMES

Italian streets form a kind of outdoor pantheon of historical figures. A jumble of artists, thinkers, politicians, generals and saints, in roughly equal proportions, intersect with each other in blind disregard for sense or chronology. The mad mix of heroes (and a very few heroines) constantly reminds the visitor of just how much Italians relish their past. Almost all of the following appear in every major Italian city.

Bassi, Ugo (1801–1849). A priest from Bologna who, as a fervent and eloquent supporter of Garibaldi and his cause, became one of its most important martyrs when he was condemned to death and shot by the Austrians.

Bellini. The name of both a talented Venetian family of fifteenth-century painters (Jacopo and sons Gentile and Giovanni) and a nineteenth-century Sicilian composer of operas (Vicenzo), best known for *Norma* and *La Somnambula*.

Bertani, Agostino (1812–1886). A Milanese doctor, who organised the medical and ambulance services for Garibaldi's campaigns and became one of his closest associates and shrewdest strategists.

Bixio, Nino (1821–1873). Loyal companion-at-arms to Garibaldi, who enlisted and disciplined civilian volunteers to fight some of the critical battles of the Unification era.

Buonarroti, Filippo (1761–1837). Tuscan revolutionary and friend of Robespierre, who was involved with Gracchus Babeuf in the short-lived Conspiracy of Equals in Paris, May 1796.

Calatafimi. First decisive battle in Garibaldi's Sicilian campaign, May 1860.

Capuccini. Monks whose characteristic brown robes and peaked white hoods have lent their names to the Italian coffee drink with hot milk.

Carducci, Giosuè (1835–1907). Patriotic poet of the Risorgimento who won the Nobel Prize for literature in 1907.

Cavour, Camillo di (1810–1861). Prime Minister of Piemonte who relied on diplomatic cunning to promote the interests of his Northern kingdom in the unification of Italy.

Crispi, Francesco (1819–1901). Reforming prime minister of the late nineteenth century.

D'Annunzio, Gabriele (1863–1938). Nationalist writer who refurbished Italy's past with sex and violence and who lived out some of his fantasies as a Fascist military ad venturer.

Dante Alighieri (1265–1321). Medieval Italian poet known for his three-part poem, *The Divine Comedy*.

Depretis, Agostino (1813–87). Italian prime minister on three occasions during the late nineteenth century. His administrations are remembered for the stagnation and corruption they engendered.

De Gasperi, Alcide (1881–1954). A prominent anti-Fascist imprisoned by Mussolini, and the first Catholic Prime Minister of modern Italy in 1945, aligning his country with the West by joining NATO.

Foscolo, Ugo (1778–1827). Nineteenth-century poet, dramatist and critic who left Venice under Austrian rule to settle in England where he became a commentator on Petrarch, Dante and Bocaccio.

Garibaldi, Giuseppe (1807–1882). Italy's unquestioned nationalist hero, and the tag on most Italian towns' most prominent boulevards or squares. Streets are full of his exploits and the supporting cast of comrades (see Bassi, Bertani, Bixio, Calatafimi, Le Mille, Turr).

Giolitti, Giovanni (1842–1928). Prime minister five times between 1892 and 1921. He sponsored an electoral reform bill which extended male suffrage and won workers the right to organise and strike.

Goldoni, Carlo (1707–1793). Venetian dramatist much influenced by Moliere, who wrote more than 250 comedies.

Gramsci, Antonio (1881–1937). One of the founders of the Italian Communist Party. Arrested by Mussolini in 1928 and held until just before his death, his influential writings from prison on the political role of culture and intellectuals remain controversial fifty years on.

Leopardi, Giacomo (1798–1837). A lyric poet plagued by ill-health and melancholy whose patriotic verses were taken up by the Unification.

Machiavelli, Nicolo (1469–1527). Political scientist and author of *The Prince* whose name outside Italy has become synonymous with unprincipled political opportunism.

Manin, Daniele (1804–1857). Leader of a revolution in Venice which proclaimed a republic in March 1948 and was overrun by the Austrians shortly thereafter.

Manzoni, Alessandro (1785–1873). Liberal Catholic writer and playwright whose historical novel *I promessi sposi (The Betrothed)*, set in seventeenth-century Milan, is still required reading in Italian schools.

Marconi, Guglielmo (1874–1937). Developer of the wireless system, sending messages across the Straits of Dover in 1899 and across the Atlantic in 1901.

Matteotti, Giacomo. A Socialist in the Italian Parliament who was murdered by Fascist thugs for his public denunciation of the 1924 elections which gave Mussolini majority control. In what has become known as Mussolini's Watergate, the incident had a brief chance of stopping Il Duce in his tracks – but didn't.

Mazzini,   Giuseppe   (1805–1872). Propagandist of Italian Unification whose influence was spread through the organisation Young Italy (*Giovine Italia*) which he founded to promote the national cause.

Le Mille (The Thousand). The name given to the largely untrained band of civilian volunteers (made up of students, workers, artists, journalists and every kind of adventurer) who were mobilised in 1860 for Garibaldi's successful Sicilian campaign.

Puccini, Giacomo (1858–1924). A member of the fifth generation of a family of professional musicians, and composer of many popular operas, including *Madame Butterfly*, *La Boheme* and *Tosca*.

Quattro Novembre (November 4). Anniversary of the 1918 victory in the war.

Ricasoli. An ancient and distinguished Tuscan family name. The nineteenth-century Baron Ricasoli (an ally of Cavour and very briefly prime minister) has been eclipsed by the relatively greater prominence of his family's vineyards, known particularly for their Chianti.

Ricci, Matteo (1552–1610). Early Italian missionary to China.

Risorgimento. The nineteenth-century movement to unify Italy and liberate the country from foreign domination.

Savanarola. A fifteenth-century Dominican friar and prophet of doom, inspired a famous book burning (which included Boccaccio's *Decameron* among the forbidden texts), and was himself burned after hanging in 1498.

Togliatti (1893–1964). Co-founder (with Gramsci and others) of the Italian Communist Party, which, in 1956, adopted his programme for an "Italian Road to Socialism".

Turr, Stefan. A Hungarian colonel in Garibaldi's army and close associate who helped acquire arms for the volunteer army (The Thousand) to mount the campaign in Sicily.

Umberto I and II. Kings of Italy, respectively, between 1878 and 1900 and for a brief period in 1946.

Vasari, Giorgio (1511–1574). The father of modern art history, whose *Lives of the Artists* traced the story of art from ancient Rome through to his own contemporary – and fellow Tuscan – Michelangelo.

Venti Settembre (September 20). The day Italian troops stormed into Rome in 1870, marking the final stage of unification.

Venti Cinque Aprile (April 25). Anniversary of the 1945 liberation.

Venti Quattro Maggio (May 24). Date in 1915 when Italy declared war on Austria-Hungary.

Verdi, Giuseppe (1813–1901). Hugely popular and prolific composer of operas who became a national hero.

Vespri Siciliani. Massacre of the Angevin French in Sicily in 1282, carried out (according to legend) while vesper bells were ringing, in retaliation for the savage colonisation of the island by the Angevin. Verdi used the story for an opera in 1855.

Vittorio Emanuele II and III. Respectively, the first king of unified Italy, from 1861 to 1878, and from 1900 until 1946. Very often the main street of towns are named after Vittorio Emanuele II – an overly grand accolade for a dull and unenlightened ruler.

Volturno. A river near Capua, and the name given to an important battle led by Garibaldi against the Bourbons in October 1860.

INDEX

HELP US UPDATE

We've gone to a lot of effort to ensure that this edition of the Rough Guide: Italy is completely up-to-date and accurate. However, things do change – hotels and restaurants come and go, especially in the larger cities, opening hours are notoriously fickle, and there's the ever-present danger of monuments being closed for long periods while under restoration. Any suggestions, comments, or corrections toward the next edition would be much appreciated. We'll credit all contributions, and send a copy of the new book (or any other Rough Guide, if you prefer) for the best letters. Send them along to:
Martin Dunford, The Rough Guides, 149 Kennington Lane, London SE11 4EZ.

BEFORE YOU TRAVEL THE WORLD, TALK TO AN EXPERIENCED STAMP COLLECTOR.

At STA Travel we're all seasoned travellers so we should know a thing or two about where you're headed. We can offer you the best deals on fares with the flexibility to change your mind as you go – without having to pay over the top for the privilege. We operate from 120 offices worldwide. So call in soon.

74 and 86 Old Brompton Road, SW7, 117 Euston Road, NW1. London.
Manchester. Leeds. Oxford. Cambridge. Bristol.
North America **071-937 9971.** Europe **071-937 9921.** Rest of World **071-937 9962**
(incl. Sundays 10am-2pm). **OR 061-834 0668 (Manchester)**
Africa Desk 071-465 0486.

WHEREVER YOU'RE BOUND, WE'RE BOUND TO HAVE BEEN. STA

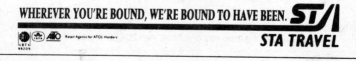

Retail Agents for ATOL Holders

STA TRAVEL